Great Lives from History

The 17th Century

1601 - 1700

The 17th Century

1601 - 1700

Volume 1
Abahai-Duchesse de Longueville

Editor
Larissa Juliet Taylor
Colby College

Editor, First Edition
Frank N. Magill

SALEM PRESS
Pasadena, California   Hackensack, New Jersey

Editor in Chief: Dawn P. Dawson

Managing Editor: Christina J. Moose   *Production Editor:* Joyce I. Buchea
Acquisitions Editor: Mark Rehn   *Graphics and Design:* James Hutson
Research Supervisor: Jeffry Jensen   *Editorial Assistant:* Dana Garey
Manuscript Editors: Desiree Dreeuws, Andy Perry   *Layout:* William Zimmerman
Assistant Editor: Andrea E. Miller   *Photo Editor:* Cynthia Beres

Cover photos: Library of Congress
(Pictured left to right, top to bottom: Thomas Hobbes, Molière, Tokugawa Ieyasu, Galileo, Massasoit, Sor Juana Inés de la Cruz, ʿAbbās the Great, Marie de Médicis, Gustavus II Adolphus)

Some of the essays in this work originally appeared in the following Salem Press sets: *Dictionary of World Biography* (© 1998-1999, edited by Frank N. Magill) and *Great Lives from History* (© 1987-1995, edited by Frank N. Magill). New material has been added.

Library of Congress Cataloging-in-Publication Data

Great lives from history. The 17th century, 1601-1700 / editor, Larissa Juliet Taylor.
    p. cm.
"Editor, first edition, Frank N. Magill."
Some of the essays in this work originally appeared in other Salem Press publications.
Includes bibliographical references and indexes.
ISBN-10: 1-58765-222-6 (set : alk. paper)
ISBN-10: 1-58765-223-4 (v. 1 : alk. paper)
ISBN-13: 978-1-58765-222-6 (set : alk. paper)
ISBN-13: 978-1-58765-223-3 (v. 1 : alk. paper)
[etc.]
    1. Biography—17th century. I. Title: 17th century, 1601-1700. II. Title: Seventeenth century, 1601-1700.
III. Taylor, Larissa. IV. Magill, Frank Northen, 1907-1997.
CT117.G74 2005
920′.009′032—dc22

2005017804

First Printing

CONTENTS

Contents

PUBLISHER'S NOTE

Great Lives from History: The Seventeenth Century, 1601-1700 is the fourth installment in the revised and expanded *Great Lives* series, initiated in 2004 with *The Ancient World, Prehistory-476 C.E.* (2 vols.) and followed in 2005 by *The Middle Ages, 477-1453* (2 vols.) and *The Renaissance and Early Modern Era, 1454-1600* (2 vols.). It will be joined by *Great Lives from History: The Eighteenth Century*, *The Nineteenth Century*, and *The Twentieth Century*. The entire series, when complete, is expected to cover more than 3,000 lives in essays ranging from 3 to 5 pages in length.

EXPANDED COVERAGE

This ongoing series is a revision of the 10-volume *Dictionary of World Biography* (*DWB*) series (1998-1999), which in turn was a revision and reordering of Salem Press's 30-volume *Great Lives from History* series (1987-1995). The expanded *Great Lives* differs in several ways from *DWB*:

• The coverage of each set has been increased significantly. In the current two volumes, 151 original essays from *Dictionary of World Biography: 17th & 18th Centuries* (1999) are enhanced by 192 new entries covering a wider geographical area and including 58 women. The result is 343 essays covering 351 historical figures (4 essays address more than one person).

• Tables and quotations from primary source documents have been added to enhance and supplement the text throughout.

• A section of maps has been added to the front matter of each volume to allow readers to locate personages geographically.

• Essays from the original *DWB* on all personages falling into the time frame are reprinted in this new series with updated and annotated bibliographies.

SCOPE OF COVERAGE

The geographic and occupational scope of the individuals covered in *Great Lives from History: The Seventeenth Century, 1601-1700* is broad. The individuals covered are identified with one or more of the following areas: Africa (1 biography), Albania (1), Australia (1),

Austria (4), Bavaria (1), Belgium (4), Bohemia (4), Brazil (1), Canada (8), China (10), Denmark (2), Egypt (1), England (126), Flanders (1), France (78), Germany (27), Hungary (1), India (4), Indonesia (1), Iran/Persia (1), Ireland (5), Italy (36), Japan (12), Manchuria (3), Mexico (2), Moravia (1), Native America (7), Netherlands (33), New Zealand (1), Norway (1), Pakistan (1), Peru (1), Poland (7), Portugal (4), Prussia (3), Russia (10), Scotland (9), Slovenia (1), Spain (22), Sweden (10), Switzerland (1), Ottoman Empire (6), Ukraine (3), American colonies (31), and Wales (1).

The editors have sought to provide coverage that is broad in areas of achievement as well as geography, while at the same time including the recognized shapers of history essential in any liberal arts curriculum. Major world leaders appear here—emperors, conquerors, kings, queens, and khans—as well as the giants of religious faith who were central to the century: popes and theologians who left their imprint on political as well as spiritual institutions. The set also includes figures who have received little or no attention in the past—from the queen Njinga of Angola to the Ottoman scholar Kâtib Çelebî. By category, the contents include figures whose achievements fall into one or more of the following areas: Architecture (13 biographies), Art (27), Astronomy (14), Business and Economics (7), Chemistry (2), Church Government and Reform (4), Diplomacy (21), Education (14), Engineering (5), Exploration (12), Geography (6), Government and Politics (139), Historiography (4), Invention (5), Law (11), Linguistics (2), Literature (66), Mathematics (19), Medicine (19), Military (34), Music (15), Patronage of the Arts (22), Philosophy (26), Physics (14), Religion and Theology (73), Scholarship (14), Science and Technology (50), Social Reform (7), Theater (28), Warfare and Conquest (41), and Women's Rights (10).

ESSAY LENGTH AND FORMAT

Each essay ranges from 1,500 to 3,000 words in length (roughly 3 to 5 pages).

Each essay displays standard ready-reference top matter offering easy access to biographical information:

• The essay title is the name of the individual; editors have chosen the name as it is most commonly found in Western English-language sources.

- The individual's *nationality or ethnicity* and *occupation or historical role* follow on the second line, including reign dates for rulers.

- A *summary paragraph* highlighting the individual's historical importance indicates why the person is studied today.

- The *Born* and *Died* lines list the most complete dates of birth and death available, followed by the most precise locations available, as well as an indication of when these are unknown, only probable, or only approximate; both contemporary and modern place-names (where different) are listed. A question mark (?) is appended to a date or place if the information is considered likely to be the precise date or place but remains in question. A "c." denotes *circa* and indicates that historians have only enough information to place the date of birth or death in a more general period. When a range of dates is provided for birth or death, historians are relatively certain that it could not have occurred prior to or after the range.

- *Also known as* lists all known versions of the individual's name, including full names, given names, alternative spellings, pseudonyms, and common epithets.

- *Area(s) of achievement* lists all categories of contribution, from Architecture and Art through Social Reform and Theater.

The body of each essay is divided into three parts:

- *Early Life* provides facts about the individual's upbringing and the environment in which he or she was reared, as well as the pronunciation of his or her name, if unfamiliar to English speakers. Where little is known about the individual's early life, historical context is provided.

- *Life's Work*, the heart of the essay, consists of a straightforward, generally chronological, account of the period during which the individual's most significant achievements were accomplished.

- *Significance* is an overview of the individual's place in history.

- *Further Reading* is an annotated bibliography, a starting point for further research.

- *See also* lists cross-references to essays in the set covering related personages.

- *Related articles* lists essays of interest in Salem's companion publication, *Great Events from History: The Seventeenth Century, 1601-1700* (2 vols., 2006).

SPECIAL FEATURES

Several features distinguish this series as a whole from other biographical reference works. The front matter includes the following aids:

- *Complete List of Contents*: This alphabetical list of contents appears in both volumes.

- *Key to Pronunciation*: A key to in-text pronunciation appears in both volumes.

- *List of Maps, Tables, and Sidebars*.

- *Maps*: The front matter of each volume contains a section of maps displaying major regions of the world during the seventeenth century.

The back matter to Volume 2 includes several appendices and indexes:

- *Rulers and Dynasties*, a geographically arranged set of tables listing major rulers and their regnal dates, covering the major regions of the world.

- *Chronological List of Entries*: individuals covered, arranged by birth year.

- *Category Index*: entries by area of achievement, from Architecture to Women's Rights.

- *Geographical Index*: entries by country or region, from Africa and Albania to the Ukraine and Wales.

- *Personages Index*: an index of all persons, both those covered in the essays and those discussed within the text.

- *Subject Index*: a comprehensive index including personages, concepts, books, artworks, terms, battles, civilizations, and other topics of discussion, with full cross-references from alternative spellings and to the Category and Geographical Indexes.

USAGE NOTES

The worldwide scope of *Great Lives from History* resulted in the inclusion of many names and words transliterated from languages that do not use the Roman alphabet. In some cases, there is more than one transliterated form in use. In many cases, transliterated words in this set follow the American Library Association and Library of Congress (ALA-LC) transliteration format for that language. However, if another form of a name or word has been judged to be more familiar to the general audience, it is used instead. The variants for names of essay subjects are listed in ready-reference top matter and are cross-referenced in the subject and personages indexes. The Pinyin transliteration was used for Chinese topics, with Wade-Giles variants provided for major names and dynasties. In a few cases, a common name that is not Pinyin has been used. Sanskrit and other South Asian names generally follow the ALA-LC transliteration rules, although again, the more familiar form of a word is used when deemed appropriate for the general reader.

Titles of books and other literature appear, upon first mention in the essay, with their full publication and translation data as known: an indication of the first date of publication or appearance, followed by the English title in translation and its first date of appearance in English; if no translation has been published in English, and if the context of the discussion does not make the meaning of the title obvious, a "literal translation" appears in roman type.

Throughout, readers will find a limited number of abbreviations used in both top matter and text, including "r." for "reigned," "b." for "born," "d." for "died," and "fl." for flourished. Where a date range appears appended to a name without one of these designators, the reader may assume it signifies birth and death dates.

CONTRIBUTORS

Salem Press would like to extend its appreciation to all who have been involved in the development and production of this work. Special thanks go to Larissa Juliet Taylor, Professor of History at Colby College, who pored over the contents list, maintaining its balance and relevance to the student audience throughout the process of acquisitions in order to ensure that the curriculum was addressed fully.

The essays were written by historians, political scientists, and scholars of regional studies as well as independent scholars. Without their expert contributions, a project of this nature would not be possible. A full list of contributors and their affiliations appears in the front matter of this volume.

CONTRIBUTORS

Patrick Adcock
Independent Scholar

Richard Adler
University of Michigan—Dearborn

Peggy E. Alford
Eastern Oregon University
Mesa Community College

Kathy Saranpa Anstine
Yale University

Sharon Arnoult
Midwestern State University

Bryan Aubrey
Independent Scholar

Tom L. Auffenberg
Ouachita Baptist University

Christopher Baker
Armstrong Atlantic State University

Renzo Baldasso
Columbia University

Carl L. Bankston III
Tulane University

John W. Barker
University of Wisconsin—Madison

Jeffrey G. Barlow
Lewis & Clark College

Alice H. R. H. Beckwith
Providence College

Graydon Beeks
Pomona College

Robert Bensen
Hartwick College

Alvin K. Benson
Utah Valley State College

Donna Berliner
Southern Methodist University

Milton Berman
University of Rochester

Charlene Villaseñor Black
University of California, Los Angeles

Carol Blessing
Point Loma Nazarene University

Julia B. Boken
Independent Scholar

Quentin Bone
Indiana State University

John Braeman
University of Nebraska

Francis J. Bremer
University of Pennsylvania—
Millersville

Jean R. Brink
Huntington Library

J. R. Broadus
University of North Carolina

William S. Brockington, Jr.
University of South Carolina—Aiken

Kendall W. Brown
Brigham Young University

Philip C. Brown
University of North Carolina at
Charlotte

David L. Bullock
Independent Scholar

William H. Burnside
John Brown University

Linnea Goodwin Burwood
State University of New York,
Binghamton

Joseph P. Byrne
Belmont University

John A. Calabrese
Texas Woman's University

Clare Callaghan
Independent Scholar

Edmund J. Campion
University of Tennessee

Allan D. Charles
University of South Carolina

Jacquelin Collins
Texas Tech University

Bernard A. Cook
Loyola University

Patricia Cook
Emory University

Christine Cornell
St. Thomas University

Loren W. Crabtree
University of Tennessee, Knoxville

Light Townsend Cummins
Austin College

Marsha Daigle-Williamson
Spring Arbor University

Thomas Derdak
Independent Scholar

Charles A. Desnoyers
LaSalle University

M. Casey Diana
University of Illinois at Urbana-
Champaign

Thomas Drucker
University of Wisconsin—Whitewater

Frederick Dumin
University of Wisconsin—Whitewater

David Allen Duncan
Tennessee Wesleyan College

Eric R. Dursteler
Brigham Young University

K. Edgington
Towson University

Mary Sweeney Ellett
Randolph-Macon Woman's College

xiii

John Roger Elliott
Pepperdine University

Robert P. Ellis
Independent Scholar

Thomas L. Erskine
Salisbury University

Randall Fegley
Pennsylvania State University

Patricia A. Finch
Independent Scholar

James Fitzmaurice
Northern Arizona University

Luminita Florea
University of California, Berkeley

George J. Flynn
*State University of New York—
    Plattsburgh*

Christopher E. Garrett
Texas A&M University

C. Herbert Gilliland
U.S. Naval Academy

Sheldon Goldfarb
University of British Columbia

Nancy M. Gordon
Independent Scholar

Larry Gragg
University of Missouri—Rolla

William C. Griffin
Appalachian State University

M. Wayne Guillory
Georgia State University

Gavin R. G. Hambly
University of Texas at Dallas

Peter B. Heller
Manhattan College

Mark C. Herman
Edison College

Sally Hibbin
Parallax Pictures, Ltd.

Sally Anne Hickson
Brock University

Anna Dunlap Higgins
Gordon College

Richard L. Hillard
University of Arkansas at Pine Bluff

Michael Craig Hillmann
Independent Scholar

John R. Holmes
Franciscan University of Steubenville

Marian T. Horvat
St. Thomas More College

W. Scott Howard
University of Denver

Ronald K. Huch
Eastern Kentucky University

Raymond Pierre Hylton
Virginia Union University

Bruce E. Johansen
University of Nebraska at Omaha

Loretta Turner Johnson
Mankato State University

Philip Dwight Jones
Bradley University

Grove Koger
Boise Public Library, Idaho

Jane Kristof
Portland State University

Paul E. Kuhl
Winston-Salem State University

Michael de L. Landon
University of Mississippi

Eugene Larson
Pierce College, Los Angeles

Anne Leader
*City College of New York, City
    University of New York*

Thomas Tandy Lewis
Anoka-Ramsey Community College

James Livingston
Northern Michigan University

Eric v.d. Luft
*State University of New York, Upstate
    Medical University*

Karl Lunde
Independent Scholar

Maxine N. Lurie
Independent Scholar

R. C. Lutz
CII

David S. Lux
Independent Scholar

M. Sheila McAvey
Becker College

Michael McCaskey
Georgetown University

Stuart McClintock
Midwestern State University

J. Sears McGee
*University of California,
    Santa Barbara*

James Edward McGoldrick
*Greenville Presbyterian Theological
    Seminary*

Caroline McManus
University of California, Los Angeles

James B. McSwain
Independent Scholar

Anne Laura Mattrella
Southeastern University

Joan E. Meznar
Eastern Connecticut State University

Mary-Emily Miller
Independent Scholar

Peter Monaghan
Independent Scholar

Gordon R. Mork
Purdue University

Barbara Mujica
Georgetown University

Terence R. Murphy
American University

Alice Myers
Simon's Rock College of Bard

John Myers
Simon's Rock College of Bard

Edwin L. Neville, Jr.
Canisius College

Brian J. Nichelson
Independent Scholar

Glenn O. Nichols
Independent Scholar

Richard L. Niswonger
Independent Scholar

Charles H. O'Brien
Western Illinois University

Joseph M. Ortiz
Princeton University

Robert J. Paradowski
Rochester Institute of Technology

Rodger Payne
Louisiana State University

Martha Moffitt Peacock
Brigham Young University

Jan Pendergrass
University of Georgia

Matthew Penney
Independent Scholar

Mark Pestana
Grand Valley State University

Susan L. Piepke
Bridgewater College

David W. Pitre
The Dunham School

George R. Plitnik
Frostburg State University

Marjorie J. Podolsky
*Pennsylvania State University—
Behrend College*

Richard H. Popkin
Independent Scholar

Clifton W. Potter, Jr.
Lynchburg College

Dorothy Potter
Lynchburg College

Shannon A. Powell
University of North Texas

Luke A. Powers
Tennessee State University

Victoria Price
Lamar University

Vinton M. Prince, Jr.
Wilmington College of Ohio

Rosemary M. Canfield Reisman
Charleston Southern University

Bernd Renner
*Brooklyn College of the City
University of New York*

Victoria Reynolds
Mandeville High School

Betty Richardson
*Southern Illinois University,
Edwardsville*

Edward A. Riedinger
Ohio State University Libraries

Victoria Rivera-Cordero
Princeton University

John O. Robison
University of South Florida

Carl Rollyson
*Baruch College of the City University
of New York*

Hilel B. Salomon
University of South Carolina

Eric Van Schaack
Independent Scholar

Randy P. Schiff
*University of California,
Santa Barbara*

Zoë A. Schneider
Georgetown University

William C. Schrader
Tennessee Technological University

Thomas C. Schunk
Independent Scholar

Roger Sensenbaugh
Indiana University

Richard M. Shaw
North Dakota State University

John C. Sherwood
University of Oregon

Neal R. Shipley
*University of Massachusetts—
Amherst*

R. Baird Shuman
*University of Illinois at Urbana-
Champaign*

Anne W. Sienkewicz
Independent Scholar

Narasingha P. Sil
Western Oregon University

Roger Smith
Independent Scholar

Ronald F. Smith
Independent Scholar

Ira Smolensky
Monmouth College

Sonia Sorrell
Pepperdine University

Robert M. Spector
Worcester State College

Joseph L. Spradley
Wheaton College, Illinois

William R. Stacy
Oberlin College

August W. Staub
University of Georgia

S. J. Stearns
*College of Staten Island of the City
University of New York*

Martha Bennett Stiles
Independent Scholar

Gerald H. Strauss
Bloomsburg University

Fred Strickert
Wartburg College

Patricia E. Sweeney
Independent Scholar

Glenn L. Swygart
Tennessee Temple University

Daniel Taylor
Bethel College

Larissa Juliet Taylor
Colby College

Thomas J. Taylor
University of Akron

Cassandra Lee Tellier
Capital University, Ohio

Leslie V. Tischauser
Prairie State College

Louis P. Towles
Independent Scholar

Andrew G. Traver
Southeastern Louisiana University

Ralph Troll
Augustana College

Carole Watterson Troxler
Elon College

Eileen Tess Tyler
United States Naval Academy

Lisa Urkevich
American University of Kuwait

William T. Walker
Chestnut Hill College

Miriam Wallraven
Universität Tübingen

Harry M. Ward
University of Richmond

Brent Waters
University of Redlands

J. Francis Watson
Grace Lutheran Church

Martha Ellen Webb
University of Nebraska—Lincoln

Marcia J. Weiss
Point Park University

Thomas Willard
University of Arizona

Michael Witkoski
University of South Carolina

Shelley Amiste Wolbrink
Drury University

Byron A. Wolverton
Southwest Texas State University

Fatima Wu
Loyola Marymount University

Kristen L. Zacharias
Albright College

Yunqiu Zhang
North Carolina A&T State University

Lilian H. Zirpolo
*Aurora: The Journal of the History
of Art*

KEY TO PRONUNCIATION

Many of the names of personages covered in *Great Lives from History: The Seventeenth Century, 1601-1700* may be unfamiliar to students and general readers. For these unfamiliar names, guides to pronunciation have been provided upon first mention of the names in the text. These guidelines do not purport to achieve the subtleties of the languages in question but will offer readers a rough equivalent of how English speakers may approximate the proper pronunciation.

Vowel Sounds

Symbol	Spelled (Pronounced)
a	answer (AN-suhr), laugh (laf), sample (SAM-puhl), that (that)
ah	father (FAH-thur), hospital (HAHS-pih-tuhl)
aw	awful (AW-fuhl), caught (kawt)
ay	blaze (blayz), fade (fayd), waiter (WAYT-ur), weigh (way)
eh	bed (behd), head (hehd), said (sehd)
ee	believe (bee-LEEV), cedar (SEE-dur), leader (LEED-ur), liter (LEE-tur)
ew	boot (bewt), lose (lewz)
i	buy (bi), height (hit), lie (li), surprise (sur-PRIZ)
ih	bitter (BIH-tur), pill (pihl)
o	cotton (KO-tuhn), hot (hot)
oh	below (bee-LOH), coat (koht), note (noht), wholesome (HOHL-suhm)
oo	good (good), look (look)
ow	couch (kowch), how (how)
oy	boy (boy), coin (koyn)
uh	about (uh-BOWT), butter (BUH-tuhr), enough (ee-NUHF), other (UH-thur)

Consonant Sounds

Symbol	Spelled (Pronounced)
ch	beach (beech), chimp (chihmp)
g	beg (behg), disguise (dihs-GIZ), get (geht)
j	digit (DIH-juht), edge (ehj), jet (jeht)
k	cat (kat), kitten (KIH-tuhn), hex (hehks)
s	cellar (SEHL-ur), save (sayv), scent (sehnt)
sh	champagne (sham-PAYN), issue (IH-shew), shop (shop)
ur	birth (burth), disturb (dihs-TURB), earth (urth), letter (LEH-tur)
y	useful (YEWS-fuhl), young (yuhng)
z	business (BIHZ-nehs), zest (zehst)
zh	vision (VIH-zhuhn)

Complete List of Contents

Volume 1

Volume 2

LIST OF MAPS, TABLES, AND SIDEBARS

VOLUME 1

VOLUME 2

AFRICA IN THE 17TH CENTURY

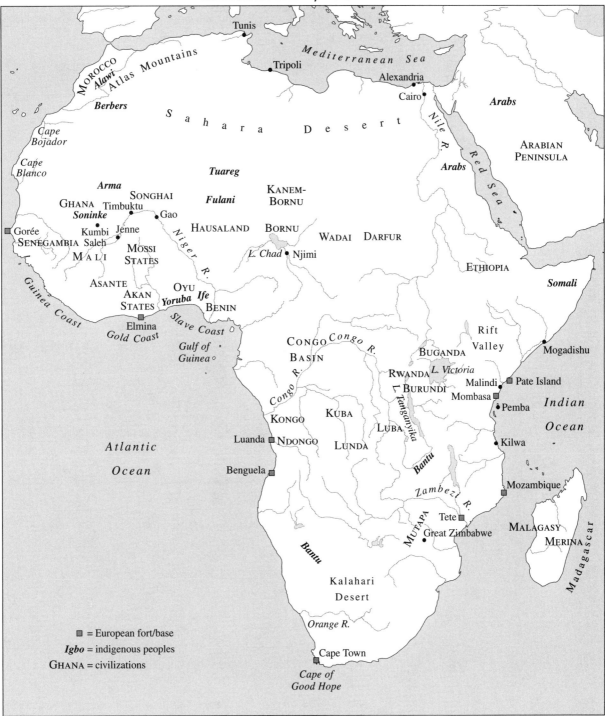

Tunis

Tripoli

Mediterranean Sea

Alexandria

Cairo

Arabs

MOROCCO
Alawi

Atlas Mountains

Berbers

Cape Bojador

Cape Blanco

S a h a r a   D e s e r t

Nile R.

Red Sea

Arabs

ARABIAN PENINSULA

Arabs

Tuareg

Arma

SONGHAI

GHANA Timbuktu

Soninke

Kumbi   Jenne
Saleh

M A L I

Gao

Fulani

KANEM-
BORNU

HAUSALAND

BORNU

L. Chad Njimi

WADAI DARFUR

ETHIOPIA

Somali

Gorée
SENEGAMBIA

MOSSI
STATES

ASANTE

Niger R.

AKAN
STATES

OYU
Yoruba *Ife*

BENIN

Elmina
Gold Coast

Guinea Coast

Slave Coast

*Gulf of
Guinea*

CONGO
BASIN

Congo R.

Congo R.

RWANDA

BURUNDI

L. Victoria

L. Tanganyika

BUGANDA

Rift
Valley

Mogadishu

Malindi
Mombasa

Pate Island

Pemba

*Indian
Ocean*

KONGO

KUBA

LUBA

Bantu

Kilwa

*Atlantic
Ocean*

Luanda NDONGO

LUNDA

Benguela

Zambezi R.

Mozambique

MUTAPA Tete

Great Zimbabwe

*MALAGASY
MERINA*

Madagascar

Bantu

Kalahari
Desert

Orange R.

Cape Town

*Cape of
Good Hope*

■ = European fort/base

Igbo = indigenous peoples

GHANA = civilizations

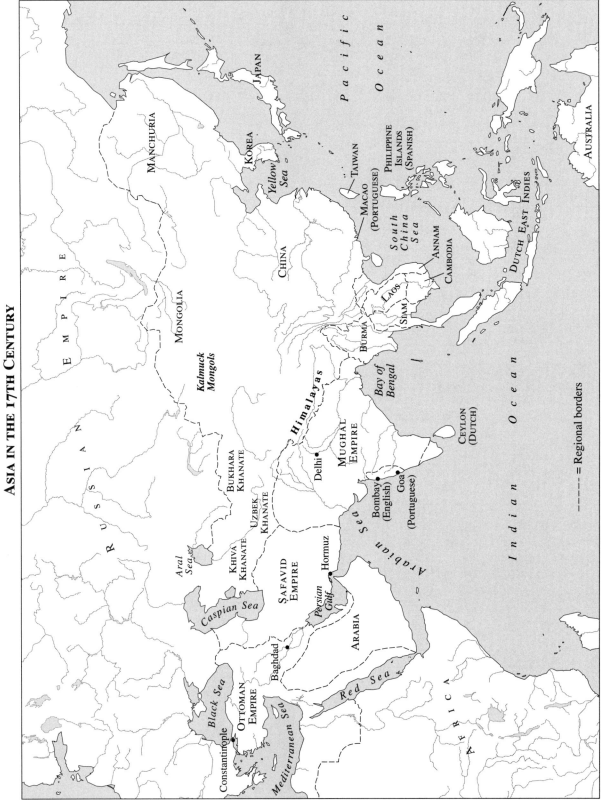

ASIA IN THE 17TH CENTURY

RUSSIAN EMPIRE

MANCHURIA

MONGOLIA

Kalmuck Mongols

JAPAN

KOREA

Yellow Sea

TAIWAN

MACAO (PORTUGUESE)

CHINA

PHILIPPINE ISLANDS (SPANISH)

Pacific Ocean

AUSTRALIA

South China Sea

ANNAM

CAMBODIA

LAOS

SIAM

BURMA

DUTCH EAST INDIES

Himalayas

Bay of Bengal

BUKHARA KHANATE

UZBEK KHANATE

Delhi

MUGHAL EMPIRE

Goa (Portuguese)

Bombay (English)

CEYLON (DUTCH)

Indian Ocean

Aral Sea

KHIVA KHANATE

SAFAVID EMPIRE

Hormuz

Persian Gulf

Arabian Sea

Caspian Sea

Baghdad

ARABIA

Red Sea

Black Sea

OTTOMAN EMPIRE

Constantinople

Mediterranean Sea

AFRICA

—— = Regional borders

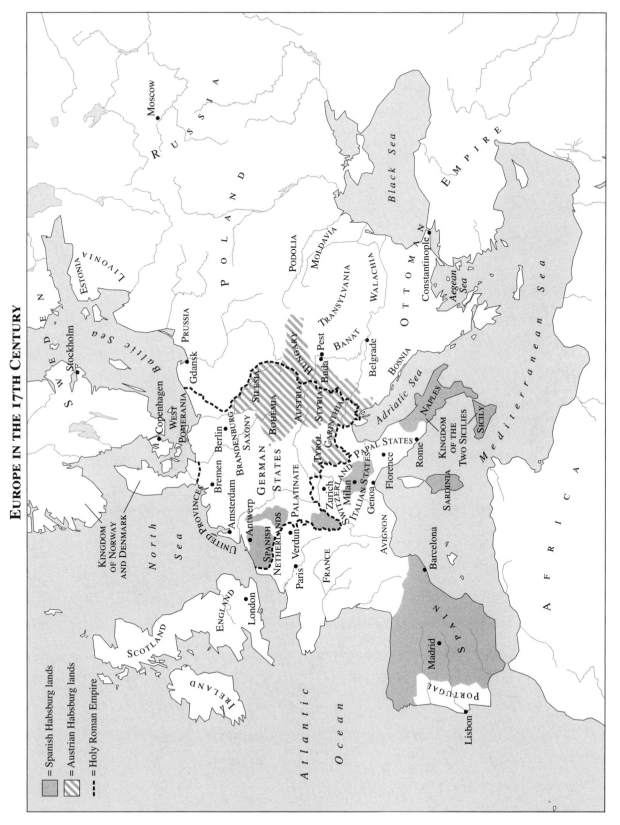

EUROPE IN THE 17TH CENTURY

= Spanish Habsburg lands

= Austrian Habsburg lands

= Holy Roman Empire

RUSSIA

Moscow

POLAND

SWEDEN

Stockholm

ESTONIA

LIVONIA

Baltic Sea

PRUSSIA

Gdansk

Copenhagen

WEST POMERANIA

KINGDOM OF NORWAY AND DENMARK

North Sea

Bremen

Berlin

BRANDENBURG

SAXONY

GERMAN STATES

Amsterdam

UNITED PROVINCES

Antwerp

SPANISH NETHERLANDS

Verdun

PALATINATE

Paris

FRANCE

AVIGNON

SCOTLAND

ENGLAND

London

IRELAND

Atlantic Ocean

Barcelona

SPAIN

Madrid

PORTUGAL

Lisbon

AFRICA

Mediterranean Sea

SARDINIA

Genoa

Florence

ITALIAN STATES

Rome

PAPAL STATES

KINGDOM OF THE TWO SICILIES

NAPLES

SICILY

Milan

Zurich

SWITZERLAND

TYROL

CARINTHIA

STYRIA

AUSTRIA

BOHEMIA

SILESIA

HUNGARY

Buda

Pest

BANAT

Belgrade

BOSNIA

Adriatic Sea

TRANSYLVANIA

WALACHIA

MOLDAVIA

PODOLIA

OTTOMAN EMPIRE

Black Sea

Constantinople

Aegean Sea

EUROPEAN COLONIZATION IN THE 17TH CENTURY

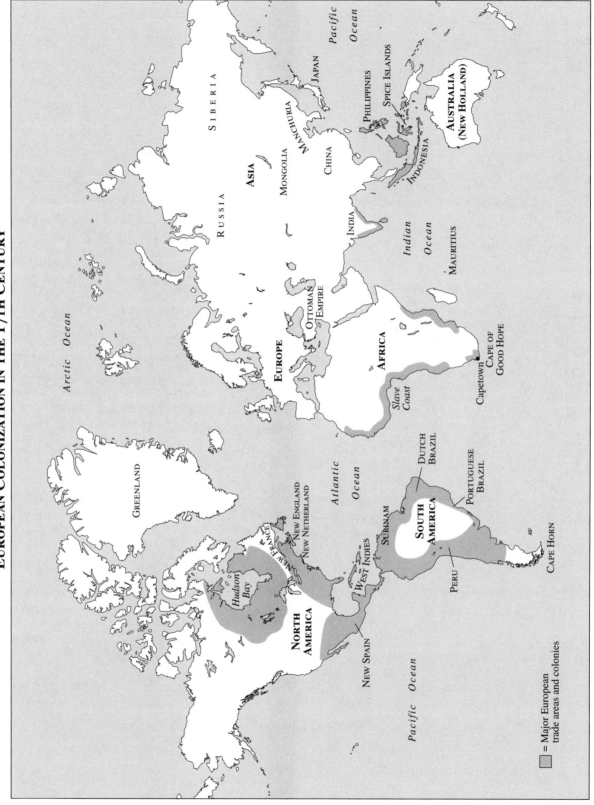

Arctic Ocean

GREENLAND

Pacific Ocean

SIBERIA

RUSSIA

ASIA

MONGOLIA

MANCHURIA

JAPAN

CHINA

PHILIPPINES

SPICE ISLANDS

INDONESIA

AUSTRALIA (NEW HOLLAND)

INDIA

Indian Ocean

MAURITIUS

OTTOMAN EMPIRE

EUROPE

AFRICA

Slave Coast

Capetown

CAPE OF GOOD HOPE

NORTH AMERICA

Hudson Bay

NEW FRANCE

NEW ENGLAND

NEW NETHERLAND

Atlantic Ocean

WEST INDIES

SURINAM

DUTCH BRAZIL

PORTUGUESE BRAZIL

SOUTH AMERICA

PERU

NEW SPAIN

CAPE HORN

Pacific Ocean

= Major European trade areas and colonies

xxx

NORTH AMERICA IN THE 17TH CENTURY

Athapascan = Native American language groups and related peoples

SOUTH AMERICA IN THE 17TH CENTURY

VENEZUELA

NEW
GRANADA

GUIANAS

San
Mateo
Bay

Amazon R.

NEW
HOLLAND

Palmares

Lima

Cuzco

PERU
Incas

PARAGUAY

Guaraní

Mato
Grosso

São Francisco R.

BRAZIL

Salvador

Pacific Ocean

Andes

Rio de Janeiro

São Paolo

Buenos Aires

PATAGONIA

Atlantic

Ocean

Cape Horn

The 17th Century

1601 - 1700

ABAHAI
Manchu leader (r. 1626-1643) and emperor of China (r. 1636-1643)

Abahai consolidated and then expanded the Manchu empire begun by his father, Nurhaci. He established the foundations for the Manchu conquest of China and the replacement of the Ming Dynasty by the Qing Dynasty.

BORN: November 28, 1592; Hetu Ala, Manchuria (now in China)

DIED: September 21, 1643; Shengjing, Manchuria (now Shenyang, China)

ALSO KNOWN AS: Nurhachi; Hong Taiji (Pinyin), Hung Taiji (Wade-Giles); Tiancong (reign name, Pinyin), T'ien-ts'ung (reign name, Wade-Giles); Chongde (reign name, Pinyin), Ch'ung-te (reign name, Wade-Giles); Qing Taizong (temple name, Pinyin), Ch'ing T'ai-tsung (temple name, Wade-Giles)

AREAS OF ACHIEVEMENT: Government and politics, warfare and conquest

EARLY LIFE
Abahai (ah-bah-hi) was the eighth son of Manchu leader Nurhaci. Little is known about his early youth, but apparently as a teen Abahai impressed his father with his fierce courage and intelligence. By the beginning of the 1600's, Nurhaci had created a unified Jurchen political state, which he originally intended to be ruled by his son Cuyen after his death. In 1613, however, when Abahai and several of Nurhaci's other sons swore that Cuyen had tried to recruit them in a conspiracy against their father, Nurhaci had Cuyen killed.

In 1616, Nurhaci reorganized his government, calling it the Later Jin, in reference to his ancestors' rule over North China during the Jin Dynasty (1116-1234). Apparently stung by the earlier ambitions of his eldest son, Nurhaci had determined to leave control of his nation to a ruling council rather than any single individual. Accordingly, in 1616, he named the four senior *beile* (or princes), who were to assist him in the administration of his growing kingdom. The four *beile* were Nurhaci's three sons Daisan, Manggultai, and Abahai, and a nephew, Amin. In 1621, the four *beile* began to take monthly turns in the administration of national affairs.

Nurhaci warned his sons against choosing a strong, vigorous leader, predicting that such a man's only goal would be to satisfy his own ambition. Upon Nurhaci's death, in September of 1626, the four *beile* nominated Abahai to become the second khan of the Later Jin. Clearly out of deference to their father's wishes, but also in keeping with their own ambitions, the *beile* expected Abahai to share power with them, and in the beginning, during all state functions, the four *beile* sat at the same level. Each prince commanded a single army banner (a military administrative unit that Nurhaci had created).

Abahai, however, having secured the title khan for himself, had no intention of sharing his power with his siblings in the long term. Sensing the group's fear of their other brother, Dorgon, Abahai convinced them to force the suicide of Dorgon's mother, the empress Hsiaolieh. In doing so, however, Abahai was able to gain control over another banner, thereby tipping the balance of power in his favor. He used this military advantage, as well as his political skills, to consolidate his rule and expand the empire that his father had begun.

LIFE'S WORK
In 1629, Abahai abolished the monthly rotation of *beile*. One year later, he imprisoned Amin for a variety of offenses, and Daisan and Manggultai "voluntarily" swore allegiance to the khan. Upon Manggultai's death, Abahai declared his brother to have been a traitor and took control of his banner as well. In consolidating his power in Manchuria and expanding his sphere of influence into China, Abahai relied on two separate sources of support: Chinese military and civilian officials serving the khan and younger Jurchen military officers who opposed the strictly hereditary power of the princes.

Abahai's relationship with the Chinese provides an interesting reflection of both his political cunning and his historical acumen. He listened carefully to the advice of Chinese officials on political and administrative policies and acted on their suggestions to centralize his government. Moreover, he cautiously paid heed to their exhortations to fight the Ming Dynasty (1368-1644) and plan the conquest of China. On May 14, 1636, Abahai proclaimed himself emperor, changing the name of his dynasty to Qing, and his reign title to Chongde. (In the Chinese dynastic chronicles, his temple name would be Qing Taizong.) Nevertheless, Abahai was exceptionally fearful of his people's being Sinicized, and he embarked on a series of measures to keep the Chinese and Manchus (a term he adopted for the Juchen in 1636) separate forever.

Abahai's special handling of the Chinese was militarily astute and politically brilliant. Although Nurhaci had also employed Chinese people, his son developed a comprehensive program for recruiting Chinese military, technical, and political experts. In warring against the Ming Dynasty, Abahai took special pains to lure the Chinese military commanders to his side. He offered them substantial rewards for abandoning the Ming Dynasty and defecting to the Manchus. Moreover, Abahai was careful to insist that his own troops refrain from looting or any other conduct that would alienate the Chinese population. Chinese officers who had previously submitted to the Manchus often appeared in Chinese towns or garrisons to relate their own good fortunes and recruit people to the Manchu side. In this manner, countless Chinese not only submitted to Manchu rule but also came to serve Abahai loyally.

Chinese soldiers not only served as crucial allies in Abahai's struggles against his brothers, but also frequently were instrumental in Manchu victories over fortified Ming towns, thanks to their mastery of artillery. Their skill in combat alone made them important members of the Manchu army. Equally important, however, was the fact that Abahai was preparing for the possible conquest of China. To this end, he needed knowledgeable officials, already familiar with the local politics and bureaucracy of the vast nation, to serve him and his successors should they become emperors. Undoubtedly, Abahai was aware of the ancient Chinese adage that "one may conquer China on horseback, but one needs learned officials to rule it." Under Chinese guidance, he established a chancellery, or literary office, which he gradually developed into a secretariat. He also borrowed from China the concept of six boards and a censorate. All these measures were intended to facilitate the eventual transfer of power from Ming China to the Manchus.

Abahai understood that many of his younger officers sought a more accessible route of advancement. He promoted young men on the basis of their courage, service, and loyalty and created a network of capable and trustworthy officers. In 1637, Abahai created the Council of Deliberative Officials, composed of lieutenant and deputy-lieutenant generals. Princes and generals were excluded on the grounds that they were too often absent and lived too far from the capital.

Abahai also sought to attract non-Chinese people into his burgeoning empire. Accordingly, he created in 1638 the Li Fan Yuan (board of colonial affairs), which would oversee the management of relations between Manchus and those Mongolians who submitted to the Qing. Eventually, the board's purview came to include Tibetans and Uighurs as well. Although not personally given to religious beliefs, Abahai sponsored Lamaism, the form of Buddhism prevalent among the Mongolians and Tibet-

ans, and established an excellent relationship with the Dalai and Panchen Lamas. Understanding the value of symbolism, he secured the great seal of the Mongol khan and began to style himself as the successor of Genghis Khan. The seal accorded Abahai enormous prestige in inner Asia and enhanced his potential claim to China.

A masterful politician and an insightful statesman, Abahai was also capable of great personal courage and strategic brilliance on the battlefield. Immediately after his ascendancy to the Later Jin throne, he had embarked on a program to defeat or at least neutralize his father's Chinese nemesis, General Yuan Chung Huan. Failing to achieve the former goal, Abahai moved, in November, 1629, through the territory of the Karacin and Tumed Mongolians, around Yuan's forces, and into China proper through the Xifeng (Hsi-feng) and Kupei Passes. Yuan was forced to hurry his troops to Beijing to defend against the invaders, who were at the capital's gates. Yuan's success in driving off the enemy did not mitigate his failure to have prevented the invasion in the first place, and the Ming court ordered him arrested and dismembered. Among the reasons for the Chinese general's demise were the rumors, planted by Abahai's spies, that Yuan was planning to defect to the Manchus.

With his Chinese adversary removed, Abahai began, in the fall of 1631, an attack upon the heavily fortified garrison complex at Daling He (Ta-ling Ho). During the complicated siege, Abahai himself led a contingent of about two hundred men and successfully routed a rescue army of seven thousand. In the end, Abahai's diplomacy and military skill secured the Chinese commander's surrender. Subsequently, many of Abahai's military maneuvers in China proper were actually designed and executed by Chinese officers in the service of the Manchus.

From 1631 to 1636, in addition to successful forays into China, Abahai's forces succeeded in subjugating the Chahar Mongolians and gained valuable horse-breeding grounds. During the closing days of 1638, the Qing emperor personally led an army into Korea and within one month secured the submission of the Korean king. In subsequent years, most of northeast Asia fell under Manchu control.

On March 18, 1642, the Manchus captured Song Shan and, shortly thereafter, Jinzhou, two strategic Chinese towns. With these victories, the fall of Beijing and the Ming Dynasty seemed inevitable. The first emperor of the Qing Dynasty, however, did not live long enough to see this transpire. On September 21, 1643, Abahai died of natural causes at Shengjing. His brother Dorgon would complete the conquest of the Ming, and his oldest son, Fulin, would become the Shunzhi emperor, the first emperor of the unified Qing Dynasty.

SIGNIFICANCE

Abahai was a rare man in the annals of history. Skillful at the politics of survival, he was equally at home on the battlefield. In the ultimate analysis, however, his genius lay in attracting capable men, earning and maintaining their loyalty, and effecting the best of their suggestions into policy. In these matters, he was even more successful than his father, Nurhaci. Not since Genghis Khan had there been such a talented leader in the steppes of northeast Asia. Though perhaps lacking the overall military genius of Genghis, Abahai was particularly strong in areas where even the "khan of khans" had been lacking. Abahai was an educated man who valued the lessons of history and had a sense of the future that bordered on prescience.

Having used Chinese advisers and military men to his advantage, Abahai nevertheless determined to keep the Manchus racially and culturally distinct from the Chinese. He repeatedly exhorted his Manchu followers to read the history of the Jin and learn from their earlier mistakes. His decision to forbid further use of the terms *Juchen* or *Chien-chou* may have been an effort to disavow the assimilation and political demise of his ancestors. Abahai predicted that the ultimate penalty for Sinicization would be the disappearance of the Manchus as a people. Having essentially guaranteed the Manchu conquest of China, he perhaps foresaw that his people might someday vanish. In a sense, the life of Abahai, as it relates to the history of the Manchus, constitutes an epilogue to a classical tragedy. Destined to create an empire that included China, the Manchus were also destined to fulfill Abahai's ominous prophesy and disappear as a people.

—*Hilel B. Salomon*

FURTHER READING

Crossley, Pamela Kyle. *The Manchus*. Malden, Mass.: Blackwell, 2002. A history of the Manchu people, including information about Nurhaci and succeeding members of the Qing Dynasty.

Hummel, Arthur W., ed. *Eminent Chinese of the Ch'ing Period, 1644-1912*. 2 vols. Washington, D.C.: Government Printing Office, 1943-1944. Volume 1 contains an excellent biography of Abahai.

Kessler, Lawrence D. *K'ang-hsi and the Consolidation of Ch'ing Rule, 1661-1684*. Chicago: University of Chicago Press, 1976. Although concentrating on the achievements of Abahai's grandson, the Kangxi emperor, the author provides an analysis of the administrative beginnings of the Qing under Abahai's direction.

Michael, Franz. *The Origin of Manchu Rule in China: Frontier and Bureaucracy as Interacting Forces in the Chinese Empire*. Baltimore: Johns Hopkins University Press, 1942. Reprint. New York: Octagon Books, 1965. A somewhat controversial but still incisive discussion of the frontier state and the processes undertaken by Nurhaci and Abahai to prepare for the conquest of China.

Oxnam, Robert B. *Ruling from Horseback: Manchu Politics in the Oboi Regency, 1661-1669*. Chicago: University of Chicago Press, 1975. In searching for the origins of the concept of regency and the nature of Oboi's policies, the author devotes considerable attention to Abahai.

Peterson, Willard J. *The Ching Empire to 1809*. Vol. 9 in *The Cambridge History of China*. New York: Cambridge University Press, 2002. Covers political, social, military, and economic developments in China from 1644 to 1809.

Roth, Gertraude. "The Manchu-Chinese Relationship, 1618-1636." In *From Ming to Ch'ing: Conquest, Region, and Continuity in Seventeenth-Century China*, edited by Jonathan D. Spence and John E. Wills, Jr. New Haven, Conn.: Yale University Press, 1979. This chapter explores the role of Chinese advisers in Abahai's consolidation of power and his establishment of the Qing.

Struve, Lynn A., ed. and trans. *Voices from the Ming-Qing Cataclysm: China in Tigers' Jaws*. New Haven, Conn.: Yale University Press, 1993. Personal accounts of Chinese life from the waning years of the Ming Dynasty through the Manchu takeover and eventual Qing rule.

Wakeman, Frederic, Jr. *The Great Enterprise: The Manchu Reconstruction of Imperial Order in Seventeenth-Century China*. 2 vols. Berkeley: University of California Press, 1985. This work is destined to be a classic in the study of Chinese history. Wakeman presents a comprehensive study of the Manchu conquest and rule over China. Volume 1 devotes much attention to Abahai's political and military activities.

SEE ALSO: Chen Shu; Chongzhen; Dorgon; Kangxi; Liu Yin; Shunzhi; Tianqi; Wang Fuzhi; Zheng Chenggong.

RELATED ARTICLES in *Great Events from History: The Seventeenth Century, 1601-1700:* 1616-1643: Rise of the Manchus; April 25, 1644: End of the Ming Dynasty; June 6, 1644: Manchus Take Beijing.

'ABBĀS THE GREAT
Persian shah (r. 1587-1629)

The most well known of all Islamic-era shahs of Persia, 'Abbās the Great was the chief architect of the modern Iranian state. His legacy includes great achievements in architecture, literature, textiles, and painting.

BORN: January 27, 1571; Herát, Persia (now in Afghanistan)

DIED: January 19, 1629; Ashraf, Mázandarán, Persia (now in Iran)

ALSO KNOWN AS: 'Abbās I

AREAS OF ACHIEVEMENT: Government and politics, warfare and conquest, military, patronage of the arts, religion and theology

EARLY LIFE

The second son of the relatively weak and incompetent Soltān Moḥammad Shāh (r. 1578-1587), 'Abbās (later known as 'Abbās the Great) spent his youth in Mashhad and Herát under the tutelage of a regional governor. Royal intrigue and strife between the royal family and Persian tribal military leaders led to the assassination of his mother, the ambitious Queen Khayronnesa Begum, and his older brother, the crown prince Hamzeh. 'Abbās himself at the age of sixteen, led by a second guardian and tutor, deposed his father after a successful march on the royal capital at Qazvīn.

On a historical note, an Iranian dynasty named for their Sufi ancestor, the Persian mystic Ṣafī od-Dīn (1252/1253-1334), established control in 1501 over the region that constitutes what is now called Iran. Known as the Ṣafavids, they made up the first native dynasty to control the region since the Arab Muslims had overthrown the Sāsānian Dynasty (224-651) nearly nine centuries earlier. Reigning for more than two hundred years, the Ṣafavids developed and expanded a middle Islamic empire between the Ottomans, centered in Turkey to the west, and the Mughals, in the Indian subcontinent to the east. Modern Iran owes to the Ṣafavids the territorial configuration of the country and its national religion, Twelver Shia Islam, which they established as the official religion, thus enhancing Iranian distinctiveness and separateness from their Sunni Muslim neighbors and contributing later to their sense of cultural and political nationalism.

In all, eleven Ṣafavid monarchs ruled over Persia, the last two in name only, from 1722, when a successful invasion and occupation by the Afghans took place, until 1736, when Nāder Shāh (r. 1736-1747) established his own short-lived dynasty. Among the Ṣafavid monarchs, the most famous and important was Shāh 'Abbās I ('Abbās the Great), who ruled for more than forty years.

At his accession, 'Abbās faced three serious tasks. First was the internal need to establish control and authority over local dynasties that had reasserted themselves during his father's reign and the tribal leaders, mostly Turkoman, who constituted a Ṣafavid military aristocracy that had developed from the dynasty's early days. Second was another internal issue, that of securing the throne against other claimants or threats from within the royal family. Third was the monumental chore of defending Persia against perennial incursions by the powerful Ottomans to the west and the troublesome Uzbeks to the east.

LIFE'S WORK

From the beginning of his reign, 'Abbās focused his attention on the organization of the military and the Ottoman and Uzbek threats. In 1590, ending a war that had begun early in his father's reign, 'Abbās signed the unfavorable Treaty of Istanbul with the Ottomans so as to avoid having to deal simultaneously with two military fronts. He was now in a position to challenge the Uzbeks, who had occupied Mashhad and Herát for a decade. He regained those two important cities.

At the same time, 'Abbās began a long-term reorganization of the corps of musketeers and the artillery corps and formed a new cavalry corps paid directly out of the royal treasury and composed of former slaves, prisoners of war, and others, many of them Georgians and Circassians, who would be loyal to the Crown rather than to regional tribal affiliations. Subsequently, he was able to quell revolts by tribal leaders and groups, to dispose of the governor-tutor who had helped him attain the throne, and to proceed to pacify various Iranian provinces. In effect, he had permanently tipped the scales in favor of the Iranian city and settled life as opposed to earlier rural and nomadic ways. He was effecting a centralized governmental administration that would be his legacy in Persia in succeeding centuries. His annexation of vassal states and his incorporation of vast amounts of territory into Crown lands were other dimensions of this policy.

By 1603, however, 'Abbās was ready to confront the Ottomans again on his own terms. In 1605, the Ṣafavid army inflicted a great defeat on them near Tabriz, regaining that important city and former Iranian capital in the process. A new treaty in 1612 reestablished old borders more favorable to Iran. In the meantime, 'Abbās had annexed the island of Bahrain in 1601-1602. Later, in 1622, with British assistance, he took Hormuz Island from the Portuguese. In 1623-1624, 'Abbās broke the peace he had made with the Ottomans and reclaimed Kurdish territory to the west. In short, as of the first quarter of the seventeenth century, 'Abbās had made the Ṣafavid Empire as large territorially as Persia would ever be.

When 'Abbās ascended the throne, the Iranian population was suffering from wretched living conditions. By the end of his reign, the economic lot of ordinary Iranians was better than it had ever been in history. One of the reasons for the improvement was the stability his military and centralizing policies achieved. Another reason has to do with the energy and resources he invested into improving communication and transportation in Persia by numerous construction projects of roads, bridges, and caravansaries. Other factors are apparent in the king's development of Eṣfahan.

In 1598, 'Abbās had moved the Ṣafavid capital from Qazvīn to Eṣfahan. He then undertook great projects of construction in his new capital, building avenues, palaces, mosques, and gardens. He established commercial and diplomatic ties with the Portuguese, the Dutch, and the British. The multiracial composition of his military corps and his relocation of several thousand Armenian families from Azerbaijan to a new Jolfa in Eṣfahan reflected a tolerant attitude on 'Abbās's part in general toward races and creeds. This led to the presence of foreign merchants and orders of Christian missionaries. He hoped, through good relations with Europe, to form an alliance against the Ottomans, which never happened. What did happen was economic growth, to which his interest in the arts also contributed. For example, 'Abbās established textile workshops for export production that were the ancestors of contemporary Iranian carpet-weaving firms.

On the negative side of the ledger, it was in dealing with the problem of royal succession and protection of his throne that 'Abbās exhibited uncharacteristic shortsightedness and instituted policies that contributed in the long run to the decline of the Ṣafavids. Plagued no doubt by the memory of the assassinations of his mother and brother, 'Abbās was suspicious to the point of paranoia about the aims of members of the royal family and

tribal leaders and princes who might rally around them or use them. After deposing his father, 'Abbās had him blinded and apparently imprisoned. He ordered the executions of many tribal princes. He had two of his brothers blinded as well. In 1615, he ordered his eldest son, the crown prince Safi Mīrzā, assassinated, and later ordered the blinding of another son and two grandsons. (According to Islamic tradition, a blind person cannot succeed to a throne.) Furthermore, he confined potential heirs to the harem, preventing them from receiving any training necessary for future leadership roles. At 'Abbās's death, because none of his brothers or sons was alive or able to ascend the throne, his grandson Sam Mīrzā became the sixth Ṣafavid monarch with the title Shāh Safi I.

SIGNIFICANCE

Without falling into the popular error of assuming that subsequent Ṣafavid rulers added no luster to the Iranian Empire and without minimizing the accomplishments of 'Abbās the Great's Ṣafavid predecessors, one can hardly

'Abbās the Great. (Library of Congress)

5

overemphasize the achievements of this astute ruler. To be sure, ʿAbbās had his major shortcomings, among them his paranoia with respect to threats to the throne and a superstitious tendency (an astrologer's warning had contributed to his decision to order the assassination of Prince Safi Mīrzā). In addition, he was a despot and hardly enlightened with respect to the rights of his subjects.

Yet ʿAbbās had uncommon vision and sense of purpose. He saw the need for secure borders, a centralized state and administrative system, and a standing army loyal to the Crown. He understood the significance of Twelver Shia Islam as the cultural core to Iranian life and paid special attention to Shia Muslim shrines, particularly those at Ardabīl and Mashhad, and to his role as a Sufi leader in the Ṣafavid order. He had a sense of the grandeur of Iranian traditions, which he expressed most forcefully in making Eṣfahan one of the world's great capitals, leading to its hyperbolic epithet as "Half the World." Yet he accomplished much more, especially in terms of his legacy to Iran. Accordingly, he stands in many Iranian minds alongside Cyrus the Great, Darius the Great, Shāpūr I, and others as one of the greatest Iranian monarchs.

ʿAbbās's manifold legacy played a significant part in the imperial government of Persia (renamed Iran in 1935) of the short-lived Pahlavi Dynasty (1926-1979) and in the Islamic Republic of Iran instituted by Ayatollah Khomeini in 1979. In the former era, Reza Shah Pahlavi and Moḥammad Reza Pahlavi strove both to carry forward ʿAbbās's policies of centralizing power and to instill in the Iranian population loyalty based primarily on obedience and respect toward the traditional institution of Iranian monarchy. They modeled their behavior as absolute monarchs on such historical forebears as ʿAbbās the Great. ʿAbbās's particular devotion to the Twelver Shia faith, which the Ṣafavids promulgated as an official religion, became the theocratic basis for the Iranian state.

Of equal significance is that Persia survived to inherit such legacies from ʿAbbās. His strengthening of the Ṣafavid state and provision of a model for Ṣafavid, Afshar, Zand, and Qajar successor monarchs were efficacious in giving Persia the means to avoid becoming directly subject to colonial powers in the nineteenth and early twentieth centuries, in contrast to the experience of most of Persia's Near Eastern, Central Asian, and South Asian neighbors.

—*Michael Craig Hillmann*

FURTHER READING

Dimand, M. S. "Ṣafavid Textiles and Rugs." In *Highlights of Persian Art*, edited by Richard Ettinghausen and Ehsan Yarshater. New York: Wittenborn Art Books, 1981. Surveys sixteenth and seventeenth century production, with emphasis on achievements during the reigns of Shah Ṭahāsp I (r. 1524-1576) and ʿAbbās.

Eskandar Beg Monshi. *The History of Shah ʿAbbās the Great*. 2 vols. Translated by Roger M. Savory. Boulder, Colo.: Westview Press, 1978. A concise, comprehensive history by the chief secretary of ʿAbbās's court and the most important source of Ṣafavid history in general. Ends with a discussion of ʿAbbās's death and funeral.

Jackson, Peter, and Laurence Lockhart, eds. *The Timurid and Ṣafavid Periods*. Vol. 6 in *The Cambridge History of Iran*. New York: Cambridge University Press, 1986. Includes four chapters dealing with ʿAbbās: "The Ṣafavid Period," a chronological treatment of the period with a biographical sketch of his life and a characterization and assessment of his reign; "Carpets and Textiles"; "Ṣafavid Architecture"; and "The Arts in the Ṣafavid Period."

Mathee, Rudolph P. *The Politics of Trade in Ṣafavid Iran: Silk for Silver, 1600-1730*. New York: Cambridge University Press, 1999. This study of the Ṣafavid silk trade contains a chapter about ʿAbbās and the Iranian economy, political situation, and anti-Ottoman diplomacy during his reign.

Melville, Charles, ed. *Ṣafavid Persia: The History and Politics of an Islamic Society*. New York: St. Martin's Press, 1996. Contains fifteen essays that examine historiography, religious policies, and the silk industry under the Ṣafavids.

Savory, Roger M. *Iran Under the Ṣafavids*. New York: Cambridge University Press, 1980. A treatment that emphasizes the monarchy and the royal court by the leading Western authority on Ṣafavid history.

Welch, Anthony. *Artists for the Shah: Late Sixteenth Century Painting at the Imperial Court of Iran*. New Haven, Conn.: Yale University Press, 1976. Describes the transitional nature of Ṣafavid painting of the period with political and historical contexts.

_____. *Shah ʿAbbās and the Arts of Isfahan*. New York: Asia Society, 1973. A catalog of an important exhibition at Asia House Gallery in New York City and Harvard University's Fogg Art Museum in Cambridge, Massachusetts.

JOHN ALDEN
English-born American colonist

One of the signers of the Mayflower Compact, Alden helped to direct the English colony at Plymouth, contributed to the business affairs of the colony, and participated in the colony's negotiations with Native Americans and other New England colonies.

BORN: c. 1599; Southampton, Hampshire, England, or Harwich, Essex, England
DIED: September 12, 1687; Duxborough, Plymouth Colony (now Duxbury, Massachusetts)
AREAS OF ACHIEVEMENT: Government and politics, diplomacy

EARLY LIFE

Very little is known about the early life of John Alden. According to some records, Alden's parents were probably George and Jane Alden of Southampton, England. Other sources suggest that Alden came from Harwich, England. An Alden family living there in the late 1500's was related through marriage to Christopher Jones, the captain of the *Mayflower*, the vessel that brought the pilgrims to Plymouth Colony in present-day Massachusetts. According to tradition, Alden was a well-educated young man.

When Alden was around twenty-one years old, he was hired at Southampton as the cooper (barrel maker) on the *Mayflower* for its journey to North America. Prior to that time, Alden had been employed to make and repair wine casks in Southampton. Alden's contract for working on the *Mayflower* gave him the option of staying in America on arrival or returning to England. Maintaining the barrels that provided the necessary drinking fluids and food for the passengers on the *Mayflower* was a job of vital importance.

The crew of the *Mayflower* intended to sail to Virginia but instead landed at the rocky coast of New England in November of 1620. Before disembarking at Plymouth Bay, the pilgrim leaders drew up the Mayflower Compact. It was signed by forty-one adult males on November 11, 1620. John Alden, the youngest man on the *Mayflower*, was the seventh man to sign the document. A strong, vigorous individual, Alden was purportedly the first person to step off of the *Mayflower* and set foot on the shore of the New World.

LIFE'S WORK

During the cold, brutal winter of 1620-1621, more than half of the 102 passengers of the *Mayflower* died. Alden helped care for the sick and the dying. One of those to succumb in January, 1621, was the wife of Captain Miles Standish. According to tradition, Standish had developed a close friendship with Alden during the voyage and asked Alden to extend a marriage proposal to Priscilla Mullins on his behalf. She had been left alone when her parents and brother died during the harsh first winter at Plymouth. As depicted in the famous, highly imaginative poem of Henry Wadsworth Longfellow, *The Courtship of Miles Standish* (1858), an ensuing relationship developed between Alden and Mullins, leading to their romance and marriage. They were married sometime during 1622 or 1623. Records indicate that they had eleven children, five sons and six daughters.

When the land was divided among the Plymouth colonists in 1623, Alden was granted an estimated four acres on the north side of Plymouth Colony. Alden soon rose to a prominent position in Plymouth. In May, 1627, he and seven other important men of Plymouth made an agreement to pay off debts that had been incurred to merchants in London, England, establishing the colony. Alden was appointed as an assistant to the governor and to Plymouth Court in 1631. He admirably carried out his duties in both appointments for many years.

In 1632, Alden, his family, and a few other families established the town of Duxborough (later called Duxbury) north of Plymouth. Alden's farm in Duxborough consisted of about 170 acres (69 hectares) of land. Alden continued to serve as the assistant governor of Plymouth Colony for most of his life, as well as serving on many different committees and councils of war, and as a surveyor of roadways. Alden served as an ensign under Captain Standish in the Duxborough Military Company and was responsible for training members of the Duxborough militia to defend their town against Native American uprisings. He was also a mediator in boundary disputes between Native Americans and settlers.

In 1634, while he was serving on a committee to oversee trade along the Kennebec River, a dispute over fur trading arose between members of the Plymouth Colony and the Massachusetts Bay Colony. The dispute escalated, shots were exchanged, and an individual from each colony was killed. Although Alden was not involved in the shootings, authorities of the Massachusetts Bay Colony had him arrested and imprisoned in Boston. Through negotiations carried out by Miles Standish, however, Alden was soon released.

During the 1640's through the 1670's, Alden's service to the Plymouth Colony continued to expand. In 1646, he served on a council of war to deal with tensions between the colonists and the Narragansett Indians. From 1656 to 1658, he served as the colony's treasurer. In 1667, he served on a council of war that made military preparations to counter threats by the Dutch and the French. In 1665 and again in 1677, he served as deputy governor of the colony. In his later years, Alden served on numerous juries, including the jury for a witch trial in which the accused was exonerated and the accuser was found guilty of libel.

As a reward for some of Alden's indispensable service to the colony, the Plymouth Court awarded him both cash and land grants in the 1660's so he could better provide for his large family. During the 1670's and 1680's, he distributed his landholdings between his sons through a series of deeds. Although not officially confirmed, existing records indicate that his wife preceded him in death. The last known mention of her being with him is at the funeral of Governor John Winslow in 1680. An unselfish man, Alden died on September 12, 1687, leaving a rather small estate. His death was commemorated in two broadsides. The only member of the Mayflower company to outlive him was Mary Allerton. Although it is known that Alden was buried in South Duxborough, the exact location of his grave remains uncertain.

SIGNIFICANCE

A founder of Plymouth Colony, Alden quickly rose from the status of a common seaman aboard the *Mayflower* to positions of prominent public leadership. He was the seventh signer of the Mayflower Compact, the cofounder of the town of Duxborough, and a negotiator in several land deals with Native Americans in New England. He was a strong supporter of the beliefs of the pilgrims and acted unselfishly to promote the welfare of the colony.

A man of high character, industry, integrity, sound judgment, and innumerable talents, Alden served Plymouth Colony in a variety of capacities for more than sixty-five years. As an assistant governor, his wisdom and administrative abilities were utilized under five different governors over a period of forty-five years. He also served as acting governor on several occasions. He helped write and review many laws for the colony, arbitrated disputes, and provided astute direction during times of conflict and impending wars with Native Americans and settlers from other countries. Alden's descendants include many noted military and professional individuals, including United States presidents John Adams and John Quincy Adams.

—Alvin K. Benson

FURTHER READING

Anderson, Douglas. *William Bradford's Books: Of Plimmoth Plantation and the Printed Word.* Baltimore: Johns Hopkins University Press, 2003. Contains a review and exploration of the writings of Governor William Bradford about the history and people of Plymouth Colony up until 1647. Extensive bibliography and index.

Banks, Charles Edward. *The English Ancestry and Homes of the Pilgrim Fathers.* New York: Society of Mayflower Descendants, 1929. Reprint. Baltimore: Genealogical, 1962. The ancestry and homes established by the pilgrims who came to Plymouth on the *Mayflower* in 1620 are traced and documented, with John Alden's father being cited as George Alden of Southampton, England.

Collier, Christopher, and James Lincoln Collier. *Pilgrims and Puritans.* New York: Benchmark Books, 1998. Written primarily for young readers, this book provides coverage of the history of Plymouth Colony. Good bibliography and index.

Deetz, James, and Patricia Scott Deetz. *The Times of Their Lives: Life, Love, and Death in Plymouth Colony.* New York: W. H. Freeman, 2000. The daily social lives and politics of the Plymouth colonists are carefully documented, including some of the leadership and service provided by John Alden to the colony. Contains maps, illustrations, bibliography, and index.

Stimson, Richard Alden. *Thirteen Generations in the New World.* Lincoln, Maine: Westchester Press, 2000. An account of the lives and contributions of John and Priscilla Alden and their family in Plymouth and Duxborough.

Stoddard, Francis Russell. *The Truth About the Pilgrims.* New York: Society of Mayflower Descendants, 1952. Reprint. Baltimore: Genealogical, 1973. An excellent

treatise about the Pilgrims who were involved in founding Plymouth Colony, including insights about John and Priscilla Alden.

SEE ALSO: William Bradford; Miles Standish.

RELATED ARTICLES in *Great Events from History: The Seventeenth Century, 1601-1700:* May 14, 1607: Jamestown Is Founded; December 26, 1620: Pilgrims Arrive in North America; March 22, 1622-October, 1646: Powhatan Wars; May, 1630-1643: Great Puritan Migration; September 8, 1643: Confederation of the United Colonies of New England.

ALEXANDER VII
Italian pope (1655-1667)

Before his rise to the Papacy, Alexander was a key if unsuccessful player at the negotiations for ending the Thirty Years' War. As pope he was a major patron of the architect Gian Lorenzo Bernini, who greatly enhanced the Roman cityscape. Largely ignored by major European powers, Alexander was a caretaker who exchanged substance for style as he helped remake Rome into a world capital.

BORN: February 13, 1599; Siena, Republic of Florence (now in Italy)

DIED: May 22, 1667; Rome, Papal States (now in Italy)

ALSO KNOWN AS: Fabio Chigi (given name)

AREAS OF ACHIEVEMENT: Architecture, art, patronage of the arts, government and politics, religion and theology

EARLY LIFE

Alexander VII, named Fabio Chigi at birth, was born into a noble family of Siena whose roots date back four centuries but whose fortunes had declined greatly. Chigi was a sickly child, and ill health would plague him his entire life. Chigi spent five years studying philosophy and law at the University of Siena and four years there earning his doctorate in theology (1626).

Pope Urban VIII presented his fellow Tuscan with a position on the Church's highest court of justice and named him vice legate to Ferrara, a position he held for five years. In 1635, Urban appointed him bishop of Nardò and inquisitor in Malta, at which point he was ordained a priest. In June, 1639, Chigi was sent to Cologne as a Papal Nuncio. On October 5, 1644, he became the Papacy's representative in the negotiations at Münster to

bring about an end to the Thirty Years' War. In the ensuing talks, the Protestant states of Germany and their ally, France, outmaneuvered or ignored Chigi and the pro-Catholic Habsburgs and framed a 1648 treaty called the Treaty (or Peace) of Westphalia, which no papal representatives signed.

Despite this failure to protect Roman Catholic interests, Chigi was named papal secretary of state in 1651 by Pope Innocent X and was named cardinal on February 19, 1652. He advanced his interests in art by cataloging all the paintings contained in Siena's churches. The College of Cardinals elected Fabio Chigi pope on April 7, 1655, after nearly three months of deliberation. He received a single vote against his candidacy—his own. Though Cardinal Jules Mazarin of France, regent for King Louis XIV, did not attend, his supporters tried to block Chigi because of his opposition to France's pro-Protestant stance in the Münster negotiations. The new pope's relationship with Europe's most significant Catholic power would always be rocky.

LIFE'S WORK

Chigi took the name Alexander in honor of the twelfth century Sienese pope, Alexander III Bandinelli (1159-1181). An enemy of nepotism, Alexander VII went so far as to ban his Sienese kin from Rome in April of 1655, but after two years, he relented and family members rushed to Rome. He rewarded many with lucrative positions in his patronage, following the standard model of the day.

Alexander preferred the company of scholars, writers, and artists, and he shared the Humanistic interests of the era. He sought to transform Rome into a true world capital whose idealized beauty would reflect the power and glory of the Church. He wrote the dedicatory inscriptions for his many building projects in Rome, some of which were the incomplete projects of earlier popes; the list includes the churches of St. Andrea della Valla, St. Ivo, and St. Peter's. He initiated another thirty-six major renovations across the city, which together changed the face of Rome. Major streets, such as the Corso, were widened and straightened, both for aesthetic reasons and for the convenience of the rapidly multiplying carriages that filled them. Alexander tried, but failed, to centralize Rome's many marketplaces, and he drove merchants away from the Pantheon. Repairs to the Pantheon's porch were completed, a project begun a century before. He had piazzas, or squares, in front of major churches or palaces expanded and regularized, with both utility and aesthetics in mind. At the northern gate into Rome—the entrance through which representatives of the great powers would pass—he created a wide piazza in which visitors were greeted by twin churches and long, straight avenues that reached deep into the city.

The most famous of Alexander's projects was St. Peter's Square. Under his patronage, the great Italian architect, sculptor, and painter Gian Lorenzo Bernini (1598-1680) designed the open space bounded by the colossal colonnade that reaches out from the church like two great arms encompassing the world. Work began in August, 1657, and was completed in 1671. Like his other piazza projects, this new space was to serve as a great open theater for church ceremonies, in the dramatic Baroque tradition. At St. Peter's, the theatrics were continued in Bernini's creation of the grand staircase known as the Scala Regia (1663-1666), which led from the square to the papal apartments at the Vatican; in the Cathedra Petri (1657-1666), a multimedia shrine for the throne of Saint Peter; and in Alexander's own tomb (1672-1678), which Alexander had ordered as soon as he became pope.

The disease-ridden pontiff (he had serious bladder and kidney problems and had lost all of his teeth to dental disease while in Münster) meditated often on death, and he slept with his own coffin in his bedroom. Given all the work proceeding at the Vatican, Alexander tended to reside in the fifteenth century Quirinal Palace in Rome, and he had it redecorated by Italian painter and architect Pietro da Cortona, one of the pope's few commissions for painting.

When, in 1659, Catholic Spain and Catholic France signed the Peace of the Pyrenees, which ended their fifteen-year-long war, they did so without having notified the pope. This was a clear sign of the political irrelevance to which the Papacy had fallen. First Cardinal

Mazarin and the young King Louis XIV (r. 1643-1715) seemed to relish Rome's decline and impotence, perhaps because of the Papacy's attempts to interfere with French diplomacy at Münster. From 1653 to 1662, the French refused to send an ambassador to the Holy See. Perhaps the ultimate insult was Mazarin's offer to landscape the area in Rome now known as the Spanish Steps. Its centerpiece would have been a fine equestrian statue of young King Louis, a gesture usually reserved for conquered cities. The offer was declined.

Alexander was, however, able to support the Poles against the Protestant Swedes and Orthodox Russians, and the Habsburgs in Vienna against the Turks. In neither case was Alexander's diplomacy or his aid of much value. It was helpful, though, in the imperial election of Leopold Habsburg, on July 18, 1658. In support of Catholic missionary efforts, Alexander expanded the Congregation for the Propagation of the Faith, and inaugurated Rome's university, the Sapienza, at which the study of non-European languages played a central role. Under his auspices a new edition of the *Index Librorum Prohibitorum* (Index of Forbidden Books) was released, and Francis de Sales, bishop of Geneva, Switzerland, and a doctor of the Church, was canonized a saint (1665). From early in 1667, Alexander suffered from kidney disease. He died peacefully on May 22 in the Quirinal Palace.

SIGNIFICANCE
Alexander VII's greatest contribution as pope was his attention to the architectural beauty of Rome. In grand baroque fashion he refashioned Rome for political and religious theater by creating the grand northern entrance at the Porta del Popolo and the terminus of the processional route in St. Peter's Square. The streets and piazzas that he cleared and widened have given visitors a vision of the Eternal City that reflects the Church universal and triumphant. Ironically, Alexander's architectural work was accomplished at a time when papal power was in many ways at its lowest ebb. Alexander was unable to make a mark on the politics of his day, however, because the era's absolutist rulers, especially Louis XIV, brushed the Church aside as a player.

—*Joseph P. Byrne*

FURTHER READING
Croxton, Derek, and Anuschka Tischer. *The Peace of Westphalia*. Westport, Conn.: Greenwood Press, 2001. A detailed reference work on the peace negotiations, including Chigi's role as papal representative.

Habel, Dorothy Metzger. *The Urban Development of*

Rome in the Age of Alexander VII. New York: Cambridge University Press, 2002. Habel concentrates on Alexander's urban planning and the execution of his plans, which she sees as being rooted in late classical, Eastern Roman models.

Kegley, Charles W., and Gregory A. Raymond. *Exorcising the Ghost of Westphalia.* Englewood Cliffs, N.J.: Prentice Hall, 2001. A close discussion of the negotiations behind the treaty in the context of modern diplomacy.

Krautheimer, Richard. *Rome in the Age of Alexander VII, 1655-1667.* Princeton, N.J.: Princeton University Press, 1985. A masterful overview of the artistic and architectural patronage of Alexander, including the projects that were completed and those of which he only dreamed.

Magnuson, Torgil. *Rome in the Age of Bernini.* 2 vols. Atlantic Highlands, N.J.: Humanities Press, 1982-

1986. Chapter 2, volume 2, contains an extended essay on Urban's pontificate entitled "The Pontificate of Alexander VII," which goes well beyond artistic considerations.

Pastor, Ludwig. *History of the Popes from the Close of the Middle Ages.* Vol. 31. Translated by Ernest Graff. St. Louis, Mo.: Herder, 1940. The fullest discussion in English of Alexander by the foremost historian of the post-medieval Papacy.

SEE ALSO: Gian Lorenzo Bernini; Christina; Ferdinand II; Innocent XI; Louis XIV; Jules Mazarin; Paul V; Urban VIII; Saint Vincent de Paul.

RELATED ARTICLES in *Great Events from History: The Seventeenth Century, 1601-1700:* c. 1601-1620: Emergence of Baroque Art; 1656-1667: Construction of the Piazza San Pietro; July 13, 1664: Trappist Order Is Founded.

ALEXIS
Czar of Russia (r. 1645-1676)

Alexis faced major social and political changes. His rule was marked by riots, an uprising, and a great schism in Russian religion. Despite these difficulties, his rule led to a professionalized Russian military, the establishment of a code of laws, and, for better and for worse, the Westernization of Russia, promoted further by his son and heir, Peter the Great.

BORN: March 19, 1629; Moscow, Russia
DIED: February 8, 1676; Moscow
ALSO KNOWN AS: Aleksei Mikhailovich Romanov (full name); Alexis Mikhailovich; Aleksei Mikhailovich; Alexei Mikhailovich; Alexis I Michaylovich Romanov
AREAS OF ACHIEVEMENT: Government and politics, law, military, religion and theology

EARLY LIFE

Alexis, whose full name is Aleksei Mikhailovich Romanov, was the oldest son of Michael Romanov, the first of the Romanov Dynasty of Russian czars. Michael had been chosen in 1613 as czar by a *zemskii sobor*, or assembly of the land, composed of Russian notables, and he reigned until 1645. The time of Czar Michael's selection was a difficult period in Russian history, known as the Time of Troubles, because the country suffered from conflicts over who was the legitimate ruler, from social disorder, and from invasions by Polish and Swedish forces. To avoid falling into the same political and social crises again, it was important that Michael produce an heir with a clear right to the throne.

In accordance with custom, Alexis spent his earliest childhood in the *terem*, or women's quarters of the family home, with his mother, Evdokia Streshneva, and other women and small children. At the age of five, Alexis was placed in the care of the politically influential noble Boris Ivanovich Morozov. Morozov introduced him to books and ideas from the European nations to the west, as well as to the religious literature that made up the entire education of most high-born Russians.

Alexis had two younger brothers, but both of them died as children. Alexis's survival was therefore a matter of considerable concern. Mortality rates were high and life was uncertain in seventeenth century Russia. If Alexis had died, there would have been no Romanov Dynasty and Russia might well have faced another Time of Troubles. Michael was trying to marry his daughter, Irina, to a Danish prince to provide an alternative heir, when the czar fell ill and died unexpectedly in July of 1645. At the age of sixteen, the same age that his father had been when chosen by the assembly of the land, Alexis became the second Romanov czar.

LIFE'S WORK

Even as czar, Alexis was still under the tutelage of Boris Morozov. The young emperor busied himself with searching for a healthy, appropriate wife to produce a future ruler, while Morozov controlled the country. Morozov sought to secure his power by encouraging Alexis to marry, in 1648, Mariya Ilinichna Miloslavskaya (d. 1669), and then by taking Mariya's sister, Anna, as his own wife. Morozov's government was unpopular, though. The tutor imposed high taxes, especially on salt, and placed administration in the hands of men who were often corrupt. Outrage at corruption and opposition to the tax on salt, a necessary item for the preservation of fish and other foods, led to rioting in the summer of 1648. Alexis was forced to dismiss Morozov, who went into exile in the Arctic north.

Alexis's problems did not end with the exile of Morozov. In 1650, a revolt broke out in the province of Pskov, which had suffered a severe famine, and spread to the neighboring city of Novgorod. The czar's troops put down the revolt through brutal suppression of the local populace. Twelve years later, riots broke out in Moscow to protest the government's minting of cheap copper coins, which had resulted in inflation and economic hardships. As in Pskov, Alexis responded by calling in his troops to massacre thousands of his subjects and to torture or disfigure others, many of whom were then sent into exile.

Public discontent led to the first of the great peasant rebellions of Romanov Russia (1667-1671). Hoping to escape serfdom and economic hardship, many peasants had fled to the Cossack region in the south and southeast of Russia. The Cossacks were warlike freebooters, organized into their own communities. A bandit chief named Stenka Razin became the leader of the peasants and the Cossacks, and turned from banditry to political rebellion. Razin proclaimed that he was fighting on behalf of the czar, and against the czar's corrupt advisers and administrators. In 1670, after a series of victories, Razin led his troops in a march on Moscow. The Romanov Dynasty could well have ended then, but Razin's mistakes and the effectiveness of Alexis's general, Prince Vasily Vladimirovich Dolgoruky (1667-1746), led to Razin's capture and public dismemberment in Moscow.

As a result of pressures from the early rebellions and complaints about the corruption and arbitrariness of his administrators, Alexis called an assembly of the land to draw up a code of laws for Russia. This produced the Sobornoye Ulozheniye (1649). While giving the country a written system of law, it also defined legal statuses, in particular the status of serfdom. Serfdom tied peasants to the land, making them in most respects slaves of those who owned the land.

During Alexis's rule, the military moved toward becoming a permanent, professional force. This was the consequence of responses to the internal rebellions, and also to external warfare. Poland and Sweden had long been enemies of Russia and had occupied Russian territory during the reign of Alexis's father. At the beginning of 1654, Russia extended its sovereignty over the Cossacks of the Dnieper region. This brought the nation into conflict with Poland in the spring of 1654. Sweden then became involved in the war against Russia from 1656 to 1661. The war with Poland did not end until January, 1667. Unlike earlier conflicts with Poland, during which Russia had lost territory, the Russians won back the cities of Smolensk and Kiev, and took the part of Ukraine east of the Dnieper River.

Perhaps the most dramatic development of Alexis's rule was the religious schism, or divide. The schism, or

Alexis. (Hulton Archive/Getty Images)

raskol, was provoked by the effort of Nikon (1605-1681), the patriarch of Moscow from 1652 to 1658, to reform religious texts and practices in Russia by bringing them into closer conformity with Greek usages. Nikon's reforms enjoyed the support of Czar Alexis, but many conservative Russian Christians saw these reforms as an attack on sacred traditions. After church councils adopted the new texts and practices in 1666 and 1667, the opponents of reform were persecuted by church and state. These persecuted religious dissenters became known as the Old Believers. This introduced a split in Russian religion and social life that continued even past the revolution of 1917. Nikon himself lost the favor of Czar Alexis because of the patriarch's insistence on the power of the church over the state.

The latter part of Alexis's reign saw a growing Westernization that reached a climax during the time of Alexis's son, Peter the Great. Alexis's socially conservative first wife, Mariya, died in 1669. A few years later, Alexis married Natalya Kirillovna Naryshkina (1651-1694). Natalya was an orphan and had been raised by the pro-West adviser of Alexis, Artamon Sergeyevich Matveyev (1625-1682), his most trusted adviser during the latter part of his reign. Under the influence of Matveyev and Natalya, Alexis forged closer cultural, military, and political ties with Western Europe.

SIGNIFICANCE

Alexis's reign was a critical time in Russian history. The Romanov Dynasty, which had begun with his father, Michael, became established as the ruling family of Russia and political stability began to emerge from the social disorders of Alexis's early years on the throne. Government greatly extended its control over the life of the nation, and a comprehensive set of laws emerged. The professionalization of the military, together with a more centralized political administration, aided Russia in its wars, particularly against Sweden and Poland. The Westernization of Russia, which would be pushed fur-

---

THE UNITY OF THE RUSSIAN ORTHODOX CHURCH

The power of the Russian Orthodox Church to overcome "tragic shortcomings and failures" is outlined here briefly. A great schism (or divide) between believers marked Alexis's reign as czar of Russia, a divide that continues to some degree into the twenty-first century.

Orthodoxy is not a national or cultural attribute of the Eastern Church. Orthodoxy is an inner quality of the Church. It is the preservation of the doctrinal truth, the liturgical and hierarchical order and the principles of spiritual life which, unchangingly and uninterruptedly, have been present in the Church since apostolic times. One should not yield to the temptation to idealize the past or to ignore the tragic shortcomings and failures which marked the history of the Church. Above all the great fathers of the Church themselves give an example of spiritual self-criticism. The history of the Church in the IV-VII [fourth to seventh] centuries [for example] knew of not a few cases when a significant proportion of believers fell into heresy. But history also reveals that the Church struggled on principled terms with the heresies that were infecting her children and that there were cases where those who had gone astray were healed of heresy, experienced repentance and returned to the bosom of the Church. This tragic experience of misunderstanding emerging from within the Church herself and of the struggle with it during the period of the ecumenical councils has taught the children of the Orthodox Church to be vigilant. The Orthodox Church, while humbly bearing witness to her preservation of the truth, at the same time remembers all the temptations which arose during her history.

Source: From "Basic Principles of the Russian Orthodox Church's Attitude to the Non-Orthodox," Russian Orthodox Church, Moscow Patriarchate, Department for External Church Relations Communication Services. http://www.mospat.ru/text/e_principles/id/5547.html. Accessed December, 2004.

---

ther in the next generation by Peter the Great, may be seen as having begun during the time of Alexis.

During Alexis's years on the throne, some of the serious divisions and conflicts that would haunt Russia throughout its history took shape. The code of laws contributed to making peasants into serfs, creating a moral and social problem that lasted for centuries. The schism that produced the Old Believers introduced a deep religious split. The introduction of Western culture and customs intensified both of these rifts. Under Peter the Great, the nobility would become Westernized and the peasants would retain older Russian traditions. The factions of Old Believers rejected Westernization as evil.

—*Carl L. Bankston III*

FURTHER READING

Kliuchevsky, V. O. *A Course in Russian History: The Seventeenth Century*. Translated by Natalie Duddington. Armonk, N.Y.: M. E. Sharpe, 1994. A translation of a classic work by one of Russia's most eminent historians. Events of Alexis's reign are dealt with throughout; Chapter 16 looks specifically at Czar Alexis.

Kotilaine, Jarmo, and Marshall Poe, eds. *Modernizing Muscovy: Reform and Social Change in Seventeenth Century Russia*. New York: Routledge Curzon, 2004. A collection of articles that provides an encyclopedic account of politics and society in Russia during the seventeenth century. Includes useful references in footnotes of each article and an index.

Lincoln, W. Bruce. *The Romanovs: Autocrats of All the Russias*. New York: Dial Press, 1981. A comprehensive history of the entire Romanov Dynasty. The first quarter of the book is devoted to the seventeenth century. Enjoyable illustrations, including a portrait of Alexis, extensive bibliography, and index.

Michels, Georg Bernhard. *At War with the Church: Religious Dissent in Seventeenth Century Russia*. Stanford, Calif.: Stanford University Press, 1999. A study of the religious dissenters involved in the schism of the Russian church during Alexis's reign.

SEE ALSO: Avvakum Petrovich; Charles X Gustav; Christina; Gustavus II Adolphus; Ivan Stepanovich Mazepa; Boris Morozov; Nikon; Stenka Razin; Michael Romanov; Sigismund III Vasa; Sophia; Lennart Torstenson.

RELATED ARTICLES in *Great Events from History: The Seventeenth Century, 1601-1700:* 17th century: Rise of the Gunpowder Empires; February 7, 1613: Election of Michael Romanov as Czar; 1632-1667: Polish-Russian Wars for the Ukraine; December, 1639: Russians Reach the Pacific Ocean; January 29, 1649: Codification of Russian Serfdom; 1652-1667: Patriarch Nikon's Reforms; July 10, 1655-June 21, 1661: First Northern War; April, 1667-June, 1671: Razin Leads Peasant Uprising in Russia; 1672-c. 1691: Self-Immolation of the Old Believers; Summer, 1672-Fall, 1676: Ottoman-Polish Wars; 1677-1681: Ottoman-Muscovite Wars; Beginning 1689: Reforms of Peter the Great; August 29, 1689: Treaty of Nerchinsk Draws Russian-Chinese Border; March 9, 1697-August 25, 1698: Peter the Great Tours Western Europe; November 30, 1700: Battle of Narva.

LANCELOT ANDREWES
English religious leader and theologian

With Jeremy Taylor and Richard Hooker, Andrewes helped establish the Anglican Church. He served, through his writings and conduct, as a model of the ideal Anglican cleric.

BORN: 1555; London, England
DIED: September 26, 1626; London
AREA OF ACHIEVEMENT: Religion and theology

EARLY LIFE

Lancelot Andrewes (LANS-uh-laht AN-drooz) was born in London in 1555. His mother and his father, a well-to-do merchant, were from Suffolk, but they had moved to London before Andrewes's birth. A healthy, gifted child, Andrewes impressed Francis Walsingham (his parents' neighbor and friend, later Queen Elizabeth's principal secretary), who convinced Andrewes's parents not to apprentice him but rather to fit him for the life of a cleric and scholar. In 1561, accordingly, Andrewes entered a free grammar school founded by the Merchant Taylors. Although he was not considered brilliant, he had a great facility for foreign languages, excelling in Latin and

Greek, and proved to be a diligent student blessed with a wonderful memory.

Because of his outstanding academic record, Andrewes was awarded a scholarship to the newly founded Pembroke Hall at Cambridge University in 1571. He was to remain at Cambridge for the next eighteen years. After he graduated in 1575, Andrewes received a competitive fellowship in 1576, was ordained deacon in 1580 and priest in 1581, and culminated his university career when he was named master of Pembroke Hall in 1589. His Cambridge years strengthened the disciplined lifestyle and the religious zeal and devotion Andrewes had already cultivated. He regularly rose early and studied until noon. His interest in theology led him to a study of patristic writings, and his linguistic abilities enabled him to learn many more foreign languages (reputedly as many as fifteen).

While at Cambridge, Andrewes also sharpened his skills as a preacher and teacher. He served as a catechist, offering well-attended weekend lectures. His sermons, then as later, were detailed explications of the biblical text under study; he subjected each word and phrase to a thorough exegesis. In addition to his considerable abilities as a lecturer, he was a spiritual shepherd to his audience and often followed his sermons with individual counsel and advice. By the time he became master of Pembroke Hall, Andrewes was the epitome of the Anglican priest, in the pulpit, in the parish, and in his private life.

Although his years at Cambridge left him a serene and devout cleric, however, Andrewes hardly found the Cambridge intellectual and theological scene idyllic. The Anglican church faced opposition from both the Catholics and the Puritans with their emphasis on the presbyterian form of government. At Cambridge, the Puritans had been especially influential, and it was not until 1570 that future archbishop of Canterbury John Whitgift triumphed over them. Yet, while the Cambridge power structure attempted to impose religious order and conformity on the students, Puritan ideas persisted, and Andrewes certainly was exposed to them. Critics and biographers differ, in fact, about the extent to which Andrewes may have inclined to Puritanism, but if he ever had Puritan leanings, they do not appear in his post-Cambridge sermons and devotional prose.

Lancelot Andrewes. (Library of Congress)

LIFE'S WORK

In 1589, Andrewes left Cambridge, though he remained master of Pembroke Hall. He moved to London, where Walsingham's intervention had secured for him a living at St. Giles. The move was symbolic, for it reflected the end of his academic life and the beginning of his life's work. Andrewes frequently preached at St. Giles and at St. Paul's, where he served as residential canon; when his pastoral duties and his exemplary lifestyle brought him to the attention of the court, he was made a chaplain to Archbishop Whitgift and to Queen Elizabeth I. Elizabeth offered him two bishoprics (at Salisbury and Ely), but he refused them, primarily as a protest against her custom of keeping sees vacant and appropriating the revenue.

Shortly before the queen's death in 1603, however, Andrewes did accept an appointment as dean of Westminster, a position that also entailed responsibility for Westminster School. There he instilled in his students, as he had at Pembroke Hall, a love for learning. Under his stewardship, moreover, the school achieved a sound financial footing, partly as a result of Andrewes's private contributions to its coffers.

After James I came to the throne, Andrewes accepted, in 1605, the bishopric of Chichester, whence he was

transferred to Ely in 1609 and to Winchester in 1619. During the reign of James, who was himself something of a theologian, Andrewes succeeded Richard Hooker as the defender of the Anglican faith and played an influential role in determining the course of Anglicanism.

When James called the Hampton Court Conference in 1605, Andrewes was a participant and a supporter of James's efforts to use the Anglican church to the power of the throne. James believed that the doctrine of divine right depended on episcopacy, or rule by bishops, with its similar emphasis on order and hierarchy, evident in the slogan, "No Bishop, No King." On the other hand, the presbytery, a much more democratic religious institution whose members voted on matters of policy and doctrine, was considered a threat to royal authority. Andrewes's support of episcopacy stood him in good stead with James, who chose him in 1607 to play a significant role in producing the new biblical translation known as the King James Bible (1611). As an expert in Hebrew, Andrewes was appointed to chair a group of scholars working on the books of the Old Testament from Genesis through the Second Book of Kings.

The year 1605 also marked the beginning of a religious controversy. In that year, a group of Catholic nobles, together with a mercenary named Guy Fawkes, conspired to kill the king and Parliament and foment a Catholic revolution. This conspiracy came to be known as the Gunpowder Plot. In the wake of the plot, an oath of allegiance to James was instituted in England, but the Roman Catholic Church, especially Cardinal Robert Bellarmine, adamantly opposed it. In response to Bellarmine's written criticism, King James published *Triplicinodo triplex cuneus: Or, An Apologie for the Oath of Allegiance* (1607), which Bellarmine answered the following year in his *Responsio Matthaei Torti* (1608; Matthew Tortus's response: Tortus was one of Bellarmine's servants).

James, an amateur though gifted theologian, was no match for Bellarmine, a Jesuit expert in religious controversy. While the king set about revising his *Apology*, he also asked Andrewes to refute Bellarmine. Both James's revised *An Apology for the Oath of Allegiance* (1609) and Andrewes's *Tortura Torti* (1609; Tortus's torment) were published soon thereafter. In his book, Andrewes explored the relationship between the oath of allegiance and the issue of royal supremacy, examined the papal claim to depose monarchs and to release Catholics from political oaths, and reviewed the circumstances surrounding the Gunpowder Plot. His discussion of civil and spiritual power in turn was answered by Bellarmine's *Apologia Roberti S.R.E. Cardinalis Bellarmini, pro responsione sua ad librum Jacobi* (1609; *Apology for the Responsio*, 1610), which occasioned another rebuttal by Andrewes. In that rebuttal, the Anglican church emerged as a church allied to Roman Catholic history and sacraments yet allowing for thought independent of Catholic dogma or papal doctrine.

While Andrewes's loyalty to James and his unswerving devotion to the Anglican cause produced *Tortura Torti*, that loyalty and religious conformity were also responsible for two acts that, from a later perspective, reflect badly on Andrewes and mark him as a product of his age. In the first instance, James, intent on enforcing religious orthodoxy, became incensed at the heretical opinions of Bartholomew Legate, who maintained that Jesus Christ was a "mere man," though "borne free from sinne." Legate was brought before the Consistory Court, which included Andrewes, in 1612, and despite the absence of laws that would justify the burning of heretics, Legate was burned to death. There is no record of Andrewes's opposition to the verdict; in fact, he mentioned the event in the context of eliminating heresy.

The second act involved Andrewes's response to the celebrated Essex divorce case of 1613, in which James sought ecclesiastical support for a divorce that would free Lady Frances Howard from her marriage to the earl of Essex. Lady Howard wanted to marry Robert Carr, Viscount Rochester, one of the king's favorites. Although Archbishop George Abbott opposed the divorce, Andrewes was among the bishops who supported James's wishes.

The same adherence to authority and compliance with "policy" affected Andrewes's later part in the inquiry into Archbishop Abbott's accidental killing of a groundskeeper while hunting deer. Although the archbishop was not subject to secular laws, there was a question about his continuation in office. Andrewes's defense, that each of the bishops could be in a similar situation, seems charitable and practical but also, unfortunately, suggests self-serving privilege.

In addition to his theological and political activities and writings, Andrewes is famous for his private devotional works, few of which were published during his lifetime. In fact, his sermons first appeared in print in 1628. What readers have since found most appealing are the three books of private prayers, which were translated from the Latin and Greek in which Andrewes wrote them. The first and most famous of the books, *The Manual of Private Devotions* (1648), was originally intended for Andrewes's exclusive use and was his constant companion up until his death on September 26, 1626, in London.

SIGNIFICANCE

To evaluate Lancelot Andrewes is to see him in three related roles—as preacher, as prelate, and as author. In an appreciative essay, T. S. Eliot, a twentieth century writer with distinctly seventeenth century affinities, terms Andrewes the "first great preacher of the English Catholic Church." Eliot's perceptive contrast between the sermons of the well-known John Donne and the relatively obscure Andrewes serves to identify the latter's strengths. Whereas Donne was a "personality" whose sermons served more as a means of self-expression, Andrewes submerged his personality as he delved into the biblical text. Whereas Donne's sermons were laden with emotion, those of Andrewes were more restrained, intellectual, and contemplative.

Biblical exegesis was Andrewes's goal, and he could, according to Eliot, "take a word and derive the world from it." Eliot's admiration for the theologian stems partly from his own stylistic similarity to Andrewes, for both are metaphysical, given to puns, figures of speech, irony, allusions, wit, and dense writing so tight that it is, unlike Donne's work, difficult to quote out of context. In a sense, while Donne is modern in his somewhat confessional style and content, Andrewes is more traditional, more concerned with the text than with himself.

As a prelate, Andrewes was theologically the model of the Anglican churchman, for he was unswerving in his pursuit of the middle way between authoritarian Catholicism and democratic Presbyterianism, the two threats to the independent yet hierarchical English church. Dedicated to his calling, his behavior was consistent with his principles and his expectations of other members of the clergy. Andrewes was, in fact, so unworldly that he did not concern himself with politics unless the church was involved. He was not, despite the power he might have wielded, ambitious for advancement—an unusual trait in his time. Controversy did not appeal to him, for he was by nature conciliatory, and he was drawn reluctantly into the Bellarmine furor that established him as spokesperson for the English church.

Andrewes never visited the Continent, choosing to remain throughout his life in the country of his birth. Because of his theological scholarship and linguistic abilities, however, Andrewes was respected by continental scholars such as Isaac Casaubon, who moved to England and became his close friend, and Hugo Grotius, who met him in London. Andrewes also enjoyed the friendship of Sir Francis Bacon and of George Herbert, the metaphysical priest and poet. In fact, despite his prominent position, itself a danger in his time, Andrewes had few contemporary detractors.

Andrewes's reputation as a writer rests on *Tortura Torti*, his sermons, and his books of prayers, but his writings are more significant in terms of their metaphysical qualities and the clues that they provide about his life, beliefs, and behavior. In a sense, for modern biographers intent on revealing their subjects "warts and all," Andrewes is a challenge, for he seems too good to be true. As a result, the private prayers, which stress his awareness of his own sin, have been read as an indication of some secret sin, and his lack of enemies and critics has been considered an indication of his unwillingness to take a stand. Such interpretations seem strained and are perhaps reactions to the saintly image perpetuated by his contemporaries.

The very absence of contemporary criticism is for some biographers a problem. Either Andrewes was so saintly that everyone loved him, or his weakness of character led him to compromise or keep silent when his voice was needed; in either case, he was not likely to make powerful enemies. Certainly, his zealous support

of the divine right of kings and his tendency to comply with his sovereign's will and caprices led him to take some positions that are questionable from a modern perspective, but he was very much a child of his age, an age that required the loyalty that was at once his strength and his weakness. It is to Andrewes's credit that his learning, scholarly reputation, and devout life made him the model Anglican prelate and that he was able to help the developing Church of England steer a course between Catholicism and Presbyterianism.

—*Thomas L. Erskine*

FURTHER READING

Andrewes, Lancelot. *Selected Writings*. Edited by P. E. Hewison. Manchester, England: Fyfield Books, 1995. A selection of Andrewes's sermons and letters, some complete and others excerpted.

Dorman, Marianne. *Lancelot Andrewes, 1555-1626: A Perennial Preacher in the Post Reformation English Church*. Tucson, Ariz.: Iceni Books, 2004. Dorman analyzes a cross section of doctrinal and religious themes contained in Andrewes's sermons.

Eliot, T. S. "Lancelot Andrewes." In *Selected Essays*. 2d ed. New York: Harcourt, Brace, 1950. An appreciation of Andrewes's sermons, particularly as they compare to those of Donne. Eliot regards Andrewes as one of the intellectual founders of the Anglican Church.

Lossky, Nicholas. *Lancelot Andrewes the Preacher, 1555-1626: The Origins of the Mystical Theology of the Church of England*. Translated by Andrew Louth. New York: Oxford University Press, 1991. An English translation of a French book defining Andrewes's significance within the mystical traditions of the Anglican Church.

Owen, Trevor A. *Lancelot Andrewes*. Boston: Twayne, 1981. A concise biographical and literary introduction, one of the biographies in Twayne's English authors series.

Welsby, Paul A. *Lancelot Andrewes, 1555-1626*. London: S. P. C. K., 1958. A well-balanced biography of Andrewes; also contains chapters on his friends, his theology, and the structure of his published prayers.

SEE ALSO: James I.

RELATED ARTICLES in *Great Events from History: The Seventeenth Century, 1601-1700:* March 24, 1603: James I Becomes King of England; November 5, 1605: Gunpowder Plot; 1611: Publication of the King James Bible.

ANNE OF AUSTRIA
Queen of France (r. 1615-1643), queen regent (r. 1643-1651)

As an outsider faced with a difficult marital relationship and caught in the maelstrom of a complex political situation at the court of France, Queen Anne of Austria overcame challenges and survived serious crises to become queen regent of France for her eldest son, King Louis XIV, securing his throne.

BORN: September 22, 1601; Valladolid, Spain
DIED: January 20, 1666; Paris, France
AREA OF ACHIEVEMENT: Government and politics

EARLY LIFE

Anne of Austria was the eldest daughter of King Philip III of Spain and his wife, Margaret of Austria. Her upbringing in the devoutly Catholic environment of her parents' court and her attachment for her native land of Spain would remain with her throughout her life.

On November 24, 1615, she married King Louis XIII of France. This marked a significant change in the foreign policy of both France and Spain. Rivalry between the two superpowers had been, for more than a century, intense, and open warfare had almost broken out only five years before. The bride and groom were only fourteen years of age, and the years of Louis XIII's minority, when France was governed by the king's mother, Marie de Médicis, and her various court favorites were unsettled years of political turbulence and economic breakdown. As a Spaniard, Anne was viewed with suspicion, generally isolated, and her husband was, for a long time, very cool and reserved in his relationship with his wife. The cause and extent of this antipathy, especially on the king's part, is a widely debated topic; some scholars have even described it as, at times, beyond bordering on hatred.

LIFE'S WORK

Anne's position was made all the more difficult with the rise to power of Cardinal de Richelieu. As France's first minister, Richelieu would retain power only if he could maintain his hold over the king, and he was wary of the queen's potential to subvert his influence. The cardinal therefore paid spies to keep a close watch on Anne, her acquaintances, and her correspondence to forestall any such threats. Thus, it was to his advantage to maintain the rift between the royal couple. The tense atmosphere was further aggravated by the injudicious decision on Anne's part (though perhaps an understandable one in view of her isolation at court) to cultivate the friendship of Marie de Rohan, duchesse de Chevreuse, an intriguer and implacable adversary of Richelieu.

A scandal sprang up around Queen Anne's alleged dalliance with the English envoy George Villiers, duke of Buckingham. While it does not seem to have been a full-blown affair, Buckingham embarrassed the queen by visiting her at inopportune times and on one occasion

Anne of Austria. (Hulton Archive/Getty Images)

publicly falling to his knees to declare his devotion to her.

In 1630, a complex plot by Anne, de Chevreuse, and Queen Mother Marie de Médicis came close to toppling Richelieu from power, before the wily prelate turned the tables on his detractors and regained royal favor (this incident was dubbed the Day of Dupes).

In 1637, the queen, through the agency of de Chevreuse, communicated with her brother, King Philip IV of Spain, although the two countries were at war and such interchanges were forbidden. Richelieu's spies amassed proof of treason against Anne, and the cardinal was thus able to blackmail her into cooperation and also noninterference in any of his future policies. In return for an amnesty from her husband, secured by the cardinal's efforts, she also was forbidden to associate further with de Chevreuse.

Anne's fortunes turned somewhat later that year when a cloudburst caused her husband to seek shelter and spend the night with her in her apartments at Saint-Maur in Paris, and by the month of March of 1638, it was common knowledge that the queen was pregnant. On September 5, 1638, at St. Germain-en-Laye, the queen gave birth to her first child, a son, who was christened Louis. So long had the marriage been without issue that the birth of the child was considered a quasi-miracle and the baby was dubbed Dieudonne (God-given). On September 20, 1640, Anne's second child, Philippe, duke of Anjou, was born, further assuring the succession and considerably strengthening the queen's political position. Her nemesis, Richelieu, died on December 4, 1642.

On May 14, 1643, Louis XIII died, and the king's will, which would have excluded the queen from all powers of regency over her four-year-old son, now Louis XIV, was turned aside by the Parlement of Paris and Anne was named coregent alongside Cardinal Jules Mazarin. Richelieu's protégé, Mazarin was now first minister and, unlike his mentor, he was quite close to the queen. They worked so closely in tandem that there was persistent talk that they were secretly married. This remains unproven, but because Mazarin had never received ordination as a priest, this would have been technically feasible.

During the dangerous years of the Wars of the Fronde (1648-1653), which saw armed nobles rise against royal power and absolutism, Anne showed a stubborn courage that astounded her contemporaries. She was highly protective of her sons, and she managed, through a combination of diplomacy and brazen defiance, to save Mazarin from the Frondist rebels and engineer his return to power. At one stage she spirited the ten-year-old king

and his brother out of Paris under the mob's very nose. She undoubtedly played a significant role in preserving the throne for Louis XIV and bringing about the eventual defeat of the Frondists.

Anne and Mazarin favored a Spanish marriage for her elder son: The queen's choice was her niece, Marie-Thérèse, eldest daughter of her brother King Philip IV. Accordingly, Louis was compelled to be betrothed to Marie-Thérèse and thus to terminate his courtship of the cardinal's niece, Marie Mancini (the young lady and her sisters were soon sent out of France). The marriage between King Louis XIV and Marie-Thérèse took place in 1660.

Cardinal Mazarin died in 1661, and Louis XIV emphatically assumed personal rule, asserting that there would be no succeeding first minister. Louis's mother was also excluded from any further political role, and though he continued to show her all outward filial respect, there is reason to believe that his resentment over her part in bringing about the Spanish marriage and Marie Mancini's banishment tinged his attitude toward her. The Queen Mother was at the center of one final controversy when she publicly condemned Molière's play *Tartuffe: Ou, L'Imposteur* (pr. 1664, pb. 1669; *Tartuffe*, 1732) about a religious hypocrite. So effective was she in her objections that King Louis banned further presentations of the play until more than one year after his mother's death. Anne herself retired to the convent of Val de Grace in Paris and died there of breast cancer on January 20, 1666.

SIGNIFICANCE

Anne of Austria is sometimes considered a passive and ineffective figure, who proved no match for the intricate political and diplomatic maneuverings of Richelieu, and who later played whatever role assigned her by Mazarin at a given time. However, she showed resolve and courage during the Wars of the Fronde and without doubt instilled in her son her devout Catholic faith, which he was to turn to so ardently in his later years—sometimes to the point of persecuting Huguenots (Protestants) and suppressing Jansenism within his domains.

—*Raymond Pierre Hylton*

FURTHER READING

Buranelli, Vincent. *Louis XIV.* New York: Twayne, 1966. The author tends to take the view that Anne had a greater influence upon the politics of the time, even after her "fall" from public life, than many have hitherto credited her with.

Cronin, Vincent. *Louis XIV*. London: Harvill Press, 1996. The first chapters give a decent, though far from extensive, treatment of Anne's role during her son's minority, including her time as regent of France.

Lewis, W. H. *The Splendid Century: Life in the France of Louis XIV*. Prospect Heights, Ill.: Waveland Press, 1997. A revealing look, originally published in 1953, at the domineering role assumed by Anne and Mazarin during Louis XIV's minority, especially regarding the king's amorous interests and eventual marriage to Marie-Thérèse.

Moote, A. L. *The Revolt of the Judges: The Parlement of Paris and the Fronde, 1643-1652*. Princeton, N.J.: Princeton University Press, 1972. Great historical detail concerning the Fronde, or the uprising of the nobility against the monarch, and the political intrigue surrounding the court.

O'Connell, D. P. *Richelieu*. Cleveland, Ohio: World, 1968. Though Anne is not portrayed unsympathetically, she is referred to—as an antagonist of the cardinal and minister—in terms of being a negative factor in the overall scheme of French history during the 1620's and 1630's.

Pitts, Vincent. *La Grande Mademoiselle at the Court of France: 1627-1693*. Baltimore: Johns Hopkins University Press, 2000. A page-turning melodrama of court intrigue as well as a major source on the period's political and social events.

SEE ALSO: Duchesse de Chevreuse; Madame de La Fayette; Duchesse de Longueville; Madame de Maintenon; The Mancini Sisters; Marie-Thérèse; Jules Mazarin; Marie de Médicis; Molière; Philip III; Philip IV; Cardinal de Richelieu; Viscount de Turenne.

RELATED ARTICLES in *Great Events from History: The Seventeenth Century, 1601-1700:* 1610-1643: Reign of Louis XIII; March 31, 1621-September 17, 1665: Reign of Philip IV; November 10, 1630: The Day of Dupes; June, 1648: Wars of the Fronde Begin; 1656: Popularizaiton of Chocolate; 1661: Absolute Monarchy Emerges in France; May 24, 1667-May 2, 1668: War of Devolution; 1673: Renovation of the Louvre; 1682: French Court Moves to Versailles; October 11, 1698, and March 25, 1700: First and Second Treaties of Partition.

ANGÉLIQUE ARNAULD
French abbess, religious reformer, and Jansenist leader

Appointed abbess of the Cistercian convent of Port Royal at age eleven, Arnauld reformed the convent according to the principles first of the Catholic reform movement and then of Jansenism. Through her actions and writings, she served as a leader of the Jansenist movement, as well as becoming the spiritual matriarch of her prominent family.

BORN: 1591; unknown
DIED: August 6, 1661; Port-Royal, Paris, France
ALSO KNOWN AS: Jacqueline-Marie-Angélique Arnauld (full name); Mother Angélique; Mère Angélique
AREAS OF ACHIEVEMENT: Religion and theology, scholarship

EARLY LIFE
Born the fourth of twenty children to Antoine Arnauld and Catherine Arnauld, possibly in Tours, France, Angélique Arnauld (ahn-zhay-leek ahr-noh) had a less than idyllic childhood. The number of her siblings (nine of whom survived to adulthood), the rise to prominence of her family, and her mother's favoritism toward her younger brother meant that Angélique received little maternal affection. In her writings, she complained bitterly of a beating she had received for inappropriate behavior on a religious holiday. Arnauld spent increasing time with her maternal grandfather, Simon Marion, the attorney general of the *parlement* of Paris. Her feeling of disconnectedness from her nuclear family can be seen in her decision to call herself "Jacqueline Marion" when she stayed with her grandfather. Headstrong from an early age, Arnauld discouraged visits from her brothers and sisters in order to keep her more demonstrative grandfather to herself. From her earliest years, Arnauld exhibited a strong sense of self that often set her at odds with her family.

LIFE'S WORK
The ascendance of the Arnauld family as members of the nobility of the robe and the large number of Arnauld children destined all but one of the girls for convent life. In consultation with the abbot of Cîteaux, Simon Marion sought to place his favorite granddaughter in the post of

abbess of Port-Royal-des-Champs upon the death of then-abbess Jeanne de Boulehart. Although both the abbess and King Henry IV agreed to the arrangement, the pope required that Arnauld first become a nun. The eight-year-old Arnauld thus entered the convent of Saint-Antoine before being sent to Maubuisson as a novice under Angélique d'Estrées, sister of the king's mistress, Gabrielle d'Estrées, duchesse de Beaufort. During the novitiate, Marion had his granddaughter's name changed to Angélique. In 1601, at the age of ten, Arnauld received approval to become the next abbess of Port-Royal; Marion had indicated her age as seventeen on the application to the pope. After the death of Boulehart in July, 1602, the young Arnauld assumed her new post.

Arnauld was ambivalent about convent life. Although pleased that she was in a position of power, she felt no calling. At the time, social status and political loyalties counted for more in the appointment of abbesses than piety. Although Arnauld continued to enjoy nature and read novels and Roman histories, she missed her grandfather and the life she had led. Angered when her eldest sister, Catherine, the most pious of the Arnauld girls, was married to a lawyer, Angélique considered running away.

Fate intervened during Lent of 1608, when the sermon of a friar inspired Arnauld. She began to reflect on the gifts God had given her and was saddened that she had not responded properly. So profound was the change that she considered resigning as abbess for a life of inward devotion. Wrestling with her feelings of pride, Arnauld began to channel her ideas toward reform. She began by fasting and imposing rigorous self-discipline, then turned to the convent in her charge. Both her parents and the families of other nuns at Port-Royal opposed the reforms that Arnauld began instituting.

During the Feast of All Saints in 1608, Arnauld received inspiration from another sermon. The preacher took his theme from the Beatitudes in Matthew 5: "Blessed are those who are persecuted for righteousness' sake, for theirs is the kingdom of heaven." To the seventeen-year-old Arnauld, the message was clear. She reimposed strict enclosure, as well as fasting, penitence, prayer, and silence, as the basis of convent life.

The turning point for Angélique and the entire Arnauld family occurred on September 25, 1609, remembered as the *journée du guichet* (Day of the Grille). When her parents and two of her siblings visited Port-Royal, Arnauld met them at the window and refused admittance. The abbess did not want her reforms endangered by her family. Heated words were exchanged for

several hours before her parents left, her mother threatening she would never again speak to Arnauld. For the young abbess, it was a pivotal moment in her resolve for reform and against hypocrisy. She had not been given a choice about becoming a nun, but now that she had power, she intended to exercise it. Arnauld's declaration of independence gave her the freedom she needed to further her program. In the process, she became one of the leading figures in the Catholic reform movement. During the next two decades, all of Arnauld's sisters and even her widowed mother would become nuns at Port-Royal. The abbess became the spiritual leader not only of a convent, but of her family as well. Soon her brothers too would be drawn to her reformed spirituality.

In the years that followed her conversion, Arnauld insisted that only novices with a vocation be admitted to Port-Royal; nuns with no calling were asked to leave. She also succeeded in making the office of abbess elective. In 1618, the head of the Cistercian Order invited her to implement her reforms at the convent of Maubuisson. The battles that followed between the ousted abbess and her soldiers and those of Arnauld and her followers seem almost comical in retrospect. The fight for control of Maubuisson typified the conflict between those who sought to protect aristocratic privilege and others who wanted real reform.

Arnauld became increasingly dissatisfied with what she viewed as the laxity of the Cistercians and considered joining the new Visitandine order of Saint Francis de Sales, briefly her confessor. Seeing her gifts as lying elsewhere, however, the future saint discouraged the change. In the meantime, Arnauld moved her nuns from Port-Royal-des-Champs's marshy site near Versailles to Paris in 1624. The community flourished, attracting increasing numbers of bourgeois women.

In the following year, Arnauld withdrew Port-Royal from the Cistercian Order and placed it under the guidance of Bishop Sébastien Zamet's new Institute of the Holy Sacrament. Trouble followed when a short treatise written by Arnauld's sister, Jeanne-Catherine-Agnès Arnauld, was declared heretical by the Sorbonne. The abbess later claimed that she and her nuns had been treated like witches. Zamet came under increasing scrutiny, and when he left to reside in his diocese of Langres (Lingones) from 1633 to 1635, he appointed Jean du Vergier de Hauranne, abbot of Saint-Cyran, as spiritual director of Port-Royal.

Friendly for many years with the Arnauld family, Saint-Cyran's influence now increased, and under his inspiration, several of the Arnauld men withdrew to a community of hermits near Port-Royal. Mother Angélique found that Saint-Cyran fulfilled her desire for a more authentic spiritual experience, but her reliance on Saint-Cyran put her on a collision course with Zamet, who returned in 1635. Recognizing Zamet's ambitious nature, Arnauld rejected his attempt to impose a new head of novices on the convent. By contrast, Saint-Cyran's penitential theology, belief in absolute predestination, and emphasis on God's grace (based on the beliefs of Cornelius Otto Jansen, bishop of Ypres) gave focus to Arnauld's religious journey.

Saint-Cyran was arrested by Cardinal de Richelieu in May of 1638 and imprisoned until the minister's death in 1642. He died of a stroke a year after his release. Mother Angéliques's Jansenist sympathies, now espoused by the entire Arnauld family, only intensified in the years that followed. She exchanged letters with supporters and wrote strong denunciations of those who "persecuted" her and others of like mind. Arnauld's steadfast beliefs and encouragement of her brothers placed her family in the forefront of opposition to royal and papal policy.

During the Wars of the Fronde (1648-1652), matters worsened, as the Jansenists became associated with sedition. The number of nuns at Port-Royal began to drop off precipitously. In 1661, in the last months of Arnauld's life, the community suffered increasing persecution from French king Louis XIV. The nuns were ordered to sign a formulary condemning Jansenist beliefs. Although she died before having to make a decision whether to sign, Arnauld was torn between belief that the formulary was wrong and unease that refusal was prideful. Announcing her willingness to suffer for the truth, and without a confessor, Arnauld looked inward, relying on what she knew to be the core of her faith.

Arnauld's work was taken up by her niece, Angélique Arnauld d'Andilly (also known as Mother Angélique de Saint-Jean), who urged her aunt to write a chronicle of her life, believing the story to be essential for the future of Port-Royal. Arnauld composed her memoirs, the *Relation écrite par la Mère Angélique sur Port-Royal* (1949; treatise written by Mother Angélique about Port-Royal), from self-imposed isolation in a small cell at the convent. Although the text contains little about her life in the period after Saint-Cyran's death, it remains an invaluable source for the history of Port-Royal, the Arnauld family, and Jansenism. Ill for many years, Arnauld died in August, 1661. Compromise and controversy involving those at Port-Royal marked the final decades of Louis XIV's reign. Port-Royal was destroyed in 1711.

SIGNIFICANCE

Mother Angélique Arnauld is not listed alongside other women in the Catholic reform movement such as Angela Merici or Teresa of Avila, because she was on the "wrong side" as defined by royal and papal authorities. Her impact, however, first on her influential and ambitious family and through them on the religious life of a great many women and men in seventeenth century France, was no less than those of her more famous contemporaries. She ultimately inspired even those in her family who had originally been against her. Armed with her belief in the value of inner reflection and the strength of the individual relationship with God, Arnauld fought to the end, upholding these views and supporting her community of nuns. Her life and her writings, including letters and an autobiography, exemplify female spirituality in early modern Catholicism.

—*Larissa Juliet Taylor*

FURTHER READING

Baxter, Carol, "Repression or Liberation? Notions of the Body Among the Nuns of Port-Royal." In *Women in Renaissance and Early Modern Europe*, edited by Christine Meek. Dublin: Four Courts Press, 2000. Using Foucault's view of the body as a social construct, Baxter examines how the austerity of Port-Royal reflected prevailing notions of behavior while at the same time it allowed the sisters to be in the vanguard of the reforming movement.

Bugnion-Secretan, Perle. *La Mère Angélique Arnauld, 1591-1661, d'après ses écrits: Abbesse et réformatrice de Port-Royal*. Paris: Cerf, 1991. French edition of autobiographical excerpts and letters of Mère Angélique.

Sedgwick, Alexander, "The Nuns of Port-Royal: A Study of Female Spirituality in Seventeenth-Century France." In *That Gentle Strength: Historical Perspectives on Women in Christianity*, edited by Lynda L. Coon, Katherine J. Haldane, and Elisabeth W. Sommer. Charlottesville: University Press of Virginia, 1990. A short study by the leading authority on the Arnauld family that examines the impact of Arnauld and her female relatives on the reform of convent life at Port-Royal and Jansenist spirituality.

_____. *The Travails of Conscience: The Arnauld Family and the Ancien Régime*. Cambridge, Mass.: Harvard University Press, 1998. The single most authoritative study of the Arnauld family, their conversion to Jansenism, and its effects on political history and family life.

SEE ALSO: Cornelius Otto Jansen; Louis XIV; Cardinal de Richelieu.
RELATED ARTICLES in *Great Events from History: The Seventeenth Century, 1601-1700*: 1625-October 28, 1628: Revolt of the Huguenots; 1638-1669: Spread of Jansenism; June, 1648: Wars of the Fronde Begin; July 13, 1664: Trappist Order Is Founded; 1685: Louis XIV Revokes the Edict of Nantes.

AURANGZEB
Emperor of India (r. 1658-1707)

Aurangzeb was the last of the great Mughal emperors who ruled north and central India after 1526. The most pious and ruthless of these rulers, he was a great conqueror, a brilliant administrator, and an extraordinarily cunning statesman who took the empire to its greatest territorial extent.

BORN: November 3, 1618; Dohad, Mālwa, India
DIED: March 3, 1707; Ahmadnagar, India
ALSO KNOWN AS: Muhī-ud-Dīn Muḥammad Aurangzeb (full name); ʿĀlamgīr I
AREAS OF ACHIEVEMENT: Government and politics, warfare and conquest, diplomacy

EARLY LIFE

Aurangzeb (ahr-ahng-zehb) was given the name Muhī-ud-Dīn Muḥammad Aurangzeb at birth. He was the third of four sons of the Mughal Emperor Shah Jahan and his wife, Mumtāz Mahal, reportedly for whom the Taj Mahal was built. The Mughals, a Muslim people descended from the Turkish and Mongol conquerors of central Asia, had ruled much of India since 1526. Aurangzeb was reared in a rich and powerful home destined to be torn by imperial intrigue and violence.

As youths, Aurangzeb and his three brothers (Dārā Shukōh, Shujah, and Murad) were taught the Qurʾān, standard works of Persian poetry, calligraphy, and the history of their great ancestors. Prince Dārā, the favorite of his father, Shah Jahan, was a liberal-minded, aesthetically inclined Muslim who believed that truth resided in a variety of traditions and could not be contained in a single religion. Aurangzeb, in contrast, from his youth displayed narrow, literalistic religious and ethnic propensities. He memorized most of the Qurʾān, became expert in Muslim law, and largely ignored poetry, music, and painting. Unlike his predecessors, he took little interest in monumental architecture and seldom patronized the arts. In the eventual struggle to succeed Shah Jahan as emperor, the two protagonists were Dārā and Aurangzeb—mystic versus puritan, unorthodox versus orthodox.

As a young man, Aurangzeb was ambitious, aggressive, and ruthless, but he was hardly more cruel than others of his time. Rather, he was more successful because of his superior skill in statecraft and intrigue. Recognizing Aurangzeb's ambitions, Shah Jahan appointed him viceroy (*nabob*) of the Deccan (central India) in July, 1636. He spent eight years there, isolated most of the time from the center of power at the Mughal court in Āgra. When he returned to Āgra in 1644, it became apparent to him that his father was discriminating against him in favor of Dārā. This conviction caused Aurangzeb to misbehave at the court, which resulted in his temporary banishment. Soon restored to favor, however, he served as the governor of Gujarat province (1645-1647) and of the northwestern Multan and Sind provinces (1648-1652). It was there that he honed his military and command skills, as his armies were sent to fight Afghan hill tribes and Persian soldiers. He suffered crushing defeats in central Asia against the Persians, however, and found himself reassigned to the Deccan in August, 1652, once again isolated from the center of power.

Aurangzeb's second viceroyalty in the Deccan (1652-1658) allowed him the opportunity to develop further his considerable administrative and military talents. His relations with his father and with Dārā continued to be contentious, however, and both of his major military campaigns in the Deccan—against two rich Muslim principalities, Golconda and Bijapur—were halted just short of victory by orders from Shah Jahan, who was influenced by anti-Aurangzeb factions at his court. In effect, Aurangzeb's attempts to expand Mughal influence in central India were nullified by the court intrigues of Dārā's supporters. It was thus a frustrated Aurangzeb who received word in September, 1657, that Shah Jahan had fallen seriously ill. This illness precipitated a struggle for succession that eventually brought Aurangzeb to the throne.

LIFE'S WORK

At the time Shah Jahan fell ill with strangury, the four brothers were widely separated. Aurangzeb was in the Deccan, Shujah was in Bengal, Murad was in Gujarat, and Dārā was at Shah Jahan's side in Delhi. Shah Jahan's

Aurangzeb. (Library of Congress)

April, 1658, the combined forces of Aurangzeb and Murad defeated a formidable imperial force, and on May 29, 1658, they confronted Dārā's main army several miles east of Āgra on the plain of Samugarh. Under his superior generalship, Aurangzeb's army overwhelmed Dārā's troops, and Dārā fled toward Āgra, leaving ten thousand of his men dead on the battlefield. On May 30, Dārā gathered about five thousand of his remaining troops and embarked for Delhi. On June 8, Āgra fell to Aurangzeb and Shah Jahan was placed under house arrest, where he would remain until his death in 1666.

Moving quickly to consolidate his power, Aurangzeb arrested his erstwhile ally, Murad, imprisoned him for the next three years, and then had him executed. Shortly after taking Āgra, his troops set out in pursuit of Dārā, but it was not until August 30, 1659, that Aurangzeb was able to capture his brother and have him executed. In the interim, he also eliminated Shujah, who eventually died a fugitive in Burma. Aurangzeb thus cemented his ascendance to the peacock throne as Ālamgīr (world conqueror) I in July, 1658. He reigned until his death in March, 1707.

Aurangzeb's nearly fifty-year reign aroused passionate support from orthodox Muslims and equally fervent opposition from some of his Hindu subjects, upon whom his policies inflicted enormous suffering. Noted mostly for his single-minded pursuit of power and territory, he brought monumental construction to an end, ceased to patronize nonreligious celebrations, and enforced Muslim puritanism in his court and realm.

His strict adherence to orthodox Islam led him to abandon the religious tolerance and preferred treatment of Hindus, which had been the hallmark of Mughal rule since the time of his grandfather Akbar the Great. The Mughals had attempted to be rulers of all Indians, irrespective of creed and ethnicity, and had welcomed Rājput warriors into the highest ranks of their armies and administration. They had also abolished the hated *jizya,* a head tax imposed on all non-Muslims. Such policies had created a large reservoir of Hindu support for the Mughal Empire.

Aurangzeb reversed these policies, despite warnings from his advisers that such action would most likely result in widespread rebellions. He began by appointing what were called censors of public morals (*muhtasibs*) in every large city, ordering the *muhtasibs* to enforce Islamic laws and customs strictly. He outlawed some Hindu festivals, prohibited repairs to Hindu temples, and in 1679 reimposed the poll tax. By refusing to treat Hindus as equals, he broke the Hindu-Mughal alliance and

illness took him to death's door and threw his court into panic over the inevitable succession struggle.

Aurangzeb began his campaign for the throne by luring his inept brother, Murad, into an alliance against Dārā, denying at first that he had any regal ambitions and then promising Murad the provinces of Punjab and Sind for his support. In the meantime, both Shujah and Murad publicly announced their own claims to the Mughal throne.

By early 1658, Shah Jahan had recovered from his illness and tried to help Dārā cope with his brother's conspiracy against him. Yet Dārā, who was always more interested in mysticism than in imperial politics, was no match for the aggressive, battle-hardened Aurangzeb. In ensured the emergence of rebellion in 1669 in the Punjab and thereafter throughout much of the empire.

The fiercest and most persistent Hindu opposition to Aurangzeb arose in the western Indian province of Maharashtra under the leadership of Śivājī, who is popularly regarded as the founder of Hindu nationalism, but whom the Mughals reviled as a "mountain rat" because of the guerrilla tactics he employed. Śivājī was a ferocious Marāthā warrior who was reared by his mother to love Hinduism and hate all varieties of Muslim rule in India. He sought self-rule and full freedom to practice his own religion. He took to the Maharashtran hills at the age of twenty to fight a guerrilla war against the Mughals and other Muslims. He soon developed a number of fortresses on mountain plateaus and gained control of much of Maharashtra. His rising power alarmed Aurangzeb, who sent a huge army against him in 1665. Śivājī was soundly defeated, but he managed to escape from the Mughals in time and by 1670 recaptured most of the ground he had lost in 1665. He remained independent of the Mughals until his death in 1680, and his sons and followers continued the battle against the Mughals thereafter.

It was the Deccan, in combination with Maharashtra, that attracted most of Aurangzeb's attention after 1680. In that year, Aurangzeb's son, Akbar, rose in rebellion against his father in alliance with two Rājput princes and Śivājī's elder son, Sambhājī, who had succeeded his father. Aurangzeb invaded the Deccan in 1681 to try to quell this potentially dangerous rebellion. Akbar's anti-Aurangzeb alliance never operated effectively, and Akbar eventually fled in 1686 to Iran, where he died in exile. In 1689, Aurangzeb captured and executed Sambhājī, who had effectively employed guerrilla tactics to frustrate Aurangzeb's completion of the Deccan conquest. In spite of Sambhājī's death, the Marāthās continued to defy the Mughals. They were the only power remaining outside Aurangzeb's control, however, as he brought Mughal power to its pinnacle. Never before or since did a single ruler control so much of India.

Yet the costs of Aurangzeb's conquest of the Deccan were enormous. At least 100,000 lives were lost, and much of the Deccan's surplus wealth was consumed by military expenditures. The military slaughter was accompanied by famine and bubonic plague, which killed countless thousands more before Aurangzeb eventually quit the Deccan and returned to the north in 1705. By then, even he seems to have regretted the carnage he had inflicted on the Deccan.

SIGNIFICANCE

Scholars disagree about Aurangzeb's character and accomplishments. His life was so dramatic and forceful that it seems to compel extreme assessments. His critics point to his bigotry against non-Muslims and his excessive military adventures as marks of monumental failure. Forgotten is that he ruled India for almost half a century and that he took the empire to its greatest territorial extent. Moreover, while he was cruel and shed much blood trying to conquer all of India, ruthless ambition was hardly unique to him in the India of that time. His archrivals, the Marāthās, matched him in their pursuit of wealth and power. Although he lacked the charisma of his father, Shah Jahan, and his grandfather, Akbar, he was a firm and capable administrator.

Although the Deccan struggles severely weakened the Mughal Empire, Aurangzeb's successor, Bahādur Shāh, was able to restore the empire's vigor within five years of Aurangzeb's death, suggesting that Aurangzeb's misgovernment may not have been as severe as some contend. It is clear to most historians that Aurangzeb was, at the least, a complex personality and an able statesman who united more of India under his personal rule than any other sovereign in history.

—*Loren W. Crabtree*

FURTHER READING

Athar Ali, M. *The Mughal Nobility Under Aurangzeb.* Rev. ed. New York: Oxford University Press, 1997. Explores the composition and role of the nobility during Aurangzeb's reign.

Azizuddin Husain, S. M. *Structure of Politics Under Aurangzeb, 1658-1707.* New Delhi, India: Kanishka Publishers, 2002. Examines various aspects of politics during Aurangzeb's rule, including his political views and theory of kingship.

Bhave, Y. G. *From the Death of Shivaji to the Death of Aurangzeb: The Critical Years.* New Delhi, India: Northern Book Center, 2000. An exploration of Mughal rule and Hindu resistance from the time of Śivājī's execution until Aurangzeb's death.

Gascoigne, Bamber. *A Brief History of the Great Moghuls.* New York: Carroll & Graf, 2002. A well-written, general history of the Mughals, first published in 1971, chronicling the empire from its founder, Bābur, through Aurangzeb. Profusely illustrated, the work presents a balanced view of Aurangzeb's reign.

Hallissey, Robert C. *The Rājput Rebellion Against Aurangzeb: A Study of the Mughal Empire in Seventeenth Century India.* Columbia: University of Missouri Press, 1977. Examines the Rājput rebellion against Aurangzeb in the light of the internal dynamics of the Rājput state and the religious differences between Hindus and Muslims. Reveals the complexity of the Mughal-Rājput relationship.

Hansen, Waldemar. *The Peacock Throne*. New York: Holt, Rinehart and Winston, 1972. Detailed history of the Mughal period, offering insights into Aurangzeb's character and style of rule. Hansen's account of the succession struggle is particularly helpful, as is his discussion of the relationship between Aurangzeb and his enemies, particularly Śivājī.

Majumdar, R. C., H. C. Raychaudhuri, and Kalikinkar Datta. *An Advanced History of India*. 4th ed. Delhi: Macmillan India, 1978. One of the most detailed histories of India by Indian scholars that is readily available in the West. The authors strike a balanced view of Aurangzeb's leadership style. However, some scholars do not support their interpretations of the Rājputs and other aspects of Indian history.

Pearson, M. N. "Shivaji and the Decline of the Mughal Empire." *Journal of Asian Studies* 35 (February, 1976): 221-236. Focuses on the relationship between Aurangzeb's nemesis, Śivājī, and the decline of Mughal power created by Aurangzeb's expeditions into the Deccan and other causes.

Sarkar, Jadunath. *A Short History of Aurangzeb, 1618-1707*. London: Longmans, Green, 1930. A distillation of Sarkar's extensive studies of the Aurangzeb era. The most detailed and scholarly work on Aurangzeb and Śivājī.

SEE ALSO: ʿAbbās the Great; Jahāngīr; Kösem Sultan; Murad IV; Shah Jahan; Śivājī.

RELATED ARTICLES in *Great Events from History: The Seventeenth Century, 1601-1700:* 1605-1627: Mughal Court Culture Flourishes; 1619-1636: Construction of Samarqand's Shirdar Madrasa; 1632-c. 1650: Shah Jahan Builds the Taj Mahal; 1639-1640: British East India Company Establishes Fort Saint George; 1658-1707: Reign of Aurangzeb; June 23, 1661: Portugal Cedes Bombay to the English; c. 1666-1676: Founding of the Marāthā Kingdom; 1679-1709: Rājput Rebellion; March 30, 1699: Singh Founds the Khalsa Brotherhood.

AVVAKUM PETROVICH
Russian religious leader

Avvakum, a major leader of the Old Believer sect in Russia, was exiled twice, imprisoned, and then burned at the stake for resisting attempts to reform Russian Orthodoxy. His autobiography, an expression of Russian nationalism in the face of foreign influences, is considered the first classic of Russian literature and also a classic document of faith.

BORN: 1620 or 1621; Grigorovo, Russia
DIED: April 14, 1682; Pustozersk, Russia
AREAS OF ACHIEVEMENT: Religion and theology, literature

EARLY LIFE

The information about the early life of Avvakum Petrovich (ahv-VAH-kihm pyih-TROHV-yihch) comes from his own autobiography. By his account, he was the son of a drunken village priest named Pëtr and a devout mother named Marija. His mother spent much of her time in fasting and prayer and gave the young Avvakum a religious upbringing. In his autobiography, *Zhitiye protopopa Avvakuma* (1672-1673; *The Life of the Arch-*

priest Avvakum, by Himself, 1924), he reports that sometime in his youth he had a spiritual awakening upon seeing a dead ox (or cow) on his neighbor's property. That night, he looked at the icons, or portraits of saints, in his own home and cried, realizing that he too would die. From that time on, according to the autobiography, he prayed every night.

At some point after seeing the ox, Avvakum's father died, and Avvakum and his mother were put out of their home by their relatives. Avvakum was apparently in late adolescence when this happened. His mother soon decided that he should marry a pious young woman in the same village who had also lost her father, a formerly rich blacksmith named Marko, who had wasted his wealth. Avvakum's mother became a nun after he had married Anastasia.

Avvakum wrote that he was driven out of the village of Grigorovo by some kind of unspecified persecution. In about 1640, he became a deacon, and two years later he became a priest. Around 1650, the Russian Orthodox bishops raised him to the rank of archpriest. He spent most of his life from the time he became a priest until 1652 preaching in various Russian communities.

LIFE'S WORK

Avvakum's eagerness to enforce religious morality led him into conflict with others. This was probably the source of the persecutions he wrote about in his autobiography. In 1652, the people of his parish in Iurevets, near the Volga River, had violently driven him out. Apparently, he had attempted to force the local population to give up drunkenness, loose sexual behavior, gambling, and nonreligious musical performances. Also, he may have tried to make the people of the village conform to tithing, the donating of funds to the church.

After leaving Iurevets, he reported to the Kremlin in Moscow, where the archpriest was unemployed for a time. He soon found a role as an outspoken opponent of a new current of reform in the Russian Church. Nikon, the metropolitan of Novgorod, had been part of a circle of religious figures who gathered around the czar's confessor, Stephen Vonifatiev. Avvakum also was connected to Vonifatiev. With the help of the Vonifatiev circle and the support of the czar, Nikon became patriarch of Moscow in 1652, the most important leader of the Russian Church. Once Nikon achieved this position, though, he began to bring about changes that angered Avvakum and some of his other associates.

Through the centuries since the Russians had been converted to Christianity from contact with the Greeks of the Eastern Roman Empire, the Russian Church had developed rituals, texts, and practices that differed from those of the Greeks. Patriarch Nikon and other reformers hoped to bring Russian Christians back to what they saw as the original and correct expressions of religious faith. Nikon brought in Greek and western Russian scholars. On their advice, he concluded that many Russian books and rites had fallen away from the correct standards, and that some of the actions of the Vonifatiev circle had introduced more corruptions. In particular, Nikon and his Greek reformers replaced the Russian method of crossing oneself with two fingers by a three-fingered crossing, they ordered that hallelujahs be sung in threes rather than in the customary twos, and they changed the prescribed

---

OLD BELIEVER AVVAKUM PETROVICH AND THE RUSSIAN ORTHODOX CHURCH

Old Belief leader Avvakum Petrovich pulls no punches in condemning those who sought to reform Russian Orthodoxy. He uses the term "mahound," meaning the Prophet in some contexts but highly contemptuous and offensive in this excerpt, to malign the reformers of the Russian Church for their "impotence," for their weakness in being oppressed over the years by Muslim Turks. Avvakum remembers the "undefiled" and "pure" orthodoxy of the Russian Church of the past.

O you Teachers of Christendom! Rome fell away long ago and lies prostrate, and the Poles [the Polish] fell in the like ruin with her, being to the end the enemies of the Christian. And among you orthodoxy is of mongrel breed; and no wonder—if by the violence of the Turkish Mahound [Muhammadan] you have become impotent, and henceforth it is you who should come to us to learn. By the gift of God among us there is autocracy; till the time of Nikon, the apostate, in our Russia under our pious princes and tsars the orthodox faith was pure and undefiled, and in the Church [there] was no sedition.

Source: From a 1924 translation of Avvakum Petrovich's autobiography, *Zhitiye protopopa Avvakum* (wr. 1672-1673). Quoted in *A History of Russia*, by Nicholas V. Riasanovsky. 2d ed. (New York: Oxford University Press, 1969), p. 217.

---

manner for bowing in church. In 1654, Nikon called a council of clergy to begin making changes in the liturgy. His agents even began going into churches and homes and taking out icons that they believed were painted according to incorrect models.

Avvakum was a leader of those who opposed Nikon's changes. He and his followers believed that the reformers were the ones corrupting pure religious practices by introducing foreign practices. Since the Greeks had agreed to a union with the Roman Catholic Church in 1439 in an attempt to preserve the remains of their empire from the Turks, Avvakum and others believed that the Russians had become the standard-bearers of the true faith. Those who opposed the new reforms became known as the Old Believers or Old Ritualists (*starovery* or *staroobriadtsy*). In 1653, even before Nikon called the council to revise the liturgy, Avvakum was exiled to Siberia with his family for his outspoken criticisms at the beginning of the reforms.

Patriarch Nikon lost the favor of the czar and the church hierarchy because of his personal arrogance and his insistence on the supremacy of the church over the state. However, Russian Church councils adopted the new texts and practices in 1666 and 1667, and the opponents of reform were persecuted by church and state.

Avvakum was recalled to Moscow from Siberia in 1660 and arrived back in that city in 1664. Although he had the opportunity to meet with Czar Alexis several times to defend his views, he was put on trial at the council of 1666. There, according to his autobiography, he not only refused to give up his beliefs but also told the high officials of the church that all of the problems of the Russian Church came from Western influences and new books. Greek models, in his view, were unreliable because they had been corrupted by the Roman Catholics and only traditional Russian practices could be regarded as Orthodox Christianity. He was again exiled, this time to Pustozersk, in the far north.

During this last period of his life, he kept in touch with his followers through his writings. Some time in the 1670's, he also wrote his autobiography, which is considered the first classic of literature in the Russian language. When the Russian novel developed in the early nineteenth century, even nonreligious writers looked back to Avvakum. His autobiography is considered an expression of Russian nationalism in the face of foreign influences, as well as the depiction of a courageous and influential life.

In 1682, Patriarch Ioakim issued a spiritual decree, which condemned the "old belief." In that same year, under Ioakim's guidance, the church completed a new council, which had begun in 1681. The council laid down a new set of measures designed to combat those who did not follow the revised rites. Avvakum was sentenced to death, part of the new effort by authorities to combat the Old Belief. He was burned at the stake in Pustozersk while making the old-style sign of the cross.

SIGNIFICANCE

Avvakum was one of the most significant leaders of those who sought to maintain the old practices of Russian religion. The Old Believers rejected the currents of change and Westernization that began during the reign of Czar Alexis and that intensified during the rule of Alexis's son, Peter the Great. Old Believers continue to practice into the twenty-first century.

Avvakum did not intend to create great literature when he wrote his autobiography, which was intended as propaganda in religious conflict and was meant to justify his own actions. Nevertheless, it is considered one of the great Russian literary works, indeed, one of the great documents in any faith, and it was the first-known Russian book to be written in colloquial Russian rather than in the formal Slavonic language of the church.

—*Carl L. Bankston III*

FURTHER READING

Avvakum Petrovich. *Archpriest Avvakum: The Life Written by Himself*. Translated by Kenneth Bostrop. Ann Arbor: Michigan Slavic Publications, 1979. An English translation of Avvakum's autobiography *Zhitiye protopopa Avvakum*, which includes translator's annotations, commentary, and historical introduction.

Bushkovitch, Paul. *Religion and Society in Russia: The Sixteenth and Seventeenth Centuries*. New York: Oxford University Press, 1992. Bushkovitch explains the fundamental changes that took place in the Russian Orthodox Church, describing how these changes were influenced by Western European ideas and how they eventually led to Peter the Great's secularization of Russia.

Kliuchevsky, V. O. *A Course in Russian History: The Seventeenth Century*. Translated by Natalie Duddington. Armonk, N.Y.: M. E. Sharpe, 1994. A translation of a classic work by one of Russia's most eminent historians. Chapter 15 examines Nikon, Avvakum, and the church schism.

Kotilaine, Jarmo, and Marshall Poe, eds. *Modernizing Muscovy: Reform and Social Change in Seventeenth Century Russia*. New York: Routledge Curzon, 2004. A collection of articles that provides an encyclopedic account of politics, society, and religion in Russia during the seventeenth century. Includes useful references in footnotes of each article and an index.

Michels, Georg Bernhard. *At War with the Church: Religious Dissent in Seventeenth Century Russia*. Stanford, Calif.: Stanford University Press, 1999. A study of the religious dissenters, including Avvakum, involved in the schism of the Russian Church. Attempts to reconstruct popular culture to understand the behavior and thought of the dissenters.

Riasanovsky, Nicholas V. *A History of Russia*. 2d ed. New York: Oxford University Press, 1969. Avvakum is discussed in a section on the relationship between Muscovite religion and culture. Maps, bibliography, appendices, index.

SEE ALSO: Alexis; Nikon; Michael Romanov.

RELATED ARTICLES in *Great Events from History: The Seventeenth Century, 1601-1700:* 1652-1667: Patriarch Nikon's Reforms; 1672-c. 1691: Self-Immolation of the Old Believers.

NATHANIEL BACON
English-born American colonist and rebel

Nathaniel Bacon died while leading a rebellion against the royally appointed governor of Virginia. A century later, on the eve of the American Revolution, he became a symbol of resistance to tyranny.

BORN: January 2, 1647; Friston Hall, Suffolk, England
DIED: October 26, 1676; Gloucester County, Virginia
AREA OF ACHIEVEMENT: Government and politics

EARLY LIFE

The eldest son of Thomas Bacon, Nathaniel Bacon was born on January 2, 1647, at Friston Hall, Suffolk, as the English Civil Wars were in their final phase. His father was a member of the cadet branch of the great Bacon family and a cousin of Francis Bacon, the lord chancellor of Elizabeth I.

At the age of thirteen, Nathaniel Bacon matriculated at Saint Catherine's College, Cambridge, but in 1663, his father withdrew him from the university. Apparently, the young Bacon, a member of one of the leading Puritan families, had ignored his studies in favor of the temptations available to a young man with money. During the next three years, Bacon, accompanied by John Ray, a noted naturalist, and two of the former Cambridge tutor's students, traveled extensively in Europe.

An attack of smallpox early in 1666 brought Bacon's grand tour to an unexpected conclusion, and he came home to recuperate. He later returned to Cambridge, where he graduated at the age of twenty-one with bachelor of arts and master of arts degrees. He then entered the Inns of Court in London, reading law at Grey's Inn to prepare himself for the place of leadership in Suffolk that was his birthright.

In 1673, he married Elizabeth Duke, daughter of Sir Edward Duke of Benhall, against her father's will. The baronet disinherited Elizabeth for her disobedience, but Bacon's troubles were just beginning. Out of either ignorance or indifference, he became involved in a plan to defraud a friend, and when the full details of the scheme became public, Bacon's father, seeking to avoid another scandal, provided this volatile and often troublesome son with eighteen thousand pounds to permit him to assume the lifestyle of a gentleman in one of England's American colonies.

Until his marriage to Elizabeth, Bacon's experiences had been typical of his class; however, his life changed forever when he emigrated to Virginia in 1673. He settled at Curles in Henrico County, a plantation on the James River about 40 miles (64 kilometers) above Jamestown. Bacon should have had a brilliant future in Virginia; his cousin, Nathaniel Bacon, Sr., was auditor-general for the colony and a councillor. Almost immediately, the younger Bacon was granted a seat on the governing council through the influence of his kinsman.

LIFE'S WORK

Sir William Berkeley, who had first been appointed governor of England's oldest colony in the New World in 1642, had been removed a decade later by the Cromwellian government because of his loyalty to the Crown. With the Restoration of Charles II in 1660, Berkeley was reappointed governor of the Old Dominion, the name the king had given the second domain to proclaim him monarch after the death of his father in January, 1649. Unfortunately, Berkeley's second term would prove a disaster, in large part because of Nathaniel Bacon.

Berkeley had devoted his years in exile to recruiting settlers for Virginia, especially members of the disgruntled royalist faction who wished to escape the restrictive policies of the Cromwellian government. Royalist migration was at its height between 1647 and 1660. Many of these immigrants were the younger sons of prominent families from the south and west of England. These new settlers changed the character of Virginia as they sought to replicate a society based upon large estates with a dependent servant class. After 1660, the policy of the impecunious government of Charles II to make large grants of land in Virginia in lieu of money payments only sped up Virginia's transformation. The vision of Berkeley and his associates, who were known as the Green Spring Faction, had no place for the small independent farmer or the indentured servant. These disgruntled and dispossessed farmers and servants formed the core of the group that Bacon would lead in open rebellion against the governor and his supporters.

In 1628, the price per pound of Virginia tobacco dropped from 24-36 pence to 2.5-3 pence, where it remained until the middle of the eighteenth century. This drop of approximately 90 percent destroyed the modest prosperity of a class of small farmers within a few years. Unable to pay the taxes levied by the Virginia government, many were forced to sell their holdings to Berkeley's newly recruited gentry and seek positions as laborers on lands that had once been their own. These men

Nathaniel Bacon. (Library of Congress)

dians, including some innocent Susquehannocks. The settlers, however, still were not satisfied.

Six months later, the Susquehannocks took their revenge by slaughtering thirty-six settlers. They were now ready to make peace, and to the disgust of his subjects living on the frontier, Berkeley agreed. The governor then levied new taxes to build a new chain of defensive forts along the frontier, but it was too late for reconciliation. By April, 1676, the planters of Charles City County began to arm, and they chose Bacon to lead them in their campaign to exterminate every Indian they could find. Governor Berkeley forbade Bacon to accept their commission, but Bacon ignored him, and for this act of defiance, he was declared a rebel on May 10, 1676.

Bacon's systematic slaughter of Indians, both friend and foe, earned him the adoration of his followers. He was elected to the House of Burgesses from Henrico County, and with an armed escort, he boldly sailed down the James River to assume his seat in the statehouse. To the surprise of friend and foe alike, Berkeley pardoned Bacon and promised him a military commission. Bacon did not trust the governor, however, and to force him to fulfill his promise, he marched on Jamestown with a force of four thousand. The governor was furious, but the terrified House of Burgesses granted the commission to "General" Bacon.

When Bacon sought more Indians to kill, Berkeley again declared him a rebel. However, the House of Burgesses was packed with Bacon's supporters. They proceeded to pass a series of measures dubbed Bacon's Laws. Although Bacon had nothing to do with their passage, these liberal measures sought to redress the balance between the small landholders and the "new" gentry while trying to correct many of the supposed abuses of Berkeley's administration. When Berkeley finally regained control over Virginia, though, these laws were quickly repealed by his supporters. Bacon then issued his Manifesto and Declaration of the People on July 29 and turned the fury of his followers on the Pamunkey tribe. Meanwhile, Berkeley recaptured Jamestown, only to lose it to Bacon again on September 19, 1676. Bacon then burned the capital.

might have recouped their losses if they had moved beyond the frontier, but this was forbidden by Berkeley. These lands were reserved by treaty for the American Indians, a policy that naturally was resented by the men whose fathers had first colonized Virginia. To make matters worse, in 1670, all freemen in Virginia who were neither householders nor landowners lost their right to vote. The colony of Virginia was therefore ripe for rebellion when Bacon arrived in the Old Dominion three years later.

The episodes that sparked Bacon's Rebellion were of secondary importance until the government overreacted. In the summer of 1675, some members of the Doeg tribe sought restitution from a Stafford County planter who owed them money. When an American Indian killed a white settler in an unrelated incident, Governor Berkeley ordered the militia to pursue the miscreants, which resulted in the deaths of a number of In-

This act of senseless destruction caused a number of Bacon's landed supporters to desert his cause. He then began actively to recruit both white and black indentured servants, to whom he promised freedom, but in so doing, he lost even more of his original adherents. The implications of Bacon's "social revolution" were never realized. On October 26, 1676, he died of "a bloody flux," or dysentery.

Governor Berkeley swiftly put an end to the rebellion by executing twenty-three of Bacon's followers. A royal commission conducted an inquiry into the affair in 1677, placing the blame on Berkeley and recommending his removal as governor. It also urged the Crown to curb the power of the House of Burgesses, thus ending for a century the possibility of a more egalitarian Virginia. Troubled by Bacon's appeal to the dispossessed, Virginia's planter aristocracy opted for a system of labor based on black slavery and thus changed forever the social and economic character of the Old Dominion.

SIGNIFICANCE

More potential demagogue than potential democrat, Bacon has nonetheless captured the imagination of those who consider him one of America's first patriot heroes. Born into one of the most respected and distinguished families in seventeenth century England, Bacon enjoyed all of the privileges of his class while fulfilling few of its responsibilities. His reputation for extravagance and reckless behavior was so well known that his clandestine marriage caused his wife to lose her inheritance.

Sent to Virginia to avoid another scandal, Bacon found himself in the midst of a crisis, which in its social implications closely resembled that which had plunged England into civil war a generation earlier. Many colonists faced economic ruin as a result of the policies of a governor who had lost touch with his constituency and of market factors beyond their control. Bacon assumed the leadership of these colonists, challenged the establishment, and almost won. His untimely death abruptly ended the social revolution that he had just begun, but his activities earned him a secure place in America's revolutionary pantheon. A century later, on the eve of the American Revolution, the legend of Bacon and his challenge to Sir William Berkeley inspired the founding fathers in their struggle against George III.

—Clifton W. Potter, Jr.

FURTHER READING

Andrews, Charles McLean. *Narratives of the Insurrections, 1675-1690.* 1943. Reprint. New York: Barnes and Noble, 1967. The first 140 pages of this volume are devoted to seventeenth century colonial America, presenting the original sources dealing with Bacon's Rebellion.

Billings, Warren M. *The Old Dominion in the Seventeenth Century: A Documentary History of Virginia, 1606-1689.* Chapel Hill: University of North Carolina Press, 1975. Examines documentary evidence from the seventeenth century for every aspect of life in colonial Virginia, placing Bacon's Rebellion in the context of the social transformation occurring after 1660.

_____. *Sir William Berkeley and the Forging of Colonial Virginia.* Baton Rouge: Louisiana State University Press, 2004. A biography of the governor who declared Bacon a rebel and crushed Bacon's Rebellion.

Carson, Jane. *Bacon's Rebellion, 1676-1976.* Jamestown, Va.: Jamestown Foundation, 1976. This slender volume not only presents a concise narrative of the events of 1676 but also deals in a critical manner with the sources, the histories, and the fictional narratives inspired by Nathaniel Bacon. The endnotes are valuable for further study.

Mouer, L. Daniel. "Digging a Rebel's Homestead." *Archaeology* 44, no. 4 (July/August, 1991): 54. Describes the causes of Bacon's Rebellion and the rebellion's implications for archaeology.

"Three Hundred Twenty-Five Years Ago." *American Heritage* 52, no. 3 (May, 2001): 96. Focuses on Governor William Berkeley's attempts to proclaim Bacon a rebel and quash Bacon's Rebellion.

Washburn, Wilcomb E. *The Governor and the Rebel: A History of Bacon's Rebellion.* 1957. Reprint. Chapel Hill: University of North Carolina Press, 1972. In this study, the roles are reversed: Bacon becomes an opportunist who exploited the gullible and the trusting in a bid for power that ended with his death, and Berkeley assumes the position of hero. Whether Sir William was Virginia's best colonial governor is debatable, but this work does provide an alternative to the usual treatment of the rebellion and those involved in it.

Webb, Stephen Saunders. *1676: The End of American Independence.* New York: Alfred A. Knopf, 1984. Reprint. Syracuse, N.Y.: Syracuse University Press, 1995. The author sees Bacon's Rebellion as one of the pivotal events in the evolution of American democracy. The revolt's failure sets in motion forces that make the rebellion of the colonies a century later inevitable. This view of the event is both new and controversial.

Wertenbaker, Thomas Jefferson. *Bacon's Rebellion, 1676.* Charlottesville: University Press of Virginia, 1957. Reprint. Baltimore: Genealogical, 1998. Wertenbaker begins his story with Governor Berkeley's return to Virginia in 1659, then recounts the events and political intrigues that led to the rebellion seven years later.

_____. *Torchbearer of the Revolution: The Story of Bacon's Rebellion and Its Leader.* 1940. Reprint. Gloucester, Mass.: Peter Smith, 1965. In the absence of a modern treatment of Bacon's life, this slender work from another generation remains the standard.

The narrative is well written and easily read, although the author's acceptance of Bacon as a precursor of American democracy is rather dated.

SEE ALSO: Charles II (of England); John Lilburne.
RELATED ARTICLES in *Great Events from History: The Seventeenth Century, 1601-1700:* May 14, 1607: Jamestown Is Founded; 1642-1651: English Civil Wars; December 16, 1653-September 3, 1658: Cromwell Rules England as Lord Protector; May, 1659-May, 1660: Restoration of Charles II; May 10-October 18, 1676: Bacon's Rebellion.

RICHARD BAXTER
English theologian and writer

Through his preaching, writing, and friendship with many political and church leaders, Baxter aided substantially in establishing an English cultural tradition of Nonconformity and freedom of conscience.

BORN: November 12, 1615; Rowton, Shropshire, England
DIED: December 8, 1691; London, England
AREAS OF ACHIEVEMENT: Religion and theology, government and politics, social reform

EARLY LIFE
Reaching maturity as the English Civil War began, Richard Baxter can be understood only with some knowledge of the historical context in which he lived. As a chaplain to the parliamentary forces, Baxter was an eyewitness of many of the battles and sieges of the war. He served as an influential minister during the years of the Puritan Commonwealth and so lost his ecclesiastical office during the Restoration of the Stuart kings. Continuing his work in a less prominent fashion, particularly by writing many books, he lived to serve freely once again after the Glorious Revolution of 1688.

Baxter was born on November 12, 1615, in the ancestral home of his mother in Rowton, Shropshire, and he lived there with his grandparents until he was ten years old. His father possessed a small estate ten miles away at Eaton Constantine. The estate had several rent-paying tenants, providing a modest income for the family. Baxter went to live with his parents at their estate at about the time of the coronation of Charles I in 1625.

An eager, sensitive, intelligent boy, Baxter was an avid reader, delighting especially in historical romances. He later wrote that he was "addicted" to playfulness and regretted stealing fruit from his neighbors' orchards. One of his father's tenants was the town piper, and Baxter recalled colorful dances in the village with bells jingling from the legs of the dancers' costumes. His schooling, however, was sporadic and inconsistent under eight different schoolmasters, most of them poorly educated and lazy.

Baxter then spent eighteen months at nearby Ludlow Castle, reading in preparation for the university, which he never attended. As a result, Baxter was largely self-taught. He loved poetry, music, art, and imaginative thought. "What is heaven to us if there be no love and joy?... Harmony and melody are the pleasure and elevation of my soul," he wrote.

Baxter was frequently ill with violent coughing, tuberculosis, and even smallpox, often fatal in the seventeenth century. He thought he would not live long but believed that his illnesses actually aided his education. As he later put it, "Weakness and pain helped me to study how to die; that set me on studying how to live; and that on studying [the Scriptures]."

Baxter grew up regularly attending the Church of England and at fifteen was confirmed in the Church along with thirty other boys his age. He thought that his spiritual awakening or conversion came gradually, particularly through the study of the Scriptures, just as his father's had earlier. The reality of the brevity of life struck home when his mother died when he was only nineteen. A year later, his father married the sister of two governors, one of Shrewsbury, the other of Banbury. Baxter always respected and admired his stepmother and found in her a kindred spirit.

In 1638, Baxter received a license to teach and an ordination certificate and spent a year at Dudley as schoolmaster. He often preached there and in neighboring villages where poor workers crowded churches, sitting even in windows and outside to hear his messages. From Dudley he moved to Bridgenorth, the second largest town of Shropshire, as assistant pastor. In April, 1641, Baxter left Bridgenorth for Kidderminster, where he began his life's work.

LIFE'S WORK

The first years of Baxter's first pastorate at Kidderminster coincided with the First English Civil War (1642-1646), and Baxter could not avoid the conflict. The issues in the war were essentially two: first, the political issue as to whether the king could govern without the consent of Parliament; second, the ecclesiastical issue as to whether the Church of England would follow an episcopal or a presbyterian form of governance. The episcopal form was hierarchical in nature, with the king and the bishops of the church essentially dictating policy and form of worship. The presbyterian form of church governance allowed for much more freedom of conscience at the grassroots level.

Baxter actually preferred a moderate episcopacy with room for the individual conscience to obey God directly, subject to one's own understanding of Scripture. The essential Reformation doctrine to Baxter was the "priesthood of all believers," or the direct relationship of each member to God through Jesus Christ. The political implications of this doctrine for representative democracy were enormous. Yet Baxter also believed in monarchy as the best form of government, a limited monarchy wherein the king would govern with the strong influence of Parliament and according to Christian principles. Baxter observed, however, that the more wicked types of men that he knew joined with the king and the more religious ones sided with Parliament, as did he.

Baxter accepted an invitation to join one of Oliver Cromwell's regiments as chaplain. In this capacity, he saw much fighting: at the Battle of Langport, the Siege of Bridgewater, and the final assaults on Bristol, Exeter, Oxford, Banbury, and Worcester. His father and many of his friends were imprisoned by the royal forces. While in prison, their houses were plundered by the king's soldiers. Baxter himself lost most of his possessions, except some books. Because of the disruption of war and its effects on morality, Baxter thought that

"it must be a very clear and great necessity that can warrant a war."

The victory of the parliamentary forces in the Civil War led to the execution of King Charles I and the establishment of a commonwealth for England, without a monarch or a House of Lords. Authority rested in the hands of the House of Commons, Lord Protector Oliver Cromwell, and his army. A presbyterian church government was established, with some allowance made for other varieties of Protestantism. Leaders from the English and Scottish churches met at Westminster and carefully prepared one of the most famous church doctrinal statements, the Westminster Confession (1646). Even Baxter, moderate Episcopalian that he was, thought it one of the most accurate statements of orthodox doctrine in church history.

Back in Kidderminster, Baxter resumed his ministerial work. Beside his regular formal preaching and administering of the sacraments of the Church, he visited every family in his church regularly, fourteen each week, to discuss the catechism they were memorizing. He was involved in evangelism, apologetics, and counseling as well and helped to organize an association of ministers of several different Protestant persuasions. One of his chief goals in life was to foster the unity of believers and yet al-

Richard Baxter. (Library of Congress)

low diversity of conscience within the English Church. To this end, he helped organize a petition drive that collected thousands of signatures in an effort to gain parliamentary support for national religious unity. He even had two private four-hour discussions on the matter with Cromwell. Although he failed in this endeavor, he acknowledged that the people had more religious freedom under the Commonwealth than they had had under any English king or queen.

The Restoration of the monarchy by parliamentary vote in 1660 brought Charles II to the throne. With several important exceptions, the new king recognized that a political partnership existed between king and Parliament and did not try to govern as arbitrarily as had his father and grandfather. Baxter welcomed this historical change and for a time was prominent in London and in the royal court. He preached both at Westminster Abbey, before members of Parliament, and at St. Paul's Cathedral in London. In June of 1660, Baxter became a chaplain to the new king and met with him personally. A month later, he preached before the king and was even offered a bishopric under the new episcopal system.

Anglicans were restored to their former positions by the Act for the Confirming and Restoring of Ministers (September, 1660), and the next year the Act of Uniformity required that all clergy not episcopally ordained and consenting to everything in the Prayer Book would lose their licenses to preach, subject to imprisonment for violations. The lawfulness of any attempt to change the form of government of either church or state was repudiated. This law affected schoolmasters and even private tutors as well as ministers. Some two thousand ministers were immediately silenced and their congregations subjected to a radical change in leadership. As a result of this violation of religious liberty, Baxter found himself in the odd position of being a Nonconformist Episcopal. He preached a farewell sermon at St. Anne's, Blackfriars, and then ceased preaching at once.

The public silencing of Baxter in 1661 (except for his occasional writing) had an unexpected consequence. Baxter was forty-six years of age at the time of the Act of Uniformity and had led such a busy life that he had decided to remain unmarried in order to give himself more completely to his work. Now, however, he had a chance to reconsider. The result was his marriage on September 10, 1662, to Margaret Charlton, an aristocratic Shropshire woman some twenty years his junior. That she married Baxter at the lowest point of his career emphasizes the depth with which she cared for her husband for the nineteen years remaining in her lifetime. Well educated,

she knew Latin, Greek, and Hebrew and conversed intelligently and with great wit. Margaret was a practical and understanding wife, of whom Baxter always spoke with the utmost tenderness. The Baxters had no children.

Religious persecution continued in the Restoration Parliament. The Conventicle Act of 1664 struck at personal liberties. Presbyterian, Quaker, and Baptist meetinghouses were destroyed. Anyone found in a religious service not conducted according to the liturgy of the Church of England could be imprisoned for three months and fined five pounds; on the third offense, he could be exiled to one of the American colonies. Hundreds of people were crammed into filthy, damp prisons merely for attending an "unauthorized" church service.

The Baxters lived in the town of Acton, where people crowded into their house on Sundays to hear Baxter preach privately. Once, a bullet, shot through his window, whizzed past him and narrowly missed his sister-in-law. In 1669, Baxter was arrested and held in jail for two weeks before being released on a technicality.

Charles II died in 1685, and his brother James II tried to reestablish Roman Catholicism in England. The heavy hand of government persecution, however, lasted for only three more years. In the process, Baxter was unfairly tried and imprisoned for eighteen months at the King's Bench Prison. Members of Parliament, Anglicans, and Nonconformists united against this renewed persecution and invited William of Orange and Mary Stuart, both related to the Stuart kings, to come from the Netherlands to rule England under a constitutionally limited monarchy. They were crowned William III and Mary II. The English Bill of Rights of 1689 followed, as did the Toleration Act of 1689, which made the Nonconformity of churches apart from the Church of England legal. Baxter was thereafter licensed as a "Nonconforming minister" and worked freely until his death, on December 8, 1691.

SIGNIFICANCE

As part of his ministerial work and political activism, Baxter wrote 141 books and literally hundreds of letters, articles, and sermons. This literary achievement staggers the imagination, particularly in view of his very active life. His writings are not polished and often were written too hastily, without proper editing and revisions. He admitted as much and used writing as a means of organizing and clarifying his thinking. He deliberately wrote in an informal and intimate tone so that his writing could substitute for and reinforce his personal counseling.

Typical of both the Puritans and the great Catholic

theologians of the Middle Ages, Baxter wrote in a clear, methodical, analytical style, building from basic axioms in a logical, deductive way. When his starting point is the existence of the universe and its form, for example, he demonstrates that there is no metaphysical necessity for the diversity seen everywhere in nature and argues that such variety could come only from a purposeful, creative, self-existing God. Similarly, when his starting point is his own existence, he observes that a human being has personality, what he calls "power," "understanding," and "will," none of which could come from an inanimate, material source.

Baxter believed in a rational faith based on Scripture, and the titles of several of his books reflect that perspective: *The Unreasonableness of Infidelity* (1655), *The Reasons of the Christian Religion* (1667), and *More Reasons for the Christian Religion* (1672). He considered himself a philosopher and had a coherent and defensible position in each of the basic categories of philosophy: the natures of reality, of the universe, of God, of human beings, and of ethics; he also had a theory of knowledge.

Baxter saw both sides of issues, the mark of a true scholar. He sought toleration toward opponents and reconciliation within the framework of adherence to basic truths of Scripture. He wanted people to accept a "mere Christianity" that included room for freedom of conscience and Christian liberty. Consequently, he recommended listening to conciliatory men of all factions, including many Episcopalians, such as Bishop James Ussher; Presbyterians, such as John Calvin; and Congregationalists, such as Giles Firmin.

Baxter's writings, too, are important as a record of the Christian experience, the searching of a sincere heart after God, and in the process the finding of meaning in life. He saw the hand of Providence in the mysteries and unanswered questions of life and thought the personal control of God far more satisfying than the concept of life being blown about by impersonal chance, fortune, or fate. His pilgrimage influenced many others and left a mark on history for good and for freedom.

—*William H. Burnside*

FURTHER READING

Baxter, Richard. *The Autobiography of Richard Baxter: Being the "Reliquiae Baxterianae" Abridged from the Folio, 1696.* Edited by J. M. Lloyd Thomas. London: J. M. Dent and Sons, 1925. Baxter's autobiography, filled with anecdotes and observations on historical events taking place around him. One cannot completely understand Baxter without reading this book.

_____. *The Practical Works of Richard Baxter, with a Preface, Giving Some Account of the Author, and of This Edition of His Practical Works: An Essay on His Genius, Works, and Times, and a Portrait.* 4 vols. London: G. Virtue, 1846. Reprint. Morgan, Pa.: Soli Deo Gloria, 2000. Contains four of Baxter's books: *The Christian Director*, *A Call to the Unconverted*, *The Saints' Everlasting Rest*, and *The Reformed Pastor*.

Cragg, Gerald R. *Puritanism in the Period of the Great Persecution, 1660-1688.* New York: Cambridge University Press, 1957. Reprint. New York: Russell & Russell, 1971. Excellent account of religious conflict during the Commonwealth and Restoration periods, charting the rise and decline of Puritan influence in England. The most complete analysis available.

Keeble, N. H. *Richard Baxter: Puritan Man of Letters.* New York: Oxford University Press, 1982. One of the more scholarly works on Baxter; focuses on his writings to discuss his worldview and philosophical presuppositions.

Lamont, William. *Puritanism and Historical Controversy.* Montreal, Que.: McGill-Queen's University Press, 1996. Focuses on the lives of Baxter and other Puritans to examine the influence of Puritanism upon capitalism, revolution, science, and other areas of seventeenth century life.

Lim, Paul Chang-Ha. *In Pursuit of Purity, Unity, and Liberty: Richard Baxter's Puritan Ecclesiology in Its Seventeenth Century Context.* Studies in the History of Christian Thought 112. Boston: Brill, 2004. Describes Baxter's concepts of the true church within the context of the second half of the seventeenth century.

Loane, Marcus L. "Richard Baxter: A Mere Nonconformist." In *Makers of Religious Freedom in the Seventeenth Century.* Grand Rapids, Mich.: Wm. B. Eerdmans, 1961. A concise and sympathetic account of Baxter's life, borrowing heavily from Baxter's autobiography. Loane views Baxter as both a witness and a participant in the growth of dissent within the Church of England.

Morgan, Irvonwy. *The Nonconformity of Richard Baxter.* London: Epworth Press, 1946. Explains the issues dividing Episcopalians from Presbyterians and discusses Baxter's advocacy of a more moderate episcopacy.

Nuttall, Geoffrey F. *Richard Baxter.* Stanford, Calif.: Stanford University Press, 1965. One of the most interesting Baxter biographies, containing detailed information, insightful anecdotes, and quotations. Shows Baxter as a conciliatory peacemaker who sought to unite the various factions in the ecclesiastical quarrel. Helpful bibliography.

Watts, Michael R. *The Dissenters.* Oxford, England: Clarendon Press, 1978. An account of dissent in England from 1641 to 1689. Discusses the wide variety of Dissenters, of whom Baxter represented only one type.

SEE ALSO: Charles I; Charles II (of England); Oliver Cromwell; James II; Mary II; James Ussher; William III.

RELATED ARTICLES in *Great Events from History: The Seventeenth Century, 1601-1700:* 1642-1651: English Civil Wars; December 6, 1648-May 19, 1649: Establishment of the English Commonwealth; May, 1659-May, 1660: Restoration of Charles II; May 19, 1662: England's Act of Uniformity; April 4, 1687, and April 27, 1688: Declaration of Liberty of Conscience; November, 1688-February, 1689: The Glorious Revolution; February 13, 1689: Declaration of Rights; May 24, 1689: Toleration Act.

PIERRE BAYLE
French philosopher

Bayle was a great skeptical arguer who criticized philosophical theories both old and new and exposed the weaknesses of Catholic and Protestant theologies. His criticisms helped pave the way for modern toleration and provided the principal arguments for the Enlightenment.

BORN: November 18, 1647; Carla-le-Comte, France
DIED: December 28, 1706; Rotterdam, the Netherlands
AREAS OF ACHIEVEMENT: Philosophy, religion and theology, historiography

EARLY LIFE

Pierre Bayle (pyehr behl) was born in the small town of Carla-le-Comte, near the Spanish border south of Toulouse, where his father was a Calvinist minister. He grew up during the increasing persecution of Protestants in France. He was first sent to a Calvinist academy at Puylaurens. Next, he attended the Jesuit college in Toulouse, because there was no advanced Protestant school left in his area.

His studies with the Jesuits led him to consider the controversial arguments used by Catholics to convert the Protestants. On the basis of intellectual considerations, he soon became a Catholic, the worst thing a son of an embattled Calvinist minister could do. He quickly redeemed himself by converting from Catholicism back to Protestantism, again on the basis of intellectual arguments. This second conversion made Bayle a relapse, someone who has returned to heresy after having abjured it. As such, he was subject to banishment or imprisonment. For his protection, he was sent to the University

of Geneva to complete his studies in philosophy and theology.

To earn his living, Bayle returned to France in disguise and was a tutor in Paris and Rouen. In 1675, he became professor of philosophy at the Calvinist academy at Sedan, where he was the protégé of the fanatically orthodox Protestant theologian Pierre Jurieu, who was to become his most bitter enemy. Bayle and Jurieu taught at Sedan until it was closed by the French government in 1681. They then went to the Netherlands as refugees and were reunited as faculty members of the new academy in Rotterdam, the École Illustre, and as leading figures in the French Reformed church in that city.

LIFE'S WORK

Bayle's career as an author began shortly after his arrival in Rotterdam. He published a work he had drafted in France, *Lettre sur la comète* (1682; *Miscellaneous Reflections Occasion'd by the Comet Which Appear'd in December, 1680*, 1708), in which he began his critique of superstition, intolerance, bad philosophy, and bad history. This was followed by *Critique générale de l'histoire du calvinisme de M. Maimbourg* (1682; general criticism of Father Maimbourg's history of Calvinism), an examination of a very polemical history of Calvinism by a leading Jesuit. In 1684, Bayle edited *Recueil de quelques pièces curieuses concernant la philosophie de M. Descartes*, a collection of articles about Cartesianism, which was then under attack by the Jesuits. The collection contained articles by Nicolas de Malebranche, Bayle, and others. From 1684 to 1687, Bayle published a learned journal, *Nouvelles de la République des Lettres*, in which he commented on the theories then appearing

BAYLE'S MAJOR WORKS

1682   *Lettre sur la comète (Miscellaneous Reflections Occasion'd by the Comet Which Appear'd in December, 1680,* 1708)

1682   *Critique générale de l'histoire du calvinisme de M. Maimbourg*

1686   *Commentaire philosophique sur ces paroles de Jésus-Christ "Contrain-les d'entrer" (A Philosophical Commentary on These Words in the Gospel, Luke XIV, 23: "Compel Them to Come In, That My House May Be Full,"* 1708)

1697   *Dictionnaire historique et critique (An Historical and Critical Dictionary,* 1710)

of Gottfried Wilhelm Leibniz, Malebranche, Antoine Arnauld, Robert Boyle, and John Locke, among others.

Because of his acute judgment, which appeared in his early writings, Bayle became one of the central figures in the republic of letters and was in direct contact with many of its leading personalities. From 1684 to 1685, Bayle devoted himself exclusively to scholarly writing. His brothers and his father died in France as a result of the religious persecution against Protestants. He declined when the Jurieu family offered the opportunity of an advantageous marriage. He rejected a position as professor at the University of Franeker, preferring to remain in Rotterdam, contending against various kinds of opponents.

In 1686, Bayle published *Commentaire philosophique sur ces paroles de Jésus-Christ "Contrain-les d'entrer" (A Philosophical Commentary on These Words in the Gospel, Luke XIV, 23: "Compel Them to Come In, That My House May Be Full,"* 1708). This essay was directed against the Catholic persecution of the Protestants in France. In it, Bayle developed the most extensive argument of the time for complete toleration, going further than Locke did in *A Third Letter for Toleration* (1692). Bayle advocated tolerating Muslims, Jews, Unitarians, and atheists, as well as Catholics (who were then persecuted in the Netherlands). Bayle's views used skeptical arguments as a basis for complete toleration of all views, claiming that an "erring conscience" had as many rights as a nonerring one, since it was impossible to tell who was right or wrong.

Bayle's tolerance brought him into conflict with his erstwhile mentor, Jurieu, who became the theorist of intolerance and a dominant figure in the French Reformed

church while in exile. Their differences became so great that Jurieu denounced his colleague as a menace to true religion and a secret atheist. During the late 1680's, Bayle began a furious pamphlet war against Jurieu and criticized the liberals who sought to develop a rational, scientifically acceptable version of Christianity. Bayle's many controversies led to his dismissal from the Rotterdam professorship in 1693. The rest of his life was devoted to skeptical, polemical scholarship.

Bayle's greatest work, *Dictionnaire historique et critique* (1697; *An Historical and Critical Dictionary,* 1710), began as an effort to correct all the errors he had found in previous dictionaries and encyclopedias and was a way of skeptically criticizing philosophical, scientific, and theological theories. The dictionary consists almost exclusively of articles about deceased people and defunct movements, with a few articles about places. Bayle decided to omit persons who had been adequately dealt with in the previous biographical dictionary of Louis Moreri from 1674. Thus, many well-known people, such as Plato and William Shakespeare and René Descartes, are missing, while many obscure people are given articles of substantial length. The format of Bayle's dictionary, in folio volumes, was to set forth a biography of a personage on the top of the page, with long footnotes below, and with notes to the notes on the side. This gives the book a look somewhat like that of an edition of the Talmud.

The core of the dictionary is in the notes and the notes to the notes, in which Bayle digressed to discuss and dissect old and new theories on a variety of subjects. He skeptically challenged Scholastic philosophy, Cartesianism, and the new philosophies of Leibniz, Malebranche, Ralph Cudworth, Baruch Spinoza, Locke, and Isaac Newton. He challenged Catholic and Protestant theologies and sought to show that they were unable to give a consistent or credible explanation of the problem of evil. Throughout *An Historical and Critical Dictionary,* Bayle claimed that his skepticism was a means of undermining or destroying reason in order to make room for faith. He cited Blaise Pascal to show this. Also throughout the work, however, Bayle questioned the moral or religious sincerity of the leading figures of the Old Testament, the Church Fathers, and the religious leaders of the Reformation. He reported all varieties of immoral sexual conduct, unethical practices, and hypocritical behavior of everyone from Noah and his children, to the heroes of Greek mythology, to kings and queens, to saints and church leaders.

An Historical and Critical Dictionary shocked the

learned and religious worlds. The French Reformed church tried to ban it; it was attacked by many, with the result that it quickly became a best-seller. In the second edition (1702), Bayle had promised his church that he would explain what they found most outrageous: his article on King David, his defense of atheists, his Pyrrhonian skepticism, and his inclusion of so much obscene material. He wrote four lengthy clarifications of these matters, which only infuriated his opponents more. The clarification on skepticism became one of his most important statements on the relationship of skepticism and religion. The material in the second edition became basic to discussions of philosophy and theology in the eighteenth century. It was used extensively by George Berkeley, David Hume, Voltaire, and many others.

In the four years after the appearance of the second edition of the dictionary, Bayle wrote several works continuing his attacks on his many opponents, particularly his orthodox, liberal, and rational opponents. Critics insisted that he was trying to undermine all philosophy, science, and religion. He insisted that he was a true believer, trying to destroy reason to buttress faith.

SIGNIFICANCE

Bayle was one of the most important skeptical arguers of the seventeenth century, who provided what was called "the arsenal of the Enlightenment." His many critical works, especially *An Historical and Critical Dictionary*, raised the central problems and questions of the time, challenging all the philosophical and theological solutions that had been offered previously. From the time that Bayle was alive and continuing after his death, there has been debate about his real intentions. Some see him as a chronic outsider, criticizing all views while apparently maintaining just a modicum of religious faith.

Regardless of his intent, Bayle influenced thinkers for the next hundred years. Leibniz wrote *Essais de théodicée sur la bonté de Dieu, la liberté de l'homme, et l'origine du mal* (1710; *Theodicy: Essays on the Goodness of God, the Freedom of Man, and the Origin of Evil*, 1952) to try and answer Bayle's skeptical attacks on religious solutions to the problem of evil. Berkeley and Hume took some of their basic argumentation from Bayle, and French Enlightenment figures from Voltaire onward built upon his criticisms. Immanuel Kant used him as a source for the antinomies of pure reason. Thomas Jefferson recommended Bayle's works as one of the initial purchases for the Library of Congress. Bayle continued to be influential until *An Historical and Critical Dictionary* was replaced by modern encyclopedias,

and his skepticism was replaced by modern scientific positivistic views. In the late twentieth century, there was a strong revival of interest in his writing and impact among scholars. He has since been recognized as one of the seminal figures in seventeenth and eighteenth century thought.

—Richard H. Popkin

FURTHER READING

Bayle, Pierre. *Historical and Critical Dictionary, Selections*. Translated by Richard H. Popkin and Craig Brush. Indianapolis, Ind.: Bobbs-Merrill, 1965. A collection of forty articles, exhibiting the range of Bayle's views.

Brush, Craig. *Montaigne and Bayle: Variations on the Theme of Skepticism*. The Hague, the Netherlands: Martinus Nijhoff, 1966. A comparison of the two thinkers, showing some profound differences as well as general points of agreement.

Labrousse, Elisabeth. *Bayle*. Translated by Denys Potts. New York: Oxford University Press, 1983. An overall view of Bayle's place in intellectual history by a leading Bayle scholar.

Lennon, Thomas M. *Reading Bayle*. Toronto, Canada: University of Toronto Press, 1999. An interpretation of Bayle's thought for modern readers.

Lieshout, H. H. M. van. *The Making of Pierre Bayle's "Dictionnaire historique et critique": With a CD-Rom Containing the Dictionaire's Library and References Between Articles*. Amsterdam: APA-Holland University Press, 2001. A detailed chronology of the dictionary's production, including a list of contributors, and a list of sources with references to their location in the book.

Mason, H. T. *Pierre Bayle and Voltaire*. London: Oxford University Press, 1963. A comparison of Bayle and Voltaire, with an effort to assess what Voltaire borrowed from Bayle.

Popkin, Richard H., ed. *The High Road to Pyrrhonism*. San Diego, Calif.: Austin Hill Press, 1980. Contains several articles dealing with Bayle's skepticism and his influence. See also the author's article on Bayle in *The Encyclopedia of Philosophy* (1967), edited by Paul Edwards.

Rex, Walter. *Essays on Pierre Bayle and Religious Controversy*. The Hague, the Netherlands: Martinus Nijhoff, 1965. A study of Bayle's views in the context of seventeenth century French Protestant theology.

Robinson, Howard. *Bayle the Skeptic*. New York: Columbia University Press, 1931. Presents Bayle as an irreligious skeptic, the precursor of Enlightenment atheism.

Sandberg, Karl C. *At the Crossroads of Faith and Reason: An Essay on Pierre Bayle*. Tucson: University of Arizona Press, 1966. An interpretation of Bayle as a sincere Calvinist.

Tinsley, Barbara Sher. *Pierre Bayle's Reformation: Conscience and Criticism on the Eve of Enlightenment*. Selingsgrove, Pa.: Susquehanna University Press, 2001. Tinsley argues that Bayle was not a religious skeptic, but a Reformed Calvinist, who devised a model for regarding religious customs and other behavior with critical skepticism.

SEE ALSO: Robert Boyle; René Descartes; Gottfried Wilhelm Leibniz; John Locke; Sir Isaac Newton; Blaise Pascal; Baruch Spinoza.

RELATED ARTICLES in *Great Events from History: The Seventeenth Century, 1601-1700:* 1637: Descartes Publishes His *Discourse on Method*; 1638-1669: Spread of Jansenism; 1651: Hobbes Publishes *Leviathan*; April 4, 1687, and April 27, 1688: Declaration of Liberty of Conscience; May 24, 1689: Toleration Act; 1690: Locke Publishes *Two Treatises of Government*; 1693: Ray Argues for Animal Consciousness.

JOHANN JOACHIM BECHER
German chemist, physician, and inventor

Becher developed ideas on the nature of physical substances that led to a new theory of chemistry. Also, his theory of the three "earths" argued that minerals grew from seeds in Earth's "bowels." As a businessperson, he would seek to capitalize financially on his ideas and inventions.

BORN: May 6, 1635; Speyer, Rhineland-Palatinate (now in Germany)
DIED: October, 1682; London, England
AREAS OF ACHIEVEMENT: Science and technology, chemistry, invention, engineering, medicine, scholarship, government and politics, physics

EARLY LIFE

Johann Joachim Becher (yoh-HAHN YOH-ahk-ihm BEHK-her) was born in a small German town along the Rhine River. Joachim, his multilingual father, was a teacher, then a Lutheran minister who married Anna Margaretha Gauss, the daughter of a Lutheran minister. He became a pastor in Speyer, his wife's hometown. After the birth of Johann, three other sons followed. Johann attended the Speyer Retscher-Gymnasium, but the premature death of his father and his mother's remarriage to an improvident and abusive man led to the end of Johann's formal schooling. During the day, Johann did manual work to help support his mother and brothers, but at night, he continued to educate himself by reading extensively.

At the age of thirteen, Becher left Speyer and began a nomadic life that took him to Sweden, Holland, France, and Italy, where he met many scientists, including alchemists. Throughout his career, he believed that the transmutation of less-valuable metals into gold (a process called alchemy) was possible, and in 1654, he edited an alchemical text.

His "wandering years" temporarily ended in 1657, when he settled at Mainz, about 48 miles north of his birthplace. In Mainz he met Maria Veronika, the beautiful daughter of an imperial councillor. Also, he would convert from Lutheranism to Roman Catholicism and, through the influence of the elector, receive his medical degree from the University of Mainz in 1661. In this same year, he published a book on medicine, and in 1663, he was appointed professor of medicine at the university. When his project of devising a universal language was unfavorably received, he felt that his talents would be better appreciated at another European court.

LIFE'S WORK

It is often difficult to determine Becher's career, given his many conflicting roles and activities: scientist/pseudoscientist, astute businessman/confidence man, inventor/charlatan. For example, at Mannheim in 1664, he devised projects for improving the manufacture of silk, glass, and paper, but, before his plans were actualized, he left for Munich, angering both merchants and the nobility.

As physician to the elector of Bavaria, he had access to the best-equipped chemical laboratory in Europe, which aided him in his alchemical writings. Becher believed that a country could be self-sufficient by efficiently exploiting domestic and foreign raw materials and by developing homebred industries, and so he was an early mercantilist. These economic interests led him, in December of 1665, to accept an appointment as councillor of commerce to Emperor Leopold I in Vienna, Austria, a position he started in 1666.

Becher, an advocate of the government regulation of the economy, pushed for a state monopoly of the silk industry and the construction of a Rhine-Danube canal to facilitate trade between Austria and the Netherlands. As a mercantilist, he urged the establishment of a colonial "New Germany" in the jungles between the Amazon and Orinoco Rivers in South America that would rival the colonies of New England, New France, and New Spain.

Becher published his most important work, *Actorum laboratorii chymici monacensis, seu, physicae subterranae libri duo* (two books of the proceedings of the Munich Chemical Laboratory, or subterranean physics) in 1669 and dedicated it to the elector of Bavaria. Best known as *Physica subterranea* from a later edition (1703) published by the chemist Georg Ernst Stahl, the book deals more with chemistry than with physics. Like many other books of the period, it blended religion and science. Indeed, *Physica subterranea* has been described as a deeply religious book, since Becher viewed the natural world as a creation of "God the Chemist" who was always and forever in contact with his creation through chemical changes.

Unlike many ancient and medieval natural philosophers, and some of his contemporaries, Becher was critical of the classic four-element theory that held that all material substances were composed of earth, air, fire, and water. He also disagreed with the *tria prima* (three principles) of the Renaissance-era alchemist Paracelsus, pointing out that the Paracelsian principles of mercury, sulfur, and salt did not share the physical properties of the actual mercury, sulfur, and salt. Becher believed mercury, sulfur, and salt were compounds, not elements.

The most influential doctrine in *Physica subterranea* was Becher's theory of the three "earths." He believed that minerals grew from seeds in the "bowels of Mother Earth." Every substance in Earth's crust is composed of *terra fluida* (fluid or mercurious earth), *terra pinguis* (fatty or flammable earth), and *terra lapidea* (stoney or vitrifiable earth). Becher maintained that the nature of metals, minerals, and stones depended on the basic earths they contained. For example, if a metal could be melted, it contained fluid earth; if a mineral could be burned, it contained flammable earth; if a stone could be neither liquefied nor burned, it contained vitrifiable earth, the principle of solidity. Using these three earths, Becher ac-

counted for the great variety of inorganic substances as well as properties such as color, shape, odor, and weight. He extended his three-earths theory to the plant and animal kingdoms. He believed in spontaneous generation, that organic life could originate spontaneously from inorganic materials.

Just as he sought economic benefits from his ideas on minerals, so he wished to realize financial rewards from his understanding of organic materials. For example, he devised a technique for producing coke and tar from coal, and he most likely prepared the flammable gas now known as ethylene by mixing alcohol and oil of vitriol (sulfuric acid).

Although some of his ideas and projects, such as the introduction of the potato into Germany, had value, others, such as a perpetual clock and a lamp that would burn forever, had no value. His suggestion of an imperial edict against French imports proved disastrous for German cities and, after a brief imprisonment, he left Vienna for Holland, where, in 1678, he persuaded the Dutch assembly to appropriate funds for his scheme of extracting gold from sand dunes. Like many of his previous proposals, his plan for recovering gold from sea sands was abandoned as impractical. This and other failures most likely contributed to his sudden departure for England without his family.

While in England during the early 1680's, he made some friends among the nobility who supported his work. He completed the final supplement to *Physica subterranea*, acquiring additional knowledge about minerals from his inspections of mines in Scotland and Cornwall. While residing at Falmouth and the Isle of Wight, he wrote other books. He returned to London in 1682, where he completed a collection of fifteen hundred chemical processes, including recipes for making the philosophers' stone, a book published in English as *Magnalia Naturæ: Or, The Philosophers-Stone Lately Exposed to Public Sight and Scale* (1680). He hoped to crown his career by becoming a member of the Royal Society. To this end he wrote a brief treatise on mechanical clocks, but the treatise's lack of originality left the society's officials unimpressed, and he was not elected.

Late in his life, he returned to the Lutheran faith of his early years. Like so many projects throughout his career, his English enterprises bore little fruit, and he died in poverty in London in 1682.

SIGNIFICANCE

Scholars have been divided over the significance of Becher and his works. Some see him as an "ingenious rogue," others as a curious combination of "sense and nonsense," and still others as the first person to construct a modern theory of chemistry. Like many of his seventeenth century colleagues who found themselves on the watershed between the medieval and modern worlds, Becher was a transitional figure. His work in science commingled alchemical and chemical ideas, and consequently, scholars disagree about his place in the history of science. Becher certainly believed in transmutation and practiced alchemy at various European courts, but he condemned astrology, finding its association of planets and metals nonsensical.

Some scholars believe that Becher only gave new names to old ideas, whereas others interpret his introduction of "fatty earth" as a step forward in the evolution of modern chemistry because his *terra pinguis* became "phlogiston" in the writings of Georg Ernst Stahl. Stahl used the idea of phlogiston, the first great generalization of chemistry, in his edition of Becher's *Physica subterranea*.

Many of Becher's financial schemes failed, but some of them involved the significant application of chemical ideas to industry. He was a prolific writer whose books and articles cover a wide variety of theoretical and practical subjects, which, with all their contradictions and outdated ideas, also contain the seeds of several modern scientific theories and techniques. Though he was not able to escape the limitations of his period—he believed in both God and science—he was a protochemist whose description of his profession can be used, mutatis mutandis, to describe his twenty-first century descendants.

> The chemists are a strange class of mortals, impelled by an almost maniacal impulse to seek their pleasures amongst smoke and vapour, soot and flames, poisons and poverty, yet amongst all these evils I seem to live so sweetly that I would rather die than change places with the king of Persia.

—Robert J. Paradowski

FURTHER READING

Brock, William H. *The Chemical Tree: A History of Chemistry*. New York: Norton, 2000. Brock tells the story of chemistry from antiquity to the twentieth century, and he discusses Becher's life and work in the second chapter, "The Sceptical Chemist." Includes an extensive forty-page bibliographic essay and an index.

Jaffe, Bernard. *Crucibles: The Story of Chemistry from Ancient Alchemy to Nuclear Fission*. 4th ed. New York: Dover, 1976. This edition of Jaffe's popular book is a revised and enlarged reprint of the book originally published in 1930. Chapter 3 covers Becher. Includes eleven pages of sources and an index.

Multhauf, Robert P. *The Origins of Chemistry*. New York: Franklin Watts, 1967. This first history of early chemistry by a professional historian of science attempts to do justice to the complexity of the many ancient and medieval disciplines that evolved into modern chemistry. Includes a forty-four-page bibliography and an index.

Partington, James R. *A History of Chemistry*. New York: St. Martin's Press, 1961. Reprint. New York: Martino, 1996. 4 vols. Volume 2 examines the period from 1500 to 1700 and analyzes Becher's life and work, an important analysis for the chapter on phlogiston theory. Volume 1 provides theoretical background to the history of chemistry. Includes indexes of names and subjects.

Smith, Pamela H. *The Business of Alchemy: Science and Culture in the Holy Roman Empire*. Princeton, N.J.: Princeton University Press, 1994. Examines the interplay between the sciences, namely alchemy, culture, and commerce. Includes illustrations, a bibliography, and index.

Strathern, Paul. *Mendeleyev's Dream: The Quest for the Elements*. New York: Berkeley Books, 2002. This book, intended for general readers, narrates the history of how humans came to understand the composition of Earth, with an emphasis on the fascinating people and ideas involved in this quest. Includes a section on further readings and an index.

Thorndike, Lynn. *A History of Magic and Experimental Science*. 8 vols. New York: Columbia University Press, 1958. Volume 3 explores the experimental science of the seventeenth century, and chapter 20 examines the "underground world" of Becher. No index in this volume, but volume 8 has a comprehensive index of the entire work.

SEE ALSO: Jakob Böhme; Robert Boyle; Jan Baptista van Helmont; Leopold I; Marin Mersenne.

RELATED ARTICLE in *Great Events from History: The Seventeenth Century, 1601-1700:* 1660-1692: Boyle's Law and the Birth of Modern Chemistry.

APHRA BEHN
English novelist and playwright

As the first commercially successful woman writer in England in the seventeenth century, Behn set an example for subsequent generations of female novelists and dramatists. Her contribution to English drama, prose, and poetry ranks alongside such contemporaries as John Dryden and William Congreve, and she is often credited as a leading figure in the emergence of the English novel.

BORN: July?, 1640; Kent, England
DIED: April 16, 1689; London, England
ALSO KNOWN AS: Aphara Amis (given name); Aphra Johnson; Aphra Bayn
AREAS OF ACHIEVEMENT: Literature, theater

EARLY LIFE
The early years of the life of Aphra Behn (AF-ruh BAYN) are not well documented and have been the subject of much speculation. A parish register in the town of Wye shows that one Aphara Amis was baptized in that town (in the county of Kent, England) on July 10, 1640, and it is likely that she was born the same year and in the same county. Aphara Amis probably became Aphra Behn. Very little about her parents is known, and most early biographers of Behn, unaware of the Wye baptismal record, established her maiden name as Johnson rather than Amis. One source indicates that Behn's father was a barber, although other scholars have speculated that she was raised as a gentlewoman, since she appears to have been educated in several languages and literatures.

Sometime between the late 1650's and the early 1660's, Behn reportedly traveled to Suriname, which was at the time under British rule. Although even the fact of this trip is disputed, many detailed descriptions of the region appear in Behn's own writings and have been adduced as evidence of her firsthand experience with British imperialism, a subject that she explored at length several years later in her most well-known novel. Behn's husband (about whom almost nothing is known) died in 1665, leaving her with very little money. However, she was reasonably well-connected in the court of Charles II, and in 1666, she traveled to the Netherlands as a government spy in order to gather information about Colonel William Scott, the son of one of the regicides who had aided the deposition and beheading of Charles I.

LIFE'S WORK
After returning to London in 1667, Behn began to establish herself in the English theater scene, and she soon began writing plays herself. In part, her venture into the commercial theater may have been a practical matter, since she had suffered serious financial problems upon returning from the Netherlands and was briefly placed in a debtors' prison in 1667. In 1670, she unsuccessfully attempted to stage her first play, *The Young King: Or, The Mistake* (pr. 1679, pb. 1683), which she had begun composing while in Suriname some years before. The play was rejected by both of the two major commercial theaters in London. Her second play, *The Forced Marriage: Or, The Jealous Bridegroom* (pr. 1670, pb. 1671), was accepted by the Duke's Theatre in

Aphra Behn. (Library of Congress)

Lincoln's Inn Fields and was first performed in December, 1670. Although the play ran for only six days, it was considered a success.

Behn enjoyed a prolific career as a London playwright throughout the next two decades. Her next play, *The Amorous Prince: Or, The Curious Husband* (pr., pb. 1671), was reasonably well received. Behn followed with a slew of other plays, including *Abdelazer: Or, The Moor's Revenge* (pr. 1676, pb. 1677), *The Town Fop: Or, Sir Timothy Tawdry* (pr. 1676, pb. 1677), *The Rover: Or, The Banished Cavaliers, Part I* (pr., pb. 1677), *The Debauchee: Or, The Credulous Cuckold* (pr., pb. 1677), *The Rover: Or, The Banished Cavaliers, Part II* (pr., pb. 1681), *The Lucky Chance: Or, An Alderman's Bargain* (pr. 1686, pb. 1687), *The Emperor of the Moon* (pr., pb. 1687), and *The Widow Ranter: Or, The History of Bacon of Virginia* (pr. 1689, pb. 1690). Most of Behn's plays can be categorized as romantic comedies, and, like her male contemporaries, she often touched on themes of sexual adventure and marital disappointment. At the same time, her plays arguably gave greater attention to the status of women in English society, and some of Behn's most memorable female characters are sharply critical of the limited options available to them.

Behn was arguably the first successful woman playwright in England, and she is often identified as the first woman to make a successful living from her writing. Her status as a woman in a male-dominated field, indeed, in a male-dominated society, made her conspicuous; Behn herself occasionally attributed much of the negative criticism of her works to the fact of her gender rather than to any inherent deficiency in her writing. In this attitude, she was probably correct. Contemporary theater critics often claimed that Behn's plays were derivative almost to the point of plagiarism; however, it was a common and accepted practice among playwrights during the Restoration period to revise existing literary works and present them as "new" plays, and the criticism was seldom leveled at equally "guilty" male playwrights.

BEHN'S MAJOR WORKS	
1670	*The Forced Marriage: Or, The Jealous Bridegroom*
1671	*The Amorous Prince: Or, The Curious Husband*
1673	*The Dutch Lover*
1676	*Abdelazer: Or, The Moor's Revenge*
1676	*The Town Fop: Or, Sir Timothy Tawdry*
1677	*The Rover: Or, The Banished Cavaliers, Part I*
1678	*Sir Patient Fancy*
1679	*The Feigned Courtesans: Or, A Night's Intrigue*
1679	*The Young King: Or, The Mistake*
1681	*The Rover: Or, The Banished Cavaliers, Part II*
1681	*The Roundheads: Or, The Good Old Cause*
1682	*The City Heiress: Or, Sir Timothy Treat-All*
1683-1687	*Love Letters Between a Nobleman and His Sister* (3 volumes)
1684	*Poems upon Several Occasions, with A Voyage to the Island of Love*
1685	*Miscellany: Being a Collection of Poems by Several Hands* (includes works by others)
1686	*La Montre: Or, The Lover's Watch* (prose and poetry)
1686	*The Case for the Watch* (prose and poetry)
1686	*The Lucky Chance: Or, An Alderman's Bargain*
1687	*The Emperor of the Moon*
1687	Translation of *Aesop's Fables* (with Francis Barlow)
1688	*Lycidus: Or, The Lover in Fashion* (prose and poetry; includes works by others)
1688	*Agnes de Castro*
1688	*The Fair Jilt: Or, The History of Prince Tarquin and Miranda*
1688	*Oroonoko: Or, The History of the Royal Slave*
1689	*The Widow Ranter: Or, The History of Bacon of Virginia*
1689	*The History of the Nun: Or, The Fair Vow-Breaker*
1689	*The Lucky Mistake*
1696	*The Younger Brother: Or, The Amorous Jilt*
1697	*The Nun: Or, The Perjured Beauty*
1697	*The Lady's Looking-Glass, to Dress Herself By: Or, The Art of Charming* (prose and poetry)
1698	*The Adventure of the Black Lady*
1698	*The Wandering Beauty*

While Behn's success in the theater was only moderate, however, she was highly regarded among London's literary circles, and she developed a warm friendship with John Dryden, the preeminent poet of the Restoration period. Behn regularly composed poems throughout most of her adult lifetime, and no less than three collections of her poems and translations were published from 1684 to 1688. Much of her poetry was erotic or amorous in nature, such as "Voyage to the Island of Love" (1684) and "On Desire: A Pindarick" (1688), and Behn often inverted conventional poetic forms and established the female figure as the narrative speaker (and, consequently, the male figure as the object of desire). For example, one of Behn's most well-known poems, "The Disappointment" (1684), has as its subject a woman's reaction to an incident of male impotence. Other poems are more political in nature, such as "A Pindaric Poem to the Reverend Doctor Burnet" (1689), and they often reveal her sympathies with Royalist politics.

In addition to her copious dramatic and poetic output, Behn achieved significant success with her prose writings. Her longest work, *Love Letters Between a Nobleman and His Sister* (1683-1687), most likely falls into the category of romance, a literary genre that is typified by a long, frequently digressive narrative and often contains heroic or fantastic plots. At the end of her career, Behn published *Oroonoko: Or, The History of the Royal Slave* (1688), which is sometimes said to be the first English novel. The tale depicts a black African prince who is captured and transported to the colonial island of Suriname (where Behn had herself traveled) as a slave. Although the work is careful not to criticize British imperialism, which it at times in fact celebrates, it is nonetheless progressive in its treatment of race and gender issues. Arguably Behn's most popular work, *Oroonoko* was widely read for several years after its publication, and it was adapted and performed on the London stage throughout the eighteenth century. Behn died on April 16, 1689, and was buried in Westminster Abbey.

SIGNIFICANCE

From a historical perspective, Behn would be an important figure to study solely because she was one of the first English women to make a successful living on the basis of her writing. However, her dramatic, poetic, and prose works are worth reading as literary works in their own right and not merely because of the historical conditions of their production. *The Rover*, for example, stands as one of the wittiest Restoration comedies, and it is still regularly performed. In the late twentieth and early twenty-first centuries, moreover, a virtual subfield of literary criticism arose around Behn's *Oroonoko*, much of it focusing on the issues of gender and British colonialism, topics which Behn's novel uniquely places in dialogue with each other. The fact that this work anticipates the rise of the novel in the eighteenth century (as well as looking back to older romance, and even epic, traditions) makes it an indispensable work for persons studying the development of the modern novel.

—*Joseph M. Ortiz*

FURTHER READING

Carnell, Rachel K. "Subverting Tragic Conventions: Aphra Behn's Turn to the Novel." *Studies in the Novel* 31 (1999): 133-151. Analyzes Behn's fiction in the context of her overall literary career. Carnell argues that, as in her poetry, Behn inverts standard literary conventions in order to undermine traditional models of male heroism.

Mendelson, Sarah Heller. *The Mental World of Stuart Woman: Three Studies*. Brighton, East Sussex, England: Harvester, 1987. Contains informative chapters on Behn's literary career, with particular attention paid to the education and literary culture to which Behn would have had access. Bibliography.

Ortiz, Joseph M. "Arms and the Woman: Narrative, Imperialism, and Virgilian *memoria* in Aphra Behn's *Oroonoko*." *Studies in the Novel* 34 (Summer, 2002): 119-140. Reconsiders Behn's contribution to the rise of the English novel with respect to modern critical theories on the relationship between colonialism and narrative. Particular attention is given to Behn's use of classical literary sources as models for imperialism.

Todd, Janet. *The Secret Life of Aphra Behn*. New Brunswick, N.J.: Rutgers University Press, 1996. Probably the most comprehensive and detailed biography of Behn. This well-written study devotes significant attention to Behn's nonliterary career as a government spy, yet it connects her activities in this area to her later career as a writer. Todd's emphasis is generally on Behn's political attitudes in relation to her cultural and social environment. Several illustrations, extensive bibliography.

Woodcock, George. *Aphra Behn: The English Sappho*. New York: Black Rose Books, 1989. A biography of Behn beginning with her travels to Suriname, this book also includes a long chapter on her activities as a government spy. Subsequent chapters are devoted to her career on the English stage and her publications of poetry and novels. Includes a short chronological bibliography of Behn's published works.

SEE ALSO: Charles I; Charles II (of England); John Dryden.

RELATED ARTICLES in *Great Events from History: The Seventeenth Century, 1601-1700:* 1642-1651: English Civil Wars; May, 1659-May, 1660: Restoration of Charles II.

GIAN LORENZO BERNINI
Italian sculptor and architect

The sculpture and architecture of Bernini are considered to be among the most complete expressions of the thought and feeling of the Counter-Reformation. He is also one of the most representative practitioners of the High Baroque style.

BORN: December 7, 1598; Naples, Kingdom of Naples (now in Italy)
DIED: November 28, 1680; Rome, Papal States (now in Italy)
ALSO KNOWN AS: Giovanni Lorenzo Bernini (full name)
AREAS OF ACHIEVEMENT: Art, architecture

EARLY LIFE

Although born in Naples, Gian Lorenzo Bernini was largely reared in Rome, where his father, Pietro, a minor Florentine sculptor, had obtained employment on the decorative program of Pope Paul V. The young Bernini was, by all accounts, a child prodigy who showed an early aptitude for his father's profession. At the age of eight, he is said to have carved a marble head that excited general admiration, and, by the time he was ten or eleven years old, he had attracted the personal attention of Pope Paul. The principal artistic influences on the young sculptor were, first, his father, who guided and encouraged the boy's early efforts with the utmost devotion, and, second, the Vatican itself, where he drew and studied the masterpieces of ancient sculpture and Renaissance painting.

Bernini's earliest surviving works are not precisely datable; early biographers and some modern scholars accept a date as early as 1610, while a majority place them around 1615. These juvenilia include a lifelike portrait of Bishop G. B. Santoni and a mythological group, *The Goat Amalthea with the Infant Jupiter and a Faun*, long regarded as an ancient Hellenistic piece because of its textural realism. Slightly later, and somewhat larger in scale, are marble figures of Saint Sebastian and Saint Laurence. The latter was Bernini's patron saint and is represented enduring martyrdom on a flaming grill. In order to achieve a convincing facial expression, the sculptor is said to have stuck his own foot into a fire while observing his face in a mirror. Although the story may be apocryphal, it does reflect Bernini's concern for psychological authenticity and his typically Baroque penchant for studying his own reactions.

More ambitious still were a series of life-size marble groups, produced between 1618 and 1625 for the great connoisseur and collector Cardinal Scipione Borghese.

The first, *Aeneas, Anchises, and Ascanius Fleeing Troy*, focuses on the physical and psychological contrast between three stages of life: manhood, old age, and childhood. A similar contrast heightens the drama of *Pluto and Persephone*, which represents the god of the underworld abducting his screaming victim. The vigorous, determined figure of the abductor is juxtaposed to the soft, vulnerable girl in his arms. The imprints of his grasping fingers on her pliant flesh are often cited as an example of Bernini's vivid illusionism. *Apollo and Daphne* again makes the most of a violent and erotic myth in which the nymph turns into a laurel tree at the moment the god seizes her. The capture of seemingly instantaneous action and reaction and the transformation of skin into bark is a tour de force of the sculptor's art.

Work on the *Apollo and Daphne* was interrupted by a new commission from Scipione Borghese for a statue of David. David had been a favorite theme of the Italian sculptural tradition, but Bernini represents him in a new way: neither before nor after the encounter with Goliath but in the very act of hurling the stone. This pose implies the presence of the opponent in the spectator's space, so that the tension and energy of the figure seem to extend into his environment, a characteristic Baroque strategy. The *David*'s face is said to be a self-portrait, based on the image in a mirror held for the artist by his close friend, Cardinal Maffeo Barbarini. While the *David* was in progress, Barbarini was elected pope and, as a result, new vistas were opened to the twenty-four-year-old Bernini.

LIFE'S WORK

When Barbarini became Pope Urban VIII in 1623, Bernini's activities were redirected to the service of the Church. Initially, the pope encouraged the artist to study painting and architecture to supplement his mastery of sculpture. Architecture did indeed become an important aspect of Bernini's career, but although he is said to have produced more than 150 paintings, only a few are identified, including several self-portraits that show him as a handsome man with a long face and prominent, dark eyes.

The major artistic challenge facing the new Papacy was the internal decoration of the newly completed St. Peter's Basilica, and this responsibility fell to Bernini. In 1629, at the age of thirty, he was officially named architect of St. Peter's, but by then he had already been at work for five years on the baldachin, the enormous bronze structure under the dome of the cathedral that marks the place where Saint Peter is believed to be buried. This monument, modeled on the canopy held over living popes, rises dynamically on its vine-covered corkscrew columns to a height of 95 feet.

Bernini also supervised the design of the four gigantic piers that surround the baldachin. Each pier contains a niche with a colossal statue of a saint, one of which, Saint Longinus, was executed by Bernini himself. Longinus's agitated robe demonstrates the sculptor's ability to make drapery convey emotional excitement, a requirement in ecclesiastical commissions.

Another of Bernini's early projects for St. Peter's was the tomb of Urban VIII, which displays a rich contrast of colors and textures between a central core in gilt bronze and peripheral figures in white marble. The artist's taste for momentary action is reflected in the presence of a skeleton shown in the process of writing the epitaph. The effigy on Urban's tomb reflects Bernini's talent for portraiture. Several busts from this period, of the pope, of Borghese, and of the sculptor's mistress, Costanza Bonarelli, re-create not only the features but also the personalities of the sitters.

One of Bernini's rare failures was a scheme to add bell towers to the facade of St. Peter's. One tower was actu-

Gian Lorenzo Bernini. (Library of Congress)

ally begun, but, because of unsound foundations, had to be demolished. This reversal coincided with the death, in 1644, of Pope Urban, and Bernini fell temporarily out of favor with the papal court. This misfortune, however, turned to his advantage by permitting him to accept private commissions, the most notable of which was the Cornaro Chapel in the Church of Santa Maria della Vittoria, executed between 1645 and 1652. The chapel is a total ensemble involving architecture, painting, and sculpture in several media, which culminates in a vision of the *Ecstasy of Saint Teresa.* Bernini regarded it as the most beautiful of all of his creations.

The artist regained papal approval with his spectacular design for the Four Rivers Fountain, constructed between 1648 and 1651, and, with the pontificate of Alexander VII, he again enjoyed the close friendship and enthusiastic patronage of a pope. It was during this period that Bernini designed the Piazza San Pietro in front of St. Peter's, shaped by two colonnades that he likened to motherly arms reaching out to embrace the faithful. For the interior of the cathedral, he constructed a climactic spectacle in the apse, the *Cathedra Petri* (chair of Peter), a characteristically multimedia amalgam of sculpture and architecture. The Scala Regia (royal stairway), incorporating an equestrian statue of the Emperor Constantine, and the dramatic tomb of Alexander VII in St. Peter's are further legacies of the collaboration between the pope and the sculptor.

Late in his career, starting about 1658, Bernini undertook a number of architectural projects. His palace designs either were not built or were substantially remodeled; nevertheless, they exerted considerable influence. His three churches are all central plan structures and, predictably, function as showcases for the sculpture and painting within. Perhaps the most remarkable of the three is San Andrea al Quirinale, built between 1658 and 1670.

Bernini left Rome only once. In 1665, at the insistence of Louis XIV, he traveled to Paris, where he spent five months engaged in various sculptural and architectural projects for the king. His bust of Louis XIV is a result of this trip, but for the most part his style was too dynamic and exuberant for the sober, classic taste of the French court.

Bernini's latest works, such as the *Angels* for the Ponte Sant'Angelo, *Beata Lodovica Albertoni*, and the portrait of Gabriele Fonseca, all dating from after the French expedition, reflect the intense spirituality of the aging artist. Bernini remained active and productive almost until his death, which occurred nine days before his eighty-second birthday.

SIGNIFICANCE

Throughout his long career Bernini demonstrated exceptional skills of hand, mind, and spirit. His almost legendary technical facility in the production of sculpture, seen particularly in his early works, was matched by an equally remarkable talent for conceiving and planning large-scale monuments and supervising their execution by others. These abilities are displayed in his many and varied ecclesiastical commissions. Bernini's particular contribution to Counter-Reformation religious art, however, consisted in his ability to make visionary experiences vividly real and to find visual and physical metaphors for spiritual states.

Another aspect of Bernini's genius was its seeming universality. An English visitor to seventeenth century Rome wrote in his diary that "Bernini . . . gave a public opera wherein he painted the scenes, cut the statues, invented the engines, composed the music, writ the comedy, and built the theatre." This ability to synthesize different art forms is characteristic of many of the artist's most impressive and distinctive monuments. Architecture, painting, sculpture, marble, bronze, stucco, and pigment are combined with the imagination of a stage director. Bernini's extraordinary versatility is seen also in the range of his production within his primary field of sculpture: mythological groups, devotional images, portrait busts, tombs, and fountains. In all of these types, he set the standard for Baroque sculpture.

Bernini was generally regarded by his contemporaries as the greatest artist of his day, and his style was widely emulated. His reputation declined rather drastically in the eighteenth and nineteenth centuries but soared again in the twentieth century. This revival was spearheaded by scholarly investigation, but his work is now widely appreciated by the art-loving public.

—Jane Kristof

FURTHER READING

Baldinucci, Filippo. *The Life of Bernini*. Translated by Catherine Enggass. University Park: Pennsylvania State University Press, 1966. An important source on Bernini's life and career, published two years after his death, by a contemporary scholar and critic. Brief, with an informative foreword.

Bauer, George C., ed. *Bernini in Perspective*. Englewood Cliffs, N.J.: Prentice Hall, 1976. A collection of essays about Bernini written between the seventeenth and twentieth centuries, with an introduction by the editor. Includes a biography by the artist's son, black-and-white illustrations, and a bibliography.

Hibbard, Howard. *Bernini*. Harmondsworth, England: Penguin Books, 1965. Scholarly but concise and highly readable text. Focuses on sculpture but touches on other areas as well. Includes black-and-white illustrations, a short bibliography, and notes.

Lavin, Irving. *Bernini and the Unity of the Visual Arts*. 2 vols. New York: Oxford University Press, 1980. A study of the interaction of the arts in Bernini's oeuvre, dealing with several of his chapels and altars and, in greatest depth, with the Cornaro Chapel. Includes a catalog of relevant works, a bibliography, and extensive color and black-and-white illustrations.

McPhee, Sarah. *Bernini and the Bell Towers: Architecture and Politics at the Vatican*. New Haven, Conn.: Yale University Press, 2002. In 1638, Bernini began to design and build twin towers atop St. Peter's Basilica. The project was a dismal failure, permanently tarnishing Bernini's reputation. McPhee recounts how and why the project failed, placing the blame not on Bernini but on the liturgical and political constraints that the Vatican imposed upon him.

Marder, T. A. *Bernini and the Art of Architecture*. New York: Abbeville Press, 1998. A chronological description of the major architectural works, including sketches, plans, and spectacular new photographs.

Morrissey, Jake. *The Genius in the Design: Bernini, Borromini, and the Rivalry That Transformed Rome*. New York: Morrow, 2005. Outlines the relationship and conflict between Bernini and Borromini, the two most significant Italian Baroque architects.

Wallace, Robert. *The World of Bernini, 1598-1680*. Alexandria, Va.: Time-Life Books, 1970. A popular and reliable survey of the life and times of Bernini. Includes lavish illustrations, many in color.

Wittkower, Rudolf. *Gian Lorenzo Bernini, the Sculptor of the Roman Baroque*. 3d ed. London: Phaidon Press, 1981. A definitive work on Bernini's sculpture, with chapters on various genres. Contains a catalog, bibliography, chronological table, and extensive illustrations.

SEE ALSO: Alexander VII; Francesco Borromini; Guarino Guarini; Louis Le Vau; Louis XIV; Paul V; Urban VIII.

RELATED ARTICLES in *Great Events from History: The Seventeenth Century, 1601-1700:* c. 1601-1620: Emergence of Baroque Art; 1656-1667: Construction of the Piazza San Pietro; 1673: Renovation of the Louvre.

THE BERNOULLI FAMILY
Swiss mathematicians

The Bernoulli family contributed to the flowering of mathematical analysis in the eighteenth century that applied advanced mathematical techniques to problems arising in physics, technology, medicine, and the emerging field of probability theory. Members of the family dominated continental mathematics from the later seventeenth to the later eighteenth centuries.

JAKOB I BERNOULLI

BORN: January 6, 1655; Basel, Swiss Confederation
(now in Switzerland)
DIED: August 16, 1705; Basel

JOHANN I BERNOULLI

BORN: August 6, 1667; Basel
DIED: January 1, 1748; Basel

DANIEL BERNOULLI

BORN: February 8, 1700; Groningen, United Provinces
(now in the Netherlands)
DIED: March 17, 1782; Basel

AREAS OF ACHIEVEMENT: Physics, mathematics, medicine, astronomy

EARLY LIVES

Jakob I, Johann I, and Daniel Bernoulli are the most important members of the Bernoulli Dynasty, but at least five other family members went on to achieve recognition from their contemporaries for their mathematical talents. There were so many Jakobs and Johanns that it has become standard to place Roman numerals after their names to help keep their identities clear. Johann I and Jakob I were brothers, and Daniel was the son of Johann I.

The Bernoullis were descended from a line of merchants. Johann I and Jakob I's grandfather moved to Basel in 1622 and continued his profession as a druggist. His son, Nikolaus, became a minor local official. Jakob received his theological degree in 1676, while studying mathematics against his father's wishes. He traveled extensively: He spent two years in Geneva as a tutor, then went to France to learn René Descartes's approach to natural philosophy. He traveled to England in 1681, meeting Robert Hooke and Robert Boyle. He settled down somewhat in 1683, giving lectures, writing papers, and teach-

ing himself more mathematics. He became a professor of mathematics at the University of Basel in 1687 and made himself master of the newly developed Leibnizian methods of infinitesimal mathematics.

Johann failed as an apprentice and received his father's permission to enter the University of Basel in 1683, where Jakob had just begun lecturing. He began to study medicine in 1685, receiving his doctorate in 1694 for a mathematical account of the motion of muscles. Before receiving an offer for a post in 1695, Johann studied mathematics with Jakob and both became quite expert at Leibnizian calculus. Johann left for the chair of mathematics at Groningen, the Netherlands. In 1700, Daniel Bernoulli was born to Johann. Daniel obtained his master's degree in 1716 and was taught mathematics by his father and his elder brother Nikolaus II. Attempts to place him as a commercial apprentice failed, and he studied medicine at several different universities, at last settling in Basel with a doctorate in 1721, his thesis concerning respiration. His first attempts to obtain a university post failed, but his *Exercitationes quaedam mathematicae* (1724; mathematical exercises) landed him a post at the St. Petersburg Academy.

LIVES' WORK

Jakob became professor of mathematics at Basel in 1687, the same year that he published a significant article on geometry. He and Johann were both soon led into problems of infinitesimal geometry. The work of the brothers over the next several years was focused on the solution of puzzles that the leading mathematicians of Europe had proposed to demonstrate their own skill. Often a problem would be devised, solved by its formulator, and presented as a challenge to other mathematicians. One such problem was the shape of the curve that represented the motion of a body in constant descent in a gravitational field. Solutions would be offered, corrected by others, or counterproblems issued. This manner of solving problems greatly expanded the class of functions that could be analyzed using the tools of Leibnizian calculus. Jakob and Johann contributed to these sometimes-peevish arguments and mild polemics that nevertheless broadened the scope of calculus.

In 1695, Johann went to Groningen. He had no hope of getting the chair of mathematics at Basel, because his brother occupied it. The brothers were antagonistic toward each other. Jakob had taught Johann mathematics and apparently could never accept his younger brother as a professional equal. Both were sensitive, critical, and in need of recognition. Their intellectual gifts differed, as can best be seen by the famous problem of the brachistochrone posed by Johann in 1696. The brachistochrone is the curve a body makes as it moves along the path that takes the least time to travel between two points. Jakob solved the problem using a detailed but formally correct technique. Johann recognized that the problem could be rephrased in such a way that existing solutions could be adapted to the solution of this problem. Johann solved the problem in a more ingenious way, but Jakob recognized that his approach could be generalized. He laid the foundations of the field of the calculus of variations, which solves a wide variety of problems by using the methods of calculus to vary terms in an expression that takes a maximum or minimum. The brothers argued in print over each other's solutions to another variational problem from 1696 to 1701.

Jakob I spent the remaining years of his life working on more problems and compiling the results of his life's work. By the time of his death, he had accumulated a significant amount of original work on series (the finite sum of an infinite number of terms), gravitational theory, and engineering applications. Nikolaus I, Jakob's nephew, helped to have Jakob's most famous and original work, *Ars conjectandi* (1713; art of conjecture), published posthumously. Though incomplete, the work contains, among other things, Jakob's final statements on probability theory. His contributions to probability theory are recognized to have been decisive in the further development of the field.

Johann broadened the scope of the new calculus in the mid-1690's by calculating the details of the application of these methods to functions in which variables appear in the exponent. It was at this time that the brothers participated in their rancorous series of exchanges in print over the brachistochrone and other variational problems. Both brothers share the credit for the early development of the calculus of variations, for although Jakob first realized the generalizability of the technique, both followed up on this idea and applied it to other problems. After his brother's death, Johann published several works that presented formal solutions to variational problems that were reminiscent of Jakob's style.

Jakob's death in 1705 was the cause of Johann's return to Basel, where he took the vacant chair of mathematics. He became involved in the priority disputes between Sir Isaac Newton and Gottfried Wilhelm Leibniz over the invention of calculus and demonstrated the superiority of Leibniz's notation in the solution of particular problems. After 1705, Johann worked primarily on theoretical and applied mechanics. He published *Théorie de la maneuvre des vaisseaux* (1714; theory of the movement of ships), dealing with navigational problems and ship design. He also won three prizes offered by scientific academies by espousing the Cartesian vortex theory to explain the motion of planets. He criticized some aspects of Cartesianism, but some scholars claim that his undisputed status and support for Descartes's vortex theory delayed continental acceptance of Newtonian physics, which banishes such vortices in favor of forces.

Daniel Bernoulli obtained a position in the St. Petersburg Academy in 1725 and remained there until 1733. In 1727, Leonhard Euler joined him. His most productive years were spent in St. Petersburg. He wrote an original treatise on probability, a work on oscillations, and a draft of his most famous work, *Hydrodynamica* (1738; *Hydrodynamics by Daniel Bernoulli*, 1968). He returned to Basel to lecture in medicine but continued to publish in the areas that interested him most—mathematics and mechanics. His father, Johann, tried to establish priority for the founding of the field of hydrodynamics by plagiarizing his son's original work and predating the publication. This is only the worst of many examples of the antagonism that Johann felt toward his son.

Daniel began lecturing on physiology, which was more to his liking than medicine, in 1743 and was offered the chair of physics in 1750. He lectured on physics until 1776, when he retired. His most important contributions center on his work in rational mechanics. He returned to probability theory in 1760 with his famous work on the effectiveness of the smallpox vaccine, arguing that the vaccine could extend the average lifespan by three years. He published a few more minor works on probability theory through 1776. Throughout his career, Daniel won ten prizes of the Paris Academy on topics involving astronomy, magnetism, navigation, and ship design.

SIGNIFICANCE

The Bernoulli family was instrumental in developing many new fields of mathematics in the eighteenth century. They mastered the Leibnizian notation of calculus and successfully applied it to a range of problems. Their contributions to probability theory, the calculus of variation, differential and integral calculus, and the theories of series and of rational mechanics dominate even introductory textbooks in physics, mathematics, and engineering. The three Bernoullis who are the most famous of the eight who achieved contemporary recognition are Johann I, Jakob I, and Daniel.

Jakob was much more interested in mathematical formalism than his more intuitive younger brother Johann. Jakob's main contribution was in the ingenious solutions to individual problems. The cumulative weight of these mounting solutions reflected on the power and scope of the newly emerging analytical techniques. He also contributed in important ways to probability theory, algebra, the calculus of variations, and the theory of series. Johann can claim similar contributions, for the brothers often worked on similar problems and criticized each other's solutions in print. Johann also contributed to theoretical and applied mechanics. Daniel's contributions include founding the field of hydrodynamics and making essential contributions to rational mechanics, probability theory, and the mechanics of physiology.

Other Bernoullis of note include Nikolaus I (1687-1759), Nikolaus II (1695-1726), Johann II (1710-1790), Johann III (1744-1807), and Jakob II (1759-1789). All received recognition from their contemporaries but did not make as many or as important contributions as their more famous relatives.

—*Roger Sensenbaugh*

FURTHER READING

Bell, Eric T. *Men of Mathematics*. New York: Simon & Schuster, 1986. Addressed to the general reader, the book recounts the history leading to the major ideas of modern mathematics.

Brett, William F., Emile B. Feldman, and Michael Sentolwitz, eds. *An Introduction to the History of Mathematics, Number Theory, and Operations Research*. New York: MSS Information, 1974. Written for undergraduates, this book describes how mathematicians are creative and inquisitive people who sometimes find solutions that are useful but inaccurate.

Brown, Harcourt. "From London to Lapland: Maupertuis, Johann Bernoulli I, and *La Terre applatic*, 1728-1738." In *On Literature and History in the Age of Ideas: Essays on the French Enlightenment Presented to George R. Havens*, edited by Charles G. S. Williams. Columbus: Ohio State University Press, 1975. Based on the voluminous collection of the Bernoullis' letters, with a significant number of excerpts from the letters used to detail the controversy over the shape of the Earth.

Dunham, William. *Journey Through Genius: The Great Theorems of Mathematics*. New York: Wiley, 1990. This popular history of mathematics includes a chapter on the Bernoullis and the harmonic series.

_____. *The Mathematical Universe: An Alphabetical Journey Through the Great Proofs, Problems, and Personalities*. New York: Wiley & Sons, 1994. Includes a chapter on the Bernoulli trials.

James, Ioan. *Remarkable Mathematicians: From Euler to von Neumann*. New York: Cambridge University Press, 2002. The chapter on Euler explains how he was influenced by the work of the Bernoullis.

Lick, Dale W. "The Remarkable Bernoulli Family." *Mathematics Teacher* 62 (May, 1969): 401-409. Presents brief biographical information on eight of the most prominent family members. Interweaves historical and technical aspects but presents only a few simple equations.

Simmons, George Finlay. *Calculus Gems: Brief Lives and Memorable Mathematics*. New York: McGraw-Hill, 1992. This collection of biographies includes a chapter on the Bernoullis' contributions to mathematics.

Turnbull, H. W. *The Great Mathematicians*. 4th ed. New York: New York University Press, 1961. Aims at revealing the spirit of mathematics without burdening the reader with technical details. Chapter 8 deals with the Bernoullis and Euler.

SEE ALSO: Robert Boyle; René Descartes; Pierre de Fermat; James Gregory; Robert Hooke; Gottfried Wilhelm Leibniz.

RELATED ARTICLE in *Great Events from History: The Seventeenth Century, 1601-1700:* c. 1670: First Widespread Smallpox Inoculations.

THOMAS BETTERTON
English actor

Betterton was the leading actor of the English Restoration period, as well as the manager of the most important acting company of the late seventeenth century. He was also instrumental in introducing women actors to the English stage and responsible for continuing the English tradition of presenting the major works of Shakespeare on stage frequently.

BORN: c. 1635; London, England
DIED: April 28, 1710; London
AREAS OF ACHIEVEMENT: Theater, patronage of the arts

EARLY LIFE

Little is known of the early life of Thomas Betterton, and there is some question as to the year of his birth, which was most likely 1635. His father was the under-cook for King Charles I. Betterton therefore had some contact as a child with the life of the court. At an early age, he was apprenticed to John Rhodes, a bookseller and theater enthusiast and manager. Apprenticeship to Rhodes doubtless introduced Betterton to literature, but more important, it laid the groundwork for a career in the theater. Rhodes, who had been the wardrobe master for the Blackfriars Theater under Charles I, trained the young actor to play serious roles.

When English theaters, after being closed by the Puritan Commonwealth, were allowed to reopen in 1660, John Rhodes had a head start on the competition, having been given special permission to stage a performance of his *The History of Sir Francis Drake* (1659) the year before. Rhodes organized a company of young actors, headed by Thomas Betterton, to play at the Cockpit theater (also known as the Phoenix after 1618). Betterton almost immediately attracted the attention of Sir William Davenant, who had been the poet laureate and producer of court plays before the Puritan Commonwealth.

Before the year was out, Betterton had been hired by Davenant, who headed the Duke's Company, and trained to be the lead actor at Davenant's new theater, Lincoln's Inn Fields. Lincoln's Inn Fields Theatre opened in 1662 with a production of Davenant's opera-like work, *The Siege of Rhodes, Part I* (1656) and *The Siege of Rhodes, Part II* (pr. 1659, pb. 1663), which introduced to the London stage the new Italian techniques in scene design and stage machinery. Betterton was featured in *The Siege of Rhodes* as Solyman (Süleyman) the Magnificent, and thus his career as a star actor commenced in his early twenties.

LIFE'S WORK

Beginning in 1662, Betterton quickly established himself as a serious actor in roles such as Hamlet in William Shakespeare's *Hamlet, Prince of Denmark* (pr. c. 1600-1601). Since Davenant had worked with actors who had also worked directly with Shakespeare, it has been assumed that Davenant passed on to Betterton some of the approaches to the Hamlet character originated by Shakespeare himself. Whatever may have been the case, Betterton quickly won a reputation as a great performer of Shakespeare, as well as of the various "heroic tragedies" such as *Love and Honour* (pr. 1634, pb. 1649) that were written by Davenant and other Restoration playwrights.

By the 1670's, Betterton was considered the greatest living actor of the English stage. Interestingly, though he won high praise for his comic performances in roles such as Sir Toby Belch in Shakespeare's *Twelfth Night: Or, What You Will* (pr. c. 1600-1602) and Falstaff in Shakespeare's *Henry IV, Part I* (pr. c. 1597-1598), Betterton never seemed to excel in the French-influenced comedies that became the high fashion of the Restoration period. This did not keep him—in his later position as theatrical manager—from aiding other actors, both men and women, in the presentation of Restoration comedies.

It was during the height of Betterton's career that women were first allowed, by order of the king himself, to perform upon the English stage. Betterton married one of the most talented of these new actresses, Mary Saunderson, and the two became an important team on stage, where, for instance, Mrs. Betterton played Ophelia to her husband's Hamlet and a much praised Lady Macbeth to Betterton's Macbeth in Shakespeare's *Macbeth* (pr. 1606). In addition to teaming with his wife, Betterton also frequently played opposite Mrs. Anne Bracegirdle, considered the greatest actress of the Restoration.

In 1668, William Davenant died and, while the Davenant family retained financial control of the Duke's Company, Thomas Betterton took up the troupe's artistic management. His management was so successful that his primary competitors, the King's Company headed by Thomas Killigrew, could not maintain financial health. In 1682, the two companies joined together and continued under the control of the Davenant family and the artistic direction of Betterton as the United Company, which occupied the Drury Lane Theatre. This was the high period of Betterton's fame and success. Both Samuel Pepys, the famous diarist, and the great writer Alexander Pope were moved to describe him as the greatest actor of their times.

Betterton was not especially well endowed physically, being short and somewhat stocky, but he was gifted with a strong, rich voice. He did not, however, rant and rage as did most performers in the popular and fashionable "heroic tragedies" such as John Dryden's *The Conquest of Granada by the Spaniards* (part 1 pr. 1670, part 2 pr. 1671, both pb. 1672). Instead, Betterton was greatly admired for his ability to bring a quiet and intense restraint to his acting and to hold audiences enraptured with his subdued power.

The king of England became so enamored of him as an actor and manager that he sent Betterton to France to study French theatrical techniques, and upon his return from France, Betterton introduced new scene-painting techniques and theatrical machinery that became the standard of the English stage for many years. He also wrote and circulated a book on acting techniques. Despite all this success, however, Betterton earned very little money. Even in his period of greatest achievement, his annual salary was equivalent to approximately $100,000 in present-day currency.

In 1695, the United Company came under the financial control of Christopher Rich, with whom Betterton did not get along. In order to escape Rich, Betterton and his wife set up a new company in the remodeled Tennis Court theater at Lincoln's Inn Fields. Other members of the new company included the playwright William Congreve and such important actresses as Anne Bracegirdle and Elizabeth Barry. The new company achieved great success and moved to the Queen's Theatre in the Haymarket, built for them in 1705 by the architect and playwright Sir John Vanbrugh. In a short time, however, Betterton was apparently forced by severe gout to retire from theatrical management. He did, though, continue to perform until his death in 1710. By that time he had created 130 new roles, as well as starring many times as such important Shakespearean characters as Hamlet, Macbeth, King Lear, and Othello. He was so admired and respected that he received the great honor of being buried at Westminster Abbey.

SIGNIFICANCE

Betterton was both the star actor and the artistic manager of the most important English acting company of the last quarter of the seventeenth century. Perhaps Betterton's most important contribution to theatrical history was his establishment of the tradition of regular revivals on the English stage of Shakespeare, Ben Jonson, and other ma-

jor Elizabethan dramatists. He also produced the works of the major playwrights of his own time, including William Congreve, John Dryden, John Lacy, Sir George Etherege, Thomas Otway, and William Wycherley.

In addition to plays, Betterton, following the lead of his mentor Davenant, continued to develop the production of French and Italianate opera in England. He also gave crucial support to the actresses in his company. Because women were not allowed on the English stage before 1660, there were no female mentors for Restoration actresses. Betterton and his wife, Mary Saunderson, provided teaching and general emotional support to these women. Finally, because of support directly from the king, Betterton was able to visit France and study the European tradition of staging both plays and operas. He returned to England and introduced new scenic practices and new elaborate and more efficient stage machinery for both plays and operas.

—*August W. Staub*

FURTHER READING

Brockett, Oscar G., and Franklin J. Hildy. *History of the Theatre*. 9th ed. Boston: Allyn and Bacon, 2002. The basic resource book in theater history; contains good general entries on the Restoration theater.

Cole, Toby, and Helen Krich Chinoy, eds. *Actors on Acting*. New York: Crown, 1970. A collection of works on acting by great actors from Greece to the present day. Betterton's theories on acting are collected herein.

Duerr, Edwin. *The Length and Depth of Acting*. New York: Holt, Rinehart, Winston, 1963. The best reference on the history of actors, their accomplishments, and their theories of the art. Includes good material on Betterton.

Fisk, Deborah Payne, ed. *The Cambridge Companion to English Restoration Theatre*. New York: Cambridge University Press, 2000. Collection of essays by noted scholars on Restoration theatrical history. Includes overview articles on each of the major genres, as well as topical essays on sexuality, profanity, politics, and other key issues in Restoration studies.

McCollum, John I., Jr. *The Restoration Stage*. Boston: Houghton, Mifflin, 1961. A collection of documents relating to the Restoration theater, including excerpts from the "Life of Thomas Betterton" by Colly Cibber.

Milhous, Judith. *Thomas Betterton and the Management of Lincoln's Inn Fields: 1695-1708*. Carbondale: University of Illinois Press, 1979. An informative and well-documented study of the practices of theatrical management by Thomas Betterton.

Murray, Barbara A. *Restoration Shakespeare: Viewing the Voice*. Madison, N.J.: Fairleigh Dickinson University Press, 2001. A book-length study of Restoration adaptations of Shakespeare's works and their place in theater history. Discusses the distinctive acting styles prevalent during the period, and the major actors employing them.

SEE ALSO: Mrs. Anne Bracegirdle; Charles I; Charles II (of England); John Dryden; Samuel Pepys.

RELATED ARTICLES in *Great Events from History: The Seventeenth Century, 1601-1700:* c. 1601-1613: Shakespeare Produces His Later Plays; December 6, 1648-May 19, 1649: Establishment of the English Commonwealth.

JOHN BIDDLE
English theologian

Biddle was a controversial lay theologian who, through his writings and strong moral leadership, became known as the father of English Unitarianism.

BORN: January 14, 1615 (baptized); Wotton-under-Edge, Gloucestershire, England
DIED: September 22, 1662; London, England
AREA OF ACHIEVEMENT: Religion and theology

EARLY LIFE

John Biddle was born in Gloucestershire and was the son of a tailor or a woolen-draper. He showed promise in the local school at an early age, impressing and allegedly surpassing his tutors with his translations of Juvenal and Vergil. He attracted aristocratic patronage, which assisted him in his preparation for university.

At the age of nineteen, he became a student in Magdalen Hall, Oxford. He took his arts degree and became a tutor there in 1638; in 1641, he was awarded the degree of master of arts. In this same year, he was elected headmaster of the Crypt Free Grammar School at Gloucester, where he was esteemed both as a teacher and for his personal character.

Biddle's interest in the study of Scripture began at a young age and continued in earnest during his tenure at Gloucester. There, he became so well versed in the New Testament that he reportedly knew most of it by heart, both in English and in Greek. As a result of his studies, however, he became convinced that the theological doctrine of the Trinity as composed of three coequal and coeternal persons—Father, Son, and Holy Spirit—had no support in Scripture. He compiled his scripturally based objections to the doctrine of the Trinity in a manuscript entitled *Twelve Arguments Drawn Out of Scripture: Wherein the Commonly Received Opinion Touching the Deity of the Holy Spirit Is Clearly and Fully Refuted* (wr. c. 1644, pb. 1647). Biddle had composed these arguments for the private use of his friends, but one of them betrayed him and reported his views to magistrates. As a result, in 1645 he was summoned before a parliamentary committee sitting in Gloucester; he would spend much of the remaining twelve years of his life in prison.

LIFE'S WORK

The parliamentary committee at Gloucester sent Biddle to prison. In the summer of 1646, Archbishop James Ussher of Ireland visited Biddle and tried to convince him of his errors, basing his arguments on Church tradition and authorities rather than Scripture. Biddle remained unmoved and was transferred to London. There he admitted that he had denied the deity of the Holy Spirit, but he also asked permission to discuss the issue with a competent theologian.

Biddle was released from prison on bail in 1647 but shortly thereafter published his *Twelve Arguments*. The publication of this work caused a sensation, as his denial of the Trinity was offensive to both the Anglican and Puritan creeds. Biddle was once again taken into custody, and his *Twelve Arguments* was seized and burned by the hangman. Nevertheless, demand for it was so great that a second edition was reprinted before the year was out. Reaction to this work's publication was severe: An ordinance of Parliament of May 2, 1648, made denial of the Trinity grounds for capital punishment.

Despite this prohibition, Biddle published two additional tracts in 1648: *A Confession of Faith Touching the Holy Trinity, According to Scripture*, and the testimonies of six church fathers and six later writers entitled *The Testimonies Concerning That One God, and the Persons of the Holy Trinity*. Both of these works refuted the belief that the three persons of the Trinity were coequal; Biddle elevated the Father and considered the other two persons subordinate. These works show a theological development in Biddle's thought and an acquaintance with the writings of the Italian anti-Trinitarian Faustus Socinus (Fausto Paolo Sozzini; 1539-1604).

Both of Biddle's later works were suppressed, but influential friends made it possible for Biddle to evade the death sentence and to live in Staffordshire under surveillance. There he preached until 1652, when he was recalled to London and again imprisoned. A sympathetic friend procured employment for him, and although in confinement, Biddle was permitted to engage in editorial work on the Septuagint, the Greek translation of the Old Testament.

Biddle was released again in 1652 under Oliver Cromwell's Act of Oblivion, which set free all who stood accused of any crime. He and his adherents, called Biddellians or Unitarians, began to meet regularly for Sunday worship and scriptural study. During these meetings, they discussed theological issues in the light of biblical interpretation, moving beyond the doctrines of the Trinity and the divinity of Christ. London ministers became incensed at these biblical study sessions, yet there was no law under which Biddle and his associates could be prosecuted.

During the period of political uncertainty and religious instability following the Act of Oblivion, many anti-Trinitarian works produced on the Continent were imported into England, translated, and circulated. Biddle himself was responsible for many of these translations, including a life of Faustus Socinus. Due to the resemblance of the views of Biddle and his companions to those of Socinus, the group was sometimes called Socinians. Biddle continued to publish throughout 1662 and 1663, advocating religious tolerance and recommending that all Christians should decide questions of scriptural interpretation by reason rather than by reference to creeds or tradition.

Toward the end of 1653, Cromwell was made protector of the Commonwealth, and he issued an Instrument of Government in forty-two articles, three of which concerned religion. While Cromwell promised complete freedom of worship for Christians professing the fundamentals of Christianity, he did not specify what these fundamentals were. Biddle took this opportunity to publish *A Twofold Catechism* (1654). This work was a catechism divided into two parts: One section was designed for adults, the other for children. In these catechisms, he examined the range of Christian doctrine and duty by citing scriptural examples; however, theologically he rejected the Trinity and the divinity of Christ, and he treated God in anthropomorphic terms.

Parliament was quick to take action in response to Biddle's *Twofold Catechism*. Both Biddle and his catechism were examined; he was imprisoned on December 13, 1654, while all copies of his catechism were ordered to be seized and burned the next day. During his stay in prison, many members of Parliament urged that he be put to death. In May, however, Parliament was dissolved, and Biddle was again set free. Biddle's popularity had grown while he was in prison, and demand for his catechism and his teachings had increased.

Less than a month after his release, Biddle was challenged to a debate by John Griffin, an illiterate Baptist preacher, on the supreme deity of Christ. During the debate, a group of fanatics managed to have Biddle arrested under the Ordinance of 1648 against denying the Trinity, which Cromwell's Instrument of Government was supposed to have superseded. Biddle was again indicted and thrown into prison. Cromwell was pursued by religious groups of all hues of the spectrum, who demanded that he either enforce the older laws concerning blasphemy or uphold his own promise of religious freedom. Reluctant to see Biddle executed but unwilling to exonerate him either, Cromwell banished him for life to St. Mary's Castle in the Isles of Scilly in October, 1655; Cromwell was also persuaded to grant Biddle a pension for sustenance. Despite numerous entreaties, Cromwell never released him.

Following Cromwell's death, a group of Biddle's friends sought and obtained his release in 1658, and he returned to the country to teach. After the Restoration of King Charles II (1660), all Nonconformist worship fell under a ban, and Biddle ceased attending public scriptural discussions, though he continued to worship privately. When detected in private worship by authorities in 1662, Biddle and some followers were hauled away to prison. As Biddle was unable to pay his fine of one hundred pounds, he was kept in prison, where he contracted a disease. Although he was permitted to be removed from the prison, he died shortly thereafter.

SIGNIFICANCE

Biddle's Unitarian congregation did not long survive him, but his influence continued in various ways. He was most noted for his great zeal in promoting life and manners. He also left a legacy of compassion and religious toleration. Finally, his works were reprinted throughout the seventeenth century, thus providing the basis of what would eventually develop into the English Unitarian tradition.

—*Andrew G. Traver*

FURTHER READING

Hill, Christopher. *The World Turned Upside Down: Radical Ideas During the English Revolution*. New York:

Viking Press, 1972. A scholarly study of the varieties of Christian thought during the English Civil Wars. Contains excellent notes.

Lindley, Keith. *Popular Politics and Religion in Civil War London*. Aldershot, Hampshire, England: Scholar Press, 1997. A good discussion about the interconnection between politics and religion in London during the English Civil Wars. Includes notes and a detailed bibliography.

McLachlan, H. John. *Socinianism in Seventeenth-Century England*. New York: Oxford University Press, 1951. An important study in the history of English Socinianism. Contains an extensive bibliography.

Spellman, W. M. *The Latitudinarians and the Church of England, 1660-1700*. Athens: University of Georgia Press, 1993. A useful study of the divergence of religious thought in England during the Restoration. Contains excellent scholarly notes and a complete bibliography.

Toulmin, Joshua. *Review of the Life, Character, and Writings of the Reverend John Biddle, M.A.* London: J. Johnson, 1789. Early biography of Biddle.

Wilbur, Earl Morse. *A History of Unitarianism in Transylvania, England, and America*. Cambridge, Mass.: Harvard University Press, 1952. Contains two excellent chapters on Biddle's place within the background of the English Unitarian tradition. Also includes a detailed bibliography.

_____. *A History of Unitarianism: Socinianism and Its Adherents*. Cambridge, Mass.: Harvard University Press, 1947. Contains an excellent theological background to the Unitarian movement in the sixteenth and seventeenth centuries. Scholarly notes.

SEE ALSO: Charles II (of England); Oliver Cromwell; James Ussher.

RELATED ARTICLE in *Great Events from History: The Seventeenth Century, 1601-1700:* May, 1659-May, 1660: Restoration of Charles II.

ROBERT BLAKE
English admiral

Combining leadership ability with deep religious faith and a strong sense of duty to his country, Blake was one of the founders and the chief admiral of the English Commonwealth Navy.

BORN: Late August?, 1599; Bridgwater, Somerset, England

DIED: August 7, 1657; at sea, off Plymouth, Devon, England

AREAS OF ACHIEVEMENT: Military, warfare and conquest, government and politics

EARLY LIFE

Robert Blake was baptized on September 27, 1599, in St. Mary's Church, Bridgwater, Somerset, England. His family came from the small farming gentry that had developed under the Tudors. His grandfather moved to Bridgwater and prospered in the shipping business. His father, Humphrey Blake, inherited a good business in 1592, adding estates to the family holdings when he married a widow, Sarah Williams. Young Robert was the eldest of twelve children, ten of whom survived.

As a youngster, Robert was a student at King James's School, an English grammar school, and in 1615, he attended St. Albans Hall, Oxford. He failed to win a scholarship to Christ Church and enrolled instead at Wadham College, which had Somerset connections. Little is known about his college life, but it may have been during these years that he developed some of his antimonarchical views. The family belonged to the Church of England, but in his beliefs Robert was a Presbyterian. He received a B.A. in 1618 but lost a fellowship bid at Merton College in 1619, reportedly because of his short, squat, ungainly figure.

Blake's father died on November 19, 1625. Blake took over the family shipping business, which was in bad shape as a result of a rise in piracy and a decline in naval defenses. For the next fifteen years, he dropped out of sight; he may have gone to sea with some of his vessels, then a fairly common practice for merchant-shippers.

In 1640, Blake emerged from this period of low profile as his nation prepared for war. Charles I had been ruling without a Parliament, but early in 1640, he called one (later known as the Short Parliament) to ask for money to finance a war with Scotland. Blake was elected a member of Parliament (M.P.) for Bridgwater, though he lost his seat in November in the election of what would be known as the Long Parliament. The next evidence of Blake appears during the First English Civil War in

March, 1643, when he served as one of twenty-six M.P.'s on the Parliamentary Committee for the Sequestration of the Estates of the Royalists in Somerset. Four months later, he was in command of a company defending Prior's Hill Fort at Bristol. The subsequent loss of Bristol to the Royalist forces of Prince Rupert, nephew of Charles I, gave the Crown control of trade to Ireland, the West Indies, and Spain.

Blake next served as a lieutenant colonel leading the defense of Lyme in 1644. The town held its ground for twenty-six days, largely thanks to the leadership, courage, and inspiration of Blake in his first independent command. He went on to capture Taunton in July, 1644. Taunton was located at the intersection of all the main roads in Somerset. Blake helped prepare it for a Royalist siege, which lasted about nine months, until the Royalist defeat at Naseby. Blake was then selected to capture Dunster Castle in Somerset, the last Royalist holdout. The surrender terms drawn up by Blake were very generous and demonstrated his humane attitude toward his foes.

With the first phase of the Civil War over, Blake was again elected to Parliament, but he was unable to take his seat until May, 1646. As a member of Parliament, Blake had to resign his military commission, but he became governor of Taunton in this period. Civil war erupted again in early March, 1648. Despite lack of funds for paying or raising troops, Blake and Edward Popham held Somerset, preventing uprisings in Devon and Cornwall. At the end of January, Charles I was executed and the Commonwealth was born, activities in which Blake took no part.

LIFE'S WORK

To replace the king, a forty-nine-member Council of State was formed. From it, the Admiralty Committee was made up and took over the duties of the lord high admiral. Sir Robert Rich, the second earl of Warwick, who held that position, was dismissed, and Edward Popham was appointed commander of the British fleet. Popham apparently spoke highly of Blake, who, along with Richard Deane, was appointed by the Admiralty Committee as a "general-at-sea." Popham, Deane, and Blake all took command of the fleet on February 23, 1649, and Blake began the most eventful part of his life.

Blake focused on settling the unrest among the nation's seamen. He met with them, listened to their grievances, and began to restore morale. A major concern was to improve the efficiency of the selling of prizes, from which crews were paid for their work. Blake and Deane

Robert Blake. (Library of Congress)

also had to get a fleet ready for sea, overseeing all the details of supplying the vessels and manning each ship with officers and crew.

Blake hoisted his flag on the ship *Triumph* at Chatham and sailed in April, 1649, to blockade Kinsale, Ireland. He declined a post as major general under Oliver Cromwell in order to remain at sea. Blake was able to restore both morale and discipline, while exhibiting great patience in patrolling. Ship conditions forced him to shift to the *Lion* and then the *Guinea*.

Blake was put in command of the winter fleet, which sailed from Cowes on March 1, 1650, to attack Prince Rupert's fleet at Lisbon. Blake's flag was in the *St. George*, which had fifty-six guns. Again, he used the blockade effectively. In July, his fleet captured or destroyed nine of the twenty-three vessels in the Portuguese Brazilian fleet. Rupert, no longer a naval threat to England, headed for the Mediterranean to raid at sea. Blake shifted his flag to the *Leopard* late in October and continued the hunt for Rupert. He was successful in destroying most of Rupert's fleet, only three ships of which safely reached Toulon. By mid-December, Blake was back at Cadiz, having maintained both morale and confidence in the fleet. He was replaced by Sir William Penn (1621-1670) and returned to England on February 10, 1651.

By March 10, 1651, Blake was on the *Phoenix* with a squadron patrolling in the Irish Seas, but on April 1, he was ordered to the Isles of Scilly to confront Admiral Maarten Tromp and a Dutch squadron. The Dutch left, and Blake took control of the Royalist strongholds in the Scilly Isles. He helped to plan and execute amphibious landings and a blockade of the Royalist forces on Saint Mary's. By early June, the Scilly Isles were under control. Generous surrender terms had been accepted and the Western Seas were safe for Commonwealth shipping, all at a cost of six men killed and no ships lost, a tribute to Blake's skill as a commander. He received new orders on August 22 and sailed for the Downs in the *Victory*, arriving on September 3, as Royalist forces were defeated at Worcester. While at Plymouth, he was busy trying to get repayment for the men who had paid discharged sailors. Shortage of funds continued to plague the Commonwealth, as it had the king.

Blake was next ordered to prepare a fleet in September, 1651, to assist in capturing the last Royalist strongholds in the Channel Islands. His flagship was the *Happy Entrance*. The amphibious operations and siege tactics were successful, and Blake returned to England late in December, where he was made a member of several committees, including the Admiralty Committee. He attended council and committee meetings regularly until early in March, 1652.

With the passage of a Navigation Act on August 20, 1651, and an English insistence on sovereignty of the seas, trouble with Holland was brewing. The Dutch were preparing a fleet to enforce their own claims to maritime sovereignty, and Blake was ordered to assemble a summer fleet. His flagship, the *James*, and the English fleet met the Dutch fleet under Admiral Tromp in the *Brederade* off Dover, England, on May 19, 1652. After this Dutch attack, Blake was ordered to capture the Dutch East India fleet and to disrupt the Dutch fishing fleet off England and Scotland. He was then to disrupt the Dutch Baltic trade while protecting that of the English. Blake sailed late in June in the *Resolution*, and war was declared on July 8, 1652. He was so successful that Tromp was blamed for Dutch losses and resigned, to be replaced by Johan de Witt and Michiel Adriaanszoon de Ruyter.

Late in September of 1652, Blake met the Dutch under Witt off Dover in the Battle of Kentish Knock, in which Blake won his first open sea battle. Although the Dutch were defeated, however, their fleet was not destroyed. Parliament dispersed the British fleet, leaving Blake with limited forces to protect the English Channel. Meanwhile, the Dutch reinstated Tromp and prepared for further action. Tromp was at sea late in November and met Blake south of Dover in the Battle of Dungeness (December 10, 1652). The English were defeated, and the Dutch controlled the channel and the Thames estuary.

This defeat forced the English to remodel their navy under Sir Henry Vane the Younger. With Blake's help, an enquiry into the defeat was made, captains were disciplined, and a new pay scale was developed. The Laws and Ordinances of the Sea, thirty-nine articles dealing with discipline, were passed on December 25, 1652. A British fleet was again prepared, and it met the Dutch fleet off Portland in the Three Days' Battle, from February 28 to March 2, 1653. The English—commanded by Blake, in the *Triumph*, Penn, and George Monck—fired low to hull their opponents, while benefiting from their own stoutly built ships. The Commonwealth was victorious, although Blake was wounded in the leg by a bar of iron.

Late in May, the English fleet was ordered out again. They met the Dutch in the Battle of the Gabbard Shoal in June. Fleet line-of-battle tactics were tried for the first time. Blake's arrival in the *Essex* with fresh forces was cheered by the crews and made possible the victory that followed. Blake did not, however, participate in the final victory of the war at the Battle of the Texel (Scheveningen) late in July, 1653. The Dutch signed a peace treaty on April 5, 1654, ending the First Anglo-Dutch War.

In August, Blake was ordered to the Mediterranean. Cruising the western portion of the sea in the *George* with a small squadron, he was instructed to carry out reprisals against the North African pirates and the French. He showed that Gibraltar cut the naval forces of both France and Spain in half.

In March, 1655, although he was then ill, Blake was again sent out to capture the Spanish Plate Fleet. He sailed in the *Naseby*, along with Edward Montagu (first earl of Sandwich), to cruise off Gibraltar. Not until September, however, were two prizes from the Plate Fleet taken by Sir Richard Stayner. Montagu returned to England in the *Naseby* with the prizes and the ships needing repairs. Meanwhile, Blake, in the *Swiftsure*, continued to blockade Cadiz, using Lisbon as a base.

In February, 1655, Blake heard that part of the Plate Fleet was heading for the Canaries. He was not able to take advantage of this information until early April, and when he did, he would not divide his fleet, instead sailing for the Canaries with most of his ships. On April 20, he attacked the forts at Santa Cruz, while Stayner attacked the galleons. All the Spanish ships were destroyed, some treasure was collected, and no English ships were lost. By early May, Blake was back off Cadiz, but he was again not well. Another commander was sent out to replace him.

Blake returned to England, arriving on the *Lizard* on August 6. He died entering the sound at Plymouth, the morning of August 7, 1657. Blake's body was taken to Greenwich to lie in state, and after a funeral procession up the Thames, he was buried at Westminster Abbey on September 4. After the Restoration, however, by order of Charles II, on September 9, 1661, Blake and other Parliamentarians were disinterred and thrown into unmarked graves north of the abbey.

SIGNIFICANCE

Blake, a hero of the English Civil War, was one of the founders of the Commonwealth's navy, and with that fleet under his command, he became a hero of the Anglo-Dutch War as well. As an admiral, he has been surpassed only by Lord Nelson in English history. He restored morale and discipline to the navy. He did not throw away the lives of his men unnecessarily, and thus they served him faithfully. An able administrator and innovator, he remodeled the navy and helped to establish the fighting instructions for the fleet and to develop new tactics of fleet line-of-battle. Blake was the first to attack land defenses from the sea, and he appreciated the use of the broadside with low firing to hull an opponent. Blake's military brilliance had influence even after he died serving his country, for he had trained many future captains and admirals. Changes in Great Britain's rocky seventeenth century political scene and Blake's service off the coasts of faraway lands hid his accomplishments, however, so that it was not until the eighteenth century that his role in history was fully appreciated.

—Mary-Emily Miller

FURTHER READING

Baumber, Michael. *General-at-Sea: Robert Blake and the Seventeenth-Century Revolution in Naval Warfare*. London: J. Murray, 1989. A biography of Blake told within the context of new developments in naval warfare occurring during his lifetime.

Blake, Robert. *The Letters of Robert Blake*. Edited by J. R. Powell. London: Navy Records Society, 1937. Most helpful in appreciating the flavor and details of naval activities of mid-seventeenth century England. The letters reveal a man of action who expressed himself well and with few words.

Bowley, R. L. *Scilly at War*. St. Mary's, Isles of Scilly, England: Bowley, 2001. The first chapter of this book recounts Blake's 1651 conquest of the Dutch in the Scilly Isles.

Curtis, C. D. *Blake: General-at-Sea*. Taunton, Somerset, England: Wessex Press, 1934. Good illustrations, maps, documentation, and extensive quotations. Contains interesting comments on the missing years, 1625-1640; contemporary accounts of Blake; extracts from Blake's wills; portraits; and his funeral program.

Gardiner, Leslie. *The British Admiralty*. London: William Blackwood and Sons, 1968. Very good on the development of British naval administration, containing interesting comments on Blake's committee work, the Articles of War, the first "Fighting Instructions," and a special code of flags for admirals.

Lewis, Michael. *The Navy of Britain: A Historical Portrait*. London: Allen and Unwin, 1948. Contains an interesting essay on Blake as embodying the transition from the old "fighting officer" type, usually a nobleman, to the modern naval officer, usually of merchant stock.

Mahan, Alfred Thayer. *The Influence of Sea Power upon History*. Boston: Little, Brown, 1890. Reprint. New York: Dover, 1987. The classic reference for a wide variety of naval matters, consistently quoted by writers on both sides of the Atlantic ever since its first publication. Discusses the state of Europe in 1660; characteristics of French, English, and Dutch ships; and the shift from melee tactics to line-of-battle naval tactics.

Padfield, Peter. *Tide of Empires: Decisive Naval Campaigns in the Rise of the West, 1481-1654*. Vol. 1. London: Routledge and Kegan Paul, 1979. This volume ends with the First Anglo-Dutch War (1652-1654). It has excellent battle descriptions and shows the connections between economic affairs and naval strengths. Deals with various naval tactics and strategy and with Blake's activities in a clear manner. Includes good battle maps and a glossary.

Phillips, C. E. Lucas. *Cromwell's Captains*. London: William Heinemann, 1938. Reprint. Freeport, N.Y.: Books for Libraries Press, 1972. This collection of four substantial essays includes an essay on Blake, focusing on his serving the Commonwealth on land and sea with courage and able administration. It also contains a portrait of Blake and maps of fleet actions at Portland and Santa Cruz.

Powell, J. R. *Robert Blake, General-at-Sea.* London: Collins, 1972. By far the best and most accurate available work on Blake. Liberally sprinkled with illustrations, maps, and battle plans. The old tales are laid to rest, and Blake is set carefully in his times. The book is well documented, with an excellent index and list of ships.

SEE ALSO: Charles I; Charles II (of England); Oliver Cromwell; George Monck; Prince Rupert; Michiel Adriaanszoon de Ruyter; Maarten and Cornelis Tromp.

RELATED ARTICLES in *Great Events from History: The Seventeenth Century, 1601-1700:* November 3, 1640-May 15, 1641: Beginning of England's Long Parliament; 1642-1651: English Civil Wars; December 6, 1648-May 19, 1649: Establishment of the English Commonwealth; October, 1651-May, 1652: Navigation Act Leads to Anglo-Dutch Wars; May, 1659-May, 1660: Restoration of Charles II.

JAKOB BÖHME
German philosopher and mystic

Böhme developed a profound metaphysical system, rich in myth and symbol, which attempted to explain the nature of God, the origin of the universe and of humans, and the fall of humanity and the way of regeneration. His complex and difficult thought influenced many German, French, and English philosophers and poets.

BORN: April 24, 1575; Altseidenberg, near Görlitz, Silesia (now in Germany)
DIED: November 17, 1624; Görlitz
AREAS OF ACHIEVEMENT: Philosophy, religion and theology, science and technology

EARLY LIFE

Jakob Böhme (YAW-kohp BOH-meh) was born in the village of Altseidenberg in what is now Germany. He was the fourth child of Jakob Böhme, a prosperous farmer, and his wife, Ursula. The family had been well established in the community for several generations, and Jakob's father was a Lutheran church elder and local magistrate.

Information about Böhme's early life is scanty. He received an elementary education at the local school, and in 1589 he was apprenticed to a shoemaker, probably for a period of three years. He then traveled as a journeyman, and in 1594 or 1595 he settled in Görlitz. In 1599, he became a citizen of that town and probably at the same time became a master shoemaker. In May, 1599, he married Catharine Kuntzschmann, the daughter of a local butcher, and they had four children.

The following year, 1600, was a highly signifi-

cant one for Böhme. It marked the arrival in Görlitz of a new Lutheran pastor, Martin Moller. Moller was well read in the German medieval mystical tradition, and he espoused a Christianity of pure and inward spirituality. Böhme was attracted to Moller's teaching and joined his Conventicle of God's Real Servants. Moller's influence

Jakob Böhme. (Hulton Archive/Getty Images)

was a lasting one. In that same year came an experience that dramatically changed Böhme's life. As he happened to glance at a pewter dish that was reflecting bright sunlight, he experienced a moment of suddenly heightened awareness. This feeling stayed with him as he went outside to the fields; he felt that he could see into the innermost essence of nature, and he later said that the experience was like being resurrected from the dead. More experiences of illumination followed over the next ten years, and these clarified and amplified what he had seen and understood in his initial experience. These experiences were the foundation of his life's work.

In 1612, he felt compelled to write, and the result was a long, rambling, but thrilling book, *Aurora: Oder, Die Morgenröthe im Aufgang* (1634; *The Aurora*, 1656). This work marked Böhme's first step on the road to be-

coming one of the most original and profound thinkers in the history of the Western religious tradition.

LIFE'S WORK

Böhme had originally written *Aurora* for his own use only, but a nobleman, Carl von Ender, found the manuscript at Böhme's house, borrowed it, and had some copies made. Unfortunately for Böhme, news of his book came to the attention of the pastor of Görlitz, Gregorius Richter, a strict defender of religious orthodoxy, who had succeeded Moller in 1606. Richter was enraged at Böhme's bold assertions and assailed him from the pulpit in virulent terms, while Böhme himself sat quietly in the congregation. The next day the town council told Böhme to hand over the manuscript of *Aurora* and to stop writing. Böhme agreed to keep silent, and for seven years he kept his promise. He became prosperous, and as a member of his trade guild he was active in the day-to-day commercial life of the town. In 1613, he sold his business and entered the linen and wool trade, which involved him in yearly journeys to Prague and possibly to the Leipzig Fair.

During this period of silence he was making some learned and influential friends, including Tobias Kober, physician of Görlitz, and Balthasar Walther, who was director of the chemical laboratory in Dresden. Böhme learned about the work of Paracelsus from Kober, and Walther introduced him to the Jewish mystical tradition embodied in the Kabbala. Both became major influences on his work, and Böhme also learned from his educated friends some Latin terms that he would later incorporate into his works. One of his friends, Abraham von Franckenberg, gave the following picture of Böhme's physical appearance: "His person was little and leane, with browes somewhat inbowed; high temples, somewhat hauk-nosed; his eyes were gray and somewhat heaven blew, and otherwise as the windows of Solomon's Temple: He had a thin beard, a small low voice. His speech was lovely."

BÖHME ON THE SOUL AFTER DEATH

On May 6, 2005, Jakob Böhme wrote the following dialogue, in which scholar-disciple Junius asks his master-teacher Theophorus about the place of the soul after death.

The scholar asked his master, "Wither goeth the Soul when the Body dieth?"

His Master answered him: There is no necessity for it to go any wither.

How not, said the inquisitive Junius, must not the Soul leave the body at death and go either to Heaven or Hell?

It needs no going forth, replied the venerable Theophorus. Only the outward Mortal Life with the body shall separate themselves from the Soul. The Soul hath Heaven and Hell within itself before, according as it is written. *The Kingdom of God cometh not with observation, neither shall they say Lo here! or Lo there! For behold the Kingdom of God is within you.* And which soever of the two, that is, either Heaven or Hell, is manifested in it, in that the Soul standeth.

Here Junius said to his Master: This is hard to understand. Doth it not enter into Heaven or Hell, as a man entereth a house; or as one goeth through a hole or casement into an unknown place; so goeth it not into another world?

The Master spoke and said: No, there is verily no such kind of entering in; forasmuch as Heaven and Hell are every where, being universally co-extended.

. . . Pray make me understand this [said Junius].

To whom the Master [replied]: Understand then what Heaven is. It is but the *turning in of the Will to the Love of God.* Wheresoever thou findest God manifesting himself in Love, there thou findest Heaven, without travelling for it so much as one foot. . . .

For *Heaven and Hell* are nought else but a *Manifestation of the Divine Will either in Light or Darkness, according to the Properties of the Spiritual World.*

Source: Jakob Böhme, *Dialogues on the Supersensual Life,* translated by William Law et al., edited by Bernard Holland (New York: Frederick Ungar, 1957), pp. 81-83, 99-100.

In January, 1619, prompted by the urgings of his friends, Böhme decided that he could no longer keep silent. Taking up his pen once more, he produced a constant stream of lengthy books over a period of nearly six years until his death. The first of these was *Von den drei Principien göttlichen Wesens* (1619; *Concerning the Three Principles of the Divine Essence*, 1648), which was quickly followed by *Vom dreyfachen Leben des Menschen* (1620; *The High and Deep Searching Out of the Threefold Life of Man*, 1650) and *Viertzig Fragen von der Seele* (1620; *Forty Questions of the Soul*, 1647). In all of these works Böhme labored to give expression to his central insights: that all life, even that of God, is composed of a dynamic interplay of opposing forces: fire and light, wrath and love. Only as a result of interaction with its opposite could anything in the universe gain self-knowledge; the clash of opposites is what drives the universe on, at every level. Within God, all opposing energies are held in a dynamic and joyful state of creative tension, a unified state that Böhme described as "eternal nature." Only in the human world ("temporal nature") does the equilibrium between the opposites of darkness and light become disturbed, and this brings with it the possibility of evil and suffering.

As Böhme's fame spread, he cultivated a large correspondence with noblemen, physicians, and others in positions of authority, who encouraged him to continue with his work. To keep up with the demand for Böhme's writings, his friend Carl von Ender employed several copyists, and because Böhme was still officially banned from writing, some of his manuscripts had to be smuggled out in grain sacks. Still they kept coming: In addition to a number of short, devotional treatises, he produced *Von der Gerburt und Bezeichnung aller Wesen* (1622; *Signatura Rerum: Or, The Signature of All Things*, 1651), a difficult but profound book full of alchemical terminology; *Von der Gnadenwahl* (1623; *Concerning the Election of Grace*, 1655), which he considered to be his greatest work; and *Erklärung über das erste Buch Mosis* (1623; *Mysterium Magnum*, 1654), a lengthy exegesis of the book of Genesis.

BÖHME ON THE CLASH OF OPPOSITES

In his work "Of the Mixed Tree of Evil and Good" (1620), Jakob Böhme shows clearly how one term in a given pair cannot exist as meaningful without the other. A principle such as "good" and a phenomenon such as "light" can only be known when distinguished by its opposite, in this case, "evil" and "dark." Also, one item in a pair always "rules," or predominates, over the other.

In God's kingdom, viz. in the light-world, no more than one principle is truly known. For the Light rules, and the other sources and properties all exist hiddenly as a mystery; for they must all serve the Light, and give their will to the Light. And therefore the wrath-essence is transformed in the Light into a desire of light and of love, into gentleness.

Although the properties, viz. sour, bitter, anguish and the sharp pang in fire remain eternally even in the light-world, yet none of them is manifest in its property; but they are all of them together only causes of life, mobility and joy.

That which in the dark world is a pang, is in the light-world a pleasing delight; and what in the dark is a stinging and enmity, is in the light an uplifting joy. And that which in the dark is a fear, terror and trembling, is in the light a shout of joy, a ringing forth and singing.

. . . What rings in the Light, knocks and thumps in the Dark.

Source: Jakob Böhme, *Six Theosophic Points and Other Writings*, translated by John Rolleston Earle (Ann Arbor: University of Michigan Press, 1958), pp. 38, 39.

In 1624, Böhme once more encountered persecution. Some of his devotional works had been printed by his friends under the title of *Der Weg zu Christo* (1622; *The Way to Christ*, 1648). The book came to the notice of Gregorius Richter, and Richter again denounced Böhme from the pulpit. Incited by the preacher, a mob stoned Böhme's house. Richter then wrote a pamphlet against Böhme, accusing him of blasphemy, heresy, and drunkenness, and of poisoning the whole city with his false doctrines. He requested that the Görlitz council imprison him. This time, however, Böhme replied to his accuser, refuting Richter point by point in writing. The town magistrates, under pressure from Richter, ordered Böhme to be banished, but the next day they rescinded their decision.

Later in the year, Böhme traveled to Dresden, where he had been called to appear before the Electoral Court. He was well received in the city by eminent men, and the several prominent Lutheran theologians who questioned him at length about his beliefs refused to condemn him. He returned to Görlitz, where he began work on *Von 177 theosophischen Fragen* (1624; *Theosophic Questions*, 1661). This work, in which Böhme's thought reached a new level of profundity, was left unfinished at his death on November 17, 1624.

SIGNIFICANCE

Böhme's achievements were many. Drawing on his own experience of enlightened states of consciousness, he took many disparate strands of thought, including Lutheranism, the German mystical tradition, Renaissance Neoplatonism, the ideas of Paracelsus and the alchemical tradition, and the Kabbala, and forged them into a new synthesis.

His work constitutes a profound exploration of the nature of existence, both human and divine; it is at once a philosophical system, a mystical vision, and a mythological drama. Perhaps its most significant aspect is Böhme's attempts to unify life without destroying its essential polarity—it is a metaphysics that includes a compelling explanation of the origin and nature of evil. His description of the process by which God comes to self-consciousness is powerful and original; his emphasis on intuitive rather than rational means of knowing is challenging, as is his insistence that humans can know, on the level of direct experience, the totality of the universe. His theory of language, which centers on a universal, paradisal "language of nature," is worth more serious consideration than some have been prepared to give it.

Böhme has had an enormous influence on the history of ideas. Georg Wilhelm Friedrich Hegel called him the father of German philosophy, and Hegel's contemporary, Friedrich Schelling, described him as "a miraculous phenomenon in the history of mankind." Arthur Schopenhauer and the twentieth century Russian philosopher Nicholas Berdyaev also felt his influence. In seventeenth century England, where Böhme's thought was readily received, there was a sect known as the Behmenists, and there was even a proposal that Parliament should set up two colleges specifically for the study of Böhme. In the nineteenth century, the English Romantic poets William Blake and Samuel Taylor Coleridge were directly inspired by Böhme's work, and Coleridge's comment that Böhme was "a stupendous human being" is not an exaggeration: The self-taught shoemaker from Görlitz made a lasting contribution to the Western philosophical and religious tradition.

—*Bryan Aubrey*

FURTHER READING

Boehme, Jacob. *The Way to Christ.* Translated with an introduction by Peter Erb. New York: Paulist Press, 1978. The most accurate and reliable translation of nine of Böhme's treatises, with an informative introduction placing Böhme's work in the context of Lutheran theology.

Brinton, H. H. *The Mystic Will: Based on a Study of the Philosophy of Jacob Boehme.* New York: Macmillan, 1930. The most reliable and perceptive study in English of Böhme's thought, particularly useful for its analysis of Böhme's concepts of the silent unmanifest Being (Ungrund) and the figure of Wisdom. Includes a chapter on the reception of Böhme's works in seventeenth century England.

Hartmann, Franz. *Jacob Boehme: Life and Doctrines.* Reprint. Blauvelt, N.Y.: Steinerbooks, 1977. An account of Böhme's life and work, including extracts and analysis of Böhme's writings, organized thematically.

Hvolbek, Russell. *Mysticism and Experience.* Lanham, Md.: University Press of America, 1998. Explains how Böhme's ideas about the individual's understanding of nature, God, and the self through feeling and connection is similar to mystical experience.

Martensen, Hans L. *Jacob Boehme (1575-1624): Studies in His Life and Teachings.* Notes and appendices by Stephen Hobhouse. Rev. ed. London: Rockcliff, 1949. Danish bishop Martensen is basically sympathetic to Böhme in this work, but he objects to some of Böhme's doctrines from the standpoint of a strongly biblical Protestant theology.

O'Regan, Cyril. *Gnostic Apocalypse: Jacob Boehme's Haunted Narrative.* Albany: State University of New York Press, 2002. O'Regan describes how Böhme's thought represents a return to medieval Gnosticism within the confines of post-Lutheran Protestantism.

Stoudt, John Joseph. *Sunrise to Eternity: A Study in Jacob Boehme's Life and Thought.* Preface by Paul Tillich. Philadelphia: University of Pennsylvania Press, 1957. Still the fullest account in English of Böhme's life. Carefully researched, accurate, and lively, it takes into account the findings of modern German scholarship that was not available to earlier biographers.

Walsh, David. *The Mysticism of Innerworldly Fulfillment: A Study of Jacob Boehme.* Gainesville: University Presses of Florida, 1983. Walsh argues that Böhme's conception of history as a dialectical process is the basis of political reality.

SEE ALSO: Johann Joachim Becher; Madame Guyon; Jan Baptista van Helmont; Marin Mersenne; Shabbetai Tzevi.

RELATED ARTICLES in *Great Events from History: The Seventeenth Century, 1601-1700:* 1637: Descartes Publishes His *Discourse on Method*; 1693: Ray Argues for Animal Consciousness.

NICOLAS BOILEAU-DESPRÉAUX
French writer and scholar

Boileau-Despréaux, a leading authority on neoclassical doctrine, wrote satire, epistles, dialogues, and literary criticism. His work became available in several languages and contributed to the rapid diffusion of French classical theory throughout Europe.

BORN: November 1, 1636; Paris, France
DIED: March 13, 1711; Paris
ALSO KNOWN AS: Nicolas Boileau des Préaux; Nicolas Boileau Despréaux; Législateur du Parnasse; Legislator of Parnassus
AREAS OF ACHIEVEMENT: Literature, scholarship

EARLY LIFE

Nicolas Boileau-Despréaux (nee-koh-lah bwah-loh-day-pray-oh) was the son of Gilles Boileau, a court clerk in the *parlement* of Paris. His mother, Anne de Niélé, died when he was eighteen months old. At the Collège de Beauvais, where he studied as an adolescent, he became familiar with the Greek and Latin classics, learned to write poetry, and received some training in theology. He also showed a keen interest in the writings of popular romance novelists such as La Calprenède and Madeleine de Scudéry, but he would later deride them as trivial authors.

Following some three and a half years of study at the Parisian Faculty of Law, he was admitted to the bar on December 4, 1656, but quickly abandoned the profession to follow his love of literature. An inheritance from his father, who died in February of the following year, offered him the financial freedom he desired. Soon, he began to attend literary circles, gaining valuable experience in matters of taste, and took to writing satire after the models of Juvenal and Horace. By the early 1660's, a number of his manuscript satires were in the hands of friends and critics. After publication of the first edition of his *Les Satires* in 1666, which had been prompted by the arrival of a pirated edition earlier that year, Boileau-Despréaux rapidly gained recognition in the French capital and went on to become one of the nation's leading social, moral, and literary critics.

LIFE'S WORK

The first edition of Boileau-Despréaux's *Satires*, preceded by a preface addressed to King Louis XIV of France, contained seven satires on various topics, ranging from life in the French capital to bad literature and boorish behavior. His criticism of Jean Chapelain's epic

poem, *La Pucelle* (1656; the maiden), notably in *satires* III and IV, sparked a series of indignant attacks on Boileau-Despréaux, to which the author quickly responded in verse and prose. Although a mediocre poet himself, Chapelain was one of the founders of the celebrated Académie Française and still had many followers in the capital willing to defend him.

Four additional satires were published during Boileau-Despréaux's lifetime, including the delightfully pessimistic *satire* VIII "Sur l'homme" (1668; on man) and a controversial *satire* X "Contre les femmes" (1694; against women). Ultimately, Boileau-Despréaux would produce a corpus of twelve satires. *Satire* XII "Sur l'équivoque" (on ambiguity) was barred from publication for its derision of Jesuit casuistry, and so did not appear until the second authoritative edition of his collected works in 1716, five years after the poet's death (*Satires*, 1711-1713).

By the end of the 1660's, Boileau-Despréaux had acquired a reputation as an unrepentant satirist. Seeking both to follow in Horace's footsteps and to reform his own public image, he diverted his attention momentarily from satire to other genres. Not surprisingly, therefore, his highly polemic *L'Arrêt burlesque* (burlesque injunction), directed against theologians at the Sorbonne, appeared anonymously in 1671. During a period covering some forty years, Boileau-Despréaux completed twelve *épîtres* (*Épîtres*, pb. 1670-1698; epistles), combining commonplace moral philosophy with praise of King Louis XIV's military exploits as well as tenets of Jansenist theology, and with reflections on life in a bucolic setting. Modern critics have remarked, however, that scathing sarcasm and irony were so deeply entrenched in the Frenchman's nature that he could hardly refrain from applying them in any genre.

Immediately following his introduction at court in January of 1674, Boileau-Despréaux received, along with the promise of a generous royal pension, a royal privilege authorizing publication of his long-awaited *Œuvres diverses* (1674; diverse works). His chief adversary, Chapelain, had used his influence to prevent the diffusion of Boileau-Despréaux's works for more than two years, but he was nearing death and could no longer sustain his opposition. In addition to *satires* I-IX and *épîtres* I-IV, this volume contained Boileau-Despréaux's important *L'Art poétique* (*The Art of Poetry*, 1683), tested and refined over the course of several years at public

BOILEAU-DESPRÉAUX ON CLEVERNESS

Nicolas Boileau-Despréaux believed that the best and most original of ideas come not from observations and articulations of the exceptional but from the common and ordinary—the universal.

What is a new, brilliant, extraordinary thought? It is not, as ignorant people think, a thought that no one has ever had or can have had before; on the contrary, it is a thought that must have occurred to everybody and that someone happens to be the first to put into words. A clever saying is clever only insofar as it expresses something that everyone was thinking and that renders it in a lively, refined, and novel way.

Source: Boileau-Despréaux, *Works* (1701), excerpted in *The Age of Reason: The Culture of the Seventeenth Century*, edited by Leo Weinstein (New York: George Braziller, 1965), p. 127.

readings in the homes of influential members of the Parisian aristocracy. Also included were the first four cantos of his mock epic *Le Lutrin* (the lectern; partial English translation, 1682) and his French translation (*Traité de sublime*) of Longinus's *On the Sublime* (first century C.E.), the first French translation of this work. From the latter, he derived his oft-discussed notion of the ineffable, "je ne sais quoi" (I know not what).

In recognition of his merit as an author and a critic, Boileau-Despréaux was appointed to the office of royal historiographer in 1677, alongside his friend Jean Racine, and was elected to membership in the prestigious Académie Française in 1684. One year later, in 1685, he became a member of the Académie des Inscriptions et Médailles (academy of inscriptions and medals) and purchased a house in nearby Auteil to escape the noise and commotion of the city. After 1690, he no longer appeared at Versailles but continued to attend meetings of the Académie Française and worked on his final *satires* and *épîtres*. He opposed fellow academic Charles Perrault in the so-called quarrel of the ancients and moderns, expressing admiration for the ancients in *Réflexions critiques sur Longin* (1694; critical reflections on Longinus).

In 1701, Boileau-Despréaux published the final edition of his *Œuvres diverses*, which included a new preface as well as *satire* IX, an "Ode sur les Anglais" (ode on the English), and various Latin translations of his writings. Translations of individual works appeared in several European languages during Boileau-Despréaux's lifetime. A major cumulative translation into English,

The Works of Monsieur Boileau, Made English by Several Hands, appeared in three separate volumes in 1711, 1712, and 1713. Two important editions of Boileau-Despréaux's collected works appeared posthumously, one in 1713 and the other in 1716.

SIGNIFICANCE

As a literary critic, Boileau-Despréaux formulated, perhaps better than any other of his generation, the basic precepts of neoclassical doctrine. In France, his *Art poétique* has been a convenient pedagogical guide used by generations of schoolchildren to acquire fundamental notions of traditional literary criticism, from the all-important Horatian precept of *placere et docere* (to please and to educate) down to the "rules" of verisimilitude and propriety as they relate to the individual genres. His work on Pseudo-Longinus, an author seldom read outside academic circles, introduced discussion of sublimity into French classical theory, fueling debate on the role of genius versus acquired skill in the process of artistic creation.

Translations of Boileau-Despréaux's work became available in several languages and contributed to the rapid diffusion of French classical theory throughout Europe. In England, *Art poétique* and *Le Lutrin* had demonstrable influence on such authors as John Dryden, Joseph Addison, and Alexander Pope. Boileau-Despréaux was, however, also one of the leading satirists of his day. His poetry not only exposed humankind's foibles but also pointed to the common virtues and values of French aristocracy during the reign of Louis XIV.

—*Jan Pendergrass*

FURTHER READING

Brody, Jules. "Nicolas Boileau." *European Writers.* Vol. 3 in *The Age of Reason and Enlightenment: René Descartes to Montesquieu*, edited by George Stade. New York: Scribner, 1984. An introduction to the author's life and works, followed by detailed analysis of his ideas.

Colton, Robert E. *Juvenal and Boileau: A Study of Literary Influence.* New York: G. Olms, 1987. This study shows the extent of Juvenal's influence on Boileau-Despréaux and how Boileau-Despréaux adapted his Roman model to seventeenth century France.

_____. *Studies of Classical Influence on Boileau and La Fontaine.* New York: G. Olms, 1996. This collection contains nine essays examining the influence of various classical Latin authors in Boileau-Despréaux's *Satires* and *Épîtres*.

Corum, Robert T., Jr. *Reading Boileau: An Integrative Study of the Early Satires*. West Lafayette, Ind.: Purdue University Press, 1998. A sequential analysis of Boileau-Despréaux's *Discours au roi* and the first nine satires points to the poet's persona as a unifying element.

Hardison, O. B., Jr., and Leon Golden. *Horace for Students of Literature: The Ars Poetica and Its Tradition*. Gainesville: University Press of Florida, 1995. This English translation and commentary of major works in the history of literary criticism, from Horace to Wallace Stevens, includes a chapter on Boileau-Despréaux.

Pocock, Gordon. *Boileau and the Nature of Neo-Classicism*. New York: Cambridge University Press, 1980. This introduction to neoclassical doctrine analyzes Boileau-Despréaux's *Satires*, *Épîtres*, and *Art poétique*, and includes basic biographical information.

White, Julian Eugene, Jr. *Nicolas Boileau*. New York: Twayne, 1969. A standard English-language reference.

Wood, Alan G. *Literary Satire and Theory: A Study of Horace, Boileau, and Pope*. New York: Garland, 1985. This work examines the relationship between the poetic work and theory of three major satirists, including Boileau-Despréaux. Discussion centers on each poet's persona.

SEE ALSO: Jean de La Fontaine; Louis XIV; François de Malherbe; Charles Perrault; Jean Racine; Madeleine de Scudéry.

RELATED ARTICLES in *Great Events from History: The Seventeenth Century, 1601-1700:* 1610-1643: Reign of Louis XIII; 1637: Descartes Publishes His *Discourse on Method*; 1638-1669: Spread of Jansenism; 1664: Molière Writes *Tartuffe*; 1682: French Court Moves to Versailles; 1689-1694: Famine and Inflation in France.

GIOVANNI ALFONSO BORELLI
Italian physicist and physiologist

Borelli, a scientist with wide-ranging accomplishments, founded the field of biophysics (iatrophysics) with his pioneering work on the mechanical basis of muscular motions, respiration, and circulation in animals. He made significant contributions to mathematics, astronomy, physics, mechanics, hydraulics, medicine, epidemiology, and physiology.

BORN: January 28, 1608; Naples, Kingdom of Naples (now in Italy)

DIED: December 31, 1679; Rome, Papal States (now in Italy)

ALSO KNOWN AS: Giovanni Francesco Antonio Alonso (given name)

AREAS OF ACHIEVEMENT: Medicine, science and technology, physics, astronomy, mathematics

EARLY LIFE
Giovanni Alfonso Borelli (jyoh-VAHN-nee ahl-FON-soh buh-REHL-lee), named Giovanni Francesco Antonio Alonso at birth, was the son of a Spanish soldier in the garrison in Naples, whose political problems led Borelli to suppress connections to his father, including his own date and place of birth. He may have had early instruction from the Catholic Humanist and empiricist Tommaso Campanella when Campanella was a prisoner of the Spanish Inquisition at Castel Nuovo in Naples, where Borelli's father was stationed. It is also thought by some scholars that Borelli attended the medical school at the University of Naples, but no records of this have been found.

In about 1628, Borelli went to Rome and became a student of one of Galileo's disciples, Benedetto Castelli. Along with Borelli was another student, a promising young scientist named Evangelista Torricelli. Perhaps at the recommendation of Castelli, Borelli took a position in 1637 as a public lecturer in mathematics at the University of Messina in Sicily. His scientific work led the senate of Messina to send him on a mission in 1641 and 1642 to Italian centers of learning to enlist lecturers for the university. He continued teaching for another fourteen years at Messina, where he became professor of mathematics in 1649. He was asked by the senate of Messina in 1647 to study a fever epidemic in the region, leading to the publication in Rome of a pamphlet entitled *Delle cagioni de le febbri maligna* (1649; on the causes of malignant fevers), which suggested contagious causes and chemical cures of fevers rather than the then-accepted astrological or meteorological causes of fevers.

LIFE'S WORK

While still at the University of Messina, Borelli began a compendium of the four surviving books of the Greek mathematician Apollonius on conic sections, although it was not published until 1679. He also wrote a concise version of Euclid's works on geometry entitled *Euclides restitus* (1658; Euclid restored), which led to his appointment as professor of mathematics at the University of Pisa in 1656 at the invitation of the Medici family.

During a decade in Tuscany, Borelli was especially active in the Accademia del Cimento (academy for experiments) and the experimental programs organized by Prince Leopold de' Medici. At the University of Pisa he became a friend and mentor of Marcello Malpighi, whose pioneering work with the microscope led him to discover the capillary veins, confirming William Harvey's theory of the circulation of the blood. The younger Malpighi stimulated Borelli's interest in applying physical laws to biology, and he conducted dissections that aided Borelli in his groundbreaking research on animal movements. He also worked on lagoons near Pisa for the grand duke of Tuscany, Ferdinand II de' Medici, and edited books on hydraulics. In 1665, he published a letter under the pseudonym Pier Maria Mutoli, which contained the first suggestion that comets travel along a parabolic path under the influence of the sun.

While still at Pisa, Borelli established an observatory in 1665 at the fortress of San Miniato outside Florence, using instruments he had designed. His most important work during this time was his research on Jupiter's moons, which helped to establish a physical framework for the Copernican system without drawing the opposition that Galileo had experienced by emphasizing Earth's motion. He introduced the idea that the planets are held in their orbits by an attractive force toward the Sun, based on a similar concept for the Galilean moons held in orbit by attraction toward Jupiter. However, he thought that this force of attraction had to be balanced by an outward centrifugal force to keep the planets in orbital equilibrium, rather than the later idea of Isaac Newton that the force of attraction prevents inertial motion in a straight line and causes orbital motion. Borelli published his ideas in an influential book entitled *Theoricae Mediceorum planetarum ex causis physicis deductae* (1666; theory of the Medicean planets deduced from physical causes).

Borelli left Tuscany in 1667 to return to his professorship at Messina. The same year, he published an expanded version of his research in physics at the Accademia del Cimento under the title *De vi percussionis* (1667; on percussion forces). The violent, historic eruption of Mount Etna in 1669 gave Borelli the opportunity to apply the laws of fluid motion to volcanic action in a pioneering contribution to volcanology. After five years in Messina, Borelli was forced to leave Sicily because of suspicions about his involvement in an anti-Spanish rebellion that had occurred in Messina in 1670.

In 1672, Borelli moved to Calabria in southern Italy and then to Rome, where in 1675 he joined the Academia Reale, established by Queen Christina of Sweden after her abdication and conversion to Roman Catholicism. Christina provided some support for Borelli, who served as her physician, and she encouraged him in his work on the movement of animals, offering to pay for the work's publication. Arrangements were being made to publish this work when all his belongings were stolen in 1677.

In financial distress, Borelli accepted the hospitality of the Clerks Regular of the Pious Schools in Rome, where he taught mathematics to novices of the order (the Piarists) during the last two years of his life (1677-1679). During this time, he completed writing his masterpiece, the two-volume *De motu animalium* (1680-1681; *On the Movement of Animals*, 1989), which was dedicated to Queen Christina and published after his death. This pioneering work used the methods of Galileo to analyze the action of muscles acting on lever arms formed by bones. The first volume examined external motions, and the second volume described the internal actions of muscles, the heart, blood circulation, and respiration.

SIGNIFICANCE

Borelli, along with Torricelli, Galileo's secretary in the last three months of his life, carried on the scientific tradition that Galileo had initiated in Italy in spite of opposition from the Roman Catholic Church. Borelli's work on the moons of Jupiter was the first to suggest that the force on an orbiting moon or planet was an attractive force toward the center of motion rather than a tangential force in the direction of motion. This extended and clarified Galileo's ideas about orbital motions and was a major step toward the work of Newton, which finally resolved the problem of planetary motion in a heliocentric system. This same idea led Borelli to offer the first explanation for the motion of comets.

Borelli's work on the movement of animals was the first application of Galileo's methods to biology and one of the first attempts to develop the view of French philosopher René Descartes that the body can be viewed as a machine subject to mechanical principles. It initiated the historical school of iatrophysics (medical physics) by demonstrating the mechanical basis of muscular contractions, blood circulation, and respiration. In this respect, Borelli can be viewed as the founder of the discipline of biophysics.

—*Joseph L. Spradley*

FURTHER READING

Boorstin, Daniel. *The Discoverers: A History of Man's Search to Know His World and Himself.* New York: Random House, 1983. This engaging book has a brief description of the work of Borelli in relation to that of Marcello Malpighi, who discovered the capillary veins, including their mutual support and friendship, and their eventual estrangement.

Borelli, Giovanni Alfonso. *On the Movement of Animals.* Translated by P. Maquet. New York: Springer-Verlag, 1989. A translation of Borelli's major work. Includes illustrations, a bibliography, and an index.

Hall, A. Ruppert. *From Galileo to Newton.* New York: Dover, 1981. Borelli's work in physiology is dis-

cussed in chapter 7, which includes diagrams of his mechanical analysis of muscle action. His work in astronomy is discussed in chapter 10 in relation to Newton's law of universal gravitation.

Koyré, Alexandre. *The Astronomical Revolution: Copernicus, Kepler, Borelli.* New York: Dover, 1992. Translated by R. E. W. Maddison. Paris: Hermann, 1961. This English translation includes excerpts and diagrams from the astronomical work of Borelli.

Rossi, Paoli. *The Birth of Modern Science.* Malden, Mass.: Blackwell, 2001. Translated by Cynthia de Nardi Ipsen. Rome: Gius, Laterza & Figli, 2000. This English translation includes a brief discussion of Borelli's mechanical physiology in chapter 9.

SEE ALSO: Tommaso Campanella; Christina; René Descartes; Galileo; William Harvey; Johannes Baptista van Helmont; Marcello Malpighi; Sir Isaac Newton; Santorio Santorio; Evangelista Torricelli.

RELATED ARTICLES in *Great Events from History: The Seventeenth Century, 1601-1700:* 1617-1628: Harvey Discovers the Circulation of the Blood; 1693: Ray Argues for Animal Consciousness.

FRANCESCO BORROMINI
Italian architect

Borromini was one of the most innovative architects of the Baroque era, but his contemporaries were highly critical of what they believed to be his fantastical instead of logical work and believed that it violated the principles of sound architectural design. For this reason, his immediate influence was slight, but he is now considered one of the giants of Baroque architecture.

BORN: September 25, 1599; Bissone, near Lake Lugano, duchy of Lombardy (now in Italy)
DIED: August 2, 1667; Rome, Papal States (now in Italy)
ALSO KNOWN AS: Francesco Castelli (given name)
AREA OF ACHIEVEMENT: Architecture

EARLY LIFE

Francesco Borromini's father, Giovanni Domenico Castelli-Brumino, and his mother, Anastasia di Leone Garovo Allio, were members of two of the many families of masons and stonecutters who lived near one another on the Swiss border near Lake Lugano. Their son

Francesco Castelli, who was later to change his name to Borromini, was born in Bissone, in what is the modern Swiss Canton of Ticino, in 1599. His early life remains a mystery. When he was fifteen, or perhaps even at the age of nine, he went to Milan, where he received a thorough grounding in the mason's and stonecarver's crafts. There was a considerable amount of building going on in Milan in the early seventeenth century, and the work on the great cathedral was in its final phases, but it is not known what, if any, work Borromini may have designed or executed.

Many of Borromini's kinsmen had gone to Rome to work on papal building projects, and two of them had achieved considerable distinction. One was Domenico Fontana, the most important architect during the papacy of Pope Sixtus V, and the other was Borromini's uncle, Carlo Maderno, who completed the construction of St. Peter's during the reign of Paul V. Borromini idolized his uncle, and it was probably about 1619 that he was able to join him in Rome.

Maderno was then Rome's leading architect, and Borromini began working for him at once, carving some of the architectural decoration for the portico of St. Peter's Basilica. Within a few years, he had established himself as Maderno's principal architectural draftsman and most trusted assistant, and he continued to work very closely with him until Maderno died in 1629. In 1621, Borromini was paid for carving some of the capitals for the drum of the dome of Sant' Andrea della Valle in Rome, and two years later Maderno let him prepare the design for the lantern of the dome. The double capitals with heads of cherubs look forward to the bizarre decorations of his maturity. He was also responsible for the design of the decorative grille of the Cappella del Santissimo Sacramento in St. Peter's.

By the mid-1620's, Borromini had begun working for Gian Lorenzo Bernini, who was designing the crossing and the apse of St. Peter's. Bernini was the great favorite of Pope Urban VIII, and during the late 1620's, he began to take on more and more work in St. Peter's. Whatever hopes Borromini may have had of ever replacing his uncle as architect in charge of the church faded during those years. Shortly after Maderno's death, however, Bernini received the coveted appointment in February of 1629.

LIFE'S WORK

Bernini was virtually an artistic dictator; in the early 1630's, Borromini had no choice but to continue to work under him, at St. Peter's and also at the Palazzo Barberini, the pope's family palace, which Maderno had begun shortly before his death. It was not until the early 1630's that Borromini was able to break with Bernini and pursue an independent architectural career.

His first commission came in 1634. The Spanish Order of the Discalced Trinitarians asked him to erect their church and monastery of San Carlo alle Quattro Fontane. Borromini built the dormitory, the refectory, and the cloisters first and, in 1638, began working on the church, which was completed in 1641 and consecrated in 1646. The facade, however, was not completed until 1665-1667. The church therefore marks the beginning as well as the end of Borromini's architectural career.

The plan of San Carlo is derived from a series of intricate geometric constructions in which two circles and an oval are inscribed within two equilateral triangles. The oval determines the shape of the dome, and the apexes of the triangles give the location of the half-oval side chapels. What is so unusual about Borromini's plan is that it contradicts what had been one of the most important principles of architectural practice from the Renaissance

onward: the concept of planning in terms of basic arithmetical units, such as the diameter of a column. By developing his plan as a series of geometric relationships, he was returning to the method of planning that had been common during the medieval period but had been largely abandoned during the Renaissance.

In 1637, the Oratorians of the Congregation of St. Philip Neri engaged Borromini to build an oratory for musical performances, a library, and living quarters for the fathers next to their church of San Maria in Vallicella. This was a major commission, and the building went up rapidly. The oratory was vaulted in 1638 and inaugurated in August, 1640. The facade is an architectural creation of great distinction. It curves slowly inward and is crowned by a pediment that for the first time combines the triangular pediment with the curved one, thus uniting in a single architectural form two motifs which had always been considered as contrasting alternatives.

No work by Borromini, though, approaches the complexity of San Ivo della Sapienza, the church of the Roman Archiginnasio, which was later the university. He had been appointed the architect of the Archiginnasio as early as 1632, but it was not until 1642 that he began work on the church. It was built at the end of a long, arcaded courtyard, and while the lower part of the facade echoes the arcaded motif, the upper part is a remarkable construction that would seem to be composed of a curved drum, a low, stepped dome, and an enormous lantern topped by a spiral ramp. The strangeness of the lantern appears to be at odds with what seems to be the rather logical division of the dome into its two parts, the drum and the dome itself. Inside the church, however, this apparent clarity is seen to be deceptive, for the dome actually extends well into the drum. Once again, Borromini insisted on creating architectural forms that his contemporaries considered to be at odds with accepted architectural practice.

Like San Carlo, the plan of San Ivo is based on a geometrical construction. This time two equilateral triangles have been joined so that, if lines are drawn to connect their points of intersection, a regular hexagon is formed, and this becomes the basis for the ground plan of the church. Hexagonal plans are virtually nonexistent in earlier Italian architecture, and Borromini's use of the figure may have been intended to represent the six-pointed Star of David, a symbol of wisdom.

While Borromini did not lack commissions, he never achieved the stature of Bernini, who for more than fifty years basked in the sun of papal patronage. Only Pope Innocent X, who was elected in 1644, favored him. Indeed, it was for Innocent that Borromini began to rebuild the family church of San Agnese in 1653. After Innocent died in 1655, work ceased, and the church was later completed by others. In 1646, Innocent had set Borromini to work on the remodeling of one of the oldest churches in Rome, the venerable church of San Giovanni in Laterano, but the vault that he planned was never built.

During the last years of his life, Borromini was finally able to complete the facade of San Carlo alle Quattro Fontane. There, where he began his career, he brought it to a climactic conclusion. The curved facade, one of the first fully curved Baroque facades on a church, is filled with contradictory elements that challenge traditional practices and concepts of design and that subsequent generations considered the antithesis of "proper" architecture. Today, however, its richness of decoration and mingling of architecture and sculpture have given it a secure place among the great monuments of Baroque architecture.

Borromini's disappointments and jealousy over Bernini's triumphs left him embittered and quarrelsome. He had few friends and lived as a recluse, devoting himself entirely to his work. As he grew older, his sense of persecution deepened, and eventually, in 1667, he tried to take his own life by falling on his sword. He lived for a few hours, taking the time to dictate to his confessor a strangely objective and dispassionate account of the reasons for his suicide.

SIGNIFICANCE

Borromini, obsessed with the problems of his art, was a shy and misanthropic bachelor who lived in sparsely furnished rooms surrounded by his library of nearly one thousand books. In his will, he asked that he be buried in the tomb of his uncle, Carlo Maderno, one of the few people with whom he ever developed a warm relationship.

His rivalry with Bernini was fueled by his conviction that Bernini was deficient in the technical knowledge that was Borromini's stock-in-trade. In the modern sense of the word, Borromini was a true professional, an expert within a limited range of concerns. Bernini, on the other hand, like his Renaissance predecessors, saw architecture as primarily a matter of design for which skill in drawing was sufficient training.

Borromini's buildings were seen by his contemporaries as new and in many ways unsettling solutions to architectural problems. His fascination with complex geometric plans, his unorthodox use of architectural motifs, his refusal to accept the traditional separation of architecture and sculpture, and his interest in architectural symbolism led his contemporaries to consider his buildings as creations of fantasy rather than reason.

From the Renaissance onward, architecture had been seen as the process by which humans, guided by reason, could create structures that reflected the rational nature of the universe. With Borromini, this process comes to an end. His architecture is so complex, so full of contradictions, that it seems to defy human reason. In reality, though, behind its apparent irrationality there lies a degree of order of such subtlety that reason can no longer understand it. His work is intended to remind people that humankind must depend upon faith, not reason, to find answers about the nature of the universe. Borromini's expression of this view makes him one of the most eloquent architectural spokespeople of the religious ideals of the Counter-Reformation.

—Eric Van Schaack

FURTHER READING

Blunt, Anthony. *Borromini*. Cambridge, Mass.: Harvard University Press, 1979. Still the best general book available in English on Borromini.

_____, ed. *Baroque and Rococo: Architecture and Decoration*. New York: Harper & Row, 1982. This work provides an excellent short chapter on Borromini's architecture.

Connors, Joseph J. *Borromini and the Roman Oratory: Style and Society*. Cambridge, Mass.: MIT Press, 1980. A detailed discussion of the Congregation of St. Philip Neri, one of Borromini's major architectural projects. Includes a catalog of drawings.

Hauptman, William. "Luceat Lux Vestra Coram Hominibus: A New Source for the Spire of Borromini's San Ivo." *Journal of the Society of Architectural Historians* 33 (1974): 73-79. An investigation of the possible sources for the lantern of Borromini's church of San Ivo della Sapienza and a detailed study of its iconographic meaning.

Hendrix, John. *The Relation Between Architectural Forms and Philosophical Structures in the Work of Francesco Borromini in Seventeenth Century Rome*. Lewiston, N.Y.: Edwin Mellen Press, 2003. Examines Borromini's work within the context of architectural theories of the Renaissance and Baroque eras.

Hopkins, Andrew. *Italian Architecture from Michelangelo to Borromini*. London: Thames and Hudson, 2002. Describes construction of a wide range of buildings to examine the changing functional demands, political forces, patronage systems, and local traditions in Italian architecture.

Morrissey, Jake. *The Genius in the Design: Bernini, Borromini, and the Rivalry That Transformed Rome.* New York: Morrow, 2005. Outlines the relationship and conflict between Bernini and Borromini, the two most significant Italian Baroque architects.

Portoghesi, Paolo. *The Rome of Borromini: Architecture as Language.* Translated by Barbara Luigia La Penta. New York: George Braziller, 1968. The author's detailed analyses of Borromini's buildings are often difficult to follow, but there are many illustrations that provide full coverage of all phases of Borromini's career.

Scott, John Beldon. "San Ivo Alla Sapienza and Borromini's Symbolic Language." *Journal of the Society of Architectural Historians* 41 (1982): 294-317. A carefully documented study of the building history, ceremonial functions, and symbolic content of Borromini's church.

Wittkower, Rudolf. *Art and Architecture in Italy, 1600-1750.* 6th ed. New Haven, Conn.: Yale University Press, 1999. The basic study of Italian Baroque art. The chapter on Borromini is an excellent introduction to his work and art theory.

_____. "Francesco Borromini, His Character and Life." In *Studies in the Italian Baroque.* Boulder, Colo.: Westview Press, 1975. The English version of a lecture delivered in 1967 at an international congress honoring the tercentenary of Borromini's death. Wittkower's essay is an incisive study of Borromini's psychological makeup.

SEE ALSO: Gian Lorenzo Bernini; Guarino Guarini; Urban VIII.

RELATED ARTICLE in *Great Events from History: The Seventeenth Century, 1601-1700:* 1656-1667: Construction of the Piazza San Pietro.

JACQUES-BÉNIGNE BOSSUET
French theologian and writer

Bossuet was one of the most eloquent orators in seventeenth century France. In his sermons and funeral orations, he expressed profound psychological insights in a very refined and effective style. His major contributions were to rhetoric and sacred oratory.

BORN: September 27, 1627; Dijon, France
DIED: April 12, 1704; Paris, France
AREAS OF ACHIEVEMENT: Religion and theology, literature, historiography

EARLY LIFE
Jacques-Bénigne Bossuet (zhahk-bay-neen boh-syew-eh) was born in the Burgundian city of Dijon, where his father, Bénigne, was a lawyer. From 1636 to 1642, he attended a Jesuit school in Dijon, where he studied rhetoric, Greek, and Latin. During his lifetime, Bossuet read an enormous amount of works written in both Latin and Greek. His lengthy study with the Jesuits would help him years later to understand the many influences of the classical tradition on the development of Christian theology.

In October of 1642, he began his preparation for the priesthood and his formal study of theology at the College of Navarre in Paris. Bossuet's major professor was the learned theologian Nicolas Cornet, who convinced Bossuet that a solid understanding of the early church fathers and Saint Thomas Aquinas was essential for the proper exposition of biblical texts. In 1652, Bossuet was ordained a priest and also received his doctorate in theology. Later in 1652, he moved to the French city of Metz, where he soon established a reputation as a very eloquent preacher. His fame would spread throughout France by the end of the 1650's. Even before he reached the age of thirty, Bossuet had enriched the cultural and spiritual life of France through his sermons.

LIFE'S WORK
Although Bossuet had a long and distinguished career as a bishop, as the private tutor for King Louis XIV's eldest son, as a respected member of the French Academy, and as a writer on such varied subjects as the history of Christianity, biblical exposition, and political theory, his fame rests largely on several well-crafted sermons and funeral orations that he delivered between the 1650's and the 1680's. Although his contemporaries greatly admired his very learned historical work *Discours sur l'histoire universelle* (1681; *A Discourse on the History of the Whole World,* 1686), this book and other of his extensive writings on the differences between Roman Catholicism and Protestantism are considered irrelevant by many contemporary theologians. Bossuet's eloquent sermons and funeral orations, however, included such universal themes as fear, despair, hope, the search for moral values, social injustice, and death that these speeches still

continue to move even those readers who may not share Bossuet's religious beliefs.

Divine Providence constituted the unifying theme in Bossuet's works. Readers since his day have revered *Sermon sur la providence* (1662; *Sermon on Providence*, 1801), *Sermon sur la mort* (1662; *Sermon on Death*, 1801), and *Oraison funèbre d'Henriette Anne d'Angleterre* (1670; *Funeral Oration for Henrietta of England*, 1801). These masterpieces of French prose illustrate Bossuet's creativity in expanding the meaning of divine Providence in order to enrich his listeners' understanding of widely different human emotions.

On March 10, 1662, Bossuet preached his *Sermon on Providence* at the Louvre, then the French royal court. Twelve days later, he delivered *Sermon on Death*. These were part of a series of fourteen Lenten sermons that he gave at the royal court in 1662. Based on the sermon titles, listeners may well have thought that these two sermons would differ significantly in perspective and in subject matter, yet these two sermons both illustrate the Christian belief that divine justice eventually rewards the just and punishes evildoers.

Bossuet argues quite sensibly that worldly success and pleasure are ephemeral. He uses a curious but effective comparison to convey this truth to his listeners. He reminds them that "pure wine" pleases the palate, whereas watered-down or "mixed wine" merely satisfies the thirst. Bossuet affirms that the pleasures of "pure wine" represent the eternal joys of the beatific vision, whereas the satisfaction from "mixed wine" symbolizes the happiness and disappointments of daily life. Bossuet begins *Sermon on Providence* by citing Saint Luke's contrast between the cruel rich man whose soul will never leave Hell and the virtuous but poor Lazarus, who is spending eternity in Paradise. Bossuet ends this sermon with an equally powerful biblical image. He tells his listeners that if they imitate Lazarus, who was never discouraged by injustice in this life, they too "will rest in the bosom of Abraham and possess with him eternal riches."

Despite its title, Bossuet's *Sermon on Death* presents a highly optimistic view of the human condition by stressing the essential grandeur and excellence of each person. This sermon develops extensively the opposition

Jacques-Bénigne Bossuet. (Library of Congress)

between appearance and reality. Bossuet makes a curious reference to chemical compounds to explain the meaning of death for Christians: "The nature of a compound is never more distinctly observed than in the dissolution of its parts." He justifies the relevance of this comment by stating that each man and woman is composed of a soul and a body that separate upon death. The body will return to dust, whereas the soul will return to Heaven. Physical death is thus both an end and a beginning. Each person possesses a dual nature: The body is mortal and the soul is immortal. In *Sermon on Death*, Bossuet explains that an acceptance of this dual nature consoles humans in their period of grieving and enables them to endure suffering in this life because of the belief that pure happiness awaits them in Paradise. In this well-structured sermon, Bossuet describes eternal life as a reality that no one should wish to deny.

Bossuet's contemporaries greatly admired the formal

beauty in his sermons and funeral orations. After his ordination in 1652, Bossuet served fifty-two years as a priest and thirty-three years as a bishop. Since he was such an influential clergyman, he was often asked to deliver funeral orations for famous French persons, including Queen Marie-Thérèse (Louis XIV's first wife) and Michel Le Tellier (chancellor of France). Although these two dignitaries were both exemplary Christians, their deaths were not personal tragedies for Bossuet himself.

In 1670, however, Bossuet had to deliver the funeral oration for Princess Henrietta Anne of England, the twenty-six-year-old wife of Louis XIV's only brother. This was an essentially painful responsibility for Bossuet. For more than a year, he had served as Henrietta's spiritual director, and he had come to admire her kindness, her virtue, and her courage. On June 29, 1670, she became suddenly ill, and she died the next morning. Bossuet himself gave her Extreme Unction, and he was at her side when she died. Such a tragic loss inspired Bossuet to compose his most moving and personal funeral oration.

Near the beginning of this oration, Bossuet describes the true paradox of death. He tells his listeners, "Madame (Henrietta) is no longer in the tomb; death, which seemed to destroy everything, has established everything." He stresses that only Henrietta's body has died and that death has freed her soul for eternity. He explains that Henrietta had grown spiritually, largely as a result of the real tragedies in her short life. The execution of her father, Charles I, in 1649 and her exile from England gave her the opportunity to reflect on eternal spiritual values that social upheavals cannot destroy. Had she enjoyed an uneventful childhood and adolescence at the English royal court, Bossuet preaches, she might have become a vain and superficial princess. Divine Providence, however, transformed her into a sincere Christian whose brief but exemplary life should inspire in others a profound love for God. Henrietta realized that "the favors of this world" are nothing in comparison to those favors that will be experienced in Heaven.

During his distinguished ecclesiastical career, Bossuet tried consistently to balance his intellectual pursuits with his responsibilities as a priest and as a bishop. He feared that worldly success would detract from his spiritual growth. In 1681, he accepted the position of bishop in the relatively small French city of Meaux. Although he continued to write and preach during the last two decades of his life, Bossuet spent most of this time tending to the spiritual affairs of his diocese. He died in Paris on April 12, 1704, at the age of seventy-six.

SIGNIFICANCE

Bossuet's contemporaries recognized and appreciated his unique contributions to the moral, political, and religious life in the France of King Louis XIV. In his sermons and funeral orations, Bossuet developed persuasive intellectual arguments to support the religious value system on which French society was then based. He convinced his listeners that it was perfectly sensible for them to accept orthodox Christian dogma.

It is difficult to overestimate Bossuet's influence on generations of French preachers who strove to imitate the eloquence and psychological depth in his sermons. His insightful remarks on divine Providence helped listeners to endure with optimism the travails and suffering of daily life. Bossuet's affirmation of universal dignity and his commitment to tolerance improved the quality of religious life in France.

Bossuet's compatriots also admired his writings on political theory. In *A Discourse on the History of the Whole World*, he argued that the French monarchy, although imperfect, was a very useful form of government because it preserved stability in society and also prevented the country from falling into the political chaos that France had experienced during its civil wars of the sixteenth and seventeenth centuries.

Since the seventeenth century, Bossuet has been admired as a brilliant orator who combined eloquence with profound erudition. Critics still admire both his skills as an orator and his keen insights into the complex motivation for human behavior. His elegant and well-structured speeches were never flowery or overly sentimental, and he expressed himself with restrained passion.

Although he wrote in a consistently formal style and never modified his acceptance of orthodox Catholic theology, he always adapted his arguments to the specific public he was addressing. He participated actively in discussions with Protestant clergymen, but he always respected the beliefs of those with whom he disagreed. He attained a stylistic perfection that no other French preacher has equaled. His speeches have often been favorably compared to the tragedies of Jean Racine and to Madame de La Fayette's psychological novel *La Princesse de Clèves* (1678; *The Princess of Clèves*, 1679). Such comparisons are both appropriate and thought-provoking. Like Racine and La Fayette, Bossuet was a profound writer whose aesthetically pleasing and yet understated works have created an enriched understanding of the human condition.

—Edmund J. Campion

FURTHER READING

Bossuet, Jacques-Bénigne. *Letters of Spiritual Direction.* Translated by Geoffrey Webb and Adrian Walker. London: Saint Austin Press, 2001. Translations of several of Bossuet's letters in which he addresses the method of prayer and other spiritual concerns.

———. *Politics Drawn from the Very Words of Holy Scripture.* Translated and edited by Patrick Riley. New York: Cambridge University Press, 1990. The first English translation of Bossuet's statement of divine right absolutism, published in 1707. Places Bossuet's work in historical and intellectual context.

France, Peter. "Bossuet: The Word and the World." In *Rhetoric and Truth in France: Descartes to Diderot.* Oxford, England: Clarendon Press, 1972. Examines the importance of rhetorical theory and practice in Bossuet's sermons and funeral orations, describing his creative use of imagery and argumentative techniques. Analyzes the emotional effect of Bossuet's speeches on contemporary listeners and modern readers.

Judge, H. G. "Louis XIV and the Church." In *Louis XIV and the Craft of Kingship,* edited by John C. Rule. Columbus: Ohio State University Press, 1969. Informative study of the indirect influence of Bossuet and other French preachers on Louis XIV's political decisions. Demonstrates that French clergymen, including Bossuet, generally supported Louis XIV's claim that clergymen possessed much independence within the Catholic Church in France.

Lockwood, Richard. *The Reader's Figure: Epideictic Rhetoric in Plato, Aristotle, Bossuet, Racine, and Pascal.* Geneva: Droz, 1996. Analyzes the ceremonial rhetoric of Bossuet and other thinkers.

Perry, Elisabeth. *From Theology to History: French Religious Controversy and the Revocation of the Edict of Nantes.* The Hague, the Netherlands: Martinus Nijhoff, 1973. Excellent study of religious controversies between French Catholic and Protestant theologians in the 1670's and 1680's. Describes Bossuet's active participation as an apologist for Catholic dogma.

Terstegge, Georgiana. *Providence as "Idée-Maîtresse" in the Works of Bossuet.* Washington, D.C.: Catholic University of America Press, 1948. Still the major English-language book on Bossuet. Argues that divine Providence is the unifying theme in his works. Examines Bossuet's numerous thematic and stylistic uses of Providence, and contains an excellent bibliography of secondary sources on Bossuet's writings.

SEE ALSO: The Great Condé; François de Salignac de La Mothe-Fénelon; Madame Guyon; Madame de La Fayette; Louis XIV; Madame de Maintenon; François de Malherbe; Marie-Thérèse; Jean Racine.

RELATED ARTICLES in *Great Events from History: The Seventeenth Century, 1601-1700:* 1661: Absolute Monarchy Emerges in France; July 13, 1664: Trappist Order Is Founded.

LOUYSE BOURGEOIS
French midwife and writer

Bourgeois was the first French woman to write treatises on midwifery, helping to establish the discipline of obstetrics. Her writings defined diseases and common problems associated with pregnancy and childbirth.

BORN: c. 1563; place unknown
DIED: December, 1636; France
ALSO KNOWN AS: Louise Bourgeois; Louyse Boursier; Loyse Bourgeois
AREA OF ACHIEVEMENT: Medicine

EARLY LIFE

Little is known about the early life of Louyse Bourgeois. The *État Civil* (records of residents in Paris of the sixteenth and seventeenth centuries) was burned during a fire that destroyed the Hôtel de Ville (Paris city hall) in 1871.

It is estimated that Bourgeois was born around 1563. Pieces of her life can be reconstructed from evidence in her writings, however. In December of 1584, Bourgeois married Martin Boursier, a barber-surgeon, after she had completed her studies in writing, reading, and needlepoint; by October, 1589, she and her husband, Martin Boursier, had three children and lived in the southern suburbs of Paris until Henry IV, king of France, captured the towns of Le Mans, Bayeux, and, temporarily, the Paris faubourgs (suburbs) on the night of October 31, 1589. In September, 1592, records place Bourgeois and her three children in Paris, while her husband was serving as a surgeon for the French army.

Bourgeois and Boursier started a legacy within their family. Future generations continued the tradition of serving the court's medical needs. One of her daughters, Françoise, married René Chartier, a physician, who served King Henry IV. Their son, Jean Chartier, was a physician to King Louis XIII.

Major figures in Bourgeois's life include Boursier, who trained her in medicine; physician Ambroise Paré, whose work Bourgeois studied for midwifery; and her clients in the French court, including Marie de Brabançon, the du Laurens family, and Marguerite de Chabot. Marie de Médicis, queen of France, played a significant role in the life of Bourgeois, as she was Bourgeois's most powerful and long-lasting client. Charles Guillemeau, who ended Bourgeois's career, is another significant person in her life.

LIFE'S WORK

Bourgeois received the majority of her medical training through her husband. The details of her training are unclear, but her own descriptions name the works of an experienced midwife, Ambroise Paré, as her teacher. It is probable that between 1594 and 1598, Bourgeois studied directly under Paré, and she passed her official examination on November 12, 1598.

A combination of factors contributed to the appointment of Bourgeois as a royal midwife to Marie de Médicis in August, 1601. Bourgeois worked her way into the French court by her knowledge of connections between the court members and the king and queen of France. The French court was a close-knit community; through word of mouth and the help of Marie de Médicis' ladies-in-waiting, Bourgeois was introduced to the queen, who appointed her royal midwife to the queen. Physicians also recommended Bourgeois to the queen's court and high-ranking officials with pregnant wives. Bourgeois's husband was known within the community of physicians, so recommendations came through him as well.

Bourgeois delivered six of the queen's children, including the future king Louis XIII. Four of the royal births took place at the Fontainebleau; two, Chrestienne in February, 1606, and Henriette in November, 1609, were born in the Louvre, where Marie de Médicis had stayed. Bourgeois was one of the highest paid midwives in seventeenth century France. As a royal midwife, she received 600 livres for every boy born and 300 livres for every girl born. In 1608, Bourgeois received a lump sum of 6,000 livres, likely in recognition of her services to the royal family.

In 1609, Bourgeois published the first book of her three-volume treatise *Observations diverses sur la sterilite', perte de fruict, foecondite', accouchements, et maladies des femmes, et enfants nouveaux naiz* (better known as *Observations diverses*), which detailed the two thousand births Bourgeois helped to deliver, deliveries assumed to have occurred between 1594 and 1598. Book 1 shows that Bourgeois had a wide range of experience in both normal and complicated childbirth. She addresses emergency births and their difficulties, and describes performing minor surgeries and autopsies resulting from childbirth. Book 2 of *Observations diverses* was published in 1617, followed by book 3 in 1626.

The end of Bourgeois's career as a midwife came in June with the death of Marie de Bourbon-Montpensier, first wife of Gaston d'Orléans and sister-in-law to King Louis XIII, one of Bourgeois's patients. Bourbon-Montpensier died on June 5, 1627, after the birth of her daughter, with a condition that modern medicine calls peritonitis. Marie de Médicis demanded an autopsy report from the court physicians on the day of the death. Five physicians and five surgeons published the report the same day. The report did not imply that Bourgeois was at fault; regardless, *Apologie . . . contre le rapport des medecins* appeared on June 8, 1627. In this rebuttal, Bourgeois argued that the autopsy commission lacked integrity and that another investigation was needed. Charles Guillemeau responded, condemning Bourgeois for incompetence.

The mutual disagreement between Bourgeois and Guillemeau makes it impossible to understand the truth behind the event. Bourgeois's disgrace is not difficult to comprehend. Members of the French court were always changing, so the court was much different in 1627 compared to 1601. The physicians and Bourgeois's past clients were not alive or present in court to support her. As a result, with no allies or powerful forces on her side, Bourgeois had no choice but to withdraw from the court and her position as a royal midwife.

After the death of her husband in 1632, Bourgeois spent the rest of her life putting together her last book, *Recueil des secrets*. This last book teaches how to heal patients using plants as remedies.

SIGNIFICANCE

Bourgeois set the standards for midwifery in seventeenth century Europe. Her books, ideas, and techniques were influential during her time, and they helped push obstetrics into the modern age.

—Shannon A. Powell

FURTHER READING

Donnison, J. *Midwives and Medical Men: A History of the Struggle for the Control of Childbirth*. 2d ed. London: Historical Publications, 1988. Examines the struggle between men and women for positions in midwifery, and discusses Bourgeois's own struggle with male physicians, which she had described in her books.

Dunn, P. M. "Louise Bourgeois (1563-1636): Royal Midwife of France." *Archives of Disease in Childhood: Fetal and Neonatal Edition* 89, no. 2 (March, 2004): 185-187. Presents a brief discussion of Bourgeois's work.

Marland, Hilary, ed. *The Art of Midwifery: Early Modern Midwives in Europe*. New York: Routledge, 1993. This work concentrates on midwifery as a practical art and discusses the general characteristics of midwifery in early modern France and Europe.

Perkins, Wendy. *Midwifery and Medicine in Early Modern France: Louise Bourgeois*. England: University of Exeter Press, 1996. The first chapter provides a biography of Bourgeois. Succeeding chapters analyze her books in detail.

Sheridan, Bridgette Ann Majella. *Childbirth, Midwifery, and Science: The Life and Work of the French Royal Midwife Louise Bourgeois (1563—1636)*. Ph.D. dissertation. Boston College, 2002. Examines Bourgeois's life and work in the context of her time, with a discussion of midwifery as a science.

SEE ALSO: Marie de Médicis; Justine Siegemundin.

RELATED ARTICLE in *Great Events from History: The Seventeenth Century, 1601-1700:* 17th century: Birth Control in Western Europe.

SAINT MARGUERITE BOURGEOYS
French-born educator and saint

Arriving in Montreal from France eleven years after the city's founding, Bourgeoys developed a community of uncloistered women, called the Congrégation de Nôtre-Dame of Montreal, dedicated to the education of indigenous peoples and French settlers. Her work critically supported the colony in its early years by providing both basic instruction and vocational training. She was beatified in 1950 and canonized in 1982.

BORN: April 17, 1620; Troyes, France
DIED: January 12, 1700; Montreal, New France (now in Canada)
AREAS OF ACHIEVEMENT: Education, religion and theology

EARLY LIFE

Marguerite Bourgeoys (mahr-gehr-reet buhr-zhwah), the seventh child born to Abraham Bourgeoys and Guillemette Garnier, grew up in a rented house in the center of Troyes. Her parents were members of the merchant class, and her father held a position in the city's mint. Marguerite was especially close to her father, who carried with him, according to Marguerite, a trinket she had made for him as a child. She spent her childhood years with other girls, pretending she was part of a community in a faraway land.

Bourgeoys received her education probably from the women of the Congrégation de Nôtre-Dame, established in Troyes in 1628. With the Congrégation, she would have learned reading, writing, arithmetic, and religion. Other than where she was likely educated, little else is known of Bourgeoys's early life. She did provide some descriptions later in life, however. A girl who was popular and had a cheerful disposition, she showed no exceptional piety until her conversion experience on Rosary Sunday, 1640. As part of a procession of women in honor of the Virgin, she passed by the portal of Nôtre-Dame-des-Nonnains. Looking up at a statue of Mary, she was struck by its beauty. Although Bourgeoys did not have a "typical" mystical experience, the moment was transformative. The Marian imagery with which Marguerite was to identify was not the passive, submissive ideal but an activism that included teaching and mission.

Bourgeoys joined the Congrégation, a loosely knit group of women who met regularly under the guidance of Louise de Chomedey, sister of the Sieur de Maisonneuve, the first governor of Montreal. Most of the women lived at their respective homes, but they took part in devotional activities and educated girls. Their compassionate ideas about teaching were advanced for the time, as they emphasized involvement of the girl's entire family. The girls would adopt positive roles in their families, society, and religious life.

Bourgeoys's work with Father Antoine de Gendret, the Congrégation's spiritual director, turned her toward the religious life. She aspired to the Carmelite Order but was rejected. Instead, she took a private vow of chastity in 1643, followed by a vow of poverty. The beginning of a project for a new kind of female ministry seems to have resulted from the interactions between Marguerite, Gendret, and the Congrégation.

LIFE'S WORK

Doors of opportunity were opened for Marguerite Bourgeoys following the arrival in Troyes of Paul de Chomedey, sieur de Maisonneuve, whose sisters Marguerite knew well. Maisonneuve, looking for a female educator, approached Marguerite about the position, an offer she discussed with Gendret and others.

In 1653, two years after the death of her father, she joined Maisonneuve on a trip to Brittany. Once again, the Virgin appeared to her, urging Bourgeoys to "go, for I will not forsake you." After an abortive embarkation from Saint-Nazaire, she and Maisonneuve, along with 108 future colonists (including a few women), finally set sail in July. During the month before the ship left port, rumors had circulated that Bourgeoys was Maisonneuve's mistress. Although he later considered marrying her, a deep friendship evolved instead.

After an arduous journey, the ship arrived in Quebec on September 22. Maisonneuve went directly to Montreal, but Bourgeoys remained behind to care for those sickened by the voyage. Although offered a place in the Ursuline convent, she instead chose to live among the settlers.

During her forty-six years in Canada, Bourgeoys devoted herself to active service. The worst of the Iroquois attacks on the colony had ended by the time she arrived in mid-November. For her first five years, she lived in the governor's residence in the center of the fort. Only fourteen women and fifteen children lived in Montreal, but 1653 marked a turning point for the settlement. The following year, three of her female shipboard companions married settlers, and soon there were births, the first French-Canadians.

As early as 1655, Bourgeoys decided to build a chapel dedicated to the Virgin. Three years later, she opened her school in a one-room stable. The building of the school, the center of the Congrégation de Nôtre-Dame of Montreal, was completed on April 30, 1658, the feast day of Saint Catherine of Siena, a woman who had actively influenced the course of political and religious events in the fourteenth century. Early teaching at the new school consisted mainly of reading and catechism.

In October, Bourgeoys returned to France with philanthropist and lay nurse Jeanne Mance, who required medical attention. Bourgeoys used the time to recruit more women for the colony in Canada. Her goal was to create not a cloistered community of women so typical of Catholic Reformation Europe but instead an active group of uncloistered women who would teach both girls and boys. Once in Troyes, she stayed not with her family but with the congregation there, enlisting four women for her new community. Along with Mance, Bourgeoys and her recruits left France on the Feast of Our Lady of the Visitation in 1659, a date she felt marked the true beginning of the Congrégation de Nôtre-Dame of Montreal. The ship arrived in Quebec on the eve of the Feast of the Nativity, and they continued on to Montreal three weeks later.

From 1659 until Maisonneuve's forced retirement and departure for France in 1665, Bourgeoys experienced some of the happiest days of her life. While Montreal's independence was under constant attack from the bishop and governor of Quebec, François Laval, the colony continued to grow, as Mance led her congregation of hospital nuns at the Hôtel Dieu, which she had founded, and Bourgeoys began in earnest to educate colonists. A census in 1663 showed about seventy children of elementary school age. In the early years, boys and girls learned reading and writing, prepared for first communion, and trained for trades and "honorable work." Bourgeoys and her companions supported themselves by taking in laundry and sewing jobs. Shoveling snow was also a regular part of their work.

In 1662, Bourgeoys obtained two new properties, one for crops and animals and the other as a temporary shelter for the *filles du roi*, the "king's girls" who were sent as partners for settlers. In 1665, with Maisonneuve's final departure for France, came the end of what is considered Montreal's "heroic era." However, Bourgeoys and her companions continued their educational and vocational training. Maisonneuve's departure had the effect of altering the vision of the congregation in Troyes; no longer would they envision a Canadian mission. As a result, Bourgeoys would place her school squarely on a secular footing. She had been encouraged to pursue an uncloistered path earlier by Gendret, and was supported later in her endeavors by the Sulpician fathers, who had taken over the work of the Society of Gentlemen and Ladies of Nôtre-Dame, the early settlers, in 1663. The Society recognized the practicality of a self-supporting school.

Bourgeoys made provisions for the continued stability of the school by elevating to power those women who were skilled in fund-raising and recruitment. The years that followed increasingly included work in the burgeoning French settlements around Montreal and with the indigenous peoples. King Louis XIV granted official recognition of the Congrégation in 1671, followed by the bishop of Quebec's recognition five years later.

Even with approval, however, interference from Quebec continued. In 1694, Jean-Baptiste de Saint-Vallier, the second bishop of Quebec, tried to force a merger between the Ursulines and the Congrégation, which would have required Bourgeoys's community to follow the Rule of Saint Augustine. Bourgeoys, however, took the fight directly to the Sulpicians in Paris, who supported her cause. In 1698, Saint-Vallier gave in, and the constitutions of the community received approval in 1698. Although the women of the community were known as "nuns" and "sisters," they had effectively broken out of the pattern of cloistering that had been established in Europe by the Catholic Reformation.

When Marguerite Bourgeoys died in January, 1700, forty sisters remained to carry on her educational and apostolic work in and around Montreal. She was beatified in 1950 and canonized by Pope John Paul II on October 31, 1982, becoming Canada's first woman saint.

SIGNIFICANCE

Saint Marguerite Bourgeoys's dynamic and assertive personality kept her from following the pattern of behavior expected of devout women in France. Aided in her efforts by Father Gendret in France and Paul de Maisonneuve and Jeanne Mance in Montreal, Bourgeoys created a school uniquely suited to a frontier territory constantly under assault from Iroquois attacks, a harsh climate, fires, and floods.

She used to her advantage the hostility between the ecclesiastical authorities in Quebec and the Jesuits and Sulpicians in Montreal to teach vocational skills, reading and writing, and catechism. The Congrégation she founded focused particularly on the plight of poor girls, teaching them the skills needed to make a living. Fighting for the right to teach and minister as secular sisters, Bourgeoys broke free of the constraints expected of women during her forty-six years in New France. More than twenty-five hundred Sisters of the Congrégation continue her work into the twenty-first century, around the world.

—Larissa Juliet Taylor

FURTHER READING

Choquette, Leslie. "'Ces Amazones du Grand Dieu.'" *French Historical Studies* 17, no. 3 (2000): 627-655. A study of how women altered the frontier society of New France to break free of Old World constraints.

Côté, Louise F. *The Writings of Marguerite Bourgeois: Autobiography and Spiritual Testament.* Montreal: Congrégation de Nôtre-Dame, 1976. An excellent collection of primary sources.

Delâge, Denys. *Bitter Feast: Amerindians and Europeans in the American Northeast, 1600-1664.* Vancouver: University of British Columbia Press, 1993. A native perspective on the history of French and Dutch colonization in northeastern North America.

Eccles, W. J. *The French in North America, 1500-1783.* East Lansing: Michigan State University Press, 1998. A general history of New France.

Moogk, Peter N. *Le Nouvelle France: The Making of French Canada, a Cultural History.* East Lansing: Michigan State University Press, 2000. Moogk traces the roots of the current conflict between English- and French-speaking Canadians to the political and social developments that occurred in New France in the seventeenth century.

Simpson, Patricia. *Marguerite Bourgeoys and Montreal, 1640-1665.* Montreal: McGill-Queen's University Press, 1997. A superb biography of Bourgeoys up to 1665. Includes extensive notes and a bibliography.

SEE ALSO: Samuel de Champlain; Pierre Le Moyne d'Iberville; Saint Isaac Jogues; Louis Jolliet; François Laval; Louis XIV; Sieur de Maisonneuve.

RELATED ARTICLES in *Great Events from History: The Seventeenth Century, 1601-1700:* March 15, 1603-December 25, 1635: Champlain's Voyages; Spring, 1604: First European Settlement in North America; 1611-1630's: Jesuits Begin Missionary Activities in New France; April 27, 1627: Company of New France Is Chartered; May, 1642: Founding of Montreal; August, 1658-August 24, 1660: Explorations of Radisson and Chouart des Groseilliers.

ROBERT BOYLE
Irish scientist

Boyle discovered Boyle's law, which describes the relationship between air pressure and volume. He promoted the experimental method in scientific study, especially in the field of chemistry.

BORN: January 25, 1627; Lismore, County Waterford, Ireland
DIED: December 31, 1691; London, England
AREAS OF ACHIEVEMENT: Chemistry, physics, science and technology

EARLY LIFE

Robert Boyle was the seventh son and the fourteenth child born to his parents. Boyle's father, Richard Boyle, was the earl of Cork, reported to be the wealthiest man in the British Isles at the time of Robert's birth. The earl's wife, Katherine Fenton, was the only daughter of Sir Geoffrey Fenton, the secretary of state for Ireland. Sadly, Robert Boyle hardly knew his mother, for she died of tuberculosis at the age of forty-four in February of 1630, when he was only four years old.

The wealth, prestige, and character traits Boyle inherited from both of his parents helped immensely in his career as a scientist. Most contemporaries of the Boyle family remark on the physical and temperamental resemblances between young Boyle and his father. Each was a tall man of wiry build with a long, thin, pale face and large eyes. Also, each was an intellectual and scholarly man who brought unusual amounts of energy and determination to the tasks he undertook. Richard Boyle had migrated to Ireland from England in 1588; he rose quickly in jobs of state in Ireland and made his fortune from land purchases. He made many friends and allies in public life—a phenomenon that would be repeated in his son's life. Each Boyle was also scrupulous about recording the details of his business, and each was an industrious worker.

Boyle was reared in the Irish countryside of Munster County, where his father had large landholdings. A peasant woman served as his nurse, and her cottage was his home during infancy. It was hoped that the simple foods, fresh air, and exercise that Robert had as a youngster would lead to good health in his adult years. He remained a frail if active person, however, all of his life. He was especially uncomfortable in cold weather and wore a series of cloaks to keep himself warm. At age twenty, he developed what was diagnosed as a kidney stone, a painful ailment. He spent much of his adult life seeking remedies for the stone and other illnesses. He often made his own medicines and tested their effectiveness on himself.

Boyle was strong enough at age eight to be sent to Eton in England to study along with his older brother, Francis Boyle. Robert's tutor at Eton, John Harrison, was highly influential in the boy's early intellectual development. Harrison first instilled in young Robert an immense passion for reading and learning that would remain with Boyle throughout his lifetime; this passion led him to read almost all day long. Since Boyle's eyes were weak, Harrison had to force him to leave his studies and play outdoors for a part of each day.

The Boyles had been without the services of Harrison at Eton for about a year when, in October of 1638, Richard Boyle sent his two sons to study in Europe. Their new tutor was a Frenchman they called Monsieur Marcombes; they lived with him for the next six years. The majority of this time the trio spent in Geneva, Switzerland, with some extended visits to Italy, especially to Rome and Florence. During these six years, Robert studied a variety of subjects, including French, mathematics, and theology. Boyle became so good at conversing in French that he could pass as a native Frenchman.

At age thirteen, in 1640, during a sudden and violent thunderstorm in Geneva, Robert believed that he was truly converted to a fervent Christianity. He was a devout believer for the rest of his life, and his studies in the physical sciences were always conducted so as to demonstrate the existence of God in the universe. The regularity of physical and chemical laws convinced Boyle that an intelligent God had created the world.

In conjunction with his religious beliefs, Boyle studied several ancient languages in order to read the Bible in its original form. These language studies especially occupied his teenage years. At fifteen, Boyle read and admired the works of Galileo, which would influence his later scientific studies. Boyle also admired Francis Bacon, the English essayist and philosopher who advocated a form of empiricism. In this system, the facts or data are observed in order to reach a theory rather than a theory being used to judge the data.

LIFE'S WORK

The civil wars in England and Ireland delayed Boyle's return home from his studies in Europe. At last, in the summer of 1644, he landed in England, where he fortunately found his older sister, Katherine, Lady Ranelagh, with whom he resided for several months. When his finances were set in order, he moved in March of 1646 to Stalbridge, England, where he spent the next six years reading and writing while maintaining his estate.

Boyle at this time began meeting regularly with a group of scientists of varied interests in London; this group became known as the Invisible College, since they had no permanent meeting place. From the influence of these men, Boyle became interested in experimental philosophy. He especially enjoyed studies in chemistry, since they were closely allied with his interest in medicine and remedies for illness.

Since Boyle's home at Stalbridge was not convenient to any major college, he consented to move to Oxford in the summer of 1654 when asked to do so by Dr. John Wilkins, the warden of Wadham College. In Oxford, Boyle set up an elaborate laboratory for scientific research on High Street. He was ably assisted by various aides, craftsmen, and secretaries, the most noted and skilled of these being Robert Hooke. This life of experimenting, recording, and discussion that Boyle established on High Street would continue for the next fourteen years. An immense amount of scientific and naturalistic data was recorded by Boyle and his staff during these years. Most of this information would be published for use by other scientists and scholars.

The first important book that Boyle published was *New Experiments Physio-Mechanicall, Touching the Spring of the Air and Its Effects* (1660). The experiments described here (in detail, as Boyle always did) were in large part related to physics rather than chemistry. Boyle had learned of an air pump invented in 1654 in Germany by Otto von Guericke. This pump created a vacuum in which scientific experiments could be performed and new physical concepts tested; it needed improvement, however, to work efficiently and consistently.

Boyle's ingenious assistant, Hooke, designed and built an improved air pump by 1659. With this new laboratory instrument, Boyle conducted numerous experiments on air pressure. From the detailed notes he kept on his work, Boyle was able to conclude in *New Experiments Physio-Mechanicall, Touching the Spring of the Air and Its Effects* that air volume always varies in inverse proportion to pressure. He further explained this important phenomenon in the second edition (1662) of the book. This physical law, known as Boyle's law, is his

most widely recognized permanent contribution to the field of physics.

Boyle's other writings would have effects on the chemical sciences in addition to physics. In his *Experiments and Considerations Touching Colours* (1664), he accurately described the physical phenomena that caused the colors black and white. This book had an impact on Sir Isaac Newton's later works in optics. The next year, Boyle published *New Experiments and Observations Touching Cold* (1665), in which he discussed how thermometers could be improved. (They were in his day a fairly new and crude piece of laboratory equipment invented by Galileo.) Boyle also studied the effects of freezing on various chemical mixtures; he was able to disprove the widely held idea that water and other liquids contract when frozen. These areas of study were also later reinvestigated by Newton.

Of all of his numerous scientific publications, Boyle is most famous for his book *The Sceptical Chymist* (1661, rev. 1679). In this work, Boyle refuted two influential schools of scientific thought popular in his era: the Aristotelian and the Paracelsian. The two schools of

Robert Boyle. (Library of Congress)

thought were similar in that both held that all matter was composed only of a certain few basic substances (and nothing else). The Aristotelians believed that air, earth, fire, and water were the four elements that made up all animate and inanimate things in nature, while the Paracelsians held that there were three basic principles that combined to form all matter: sulfur, salt, and mercury.

Boyle demonstrated, by experimentation (something the other two systems did not employ), that these theories were incorrect. Instead, he argued that the universe was composed of numerous small particles, or corpuscles, of various shapes and sizes. Their alignments and combinations, and even their motion, determined what element would be formed. Boyle's conception of matter is known as corpuscular philosophy; it was greatly influenced by the mechanistic theory of Francis Bacon.

In the summer of 1668, Boyle returned to live in London at Pall Mall with his sister, Katherine, Lady Ranelagh. The two kept a house together, for Boyle never married, and his sister was separated from her husband. Boyle and Katherine were very popular and famous persons in their era. They entertained frequently, and Boyle even had to post a sign on their door to state when visitors were not allowed. Only in this way could he conduct his studies; he also maintained an extensive correspondence with scientists throughout England and Europe. Boyle continued his scientific work even after suffering a stroke in June of 1670, which left him partially paralyzed. He died on December 31, 1691, exactly one week after his sister had died. Both were buried in London.

SIGNIFICANCE

Boyle made two important contributions to science, particularly physics and chemistry. The first is a tangible contribution: He was a founding member of the Royal Society of England in 1662. This group of eminent scientists, including William Brouncker, Robert Murray, Paul Neile, John Wilkins, and Sir Christopher Wren, met regularly to present papers on scientific thought and to discuss the results of experiments. The society also kept meticulous records of their proceedings (perhaps a direct result of Boyle's participation) and published the first science journal in England. The Royal Society promoted excellence and dedication in the sciences and attracted such men as Sir Isaac Newton to careers in science. Boyle, solidly a member of the British aristocracy and noted for his hard work on behalf of experimentation, did much to raise the science of chemistry to a high level of respectability (something it previously lacked in English

society and culture). King Charles II officially chartered the Royal Society in 1662 and himself did some amateur experiments.

Boyle's second contribution is less concrete but nevertheless vital. Boyle's experimental approach to chemistry helped to bring it into the realm of modern scholarship. Previously, a mystical or mysterious element was associated with chemistry. Alchemy, or the alleged changing of one substance into another (most often a base metal into a precious one), was almost the only chemical investigation done until Boyle's day. Fraudulent claims, farfetched speculation, and outright trickery made alchemy an unrespectable method of study. By replacing quasi-scientific work with the experimental method, Boyle did a great service for future generations of chemical researchers.

Ironically, Boyle made no specific discoveries that remain as part of modern chemistry, although he is frequently called the father of modern chemistry. In his experiments with air, he came close to discovering oxygen, but Joseph Priestly would actually do that many years later. Similarly, Boyle's work on the nature of colors was less influential than that of Newton, who worked with a prism in his experiments. Boyle himself acknowledged his lack of acumen in experiments requiring complex mathematical calculations. He thought that his greatest contribution to future scientists would come from the mass of naturalistic data he had accumulated in his lifetime. That data, if one includes his published scientific treatises in it, did prove to be Boyle's most important legacy. He provided for others an essential foundation on which to build their own scientific accomplishments.

—*Patricia E. Sweeney*

FURTHER READING

Anstey, Peter R. *The Philosophy of Robert Boyle*. New York: Routledge, 2000. An overview of Boyle's philosophy, including his theories of matter, causation, and the laws of nature.

Boas, Marie. *Robert Boyle and Seventeenth-Century Chemistry*. Cambridge, England: Cambridge University Press, 1958. The leading authority on Boyle, Boas was the first person thoroughly to study his papers at the Royal Society. She is both scholarly and fair in her assessment of his contributions to chemistry.

Boyle, Robert. *The Sceptical Chymist*. London: F. Cadwell, 1661. Reprint. New York: E. P. Dutton, 1911. This is not an easy book to read, for the language and style are from the seventeenth century. Nevertheless, the dialogue Boyle sets up among characters decisively refutes earlier chemical theories. He also provides his own empirical approach to science studies.

Conant, James B., ed. *Robert Boyle's Experiments in Pneumatics.* Cambridge, Mass.: Harvard University Press, 1950. Detailed explanations of Boyle's air pump experiments, with illustrations to help the reader visualize the numerous steps in important experiments. Offers excellent background material on Boyle's life and the work at his laboratory.

Hall, A. Rupert. *From Galileo to Newton, 1630-1720: The Rise of Modern Science.* New York: Harper and Row, 1963. Hall discusses the major developments in this fertile period of scientific achievement. Provides an excellent understanding of Boyle's contributions to the advancement of chemistry.

Hall, Marie Boas. *Robert Boyle on Natural Philosophy.* Bloomington: Indiana University Press, 1965. In her second major book on Boyle, Hall continues to explicate his work clearly and concisely. She provides edited selections from some of Boyle's most important writing and an informative introductory essay.

Maddison, R. E. W. *The Life of the Honourable Robert Boyle, F.R.S.* New York: Barnes and Noble Books, 1969. Maddison details Boyle's life, career, and interactions with other seventeenth century scientists but does not analyze the impact or influence of Boyle's work.

More, Louis T. *The Life and Works of the Honourable Robert Boyle.* New York: Oxford University Press, 1944. More divides this biography into two parts: The first deals with Boyle's personal and social life, while the second offers an in-depth description of his writings. More analyzes all of Boyle's books and articles, including his youthful meditations and religious tracts.

Principe, Lawrence. *The Aspiring Adept: Robert Boyle and His Alchemical Quest.* Princeton, N.J.: Princeton University Press, 1998. Reveals Boyle's lifelong but carefully hidden pursuit of alchemy. Principe reconstructs fragments of Boyle's unpublished manuscript, *Dialogue on the Transmutation and Melioration of Metals*, to demonstrate Boyle's enthusiasm for alchemy. Principe maintains that interest in alchemy was common among seventeenth-century scientists and argues that alchemy played an important role in the scientific achievements of this era.

Sargent, Rose-Mary. *The Diffident Naturalist: Robert Boyle and the Philosophy of Experiment.* Chicago: University of Chicago Press, 1995. Sargent explains how English common law, alchemy, medicine, Christianity, and other influences shaped Boyle's philosophy of experimentation.

Toulmin, Stephen, and June Goodfield. *The Architecture of Matter: The Physics, Chemistry, and Physiology of Matter, Both Animate and Inanimate.* New York: Harper and Row, 1962. This is an extremely well-written survey of the history of physics and chemistry. The authors combine their scholarship with a lively narrative of the major developments in these sciences.

Wojcik, Jan W. *Robert Boyle and the Limits of Reason.* New York: Cambridge University Press, 1997. A study of Boyle's theory of knowledge, examining his views on the limitation of reason within the context of seventeenth-century English theological controversies.

SEE ALSO: Otto von Guericke; Robert Hooke; Sir Isaac Newton; Sir Christopher Wren.

RELATED ARTICLES in *Great Events from History: The Seventeenth Century, 1601-1700:* 1601-1672: Rise of Scientific Societies; 1660-1692: Boyle's Law and the Birth of Modern Chemistry.

MRS. ANNE BRACEGIRDLE
English actress

Because of her talent and her wit, as well as a reputation for chastity that was exceptional in her profession, Mrs. Anne Bracegirdle was one of the most admired actresses of the Restoration period. An excellent businesswoman, she became one of the first women in history to assume a managerial role in an acting company.

BORN: c. 1663; Northamptonshire, England
DIED: September 12, 1748; London, England
AREAS OF ACHIEVEMENT: Theater, women's rights, business and economics

EARLY LIFE

Mrs. Anne Bracegirdle was born about 1663, the daughter of Justinian Bracegirdle and Martha Bracegirdle of Northamptonshire. Her father was believed to have been a coachman, coach maker, or coach renter in Northampton, though a poem written in 1700 by one of Anne's admirers describes him as keeping an inn for carriers. Anne had a sister, Frances, and two brothers, Hamlet and John. However, Anne did not remain at home for long. Her father's financial situation deteriorated to the point that he had to place Anne with another family.

In 1668 or thereabout, Bracegirdle went to live with Thomas Betterton and his wife, Mary Betterton, who as Mary Saunderson had been one of the first professional actresses on the English stage. In 1662, she had married Betterton, another member of her company who was also rapidly advancing in his profession. The childless young couple welcomed Anne into their family and, it is assumed, almost immediately began teaching her their craft. Though an account of her making an appearance on stage at the age of six is almost certainly erroneous, from 1676, the Bettertons' company produced playbills that refer to "a little girl" who might have been Bracegirdle. There is also speculation that she was the "little girl" who in 1680 played the role of the page Cordelio in Thomas Otway's *The Orphan: Or, The Unhappy Marriage* (pr., pb. 1680), though her name did not appear in the lord chamberlain's records as a member of the United Company until 1688. What is certain is that by the time Bracegirdle appeared in her first major role, her adoptive parents had fully prepared her for success.

LIFE'S WORK

On February 6, 1688, Mrs. (Mistress) Anne Bracegirdle was listed as playing Atelina in *The Injured Lovers: Or, The Ambitious Father* (pr. 1688), by the actor-playwright

William Mountfort. In November, 1689, she appeared as Semernia in *The Widow Ranter: Or, The History of Bacon of Virginia* (pr. 1689, pb. 1690), by Aphra Behn, a woman playwright. This was Bracegirdle's first "breeches" part, in which she was presented as a woman disguised as a man. The audience was so impressed by her shapely legs that thereafter she was often cast in parts that enabled her to display them.

Though Bracegirdle might have aroused the passions of the male members of her audiences, however, she had no intention of satisfying them. Indeed, as her contemporaries pointed out, her very reputation for chastity merely served to increase the number of her admirers. Their infatuation could have tragic results. In 1692, after Bracegirdle had rejected his proposal of marriage, Captain Richard Hill attempted to abduct her. After she evaded him, Hill waited for Mountfort, whom Hill supposed to be his rival, and when the actor arrived, Hill ran him through before Mountfort could draw his weapon. The death of her friend so distressed Bracegirdle that she did not appear on stage for several months.

The parts Bracegirdle played on stage were appropriate for a woman known for her exemplary behavior offstage. While she was still in her twenties, she had been assigned major roles in William Shakespeare's plays, but the characters that suited her talent for pathos were those who were innocent victims. In the 1690's, she was Lady Anne in *Richard III* (pr. c. 1592-1593, revised 1623) and Desdemona in *Othello, the Moor of Venice* (pr. 1604, revised 1623), and in the following decade, she appeared as Cordelia in *King Lear* (pr. c. 1605-1606) and Ophelia in *Hamlet, Prince of Denmark* (pr. c. 1600-1601). During the Restoration period, rapes became a standard plot element for the first time; it is hardly surprising, then, that Bracegirdle was often called upon to play the chaste victim of sexual brutality.

As the heroine of a comedy, however, Bracegirdle never lost control of the situation; though she flirted with her suitors, teased them mercilessly, and made them the targets of her wit, she never acceded to their demands. The playwright William Congreve was not immune to her charms. Not long after she appeared as Araminta in his first play, *The Old Bachelor* (pr., pb. 1693), he began writing plays with Bracegirdle in mind. One of these was the comedy *Love for Love* (pr., pb. 1695), which opened the new theater in Lincoln's Inn Fields on April 30, 1695. A series of brilliant plays followed, but Bracegirdle's finest role was probably that of the sophisticated, tantalizing Millamant in Congreve's *The Way of the World* (pr., pb. 1700), first performed on March 5, 1700. During her lifetime, it was believed that Bracegirdle was Congreve's mistress or perhaps even his wife, but there is no evidence that the playwright was any more successful in winning her favors than were any of her other admirers.

Meanwhile, Bracegirdle had become involved in theatrical management. From the time the United Company was formed in 1682, Thomas Betterton had made many of the company's business decisions. By 1695, however, Christopher Rich had seized control, so infuriating the more established members of the company that they took their grievances to the lord chancellor. After Betterton, Bracegirdle, and the actress Elizabeth Barry met privately with King William III, he granted them a license to start a new company. As one of the three managers, Bracegirdle received a substantial share of the company's net profits. In addition, she was so popular that her acting salary alone equaled that of the leading male actors.

Although other members of the company objected to the managers' handling of company finances, Bracegirdle had made enough during her career that she could retire whenever she liked. As long as she was sharing the boards with Barry, who played women led astray by their passions, Bracegirdle did not feel threatened. However, in 1707, when a new manager began giving her roles to the young actress Anne Oldfield, Bracegirdle left the company in mid-season, returning only once, when she performed in a 1709 benefit for Betterton.

During the remaining forty years of her life, Bracegirdle lived quietly, entertaining friends, discussing the theater, and attending plays. She died on September 12, 1748, and was buried at Westminster Abbey.

SIGNIFICANCE

Bracegirdle was largely responsible for elevating the status of English Restoration actresses, who had entered the theatrical world as poorly paid novelties, until they were considered the equals of their male counterparts. Her brilliant performances onstage and her business skills offstage, along with the decorum she displayed in her personal life, combined to gain her the respect of her contemporaries. Thus, she proved that if they chose to do so, women could indeed make acting not just a way to attract the attention of wealthy men but instead a legitimate profession to be pursued until retirement. The comedies she inspired Congreve to write for her all reflect Bracegirdle's own intelligence and strength of character; these plays reinforced the idea that a woman who had control

over her own emotions could have immense power over men. Thus, long after she was the toast of London, Bracegirdle is remembered not only for her valuable contributions both to her profession and to the literary canon but also as an important figure in women's history.

—*Rosemary M. Canfield Reisman*

FURTHER READING

Highfill, Philip H., Kalman A. Burnim, and Edward A. Langhans. "Bracegirdle, Anne." In *Belfort to Byzand.* Vol. 2 in *A Biographical Dictionary of Actors, Actresses, Musicians, Dancers, Managers, and Other Stage Personnel in London, 1660-1800.* Carbondale: Southern Illinois University Press, 1973. An admirable scholarly study in which a mass of relevant documents and contemporary comments about the actress are presented and evaluated.

Howe, Elizabeth. *The First English Actresses: Women and Drama, 1660-1700.* New York: Cambridge University Press, 1992. Describes the Restoration theater and focuses on the changes brought about by the substitution of women for boy actors and especially on the links between the stage roles of the actresses and their offstage conduct. An appendix lists plays in which Barry and Bracegirdle appeared together. Illustrated. Extensive notes, bibliography, and index.

Kavenik, Frances M. *British Drama, 1660-1779: A Critical History.* New York: Twayne, 1995. An excellent overview, with one chapter devoted to each of four historical periods. The introduction includes such topics as stagecraft, financial policies, and acting conventions. Chronology, notes, bibliography, and index.

Lowenthal, Cynthia. *Performing Identities on the Restoration Stage.* Carbondale: Southern Illinois University Press, 2003. A feminist critic looks at the challenges to conventional identity boundaries that followed the introduction of women into the acting profession. Bibliography and index.

Wilson, John Harold. *All the King's Ladies: Actresses of the Restoration.* Chicago: University of Chicago Press, 1958. A thoughtful examination of the problems actresses faced in what was still a man's world. An appendix contains biographies of the major actresses, including a lengthy entry on Anne Bracegirdle. Brief bibliography and index.

SEE ALSO: Thomas Betterton; William III.
RELATED ARTICLE in *Great Events from History: The Seventeenth Century, 1601-1700:* February 24, 1631: Women First Appear on the English Stage.

WILLIAM BRADFORD
English-born American colonist

Bradford was the leader of the Pilgrims once they settled in America, and he was the author of a history of Plymouth Colony, one of the great works of early American literature.

BORN: March, 1590; Austerfield, Yorkshire, England
DIED: May 9, 1657; Plymouth, Massachusetts Bay
    Colony (now in Massachusetts)
AREAS OF ACHIEVEMENT: Government and politics,
    literature

EARLY LIFE

William Bradford was born in March, 1590 (baptized on March 29), at Austerfield, Yorkshire, England, one of three children and the only son of William Bradford, a yeoman farmer, and Alice Hanson. His father died when he was sixteen months old. Upon his mother's remarriage when Bradford was four, he was placed in the custody of his grandfather, after whose death in 1596 he went to live with his uncles, Robert and Thomas Bradford. Like his ancestors, William Bradford pursued "the affairs of husbandry."

At age twelve, Bradford started attending religious services conducted by Richard Clyfton at Babworth, eight miles from Austerfield. The group was made up of Separatists, who believed in the sovereign authority of the Scriptures and the autonomy of each church. The Separatists had spun off from the Puritan movement, which sought reform toward greater simplicity in the worship and practices of the Church of England. When Clyfton's own congregation split, he took part of the original group to hold services at the bishop's manor house in Scrooby. William Brewster, who became a mentor and tutor for Bradford, was the local bailiff and postmaster and resided at the bishop's decaying mansion. John Robinson, who later would be the leader of the group when they went to Holland, was teacher of the congregation. Bradford had only to walk three miles to attend services at Scrooby, which was in Nottinghamshire, 150 miles (241 kilometers) north of London.

The Scrooby Separatists, completely at odds with the national church and fearing further persecution after King James I ascended the throne, sought refuge in the Netherlands. They failed in their first attempt to leave England in 1607, having been betrayed by the ship's captain. The following year, however, a Dutch vessel took them to Amsterdam, where they stayed briefly before moving to the university town of Leyden. The Nether-

lands offered the refugees full freedom of conscience. Their new home proved a relief, as Bradford said, from the situation which the Pilgrims (as they were to be called) had faced in England, where they were "hunted and persecuted on every side, so that their former afflictions were but as flea-bitings in comparison of those which now came upon them."

At Leyden, the Pilgrims worked as artisans, with Bradford becoming a maker of fustian (a twilled cloth of cotton and linen). While in Leyden, Bradford learned some Latin and Hebrew. Coming of age in 1611, he gained an inheritance from his uncles, which he applied to buying a house; he also became a Dutch citizen. In December, 1613, Bradford married Dorothy May. The Pilgrims, however, were unhappy in their new home for a variety of reasons, chiefly because they were an alien people in a strange land. In 1617, therefore, Bradford was one of a committee to make arrangements to take the congregation to America.

William Bradford. (Library of Congress)

The Pilgrims secured financing for their expedition through a joint stock company formed by English merchants. They also secured a patent from the Virginia Company, which was to prove invalid when they settled in Massachusetts and was replaced a year later with one from the Council of New England. Thus armed, the Pilgrims set out for America. Shares in the company were ten pounds each, with each settler receiving one share free. Bradford was among the 102 persons who crossed the Atlantic in the *Mayflower* and was a signer of the Mayflower Compact in November of 1620 as the ship anchored off the tip of Cape Cod.

The compact, as John Quincy Adams later observed, was "the first example in modern times of a social compact or system of government instituted by voluntary agreement conformably to the laws of nature, by men of equal rights and about to establish their community in a new country." Bradford led exploring parties, and the colonists chose a site at what is now Plymouth, Massachusetts. On December 17, 1620, Bradford's wife fell overboard and drowned, possibly a suicide. In August, 1623, he married Alice Carpenter, widow of Edward Southworth.

THE PILGRIMS ARRIVE IN THE NEW WORLD

The Pilgrims had intended to land in Virginia, where their fellow Englishmen had founded Jamestown in 1607. Instead, they were blown farther north, landing at Cape Cod, Massachusetts, where they could expect no friendly European faces to greet them. In the following excerpt from William Bradford's account of the Mayflower*'s voyage and the settlement of Massachusetts, he describes the experience of arriving in an unsettled and unfamiliar land.*

But here I cannot but stay and make a pause, and stand half amazed at this poor peoples present condition; and so I think will the reader too, when he well considers the same. Being thus past the vast ocean, and a sea of troubles before in their preparation (as may be remembered by the [*sic*] which went before), they had now no friends to welcome them, nor inns to entertain or refresh their weather-beaten bodies, no houses or much less towns to repair to, to seek for succor. It is recorded in Scripture as a mercy to the apostle and his shipwrecked company, that the barbarians shewed them no small kindness in refreshing them, but these savage barbarians, when they met with them (as after will appear) were readier to fill their sides full of arrows than otherwise. And for the season it was winter, and they that know the winters of that country know them to be sharp and violent, and subject to cruel and fierce storms, dangerous to travel to known places, much more to search an unknown coast. Besides, what could they see but a hideous and desolate wilderness, full of wild beasts and wild men? And what multitudes there might be of them they knew not.

Source: From *Living History America: The History of the United States in Documents, Essays, Letters, Songs, and Poems*, edited by Erik Bruun and Jay Crosby (New York: Tess Press, 1999), p. 48.

LIFE'S WORK

Upon the death of John Carver in 1621, Bradford was elected governor of the colony, remaining in that office until his death in 1657, with the exception of the years 1633-1634, 1636, 1638, and 1644. He received no salary until 1639, when he was paid twenty pounds annually. Bradford virtually dominated the colony's government, which had no standing under English law and had no charter from the king. Bradford, however, shared executive, legislative, and judicial powers with a court of assistants, which by the 1640's numbered eight people. The governor and assistants were elected annually by the freemen at large. Beginning in 1638, legislative powers were divided with a lower house of two representatives from each town, starting with those from Plymouth town, Duxborough, and Scituate. Bradford assisted in the codification of Plymouth's laws in 1636, significant as the first such embodiment of statutes in the American colonies and also noteworthy for setting forth basic rights.

Bradford and his colony faced many hardships. The people who emigrated to the settlement were poor, and for the most part the land was of poor quality. Lacking means for capital investment, the Pilgrims made little progress in establishing shipping and fishing industries. For a while they enjoyed success in the fur trade, but they had to compete with the Dutch, the French, and the English in that pursuit. The colony struggled to pay off its indebtedness. Bradford, believing that the communal system discouraged initiative, had it abandoned in 1623.

In 1627, Bradford, seven other colonists, and four Londoners associated as the Undertakers to pay off the colonists' eighteen-hundred-pound debt to the English members of the joint stock company, which was then dissolved. Bradford and the other Undertakers were given a monopoly on the fur trade and offshore fishing. Still, it was not until the 1640's that the debt was paid. Also at the time of dissolving their connection with the English merchants, all property in the colony, real and personal, was divided equally among heads of families and free single men.

BRADFORD'S MAJOR WORKS	
1622	*Mourt's Relation*, 1622 (with Edward Winslow)
1630-1650	*History of Plymouth Plantation* (pb. 1856)
1648-1652	*Dialogue Between Some Young Men Born in New England and Sundry Ancient Men That Came out of Holland* (third dialogue pb. 1871, first dialogue pb. 1920)
1650's	"Of Boston in New England" (pb. 1838)
1650's	"A Word to New England" (pb. 1838)
1669	"Epitaphium Meum"

Bradford and the Pilgrims had scant troubles with American Indians. The Pawtuxet Indians, who had lived in the vicinity of Plymouth town, had died off from European diseases, principally the plague (typhus) brought over by English fishermen. Two Indians, Samoset and Squanto, who had themselves been to Great Britain and spoke English, served at the outset as vital liaisons with other Indians in the area. Bradford was successful in keeping the friendship of Massasoit, chief of the Wampanoags, the only strong tribe in close proximity to the colony.

Indeed, though troops were mustered on several occasions to be sent against the local Native American tribes (for example, during the Pequot War of 1636-1637), the colony under Bradford's administration contended with no significant Indian hostility. Miles Standish's butchery of several Massachusetts Indians at Wessagusett can, however, be charged to Bradford's blame.

The latitude of personal freedom at Plymouth was great in comparison with the Puritan colonies. Although seeking at first to oust dissenters, Bradford came to favor a policy of tolerance, allowing persons of other faiths to settle in the colony. Yet Bradford was thin-skinned with those who put the Pilgrims in a bad light in England, and once, upon intercepting the letters of two such individuals, he forced them to return to England. A major blotch on Bradford's career was his overreaction to the "wickedness" of the times, especially during the alleged sex-crime wave of 1642. During this brief hysteria, induced largely by anxiety over an Indian crisis, a teenager was hanged for buggery. Otherwise, to the Pilgrims' credit, there were executions only for murder. In addition to serving as governor, Bradford was a commissioner of the Puritan defensive confederation, the United Colonies of New England, in the years 1647 to 1649, 1652, and 1656.

History of Plymouth Plantation (wr. 1630-1650, pb. 1856) is Bradford's masterpiece. Probably intended only for the enlightenment of his family, it was not published in its entirety until 1856. For a long time, the manuscript was lost, probably taken out of the country by a British soldier during the Revolution; it resurfaced at the Bishop of London's Library at Fulham Palace. In the late nineteenth century, as a goodwill gesture, it was returned to the United States. Bradford worked on it at various times, from 1630 to 1650, writing from notes, correspondence, and memory. The work traces the entire Pilgrim story from their English exile to 1646.

Other writings of Bradford include admonitory poems and *Dialogue Between Some Young Men Born in New England and Sundry Ancient Men That Came out of Holland* (wr. 1648-1652, pb. 1871 [third dialogue], 1920 [first dialogue]). Bradford was also the coauthor with Edward Winslow of the promotional tract *Mourt's Relation* (1622) and letters, printed as *Governor Bradford's Letter Book* (1794; reprinted in 1968).

Besides his home in Plymouth, Bradford had a 300-acre (121-hectare) farm on the tidal Jones River and scattered real estate elsewhere, which made him the largest landowner in the colony. Bradford died during the evening of the day in which he dictated his will, May 19, 1657. He was buried on the hills overlooking Plymouth. He left four children: John (by his first wife), William, Mercy, and Joseph.

SIGNIFICANCE

Bradford's life epitomized the plain and simple virtues of a people longing to be free. From yeoman farmer in England to artisan in Leyden to immigrant in an unexplored land, he displayed the courage and faith of one who believed that there was a better way. With skill, a sense of fair play, and open-mindedness, he guided his people in founding a successful community, which would eventually grow into some twenty towns. Bradford's colony was unable to secure a charter, largely because of the lack of resources needed to support a lobbying effort in England. Plymouth Colony would later be incorporated into the royal colony of Massachusetts Bay, an event that Bradford probably would not have celebrated, considering the differences between the Puritans and the Pilgrims. While Bradford discouraged people from leaving the colony to form new settlements, he himself became a suburbanite, tending his farm outside Plymouth.

Bradford's administration brought peace and stability to Plymouth, and the Pilgrim experience in founding government served as a model for the establishment of other colonies. In Plymouth Colony, under Bradford, there was a rigid separation of church and state as to officeholding, though between them there was a mutuality of action. Bradford's history of Plymouth exemplifies high standards of clarity and straightforward prose; at the same time, it is enlivened by an understated humor that belies the popular image of the Pilgrims. It is regarded as one of the major works of colonial American literature.

—Harry M. Ward

FURTHER READING

Anderson, Douglas. *William Bradford's Books: Of Plimouth Plantation and the Printed Word.* Baltimore: Johns Hopkins University Press, 2003. Anderson argues that Bradford's history of the Plymouth colony is not a gloomy elegy but a graceful and ambitious work that describes the successful adaptation of a small community of religious exiles to life in a new country.

Bartlett, Robert M. *The Pilgrim Way.* Philadelphia: United Church Press, 1971. Discusses the Pilgrims only through the early years in America. Though emphasizing the role of John Robinson and religious issues, it probes the thinking and actions of the Pilgrim leaders, including Bradford.

Bradford, William. *Of Plimmoth Plantation, 1620-1647: The Complete Text, with Notes and an Introduction by Samuel Eliot Morison.* Boston: Massachusetts Historical Society, 1856. Rev. ed. New York: A. A. Knopf, 2001. This is the latest edition of the work, which has been reprinted numerous times since its initial publication in 1856. The 2001 reprint includes Samuel E. Morison's notes and introduction to the 1952 edition.

Dillon, Francis. *The Pilgrims.* Garden City, N.Y.: Doubleday, 1975. Popularly written and well researched, this narrative traces the Pilgrim story to the time of the death of Bradford. Views the Pilgrim experience through Bradford's eyes.

Langdon, George D., Jr. *Pilgrim Colony: A History of New Plymouth, 1620-1691.* New Haven, Conn.: Yale University Press, 1966. A scholarly and perceptive examination of the Plymouth Colony until its union with Massachusetts Bay Colony. Emphasis is on the government and institutions.

Pafford, John M. *How Firm a Foundation: William Bradford and Plymouth.* Bowie, Md.: Heritage Books, 2002. Examines Bradford's life in conjunction with the history of the Plymouth colony, from Bradford's birth through 1691, the year Plymouth became part of the Massachusetts Bay colony.

Runyan, Michael G., ed. *William Bradford: The Collected Verse.* St. Paul, Minn.: John Colet Press, 1974. Contains the seven items of verse attributed to Bradford. Places the poems in their historical context and in the context of Bradford's life as well as discussing their literary qualities.

Sargent, Mark L. "William Bradford's 'Dialogue' with History." *New England Quarterly* 65, no. 3 (September, 1992): 389-422. An examination of Bradford's *Dialogue* and its place in the American Colonial canon.

Shurtleff, Nathaniel Bradstreet, ed. *Records of the Colony of New Plymouth in New England.* Boston: Press of W. White, 1861. Reprint. 2 vols. Bowie: Md.: Heritage Books, 1998. All of Bradford's service as governor can be discerned from this collection, which contains the records of the General Court (governor, assistants, and deputies).

Smith, Bradford. *Bradford of Plymouth.* Philadelphia: J. B. Lippincott, 1951. The only full-scale biography of Bradford. It is well researched but glosses over many topics.

Westbrook, Perry D. *William Bradford.* Boston: Twayne, 1978. Examines all of Bradford's writings from the point of view of literary criticism. Contains a chronology of Bradford's life.

SEE ALSO: James I; Massasoit; Squanto; Miles Standish.

RELATED ARTICLES in *Great Events from History: The Seventeenth Century, 1601-1700:* March 24, 1603: James I Becomes King of England; December 26, 1620: Pilgrims Arrive in North America; July 20, 1636-July 28, 1637: Pequot War.

ANNE BRADSTREET
English-born colonial American poet

Anne Bradstreet ranks as the first true American poet, occupying a central place in the definition and history of distinctively American literature.

BORN: 1612?; Northampton, Northamptonshire, England

DIED: September 16, 1672; Andover, Massachusetts Bay Colony

ALSO KNOWN AS: Anne Dudley (given name)

AREA OF ACHIEVEMENT: Literature

EARLY LIFE

Although no record of her birth survives, Anne Bradstreet is known to have been the daughter of Thomas and Dorothy Dudley of Northampton, England, and according to a reference in one of her poems, she must have been born in 1612. Her father, though not highly educated, was a substantial man who valued books and learning. Dorothy, apparently also literate, probably taught her daughter religion, and the Dudley children grew up with books.

The Dudleys claimed kinship to a much more prominent group of Dudleys: Robert Dudley, earl of Leicester, was a favorite of Queen Elizabeth I, while John Dudley, duke of Northumberland, was the grandfather of Philip Sidney, famed courtier and important English poet. Several other members of the Sidney family had literary talent, including Philip's sister Mary, countess of Pembroke, and his niece, Lady Mary Wroth. It is clear that early in life Anne Dudley became acquainted with the poetry of Philip Sidney. Another favorite was the Protestant French poet Guillaume Du Bartas.

In a letter to her own children years later, Bradstreet related that she was an obedient child who took comfort in reading the Bible, but she confessed that at the age of fourteen or fifteen she was beset by "carnal" desires. Meanwhile, the family had moved to the coastal town of Boston in Lincolnshire, where Thomas Dudley served as a steward to the earl of Lincoln. At the age of sixteen, Anne suffered from a common but potentially deadly disease, smallpox; her face may well have been scarred for life as a result. Also at sixteen, she married Simon Bradstreet, a Lincolnshire man and Cambridge graduate.

The Dudleys were Puritans, oppressed by religious authority and eager to make a new livelihood abroad, and Thomas Dudley became one of the founders of the Massachusetts Bay Company. Still much under the influence of her father, the eighteen-year-old Anne Bradstreet and her husband sailed from Old World Boston in 1630 to settle a new Boston across the Atlantic.

LIFE'S WORK

It is well to remember that the work of Bradstreet existed on two fronts. When she arrived as part of the earliest wave of Massachusetts Bay settlers, she was a young wife who, in the years that followed, became the mother of eight children. The duties implicit in such a life in a newly planted colony represented all the work that even a healthy woman might reasonably be expected to perform, and Bradstreet suffered frequent illnesses. This work would not of itself have made her famous, but the work for which the world knows her is intimately connected with her status as colonial wife and mother.

Bradstreet's earliest poems cannot be dated precisely, but by 1647, when she was thirty-five, someone, generally conceded to be the Reverend John Woodbridge, her brother-in-law, returned to England with a stack of her poems in manuscript. Three years later the first book of

---

BRADSTREET'S "TO MY DEAR AND LOVING HUSBAND"

Anne Bradstreet's poetry is dominated by two themes, family and religion. In "To My Dear and Loving Husband," she characteristically combines these themes, paying tribute to her marital relationship in the context of devout Christianity.

> If ever two were one, then surely we.
> If ever man were loved by wife, then thee;
> If ever wife was happy in a man,
> Compare with me, ye woman, if you can.
> I prize thy love more than whole mines of gold,
> Or all the riches that the east doth hold.
> My love is such that rivers cannot quench,
> Nor aught but love from thee, give recompense.
> Thy love is such I can no way repay,
> The heavens reward thee manifold, I pray.
> Then while we live, in love let's so perservere
> That when we live no more, we may live ever.

Source: From the Electronic Texts for the Study of American Culture database. http://xroads.virginia .edu/~HYPER/Bradstreet/bradstreet.html. Accessed April 20, 2005.

original poetry by an American, *The Tenth Muse Lately Sprung up in America: Or, Several Poems Compiled with Great Variety of Wit and Learning, Full of Delight* (1650, rev. 1678), appeared in London. Most of the poems now considered Bradstreet's best had presumably not yet been written, but the book has nonetheless become justly famous.

The poems in this first volume represented an apprenticeship rendered long by circumstances. Even the bookish Dudleys and Bradstreets could not have carried any great library to Massachusetts. For a number of reasons, poets thrive on fruitful contacts with other poets, and, the possibility of a few amateur versifying friends aside, Anne Bradstreet had no such contacts. The time and energy she could devote to the lonely task of composing poetry must have been severely limited as well. Few poets can have learned their craft under more trying conditions.

Bradstreet's book, which in a later poem she claimed to have been "snatched" from her in an "unfit" state by friends "less wise than true," consists mainly of long poems, primarily quaternions, or four-part poems. There are four of these interrelated quaternions, on the four elements, the four humors, the four ages of man, and the four seasons, respectively. The subject matter is traditional, the "elements" being the classification of the physical universe into fire, air, earth, and water, which goes back at least as far as Plato. The four humors represented four different mixtures of the elements in humans which determined their physiological and temperamental types. Modern English vocabulary still retains the adjectives—choleric, sanguine, melancholy, and phlegmatic—used to describe the four basic types. The poems, varying in length from 264 to 610 lines, are all written in rhymed pentameter couplets. These poems hardly show Bradstreet at her best, nor does her unfinished *The Four Monarchies* in 3,572 lines, many of which paraphrase Sir Walter Ralegh's *The History of the World* (1614).

The Tenth Muse contains a few other poems. "A Dialogue between Old England and New" indicates that Bradstreet maintained a strong interest in contemporary

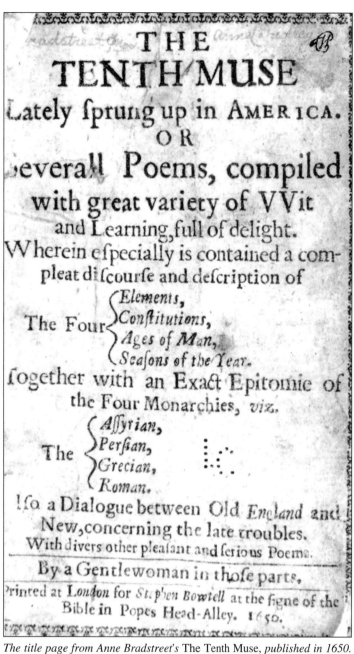

The title page from Anne Bradstreet's The Tenth Muse, *published in 1650.* (Library of Congress)

events in the early 1640's, when the policies of King Charles I that had sent people such as the Dudleys and Bradstreets to Massachusetts were leading toward civil war in England. Yet the most interesting poem in the collection for most people is the first one, appropriately called "The Prologue," in which Bradstreet writes in a personal vein about her vocation as poet.

"The Prologue" is essentially a plea to accept the work of a woman invading a man's province. Most critics have taken its humility at face value, and it is true that Bradstreet is often humble and even apologetic about her poetry, but it is also true that talented people usually recognize that they *have* talent, and it is possible to read some passages as ironical needling of the "superior" men. Her wit cannot be disputed. Instead of the "bays" (laurels) that men poets receive, she asks for "thyme or parsley wreath." She surely knew (as doubtless many men did not) that laurel is indeed a botanical cousin to the housewife's kitchen spice, the bay leaf. Whether ironical or not, Bradstreet displays in "The Prologue" a sincere desire for "some small acknowledgement" of women's artistic capacity and a discernible indignation that such recognition has been so long in coming.

Because *The Tenth Muse* was presumably published without her consent, in "The Author to Her Book," written for a possible second edition, she compared her book to an "ill-formed" child, an embarrassment to its mother. Of her literal children, however, Bradstreet was proud. In a poem of 1659, they become "eight birds hatched in one nest, of whom five have flown, while three remain in the nest." In most of her later poems—some included in a posthumous 1678 edition of her book, some unpublished until 1867—the long, earnest, and fairly dull poems on set subjects have given way to highly personal domestic poems.

Several of Bradstreet's poems take the form of letters to her husband, who, as a figure of some consequence in the colony, made frequent business trips. Although her marriage most likely was an arranged one, these poems attest that a deep love had developed between them. She depicts Simon as her "mine of gold" or her "Sun" whose absence is her "winter." She writes also of her illnesses, of her children, and, as time goes on, of the deaths of grandchildren, several of whom proved less hardy than their parents. One poem tells of a 1666 fire that destroyed their home.

Some of her poems refer to events that are dated or datable; one of her most admired, "Contemplations," does not. She may well have begun it relatively early in her career, but it was not published until after her death. It is a mature poem in thirty-three stanzas, all but the last containing seven lines. Various critics have described it as a religious meditation, as an example of the seventeenth century emblem poem, even—because of its interest in landscape and vegetation—as an anticipation of romantic nature poetry. It blends elements of the "public" quaternions and of the more personal family poems. She

also composed for her son Simon a series of prose *Meditations Divine and Moral* (1678), urging that his appreciation of "mortal things" ultimately yield, like hers, to a Puritan faith in eternal ones.

Bradstreet died on September 16, 1672, at the age of sixty.

SIGNIFICANCE

Bradstreet was both a meditative and a lyric poet. The scope of her work was circumscribed by religious and domestic boundaries beyond which modern women poets have plunged successfully. Yet as an artist, she not only was unique in her time and place but also progressed far beyond the level reached by the numerous religious and domestic female writers who flourished two centuries later. In culturally limited Massachusetts of the middle decades of the seventeenth century, she was able to apply the techniques she had learned from English and French Renaissance poets to the raw material of her own life. In her time, for a woman to be an original meditative and lyric poet was a bold step, "obnoxious," as she put it, to men in general and probably more intensely so to the men who were fashioning the New England Puritan Commonwealth.

So in her way Bradstreet was a torchbearer for women. She apparently took no initiative in publishing her work, but she persisted in writing original poems, her last datable one, "As Weary Pilgrim," coming in 1669, only three years before her death. Virtually all English women writers before her had concentrated their efforts on translations of works by men. The next woman to challenge men's poetic hegemony pointedly, Anne Finch, countess of Winchilsea, was born the year before Bradstreet died.

In 1956, an important twentieth century poet, John Berryman, composed a major poem called *Homage to Mistress Bradstreet*. Although male critics had come to credit her achievement over the intervening centuries, Berryman's poem, an imagined dialogue, even an imaginative identification, with this woman who had lived three centuries earlier, symbolizes the full, ungrudging recognition of her as a sensitive victor in the dual struggle with environment and language—in other words, as a poet.

—*Robert P. Ellis*

FURTHER READING

Bradstreet, Anne. *The Works of Anne Bradstreet*. Edited by Jeannine Hensley. Cambridge, Mass.: The Belknap Press of Harvard University Press, 1967. The best modern edition of Bradstreet's poems, Hensley's boasts several attractive features: a foreword by Adrienne Rich, an informative introduction by the editor, and an index of proper names in Bradstreet's poems. Hensley orders the poems chronologically insofar as this order is known or can be inferred.

Cowell, Pattie, and Ann Stanford, eds. *Critical Essays on Anne Bradstreet*. Boston: G. K. Hall, 1983. A selection of colonial and nineteenth century essays followed by twenty-one modern ones from a variety of critical perspectives with emphasis on the feminist. An unusual and useful feature in an anthology of this type is its thorough index.

Latta, Kimberly. "'Such Is My Bond': Maternity and Economy in Anne Bradstreet's Writing." In *Inventing Maternity: Politics, Science, and Literature, 1650-1864*, edited by Susan C. Greenfield and Carol Barash. Lexington: University Press of Kentucky, 1999. Describes how Anne Bradstreet's poetry treats maternity and paternity in relation to economic issues.

Martin, Wendy. *An American Triptych: Anne Bradstreet, Emily Dickinson, Adrienne Rich*. Chapel Hill: University of North Carolina Press, 1984. Martin regards Bradstreet as the initial figure in a "female counter-poetic" linked to traditional Puritan values. For the most part the three essays are separate entities, with the one on Bradstreet emphasizing her struggles with religious faith and her numerous illnesses.

Merrim, Stephanie. *Early Modern Women's Writing and Sor Juana Inéz de la Cruz*. Nashville, Tenn.: Vanderbilt University Press, 1999. A feminist interpretation of Bradstreet's poetry, comparing her to two other seventeenth century women writers: Mexican poet Juana Inéz de la Cruz and Spanish writer Catalina de Erauso.

Rosenmeier, Rosamond. *Anne Bradstreet Revisited*. Boston: Twayne, 1991. Intended to supersede Josephine K. Piercy's study for the same publisher, this work's format is unusual in a Twayne book. Its approach is suggested by the titles of the three main chapters: "Daughter-Child: Actualities and Poetic Personas," "Sister-Wife: Conflict and Redefinitions," and "Mother Artist: A Typology of the Creative."

Stanford, Ann. *Anne Bradstreet: The Worldly Puritan*. New York: Burt Franklin, 1975. A biography with criticism by a leading Bradstreet scholar. The subtitle alludes to the conflict between the "invisible world" of Bradstreet's Puritan heritage and the "visible world" of her poetic vision. Stanford also casts light on Bradstreet's reading and her interest in American landscape.

White, Elizabeth W. *Anne Bradstreet*. New York: Oxford University Press, 1971. The most thorough Bradstreet biography. White includes useful discussions of the religious and political influences on Bradstreet's family, of the difficulties faced by the first wave of Massachusetts immigrants, and of the way Bradstreet transmuted these difficulties and numerous family griefs into impressive poems.

Wilson, Douglas. *Beyond Stateliest Marble: The Passionate Femininity of Anne Bradstreet*. Nashville, Tenn.: Highland Books, 2001. Wilson's biography examines Bradstreet's personality, her poetry, and her contributions to the life of the Massachusetts Bay Colony.

SEE ALSO: Anne Hutchinson; John Winthrop.

RELATED ARTICLE in *Great Events from History: The Seventeenth Century, 1601-1700:* May, 1630-1643: Great Puritan Migration.

MARGARET BRENT
English-born colonial American lawyer and activist

A powerful Maryland landholder, Brent saved the Catholic colony from a mutinous military uprising and Protestant revolt. As the first colonial female lawyer, she represented the second Lord Baltimore and appeared at the Maryland Assembly as the first woman to demand the right to vote.

BORN: c. 1600; Gloucestershire, England
DIED: c. 1671; Westmoreland county, Virginia
AREAS OF ACHIEVEMENT: Government and politics, law

EARLY LIFE

Margaret Brent was born about 1600 in Gloucestershire, England, into an important Catholic family. Like many ladies, she received a basic education and learned from her father the business of running an estate, a skill that was to serve her well throughout her life. In this era, England was a Protestant country, and to be a member of the Catholic Church was politically dangerous and financially perilous. Since the Protestant Queen Elizabeth I had succeeded to the throne after the death of Catholic Queen Mary I in 1557, English Catholics had continually experienced religious persecution. In addition, the advance of the Puritans during the 1630's increased political pressure on Catholic families and increasingly limited their rights.

This persecution caused the Brent family's wealth to decline, and the birth of twelve siblings ensured the eventual failure of the family fortune. As a child, Margaret Brent's future looked bleak. Immigration to Maryland—a colony created by George Calvert, first Lord Baltimore, specifically as a refuge for Catholics—seemed to provide a reasonable, albeit risky, method of survival. In short, Margaret Brent would have experienced a very different, and indeed easier, life had she not been born a Catholic.

Seeking out religious freedom and economic opportunity, Brent, her sister Mary, and their brothers Giles and Fulke left England in 1638 and arrived in Maryland in November of that year. Calvert's son Cecilius, the second Lord Baltimore, was a distant cousin of the Brents and was known at the time as the proprietor of Maryland. He had written a letter to the Maryland colonists on the Brents' behalf, asking that they be allowed to purchase land for the same reduced price he had offered to the first settlers in 1634.

Margaret Brent blossomed in Maryland. She and her sister Mary struck out on their own for the Maryland wilderness and settled on what came to be known as the Sisters Freehold, a 70-acre (28-hectare) parcel of land in Saint Marys, the capital of the colony. A short while later, she obtained another 1,000 acres (405 hectares) of land from her brother Giles. She also gained the friendship of her distant cousin, Maryland governor Leonard Calvert (the first Baron Baltimore's second son), and shared with him the guardianship of Mary Kittamaquund, the daughter of a Piscataway chief, who lived in the colony.

LIFE'S WORK

Both the first and second barons Baltimore had envisioned the Maryland colony as a place of religious toleration and political participation for all settlers, and they had attempted to design the colony's royal charter to ensure that it would remain so. This proved to be an extremely difficult task, however. In 1644, the colony's Protestants, led by Richard Ingle, revolted against its Catholic government in what became known as Ingle's Rebellion. The Protestants seized control of the Maryland colony, driving Governor Calvert into Virginia. Calvert managed to hire mercenary soldiers in Virginia, however, and in 1646, he regained control of Maryland. Brent aided Calvert in his campaign, raising a troop of volunteers to help fight the Protestants.

In the aftermath of Ingle's Rebellion, a new problem developed: Although Governor Calvert had plenty of land, he didn't have the actual currency to pay the Virginia mercenaries the money he owed them. He pledged his family's estates as security. Then, in the very midst of this crisis, Calvert died suddenly, leaving the government without a leader and with a troop of mutinous mercenaries on its hands. Before he died, however, Calvert had the wherewithal to declare Thomas Green his successor and to name Brent to take charge of the rising military unrest: "I make you my sole Exequtrix. Take all, pay all."

Brent quickly realized the enormity of the situation. The Catholic rule of Maryland depended upon the Calverts, as the governing family. She realized that in order to avoid further Protestant uprisings and preserve Catholic freedom, she would have to save the colony from the angry soldiers. Such huge responsibility was almost unheard of for a woman in this era, but Brent, who had never married, had been forced from an early age into making considerable decisions as a responsible landowner. Indeed, Brent's business acumen prompted her to make loans to new arrivals in the colonies, and if they failed to pay her, she prosecuted them herself. She claimed "The Courtroom—It's my life." As the first colonial woman lawyer, she appeared in court at least 134 times to file suits against debtors, and she pleaded cases in the Provincial Court for her brother and for otherwise unrepresented women.

Brent swiftly took control of the explosive situation. Since food was scare, she arranged for corn to be imported from Virginia to feed the hungry soldiers camped throughout Saint Marys. Then, she used her power of attorney over Governor Calvert's estate to sell his cattle and pay the troops. Her quick, skilled decision making diffused the tense military situation, and the soldiers either left quietly or stayed behind as settlers.

In an era when women were denied the vote, Brent claimed not one but two votes in the 1648 Maryland Assembly, asserting that she was entitled to a personal vote as an independent landowner, as well as a vote as Lord Baltimore's attorney. However, the court opposed her claim, denying her any vote at all because she was a woman. Although it declined to grant her a vote, however, the Assembly defended Brent's rights as Lord Baltimore's steward and publicly recognized her heroic actions in ensuring the safety of the colony. However, she fell out of favor with Lord Baltimore the following year.

In 1649, although the colony was becoming increasingly Protestant, Lord Baltimore preserved Maryland as a refuge for Catholics by establishing the Toleration Act, which allowed for the free exercise of religion for all Christians. Despite her contributions to the political, financial, and military stability that made the Toleration Act possible, however, Brent's decisions caused her ongoing problems. Baltimore was furious that she had sold his family's cattle to pay the mercenary soldiers. Moreover, he was a renowned defender of Catholics in a nation that had just established a Puritan Commonwealth. In an attempt to gain favor with the new Puritan government of England, Baltimore publicly denounced Brent and accused her of mishandling his finances.

Ironically, by defending his land, Brent became Lord Baltimore's enemy, and as a result, she was forced to move to the Northern Neck region of Virginia in 1651, where she established an estate named Peace. She died in 1671, leaving a large amount of property in Virginia and Maryland to her brother and his children.

SIGNIFICANCE

Brent is often recognized as an early feminist, the first colonial female lawyer and the first colonial woman to demand the right to vote. Beyond these firsts, however, Brent saw in the American colonies a way not only to ensure her freedom of religion but also to gain a foothold in a land that offered unprecedented opportunity. In America, she could design a life where she could own a large plantation of her own, something absolutely impossible in England. In America, she could, as it were, live up to her potential.

Throughout her life, Brent was determined not to fall socially. She found a way to remain in the highly regarded gentry class by becoming a woman of wealth and property without the aid of a man. In a land filled with men in need of wives, she and her sister withstood the social pressure to marry and in this way guaranteed their freedom to live independent lives. If Brent had married, she would have had to transfer ownership of her land to her husband. She never could have appeared in court, since women could not conduct business affairs. Moreover, by not marrying, she was able to take an active role in the defense of her land, her town, and her colony against mutinous soldiers and a religious revolt, and also to protect her rights as a lawyer in one of America's first courts of law.

—*M. Casey Diana*

FURTHER READING

Collins, Gail. *America's Women: Four Hundred Years of Dolls, Drudges, Helpmates, and Heroines*. New York: William Morrow, 2003. Discusses Brent's role as a landowner, lawyer, and manager in the seventeenth century Maryland colony.

Henretta, James, et al. *America's History*. New York: Worth, 1997. Contains a comprehensive essay on Margaret Brent and her contributions to the Maryland colony and her role as the first woman lawyer in the American colonies.

Leon, Vicki. *Uppity Women of the New World*. New York: Conari Press, 2001. In the chapter titled "The Courtroom—It's My Life," Brent is one of this book's two hundred women in North and South America and Australia who took their destinies into their own hands.

SEE ALSO: George Calvert.

RELATED ARTICLES in *Great Events from History: The Seventeenth Century, 1601-1700:* December 6, 1648-May 19, 1649: Establishment of the English Commonwealth; April 21, 1649: Maryland Act of Toleration.

SIR THOMAS BROWNE
English physician, scholar, and writer

Browne became a public figure in 1642 with the unauthorized printing of Religio Medici. *He became famous for a skeptical prose style and a freethinking perspective, evident in his eight published works, as well as a singular, eclectic, unorthodox, and interdisciplinary approach to the mind, body, and spirit.*

BORN: October 19, 1605; London, England
DIED: October 19, 1682; Norwich, Norfolk, England
AREAS OF ACHIEVEMENT: Medicine, scholarship, philosophy

EARLY LIFE

Sir Thomas Browne was born in London on October 19, 1605, the only son of Thomas Browne, a silk mercer from Chester. After the death of his father in 1613, Browne's mother married Sir Thomas Dutton, a soldier. In 1616, Browne began his education at Winchester College. At eighteen, he continued his studies at Broadgates Hall, Pembroke College, Oxford, where he matriculated in 1623 and graduated with a B.A. in 1626. He received an M.A. in 1629. Although he first gained distinction at Pembroke as a classical scholar, Browne's future inclinations toward medicine, philosophy, metaphysics, and religion were influenced greatly by two men: Thomas Clayton, principal at Pembroke and professor of physics, and Browne's tutor, Thomas Lushington, a liberal-minded cleric who later moved to Norwich.

It is not known when exactly Browne first began the study of medicine. Following his graduation, Browne visited Ireland with his stepfather on a tour of English military installations. Between 1630 and 1633, he traveled in France, Italy, and Holland, and studied at the medical schools in Montpellier, Padua, and finally Leyden, where he received his M.D. in 1633. There is general disagreement as to what happened next for Browne. According to some scholars, he returned to London in 1634, then resided at Shipden Hall, near Halifax. Others maintain that, after leaving Leyden, Browne worked as a doctor's assistant in Oxfordshire until he was incorporated M.D. at the university.

Browne settled in Norwich in 1636 or 1637, where he practiced medicine (as a family doctor) for the rest of his life, never again leaving East Anglia. Between 1635 and the end of his first year in Norwich, Browne spent his leisure time composing *Religio Medici* (1642, authorized ed. 1643; the religion of a doctor). The book was written for his own private satisfaction and exercise, as Browne tells his readers in the preface, "To the Reader," that accompanies the 1643 revised edition of his text.

LIFE'S WORK

In 1641, Browne married Dorothy Mileham, the daughter of Edward Mileham of Burlingham St. Peter, a village not far from Norwich. By all accounts, the Brownes were happily married. They had twelve children; eight died in infancy or youth, while four survived into adulthood. Edward, their eldest son, became a distinguished medical practitioner in London. Before the unexpected success of *Religio Medici* in 1642, Browne had already become the leading botanist and naturalist of Norfolk and Suffolk. As a physician he was highly regarded. Browne was also popular for his characteristic modesty: He was known to blush visibly when receiving a compliment.

By 1671, Browne's celebrity had grown to the extent that King Charles II bestowed a knighthood upon him. As the story goes, Charles II (accompanied by the Royal Court) visited Norwich. The king called upon Browne at his home and was impressed to find father and son (Edward) busily dissecting a dolphin. Later, at the royal banquet, the king—obliged by his visit to honor a local citizen—first approached the mayor of Norwich, who declined, but suggested Browne instead. Browne, a passionate Royalist, accepted.

Andrew Crooke printed a copy of *Religio Medici* in 1642 without Browne's knowledge. Once he discovered the text, Browne was initially furious, because the edition was riddled with errors. He soon forgave Crooke, however, then partially revised the work for a second edition, published in 1643. No manuscript copy of *Religio Medici* in Browne's own hand survives, but the book was issued in many versions during the seventeenth century and was translated into Dutch, French, and German. A 1644 Latin translation, published in Leyden, was widely read on the Continent.

The Roman Catholic Church condemned the text and, in March, 1645, placed *Religio Medici* on the Index of Prohibited Books due to the author's freethinking spirit. Although Parisians considered Browne a Roman Catholic, Church authorities in Rome found him to be an atheist because of his book's skeptical inquiry into relationships between reason and faith, body and soul, medicine and religion. Browne's arcane, capacious, and erudite style in *Religio Medici* established his reputation as a literary master.

Browne's most ambitious work, *Pseudodoxia Epidemica: Or, Enqueries into Very Many Received Tenets, and Commonly Presumed Truths* (1646; commonly known as *Browne's Vulgar Errors*), investigates diverse superstitious beliefs held during the seventeenth century, such as the notion that a man's skeleton contains one less rib than a woman's. In 1658, Browne published *Hydriotaphia Urne-Buriall: Or, A Discourse of the Sepulchrall Urnes Lately Found in Norfolk* together with *The Garden of Cyrus: Or, The Quincunciall Lozenge, or Net-Work Plantations of the Ancients*. Each text was dedicated to a friend living in the Norwich area: the first to Thomas le Gross, the second to Nicholas Bacon. *Hydriotaphia Urne-Buriall* offers, by way of four sepulchral urns recently discovered in Norfolk, a meditation on burial customs and the human desire for immortality. *The Garden of Cyrus* pursues the Platonic ideal through studies in architecture, botany and horticulture, geometry and mathematics, music, and verbal imagery.

Browne's four remaining primary works were printed posthumously. *Miscellany Tracts* (1684) addresses various topics in archaeology, botany, theology, music, and philology that were originally prompted for Browne's inquiring mind by friends and distinguished correspon-

dents, such as Nicholas Bacon and John Evelyn. *A Letter to a Friend, upon Occasion of the Death of His Intimate Friend* (1690)—probably composed early in 1657—elaborates upon a clinical report on an actual patient of Browne who died of phthisis (pulmonary tuberculosis). *Repertorium* (1712) reflects upon the monuments and tombs in Norwich Cathedral. A collection of short essays, *Christian Morals* (1716), illustrates the proximity of Browne's unorthodox religious philosophy to deism and atheism.

In addition to these eight major works, Browne authored three minor texts—*Nature's Cabinet Unlock'd* (1657); a poem, "Animae brutorum sunt corporeae" (1680); and "A Discourse on the Fishes Eaten by Our Saviour" (1684)—and coauthored at least two others: *Mercurius Centralis* (1664) and "A Discourse of Subterraneal Treasure" (1668). He also produced a collection of notes on a range of subjects, a short essay "On Dreams," several poems, and numerous letters.

Browne died in 1682 of natural causes on his seventy-seventh birthday and was buried at St. Peters, Mancroft, Norwich. His coffin was inadvertently disturbed in 1840 by a workman's pickax; Browne's skull was subsequently taken into the care of Norwich Hospital, where the relic is preserved to this day.

SIGNIFICANCE

Browne's literary achievement has overshadowed his accomplishments in medicine, natural history, occult philosophy, and other fields of knowledge, including religion, philology, archaeology, botany, and anthropology. His catholic intellectual interests, the breadth and depth of his knowledge, and the idiosyncrasies of his methods make Browne the epitome of the Renaissance Humanist. These eclectic characteristics garnered both praise and protest for Browne, however, as his autonomous, skeptical stance on religious and political matters, in particular, engendered strong criticism.

In an age of vituperative rhetoric, Browne's quietist voice was unique, compelling, and suspicious. Browne's pursuit of the natural and the metaphysical, the worldly and the transcendental, was ultimately driven by his fascination with a combination of Neoplatonic, hermetic, pagan, and scientific traditions. He believed in Christianity as well as in the occult writings of Hermes Trismegistus and also defended various tenets from Zoroastrianism, alchemy, astrology, and witchcraft.

Browne's singular qualities are matched by his manner of writing. His prose, which combines the Ciceronian and Senecan styles popular during the seventeenth cen-

Sir Thomas Browne. (Hulton Archive/Getty Images)

tury, demonstrates deft spontaneity and elegant digression. Browne's works have been admired by many great writers, including Samuel Taylor Coleridge, Herman Melville, Virginia Woolf, Jorge Luis Borges, Max Sebald, and Stephen Jay Gould.

—W. Scott Howard

FURTHER READING

Bennett, Joan. *Sir Thomas Browne: A Man of Achievement in Literature*. Cambridge, England: Cambridge University Press, 1962. Bennett interprets the literary significance of Browne's major, minor, and posthumous works in terms of his life and cultural milieu.

Dunn, William P. *Sir Thomas Browne: A Study in Religious Philosophy*. Minneapolis: University of Minnesota Press, 1950. Dunn's biographical and formal analysis consists of four thematic sections (Renaissance worldviews, faith and reason, the art of God, and literary themes), each addressing a range of Browne's texts.

Havenstein, Daniela. *Democratizing Sir Thomas Browne*. Oxford. England: Clarendon Press, 1999. Havenstein's monograph investigates the reception and influence (both literary and cultural) of Browne's *Religio Medici* through the seventeenth and eighteenth centuries.

Merton, Egon Stephen. *Science and Imagination in Sir Thomas Browne*. New York: Columbia University Press, 1949. Merton's biographical and formal study follows three primary topics (science, philosophy, and art) across the spectrum of Browne's works.

Patrides, C. A., ed. *Approaches to Sir Thomas Browne*. Columbia: University of Missouri Press, 1982. This edited collection of fifteen original essays by leading scholars in the field presents an array of perspectives on the life and work of Sir Thomas Browne, such as Browne's prose style and the essay tradition, and *Religio Medici*, and the English civil wars.

Wise, James N. *Sir Thomas Browne's "Religio Medici" and Two Seventeenth-Century Critics*. Columbia: University of Missouri Press, 1973. Through the critical writings of Browne's contemporaries, Sir Kenelm Digby and Alexander Ross, Wise examines the literary and cultural history of *Religio Medici* in the seventeenth century.

Wong, Samuel Glen. "Constructing a Critical Subject in *Religio Medici*." *Studies in English Literature* 43, no. 1 (2003): 117-121. Wong's article studies the authorship and textual production of *Religio Medici* by way of Kenelm Digby's observations upon the work and Browne's replies to Digby in private correspondence.

SEE ALSO: Charles II.

RELATED ARTICLES in *Great Events from History: The Seventeenth Century, 1601-1700:* March, 1629-1640: "Personal Rule" of Charles I; November 3, 1640-May 15, 1641: Beginning of England's Long Parliament; 1642-1651: English Civil Wars.

FIRST DUKE OF BUCKINGHAM
English politician

As the personal favorite of James I and Charles I, Buckingham was the most powerful political figure in Britain in the 1620's. Under his leadership, British participation in the Thirty Years' War resulted in embarrassing military defeats, causing a dangerous political and constitutional rupture between the Crown and Parliament.

BORN: August 28, 1592; Brooksby, Leicestershire, England
DIED: August 23, 1628; Portsmouth, Hampshire, England
ALSO KNOWN AS: George Villiers (given name)
AREA OF ACHIEVEMENT: Government and politics

EARLY LIFE

The first duke of Buckingham (BUHK-ihng-uhm) was born George Villiers on August 28, 1592. He was the second son of the second marriage of a rather obscure country squire, Sir George Villiers, who died in 1605, leaving the boy to the care of his ambitious and formidable mother. The future duke was sent to France in 1611 to polish his courtly skills. He turned up at the English court in August, 1614, in a threadbare suit, without powerful friends, connections, or prospects, hopeful of making his way on the basis of the charm and good looks with which he was plentifully supplied.

Villiers was fortunate in catching the eye of King James I, who delighted in the intimate company of attractive young men. The king's current favorite, the earl of Somerset, had grown insolent, though the king had long been patient with him, and he had made many enemies, public as well as private. Once the king noticed Villiers, he appointed him cupbearer, over Somerset's objections, which appointment kept Villiers constantly in the royal presence. The archbishop of Canterbury encouraged Villiers's rapid rise, hoping to reorient the country's foreign policy against Spain. In April, 1615, Villiers was made a gentleman of the king's bedchamber, again over Somerset's objections, and was knighted. As the relationship ripened, the king, always generous to his friends, began to shower gifts of land and money on his young protégé. Villiers won the support of the queen with his charm and eventually of young Prince Charles, who became devoted to him. Somerset, mired in scandal, was dismissed, utterly routed.

In rapid succession, between June, 1616, and January, 1619, Villiers was made master of the horse, a knight of the Order of the Garter, Lord Waddon, Viscount Villiers, earl of Buckingham, marquess of Buckingham, and lord high admiral. In May, 1620, with King James's blessing, Buckingham married Katherine Manners, daughter of the earl of Rutland, one of the richest peers in England.

Buckingham now became the sole dispenser of royal patronage. Without his approval, it was impossible to obtain the king's assent to anything. Both the swiftness of his rise and his monopoly of royal favor were naturally deeply resented at court, but Buckingham, secure in his relationship with the king, withstood all attempts to supplant him. The king treated him, as he did Prince Charles, as an apprentice at governing, but Buckingham did not interest himself in the management of royal policy so long as he was consulted about appointments.

Early in his startling ascent to the heights of power, Buckingham showed that he possessed quick wit, great charm, and considerable daring. He was an adventurer who had risen far beyond what was thought possible for someone of his background, but he did not allow resentment at his astonishing rise to unnerve him. He also made every effort to provide for the members of his extended family. To his friends and family, he showed loyalty and boundless generosity; to rivals and enemies, implacable hostility, albeit hidden beneath courtesy.

LIFE'S WORK

The central political problem of the day was how Great Britain should deal with the Thirty Years' War, which had just broken out in Europe. The king's inclinations were, as always, peaceful, but it proved impossible to re-

First Duke of Buckingham. (Library of Congress)

main aloof. James's son-in-law, Frederick V, the Protestant elector of the Palatinate in Germany, had accepted the crown of Bohemia in defiance of Catholic Austria. This decision had set off the war, and Frederick promptly lost both of his crowns. James could not sit idly by and allow his daughter's husband and their children to be dispossessed, but the military power of the Catholic states Austria and Spain was formidable. The king found, on summoning Parliament late in 1620, that the cost of recovering the Palatinate would be far more than he could afford or Parliament would grant. He therefore tried to pursue a diplomatic solution. What England, as the strongest Protestant power, had to offer in return for a restored Palatinate was a valuable promise of neutrality in the widening European war and a marriage alliance with Spain.

Buckingham and Prince Charles grew impatient with the slow pace of negotiation, in which Spain and Austria seemed to be gaining from the delay. In the spring of 1623, they pressed the aging king to allow them to go to Spain themselves to force a conclusion to the negotiations. Although it was extremely dangerous, they would not be denied. Traveling in disguise and almost unaccompanied, they descended on Madrid without warning and then spent six fruitless months trying to conclude the talks. While in Spain, Buckingham was made a duke, the first nonroyal English duke in more than fifty years. Ultimately, Buckingham and Charles concluded that Spain had never been serious about restoring the Palatinate, whatever had been promised or implied, and they returned home to a chorus of popular approval and demands for war, which they did much to inflame.

King James was no longer fully in control of the situation and reluctantly summoned Parliament. Buckingham won from them some funds, inadequate for a full-scale war but sufficient for the beginning of a vigorous military action against Spain. As lord admiral, Buckingham had done much to revitalize the Royal Navy, which had been allowed to decay during the Jacobean years of peace. Buckingham now set about trying to assemble a coalition of Protestant powers to oppose Austria and Spain in Germany and to secure the indispensable assistance of Catholic France by offering it a marriage alliance. Without French help, the Protestant powers were not strong enough to prevail over Spain and Austria. France was reluctant, however, to commit resources to recover the Palatinate. Buckingham raised an army, led by the German adventurer Count Peter Ernst Mansfeld (1580-1626), but it came to grief. Badly paid and supplied, the troops melted away when the expected French aid was not forthcoming. At this juncture, the old king died.

In 1625, the newly crowned King Charles I was forced to summon Parliament, the money granted for the war effort the previous year having been squandered. Parliament, which had been uninterested in, if not hostile to, the plan for a war in Europe, could not be expected to produce money for more of the same. Buckingham, seeing the difficulty, proposed that if Parliament produced the funds, it should have the war it preferred, a naval war in the best Elizabethan manner, directly against Spain and the riches of her Indies. Under this pressure, Parliament voted some additional money, though not enough, and a naval expedition against Spain was launched in the fall of 1625. It returned home in disgrace, having accomplished nothing. The new Parliament, summoned in 1626, responded to Buckingham's mismanagement of the situation by impeaching him. The king could save him only by hastily dismissing Parliament.

Having narrowly escaped disaster on the domestic front, Charles and Buckingham now compounded their foreign policy difficulties. Because Charles had married a French princess, they were still hopeful of getting some

help from their French alliance, but they managed matters so clumsily that, on the contrary, they blundered into war with France.

Hoping to force the French to help in Germany, Buckingham applied pressure by providing aid to the French Huguenots, the country's Protestant minority, in their intermittent civil wars. In the summer of 1627, Buckingham took personal charge of an expedition to the Isle of Re, off Rochelle, the principal Huguenot stronghold. Here the duke spent many months besieging a French fortress until, exhausted, outnumbered, and on the point of being besieged themselves, the English were forced to withdraw.

When Buckingham returned with the remnants of his defeated army, he was the object of great public hatred, though he continued to possess the king's confidence. Buckingham insisted on pursuing the French war, but a new Parliament raised a storm of objections to the measures the Crown had taken—without its approval—to finance the previous campaigns. These, embodied in the Petition of Right, provoked another dissolution of Parliament. Undeterred, Buckingham pressed forward on provisioning a relief fleet for Rochelle. He was at Portsmouth overseeing the work when, on August 23, 1628, a disgruntled officer who had survived the expedition against Spain assassinated him.

SIGNIFICANCE

The first duke of Buckingham's brief and astonishing career is difficult for modern historians to assess fairly, though the utter failures of his public policy make it easy to condemn him. His contemporary rivals for power regarded him with all the jealousy that only a rank upstart could excite. As an opponent of Parliament, he wins little retrospective sympathy from modern students. Like Cardinal de Richelieu in France and Gaspar de Guzmán y Pimental, count-duke of Olivares, in Spain, he was a practitioner and a great example of a form of government long vanished, the rule of the royal favorite. A proper scholarly assessment of what he was trying to do, in his own terms, has always been difficult because few of his papers seem to have survived.

There can be little question that Buckingham's failure had powerful consequences in British domestic politics, for the disgrace of the defeats and the huge costs of the war generated a parliamentary uproar that poisoned the political atmosphere in the 1620's, making cooperation between king and Parliament impossible. Whether these grave difficulties were a major precipitant of the English Civil War, which followed a dozen years later, is still a matter of controversy, but it is difficult to imagine that they played no role at all.

Buckingham rose swiftly, because he was attractive and charming and devoted himself successfully to holding the favor of two successive kings. His youth and inexperience brought him to grief, and for the disasters of the 1620's he has received much blame. The seventeenth century made of his swift rise and fall a moral tale about the wickedness of a subject misleading his king and an object lesson about the folly of letting an upstart "crow" rise from obscurity to the highest level of society and politics.

—*S. J. Stearns*

FURTHER READING

Cooper, J. P., ed. *The Decline of Spain and the Thirty Years' War, 1609-1648/59.* Cambridge, England: Cambridge University Press, 1971. An authoritative collaborative survey of the world in the early seventeenth century, with good bibliographies for further study. A basic introduction for serious students seeking the general historical background for the period.

Dalton, Charles. *Life and Times of General Sir Edward Cecil, Viscount Wimbledon.* 2 vols. London: Sampson, Low, Marston, Searle and Rivington, 1885. Cecil commanded the failed attack on Spain in 1625. This biography, despite its age and protectiveness toward its subject, prints many documents and gives much detail on the political and military difficulties facing Buckingham.

Elliott, J. H. *Richelieu and Olivares.* New York: Cambridge University Press, 1984. A concise and highly suggestive comparative study of two other royal favorites, contemporaries and rivals of Buckingham. Useful as a measure of Buckingham's failure.

Gardiner, S. R. *History of England from the Accession of James I to the Outbreak of the Civil War, 1603-1642.* 10 vols. London: Longman, 1883-1884. Despite its age, still the best narrative history of the period, though under growing scholarly attack (see Russell and Sharpe works below). Extremely critical of Buckingham and the Stuart administration generally.

_____, ed. *Documents Illustrative of the Impeachment of the Duke of Buckingham in 1626.* London: Camden Society, 1887. A central collection of documents on the greatest political crisis of Buckingham's career, assembled and introduced by the greatest historian of the period. Virtually all the other volumes of documents assembled and edited by Gardiner for the Camden Society are relevant here. They were the by-product of his great history.

Lockyer, Roger. *Buckingham: The Life and Political Career of George Villiers, First Duke of Buckingham, 1592-1628.* London: Longman, 1984. Has replaced all previous biographies in its completeness and thoroughness of research. Has been criticized for its strong and rather one-sided defense of Buckingham. Though now the standard biography, its exoneration of Buckingham remains controversial.

Russell, Conrad. *Parliaments and English Politics, 1621-1629.* New York: Oxford University Press, 1979. A key work in the attempt to revise the history of the politics of the 1620's. Since Gardiner's views can be seen as partisan, Buckingham's difficulties appear more sympathetically.

Sharpe, Kevin, ed. *Faction and Parliament: Essays on Early Stuart History.* Reprint. New York: Methuen, 1985. With Russell, one of the most influential revisionist works attempting to see the history of the 1620's not, as Gardiner did, essentially in the terms set by Parliament, but with attention to the Stuart position.

Treadwell, Victor. *Buckingham and Ireland, 1616-1620: A Study in Anglo-Irish Politics.* Portland, Oreg.: Four Courts Press, 1998. Explores the influence of Buckingham on Ireland in the early years of the 1600's, and concludes that his influence was invariably for the worse.

SEE ALSO: Robert Carr; Charles I; James I.

RELATED ARTICLES in *Great Events from History: The Seventeenth Century, 1601-1700:* March 24, 1603: James I Becomes King of England; 1618-1648: Thirty Years' War; 1620: Bacon Publishes *Novum Organum*; 1625-October 28, 1628: Revolt of the Huguenots; May 6-June 7, 1628: Petition of Right; March, 1629-1640: "Personal Rule" of Charles I.

JOHN BUNYAN
English writer

Drawing on the popular culture of England's socially most turbulent period, Bunyan preserved in much of his writing the idiom and images of the less articulate levels of society. As a religious allegory, his The Pilgrim's Progress *appeals beyond creed to the vision of a life transcending the ordinary.*

BORN: November 30, 1628 (baptized); Elstow, Bedfordshire, England

DIED: August 31, 1688; London, England

AREAS OF ACHIEVEMENT: Literature, religion and theology

EARLY LIFE

John Bunyan was the eldest child of Thomas Bunyan, Jr., and Margaret Bentley Bunyan of Bunyan's End, between Harrowden and Elstow in Bedfordshire, where the Bunyans had been landowners since the twelfth century. From his father, the young Bunyan learned the trade of a brazier, tinker, or whitesmith (one who mends and sells various small household utensils), and he learned to read and write in a local school. When Bunyan was fifteen, his

John Bunyan. (Library of Congress)

mother and sister died and his father remarried, a circumstance to which biographers have credited John's subsequent rebellious behavior, which he later regretted and indeed may have exaggerated.

Parliamentarians dominated Civil War Bedfordshire, and Bunyan was drafted when he reached the militia age of sixteen years. He served for two and one-half years in a regiment that formed part of the garrison of Newport Pagnell.

LIFE'S WORK

Bunyan married in 1648 or 1649 and took on the outward forms of religious practice. His wife, whose name has not survived, possessed two books: Lewis Bayley's *The Practice of Piety* (1612) and Arthur Dent's *The Plaine Man's Pathway to Heaven* (1601). Although far less important to Bunyan than the King James version of the Bible, these books interested him when his religious searching began. In his spiritual autobiography, Bunyan related the origin of his awakening to what he called "inner" faith, as opposed to outward practices: While working in Bedford, he overheard a few poor women enjoying the sun and talking about religion. Feeling that they were discussing something he had not experienced, Bunyan conversed with them, and they invited him to attend their Nonconformist congregation, which met in St. John's Church, Bedford.

Their Particular Open Communion Baptist congregation apparently had been organized by its first minister, John Gifford, a physician who had served in the Royalist army. In 1653, the Bedford town council, acting under Oliver Cromwell's Broad Church policies, presented Gifford to the living of St. John's Church. By that time, the minister had seen Bunyan through three or four years of alternating doubt and ecstasy. Better educated than Bunyan, Gifford was for Bunyan a source of books as well as conversations and sermons. Bunyan later declared that, except for the Bible, the book that had had the greatest influence on him had been Martin Luther's *In epistolam sancti Pauli ad Galatas commentarius* (1519; *Commentary on St. Paul's Epistle to the Galatians*, 1575). He joined Gifford's congregation in 1653 or shortly thereafter and moved his family from Elstow to Bedford about 1655.

Soon after the move to Bedford, both Bunyan's wife and his minister died, and Bunyan himself contracted tuberculosis. By this time, Bunyan had been chosen a deacon, and he began preaching, privately at first and then publicly following his ordination in 1657. He continued to travel as a brazier but combined his secular work with preaching, occasionally in parish churches and frequently on village greens and in barns and woods. During the repression of Nonconformity that accompanied the Restoration, Bunyan was first warned and then arrested and indicted under the Elizabethan Conventicle Act. The charge was conducting a conventicle and not conforming to the worship of the Church of England.

After his arrest, Bunyan refused to allow bonds to be made against his renewed preaching. He maintained that the laws against conventicles were aimed only at persons who used religious meetings as a disguise for sedition and so did not apply to him: an unsuccessful defense frequently made by Nonconformists. He was indicted in Quarter Sessions in January, 1661, and was lodged in the Bedford county jail for the following twelve years, with occasional releases after 1668. He learned to make laces and sold them for his family's support. His second wife, Elizabeth, whom he had married in 1659, managed the family and made numerous petitions for his release, even appearing before the House of Lords.

In prison, Bunyan produced much of the writing for which he is now remembered. *Grace Abounding to the Chief of Sinners* was published in 1666, and it went through five more editions in Bunyan's lifetime. It was typical of the Puritan spiritual autobiographies of the second half of the sixteenth century, in which a preacher described his conversion, calling, ministry, and persecutions and sought to convert and guide others. Bunyan's treatment surpasses others, however, in its literary grace and sense of drama. It is the chief source for the meager information about Bunyan's early life.

Bunyan was pardoned under the authority of Charles II's 1672 Declaration of Indulgence. Prior to his pardon, he had been called as pastor to his congregation in Bedford and had received a royal license to preach in May,

	BUNYAN'S MAJOR WORKS
1656	*Some Gospel Truths Opened*
1657	*A Vindication . . . of Some Gospel Truths Opened*
1658	*A Few Signs from Hell*
1659	*The Doctrine of the Law and Grace Unfolded*
1661	*Profitable Meditations Fitted to Man's Different Condition*
1663	*I Will Pray with the Spirit*
1664	*A Mapp Shewing the Order and Causes of Salvation and Damnation*
1664	*A Caution to Stir Up to Watch Against Sin*
1665	*One Thing Is Needful*
1665	*The Holy City: Or, The New Jerusalem*
1666	*Grace Abounding to the Chief of Sinners*
1671	*A Confession of My Faith and a Reason for My Practice*
1672	*A New and Useful Concordance to the Holy Bible*
1672	*A Defence of the Doctrine of Justification by Faith*
1676	*The Strait Gate: Or, The Great Difficulty of Going to Heaven*
1676	*Saved by Grace*
1678	*The Pilgrim's Progress from This World to That Which Is to Come, Part I*
1679	*A Treatise of the Fear of God*
1680	*The Life and Death of Mr. Badman*
1682	*The Holy War*
1684	*The Pilgrim's Progress from This World to That Which Is to Come, the Second Part*
1684	*A Holy Life, the Beauty of Christianity*
1686	*A Book for Boys and Girls: Or, Country Rhymes for Children*
1688	*Discourse of the Building, Nature, Excellency, and Government of the House of God*
1688	*Solomon's Temple Spiritualized: Or, Gospel Light Fecht Out of the Temple at Jerusalem*
1688	*The Jerusalem Sinner Saved*

1672. The building and grounds of St. John's Church having been returned to the ownership of the Church of England, Bunyan's congregation met at a barn in an orchard belonging to one of its members. Within three years of Bunyan's release, the owner gave the land to the congregation, and it remains the site of the Bunyan Meeting.

As a result of Parliament's pressuring Charles II to annul the Declaration of Indulgence, Bunyan was imprisoned again, this time in the Bedford town jail, located on the bridge over the Ouse River. There he began writing *The Pilgrim's Progress from This World to That Which Is to Come* (Part I, 1678; Part II, 1684), according to John Brown, his most influential biographer, and he completed it following his release in 1676. When Part I was published in 1678, it was the twenty-fourth of what

would be Bunyan's sixty publications, and it was repub-
lished eleven times during his lifetime alone. *The Pilgrim's Progress* was a natural sequel to *Grace Abounding to the Chief of Sinners*. In *The Pilgrim's Progress*,
Bunyan generalized the personal experiences he had related in the earlier work. In both works, the inner world
of the spirit is real; the outer world, insubstantial.

Both works were drawn from the same popular culture that supported works by less graceful and now forgotten artisan preachers. Allegory and pilgrimage were
familiar to English readers, and many of Bunyan's characters and adventurers had their models in medieval romances. Some scenes in Christian's pilgrimage were
drawn realistically from seventeenth century life, particularly that of rural Bedfordshire. The story in *The Pilgrim's Progress*, what Bunyan called the "outside" of his
dream, appealed to and reflected the interests and out-
looks of Restoration readers from the middle and lower
ranks of society, where the Puritan impulse after 1660
was strongest.

In the effect of its drama, its storytelling charm, and its
allegorical vision, *The Pilgrim's Progress* qualifies Bunyan as a founder of the English novel. The power of the
work, however, derives from its moral conception as an
ideal of life, what Bunyan referred to as the "inner side"
of his dream. The second part of *The Pilgrim's Progress*,
the account of the pilgrimage of Christian's wife and
children, was completed in 1684 and reprinted six times
by 1693. A response to the popularity of *The Pilgrim's
Progress*, the sequel can stand alone and reflects the
more relaxed tone of Bunyan's mature ministry. Beginning in 1676, he obtained licenses for preachers and
preaching places under his supervision and directed cir-
cuits from Bedford. He frequently preached to huge
crowds in London and in 1688 was serving as chaplain to
the lord mayor of London, Sir John Shorter.

Meanwhile, Bunyan had also published *The Life and
Death of Mr. Badman* (1680) and *The Holy War* (1682).
Concern for the powerless and oppressed was registered
in many of Bunyan's writings, but particularly in *The
Life and Death of Mr. Badman*, in which Bunyan spoke
more as a compassionate champion of the oppressed than
as a discontented workman. *The Holy War* treated allegorically the fall and redemption of humankind and the
struggle for humanity's soul. Its millenarian imagery reflected Bunyan's familiarity with the aspirations of the
Fifth Monarchy Men. When James II sought to build an
alliance between Nonconformists and the court, some of
Bunyan's congregation accepted seats on the remodeled
corporation of Bedford, but Bunyan held aloof. Sir

Charles Firth has explained this reticence as a fear of Catholicism, but William York Tindall has interpreted Bunyan's apparent aloofness from politics as distrust and distaste for monarchy, an attitude profoundly political.

Bunyan never saw the denouement of toleration for
Nonconformists, dying some two months before the
landing of William III of Orange. Almost sixty, he had
been ill in the spring and had caught cold riding in a
heavy rain on a pastoral mission. He died at the home of a
friend, John Strudwick, a grocer and chandler near Holborn Bridge in London, and was buried in Bunhill Fields
cemetery. Most of his unpublished material was printed
at the direction of his friend Charles Doe, a London
comb-maker, in 1692 and 1698. Elizabeth Bunyan died
in 1691. They had two children, Sarah and Joseph. Bunyan had four children by his first wife: Mary, John,
Thomas, and Elizabeth.

SIGNIFICANCE

Bunyan's main significance is as a writer, and his most
important creation is *The Pilgrim's Progress*. The initial
popularity of the work accounts for much of its influence. As a precursor of the English novel, it was outstanding for its literary and narrative merit, and by the
time the novel evolved in the eighteenth century, *The Pilgrim's Progress* had become an established part of the
literary and cultural environment of writers such as Daniel Defoe, Henry Fielding, and Laurence Sterne. There
were 160 editions of *The Pilgrim's Progress* by 1792.

Outside the ranks of Nonconformity, however, Bunyan was dismissed by his contemporaries as a tradesman-
preacher whose literary popularity bespoke only the ignorance of his coreligionists. In historical perspective,
this disdain and the class divisions it reflects give Bunyan's works special interest for the social historian. Not
only his beliefs and values but also his literary character-
izations, his descriptions, and even his vocabulary are
valued as the surviving expressions of seventeenth century common people who otherwise have been largely
unrepresented in the historical records.

Literary critics were slow to appreciate Bunyan or to
see anything in his writings except his fervent faith and
its inspirational effects. Jonathan Swift and Ben Jonson
were the first secular writers to praise *The Pilgrim's
Progress*; not until the 1830's, with Robert Southey's
edition of the work and a subsequent essay by Thomas
Babington Macaulay, was there general critical acceptance of Bunyan as a writer. In 1880, Bunyan was entered
into the English Men of Letters series in a biography by
James Anthony Froude. By that time, *The Pilgrim's*

Progress had been published in more than seventy languages. As a statement of religious faith, *The Pilgrim's Progress* for centuries has symbolized the simple but profound human desire to live to one's fullest capacity.

—*Carole Watterson Troxler*

FURTHER READING

Brown, John. *John Bunyan: His Life, Times, and Work*. Boston: Houghton Mifflin, 1888. Reissued with addenda, edited by Frank Mott Harrison, London: 1928. The most detailed biography, by the minister of Bunyan Meeting, Bedford, whose thorough research has not yet been surpassed.

Bunyan, John. *"The Pilgrim's Progress from This World to That Which Is to Come," and "Grace Abounding to the Chief of Sinners."* Edited by John F. Thornton and Susan B. Varenne. New York: Vintage Books, 2004. One of the more recent editions of Bunyan's best-known works, with introductory comments and analysis.

Greaves, Richard L. *Glimpses of Glory: John Bunyan and English Dissent*. Stanford, Calif.: Stanford University Press, 2002. Focuses on the interplay of literature, history, psychology, and religion in Bunyan's life and work.

_____. "Organizational Response of Nonconformity to Repression and Indulgence: The Case of Bedfordshire." *Church History* 44 (December, 1975): 472-484. Describes the successful network of teachers and preachers organized to withstand persecution in the 1670's.

Harrison, Frank Mott. *A Bibliography of the Works of John Bunyan*. Supplement to the Bibliographical Society's "Transactions," No. 6. Oxford, England: Clarendon Press, 1932. Reprint. Norwood, Pa.: Norwood Editions, 1977. The standard reference source for Bunyan's works in their myriad editions.

Hill, Christopher. *A Tinker and a Poor Man: John Bunyan and His Church*. New York: W. W. Norton, 1990. In Hill's opinion, Bunyan was a lower-middle-class Calvinist, whose works spoke to "millions of poor and oppressed people whom Bunyan wished to address."

Miller, Perry. "John Bunyan's *Pilgrim's Progress*." In *Classics of Religious Devotion*. Boston: Beacon Press, 1950. The religious nature of the work is here explained by an astute analyst of Puritanism.

Millett, Michael A. *John Bunyan in Context*. Pittsburgh, Pa.: Duquesne University Press, 1997. Examines Bunyan's life and work to describe how he combined English culture with Calvinist doctrine.

Tindall, William York. *John Bunyan: Mechanick Preacher*. 1934. Reprint. New York: Russell & Russell, 1964. Explores the popular culture that produced Bunyan and numerous lay preachers and emphasizes class consciousness, particularly that of the Baptists.

White, Barrington R. *The English Baptists of the Seventeenth Century*. London: Baptist Historical Society, 1983. Rev. ed. Northampton, England: Baptist Historical Society, 1996. Explores the changing relationship between Baptists and the state from 1640 to 1689 and emphasizes associations among congregations.

Winslow, Ola Elizabeth. *John Bunyan*. New York: Macmillan, 1961. Solidly based on secondary historical and literary studies, this is a balanced and highly readable introduction.

SEE ALSO: Charles II (of England); Oliver Cromwell; James II.

RELATED ARTICLES in *Great Events from History: The Seventeenth Century, 1601-1700:* May 19, 1662: England's Act of Uniformity; February 18, 1678: Bunyan's *The Pilgrim's Progress* Appears.

RICHARD BURBAGE
English actor

Actor and shareholder with Shakespeare in the Lord Chamberlain's Men, Burbage created many of Shakespeare's most striking characters, including Richard III, Hamlet, Lear, and Othello.

BORN: c. 1567; London, England
DIED: March 13, 1619; London
AREA OF ACHIEVEMENT: Theater

EARLY LIFE

Richard Burbage (BUR-bihj) literally grew up with the Elizabethan theater. His father, theatrical entrepreneur James Burbage (c. 1530-1597), built what was perhaps the first private theater in London, the Red Lion, in 1567, about the time Richard was born. Nine years later, with capital from his brother-in-law John Brayne and his professional skill as a joiner (carpenter), James Burbage built the much larger theater called—with a bravado contemporary accounts imply was justified—simply The Theatre. Richard's only brother, Cuthbert, would become a partner in his own theatrical enterprises; of their three sisters, Joan, Helen, and Alice, only Alice would survive to own a share of the theaters.

James Burbage, who had himself been an actor, encouraged his sons Richard and Cuthbert to enter the profession. Cuthbert's participation in the theatrical boom of the period was limited to the business end, but Richard must have been a boy actor from the start, because by the 1580's, he was already known as one of the premier actors of his day. The earliest surviving credit for a role was the printed version of an interlude by Richard Tarleton called *The Seven Deadlie Sins* (1585), listing "R. Burbadg" as playing both King Gorboduc and Tereus. The following year, James Burbage purchased a house in the Blackfriars district (so called because it had been owned by the Dominican order before Henry VIII seized all Catholic holdings). He converted the house to a theater, which Richard would later inherit. In 1588, Richard created the most celebrated role of the pre-Shakespearean Elizabethan stage: that of Hieronymo in Thomas Kyd's *The Spanish Tragedy* (pr. c. 1585-1589, pb. 1594?).

LIFE'S WORK

By 1590, Richard Burbage, by then an actor in the Lord Admiral's Men, saw his interest in The Theatre sufficiently established to defend its profits. In November of that year, Nicholas Bishop, legal agent for Burbage's aunt, John Brayne's widow, burst into The Theatre de-

manding the receipts for that day's performance in the widow's name. A legal deposition concerning the brawl testifies that Burbage grabbed Bishop by the nose and threatened to beat him if he did not leave. The following year, James Burbage severed his connection with the Lord Admiral's Men, which merged with Strange's Men and moved, apparently without Richard, to the Rose Theatre.

Despite his separation from this popular company, Burbage in 1592-1593 scored another hit with a role that became associated with him for the rest of his career, the title role of William Shakespeare's *Richard III* (pr. c. 1592-1593, rev. 1623). As M. C. Bradbrook observed in 1962, the hypocrite Richard is the consummate actor, a role seemingly tailor-made for Burbage—which indeed it was, for Shakespeare wrote it with his fellow actor in mind.

In the spring of 1594, the major players of the amalgamated Lord Admiral's/Strange's company formed the Lord Chamberlain's Men, in which both Burbage and Shakespeare were major stockholders. That Christmas, Burbage was summoned, with Shakespeare and the comic actor Will Kempe, for the first of many command performances before Queen Elizabeth I herself. If Shakespeare's *Romeo and Juliet* (c. 1595-1596) had been finished by then, it might have been among the plays in which Burbage performed on December 27 and 28 for the queen, for the playwright John Marston records in a 1598 satire that Burbage was the first to act the role of Romeo.

In 1597, James Burbage's lease on the land on which The Theatre stood lapsed. The elder Burbage was negotiating for a renewal of the lease when he died in the spring of 1597. The suit was taken up by Richard and his brother Cuthbert. The brothers Burbage had undisputed right to The Theatre itself, since their father had built it, but the land was owned by Giles Allen, who, attracted to the lucrative gate of The Theatre, was not about to renew the lease without some part of the profit.

A year into the suit, in December, 1598, or January, 1599, the brothers boldly outmaneuvered Allen, dismantling The Theatre and reassembling it across the river on land they had secured at Bankside. The Theatre was now indisputably theirs (in partnership with their sister Alice), as was the Blackfriars Theatre, which they leased to one of the companies of child actors, the Queen's Majesty's Children of the Chapel. While most of Burbage's acting successes were at the Globe Theatre, built for Chamberlain's company in 1599, Burbage also appeared in most of the major plays Ben Jonson and John Marston premiered at the Blackfriars Theatre, indicating his prestige as an actor.

The roles that Burbage premiered in the following years were some of the most celebrated of the Elizabethan stage: comic roles in Jonson's *Every Man in His Humor* (pr. 1598, pb. 1601, revised pr. 1605, revised pb. 1616) and *Every Man Out of His Humour* (pr. 1599, pb. 1600), and the tragic title characters of Jonson's *Sejanus His Fall* (pr. 1603, pb. 1605; commonly known as *Sejanus*) and *Catiline His Conspiracy* (pr., pb. 1611; commonly known as *Catiline*). Jonson's most famous character, the eponymous protagonist of *Volpone; Or, The Fox* (pr. 1605, pb. 1607), was also first realized by Burbage. For Shakespeare, Burbage gave the first life to the title characters of *Hamlet, Prince of Denmark* (pr. c. 1600-1601), *Othello, the Moor of Venice* (pr. 1604, rev. 1623), and *King Lear* (pr. c. 1605-1606). With the death of Queen Elizabeth in 1603, her successor, King James I, gave tribute to the preeminence of Chamberlain's company by becoming its patron and changing the group's name to the King's Men.

Richard Burbage. (The Folger Shakespeare Library)

Burbage's share of the profits of the company matched his "box office" value, and by 1601, he could afford to marry. His wife, Winifred, bore him five daughters and two sons, of whom only two daughters and a son survived him.

In the second decade of the seventeenth century, a new dramatic vogue known as tragicomedy (for which Shakespeare had laid the groundwork with his romance plays, including *The Winter's Tale* [pr. c. 1610-1611] and *The Tempest* [pr. 1611]) took the London stage, and the leading playwrights of the genre, Francis Beaumont (c. 1584-1616), who wrote for the children's company at Blackfriars, and John Fletcher (1579-1625), turned to Burbage to ensure the success of their plays. He had lead roles in all of the plays written by Beaumont and Fletcher between 1611 and 1618. In 1609, Burbage bought out the lease of the Blackfriars from the children's company, giving him an interest in the three most successful theaters of the era: The Theatre, the Globe, and the Blackfriars.

On June 29, 1613, Burbage was acting in the Globe, in a play recorded as "All Is True" but assumed by scholars to be Shakespeare's *Henry VIII*, when the theater caught fire. Burbage barely escaped with his life, and the theater was rebuilt the following year.

On March 13, 1619, Burbage died, leaving a sizable estate to his widow and children. His will is not specific as to the amount, but a contemporary of Burbage named Chamberlain attests that he left behind three hundred pounds in land, no small sum in the seventeenth century.

SIGNIFICANCE

Burbage became the most famous actor of his day with an acting style that was probably close to the ideals of more modern times: realism, an avoidance of extremes of emotion and gesture, and identification with the role. These qualities are summarized by Hamlet's famous "advice to the players," a speech that Burbage was the first to speak on stage. Those values were also attributed to Burbage himself by Irish poet Richard Flecknoe (c. 1600-c. 1678), who as late as 1660 wrote in admiring memory of the acting style he had seen in his teen years in London. Flecknoe praised Burbage for not dropping character until he had returned to the "tiring house" or dressing room, and for reacting in character even when he had no lines to speak. Flecknoe called Burbage "Proteus," after the Greek god who could assume any form he wished, and objected to calling Burbage a "player," because to him acting was not play, but business.

—*John R. Holmes*

FURTHER READING

Bradbrook, M. C. *The Rise of the Common Player: A Study of Actor and Society in Shakespeare's England.* Cambridge, Mass.: Harvard University Press, 1962. An excellent introduction to the nature of Elizabethan acting, recording many sixteenth and seventeenth century anecdotes about Burbage.

Chambers, E. K. *The Elizabethan Stage.* Oxford, England: Clarendon Press, 1923. This standard reference work on the subject, in four volumes, contains thorough documentation of the era, including in volume 2 a biography of all the major actors, of which Burbage's (pages 306-310) is the longest.

Gurr, Andrew. *The Shakespeare Company, 1592-1642.* New York: Cambridge University Press, 2004. An exhaustive reconstruction of Burbage's theatrical company, with invaluable appendices offering biographies of Burbage and his fellow actors, and all of their shareholders' documents.

Stopes, Charlotte Carmichael. *Burbage and Shakespeare's Stage.* New York: Haskell House, 1970. A reprint of the most thorough documentation of Burbage's career, originally published in London in 1913.

SEE ALSO: James I.

RELATED ARTICLES in *Great Events from History: The Seventeenth Century, 1601-1700:* c. 1601-1613: Shakespeare Produces His Later Plays; June 29, 1613: Burning of the Globe Theatre.

THOMAS BURNET
English theologian and geologist

Burnet composed what he believed to be a scientific description of the early geological history of the earth that would explain the biblical account of Creation. He is notable for attempting to establish a bridge between the science and religion of his day.

BORN: c. 1635; Croft, Yorkshire, England
DIED: September 27, 1715; London, England
AREAS OF ACHIEVEMENT: Religion and theology, science and technology

EARLY LIFE

Thomas Burnet earned early recognition as an excellent student and entered Cambridge in 1651, studying under John Tillotson (archbishop of Canterbury from 1691 to 1693) and the Cambridge Platonist Ralph Cudworth. Burnet received an M.A. from Christ's College (John Milton's alma mater) in 1658, becoming a proctor in 1667. He visited the Continent, serving as a tutor to the young James Butler, Lord Wiltshire, the grandson of James Butler, twelfth earl, first marquis, and later first duke of Ormonde.

In 1685, Ormonde was influential in helping Burnet to gain the position of master of Charterhouse School in London. In 1686-1687, Burnet and others successfully resisted illegal efforts by James II to make the Catholic Andrew Popham a pensioner of the school; Burnet remained its master until his death. In 1691, he became chaplain in ordinary and clerk of the closet to King William III of Orange. Burnet was regarded as a possible successor to Tillotson as archbishop, but his theology was thought too unorthodox, and he advanced no further in the Church. Toward the end of 1695, Burnet resigned his duties at court, largely under pressure brought against his writings, and thereafter he lived at Charterhouse as a lifelong bachelor. He died there on September 27, 1715, and is buried in the chapel.

LIFE'S WORK

Burnet's most famous work, *Telluris theoria sacra* (1681; *The Sacred Theory of the Earth*, 1684-1690), offered a theory of the development of the earth since Creation that would be rationally plausible yet support the biblical account given in Genesis. Burnet believed that Creation had been divinely caused, but he felt it should be possible to explain in physical terms the processes by which the globe achieved its present form. Because science in Burnet's day had not yet become a distinctly defined discipline, later practitioners of formal science would evaluate his theory harshly, categorizing it as speculation lacking in hard evidence (he completely ignored the known fossil record). Nevertheless, his effort to propose an explanatory hypothesis is a significant step toward the later growth of empirical geology.

Burnet posited that the earth's original form, owing to the perfection of creation, was a smooth sphere unbroken by mountains or valleys. He calculated that the biblical Deluge would have been insufficient to cover the continents, and therefore the Flood must have sprung from a subterranean layer of water that cracked through the surface from an underground abyss. Mountain ranges were the result of this breakup of the surface; they stood as evidence of the imperfect nature of the world after the Fall (the earth was now "a hideous ruin"), yet they possessed a profound grandeur that moved Burnet deeply. "There is nothing that I look upon," he wrote, "with more pleasure than the wide Sea and the Mountains of the Earth. There is something august and stately in the Air of these things that inspires the mind with great thoughts and passions."

Burnet also offered a physical explanation of the final destruction of the world by fire. Interestingly, Sir Isaac Newton disagreed with Burnet's account of the Flood and supported the authority of the Genesis account rather than Burnet's more "rational" analysis. Burnet's assumptions about the relationship of human reason to divine authority are perhaps more significant than the details of his theory, for he believed that if human reason and biblical truth were both the works of God, they could not finally contradict each other: "He that made the Scripture made also our Faculties, and 'twere a reflection upon the Divine Veracity, for the one or the other to be false when rightly us'd. We must therefore be careful and tender of opposing these to one another, because that is, in effect, to oppose God to himself."

Burnet's *Archaeologiae philosophicae* (1692) is the work credited with earning him the label "unorthodox," thus ending his position at court. Burnet supported the concept of accommodation in biblical language. In other words, he asserted that the truths of Scripture were framed in language adapted to the imperfect understanding of its human readers, not necessarily in ways that rendered its ideas factually (rather than spiritually) true. Burnet held that Moses had simplified the account of Creation to better enable the ancient Hebrews to comprehend it, a view that prompted a satirical poem of the 1690's accusing him of stating "That all the books of Moses/ Were nothing but supposes."

Burnet also anonymously issued a series of three responses in 1697 and 1699 in answer to John Locke's *An Essay Concerning Human Understanding* (1690). Burnet argued against Locke's concept of learned ideas, asserting that humans instead possess at birth a native moral sense allowing them to distinguish right from wrong. Two of Burnet's theological works were published posthumously, *De statu mortuorum et resurgentium liber: Accesserunt epistolae duae circa libellum de archaeologiis philosophicis* (1723; *A Treatise Concerning the State of Departed Souls, Before, and at, and After the Resurrection*, 1730) and *De fide et officiis Christi-*

anorum liber (1723; *The Faith and Duties of Christians*, 1728?).

SIGNIFICANCE

Though his ideas have in the past been generally deemed eccentric, Burnet now tends to be viewed as a precursor of modern attempts to form a unified conception of scientific and religious truth, specifically to reconcile the claims of empirical research with the biblical narrative of Creation. He is also a significant figure in the development of the aesthetics of the sublime, the effort to portray verbally or pictorially the grandeur of natural vistas that seem too exalted for human expression. Such scenes, he felt, "fill and overbear the mind with their Excess and cast it into a pleasing kind of stupor and imagination."

Burnet's writing style impressively conveys his theories in graceful, rhythmic sentences. His ideas prompted both vigorous support and angry criticism after his death. Among his English supporters were Richard Steele, who compared Burnet favorably to Cicero and praised *The Sacred Theory of the Earth* in the August 17, 1711, issue of *The Spectator*, and Steele's partner, Joseph Addison, who composed a Latin ode in praise of him. Others, however, suggested that Burnet might even have been an atheist. His work contributed to the strong eighteenth century interest in the aesthetic appeal of nature and thus distantly influenced Edmund Burke's important essay *A Philosophical Enquiry into the Origin of our Ideas of the Sublime and Beautiful* (1757). The English Romantic poets William Wordsworth, Samuel Taylor Coleridge, and Percy Bysshe Shelley refer in passing to Burnet's ideas, and Coleridge used a passage from the *Archaeologiae Philosophicae* as the epigram to later editions of *The Rime of the Ancient Mariner* (1798).

—*Christopher Baker*

FURTHER READING

Almond, Philip C. *Adam and Eve in Seventeenth-Century Thought*. New York: Cambridge University Press, 1999. Contains several brief discussions of Burnet's skeptical, nonliteral interpretations of Genesis in *The Sacred Theory of the Earth*.

Bevenga, Nancy. "On Holy Ground: Mountains and Their Significance for Samuel Taylor Coleridge." *Anglican and Episcopal History* 67, no. 1 (1998): 49-68. Examines the sources of Coleridge's fascination with mountains, among which *The Sacred Theory of the Earth* is significant.

Davenport-Hines, Richard. *Gothic: Four Hundred Years of Excess, Horror, Evil, and Ruin*. New York: Farrar, Straus, and Giroux, 1998. Contains a brief popular discussion of Burnet's place in the development of the Gothic movement in art, placing him in the context of the paintings of Salvator Rosa (1615-1673) and the aesthetics of Anthony Ashley Cooper, third earl of Shaftesbury (1671-1713).

Gould, Stephen Jay. *Time's Arrow, Time's Cycle*. Cambridge, Mass.: Harvard University Press, 1987. Sees Burnet as a key figure in the development of the modern concept of "deep" geological time, paving the way for the more influential geologists James Hutton and Charles Lyell, who dispensed with religious considerations entirely. Gould also discusses Burnet briefly in his *Ever Since Darwin* (1977).

Grave, S. A. *Locke and Burnet*. [Perth]: Philosophy Society of Western Australia and Department of Philosophy, University of Western Australia, 1981. A philosophical study comparing Burnet and John Locke on issues of morality, religious revelation, and the immortality of the soul, as well as addressing Burnet's concept of the conscience.

Jacob, M. W., and W. A. Lockwood. "Political Millenarianism and Burnet's Sacred Theory." *Science Studies* 2, no. 3 (July, 1972): 265-279. Argues that Burnet's original intention in writing *The Sacred Theory of the Earth* was to assert the final authority of the Anglican Church in the coming millennium.

Mandelbrote, Scott. "Isaac Newton and Thomas Burnet: Biblical Criticism and the Crisis of Late Seventeenth-Century England." In *The Books of Nature and Scripture: Recent Essays on Natural Philosophy, Theology, and Biblical Criticism in the Netherlands of Spinoza's Time and the British Isles of Newton's Time*, edited by James E. Force and Richard H. Popkin. Boston: Kluwer Academic, 1994. A detailed discussion of Burnet's work within the larger seventeenth century debate over the nature of scientific evidence and its relationship to scriptural authority; also examines Newton's response to Burnet.

Nicholson, Marjorie Hope. *Mountain Gloom and Mountain Glory: The Development of the Aesthetics of the Infinite*. Reprint. New York: W. W. Norton, 1963. Devotes chapters 5 and 6 to Burnet's ideas, the debates they sparked, and the broad influence they had.

Rappaport, Rhoda. *When Geologists Were Historians, 1665-1750*. Ithaca, N.Y.: Cornell University Press, 1997. Summarizes Burke's methodology and contains a detailed summary of reactions to Burnet's theories by British and European thinkers of his own day. Extensive bibliography and index.

Watson, George, ed. *Remarks on John Locke by Thomas Burnet with Locke's Replies*. Doncaster, South Yorkshire, England: Brynmill Press, 1989. A complete edition of Burnet's responses to Locke, with a helpful introductory essay.

SEE ALSO: James II; John Milton; Sir Isaac Newton; William III.

RELATED ARTICLE in *Great Events from History: The Seventeenth Century, 1601-1700:* 1669: Steno Presents His Theories of Fossils and Dynamic Geology.

ROBERT BURTON
English writer

Burton's major work was The Anatomy of Melancholy, *a large book full of learning presented in an informal and engaging prose style, which provided entertainment and education to readers in his own day and in subsequent centuries.*

BORN: February 8, 1577; Lindley, Leicestershire, England

DIED: January 25, 1640; Oxford, England

AREAS OF ACHIEVEMENT: Literature, astronomy, medicine, philosophy, religion and theology, science and technology

EARLY LIFE

Robert Burton was born on February 8, 1577, the fourth of nine children of the landowner Ralph Burton and his wife, Dorothy. Young Robert was educated at two grammar schools in the neighboring county of Warwickshire, one at Nuneaton and one at Sutton Coldfield. He then went on to Oxford University, enrolling in Brasenose College in 1593 and transferring to Oxford's Christ Church College in 1599. He received a bachelor of arts degree in 1602, a master of arts in 1605, and a bachelor of divinity in 1614.

Because of the long time it took him to obtain his first degree, there has been speculation that Burton withdrew from Oxford for a time owing to illness, perhaps appropriately enough because of a bout of melancholy. There is a record of a twenty-year-old Robert Burton receiving treatment for melancholy in London in 1597, but it is not certain that this was the same Robert Burton.

LIFE'S WORK

Burton lived a quiet, uneventful life. He never married or traveled or took part in the political controversies of his day. Once he entered Oxford's Christ Church College, he remained there the rest of his life. He became librarian for the college's library in 1626. He also served as vicar of an Oxford church, the Church of St. Thomas the Martyr, from 1616 until his death. He had two other clerical appointments outside Oxford but delegated the duties and did not attend to either of them in person. One of these was at Walesby in Lincolnshire, from 1624 to 1631, and the other was at Seagrave in Leicestershire, from the 1630's on.

Burton's life as an adult consisted mostly of reading and writing. Besides the library in Christ Church College, he spent time in Oxford's Bodleian Library and also amassed a sizable private library of his own, approximately fifteen hundred volumes, at a time when books were expensive. His earliest published writing was a Latin poem, which he contributed to a collection celebrating the accession of James I to the throne of England in 1603. Two years later he contributed another Latin poem to a similar collection celebrating a visit of King James to Oxford. He also contributed to a not very successful play, *Alba* (pr. 1605), performed for James during his visit. The following year he began work on another play, *Philosophaster* (pr. 1618, pb. 1862; the false philosopher), a satire in Latin about life at a Spanish university. It was not performed until a decade later.

At three different times in the 1610's, Burton served in an administrative position as clerk of the Oxford Market. During this same decade he must also have been at work on his masterpiece, *The Anatomy of Melancholy* (1621). Throughout the rest of his life, Burton continued to work on this major project, issuing revised and greatly expanded editions in 1624, 1628, 1632, and 1638. A final edition worked on by Burton, but not published until after his death, appeared in 1651. During these revisions, *The Anatomy of Melancholy* grew from an already sizable 300,000 words to nearly 450,000 words, or approximately twelve hundred pages. It also quoted approximately thirteen hundred different authors.

The Anatomy of Melancholy has a quite formal structure, which, however, is continually undermined by Burton's tendency to digress. It is divided into three major "partitions" and subdivided into sections, subsections, and "members," all of which are laid out in synopses at the beginning of each partition. Before the first partition, there is an extended preface, almost a book in itself, called "Democritus Junior to the Reader," in which Burton adopts the persona of a descendant of the original Democritus, an ancient Greek known as the Laughing Philosopher, and surveys the sad state of humanity. He scoffs at human foibles in the preface but also reveals compassion for sufferers. The preface also contains a depiction of his ideal, Utopian society.

Although his ostensible aim is to analyze and suggest remedies for melancholy, the seventeenth century term for what later became known as depression, Burton says in his preface that everyone and all of society suffers from melancholy, and in the rest of his book he feels free to discuss a wide variety of topics only tangentially connected to psychological problems, from geography and climate to the nature of beauty to astronomy, astrology, religion, lawyers, and love. He does so both learnedly and casually, quoting a variety of authorities, many of them in Latin, but writing in a very informal, colloquial manner, always ready to digress from the supposed subject at hand, and somehow making all the quotations his own.

Always interested in astrology, Burton cast his own horoscope, which appears on his tombstone. After he died, on January 25, 1640, there was a rumor that he had predicted his own death based on his horoscope and had committed suicide in order to make the prediction come true. However, there is no evidence that he died of anything other than natural causes.

SIGNIFICANCE

Burton's *The Anatomy of Melancholy* was quite popular in his own day, selling so well that it made his publisher rich. It owed some of its popularity to its subject matter, because melancholy was a popular topic in the early seventeenth century, but Burton went far beyond other writers on the subject in his comprehensiveness and learning. The poet John Milton drew on Burton's work for his companion poems "L'Allegro" and "Il Penseroso" (wr. c. 1631, pb. 1645).

The book fell out of favor in the eighteenth century, though it influenced Laurence Sterne's digressive novel *The Life and Opinions of Tristram Shandy, Gent.* (1759-1767) and was a favorite of the dictionary maker Samuel Johnson. It returned to favor after 1800 and was much admired by Romantic writers such as John Keats, Charles Lamb, and Lord Byron. The nineteenth century saw it mainly as a literary curiosity and a useful repository of quotations; one early twentieth century writer, the physician Sir William Osler, saw it as a serious discussion of depression. In the late twentieth century, postmodernist critics saw Burton's book as a forerunner of postmodernism because of its internal contradictions and its tendency to create uncertainties instead of providing easy answers.

There is no agreement on the nature of Burton's achievement in his book, but except for the eighteenth century, which saw it as lacking in order, there has been general agreement through the years that *The Anatomy of Melancholy* has been an important and entertaining work dealing in a lively way with the complexities of life.

—Sheldon Goldfarb

FURTHER READING

Babb, Lawrence. *Sanity in Bedlam: A Study of Robert Burton's "Anatomy of Melancholy."* East Lansing: Michigan State University Press, 1959. An older study providing useful information about Burton's life, the contents of the *Anatomy*, and Burton's revisions to it.

Breitenberg, Mark. "Fearful Fluidity: Burton's *Anatomy of Melancholy*." In *Anxious Masculinity in Early Modern England*. New York: Cambridge University Press, 1996. Sees the *Anatomy*'s incessant digressiveness as an example of the impossibility of imposing limits on the passions. Also sees Burton as misogynistic.

Burton, Robert. *The Anatomy of Melancholy*. Edited by Holbrook Jackson. Reprint. London: Dent, 1972. One-volume edition with a wide-ranging introduction by Jackson.

_____. *The Anatomy of Melancholy*. Edited by Thomas C. Faulkner, Nicolas K. Kiessling, and Rhonda L. Blair, with commentary by J. B. Bamborough. 6 vols. Oxford, England: Clarendon Press, 1989-2000. A scholarly edition of Burton's text. Introductory material includes biographical details and information on the growth of the work.

Fish, Stanley E. "Thou Thyself Art the Subject of My Discourse: Democritus Jr. to the Reader." In *Self-Consuming Artifacts: The Experience of Seventeenth-Century Literature*. Berkeley: University of California Press, 1972. Argues that the *Anatomy* creates uncertainty by means of ambiguity and contradiction and by refusing to provide easy answers.

Nochimson, Richard L. "Studies in the Life of Robert Burton." *Yearbook of English Studies* 4 (1974): 85-111. Detailed study of various biographical issues in Burton's life.

O'Connell, Michael. *Robert Burton*. Boston: Twayne, 1986. Useful study of Burton's life and work. Includes bibliography, chronology, and index.

Renaker, David. "Robert Burton and Ramist Method." *Renaissance Quarterly* 24 (1971): 210-220. Discusses Burton's methods in the *Anatomy*.

Sawday, Jonathan. "Shapeless Elegance: Robert Burton's Anatomy of Knowledge." In *English Renaissance Prose: History, Language, and Politics*, edited by Neil Rhodes. Tempe, Ariz.: Medieval & Renaissance Texts & Studies, 1997. Sets Burton in the context of seventeenth century science and notes his appeal for postmodernists.

Trevor-Roper, Hugh. "Anatomist of Melancholy." *The Listener* 97 (February 10, 1977): 187-189. Discusses Burton's character and his aim in the *Anatomy*.

SEE ALSO: James I; John Milton.

RELATED ARTICLE in *Great Events from History: The Seventeenth Century, 1601-1700:* Beginning c. 1615: Coffee Culture Flourishes.

FRANCESCA CACCINI
Italian composer, singer, and teacher

Caccini was one of the most successful musicians of early seventeenth century Europe and the first woman to have composed an opera, one which became the first opera by any composer to be performed outside Italy.

BORN: September 18, 1587; Florence (now in Italy)
DIED: After June, 1641; place unknown
ALSO KNOWN AS: Francesca Signorini; Francesca Signorini-Malaspina; Francesca Raffaelli; La Cecchina
AREA OF ACHIEVEMENT: Music

EARLY LIFE

Francesca Caccini (frahn-CHAYS-kah kaht-CHEE-nee) was the eldest daughter of the great composer Giulio Caccini (c. 1545-1618), who is credited with writing the first operas. Francesca received a literary education at an early age and wrote poetry in Italian and Latin. Her childhood was ensconced in music, and she was given lessons in guitar, harp, keyboard, composition, and singing.

It is believed that at the age of thirteen, Caccini was a performer in the group known as *donne di Giulio Romano*—the ladies of Giulio Romano (Giulio Caccini). Her sister Settimia and her stepmother Margherita della Scala were also in the ensemble, which in 1600 performed in the first complete opera that survives intact, *Euridice* (parts of which were rewritten by Guilio Caccini), by Jacopo Peri. That same year, the singers performed in Giulio's *Il rapimento di Cefalo*. The group dominated chamber music activities at the Medici court in the early years of the seventeenth century. They were replaced in 1611 by a group apparently headed by Caccini known as *la sig. a Francesca e le sue figliuole* (Francesca and her pupils), which performed regularly at court until the late 1620's.

Caccini's talent was recognized by many when she was still very young. Queen Marie de Médicis of France and her husband, King Henry IV, offered Caccini a position at the French court in 1604-1605, and in 1606, Princess Margherita della Somaglia-Peretti likewise offered her a salaried post, but she took neither position.

LIFE'S WORK

In 1607, Caccini made her compositional debut with *La stiava*, a carnival entertainment that was well received and described as *una musica stupenda*, a marvelous music. That same year, upon the order of Grand Duchess Christine of Lorraine, Caccini accepted a post with the Medici court. In addition to serving as a composer, her duties included singing at liturgical services, specifically the Offices during Holy Week. This was unusual during a time when women were usually barred from church singing. (At one point, she and her sister were invited soloists at the Cathedral of Pisa.) She also sang at receptions and taught singing, instrumental performance, and composition to the princesses, ladies-in-waiting, and younger female attendants. She was appreciated for her skills and by 1620 was the highest paid musician in Medici service. She would work for the Medici family until 1627 and again from 1633 to 1637.

Caccini wrote or contributed to at least thirteen court entertainments—shows with singing and dance—including poet Ottavio Rinuccini's *La mascherata delle ninfe di Senna* (1611) and Jacopo Cicognini's *Il martiro di S Agata* (1622). One of Caccini's most famous works was her sole surviving opera, the first extant opera by a woman composer, *La liberazione di Ruggiero dall'isola d'Alcina* (the freeing of Ruggiero from the island of Alcina), billed as a ballet but actually an opera, complete with prologue, recitatives, arias, choruses, and instrumental ritornellos. The work was commissioned in 1625 by Florence's regent archduchess Maria Magdalena of Austria in honor of a visit by the Polish prince Władysław (who became King Władysław IV Vasa in 1632). The prince enjoyed the work immensely and, consequently, it was performed at the court of Poland three years later, thus becoming the first Italian opera—by a woman or a man—performed outside Italy. Moreover, in 1626, Władysław commissioned two new operas from Caccini: one about Saint Sigismund and the other on a subject of her choice.

La liberazione di Ruggiero dall'isola d'Alcina is unique among contemporary works. Gender plays a significant role in the actual music. For instance, gender is depicted with tonal keys. Alcina and her ladies-in-waiting sing in keys with flats, and Ruggiero and other men sing in keys with sharps. The androgynous sorcerer figure, Melissa, sings in the key of C major, which has no sharps or flats.

First, women and men are portrayed as experiencing the action from different points of view, while juxtapositions of gender-identified key areas are frequent and striking enough to create a musical subtext exploring the relationship between social status and cross-gender behavior. Second, Caccini's intense, chromatic setting of Alcina's long complaint to the unfaithful Ruggiero gradually dis-

solves the union between poetic and musical form as the
woman retreats from the treachery behind Ruggiero's
courtly promises. This formal disjunction combines with
Alcina's retreat to the furthest reaches of the flat keys to
create a haunting image of an abandoned woman whose
grief turns to unreconciled anger. Lingering memory of
this scene undermines the moralizing at the conclusion of
the opera and challenges the stereotypical treatment of
the lamenting woman in most early opera.

In 1618, Caccini published *Il primo libro delle mu-
siche*, a book of thirty-two solo songs and four duets for
soprano and bass (it is possible the bass parts were written for her husband). This volume, which has pedagogical characteristics, is one of the largest and most diverse
collections of early monody, which was a new style of musical texture, one innovated by her father, Giulio. Monody emphasizes a solo line with chordal accompaniment.
This style was extremely significant since it distinguished
music of Caccini's era from that of the Renaissance.

Caccini was among the first musicians to go on tour,
something that would become common for professionals
in later times. She performed in Rome in 1616; toured
Genoa, Savona, and Milan in 1617; and performed in
Rome again in the winter of 1623-1624. She was accompanied by others from Florence, including her husband,
who was a singer.

Caccini had married years before, in November, 1607,
after she initially assumed her post with the Medici. Her
husband, Giovanni Battista Signorini, was a court singer,
and, like Caccini, he was working for the grand duchess
and for the grand duke Cosimo II de' Medici. He had little wealth, but with Caccini's dowry of 1,000 scudi, he
bought two neighboring houses in the via Valfonda in
1610. They lived there until his death in 1626. Margherita (born 1622) was their only child, and she would become a nun and an active singer.

A year after Signorini's death, Caccini left Florence,
married an aristocrat and amateur singer of Lucca,
Tomaso Raffaelli, and entered into the service of a
wealthy banker. In 1628, she had a son, Tomaso. Her second husband died in 1630, leaving her wealthy. She was
quarantined for three years in Lucca because of the
plague, but in 1633 returned to Florence to serve the
Medici. There, she sang chamber music with her daughter, taught nuns singing, and composed for the court. She
left the Medicis for a second time in 1641 and may have
died in 1645, since this was the year her son's guardianship was issued to his uncle Girolamo Raffaelli. She is
entombed with her father, her sister, and an otherwise unidentified person named Dianora.

SIGNIFICANCE

Caccini was one of the most successful female musicians, composers, and music teachers of the early seventeenth century. She composed the first extant opera by a
woman, the first opera by a woman or a man to be performed outside Italy. She went on tour before doing so
was commonplace.

Her compositions are more abundant than those of her
female contemporaries, and her works were composed
over a longer period of time. She was a leader in presenting and composing monody, a new style of music innovated by her father that would be dominant throughout
the era.

—*Lisa Urkevich*

FURTHER READING

Bowers, Jane, and Judith Tick, eds. *Women Making Music.* Urbana: University of Illinois Press, 1987. Contains a chapter on the emergence of women composers in Italy, 1566-1700, that places Caccini in cultural
context among her female peers.
Cusick, Susan G. "'Who Is This Woman . . . ?': Self-
Presentation, *Imitatio Virginis*, and Compositional
Voice in Francesca Caccini's *Primo libro* of 1618." *Il
saggiatore musicale* 5, no. 1 (1998): 5-41. An interpretation of Caccini's 1618 music book and its symbolism.
Kirkendale, Warren. *The Court Musicians in Florence
During the Principate of the Medici: With a Recon-
struction of the Artistic Establishment.* Firenze, Italy:
Olschki, 1993. Discusses the lives and activities of the
salaried musicians of the Medici grand dukes and
duchesses, including Caccini's.
Pendle, Karin. *Women and Music.* Bloomington: Indiana
University Press, 1991. Contains a section on the
Caccini women, specifically Francesca.
Silbert, Doris. "Francesca Caccini, Called La Ceccinna."
Musical Quarterly 32, no. 1 (1946): 50-62. Details on
Caccini's life with examples of her music. Includes
translated primary sources.

SEE ALSO: Arcangelo Corelli; Girolamo Frescobaldi;
Jean-Baptiste Lully; Marie de Médicis; Cosimo II
de' Medici; Claudio Monteverdi; Heinrich Schütz;
Barbara Strozzi.
RELATED ARTICLES in *Great Events from History: The
Seventeenth Century, 1601-1700:* c. 1601: Emer-
gence of Baroque Music; February 24, 1607: First
Performance of Monteverdi's *La favola d'Orfeo*.

PEDRO CALDERÓN DE LA BARCA
Spanish dramatist

Calderón continued the Golden Age of drama after the death of Lope de Vega Carpio, bringing to Spain some of the greatest dramatic literature and autos sacramentales *in the seventeenth century.*

BORN: January 17, 1600; Madrid, Spain
DIED: May 25, 1681; Madrid
AREA OF ACHIEVEMENT: Theater

EARLY LIFE

The bright Spanish cultural renaissance had its center in the *fin de siècle* spirit, and Pedro Calderón de la Barca (PAY-throh kol-day-ROHN day lah BAHR-kah) was born into it, in 1600, in Madrid. His parents were very much part of the establishment; his father, strong-willed and demanding, was secretary to the Council of the Royal Treasury. It was his mother's wish before her death in 1610 that Pedro enter the priesthood; his father, on his deathbed when Calderón was fifteen, turned her request into an order, a dying command that was to plague Calderón throughout his career, until he finally took holy orders at the age of fifty-one. Without his parents to guide him, Calderón was forced to examine his life alone, with the guilt of disobedience mixed with a sense of not knowing who he was. No early portrait of Calderón exists, but a graphological analysis of his handwriting done by one scholar reveals a shy, nervous, and sensitive young man, not so much challenging his faith or loyalty to the Catholic church as questioning his own place in it. This combination of an inquiring mind together with a mandate by his dead parents confused Calderón during his youth and possibly led him to explore answers to his dilemma in the dramatic mode, dramatizing over and over the conflict between predestination and free will.

Calderón's schooling, however, was not neglected. From 1614 to 1620, his academic virtuosity reflected his internal confusion and indecision. At the imperial Jesuit College, he received an excellent education in the classics, religion, and (later, at the University of Alcala) rhetoric and logic. In Salamanca he studied law. It was, however, a minor poetry contest in 1620, part of a celebration in honor of Saint Isadore, patron saint of Madrid, that was to turn Calderón's life away from the traditional pursuits of priesthood or law to writing. Lope de Vega Carpio, the acknowledged master dramatist of the Spanish Golden Age, was a judge and saw fit to praise Calderón's entry. Inspired, Calderón began to write plays at a rate that rivaled Lope de Vega's (who is said to have written fifteen hundred plays in his lifetime).

His first play (discounting youthful efforts), *Amor, honor y poder* (love, honor, and power), was performed in Madrid at the court of Philip IV in 1623 and was immediately followed by *La selva confusa* (the entangled forest) and *Judas Macabeo* (Judas Macabee), both in 1623. Calderón's military service in Italy and Flanders interrupted his dramatic writing for a short time. Returning from Spain's triumph at Breda, Calderón wrote *El sitio de Breda* (the siege of Breda), performed in 1625 and, judging from accurate geographical details in the play, conjectured to be based on his own experiences in battle.

The court life of the Spanish Golden Age could only emerge from more than one hundred years of relatively peaceful royal succession since Ferdinand and Isabella, who united Spain and defeated the Moors in a decisive battle at Granada in 1492. When Lope de Vega died in 1635, Calderón was his successor at the court of Philip IV, during the construction of the king's great court theater, El Coliseo del Buen Retiro.

Pedro Calderón de la Barca. (Library of Congress)

LIFE'S WORK

"The sober celebration of order triumphant"—this phrase, from James E. Maraniss's study, *On Calderón* (1978), summarizes Calderón's life's work, manifested in his dramatic approach to his secular plays (1630 to 1651) as well as his religious attitudes expressed in the *auto sacramentale* form he favored after 1651. Throughout his career, which lasted more than fifty years, Calderón viewed the function of the stage as the reestablishment of order in the face of the constant threat of political, moral, and spiritual rebellion. By 1635, at the beginning of Calderón's succession as director at the court of Philip IV, he had written thirty plays, of which three—*La dama duende* (wr. 1629, pr. 1636; *The Phantom Lady*, 1664), *El príncipe constante* (1629; *The Constant Prince*, 1853), and *La vida es sueño* (1635; *Life Is a Dream*, 1830)—have joined the permanent repertory of classical world drama, performed, adapted, and modernized in many countries. The latter play, considered his masterpiece, embodies the themes and the style of virtually all the secular plays: A hero, wrongly deprived of his royal honor, examines his own consciousness to recover his station and his free will. The gongoristic style of bombast and exaggeration, together with the insertion of poetic monologues, denotes the dramatic style of the period, of which Calderón and Lope de Vega, along with Tirso de Molina, were masters.

Calderón's appointment coincided with the construction and occupation of the royal palace, Buen Retiro, begun in 1629 and opened in 1634, featuring the Coliseo del Buen Retiro, a special theater space expressly designed for the performance of his plays. It was this permanent home and captive audience of sympathetic courtiers, together with encouragement of his early work, that allowed the prolific Calderón to continue his career as playwright well into midlife. The theatrical companies of that day, licensed by the king, gave private performances to the royal court, usually before their public debut; consequently, Calderón's position at court gave him easy access to the commercial theater outside the royal palace. One memorable evening performance of *El mayor encanto, amor* (1635; *Love, the Greatest Enchantment*, 1870) took place on an island in the garden lake, with the audience attending from gondolas; a sudden storm toppled several vessels and blew out the candles, causing the six-hour play to be postponed.

The many performances at court in the years between 1635 and 1650, described by one biographer as "counted among the rare blissful hours in theatrical history," perfected Calderón's dramaturgical skills and gave the theater world such masterpieces as *El alcalde de Zalamea* (1643; *The Mayor of Zalamea*, 1853), *El mágico prodigioso* (1637; *The Wonder-Working Magician*, 1959), *El médico de su honra* (1637; *The Surgeon of His Honor*, 1853), and *A secreto agravio, secreta venganza* (1637; *Secret Vengeance for Secret Insult*, 1961); these plays were collected from time to time during this period and published in several volumes under Calderón's supervision.

A series of personal blows, including the death of his brothers and mistress in 1650, forced him to retreat into a monastic life. Calderón's retreat into priesthood did not end his perpetual examination of the idea of free choice as moral basis. The *autos sacramentales* of his later pe-

---

CALDERÓN'S MAJOR WORKS

1623	*Amor, honor y poder*
1625	*El sitio de Breda*
1629	*El príncipe constante* (*The Constant Prince*, 1853)
1629	*La dama duende* (*The Phantom Lady*, 1664)
1629	*Casa con dos puertas, mala es de guardar* (*A House with Two Doors Is Difficult to Guard*, 1737)
c. 1634	*Los cabellos de Absalón* (pb. 1684; *The Crown of Absalom*, 1993)
1634	*La devoción de la cruz* (*The Devotion to the Cross*, 1832)
1635	*El gran teatro del mundo* (pr. 1649; *The Great Theater of the World*, 1856)
1635	*El mayor encanto, amor* (*Love, the Greatest Enchantment*, 1870)
1635	*La vida es sueño* (*Life Is a Dream*, 1830)
1637	*El médico de su honra* (*The Surgeon of His Honor*, 1853)
1637	*A secreto agravio, secreta venganza* (*Secret Vengeance for Secret Insult*, 1961)
1637	*El mágico prodigioso* (*The Wonder-Working Magician*, 1959)
1640-1642	*El pintor de su deshonra* (pb. 1650; *The Painter of His Dishonor*, 1853)
1643	*El alcalde de Zalamea* (*The Mayor of Zalamea*, 1853)
1653	*La hija del aire, Parte I* (*The Daughter of the Air, Part I*, 1831)
1653	*La hija del aire, Parte II* (*The Daughter of the Air, Part II*, 1831)
1659	*El laurel de Apolo*
1660	*La púrpura de la rosa*
1680	*Hado y divisa de Leonido y Marfisa*

riod reflect once again the metaphysical struggle between earthly desires and the willful renunciation (a word used often by Calderón's biographers) of those desires by the Christian soul. The *autos sacramentales* were allegorical pieces in which abstractions such as Everyman, Error, and the World were personified in Manichaean battles with temptations to sin and moral compromise. By far the most frequent figure was the World, whose tribulations on the stage actually continued for Calderón his never-ending struggle to reconcile his ethical standards with his own human weaknesses, as he saw them. His most popular *auto sacramentale, El gran teatro del mundo* (wr. 1635, pr. 1649; *The Great Theater of the World*, 1856), was written before his investiture and contains all the elements of the genre: A Director in gaudy symbolic costume of stars and rays calls together the World, the Law of Grace, and various actors in the Play of Life to "celebrate / My power infinitely great." As the play-within-a-play moves to its patrological conclusion, the Poor Man retreats to a subservient position and the Rich Man justifies his place in the importance of historical events, thus reinforcing the conservative view. Despite modern reservations about the outcome, the play is studied as a model of the type.

During his most fruitful years at court, Calderón kept careful accounts of his work, publishing them in several volumes under the editorship of his brother and other friends, rejecting publicly the imitations and acknowledging the authentic works as his own. Near the end of his life, after publishing five volumes of his work, he provided an official list of his secular and religious pieces. Thus, despite the paucity of biographical documentation of Calderón's life—caused in large part by his habit of keeping secret his social and private activities—his canon is definitive and relatively uncontested, and includes some 180 plays.

SIGNIFICANCE

Spanish literature, with the exception of a few masterpieces, is not nearly as widely known in Western culture at large as are French and English literature. Spain, while flourishing in its own cultural climate, did not export its ideas and creative artists. Spain's participation in the Thirty Years' War (1618-1648) promoted more crossbreeding of cultures, but it remained for the scholars of the nineteenth and twentieth centuries to renew the world's interest in Miguel de Cervantes, Lope de Vega, Tirso de Molina, and the other giants of Spanish literature.

Although his works were performed in some Euro-

pean countries during the eighteenth century, Pedro Calderón de la Barca's contributions to world literature have been only lately appreciated. His defense of royalist principles, in a time when the rising middle class was questioning monarchies elsewhere, makes even more remarkable his popularity and the currency of his ideas in today's humanistic studies. Furthermore, the dramatization of the philosophical question of free will versus predestination had found no greater craftsperson since the Greek tragedians. Finally, the *autos sacramentales* provide a religious continuity from the medieval pageant plays of all European countries to the modern work of T. S. Eliot and Christopher Fry. Calderón should not be considered a minor local phenomenon isolated by the Pyrenees from the mainstream of Western ideas, but rather a gifted, prolific, and articulate spokesperson for the universal themes of the late European Renaissance: man's relation to his God, his country, and his fellowman, and the nature of his being.

—Thomas J. Taylor

FURTHER READING

Aycock, Wendell M., and Sydney P. Cravens, eds. *Calderón de la Barca at the Tercentenary: Comparative Views*. Lubbock: Texas Tech Press, 1982. An important collection of papers published on the three-hundredth anniversary of Calderón's death. The essayists compare some of Calderón's contributions with other artistic impulses, such as German Idealist philosophy, Euripides, Mexican cleric characters, and William Shakespeare.

Cascardi, Anthony J. *The Limits of Illusion: A Critical Study of Calderón*. New York: Cambridge University Press, 1984. Valuable for the breadth and variety of its inquiry. Concentrates on Calderón's unique notion of the universal dramatic theme of illusion.

Fox, Dian. *Refiguring the Hero: From Peasant to Noble in Lope de Vega and Calderón*. University Park: University of Pennsylvania Press, 1991. Fox reevaluates nine plays by Lope de Vega and Calderón within the larger context of European literary heroism.

Gerstinger, Heinz. *Pedro Calderón de la Barca*. Translated by Diana Stone Peters. New York: Frederick Ungar, 1973. The first section features a description of Spain's Golden Age and its theater, and focuses on Calderón's dramaturgy, worldview, religious attitudes, modern interpretations, and permanent legacy. The second section provides analysis of nine plays.

Greer, Margaret Rich. *The Play of Power: Mythological Court Dramas of Calderón de la Barca*. Princeton,

N.J.: Princeton University Press, 1991. Some critics have denounced the plays Calderón wrote for the Habsburg court as servile flattery of royalty. Greer refutes this criticism, analyzing seven plays to demonstrate how they explore human life and social organization with artistic and thematic complexity.

Hesse, Everett W. *Calderón de la Barca*. Boston: Twayne, 1967. Treats the Spanish theater of the Golden Age, the political and social arena, the structure of Calderón's work, the works in which he excelled, and his critical reception. Particularly valuable is Hesse's discussion of such subgenres as cloak-and-sword plays, honor tragedies, and mythological plays.

Honig, Edwin. *Calderón and the Seizures of Honor*. Cambridge, Mass.: Harvard University Press, 1972. These essays were generated from Honig's translations of Calderón's plays in 1961 and 1970 and constitute the clearest, most easily accessible overviews of the plays available to readers.

Maraniss, James E. *On Calderón*. Columbia: University of Missouri Press, 1978. Stressing Calderón's sense of "order triumphant," Maraniss moves through his work, examining the structural integrity of each play, the symmetry and careful alternation of the plots, and the dramatic restatement of acknowledged social principles.

Mujica, Barbara Louise. *Calderón's Characters: An Existential Point of View*. Barcelona: Puvill, 1980. A strong work that examines the characters of Calderón's plays with an eye toward their existential choices and the sense of free will in the face of despair. Mujica claims that "the type of character—free and *en situation*—which is the hallmark of existentialist fiction is also the hallmark of seventeenth century Spanish theater, in particular, Calderón's."

Wardropper, Bruce W., ed. *Critical Essays on the Theatre of Calderón*. New York: New York University Press, 1965. Essays on Calderón's themes, characters, structure, political viewpoint, and theoretical perspectives. The opening article, by A. A. Parker, is a good summary of the justifications for ranking Calderón among the great writers of a great literary age.

SEE ALSO: Philip IV; Tirso de Molina; Lope de Vega Carpio.

RELATED ARTICLES in *Great Events from History: The Seventeenth Century, 1601-1700:* c. 1601-1682: Spanish Golden Age; 1605 and 1615: Cervantes Publishes *Don Quixote de la Mancha*; March 31, 1621-September 17, 1665: Reign of Philip IV; February, 1669-January, 1677: John of Austria's Revolts.

JACQUES CALLOT
French engraver and painter

Callot's technical innovations revolutionized etching and transformed it into an independent art. Etching became the preferred print medium of famous artists such as Rembrandt and Francisco Goya. Callot's genius was recognized during his lifetime, and his prints were sought after by art collectors and wealthy patrons.

BORN: 1592; Nancy, France
DIED: March 25, 1635; Nancy
AREAS OF ACHIEVEMENT: Art, patronage of the arts, science and technology

EARLY LIFE

Jacques Callot (zhahk kah-loh) was the son of Jean Callot, a courtier of the duke of Lorraine, Charles III, who was responsible for organizing and overseeing the court's festivities. When the duke died in 1608, Jean supervised the pompous funerary ceremonies. These activities integrated theatrical, visual, and musical components, proving an excellent introduction to the world of the arts for the young Callot.

In 1607, Callot began an apprenticeship in the shop of a Nancy medalist and goldsmith. In that year he produced his first signed print, an engraving portraying Duke Charles. It is not known whether Callot completed his apprenticeship, which would have lasted four years. It is quite possible that during the autumn of 1608 he moved to Rome; he was certainly there in 1611, working for the engraver Philippe Thomassin. In the eternal city, he came in direct contact with and was influenced by Antonio Tempesta and Francesco Villamena, two accomplished graphic artists. Among their various collaborative projects, Callot helped Tempesta with the series of prints commissioned for the funeral of the queen of Spain. For Thomassin, Callot reproduced several series of prints by famous artists, including *The Seasons*, engraved by Johan Sadeler after the sixteenth century paintings of Jacopo Bassano. Generally, Callot's 1611 prints demonstrate the progressive confidence he gained in handling the burin—the tool used to engrave copper plates. At the end of 1611, he traveled to Florence to deliver prints he had produced with Tempesta, and in Florence he remained.

LIFE'S WORK

Callot worked independently in Florence, becoming a Medici court artist formally in October of 1614. He was given a studio in the Uffizi and a generous monthly stipend, a salaried position that freed him from having to produce works for the art market and allowed him to concentrate on more creative projects. During his time in Florence, he made his most important prints, including the following series: *The Life of Ferdinand de' Medici*, *The Caprices*, *The War of Love*, and *The War of Beauty*. The latter two prints represent court festivals directed by Giulio Parigi. Also from this period are Callot's famous single prints, such as his first version of *The Temptation of Saint Anthony*, and finished drawings that would inspire the rest of his career.

The technical and artistic innovations presented in these prints are numerous, and they had a profound influence on graphic artists for centuries after Callot's time. Although etching was a technique developed around 1510 and successfully employed by masters such as Albrecht Dürer and Parmigianino, Callot devised several solutions that virtually revolutionized etching, expanding its range of expressiveness and making it the preferred graphic mode of expression for Rembrandt and Goya.

Callot's three crucial innovations include the instrument used to make the incisions, the preparation of the ground, and the perfecting of the multiple "biting" process, that is, the multiple immersions of the incised coated plate into an acid bath. His first innovation—the incising instrument—was developed out of Callot's interest in achieving the same variation in the breadth of the incised line procured by the rotation of the burin in engravings. To produce a swelling and tapering line, Callot replaced the etching needle with an instrument that had an oval-shaped point, allowing the needle to modulate the width of the furrow. Realizing line virtuosity depended upon Callot's new mixture for coating the copper plate. In fact, only a ground harder than the one that was commonly in use would have avoided cracks and retained the incised marks with precision. Thus, for his second innovation—preparing the ground—he sub-

Jacques Callot. (Hulton Archive/Getty Images)

stituted the traditional wax-based ground for one made of oil and mastic, similar to the varnish used by lute makers. His third innovation—perfecting the multiple biting of the etched plate—was a way to create printed lines of different intensity: Those lines etched last and exposed only to the last biting would be soft. Inked lines were created through repeatedly exposing the etched lines to acid baths, because the acid deepens the furrows. The deeper furrows, in turn, would retain more ink and thereby create a blacker line.

The etchings Callot produced in the early 1600's were revolutionary also from an artistic perspective: At this time his innovations concerned the character of the line, the rendition of space, and the choice of subject. Recalling painter Il Guercino's (Giovanni Francesco Barbieri) nervous strokes but maintaining a measured command of the line, Callot's etching style mixed spontaneity and academic virtuosity, eloquently demonstrating that a small number of marks is sufficient not only to define a figure but also to perfectly capture its character. Thus, the vivacity of his line infuses energy into figures and their surrounding, while the economy of his line allows for minute silhouettes to live next to the monumental figures without losing their identity.

Rather than simply filling space, the multitude of minuscule figures that populates Callot's prints delights the beholder, inviting him or her to peruse the print. This appreciation of prints reflects Callot's choice of not pursuing a powerful Baroque naturalism, which often requires the viewer to empathize with the scene portrayed. On the contrary, Callot intended his audience to remain emotionally detached so that he could represent charged subjects without being offensive or moralistic. This is epitomized by the prints in the famous series titled *Miseries of War*, published in 1633. In these prints the artist depicts with detached but poignant naturalism the horrific deeds of soldiers killing, raping, and pillaging; he documents timeless truths while exposing the dark side of human nature. Callot's creation of a detached but privileged position for the viewer of his etchings is predicated on an accurate construction of perspective. His compositions incorporate a distant theatrical space that is separated from the immediate foreground; this latter is often defined by a boundary figure with whom the beholder shares the view of the main scene presented at a distance.

Callot lost his Medici court appointment in 1621, following the death of Grand Duke Cosimo II de' Medici. He returned to Nancy, where he struggled for more than a year despite producing his best, and certainly most famous, print series, the *Gobbi and Other Bizarre Figures* (hunchbacks) and *Balli di Sfessania* (Sfessania dances). The *Gobbi and Other Bizarre Figures* are comic depictions of dwarfs and hunchbacks with grotesque faces, and the *Balli di Sfessania* represent pairs of figures from the *commedia dell'arte*. Beginning in 1623, Callot received the patronage of Henry II, the duke of Lorraine, and in the following years, as his fame grew, he accepted commissions from many important dignitaries, including Louis XIII, the king of France. Most of these commissions were large, celebratory scenes, most often sieges, military victories, or court festivals.

In 1635, Callot produced his second version of *The Temptation of Saint Anthony*, considered by many to be his final masterwork. This large print embodies all of his technical innovations, and it perfectly displays his artistic mastery of etching. The scene is set in a deep space that is given an atmospheric perspective, and it is populated by innumerable minute and several large demoniac creatures; despite their monstrous appearance, they do not threaten but instead delight the beholder. The beholder can safely peruse the creatures' horrific shapes and actions because the expansive center ground, where

the action is taking place, is framed by a backlighted, rocky cornice closer to the viewer's perceived space. Callot, by this time a famous etcher with more than fourteen hundred prints bearing his signature, died shortly after *The Temptation of Saint Anthony* was finished.

SIGNIFICANCE

Jacques Callot was the first artist to achieve international fame producing prints alone. Baroque connoisseurs recognized his inventive genius; they equally appreciated his mastery of the technical aspects of etching. His achievements and his legacy perhaps are best measured by recognizing the debts owed to Callot by the greatest etchers who followed him. Although he had accomplished followers by the middle of the seventeenth century, including Stefano della Bella, Giovanni Benedetto Castiglione, and Salvator Rosa, his best students remain Rembrandt and, in the nineteenth century, Goya. Rembrandt learned and expanded the range of Callot's technical subtleties, and he also found inspiration in Callot's *Caprices*. Goya's fame as a graphic artist derives primarily from his emulation of Callot's *Miseries of War*, which influenced his own *Disasters of War*, an even more moving series of prints.

—Renzo Baldasso

FURTHER READING

Howard, Daniel. *Callot's Etchings*. New York: Dover, 1974. An excellent introduction to the artist's most famous prints.

Hults, Linda. *The Print in the Western World: An Introductory History*. Madison: University of Wisconsin Press, 1996. Clear and comprehensive guide to the history of printmaking, with a section on printing techniques and processes. Extensive bibliography.

Jacques Callot, 1592-1635. Nancy, France: Musée Historique Lorrain, 1992. An exhibition catalog dedicated to the artist, with hundreds of fine reproductions of his prints and drawings.

Kahan, Gerald. *Jacques Callot: Artist of the Theater*. Athens: University of Georgia Press, 1976. A short but good introduction to the art of Callot's etchings.

Lieure, Jules. *Jacques Callot*. 2 vols. San Francisco, Calif.: Alan Wofsy Fine Arts, 1989. The reference catalogue raisonné for the artist's oeuvre. Includes chronology and biography.

Pellegrini, Franca. *Capricci Gobbi Amore Guerra e Bellezza*. Padua, Italy: Il Poligrafo, 2002. An exhibition catalog on the artist with an insightful introductory essay and other entries.

Reed, Sue Welsch, and Richard Wallace. *Italian Etchers of the Renaissance and Baroque.* Boston: Museum of Fine Arts, 1989. Exhibition catalog that is useful for its comparative material. Includes a separate section on Callot. Extensive bibliography.

Russel, Diane H. *Jacques Callot: Prints and Related Drawings.* Washington, D.C.: National Gallery of Art,

1975. Organized thematically, this exhibition catalog is perhaps the best volume in English on the artist.

SEE ALSO: Hishikawa Moronobu; Rembrandt.
RELATED ARTICLE in *Great Events from History: The Seventeenth Century, 1601-1700:* 1610-1643: Reign of Louis XIII.

GEORGE CALVERT
English statesman

Calvert served King James I as secretary of state and as a privy councillor until 1625, when he converted to Catholicism. James created him Lord Baltimore, and he spent the remaining years of his life gaining approval for a charter for the Maryland colony, a refuge for English Catholics.

BORN: 1579 or 1580; Kipling, Yorkshire, England
DIED: April 15, 1632; London, England
ALSO KNOWN AS: First Lord Baltimore
AREA OF ACHIEVEMENT: Government and politics

EARLY LIFE
George Calvert was born in 1579 or 1580 to Leonard and Grace Crossland Calvert in Kipling, Yorkshire. The Calvert family first appears in the records of Yorkshire in the mid-fourteenth century. In 1594, this successful merchant family had adequate resources to send George to Trinity College, Oxford University, where he graduated in 1597; he later received an honorary M.A. in 1605.

Calvert was married twice. His first marriage was to Anne Mynne (November 22, 1604); she was born on November 20, 1579, in Hertfordshire, England. Anne Mynne was the daughter of George Mynne and Elizabeth Wroth Mynne. The Wroth family had been prominent in English political life since the second half of the fourteenth century: Wroths had served as lord mayor of London and as political advisers to Henry VIII and Edward VI. Anne and George Calvert had eleven children together, several of whom became influential in the political and economic histories of England and Maryland.

Anne died on August 12, 1622. Shortly thereafter, Calvert married a second time to a person known only as Joan—no additional information has been found about the woman who would become the first Lady Baltimore. Calvert had one additional son with his second wife in 1626. Calvert traveled throughout Western and northern Europe in his years after Oxford; his intelligence and am-

bition attracted the attention of the future first earl of Salisbury, Robert Cecil; with Salisbury's influence and protection, Calvert would ascend quickly in the Jacobean government.

LIFE'S WORK
With family support and connections, Calvert gained access to Parliament in 1603 as a member for Bosmay, Cornwall (later in his political career, Calvert would represent Yorkshire and Oxfordshire). He came to Parliament the year of Elizabeth I's death and of the accession of a new dynasty and king—the Stuart, James I. The transition of monarchs and dynasties also coincided with the beginning of a new age that reflected the developing polarization of English society. On one hand, those who identified with the monarchy tended to be Anglicans, clandestine Catholics, the traditional landed aristocracy, and others whose interests or beliefs supported a strong monarchical power. On the other hand were those who supported a strong Parliament that would share power with the monarch, a new merchant class that wanted access to power for itself, and Puritans and other Calvinists. The beginning of the seventeenth century was also a period of exploration and colonization for England. The failure of Sir Walter Ralegh's Roanoke colony was followed by the difficult but ultimately successful colony at Jamestown in Virginia.

Calvert was industrious, ambitious, and loyal to James I and his ministers. He served as clerk of the Privy Council (1613) and as clerk of the Crown and assizes in County Clare, Ireland (1615-1617). He was knighted by James I as a reward for his work (1617); served as treasurer, appointed by James I as principal secretary of state (1619); and served as a member of the Virginia Company. As secretary of state (1619-1625), Calvert reached the zenith of his political power; during most difficult years in foreign and domestic politics, Calvert served as James I's primary adviser and minister. While the political environment did not improve—indeed, the fundamental differences between king and the Parliamentarians only deepened—James rewarded Calvert for his loyalty and service by granting him a manor house and 2,300 acres (931 hectares) in County Longford, Ireland, on February 18, 1621.

Throughout his life, Calvert had indicated repeatedly his interest in colonization. In 1609, he joined the Virginia Company, and in 1622, James granted his secretary of state the Avalon Peninsula, in Newfoundland. Calvert spent considerable resources attempting to develop Avalon; after visiting Avalon in 1627, he returned in 1628 and spent the winter of 1628-1629 along with about one hundred others. Calvert was devastated by the long Newfoundland winter and the deaths of ten colonists; he determined that the location did not warrant any further investment.

During the early 1620's, Calvert was moving to the right in his religious thinking and beliefs; his move toward Catholicism paralleled and opposed the growth of Puritanism. In 1625, Calvert announced his conversion to Catholicism and offered his resignation; at first, the

dying James I refused to accept it, but Calvert withdrew from active involvement in the life of the government. James, in response, augmented his gift of Irish land to his trusted adviser: Calvert formally entered the Irish peerage on February 12, 1625, when James created him Baron Baltimore of Baltimore, County Longford, Ireland.

After the failure of his efforts to develop a colony in Avalon, Calvert traveled to Virginia, where he hoped that he could identify a suitable location for a new settlement. By this time, he intended to establish a sanctuary for English Catholics, who were encountering increased persecution from the Puritans. The English governor of Virginia, John Harvey, welcomed Calvert but declared that Virginia was not a locale that Calvert could pursue: As a royal colony, Virginia required all colonists to take an oath recognizing the monarch as head of the Church in England.

During this same trip, however, Calvert became familiar with the Chesapeake Bay and the land north of the Potomac River to Delaware Bay. It was that area that he requested of King Charles I in a charter for a new colony.

Calvert worked on the charter and modeled it on a medieval palatinate. All powers were retained by the colony's founders, but, while the colony was intended to be a place where Catholics could worship in peace, there was no mention of a preferred denomination of Christianity in the charter. As a result, the declarations relating to Christianity in the colony effectively created safeguards guaranteeing religious freedom for all Christians. After a lengthy process, the formal charter for the Maryland Colony, named after Charles I's Catholic queen, Henrietta Maria, was granted on June 20, 1632, two months after Calvert's death on April 15. Calvert had died in London at the age of around fifty-three. The Charter was therefore granted to Calvert's son, Cecilius, who became the sole owner of the Maryland Colony. Cecilius Calvert, the second Lord Baltimore (1605-1675), is considered the founder of Maryland, even though he never visited it.

SIGNIFICANCE

The significance of the life and work of George Calvert, first Lord Baltimore, rests both on his years of service to King James I and on his later conversion to Catholicism and founding of the Maryland Colony as a haven for English Catholics. Baltimore effectively defended the policies and

George Calvert. (Hulton Archive/Getty Images)

practices of James I's government and served his king in several positions, including principal secretary of state, but he could not reverse the historical trends that threatened the Stuart monarchy.

Becoming a Catholic, Baltimore reflected the sentiments of a growing number of English aristocrats and, while he never visited Maryland nor lived long enough to receive the royal charter granting the Calverts a proprietary right to establish a colony north of the Potomac, he set in motion the process of establishing the Maryland Colony, intended for Catholic émigrés but also open to all Christians. Calvert's vision of religious toleration was progressive and at odds with the thought of most during the early seventeenth century.

—*William T. Walker*

FURTHER READING

Andrews, Charles M. *Our Earliest Colonial Settlements: Their Diversities of Origin and Later Characteristics.* Ithaca, N.Y.: Cornell University Press, 1966. Includes an excellent chapter on "Maryland: A Feudal Seignory in the New World," in which the role of Lord Baltimore in the founding of the colony is amply introduced.

Foster, James W. *George Calvert: The Early Years.* Baltimore: Maryland Historical Society, 1983. An excellent study of Calvert's life that addresses his childhood, his education at Oxford, and the early years of his career.

Krugler, John D. *English and Catholic: The Lords Baltimore in the Seventeenth Century.* Baltimore: Johns Hopkins University Press, 2004. A scholarly examination of George Calvert and his seventeenth century descendants; this is a critical and important study that should be of interest to the general reader, as well as students of history.

Lough, Loree, and Arthur M. Schlesinger, Jr. *Lord Baltimore: English Politician and Colonist.* New York: Chelsea House, 2000. A very good introduction to Calvert; raises a series of questions that may be of interest to students who are studying colonial American history. The best introduction for younger readers.

Nicklin, J. B. C. "The Calvert Family." *Maryland Historical Magazine* 16 (1921): 50-59. A reliable account of the life of George Calvert, first Lord Baltimore.

SEE ALSO: Charles I; Henrietta Maria; James I.

RELATED ARTICLE in *Great Events from History: The Seventeenth Century, 1601-1700:* March 24, 1603: James I Becomes King of England.

RICHARD CAMERON
Scottish religious leader

Although Cameron prepared for ordination in the Church of Scotland, he became a zealous Covenanter during the Restoration period in Britain. He was killed during a revolt against the established order, but his followers, the Cameronians, later established the Reformed Presbyterian Church.

BORN: c. 1648; Falkland, Fife, Scotland
DIED: July 22, 1680; Airds Moss (or Ayrsmoss), near Auchinleck, Ayrshire, Scotland
AREA OF ACHIEVEMENT: Religion and theology

EARLY LIFE

Virtually nothing is known of Richard Cameron's early life, but the world in which young Richard came of age was one of religious zealotry and war. In 1637, Charles I of England demanded that the Scottish Kirk use a new Book of Canons in all worship services. Scottish religious leaders declared the new liturgy to be "popish" and proposed a "Covenant" that bound Scots together in op-

position to the monarch's religion. This Covenant also purged the Kirk of the bishops that had been imposed upon Scottish Presbyterians by the episcopalian James I and established a theocratic government. Charles called upon Parliament to suppress the Scots, but disagreements between the king and Parliament ultimately led to the First English Civil War in 1642.

The Scots initially sided with Parliament against the king, but they joined the Royalist side in 1647. The Parliamentary army of Oliver Cromwell crushed the Scottish forces, however, and Scotland was placed under martial law. Cromwell's death in 1658 led to the Restoration of the monarchy, and Charles II acceded to the throne in 1660. The new government restored the official church and implemented the Clarendon Code, a series of laws that virtually disestablished Puritans and Presbyterians. The Act of Uniformity (1661) required all clergy and schoolmasters to accept the Book of Common Prayer. Those who refused to accept the Act of Uniformity were named Nonconformists, and the Conventicle Act (1664) prohibited them from having public religious meetings. Parliament did issue an Act of Indulgence (1667) permitting clergy to continue privately as Nonconformists if an outward appearance of conformity were retained. These religious decisions, which deeply divided the Scottish nation, provided the backdrop for Richard Cameron's revolutionary activities.

Cameron himself was born about 1648 to Allan Cameron, a general merchant in Falkland, and his wife, Margaret Paterson. He had at least two younger brothers, Michael and Alexander. In 1662, Richard Cameron's father borrowed £40 against his home so that his son could attend the University of St. Andrews. "Ricardus Camero[n]" was graduated in July, 1665, with a master of arts degree, and he likely pursued further theological studies until at least 1667. His first position was that of parish schoolmaster at Falkland, where he also served as precentor, or choir director, in the parish church.

At this time, in defiance of the Conventicle Act, public "field meetings" of devout Presbyterians were being held throughout Fifeshire. It is probable that Richard attended some of these meetings and was profoundly influenced by the religious fervor of the preachers. It is also likely that he then refused to accept either the Act of Uniformity or an indulgence, as church records indicate that the positions held by Cameron were vacant in 1674.

Cameron moved to Borthwick, near Edinburgh, where he served as chaplain to Lady Cavers and later as chaplain to the family of Sir William Scott. These private positions allowed him to follow his religious convictions in secret, but at some point in 1677, Cameron publicly refused to attend the local church. He resigned his position and began his public career.

LIFE'S WORK

By 1677, Cameron perceived his life's mission to be crusading against two major trends of seventeenth century Britain: religious conformity and political absolutism. A devout Covenanter, he believed that the religious principles for which Scots had died were being compromised by those who were interested only in political gain. He could not agree to a conciliatory policy with the official religious establishment and opposed any action that returned the Church of Scotland to pre-Covenant status. Cameron believed that the restoration of episcopacy (bishops), accomplished at the order of Charles II, was sinful, as were the offering and accepting of indulgences. Opposition to these policies was therefore the only course he could take to ensure his own personal salva-

tion. Just as important to Cameron was his belief that no church could have a secular ruler as head. To him, caesaropapism was anathema, and minions of the king, be they government agents, bishops, or clergy, were profane and tyrannical. His Covenanter conscience required that he not submit to what, to him, was clearly false doctrine.

It was not an age of toleration, and those who refused to conform to the official state church were subject to ruthless persecution by the government. Approximately one-fourth of the ministers in Scotland were deprived of their positions because of their refusal to accept the Act of Uniformity. Their replacements were generally inadequate, resulting in widespread disaffection for the established church. The government crushed one uprising in November, 1666, and many malcontents were hanged or banished to Barbados. In an effort at conciliation, the government offered indulgences, but most of the deprived ministers refused them, preferring instead to preach in the fields. Cameron was but one of many who became a field preacher, although he was one of the most eloquent. Cameron's passionate delivery often stirred strong emotions in the large crowds to which he spoke. Unfortunately, his strident denunciations of those who accepted indulgences or any who worked with the government alienated him from the majority of Presbyterians.

The brutal murder on May 3, 1679, of James Sharp, archbishop of St. Andrews and leader of the conciliation wing of Presbyterianism, precipitated a revolution against the government. The rebels issued the Rutherglen Declaration, which declared invalid any religious legislation enacted by the government since the Covenant of 1637. The rebellion was broken at Bothwell Bridge on June 22, but the victorious duke of Monmouth was deliberately generous to the rebels. He hoped to bring peace by allowing the rival religious groups to focus on their differences rather than by providing a unifying force in the form of a vindictive government.

Cameron himself was absent from Scotland during these events, having gone to Holland in late 1678 to meet with other refugees from the government's religious policy. While there, he was ordained by Separatist (those who desired a separation of church and state) ordained ministers in the old Scots Church in Rotterdam. Upon his return to Scotland in 1680, he found the Covenanter movement in disarray and the countryside under close watch by the government.

Undismayed, Cameron and his friends, including Donald Cargill, Thomas Douglas, and David Hackston, acted against the government. The Queensferry Paper, later called the Cameron's Covenant, bound subscribers to strict religious beliefs regarding doctrine, worship, and church government. On June 22, 1680, Cameron and twenty armed men marched to the market cross at Sanquhar and called for war against Charles II as monarch and for the exclusion of his brother James, duke of York, from the succession to the throne. The Sanquhar Declaration announced Cameron's rebellion against the Crown, but it was hardly a considerable threat to the government. It could not be ignored, however, and a price of five thousand merks was placed on Cameron's head. An additional bounty of three thousand merks was offered for the head of either Cargill or Douglas.

Cameron continued preaching in the fields south of Glasgow, exhorting his listeners to act against the government. On July 22, a Royalist troop caught his party at Airds Moss in Ayrshire. Before the short fight, Cameron is reputed to have prayed, "Lord spare the green and take the ripe." Cameron, his brother Michael, and most of his men were either killed in the combat that followed or captured and executed at the site. Cameron's head and hands were cut off and displayed in Edinburgh; the captured Hackston was tried and publicly executed in Edinburgh in much the same fashion as William Wallace had been almost three centuries earlier.

SIGNIFICANCE

The life's work of Cameron, the Lion of the Covenant, spanned only three short years and touched but few people during that time. His ministry is sparsely documented, for he left no written material of his own, and what written accounts exist are generally antithetical to his cause. He died a traitor to the Crown, and his cause was understood by few Presbyterians of his day. He was, to many, an uncompromising fanatic who challenged church and state at the same time. Yet this very unwillingness to compromise guaranteed his place in history.

Five years after Cameron's execution, Charles II died, leaving his Catholic brother James II as monarch. Within three years, James alienated significant elements within Britain, and in the Glorious Revolution of 1688, he was replaced by William III of Orange and Mary II Stuart. The Revolution Settlement that followed ended forever the concept of absolutism in Britain by establishing a separation of powers and a system of checks and balances within the government. A religious settlement separated church and state and provided for toleration of all religions except Catholicism. In some ways, the Sanquhar Declaration foreshadowed the political and reli-

gious events that took place within a decade, although it seems doubtful that Cameron would have agreed with some of the ensuing compromises.

Cameron's legacy may also be seen in two other areas: Scottish nationalism and Presbyterianism. In the nineteenth century, Scottish nationalists recalled Cameron and his tiny band as saints slaughtered for their religious beliefs. Cameron became a folk hero, portrayed as a defender of freedom against a ruthless government, as well as a Scot who defied the English. Again, it is doubtful that Cameron would have accepted such a role, for he was as intolerant as those who dispatched him. It is also significant that Cameron is considered but a footnote in modern Scottish historiography.

Cameron's religious bequest is perhaps more substantive than his political legacy, although much of the work was done by others. Cameronians were the most uncompromising and fundamentalist Presbyterians in Scotland. Later, under the leadership of John Macmillan, the Reformed Presbytery was established in 1743 and continued as a separate conservative voice in religious affairs until the late nineteenth century. Scottish Reformed Presbyterians were ultimately absorbed into a reunited Church of Scotland in 1929. Emigrant Reformed Presbyterians, particularly those in the American South, refused to participate in the civil affairs of an uncovenanted state. The religious descendants of Cameron continue as small, fundamentalist synods.

—*William S. Brockington, Jr.*

FURTHER READING

Cowan, Ian B. *The Scottish Covenanters, 1660-1688.* London: Victor Gollancz, 1976. Focuses on religious issues in Scotland following the restoration of Charles II. Cowan's primary emphasis is on those Scottish Presbyterians who refused to accept the established church, but background information regarding the controversies is included.

Foster, Walter Roland. *Bishop and Presbytery: The Church of Scotland, 1661-1688.* London: Spottiswoode, Ballantyne, 1958. Primarily a survey of the religious issues faced by the Kirk of Scotland in the Restoration era. Cameron's "radical" movement is dismissed with the observation that it attracted little support from religious moderates.

Henderson, Thomas Finlayson. "Richard Cameron." In *Dictionary of National Biography*, edited by Sir Leslie Stephen and Sir Sidney Lee. London: Oxford University Press, 1967. This reference work of significant British historic personages provides basic information on Cameron and is the least biased source of biographical data.

Herkless, John. *Richard Cameron.* Famous Scots Series. Edinburgh: Oliphant, Anderson, and Ferrier, 1896. The only biography of Cameron, the work suffers from the Scottish nationalistic attitude of the author. Cameron is viewed more as a martyr for Scottish freedom than as a religious zealot, but Herkless provides significant information and sources regarding the life of Cameron.

Howie, John. *The Scots Worthies.* Edited by W. H. Carslaw. Edinburgh, Scotland: Oliphant, Anderson, and Ferrier, 1870. Provides hagiographic biographies of Cameron, Cargill, and Hackston. Important only for understanding the evolution of Scottish nationalism.

Orr, Brian J. *As God Is My Witness: The Presbyterian Kirk, the Covenanters, and the Ulster Scots.* Bowie, Md.: Heritage, 2002. A history of the Scottish Covenanters, including biographies of Cameron and other people who were pivotal in the conflict between Scottish church and English crown.

Paterson, Raymond Campbell. *A Land Afflicted: Scotland and the Covenanter Wars, 1638-1690.* Edinburgh, Scotland: J. Donald, 1998. A study of religious dissent in seventeenth century Scotland.

Smellie, Alexander. *Men of the Covenant: The Story of the Scottish Church in the Years of the Persecution.* London: Billing and Sons, 1975. A reprint of an edition originally published in 1903. Surveys the period 1661-1688 from the perspective of those who opposed Charles II. Cameron is portrayed as a martyr to the Covenant.

Stevenson, David. *Union, Revolution, and Religion in Seventeenth Century Scotland.* Brookfield, Vt.: Variorum, 1997. Focuses on the Covenanters and their attempts to create a Scottish regime strong enough to be granted autonomy from England.

Stewart, Duncan. *The Covenanters of Teviotdale and Neighbouring Districts.* Edited by John Smith. Galashiels, Scotland: A. Walker & Son, 1908. Cameron's career in southeastern Scotland is surveyed in a brief synopsis of his life. Stewart, a Presbyterian minister, views Cameron as heroic, willing to lose everything for his conscience.

SEE ALSO: Charles I; Charles II (of England); Oliver Cromwell; James I; James II; Mary II; Duke of Monmouth; William III.

RELATED ARTICLE in *Great Events from History: The Seventeenth Century, 1601-1700:* March-June, 1639: First Bishops' War.

TOMMASO CAMPANELLA
Italian philosopher, theologian, and poet

Despite many years of imprisonment for religious and political nonconformity, Campanella wrote voluminous works promoting both philosophical speculation and scientific explorations. His book City of the Sun *is recognized as one of the classics in utopian literature.*

BORN: September 5, 1568; Stilo, Kingdom of Naples (now in Italy)
DIED: May 21, 1639; Paris, France
ALSO KNOWN AS: Giovanni Campanella
AREAS OF ACHIEVEMENT: Philosophy, literature, religion and theology

EARLY LIFE
Tommaso Campanella (tohm-MAHZ-oh kahm-pah-NEHL-lah), baptized with the name Giovanni Campanella, was the son of an illiterate shoemaker in a small town of southern Italy. At a young age, he impressed adults with his remarkable memory, and when five years

old, he was able to repeat the sermons of the priests at church. Too poor to attend the local school, he first learned to read and write by listening outside the window of the school. By the age of thirteen, he had read all the Latin works available in his town.

Campanella was attracted to the Dominicans because of the great value they placed on preaching and on the scholarship of Saint Thomas Aquinas. In 1582, before his fifteenth birthday, he entered the nearby Dominican monastery as a novitiate. He later said that he entered the priesthood because there was no other way for a poor boy to pursue an intellectual career. When taking his priestly vows in 1583, he adopted the name Tommaso. He was then sent to the monastery of San Giorgio to study philosophy, which at that time concentrated almost entirely in the study of Aristotle. Soon he was demonstrating an independent spirit and resisting the efforts of his teachers at indoctrination.

In 1586, Campanella was transferred to the monastery at Nicastro. Increasingly, he grew dissatisfied with Aristotelian philosophy, particularly the doctrine of hylemorphism, which explained objects of nature as based on their underlying forms. He irritated his teachers with his constant arguments. Imbued with the questioning spirit of the late Renaissance, he read voraciously in the writings of ancient and contemporary philosophers, and he was particularly influenced by Plato and the Neoplatonic works of Marsilio Ficino. He also studied skeptical writers such as the ancient Greeks Pyrrho and Democritus. One night he cried as he thought about the logical weaknesses of the arguments for immortality of the soul.

Admitted to the theological seminary at Cosenza in 1588, Campanella became familiar with the writings of a local Humanist, Bernardino Telesio, whose views corresponded to his own. Telesio advocated the empirical study of nature rather than appealing to authority, and he accepted the validity of spiritual illumination. When the aging Humanist died before he could arrange a meeting, Campanella composed a Latin eulogy to the memory of "the prince of philosophers." Transferred to the rural monastery at Altomonte, Campanella became indignant when he read Giacomo Marta's book attacking Telesio's principles. He felt compelled to write a response.

LIFE'S WORK

In 1589, Campanella composed his first book, *Philosophia sensibus demonstrata* (pb. 1591; philosophy demonstrated by the senses). Defending Telesio as a Christian philosopher worthy of esteem, Campanella attacked Aristotle as an impious pagan who did not believe in an afterlife. He also asserted that contemporary Peripatetics, or Aristotelians, were heretics. Although the work did not deny any basic Christian doctrines, leaders of the Dominican order viewed it as an attack on their authority. Finding life at the monastery unpleasant, Campanella moved to the city of Naples, where he was received in the home of a nobleman, Mario del Tufo.

Naples was an exciting place for a curious young person from a small town. Campanella became actively associated with a famous author, Giambattista della Porta, whose circle conducted simple experiments in physics and magic. By the end of 1590, Campanella had written *De sensu rerum et magia* (pb. 1620; on the sense and feeling of all things and on magic), which became the most influential and widely ready of his philosophical works. It was here that he first recorded his developing pansensism, the speculative theory that the entire universe is alive and sentient. At the same time, he began to write a projected series of twenty books devoted to the philosophy of nature.

In May of 1592, Campanella was arrested after a fellow friar denounced him as a heretic practicing demoniac magic. Following a four-month trial, Dominican authorities in Naples pronounced a mild sentence, which included penitential prayer, affirmation of Aquinas's theology, repudiation of Telesio, and a return to the monastery in Calabria. Instead of returning, however, Campanella traveled to Rome, Florence, and Padua in an unsuccessful effort to obtain a professorship in philosophy. In Padua in 1593, he established a friendship with Galileo and would later write a defense of Galileo's investigations. Also, he was prosecuted in Padua on charges of homosexuality, but he was acquitted, His later poetry, however, suggests there might have been some truth to the "accusation."

In this age of Counter-Reformation and Inquisition, Campanella's views were considered dangerous. Although he defended basic Catholic doctrines on matters such as salvation, biblical miracles, and the seven sacraments, he tended to interpret doctrines metaphorically rather than literally. Inspired by Renaissance Neoplatonism, he asserted a form of pantheism, the idea that all reality is infused with a spiritual essence. Every human mind, moreover, makes up part of a larger whole, and spiritual knowledge comes not from the senses but from an innate self-awareness. This worldview was somewhat difficult to harmonize with the claims that Christianity possesses ultimate truth based on a unique revelation. In 1594, the Holy Office in Padua arrested Campanella and sent him to Rome for trial, where he was condemned to make a public adjuration. After another imprisonment in 1597-1598, he returned to the monastery of his native Stilo.

As the new century approached, Campanella began preaching that signs and prophecies were pointing to the coming of a millenarian government under the authority of the pope. To bring about this universal cleansing, he said it would be necessary to end Spanish rule in Naples and Calabria. The political and religious authorities of Italy would not tolerate such talk.

On September 6, 1599, Campanella, betrayed by friends, was arrested and taken to Naples in chains. During a series of trials, he was tortured four times on the rack—once for thirty-six hours. His feigning of insanity probably saved his life. On November 13, 1602, the Holy Office sentenced him to life imprisonment. He would spend twenty-seven years in prison, much of the time in dark dungeons.

During the trial, Campanella completed the most famous of his works, *La città del sole* (pb. 1623; *City of the Sun*, 1886), in which the captain of a merchant vessel describes a utopian society where everyone was happy and had the equal obligation to work four hours each day. The society had no nuclear families or private property, and it fused secular and religious authority. Campanella apparently envisioned the utopia as a model for a universal monarchy ruled by a priest-king.

After making numerous appeals to Rome for clemency, he was finally released by Pope Urban VIII in 1626. Campanella then moved into the monastery at Frascati, where he continued to write books that attracted the attention of the Inquisition. He was jailed once again in 1628-1629. When faced with even more accusations in 1634, King Louis XIII and Cardinal de Richelieu agreed to give him refuge in France, where he was awarded a pension and allowed to continue his writing. Occasionally, he praised Richelieu as possibly a universal ruler, but few people paid much attention. He was seventy years old when he died at the Dominican convent of St.-Honoré in Paris.

SIGNIFICANCE

Sometimes called "the last great philosopher of the Renaissance," Campanella was a major participant in the intellectual debates of his day, and he anticipated several philosophical currents of the next two centuries, including René Descartes's method of universal doubt in the pursuit of knowledge. His challenges to the orthodoxies of his time encouraged others to question religious authority. Even though he practiced magic, his emphasis on empirical investigation of nature probably had some influence on the development of modern science.

His best-known work, *City of the Sun*, was not especially original, but it has attracted many admirers over the centuries. It is possible that Francis Bacon read the work before developing his own utopian vision.

—*Thomas Tandy Lewis*

FURTHER READING

Bonansea, Bernardino. *Tommaso Campanella: Renaissance Pioneer of Modern Thought*. Washington, D.C.: Catholic University of America Press, 1969. Gives an adequate account of Campanella's life and a useful analysis of his writings.

Campanella, Tommaso. *The City of the Sun*. Translated by A. M. Elliott and R. Millner. Introduction by A. L. Morton. West Nyack, N.Y.: Journeyman Press, 1981. Campanella's best-known literary work, a utopian text.

Copenhaven, Brian, and Charles Schmitt. *Renaissance Philosophy*. New York: Oxford University Press, 1992. A favorable analysis of Campanella that emphasizes his scientific and anti-Aristotelian views.

Garber, Daniel, and Michael Ayers, eds. *The Cambridge History of Seventeenth-Century Philosophy*. 2 vols. New York: Cambridge University Press, 1998. A standard work organized into broad philosophical themes, but not particularly helpful for the study of individual philosophers.

Headley, John. *Tommaso Campanella and the Transformation of the World*. Princeton, N.J.: Princeton University Press, 1997. An excellent examination of Campanella's political and religious writings, within the context of the intellectual life of the century.

Manuel, Frank, and Fritzie Manuel. *Utopian Thought in the Western World*. Oxford, England: Basil Blackwood, 1979. A detailed account of the significant utopian writers from Plato to the late twentieth century. Highly recommended.

Tod, Ian, and Michael Wheeler. *Utopias*. New York: Harmony Books, 1977. Provides a good but relatively short summary of Campanella and other utopian thinkers, with many beautiful illustrations.

Walker, D. P. *Spiritual and Demonic Magic: From Ficino to Campanella*. University Park: Pennsylvania State University Press, 2000. Demonstrates that magic was considered a respectable science from the fifteenth through the seventeenth centuries.

SEE ALSO: René Descartes; Galileo; Louis XIII; Marin Mersenne; Nicolas-Claude Fabri de Peiresc; Cardinal de Richelieu; Urban VIII.

RELATED ARTICLE in *Great Events from History: The Seventeenth Century, 1601-1700:* 1610-1643: Reign of Louis XIII.

THOMAS CAMPION
English poet and composer

A talented poet and musician, Campion became an important figure in the development of the English song in the early seventeenth century. As one of the most successful English composers of the court masque, Campion continued the development of a style of English music initiated by John Dowland.

BORN: February 12, 1567; London, England
DIED: March 1, 1620; London
AREAS OF ACHIEVEMENT: Literature, music

EARLY LIFE

Thomas Campion (CAMP-ee-uhn) was born in London on February 12, 1567, to John and Lucy Campion. John Campion was a successful law clerk who had been appointed to the Chancery Court in 1565. Although John Campion died when Thomas was only nine years old, his professional interests seem to have had an early influence on his son, who ten years later entered Gray's Inn, one of the leading law schools in London. Lucy Campion, Thomas's mother, died only a few years after her husband, in 1580, and Thomas was subsequently sent to Cambridge University in 1581. He left Cambridge in 1584 without a degree, although the reason for his leaving the university is unknown.

When Campion entered Gray's Inn in 1586, he made several important acquaintances among his fellows, many of whom were aspiring poets and writers. Campion's study of law (if, indeed, he studied it at all) was unremarkable, but while at the school, he participated in and organized several entertainments. It was during his tenure at Gray's Inn, for example, that Campion coauthored his first masque, *The Masque of Proteus and the Adamantine Rock* (1594), with Francis Davison. The work was performed before Queen Elizabeth. In 1592, Campion traveled to Rouen, France, as part of an expedition against Spanish invaders commanded by the earl of Essex. Campion returned to England shortly thereafter, and, still living on the inheritance following the death of his mother, he devoted himself to a literary career in earnest.

LIFE'S WORK

Before Campion had traveled to France as part of Essex's expedition, he had written only a few poems, many of which were composed as exercises in Latin poetry. In 1591, five of Campion's poems were published in a vol-ume devoted to Philip Sidney's *Astrophel and Stella* (pirated ed. 1591, authorized ed. 1598), an important collection of sonnets that had already been circulating among London's literary circles. Four years later, Campion published his own volume of poetry, the *Poemata* (1595), which contained several types of Latin poems, many of which were dedicated to the leading English poets of the day (George Chapman, Philip Sidney, and Edmund Spenser).

While Campion was relatively productive as a poet (mostly in Latin genres) through the end of the sixteenth century, he became increasingly adept as both a poet and a musical composer after 1600. It was around this time that Campion became close friends with Philip Rosseter, one of England's leading lutenists. Campion's public contribution to the tradition of English poetry and music had its start in 1601, when several of his songs appeared in *A Booke of Ayres* (1601). The book was published as a collaborative effort with Rosseter, and it contained approximately an equal number of songs by each.

English music had undergone a major development throughout the 1590's, as the lyric song had begun to replace the madrigal as the dominant musical form, in large part because of the contributions made by John Dowland. The English madrigal was typically a polyphonic composition, with relatively complex harmonies and often including word-painting (a musical device in which words in the text are musically depicted or "illustrated"). Songs, or airs, on the other hand, were lighter in texture and placed more significance on the verbal text; they tended to be more homophonic using only a single musical note in correspondence with each single word or syllable. Campion's music very much followed the tradition that had been inaugurated by Dowland, and Campion eventually became one of the most prolific publishers of songs in seventeenth century England. His most well-known collections include *Two Bookes of Ayres* (1613) and *The Third and Fourth Booke of Ayres* (1617).

Campion traveled again to the Continent in 1602 to study medicine, and in 1605, he received a medical degree from the University of Caen. Campion's motives for taking up medicine are not clear, although it has been speculated that his inheritance had run out by this time and that he was attempting to find a regular source of income. When he returned to England, in addition to practicing medicine, Campion composed several masques that were performed before the court, including *Lord*

CAMPION'S MAJOR WORKS

1595	*Poemata*
1601	*A Booke of Ayres* (with Philip Rosseter)
1602	*Observations in the Art of English Poesie*
1607	*Lord Hay's Masque*
1613	*The Lord's Masque*
1613	*The Caversham Entertainment*
1613	*The Somerset Masque*
1613	*Two Bookes of Ayres*
1613	*Songs of Mourning*
c. 1617	*A New Way of Making Fowre Parts in Counter-point*
1617	*The Third and Fourth Booke of Ayres*
1618	*The Ayres That Were Sung and Played at Brougham Castle*
1619	*Thomae Campiani Epigrammatum Libri II*

madrigal as the principal musical form among English composers.

From a historical or critical standpoint, Campion is a fruitful case study for the relationship between poetry and musical thought in Renaissance England, since he not only composed both poetry and music but also wrote two significant treatises dealing directly with versification and musical counterpoint. Although his call for a return to Latin versification was not heeded (even by himself), his interest in continental theories of poetry made him an important conduit for the transfer of ideas about poetry and music to England in the seventeenth century. Campion died in London on March 1, 1620. He never married or had children; at his death, he bequeathed all his possessions to his longtime friend Philip Rosseter.

—*Joseph M. Ortiz*

FURTHER READING

Bevington, David, and Peter Holbrook, eds. *The Politics of the Stuart Court Masque.* New York: Cambridge University Press, 1998. Includes several articles on the court masque and its political functions in Renaissance England. Campion is mentioned throughout, and Bevington's essay on Shakespeare's *The Tempest* in this volume considers at length Campion's influence on Renaissance drama. Illustrations, musical examples, bibliography.

Campion, Thomas. *The Works of Thomas Campion.* Edited by Walter R. Davis. New York: Doubleday, 1967. The best single-volume collection of Campion's works, with selections from the early poems, the four books of *Ayres*, Latin poems, songs (some reproduced with the original music), and the two treatises. Includes a brief introduction, biographical outline, illustrations, and bibliography.

Davis, Walter R. *Thomas Campion.* Boston: Twayne, 1987. A concisely written study of Campion's life work, including an introductory biographical chapter. Subsequent chapters focus separately on Campion's songs, poems, musical compositions, treatises, and masques, and the final chapter treats Campion's reputation and influence from his lifetime to the present. Includes a short chronology and selected bibliography.

Lindley, David. *Thomas Campion.* Leiden: E. J. Brill, 1986. A well-written study of Campion's poetry and musical compositions, as well as their interrelationship. The first two chapters cover Campion's poetry and music, respectively, while the third chapter considers how the poetry and music inform each other.

Hay's Masque (1607), *The Lord's Masque* (1613), *The Caversham Entertainment* (1613), and *The Somerset Masque* (1613).

In addition to his poetry and music, Campion wrote two significant theoretical works during his lifetime. His *Observations in the Art of English Poesie* (1602) criticized the popular English habit of rhyming in poetry, and it argued for a return to classical methods of versification. The book inspired vehement criticism by another well-known poet, Samuel Daniel, who published *A Defense of Rhyme* (1603) largely as a rebuttal to Campion's treatise. Campion also wrote *A New Way of Making Fowre Parts in Counter-point* (c. 1617), a musical treatise that established methods for composing harmonic sequences with the standard four-part structure. The treatise was considered innovative among English theories of composition, and it introduced into England ideas about music that Campion had learned from Continental theorists (most notably Sethus Calvisius of Leipzig).

SIGNIFICANCE

Even among the finest examples of Renaissance poetry, Campion's poems are exceptional for their lyricism and lightness. His musical compositions, although perhaps not as highly celebrated as his poems, are themselves excellent examples of the English lyric song in the early seventeenth century, and Campion's lute songs (along with John Dowland's) are frequently regarded as the finest examples of the genre. In this respect, Campion was a leading figure in the development of the English song, which at the turn of the century had begun to replace the

The final chapter is devoted to Campion's contribution to the masque. Several musical examples, short bibliography.

_____, ed. *Court Masques: Jacobean and Caroline Entertainments, 1605-1640*. Oxford, England: Clarendon Press, 1995. Includes a number of Campion's masques, as well as a general introduction that discusses the form and function of court entertainments in seventeenth century England. Illustrations, bibliography.

Wilson, Christopher. *Words and Notes Coupled Lovingly Together: Thomas Campion, a Critical Study*. New York: Garland, 1989. An analysis of Campion's poetic, musical, and theoretical works with respect to their historical context. As with most single-volume studies of Campion, this book includes individual chapters on the poetry, music, theory, and masques. Includes an overview of previous commentary on Campion. Illustrations, musical examples, bibliography.

SEE ALSO: Arcangelo Corelli; Girolamo Frescobaldi; Orlando Gibbons; Henry Lawes; Claudio Monteverdi; Henry Purcell.

RELATED ARTICLES in *Great Events from History: The Seventeenth Century, 1601-1700:* c. 1601: Emergence of Baroque Music; February 24, 1607: First Performance of Monteverdi's *La favola d'Orfeo*; 1619-1622: Jones Introduces Classicism to English Architecture; February 24, 1631: Women First Appear on the English Stage; September 2, 1642: Closing of the Theaters.

CANONICUS
Grand sachem of the Narragansett tribe (r. before 1600-1647)

Leader of the Narragansetts when the first English colonists arrived at Plymouth in 1620, Canonicus was one of the most influential political figures during New England's formative years. Despite English provocations, he refused to join the Pequots in their war against the colonists, and he provided aid to the Rhode Island exile Roger Williams.

BORN: c. 1565; place unknown
DIED: June 4, 1647; place unknown
AREAS OF ACHIEVEMENT: Government and politics, diplomacy, warfare and conquest

EARLY LIFE
Canonicus (kuh-NAHN-ih-kuhs) is believed to have been born sometime around 1565, and his first known dwelling place was on the western shore of Narragansett Bay, in what is now Rhode Island. Narragansett Bay is thus the most likely location of his birth, but no reliable evidence as to his actual birthplace exists. He was born to wealth and status: His grandfather Tashtassuck, the earliest recorded Narragansett sachem (the political, military, and spiritual leader of the tribe), was still legendary for his wisdom and courage when Canonicus was an old man. The status of the other tribes of the region—the Pequots to the west and the Wampanoags across the bay to the east—among the Narragansetts is indicated by the tradition that when the time came for Tashtassuck to marry his son and daughter, he could find no suitable matches among the neighboring tribes. Consequently, he was said to have married the siblings to each other.

Canonicus, the eldest of four sons of this match, probably ruled jointly with his father or grandfather as soon as he came of age, a Narragansett practice that ensured dynastic continuation while providing youth and strength in tribal leadership. The Narragansett nation had a hierarchical system of sub-sachems, each ruling at the pleasure of the great sachem. By 1600, Canonicus held this position, ruling a nation of some thirty thousand. Later in his reign, Canonicus continued the practice of joint rule with a younger kinsman, but, although Canonicus had a son named Mriksah or Meika, it was his nephew Miantonomo, son of his younger brother Mascus, whom Canonicus made his heir apparent and junior sachem.

LIFE'S WORK
Canonicus appears in the records of the Plymouth Colony from its inception, though the colony's relations with Massasoit (also known as Ousamequin) of the Wampanoags are better known. In 1621, Canonicus sought a treaty with the struggling colony, which instead signed a "covenant" with the Wampanoags that included a mutual defense pact. Since the Wampanoags had formerly held allegiance to Canonicus, this was a potentially belligerant act.

The affront may have resulted in a war threat from Canonicus in 1622, though the previously accepted facts of the case have now been called into question by historians. William Bradford's *History of Plymouth Plantation* (wr. 1630-1650, pb. 1856) asserts that the Narragansetts sent a bundle of arrows wrapped in a snake skin to Plymouth as a threat of war and that the governor (then Bradford himself) returned the same skin filled with powder and shot. It is unlikely that such a response would have deterred Canonicus had he really sought war; Plymouth gunpowder notwithstanding, the hundred or so colonists could not have prevailed against a nation of thirty thousand.

When the more organized and much larger Massachusetts Bay Colony was established in 1630, Canonicus sought a covenant with them as well. His name first appears in the colony's records in 1633, when a Boston inquest found him and his nephew Miantonomo innocent of the murder of Captain John Oldham at the hands of the Pequots, though a few Narragansetts were implicated in the death. Oldham had taken an exploration party deep into Pequot territory on the upper Connecticut River, apparently carrying the smallpox virus, to which Native Americans were more susceptible than the Europeans who had generations of exposure to it. Canonicus lost more than seven hundred of his subjects to the disease that winter.

The following year, the Pequots, increasingly displaced by the new colonists, encroached on Narragansett hunting grounds, and Canonicus declared war with them. Massachusetts brokered a peace between the tribes, but by 1635, the Wampanoags threatened the Narragansett from the other side, and Canonicus went to war again. The following year, dissenters against the Massachusetts Bay orthodoxy, Roger Williams foremost among them, looked to Canonicus to provide them living space denied them by the Puritan authorities. These founders of what would become Rhode Island started a new precedent by paying for the lands they were granted. On March 24, 1637, William Coddington bought Aquidneck Island for 40 fathoms of white wampum; the deed names Canonicus and Miantonomo. That summer, English troops marched into the Mystic River Valley, where the Pequots held a fortified settlement. Canonicus sent one hundred warriors with the English, since he was still at war with the Pequots, but they were sickened by the massacre of their starving and diseased former enemies.

In 1642, a son of Canonicus, perhaps the Mriksah mentioned in early chronicles, died. While he had passed over his son to name his nephew junior sachem of their people, Canonicus clearly loved his son. Indeed, the elder Sachem's love for his son was great enough for the incident to be recorded in Narragansett oral tradition. Af-

ter burying his son, Canonicus registered his grief by burning his lodge, along with all of the son's belongings. His grief increased in 1643, when the Mohegans, the larger nation of whom the Pequots were a sept, moved into Pequot territory and harried the Narragansett, and the Mohegan sachem Uncas killed Miantonomo. Knowing that the Boston authorities were complicit in the younger sachem's death (they had promised Miantonomo protection then turned him over to Uncas), Canonicus responded in a bold move that demonstrated the depth of his comprehension of the colonial political situation. He renounced all ties with Boston and declared the Narragansetts to be under the direct protection of the king of England.

Unfortunately, he had no way of knowing that King Charles I had problems of his own with Puritans in England, who had seized control of Parliament and kept him under house arrest. Nevertheless, Canonicus had had enough of Boston's claims of authority in the region. When the governor called him to Boston in the spring of 1644, he refused to go. When Boston magistrates came to his village to investigate, Canonicus kept them waiting for two hours in the rain before letting them into his lodge. On April 19, 1644, he signed a treaty acknowledging Great Britain as the only sovereign authority in the colonies.

The last years of Canonicus's life saw a waning of Narragansett authority. Canonicus mostly deferred to the new junior sachem, Miantonomo's brother Pessecus, who ruled solely upon the death of Canonicus on June 4, 1647.

SIGNIFICANCE

Despite the preferential treatment the New England colonies gave to the enemies of Canonicus, colonial writers paint a surprisingly flattering portrait of the great sachem's pacifism, his honesty, and his generosity. Roger Williams credited Canonicus with saving his life with his hospitality in Rhode Island, and more than fifty years before Henry Wadsworth Longfellow's *The Song of Hiawatha* (1855), John Lathrop, Jr., made the sachem the hero of an epic poem, *The Speech of Caunonicus: Or, An Indian Tradition* (1802). Thus, more than 150 years after the death of Canonicus, a minor Boston poet remembered him as the sachem who had met the first colonists. Lathrop likened Canonicus to Moses, leading his people through the oppression of a more powerful and alien king.

Two hundred years after the passing of Canonicus, Henry David Thoreau recalled New England traditions of the great sachem serving boiled chestnuts at council feasts. A modern historian of Rhode Island, Sydney V. James, has attributed the form of the Rhode Island colony largely to the policies of Canonicus. Canonicus showed himself an able military leader against the Wampanoags and Pequots, but equally skilled in peacemaking, even in the face of Puritan belligerence.

—*John R. Holmes*

FURTHER READING

Doherty, Craig A. *The Narragansett*. Vero Beach, Fla.: Rourke, 1994. This very brief (31 pp.) pamphlet provides an overview of the tribe led by Canonicus; includes maps and period illustrations.

James, Sydney V. *Colonial Rhode Island: A History*. New York: Scribner, 1975. A thorough treatment of the early history of Narragansett Bay, with a relatively sympathetic account of Canonicus's role in the English settlement of the area.

_____. *Three Visitors to Early Plymouth: Letters About the Pilgrim Settlement in New England During Its First Seven Years*. Plymouth, Mass.: Plimoth Plantation, 1963. Primary documents from the time of the first English contacts with Canonicus.

Lathrop, John, Jr. *The Speech of Caunonicus*. Calcutta, India: Hircirrah Press, 1802. This brief epic, though a fictionalized account of the sachem's first encounter with Europeans, shows how his memory was preserved in early republican New England.

Rubertone, Patricia E. *Grave Undertakings: An Archaeology of Roger Williams and the Narragansett Indians*. Washington, D.C.: Smithsonian Institute Press, 2001. While this is a work of archaeology rather than history, it provides useful sociological background to the Narragansetts of the time of Canonicus.

SEE ALSO: Charles I; Massasoit; Roger Williams.

RELATED ARTICLES in *Great Events from History: The Seventeenth Century, 1601-1700:* 1617-c. 1700: Smallpox Epidemics Kill Native Americans; December 26, 1620: Pilgrims Arrive in North America; June, 1636: Rhode Island Is Founded; July 20, 1636-July 28, 1637: Pequot War; 1642-1651: English Civil Wars.

ROBERT CARR
Scottish politician

A favorite of King James I of England, Carr steadily gained political power and wealth, until he was implicated in one of the most famous murders in English history.

BORN: c. 1587; Scotland
DIED: July 17, 1645; London, England
ALSO KNOWN AS: Robert Ker; Robert Kerr; Earl of Somerset; Viscount Rochester
AREA OF ACHIEVEMENT: Government and politics

EARLY LIFE

Little is known of Robert Carr before his emergence as a favorite of King James I. Born about 1587, Carr was the son of Sir Thomas Ker of Ferniehurst, near Edinburgh, Scotland, who had attempted to assist James's first favorite, Esmé Stuart, duke of Lennox, and James's mother, the Catholic Mary, Queen of Scots. James did not forget such loyalty, although he had tacitly consented to his mother's execution in order to gain the English throne. Carr also had the protection of the earl of Dunbar, by whom he had probably been employed. First a page at James's English court, Carr then apparently spent some time in France. On his return, possibly with Dunbar's help, he became a groom of the royal bedchamber, a post that brought him continually into the presence of the king. What James saw was a personable, handsome young man. The weaknesses that would end Carr's career—his lack of education, stupidity, vanity, stubbornness, insensitivity, and pride—were not yet important.

Carr was not the king's first male favorite, but the king's uninhibited display of affection for him drew considerable attention. It is not known whether the king was actively homosexual, then an offense that could be punished by death. Separated from his mother in infancy and witness to the bloody shooting death of one grandfather, James, as infant king, lived under three regents in his first five years. Insecure and surrounded by strong, violent men and subservient, dependent women, James certainly, with some desperation, sought emotional support from other men. Whatever his sexual life, James's behavior brought down public censure on both himself and his favorites.

LIFE'S WORK

Despite England's weak economic condition, James lavished wealth and titles on his favorites, again incurring public displeasure. Carr rapidly gained both. In 1607, now a knight, he was made gentleman of the bedchamber. In 1608, after several substantial gifts of money, James, extremely short of funds, gave Carr the estate of the popular Sir Walter Ralegh, who had been condemned (if temporally reprieved) and whose property consequently was seized by the crown. Ralegh wrote an impassioned letter begging Carr not to deprive his family of this estate, but James refused to reconsider.

In 1611, Carr was made Viscount Rochester; this made him the first Scottish member of the English House of Lords. That same year, he was made knight of the garter and, in 1612, privy counselor. Although resident in England, he was appointed to Scotland's Privy Council and named lord treasurer of Scotland in 1613. He also was made warden of the cinque ports and lord privy seal. Most of his appointments offered opportunity for financial gain.

After the 1612 death of James's principal secretary, Sir Robert Cecil, earl of Salisbury, the king did not appoint a new secretary. Instead, Carr assumed the responsibility for serious government decisions, a responsibility he was not intellectually equipped to bear. In his need, he relied on an old friend, Sir Thomas Overbury, to handle correspondence and make decisions. Overbury was a minor writer whose death made him famous. His poem *The Wife* (1614), licensed for publication in 1613 while Overbury yet lived, went through five editions the following year. It was published with a collection of character sketches, the *Characters*, some of which were written by Overbury and others of which have been attributed to John Webster, Thomas Dekker, and John Donne. Overbury was tactless, ambitious, and argumentative; his new power badly affected his judgment. If Carr ruled the king, Overbury believed that he ruled Carr.

Overbury and Carr were brought into conflict in 1612, when Carr was attracted to Frances Howard, daughter of the powerful earl of Suffolk. The Howards were a powerful, traditionally Catholic family. (Although the practice of Catholicism was illegal under James I, there were many clandestine Catholics in England, probably including James's queen, Anne of Denmark.) At age thirteen, Frances Howard had been married to Robert Devereux, third earl of Essex, the son of Queen Elizabeth I's favorite. Howard was determined, however, to escape her marriage to Essex and to marry Carr. She moved to have the marriage annulled on the grounds that her husband was impotent with her.

James, who would deny his favorites nothing, put pressure on the clerics who were to hear the case, and the annulment was granted, creating another scandal. Overbury, who had approved of Carr's affair with Howard, was appalled at the thought of a marriage; the marriage and the patronage of the Howard family would inevitably reduce Overbury's own power. To get Overbury out of the way, James had him imprisoned in the Tower of London on April 21, 1613; he died there on September 15, 1613. In October, 1613, Carr became earl of Somerset, so that his wife, formerly countess of Essex, could remain a countess. Their marriage took place on December 26, 1613, with great celebration funded by the king.

Like Overbury, Carr allowed his newfound power to affect his judgment. He became cold and insulting to the king. By 1615, when rumors about Overbury's death led to a formal investigation, Carr had been replaced by a new favorite, George Villiers, first duke of Buckingham. In September, 1615, Sir Gervase Elwes, lieutenant of the tower, confessed that, while he had managed to keep Richard Weston, deputy tower keeper, from poisoning Overbury, Sir Thomas had indeed been poisoned. Implicated were Anne Turner, a Catholic friend of Frances Howard, and the countess herself, who had hated Overbury for his opposition to her marriage.

Turner admitted she had consulted with Simon Forman, a physician, astrologer, and wizard, who died in 1611, before he could be involved in Overbury's death. Famed legal authority Edward Coke, a fanatic in his hatred of Catholicism, attempted to link the plot against Overbury with a Catholic plot against the throne itself, reminiscent of the Gunpowder Plot of 1605. Coke was in charge of establishing the cases against the suspects, and he served as judge at the trials after which Turner, Elwes, Weston, and James Franklin—an employee of the countess and of Turner—were executed. Somerset, who maintained his innocence, and his wife, who confessed to the poisoning, were imprisoned, but their trials were postponed until May 24 and 25, 1616. Sir Francis Bacon, not the zealous Coke, conducted the trials, at which both Somersets were found guilty.

Although the Somersets received death sentences, James did not want them executed. Instead, they were exiled from London and the court. According to rumor, their marriage failed. They had one daughter, Anne, who married into the important Russell family. Frances Carr—no longer countess of Somerset—died painfully of cancer on August 22, 1632. Her husband lingered on until 1645, deprived of wealth, titles, glamour, and power. Long before then, much of the public had been aroused against them. Carr was a Scottish favorite upon whom much English money had been wasted, despite England's poor financial condition; he was from a Catholic background, allied with the house of the Howard, and had urged a Catholic Spanish marriage upon the king's son at a time when anti-Catholic fervor was intense.

SIGNIFICANCE

Carr is best remembered for his role in Overbury's death. Once it was revealed that Overbury had been murdered, the ensuing scandal became a focal point for English hatred of the Scottish king James and his favorites, especially Carr, both because of the waste of English money on favorites and because of the suggestion that the Stuart court was a hotbed of vice. It also became a focus for Puritan hatred of anything savoring of Catholicism. Overbury's death was, arguably, the most important single scandal involving the court in English history, since the ferment stirred up by the Overbury affair became part of the contempt for and hatred of the Stuarts, their behavior, and their policies that erupted into revolution in the 1640's and resulted in the execution of James's son, Charles I, in 1649.

Popular writers, as well as historians, have repeatedly returned to the subject. In his notes to *The Fortunes of Nigel* (1822), the influential novelist Sir Walter Scott admitted modeling one of his characters on Anne Turner, while equally influential novelist and journalist Charles Dickens included the affair in *A Child's History of England* (1852-1854). The case has also attracted the attention of distinguished true crime writers, including William Roughead in *The Fatal Countess and Other Studies* (1924) and Miriam Allen deFord in *The Overbury Affair* (1960). The latter is still sometimes cited as one of the finest works of its kind.

—*Betty Richardson*

FURTHER READING

Bellany, Alastair. *The Politics of Court Scandal in Early Modern England: News Culture and the Overbury Affair, 1603-1660.* New York: Cambridge University Press, 2002. The only comprehensive source for information about how media of the time influenced public reaction to Overbury's death; extremely detailed, however, and designed for a scholarly audience.

Bergeron, David M. *Royal Family, Royal Lovers: King James of England and Scotland.* Columbia: University of Missouri Press, 1991. Shows the cool and distant relationships between King James and members of his family, as contrasted with his highly emotional relationships with male favorites.

Croft, Pauline. *King James.* New York: Palgrave Macmillan, 2003. A brief study emphasizing the king's strengths, while acknowledging weakness involving such favorites as Somerset.

Somerset, Anne. *Unnatural Murder: Poison at the Court of James I.* London: Weidenfeld & Nicolson, 1997. Comprehensively researched and clearly written study of crime and trials, with background of those involved; sympathetic to Frances Howard.

Stewart, Alan. *The Cradle King: The Life of James VI and I, the First Monarch of a United Great Britain.* New York: St. Martin's Press, 2003. Views Somerset in the context of the king's insecurity, born of the brutal conditions that surrounded him during his early years.

SEE ALSO: Sir Edward Coke; Thomas Dekker; John Donne; James I; John Webster.

RELATED ARTICLES in *Great Events from History: The Seventeenth Century, 1601-1700:* March 24, 1603: James I Becomes King of England; 1642-1651: English Civil Wars.

GIAN DOMENICO CASSINI
Italian astronomer

Cassini accurately determined the rotation periods of Jupiter and Mars, observed a gap in the rings of Saturn, and observed the phases of Venus. He also discovered that Jupiter and Saturn were not spherical but were slightly flattened at their poles. His astronomical measurements, dismissed as inaccurate by Cassini himself, were nevertheless used by Danish astronomer Olaus Rømer in 1676 to calculate the speed of light.

BORN: June 8, 1625; Perinaldo, Imperia, Republic of Genoa (now in Italy)
DIED: September 14, 1712; Paris, France
ALSO KNOWN AS: Jean Dominique Cassini
AREAS OF ACHIEVEMENT: Astronomy, mathematics

EARLY LIFE

Gian Domenico Cassini (zhyahn doh-MAY-nee-koh kah-SEE-nee) was born in Perinaldo on the Mediterranean coast, near Nice, France. His father, Jacopo Cassini, was from Tuscany, and his mother was Julia Crovesi. Cassini was raised by an uncle, his mother's brother.

Cassini studied poetry, mathematics, and astronomy at the Jesuit College in Genoa. Initially, Cassini was interested in astrology, but he soon became convinced that astrological predictions were not accurate. Nonetheless, Cassini's knowledge of astrology led to his first professional employment. In 1644, a senator from Bologna, the marquis Cornelio Malvasia, who had a deep interest in astrology and was familiar with Cassini, offered him a position at the new Panzano Observatory in Bologna. Beginning in 1648, Cassini would observe there, using instruments purchased with money obtained by Malvasia. Moving to Bologna was important for Cassini, since he had the opportunity to learn from two outstanding Jesuit scientists: Giovanni Battista Riccioli, an astronomer who made highly detailed telescopic observations of the Moon, and Francesco Maria Grimaldi, a physicist who discovered the diffraction of light.

LIFE'S WORK

In 1650, at the age of twenty-five, Cassini became a professor of mathematics and astronomy at the university in Bologna, Italy. While at Bologna, from 1650 to 1671, Cassini made many planetary observations using telescopes built by two contemporary Italians, Eustachio Divini and Giuseppe Campini.

His first serious astronomical observations were of the Sun, and he measured its position with an instrument called a gnomen, a device that used a small hole to allow the Sun's rays to form an image on the floor and, thus, allow Cassini to chart its position accurately. He had this gnomen built to replace an older device that was in the church of San Petronio in Bologna. Cassini was able to determine the precise times of the solstices, that is, the time the Sun reaches its farthest north and farthest south positions in the sky, marking the beginning of winter and summer respectively. In 1652-1653, Cassini observed a comet.

Cassini had initially believed in an Earth-centered solar system. In 1659, however, he presented his own version of an Earth-centered system, in which the Moon and the Sun orbited Earth while the other planets orbited the Sun. He would later come to accept the Copernican

Gian Domenico Cassini. (Library of Congress)

model, in which all the planets, including Earth, orbit the Sun.

In July of 1664, using a telescope built by Campini, Cassini observed that Jupiter was not a perfect sphere, as first believed, but instead was flattened at its poles; he also saw that there were bands and spots on the planet. He measured Jupiter's period of rotation by determining how long it took for the large red spot in Jupiter's atmosphere to circle the planet. His value for the rotation period of 9 hours and 56 minutes, published in 1665, is within a few minutes of the best value obtainable with modern instruments.

Cassini observed the moons of Jupiter between 1666 and 1668, and discovered discrepancies in his own measurements that, at first, he attributed to light having a finite speed. However, he appears to have rejected his own idea. In 1676, Danish astronomer Olaus Rømer used Cassini's measurements to calculate the speed of light.

In 1666, he observed surface features on Mars, including Syrtis Major, a feature discovered by Christiaan Huygens in 1659. As with Jupiter, Cassini observed these features as they rotated around the planet and measured the red planet's rotation period. His value of 24 hours and 40 minutes is within 3 minutes of the number accepted in the early twenty-first century.

Cassini also attempted to determine the rotation period of Venus: 23 hours, 20 minutes. However, it is not clear what Cassini observed or what he interpreted as surface features. Modern telescopes show no features on Venus, which is entirely covered by bright clouds, and its rotation period, which can be determined only by mapping surface features with radar that penetrates the clouds, is about 243 days.

Cassini's measurements made him famous in scientific circles throughout Europe, and his work came to the attention of Jean-Baptiste Colbert, the French minister of finance during the reign of King Louis XIV. Colbert had been attempting to strengthen science in France, so, at Colbert's suggestion, the king invited Cassini to Paris to head the new Paris observatory. Cassini arrived in Paris on April 4, 1669, and immediately joined the new Académie Royale des Sciences (Royal Academy of Sciences), which Colbert had founded. When Cassini moved to France, he adopted the French version of his name, Jean Dominique Cassini.

Saturn was a major focus of Cassini's efforts at the Paris observatory. Huygens had discovered Titan, the largest moon of Saturn in 1655. Cassini discovered two other moons, Iapetus in 1671 and Rhea in 1672. In 1675,

he recognized that Saturn's ring, discovered by Huygens in 1656, was divided into two parts, separated by a dark gap that is now known as the Cassini Division. In 1677, Cassini demonstrated that Saturn was not a perfect sphere but was flattened at its poles, and he discovered two more moons, Dione and Thetys, in 1684. In 1705, he suggested that Saturn's ring might not be a solid disk, but rather a swarm of objects moving around the planet, objects so small that they could not be seen individually.

Cassini also observed several comets between 1672 and 1707. From December 5 to December 23, 1690, Cassini observed a feature that appeared in the atmosphere of Jupiter. That feature is similar to the features observed in 1994, when more than twenty observable fragments of Comet Shoemaker-Levy 9 impacted Jupiter. Amateur astronomer Isshi Tabe and professional astronomer Junichi Watanabe, both Japanese, believe that Cassini's drawings show that he observed the effects of a similar comet impact in 1690. Watanabe and colleagues published the findings in a 1997 journal article.

During his years at the Paris observatory, Cassini served as the organizer of a renowned group of astronomers called the Paris School, and it included Jean Picard, Huygens, Rømer, Giacomo Felippo Maraldi, and Philippe de La Hire. Cassini was also trained in engineering and published several manuscripts on flood control. He served as inspector of water and waterways and as superintendent of the fortifications of Fort Urban.

In 1673, Cassini became a naturalized French citizen and married Geneviève Delaître, the daughter of an adviser to the king. They had two sons. The younger son, Jacques Cassini (1677-1756), followed in his father's footsteps, taking over his duties as head of the Paris observatory in 1712. Cassini's grandson César-François Cassini de Thury (1714-1784) and his great-grandson, Jacques-Dominique de Cassini (1748-1845) also became noted astronomers. By 1711, Cassini was blind, and he died in Paris on September 14, 1712.

SIGNIFICANCE

Cassini's improvement of the gnomen in the church of St. Petronius allowed him to determine precisely the times of the solstices. His measurements were influential in the adoption of the Gregorian calendar in the Protestant countries in 1700, by which time the Julian calendar was eleven days behind the actual beginning of each season. The Gregorian calendar, which corrected errors in the earlier Julian calendar, had been introduced in the Catholic countries of Europe in 1582.

Civil and Jesuit missionaries came to the Paris observatory to be trained in Cassini's methods of observing the eclipses of the moons of Jupiter. In 1668, Cassini had published tables listing the times of future eclipses of Jupiter's moons. The missionaries would go on to make their own observations while in Africa, the Americas, and China, and they used Cassini's tables to determine the longitudes of their remote sites. Also, other astronomers of his and later times used Cassini's methods to determine the longitudes of astronomical observation sites around the world.

Although Cassini never followed up on his own speculation that the apparent errors in the timing of the eclipses of the moons of Jupiter were a result of the finite speed of light, his measurements were used by Rømer, who announced in 1676 that he had determined the speed of light.

Cassini's achievements were so notable that the National Aeronautics and Space Administration (NASA) named its Saturn orbiter after him; the orbiter was launched in October, 1997. In addition, named in his honor are a crater on the Moon, a crater on Mars, and the Cassini Regio region on Saturn's moon Iapetus.

—*George J. Flynn*

FURTHER READING

Alexander, A. F. O'Donel. *The Planet Saturn: A History of Observation, Theory, and Discovery*. New York: Dover, 1980. This work describes Cassini's many contributions to the understanding of Saturn, its rings, and his discovery of the moons Iapetus, Rhea, Dione, and Thetys.

Beatty, J. K. "A Comet Crash in 1690?" *Sky and Telescope* 93 (April, 1997): 111. Beatty summarizes a new Japanese interpretation of Cassini's 1690 sketches of Jupiter, suggesting Cassini saw the results of a comet impact.

Débarbat, S., and C. Wilson. "The Galilean Satellites of Jupiter from Galileo to Cassini, Rømer, and Bradley." In *Planetary Astronomy from the Renaissance to the Rise of Astrophysics*, edited by René Taton and Curtis Wilson. New York: Cambridge University Press, 1989. Part A of this edited volume provides an excellent account of Cassini's contributions to the measurement of the positions and eclipses of the moons of Jupiter.

Schorn, Ronald A. *Planetary Astronomy: From Ancient Times to the Third Millennium*. College Station: Texas A&M University Press, 1999. This work describes Cassini's numerous contributions to the observations of the planets, particularly Jupiter and Saturn.

SEE ALSO: Giovanni Alfonso Borelli; Jean-Baptiste Colbert; Galileo; Francesco Maria Grimaldi; Christiaan Huygens; Johannes Kepler; Hans Lippershey; Marin Mersenne; Nicolas-Claude Fabri de Peiresc.

RELATED ARTICLES in *Great Events from History: The Seventeenth Century, 1601-1700:* September, 1608: Invention of the Telescope; 1610: Galileo Confirms the Heliocentric Model of the Solar System; 1632: Galileo Publishes *Dialogue Concerning the Two Chief World Systems, Ptolemaic and Copernican*; February, 1656: Huygens Identifies Saturn's Rings; 1665: Cassini Discovers Jupiter's Great Red Spot; December 7, 1676: Rømer Calculates the Speed of Light.

CATHERINE OF BRAGANZA
Queen consort of England (r. 1662-1685) and regent of Portugal (r. 1704-1705)

Catherine's marriage to English king Charles II conferred commercial advantages on England, renewing the fortunes of the British East India Company. Although she and Charles were unable to produce an heir, Catherine's thirty years at court benefited Portugal, to which she returned in 1692. In 1704-1705, she acted as regent for her brother Pedro II while Portugal was at war with Spain.

BORN: November 25, 1638; Vila Viçosa Palace, Portugal
DIED: December 31, 1705; Lisbon, Portugal
AREA OF ACHIEVEMENT: Government and politics

EARLY LIFE

Catherine of Braganza (bruh-GAN-zuh), first daughter and third child of John, duke of Braganza, and his wife, Donna Luisa, was born on November 25, 1638, at the Vila Viçosa Palace, about 300 miles (483 kilometers) from Lisbon. By this time, Spain had controlled Portugal for sixty years. Duke John, Portugal's wealthiest and most powerful noble, led a successful struggle for independence. In December, 1640, he became King John IV the Fortunate at his coronation in Lisbon.

Like many royal females, Catherine received a convent education, spending most of her time in devotions and needlework, secluded from the outside world. This experience reinforced her piety and gentle, trusting nature. The search for a suitable husband for her, and a powerful ally for Portugal, began when she was eight. One candidate was the young Louis XIV, who was the same age and who had become king of France before his fifth birthday. Negotiations, however, were unsuccessful.

John IV's ambassadors were better received by Charles I. A commercial treaty between England and Portugal was signed in 1642. As the First English Civil War began, the Portuguese secretary António de Sousa Macedo helped procure arms for the English Royalist cause. In 1644, he and some of Charles I's advisers discussed a marriage between Prince Charles, then fourteen, and one of the Portuguese Infantas. The defeat, imprisonment, and execution of Charles I in 1649, and his family's exile on the Continent during the Commonwealth led by Oliver Cromwell, halted these proposals.

Cromwell's death in 1658 renewed hopes of a Stuart restoration. Negotiations between the Commonwealth's most powerful general, George Monck, and agents for Charles II culminated in the Declaration of Breda (1660), in which the king issued a general amnesty, recognized the rights of Parliament, and promised religious toleration. On May 18, 1660, Charles was proclaimed king by Parliament, and on his birthday, May 29, he entered London in triumph and still unmarried.

The Portuguese reminded the English about Catherine, offering as her dowry the African fortress of Tangier, the island of Bombay, trading rights with Brazil and India, and £500,000. These commercial advantages would soon revitalize the East India Company, opening new opportunities to British trade. The monetary sum also made a Catholic princess more acceptable to the average Englishman. In frustration, the Spanish ambassador told Charles that Catherine was deformed and could not bear children. His first assertion was untrue; Catherine, a short, dark-eyed brunette, with small hands and feet, was not misshapen. Charles at any rate ignored his advice. Catherine left Portugal in April, 1662, and a month later, the fleet sent to conduct her to Britain reached Portsmouth. However, when she met her husband for the first time, she was ill and could not yet speak English. Whatever doubts Charles may have had at that moment, the marriage was promptly celebrated, first in a private Catholic ceremony, and then in a public Protestant service.

LIFE'S WORK

Though not conventionally handsome, Charles II was tall, witty, athletic, and fond of women. He had enjoyed several liaisons during his fourteen-year exile; in 1662, he was infatuated with Barbara Villiers Palmer, countess of Castlemaine, beautiful, amoral, ill-tempered, and pregnant with his child. Other problems for the new bride included the language barrier and Catherine's natural shyness. The informality of the Restoration court differed markedly from Portuguese courtly etiquette. The dress and manners of the elderly ladies in waiting selected by her mother were sources of amusement to English observers. Charles sent them home, to be replaced by Englishwomen, among whom was Lady Castlemaine. The queen knew of Castlemaine, however, and angrily refused to accept her.

Caught between a termagant mistress and an outraged queen who threatened to return home, Charles insisted it was Catherine's wifely duty to obey his wishes. This directive may have been influenced not only by his passion for the mother of his new son, but also the realization that the monetary portion of the dowry had been supple-

Catherine of Braganza. (Hulton Archive/Getty Images)

Many people respected Catherine as a good woman, and she had never tried to promote her faith. To allay fears of a series of Catholic kings, Charles directed that James's daughters, Mary and Anne, be raised as Protestants.

The death of Charles II on February 6, 1685, grieved Catherine. Despite his infidelities, she loved him, and he increasingly honored and respected her judgment. Unfortunately, the new King James II had none of his brother's political acumen; his bigotry and arrogance offended almost everyone. When his second wife, Mary of Modena, gave birth to a son on June 10, 1688, much of the nation rejected the idea of a Catholic dynasty. Prince William III of Orange, husband of James's elder daughter Mary, was invited to come to England, and following his successful invasion, James, his wife, and their infant son fled to France.

Catherine remained in England, but as the only Catholic in the English royal family she felt increasingly isolated. On several occasions she petitioned William and Mary to be allowed to return to Portugal. In May, 1692, her wish was granted. After a brief visit to her exiled brother-in-law and his family in France, she and her entourage reached Portugal in January, 1693. During the last years of her life, Catherine remained interested in English affairs and was on good terms with the English ambassador in Lisbon. In May, 1704, her brother Pedro II, at war with Philip IV of Spain, chose Catherine as regent. During this time she conducted state business, and implemented the recruitment of Portuguese troops. Suddenly stricken with colic, Catherine died on December 31, 1705.

SIGNIFICANCE

Catherine is often remembered for being unable to give Charles II a legitimate heir and thus contributing involuntarily to events that led to the deposition of James II. However, her importance to English history is more than just a negative. She brought exotic goods from the Far East that soon became part of English life and were later incorporated into British colonial life and the history of American culture as well. These goods included Indian cottons, silks, lacquer work, cane chairs, porcelain, and, most popular of all, tea. It is perhaps ironic that this shy princess's most valuable gifts to her adopted country enhanced a more gracious ways of living.

—Dorothy Potter

mented by spices, silks, tea, and other exotic delights. Eventually, Catherine accepted the inevitable. Castlemaine and other mistresses, including the actress Nell Gwyn, gave Charles, an indulgent father, the children he enjoyed. Despite medicinal remedies, visits to spas, and many prayers, Catherine remained barren. Charles's legitimate heir was, of necessity, his brother James, duke of York, who was rumored to be a secret Catholic.

Some courtiers and politicians suggested Catherine be divorced. The king refused to consider such a step, however, even during the Popish Plot of 1678, a scheme hatched by an adventurer named Titus Oates. Among the outlandish charges leveled by Oates and his associates was that the queen's physician had agreed to poison Charles. The king and the more perceptive of his advisers quickly recognized the plot as a sham, but the Whig opposition in Parliament supported Oates's story, hoping to limit the power of the Crown and to remove the Catholic duke of York from the succession. Charles II steadfastly defended his wife and his brother, and gradually public opinion rallied to the monarchy in the early 1680's.

FURTHER READING

Bowle, John, ed. *The Diary of John Evelyn*. New York: Oxford University Press, 1985. Evelyn, a conservative Royalist and minor politician, chronicled public and private events from 1640 to 1706. Court life was often included in his narrative.

Coote, Stephen. *Royal Survivor: The Life of Charles II*. New York: St. Martin's Press, 2000. Focusing on Charles II's personality, political difficulties, and survival skills, this book details life at the Restoration court.

Davidson, Lillias Campbell. *Catherine of Bragança: Infanta of Portugal and Queen-Consort of England*. London: John Murray, 1908. Probably the earliest English biography of Catherine. Useful for details about her life before marriage and later as queen regent in Portugal. Includes letters related to Catherine and her will.

Elsna, Hebe. *Catherine of Braganza: Charles II's Queen*. London: Robert Hale, 1967. A sympathetic account of Catherine's life.

Fraser, Antonia. *King Charles II*. London: Phoenix, 2002. An exhaustive (more than six-hundred-page) account, including numerous illustrations and an extensive bibliography.

Latham, Robert, and William Matthews, eds. *The Diary of Samuel Pepys*. 11 vols. London: Bell & Hyman, 1983. The complete and unexpurgated edition of Pepy's secret diary. As clerk of the acts at the Admiralty, Pepys had access to the court and wrote about everything he saw, heard, or experienced. This period (1660-1669) included many important events in Catherine's early career as Charles II's queen.

Sousa, Manuel Andrade e. *Catherine of Braganza: Princess of Portugal, Wife to Charles II*. Lisbon: Edições Inapa, 1994. An illustrated biography of Catherine, with numerous portraits of her and her contemporaries, as well as documents and devotional objects associated with her.

Thomas, Gertrude Z. *Richer than Spices: How a Royal Bride's Dowry Introduced Cane, Lacquer, Cottons, Tea, and Porcelain to England, and So Revolutionized Taste, Manners, Craftsmanship, and History in both England and America*. New York: Knopf, 1965. Focuses on the decorative arts and offers a unique perspective on the value of Anglo-Portuguese trade. Extensive illustrations and bibliography.

SEE ALSO: Charles I; Charles II (of England); Oliver Cromwell; James II; John IV; Louis XIV; Mary of Modena; Mary II; George Monck; Titus Oates; Philip IV; William III.

RELATED ARTICLES in *Great Events from History: The Seventeenth Century, 1601-1700:* 1606-1674: Europeans Settle in India; 1609: China Begins Shipping Tea to Europe; May, 1640-January 23, 1641: Revolt of the Catalans; June 23, 1661: Portugal Cedes Bombay to the English; December 19, 1667: Impeachment of Clarendon; February 13, 1668: Spain Recognizes Portugal's Independence.

SAMUEL DE CHAMPLAIN
French-born colonial Canadian explorer

Widely considered to be the father of New France, Champlain now represents the French attempt to acquire and settle North America, one of the great might-have-beens of American history.

BORN: c. 1567/1570; Brouage, Saintonge, France
DIED: December 25, 1635; Quebec, New France (now in Canada)
AREAS OF ACHIEVEMENT: Exploration, government and politics

EARLY LIFE
Little is known of the early life of Samuel de Champlain (sahm-wehl duh shahm-plan), not even his date of birth. Scattered evidence and informed speculation have

placed it as early as 1564 and as late as 1573; authorities seem to be divided fairly equally between 1567 and 1570. Champlain was born and reared on the Atlantic coast of France in the town of Brouage, a small seaport important for the salt trade. During the years of his youth, Brouage was a minor prize in the bitter religious wars between the Catholics and the Calvinist Huguenots. He may well have come from a Huguenot family, though as an adult he was a staunch Catholic.

As he climbed the social ladder, Champlain officially described his father as a captain in the merchant marine, attributing to him the "de" before Champlain, implying nobility. As a young man, however, the explorer was simply Samuel Champlain, and there is no record of a patent of nobility for the family. He had little formal education, but he learned the practical skills of seamanship and navigation from an early age and developed a straightforward and effective writing style, unembellished by Latinisms.

Like many of the other pioneers of the New World, therefore, Champlain was a self-made man. He was strongly religious, justifying his projects by a desire to save heathen souls for Christ as well as by arguments for the economic and political benefits to the kingdom of France. Personally, he was ascetic and self-denying, enduring the hardships of ocean voyages and frigid winters without complaint and ignoring the Native American women that other Europeans often molested or married. He was a courageous soldier and an honest administrator. He married late in life and had no children. No authentic contemporary portrait of him survives; he was described as modest in stature but tough in both mind and body.

LIFE'S WORK

Champlain made his first voyage to the Americas in 1599, signing on with a Spanish fleet to the Caribbean. His skill as an observer, author, cartographer, and sketch artist produced a detailed record of this voyage into the Spanish Americas. He described the Spanish empire, speculated on the possibility of building a canal in Panama, and noted the injustices of the heavy-handed Spanish rule over the native peoples. His handwritten and illustrated account brought him to the attention of Henry IV, king of France, under whom he had served as a soldier, and he received an appointment as a royal geographer.

In 1603, he accompanied François Pont-Gravé, a sea captain, to North America with a royal commission to establish a French colony. The Saint Lawrence River valley had been visited and claimed for France by Jacques Cartier in 1534-1536, but the forbidding winters and the lack of either precious metals or an obvious passage to the Pacific Ocean (the elusive Northwest Passage) had discouraged French settlement. Each year, nevertheless, French, Basque, and assorted other European fishermen had braved the North Atlantic to fish in the teeming waters and engage in some trade with the North American Indians. After a stormy voyage of ten weeks, Champlain first set foot on North American soil. In the course of his sixty-odd years of life, he would cross the Atlantic no less than twenty-five times, tirelessly working to establish his dream of New France in America.

In 1604-1605, Champlain spent his first winter in America, at Saint Croix Island, which eventually became a United States National Monument along the border of Maine and New Brunswick, Canada. It was a disastrously cold winter, and thirty-five of the seventy-nine expedition members died. The settlement was abandoned the following spring. The next year Champlain and his men, reinforced by newcomers and supplies from France, tried an alternate site, Port

Samuel de Champlain. (Library of Congress)

Royal, on the protected inner coast of present-day Nova Scotia, which the French called Acadia. From this base, Champlain led exploratory expeditions down the American coast as far south as Cape Cod. He wrote descriptions and sketched navigational maps and charts of the New England coast that are remarkable for their accuracy.

The Port Royal colony proved unsatisfactory because of its high cost and modest return to the investors of the French colonial company. The French monarchy itself was disinclined to bear its costs, and there were no precious metals and few furs to be acquired. Champlain returned to France and laid a plan before Henry IV for a new colonial venture. The vast watershed of the Saint Lawrence River offered two attractive possibilities. It funneled the trade in Canadian furs to a single point, the natural fortress of Quebec, making it possible for France to institute a monopoly on the fur trade similar to Renaissance Portugal's monopoly on East Indian spices. It also held the promise of a passage to Asia, because Canadian Indian tales spoke of vast seas that could be reached by following river routes to the west and north.

The king approved Champlain's new plan, and in 1608, three ships sailed from Honfleur, France, to establish a permanent settlement at Quebec. Had Champlain pressed his New England exploration south of Cape Code, charted the natural harbor to be known later as New York and the lower Hudson River, and petitioned the French monarch to establish his settlement there, the history of North America might have been very different indeed. New France, however, remained centered at Quebec to the north.

Champlain and his men built a small settlement on the site of what is today the lower town of Quebec City. For himself, Champlain constructed an elaborate "habitation," part fortress and part château. His sketch of this three-story building, complete with a moat and a tower, bears an extraordinary resemblance to the Lieutenance, the royal headquarters building at Honfleur, from which he sailed. The first winter at Quebec was a very rough one: Of the twenty-four Frenchmen who stayed on when the ships sailed for home, only Champlain and seven others survived. The settlement was reinforced from the mother country in the spring. Champlain constantly tried to encourage French families to settle in Quebec and establish farms, but with little success. He brought his young wife, Hélène, with him in 1620; she disliked the isolation of Quebec and went back to Paris in 1624, never to return. By the time Champlain died at Quebec in 1635, the number of European settlers in the colony still would not surpass two hundred.

Recalling his skirmishes with local Indians along the New England coast and the repressive Spanish rule he had seen, Champlain strove to establish and maintain good relations with the Indians of the Saint Lawrence Basin, the Montagnais, the Algonquians, and the Hurons. He respected their way of life and nurtured the hope that they could be converted to Christianity gently rather than by force. The goodwill of the Canadian Indians was essential to the colony, because they controlled the sources of the beaver pelts on which Quebec's economy was based. Champlain cemented relations with them by promising military aid in their wars against their traditional rivals, the Iroquois.

In 1609, Champlain accompanied a war party of Montagnais and their allies against the Mohawk Iroquois. They traveled south from the Saint Lawrence River to Lake Champlain, in modern New York State, and met their enemy near the site of Fort Ticonderoga. Champlain and two other Frenchmen, protected by armor and firing harquebuses, quickly scattered the Iroquois. The victory was by no means decisive, however, and traditional enmity remained. In 1615, Champlain led another war party west to Lakes Huron and Ontario and then southward, where he fought a battle near modern-day Syracuse, New York. The Iroquois were now better informed about the limitations of the harquebus and turned back the invaders. Champlain was wounded and the myth of European invincibility was broken. Throughout the history of Quebec, the French maintained their alliance with the local tribes, but paid for it with the hostility of the Iroquois in the British American Colonies to the south.

From time to time, Champlain would return to France to lobby for governmental and commercial support for the struggling colony. The situation in Europe was volatile, a residual effect of the wars of religion. King Henry IV was assassinated in 1610 and followed to the throne by Louis XIII, a mere boy. During the 1620's, Cardinal de Richelieu stabilized the government of France by becoming the young king's first minister. In 1627, he founded a company called the Hundred Associates, a royally chartered monopoly to develop the Canadian colony. Champlain was confirmed as the company's and the king's lieutenant in Canada, strengthening his authority. Nevertheless, direct government aid to New France was meager, and without the profits from the fur trade, the whole enterprise would have collapsed.

In 1628 and 1629, France and Britain were briefly at war, and Champlain was besieged at Quebec by British privateers and forced to surrender the colony to them.

Canada was returned to France by the Treaty of Saint-Germain-en-Laye in 1632, and Champlain sailed from France for the last time to reestablish the colony and govern it in 1633. He died on Christmas Day, 1635, and was buried beneath the little Catholic church he had founded, Notre Dame de la Recouvrance, much lamented by Europeans and Native Americans alike.

SIGNIFICANCE

Like the other hardy explorers who established the European presence on the North American continent during the sixteenth and seventeenth centuries, Champlain combined the virtues of fortitude to resist the hardships of the time and the vision for the possibilities of the future. Like many, though by no means all, Europeans, he also was a man of strong Christian convictions, which he sought to bring to the Canadian Indians even as he used them to discipline fellow Europeans who were given to brutal and exploitative behavior. He sought honest alliances with the Native Americans, using his superior military technology to aid them in their traditional battles. He sought to turn a fair profit for French merchants through the fur trade, but he constantly argued that what America needed most was families of settlers who would clear and work the land. He realized that a purely commercial, missionary, and military colony could never create a permanent New France in the Americas.

The British colonies in New England and Virginia grew into thriving settlements, based on agriculture and artisan manufacturing as well as trade. By the 1750's, Champlain's New France had extended its net of military and trading posts over thousands of miles from the Saint Lawrence River to the lower Mississippi River, laying the foundations of Detroit, Chicago, Saint Louis, and New Orleans, yet the thinly spread French were outmanned and outgunned by the more populous and more densely distributed British and their American settlers. By 1763, New France was no more. The Acadians, refusing to swear an oath of allegiance to the British who took control of their territory, were forcibly deported from the region. Many of these Acadians became known as Cajuns and settled in Louisiana and elsewhere in the modern United States. Moreover, a francophone culture continues to thrive at Champlain's Quebec, a culture strong enough to motivate many Quebecois to seek to secede from the rest of Canada.

Champlain, like Christopher Columbus, reminds Anglo-Americans that their ancestors were not the only ones whose daring and foresight served to bring Western civilization to North America. Champlain is justly recognized as the father of New France and ranks also as one of the great American discoverers.

—Gordon R. Mork

FURTHER READING

Bishop, Morris. *Champlain: The Life of Fortitude*. New York: Alfred A. Knopf, 1948. Reprint. New York: Octagon Books, 1979. A solidly written biography organized around Champlain's many voyages to the New World. There are lengthy quotations from Champlain's own colorful descriptions of the country and people he found and several of his own sketches, as well as excellent modern maps and several appendices on some of the more controversial aspects of his life and times.

Champlain, Samuel de. *Algonquians, Hurons, and Iroquois: Champlain Explores America, 1603-1616*. Translated by Annie Nettleton Bourne. Edited by Edward Gaylord Bourne. Dartmouth, N.S.: Brook House Press, 2000. The Bournes originally published a two-volume translation of Champlain's *Voyages de la Nouvelle France* in 1906, with the title *The Voyages and Discoveries, 1604-1616*. This book is a revised edition of the earlier translation.

Eccles, William J. *France in America*. New York: Harper and Row, 1972. Rev. ed. East Lansing: Michigan State University Press, 1998. Originally a volume in Henry Steele Commager's New American Nation series, this standard history covers French colonization in North America and the Caribbean from the earliest contact until the American Revolution. In his first chapters, Eccles puts the contributions of Champlain in a broader context.

Heidenreich, Conrad E. "The Beginning of French Exploration out of the St. Lawrence Valley: Motives, Methods, and Changing Attitudes Towards Native People." In *Decentering the Renaissance: Canada and Europe in Multidisciplinary Perspective, 1500-1700*, edited by Germaine Warkentin and Carolyn Podruchy. Toronto: University of Toronto Press, 2001. Compares Champlain's exploration of Canada to exploration by Jacques Cartier and Jean-François de la Rocque, sieur de Roberval.

Morison, Samuel Eliot. *Samuel de Champlain: Father of New France*. Boston: Little, Brown, 1972. This prolific and esteemed naval historian has combined in this biography both scholarship and graceful prose. Morison was himself a sailor and navigated many of the waters along the New England and Canadian coasts with Champlain's descriptions and charts at hand. In the appendix is a translation of Champlain's "Treatise on Seamanship" of 1632.

Parkman, Francis. *France and England in North America*. 1856. Edited by David Levin. Vol. 1. New York: Viking Press, 1983. Parkman favors the British and the Protestants, but he nevertheless gives a vivid and not unfavorable picture of Champlain. For those with the patience to savor the style of Victorian prose, this well-known book can still pay substantial dividends.

Rudin, Ronald. *Founding Fathers: The Celebration of Champlain and Laval in the Streets of Quebec, 1878-1908*. Toronto: University of Toronto Press, 2003. From 1878 to 1908, Quebec City celebrated its founding at four commemorative events. While Rudin's book focuses on the staging of these celebrations, it describes Quebeckers' perceptions of the historical significance of Champlain and Laval.

SEE ALSO: Henry Hudson; Louis Jolliet; Sieur de La Salle; Louis XIII; Jacques Marquette; Pierre Esprit Radisson; Cardinal de Richelieu.

RELATED ARTICLES in *Great Events from History: The Seventeenth Century, 1601-1700:* March 15, 1603-December 25, 1635: Champlain's Voyages; Spring, 1604: First European Settlement in North America; 1610-1643: Reign of Louis XIII; Beginning June, 1610: Hudson Explores Hudson Bay; 1611-1630's: Jesuits Begin Missionary Activities in New France; December 26, 1620: Pilgrims Arrive in North America; 1625-October 28, 1628: Revolt of the Huguenots; April 27, 1627: Company of New France Is Chartered; May, 1630-1643: Great Puritan Migration; 1642-1684: Beaver Wars; May, 1642: Founding of Montreal; May 1, 1699: French Found the Louisiana Colony.

CHARLES I
King of England (r. 1625-1649)

As king of England, Charles I became involved in a dispute with Parliament over the extent of his prerogative and the ordering of religion, a dispute that resulted in civil war, in Charles's execution, and, ultimately, in the development of limited constitutional monarchy in England.

BORN: November 19, 1600; Dumferline Castle, Fife, Scotland
DIED: January 30, 1649; London, England
AREA OF ACHIEVEMENT: Government and politics

EARLY LIFE

Charles I was the second son of the Scottish king James VI and his queen, Anne of Denmark. Charles's grandmother was Mary, Queen of Scots, whose lineal relationship to the Tudor monarchs resulted in James's succession to the English throne in 1603.

A sickly child, Charles did not walk until he was almost four years old, the weakness in his legs probably resulting from rickets. He was also slow in learning to talk, and he spoke with a stammer to the end of his life. As he grew to young manhood, he did strengthen his physical stamina by rigorous exercise and equestrian pursuits, but he always remained short in stature, never attaining a height beyond five feet, four inches. His education was closely supervised by his father. He learned to read and

write Greek and Latin, and he was said to have spoken French, Spanish, and Italian fluently.

On the death of his brother, Prince Henry, in 1612, Charles became heir apparent to the English throne. In the following year, his sister Elizabeth married a German prince, Frederick V, elector of the Palatinate. King James had long dreamed of a Spanish marriage for his heir, and when Prince Frederick's patrimony was seized by Spanish forces in 1619, the king had all the more incentive to promote a dynastic alliance that would lead to the restoration of his son-in-law.

At the urging of his favorite, George Villiers, duke of Buckingham, the aging king granted Buckingham and Charles permission to travel incognito to Spain, there to woo the Infanta Dona Maria. After enduring the dalliance of the Spanish negotiators for eight months, the two young men returned to England without the infanta and determined on war against Spain. A strongly Protestant Parliament proved willing to declare war against Catholic Spain but reluctant to vote sufficient revenue for a land war. It was amid this situation that James died in March, 1625.

LIFE'S WORK

As his father's successor, King Charles I imparted a different character to the throne from that which had prevailed under James I. He rid the royal presence of drunkards and catamites, so that his court was dignified and well-ordered. He patronized the arts and was an excellent judge of artistic merit. He was temperate, chaste, and serious, slow of thought and sparing of words; his greatest fault was his deviousness in public matters. Charles soon welcomed his new queen, Henrietta Maria, the youngest sister of King Louis XIII of France. From the time Charles and Buckingham had left Spain, secret marriage negotiations had been conducted with France, and despite the difficult terms of a Catholic marriage, they were concluded not long before the late king's death.

Between 1625 and 1629, Charles convened Parliament every year but one. From the outset, the king and Parliament fell into dispute over taxation, the influence of Buckingham, and ritual in the Church of England. In 1625, Parliament granted tonnage and poundage, a customs tax, for only one year, though it had been traditional to accord this revenue to a new monarch for the duration of his reign. In 1626, Charles dissolved his second parliament to save Buckingham from trial after he had been impeached in the Lower House.

Since Parliament had not voted sufficient money to conduct the war, Charles contin-

Charles I. (Library of Congress)

ued to collect tonnage and poundage and in addition imposed forced loans on affluent landowners. Those who refused to pay were thrown into prison. Meanwhile, Buckingham, the leader of repeated military expeditions that invariably ended in ignominious defeat, blundered into another war, this one against France. The Parliament of 1628 brought the king to account, compelling him to sign the Petition of Right; Charles pledged himself not to imprison any subject without cause, not to collect taxes unauthorized by Parliament, not to billet soldiers on his subjects' property, and not to declare martial law in time of peace.

Buckingham was assassinated by a disappointed office-seeker in August, 1628. It was at this time that the king fell in love with his queen. Henceforth, he was to be that rarity among monarchs of his day, an affectionate and loyal husband.

When Parliament reconvened in 1629, it turned at once to grievances. Believing that he had nothing to expect from this session, Charles ordered both houses dissolved, but before allowing themselves to be sent away,

the Commons passed resolutions declaring anyone who supported the collection of tonnage and poundage, or who advocated innovations in the Church of England, to be a capital enemy of the realm. For the next eleven years, Charles did not call a Parliament. Without parliamentary revenues, he was forced to withdraw from expensive wars, signing peace treaties with France in 1629 and with Spain in 1630.

Charles had to raise money by any means he could devise under the royal prerogative. He revived old feudal dues and fines, such as penalties for infringement on the royal forests. He also continued to collect tonnage and poundage. The measure that raised the greatest protest, however, was the king's decision to extend "ship money" (a rate levied for upkeep of the royal fleet) from coastal towns to inland counties. In the celebrated Ship Money Case, a panel of judges narrowly upheld the king's right to collect the assessment from John Hampden, a wealthy landowner who had refused to pay. By reduction of expenses and the use of such expedients as were available, Charles collected sufficient revenue to meet current costs of his government, but not enough to defray extraordinary demands on the treasury.

Another troublesome issue in the 1630's was what Puritans took to be a trend toward Catholicism in the Church of England. In 1633, Charles appointed William Laud archbishop of Canterbury. Laud was the leader of that group of clergy who supported a more elaborate church ritual and emphasized episcopacy. Practices such as bowing at the name of Jesus and placing of the Communion table at the east end of the church suggested a drift toward Rome. Despite the misgivings of the Puritans, however, neither Charles nor Laud entertained any idea of returning to Catholicism.

Charles might have continued indefinitely to rule without Parliament had his Scottish subjects not rebelled. When, in 1636, he imposed episcopal control on the Scottish Church, the Presbyterian Scots resolved to defend their religion whatever the cost. After a futile attempt to send the militia against Scotland and an abortive Parliament in April and May, 1640 (afterward referred to as the Short Parliament), Charles convened the Long Parliament on November 3, 1640. Meanwhile, Scottish troops occupied two northern counties of England and held the king liable for the expense of occupation.

Parliament appeared little worried about the Scottish occupation but proceeded forthwith to reduce the royal prerogative. First, it condemned Thomas Wentworth, first earl of Strafford, by a bill of attainder for giving the king evil advice. Next, the king was shorn of his offending prerogative powers. The prerogative courts were abolished, ship money was declared illegal, feudal exactions were forbidden, and Parliament was to be dissolved only with its own consent.

On November 3, 1641, the members of Parliament were stunned when news arrived that the Catholic Irish had revolted and were slaughtering English settlers in Ireland. An army to quell the uprising would have to be raised, and it was the issue of who would control these forces, the king or Parliament, that proved to be the breaking point between the two. In violation of parliamentary privilege, Charles, accompanied by a body of guards, entered the House of Commons and attempted to arrest several of its members. A week later, on January 10, 1642, Charles and his family left London. The following August, he raised his royal standard near Nottingham. The First English Civil War began.

The Houses of Lords and Commons divided according to no particular pattern, some of them supporting the king and others the Parliamentary cause. The civil war

dragged on for four years, at the conclusion of which Royalist arms had been defeated by Parliamentary forces and by the Scots, who had joined Parliament against the king in 1644. In the spring of 1646, Charles surrendered himself into the hands of the Scottish army. Negotiations for the restoration of the monarchy stalled on the questions of control over the army and the church. In 1647, the Scots gave their royal prisoner to the keeping of Parliament and marched back north of the border. During the following year, Charles temporarily escaped imprisonment. He reached an agreement with the Scots, who undertook his restoration in return for the establishment of Presbyterianism in England. Scottish designs to place Charles back on the throne were foiled, however, when Oliver Cromwell crushed their army at Preston.

To Cromwell and the remnant of members still sitting in Parliament, there appeared to be no future for Charles in the government of England. He was deceptive; he could not be trusted to keep even the most solemn promise. A special court, whose jurisdiction Charles refused to recognize, was established to try the king on charges of tyranny and subversion of the rights of the people. He conducted himself with calm dignity throughout the proceedings, which ended with a sentence of death.

Noble in adversity, Charles proved serene in the face of death. On January 30, 1649, he was taken to a scaffold built to extend from one of the windows of the banqueting hall at Whitehall Palace and was beheaded before a sympathetic crowd of onlookers.

SIGNIFICANCE

Since the execution of Charles I, historians have variously interpreted the origins and underlying socioeconomic meaning of the English Civil War. If England was undergoing basic change, Charles I was hardly the person to lead his country through a transformation. He lacked breadth of understanding and imagination. He stubbornly resisted adaptation and connived to win out over his opposition. Despite the fine qualities he displayed in his private life, his public endeavors did not directly lead to any positive achievement.

Charles was more than a man who held the office of king of England, however. He was, as all monarchs are, a symbol of the royal office itself. His execution, in retrospect, can be seen to have been a traumatic event for the English people, who were not as ready to dispense with royalty as they may have seemed in the midst of the English Civil War. The execution left the English people with lasting feelings of uncertainty about the nature of government, as well as feelings of guilt over their willingness to kill a man who, in the eyes of some, had a divine right that should have placed him beyond their reach.

—Quentin Bone

FURTHER READING

Ashton, Robert. *The City and the Court, 1603-1643.* New York: Cambridge University Press, 1979. Probably the main reason Charles I lost the military conflict of 1642-1646 was that London, the nexus of English commerce and wealth, fell under the control of Parliament. Ashton explains how growing radicalism late in 1641 and early in 1642 led to the extremists' seizure of power in the city.

Bowle, John. *Charles I: A Biography.* Boston: Little, Brown, 1975. Engagingly written, this is a narrative history without pretense of sociological or psychological analysis. Charles I is presented just as he appears from evidence gleaned by modern research.

Carlton, Charles. *Charles I: The Personal Monarch.* 2d ed. New York: Routledge, 1995. A highly praised, well-written biography that challenges conventional interpretations of Charles's life and the origins of the English Civil War.

Durston, Christopher. *Charles I.* New York: Routledge, 1998. Analyzes Charles's personality and the effects of his decisions as monarch.

Gregg, Pauline. *King Charles I.* London: J. M. Dent and Sons, 1981. The best biography of Charles I, this work presents a balanced and judicious view of his kingship. The author writes understandingly of Charles's motives but is not blind to his faults.

Hibbard, Caroline M. *Charles I and the Popish Plot.* Chapel Hill: University of North Carolina Press, 1983. Explores the efforts of Catholics at Charles's court to mitigate recusancy laws against English Catholics and possibly to align England with Catholic powers in the religious struggle of the seventeenth century. The fear of "popery" engendered deep distrust of the king and court among the populace.

Stone, Lawrence. *The Causes of the English Revolution.* New York: Harper and Row, 1972. The author shows that the monarchy in England, having no standing army, well-established bureaucracy, or independent source of royal revenue, governed by consent; this delicate balance was upset when economic and religious developments brought about a loss of confidence in the king's leadership.

Wilson, Derek. *The King and the Gentleman: Charles Stuart and Oliver Cromwell, 1599-1649.* New York: St. Martin's Press, 1999. Examines the formative years and religious convictions of Charles and Cromwell to explain their opposing visions of England and how these visions led to the English Civil War. The book is intended for readers with some knowledge of British history.

Zagorin, Perez. *The Court and the Country.* New York: Atheneum, 1969. In this analytical and interpretive work, the author does not attempt an extensive narrative of events but rather delineates the main social, political, and religious interests that were significant elements in the seventeenth century conflict. He concludes that the decisive factor in the conflict were constitutional issues rather than religious differences.

SEE ALSO: First Duke of Buckingham; Oliver Cromwell; Frederick V; Henrietta Maria; James I; William Laud; First Earl of Strafford.

RELATED ARTICLES in *Great Events from History: The Seventeenth Century, 1601-1700:* 1625-October 28, 1628: Revolt of the Huguenots; May 6-June 7, 1628: Petition of Right; March, 1629-1640: "Personal Rule" of Charles I; May, 1630-1643: Great Puritan Migration; March-June, 1639: First Bishops' War; November 3, 1640-May 15, 1641: Beginning of England's Long Parliament; October 23, 1641-1642: Ulster Insurrection; 1642-1651: English Civil Wars; September 2, 1642: Closing of the Theaters; August 17-September 25, 1643: Solemn League and Covenant; July 2, 1644: Battle of Marston Moor; Spring, 1645-1660: Puritan New Model Army; 1646-1649: Levellers Launch an Egalitarian Movement; December 6, 1648-May 19, 1649: Establishment of the English Commonwealth; 1651: Hobbes Publishes *Leviathan*; December 16, 1653-September 3, 1658: Cromwell Rules England as Lord Protector; April 4, 1687, and April 27, 1688: Declaration of Liberty of Conscience.

CHARLES II (OF ENGLAND)
King of England (r. 1660-1685)

Charles II played a crucial role in the restoration of stable government in the aftermath of the English Civil War and the Interregnum. At ease in any company, he gave the monarchy a human dimension, and his understanding of the forces that motivated his subjects helped him steer the nation through troubled times.

BORN: May 29, 1630; London, England
DIED: February 6, 1685; London
AREA OF ACHIEVEMENT: Government and politics

EARLY LIFE

When Charles II was born on May 29, 1630, astrologers celebrated the event by predicting a brilliant future for this son of King Charles I and his queen, Henrietta Maria. For the first twelve years of his life, it seemed that all their glowing prophecies were correct. Blessed with parents who were genuinely fond of their children, Charles mastered all the princely arts under the watchful eye of his tutor, the duke of Newcastle. Then the First English Civil War erupted, and every member of the royal family was caught up in the struggle.

At the age of fifteen, Charles was sent to the west of England and assigned his first military command. Luckily, he was guided by prudent counselors such as Edward Hyde, first earl of Clarendon, who later became his chancellor. A boy could not hold back the hosts of Parliament, however, and in 1646 he was forced to retreat to the Scilly Isles, then to Jersey, and finally to exile in Paris, where his mother was desperately trying to raise support for her beleaguered husband. There Charles II remained for two years, under the instruction of Thomas Hobbes.

Charles II was in the Netherlands with his sister, Mary, and his brother-in-law, William II of Orange, in January, 1649, when his father was executed, and thus, at the age of eighteen, he inherited a crown without a kingdom. Nevertheless, Charles was proclaimed king in the Channel Islands, Scotland, parts of Ireland, and Virginia. In September, he sailed to Jersey, but the following February, he was forced to return to the Netherlands.

Against the warnings of some of his advisers, Charles II came to terms with the Scots, accepting their conditions in exchange for the crown of Scotland. This acquiescence on his part resulted in the failure of the efforts of James Graham Montrose to make military gains for the Royalist cause. To blame a youngster of nineteen for the judicial murder of the first marquess of Montrose, how-

ever, is to assign a depth of subtlety and understanding to the king that he did not yet possess. In time, Charles would avenge the death of Montrose, but in 1650 he was a virtual prisoner of the earl of Argyll and the Scottish Covenanters.

On January 1, 1651, Charles was crowned king of Scots at Scone, but he was a monarch in name only. Argyll and his associates used him as a pawn in a deadly game of politics with Oliver Cromwell. When the Royalist army marched south late in the summer of 1651, the king believed that he was on his way to liberate England, but the Covenanters had other plans for him. Trapped in Worcester on September 3, Charles had to fight his way out of the city without the help of the Scots, who refused to engage the enemy. Barely escaping with his life, the king found himself a fugitive in his own kingdom, and for the next six weeks he experienced a series of adventures that changed him and his perception of kingship forever.

At grave personal risk to themselves and their families, a number of ordinary Englishmen gave shelter to their sovereign. Some of them were Roman Catholics and therefore faced a double danger if they were caught. Charles, for his part, gained an intimate knowledge and a deep appreciation of his subjects; no other English monarch has enjoyed such an advantage. During the remaining years of his exile, he never betrayed any of the names, places, or actual details of his escape. Only after his restoration did he tell the truth. Each person who aided him was rewarded generously.

While eluding Cromwell's troops, Charles had at one point found refuge in an oak tree; during the nine years of exile that remained to him, that bed of leaves and boughs seemed soft indeed compared to some of the privations he suffered. In 1654, France and Commonwealth England settled their differences, and Charles was deprived of an ally. He was forced to wander through Germany, existing on the charity of friends and relatives. Finally, in 1656, the Spanish crown provided him with a small pension and a place of residence at Bruges in Belgium, but his poverty was a topic of discussion in European courts.

Cromwell's death in 1658 set in motion a chain of events beyond Charles's control that would, within two years, see him restored to his father's throne. It became increasingly obvious that England was on the verge of another civil war as rival generals and politicians jockeyed for a positions of power. Catching his opponents by

Charles II. (Library of Congress)

surprise, General George Monck marched on London, seizing the capital and then restoring parliamentary government, step by step. The members of the Long Parliament who had been expelled were recalled, and then that legislative body, which in theory had existed for almost twenty years, was dissolved.

The Free Parliament was then summoned to meet in April, 1660, and it proved decidedly Royalist in sentiment. While Monck had been outwardly observing the laws and customs governing the nation, he was quietly negotiating with the king. On Monck's advice, Charles issued the Declaration of Breda, promising that Parliament would ultimately declare a general amnesty, allow liberty of conscience, transfer property, and settle arrears in pay to all ranks of the army. Parliament immediately accepted the declaration, and on May 8, Charles II was proclaimed king of England. He landed at Dover on May 26, and on his thirtieth birthday he entered London.

LIFE'S WORK

In forming his first ministry, Charles II sought to include both former rebels and Royalists; to hasten the healing of the nation's wounds, he sought to pardon most of those who had overthrown his father's government. Only thir-

teen regicides were executed, and twenty-five were imprisoned for life. The land settlement was also quickly made, and although not universally popular, it was final. All property seized by the successive rebel governments was returned to its former owners, but those persons who sold their land to pay taxes or fines received no compensation. Within a year of the Restoration, the army had been paid and disbanded.

Charles II favored a policy of religious toleration, but his new Parliament, which assembled on May 8, 1661, did not share his enlightened views. Instead, they devoted their attention to restricting further the liberties of the very groups the king was trying to help. Their efforts were embodied in a series of acts known as the Clarendon Code, although the hapless Chancellor Hyde was certainly not the author of those repressive laws. Throughout his reign, Charles tried to alleviate the difficulties of his non-Anglican subjects, but with limited success. In 1673, the Test Act further restricted the rights of Roman Catholics. Recognizing that he was a parliamentary monarch, Charles did not openly oppose the will of the legislature, but he tried by personal example to alter the attitudes of those governing the nation in regard to religious toleration.

The king's foreign policy was more difficult to define than his approach to religion, and it has often led to a misunderstanding of his motives. Many of the decisions made by Cromwell were not reversed, including the Navigation Act of 1651, which restricted colonial commerce. Although peace was made with Spain, Jamaica was not returned, and Charles married a Portuguese princess, Catherine of Braganza, in 1662. Despite these seemingly contradictory decisions, Charles's England maintained cordial relations with Spain, as it was no longer a rival.

On the other hand, the similarity of English and Dutch colonial and commercial ambitions was a constant source of friction between those two nations. England had already battled the Netherlands from 1652 to 1654. In 1665, war again erupted between them. The conflict abated two years later, but it ended indecisively and made another war inevitable. During the course of this Second Anglo-Dutch War, England suffered a series of three national disasters. In London during 1665, the Great Plague wiped out many thousands, and the following September, the Great Fire of London burned much of the capital. In 1667, the Dutch in a daring raid crippled the English fleet while it lay at anchor. The results of these events were three: the Treaty of Breda, signed in 1667; the dismissal of Clarendon, who was blamed for everything; and the acquisition of two new colonies, New York and New Jersey.

Freed at last from the vigilance of his chancellor, Charles was able to follow his own policies. The one principle that guided him in foreign affairs was simple: England first. Unfortunately for his reputation, this maxim often led him to make decisions that provoked not only debate but also, at times, strong opposition. Charles accepted thousands of pounds from his cousin Louis XIV of France in exchange for promises he never intended to keep. Charles was a good-natured cynic who could promise to become a Roman Catholic in the secret Treaty of Dover in 1670 with the intention of doing nothing but spending the subsidy Louis paid him. He used France in 1672 to help England wage another war against the Dutch, and when he was obliged to make peace in 1674, he did so, deserting France in the process. Three years later, Charles enraged the French by arranging the marriage of his niece, Mary, the eldest daughter of James, duke of York, to his nephew, William III of Orange. At the end of his reign, Charles was still taking money from Louis and ignoring his promises. Unfortunately, domestic problems were not so easily handled.

Political parties began to evolve during Charles's reign, but their growth was erratic and at times violent. After the fall of Clarendon, the king tried to govern with the advice of five men (Sir Thomas Clifford; Sir Henry Bennet, earl of Arlington; George Villiers, second duke of Buckingham; Anthony Ashley Cooper, known as Lord Ashley; and John Maitland, duke of Lauderdale) whose initials spelled the name "Cabal," by which they came to be known. Religious conflicts dissolved this body, however.

Clifford and Arlington were Roman Catholics. Ashley, now the first earl of Shaftesbury, went into opposition, collecting about him a faction that included remnants of the revolutionary groups that had destroyed the government of Charles I. From these unlikely elements would emerge the Whigs. Thomas Osborne, later earl of Danby and duke of Leeds, formed the nucleus of a court party that appealed to the more conservative elements in English society. In time, its members would be designated with the name Tory. As these two factions struggled with each other, they used bribery, corruption, patronage, and intimidation to gain control of the government. The most ambitious of these devices was the so-called Popish Plot, by which Shaftesbury sought to make himself master of the state.

The events of the Popish Plot began in August, 1678, when an adventurer named Titus Oates presented Shaftes-bury with evidence that there was a Roman Catholic plot to murder Charles II and overthrow the government. The fact that Oates's story was demonstrated to be composed of lies did nothing to calm a national panic. Before the resulting anti-Roman Catholic hysteria subsided, thirty-five innocent men were executed and hundreds of lives had been ruined.

Refusing to subvert the laws of the realm even in the name of mercy, Charles was finally able to stop Oates when he accused the queen of involvement in the plot. Oates was jailed, Shaftesbury fled abroad, and Parliament, which had been in session since 1661, was dissolved in January, 1679. Charles summoned two other Parliaments, one in 1680 and the Oxford Parliament of 1681. Both were dissolved because they insisted on ignoring the affairs of the nation to concentrate their energies on excluding James, duke of York, a Roman Catholic, from the throne in favor of the king's eldest illegitimate son, James, duke of Monmouth.

During the first twenty-one years of his reign, Charles had governed in partnership with Parliament. Now, at the end of his life, he chose to rule without the advice of Parliament, because he realized that the tyranny of many can often be more destructive to the fabric of the state than the supposed subversion of one man. Save for the Rye House Plot in 1683, an abortive attempt by some of Shaftesbury's associates to murder the king and the duke of York, the last four years of Charles's life were peaceful. He died February 6, 1685, after suffering a stroke.

SIGNIFICANCE

Schooled in adversity and familiar with all strata of his society, King Charles II was a professional politician in an age of amateurs. No English monarch before him had so complete an understanding of the ordinary citizen. Feigning an air of laziness and ease of manner, he masked a determined will and boundless energy. Coming to the throne in 1660, he restored the confidence of the English people in their system of government by striking a partnership with Parliament. As a result, he was the last English monarch who both reigned and ruled.

—Clifton W. Potter, Jr.

FURTHER READING

Bryant, Arthur. *King Charles II*. London: Longmans, Green, 1931. This remains the best-balanced biography of the king and his time.

_____. *Restoration England*. London: Collins, 1960. Provides an overview of society in the reign of

Charles II without being dull and fact-ridden. It is an excellent introduction to the period.

_____, ed. *The Letters of King Charles II*. London: Cassell, 1935. A valuable resource for the general reader that provides a personal glimpse of the most charming of the Stuart monarchs.

Fraser, Antonia. *Royal Charles: Charles II and the Restoration*. New York: Alfred A. Knopf, 1979. Popular biography, which at times betrays the author's fondness for her subject.

Hutton, Ronald. *Charles the Second: King of England, Scotland, and Ireland*. New York: Oxford University Press, 1989. Scholarly biography providing a well-written, chronological treatment of Charles's life, personality, and attempts to rule a unified Great Britain.

Matthews, William, ed. *Charles II's Escape from Worcester: A Collection of Narratives Assembled by Samuel Pepys*. Berkeley: University of California Press, 1966. Modern edition of the king's account of his escape after the Battle of Worcester. It is a must for students of the period, but is also exciting reading for anyone who loves a good adventure story.

Miller, John. *After the Civil Wars: English Politics and Government in the Reign of Charles II*. London: Longman, 2000. Comprehensive study of English politics during Charles's reign, based upon original research. Miller outlines the development of Parliament and local governments, changes in the Anglican church, and attempts to heal divisions created by the civil wars.

_____. *Charles II*. London: Weidenfeld and Nicholson, 1991. Comprehensive biography by a recognized expert in late seventeenth century British history.

Ogg, David. *England in the Reign of Charles II*. 2 vols. Oxford, England: Oxford University Press, 1963. The standard work on the period and likely to remain so. The scholarship is thorough, and while the style is not inspired, the work is nevertheless worthy of inclusion in any bibliography of the Restoration.

Pepys, Samuel. *The Diary of Samuel Pepys*. Edited by Robert Latham and William Matthews, 11 vols. London: Bell and Hyman, 1970-1983. A masterful edition of a classic that will long remain the standard rendition of Pepys's diary. The notes alone are worth the price of the eleven volumes.

Scott, Eva. *The King in Exile: The Wanderings of Charles II from June 1646 to July 1654*. London: Archibald Constable, 1905. Chronicles the crucial years in which Charles Stuart became a king without a throne. Based on an impressive collection of manuscripts, it has served as a source for other historians.

SEE ALSO: Catherine of Braganza; First Earl of Clarendon; Oliver Cromwell; Thomas Hobbes; First Duke of Leeds; Louis XIV; George Monck; Titus Oates; First Earl of Shaftesbury; William III.

RELATED ARTICLES in *Great Events from History: The Seventeenth Century, 1601-1700:* 1601-1672: Rise of Scientific Societies; 1642-1651: English Civil Wars; 1651: Hobbes Publishes *Leviathan*; March 12-14, 1655: Penruddock's Uprising; May, 1659-May, 1660: Restoration of Charles II; September 13, 1660-July 27, 1663: British Navigation Acts; 1661-1665: Clarendon Code; June 23, 1661: Portugal Cedes Bombay to the English; 1662-May 3, 1695: England's Licensing Acts; May 19, 1662: England's Act of Uniformity; March 4, 1665-July 31, 1667: Second Anglo-Dutch War; Spring, 1665-Fall, 1666: Great Plague in London; September 2-5, 1666: Great Fire of London; May 24, 1667-May 2, 1668: War of Devolution; December 19, 1667: Impeachment of Clarendon; January 23, 1668: Triple Alliance Forms; February, 1669-January, 1677: John of Austria's Revolts; April, 1670: Charles Town Is Founded; May 2, 1670: Hudson's Bay Company Is Chartered; 1673-1678: Test Acts; 1675-1708: Wren Supervises the Rebuilding of St. Paul's Cathedral; August 13, 1678-July 1, 1681: The Popish Plot; 1679: Habeas Corpus Act; March 4, 1681: "Holy Experiment" Establishes Pennsylvania; August, 1682-November, 1683: Rye House Plot.

CHARLES II (OF SPAIN)
King of Spain, r. 1665-1700

Charles II, who suffered serious mental and physical disabilities as a result of generations of close marriages in the Habsburg Dynasty, ruled the vast but rapidly declining Spanish Empire. Although married twice, Charles produced no heirs, which created the problem of the Spanish Succession. European powers negotiated treaties to partition the empire upon his death in an attempt to maintain a balance of power and preclude war.

BORN: November 6, 1661; Madrid, Spain
DIED: November 1, 1700; Madrid
ALSO KNOWN AS: Charles the Mad; Carlos II; El Hechizado (the bewitched)
AREA OF ACHIEVEMENT: Government and politics

EARLY LIFE

Charles II became king of Spain at the age of four upon the death of his father, King Philip IV (r. 1621-1665). Because of generations of consanguineous marriages within the Habsburg family, Charles suffered severe physical and mental disabilities. Among the physical problems that plagued him was a severe underbite because of the protruding "Habsburg jaw." The protrusion made it impossible to chew properly, so he suffered from chronic indigestion. He also had a large tongue, suffered bouts of epilepsy, rashes, and dizziness, had poor eyesight and had ulcers on his legs, and his hearing became impaired. He suffered from melancholy, lacked normal emotional development, and was extremely superstitious. Charles II was not weaned until he was four years old, about the same time that he learned to walk; this was only after his father's death.

The will of Philip IV set up a Regency Council that was to be headed by the Queen Mother, Mariana de Austria, until Charles was fourteen years old. The king's minority, dominated by the Queen Mother and her favorites, coincided with several economic problems and military setbacks for Spain in European wars. Less than two years into his reign, Louis XIV attacked the Spanish Netherlands in the War of Devolution (1667-1668) to claim his wife's inheritance. His wife, Marie-Thérèse, was the oldest daughter of Philip IV, thus Louis and Charles were brothers by marriage. This war led Louis and Austrian Habsburg emperor Leopold I to create a secret partition treaty in 1668 to dispose of the Spanish Empire upon the death of Charles. Leopold I would gain

Spain, Milan, and the colonies in the Americas, while Louis would obtain the Spanish Netherlands, Naples, Navarre, Franche-Comté, and the Philippines. The fate of the Spanish Empire upon the death of Charles II would be a recurring issue.

On November 6, 1675, Charles officially came of age, and the Regency Council established by Philip's will expired. The Queen Mother tried to have Charles sign a document extending the regency two years, but he refused. Poorly educated, the pawn of factions, caught up in stifling court etiquette, and lacking the capacity to govern, Charles was to embark on "ruling" in his own name. One problem for Charles and his mother was the political ambitions of John of Austria, an illegitimate son of Philip IV and Charles's half brother.

LIFE'S WORK

Once Charles II reached his teenage years, it became important to discuss prospective brides, and this led to a heightening of factional tensions with the bringing forth of French and Austrian "candidates." John had suggested as a possible bride the daughter of Philippe I, the duke of Orléans of the Bourbon Dynasty, Marie Louise, whom he believed would counterbalance the Queen Mother's influence. This sat well with Louis XIV and with Charles, who fell in love with Marie Louise. The Queen Mother's candidate, the Austrian princess, Maria Antonia, was only six years old, which was a major drawback because the production of an heir was paramount and the Spanish could not wait until she reached reproductive age.

John's death on September 17, 1679, allowed the Queen Mother to be reconciled with Charles and to help reassert his influence. Marie Louise, pretty, vivacious, and charming, married Charles in 1679, but the marriage was childless because Charles was impotent. As queen of Spain, Marie Louise had to attend with Charles an *auto-da-fé* (act of faith) on June 30, 1680, in Madrid. The king and queen attended, for an entire hot summer day, the burning to death at the stake of nineteen individuals, and witnessed numerous others receiving lesser penalties. The royal couple sat almost motionless and expressionless, with only short breaks for meals, as the elaborate spectacle played out before them.

Ten years later, Marie Louise had put on a tremendous amount of weight and died from possible poisoning, on February 12, 1689. Just ten days after her death, the Spanish council sent Charles a note requesting that he marry and produce heirs. Maria Anna of Bavaria-Neuburg was selected in May of 1689, but there was extreme difficulty in getting her to Spain because of war in Europe and because of bad weather. The marriage was finalized within the year. The new queen came from a large family and felt compelled to find places for her relatives, which resulted in quarrels between her and the Queen Mother over government positions. During the struggles, Charles was caught in the middle, as his mother and his wife sought his support. The queen became withdrawn and depressed, but her fortunes appeared to improve when the Queen Mother died in May of 1696.

The Treaty of Rijswijk (1697) allowed the Spanish Succession issue to re-emerge, especially after Charles became ill around February or March, 1698. The Spanish called him El Hechizado (the bewitched), a characterization with which Charles agreed. Some clergy felt compelled to ask the devil the circumstances of Charles's bewitching. Louis and William III of Orange, king of England, Scotland, and Ireland and leader of the Netherlands, negotiated the First Treaty of Partition on October 11, 1698, which apportioned the vast Spanish Empire. Joseph Ferdinand, electoral prince of Bavaria, became king of Spain and the Austrians and French gained territory. The Spanish were outraged, and Charles signed a will designating the young electoral prince as his sole heir, seeking to keep the Spanish Empire intact. After Ferdinand died in 1699, Louis XIV and William III produced a Second Treaty of Partition (March 25, 1700), which was more complicated than the first. The Austrian candidate, Archduke Charles, would become king of Spain as Charles III (and, later, Holy Roman Emperor as Charles VI), and the French would gain Naples, Sicily, and Lorraine. They then exchanged Naples and Sicily for Savoy-Piedmont. The duke of Lorraine would be given Milan.

Once again, this arrangement upset Spanish sensibilities, and the Spanish council, on June 6, 1700, rejected the treaty, deciding instead to keep the empire under a single ruler and offer it to the prince who was best able to protect its territorial integrity. Because of pressure from Spanish clergy, Charles signed a will on October 2, 1700, presenting the entire empire to Louis XIV's grandson, Philip of Anjou, and then to the duke of Berry if Philip did not accept. If both French candidates rejected the will, it was to be offered to Archduke Charles. Contemporary gossip held that Charles visited the graves of his ancestors in the palace basement to ask for their pardon for such a heinous act—offering the French the Spanish Empire. Charles did not have long to live, and the bizarre act of placing freshly killed animals on his body to keep him warm did not suffice to prevent his death on November 1, 1700.

SIGNIFICANCE

Spanish history during the seventeenth century presents a cautionary tale of the consequences of consanguineous marriages and the failure to make needed reforms; both were especially true during the reign of Charles II. His death and the accession of Philip of Anjou as Philip V (r. 1700-1724, 1724-1746) marked the end of the Habsburg rule of Spain, the beginning of the Bourbon Dynasty, and the start of the War of Spanish Succession (1700-1714).

The Spanish desire to preserve the territorial integrity of Spain's vast empire and prevent its division through the designation of Philip of Anjou as heir by Charles's will, and Louis's acceptance of the will, stand as the immediate causes of the war of succession. Although Philip retained the Spanish throne, the war ended with a partition, as all the major participants received some territorial or commercial concessions. Austrian Habsburg emperor Charles VI (r. 1711-1740) gained Naples, Sardinia, Milan, Tuscan ports, and the Spanish Netherlands.

The major shift in the "balance of power" in Europe was England's emergence as the preeminent power, eclipsing France, which was financially exhausted and having to relinquish significant territories—Nova Scotia and Newfoundland—to England. The Spanish accorded to England the *asiento* contract to supply Spanish colonies with slaves, and enabled the English to have greater trade, legitimate and illegitimate, with the Spanish American possessions. A declining empire "ruled" by a physically and mentally defective king who clung to a strong sense of duty along with a lack of effective government ministers was a combination that proved too much for Spain to overcome.

—*Mark C. Herman*

FURTHER READING

Frey, Linda, and Marsha Frey, eds. *The Treaties of the War of the Spanish Succession.* Westport, Conn.: Greenwood Press, 1995. An excellent reference source with short articles on Charles, his will, other European rulers, and the partition treaties.

Kamen, Henry. *Empire: How Spain Became a World Power, 1492-1763.* New York: Harper Collins, 2003. An excellent analytical survey of Spain's rise to global prominence, placing the reign of Charles within the broader context of Spanish history and underscores how his reign was an important turning point.

Langdon-Davies, John. *Carlos: The King Who Would Not Die*. Englewood Cliffs, N.J.: Prentice-Hall, 1963. An entertaining, if not overly critical, biography of Charles, which focuses on the king's personality and the intrigues at court rather than on government policy.

Lynch, John. *The Hispanic World in Crisis and Change, 1598-1700*. Oxford, England: Blackwell, 1992. The importance of Charles's reign for Spain's possessions in the Americas is a strong feature of this analytical study.

Pierson, Peter. *The History of Spain*. Westport, Conn.: Greenwood Press, 1999. A noted historian explains the significance of Charles's reign for Spain and Europe.

SEE ALSO: Anne of Austria; John of Austria; Leopold I; Louis XIV; Marie-Thérèse; Philip IV; William III.

RELATED ARTICLES in *Great Events from History: The Seventeenth Century, 1601-1700:* 17th century: Rise of the Gunpowder Empires; c. 1601-1682: Spanish Golden Age; March 31, 1621-September 17, 1665: Reign of Philip IV; May, 1640-January 23, 1641: Revolt of the Catalans; May 24, 1667-May 2, 1668: War of Devolution; January 23, 1668: Triple Alliance Forms; February 13, 1668: Spain Recognizes Portugal's Independence; February, 1669-January, 1677: John of Austria's Revolts; June 30, 1680: Spanish Inquisition Holds a Grandiose *Auto-da-fé*; 1689-1697: Wars of the League of Augsburg; June 2, 1692-May, 1693: Salem Witchcraft Trials; October 11, 1698, and March 25, 1700: First and Second Treaties of Partition.

CHARLES X GUSTAV
King of Sweden (r. 1654-1660)

Charles X fought expensive wars against Poland and Denmark, and although his aggressive policies united the opposition of several Baltic countries against Sweden, his ultimate successes secured for Sweden—in the months after his death—substantial territory through three treaties with four different countries in 1660.

BORN: November 8, 1622; Nyköpering Castle, Sweden

DIED: February 13, 1660; Göteborg, Sweden

AREAS OF ACHIEVEMENT: Government and politics, warfare and conquest

EARLY LIFE

Charles X Gustav (GEHS-tahv) was the son of a German nobleman, John Casimir of the Palatinate, and Katarina, daughter of Charles IX and half sister of Gustavus Adolphus. Born and raised in Sweden, Charles X studied at the University of Uppsala. During his youth, he traveled widely and reportedly was something of a playboy. Trained as a military officer, he was a man of action more than reflection. Although strong-willed, physically powerful, and competent, he had a reputation for excessive consumption of food and alcoholic beverages, and he tended to dream about grand schemes.

For many years it was widely expected that Charles would marry his cousin, Queen Christina of Sweden, and

they were secretly engaged for a time. About the time the queen came of age in 1644, however, she became more interested in others, most notably the courtier Count Magnus Gabriel De la Gardie (1622-1686)—the son of a soldier and statesman—and Countess Ebba Sparre (1626-1662). Charles, primarily because of his ambition for political power, was greatly disappointed.

Charles accompanied the Swedish army to Germany during the later years of the Thirty Years' War (1618-1648). He learned the art of warfare under Lennart Torstenson, taking part in battles at Breitenfeld and Jankowitz. In 1648, he was appointed commander of the forces in Germany, but the war's end in the Treaty of Westphalia prevented him from pursuing the military glory he desired. Serving as the Swedish ambassador at the executive congress of Nuremberg, he defended Swedish interests skillfully.

In 1649, Christina designated Charles as her successor, despite the strong opposition of the venerable Axel Oxenstierna, who headed the Privy Council. The next year, Sweden's representative assembly, the Riksdag, approved her choice. Charles had to sign a document pledging to follow the laws and respect the traditional privileges of citizens, including the nobility. As discontent with Christina increased, there were rumors about a possible coup d'état. Avoiding the appearance of intrigue, Charles withdrew to the island of Öland. Christina's conversion to Catholicism, which was illegal in Sweden, made it impossible for her to continue as monarch. When she abdicated on June 6, 1654, Charles ascended to the throne.

LIFE'S WORK

As Charles X took his coronation oath, Sweden was facing a serious economic crisis. He and many other Swedes hoped to improve conditions by expanding into territories held by one of the neighboring countries. The most inviting target was Poland, which had a notoriously weak central government and faced a Cossack uprising. Charles was also motivated by a belief that the existence of a Polish king belonging to the Vasa Dynasty was a potential threat to his rule. In October, Charles married Hedwig Leonora, daughter of the duke of Holstein-Gottorp, partly because of desire for a dependable ally. Three months later, Charles's council agreed to support a war with Poland.

In January, 1655, Charles made definite preparations for the coming conflict. He began in earnest to hire mercenaries and to take the financial measures necessary. When the Riksdag met in Stockholm in March, 1655, he already had spent much money on war preparations. For the Riksdag to oppose his project would have meant considerable financial loss. With Oxenstierna's enthusiastic encouragement, the delegates authorized the king to initiate a preemptive war against Poland, They refused, however, to provide all the funding he requested, making it necessary for him to borrow large sums of money.

On July 10, 1655, Charles personally led an attack on Poland with an army of fifty thousand, thus beginning the First Northern War (1655-1660). The Swedes were victorious in the early engagements and soon occupied Warsaw, Kraków, and most of Poland proper. The king of Poland, John II Casimir Vasa (r. 1648-1668), fled to Silesia. Swedish mercenaries pillaged cities and looted the countryside. The Swedish failure to take the fortress-monastery near Czestochowa triggered a general uprising. Polish guerrillas harassed the occupying army, while Russian troops occupied Polish lands in the east.

At the start of the war, Elector Frederick William of Brandenburg was a Polish ally, but after suffering a defeat, he joined the Swedish side in the Treaty of Königsberg. In early 1656, John II returned from exile, won several battles, and temporarily reclaimed Warsaw. In July, however, the Swedes and Brandenburgers rebounded in the Battle of Warsaw. Then Russia declared war on Sweden and invaded Swedish Livonia. Poland's strategy of wearing down the invaders was increasingly successful. With aid from the Holy Roman Emperor, Polish forces took control of most of the south. By the summer of 1657, the Swedish-Brandenburg invaders were on the defensive.

On June 1, 1657, Denmark's declaration of war against Sweden forced Charles to withdraw most of his troops from the Polish quagmire. Brandenburg switched sides. Still, Charles's army rather quickly overwhelmed the Danes. Swedish troops led by Karl Gustav Wrangel (1613-1676) took advantage of Danish weaknesses along the southern boundary and moved into Bremen. Shortly thereafter, Charles successfully overran Jutland. In January, 1658, because of unusually cold weather, Charles took five thousand troops across the ice of the Little and Great Belts (the Sound Strait) to surprise Danish defenses on Fyn Island. The rare weather continued into February, allowing two thousand Swedes to continue an island-hoping operation over the Great Belt, eventually reaching the outskirts of Copenhagen, which had no land defenses. The Danes sued for peace.

In the resulting Treaty of Roskilde (1658), Denmark agreed to give up almost half of its territory, including the rich southern provinces of Halland and Blekinge, which,

Charles X Gustav. (Hulton Archive/Getty Images)

however, was not enough for Charles. When the Danish government refused to join him in an alliance against Brandenburg, he responded angrily with a siege of Copenhagen. Again, he had miscalculated. The war's interruption of the grain trade was doing great harm to the Dutch Republic. Both the Dutch and English governments dispatched their fleets in support of Denmark. The siege of Copenhagen failed. Meanwhile, the Poles liberated almost all their lands. During the next year, Sweden suffered so many defeats that it appeared briefly as if its Baltic empire would be partitioned.

Living outside Sweden during most of his reign, Charles was unable to have much impact on the country's domestic development. He did reorganize the University of Uppsala and stopped the large-scale alienation of royal lands. Although he encouraged the Riksdag to reduce the holdings of the nobility, the war prevented any real accomplishment toward that result. Major social and economic problems were largely ignored. The constitutional system continued almost unchanged.

In early 1660, Charles made one of his few return visits to Sweden to make plans for a new campaign against Norway. Hoping to get approval for additional funding, he opened a meeting of the Riksdag in Göteborg. Suddenly, the king became ill and died on February 13 at the age of thirty-eight. His four-year-old son succeeded him as Charles XI. Political power was turned over to a regency of nobles in the royal council.

SIGNIFICANCE

Within a few months of Charles's death, Sweden's new government ended the First Northern War in the treaties of Oliva (with Poland and Brandenburg), Kardis (with Russia), and Copenhagen (with Denmark). Although Sweden had to give up Bornholm and the Trondheim region, it retained possession of the rich provinces of Halland, Scania, and Blekinge. Because of Dutch demands, Sweden was forced to give up its colony of Delaware in North America.

In the First Northern War, the aggressive policies of Charles X alarmed and united most of the powers of the Baltic region. Although his rather impetuous attack on Poland at first succeeded militarily, he aroused a popular uprising that he was unable to subdue. Then, in continuing the conflict with Denmark, again he made the mistake of not putting a limit to his ambition. Yet, Charles's war achieved the annexation of the southern "breadbasket," which is considered his lasting contribution to Sweden.

—Thomas Tandy Lewis

FURTHER READING

Akerman, Susanna. *Queen Christina of Sweden and Her Circle: The Transformation of a Seventeenth-Century Philosophical Libertine*. New York: E. J. Brill, 1991. A fascinating biography that provides considerable information about the background and life of Charles before 1654.

Conforti, Michael. *Sweden: A Royal Treasury, 1550-1700*. Chicago: University of Chicago Press, 1988. The story of the monarchy told by way of the country's art, textiles, weapons, and other technological artifacts.

Lisk, Jill. *The Struggle for Supremacy in the Baltic, 1600-1725*. New York: Funk and Wagnalls, 1968. This work examines the complex and often violent rivalry in the Baltic region, and it provides an excellent summary of the First Northern War.

Nordstrom, Byron. *The History of Sweden*. Westport, Conn.: Greenwood Press, 2002. The place to begin for the reader who wants a broad overview of the country's story.

Roberts, Michael. *From Oxenstierna to Charles XII: Four Studies*. New York: Cambridge University Press, 2002. Two of the studies in this work look at Charles X's policies, one on his foreign policy and the other on his domestic policies.

_____. *Sweden's Age of Greatness, 1633-1718*. New York: Macmillan, 1973. Dahlgren Stellan's essay on Sweden's constitutional system during the reign of Charles X is especially helpful.

_____. *The Swedish Imperial Experience*. New York: Cambridge University Press, 1979. Includes the best and most complete account in English of Charles X's reign.

Scott, Franklin. *Sweden: The Nation's History*. Minneapolis: University of Minnesota Press, 1977. A good standard account of Swedish history, although somewhat dated.

SEE ALSO: Alexis; Christina; Frederick William, the Great Elector; Gustavus II Adolphus; John III Sobieski; Leopold I; Axel Oxenstierna; Michael Romanov; Lennart Torstenson.

RELATED ARTICLES in *Great Events from History: The Seventeenth Century, 1601-1700*: 1632-1667: Polish-Russian Wars for the Ukraine; 1640-1688: Reign of Frederick William, the Great Elector; July 10, 1655-June 21, 1661: First Northern War; November 30, 1700: Battle of Narva.

CHEN SHU
Chinese painter

An accomplished painter of landscapes and flowers, Chen Shu belongs among the elite of Qing Dynasty painters. Her conservative style appealed greatly to imperial society, and as an important teacher of male and female art students, Chen Shu established an artistic tradition that influenced future generations.

BORN: March 13, 1660; Jiaxing, Zhejiang province, China
DIED: April 17, 1735; Beijing, China
ALSO KNOWN AS: Ch'en Shu (Wade-Giles)
AREA OF ACHIEVEMENT: Art

EARLY LIFE

Chen Shu (chehn shew) was born to an illustrious upper-class family in Jiaxing, about 50 miles (80 kilometers) southwest of Shanghai, in the early years of the new Qing Dynasty. Her family traced its origins to the twelfth century, and her father, Chen Yao Xun, had gone to university. According to family legend, Chen's artistic success was related to her father's relationship with the god of literature. When her mother was pregnant with Chen, a monk told her father that the god had told him to ask Chen Yao Xun for money to restore his temple in town. Chen's father agreed to pay, and just before Chen was born, he dreamed that the god visited his house. The baby was given the name Shu, which means "writing" or "book" in Chinese.

As a young girl, Chen was not sent to school along with her brothers. At seven, however, she began to ask them about their school readings, which she learned by heart. She also began to copy paintings and scrolls of calligraphy. Her traditional mother ordered her to stop these activities, which she saw as a distraction from her education as future housewife. Chen disobeyed her mother, copying one of the paintings in her father's study, and was beaten for it by her mother. That night, the god of literature appeared to Chen's mother in a dream and told that her daughter would become famous and must be allowed to study. The dream caused a change of heart in Chen's mother, and she hired a tutor to instruct Chen in classical literature. In turn, Chen often painted literary scenes and decorated her bedroom with her work.

Chen's father died when she was still a teen. She helped her bereaved family, selling the products of her sewing and teaching her younger brother classical literature.

LIFE'S WORK

Chen Shu was fortunate to marry an unconventional man who appreciated her art and shared similar interests, supporting her work and professional development. Qian Long Guang, a teacher, was five years her elder and had recently been widowed. He, too, came from a respected family. Chen fully accepted her integration in his family and continued to honor his deceased first wife, attending her altar in the family home. She also received positive artistic feedback and support from her father-in-law, Qian Rui Cheng, an official and specialized painter of pines and rocks as well as a calligrapher, whose ill wife Chen helped to nurse.

Soon, Chen found herself in a vibrant artistic, literary, and intellectual circle, and her paintings were widely admired. Her home became the location of many artistic meetings, and the sale of her work helped to sustain her lifestyle in spite of her husband's relatively low income. Indicative of Chen Shu and Qian Long Guang's artistic collaboration is a series of undated landscape paintings by Chen, idealizing scenes on the Yangzi River, that are inscribed with the poems of her husband in the sky.

The birth of her five children also inspired Chen as a teacher. Her first son was born in 1683, when Chen was twenty-three years old; he died of smallpox in 1687. To save her second son, Qian Chen Qun (1686-1774), from this epidemic, Chen sent him to live with her mother-in-law for the next seven years. Chen bore two more sons, Qian Feng (1688-1718) and Qian Jie (1691-1758), and one daughter whose year of birth is unknown. In 1695, Chen's husband went home to his ailing parents. Failing to find a satisfactory teacher, Chen decided to educate her four children herself, an unusual act concerning her boys.

While raising her children, Chen continued to paint. Her favorite subjects were flowers, landscapes, and figures. Artistically, Chen employed a conservative style and modeled her work on that of classical masters. Her orthodox style earned her the admiration of her society, which saw in her works a vigor generally deemed absent from the paintings of women who employed a more contemporary, decorative style.

Chen's flower paintings drew inspiration from the Ming painters of the Wu School of Suzhou. Among Chen's best surviving works in this genre are the ten leaves of the *Sketches from Life* (1713) album, held by the National Palace Museum in Taipei, Taiwan, like much of her existing work. The brush strokes of the leaf *Vegetables, Fruit, and Asters* show an expressive yet also relaxed quality, and the colors are applied directly, without outlining in the so-called boneless style of the Wu School. Similarly, *Iris and Roses* shows long ink brushstrokes tracing the veins of the leaves and petals of the iris, whose colors are depicted in classical hues.

After her husband Qian and her third son Feng both died in 1718, when she was fifty-eight years old, Chen maintained a close relationship with Qian Chen Qun, who stayed home with her for the official two-year mourning period following Qian Long Guang's death. When Qian Chen Qun returned to Beijing in 1721 and rose high in the imperial bureaucracy, he invited Chen to join him, and she stayed in Beijing from 1722 to 1725. This visit enlarged Chen's artistic reputation and introduced her to the artistic life of the capital.

Eventually, however, Chen asked for leave to return to Jiaxing, where she would stay and work until 1735. Two of her most famous landscape paintings were created there in 1734. *Imitating Tang Yin's "Dwelling in the Summer Mountains"* offers a vast view onto a pastoral southern Chinese river scene. On the left of the river, weeping willows are executed in exact strokes, along with shelter houses with open windows through which figures are seen and white rocks crowned by three pines rise against a summer sky. On the right, pine ridges traverse hills before distant mountains. It is a picture of serenity, created with formal rigor.

In 1735, her second son wanted to visit Chen in Jiaxing, but she traveled instead to see him in Beijing. The journey weakened the old artist, and she became ill. For the new year, Chen Shu may have created her last works, if her seals are authentic on the two hanging scrolls depicting a flower planter and a vase with flowers.

Chen Shu died on April 17, 1735. Her brother and the husband of her daughter were at her side as death ended a long, artistically productive and highly esteemed life.

SIGNIFICANCE

Chen Shu's flower, landscape, and figure paintings were valued by her contemporaries for their orthodoxy and mastery of classical conventions. Critics praised Chen for creating her art based on references to past masters. Her adherence to classical styles and rejection of fashionable, decorative techniques was interpreted at the time as displaying "masculine" virtues and eschewing "inferior, feminine" aesthetics.

Traditionally, part of Chen Shu's artistic fame in China was based on her exemplary personal lifestyle. Exhibiting the desired virtues of model daughter, wife, and mother, her personal life contributed to her lasting artistic reputation, yet her paintings do not show any signs of subordination or compromise.

Her son Qian Chen Qun, who wrote a glowing biography of his mother, aided Chen's reputation. As Qian rose at the imperial court, he made gifts of his mother's paintings to the Qian Long emperor and his court. Thus, many of Chen's works became part of the imperial collection. The emperor appreciated Chen Shu's paintings so much that he adorned them with his own poetry. On Chen's painting *Imitating Wang Meng's "Dwelling in the Mountains on a Summer Day,"* Qian Long wrote poems five times, from 1782 to 1793, affixing his seal every time and filling most of the painting's sky.

Chen Shu's artistic impact reached beyond her immediate work. As a respected teacher of male and female art students, including prominent members of her family, she founded an artistic tradition of her own. Her youngest son, Qian Jie, and the famous Qing painter and art historian Zhang Geng both learned life sketching from Chen. Zhang's *Landscape After Wang Meng* (1732) clearly reveals the depth of Chen's influence upon his artistic development. Chen's work, no less than her teaching, served to inspire future artists, such as when the court painter Chin Deng Biao created the album *Imitating Chen Shu* (no date). Chen's poetry was collected but never printed, and it has been lost.

—*R. C. Lutz*

FURTHER READING

Barnhart, Richard, et al. *Three Thousand Years of Chinese Painting*. New Haven, Conn.: Yale University Press, 1997. Standard introduction to the subject; places Chen's artistic achievement into the context of China's national art. Illustrated, notes, bibliography, index.

Sullivan, Michael. *The Three Perfections: Chinese Painting, Poetry, and Calligraphy*. 2d rev. ed. New York: George Braziller, 1999. Sheds welcome light on the artistic practice of adorning paintings with poems written in calligraphy, as happened to Chen Shu's works. Illustrated, bibliography.

Weidner, Marsha. "The Conventional Success of Ch'en Shu." In *Flowering in the Shadows: Women in the History of Chinese and Japanese Painting*, edited by Marsha Weidner. Honolulu: University of Hawaii Press, 1990. Thorough discussion of Chen's life and work; reproduces many of her paintings. Uses Wade-Giles. The same book has a chapter on "Women Painters in Traditional China" by Ellen Johnston Laing, providing background for Chen's life and art. Illustrated, notes, bibliography, glossary of Chinese names.

Weidner, Marsha, et al. *Views from the Jade Terrace: Chinese Women Artists, 1300-1912.* Indianapolis: Indianapolis Museum of Art, 1988. Catalog of an American exhibition, contains primary and background in-

formation on Chen and places her in a larger tradition. Illustrated, notes, bibliography, index.

SEE ALSO: Abahai; Chongzhen; Dorgon; Kangxi; Liu Yin; Shunzhi; Tianqi; Wang Fuzhi; Zheng Chenggong.

RELATED ARTICLES in *Great Events from History: The Seventeenth Century, 1601-1700:* June 6, 1644: Manchus Take Beijing; February 17, 1661-December 20, 1722: Height of Qing Dynasty.

DUCHESSE DE CHEVREUSE
French princess

During her long and colorful life, de Chevreuse gained great power as an intimate of Queen Anne of Austria. She became powerful also by conspiring against governmental ministers during the reigns of Louis XIII and the regency for Louis XIV.

BORN: December, 1600; place unknown
DIED: August 12, 1679; Gagny, France
ALSO KNOWN AS: Marie de Rohan (given name)
AREA OF ACHIEVEMENT: Government and politics

EARLY LIFE

Not much is known about the early life of Marie de Rohan, duchesse de Chevreuse (shehv-rayz). She was born in December of 1600, the daughter of the governor of Paris, Hercule Rohan, duc de Montbazon. In 1617, she was married to Charles d'Albert, who later became the duc de Lynes. Almost immediately after her marriage, she departed for the royal court, where she became an important member of the royal household as the superintendent for Queen Anne of Austria, the unhappy and much-neglected wife of King Louis XIII. Rohan became Queen Anne's mistress, and Anne, who figures centrally in Alexandre Dumas's famous novel *Les trois mousquetaires* (1844; *The Three Musketeers*, 1846), was to become one of the most influential people in Rohan's life. Rohan, in turn, was to play a major friendly and political role in the life of the queen and her son, Louis XIV, who became one of the most popular French kings.

In 1621, Rohan became a widow. She married Claude de Lorraine, duc de Chevreuse, in 1625. After her second marriage, Rohan came to be known as the duchesse de Chevreuse. It was around this time that she set in motion her never-ceasing quest for power by conspiring to control royal states of affairs and to manipulate international

events. She was known far and wide for her great beauty and attracted a range of high-standing and, ultimately, very politically useful lovers.

LIFE'S WORK

Chevreuse came to be recognized as one of the great French politicians of the mid-seventeenth century. She was at times a friend to the powerful royal cardinal ministers, Cardinal de Richelieu and Cardinal Jules Mazarin and at other times when it served her purposes, she became their sworn enemy. Regardless, both no doubt came to respect her highly.

In 1625, Rohan attempted to promote a relationship between Queen Anne, who was sorely neglected by her cold husband Louis XIII, and the dashing British lord George Villiers, first duke of Buckingham. Her intentions failed miserably, however, when Buckingham openly declared his love for the queen to the shocked French court. This daring action, in turn, cast a shadow on Queen Anne's reputation. Rohan, for some unknown reason, also bore the blame when the queen suffered a miscarriage during her first pregnancy. The following year, the duchesse de Chevreuse was exiled to Poitou, for her continuous intrigues in opposition to King Louis XIII's powerful minister, Richelieu. However, she failed to learn a lesson and soon left for her own duchy of Lorraine, where she conspired against the king by aiding Buckingham. Two years later, in 1628, Richelieu found her information useful and gave permission for her to return to France.

However, Chevreuse continued her ways and found herself exiled once more to Touraine in 1633 for providing Spain with French state secrets gleaned from her lover, the marquis de Châteauneuf.

In 1635, France went to war with Spain, and Chevreuse and her lover Queen Anne were accused of providing treasonous information to the Spanish court. Queen Anne's loyalty to Spain (she was born there) and her strong Roman Catholic background made her a natural suspect. Once more, the duchesse de Chevreuse had to flee into exile to Spain, where she remained until the death of the French monarch, Louis XIII. During her exile, Chevreuse traveled to England and Brussels (now in Belgium), where she entered into various espionage adventures. She was allowed to return to France only after Queen Anne became regent upon the accession of her minor son, Louis XIV, who came to be known as both the Sun King (Le Roi de Soleil) and Louis the Great (Louis le Grand). He ruled France for seventy-two years.

At this point, it becomes clear how brilliant Rohan was as a politician. Some scholars call her one of the brightest politicians of the seventeenth century. She proved to be even more dangerous when in exile because of her plotting with France's enemies, notably Duke Charles IV of Lorraine. Upon her return to France, she became involved in the failed conspiracy of Les Importants, a group of aristocrats intent on assassinating the queen's first minister, Jules Mazarin. Mazarin was a cardinal of the Roman Catholic Church and Richelieu's successor. Some scholars maintain that Mazarin was secretly married to the widowed Queen Anne and indeed others think he was the father of Louis XIV.

For Rohan's political indiscretion, Anne sent Rohan once more into exile. However, in 1649, she was allowed to return to France during the first phase of the Wars of the Fronde (1648-1653), the aristocratic uprising caused by the efforts of the *parlement* (the chief judiciary body) and by angry and ambitious nobles to restrict the monarch's authority and overspending. Serving as a link with Spain, Rohan's great midlife achievements included her designation as a major player in the first Fronde (Fronde of the *parlementaires*) and the second Fronde (Fronde of the princes).

In the second Fronde, Rohan helped organize a group of aristocrats that supported the prince de Condé (the Great Condé) in 1651. The Fronde of the princes came about as a conflict between Condé and Cardinal Mazarin. Condé was a brilliant French general in the Thirty Years' War (1618-1648) and came to the royal family's assistance during the first Fronde. However, the prince expected to control Queen Regent Anne, her eleven-year-old son, Louis XIV, and Cardinal Mazarin. After Condé

Duchesse de Chevreuse. (Hulton Archive/Getty Images)

failed to follow through on his promise and broke his agreement to marry his brother to her daughter Charlotte, Rohan reunited with Mazarin and, thus, helped bring about the end of what came to be known as the Wars of the Fronde. After the defeat of the Fronde, Mazarin remained in control of France. A compromise was finally reached between *parlement* and the royal family in March of 1649. With the Fronde defeated, Louis XIV established an undisputed monarchy.

In 1652, Rohan retired to Dampierre. Little is known of her life between this time and her death in Gagny, France, in 1679.

SIGNIFICANCE

Marie de Rohan's colorful life and brilliant mind ensured she would be remembered not only as a figure in fiction and art but also as a real-life, key seventeenth century political player. In an era when women did not wield much public power, Rohan became a major politician in the

French court in a time when the aristocracy battled the monarch for more power. Because of the insights she gained from her many travels, intrigues, and connections, she was able to encourage rebellion and effect resolution.

In fiction, there is little doubt that Rohan is characterized as the French literary prototype, the seductive villainess Milady de Winter of *The Three Musketeers*. Instead of a helpless female, Milady is portrayed by Alexandre Dumas as a powerful woman intent on success at any price.

In addition, through close analyses of the sitter's costumes and attributes in view of seventeenth century decorum, Marie de Rohan has been credited as the model for the master artist Diego Velázquez's painting *Lady with a Fan*, painted during Rohan's time of exile in Madrid in 1638.

—M. Casey Diana

FURTHER READING

Menzies, S. "La Duchesse de Chevreuse (1600-1679)." In *Famous Women Described by Great Writers*, edited by Esther Singleton. New York: Nova Science, 2002. Informative account of Marie de Rohan's colorful life, with an illustration of the famous duchess.

Moote, A. L. *The Revolt of the Judges: The Parlement of Paris and the Fronde, 1643-1652*. Princeton, N.J.: Princeton University Press, 1972. Provides great historical detail concerning the uprising of the nobility against the monarch and the political intrigue surrounding the court in which Marie de Rohan participated.

Pitts, Vincent. *La Grande Mademoiselle at the Court of France: 1627-1693*. Baltimore, Md.: Johns Hopkins University Press, 2000. Makes many mentions of Marie de Rohan and, although she isn't central, the book remains a major source of information on the period's political and social events as well as a page-turning melodrama of court intrigue.

Prawdin, Michael. *Marie de Rohan, Duchesse de Chevreuse*. New York: Allen & Unwin, 1971. This is the only English-language biography of Marie de Rohan and serves as a wonderful introduction to the era.

SEE ALSO: Anne of Austria; The Great Condé; First Duke of Buckingham; François de La Rochefoucauld; Louis XIV; Jules Mazarin; Cardinal de Richelieu; Viscount de Turenne.

RELATED ARTICLES in *Great Events from History: The Seventeenth Century, 1601-1700*: 1610-1643: Reign of Louis XIII; November 10, 1630: The Day of Dupes; 1661: Absolute Monarchy Emerges in France; 1682: French Court Moves to Versailles.

CHONGZHEN
Emperor of China (r. 1628-1644)

Chongzhen presided over the demise of the Ming Dynasty. He managed to stay on the throne while battling various problems in the country until the seventeenth year of his reign, when the Ming Dynasty came to an end.

BORN: February 6, 1611; Beijing, China
DIED: April 25, 1644; Beijing
ALSO KNOWN AS: Ch'ung-chen (reign name, Wade-Giles); Zhu Youjian (given name, Pinyin), Chu Yu-chien (given name, Wade-Giles); Huaizong (temple name, Pinyin), Huai-tsung (temple name, Wade-Giles); Xizong (temple name, Pinyin), Ssu-tsung (temple name, Wade-Giles); Zhuang Liedi (posthumous title, Pinyin), Chuang Lieh-ti (posthumous title, Wade-Giles)
AREA OF ACHIEVEMENT: Government and politics

EARLY LIFE

The Ming emperor Tianqi (also known as Zhu Youjiao) had five children, but they all died in infancy. Thus, when Tianqi passed away in 1627 at the age of twenty-two, he left no heir. Zhu Youjian, the emperor's oldest surviving brother, came to the throne. The seventeen-year-old successor was the fifth son in the imperial family, and he took the reign name Chongzhen, meaning "lofty and auspicious." His mother, Consort Liu had died in 1615, when he was four.

Chongzhen inherited from his brother a discredited country, void of hope and future. In the 1620's, China had been troubled by both domestic and foreign issues, all of which the new emperor decided to overcome. In the foreign sphere, the Manchus' threatening presence in the northeastern part of the country was a sore that never healed. At home, the ministers at court were engaged in factional power struggles, while Wei Zhongxian (Wei Chong-hsien, 1568-1628), the powerful eunuch from Tianqi's era, continued to conspire against his enemies. Chongzhen, being a hardworking and conscientious young man, attempted to start a new age for himself and his people.

LIFE'S WORK

Chongzhen's first and most important priority was to rid the court of the vicious eunuch Wei Zhongxian. Wei had been promoted to be the director of Eastern Depot, a secret service of the Ming, by the previous emperor. Before Chongzhen came to the throne, Wei and the late emperor's wet nurse, Madame Ke, had wreaked havoc at court, abusing the power bestowed on them by the emperor. Together, Wei and Ke intercepted memorials meant for the emperor and made decisions using the imperial seal. Any opponents or critics of the duo met with imprisonment and persecution.

When Chongzhen came on the scene on October 2, 1627, all were wary of the new ruler's attitude. In three months' time, Chongzhen issued an order to Wei, ordering him to serve at the imperial tombs at Nanzhili. Wei, aware of his imminent demise, committed suicide en route. The other culprit, Madame Ke, was stripped of her power and beaten to death. This first move by the new emperor was applauded by the whole court, which had been oppressed by the infamous duo for years. Soon after Wei's demise, the Donglin (Eastern Grove) faction returned to power, bringing a partisan structure back to the imperial court.

Being a daring and curious young man, Emperor Chongzhen was open to new ideas and knowledge. Intellectual life at court was revived, and the emperor allowed the important task of reforming the imperial calendar to be given to two Jesuits, Adam von Schall and John Schreck. The two foreigners had predicted an eclipse more accurately than the court astronomers. The importance of an eclipse cannot be slighted in Chinese culture, where the natural phenomenon was believed to have ties with the imperial fortune.

In the mid-1620's, maritime trade in China was severely affected by piracy along the southeast coastline. Both Dutch and Chinese pirates harassed the Taiwan Strait and South China Sea. Only after the capture of the pirate leader Zheng Zhilong (Cheng Chih-lung, 1604-1661) did the situation improve. At the same time, trading with the Spanish through Manila increased. Sino-Japanese commerce blossomed, while the Portuguese brought silver to China via Macao. Thus, the sagging Ming economy received a temporary boost during the early years of Chongzhen's reign in the 1630's, yet the maritime situation took a drastic turn in 1639, when Japan blocked Portuguese merchants in Macao from trading in Nagasaki. In the same year, the Chinese in Manila were involved with the Spanish and violence exploded. Hence, Sino-Japanese trade came to an end. The lucrative profits from maritime trade were important to the Ming economy, and their absence contributed to the end of the dynasty.

Soon, the domestic and foreign plagues that had almost devoured the Ming administration during the previous emperor's reign began to reemerge. The Manchus' constant invasions in the Liaodong area and the partisan disputes and conspiracy at court were intensified by the famine of 1628 in Shaanxi province, brought on by a severe drought. The government lacked the funds to provide food for the people. The situation went from bad to worse as wives and children were being sold for survival. Cannibalism was not unheard of, and groups of bandits began raiding the countryside for food. Without sustenance, soldiers deserted to join the bandits for a chance to live.

To counter this situation, Chongzhen decided to raise money by cutting government expenditures and reducing imperial posts. The dismissed attendants had no place to turn but to join the rebels, however, and the situation snowballed. When bad weather in the 1630's and 1640's brought another series of droughts, floods, and locust attacks, the provinces of Shanxi, Shaanxi, Henan, Zhejiang, and Sichuan were devastated by mass starvation, infanticide, cannibalism, and epidemic diseases. Hordes of beggars were seen everywhere, snatching food wherever it was available. The rebels, led by Li Zicheng (Li Tzu-Ch'eng), were joined by thousands of volunteers; together they raided from city to city, taking over government institutions.

To battle the rebels, the Chongzhen administration raised funds by taxing landowners. Between 1618 and 1637, the land tax was increased six times. These funds were used entirely to fight the bandits and feed the military: Ordinary people found no relief, and the landowner class declined. Li Zicheng, supported by the poor masses and spurred by the misfortunes of the Ming, roared across the north China plain, defeating the Ming generals sent by Chongzhen. By November of 1643, Li, calling himself "The Prince of Shun," controlled the northwest and central provinces. With the Manchu forces in the northeast, Li now aimed at the capital at Beijing.

The danger of their position was felt at the Ming court, where Emperor Chongzhen consulted his ministers for a possible solution. Some loyal officials suggested the imperial family move south, where there were Ming supporters. The emperor lacked the funds to move his capital, however. Many soldiers in the capital had not been paid for three months. When even Chongzhen's son-in-law refused to let his private guards accompany the emperor, the son of heaven realized the end was near.

Doomsday came in April, 1644, when the Manchu army was marching toward Beijing, and Li's rebel groups had sacked the imperial tombs. On the 24th, Chongzhen called the last meeting at court, during which emperor and ministers wept. Meanwhile, the imperial troops fled or surrendered. Chongzhen disguised his two sons in ordinary clothes and made sure they left for the south. Then, the intoxicated emperor ordered the women of the palace to commit suicide. The empress and Tianqi's widow submitted, while Chongzhen finished off his concubines and daughters with his sword. He left one daughter with her arm cut off moaning in blood. At dawn, without his crown, the despondent ruler ran outside of the palace. With bloodstains in his hands, Chongzhen used his belt to hang himself on a tree. Only one eunuch, the loyal Wang Chengen, followed the emperor to death in the same manner.

SIGNIFICANCE

Chongzhen was the sixteenth and last emperor of the Ming Dynasty. After his death, the Manchu army moved in, overcame Li Zicheng and set up the Qing Dynasty (Ch'ing, 1644-1911) on the imperial throne. Chongzhen did his best to counter the damage done to the empire and to his dynasty by his weak predecessors, but his efforts were in vain. At the onset of Chongzhen's reign, the dynasty was already beyond saving, and the emperor could only stave off the inevitable. Chongzhen was given the time, but he was never given the chance.

—*Fatima Wu*

FURTHER READING

Chan, Albert. *The Glory and Fall of the Ming Dynasty.* Norman: University of Oklahoma Press, 1982. Has analytical discussions on the failure of the Ming Dynasty and the last ruler Chongzhen.

Mote, Frederick W., and Denis Twitchett, eds. *The Ming Dynasty, 1368-1644, Part 1.* Vol. 7 in *The Cambridge History of China.* New York: Cambridge University Press, 1988. Problems for the last emperor of the Ming Dynasty include civil rebellions due to economic decline, Manchu invasions, natural disasters as well as a corrupted and factional government.

Paludan, Ann. *Chronicles of the Chinese Emperors.* London: Thames and Hudson, 2001. A comprehensive chronicle of Chinese emperors, beginning with Qin Shihuangdi, the first emperor of China, and ending with the last emperor, Puyi of the Qing. Beside biographical details for each emperor, Paludan also presents cultural and political highlights for each dynastic era. Portraits, illustrations, and maps are helpful.

Perkins, Dorothy. *Encyclopedia of China: The Essential Reference to China, Its History and Culture.* New York: Round Table Press, 1999. A good source on biographical and cultural data for classical China. Read entries on Chongzhen, Ming Dynasty, Wei Zhongxian and eunuchs.

Twitchett, Denis, and Frederick W. Mote, eds. *The Ming Dynasty, 1368-1644, Part 2.* Vol. 8 in *The Cambrdge History of China.* New York: Cambridge University Press, 1998. Chapter 2 discusses the issues on fiscal administration of the late Ming government that led to the final collapse of the dynasty.

SEE ALSO: Abahai; Chen Shu; Dorgon; Kangxi; Liu Yin; Shunzhi; Tianqi; Wang Fuzhi; Zheng Chenggong.

RELATED ARTICLES in *Great Events from History: The Seventeenth Century, 1601-1700:* 1616-1643: Rise of the Manchus; 1631-1645: Li Zicheng's Revolt; April 25, 1644: End of the Ming Dynasty; June 6, 1644: Manchus Take Beijing.

CHRISTINA
Queen of Sweden (r. 1644-1654)

Under Christina's rule, Sweden benefited politically through the Treaty of Westphalia, which brought an end to the devastating Thirty Years' War, and it benefited culturally by the importation of many works of art and manuscripts from throughout Europe. During her residence in Rome, Christina was an enthusiastic patron of the arts and scholarship, founding the learned society Accademia Reale, a precursor to the Accademia dell'Arcadia of eighteenth century Italy.

BORN: December 8, 1626; Stockholm, Sweden
DIED: April 19, 1689; Rome, Papal States (now in Italy)
AREAS OF ACHIEVEMENT: Government and politics, patronage of the arts

EARLY LIFE

Christina was the daughter of the beloved King Gustavus II Adolphus of Sweden and Maria Eleonora, daughter of the elector of Brandenburg. Gustavus not only was a war hero of epic proportions but also was the famed Protestant king and commander of the Swedish troops in the Thirty Years' War as well as the last male member of the Protestant branch of the royal Wasa family.

Christina was the only one of the couple's children to survive beyond her first year and was convinced that she was hated by her mother because of her gender—both mother and father had hoped for a male heir to the throne. Yet Gustavus accorded all the ceremony and honor to his daughter that a prince would have received, and he made her his heir before the Riksdag in 1630. When Gustavus was killed at the Battle of Lützen in 1632, his five-year-old princess became queen, although she did not begin ruling until she reached eighteen years of age.

The young Christina showed an intellectual bent thought to be unusual for females of her time; she spent long hours studying and, apparently, preferred this activity to all others. The young queen displayed the same talent for languages that her father had possessed; she learned German, French, and Latin rapidly, reading Livy, Terence, Cicero, and Sallust. Soon she developed a liking for Cornelius Tacitus, who was one of her father's favorite writers and not an easy one to comprehend.

Christina's appearance also set her apart from other women. Her gait was confident; she spoke in a deep, booming voice; and she showed a lack of interest in fine clothing and adornment. This latter trait developed in later years into a penchant for wearing (often shabby or dirty) men's clothes with little or no jewelry. She was decidedly homely, though portraits reveal large, beautiful eyes. In addition, her exceptional skill in horseback riding surpassed that of most men of her court.

Major figures in the young queen's life included the chancellor Axel Oxenstierna, her tutor in statesmanship, who essentially ruled in her minority; Bishop John Matthiae, her religious instructor, who was primarily responsible for teaching her tolerance of other religions; and Countess Catherine Palatine, her paternal aunt, who came closest to providing the young girl with a normal mother figure until Christina's mother sent her away. Maria Eleonora seems to have been too warped by grief to be able to nurture her child properly; in addition, the Queen Mother kept so-called dwarves and buffoons at court, characters that frightened Christina, who was also misshapen. Oxenstierna and other advisers to the late king removed Maria Eleonora to Uppsala, fearing that her mental instability and prolonged, ostentatious grief

Christina. (Library of Congress)

CHRISTINA QUESTIONS RENÉ DESCARTES

Queen Christina invited philosopher René Descartes to Stockholm in 1649, requesting that he be her tutor. He agreed. In the following excerpt, Christina calls into question his views of the infinite nature of the universe and of God, that humans are but specks in a vast realm that could include other "earths" and creatures, some of whom could be more intelligent and worthy than those on planet Earth. Christina seems to conclude that humans would lose hope if the universe were infinite and if it were not a realm only for humans on Earth.

[I]f we conceive the world in that vast extension you [Descartes] give it, it is impossible that man conserve himself therein in this honorable rank, on the contrary, he shall consider himself along with the entire earth he inhabits as but small, tiny and in no proportion to the enormous size of the rest. He will very likely judge that these stars have inhabitants, or even that the earths surrounding them are all filled with creatures more intelligent and better than he, certainly, he will lose the opinion that this infinite extent of the world is made for him or can serve him in any way.

Source: "Kristina Wasa, Queen of Sweden," by Susanna Åckerman. In *Modern Women Philosophers, 1600-1900*. Vol. 3 in *A History of Women Philosophers*, edited by Mary Ellen Waithe (Boston: Kluwer Academic, 1991), p. 30.

would prove harmful to her daughter. Christina's childhood was therefore essentially lonely and devoid of a proper family environment.

An early romantic interest blossomed for Christina in her early teens, and she and her cousin Charles Gustav (later King Charles X Gustav of Sweden) became secretly engaged. By the time she reached the throne, however, her feelings for him had cooled, possibly as a result of her passionate if unanswered affection for the courtier and count Magnus Gabriel De la Gardie; they never married. During this time, she also made the acquaintance of Countess Ebba Sparre, her best female friend, who may have been Christina's lover.

LIFE'S WORK

Christina's adult life lends itself to a discussion of two distinct time periods: her Swedish reign and her post-abdication travels and eventual permanent residence in Rome. She came to power in Sweden during a particularly difficult time. The Thirty Years' War had been raging for twenty-six years, a situation that had taxed the Swedish population in terms of both people and money. In addition, the politics at the court itself featured a strengthened nobility worried about possible land confiscations to improve the royal finances.

Christina proved herself to be an astute politician and strategist but a profligate spender with little comprehension of economic affairs. She improved Sweden's diplomatic relations with France, to some degree through her personal friendship with the French minister (later ambassador) Pierre-Hector Chanut, and brought her country to temporary, welcome peace by the Treaty of Westphalia. She strengthened the power of the Crown vis-à-vis the nobility by means of clever strategies, aligning herself with the estates of the bourgeoisie and the peasantry. Yet the royal finances continued to deteriorate.

For all of her enjoyment of diplomatic intrigues and political power (things she did not cease to seek even after her abdication), her spiritual life was apparently lacking. She had been reared in the Lutheran faith but had been repelled by its austerity and sternness; her religious instructor, Matthiae, had taught her religious tolerance. The war booty from the Continent, which boasted sumptuous Italian paintings, vibrant tapestries, and volumes of hitherto (in Sweden) unknown literature, introduced her to the cultural wealth, lacking in her native land, that the more southerly countries of Europe had to offer. Although Christina called, among others, foreign artists, musicians, doctors, and philosophers (including René Descartes) to her court to try to fill the cultural void, she soon realized that she could not remain in spartan Sweden. She chose to abdicate, a decision to which her unrequited love for De la Gardie may have contributed.

She prepared for this step with great care, ensuring that her own candidate for the succession, her cousin and former fiancé Charles Gustavus, was officially accepted by the Riksdag as the heir to her throne. During this time, she became attracted to the Catholic religion, a faith with greater appeal to her aesthetic sense than Protestantism (it is recorded that she actually subscribed to her own private religion), and received instruction in secret from Italian Jesuit priests, for Catholicism was still illegal in Sweden at the time. Although the Riksdag refused initially to accept her bid for abdication, she persisted, citing as grounds her intention never to marry, her "weaker" gender, and her wish to retreat into private life. She also probably allowed an inkling of her Catholic interest to be perceived. It would have been a terrible embarrassment to Sweden if the daughter of its Protestant hero had converted to the opposing religion. To retain her on the throne would have been unthinkable. Her decision was accepted, and she abdicated on June 6, 1654.

After her abdication, Christina left in disguise for the Spanish Netherlands; the sponsor of her conversion to Catholicism was King Philip IV of Spain. After a stay in Brussels, she continued to Innsbruck, where she made her formal profession of the Catholic faith on November 3, 1655; Pope Alexander VII received her in Rome with lavish ceremonies on December 23 of the same year. There she met Cardinal Decio Azzolino, who later became her closest friend and, some believe, her paramour; he supported her with advice and friendship for the remainder of her life, dying two months after she did as her sole heir.

Christina was not content to live quietly in Rome, practicing her new faith. Her interest in politics kept her in touch with the most powerful figures of Europe; on a more prosaic level, she needed money to maintain her extravagant lifestyle. Although she thought that she had provided for steady financial support by securing for herself the income from Sweden's Baltic possessions and other lands, political unrest and poor or dishonest administration of these areas made her financial situation shaky at best. For these reasons, she went to France in 1656 and entered into secret negotiations with Cardinal Jules Mazarin to place her on the throne of Naples, a political dream that was foiled, partially through the treachery of a member of her entourage, Gian Rinaldo Monaldeschi. She had him murdered at Fontainebleau on November 10, 1657, an act that later prevented her from ascending the Polish throne (to which she actually had some claim) and which gave her a reputation for bloodthirstiness. In 1660 and 1667, Christina made trips to Sweden, primarily to protect her financial interests. Finally, in 1668, she returned to Rome, where she remained until her death.

In her adopted home, the now-round, stout queen, eccentric as ever, continued her involvement in politics and culture; she supported certain papal candidates during conclaves and founded learned societies, in particular the Accademia Reale. She invited singers and other musicians to her rented palace, the Palazzo Riario, and bought works of art that were displayed there. Christina worked on her autobiography (of which there are several drafts extant) and began writing aphorisms, which are often rather unoriginal but occasionally revelatory of her feelings toward Azzolino. She died as a result of a stroke on April 19, 1689.

SIGNIFICANCE

Christina has never quite died in terms of controversy over her reputation. She has been by turns slandered and revered, seen as a murderer of her lovers and as a saint who sacrificed her crown for religion. Clearly, that she was female and was never married contributes to the fascination surrounding her. She was an anachronism in some ways; a woman with a strong personality and a sharp intellect would fit into the modern world much more smoothly than into the Baroque Age. It was perhaps partly her own inability to feel comfortable in her time that made her restlessly give up one crown, go on to seek two or three others, and change religions and homelands.

Her attractive personality reaches across time to pull modern readers and historians into her sphere, as the physically plain queen was able to attract young courtiers, cardinals, and even noblewomen to her. Christina remains enigmatic, and perhaps this is why much of what has been written about her has focused on the questions of whether she had sexual relations with Sparre, Azzolino, Monaldeschi, or other members of her court, or on questions of her alleged hermaphroditism or lesbian sexuality.

Yet Christina made a lasting contribution to Swedish and Italian cultural life. She commanded that libraries from the Continent be bought and shipped to Sweden, modeled the Swedish court on that of Louis XIV, and surrounded herself with many talented minds. In Rome, she continued to support the arts to the extent that her reduced means allowed, making her home a meeting place for culture and scholarship.

—*Kathy Saranpa Anstine*

FURTHER READING

Åkerman, Susanna. *Queen Christina of Sweden and Her Circle: The Transformation of a Seventeenth-Century Philosophical Libertine*. New York: E. J. Brill, 1991. Åkerman discusses Christina's abdication, her conversion to Catholicism, and her attempt to become queen of Naples as the consequence of her heretical religious beliefs.

Buckley, Veronica. *Christina, Queen of Sweden: The Restless Life of a European Eccentric*. New York: Fourth Estate, 2004. A portrait of Christina, focusing on her decision to abdicate. Buckley argues that Christina did not renounce the Swedish throne for religious reasons but because she loved art and ancient Roman culture.

Findlen, Paula. "Ideas in the Mind: Gender and Knowledge in the Seventeenth Century." *Hypatia* 17, no. 1 (Winter, 2002). Using modern critical editions of the writings of women in the seventeenth century, Findlen analyzes the works to explore the connections between gender and knowledge in that time period.

Garstein, Oskar. *Rome and the Counter-Reformation in Scandinavia: The Age of Gustavus Adolphus and Queen Christina of Sweden, 1622-1656.* New York: E. J. Brill, 1992. This work completes Garstein's earlier study of the Counter-Reformation in Scandinavia from 1537 until 1622. The book recounts an underground campaign, funded by the Holy See, to lure Scandinavian students to attend Jesuit colleges. Campaign supporters hoped the students would return to Scandinavia and infiltrate the area's political and religious life. Garstein evaluates the success of this campaign.

Goldsmith, Margaret. *Christina of Sweden: A Psychological Biography.* Garden City, N.Y.: Doubleday, Doran, 1933. A straightforward biography that is, despite its title, not particularly psychological. The thesis and conclusion, that Christina left no mark on history, leads one to wonder why the author decided to write about this important figure.

Gribble, Francis. *The Court of Christina of Sweden and the Later Adventures of the Queen in Exile.* New York: Mitchell Kennerley, 1913. A biography of Christina with a good discussion of her aphorisms

presented in the last two chapters. Gribble sees Christina's relationship with Azzolino as the most important aspect of Christina's life.

Masson, Georgina. *Queen Christina.* New York: Farrar, Straus & Giroux, 1968. An excellent, informative introduction that proceeds chronologically from a brief overview of Gustavus's career to Clement XI's funding a monument to Christina in 1701. Masson gives succinct and helpful explanations of the often confusing historical events of the seventeenth century.

Woodhead, Henry. *Memoirs of Christina, Queen of Sweden.* London: Hurst and Blackett, 1863. This standard, two-volume work is indispensable for the interested student. It is well documented and gives a full picture of the political and historical climate surrounding Christina. The author takes the view that, despite her personal flaws, Christina made a considerable contribution to society. Contains a selection of her aphorisms translated into English.

SEE ALSO: Alexander VII; Giovanni Alfonso Borelli; Charles X Gustav; Arcangelo Corelli; René Descartes; Gustavus II Adolphus; Jules Mazarin; Axel Oxenstierna; Philip IV.

RELATED ARTICLES in *Great Events from History: The Seventeenth Century, 1601-1700:* November, 1602: First Modern Libraries in Europe; 1625: Grotius Establishes the Concept of International Law.

FIRST EARL OF CLARENDON
English statesman

The adviser to two kings of England during the English Civil Wars, Clarendon laid the theoretical and the practical bases for the restoration of both the monarchy and traditional English society. He also wrote a masterpiece of historical literature, based on his experiences.

BORN: February 18, 1609; Dinton, Wiltshire, England
DIED: December 9, 1674; Rouen, France
ALSO KNOWN AS: Edward Hyde (given name)
AREAS OF ACHIEVEMENT: Government and politics, literature

EARLY LIFE

Edward Hyde, the future first earl of Clarendon, was born February 18, 1609, the son of Henry Hyde of Dinton, Wiltshire, and his wife, Mary, daughter of Ed-

ward Langford of Trowbridge. His was a prosperous gentry family long established in Wiltshire and Cheshire. He was born a younger son but by young manhood had become his father's heir through the deaths of his elder brothers.

Hyde attended Magdalen Hall, Oxford, and received a bachelor of arts degree in 1626. The previous year, he had become a member of Middle Temple, one of the four Inns of Court that formed the heart of English legal society, and he prepared for a career at the bar. He married twice, both times most advantageously. His first wife was Anne Ayliffe, a relative of the influential Villiers family, by which Hyde first attracted the notice of the late duke of Buckingham's friend Charles I. On his first wife's early death, Hyde married the daughter of Sir Francis Aylesbury, a master of requests, and thus strengthened his links to the court and to the legal profession.

In addition to these connections, Hyde's uncle was Sir Nicholas Hyde, chief justice of the Court of Common Pleas, so the stage was set for his rapid advance. During his early years in London, however, Hyde was more interested in polite society and letters than in law or politics, and he was more intimate with figures such as Ben Jonson, John Selden, and especially Lucius Cary, second Viscount Falkland, than with his colleagues at the bar. Years later, Hyde singled out Falkland as one of the decisive influences in his life, and the effect of that early association can be seen in Hyde's *The History of the Rebellion and Civil Wars in England* (wr. 1647-c. 1671, pb. 1702-1704) and his autobiography, *The Life of Edward, Earl of Clarendon* (pb. 1759). Starting about 1633-1634, though, Hyde began to apply himself with increasing seriousness to the law, and, aided by family, connections, the favor of Archbishop William Laud, and his outstanding natural abilities, he advanced rapidly. By 1640, Hyde was a leading lawyer in the capital.

LIFE'S WORK

Hyde was elected to the Short Parliament in May, 1640, and, according to his own account, attempted to pursue a moderate and conciliatory course during that tumultuous session. He sat also in the Long Parliament in November, 1640, when his displeasure at the Crown's manipulation of the legal system during Charles I's period of personal rule led him at first to align himself with the anti-Royalist elements in the House of Commons.

In the House of Commons, Hyde specialized in the investigation of abuses in the legal system and was responsible for the virtual extinction of the Earl Marshal's Court (the institution for arbitrating disputes over coats of arms). Hyde also investigated the councils of Wales and the north, key targets in Parliament's attack on the Crown's prerogative powers, and reviewed charges of judicial misconduct. He joined the anti-Royalist cause during the trial and impeachment of the first earl of Strafford and actually helped draft the articles of impeachment by which Strafford was convicted and executed. Hyde appears to have voted for Strafford's execution in May, 1641. By mid-1641, Hyde was one of the most influential members of the Commons and appeared to be firmly allied with the radical wing.

First Earl of Clarendon. (Library of Congress)

Like many others, however, Hyde parted company with Parliamentary radicalism over the so-called Root and Branch Bill (1641), which called for the extinction of the episcopal system and the radical reconstruction of the Church of England. Hyde's disaffection from the Royalist cause, it soon became clear, was specific, not general: He disapproved of the Crown's policy toward the courts and the common law in the 1620's and 1630's, but he had no desire whatsoever to alter the established order in either church or state. Through skillful parliamentary and political maneuvering, Hyde managed to block the Root and Branch Bill, and by so doing he attracted the favorable notice of Charles I, who desperately needed trustworthy advice on parliamentary and legal issues.

Hyde's alienation from the Parliamentary cause, which began when he blocked the Root and Branch Bill, was increased and then completed by Hyde's response to two further measures: John Pym's Irish policy would have severely curtailed the king's military authority, and the Grand Remonstrance was, in effect, a comprehensive indictment of Stuart rule. By the fall of 1641, Hyde was firmly Royalist, though the full extent of his commitment to the king was necessarily and skillfully concealed from his colleagues in the Commons for the greater part of a year. Beginning by that fall, Hyde wrote most of Charles I's public pronouncements on parliamentary and other public issues, and on at least one occasion the king went so far as to copy a draft proclamation by Hyde in his own hand in order to conceal the true author's identity.

Hyde consistently recommended a cautious and circumspect policy to the king and never supported, or even knew in advance, of the king's ill-fated plan to arrest five members of the House of Commons on January 4, 1642. Hyde was appalled by this blunder, which effectively lost for the king the City of London, but he rallied after the event and prepared the king's official responses to the public outcry that followed. The royal family fled London on January 10, 1642; Hyde eventually left the capital and joined the king at York in June, 1642. Thereafter, he was regarded as a deadly enemy by Parliament and excluded from all proposals for amnesty.

Between 1642 and 1645, Hyde was one of Charles I's most intimate and trusted advisers. In the Royalist councils, Hyde advocated a cautious and conservative policy, urging the king to represent himself as the defender of the common law, traditional usages, and ancient and approved practices and to embody "the old foundations in church and state." Hyde argued, in effect, that in the rapidly worsening situation the king should stand firm, make no concessions, and wait for Parliament to discredit itself by radicalism and by innovation. With the king as the symbol of tradition and stability, Hyde said, the Royalist cause would ultimately triumph—as, indeed, it did, under Hyde's supervision, though not until 1660. There were others in the king's councils who thought Hyde's policy passive, legalistic, and unrealistic and argued for vigorous military and political initiatives. Most prominent among the latter was the queen herself, Henrietta Maria, whose dislike of Hyde and resentment of his influence over Charles I, and later over Charles II as well, were fierce and unremitting.

Hyde entered the Privy Council in February, 1643, and the following month became chancellor of the exchequer; he was soon a member of the inner group of five that reviewed and discussed all matters before referral to the full Privy Council. As chancellor of the exchequer, Hyde was primarily responsible for financing the Royalist effort, for which he was obliged to maintain complex negotiations with institutions, such as Oxford University, and individuals in order to maintain even an inadequate flow of revenue. He continued to be responsible for

all major Royalist policy statements and was the king's principal strategist and negotiator in all dealings with the Scots and Parliament. The king repeatedly demonstrated his complete confidence in Hyde, though he continued to develop initiatives without Hyde's knowledge (and did so with increasing frequency as the Royalist position worsened).

When the king's fortunes began to deteriorate rapidly in early 1645, he sent Hyde to Bristol and gave him charge of the prince of Wales, the clearest possible sign of the royal confidence. Neither Hyde nor the prince ever saw Charles I again. When the Royalist cause collapsed in 1646, Hyde moved the prince to the Scilly Isles, then to Jersey, and finally, reluctantly, permitted his charge to rejoin his mother in France.

Hyde was retained by Charles II on his father's death in 1649, though his influence was at first uncertain. Hyde strongly opposed the various military ventures against England that many around the young king proposed, and he was adamantly opposed to any form of negotiation or compromise with the Scots, now disillusioned with Cromwellian England. Yet Charles II decided at first on a bold and venturous policy. He made humiliating concessions to the Scots and with their help invaded England. At that point, Hyde withdrew to Spain on a mission for the better part of two years. When Charles II returned, chastened, to the Netherlands in 1651 after the debacle of the Battle of Worcester, however, he was rejoined by Hyde, whose influence was thenceforth paramount.

Hyde clearly perceived the unique role of Oliver Cromwell in the Commonwealth Protectorate regime and realized that the king's turn would come after Cromwell had somehow been removed from the scene. Accordingly, Hyde strove consistently to keep the king free of all compromising entanglements and to represent him as a figure above faction. Thus, it was Hyde who developed the policy finally expressed in the Declaration of Breda, which paved the way for Charles II's return to England. In particular, it was Hyde who devised the tactic of having the king, while in exile, defer all complex or potentially controversial questions to the decision of a free Parliament, thus at once deflecting danger and encouraging hope. When the king arrived at Dover in May, 1660, he came not as a conqueror or as the vindictive head of a faction, but as the traditionalist alternative to a discredited Commonwealth regime, as the symbol of conciliation, stability, and peace. In effect, after all the vicissitudes of war and exile, Hyde's unheroic policies had triumphed at last.

Charles II named Hyde lord chancellor in January, 1658, and after the Restoration, he continued as the principal figure in the government. In 1661, he was created earl of Clarendon. In September, 1660, Hyde's daughter Anne had married James, duke of York, younger brother and heir presumptive of Charles II, and in this manner Hyde eventually became grandfather of two queens of England, Mary II Stuart and Anne I.

Between 1660 and 1667, Clarendon's influence extended to all branches of government. He was one of the crucial participants in the protracted negotiations about the eventual shape of the restored Church of England and in the end joined in the refusal to include Nonconformists in the reconstructed church; he generally supported the series of punitive measures against religious dissidents that came to be known as the Clarendon Code. In this, he was out of step with the king, who favored toleration, and Clarendon became a deeply hated figure among non-Anglicans.

Clarendon was also closely associated with the controversial Act of Indemnity, by which, by and large, only confiscated land was returned to Royalists and land conveyed in any other way, even as a result of punitive taxation under Cromwell, was secured to its new owners. Thus, many of the king's most loyal and hard-pressed supporters lost heavily, and again, Clarendon was widely held responsible. Clarendon was also interested in the English colonies and began to organize bureaucratically the relationship between colonies, especially those in America.

Clarendon was clearly least successful in the conduct of foreign policy, as he was not very skilled in his dealings with France and the Netherlands. He was held to be primarily responsible for the unpopular sale of Dunkirk to France, and the magnificent residence Clarendon built for himself in London was popularly known as Dunkirk House, an allusion to alleged bribes. The Second Anglo-Dutch War (1665-1667), which Clarendon had in fact opposed, was blamed on him, and its inept conduct increased opposition to him in the government and stirred up great animosity in the country at large. When Dutch ships were so bold as to sail up the Thames and burn English ships in the Medway, national anger focused on Clarendon.

Opposition mounted steadily, and it soon became clear that the beleaguered minister no longer had the confidence of the king. Charles II had grown tired of Clarendon's tutelage, apparently saw in him a convenient whipping boy for the various failures of the regime, and abandoned him without a qualm, making it clear that he

preferred Clarendon to flee rather than answer the charges against him. Clarendon fled to France in December, 1667, and spent the remainder of his life in exile. He later requested permission to return, but it does not appear that either his family or the king paid any attention. Clarendon spent these last years working on his *The History of the Rebellion and Civil Wars in England*, which he had begun in Jersey in 1647, and his autobiography. He suffered from rapidly worsening health, primarily gout, and died at Rouen on December 9, 1674. His body was returned to England for burial in Westminster Abbey.

The History of the Rebellion and Civil Wars in England, which Clarendon completed in exile, is a classic of historical writing. Admittedly, it has its faults: Clarendon included many documents and digressions that impede the flow of the narrative but that he thought necessary for a full explanation of events, and he attributed causation of the mighty events he had witnessed primarily to personal factors, rather than to the social and economic issues in favor today. Yet the work transcends these qualifications by its authority as the first-person account of a major participant and by the frequent magnificence of its prose. All profits from *The History of the Rebellion and Civil Wars in England* were assigned to Oxford University, and Clarendon's great-grandson left all of his other manuscripts to the university as well, the profits from which led to the building of the Clarendon Laboratory in 1868.

SIGNIFICANCE

The first earl of Clarendon had, in effect, three careers: from 1641 to 1660, the adviser in adversity; from 1660 to 1667, the head of the Restoration government, second only to the king himself, with whom he became allied by marriage; and then from 1667 to 1674, the lonely exile, who filled up his time reviewing and writing about his previous busy life. The first and third careers were virtually unqualified successes. As adviser to Charles I and then to the prince of Wales, eventually Charles II, Hyde peaceably laid the foundations not only for the Restoration of the king himself but also for an entire traditional ruling class, without significant bloodshed. The peaceful Restoration of Charles, of the Anglican Church, of Parliament, and of the common law, all were attributable more to Hyde than to any other person. Though the years in exile were sad and weary for him, Clarendon used them to good purpose: His history of his own era is one of the classics of historical writing and is an invaluable source for the revolutionary era.

Only in his second career, as royal minister, did Clarendon falter. He failed to resolve the long-standing religious divisions in the country, although reconciliation might have been impossible for anyone at the time, and he bore the brunt of Royalist outrage over Restoration property settlements. He was, on the whole, one of those who made a great mark on seventeenth century English history, and he did it through means of peace and reconciliation.

—Neal R. Shipley

FURTHER READING

Harris, Ronald W. *Clarendon and the English Revolution*. Stanford, Calif.: Stanford University Press, 1983. Attempts to study Clarendon's public life through his own writings, especially his history. Views Clarendon as the greatest Royalist statesman of the seventeenth century, but the sections dealing with Clarendon's literary and intellectual contributions are the strongest.

Hicks, Philip Stephen. *Neo-classical History and English Culture: From Clarendon to Hume*. New York: St. Martin's Press, 1996. This analysis of English historical writing contains a chapter on Clarendon, whom the author describes as "the English Thucydides."

Hyde, Edward, earl of Clarendon. *The History of the Rebellion and Civil Wars in England Begun in the Year 1641*. Edited by W. Dunn Macray. 6 vols. 1888. Reprint. New York: Oxford University Press, 1993. The standard edition of Hyde's masterpiece.

Miller, George. *Edward Hyde, Earl of Clarendon*. Boston: Twayne, 1983. A prominent attempt to reevaluate the traditional picture of Clarendon as a politician and to emphasize his contribution to revolutionary politics.

Ollard, Richard Lawrence. *Clarendon and His Friends*. New York: Atheneum, 1988. A biography of Clarendon, focusing on his relationships with Ben Jonson, Thomas Hobbes, and others.

Trevor-Roper, H. R. "Clarendon and the Practice of History." In *Milton and Clarendon: Two Papers in Seventeenth-Century English Historiography*, by F. R. Fogle and H. R. Trevor-Roper. Los Angeles: Clark Memorial Library, 1965. A warm defense of Clarendon's contribution to English historical literature, praising the high quality and accuracy of his historiography.

Wormald, B. H. *Clarendon: Politics, Historiography, and Religion, 1640-1660*. 1951. Reprint. New York: Cambridge University Press, 1989. An important work of reassessment.

SEE ALSO: First Duke of Buckingham; Charles I; Charles II (of England); Oliver Cromwell; Henrietta Maria; James II; William Laud; John Pym; First Earl of Strafford.

RELATED ARTICLES in *Great Events from History: The Seventeenth Century, 1601-1700:* November 3, 1640-May 15, 1641: Beginning of England's Long Parliament; 1642-1651: English Civil Wars; December 6, 1648-May 19, 1649: Establishment of the English Commonwealth; December 16, 1653-September 3, 1658: Cromwell Rules England as Lord Protector; May, 1659-May, 1660: Restoration of Charles II; 1661-1665: Clarendon Code.

CLAUDE LORRAIN
Italian painter

Claude Lorrain established landscape in Roman and French painting as a subtle and varied means of artistic expression on an equal level with the older genres of religious and historical painting. He is one of the greatest masters of all time in the painting of the ideal landscape.

BORN: 1600; Chamagne, Lorraine, France
DIED: November 23, 1682; Rome, Papal States (now in Italy)
ALSO KNOWN AS: Claude Gellée (given name)
AREA OF ACHIEVEMENT: Art

EARLY LIFE

Claude Lorrain (klohd law-rahn), known to the French as le Lorrain, was born the third of five sons. In 1612, his parents died and he went to Freiburg im Breisgau to live with an elder brother, Jean, a wood-carver. In 1613, he accompanied a relative to Rome and remained there to become a pastry cook. In this capacity, he obtained employment in the house of Agostino Tassi, the landscape painter. Gradually he learned the rudiments of painting from Tassi, who became his principal master at this time. Claude may have been one of the apprentices employed by the Cavalier d'Arpino and Tassi on the decoration of the Villa Lante, Bagnaia, which was completed by 1616.

At some time between 1616 and 1622, Claude went to Naples to work under the Flemish artist known in Italy as Goffredo Wals. This visit had a lasting effect on Claude. He was haunted by the beauty of the Gulf of Naples and reproduced to the end of his life the coast from Pozzuoli to Sorrento. In April, 1625, Claude departed from Rome for Nancy, the capital of Lorraine. There he worked as assistant to the Lorrainese court painter Claude Deruet painting architectural backgrounds to his vault frescoes for the Carmelite church. By the beginning of 1627, Claude returned to Rome. He remained in Rome until his death, with only one recorded absence, in 1660.

In 1627, Claude painted for both Italians and foreigners and was commissioned by Cardinal Guido Bentivoglio to make two landscapes, but no certain works by him survive from before 1630. During the early 1630's, he was active chiefly as a fresco decorator in the Palazzi Crescenzi and Muti. Although the fine quality of the Muti frescoes was a major factor in establishing his artistic reputation, he never again worked in the fresco medium.

LIFE'S WORK

Still comparatively unknown in 1633, by 1638 Claude was the leading landscape painter in Italy, with commissions to his credit from the pope, several cardinals, the king of Spain, and the French ambassador. From that time, patrons were never lacking, and his paintings, which fetched high prices, were in demand by both Italian and foreign collectors. At this time, Claude's style began to attract the attention of imitators and forgers. In 1634, the artist Sébastien Bourdon thought it profitable to copy Claude's style and pass off one of his own paintings as a work of Claude. As a measure of his artistic reputation, in 1635 Claude began to record his compositions in the *Liber veritatis* (book of truth). Though incomplete at first, the *Liber veritatis*, from 1640 onward, formed a virtually complete inventory of Claude's production.

In addition to the influence of his early master Tassi, the roots of Claude's landscape style can be traced to the Dutchman Paul Brill and the German Adam Elsheimer. In Rome, Brill and Tassi had developed the late mannerist landscape tradition. This style, with its artificial nature, consists of the division of the picture into areas of dark greenish-brown foreground, light green middle distance, and blue hills on the far distant horizon. Each area of the composition is set out in coulisses, side pieces at either side of a stage arranged to give room for exits and entrances, starting from a dark tree in the foreground to create a sense of infinite distance. This artificiality of design is combined with stylized treatment of the trees, painted in a set formula of feathery fronds in silhouette. In paintings of the early 1630's, such as *The Mill* (1631), Claude followed Brill closely. The influence of Elsheimer is more evident in Claude's etchings of this period.

As a result of these influences, Claude developed a style that is neither as heroic nor as classical as that of his great contemporary Nicolas Poussin, but rather is capable of expressing both a more poetic mood and a livelier sense of the beauty and variety of nature. The most significant element of this style is his varied treatment of atmosphere and light: the calm glow of evening, the brilliance of noon, the cool light of early morning. Claude studied these carefully on his frequent sketching excursions into the Roman countryside using pen, wash, and even oils. He represented these lights with a subtlety unparalleled in his time and not excelled before Impressionism. Whereas Elsheimer explored the strong dramatic effects of moonlight or dark twilight, Claude aimed at serenity, minimizing value contrasts to preserve the calm unity of the whole.

The light of Claude's paintings usually emanates from an area of the sky immediately above the horizon, so that the viewer may gaze directly or almost directly into it. It spreads forward and outward through the composition, permeating the whole landscape with its radiance and joining background and foreground in one continuous spatial unity. By the late 1630's, Claude had carried these effects almost to the point of exaggeration. Shadowy masses of trees in the foreground are contrasted with a misty sunlit vista. In several of the seaport scenes, a corridor of light emanates from the sun, just visible above the horizon. The *Harbor Scene* (1634) is one of the earliest examples of this phenomenon in the history of painting.

Claude was intrigued by the pastoral life described in the poems of Vergil as well as by the mythic age when Aeneas founded Rome. Some works even depict themes from this early phase of the *Aeneid*. His knowledge of Vergil came through translations and conversations with learned friends, since he was not a Latin scholar. The pastoral illustrations from the *Vatican Virgil*, which was studied by his friends, along with actual Roman frescoes of country landscapes and architectural scenes, also in-

fluenced his development. Claude's painting at times included ruins, and it was an essential part of his intention to create a feeling of nostalgia for the past.

Claude did not develop a composition logically from the particular theme of a painting. His concern, which went beyond the theme of any given work, was the beauty of the Roman landscape, which, in its pictorial possibilities, had gone unnoticed. The scenes he painted were given significance by his understanding of the particular light that bathes them. In short, the content of Claude's paintings is actually a poetic rendition of the subtle, changing light and atmosphere of the countryside.

Between 1640 and 1660, Claude refined his complete mastery over every type of landscape painting. His style became calmer and the lighting more diffused as in *The Marriage of Isaac and Rebecca* (1648). An idyllic pastoral mood permeates many of these mature landscapes. He turned to both sacred and classical literature for subject matter and included a conventional type of Arcadian shepherd for the pastoral scenes. He selected and combined all the familiar pictorial elements—tall trees against the sky, villages, distant hills, winding streams, fragments of classical architecture, large bodies of water—in such a way as to convey a sense of repose and enchantment.

In Claude's late phase, 1660-1682, the earlier process of idealization, of setting the imaginary world of the painting at a distance from the real world, was taken much further. The human figure, never very important, was reduced to insignificance, totally dominated by the scenery. His last paintings, such as *Ascanius and the Stag* (1682), represent a dreamland in which the forms are so shadowy that they hardly interrupt the continuity of the air in which light has a mysterious magical property.

Claude was a respected member of the colony of foreign artists in Rome. He remained on good terms with Poussin until his death in 1665. Claude never married but had a daughter, Agnese, born in 1653, who lived with him until his death. Though he amassed a small fortune, he lived frugally and quietly and had no ambitions beyond the pursuit of his art. He was seriously ill in 1663, suffered from gout in his later years, and died on November 23, 1682. He was buried in the French Church of Trinità dei Monti, above Piazza di Spagna in Rome. Biographies of him were first published by his friend Joachim von Sandrart in 1675 and by Filippo Baldinucci in 1728.

SIGNIFICANCE

Claude Lorrain brought to its limit the study of light and atmosphere as a means of creating imaginative, pictorial unity. The experience of drawing had major significance

Claude Lorrain. (Library of Congress)

for his paintings. He made many finished preparatory sketches and etchings for paintings that often reveal the evolution of his design. Claude's drawings illustrate the wide range and intensity of his observations. There is an endless variety to his sketches made from nature, and they are often bolder than his paintings. Most of the nature drawings, which include rapid pen sketches, black chalk, washes, and oils, were done before 1645. The majority of these embody some unexpected effect of light: changing light in a valley, a path through a sunlit wood, a tree seen *contre-jour*—pointed toward or nearly toward the chief source of light. To render precisely, for example, the complexity of light effects with reflections in a valley, he, at times, permitted the solidity of the hills to disappear. No artist before Claude had attempted such a subject. Claude was able to capture the infinity of nature within the narrowly defined boundaries of classical composition, that is, art derived from the study of antique exemplars. His methods showed that French classicism, best exemplified in the disciplined, rational approach of Poussin, could be softened to reveal the poetic side of nature.

Poussin constructs hollow, boxlike space filled with solid objects that recede in clearly defined steps. Claude creates looser space almost always leading the eye to infinity on the horizon. Atmosphere fills and unifies this space. Recession occurs by the subtle gradation of color, usually in trees that have no sharp outline. Poussin rarely represents water, but when he does it is the static surface of a river that clearly reflects the surrounding scene. Claude chooses to render the constant motion of the sea. The eye is led over the continuous surface of the sea to the horizon by no means other than color, tone changes, and minute variations in the surface of wave patterns that reflect light. Poussin's buildings are simple solid blocks; Claude's porticoes, facades, and towers are seen against the Sun and lose their substance in the atmosphere. Poussin's trees are marble, Claude's reflect light.

Claude is rightly regarded as one of the greatest landscape painters in history. It is his stress on the subjective side of nature, the attempt to capture a mood, that made his work so popular with the early Romantics, most notably Joseph Mallord William Turner. From his own time to the present, Claude has enjoyed a great reputation, especially in England, and his popularity has remained undimmed.

—*John A. Calabrese*

Further Reading

Lagerlöf, Margaretha Rossholm. *Ideal Landscape: Annibale Carracci, Nicolas Poussin, and Claude Lorraine*. New Haven, Conn.: Yale University Press, 1990. A study of landscape paintings created by three sixteenth and seventeenth century artists.

Manwaring, Elizabeth Wheeler. *Italian Landscape in Eighteenth Century England*. Reprint. New York: Russell & Russell, 1965. Examines how the literary and poetic appeal of the Italian landscapes of Claude Lorrain and Salvator Rosa shaped English taste and concepts of landscape beauty.

Röthlisberger, Marcel. *Claude Lorrain: The Drawings*. 2 vols. Berkeley: University of California Press, 1968. Catalog of the artist's almost twelve hundred known drawings, with information on drawing types, styles, and techniques. Volume 1 contains precise information to correspond with each black-and-white plate in volume 2.

_____. *Claude Lorrain: The Paintings*. 2 vols. New Haven, Conn.: Yale University Press, 1961. Catalog of Claude's existing output as a painter, nearly 250 oils. The introduction to volume 1 includes a basic summary of artistic influences and stylistic development. Each black-and-white plate in volume 2 has a corresponding text in volume 1.

Russell, H. Diane. *Claude Lorrain, 1600-1682*. Washington, D.C.: National Gallery of Art, 1982. This comprehensive volume is excellent in every respect. Illustrations of paintings and drawings are in color, two-tone, and black-and-white. Contains historical commentaries, an intricate chronology, a glossary, a fine bibliography, and appendices.

Schade, Weiner, ed. *Claude Lorrain: Paintings and Drawings*. Munich, Germany: Schirmer Art Books, 1998. Critical study of Claude Lorrain's artwork, illustrated with reproductions of his paintings and drawings.

Whiteley, J. J. L. *Claude Lorraine: Drawings from the Collections of the British Museum and the Ashmolean Museum*. London: British Museum Press, 1998. Catalog of an exhibition held at the British Museum from October 9, 1998, through January 10, 1999.

Wine, Humphrey. *Claude: The Poetic Landscape*. London: National Gallery Publications, 1994. Catalog of an exhibition held at the National Gallery in London from January 26 through April 10, 1994.

See also: Nicolas Poussin.

Related article in *Great Events from History: The Seventeenth Century, 1601-1700:* c. 1601-1620: Emergence of Baroque Art.

SIR EDWARD COKE
English lawyer, judge, politician, and scholar

As a barrister, member of the House of Commons, attorney general, and chief justice, Coke was a leading defender of the rights of individuals and of Parliament. He was instrumental in creating the Petition of Right in England and in developing a theory of judicial review that would shape the United States Constitution.

BORN: February 1, 1552; Mileham Manor, Norfolk, England

DIED: September 3, 1634; Stoke Poges, Buckinghamshire, England

AREAS OF ACHIEVEMENT: Law, government and politics

EARLY LIFE

Sir Edward Coke was the son of Robert Coke, a prosperous barrister and member of the English gentry who owned several estates. His mother, née Winifred Knightley, was herself the daughter of a Norwich attorney and descended from a family as respectable and prosperous as her husband's. Edward had seven sisters but no brothers. He received his early education at home. When he was nine, the same year that his father unexpectedly died, he was sent to the Free Grammar School in Norwich, where his classmates were the sons of other local prosperous families. Coke studied Latin and Greek and read the classic works in those languages. What written English language and history he knew, he had learned on his own. Norwich had been a free city since the fourteenth century with its own constitution and a history of competitive elections for mayor and sheriff. Coke absorbed something of the free, individualistic spirit of the city, and it remained his favorite place in England.

In 1563, Coke's mother remarried, but little changed in his life until the fall of 1567, when, at age fifteen, he entered Trinity College, Cambridge University. There was turmoil during his three and one-half years there between Puritan reformers and those committed to the Church of England. In spite of the religious distractions and the medieval curriculum, however, Coke learned some things of use to his later career. He became adept at debate, did well in the study of logic, and improved his knowledge of Latin. His mother had died in 1569, and Coke was head of his family when he left Trinity.

Coke decided to follow his father in law and on January 21, 1571, he joined Clifford's Inn, where he received preliminary legal training. After the customary one year, he moved to the Inner Temple, one of the Inns of Court, where he endured a rigid, traditional apprenticeship. He remained seven years, mastering the difficult and extensive vocabulary of the law. The major text was Judge Thomas Littleton's *Treatise on Tenures* (1481), which focused on land law. Yet, like the whole curriculum during his years at Inner Temple, the text was obtuse, jumbled, and incoherent, and only the stubborn and determined learned to make sense of it.

Criminal law, on the other hand, was much easier, and while English sentences for criminal offenses were harsh by comparison with the more advanced continental European nations, English trials were the fairest. This was the result of English laws and procedures that protected the rights of the accused to make habeas corpus petitions, to a trial by jury, and to speak in their own defense, hear their accusers, and challenge jurors. Nowhere else in Europe were there equivalents to these English concepts, and Coke became justly proud of them and of the concept of the law of the land.

LIFE'S WORK

On April 20, 1578, Coke was called to the bar, which meant that he could return to his family home and begin practicing law. In these early years, he traveled extensively in Norfolk and the surrounding shires, was elected to a number of local minor public offices, and attended court sessions at Westminster. On April 30, 1582, at the age of thirty, Coke married the seventeen-year-old Bridget Paston, who came from a wealthy and distinguished Norfolk family. They moved shortly after their marriage to Huntington Manor in Suffolk, one of Bridget's mother's estates. Coke and his wife had ten children. Coke's home was a happy place, and he prospered and began acquiring land and property, a habit he kept the rest of his life.

During these years, Coke acquired another more important habit. From the beginning of his career as a lawyer and for the next forty years, Coke kept extensive notes of all the law cases he participated in or witnessed. He published these notes in eleven parts as *Reports* (1600-1615), which contained almost six hundred cases. Two additional volumes were published posthumously. The *Reports* cover all types of cases and contain not only a wealth of legal information but social history as well. Since judicial decisions of this period were recorded only haphazardly, Coke's *Reports* had no peer, and they were the basis of his lectures on the law given at the Inner Temple.

Coke soon gained recognition as an energetic and knowledgeable lawyer, although outspoken and rarely subtle. In Parliament, these traits gained for him admiration and respect from many, including Queen Elizabeth's chief minister, William Cecil, lord treasurer Burghley. As Cecil's protégé, Coke began his career in public office as solicitor general and was later appointed by the queen as speaker of the House of Commons in 1593. The speaker's job was difficult, because he had to please both the queen and the members of the Commons. Coke cut an imposing figure before that assembly. He was tall, large-boned, and spare, with a handsome oval face, dark hair, and a high forehead. His eyes were large, dark, and penetrating. Coke always dressed fashionably and carried himself with style. He performed his duties with sufficient merit that the queen appointed him to the lucrative post of attorney general on April 10, 1595. The vacancy occurred while he was speaker, and Coke spent considerable effort campaigning for it against the opposition of Sir Walter Ralegh, who promoted Francis Bacon.

During his twelve years as attorney general, Coke participated in a number of famous treason trials, including those of Dr. Roderigo Lopez; Robert Devereux, second earl of Essex; Essex's numerous associates; Sir Walter Ralegh; and those involved in the Gunpowder Plot. Although he claimed to be proud of England's enlightened criminal laws and procedures, Coke's loyalty as attorney general was to the Crown, and he was willing to violate the rules to gain convictions.

During Coke's tenure as attorney general, Bridget, his wife of fifteen years, died, on June 26, 1598, six months after delivering her eleventh child and seventh son. By the time of her death, only eight of her children still lived. Bridget had been a quiet, loving, dutiful wife. Lady Elizabeth Hatton, the wealthy widow and granddaughter of William Cecil, whom Coke married on November 7, 1598, was dramatically different. The marriage was a disaster, and Coke never again knew domestic peace. Lady Hatton, twenty years old at the time of her marriage to a man more than twice her age, was clever, vivacious, and stylish, loved parties, and was notorious for her willful temperament.

Queen Elizabeth I died March 24, 1603, and was succeeded by James I (King James VI of Scotland). Coke's world began to change dramatically. During the first months of his reign, James I granted titles and knighted men on a scale not seen before in England. Among the new knights was Coke, now Sir Edward. When the position of chief justice of the Court of Common Pleas became vacant, Coke was the obvious choice and took the oath of office in the early summer of 1606. As attorney general, Coke had always served the interest of the Crown and guarded the royal prerogative. As chief justice of the Court of Common Pleas, he served the law and felt compelled to use it to set limits to the royal prerogative. The change in attitude came mainly because by the time he was appointed chief justice, Coke had concluded that James I meant to govern England from a position above the law, and Coke was determined to prevent that, using the only means at hand, the common law of England.

Sir Edward Coke. (Library of Congress)

English common law grew out of ancient custom and usage and was gradually systematized during the medieval period into a body of legal rules and precedents by the decisions of judges and by Parliament in its role as the High Court of Parliament. In time, three superior courts of the common law were established at Westminster, the Court of Common Pleas for suits between private individuals, the King's Bench for cases involving public issues such as murder, and the Exchequer for tax cases. Cases involving religious issues were heard by the High Commission and those involving the Crown's prerogative, by the Court of Chancery. Both High Commission and Chancery were by their nature willing to do the king's bidding and were known as the prerogative courts.

James I, who wished to expand his authority and govern England as an absolute monarch, sought a much broader interpretation of his prerogative from all the courts. Coke thought James I would upset the balance of English government, and as chief justice of Common Pleas, he acted to thwart the king's ambitions. He issued numerous writs of prohibition to remove cases from the prerogative courts on the ground that they lacked jurisdiction. The prerogative courts were furious and claimed the king had the right to intervene personally in questions of jurisdiction and even decide cases himself if he chose. When Coke denied such royal authority, James I became enraged: Coke was forced to kneel to the king in November of 1608 and ask forgiveness to avoid being sent to prison in the Tower of London. Coke did not, however, stop issuing writs of prohibition to remove more cases from the prerogative courts. There were numerous meetings to dissuade Coke, but he would not change his position.

Coke got away with his defiance, because he had a reputation as learned, fair, and incorruptible. Further, in several famous cases Coke's decisions were clearly popular. In one case that he removed from the Court of High Commission, he acquitted a man of libel charges, because the accused was forced to testify under oath on the meaning of words and symbols he had used in a letter concerning a bishop who had interpreted the letter as derogatory. Coke claimed the case violated the common law rule that the law cannot hold people accountable for their private thoughts, only for their public speech. James I was opposed to Puritans and Catholics alike and used the High Commission to harass and suppress religious dissent.

Dr. Thomas Bonham's case was Coke's most celebrated decision. The case arose out of a law of Parliament giving the Royal College of Physicians the right to regu-

late all London physicians and punish infractions with fines and imprisonment. Dr. Bonham, a Cambridge graduate who had refused to obtain the proper certificate before practicing in London, was fined and imprisoned by the Royal College. When he appealed, Coke ruled the law allowing his sentence null and void, because the Royal College received half of all fines collected and were, therefore, at once judge and party to the case. Coke was following the common law dictum that no man should be judge in his own cause.

In the Bonham decision, Coke went on to say that the common law could set limits to Parliament's authority. Because Coke had strong connections with the leadership in Parliament and they approved of his efforts to limit the king's ambitions, Parliament chose in this instance to ignore Coke's statement. The idea of judicial voidance (that is, the ability of courts to void laws passed by legislative bodies) never received serious consideration in England, but across the Atlantic, in England's colonies, the Americans would one day make great use of the principle.

Another strategy James I used to expand his prerogative was dramatically increasing the number and scope of royal proclamations in general. When Parliament sent the king a petition in 1610 complaining of the practice, Coke was summoned to a meeting of the Privy Council to give an opinion on their legality. Coke argued that the king's proclamations were not the same as law and that James I had no authority on his own to create offenses by proclamation. The king promised to restrain his use of proclamations but did not.

The confrontations continued, and the king wished to be rid of Coke but could think of no way to overcome Coke's popularity and prestige. Francis Bacon, James I's brilliant and power-hungry solicitor and Coke's most dangerous enemy, advised the king to promote Coke to chief justice of the King's Bench when the post fell vacant in 1613. From that position, Bacon reasoned that Coke would not dare oppose the king. Coke wanted to stay on the Common Pleas bench and protested, but the king insisted, and Coke took the oath of his new office October 25, 1613.

For a time, Coke justified Bacon's prediction that Coke's attacks on the royal prerogative would cease once he was on the King's Bench, but events precluded a long retreat. In a case involving Edmund Peacham, a country parson of Puritan sympathies who had written some notes for a sermon that seemed treasonous, the justices of the King's Bench were asked for opinions on Peacham's guilt before the trial was held. James I wanted him tried but knew that Peacham had friends in Parliament and feared the embarrassment of an acquittal. At first Coke refused, but his colleagues, being more timid, gave in and, ultimately, so did Coke. The opinion Coke gave, however, was that Peacham was innocent. While the parson's notes were insulting to the king, they were not treasonous, because they were neither made public nor included any specific proposal. This effectively blocked the big public trial that the king had desired. James I was not willing to provide Coke with a forum for another popular dictum against him.

There were other cases in which Coke thwarted James I's arbitrary actions, but the case that caused the most trouble and led to his dismissal from the bench was the case of Commendams of 1616. For various reasons, James I wanted the King's Bench to halt proceedings in a particular case involving the king himself until after consulting with him in person. Coke refused, and this time he prevailed upon each of his colleagues to sign a letter to the king explaining why his order to recess was an unlawful interference.

Coke and his colleagues were summoned for a royal harangue, and all but Coke yielded to the king's opinion. James I was by then convinced that he must remove Coke from the bench. Weak charges were brought by Bacon, and Coke was stripped of his position in November of 1616. Coke was devastated by his removal. He believed that his career was over, but he would yet perform important services to his country. In an odd turn of events, the king invited him back as a privy councillor after the marriage of Francis, his daughter and only child by Lady Hatton, to John Villiers, the brother of the duke of Buckingham, the king's new palace favorite. The wedding took place September 29, 1617, as a state occasion.

By 1620, James I was desperate again for money and called a Parliament to meet in January of 1621. It was a vigorous session, and before it was dissolved in December of that year, it had impeached Chancellor Bacon and numerous other officials for accepting bribes and other corrupt acts. The Commons also launched a major attack on monopolies, ending many of them. While the king accepted these actions, he was not willing to allow Parliament to discuss his foreign policy and warned the Commons to this effect several times. Thwarted in their desire to petition the king directly on these matters, the Commons entered their grievances in their official journal, an event that came to be known as the Great Protestation.

Throughout this Parliament, Coke was the most prominent leader of the House of Commons, taking special care to guard what he perceived as the ancient rights and liberties of the Commons. He was largely responsible for the inclusion of a definitive claim to these rights and liberties in the grievances entered into the journal. When James I heard of the parliamentary grievances, he dismissed Coke from the Privy Council and sent him to the Tower of London under close confinement for seven months for what James I interpreted as an attack on the royal prerogative. The king then personally tore out the pages of the House of Commons journal containing the grievances and dissolved Parliament. Coke's personal and professional papers were searched by the Privy Council in an effort to obtain evidence of treason; they found nothing, and at his trial, Coke was acquitted. Coke, now seventy years old, was released from the Tower and the public's perception of him as the champion of liberties and the oracle of the law grew significantly.

James I had been promoting a marriage between his only son, Prince Charles, and a daughter of the Spanish king. While it might have been a good diplomatic move to make peace with Spain, it was very unpopular in England. When the negotiations failed, celebrations were held throughout much of the realm. Buckingham's popularity rose because he was erroneously given the credit. Seizing the moment, Buckingham called for war with Spain. James I glumly called a parliament for February of 1624 to provide funds for the navy. Parliament, pleased with the shift in policy toward Spain, voted James the money he needed. Relations were so cordial that the king also accepted a bill drafted by Coke to end all monopolies forever. Some historians have called the monopoly bill Parliament's greatest achievement during James I's reign.

On March 27, 1625, James I died, and his son became King Charles I. The general public was initially indifferent. When Charles I kept Buckingham on as his principal adviser and Buckingham's conduct of the war with Spain and other foreign affairs went poorly, however, the public mood turned angry. The new king was obliged by custom to call a Parliament, and when it met in April of 1625, grievances against Buckingham surfaced immediately. Coke, now seventy-two, was at the forefront of the leadership of the Commons. He spoke strongly in favor of impeaching Buckingham. To save his adviser, Charles I dissolved Parliament, even though this meant that the money customarily given a new king could not be voted. In 1625, Charles I called another Parliament, which he hoped would be more sympathetic, partly because he had forced Coke to accept the post of high sheriff of Buckinghamshire, which kept him from serving in the Commons. The ploy gained the king little, however.

Once again, Parliament sought to impeach Buckingham, and the king had to dissolve it.

The king's problem was how to raise money without Parliament, whose approval was required for any taxes to be levied. Charles I tried many schemes, but the results were insufficient, and he had no alternative by January of 1628 but to call a Parliament to meet in March. The election results were the worst that the king had yet experienced. The Parliament of 1628 was to be one of the most famous ever assembled, and Coke, with his extensive experience in previous Parliaments and the law, played a leading role.

The Commons' leaders held private meetings early on. They decided that, in view of the extraordinary attacks on personal liberties suffered by all English citizens during the last two years, instead of attacking particular abuses and officers of the Crown as in earlier Parliaments, this time they must pass a new fundamental law protecting their liberties. Coke's goal was to limit the royal prerogative. The result was the Petition of Right, of which Coke was a principal author, one of the great documents of English constitutionalism. It included four major provisions: first, no taxation without Parliament's consent; second, no soldiers could be billeted in a private home without consent of the owner; third, military officers could not execute martial law in time of peace, and fourth, no one could be imprisoned without cause or denied the protection of habeas corpus.

The king had little choice but to agree to the petition, because Coke and others had established a common front with the House of Lords and, more important, stood firm by the decision not to release any money to the king unless he did agree. There were great celebrations in London and throughout much of England on June 7, 1628, when King Charles I announced formally his assent to the Petition of Right. Parliament adjourned a few days later, and the seventy-six-year-old Sir Edward Coke went home to Stoke House, having served in his last Parliament.

The project that Coke set for his remaining years was to finish his *Institutes* (1628-1644) and edit the last two volumes of his *Reports*. When completed, the *Institutes* comprised four volumes, one each on English land law, fundamental charters and statutes, criminal law, and court procedures and jurisdiction. Collectively, they formed the greatest treatise yet written on English law and remained, with his *Reports*, the most important authority on the subject for nearly three centuries, especially in England's American colonies.

Coke packed the *Institutes* with every detail and ex-

ample that he could find. His style made the *Institutes* somewhat disorganized and difficult to read, but they were rewarding to those who persevered. Coke argued that the common law limited both royal prerogative and parliamentary acts. While England never accepted his views on the supremacy of common law, his work was a major contribution to English constitutionalism and the concept of a limited executive branch. In 1628, the first volume was already published and volumes 2 and 3 were in manuscript form. The fourth had yet to be written. Coke set to work and finished the entire treatise several years before he died.

When Charles I heard that Coke had nearly finished volume two of the *Institutes*, he ordered that it not be printed. He rightly feared an attack on the royal prerogative. The second volume was not printed until 1642, and volumes 3 and 4 in 1644. By this time, Parliament had the power to overrule the king.

Stoke House, where Coke spent his last years, was a cheerful, large, rambling stone structure. Coke owned about sixty great manors and was considered a very wealthy man. A major portion of the income from his properties, however, went to keep his sons out of financial trouble. None of them could manage money. His daughters were more comfort to him in his old age, especially Francis. She seemed quite devoted to her father and came to live at Stoke House and look after him. He remained in good health until near the end. In 1632, at age eighty, his horse fell on him, but he walked away from it virtually unhurt. At every illness rumors flew to London that he was dead or dying. The king's agents kept watch on him, because they feared his unpublished manuscripts. On September 3, 1634, in his eighty-second year, Coke died in his sleep while the king's agents were in the act of confiscating his manuscripts. He was buried in a marble tomb next to his first wife, Bridget.

SIGNIFICANCE

During his long and active professional life, Coke held a remarkable variety of political positions in all branches of government. Through this experience and his work as a legal scholar, he was well prepared for the great work of his later years as judge, parliamentarian, and legal commentator. When the Stuart kings James I and Charles I attempted to implement the divine right theory of kingship, Coke first attempted to limit the expansion of their prerogative through the common law and then developed the theory eventually known as judicial review.

After James I removed Coke from his position as judge, Coke shifted his battleground to Parliament, using the ancient authority of that body to impeach corrupt officials. When that proved insufficient to stop the expansion of royal power, he helped devise a new strategy for Parliament: withholding funds from the king until he recognized an expanded definition of the rights and privileges of Parliament and all English citizens. The result was the Petition of Right of 1628. Coke was instrumental in the evolution of Parliament from a medieval assembly into a legislature. The work of Coke and his Parliamentary colleagues laid the groundwork and determined much of Parliament's agenda for its civil war with the king in the 1640's.

In his last years, Coke finished his thirteen-volume *Reports*. This compilation of legal cases and commentary was the most comprehensive in England and contributed greatly to the stabilization of English law. He also finished his *Institutes*, the four-volume treatise on English law. These works were the principal texts in the education of lawyers in England and its colonies for nearly three centuries. Coke's bias toward the common law and against arbitrary royal government remained a constant reminder to English and colonial politicians of the alternative to royal absolutism and contributed significantly to the growth of liberty on both sides of the Atlantic.

—Richard L. Hillard

FURTHER READING

Allen, J. W. *English Political Thought, 1603-1644*. London: Methuen, 1938. Reprint. Hamden, Conn.: Archon Books, 1967. A scholarly exposition of English political thought during the early Stuart era. Allen's work is considered a classic in its field. Coke's views are included.

Baker, J. H. *An Introduction to English Legal History*. 3d ed. London: Butterworths, 1990. One of the great standard survey texts on the history of English law. Baker's well-written study deals with a complex and often confusing subject in an organized manner. Numerous references to Coke.

Bowen, Catherine Drinker. *The Lion and the Throne: The Life and Times of Sir Edward Coke, 1552-1634*. 1956. Reprint. Boston: Little, Brown, 1990. A popular, rather than scholarly, biography of Coke. Should be read together with other more scholarly works.

Boyer, Allen D. *Sir Edward Coke and the Elizabethan Age*. Stanford, Calif.: Stanford University Press, 2003. The first volume in a two-volume biography, examines Coke's early life and legal career until 1603, the last year of Elizabeth I's reign.

_____, ed. *Law, Liberty, and Parliament: Selected Essays on the Writings of Sir Edward Coke*. Indianapolis, Ind.: Liberty Fund, 2004. A collection of essays analyzing Coke's judicial decisions, legal theories, and the relation of Crown and court in seventeenth century England.

Hostettler, John. *Sir Edward Coke: A Force for Freedom*. Chichester, West Sussex, England: Barry Rose Law, 1997. A more recent biography of Coke written by a British legal historian and former magistrate.

Keir, Sir David Lindsay. *The Constitutional History of Modern Britain Since 1485*. 9th ed. London: Adam and Charles Black, 1969. An excellent, well-written, and scholarly constitutional history of England since the Tudor monarchs that includes a detailed interpretation of the Stuart era. Coke is mentioned several times.

Sabine, George H. *A History of Political Theory*. 4th ed. Revised by Thomas Landon Thorson. Hinsdale, Ill.: Dryden Press, 1973. A historical survey of political thought from earliest times. Standard text in the field. Provides excellent background to appreciate the significance of political developments in England under the early Stuart kings. Includes brief discussions of Coke.

Smith, Lacey Baldwin. *This Realm of England, 1399-1688*. 8th ed. Boston: Houghton Mifflin, 2001. A readable and scholarly general history of England from the end of the medieval period to the Glorious Revolution. Part of a four-volume series. Excellent both for narrative and interpretation. Mentions Coke briefly.

White, Stephen D. *Sir Edward Coke and "The Grievances of the Commonwealth," 1621-1628*. Chapel Hill: University of North Carolina Press, 1979. A detailed and scholarly examination of Coke's work in the parliaments of 1621-1628 and of his critical role as promoter of the 1628 Petition of Right.

SEE ALSO: First Duke of Buckingham; Charles I; James I.

RELATED ARTICLES in *Great Events from History: The Seventeenth Century, 1601-1700:* February 7-19, 1601: Essex Rebellion; November 5, 1605: Gunpowder Plot; December 18, 1621: The Great Protestation; May 6-June 7, 1628: Petition of Right; 1642-1651: English Civil Wars.

JEAN-BAPTISTE COLBERT
French politician and administrator

Colbert contributed to the reform of the administrative, economic, legal, and cultural foundations of the French monarchy. Historians consider him the founder of the economic and political idea of mercantilism, which predominated in eighteenth century Europe. His founding of several academies of arts, letters, and sciences is perhaps his most enduring legacy.

BORN: August 29, 1619; Reims, France
DIED: September 6, 1683; Paris, France
ALSO KNOWN AS: Le Nord (the North)
AREAS OF ACHIEVEMENT: Business and economics, government and politics, patronage of the arts

EARLY LIFE

Jean-Baptiste Colbert (zhahn-baw-teest kohl-behr) was born in the city of Reims in the Champagne region of France. Little is known of Colbert's childhood or education beyond that he sprang from a family of wholesale cloth merchants turned financiers and that he attended the Jesuit college in Reims. Changes in trading routes and European economic patterns had dramatically reduced Reims's commercial significance by the 1620's, and the once prosperous Colbert family moved to Paris in 1629, seeking wider opportunities as bankers and financiers. Apparently, young Colbert remained behind in Reims to complete his education and in 1634 took up a position at a banking house in Lyons. Shortly afterward, however, he moved to Paris and took employment as an assistant to a notary. Sometime before 1640, he obtained a position as a royal war commissioner, a minor venal office his father probably purchased for him.

Colbert took his first real steps up the political and social ladders in the early 1640's. First, family connections allowed him to attach himself to the entourage of Michel Le Tellier, France's war minister. Then, with deliberate calculation he married Marie Charon, the daughter of a wealthy financier, who brought a very large dowry (100,000 livres) to the marriage. Sometime after Le Tellier acquired the post of secretary of state for war in 1643, Colbert became an assistant to the secretary and then his personal emissary to Jules Mazarin. From that point until early 1651, when he entered Mazarin's service, Colbert's loyalty to Le Tellier's cause and his aptitude for political and financial dealings proved themselves time and again. Indeed, despite his initial dislike for Colbert, it was those very qualities of loyalty, service,

and efficiency that prompted Mazarin to request Le Tellier to release Colbert to enter his own service.

From 1651 until Mazarin's death in 1661, Colbert served Mazarin faithfully. During the turbulent years of civil war (the Wars of the Fronde, 1648-1653) and Mazarin's two political exiles (1651-1653), Colbert acted as the minister's personal financial agent in Paris and as his representative at court. So great was his skill for these tasks that he managed to amass a fortune in Mazarin's name. Following the end of the Fronde and Mazarin's return to Paris, Colbert once again proved himself the loyal servant of his patron's interests, advising the minister on political matters and continuing to enlarge Mazarin's fortune (and his own) through the traffic in venal offices, manipulation of the monarchy's debts, and financial speculations. On his deathbed, Mazarin commended Colbert to Louis XIV's service.

LIFE'S WORK

Following Mazarin's death, Louis XIV's dramatic announcement of the plan to act as his own first minister meant that Colbert would never rise to the heights of political power or personal wealth that Cardinal de Richelieu and Mazarin had attained. Nevertheless, as a member of the king's financial council (from 1661), as controller general of finance (from 1665), as secretary of state for the navy (from 1668), and as secretary of state for the king's household (from 1669), Colbert made his mark on the first half of Louis's reign in ways so profound as to set the political form of Louis's absolutism as the European model for centralized monarchy.

Colbert's rise in the power structure of Louis's government resulted from his zeal in pursuing reforms aimed at eradicating the very same ministerial abuses of power and finance he himself had helped Mazarin practice during the 1650's. With Mazarin's death, the greatest threat to Louis XIV's power and to his resolution to act as his own first minister came from Nicolas Fouquet, the king's powerful superintendent of finance. Fouquet was, in fact, the most logical successor to Mazarin's ministry. Clearly the richest man in France, Fouquet's willingness to finance the monarchy through loans and pledges based on his personal fortune had allowed Louis to pursue war against Spain to a successful conclusion in 1659. In short, Fouquet had personally acted as one of the monarchy's chief bankers throughout the 1650's. Such open-handedness in financing the monarchy was only possible because Fouquet had used his position in the government to enrich himself beyond all measure.

Within months after Mazarin's death, Louis and Colbert had spun an elaborate trap for Fouquet, which culminated in a dramatic arrest on charges of treason and financial peculation (embezzlement). Fouquet not only held a stranglehold on Louis's finances but also maintained private fortresses, troops, and a personal navy stronger than the king's. Additionally, Fouquet enjoyed tremendous popular support. Colbert, formerly on close terms with Fouquet, undertook personal charge of the prosecution and succeeded in gaining a conviction on the charges of financial misconduct. Many condemned Colbert as a hypocrite, claiming that Fouquet's crimes in the 1650's had been no worse than those of Mazarin (or Colbert's own). At a personal level Fouquet was treated unfairly, but this case actually concerned crimes of the past less than it did the future direction of the monarchy. Through the Fouquet prosecution, Louis signaled his absolute determination to subordinate the machineries of royal finance, administration, and justice to his personal will. Henceforth, the king would tolerate no overly ambitious or powerful subjects. Breaking Fouquet was an object lesson to anyone who might try to emulate the models of either the Cardinal de Richelieu or Mazarin.

Colbert himself belonged to that group of financiers and political actors who had risen to power under Richelieu and Mazarin. His own part in the Fouquet prosecution signaled his acceptance of Louis's lesson—the rules of high politics had changed. From his first efforts to assist the king in laying his trap for Fouquet through his death in 1683, Colbert never forgot that lesson. Beginning with the dismantling and royal seizure of Fouquet's financial empire, then moving on to the establishment of special chambers of justice to investigate, punish, and fine wrongdoers among the entire class of royal financiers, Colbert launched a financial reform that reversed Louis's kingdom from its position as the greatest debtor state in Europe to a status as the richest and most rationally administered.

Colbert proved tireless in his efforts to reform and regularize royal taxation, government contracting, financial administration, and economic regulation. He also showed himself equally willing to employ the monarchy's resources to build new manufacturing, to establish colonies and trading companies, and to reform the legal system. Al-

together, this complex of reforms and royal initiatives constituted a whole that historians have labeled "Colbertisme" in its particular application to France and mercantilism in its more general application as the model for the economic and political thinking that dominated Europe in the eighteenth century.

The specifics involved in Colbert's mercantilism defy easy summary, but the main theoretical lines can be delineated. The state was to foster and support new manufacturing, both through direct subsidies and the establishment of prohibitive import duties. Regulating everything concerning the quality, type, and quantities of goods, France would become an economically independent state enjoying a surplus in the value of trade export over the value of imports. Colonies would provide raw materials and markets for finished goods. Trade with other European states was to be limited to exports paid in cash. Other trading nations such as the Dutch and the English constituted France's natural enemies, and France's greatness depended on undercutting or destroying these enemies' ability to compete economically. Finally, the success of the entire system must depend on a debt-free, centrally organized economy.

Jean-Baptiste Colbert. (Library of Congress)

In practice, this theoretical framework called for a massive overhaul of the French economy and political administration. The task was obviously beyond the reach of Colbert's lifetime, and his success must be measured in terms of progress rather than actual accomplishments. France was an overwhelmingly agricultural nation, but Colbert did lay the basis for a new system of state-controlled manufacturing establishments, especially in the luxury trades. Moreover, despite hindrances to trade, the government regulations gained for French goods an unparalleled reputation for quality and value. His efforts to build a new navy and the merchant ships necessary for colonization and the protection of trade made considerable gains—enough so, in fact, that the French navy seriously challenged English/Dutch supremacy for a time. Most important, his efforts at reforming the tax collection system (not the actual tax burdens on the population), the management of debt, and the administration of the kingdom's finances yielded dramatic results in reestablishing the state's solvency.

Within the new political order Louis XIV's personal reign created, Colbert was only one of several powerful ministers who acted strictly in the king's name while serving at his pleasure. Such a system was bound to create disagreements and conflicts among these ministers, and Colbert was involved in his share. The most important of these long-running political enmities put him in conflict with Le Tellier, his former patron, and Le Tellier's son the marquis de Louvois. Le Tellier and Louvois, as successive secretaries of state for war, pushed relentlessly for turning the royal treasury to the purposes of strengthening the French army. They also urged a militarist foreign policy on Louis as the best approach to building the monarchy. Colbert opposed both of these policies, urging economic warfare instead.

Initially successful in winning the king's ear, Colbert progressively lost ground to the Le Tellier/Louvois faction as the reign unfolded. Louis did indeed pursue an increasingly militaristic policy, and as he did Louvois's influence waxed, while Colbert's waned. Nor was this basic policy issue the only one on that Colbert suffered reverses. Although he was the superintendent of the king's buildings, he strongly opposed the lavish building program Louis launched in renovating the palace at Versailles. Colbert wanted Louis to make Paris itself his capital and the Louvre his principal residence. He did succeed in making dramatic improvements in the sanitation, police, and public works of Paris, but here, too, his basic policy was at odds with the king's wishes. Despite Colbert's efforts to make Paris the modern Rome, his death really marked the eclipse of the city of Paris as the focal point of French absolutism. Similarly, as a proponent of religious toleration, Colbert failed to sway the king from his policy of increasing persecution of French Protestants. Although he did not live to see the results, the revocation of the Edict of Nantes was to prove his views correct.

In another realm, Colbert fared better. As superintendent of the king's buildings, Colbert assumed responsibility for establishing Louis as the greatest patron of the arts, letters, and science that Europe had ever seen. Starting in 1662 with a European-wide system of French royal patronage for artists and intellectuals, Colbert went on to found the Academy of Inscriptions (1663), the Académie Royale des Sciences (1666), the Académie de France de Rome (1667), the Academy of Architecture (1671), and the first of the formal royal academies in the provinces. Colbert also reorganized and recharted the two existing royal academies, the Académie Française and the Academy of Painting and Sculpture, making them true state-supported institutions. The system of royal academies Colbert created not only served to glorify Louis's reign but also served the important political purpose of bringing France's most noted artists, intellectuals, and scientists under royal control. Colbert's academies survived until the Revolution and as reconstituted under Napoleon still form the basis for the Institut de France. To the extent that French arts, literature, and science have dominated various cultural periods in the three centuries since Colbert's death, these academies may be claimed as his most enduring legacy to the world.

SIGNIFICANCE

Colbert's life remains particularly difficult to summarize. He was intensely private, noted for his formidable and chilling personality. Moreover, the circumstances under which he served Louis XIV made it difficult for him to give free rein to his ambitions and personality. Historians long debated whether he may have been the actual architect behind the major policies of Louis's reign; while that interpretation has been rejected, the fact remains that he exercised primary responsibility for implementing the reforms and administrative machinery of Louis's reign. In that sense, he was the primary "contractor" building the edifice of absolutism that Richelieu, Mazarin, and Louis had designed.

A complex figure, Colbert defies easy categorization in the modern terms of government service. His career spanned a crucial transitional period in the development of political forms, and perhaps his greatest virtue lay in his ability to adjust to and then support inevitable changes.

He died a bitter and cynical man; indeed, his strict, calculating, and rather cold personality had earned him the sobriquet Le Nord (the North) from the fashionable Madame de Sévigné. His influence clearly on the wane, he was acutely conscious of his failure to sway the king from policies he considered destructive to the monarchy's future. Although he was little mourned at his death, his legacies to France proved themselves of incalculable value.

—*David S. Lux*

FURTHER READING

Beik, William. *Louis XIV and Absolutism: A Brief Study with Documents.* Boston: Bedford/St. Martin's Press, 2000. A collection of newly translated documents that demonstrate how Louis XIV became an absolute monarch. Includes some of Colbert's memos and letters regarding financial administration, reform in the provinces, and other subjects.

Cole, Charles Woolsey. *Colbert and a Century of French Mercantilism.* 2 vols. New York: Columbia University Press, 1939. This classic treatment of Colbert's economic ideas and financial reforms is the best starting point for understanding Colbert's impact on France.

Dent, Julian. *Crisis in Finance: Crown, Financiers, and Society in Seventeenth-Century France.* New York: St. Martin's Press, 1973. A solid exposition of the financial workings of the seventeenth century French monarchy, starkly exposing the weaknesses of the financial administration Colbert set out to reform. Detailed and scholarly, this work offers a strong portrait of the political and social world of the financiers.

Levi, Anthony. *Louis XIV.* New York: Carroll & Graf, 2004. This biography contains a great deal of information on Colbert's administration and relationship with Louis XIV.

Maland, David. *Culture and Society in Seventeenth-Century France.* New York: Charles Scribner's Sons, 1970. An excellent survey examining French high culture, political involvements with patronage, and the institutional development of the academies. Treats personalities and conflicts as well as more traditional historical facts.

Ranum, Orest. *Artisans of Glory: Writers and Historical Thought in Seventeenth-Century France.* Chapel Hill: University of North Carolina Press, 1980. Despite the seemingly narrow focus on historical writing, this work offers many general insights into the world of patronage and letters that Colbert sought to control. More importantly, Ranum's work suggests why such control was important to Colbert and the monarchy.

_____. *Paris in the Age of Absolutism.* New York: John Wiley & Sons, 1968. Ranum traces the cultural, social, and political history of Paris from the reign of Henry IV through Colbert's death. Invaluable as a guide to understanding the aims and purposes of Colbert's cultural ideas and Louis's policies.

Root, Hilton L. *Peasants and King in Burgundy: Agrarian Foundations of French Absolutism.* Berkeley: University of California Press, 1987. Focused primarily on developments in eighteenth century France, demonstrating the profound effects of Colbert's financial and administrative reforms. Tracing the development of village corporatism in Burgundy, this work shows many connections between Colbert and struggles over political reform in the next century.

Wolf, John B. *Louis XIV.* New York: W. W. Norton, 1968. A scholarly biography of Louis XIV, this work contains invaluable material concerning Colbert's relations with the king. Particularly strong in explaining the political significance of Louis's decision to rule in his own right and the development of a new ministerial system in the 1660's.

SEE ALSO: Gian Domenico Cassini; Christiaan Huygens; Louis XIV; François Mansart; Jules Hardouin-Mansart; Jules Mazarin; Charles Perrault; Cardinal de Richelieu; Madame de Sévigné; Duke de Sully.

RELATED ARTICLES in *Great Events from History: The Seventeenth Century, 1601-1700:* 17th century: Europe Endorses Slavery; 1601-1672: Rise of Scientific Societies; December, 1601: Dutch Defeat the Portuguese in Bantam Harbor; 1606-1674: Europeans Settle in India; 1610-1643: Reign of Louis XIII; 1661: Absolute Monarchy Emerges in France; 1661-1672: Colbert Develops Mercantilism; 1665-1681: Construction of the Languedoc Canal; May 24, 1667-May 2, 1668: War of Devolution; 1673: Renovation of the Louvre; 1682: French Court Moves to Versailles; 1689-1694: Famine and Inflation in France.

THE GREAT CONDÉ
French military leader

Condé played an important role in the struggle for royal absolutism, initially supporting the royal cause during the Fronde, then rebelling against the king. After reconciliation, he continued to serve as a successful and innovative military commander. He was part of the movement to abandon the old feudal levies in exchange for a tightly organized and highly trained and disciplined standing royal army. Condé was an expert tactician in the field.

BORN: September 8, 1621; Paris, France
DIED: December 11, 1686; Fontainebleau, France
ALSO KNOWN AS: Louis II de Bourbon (given name); Duke of Enghien
AREAS OF ACHIEVEMENT: Military, warfare and conquest

EARLY LIFE

The princes of Condé (kohn-day) were members of the most important cadet branch of the ruling Bourbon family of France, descended through Duke Charles IV of Bourbon. Two sixteenth century ancestors were Huguenot leaders, but Henri I renounced Calvinism during the St. Bartholomew's Day Massacre of 1572 to save his life. The family continued to play important roles until the dethronement of Charles X in 1830, when Louis-Henri-Joseph committed suicide. The son of the above, Louis-Antoine-Henri, the duke of Enghien, had been executed on Napoleon I's orders in 1804, ending the Condé line.

Louis II de Bourbon, the duke of Enghien, a title the line's oldest male member held from birth, was a youth of such violent and moody temper that some questioned his sanity and his ability to function as an adult. By age twenty, however, he appeared to have outgrown the worst of these shortcomings, though he continued to be an extremely arrogant and undiplomatic individual, showing little tolerance for persons of lesser ability. Following the death of his father in 1646, he inherited the rank of "Premier Prince of the Blood," becoming the fourth prince of Condé. As a young boy, he received a thorough education from the Jesuits at Bourges in central France and at the Royal Academy in Paris, where he was taught mathematics and horsemanship.

Though of high nobility, Louis, twenty years old, had to enter into an unhappy marriage with the thirteen-year-old hunchbacked Claire-Clémence de Maillé-Brézé, a niece of Cardinal de Richelieu, Louis XIII's prime min-ister, to gain a military command. Richelieu believed him to be more trustworthy than most of the king's generals and named him commander in chief of an ill-trained and poorly disciplined French force on the Flemish frontier late in the Thirty Years' War (1618-1648). At this point, the emphasis in the Thirty Years' War had shifted from Germany to northeastern France. Louis, though he had no prior military experience or formal military training, immediately set about to train and instill discipline in his force, a task in which he was ably supported by two officers who had earlier served under King Gustavus II Adolphus of Sweden.

LIFE'S WORK

Condé won his first major victory in defeating a Spanish army that had besieged the border fortress of Rocroi, near Sedan, only five days after Louis XIV's accession to the throne. Rocroi, often considered the most important French victory of the seventeenth century, was won by the French cavalry, well supported by field artillery (though the French had only twelve, as opposed to twenty-eight, Spanish guns), over the famous Spanish infantry, marking the beginning of the end of Spain's military prestige. Of the eighteen thousand Spanish infantry involved in the battle, eight thousand were killed and seven thousand captured (total Spanish casualties amounted to twenty-one thousand out of twenty-seven thousand men). French casualties numbered four thousand of about twenty-three thousand men engaged. The Spanish never again fielded infantry as good as the troops lost there. Condé continued to enhance his martial reputation during the last years of the Thirty Years' War, winning several significant victories in southwestern Germany. During this period, he served alongside his famous contemporary and sometime rival, Henri de La Tour d'Auvergne, viscount de Turenne.

It was during this period that the French army adopted the new tactics of concentrated fire and rapid movements. Condé became a master of these tactics, which supplemented Turenne's strategic ability. Condé was instrumental in furthering the new concepts of a rigidly disciplined and thoroughly trained army, as opposed to the old, poorly organized, and inadequately equipped and trained feudal levies. The old matchlock musket was replaced with the flintlock musket, and the formerly rather independent artillery was more fully integrated into the army, which was now composed of about 75 percent infantry, deemphasizing cavalry. Condé employed his rather mobile field artillery in a more concentrated fashion, following the example of Gustavus, providing more effective support for both infantry and cavalry. The number of camp followers, especially women, was substantially reduced, and the army became more national in makeup and spirit. Increasingly, the power and security of the state depended on the new royal standing army, which in France was carefully and strictly supervised by the war office, progressively replacing the formerly powerful feudal levies, largely controlled by the high nobles of the realm.

France emerged from the Thirty Years' War with the most powerful European army and with expanded borders, though the war with Spain continued until 1659. During the final phase of the Thirty Years' War, however, France faced a most serious internal challenge to royal power and national unity in the form of the Fronde (1648-1653).

The initial phase of the Fronde was supported primarily by the middle class and the *parlementaires* (judges and lawyers of the Paris law court), who were struggling to maintain traditional power distributions within government against the growth of royal absolutism. Condé, still serving in Germany until the Treaty of Westphalia (October, 1648), which ended the Thirty Years' War, initially supported the royal cause. Following the peace in Germany, Cardinal Jules Mazarin, Richelieu's successor, fearing the power and following of the ambitious Condé, sent him first against Spain and then against the Spanish Netherlands. The war with Spain continued until 1659. Upon his return, Condé besieged rebellious Paris with an army of fifteen thousand and was instrumental in ending the first Fronde in the king's favor. As a result of disagreements with Mazarin, Condé fell into royal disfavor. Condé believed that he, not Mazarin, was the true savior of the king's power and demanded a greater role in government as well as high rewards. Condé was arrested in January, 1650, and imprisoned for about a year.

Pressure from the noble party forced his release, but bitter disagreements continued, and Condé led the second Fronde, the Fronde of the Princes, believing that he should replace Mazarin as the king's chief minister. Because of his undiplomatic arrogance and his quarrel with Queen Anne of Austria (the widow of Louis XIII and regent for her young son Louis XIV), Condé's opponents were able to maneuver him into open rebellion against Louis XIV, who had recently been declared of age. At this time, the monopoly of military power had not yet fully shifted to royal hands, and the great nobles of the realm still held large estates with great wealth and their own powerful military forces.

Condé raised an antiroyal army in southern France, while Turenne, who had briefly joined the Fronde, returned his loyalties to the Crown. The Fronde of the Princes, similar to the earlier Fronde, failed to gain popular support and brought France to the brink of anarchy. The frondeurs' goals were selfish and designed to benefit the aristocracy, rather than establish true constitutional government, in imitation of the English model, as frequently claimed. The frondeurs were also hindered in their struggle by their own, typically feudal inability to form a clear and lasting alliance, and by Condé's frequent shifts of allegiance and his lack of clear objectives. This was, in fact, the last serious attempt by the feudal aristocracy to halt the development of divine right royal absolutism. When Condé realized that power was slipping away from him, he fled to the Spanish Netherlands and for the next eight years served the Spanish. He served first in southern France and then in Flanders, though without notable success, partly because the Spanish never fully trusted him. Meanwhile Condé was sentenced in absentia to death for rebellion.

The Great Condé. (Library of Congress)

Following Condé's desertion, the Fronde came to an inglorious end. Louis XIV had broken the power of the *parlementaires* and of the nobles in general, and had firmly established royal absolutism. Condé and other rebels received a general amnesty following the Treaty of the Pyrenees in 1659. Condé regained all of his possessions and titles, though the king was initially reluctant to trust him fully. For the next few years, Condé lived at his estate of Chantilly about fifteen miles north of Paris and made it a center of the arts. Throughout his life, he had been a patron of the arts, and Chantilly attracted a literary circle that included Jean de La Fontaine, Molière, Jean Racine, and Jacques-Bénigne Bossuet. In 1667, when John II Casimir Vasa abdicated as king of Poland, Condé was advanced as his successor, a proposal that alarmed the Prussians in particular, and Louis was able to use this threat to keep Prussia out of the War of Devolution.

Condé returned to military service in 1668, when he led the French forces that captured Franche-Comté in a swift, two-week campaign. In 1672, in the war against Holland, he commanded the French forces in the Rhineland and the Netherlands. Following the death in battle of Turenne on July 27, 1675, Condé, now in overall command of the French forces, successfully defended Alsace against imperial forces. Later that year, ill with gout, he retired to Chantilly, where he spent his remaining years. He died in 1686, following a religious deathbed conversion, after a life without religion, in which he had rebelled against religious as well as worldly authority. He is at times described as an aggressive atheist, though he favored religious tolerance.

SIGNIFICANCE

The Great Condé, along with Turenne, was among the most outstanding and innovative military commanders of the seventeenth century, though he, contrary to most of his contemporary military geniuses, had no formal military training or apprenticeship. He was an enterprising and daring tactician, who inspired his troops. Condé adopted military concepts, developed by Gustavus II Adolphus and by Oliver Cromwell, which emphasized mobility and the more flexible use of field artillery, especially in combination with cavalry. Condé employed these methods as early as the Battle of Rocroi, which resulted in a stunning victory over Spain's famous infantry. Following that battle, Condé was viewed as a model commander and teacher of these new concepts. During this period, however, strong fortifications increasingly dominated warfare, and it was in this latter area that

Turenne's greater strategic skills, based on patience and planning, gained greater success and reputation. The reforms introduced by these two great captains were ably advanced by the marquis de Louvois, one of France's greatest ministers of war, who held that office from 1677 to 1691.

Condé's role in the Fronde was designed to reverse the growth of royal absolutism and centralization of power in France and to preserve, or reestablish, traditional noble rights. His efforts failed, and he has to share in the blame for bringing France close to anarchy. His loyalty to the Crown, however, was firm and unchallenging following the amnesty of 1659.

—Frederick Dumin

FURTHER READING

Bannister, Mark. *Condé in Context: Ideological Change in Seventeenth-Century France.* Oxford, England: European Humanities Research Centre, 2002. Examines Condé's significance to his contemporaries, who considered him a hero of the age.

Briggs, Robin. *Early Modern France, 1560-1715.* 2d ed. New York: Oxford University Press, 1998. A general introductory history with several charts, an index, a glossary, and a six-page annotated bibliography.

Lynn, John A. *Giant of the Grand Siècle: The French Army, 1610-1715.* New York: Cambridge University Press, 1997. A comprehensive overview of army administration and tactics, including information about Condé and other military officials.

_____. *The Wars of Louis XIV, 1667-1714.* London: Longman, 1999. A history of French military campaigns during the final years of Louis XIV's reign, including information on Condé's participation in these battles.

Montgomery of Alamein, Viscount. *A History of Warfare.* Cleveland, Ohio: World, 1968. A general history of warfare, which places Condé and his times in a larger framework. Includes illustrations, maps, index, and short bibliography.

Ogg, David. *Europe in the Seventeenth Century.* 9th ed. London: A. C. Black, 1971. A standard history that still is of great value. Contains several maps, an index, and a ten-page bibliography.

Ranum, Orest. *Paris in the Age of Absolutism.* Bloomington: Indiana University Press, 1979. Chapter 10, "The Frondeurs," is entirely devoted to the Fronde.

Wedgwood, C. V. *The Thirty Years' War.* New Haven, Conn.: Yale University Press, 1939. A standard history of the war, and an excellent treatment.

ANNE CONWAY
English philosopher

One of the few English women philosophers of the seventeenth century, Conway's posthumously published work proposes a spiritualistic cosmology that attempts to reconcile theories of emanation and vitalism with Christian theology and modern philosophy. An important early proponent of monism and idealism, she influenced the later philosophy of Leibniz and through him the German Idealists of the nineteenth century.

BORN: December 14, 1631; London, England
DIED: February 18, 1679; Ragley, Warwickshire, England
ALSO KNOWN AS: Lady Conway (honorific), Viscountess Conway (honorific), Anne Finch (given name)
AREA OF ACHIEVEMENT: Philosophy

EARLY LIFE

The youngest of eleven children, Lady Anne Conway, née Finch, was the posthumous daughter of Sir Heneage Finch, the speaker of the House of Commons, and his second wife, Elizabeth Cradock. Anne was tutored at home but received no formal education, as was customary for girls at that time. However, she seems to have exhibited intellectual curiosity and ability very early on: Being an avid reader, she taught herself French, Greek, and Latin and read extensively about mathematics and philosophy.

Anne Finch was particularly close to her half brother, John Finch, who attended Christ's College, Cambridge, and was a pupil of the Cambridge Platonist philosopher Henry More (1614-1687). As a woman, Anne was denied a university education, but her brother arranged for her to receive instruction from Henry More by correspondence from 1650 onward. More provided her with intellectual stimulation, introducing her to many philosophers and scientists, and they remained close friends throughout her life.

In 1651, a marriage was arranged between Anne and Edward, third Viscount Conway. Anne's husband, having been a pupil of Henry More himself, encouraged his wife's intellectual occupations. However, from her teens onward, Anne had suffered from an illness that made it impossible for her to live with her husband until 1655 or 1656, because of her need for constant medical attention. At the age of twelve, Anne had caught a fever that left her with debilitating and recurring headaches, which tormented her for the rest of her life. The headaches proved to be untreatable, and the pain became so severe that she nearly died on several occasions. Due to her illness, Conway led a withdrawn life, which, however, did not deter her from philosophical studies and from participating in intellectual circles.

LIFE'S WORK

While Conway's personal life was limited by her pain and illness, her studies and her participation in England's intellectual circles never ceased. These circles included such members as the Cambridge Platonists Henry More, Ralph Cudworth, Joseph Glanvill, George Rust, and Benjamin Whichcote. In 1658, Conway gave birth to her only child, a son named Heneage. In 1660, both mother and son contracted smallpox. While Anne was able to survive (barely), her son died of the disease.

Conway tried many, sometimes very dangerous, potential cures for her headaches. In 1656, the excruciating pain forced her to travel to France to undergo an operation known as a trepan, in which the skull is opened to release pressure—at that time without anaesthetics, of course. However, the French surgeons seem to have been afraid to perform this surgery and opened her jugular arteries instead, but again without success.

Conway's correspondence with Henry More, who was also a frequent visitor at the Conway home, indicates that she was schooled in a critical version of Cartesianism. In 1670, during the search for a cure for her headaches, she also encountered the Flemish philosopher and physician Franciscus Mercurius van Helmont. Although he failed to cure her, he was impressed by her personality and stayed with Conway in Ragley from 1670-1679 (with minor absences). Helmont introduced Conway to alchemical thought and the Jewish Kabbala, which finally caused her to depart from the Cartesian dualism of her Cambridge-Platonist schooling.

Helmont also proved influential in fostering Anne Conway's interest in the Quakers, an interest that progressed from detached intellectual curiosity to close personal contact with Quakers who visited her frequently between 1675 and 1677. In 1677, she finally converted to Quakerism—a courageous decision, since the Quakers were much feared and loathed for their political and social radicalism (which included a belief in the equality of men and women). Conway died in 1679 after torturous suffering. Her epitaph only reads "Quaker Lady."

After Conway's death, Helmont took a notebook with him from Ragley in which Conway had written a philosophical treatise. The treatise was eventually translated into Latin and published in Holland under the title *Principia philosophiae anti-quissima et recentissimae* (1690; *The Principles of the Most Ancient and Modern Philosophy*, 1692). The 1692 English edition of the work was actually a retranslation of the Latin version, since the notebook containing Conway's original manuscript had been lost. The only other surviving source of Conway's philosophical theories is her correspondence with Henry More and others.

Conway's theory is both monist and vitalist and sharply criticizes mechanism. That is, she believes that each thing in the world is a monad, which means that it has a single, total, and indivisible nature. This belief opposes that of René Descartes, who put forward a dualism that distinguishes between physical reality and spiritual or mental reality, thereby positing an absolute distinction between mind and body. Conway, as an antimechanistic vitalist, sees the world as fundamentally spiritual or organic, rather than controlled by inorganic, mechanical processes.

The basis of her work lies in the distinction between three different kinds of beings: God, Christ, and creation. These differ mainly in their changeability: God is essentially unchangeable, Christ—as a mediator between God and creation—can only change for the better, whereas creation is changeable for the better or for the worse. All created beings are constituted by one single spiritual substance, which is arranged into an infinite, hierarchically ordered number of monads (that is, indivisible particles of spirit). All creation is alive and endowed with perception and motion. Conway claims that there is no body in the sense of inert matter. She argues that matter and spirit are essentially the same and differ from one another only in mode—matter is made up of congealed spirit.

Conway's system is presented as a response to the predominant philosophical approaches of her time—in particular, it rejects the dualism of Descartes. According to Conway, philosophical theories that argue for an absolute separation of matter and spirit fail to explain the interaction of body and mind. She believes her system is better equipped to answer the question: Why is it that the spirit also suffers when the body is in pain? Conway also criticizes the pantheist materialism of Thomas Hobbes and Baruch Spinoza, since their approach does not acknowledge a difference between God and creation.

Conway's natural philosophy is thus at the same time a work of metaphysics, in that it posits a fundamental nature of the universe, rooted in the nature of God, that stands as the explanation for all things, and also a theodicy—an attempt to explain why suffering exists in the world despite God's benevolence. Consequently, Conway denies the eternity of hell and explains suffering as a process of purification by which a creature achieves a more spiritual and divine state. Her work is also based on the Neoplatonic theory of creation by divine emanation and influenced by the Kabbala and the Jewish mystic Isaac ben Solomon Luria (1534-1572), whose vision of a perfect universe proved to be influential for Conway. It seems likely, moreover, that Gottfried Wilhelm Leibniz appropriated the term *monad* from Conway, whose work he became acquainted with via Helmont.

SIGNIFICANCE

In an age when philosophy and indeed all learned discourses were the almost exclusive province of men, Conway managed to participate in intellectual exchanges and even to produce her own distinctive metaphysical system. Although women's opportunities were restricted to the private sphere, Conway occupies an important place in modern philosophy. She is also exceptional in having received the equivalent of a university education, a privilege usually denied to women. Her work has suffered from the same neglect as texts by other modern women philosophers, which is partly because of the anonymous and posthumous nature of her treatise's publication. However, renewed feminist scholarly interest in female biographies, texts, and philosophies from the 1970's onward has made Conway's work accessible once again. While she occupies an important place within modern philosophical discourse, she is now also read in her own right as a woman leading an exceptional life. Her scandalous conversion to Quakerism is only one example that testifies to her mental independence and determination.

—Miriam Wallraven

FURTHER READING

Conway, Anne. *The Conway Letters: The Correspondence of Anne, Viscountess Conway, Henry More, and their Friends, 1642-1684*. Edited by Sarah Hutton and Marjorie Hope Nicholson. Oxford, England: Clarendon Press, 1992. Includes detailed introductions to Conway's intellectual connections and provides information about religious, scientific, and biographical matters.

_____. *The Principles of the Most Ancient and Modern Philosophy*. Edited by Allison P. Coder and Taylor Corse. New York: Cambridge University Press, 1996. Accompanied by an accessible introduction focusing on Conway's critique of Cartesian philosophy, as well as the influence of the Kabbala and Quakerism.

Frankel, Lois. "Anne Finch, Viscountess Conway." In *Modern Women Philosophers, 1600-1900*. Volume 3 in *A History of Women Philosophers*, edited by Mary Ellen Waite. Boston: Kluwer Academic, 1991. Compares Conway's work to that of Leibniz and analyzes her principles of motion and emanation.

Gilbert, Pamela K. "The 'Other' Anne Finch: Lady Conway's 'Duelogue' of Textual Selves." *Essays in Arts and Sciences* 26 (1997): 15-26. A feminist reading of *The Principles of the Most Ancient and Modern Philosophy*.

Hutton, Sarah. "Anne Conway, Margaret Cavendish, and Seventeenth-Century Scientific Thought." In *Women, Science, and Medicine, 1500-1700: Mothers and Sisters of the Royal Society*, edited by Lynette Hunter and Sarah Hutton. Stroud, Gloucestershire, England: Sutton, 1997. Comparison of Conway's philosophy with Margaret Cavendish's approach to spirit and matter. Whereas both are vitalists and monists, for Cavendish this single substance is body, while Conway focuses on spirit.

Merchant, Carolyn. "The Vitalism of Anne Conway: Its Impact on Leibniz's Concept of the Monad." *Journal of the History of Philosophy* 17 (1979): 255-269. Argues that Conway's treatise influenced Leibniz's famous concept of the "monad."

Popkin, Richard H. "The Spiritualistic Cosmologies of Henry More and Anne Conway." In *Henry More, 1624-1687: Tercentenary Studies*, edited by Sarah Hutton. Boston: Kluwer, 1990. Analyses the spiritual cosmologies of More and Conway (and their influence on Leibniz and Newton) as a rejection of seventeenth century materialism.

SEE ALSO: René Descartes; Thomas Hobbes; Gottfried Wilhelm Leibniz; Duchess of Newcastle; Baruch Spinoza.

RELATED ARTICLES in *Great Events from History: The Seventeenth Century, 1601-1700:* 1637: Descartes Publishes His *Discourse on Method*; 1652-1689: Fox Organizes the Quakers.

ARCANGELO CORELLI
Italian musician and composer

Corelli was one of the most significant violin virtuosos of the late Baroque period. He composed sonatas and concertos for string instruments, which became famous throughout Europe for their pedagogical and musical value.

BORN: February 17, 1653; Fusignano, Papal States (now in Italy)
DIED: January 8, 1713; Rome, Papal States (now in Italy)
AREA OF ACHIEVEMENT: Music

EARLY LIFE

Arcangelo Corelli (ahr-KAHN-jay-loh koh-REHL-lee) was born in Fusignano, a small village midway between Bologna and Ravenna. Corelli became the only accomplished musician in a family of wealthy landowners who generally preferred other professions, such as medicine and law. The high social status of the wealthy Corelli family definitely helped Corelli as he matured musically during his early years. He received his first music lessons from a priest in the nearby town of Faenza; other music lessons followed at Lugo. Since his early teachers and their qualifications are unknown, these music lessons could have been devoted to the rudiments of music rather than to violin playing, as has often been assumed.

In 1666, Corelli moved to Bologna, one of the most important centers for instrumental music in seventeenth century Europe. From his studies in Bologna, he acquired an excellent violin technique and a knowledge of improvisation. It is likely that his teachers included some of the most significant Bolognese musicians of the day (Giovanni Benvenuti, Leonardo Brugnoli, and B. G. Laurenti). Corelli's improvement on the violin is attested by the fact that he was admitted as a member of Bologna's Accademia Filarmonica in 1670. Nothing is known of his activities between 1670 and 1675; he may have left Bologna for another Italian town in 1670, but he probably did not arrive in Rome until 1675, the year in which he began his career as a professional violinist.

LIFE'S WORK

Beginning in 1675, Corelli rapidly became one of the most important violinists in Rome. He performed for various local church functions, including the Lenten oratorios in the church patronized by Cardinal Pamphili. In 1679, Corelli became chamber musician to Queen Christina of Sweden, who hosted well-known musical gather-

ings at her palace in Rome. Two significant events of the year 1684 indicate his growing stature as a violinist: He was accepted as a member of the prestigious Congregazione dei Virtuosi di Santa Cecilia and he began to play every Sunday for musical functions at Cardinal Pamphili's palace.

Corelli formally entered the service of Cardinal Pamphili as his music master on July 9, 1687. Three years later, when Cardinal Pamphili moved to Bologna, Corelli became first violinist and music director to the young Cardinal Pietro Ottoboni, nephew of Pope Alexander VIII. At Cardinal Ottoboni's palace, concerts were normally held every Monday evening. Corelli was thus an important part of Roman musical life, an accomplished violinist patronized by two wealthy Roman church officials, and a musician whose talents were esteemed so highly that he served as music director to these officials and was allowed to take up residence in their respective palaces.

While his reputation was increasing during the last two decades of the seventeenth century, Corelli published four books of trio sonatas for two violins and continuo (1681, 1685, 1689, 1694). Each of these books consists of twelve sonatas, distributed equally between major and minor keys. The first and third books of these publications belong to the more contrapuntal and learned church type of sonata, while the second and fourth books belong to the lighter and more dancelike chamber type of sonata. While Corelli's church and chamber sonatas can still be distinguished from one another, one of Corelli's major achievements was the intermingling of church and chamber styles to the point where his church sonatas begin to acquire some dancelike traits, while his chamber sonatas became more contrapuntal.

More than half of Corelli's church trio sonatas have four movements that alternate between slow and fast tempos. The opening slow movements all achieve variety by the use of several standard devices (motion in parallel thirds, close points of imitation, dissonances at cadential preparations, and chains of suspensions). The second movements are quicker, with three-part imitation between the two violins and bass. Usually the third movements are in a slower meter, which suggests the influence of the saraband dance. The inclusion of dance elements in these church sonatas is seen most clearly in the fast finales, which are reminiscent of a gigue in compound meter or another type of dance in a quick triple meter. The finales often juxtapose imitative sections with homophonic sections, and some finales have the binary form associated with dance pieces.

Corelli's chamber trio sonatas may have three or four movements. In those sonatas that open with slow preludi, the influence of the church sonata is evident in their use of through-composed form, active bass lines, and interweaving polyphonic lines. In addition to the polyphony of the preludi, these dance movements occasionally show church sonata influence by having sections that begin with imitation. The prevailing dancelike style is retained, however, through the use of the following stylistic features: movements in binary form, sections where the two violins move in similar rhythms and/or parallel thirds, an active bass part with two sustained violin parts, and a dominant first violin part over a slower-moving second violin part and bass line. Despite the intermingling of church and chamber sonatas in Corelli's sonatas, all these devices tend to make his chamber sonatas lighter and less complex than his church sonatas.

Corelli's most famous work is his fifth book of sonatas (1700), written for solo violin and continuo. Six of these sonatas are church sonatas, while five are chamber sonatas (the final piece is a set of variations). The church sonatas have five rather than four movements. Their opening slow movements have an active dialogue between violin and bass, and their quick second movements incorporate two melodic lines within the solo violin part to create a three-part imitative texture. Of the third and fourth movements, one will be slow and tuneful, while the other will be a virtuosic fast movement, using rapid scales and arpeggios. The finales will often show the influence of a quick dance, such as the gavotte or the gigue. The chamber sonatas have either four or five movements and open with the usual slow, contrapuntal preludi. They also have one interior slow movement and fast movements that are based on the rhythms of the allemanda, gavotte, or gigue. Their lighter, dancelike style is shown in the use of two-part rather than three-part imitation, the predilection for binary forms, and the frequent dominance of either the violin or bass part over the other. In all the sonatas in this fifth book, the presence of only one violin part leads Corelli to compose movements that are much more virtuosic, movements that became well known throughout the eighteenth century for both their musical and pedagogical value.

During his later years, Corelli was admitted to the Arcadian Academy, the most exclusive society in Italy. Since he published no more books of sonatas after 1700, his later years must have been devoted to his concertos,

which were published posthumously in 1714. These may have been partially revised from earlier works, but the overall style suggests that they were primarily late creations. In general, Corelli's concertos are not innovative because they use the forms and textures of his trio sonatas. They are, however, significant for their mingling of church and chamber styles, for their increased tendency toward homophonic writing, and for their virtuosic display.

Corelli did not perform in public during the last few years of his life. After a period of failing health, he died on January 8, 1713. He was buried in the Pantheon, where his concertos were performed annually for some years to commemorate the anniversary of his death.

SIGNIFICANCE

Corelli's great reputation has created considerable disagreement over his personality, the attribution of additional works to him, and the performance of his music. Despite his fame and wealth, Corelli, many biographers claim, was courteous, modest, and mild-tempered; other biographers claim that he was more passionate and ag-

Arcangelo Corelli. (Library of Congress)

gressive. Of the many manuscripts and prints that contain additional music attributed to him, only a few have sonatas that may actually have been composed by Corelli (a trumpet sonata, four solo sonatas, and eight trio sonatas have been included in the new edition of Corelli's works, although the authenticity of at least four of these pieces is in doubt). His solo sonatas are found in numerous manuscripts and prints with many ornaments added, and although these ornaments differ considerably, many sources claim that they are based on Corelli's own performances.

Corelli had a tremendous impact on his contemporaries and eighteenth century successors. By the end of the eighteenth century, his various books of sonatas had been reprinted more than one hundred times. Some sonatas were arranged for other instruments or as concertos for strings. Many composers wrote works dedicated to Corelli or wrote original pieces that adopted many of his stylistic features. His music influenced composers in Italy (Antonio Vivaldi), France (François Couperin), Germany (Johann Sebastian Bach), and other European countries. Eighteenth century violin methods were based on his principles and recommended the daily study of his music for didactic purposes. He was the most outstanding violin teacher of his day, and many of his students had successful careers in Germany, France, and England (Francesco Geminiani, Michele Mascitti, and others).

The tremendous impact of Corelli's music stems from a number of factors—the mixture of church and chamber styles, the balance between contrapuntal and homophonic textures, the clear-cut sense of tonality, and the tendency toward thematic unity. Because of these stylistic features, his music became the basis for all other late Baroque sonatas and was widely disseminated during the eighteenth century.

—John O. Robison

FURTHER READING

Allsop, Peter. *Arcangelo Corelli: New Orpheus of Our Times*. New York: Oxford University Press, 1999. A reassessment of Corelli's life and work, disputing eighteenth century critics who viewed the composer as a consolidator of past trends, not an initiator of new styles. Allsop provides a more balanced portrait of Corelli's role in the development of instrumental music.

Deas, Stewart. "Arcangelo Corelli." *Music and Letters* 34 (January, 1953): 1-10. A good summary of Corelli's early life and years in Rome. Recounts various anecdotes that suggest Corelli was modest and mild-tempered. The general description of Corelli's works indicates some prejudice against his chamber sonatas and emphasizes his sense of balance and proportion.

Libby, Dennis. "Interrelationships in Corelli." *Journal of the American Musicological Society* 26 (Summer, 1973): 263-287. A detailed, valuable study of Corelli's style that stresses his overall sense of harmonic progression and tonality, and his tendency toward thematic unity within and between movements.

Marx, Hans Joachim. "Some Corelli Attributions Assessed." *Musical Quarterly* 56 (January, 1970): 88-98. Discusses five manuscripts with works attributed to Corelli, noting these pieces are by other composers. Also lists ten manuscripts and three prints with works attributed to Corelli, arguing only one or two of these sources may contain authentic works.

_____. "Some Unknown Embellishments of Corelli's Violin Sonatas." *Musical Quarterly* 61 (January, 1975): 65-76. Discusses some embellished versions of Corelli's solo sonatas, suggesting that some may have a didactic as well as artistic purpose. Concludes with a valuable list of sources that have embellished versions of Corelli's opus five sonatas.

Pincherle, Marc. *Corelli: His Life, His Work*. Translated by Hubert Russell. New York: W. W. Norton, 1956. A detailed account of Corelli's life and work. The biographical account is somewhat romanticized, but the description of Corelli's works and influence is thorough. Includes a valuable bibliography of the various seventeenth and eighteenth century editions and arrangements of Corelli's sonatas and concertos.

Talbot, Michael. "Arcangelo Corelli." In *The New Grove Italian Baroque Masters*, by Denis Arnold et al. New York: W. W. Norton, 1984. An objective summary of Corelli's life, style, and influence. Focuses mostly on known biographical details but also includes useful information on Corelli's influence and style, without discussing specific works in detail. Includes a brief list of Corelli's known and probable works, and an excellent bibliography.

SEE ALSO: Francesca Caccini; Christina; Girolamo Frescobaldi; Claudio Monteverdi; Johann Pachelbel; Heinrich Schütz; Barbara Strozzi.

RELATED ARTICLES in *Great Events from History: The Seventeenth Century, 1601-1700:* c. 1601: Emergence of Baroque Music; c. 1666: Stradivari Makes His First Violin; c. 1673: Buxtehude Begins His Abendmusiken Concerts.

PIERRE CORNEILLE
French playwright

Corneille wrote or collaborated on more than thirty plays during a career spanning forty-five years. His masterpiece, The Cid, *is the first classical tragedy in French. His work dominated the French stage during the first half of the seventeenth century and helped to define the character of classical theater.*

BORN: June 6, 1606; Rouen, France
DIED: October 1, 1684; Paris, France
AREA OF ACHIEVEMENT: Theater

EARLY LIFE

Although Pierre Corneille (pyehr kohr-nay) wrote the first French classical tragedy and established the classical theater in France, relatively few details of his personal life are known. Born in Rouen, France, to provincial bourgeois parents, Corneille enjoyed the pleasures afforded by a stable family life. His Jesuit education, with its emphasis on the Latin classics and on the importance of the role of free will in humankind's search for a moral life, profoundly affected the dramatist's later works.

In 1622, following his father's example, he chose to study law and was admitted to the bar in 1624. Timid by temperament, Corneille lacked the verbal eloquence and aggressiveness required for success in the legal profession. In 1641, he married Marie Lampérière; they had six children. Throughout his life, Corneille preferred the pleasures of an uncomplicated, provincial family life to the preciosity of Paris literary salons. As portraits of him in later life reveal, he was attractive and physically robust.

Corneille's early literary career began with the production of *Mélite: Ou, Les Fausses Lettres* (1630; English translation, 1776) when he was in his early twenties. After this early success, Corneille produced four comedies in quick succession: *La Veuve: Ou, Le Traître trahi* (1631; the widow), *La Suivante* (1633; the waiting-maid), *La Place royale: Ou, L'Amoreux extravagant* (1634; the royal square), and *L'Illusion comique* (1636; *The Illusion*, 1989). At about this time Cardinal de Richelieu, the great minister of Louis XIII, engaged Corneille and four other dramatists, known collectively as "the five authors," to write plays for the royal court. Corneille found the restrictions of the collaboration oppressive and soon abandoned the group.

LIFE'S WORK

In 1636-1637, Corneille produced his masterpiece, *Le Cid* (*The Cid*, 1637). The play is based in part on a historical Spanish character, Rodrigo de Bivar (1040?-1099). As the play opens, Chimène, daughter of Don Gomez, learns of her father's approval of her marriage to Rodrigue, the Cid. Simultaneously, Rodrigue's father, Don Diègue, engages in an argument with Don Gomez and in the course of the argument Don Gomez strikes Don Diègue. Following the code of the times, Don Diègue demands that his son avenge his disgrace. Rodrigue is thus caught in a conflict between his love for Chimène and his duty to defend the honor of his family. By resolving to fulfill his family duty by killing Don Gomez, Rodrigue announces the fundamental tension that will resonate throughout all Corneille's great tragedies: the eternal

Pierre Corneille. (Library of Congress)

human struggle to balance personal sentiment with duty to family and society.

Chimène's dilemma is equal to that of Rodrigue: How can she accept marriage to the man who has slain her father? Like Rodrigue, she chooses to uphold her family's honor and implores the king Don Fernando for vengeance. Ultimately, she confesses her love, and the king decrees that Rodrigue shall lead his armies in battle for a year while Chimène mournsher father's death; then the two shall be married. The dramatic power of the play resides in Corneille's skillful manipulation of the conflict of honor and love.

Despite its popular success, the play angered many of the conservative critics of the day. The ensuing stormy Quarrel of the Ancients and the Moderns lasted for nearly a year, and it was officially resolved at the request of Richelieu by the forty *doctes* (learned men) of the newly formed French Academy. The largely negative judgment of the Academy dealt Corneille a severe blow. Although the Academy quibbled with some of Corneille's versification and with his laxity in strictly maintaining the classical Unities of time, place, and action, the central issue involved a rather academic determination of what was tragic, thus establishing those elements that could be properly included in a tragedy and those which could not.

CORNEILLE'S MAJOR WORKS	
1630	*Mélite: Ou, Les Fausses Lettres* (English translation, 1776)
1631	*Clitandre*
1631	*La Veuve: Ou, Le Traître trahi*
1632	*La Galerie du palais: Ou, L'Amie rivale*
1633	*La Suivante*
1634	*La Place royale: Ou, L'Amoureux extravagant*
1635	*Médée*
1636	*L'Illusion comique* (*The Illusion*, 1989)
1637	*Le Cid* (*The Cid*, 1637)
1640	*Horace* (English translation, 1656)
1640	*Cinna: Ou, La Clémence d'Auguste* (*Cinna*, 1713)
1642	*Polyeucte* (English translation, 1655)
1643	*La Mort de Pompée* (*The Death of Pompey*, 1663)
1643	*Le Menteur* (*The Liar*, 1671)
1644	*La Suite du menteur*
1645	*Rodogune, princesse des Parthes* (*Rodogune*, 1765)
1645	*Théodore, vierge et martyre,*
1647	*Héraclius* (English translation, 1664)
1649	*Don Sanche d'Aragon* (*The Conflict*, 1798)
1650	*Andromède*
1651	*Nicomède* (English translation, 1671)
1651	*Pertharite, roi des Lombards*
1656	*Imitation de Jésus-Christ* (translation of Thomas à Kempis's poetry)
1659	*Œdipe*
1660	*Trois Discours sur le poème dramatique*
1660	*Examens*
1660	*La Toison d'or*
1660	*Théâtre* (3 volumes)
1662	*Sertorius* (English translation, 1960)
1663	*Sophonisbe*
1664	*Othon* (English translation, 1960)
1666	*Agésilas*
1667	*Attila* (English translation, 1960)
1670	*Tite et Bérénice*
1670	*Office de la Sainte Vierge* (translation of Saint Bonaventure's poetry)
1672	*Pulchérie* (English translation, 1960)
1674	*Suréna* (English translation, 1960)

The classicists, or ancients, of the Academy supported the Aristotelian distinction between *le vrai* (the real) and *le vraisemblance* (having the simple appearance of the real, or the verisimilar). History, the *doctes* maintained, is full of true events that conflict with common moral decency and thus are not the proper basis of art. Thus from the perspective of the *doctes*, Chimène's marriage to her father's killer, though based in fact, was morally reprehensible and consequently an improper use of the real.

After receiving the Academy's judgment, Corneille

did not produce another play for three years. Despite the distress that the debate caused Corneille, it resulted in the establishment of a clearer sense of the definition of tragedy and comedy, thus setting the stage for the creation of the mature masterworks of Corneille himself as well as those of Jean Racine and Molière later in the century.

Corneille's three-year silence ended in May, 1640, with the presentation of his second tragedy, *Horace* (English translation, 1656), quickly followed by two more tragedies, *Cinna: Ou, La Clémence d'Auguste* (1641; *Cinna*, 1713) and *Polyeucte* (1642; English translation,

1655). Corneille's reputation rests largely on these three great works and on *The Cid*.

Horace continues the theme first broached in *The Cid*. Horace must ultimately choose between his duty to Rome and his love for his wife and family. Despite the grandeur of the subject, Corneille's strict adherence to the unities, partly in response to the Academy's earlier critiques, attenuates the potential power of the work. *Cinna*, a political tragedy, and *Polyeucte*, a religious tragedy, both based on Roman sources, definitively established Corneille's literary reputation. *Cinna* has often been argued to be Corneille's finest play after *The Cid*, principally because of its strict faithfulness to classical form and the depiction of the slow evolution of Augustus's character from apparent tyrant to magnanimous hero. The language of the play, however, does not equal that of *The Cid*, often bordering on the grandiloquent. The weakness of plot and absence of fully developed characters have also evoked criticism.

In contrast with *Cinna*, *Polyeucte* incorporates a relatively complex plot with equally complex relationships between pagan and Christian characters of third century Rome. Polyeucte, recently converted to Christianity, is imprisoned and then killed for having destroyed pagan idols at a public sacrifice. As a result of Polyeucte's martyrdom, his wife, Pauline, and her weak father, Felix, who had ordered Polyeucte's death, convert to Christianity. The beauty of the play lies largely in the touching relationship of Polyeucte and Pauline, as the latter comes to realize her true love for her husband. The noted French poet/critic Charles-Pierre Péguy discovered in *Polyeucte* Corneille's most eloquent poetic voice, a triumphant evocation of the heroic and mystical registers of the human spirit.

Between 1643 and 1650, Corneille produced seven tragedies and three comedies with varying degrees of success. The works of this period, while always reflecting Corneille's genius for invention and versification, suffer from an absence of human interest, overuse of mechanical *coups de théâtre*, complicated intrigues, and mistaken identities—all techniques more typical of the later melodrama than of classical theater. The singular success of these years was his election to the French Academy in 1647.

Corneille's last triumph, *Nicomède* (1651; English translation, 1671), was followed by the complete disaster of *Pertharite, roi des Lombards* (1651). The public's absolute rejection of this last work sent Corneille into a seven-year retirement from the theater. From 1652 until 1659, he published a thirteen-thousand-line verse translation of the *Imitation de Jésus-Christ* (1652-1656) and completed *Trois Discours sur le poème dramatique* (1660; three discourses on dramatic poetry) and a series of critical evaluations of his plays. Between 1659 and 1674, when he produced his final tragedy, *Suréna* (pr. 1674, pb. 1675; English translation 1960), Corneille wrote six more tragedies and four comedies, works that he viewed as "the last spark of a fire about to die out." Having moved his family from Rouen to Paris in 1662, to secure his seat in the Academy, he died there in 1684.

SIGNIFICANCE

Although Corneille's reputation among the larger public continues to rest on the four great tragedies written between 1636 and 1642, modern scholarship suggests that both his early comedies and late tragedies, taken in context and viewed as a whole, reveal a continuous movement toward experimentation, on both poetic and thematic levels. Such works as the early *L'Illusion comique* and the late *Suréna* testify to the dramatist's persistent attempts to dazzle his public with innovative responses to old dilemmas. Often going against the grain of established literary conventions of the time, Corneille's genius for invention led him both to great success and to total failure.

Corneille's great tragic personages, the grandeur of his style, and his relentless focus on the conflict between passion and moral obligations to society have established his place in world literature. What defines humankind's dignity in the Corneillian universe is the human freedom to choose. Corneille succeeded in presenting this conflict in a style marked by forcefulness, clarity, lyricism, and dignity. Thus Racine's words, pronounced before the Academy shortly after Corneille's death, are as accurate in their assessment of Corneille's work today as they were in 1684: "You know in what condition was the French stage when he began his work. Such disorder! such irregularity! No taste, no knowledge of the real beauties of the theater. . . . In this chaos . . . [Corneille] against the bad taste of the century, . . . inspired by an extraordinary genius, . . . put reason on stage."

—*William C. Griffin*

FURTHER READING

Abraham, Claude. *Pierre Corneille*. Boston: Twayne, 1972. Written for the general reader, Abraham's book is the most accessible introduction to Corneille's principal works and to the times in which he created them. All French text has been translated into English.

Carlin, Claire L. *Pierre Corneille Revisited*. New York:

Twayne, 1998. Carlin explores how other critics have approached Corneille's plays, and he interprets the relationship between the plays and the Baroque and discusses the validity of modern psychoanalytical insight into the plays.

Corneille, Pierre. *Le Cid.* Translated by Vincent J. Chang. Newark: University of Delaware Press, 1987. In addition to the most faithful English translation of *The Cid*, the text includes five elegantly written chapters on Corneille's life and times and an analysis of the play. Chang directs his work toward the non-French-speaking reader, distilling the best of French and English scholarship into seventy-five tightly argued pages.

_____. *Le Cid.* Edited by Peter H. Nurse. New York: Basil Blackwell, 1988. Edited by one of the foremost Corneillian scholars, this edition provides one of the most complete introductions to Corneille's masterpiece. Designed for the serious student, the text contains all the variants of the 1682 edition of *The Cid*.

Elmarsafy, Ziad. *Freedom, Slavery, and Absolutism: Corneille, Pascal, Racine.* Lewisburg, Pa.: Bucknell University Press, 2003. Examines the concept of freedom in the work of Corneille, Racine, and Pascal, who shared the belief that freedom could be ensured only by absolute authority.

Mallison, G. J. *The Comedies of Corneille: Experiments in the Comic.* Manchester, England: Manchester University Press, 1984. Copiously documented with extracts from the French texts, this volume defines comedy in its seventeenth century context, then evaluates Corneille's concept of the genre in this light.

Nelson, Robert J. *Corneille, His Heroes, and Their Worlds.* Philadelphia: University of Pennsylvania Press, 1963. The standard critical text dealing with the complex composition of Corneille's heroes, written by one of the most eminent Corneillian scholars. Detailed and reasoned analysis of all works is complemented by a vivid picture of the seventeenth century literary world.

Pocock, Gordon. *Corneille and Racine: Problems of Tragic Form.* New York: Cambridge University Press, 1973. Pocock's work is among the most readable scholarly studies centering on the contrasts between Racine and Corneille. The first ten chapters are devoted exclusively to an analysis of Corneille's principal works and his inventive versification. Although citations are in the original French, the author's lucid argument is accessible to the serious reader.

SEE ALSO: Pedro Calderón de la Barca; Cyrano de Bergerac; Molière; Jean Racine; Cardinal de Richelieu; Tirso de Molina; Lope de Vega Carpio.

RELATED ARTICLES in *Great Events from History: The Seventeenth Century, 1601-1700:* 1610-1643: Reign of Louis XIII; 1664: Molière Writes *Tartuffe.*

JOHN COTTON
English-born colonial American religious leader

One of the foremost clergymen who defined the religious practices of early New England colonists, Cotton was a key architect of Congregationalism.

BORN: December 4, 1584; Derby, England
DIED: December 23, 1652; Boston, Massachusetts Bay Colony (now in Massachusetts)
AREA OF ACHIEVEMENT: Religion and theology

EARLY LIFE

John Cotton was the son of Roland Cotton, an attorney in Derby, England. Cotton attended the Derby Grammar School and entered Trinity College, Cambridge University, at about the age of thirteen. He received a B.A. in 1602. In 1603, he was elected a fellow (a member of the faculty) at Cambridge's Emmanuel College, from which he received an M.A. in 1606. While at Emmanuel, Cotton served at various times as tutor, catechist, and dean. He developed close friendships with several Cambridge contemporaries, with whom he cooperated later in his career, including Thomas Hooker, Richard Sibbes, Thomas Goodwin, and Thomas Weld. These men were in part responsible for Cotton's conversion to Puritanism and his transformation into a zealous Calvinist reformer working within the Church of England. Emmanuel College was a center of Puritan activity at Cambridge, and Cotton was soon recognized as one of the movement's key spokespeople.

Cotton was ordained into the ministry in 1610, and in 1612, the corporation of Saint Botolph's Church in Boston, Lincolnshire, chose him as their vicar. He was an active preacher whose popularity attracted many believers, including both laypersons such as Anne Hutchinson and fellow English clergymen, who traveled to Boston to hear him and study under him. His Puritan stand began to involve him in clashes with the authorities, however, including an incident in which he was suspected of having inspired iconoclastic vandalism against some of the statues and stained glass in the church.

The support of prominent laymen, such as the earl of Lincoln, protected Cotton for a while. In 1632, however, he was called to defend himself before William Laud's Court of High Commission. Cotton was in contact with the leaders of the Puritan exile community in the Netherlands, and he had supported the Puritan migration to Massachusetts, preaching the farewell sermon to the Winthrop fleet in 1630. Fearing that Laud and others would effectively silence him if he remained in England, Cotton decided to emigrate to New England in 1633.

LIFE'S WORK

Upon his arrival in the Massachusetts Bay Colony town of Boston, Cotton was elected by the congregation of Boston's church to be their teacher, one of the two ministerial positions in the church. His evangelical preaching in the months that followed stirred a religious revival in which many were "born again" and shared the stories of their spiritual rebirth with their fellow believers. From this phenomenon, a requirement evolved for anyone who sought full membership in the colony's churches to produce a narrative of his or her personal conversion.

The Puritan settlers were attempting gradually to shape an orthodox system of faith and a unified church structure that would be a model for England and the rest of the world. To achieve this goal, the settlers needed to achieve consensus on matters that had been subjects for speculation and debate when the Puritans were a dissenting and largely powerless minority within the established Church of England. There were, however, continual doctrinal disputes within the Church in New England. Cotton's conflicts with Roger Williams and Anne Hutchinson are both examples of such disputes, the eventual resolution of which further defined the colonial polity.

Cotton was a key figure in this ongoing definition of Massachusetts's religious orthodoxy. In his dispute with Roger Williams, which was carried on in print into the 1640's, Cotton was the foremost spokesperson for the New England belief that the state, while institutionally separate from the church, had a responsibility to safeguard religion by acting against those whose beliefs threatened the order of the churches.

In the Antinomian controversy, Anne Hutchinson (who had followed Cotton to the New World) claimed

John Cotton. (Library of Congress)

Cotton as her inspiration when she argued that there was no connection between saving grace and human works. Hutchinson argued that because the elect had been sanctified by God, there was no need for them to devote themselves to good works in order to ensure their salvation. Salvation was contingent not upon a Covenant of Works but rather upon a Covenant of Grace. Cotton tried to maintain a middle ground that asserted God's freedom to act in various ways on people's souls. When Hutchinson's increasing radicalism threatened to divide and hence to destroy the newly established church, Cotton joined his clerical brethren in their decision to denounce her.

Despite suspicions aroused by his ambiguous position in the early phases of the Antinomian controversy, Cotton maintained and expanded his position as the foremost interpreter of Puritanism in New England. He was a principal architect of the Congregational ecclesiastical polity, which allowed each congregation of believers to control its own affairs, in consultation with neighboring churches but free from the supervision of any hierarchical church authority. Cotton argued for the value of this system in a series of tracts: *The True Constitution of a Particular Visible Church* (1642), *The Way of the*

Churches of Christ in New England (1645), and *The Way of the Congregational Churches Cleared* (1648).

Cotton's books were directed at an English audience that was in the process of restructuring its own church order as part of the Puritan Revolution. They were published in London through the efforts of English friends, such as Thomas Goodwin and Philip Nye, who were advocates of New England Puritanism. As the unity of English Puritanism fragmented in the 1640's, Cotton identified himself with the Congregational faction of the Independent coalition that opposed the imposition of a national Presbyterian system. His publications and those of other colonial clergymen were intended to support Congregational Independency as advanced by clergymen such as Goodwin and by civil leaders such as Oliver Cromwell.

In 1651, Cotton gave evidence of his continued support for the revolutionary cause in England when he preached a sermon explaining and justifying the 1649 execution of King Charles I. In his sermon, Cotton set forth his belief in the limits of civil authority and the right of the people to resist tyranny. He believed that the events in England signaled the approach of the millennium as foretold in Scripture. Cotton died on December 23, 1652, still hopeful that New England Puritanism would prevail in England and that the millennium would soon follow.

SIGNIFICANCE

Cotton was one of the most influential members of the founding generation of New England Puritans, a position he achieved by his abilities but which was reinforced by his status as one of the ministers of the Boston church. He helped to define the Congregational system of church governance, and he persuaded New England to accept the Calvinist belief in humankind's dependence on God's grace. He defended colonial religious practices against domestic critics such as Roger Williams and against English Presbyterian authors. He was one of the clergymen who shaped New Englanders' belief that they were a people in covenant with God, a people whose example would transform the world. His views were carried on and defended to later generations by his grandson, Cotton Mather.

—*Francis J. Bremer*

FURTHER READING

Bremer, Francis J. "In Defense of Regicide: John Cotton on the Execution of Charles I." *William and Mary Quarterly*, 3d ser. 37 (January, 1980): 103-124. Contains Cotton's 1651 sermon justifying the execution

of Charles I, prefaced by an introduction discussing Cotton's political theory and his views on the English Puritan Revolution.

Bush, Sargent, Jr., ed. *The Correspondence of John Cotton*. Chapel Hill: University of North Carolina Press, 2001. Bush, a prominent scholar of early American literature, edited and annotated this collection of Cotton's extant correspondence.

Cotton, John. *John Cotton on the Churches of New England*. Edited by Larzer Ziff. Cambridge, Mass.: Harvard University Press, 1968. A well-introduced and annotated edition of some of Cotton's major works on church organization.

Emerson, Everett H. *John Cotton*. New Haven, Conn.: College and University Press, 1965. A volume in Twayne's United States Authors Series, this study focuses on Cotton's published works, summarizing them and providing worthwhile analysis.

Fichte, Joerg O. "The Negotiation of Power in John Cotton's Commentaries on Revelation." In *Millennial Thought in America: Historical and Intellectual Contexts, 1630-1860*, edited by Bernd Engler, Joerg O. Fichte, and Oliver Scheiding. Tübingen, Germany: Wissenschaftlicher, 2002. Examines how Cotton analyzed the Book of Revelation to determine the proper relationship of church and state.

Hall, David D. *The Faithful Shepard: A History of the New England Ministry in the Seventeenth Century*. Chapel Hill: University of North Carolina Press, 1972. The best study of the Colonies' clergy, showing the problems faced by Cotton and his colleagues and how they responded to those challenges.

Rosenmeier, Jesper. "'Clearing the Medium': A Reevaluation of the Puritan Plain Style in Light of John Cotton's *A Practicall Commentary upon the First Epistle Generall of John*." *William and Mary Quarterly*, 3d ser. 37 (October, 1980): 577-591. Examines and explains Cotton's preaching style and relates it to his views on personal relationships.

_____. "The Teacher and the Witness: John Cotton and Roger Williams." *William and Mary Quarterly*, 3d ser. 25 (July, 1968): 408-431. Examines the debate between Cotton and Williams and relates their differing views to different forms of scriptural interpretation.

Smolinski, Reiner. "'The Way to Lost Zion': The Cotton-Williams Debate on the Separation of Church and State in a Millenarian Perspective." In *Millenial Thought in America: Historical and Intellectual Contexts, 1630-1860*, edited by Bernd Engler, Joerg O.

Fichte, and Oliver Scheiding. Tübingen, Germany: Wissenschaftlicher, 2002. Compares the positions of John Cotton and Roger Williams on church-state relations.

Ziff, Larzer. *The Career of John Cotton: Puritanism and the American Experience*. Princeton, N.J.: Princeton University Press, 1962. The best biography, though its interpretations should be supplemented by those in the articles above.

SEE ALSO: Charles I; Oliver Cromwell; Thomas Hooker; Anne Hutchinson; William Laud; Roger Williams.

RELATED ARTICLES in *Great Events from History: The Seventeenth Century, 1601-1700:* December 26, 1620: Pilgrims Arrive in North America; May, 1630-1643: Great Puritan Migration; June, 1636: Rhode Island Is Founded; 1642-1651: English Civil Wars; September 8, 1643: Confederation of the United Colonies of New England.

ABRAHAM COWLEY
English poet

A published poet by the age of fifteen, Cowley ultimately emerged as the premier English poet of his generation. He also supported the Royalist cause during the English Civil War, and his influential essays helped pave the way both for modern prose style and for the creation of the Royal Society.

BORN: 1618; London, England
DIED: July 28, 1667; Chertsey, England
ALSO KNOWN AS: The Muse's Hannibal (moniker)
AREA OF ACHIEVEMENT: Literature

EARLY LIFE

Abraham Cowley (KEW-lee) was born in London in 1618, the seventh child of Thomas Cooley, a prosperous stationer, who died before Cowley was born. Around 1630, Cowley was enrolled as a student at Westminster School, where he received a solid grounding in the Greek and Roman classics. However, Cowley had already begun his literary career, ensuring for himself a reputation as a child prodigy in the canon of English literature.

At the age of ten years, Cowley composed a poem entitled *The Tragicall History of Piramus and Thisbe* (pb. 1633). Around 1630, Cowley wrote another lengthy poem, *Constantia and Philetus* (pb. 1633), and in 1631 he composed *Elegy on the Death of Dudley, Lord Carlton* (pb. 1633). These three poems were published in a collection entitled *Poeticall Blossomes* (1633), which was dedicated to the headmaster at Westminster School. As his youthful work was well received, Cowley obtained literary fame by the age of fifteen.

Cowley next composed a pastoral comedy entitled *Loves Riddle* (wr. 1634, pb. 1638). In 1637, Cowley enrolled in Trinity College, Cambridge, from which he received a B.A. in 1639. While he was at Cambridge, Cowley's *Naufragium Joculare* (pr., pb. 1638), a comedy composed in Latin, was printed, as was *Loves Riddle*. In 1640, Cowley was elected as a fellow of Trinity College, and he received an M.A. in 1643. According to Cowley's preface to the 1656 edition of his works, many of the poems printed later in his life, such as the celebrated elegies *On the Death of Mr. Crashaw* (pb. 1656) and *On the Death of Mr. William Hervey* (pb. 1656), were composed during his years as a student at Cambridge.

LIFE'S WORK

Throughout the First English Civil War (1642-1646), Cowley linked himself with the Royalist cause. In 1644, Cowley, who had published two anti-Puritan pamphlets, *Puritan's Lecture* (1642) and *The Puritan and the Papist* (1643), had his Cambridge fellowship taken away by commissioners in Parliament allied to Oliver Cromwell. Cowley had already moved to Oxford in 1643, where the embattled King Charles I and a cadre of royalist supporters were residing. In Oxford, Cowley became friends with Lucius Cary, second Viscount Falkland, who introduced the poet into the circle of the royal family.

After the Parliamentarian victory in the Battle of Marston Moor (1644), Cowley went to Paris, where Queen Henrietta Maria had established a residence for her Royalist supporters. Cowley became secretary to Henry Jermyn, the queen's vice chamberlain and master of horse, and he was engaged in a number of secret diplomatic missions necessitating his travel to such places as the Netherlands and Scotland. Cowley also became the cipher secretary to the queen, taking upon himself the painstaking task of encoding and decoding messages sent from Henrietta Maria to her husband, Charles.

From France, Cowley published *The Mistress: Or, Several Copies of Love Verses* (1647), a collection containing almost one hundred poems. In the volume, the

Early nineteenth century engraving of Abraham Cowley by James Basire. (Hulton Archive/Getty Images)

poet reports on his unsuccessful pursuit of an unnamed woman of a higher social status than he, offering much commentary on the arbitrariness of women and the cruelty of love. The collection, which is heavily influenced by the metaphysical style of John Donne, gained for Cowley a very high degree of literary celebrity.

In 1654, upon returning to England, Cowley was imprisoned as a Royalist spy by the Cromwell regime. After being released on bail, Cowley proved to be a hapless practitioner of politics, managing both to remain a suspected Royalist and to raise suspicions in the regime of Charles II that he was in fact a Parliamentarian double agent.

In 1656, *Poems*, a collection of Cowley's work that included *The Mistress, Miscellanies, Anacreontics, Pindaric Odes*, and four books of *Davideis*, was printed. Cowley's *Pindaric Odes* proved to be quite popular, triggering a vogue for its eccentric style of composition: Eschewing any attempt to mimic the meter of the Greek

poet Pindar for which he named the work, Cowley instead used very irregular rhythms while still retaining regular rhyme patterns. The books of *Davideis* are all that remains of Cowley's attempt, begun in the 1630's, to write an epic in couplets on the subject of the biblical King David.

Cowley next applied himself to the study of medicine, demonstrating his enthusiasm for the contemporary movement toward scientific progress. On December 2, 1657, Cowley earned from Oxford University the degree of Doctor of Physic. In 1658, Cowley prepared for print a play, *The Cutter of Coleman Street*, which was not published until 1663.

After the death of Oliver Cromwell in 1658, Cowley traveled again to Paris, returning to England after the Restoration of Charles II. In 1661, Cowley's fellowship at Cambridge was restored, and he was given a grant of land in Chertsey. He published a pamphlet entitled *A Proposition for the Advancement of Experimental Philosophy* (1661), in which he endorsed the creation of an academy dedicated to the advancement of science. Cowley's last collection of poetry was entitled *Verses Lately Written upon Several Occasions* (1663).

Cowley passed the remainder of his life at Barn's Elm, his country residence in Chertsey, devoting most of his intellectual endeavors to the writing of essays. Cowley's essays, such as his *Of Myself* (pb. 1668), are often highly personalized studies, revealing the influence of the French essayist Michel Eyquem de Montaigne. Cowley's interest in science endured for the rest of his life, much of which was spent upon the study of botany. Cowley wrote a number of poems in Latin on the subject of plants, works that were first published in part as *Libri Plantarum* (1662) and later printed as a collection entitled *Poemata Latina* (1668).

On July 28, 1667, Cowley died, apparently of complications brought about by a common cold, at his country residence in Chertsey. On August 3, 1668, Cowley's esteemed status as a national poet was confirmed when he was buried beside Chaucer and Spenser in Westminster Abbey. Cowley's works were collected in 1668 by Thomas Sprat, who also produced a biography of the poet.

SIGNIFICANCE

Though his literary fame would not be long lasting, Cowley was revered by many of his contemporaries as the premier poet of England. Cowley thus had many imitators, and echoes of his work resonate throughout the seventeenth century. Cowley's *Pindaric Odes* was particularly influential, with poets such as John Dryden producing compositions in the innovative form Cowley had introduced. Cowley's *Davideis*, though it is often criticized as artificial, stands as a significant attempt at an English epic, and may well have influenced John Milton in his decision to avoid rhyme in his later *Paradise Lost* (1667, 1674).

Cowley's vigorous endorsement of experimental science contributed to the successful foundation of the Royal Society (c. 1661), an academy to which he would give advice until the end of his life. Perhaps more important, Cowley's numerous essays helped fashion a prose style more fit for the progressive science in which he was so interested. Cowley's essays were influential as models of composition and have been cited as a key factor in the transition from the highly rhetorical prose style of the Renaissance to a more concise, modern style of prose.

—*Randy P. Schiff*

FURTHER READING

Cummings, Robert, ed. *Seventeenth-Century Poetry: An Annotated Anthology*. Oxford, England: Blackwell, 2000. Offers a diverse selection of poems by Cowley and his contemporaries with very full notes on literary and historical context. Includes bibliographical data.

Gough, Alfred B., ed. *The Essays and Other Prose Writings of Abraham Cowley*. Oxford, England: Clarendon Press, 1915. Includes prefaces Cowley wrote as introductions to his collections of poems and to his plays.

Griffin, Julia, ed. *Selected Poems of Abraham Cowley, Edmund Waller, and John Oldham*. New York: Penguin, 1998. Generous selection of Cowley's verse, offering full notes on cultural and historical context. The inclusion of texts by Waller and Oldham allows for a broad understanding of seventeenth century English verse.

Martin, L. C., ed. *Abraham Cowley: Poetry and Prose, with Thomas Sprat's "Life," and Observations by Dryden, Addison, Johnson, and Others*. Oxford, England: Clarendon Press, 1949. Includes selections from Cowley's poems and essays, as well as the earliest biography of the poet. Extracts from later poets offer insight about the reception of Cowley by key players in the English literary canon.

Nethercot, Arthur Hobart. *Abraham Cowley: The Muse's Hannibal*. 2d ed. New York: Russell and Russell, 1967. Biography of the poet, offering comparisons of Cowley's work with that of other canonical authors. Includes plates of pictorial depictions of Cowley.

Taafe, James G. *Abraham Cowley*. New York: Twayne, 1972. Biography of the poet. Includes a bibliography.

Trotter, David. *The Poetry of Abraham Cowley*. Totowa, N.J.: Rowman and Littlefield, 1979. Offers extended analysis of Cowley's verse, providing full treatment of the literary historical background for Cowley's compositions.

SEE ALSO: Charles I; Charles II (of England); Richard Crashaw; Oliver Cromwell; John Dryden; Henrietta Maria.

RELATED ARTICLES in *Great Events from History: The Seventeenth Century, 1601-1700:* 1601-1672: Rise of Scientific Societies; 1642-1651: English Civil Wars; July 2, 1644: Battle of Marston Moor; May, 1659-May, 1660: Restoration of Charles II.

RICHARD CRASHAW
English poet

Crashaw was a member of the Metaphysical movement in English poetics in the early seventeenth century. Unlike other prominent Metaphysical poets, however, his poetry was strongly marked by his conversion to Catholicism. He was also heavily influenced by Spanish mysticism and the style of the Italian poet Marini.

BORN: c. 1612; London, England
DIED: August 21, 1649; Loreto (now in Italy)
AREA OF ACHIEVEMENT: Literature

EARLY LIFE

Richard Crashaw's father, William Crashaw, was an Anglican priest in London noted for his strong anti-Catholic (and possibly Puritan) convictions; his surviving writings document his hatred of the Jesuits. Richard's mother died when he was six or seven years of age; his father remarried in 1619. Richard's stepmother seems to have been a loving parent, but she died in childbirth the year after her marriage. William Crashaw died in 1626, but he left Richard no inheritance. Two lawyers who were friends of his father paid for Richard's education at Charterhouse School, to which he was admitted in 1629. The master of Charterhouse, Robert Brooke, most likely had a formative influence on the poet, contributing to his later Royalist politics.

Crashaw was a promising student, and on July 6, 1631, he was admitted to Pembroke College, Cambridge University. Cambridge was a center of High Anglicanism, that branch of the Church of English that—though opposed to the authority of the Pope—adhered to rites and liturgical practices regarded by Puritans as too close to those of the Roman Catholic Church. The great Anglican preacher Lancelot Andrewes had been a master of Pembroke, and his influence continued while Crashaw was in attendance. Crashaw received a B.A. in 1634 and proceeded to Peterhouse College, where he was granted a fellowship in 1635. While at Peterhouse, certainly by 1639, he was ordained to the priesthood. The High Anglican climate Crashaw experienced at Pembroke continued at Peterhouse, whose master, John Cosin, was the author of an influential book of prayers, *A Collection of Private Devotions* (1627).

During these years, Crashaw also maintained a close association with Little Gidding, an Anglican religious community established in 1626 by Nicholas Ferrar for his family and friends. Crashaw enjoyed worshipping in the chapel established by Ferrar, a place visited by King Charles I and, much later, by the modern poet T. S. Eliot, for whom it became the inspiration for the last of his *Four Quartets* (1943). As the influence of Puritanism spread throughout England, High Church Anglicans came increasingly under threat. In 1644, Crashaw, Cosin, and other leaders at Peterhouse were expelled by order of Parliament, and in 1646, a year after the king's visit, Little Gidding was raided by a group of Puritan soldiers who stripped it of its "Popish" crosses, altar vessels, and cloth hangings.

LIFE'S WORK

By the time Crashaw reached Cambridge, he was already a published poet, having contributed poems to Lancelot Andrewes's *XCVI Sermons* (1629). He continued to write while at the university, and soon published *Epigrammatum Sacrorum Liber* (1634), which contains 178 Latin epigrams, brief poems of several lines each that offer concise observations. Crashaw's epigrams focus mostly on religious topics. The epigram has a history reaching back to such classical practitioners as the first century Roman poet Martial; it relies for effect on wittily inventive turns of phrase, an often sarcastic tone, and the use of striking paradox, devices frequently seen in the Metaphysical poetry of John Donne. Unlike the socially scathing epigrams of Martial, however, Crashaw's poems are focused on the theological contradictions of Christian faith and mock those persons who seem unable to accept those contradictions.

Around 1637, Crashaw completed a translation of the first book of Italian poet Giambattista Marini's *La strage degli innocenti* (1632; *The Slaughter of the Innocents*, 1675). Like the rest of the work, *Sospetto d'Herode* (*The Suspicion of Herod*, 1637) explored the New Testament theme of the massacre of innocents. Marini (1569-1625) has given his name to Marinism, a mannered and self-consciously witty style of poetry that bears some parallels with the English Metaphysical style. Crashaw freely imitated Marini's farfetched ingenuity and extravagantly sensual ornamentation, stylistic features that contribute to Crashaw's reputation as one of the most Baroque English poets of his day.

Crashaw actually left Cambridge in 1643, the year before his official explusion was announced, fleeing to the safety of Holland. At some point shortly after his departure from Cambridge, he met Queen Henrietta Maria, who wrote a letter of introduction for him in 1646 to the pope. By this time, he had done something which would have scandalized his father—Crashaw had become a Roman Catholic. His travels took him from Holland to Paris, where he was discovered living in poverty by the poet Abraham Cowley, a friend from his Peterhouse days. In late 1646, he reached Rome, where he gained a clerical appointment from Cardinal Pallota.

Also in 1646, Crashaw first published *Steps to the Temple: Sacred Poems, with Other Delights of the Muses* (1646, 1648). The volume's title pays tribute to George Herbert's volume of Metaphysical religious verse *The Temple* (1633), published thirteen years earlier. Among the secular "delights" in this volume are a number of elegies, an assortment of poems in praise of the monarchy and Charles I, and several love poems. The book also contains one of Crashaw's most characteristically Baroque poems, "Musicks Duell," which depicts a contest between a nightingale and a lutenist.

The 1648 edition of *Steps to the Temple* added several new religious poems, notably "The Flaming Heart," Crashaw's verse rendition of Saint Teresa of Ávila's moment of religious ecstasy as recorded in her autobiography. (It is not known whether Crashaw, when in Rome, saw Bernini's famous sculpture of this event.) The careful balancing of religious and erotic imagery in the poem is typically Baroque in its intensity: Crashaw refers to Teresa as "thou undaunted daughter of desires!"—just the sort of emotional "excess" condemned by the Puritans.

Three years after his death, Crashaw's *Carmen Deo Nostro* (1652) was published. It was composed almost exclusively of previously published religious verse, but it did contain a significant new poem, "To the Noblest and Best of Ladies, the Countess of Denbigh." The countess's husband had been killed in 1643, fighting in the Royalist army; she visited Paris with the Catholic Queen Henrietta Maria the following year, and Crashaw's poem represents his attempt to convert her from her Anglicanism to the Roman Catholic faith. It is one of many literary works of Crashaw's day addressing the religious doubts of persons caught in the denominational quarrels of the time and attempting to resolve their theological questions. The poem is a parody of a seduction verse, seeking to convince the countess through sensual imagery that nevertheless carries a religious intent ("Unfold at length, unfold, fair flower,/ And use the season of love's shower").

In April of 1649, Crashaw was given a position at the shrine at Loreto, but shortly after arriving there in August, he contracted a fever and died.

SIGNIFICANCE

Next to the compact metaphors of Donne or the more accessible yet still surprising conceits of Herbert, Crashaw's verse often seems exaggerated, emotionally intense, or even obsessive in its attention to images of blood, fire, tears, and physical sensation. Crashaw's poetry, however, is a noteworthy English contribution to the broad European movement of Baroque art, which sought to hold in delicate tension strongly contradictory feelings, forces, or intellectual convictions. While much of Crashaw's verse was written before his conversion, he represents a valuable Roman Catholic element within the dominantly Anglican outlook of English poetry during the Caroline monarchy, underscoring the fact that English poetry of this era was as varied as the culture that produced it.

—*Christopher Baker*

FURTHER READING

Davidson, Clifford. "The Anglican Setting of Richard Crashaw's Devotional Verse." *Ben Jonson Journal* 8 (2001): 259-76. Calls attention to the significant poems Crashaw wrote while still an Anglican and challenges Crashaw's usual categorization as simply a Catholic poet.

Netzley, Ryan. "Oral Devotion: Eucharistic Theology and Richard Crashaw's Religious Lyrics." *Texas Studies in Literature and Language* 44, no. 3 (Fall, 2002): 247-272. Counters criticism of Crashaw's seeming obsession with mouths and bodily orifices by arguing that he is deeply concerned with poetic variations upon the Catholic Eucharist, a sacrament of oral communion with God.

Parrish, Paul. *Richard Crashaw.* Boston: G. K. Hall, 1980. A concise overview of the poet's life and work, with a chronology and selected bibliography.

Roberts, John R., ed. *New Perspectives on the Life and Art of Richard Crashaw.* Columbia, Mo.: University of Columbia Press, 1990. Twelve essays explore aspects of Crashaw's life, poetry, and education. Contains a bibliography of modern studies of Crashaw.

Sabine, Maureen. *Feminine Engendered Faith: The Poetry of John Donne and Richard Crashaw.* Basingstoke, Hampshire, England: Macmillan, 1992. Chapters 4 through 7 discuss the feminine aspects of divinity as expressed through Crashaw's verse, as well as female personages contained in it, such as the Virgin Mary, Saint Teresa of Ávila, and the Countess of Denbigh. Contains a useful bibliography.

Warren, Austin. *Richard Crashaw: A Study in Baroque*

Sensiblity. Baton Rouge: Louisiana State University Press, 1939. Reprint. Ann Arbor: University of Michigan Press, 1957. Still one of the best studies of Crashaw's links to the Baroque movement in European culture.

Young, R. V. *Doctrine and Devotion in Seventeenth-Century Poetry*. Woodbridge, Suffolk, England: D. S. Brewer, 2000. A study of the theological themes present in the work of Donne, Herbert, Crashaw, and Vaughan. Comments in most detail upon "A Letter to the Countess of Denbigh" from *Carmen Deo Nostro*, with shorter discussions of several other poems.

SEE ALSO: Lancelot Andrewes; Charles I; John Donne; Nicholas Ferrar; Henrietta Maria; George Herbert.

RELATED ARTICLES in *Great Events from History: The Seventeenth Century, 1601-1700:* c. 1601-1620: Emergence of Baroque Art; 1642-1651: English Civil Wars.

OLIVER CROMWELL
Lord protector of England (1653-1658)

Cromwell was the dominant figure in the English Civil Wars, first as a military commander, then as an advocate of the trial and execution of Charles I, and finally as a political leader trying unsuccessfully to restore stability to his nation.

BORN: April 25, 1599; Huntingdon, Huntingdonshire, England

DIED: September 3, 1658; London, England

AREAS OF ACHIEVEMENT: Government and politics, warfare and conquest

EARLY LIFE

Oliver Cromwell's father, Robert, was descended from the Williamses, a Welsh family that had profited from the dissolution of the monasteries under Henry VIII and from a fortuitous marriage to the sister of that monarch's secretary, Thomas Cromwell. Oliver's great-grandfather, Thomas Cromwell's nephew, changed the family name from Williams to Cromwell to show his gratitude. Oliver's mother was Elizabeth Steward of Ely.

Cromwell's early life was typical of the English gentry. His family's Puritanism was reinforced by his education at Huntingdon under Thomas Beard and at Sidney Sussex College, Cambridge (1616-1617), where it seems he was more interested in horses than scholarship. He probably attended the Inns of Court in London, learning enough law for a country gentleman. After his father's death in 1617, Cromwell returned to Huntingdon and the family estate. In 1620, he married Elizabeth Bourchier, the daughter of a London merchant. Their long and happy marriage produced four sons and four daughters. In 1631, he sold the family property at Huntingdon and rented land at Saint Ives, and in 1636, he inherited property from an uncle and moved to Ely. There, he played a modest but noteworthy role in public affairs.

In 1628, Huntingdon elected Cromwell to Parliament, where he made a speech on Puritanism, participated in the creation of the Petition of Right and, in 1629, witnessed the session's tempestuous conclusion, in which Parliament was dissolved by King Charles I. In 1630, as a justice of the peace for Huntingdon, Cromwell supported the rights of commoners. In 1637, he defended the rights of men who could be hurt by a project to drain the Fens. Cromwell's Puritanism became a deep, abiding faith with a Calvinist sense of sin and of salvation by grace. He sought earnestly to do the work of God, not in order to earn salvation but out of gratitude to his Maker (although success, as Beard had taught him, could also be a welcome assurance of one's membership in the elect).

LIFE'S WORK

Had there been no Puritan Revolution, it is unlikely that Cromwell's potential would ever have been realized. In 1640, Cambridge elected Cromwell to the Short Parliament and then to the Long Parliament. He supported the Root and Branch Bill to end episcopacy, limits on the king's command of the army, and the Grand Remonstrance (1641), an extended list of Parliament's grievances against the king. His rise began in 1642, when both the king and Parliament became increasingly militant in their dispute. Cromwell raised a troop of cavalry, gave money for the defense of Parliament, and militarized his constituency in Cambridge.

At the indecisive Battle of Edgehill (October 23, 1642), Cromwell saw the army's need for men such as himself, who knew what they believed and were willing to fight for it. In 1643, while Parliament was negotiating the Solemn League and Covenant, obtaining the support of the Scottish army in exchange for a promise to reform religion in England along Presbyterian lines, Cromwell's cavalry grew to a regiment of more than one thousand men and gained experience in a number of skirmishes. The Ironsides, as they were soon called, were unique for their religious and fighting spirit, for their discipline, and for the devastating effect of their charge. It was Cromwell's Ironsides that turned the tide at the Battle of Marston Moor (July, 1644), giving Parliament its first major victory.

Cromwell urged Parliament to create a national, professional army and advocated the removal of any officers who were reluctant to defeat the king. The fighting force that subsequently developed came to be known as the New Model Army. In order to rid it of incompetent amateurs, the Self-Denying Ordinance was enacted in April, 1645, ordering members of Parliament from both houses to surrender their military commissions. As a member of Parliament, Cromwell was technically covered by this ordinance, but Parliament delayed his resignation and then made him lieutenant general and commander of cavalry of the New Model Army under Thomas Fairfax, the future third Baron Fairfax. The success of these reforms and of Cromwell's enlarged cavalry was seen in Parliament's victory at Naseby in June, 1645.

In 1646, when the initial phase of the English Civil War was over, Cromwell resumed his seat in Parliament, which was attempting to reestablish order in England. Stability was not achieved, however: Charles I was intransigent, and the victorious Parliamentarians were themselves deeply divided. Cromwell, an Independent, or Congregationalist, opposed the Presbyterian settlement favored by Parliament and the Scots. Differences between Cromwell and his fellow M.P.'s were aggravated by Parliament's 1647 proposal to disband the army without paying the soldiers. Cromwell, disgusted with Parliament's poor treatment of the men who had bravely defended England, threw in his lot with the army. The army occupied London and overawed Parliament.

Rejecting entreaties by Cromwell and his son-in-law Henry Ireton to agree to a constitutional settlement, Charles I escaped from Hampton Court Palace. When, in December, 1647, Charles began negotiations with his fellow Scotsmen for military support, the Second Civil War erupted. The army and Parliament resolved their differences and agreed to cease negotiating with the king.

Oliver Cromwell. (Library of Congress)

Cromwell defeated Royalist forces in Wales and then crushed the Scottish army at Preston in August, 1648. Returning to London, he acquiesced in Colonel Thomas Pride's purge of Parliament, leaving only the small Rump of members who supported the army. Cromwell became the chief advocate of the king's trial and of his execution on January 30, 1649.

While the Rump and a council of state were turning England into a commonwealth without king or House of Lords, Cromwell was ridding the government of its enemies. At Burford, in May, 1649, he removed the Levellers (a Puritan group that aimed to level the differences between the classes) from the army. He then subdued Ireland, preventing it from becoming a base for the restoration of monarchy. When the fortified town of Drogheda refused to surrender, Cromwell ordered all defenders put to the sword (September 11, 1649). Wexford received much the same treatment. In 1650, Cromwell was recalled to London to deal with the Scots, who had recognized Charles II, Charles I's son, and were preparing to invade England. On September 3, 1650, Cromwell defeated the Scots at Dunbar, Scotland, and destroyed Charles II's Scottish army a year later in Worcester.

Cromwell, his fame greater than ever, returned to his

place in Parliament, which was still no closer to a permanent settlement of the government. On April 20, 1653, by which time the Rump had proved its intransigence, Cromwell and a troop of soldiers expelled its members, thereby eliminating the last vestige of legitimate rule. The Church and the army selected members for the Barebones Parliament, but when it became rancorous, its more moderate members dissolved Parliament and gave Cromwell its powers.

In December, 1653, Cromwell accepted the Instrument of Government, a written constitution granting power to a one-house Parliament and to himself as lord protector of England. This arrangement, too, worked poorly. Cromwell quarreled with his first Parliament (1654-1655). After the Royalist Penruddock's Uprising (1655), Cromwell instituted martial law. He appointed eleven major generals to oversee local government and prevent disorder. This action more than anything else made Cromwell's Puritan rule hateful and confirmed the people's conviction that standing armies were dangerous to their rights. Cromwell accepted the Humble Petition and Advice (1657), recommended by his second Parliament, by which he could name his successor and create a second house of Parliament but would not become king.

Cromwell aimed not only for a stable government but also for a Puritan church settlement with toleration of dissent. By ordinance, he established what had been the status quo, a Presbyterian church with toleration for Protestant dissenters. Politically dangerous Catholics and Episcopalians were excluded from the church, but they were not actively pursued. Though the Quakers at times suffered under Cromwell's regime, their survival proves the degree of toleration he allowed. In 1655, Cromwell allowed Jews to return to England and to have a synagogue, ending the banishment begun in 1290. In all this, Cromwell took the lead; few were willing to go so far.

Cromwell restored England's respect among its neighbors. Though he at times spoke as if he would champion a Protestant crusade in Europe, in fact his actions always served England's national interests. English ships became a force in the Mediterranean, and they seized Spanish treasure fleets in the Atlantic. In 1655, an English expedition captured Jamaica. In 1657, a treaty with France gained for England an ally in its war with Spain. In 1658, the Battle of the Dunes, which won Dunkirk for England, demonstrated to a French ally and a Spanish enemy the quality of the New Model Army.

Cromwell died on September 3, 1658, and was buried in Westminster Abbey. His son Richard succeeded him as lord protector.

SIGNIFICANCE

For two-thirds of his life, Cromwell was an obscure country gentleman. Then, for almost two decades, he rose to heights equaled by few others in English history. Afterward, he, or rather his reputation, fell more rapidly than he had risen. Within nine months, his reluctant successor had resigned, and England fell into a state of confusion that could well have become anarchy had not General George Monck and the English people decided to restore the old order. The revolution was repudiated, as was Cromwell. Already dead, he could not be punished with the other regicides, but his body was exhumed and hanged, his head then placed on a pole above Westminster Hall.

It was almost two centuries before historians could begin to think favorably of Cromwell. To Royalists, he was the chief of those who had killed the royal martyr. To radicals and republicans, he was the traitor to the cause of revolution. There is no doubt of his ability to lead an army; he is, perhaps, unparalleled as a cavalry commander. His role in furthering the power of England and its empire also seems beyond doubt. His religion and the role it played, for good or ill, will always be difficult to evaluate. The nineteenth century Whigs, who resurrected his reputation, saw him as an early champion of parliamentary democracy. Twenty-first century observers tend to see him either as a counterpart to contemporary European dictators or as an important contributor to an English revolution.

Cromwell failed in his attempts to establish a parliamentary government and a tolerant church. His ideas about government, society, religion, and economics, however, eventually triumphed. If Cromwell's will and power were insufficient to achieve what he sought in his own day, he at least provided a relatively stable environment where ideas could grow, and his regime was sufficiently moderate that neither did it destroy everything old nor did the reaction to it destroy everything new.

—Jacquelin Collins

FURTHER READING

Abbott, Wilbur Cortez, ed. *The Writings and Speeches of Oliver Cromwell, with an Introduction, Notes, and a Sketch of His Life.* 4 vols. Cambridge, Mass.: Harvard University Press, 1937-1947. Reprint. New York: Russell & Russell, 1970. The place to begin any serious study, though the evaluation of Cromwell is somewhat influenced by the rise of Fascism at the time the book was produced.

Ashley, Maurice. *The Greatness of Oliver Cromwell.*

London: Hodder and Stoughton, 1957. A good biography concerned with the paradoxes of Cromwell's character and finding greatness in his religious toleration.

Carlyle, Thomas, and S. C. Lomas, eds. *Oliver Cromwell's Letters and Speeches, with Elucidations.* 4 vols. New York, 1845. Reprint. New York: AMS Press, 1974. This work played an important role in presenting a more sympathetic understanding of Cromwell.

Coward, Barry. *The Cromwell Protectorate.* New York: Palgrave, 2002. Coward, a Cromwell biographer, refutes historians who have depicted Cromwell's rule as a reactionary military dictatorship. Instead, this selection of essays points out the positive achievements of Cromwell's government.

Davis, J. C. *Oliver Cromwell.* New York: Oxford University Press, 2001. Examines Cromwell's life and the familial, religious, and political alliances on which his career depended.

Firth, C. H. *Oliver Cromwell and the Rule of the Puritans.* New York: G. P. Putnam's Sons, 1901. Reprint. New York: Oxford University Press, 1953. The standard biography written in the Whig tradition, but perhaps still the best.

Fraser, Antonia. *Cromwell: Our Chief of Men.* New York: Alfred A. Knopf, 1973. Reprint. London: Weidenfeld and Nicolson, 1997. A biography intended for a popular audience.

Gaunt, Peter. *Oliver Cromwell.* Cambridge, Mass.: Blackwell, 1996. Reprint. New York: New York University Press, 2004. A concise and accessible biography detailing Cromwell's life and career.

Hill, Christopher. *God's Englishman: Oliver Cromwell and the English Revolution.* London: Weidenfeld and Nicolson, 1970. A good biography that attempts to escape from the Whig viewpoint of Firth and to see Cromwell in his own time, involved in a revolution that was economic and social as well as religious and political.

_____. *Oliver Cromwell.* London: Historical Association, 1958. An excellent, twenty-eight-page discussion of Cromwell and his important place in history.

Paul, Robert S. *The Lord Protector: Religion and Politics in the Life of Oliver Cromwell.* 2d ed. Grand Rapids, Mich.: Wm. B. Eerdmans, 1964. An excellent biography by an author trained as a theologian as well as a historian. A sympathetic presentation of Cromwell's religious belief and its influence.

Smith, David L., ed. *Cromwell and the Interregnum: The Essential Reading.* Malden, Mass.: Blackwell, 2003. Collects eight of the most frequently cited essays about Cromwell. Among other topics, the essays focus on Cromwell's religiousness and the workings of British government during the 1650's.

SEE ALSO: Charles I; Charles II (of England); Third Baron Fairfax; George Monck; Thomas Pride.

RELATED ARTICLES in *Great Events from History: The Seventeenth Century, 1601-1700:* May 6-June 7, 1628: Petition of Right; March, 1629-1640: "Personal Rule" of Charles I; November 3, 1640-May 15, 1641: Beginning of England's Long Parliament; 1642-1651: English Civil Wars; August 17-September 25, 1643: Solemn League and Covenant; July 2, 1644: Battle of Marston Moor; Spring, 1645-1660: Puritan New Model Army; 1646-1649: Levellers Launch an Egalitarian Movement; December 6, 1648-May 19, 1649: Establishment of the English Commonwealth; 1652-1689: Fox Organizes the Quakers; December 16, 1653-September 3, 1658: Cromwell Rules England as Lord Protector; March 12-14, 1655: Penruddock's Uprising; May 10, 1655: English Capture of Jamaica.

SOR JUANA INÉS DE LA CRUZ
Colonial Mexican poet and playwright

Sister Cruz was an outstanding poet of Mexico's colonial period. A key figure in Latin American literature and in seventeenth century Spanish poetry, Cruz was an intellectual woman in a culture in which learning was considered a properly masculine pursuit.

BORN: November, 1648 (baptized December 2, 1648); San Miguel Nepantla, New Spain (now in Mexico)
DIED: April 17, 1695; Mexico City, New Spain (now in Mexico)
ALSO KNOWN AS: Juana Inés de Asbaje y Ramírez de Santillana (given name); Sor Juana
AREA OF ACHIEVEMENT: Literature

EARLY LIFE

Sor Juana Inés de la Cruz (SAWR KHWAHN-ah ee-NAYS thay lah KREWS) was born Juana Inés de Asbaje y Ramírez de Santillana in San Miguel Nepantla, New Spain, a small village in the foothills of the Popocatépetl volcano, probably in November, 1648. The traditional

Sor Juana Inés de la Cruz. (Library of Congress)

date of her birth, based on a biography by the Jesuit Diego Calleja, was November 12, 1651, but scholars have found a baptismal record for her parish for a female child dated December 2, 1648, which is believed to be hers. She is recorded as a "daughter of the Church," since her parents, Isabel Ramírez de Santillana and Pedro Manuel de Asbaje, were not officially married.

Juana Inés was one of six children, all illegitimate. Her father seems to have left when Juana Inés was very young, and she scarcely mentions him in her writings. After Captain Diego Ruiz Lozano entered the household, Juana Inés was sent to the house of her maternal grandfather, where she was reared and where she had access to a library. She learned to read at the age of three, and at the age of eight, she composed a dramatic poem (*loa*) to the Eucharist. Eager to learn, she mastered Latin in about twenty lessons.

When she was sixteen, Juana Inés went to the Spanish viceroy's court as a lady of the viceroy's wife, the marquesa de Mancera. She very soon became a favorite of the marquesa, as the two apparently shared a love of learning and of the intellectual life. At one point, the viceroy invited a group of about forty professors to question Juana Inés on her knowledge, and she astounded everyone with her answers. At this age, Juana was also a strikingly beautiful young woman.

A life at court did not provide a young woman in Juana Inés's circumstances with an opportunity for marriage, and she herself refers to a "total disinclination to marriage." Considering the options available to her, especially with her desire to continue studying, she chose, in 1667, to enter the Convent of the Discalced Carmelites. The order was too severe for her, however, and she became ill and left after three months. A year later, she entered the Order of Saint Jerome, where she remained for the rest of her life.

LIFE'S WORK

When Juana Inés took the veil in the Convent of Saint Jerome (San Jerónimo) on February 24, 1669, and officially became Sor Juana Inés de la Cruz, she was not yet twenty-one. She was from then on bound to the regulations and activities of the convent, which were not especially strict, but the communal life did provide interruptions that sometimes took her away from her studies. Nevertheless, she read broadly to fill in the many gaps in her education—she was essentially self-taught—and she also wrote extensively. From 1669 to 1690, she built up a considerable library collection at the convent, primarily for her own use.

Cruz refers to her frail health on several occasions, and she was seriously ill with typhoid fever in 1671 or 1672. As a result, she wrote about the experience of death in a sonnet dedicated to "Laura" and a *romance* (a poem in octosyllabic verse with alternate lines of assonance) addressed to Fray Payo Enríquez de Rivera. Even her early writings show a sure skill in using the styles and forms of her times, and her own intelligence and sensitivity for nuances of meaning are evident.

Throughout her life, Cruz wrote many poems, but it is impossible to date them accurately, since the originals have been lost and her style did not evolve. From the beginning, she showed a control of chiaroscuro and a sense of form and proportion. As is true of other works of the Baroque period, Cruz's poems are not personal revelations but rather demonstrations of talent in using correct form. Within a given form, individual talent emerges through ingenious use of well-known comparisons and images or in the particular emphasis or tone.

In 1680, the marqués de la Laguna was appointed viceroy of New Spain, and the period of his reign, 1680-1688, was a very rich period in Cruz's intellectual life. She even heralded his arrival with a symbolic work entitled *El Neptuno alegórico* (1680; allegorical Neptune). Completely in tune with Baroque tradition, Cruz skillfully draws an allegorical portrait of the new viceroy, using the device of an emblem or enigma. *Primero sueño* (1692; *First Dream*, 1983) begins with a poetic rendering of a slumbering world through mythology and imagery but develops into a philosophical argument on the relation of the intellect to the senses using the vocabulary and reasoning of Scholasticism. *El divino Narciso* (pr. c. 1680, pb. 1690; *The Divine Narcissus*, 1945) is a sacramental play employing allegorical characters and representing the search of Human Nature (a woman) for Christ (in the form of Narcissus). Much of her other work consists of poems for special occasions.

Cruz's *Carta atenagórica* (1690; the Athenagoric letter) was published as a small pamphlet. The work, in the

---

CRUZ'S MAJOR WORKS

1668	*Amor es más laberinto* (pr. 1689; with Juan de Guevara)
c. 1680	*El divino Narciso* (*The Divine Narcissus*, 1945)
c. 1680	*Los empeños de una casa* (adaptation of on Lope de Vega Carpio's play *La discreta enamorada*; *A Household Plagued by Love*, 1942)
1689	*Inundación castálida*
1692	*El cetro de José*
c. 1692	*El mártir del Sacramento, San Hermenegildo*
1692	*Segundo volumen de las obras*
1700	*Fama y obras póstumas*
1700	*Respuesta de la poetisa a la muy ilustre Sor Filotea de la Cruz* (*Reply to Sor Filotea de la Cruz*, 1982)

---

form of a letter, is a critique of a sermon given by the Portuguese Jesuit Antonio de Vieyra on Holy Thursday in 1650. She put her thoughts on paper at the request of someone with whom she had discussed the topic in casual conversation, and the letter came into the hands of Manuel Fernández de Santa Cruz, bishop of Puebla, who wrote a brief prologue and had it published. This prologue, in the form of a letter signed Sor Filotea de la Cruz and dated November 25, 1690, did not forbid Cruz from studying but did suggest that she study more in the area of sacred letters.

Three months later, on March 1, 1691, Sor Juana wrote her *Respuesta de la poetisa a la muy ilustre Sor Filotea de la Cruz* (pb. 1700; *Reply to Sor Filotea de la Cruz*, 1982). In this famous manuscript, she defends her thirst for knowledge. First, she recognizes her overpowering yearning to know and says that she learns not only from books but also from nature and everyday life. In essence, she defines herself as an intellectual. She then addresses the question of whether women should study. Since she is writing to the bishop, she readily agrees that she should study sacred works more, but the letter itself reveals a considerable knowledge of the Bible and religious writers. In her argument, she reviews her own background and learning and even her decision to become a nun.

Within the convent, there was much opposition to her studies, and, although Cruz does not mention people by name, it is clear that she suffered because she could not quiet her intellect. The letter is a clearly considered and well-formulated argument, bringing to bear the use of reason, as well as authority (a weaker form of justification). The letters of Cruz and the bishop caused some disagreement with the Church, and although the bishop favored Cruz, her own confessor, Jesuit Padre Antonio Núñez de Miranda, broke ties with her. Cruz then decided to renounce the world by selling her library and giving the money to the poor. In addition, she signed an affirmation of faith in her own blood. When an epidemic struck the convent in 1695, Cruz helped the sick members of the community until she herself became ill. She died from the disease on April 17, leaving unanswered the mystery of her renunciation.

SIGNIFICANCE

Cruz is a key figure in the history of Latin American literature, not only for her poetry but also for her important prose works *Reply to Sor Filotea de la Cruz* and *Carta atenagórica*, for which she is considered an early defender of women's emancipation. She believed that women, like men, should be allowed full intellectual development.

Cruz's poetic accomplishments, however, are what secure her place in Latin American literary history. While her poems were not original in the modern sense, wherein personal experience is important in poetry, she skillfully followed the tradition of the great Spanish writers Luis de Góngora y Argote and Pedro Calderón de la Barca. Her work is not distinctly American as opposed to peninsular Spanish, but she is honored as a Mexican poet nevertheless, because she was a part of the literature written in the New World and because she herself was a product of a criollo family. Her writings include an important body of lyric poetry, two stage comedies, and three religious allegories. The range of her abilities is reflected in her poetry, which could be intellectual or passionate, complicated or in popular style, witty or serious. Although she lived at the end of the Baroque period, the literature of which has been criticized as imitative and often extravagant, Cruz's poetry demonstrates a skill and clarity of design that is exceptional and merits for her a distinguished place in the history of Spanish and Latin American literature.

—*Susan L. Piepke*

FURTHER READING

Cruz, Sister Juana Inés de la. *A Woman of Genius: The Intellectual Autobiography of Sor Juana Inés de la Cruz.* Translated with an introduction by Margaret Sayers Peden. Salisbury, Conn.: Lime Rock Press, 1982. An English translation of Cruz's memoirs.

Flynn, Gerard. *Sor Juana Inés de la Cruz.* Boston: Twayne, 1971. Introduction to Cruz and her work. Includes biographical information, review and criticism

of her poetry and drama, and quotations from her work with English translations.

Gonzalez, Michelle A. *Sor Juana: Beauty and Justice in the Americas.* Maryknoll, N.Y.: Orbis Books, 2003. A recent biography of Cruz, examining her life, work, and theology. The author argues that by joining aesthetics with the quest for truth and justice, Cruz was a forerunner of the contemporary liberation theology movement.

Merrim, Stephanie. *Early Modern Women's Writing and Sor Juana Inés de la Cruz.* Nashville, Tenn.: Vanderbilt University Press, 1999. Situates the work of Cruz within the field of seventeenth century women's writing in Spanish, English, and French. The protofeminist writings of Cruz are used as a benchmark for the examination of the literary production of her female contemporaries.

_____, ed. *Feminist Perspectives on Sor Juana Inés de la Cruz.* Detroit, Mich.: Wayne State University Press, 1991. A collection of essays by literary critics and translators of Cruz. Discusses her life, time, and work in the context of feminist criticism.

Montross, Constance M. *Virtue or Vice? Sor Juana's Use of Thomistic Thought.* Washington, D.C.: University Press of America, 1981. Examines Cruz's use of Scholastic doctrine and methodology, specifically the ideas of Saint Thomas Aquinas. The author analyzes the combination of belief and questioning in the *Carta atenagórica*, the *Reply to Sor Filotea de la Cruz*, and *First Dream.*

Paz, Octavio. *Sor Juana: Or, The Traps of Faith.* Translated by Margaret Sayers Peden. Cambridge, Mass.: Harvard University Press, 1988. A biography of Cruz by a leading Mexican poet, essayist, and cultural critic. Paz emphasizes Cruz's uniqueness as a poet and focuses on her struggle for an intellectual and creative life. Includes portraits of Cruz and other illustrations plus a helpful listing of Spanish literary terms.

_____, ed. *Mexican Poetry: An Anthology.* Translated by Samuel Beckett. Reprint. New York: Grove Press, 1985. Paz's introduction to the history of Mexican poetry includes a discussion of Cruz's work. Also contains translations of twelve of Cruz's poems.

SEE ALSO: Pedro Calderón de la Barca; Luis de Góngora y Argote.

RELATED ARTICLE in *Great Events from History: The Seventeenth Century, 1601-1700:* 1604-1680: Rise of Criollo Identity in Mexico.

CYRANO DE BERGERAC
French writer

Although the real-life Cyrano de Bergerac was a gallant soldier, a fine swordsman, a playwright, and an author, he is best remembered as the hero of numerous romantic but unhistorical legends. Since the nineteenth century, many readers have known him only as the protagonist of a poetic drama by Edmond Rostand.

BORN: March 6, 1619; Paris, France
DIED: July 28, 1655; Paris
ALSO KNOWN AS: Savinien de Cyrano de Bergerac (given name)
AREAS OF ACHIEVEMENT: Literature, military

EARLY LIFE

Savinien Cyrano became famous as Cyrano de Bergerac (see-rah-noh deh buhr-zheh-rahk), an appellation he took from the name of an estate near Paris. When Cyrano was born, France was entering a turbulent but exciting period. Young Louis XIII was on the throne, and Cardinal de Richelieu was consolidating his power behind that throne. The great philosophers René Descartes (1596-1650) and Blaise Pascal (1623-1662) flourished during this period. Pierre Corneille (1606-1684) became the era's great tragic dramatist, abandoning the comic stage to Jean-Baptiste Poquelin, known by the pseudonym Molière (1622-1673). Corneille's even greater successor, Jean Racine, was born in 1639. The French Academy had been established only four years earlier.

The first half of the seventeenth century was a time of revivification in France, and Paris was the scene of furious activity when, as legend has it, a brilliant, impudent nineteen-year-old Gascon, Cyrano de Bergerac, arrived in the capital. Although Cyrano certainly fit the Gascon stereotype of a swaggering boaster, most sources list Paris as his birthplace, which means that the appealing story of a young fire-breather from the provinces who takes the capital by storm is probably fiction. However, Cyrano could outswagger and outboast anyone in France, and his fearsome sword arm supported his bravest words. In Edmond Rostand's play *Cyrano de Bergerac* (1897), the author presents a hero whose swordplay is a match for that of a hundred men. Although this characterization suits Rostand's romantic purposes, it also is historically accurate. Cyrano's capacity for dazzling violence was larger than life, even in a violent age. His personality utterly charmed his friends, embittered his enemies, and assured him of having plenty of both.

Cyrano's most prominent physical feature was his long nose—so long, indeed, that it was thought to be disfiguring. A modern historian might be tempted to attribute Cyrano's disdain for the nobility, the clergy, artistic dilettantes, and the reigning beauties of the day to a neurotic compensation for his facial disfigurement. Regardless of the source of his motivation, he was a force with which to be reckoned during the stormy seventeenth century.

As a very young man, Cyrano had joined a company of guards, and he was a soldier up to the age of twenty-three. During his distinguished military career, he was twice wounded, suffering one of these injuries while serving gallantly at the Siege of Arras.

LIFE'S WORK

In 1642, Cyrano left military life to study science and literature. His teacher was the philosopher and mathematician Pierre Gassendi. Cyrano was strongly influenced by his tutor's scientific theories and libertine philosophy and, as a result, had become a skeptic and a materialist by the time he began his writing career.

He published works in several genres. His writings for the stage include a comedy, *Le Pédant joué* (1653; *The Ridiculous Pedant* or *The Pedant Imitated*), and a tragedy *La Mort d'Agrippine* (1654; *The Death of Agrippina*). His best-known works, however, were collected and published after his death by his friend Le Bret. These two science fiction books are *L'histoire comique des états et empires de la lune* (1657; *The Other World, or the States and Empires of the Moon*)—the complete text of which appeared for the first time in 1921 as *L'Autre Monde*—and *L'histoire comique des états et empires du soleil* (1662; *The States and Empires of the Sun*). His other writings, the *Lettres* and *Le ministre d'état flambé*, are difficult, if not impossible, to find in English translations.

Cyrano was a free thinker who questioned traditional religious beliefs and challenged the authority of the church. He was ahead of his time in arguing that animals possess intelligence and in stating that matter is made up of atoms. His science fiction is sometimes prescient; for example, it predicts the invention of the phonograph and Esperanto, an artificial language that was not created until 1887. His writings in this genre satirize seventeenth century religious and astronomical beliefs, which placed humans and their world at the center of the universe. Cyrano was not, however, a rigorous, systematic thinker.

Cyrano de Bergerac. (Library of Congress)

Rather, his mind was that of a brilliant poet, capable of achieving inspired insights.

His earlier dramatic work *The Ridiculous Pedant* was ebullient but was considered too frivolous for the established taste of classicism. The value of its liveliness and high spirits was recognized first by Molière, who based two scenes in one of his plays on it, and later by modern readers. *The Death of Agrippina* is a fine, intellectually impressive play that advances daring ideas through impassioned tragic dialogue. Among Cyrano's political writings—he was a fearless political satirist—was a violent pamphlet against the men of the Fronde (opposition)—a series of political disturbances between 1648 and 1653 during the minority of King Louis XIV. In this pamphlet, he defends Cardinal Jules Mazarin, prime minister to Louis XIV, as a political realist in the tradition of Niccolò Machiavelli. Cyrano's *Lettres*, filled with bold and original metaphors, are among the finest examples of baroque prose, an elaborate and ornate style. His works inspired a number of later writers.

Despite the quality of these works, Cyrano's colorful life consistently evokes more interest than does his work, largely because of the continuing popularity of Rostand's play. When the name Cyrano de Bergerac is mentioned, it is the Cyrano of Rostand's somewhat fanciful account that usually comes to mind. In the plot of this play, the gallant soldier and brilliant poet becomes a shy lover because of his remarkably large nose (a period portrait of the historical Cyrano attests to the reality of this facial feature).

Because no satisfactory biography of Cyrano is to be found in English and because multiple translations of Rostand's play, ranging over a period of many years, are still in print, Cyrano's life story has become Rostand's version. This version reflects a poetic, if not a literal, truth. For example, Cyrano was an unorthodox and daring, yet essentially minor, dramatist. In histories of French drama, even of seventeenth century French drama, Cyrano's career is summarized in paragraphs, whereas whole chapters are devoted to the comedies of Molière and the tragedies of Racine. Yet Rostand seizes upon Cyrano's independence and iconoclasm as a dramatist and heightens those qualities for theatrical effect. In Act I, he has Cyrano interrupt the performance of a classical play that has just begun before a full house. A fat and windy actor, in the costume of a rustic shepherd, is driven from the stage by the high-handed hero because his acting has offended Cyrano's artistic sensibilities.

Likewise, Rostand takes the florid baroque style for which Cyrano was known and creates one of the most memorable scenes in his play. When a young nobleman seeks to goad the hero into a duel with swords by telling him his nose is "rather large," Cyrano chides him for wasting his opportunity to insult imaginatively and reels off twenty outrageously witty metaphors for the hugeness of his nose. The dim-witted nobleman is a stereotype of the aristocracy that the writer scorned.

Next, the playwright charmingly combines Cyrano's audacity with his facility in composition. As he fights the young man who insulted him, he composes an extemporaneous ballade—three stanzas of eight lines each and a refrain of four. As he declaims the last line of the refrain, he runs his opponent through.

Rostand dramatizes Cyrano's well-documented contempt for clerics by introducing, in Act III, a vain, greedy, and rather stupid Capuchin monk who is easily duped into marrying young lovers. While the marriage is being performed, Cyrano distracts an unwanted suitor by dropping from a branch, as from a great height. He confronts the man, disguising his face. He claims to have fallen from the Moon and dazzles his victim by recounting vivid details of his journey through the constellations. When the ceremony has been completed and the importunate lover can no longer interfere, Cyrano reveals his true identity. The interloper sarcastically suggests that Cyrano some day write a book about his experiences on the Moon. He replies that he has engaged himself to do so. Of course, the historical Cyrano did write such a book.

Other scenes are pure invention. The historical Cyrano died young, at the age of thirty-six. Rostand sets the romantic death in the park of a Parisian convent after Cyrano has declared his long-concealed love for his beautiful cousin Roxane. He has suffered a mortal head wound, inflicted in a cowardly sneak attack by his enemies. In the delirium resulting from his injury, he composes his epitaph, grandiloquently identifying himself as Hercule-Savinien de Cyrano de Bergerac—philosopher, scientist, poet, musician, duelist, wit, and lover. He dies still speaking brilliant dialogue. This is the legendary Cyrano, the Cyrano who has largely absorbed and mythologized the historical person.

SIGNIFICANCE

Cyrano's short life was marked by imprudence and misfortune. His was a genius that perhaps revealed itself only in snatches. He was a writer fated to be remembered less for his own works than as a precursor or inspiration to other writers. His "imaginary voyages" influenced Bernard le Bovier de Fontenelle, Jonathan Swift, and Voltaire—all of whom improved on his ideas. Molière in his farcical *Les Fourberies de Scapin*, first performed on May 24, 1671, borrows from Cyrano's *The Ridiculous Pedant* the idea of the famous galley scene as well as the account of the trick Scapin plays on Géronte.

However, Cyrano's persona has become more comparable to a character from Alexandre Dumas's *Les trois mousquetaires* (1844; *The Three Musketeers*, 1846) than to Molière or Racine. His image has been molded by the many actors who have portrayed him in Rostand's charming vehicle. The first actor to play the role was Constant Coquelin. His performance so pleased the playwright that the published version of the play was dedicated to him. According to Rostand, the soul of Cyrano

was reborn in Coquelin. Actor José Ferrer won an Academy Award for his portrayal of Cyrano in a 1950 film adaptation of the play. The French leading-man Gérard Depardieu won praise for his rendition of the role in another film version released in 1990.

The prolific novelist, screen writer, and essayist Anthony Burgess translated and adapted *Cyrano de Bergerac* as a play with music. His version was published in 1971 and produced on Broadway as *Cyrano* in 1973. The dramatic character and the charismatic real person from whom he was created continue to fascinate.

—Patrick Adcock

FURTHER READING

Butler, Kathleen T. *A History of French Literature: From the Earliest Times to the End of the Eighteenth Century*. Vol. 1. New York: Russell & Russell, 1966. In Chapter II, "Literature Under Richelieu and Mazarin (1610-1661)," the author refers to Cyrano's comedy as burlesque, reflecting a freedom that preceded the standard of taste to which the next generation of writers conformed.

Cazamian, L. *A History of French Literature*. Oxford, England: Clarendon Press, 1955. Discusses the smoothness of Cyrano's style and characterizes him as the most intellectually fertile of the "irregulars" preceding the marshaled ranks of the classics.

Dowden, Edward. *A History of French Literature*. London: William Heinemann, 1911. Describes Cyrano's taste, under the influence of the mannerisms of Italy and Spain, as "execrable" but also notes the satiric truth to be found within his wild fantasies.

Lloyd, Sue. *The Man Who Was Cyrano: A Life of Edmond Rostand, Creator of Cyrano de Bergerac*. Bloomington, Ind.: Unlimited, 2002. The first full-length English biography of Rostand, the book recounts the origins of *Cyrano de Bergerac* and describes how he expressed his own character and ideals in the character of Cyrano.

Romanowski, Sylvie. "Cyrano de Bergerac's Epistemological Bodies: 'Pregnant With a Thousand Definitions.'" *Science Fiction Studies* 25, no. 3 (November, 1998): 414-432. Examines the scientific imagery and treatment of the human body in Cyrano's science fiction novels, *L'Histoire comique des états et empires de la lune*, and *L'Histoire comique des états et empires du soleil*.

Rostand, Edmond. *Cyrano de Bergerac*. New York: Three Sirens Press, 1931. A translation by Helen B. Dole, illustrated with pen-and-ink drawings by Nino

Carbe. Valuable because of W. L. Parker's introduction, which compares the historical Cyrano with the hero of the play. Parker concludes that Cyrano's skill with the sword is "no metaphor." Also contains critical commentary on the play by W. P. Trent.

_____. *Cyrano de Bergerac*. Translated by Brian Hooker. New York: Modern Library, 1923. In a lengthy foreword, Clayton Hamilton comments upon the romantic power of the play and the quality of this translation. Most interestingly, he compares the opening performance (October 3, 1898) of Richard Mansfield, the first American actor to play Cyrano, with a 1900 performance by Constant Coquelin, the French actor who originated the role in Paris. Hamilton writes that Mansfield "acted the part admirably" but that Coquelin "was Cyrano."

SEE ALSO: Pierre Corneille; René Descartes; Louis XIII; Molière; Blaise Pascal; Jean Racine; Cardinal de Richelieu.

RELATED ARTICLES in *Great Events from History: The Seventeenth Century, 1601-1700:* 1610-1643: Reign of Louis XIII; 1637: Descartes Publishes His *Discourse on Method*.

WILLIAM DAMPIER
English scientist and explorer

Dampier was the most accomplished of the British sailor-scientists in the era of transition between the great Elizabethan voyages of discovery and the planned scientific expeditions of the mid-eighteenth century.

BORN: August?, 1651; East Coker, Somerset, England
DIED: March, 1715; London, England
AREAS OF ACHIEVEMENT: Exploration, science and technology

EARLY LIFE

William Dampier (DAMP-yuhr) was a curious mixture of adventurer, navigator, buccaneer, and outstanding author of the prescientific era. He was the son of a tenant farmer, George Dampier, and his wife, Ann, who had both died by the time Dampier went to sea at age sixteen with a Weymouth trader bound for Newfoundland. After discovering his distaste for cold weather, he returned to London and sailed aboard an East Indiaman to Bantam, Java, the first of Dampier's many voyages to tropical regions. He returned to England in 1672 and, at the outbreak of the Third Anglo-Dutch War (1672-1674), Dampier joined the navy. He saw action, though largely from a sickbed, as an able seaman at the Battle of the Texel.

After recovering his health in Somersetshire, Dampier sailed in 1674 for Jamaica, where he had been offered a position by his father's former landlord as assistant manager of a plantation. He quit that employment after only a few months, however, to work on board coastal traders. In 1675, he joined a logwood vessel called a ketch bound for Campeche, in southeast Mexico. The ketch was, in fact, a buccaneer ship on which life was hard, unfettered, drunken, and dangerous as a result of frequent clashes with Spanish ships. Dampier began here the journal that would form the basis of his later publications. In addition to recording the way of life on board, he carefully noted points on hydrography and pilotage.

For several years, Dampier sailed in the West Indies and Central America with traders and buccaneers. In 1678, he returned to England, where he married a young woman named Judith, of whom virtually nothing else is known. Dampier sailed for Jamaica in 1679. There, he again joined a crew of buccaneers, who captured Spanish ships and plundered settlements in Panama before the band split up on Drake's Island amid disputes. Dampier and about fifty others remained on the island when their ship departed. They made their way back across the Isthmus of Panama and joined a party of pirates. Dampier sailed with these pirates until July, 1682, when he spent more than a year in Virginia. In August, 1683, he enlisted as the assistant paymaster on the buccaneer ship the *Revenge*, whose crew traveled to the Pacific Ocean via Cape Horn, capturing a thirty-six-gun Danish ship and plundering the coast of Peru en route to Panama. The expeditions were so successful that at times Dampier's leaders commanded as many as ten ships and a thousand English and French buccaneers.

One ship, the *Cygnet*, broke away from the group in 1686. With Dampier aboard as navigating officer, it crossed the Pacific Ocean and traded in the East Indies. The crew then spent three months on the coast of Western Australia at King Sound in 1688 in order to make repairs, the first recorded landing on Australian soil of a British vessel.

LIFE'S WORK

In May, 1688, Dampier and seven companions were left behind in the Nicobar Islands after a quarrel with their mates. Relying on Dampier's skills as a navigator, they sailed to Sumatra in an improvised outrigger. Dampier recorded that during the perilous voyage, he contemplated his buccaneering life and resolved to correct its shortcomings.

After recovering from an illness brought on by the ordeal, Dampier worked for two years on trading ships, was forced into service as a gunner at the fort at Bencoolen, escaped in January, 1691, aboard an Indiaman, and eventually made his way to back to England. He arrived in his native country in 1691, after an absence of twelve years that had seen him complete a circumnavigation of the globe. He was penniless and was forced to sell his only possession, a slave from Miangas, Indonesia, named Prince Jeoly. Jeoly was exhibited as a curiosity for his tattoos, and he eventually died of smallpox in Oxford.

After several years of anonymity, Dampier won influential friends, such as scientists Sir Hans Sloane and Sir Robert Southwell, by writing a highly popular book about his adventures, *A New Voyage Round the World* (1697). A second volume, *Voyages and Descriptions* (1699), appeared two years later and contained "A Supplement for the Voyage Round the World" and "Two Voyages to Campeachy." The books won for Dampier a reputation as an authority on the South Seas.

His unexpected fame also attracted the attention of the Admiralty. In January, 1699, Dampier was named captain of HMS *Roebuck*, with orders to explore the east coast of Australia, which had never been visited by Europeans. Dampier captained fifty men and boys but appears to have acquitted his charge poorly. He put his first mate, George Fisher, ashore in Brazil after quarreling with him. He then sailed east across the Indian Ocean, arriving in August, 1699, at Shark's Bay, Western Australia. Seeking fresh water, he sailed up the coast to Roebuck Bay, near modern Broome. In September, having failed to find water and facing the spread of scurvy, he headed north to Timor, then east round the north coast of New Guinea, and discovered and named New Britain and New Ireland in 1700.

Dampier's ship needed repairs, so he returned to England rather than fulfill his ambition of sailing south to explore the east coast of Australia, which would remain unvisited by Europeans until Captain James Cook sailed its length in 1770.

In July, Dampier reached Batavia, made repairs, and embarked for England in October, 1700. After rounding Cape Horn, the *Roebuck*, already in exceedingly poor shape, began to leak badly, and Dampier was forced in February, 1701, to beach it at Ascension Island. He and his crew found ample supplies of fresh water and food and were soon rescued by a fleet of British warships and trading vessels. These brought Dampier to England, where he found he would face a court-martial for, among other charges, cruelty toward his second-in-command, Fisher. In June, 1702, the court declared Dampier unfit for command, finding that he had beaten Fisher with a cane, chained him, and then left him in a jail in Bahia, Brazil.

Despite the verdict, Dampier was introduced to Queen Anne by the lord high admiral the following April, after being given another commission as captain of the privateer *St. George*. He was directed to wage battle against French and Spanish ships in the South Seas, aided by another warship, the *Cinque Ports*. The expedition, which began in April, 1703, was disastrous because of Dampier's lack of control over his men and the poor condition of his ships. A series of defeats led to the breakup of the expedition. After a series of misadventures, Dampier returned to England in 1707, again impoverished and with his reputation further damaged by an account of the voyage written by one of those aboard, Funnell, who accused Dampier of such wrongs as quarreling with his officers, drunkenness, and cowardice. Dampier tried to answer these charges in his

William Dampier. (Library of Congress)

brief, poorly written *Captain Dampier's Vindication of His Voyage to the South Seas in the Ship St. George* (1707).

Dampier was now about fifty-seven and was not to lead another expedition, but from 1708 to 1711 he completed another circumnavigation of the globe as the pilot of the ships *Duke* and *Duchess*, captained by Woodes Rogers. It was during these voyages that Alexander Selkirk, the master of the Cinque Ports who had been marooned after the breakup of the 1703 expedition, was rescued from Juan Fernandez Island. Selkirk's solitary confinement served as the model for Daniel Defoe's novel *The Life and Strange Surprizing Adventures of Robinson Crusoe, of York, Mariner, Written by Himself* (1719; commonly known as *Robinson Crusoe*). Rogers was a far more capable leader than Dampier had proven. His skills as a buccaneer would have greatly enriched Dampier had the expedition's dividends been paid before Dampier's death in March, 1715. Dampier appears, however, to have lived comfortably in London on advances and credits. He stated in his will that he would go to his grave "diseased and weak of body, but of sound and perfect mind."

SIGNIFICANCE

Dampier's thoroughly observed, unaffected descriptions of natural phenomena exemplified the surge of scientific enlightenment in the late seventeenth century. His chronicles are all the more extraordinary in that he had had little schooling and compiled his writings while traveling in rough company hardly conducive to contemplation.

All of Dampier's works laid the groundwork for the great planned scientific explorations pioneered by Captain James Cook in 1770. Particularly influential and useful was his 1699 study of winds and currents, which is still praised as the most skillfully written treatise on those subjects of its time. That work typifies Dampier's extraordinary curiosity and the attention to detail it produced. Also a hallmark of his writing is its modesty and clarity. Its literary merit recommended it to a whole generation of writers. Dampier's highly successful books were, for example, influential in the history of travel literature and the novel; his descriptions of foreign lands strongly influenced such works as Daniel Defoe's *Robinson Crusoe* and Jonathan Swift's *Gulliver's Travels* (1726; originally entitled *Travels into Several Remote Nations of the World, in Four Parts, by Lemuel Gulliver, First a Surgeon, and Then a Captain of Several Ships*) and are thought to have provided background information for Samuel Taylor Coleridge's *The Rime of the Ancient Mariner* (1798).

In viewing Dampier's life as a whole, many commentators have cautioned readers to bear in mind that the navigator was, for several years, tantamount to a pirate. They note, for example, that Dampier commonly glossed over the nature of privateering voyages, presenting them as voyages of discovery. It is also noted, however, that Dampier stated that he joined bands of buccaneers "more to indulge my curiosity than to get wealth." For most of his life, Dampier was a writer posing as a buccaneer. He first commanded a ship at age forty-seven as a result of his growing fame as an observer, not as a sailor, and that undoubtedly provides a clue to his failure as a leader; on both the expeditions he led, Dampier returned to England without his ship. His works of observation as a seaman and scientist, however, remain unimpugned.

—*Peter Monaghan*

FURTHER READING

Bonner, Willard Hallam. *Captain William Dampier: Buccaneer-Author*. Stanford, Calif.: Stanford University Press, 1934. Describes the influence that Dampier's travels and writing had on the burgeoning travel literature of his day.

Dampier, William. *A New Voyage 'Round the World*. London: James Knapton, 1697. Rev. ed. New York: Dover, 1968. Highly successful in its time, this and Dampier's other works are the best resources for his life and mind. Offers a detailed account of the places and natural phenomena he encountered during his first, long circumnavigation. A companion volume, *Voyages and Descriptions* (1699), includes "A Supplement to the Voyage Round the World," "Two Voyages to Campeachy," and "A Discourse of Trade-Winds, Breezes, Storms, Seasons of the Year, Tides, and Currents of the Torrid Zone Throughout the World."

_____. *A Voyage to New Holland: The English Voyage of Discovery to the South Seas in 1699*. 2 vols. London: James Knapton, 1703-1709. Rev. ed. Gloucester, Gloucestershire, England: Alan Sutton, 1981. A two-part account of the author's command of the *Roebuck*, including the earliest English portrayals of Australia's flora and fauna, as well as its aboriginal inhabitants. Dampier's description of the latter as wretched is seen variously as an accurate description and as a classic statement of bigotry.

George, Alex S. *William Dampier in New Holland: Australia's First Natural Historian*. Hawthorn, Vic.: Bloomings Books, 1999. Describes the observations of flora and fauna that Dampier recorded during his expedition to Australia.

Gill, Anton. *The Devil's Mariner: A Life of William Dampier, Pirate and Explorer, 1615-1715*. Salisbury, Wiltshire, England: Michael Joseph, 1997. A useful biography of Dampier.

Lloyd, Christopher. *William Dampier*. Hamden, Conn.: Archon Books, 1966. Places Dampier in the context of the mid-seventeenth century Age of Observation, and describes how his inexhaustible curiosity made him more adventurous than more famous men of science such as Sir Isaac Newton, Robert Boyle, and Robert Hooke.

Preston, Diana, and Michael Preston. *A Pirate of Exquisite Mind: The Life of William Dampier*. New York: Walker, 2004. The Prestons drew on Dampier's writings to provide this exhaustively detailed biography.

Russell, W. Clarke. *William Dampier*. London: Macmillan, 1894. An often compelling but rather melodramatic account of Dampier's adventures and stature.

Shipman, Joseph C. *William Dampier: Seaman-Scientist*. Lawrence: University Press of Kansas, 1962. Describes the reception and assesses the significance of Dampier's writings and observation of a variety of natural phenomena.

Wilkinson, Clennel. *William Dampier*. London: Argonaut Press, 1922. Generally considered the best biography of Dampier. A thorough account of his life and influence, with relatively little attention to his scientific contributions.

SEE ALSO: Samuel de Champlain; Henry Hudson; Louis Jolliet; Sieur de La Salle; Jacques Marquette.
RELATED ARTICLE in *Great Events from History: The Seventeenth Century, 1601-1700:* April 6, 1672-August 10, 1678: French-Dutch War.

JOHN DAVENPORT
English and colonial American clergyman

A controversial clergyman who embraced Calvinism and Puritanism, John Davenport immigrated to the Massachusetts Bay Colony in 1630. He helped to establish the New Haven Colony in what became Connecticut.

BORN: April, 1597; Coventry, Warwickshire, England
DIED: March 15, 1670; Boston, Massachusetts Bay Colony (now in Massachusetts)
AREAS OF ACHIEVEMENT: Religion and theology, government and politics

EARLY LIFE

The fifth son of Henry Davenport and Winifred Barnabit Davenport, John Davenport came from a socially conscious, politically involved family. His father was chamberlain and sheriff of Coventry before becoming its mayor in 1613, the year in which sixteen-year-old John enrolled as a student at Merton College, Oxford. Two years later, the young man moved from Merton to Magdalen College, but lacking funds to continue his studies, in 1615 he left school and began preaching in the private chapel of Hilton Castle.

In 1619, he became a curate in London's Church of Saint Lawrence Jewry, where he was first attracted to the tenets of Puritanism and Calvinism. Davenport was reputed to be a riveting preacher, although the highly controversial ideas he expressed often raised hackles within his congregation.

In 1624, when he was a candidate for the vicarage of Saint Stephen's Church, several church leaders opposed his appointment because they considered his Puritan views dangerously extreme. He was appointed vicar, however, after writing persuasive letters to the congregation in which he denied having Puritan leanings. He gained the support and confidence of his congregation, especially after he chose to remain in London to minister to his parishioners during the plague of 1625, the same year in which he completed a bachelor's degree in divinity at Magdalen College.

LIFE'S WORK

Still wrestling to formulate his religious philosophy, Davenport fell under the influence of Lady Mary Vere and John Cotton, both discontented with what they considered England's religious oppression. In 1629, they convinced him to contribute money to the movement petitioning the king to obtain a charter for the Massachusetts Bay Colony. Many supporters of this movement had Puritan leanings. They felt compelled to leave England, which was then suffering the dire consequences of the Thirty Years' War that raged from 1618 to 1638, virtually destroying the economically crucial English textile industry. This situation, combined with a series of crop failures, resulted in famine and crippling poverty throughout much of England.

The anti-Puritan William Laud, who became archbishop of Canterbury in 1629, used his powerful office to discriminate against clergymen with Puritan leanings and went so far as to have some of them imprisoned. The following year, when the Massachusetts Bay Colony was granted its charter, some twenty thousand people fled from the religious persecution of England to the New England colony. John Davenport, however, was not among them.

Davenport continued preaching in London until August, 1633, when, pressured by Archbishop Laud's disapproval, he finally fled to the Netherlands, where he remained until 1637. Because his radical religious views were shunned by the Dutch, Davenport could not preach in the Netherlands. Therefore, after almost three years in Amsterdam, he and his wife, Elizabeth, set sail for the New England colony, accompanied by John's friend from his childhood, Theophilus Eaton, and a group of his followers whose passage was subsidized by Eaton. This group arrived in Boston in June, 1637.

The new arrivals quickly discerned that the Massachusetts Bay Colony was being torn apart, both by internal strife and by disputes with its neighbors. More liberal groups within the colony complained that the religious strictures placed upon them were too severe and sought to have them relaxed. Davenport, Eaton, and their followers, on the other hand, were convinced that the colony's rules and regulations were too lax and needed to be intensified.

Finally, in April, 1638, Davenport and Eaton, realizing that they were fighting a losing battle in the Massachusetts Bay Colony, defected. They traveled south to modern-day Connecticut, where they established the New Haven Colony on the Quinnipiac River. The new colony, a strict theocracy based upon Puritan and Calvinist principles, was well situated for trade with New Amsterdam to the south and Massachusetts to the north, yet it was sufficiently isolated geographically that its inhabitants could function independently.

The New Haven Fundamental Principles of 1639, made it clear that the new colony was Bible-based and that secular laws were considered secondary to biblical laws. Only church members, freemen, were permitted to vote. Church membership was extended only to a select few. Jury trials were banned as antibiblical.

Davenport was the most influential clergyman in the new colony and Eaton was elected governor by the freemen, most of whom were prosperous traders and mer-

John Davenport. (Hulton Archive/Getty Images)

chants. Davenport and Eaton based their fledgling colony on John Cotton's strict, Calvinist legal system, as outlined in his *Model of Moses His Judicials* (1636), which the Massachusetts Bay Colony had declined to use, considering it too repressive. Because church and state were virtually one in the new colony, Davenport's role as a leading clergyman was highly political. He and Eaton ran the colony for the next twenty-four years.

Davenport was a prolific writer. Notable among his publications were such pamphlets as *An Answer of the Elders of the Severall Churches in New England* (1643) and *Another Essay for Investigation of the Truth* (1663). The former sought to systematize the religious principles by which Davenport thought his church should be guided. The latter was a strong protest against the "Half-Way Covenant" that, after its approval by the synod in 1662, permitted children of members of the congregation who had not professed their faith to be baptized nevertheless.

In 1662, John Winthrop, Jr., asked King Charles II to grant him a charter to establish a new colony that would include the whole of Connecticut, including the New Haven Colony. Contending that the New Haven Colony was an autonomous entity that could not be annexed legally, Davenport protested vehemently against granting the charter for which Winthrop had petitioned. He coauthored a detailed, carefully reasoned protest entitled *New Haven's Case Stated* (1662).

In the previous year, however, Davenport had provided refuge to two regicide judges, Edward Davenport and William Goffe, who had served during the reign of King Charles I. The two fled to the New Haven Colony seeking asylum. Davenport's willingness to allow them sanctuary presumably did not pass unnoticed when Charles II reviewed and approved Winthrop's petition for a charter.

Distressed by the king's decision, Davenport vowed to leave Connecticut. In 1667, he decided to accept a call to become the minister of Boston's First Church. It was, however, incumbent on ministers making such a move to be formally released by their former church. When Davenport's congregation in New Haven declined to grant him the release he sought, he arranged to have letters from his Connecticut congregation suppressed, so that church leaders in Boston could not take them into account.

Davenport was duly appointed to the ministry in Boston. Late in 1669, however, his deception was revealed, bringing considerable calumny upon him. As this scandal unfolded, Davenport fell into a depression. He died in Boston in March of the following year.

SIGNIFICANCE

Davenport's was a life of service, but it was lived within such narrow religious confines that in time it became a life that was clouded by shame. A breathtaking preacher and persuasive apologist for his religious and political beliefs, Davenport could function effectively only with people who shared his dogma and who were willing to lead the austere life that his Puritan and Calvinist religious philosophy mandated.

Davenport was, however, instrumental, along with Theophilus Eaton, in establishing a thriving colony in southern Connecticut. Under their guidance, the colony was constructed rapidly and encouraged the prosperity of its members. Considerable effort went into structuring this community both physically and morally. Davenport was the chief impetus behind creating the New Haven Colony, which in time became the city of New Haven, Connecticut. He deserves credit for his efforts, but his life also emphasizes the futility of attempting to control stringently the religious lives of a diverse populace.

—*R. Baird Shuman*

FURTHER READING

Dexter, Franklin B. *Life and Writings of John Davenport*. New Haven, Conn.: New Haven Colony Historical Society Papers, 1877. This compilation of Daven-port's most crucial writings is essential to serious Davenport scholars. Quite specialized. Not for the in-experienced.

Girod, Christina M. *Connecticut*. San Diego: Lucent Books, 2002. This book will provide useful background for adolescent readers. It offers a snapshot of John Davenport and Theophilus Eaton as founders of the New Haven Colony. Accurate, enticing, and accessible.

Johnson, Paul. *A History of the American People*. New York: HarperCollins, 1997. One of the best sources on life in colonial New England in the seventeenth century. The presentation is interesting and direct.

Sherrow, Victoria. *Connecticut*. New York: Marshall Cavendish, 1998. This profusely illustrated book, although it does not mention Davenport directly, offers useful background information in an appealing format.

SEE ALSO: Charles I; Charles II (of England); John Cotton; William Laud.

RELATED ARTICLES in *Great Events from History: The Seventeenth Century, 1601-1700:* 1618-1648: Thirty Years' War; May, 1630-1643: Great Puritan Migration; Fall, 1632-January 5, 1665: Settlement of Connecticut.

LADY ELEANOR DAVIES
English writer and prophet

Believing herself to be inspired by the prophet Daniel, Lady Eleanor addressed more than sixty religious and political tracts to the king, Parliament, and the public, alarming the authorities, who imprisoned her in the Tower of London and Bedlam.

BORN: 1590; England
DIED: July 5, 1652; London, England
ALSO KNOWN AS: Eleanor Touchet (given name)
AREAS OF ACHIEVEMENT: Literature, religion and theology

EARLY LIFE

Lady Eleanor Davies (DAY-vihs) was born Eleanor Touchet, the fifth daughter of George Touchet, eleventh Baron Audeley, and his wife, Lucy, daughter of Sir James Mervin of Fonthill Gifford, Wiltshire. Her family home was in Stalbridge, Dorset. She had four sisters, Anne, Elizabeth, Mary, and Christian, and two brothers, Ferdinando and Mervin. Eleanor prided herself on her lineage and on her vocation as a prophet: In *The Appearance or Presence of the Son of Man* (1650), she insisted that the Audeley title was not a modern invented peerage but predated the Norman Conquest. She claimed that the family name derived from the Old Saxon title *Audleigh* or Old field. She explained that the letters A and O, standing for audleigh and old field, represented Alpha and Omega, the first and last, and so signified her ancient origins and the approaching judgment of her prophecies.

Nothing is known about Eleanor's education, but one can deduce that she received some training in languages because of her discussions of Latin, Greek, and Hebrew in her tracts. It is likely that she depended upon a polyglot Bible for her discussion of Greek and Hebrew, but she may have composed the Latin text of her tract *Prophetia de die Novissimo novissimis hisce temporibus manifes-tando: Item de excisione Ecclesiae and Redemptione Ex inferis* (1644; *A Prophesie of the Last Day to Be Revealed in the Last Times, and Then of the Cutting Off the Church and of the Redemption Out of Hell: The Word of God,* 1645). Sometime between her tenth and her fifteenth birthday, Eleanor accompanied her mother to Ireland, where they rejoined her father. Baron Audeley had taken part in the Siege of Kinsale in 1601, but it was not until 1605 that he succeeded in obtaining lands in Ireland; he was created earl of Castlehaven in 1616.

LIFE'S WORK

By 1609, Lord Audeley had amassed enough property that he could provide even his fifth daughter with six thousand pounds in money and land and, according to his discussion of her dowry, also supply her with valuable household plate and linen. At nineteen, Eleanor married Sir John Davies (1569-1626), attorney general of Ireland and a distinguished poet as well as a successful barrister and civil servant. More than twice her age, Davies was the coauthor with Christopher Marlowe of *Epigrammes and Elegies* (1590?). Eleanor would have been attracted to the acrostic format of his *Hymns of Astraea* (1599), because her own work reveals an interest in word play, particularly in anagrams. She would also have been interested in the subject matter of *Nosce Teipsum: This Oracle Expounded in Two Elegies* (1599), a verse explaining the nature of the soul and arguing for its immortality.

Eleanor's marriage to Davies resulted in the birth of two sons, Richard, who probably died in infancy, and John, who was alive on May 13, 1617, because he is mentioned in a letter written by Sir Robert Jacob. Clearly a diagnostic letter, it states that Jack can understand spoken language, indicating that his hearing is not defective but that his tongue may be. Her son's apparent disabilities may have led Eleanor to sympathize with George Carr, a mute thirteen-year-old Scot who gained celebrity as a fortuneteller and whom she took into her home in 1625. Davies's son John was drowned in Ireland sometime between 1617 and 1619. A daughter, Lucy, was born on January 20, 1613, in Dublin and named after her maternal grandmother. On October 31, 1619, Davies was relieved of his official responsibilities as attorney general, and he and Eleanor returned to England.

Eleanor attracted public attention in 1622, when she became involved in a quarrel with Lady Jacob. In a personal letter preserved among the domestic state papers for 1622, Kit Brooke, Lady Jacob's husband, threatens Eleanor that if she does not leave his wife and child

alone, he will scratch a mince pie out of her and curses her with the wish that she remain ever what she is.

In 1623, Sir John Davies purchased the manor of Englefield in Berkshire, not far from London. Also in 1623, he supplied his daughter, Lucy, with a dowry of sixty-five hundred pounds and arranged her marriage to Ferdinando Hastings, heir to the earl of Huntington; they were married on July 7 at Harefield, the home of Ferdinando's maternal grandmother, Alice, countess of Derby. Lucy, who was only eleven, remained with her parents until going to live with the Hastings family in 1625.

Eleanor began her prophetic career on July 28, 1625, when she received her first vision from Daniel and wrote a prophetic text, probably an early version of the text later published as *Warning to the Dragon and All His Angels* (1625). Illustrating how her prophecy would act as a mirror, she printed her own name, Eleanor Audeley backward and her anagram of it, REVEALE O DANIEL forward. She personally delivered her prophecy to Archbishop Abbot of Canterbury in Oxford, where he was attending Parliament. Eleanor was fiercely anti-Catholic and unwisely warned King Charles I that he must guide his wife Henrietta Maria away from popery.

Lady Davies reported in *The Lady Eleanor Her Appeal: Present This to Mr. Mace the Prophet of the Most High, His Messenger* (1646) that her husband burned the book containing her first prophecy. She retaliated by using an anagram of his name to prophesy his death: JOHN DAVES, JOVES HAND. She told Davies that he would die within three years, and she began wearing mourning immediately. When they were at dinner in December, 1626, she began to cry, and Davies told her, "I pray weep not while I am alive, and I will give you leave to laugh when I am dead." He died three days later, and Eleanor remarried Sir Archibald Douglas after only three months in March, 1627. This remarriage weakened her claim to Davies's estate, which the Huntingdon family claimed through Lucy. Records of the litigation over Davies's estate are preserved at the Huntington Library, San Marino, California.

By 1631, another member of Eleanor's family had attracted public attention. On May 14, 1631, after a notorious trial, her brother, Mervin, eleventh Baron Audeley and second earl of Castlehaven, was executed for sodomy and for being an accessory to the rapes of his wife and his stepdaughter by a servant. Anne Stanley, the aggrieved wife of Castlehaven, was the sister of Eleanor's daughter Lucy's mother-in-law, making Eleanor's relationship with the Hastings family even more difficult.

For the rest of her life, Eleanor concentrated upon publishing her prophetic writing, amounting to more than sixty pamphlets. The first serious repercussion occurred in October 23, 1633, when she was called before the Court of High Commission after she returned from publishing several tracts in the Netherlands. Her books were burned in front of her, and in 1635, after she destroyed altar hangings, which she regarded as too popish, she was committed to Bedlam. She was released by 1640, but she continued to prophesy the end of the world. She was imprisoned off and on until her death in 1652, because she continued to foresee retribution overwhelming government officials. Her daughter Lucy buried her in Saint Martin-in-the-Fields with an epitaph describing her as "learned above her sex" and "in a woman's body, a man's spirit."

SIGNIFICANCE

Lady Eleanor Davies, though previously ridiculed as a madwoman and dismissed because of her unconventional style, is now regarded as an important seventeenth century author. Prolific, extremely clever, and highly literate, Davies's work portrays and comments upon both the turbulent public events of her time and her own private, domestic, and religious experience, juxtaposing the one with the other. This juxtaposition of public and private, often characteristic of women writers in patriarchal societies, places her as an important member of a tradition extending from Julian of Norwich through Virginia Woolf and beyond. It also renders her texts invaluable as sources in the cultural history of seventeenth century England.

—Jean R. Brink

FURTHER READING

Cope, Esther. *Handmaid of the Holy Spirit: Dame Eleanor Davies, Never Soe Mad a Ladie*. Ann Arbor: University of Michigan Press, 1992. A revisionary biography of Lady Eleanor offering a sympathetic view of her life and works. Supplies a useful seventeenth century context for female prophets.

_____, ed. *Prophetic Writings of Lady Eleanor Davies*. New York: Oxford University Press, 1995. Selections from the prophetic tracts of Lady Eleanor.

Herrup, Cynthia B. *A House in Gross Disorder: Sex, Law, and the Second Earl of Castlehaven*. New York: Oxford University Press, 1999. Account of the politics of the trial and execution of Lady Eleanor's brother for rape and sodomy.

Pickard, Richard. "The Anagrams, Etc.: The Interpretive Dilemmas of Lady Eleanor Douglas." *Renaissance and Reformation* 20, no. 3 (1996): 5-22. Study of the unusual prose style favored by Lady Eleanor.

Porter, Roy. "The Prophetic Body: Lady Eleanor Davies and the Meaning of Madness." *Women's Writing* 1, no. 1 (1994): 51-63. Approaches Lady Eleanor from a feminist perspective.

Travitsky, Betty. "The Possibilities of Prose." In *Women and Literature in Britain, 1500-1700*, edited by Helen Wilcox. New York: Cambridge University Press, 1998. Excellent overview of Lady Eleanor in the context of other seventeenth century women writers.

SEE ALSO: Charles I; Henrietta Maria.

RELATED ARTICLE in *Great Events from History: The Seventeenth Century, 1601-1700:* February 7-19, 1601: Essex Rebellion.

THOMAS DEKKER

English playwright

An Elizabethan and Jacobean dramatist, Dekker was one of the most prolific and versatile playwrights of the late Renaissance and early seventeenth century. Working both alone and in collaboration, he wrote dramas that represented an unusual synthesis of romance, realism, and Christian morality.

BORN: c. 1572; London, England
DIED: August, 1632; London
AREAS OF ACHIEVEMENT: Literature, theater

EARLY LIFE

Though no documents have been found to corroborate the date or place of birth of Thomas Dekker, the fact that in 1632 Dekker mentioned being three score years old makes 1572 a plausible birth year, and there are references in his works to London as the place where he was born and bred. He must have had a Dutch heritage, for his surname is Dutch, and Dekker had a good knowledge of the Dutch language.

Dekker evidently attended an excellent grammar school, for he often quotes from Latin writers, and he demonstrates an easy familiarity with classical mythology, English history, European politics, and even economic theory. His knowledge of the Bible and his reverence for it, his consistently moral view of life, and his lifelong attachment to Anglicanism suggest all that his parents were faithful members of the Church of England. Dekker may have gone to sea after leaving grammar school, for his plays are filled with nautical terms. He probably married a woman named Mary in 1592 or 1593, and their first child may have been born in 1594. However, as far as verifiable history is concerned, Dekker's public life began in January, 1598.

LIFE'S WORK

One of the best sources of information about the seventeenth century theater is a business journal kept by Philip Henslowe, a theater owner and entrepreneur. On January 8, 1598, and again on January 15, Henslowe recorded payments to Dekker for writing the play *Phaethon* (pr. 1598). However, Dekker must have been writing for Henslowe for several years, for when the playwright was put in debtors' prison in February, Henslowe loaned him the money for his release, as he would do again in January, 1599.

During this early period, Dekker wrote his most popular play, *The Shoemaker's Holiday: Or, The Gentle Craft*

(pr., pb. 1600), the story of a lowly shoemaker who becomes lord mayor of London. *The Shoemaker's Holiday* shows Dekker at his best, writing a mixture of sentimental romance and realistic comedy. Although based on a narrative by Thomas Deloney, the text of *The Shoemaker's Holiday* was altogether Dekker's own invention. However, Henslowe's playwrights were often expected to collaborate on their plays, sometimes with as many as four other writers. Henslowe's records indicate that, writing alone or with others, Dekker was one of his most prolific playwrights. In 1602 alone, Dekker rewrote two old plays, composed two of his own, and collaborated on four more. Dekker was also an amazingly versatile writer: He could write tragedies of all varieties as easily as he turned out his realistic urban comedies, and he was as skilled in evoking the atmosphere of ancient Greece or of European courts as he was in depicting daily life in his beloved London.

Dekker was least adept at writing dramatic satire. Unfortunately, after 1600, when two companies of boy actors reappeared on the London stage, that became the genre most popular with London's most sophisticated audiences. Those dramatists who excelled in satirical writing embraced the opportunity presented by satire's rise in popularity, but before long dramatic competition and satiric writing proved a vitriolic combination. The satirists began openly to ridicule each other, and former friends became bitter enemies.

A feud between two such playwrights, Ben Jonson and John Marston, began the so-called War of the Theaters: Marston skewered Jonson in *Histriomastix: Or, The Player Whipd* (pr. 1599, pb. 1610), and Jonson returned fire in his *Poetaster: Or, His Arraignment* (pr. 1601, pb. 1602). The malicious delight of his audiences, in fact, caused Jonson to attack several of those who wrote for the popular theater, including Dekker, whom Jonson depicted in *Poetaster* as an ignorant, venal hack. Dekker responded by disparaging Jonson in his play *Satiromastix: Or, The Untrussing of the Humourous Poet* (pr. 1601, pb. 1602). Critics agree that Dekker's work was inferior to that of Jonson, but in any case, the war ended, though it took some time for it to be forgotten.

When the theaters were closed in 1603 because of an outbreak of plague, playwrights had to seek other ways to make a living. Dekker and Ben Jonson were fortunate in that they were commissioned to write the speeches for a show in honor of the new monarch, King James I.

DEKKER'S MAJOR WORKS

1599	*The Whole History of Fortunatus*
1600	*The Shoemaker's Holiday: Or, The Gentle Craft* (based on Thomas Deloney's narrative *The Gentle Craft*)
1600	*Patient Grissell* (with Henry Chettle and William Haughton)
1601	*Satiromastix: Or, The Untrussing of the Humourous Poet*
1602	*Sir Thomas Wyatt* (pr. as *Lady Jane*)
1603	*The Magnificent Entertainment Given to King James* (with Ben Jonson and Thomas Middleton)
1603	*The Wonderful Year*
1604	*The Honest Whore, Part I* (with Thomas Middleton)
1604	*Westward Ho!* (with John Webster)
c. 1605	*The Honest Whore, Part II*
1605	*Northward Ho!* (with Webster)
1606	*The Double PP*
1606	*The Seven Deadly Sins*
1606	*News from Hell*
c. 1606-1607	*The Whore of Babylon*
1608	*The Bellman of London*
1608	*Lanthorn and Candlelight* (revised as *O per se O*, 1612; *Villanies Discovered*, 1616)
1609	*Four Birds of Noah's Ark*
1609	*The Gull's Hornbook*
1609	*A Work for Armourers*
c. 1610	*The Roaring Girl: Or, Moll Cutpurse* (with Middleton)
c. 1610-1612	*If This Be Not a Good Play, the Devil Is in It*
c. 1611-1612	*Match Me in London*
1620	*English Villanies*, 1632, 1638, 1648
1620	*Dekker, His Dream*
c. 1620	*The Virgin Martyr* (with Philip Massinger)
1621	*The Witch of Edmonton* (with William Rowley and John Ford)
c. 1622-1631	*The Noble Soldier: Or, A Contract Broken, Justly Revenged* (with John Day; thought to be the same as *The Spanish Fig*, 1602)
c. 1623	*The Wonder of a Kingdom*
1624	*The Sun's Darling* (with John Ford)
c. 1624	*The Welsh Embassador: Or, A Comedy in Disguises* (revison of *The Noble Soldier*)
1631	*Penny-Wise, Pound-Foolish*

Dekker's contribution was published in 1604 as *The Magnificent Entertainment Given to King James* (pr. 1603, pb. 1604); Jonson's work was published separately, probably because of their earlier antipathy. In order to support himself, at this time Dekker began writing prose tracts on moral and religious subjects. He would continue to do so for the remainder of his life.

Meanwhile, with the aid of Thomas Middleton, Dekker had written a play called *The Honest Whore* (pr.,

pb. 1604; now known as *The Honest Whore, Part I*), a moving story about the attempts of a prostitute to reform. That play and its sequel, *The Honest Whore, Part II* (pr. c. 1605, pb. 1630), are considered two of Dekker's best works. Another of Dekker's serious plays demonstrates both his commitment to his faith and his patriotism. *The Whore of Babylon* (pr. c. 1606-1607, pb. 1607) was written in the wake of the Gunpowder Plot of 1605, a conspiracy by Roman Catholics to blow up both houses of Parliament and kill the royal family. Dekker portrays the conflict between Roman Catholicism and Anglican Protestantism as a clear case of a battle between good and evil.

After *The Whore of Babylon*, Dekker devoted four or five years to producing prose tracts. He took up drama again around 1610, producing three minor plays between 1610 and 1612. In 1612, he was commissioned to write the pageant for the annual inauguration of the new lord mayor of London. In 1613, however, Dekker was arrested for debt, and he spent the next seven years in prison. During his confinement, his wife, Mary, died.

By the time Dekker emerged from prison, romantic tragicomedy had become the fashion, inspired in part by William Shakespeare's romance plays, such as *Pericles, Prince of Tyre* (pr. c. 1607-1608) and *The Winter's Tale* (pr. c. 1610-1611). Dekker could not seem to master the new genre, however. Perhaps for that reason, during the last years of his life, he almost always worked in collaboration with others. When an outbreak of plague in 1625 again caused the theaters to be closed, Dekker returned to writing tracts. In 1627, he was again commissioned to write the pageant for the lord mayor's inauguration. However, the fact that in both 1626 and 1628 this devout man was indicted for recusancy, or failure to attend services of the Church of England, suggests that he avoided public places for fear of being arrested for debt. Dekker died in August, 1632, leaving only debts to his second wife, Elizabeth. On August 25, he was buried in the parish of Saint James's, Clerkenwell.

SIGNIFICANCE

Although most critics agree that on occasion Dekker had problems with dramatic structure, he is admired for his skill in maintaining suspense by alternating tone from scene to scene, moving from sentiment to pathos to broad humor and back again. He also excelled in the use of language. He was as adept at writing lyrical speeches for his sentimental lovers as he was at reproducing the dialogue of comic characters from the streets of London.

Dekker is also important because, just when playwrights were becoming increasingly pessimistic, he maintained his belief that, with the grace of God, human beings could correct their moral flaws. Modern students of Renaissance literature have found in Dekker's work not only the realistic picture of London life for which he has long been known but also an admirable seriousness, united with optimism, that links his work to the medieval morality play. As a result, after being largely neglected for centuries, this brilliant playwright began to achieve some level of serious recognition in the early twenty-first century.

—*Rosemary M. Canfield Reisman*

FURTHER READING

Adler, Doris Ray. *Thomas Dekker: A Reference Guide*. Boston: G. K. Hall, 1983. The introduction to this useful book provides an excellent overview of Dekker criticism. Annotated bibliography and index.

Baston, Jane. "Rehabilitating Moll's Subversion in *The Roaring Girl*." *Studies in English Literature, 1500-1900* 37 (1997): 317-336. A feminist critic argues persuasively that though it begins by challenging social norms, *The Roaring Girl* ends in acquiescence.

Champion, Larry S. *Thomas Dekker and the Traditions of English Drama*. American University Studies, Series IV, English Language and Literature 27. New York: Peter Lang, 1985. Contends that for stagecraft as well as content, Dekker should be ranked among the most important playwrights of his time. Bibliography and index.

Franssen, Paul. "Horace the Second: Or, Ben Jonson, Thomas Dekker, and the Battle for Augustan Rome." In *The Author as Character: Representing Historical Writers in Western Literature*, edited by Paul Franssen and Ton Hoenselaars. Madison, N.J.: Fairleigh Dickinson University Press, 1999. A lucid explanation of the War of the Theaters, demonstrating how first Jonson, then Dekker, used the Roman writer Horace in verbal attacks on each other.

Gasper, Julia. *The Dragon and the Dove: The Plays of Thomas Dekker*. Oxford, England: Clarendon Press, 1990. Focuses on how the political and religious history of the period is reflected in several of Dekker's plays.

Hoy, Cyrus Henry. *Introductions, Notes, and Commentaries to Texts in "The Dramatic Works of Thomas Dekker," edited by Fredson Bowers*. 4 vols. New York: Cambridge University Press, 1980. Contains close readings and useful annotations of all the plays.

McLuskie, Kathleen. *Dekker and Heywood*. New York: St. Martin's Press, 1994. Addresses such issues as the demands of the marketplace, the infuence of the new theatergoing elite, the question of gender, and the difference between the play as written and the play as staged.

Price, George R. *Thomas Dekker*. New York: Twayne, 1969. A thoroughly researched and well-written book on Dekker's life, his dramatic and nondramatic works, and his religious and social thought. Includes chronology, notes, bibliography, and index.

SEE ALSO: James I; Ben Jonson; Thomas Middleton.

RELATED ARTICLES in *Great Events from History: The Seventeenth Century, 1601-1700:* c. 1601-1613: Shakespeare Produces His Later Plays; March 24, 1603: James I Becomes King of England; November 5, 1605: Gunpowder Plot.

RENÉ DESCARTES
French philosopher and mathematician

Descartes extended mathematical method, the erasure of doubt by reaching certainty, to all fields of knowledge, and argued that "I think, therefore I am" is the only undoubtedly true statement that can be made. His radical distinction between mind and body and his revolutionary method of metaphysical inquiry have had a profound effect on the history of philosophy.

BORN: March 31, 1596; La Haye, Touraine, France
DIED: February 11, 1650; Stockholm, Sweden
AREAS OF ACHIEVEMENT: Mathematics, philosophy, physics, science and technology

EARLY LIFE

René Descartes (reh-nay day-kahrt) was born to one of the most respected families among the French-speaking nobility in Touraine. His father, Joachim, held the post of counselor to the Parlement de Bordeaux. Descartes's mother died of tuberculosis only a few days after giving birth to her son, leaving a frail child of chronically poor health to the sole care of his father. René's physical condition remained delicate until he was in his twenties.

Joachim Descartes was a devoted and admiring father, determined to obtain the best education for "his philosopher." When Descartes was ten, he was sent to the College of La Flèche, newly established by the Jesuits under the auspices of Henry IV. Descartes was an exemplary student of the humanities and of mathematics. When, at the age of sixteen, he began his study of natural philosophy, he came to the insight that would later give rise to his revolutionary contributions to modern thought. Uncertainty and obscurity, he discovered, were hallmarks of physics and metaphysics. These disciplines seemed to attract a contradictory morass of opinions that yielded nothing uniform or definite. By contrast, Descartes's studies in mathematics showed him something firm, solid, and lasting. He was astonished to find that while mathematical solutions had been applied to scientific problems, the method of mathematics had never been extended to important practical matters. At La Flèche, Descartes concluded that he would have to break with the traditions of the schools if he were to find knowledge of any worth.

Descartes left his college without regret, and his father subsequently sent him to Paris. Social life there failed to amuse him, and he formed his most intimate friendships with some of France's leading scholars and teachers. When he was twenty-one, he joined the army but spent little time campaigning. In his spare time, he wrote a compendium of music and displayed his mathematical genius by instantaneously solving puzzles devised for him by soldiers in his company.

Descartes was housed with a German regiment in winter quarters at Ulm, waiting for active campaign, when the whole core of his subsequent thought suddenly took shape. On the night of November 10, 1619, after a day of intense and agitated reflection, Descartes went to bed and had three dreams. He interpreted these dreams as a divine sign that he was destined to found a unified science based on a new method for the correct management of human reason. Descartes's sudden illumination and resolve on that night to take himself as the judge of all values and the source of all certainty in knowledge was momentous for the world of ideas.

René Descartes. (Library of Congress)

DESCARTES'S MAJOR WORKS

1633   *Le Monde* (*The World*, 1998)
1637   *Discours de la méthode* (*Discourse on Method*, 1649)
1641   *Meditationes de prima philosophia* (*Meditations on First Philosophy*, 1680)
1644   *Principia philosophiae* (*Principles of Philosophy*, 1983)
1649   *Les Passions de l'âme* (*The Passions of the Soul*, 1950)
1701   *Regulae ad directionem ingeni* (*Rules for the Direction of the Mind*, 1911)

LIFE'S WORK

Descartes spent the next ten years formulating his method while continuing scientific researches and occupied himself with travel in order to study what he called "the great book of the world." He had come to the view that systems of human thought, especially those of the sciences and philosophy, were better framed by one thinker than by many, so that systematizing a body of thought from the books of others was not the best method. Descartes wanted to be disabused of all the prejudices he had acquired from the books of others; thus, he sought to begin anew with his own clear and firm foundation. This view was codified in his *Regulae ad directionem ingenii* (1701; *Rules for the Direction of the Mind*, 1911). In this work, Descartes set forth the method of rational inquiry he thought requisite for scientific advance, but he advocated its use for the attainment of any sort of knowledge whatever.

Descartes completed a scientific work entitled *Le Monde* (*The World*, 1998) in 1633, the same year that Galileo was condemned by the Inquisition. Upon hearing this news, Descartes immediately had his own book suppressed from publication, for it taught the same Copernican cosmology as did Galileo and made the claim that indicted Galileo's orthodoxy: that human beings could have knowledge as perfect as that of God. A few years later, Descartes published a compendium of treatises on mathematics and physical sciences that were written for the educated but nonacademic French community; this work obliquely recommended his unorthodox views to the common persons of "good sense" from whom Descartes hoped to receive a fair hearing. This work was prefaced by his *Discours de la méthode* (1637; *Discourse on Method*, 1649) and contained the *Geometry*, the *Dioptric*, and the *Meteors*.

Discourse on Method provided the finest articulation of what has come to be known as Descartes's method of doubt. This consisted of the four following logical rules: to admit as true only what was so perfectly clear and distinct that it was indubitable; to divide all difficulties into analyzable elements; to pass synthetically from what is easy to understand to what is difficult; and to make such accurate enumerations of the steps of reasoning so as to be certain of having omitted nothing.

The method is fundamentally of mathematical inspiration, and it is deductive and analytical rather than experimental. It is a heuristic device for solving complex problems that yields explicit innovation and discovery. Descartes employed his method to this end in the tract on geometry when he discovered a way to resolve the geometric curves into Cartesian coordinates. Such an invention could hardly have come from the traditional Euclidean synthetic-deductive method, which starts from assumed axioms and common notions in order to generate and prove logically entailed propositions.

Descartes's new method was akin to those found in the writings of Francis Bacon and Galileo, and it was the architectonic of the new science. "Old" science, leftover from ancient and medieval researches, merely observed and classified, and explained its findings in terms of postulated natural purposes of things. The new science inaugurated in the seventeenth century sought, in Descartes's words, to make humans the "masters and possessors of nature." This goal involved invention and discovery, the generation of new and nonspeculative knowledge, to be put in the service of practical ends. For Descartes and the other seventeenth century "new" scientists, human wonder and understanding were without intrinsic value; what was without practical use or application for humankind, Descartes remarked in *Discourse on Method*, was absolutely worthless. The new science aimed to create effects, not merely to understand causes.

Descartes intended his method not for mathematics and science only. He envisioned the unity of all knowledge. He employed his method in a purely metaphysical inquiry in *Meditationes de prima philosophia* (1641; *Meditations on First Philosophy*, 1680) to "establish something firm and lasting in the sciences." He fashioned in this a primary certainty by rejecting at the outset everything about which it was possible to have the least doubt.

He set aside as false everything learned from or through the senses, and the truths of arithmetic and geometry. Only the proposition, "I think, therefore I am," remained an indubitable truth. One cannot doubt one's existence, Descartes reasoned, without existing while

DESCARTES THINKS, THEREFORE HE IS

René Descartes doubted the existence of everything that could be doubted, and given the power of the mind, the doubtable could include everything. He famously noted, however, that the only thing that cannot be doubted is that one thinks, that one exists as a thinking thing.

I shall proceed by setting aside all that in which the least doubt could be supposed to exist, just as if I had discovered that it was absolutely false; and I shall ever follow in this road until I have met with something which is certain, or at least, if I can do nothing else, until I have learned for certain that there is nothing in the world that is certain. . . .

What of thinking? I find here that thought is an attribute that belongs to me; it alone cannot be separated from me. I am, I exist, that is certain. But how often [do I exist]? Just when I think; for it might possibly be the case if I ceased entirely to think, that I should likewise cease altogether to exist. I do not now admit anything which is not necessarily true: to speak accurately I am not more than a thing which thinks, that is to say [I am not] a mind or a soul, or an understanding, or a reason, which are terms whose significance was formerly unknown to me. I am however, a real thing and really exist; but what thing? I have answered: a thing that thinks.

Source: Descartes, *Meditations on First Philosophy* (1641), in *Descartes: Selections*, edited by Ralph M. Eaton (New York: Charles Scribner's Sons, 1927), pp. 95-96, 99.

one doubts. Thus, *cogito ergo sum* became his first and most certain principle. Further days of meditation on this principle revealed the certitudes that he was a substance whose whole essence it was to think, entirely independent of his body and of all other material things. His primary truth also made him believe he had proven the existence of God.

In this one epochal week of meditations, Descartes made privacy the hallmark of mental activity, moved the locus of certitude to inner mental states, and rejected faith and revelation in favor of clarity and distinctness. Reason itself had previously governed the coherence of what had to be taken as truth; now inner representation, and its correspondence with the external, material world, governed the kingdom of relevant truth. Most philosophers after Descartes have followed his conception of inner representations as the foundation of knowledge of all outer realities. Only in the twentieth century has this position, and its attendant problems, been systematically examined and contested.

The years that followed the publication of *Meditations on First Philosophy* were marked by controversies resulting from attacks by theologians. Descartes's orthodoxy was impugned and his arguments were assailed. In 1647, formal objections to the Cartesian metaphysics, along with the author's replies, were published as a companion volume to a second edition of the *Meditations on First Philosophy* in French translation.

Descartes's next project was to be his last. *Les Passions de l'âme* (1649; *The Passions of the Soul*, 1950) was a treatise of psychology that explained all mental and physiological phenomena by mechanical processes. This work has striking moral overtones as well. Descartes's implicit prescription for the best human life is reminiscent of that of the ancient Stoics: Humans should strive to conquer their passions in order to attain peace of mind. Descartes maintained in *The Passions of the Soul* that while people who feel deep passions are capable of the most pleasant life, these passions must be controlled with the intervention of rational guidance. In the end, he claimed that teaching one to be the master of one's passions was the chief use of wisdom.

In 1649, Descartes responded to the request of Queen Christina of Sweden to join a distinguished circle of scholars she was assembling in Stockholm to instruct her in philosophy. The cold Swedish climate and the rigorous schedule demanded by the queen took their toll; Descartes caught pneumonia and died the following year.

SIGNIFICANCE

Descartes's thought epitomizes the transition from the medieval epoch of the Western world to the modern period, in which personal freedom was deified. This tendency originated with the privatization of consciousness and the drive to overcome the rigors of nature. For Descartes, only absolutely certain knowledge counted as wisdom. Descartes envisaged wisdom as having practical benefits for the many, as opposed to being a mere cerebral exaltation for the educated few. Descartes saw the improvement of the mental and physical health of humankind as being the best of these benefits of wisdom. This prospect was ratified by the enterprises of centuries to come.

Descartes was one of the pioneers of modern mathematics. He conceived the possibility of treating problems of geometry by reducing them to algebraic operations and devised the necessary means for making geometric operations correspond to those of arithmetic. He also introduced the notion of deducing solutions from the assumption of the problem's being solved. This has become such a fundamental technique in algebra and higher mathematics that one can scarcely imagine its having had a genesis.

—Patricia Cook

FURTHER READING

Alanen, Lilli. *Descartes's Concept of Mind*. Cambridge, Mass.: Harvard University Press, 2003. Examines Descartes's influential ideas about the mind and the relation of mind and body.

Balz, Albert G. A. *Descartes and the Modern Mind*. New Haven, Conn.: Yale University Press, 1952. Balz analyzes the pervasive influence of Cartesianism on the last three centuries. The analysis proceeds topically, with exposition of a particular facet of Descartes's thought followed by analysis of its legacy.

Bordo, Susan, ed. *Feminist Interpretations of René Descartes*. University Park: Pennsylvania State University Press, 1999. Collection of essays offering a feminist perspective of Descartes's philosophy. Includes a select bibliography on Descartes, Cartesianism, and gender.

Cottingham, John G. *Descartes*. New York: Basil Blackwell, 1986. Most commentators focus on Descartes's theory of knowledge; Cottingham takes a broader view of Cartesian philosophy and offers a profound Cartesian understanding of human nature. Excellent for beginning students; clear on, and faithful to, Descartes's texts.

Davies, Richard. *Descartes: Belief, Skepticism, and Virtue*. Studies in Seventeenth Century Philosophy 3. New York: Routledge, 2001. Analyzes Descartes's thoughts on credulity, skepticism, and the search for reason and eternal truth.

Gaukroger, Stephen, ed. *Descartes: Philosophy, Mathematics, and Physics*. Totowa, N.J.: Barnes & Noble Books, 1980. Ten authors offer different perspectives on Descartes's interest in providing a philosophical foundation for mathematical physics. Thorough index.

Haldane, Elizabeth S. *Descartes: His Life and Times*. New York: American Scholar Publications, 1966. An artfully crafted and detailed (nearly 400 pages) biography. Haldane is especially good at providing historical notes on circumstances that influenced Descartes's thought and development.

Keeling, S. V. *Descartes*. New York: Oxford University Press, 1968. Still one of the best overviews of Descartes's thought and influence, this book connects Descartes's development to his ideas, gives a systematic reading of his work, and critically analyzes the merits and defects of Cartesianism.

Kenny, Anthony. *Descartes: A Study of His Philosophy*. New York: Random House, 1968. A standard commentary for beginning students of Descartes that emphasizes his epistemology (theory of knowledge). Treats philosophical issues topically in brief, clear chapters.

Moriarty, Michael. *Early Modern French Thought: The Age of Suspicion*. New York: Oxford University Press, 2003. Examines the philosophy of Descartes, Blaise Pascal, and Nicolas Malebranche.

SEE ALSO: Pierre Bayle; The Bernoulli Family; Robert Boyle; Tommaso Campanella; Christina; Anne Conway; Elizabeth of Bohemia; Pierre de Fermat; Galileo; Pierre Gassendi; Thomas Hobbes; Gottfried Wilhelm Leibniz; John Locke; Duchess of Newcastle; Sir Isaac Newton; Blaise Pascal; Wilhelm Schickard; Anna Maria van Schurman; Baruch Spinoza; Wang Fuzhi.

RELATED ARTICLES in *Great Events from History: The Seventeenth Century, 1601-1700:* 1601-1672: Rise of Scientific Societies; 1610-1643: Reign of Louis XIII; 1615-1696: Invention and Development of the Calculus; 1617-1628: Harvey Discovers the Circulation of the Blood; 1618-1648: Thirty Years' War; 1637: Descartes Publishes His *Discourse on Method*; 1651: Hobbes Publishes *Leviathan*; 1654: Pascal and Fermat Devise the Theory of Probability; 1660-1692: Boyle's Law and the Birth of Modern Chemistry; 1664: Willis Identifies the Basal Ganglia; 1669: Steno Presents His Theories of Fossils and Dynamic Geology; Late December, 1671: Newton Builds His Reflecting Telescope; Summer, 1687: Newton Formulates the Theory of Universal Gravitation; 1690: Locke Publishes *Two Treatises of Government*; 1693: Ray Argues for Animal Consciousness.

JOHN DONNE
English poet

Capturing the restless, questioning spirit of the early seventeenth century, Donne established the Metaphysical poetic style—witty, colloquial, and dramatic—in love poetry that was both devotional and erotic.

BORN: Between January 24 and June 19, 1572; London, England
DIED: March 31, 1631; London
AREA OF ACHIEVEMENT: Literature

EARLY LIFE
The early life of John Donne (DUHN) set the stage for a lifelong tension that is reflected in his poetry: On the one hand, he carefully cultivated the skills necessary for political success as a courtier; on the other, he embraced a religion and entered into an imprudent marriage that impeded his political career. Donne was born in 1572, the son of John Donne, a successful London merchant and member of the Ironmongers' Company, and Elizabeth, the daughter of epigrammatist John Heywood, and the great-niece of the martyred Sir Thomas More. Consequently trained in the Catholic faith, Donne learned early of the dangers to Catholics in Anglican Elizabethan England. Two of his uncles were Jesuits, one of whom headed a clandestine mission in England and was imprisoned, sentenced to death, and exiled. In addition, Donne's brother Henry died of plague in Newgate Prison in 1593, having been arrested for harboring a seminary priest.

Being Catholic, Donne could not be granted a university or law degree, even though he matriculated at Hart Hall, Oxford, in 1584 and was probably at Cambridge in 1588-1589. After traveling abroad (probably from 1589 to 1591), Donne entered Thavies Inn in 1591 and spent 1592 to 1594 at Lincoln's Inn, studying law, the classics, divinity, and perhaps medicine. During this time, Donne lived the life of a young man about town, frequently attending plays and cultivating the persona of a witty, cynical rake. In 1596-1597, he sailed with the English expeditions to Cádiz and the Azores under Robert Devereux, second earl of Essex, and Sir Walter Ralegh, thus aligning himself with energetic and aspiring but doomed political forces (Raleigh was later imprisoned and Essex beheaded).

Donne's poetry of the 1590's communicates a sense of daring rebellion, restless talent, and spiritual exploration. Defying Elizabethan literary tradition, Donne wrote several Ovidian elegies. The elegies' harsh realism, especially regarding sexual relationships, is a reaction against Golden Age idealism; their immediacy of situation and dominant, ironic speaking voice reflect the theater's influence on Donne as well as his powers of self-dramatization as a "forward wit."

In addition to challenging literary tradition, Donne questions religious authority, especially in his third satire. Again, Donne's compelling speaking presence dictates the poem's meter—so unlike mellifluous Elizabethan verse with its patterned "flowers of rhetoric"—and his twisted, complex syntax mirrors the convoluted theological issues being explored. Donne urges readers to "doubt wisely" while pursuing a vigilant intellectual quest for personified Truth, which stands "on a huge

John Donne. (Library of Congress)

hill,/ Cragged, and steep . . . and he that will/ Reach her, about must, and about must go."

Even his frankly amatory verses, written approximately between 1590 and 1617 and published posthumously as *Songs and Sonnets* in *Poems, by J. D.: With Elegies on the Authors Death* (1633, 1635, 1639, 1649, 1650, 1654, 1669) are touched by Donne's searching religious sensibility. While frequently interpreted as a typically Metaphysical "forcible yoking together" of sacred and profane opposites, Donne's technique derives from an incredible flexibility of mind that balances the physical and spiritual simultaneously. For example, "The Ecstasy," with its steady movement from body to soul to body, can be interpreted both as a sophisticated verbal seduction, soon to be translated into the language of the body, and as a reverent celebration of the transcendent unity experienced by spiritual lovers.

Even "The Flea," typically viewed as one of Donne's wittiest seduction poems, draws on religious imagery to create Christian undercurrents. The poem's recurring wordplay on life and death is not merely a bawdy pun; the Eucharistic implications of drinking blood and the Crucifixion echoes suggested by the purpled nail that has killed the flea both point to the body's importance in Christ's life-giving sacrifice as well as in sexual intercourse.

LIFE'S WORK

In many ways, Donne's life's work was searching for work, for a position suited to a person of his tremendous intelligence and talent. His elegies, satires, songs, and sonnets were not published during his lifetime but circulated instead in handwritten manuscript, primarily because the radical style, tones, and themes of these poems might have endangered Donne's chances for political advancement. Donne's prospects seemed promising in 1597-1598, when he was appointed secretary to Sir Thomas Egerton, lord keeper of England; in 1601, Donne also served as a member of Parliament in the final gathering of that body under Queen Elizabeth I.

In December of 1601, however, Donne secretly married Anne More, the seventeen-year-old niece of Lady Egerton. Anne's father, Sir George More, had Donne imprisoned and then dismissed from Egerton's service, which essentially ruined the young man's career. Despite the devastating effects of the marriage, the sincere love

DONNE'S MAJOR WORKS	
1610	*Pseudo-Martyr*
1611	*An Anatomy of the World: The First Anniversary*
1611	*Ignatius His Conclave*
1612	*Of the Progress of the Soule: The Second Anniversary*
1624	*Devotions upon Emergent Occasions*
1632	*Death's Duell*
1633	*Juvenilia: Or, Certaine Paradoxes and Problems*
1633	*Poems, by J. D.: With Elegies on the Authors Death,* (revised editions 1635, 1639, 1649, 1650, 1654, 1669)
1634	*Six Sermons on Several Occasions*
1640	*LXXX Sermons*
1646	*Biathanatos*
1649	*Fifty Sermons*
1651	*Essayes in Divinity*
1651	*Letters to Severall Persons of Honour*
1660	*XXVI Sermons*
1660	*A Collection of Letters*

Donne shared with Anne seems remarkable in an age of arranged marriages, and Donne's powers to express the many facets of the love experience, particularly the mutually sustaining love of equals, are phenomenal.

Poems such as "The Canonization" and "A Valediction: Forbidding Mourning," usually assumed to portray John and Anne's love, again combine the physical and the spiritual and demonstrate the force of Donne's dramatic imagination. "The Canonization" begins abruptly with the command, "For God's sake hold your tongue, and let me love," as though the speaker is reacting to another's words. Even as he celebrates the mystery and uniqueness of his love, the speaker comments on its potentially destructive nature by alluding to the phoenix, which must die before rising anew from its ashes, and by punning, "We can die by it, if not live by love,/ And if unfit for tombs and hearse/ Our legend be, it will be fit for verse."

Similarly, "A Valediction: Forbidding Mourning" dramatizes a scene of the lovers parting and distinguishes between "Dull sublunary lovers' love/ (Whose soul is sense)" and lovers like the speaker: Refined and spiritual, the souls of such lovers undergo not "A breach, but an expansion,/ Like gold to aery thinness beat," suggesting a painful process of purification. Donne's use of religious imagery to describe his love affairs implies that he perceived and valued the mystical potential of human love as well as its physical pleasures.

The early years of Donne's marriage were characterized by frequent moves and unsuccessful requests for employment. He was denied a position in the queen's household and later denied secretaryships in Ireland, with the Virginia Company, and with the state. During these disillusioning years of the early seventeenth century, Donne wrote *Biathanatos* (pb. 1646), a treatise challenging "right reason's" condemnation of suicide. Donne used his literary talent in his attempts to secure a place; from 1606 to 1610, he assisted Thomas Morton (later dean of Gloucester) by producing the anti-Catholic polemics *Pseudo-Martyr* (1610) and *Ignatius His Conclave* (1611). In 1607, Morton urged Donne to take holy orders, but Donne pleaded unworthiness. Although he had converted to an uneasy Anglicanism sometime in the 1590's, Donne was probably clinging tenaciously to a hope for political preferment and considered the Church only a last resort for advancement.

From 1610 onward, Donne's career outlook began to brighten, though not, perhaps, in the manner he had hoped. He received an honorary M.A. from Oxford in 1610; in 1611, he accompanied Sir Robert Drury to the Continent, and upon his return in 1612, Donne moved with his large family to a house in Drury Lane, on the Drury estate. He published his first book of verse, *An Anatomy of the World: The First Anniversary* (1611), followed a year later by *Of the Progress of the Soule: The Second Anniversary* (1612). Known collectively as the Anniversaries, these companion poems are formal funeral elegies commemorating the death of Drury's fifteen-year-old daughter, Elizabeth (whom Donne, incidentally, had never met). Symbolizing innocence, vitality, and virtue, Elizabeth takes with her all order and harmony, leaving the earth in a chaotic state of sin, corruption, and death. The first Anniversary is usually said to reflect Jacobean melancholy, that early seventeenth century questioning of the once-stable universal hierarchy; contemporary economic, political, theological, and scientific thought is summarized in Donne's famous line, "new philosophy calls all in doubt."

Although only a satellite of the court, Donne maintained friendships and exchanged verse letters with an influential group of courtiers, politicians, poets, and clergy. In 1613, for example, he paid visits to Sir Henry Goodyer and Sir Edward Herbert (whose brother George was to become a Metaphysical poet and whose mother, Magdalen, was one of Donne's patronesses). This visit occasioned the poem "Good Friday, 1613: Riding Westward," which reveals Donne's concern with vocation and his ultimate willingness to imitate Christ's sacrifice. In 1615, Donne was finally ordained as a priest at Saint

Paul's Cathedral and received an honorary doctorate in divinity from Cambridge at King James's command.

Two years later, Anne Donne died, having borne twelve children (five of whom predeceased Donne). Ironically, Donne's public stature and responsibilities increased after Anne's death; for the next fifteen years, he preached frequently to the court and various nobles, demonstrating great intellectual and dramatic talent, while also serving as reader in divinity at Lincoln's Inn. He traveled to Germany as chaplain with the embassy of James Hay, Viscount Doncaster, in 1619-1620 and was installed as the dean of Saint Paul's in 1621. Throughout the 1620's, Donne heard cases in ecclesiastical courts and the Court of Delegates and served as a justice of the peace and as the governor of the Charterhouse School.

During a severe illness in 1623, Donne produced several prayers and devotional poems, which were published the next year as *Devotions upon Emergent Occasions* (1624). One such poem, "Hymn to God My God, in My Sickness," reveals Donne's preoccupation with the essentials of Protestant drama—sin, death, faith, resurrection—and his keen introspective ability. Using, as usual, striking conceits (complex intellectual comparisons of seemingly dissimilar objects), Donne ingeniously compares his body to a lute, a map, and the two Adams. Donne also wrote numerous holy sonnets; many of these incorporate erotic imagery to emphasize the soul's passionate desire for God, as evidenced in "Batter My Heart, Three-Personed God" and "Show Me, Dear Christ, Thy Spouse."

Taken ill late in 1630, Donne instinctively began to dramatize his death, preaching his own "funeral" sermon (published posthumously in 1632 as "Death's Duel") to the court on February 25, 1631. Sometime in February or March, he dressed in a shroud and posed for a portrait, making himself an emblem of mortality upon which to meditate. He transacted final Cathedral business on March 21, and on March 31, he died, a well-known and respected divine. He was buried on April 3, at St. Paul's.

SIGNIFICANCE

There survive approximately 160 of Donne's sermons, some of which were published during his life; in 1633, the first collected edition of Donne's verse was published. Donne's work exerted a tremendous influence on other seventeenth century poets, including George Herbert, Richard Crashaw, Henry Vaughan, Andrew Marvell, and Abraham Cowley. While not a self-styled group, as were Ben Jonson's cavalier poets, the Sons of Ben, this Metaphysical school of poets (a term coined by

John Dryden and Samuel Johnson) practiced Donne's roughly vigorous, colloquial, and wittily "conceited" style. Donne's innovative talent popularized the use of realistic, homely imagery, a concentration of thought, and a precision of diction.

Donne's popular reputation languished in the eighteenth and nineteenth centuries. With the publication of Sir Herbert Grierson's edition of Donne's poetry in 1921, however, his influence was revived. Early twentieth century poets, themselves struggling to find truth and meaning in a rapidly changing world, found in Donne a kindred soul and a fitting model.

The parallel drawn by Izaak Walton in his hagiographic *Life and Death of Dr. John Donne* (1640) between Donne and Saint Augustine (whose lives are both neatly divided into sensual and ascetic halves) is, although to some extent encouraged by Donne himself, ultimately a false one. Unlike Saint Augustine, Donne's two halves actually cohere comfortably in one and the same identity. Both Donne's amatory and religious experiences are characterized by a troubled restlessness, a sense of struggle intermingled with joyous union. His poetry powerfully combines the emotional and the intellectual, fusing song, drama, argument, and theological discourse. Though artfully crafted, Donne's poetry achieves an effect of spontaneity and psychological truth as it probes skeptically, perceptively, boldly into man's heart and soul.

—Caroline McManus

FURTHER READING

Bald, R. C. *John Donne: A Life*. New York: Oxford University Press, 1970. Corr. ed. Oxford, England: Clarendon Press, 1986. Bald draws on anecdotes, poems, letters, and earlier biographies. Includes useful appendices providing information on Donne's children, his library, his will, and other relevant documents.

Carey, John. *John Donne: Life, Mind, and Art*. New York: Oxford University Press, 1981. New ed. Boston: Faber and Faber, 1990. Carey approaches Donne from a somewhat psychoanalytic perspective, focusing on Donne's anxiety about the permanence of human relationships, his apostasy as a major influence on his verse, and his fascination with power. Carey's observations are, at times, outrageous, but he is frequently perceptive and always entertaining.

Edwards, David Lawrence. *John Donne: Man of Flesh and Spirit*. Grand Rapids, Mich.: William B. Eerdmans, 2002. A biography written by a theologian, especially good for its analyses of Donne's sermons.

Eliot, T. S. "The Metaphysical Poets." In *Selected Essays, 1917-1932*. New York: Harcourt Brace Jovanovich, 1932. A seminal essay in Donne's critical history. Eliot's work originated as a review of Grierson's edition of the poems. Discusses the "direct sensuous apprehension of thought" and the "dissociation of sensibility."

Gardner, Helen, ed. *John Donne: The Divine Poems*. Oxford, England: Clarendon Press, 1952. Reprint. New York: Oxford University Press, 2000.

_____. *John Donne: The Elegies and the "Songs and Sonnets."* Oxford, England: Clarendon Press, 1965. An eminent critic of Donne, Gardner provides in these two books excellent general introductions to the love poems and the devotional poems, commentary, and detailed textual analysis of manuscript dating.

Leishman, J. B. *The Monarch of Wit: An Analytical and Comparative Study of the Poetry of John Donne*. 7th ed. London: Hutchinson, 1965. A good one-volume overview with chapters on Donne's life, seventeenth century poetry, and analyses of Donne's poems.

Lewalski, Barbara Kiefer. "John Donne: Writing After the Copy of a Metaphorical God." In *Protestant Poetics and the Seventeenth-Century Religious Lyric*. Princeton, N.J.: Princeton University Press, 1979. Lewalski argues that Donne relied increasingly on genres important to Protestant devotion and biblical poetics theory, instead of forms that were secular, liturgical, or meditational. Focuses on typology and the Protestant "application to the self." Her first two sections, "Biblical Poetics" and "Ancillary Genres," are also useful.

Martz, Louis L. "John Donne in Meditation." In *The Poetry of Meditation: A Study in English Religious Literature of the Seventeenth Century*. Rev. ed. New Haven, Conn.: Yale University Press, 1962. Martz argues that Donne's poetry is modeled on formal religious meditations such as those practiced by St. Bernard and St. Ignatius of Loyola. Places Donne's work in a religious cultural context.

Parfitt, George A. E. *John Donne: A Literary Life*. Basingstoke, England: Macmillan, 1989. Focuses on Donne's life and work between his marriage at age 30 and his ordination 15 years later.

Walton, Izaak. *The Lives of John Donne, Sir Henry Wotton, Richard Hooker, George Herbert, and Robert Sanderson*. London: Oxford University Press, 1973. Walton's *Life and Death of Dr. John Donne* is hagiography rather than biography. His facts are inaccurate, but his testimony as a contemporary of Donne is valuable.

Whalen, Robert. *The Poetry of Immanence: Sacrament in Donne and Herbert.* Buffalo, N.Y.: University of Toronto Press, 2002. An exploration of the importance of sacrament to seventeenth century British identity and of sacramental imagery and tropes in the poetry of Donne and of George Herbert. Attempts to discuss the poets in terms of a "sacramental Puritanism."

SEE ALSO: Abraham Cowley; Richard Crashaw; John Dryden; George Herbert; James I; Ben Jonson; Andrew Marvell.
RELATED ARTICLES in *Great Events from History: The Seventeenth Century, 1601-1700:* February 7-19, 1601: Essex Rebellion; March 24, 1603: James I Becomes King of England.

DORGON
Manchu prince and imperial regent

Dorgon devised and implemented the political and military policies that led to the Manchu conquest of China. As regent for Shunzhi, the first Qing emperor, his measures contributed to the longevity of Manchu rule.

BORN: November 17, 1612; Mukden, Manchuria (now Shenyang, China)
DIED: December 31, 1650; Kharahotun, China ·
AREAS OF ACHIEVEMENT: Government and politics, warfare and conquest

EARLY LIFE

Dorgon was the fourteenth son of Nurhaci and one of three sons the Empress Hsiaolieh bore to the Manchu ruler. Early in his life, there was a rumor that he was a favorite of Nurhaci and was slated to become his heir. More likely, Dorgon was one of the young men whom Nurhaci had chosen to participate in a leadership rotation. Not long after Nurhaci's death in 1626, however, one of the four senior administrators, Abahai, forced the suicide of Dorgon's mother in a successful effort to garner complete power for himself.

Abahai chose not to punish the sixteen-year-old Dorgon or his brothers but instead treated them well, with Dorgon and his brother, Dodo, each gaining control of a banner (a military unit). In return, Dorgon served Abahai with dedication and courage and, during the period 1627-1636, participated in almost every military campaign undertaking by the Manchu leader. In 1636, when Abahai declared himself emperor of the Qing, Dorgon became a prince of the first degree with the designation *jui*. Two years later, he assumed command of one of two giant armies that invaded China.

Besides his military successes, Dorgon also possessed considerable diplomatic skills and was apparently admired by Chinese Mongols and Koreans. Abahai en-

trusted Dorgon with important administrative posts, and Dorgon was instrumental in the establishment of the Six Boards in 1631. Dorgon encouraged Abahai to treat the Chinese under Manchu control well in order to facilitate a future Manchu conquest of China. While Abahai accepted this advice, it apparently kindled the Manchu monarch's suspicions concerning Dorgon's ultimate agenda. Nevertheless, Dorgon served Abahai faithfully and continued to assume major responsibilities up until the death of the Qing emperor in September, 1643.

LIFE'S WORK

Upon the death of Abahai, his eldest son, Haoge, competed with Dorgon for the Manchu throne. The successional dispute threatened to erupt into a civil war, with Haoge holding a slight military advantage. Dorgon, however, succeeded in obtaining a compromise. Abahai's five-year-old son, Fulin, would become the heir and rule under the reign title Shunzhi. Until Shunzhi came of age, however, Dorgon and another Manchu prince, Jirgalang, were to act as regents.

Haoge and his supporters were mollified, expecting Jirgalang, who had enjoyed an outstanding military career, to be an effective deterrent to Dorgon's ambitions. They had not, however, counted on either Dorgon's political acumen or Jirgalang's distaste for civilian matters. Within months, Jirgalang was referring most important governmental affairs to Dorgon, and the latter was laying the foundations for Haoge's demise. By May of 1644, Dorgon had Haoge impeached for sedition and demoted to commoner. In 1647, Dorgon deposed Jirgalang, who had already been demoted to assistant regent, and had his own brother, Dodo, take his place. Finally, in 1648, Haoge himself was imprisoned and encouraged to commit suicide. Later, in 1650, upon the death of his own wife, Dorgon would marry Haoge's widow as a symbolic gesture of victory over his former rival.

During the course of this consolidation of power, Dorgon had himself repeatedly promoted in rank, starting out as uncle prince regent and culminating in 1648 with the title of imperial father regent. In the same year, he was excused from prostrating himself before the emperor at audiences. Even as he was effecting a complete domination of the Manchu court, Dorgon was also leading the Manchus in their conquest of China and in the establishment of the Qing Dynasty (Ch'ing, 1644-1911). Dorgon proved to be as clever at military diplomacy and administrative reform as he had been at conspiratorial court politics.

Within days of consolidating his power at Mukden, Dorgon had begun a massive invasion of Ming China, which had been weakened by a decadent court and constant internal upheavals. In April, 1644, Beijing fell to a brutal bandit-rebel, Li Zicheng, with the Ming emperor, Chongzhen, hanging himself near the palace. During this time, the Manchus were preparing an attack on Shanhaiguan (Shan-hai-kuan), which was being defended by General Wu Sangui (Wu San-kuei). News of the fall of Beijing prompted Wu to invite Dorgon to participate in a joint venture to punish the bandit Li and to profit from captured booty.

Dorgon, however, following the advice of several of his Chinese followers, agreed to help punish Li but also made it clear that the Manchus intended to take over the Dragon throne. Dorgon called upon General Wu to surrender his troops and join the Manchus in recapturing Beijing and eliminating Li. Using flowery sentences that promised vengeance for the late Ming emperor's death, Dorgon's messages also pointed out the historical validity of the so-called Mandate of Heaven's being passed from the unworthy Ming to the worthy Qing.

Unquestionably, these polished Chinese sentences were not the products of Dorgon himself but rather of advisers such as Fan Wencheng and Hong Chengchou. Ultimately, however, it was Dorgon who realized the usefulness of ensuring that the Manchu invasion would not simply be another barbarian raid. Accordingly, Dorgon issued strict instructions to his officers and men to refrain from looting. After rushing to Shanhaiguan and accepting Wu Sangui's surrender and subordination, Dorgon marched to Beijing.

Li Zicheng had begun to attack Shanhaiguan but had retreated to Beijing on news of the Manchu-Wu alliance. There, he crowned himself the Yong Chang emperor as his troops savagely pillaged the capital. On June 4, 1644, however, Li left after setting the palace and much of Beijing ablaze. On the next day, to the amazement of those officials and residents who were anticipating a Chinese rescue army, Dorgon appeared and announced that the Manchus were there to receive the Mandate of Heaven. He promised Beijing's residents and all Chinese that the Manchus would rule wisely and justly. Thus, with Dorgon as regent, Shunzhi began his rule over Qing China.

During the rest of his regency, Dorgon consolidated Manchu control, both through military force and by seducing former Ming military and civilian officials into his government. Slowly but methodically, Qing rule over China spread, and the waning hope of a Ming revival expired. In battle, Dorgon not only used his own trusted kin and supporters, but also cautiously employed some of Haoge's former allies, as well as Chinese soldiers. Dorgon was very successful at enlisting the allegiance of former Ming military officials, and he was able to employ civilian officials and draw good service from them as well.

Perhaps Dorgon's most impressive achievement was his ability to clean up the corruption that had characterized the Ming and yet do so with many of the same officials who had served in the corrupt administration. He did much to improve morale among the Chinese officials and helped reduce corruption throughout the empire by eliminating the power and influence of the palace eunuchs. Dorgon ordered that anyone who voluntarily castrated himself in order to become a palace eunuch should be decapitated.

The regent also reduced taxes and fought against venality, both at the court and in the countryside. He strove to maintain the examination system as a principal means of recruiting honest and conscientious Chinese officials to the Qing administration. Areas that had suffered from the civil wars of the last generation were often temporarily excused from taxes. Clearly, Dorgon was intent upon making Manchu rule as smooth and as acceptable to the Chinese population as possible. Yet, like his brother Abahai before him, Dorgon struggled with the question of the assimilation of the Manchus by the Chinese. Ultimately, his solution was a form of apartheid.

Initially, Dorgon vacillated over the previous policy of ordering Chinese under the Manchus to shave the front of their heads and wear their hair in queues, a very controversial demand designed to make the Chinese conform with a Manchurian cultural tradition. By 1645, however, Dorgon decided to demand this conformity of all Chinese under the Qing as a means of separating the conquerors from the conquered. Dorgon rationalized that this policy would actually reduce tensions, but it was clear that he wished to avoid having his people assimilated by the Chinese. He gave much of the rich farmland surrounding Beijing to Manchu troops and princes and even had the Chinese population moved from the northern part of Beijing to the south. While he recruited Chinese officials, he was also careful to leave the major positions in Manchu hands.

Having eliminated his major enemies and having achieved much success in ensconcing the Manchus in China, Dorgon began in the late 1640's to give up some of his previously rigorous regimen. He began to build a magnificent palace in Southern Jehol and was already at work stockpiling luxuries and concubines. It was not clear whether he intended to retire from active politics or to shift the focus of Manchu power from Beijing to his future palace. In any case, while not quite recovered from an illness, Dorgon went on a difficult hunting trip, took ill at Kharahotun, and died on the last day of 1650. He was buried with great honor, but his reputation would not last long after his death. By March of 1651, some of his former enemies assumed the regency and proceeded to withdraw most of Dorgon's honors and titles. His adopted son was forced to return to his previous family, and the records of Dorgon's achievements were rewritten in an unflattering manner. In 1773, however, the Qianlong emperor restored most of Dorgon's honors, and his name was celebrated in the Imperial Ancestral Temple.

SIGNIFICANCE

A consummate factionalist player, Dorgon survived the deadly game of court politics resulting from the refusals by both Nurhaci and Abahai to designate heirs before they died. Had this been his only achievement, his career would have been historically insignificant. His legacy, however, was much more considerable. Dorgon surrounded himself with talented advisers and implemented their advice. He was thus instrumental in establishing Qing rule over China in a manner that would facilitate the longevity of the dynasty. His insistence upon a form of dyarchy allowed the relatively unsophisticated Manchus an opportunity to mature into their role as overseers of a traditional Chinese government. Dorgon's policy with respect to eunuchs also prevented an endemic problem of the previous regime from ever developing to hinder Chinese Manchu rule.

Ultimately, however, Dorgon's hope that the Manchus would forever remain a separate people failed. In measure, this was a consequence of his land policies: By distributing confiscated land among Manchus, Dorgon essentially laid the foundations for his people's eventual abandonment of hunting and pastoralism, the absence of which opened the door to rapid Sinicization. The Manchus would continue to rule China for more than two and a half centuries, but by becoming agriculturalists, they could not, as their Mongol neighbors had done, avoid assimilation and remain a separate people.

—Hilel B. Salomon

FURTHER READING

Crossley, Pamela Kyle. *The Manchus*. Malden, Mass.: Blackwell, 2002. A history of the Manchu people, including information about Nurhaci and succeeding members of the Qing Dynasty.

Des Forges, Roger V. *Cultural Centrality and Political Change in Chinese History: Northeast Henan in the Fall of the Ming*. Stanford, Calif.: Stanford University Press, 2003. Recounts the Li Zicheng Rebellion in Beijing and the rise of the Shunzhi emperor.

Hummel, Arthur W., ed. *Eminent Chinese of the Ch'ing Period, 1644-1912*. 2 vols. Washington, D.C.: Government Printing Office, 1943-1944. Volume 1 contains an excellent biography of Dorgon.

Kessler, Lawrence D. *K'ang-hsi and the Consolidation of Ch'ing Rule, 1661-1684*. Chicago: University of Chicago Press, 1976. Although concentrating on the achievements of the Kangxi emperor, the author provides some insight into the administrative beginnings of the Qing Dynasty during the Dorgon regency.

Lee, Robert H. G. *The Manchurian Frontier in Ch'ing History*. Cambridge, Mass.: Harvard University Press, 1970. Essential reading for an understanding of frontier politics during Dorgon's life.

Michael, Franz. *The Origin of Manchu Rule in China: Frontier and Bureaucracy as Interacting Forces in the Chinese Empire*. Baltimore, Md.: Johns Hopkins University Press, 1942. Reprint. New York: Octagon Books, 1965. A somewhat controversial, but still-incisive discussion of the frontier state and the processes undertaken by the early Manchu leaders to prepare for the conquest of China.

Oxnam, Robert B. *Ruling from Horseback: Manchu Politics in the Oboi Regency, 1661-1669*. Chicago: University of Chicago Press, 1975. In searching for the origins of the concept of regency and the nature of Oboi's policies, the author devotes considerable attention to the model provided by the Dorgon regency.

Struve, Lynn A., ed. and trans. *Voices from the Ming-Qing Cataclysm: China in Tigers' Jaws*. New Haven, Conn.: Yale University Press, 1993. Personal accounts of Chinese life from the waning years of the Ming Dynasty through the Manchu takeover and eventual Qing rule.

Wakeman, Frederic, Jr. *The Great Enterprise: The Manchu Reconstruction of Imperial Order in Seventeenth-Century China.* 2 vols. Berkeley: University of California Press, 1985. A classic in the study of Chinese history. Wakeman presents a comprehensive study of the Manchu conquest and early rule over China. Volumes 1 and 2 devote much attention to Dorgon's career.

Wang, Chen-main. *The Life and Career of Hung Ch'eng Chou, 1593-1665: Public Service in a Time of Dynastic Change.* Ann Arbor, Mich.: Association for Asian Studies, 1999. A biography of Hong Chengchou, a Ming court advisor who became the most powerful minister of the new Qing government.

SEE ALSO: Abahai; Chen Shu; Chongzhen; Kangxi; Liu Yin; Shunzhi; Tianqi; Wang Fuzhi; Zheng Chenggong.

RELATED ARTICLES in *Great Events from History: The Seventeenth Century, 1601-1700:* 1616-1643: Rise of the Manchus; 1631-1645: Li Zicheng's Revolt; April 25, 1644: End of the Ming Dynasty; June 6, 1644: Manchus Take Beijing.

MICHAEL DRAYTON
English poet

A prolific English poet with laureate ambitions, Drayton published sonnets, satires, pastorals, historical poems, biblical poems, and Poly-Olbion, *a topographical survey of Great Britain.*

BORN: 1563; Hartshill, Warwickshire, England
DIED: December 23, 1631; London, England
AREA OF ACHIEVEMENT: Literature

EARLY LIFE

Modern biographies of Michael Drayton have largely been fictionalized accounts inspired by autobiographical statements found in Drayton's poetry and dedications. The principal source for such accounts of Drayton's early life is a passage in his poem, "Of Poets and Poesie" (1627), written when he was 64. He reports that he was a "goodly page" and that he asked his tutor what sort of men poets were; his Renaissance tutor naturally directs him to read Latin classics to answer the question. In the late nineteenth century, this allusion to a tutor was interpreted by Drayton's biographers as a reference to Sir Henry Goodere of Polesworth (1534-1595), and Drayton was posthumously provided with a genteel background and a classical education in the Goodere household.

In actuality, Drayton was a servant in the household of Sir Henry's younger brother. He is specifically identified as a servant in a deposition given on August 16, 1598, during a court case involving the Thomas Goodere estate. There is no evidence that Drayton attended a university, but his work, like that of Shakespeare, shows that he had read classical and English authors. His early works were dedicated to members of the gentry who had estates near his home in Warwickshire. Although he wrote intermittently for the theater, Drayton was dependent upon the patronage system, so the dedications of his many publications offer a record of his attempts to establish himself as a client in that system.

LIFE'S WORK

His *Idea, the Shepheards Garland* (1593), consisting of nine pastoral eclogues, was intended as Drayton's early poetic manifesto and was aimed at attracting the clientage of Mary Sidney Herbert, countess of Pembroke. In the fourth eclogue, he mourns the death of Mary's brother, Sir Philip Sidney, portraying him as Elphin, god of poetry. He follows this pastoral eclogue with a panegyric on the countess, who is praised as Pandora, the true patroness of poetry.

Drayton followed these early pastorals with a sonnet sequence. He addressed his mistress in these sonnets as Idea, emphasizing his interest in Neoplatonism, but early literary criticism insisted that Idea was Anne Goodere, the daughter of his patron, Sir Henry Goodere. Drayton dedicated the first of many versions of this sonnet sequence, *Ideas Mirrour* (1594), to the countess of Pembroke. Later in 1594, however, he turned to Lucy Harington as a possible patron, dedicating to her *Matilda* (1594), *Endimion and Phoebe* (1595), and *Mortimeriados* (1596), his first attempt at epic. Signaling his interest in being taken seriously as a laureate poet, Drayton adopted Rowland as his pen name; Rowland is probably an anglicized allusion to the title character of Ludovico Ariosto's *Orlando furioso* (1516, 1521, 1532; English translation, 1591), himself based on the medieval French folk hero Roland.

Drayton's *Englands Heroicall Epistles* (1597) was an emphatic bid for patronage, appearing with nine dedications. This collection of verse epistles is modeled upon Roman poet Ovid's *Heroides* (before 8 C.E.; English translation, 1567), but Drayton introduces figures from English history as the lovers who exchange letters. *Englands Heroicall Epistles* was a popular success and went through five separate editions between 1597 and 1602. Drayton took advantage of these editions to revise and add to the collection, but he seems to have recognized that it was already largely a success: Although he supplemented the collection, he did not subject it to the meticulous revision that he devoted to his pastorals, sonnets, and historical verse.

In 1598, Drayton began to write for the professional theater, and he has been identified as a collaborator on twenty-one plays between 1598 and 1604. Only one of these plays, *The First Part of the True and Honorable Historie of the Life of Sir John Old-Castle the Good Lord Cobham* (pr. 1599), was printed and has survived. This play appears to have been commissioned by the Cobham family to defend the reputation of their ancestor. The character Falstaff in William Shakespeare's *Henry IV, Part I* (pr. c. 1597-1598), *Henry IV, Part II* (pr. c. 1598), and *The Merry Wives of Windsor* (pr. 1597, revised c. 1600-1601), was originally called Sir John Oldcastle.

In 1602, Drayton seems to have succeeded in establishing himself as the client of Sir Walter Aston (1583-1639), a wealthy landowner with estates in Stafford, Derby, Leicester, and Warwick. Although we know that the 1619 folio of Drayton's collected verse is dedicated to Sir Walter Aston, we do not know what kind of patronage or how much Drayton received from Aston. From Drayton's verse, we know that he felt ill-used by the court and resented the patronage extended to poets who were less ambitious. In his revised pastorals of 1606, he takes to task his early patroness, Lucy Harington, by then Lucy Russell, countess of Bedford, for her ingratitude. He calls for time to devour any mention of her name and hopes that age will sit soon and ugly on her brow. He removed the passages cursing Lady Bedford into oblivion from *Poems* (1619), a folio edition of his works, but he also removed all of his earlier dedications and compliments addressed to her.

In 1612, Drayton published the first part of *Poly-Olbion* (1612-1622) with a dedication to Henry, prince of Wales, and Henry's household accounts record that Drayton was given a pension of ten pounds. Fate inter-

vened to thwart Drayton's hopes, however, as Henry died on November 6, 1612. *Poems* contains revisions of Drayton's earlier work; this major publication appeared with a frontispiece of a stern-faced Drayton, crowned with a laurel wreath but disapproving of seventeenth century England. *Poly-Olbion* was not a popular success. Drayton finished the second part in 1618, but he was not able to find a printer until 1622.

He published two more folio collections of his poetry: *The Battaile of Agincourt* (1627) and *The Muses Elizium* (1630). *The Battaile of Agincourt* contains a twenty-five-hundred-line poem celebrating the English victory over the French in 1415. The volume also contains a number of verse epistles, which Drayton called elegies. His extremely important elegy addressed to Henry Reynolds, "Of Poets and Poesie," defines a canon of English poetry. The title poem of *The Muses Elizium* was Drayton's last pastoral. Elizium is an idealized golden world, and this paradise for poets is contrasted to Felicia, the actual world of seventeenth century England. The old Satyr is Drayton's persona, and he remains bitterly critical of contemporaries who are defacing the land and ravaging the forests.

Drayton concludes *The Muses Elizium* with three divine poems, including *Moses His Birth and Miracle* (wr. 1604), *Noahs Floud*, and *David and Goliah*. These divine poems, like all of Drayton's seventeenth century poems, lament the loss of heroic aspiration in life and art. When he died in 1631, his brother Edmund reported that he had an estate of less than twenty-five pounds. Drayton's contemporaries, however, praised his learning and called him "golden-mouthed." He was buried in Westminster Abbey, and a statue of him was later erected in the poet's corner near Geoffrey Chaucer and William Shakespeare.

SIGNIFICANCE

Drayton was regarded by his contemporaries as a major poet, particularly because of his sonnets, historical poetry, and satires. In modern criticism, the verdict has been more critical, perhaps because less attention has been paid to his sonnets and satires than to *Poly-Olbion*. In addition to his poetic work, Drayton was an important literary critic, commenting upon the works of others and formulating his own theory of poetics. In *Poly-Olbion*, he differentiated public from private, or coterie, poetry; in *Poems*, he defined a number of genres, and in his elegy, "Of Poets and Poesie," he evaluated English and Scottish poets, beginning with Chaucer and concluding with William Browne. Drayton's widely acknowledged masterpiece, "Since there's no help, Come let us kiss and part," (1619) is so magnificent a sonnet that there have been attempts to claim it for Shakespeare.

—*Jean R. Brink*

FURTHER READING

Brink, Jean R. *Michael Drayton Revisited*. Boston: G. K. Hall, 1990. Substantially revises Drayton's biography and offers an analysis of each of his major poems and a comprehensive annotated bibliography.

Hebel, J. William, Kathleen Tillotson, and Bernard H. Newdigate, eds. *The Works of Michael Drayton*. 5 vols. Oxford, England: Basil Blackwell for the Shakespeare Head Press, 1961. Standard edition of Drayton's work, but difficult to use. Editors use the 1619 folio as copy text for the Elizabethan verse, and so Drayton's many revisions to his verse are printed only as variants in the fifth volume, where the notes are printed in very small type.

Klein, Bernhard. "The Imaginary Journeys: Spenser, Drayton, and the Poetics of National Space." In *Literature, Mapping, and the Politics of Space in Early Modern Britain*, edited by Andrew Gordon and Bernhard Klein. New York: Cambridge University Press, 2001. Examines *Poly-Olbion* in relation to maps and a developing sense of nationhood.

Lewalski, Barbara. "Lucy, Countess of Bedford: Images of a Jacobean Courtier and Patroness." In *Politics of Discourse: The Literature and History of Seventeenth-Century England*, edited by Kevin Sharpe and Steven Zwicker. Berkeley: University of California Press, 1987. Excellent biographical study of Lucy, countess of Bedford, the patroness whom Drayton spurned.

Lyne, Raphael. *Love's Changing Worlds: English Metamorphoses, 1567-1632*. New York: Oxford University Press, 2001. Study of Drayton's handling of Ovidian themes.

Speed, Stephen. "The Cartographic Arrest: Harvey, Raleigh, Drayton, and the Mapping of the Sense." In *At the Borders of the Human: Beasts, Bodies, and Natural Philosophy in the Early Modern Period*, edited by Erica Fudge, Ruth Gilbert, and Susan Wiseman. New York: Palgrave, 2002. Analyzes *Poly-Olbion* in relation to natural philosophy.

SEE ALSO: Abraham Cowley; Richard Crashaw; John Donne; John Dryden; George Herbert; Robert Herrick; Richard Lovelace; Andrew Marvell; John Milton; Katherine Philips.

RELATED ARTICLES in *Great Events from History: The Seventeenth Century, 1601-1700:* Early 17th century: Revenge Tragedies Become Popular in England; c. 1601-1613: Shakespeare Produces His Later Plays; March 24, 1603: James I Becomes King of England; 1611: Publication of the King James Bible; March, 1629-1640: "Personal Rule" of Charles I.

JOHN DRYDEN
English poet and playwright

Poet, playwright, satirist, translator, and critic, Dryden was the central literary figure of the English Restoration period.

BORN: August 19, 1631; Aldwinkle, Northamptonshire, England
DIED: May 12, 1700; London, England
AREAS OF ACHIEVEMENT: Literature, theater

EARLY LIFE
John Dryden's mother was Mary Pickering, the niece of the substantial landholder Sir John Pickering. His father was Erasmus Darwin, who, although the youngest son of his family, had been given a considerable parcel of land in Northamptonshire. Although members of the Church of England, both the Drydens and the Pickerings were Puritans.

The oldest of fourteen children, John may have begun his education in a village school or at home, continuing at Westminster School and at Trinity College, Cambridge. He wrote poems even as a schoolboy, and although they are not impressive, their existence does indicate that the creative impulse was present at an early age. His university record was not distinguished, yet his presence at Cambridge during a time when it was the center of philosophical and religious speculation, led by the Cambridge Platonists, obviously stimulated Dryden's own questionings, which were to lead him to Roman Catholicism.

After the death of his father in 1654, Dryden left Cambridge to take up his responsibilities as the new head of the family. It is unclear whether he held a minor post in Oliver Cromwell's government; he may simply have been preoccupied with family matters. At any rate, he must have been practicing his craft, as he produced his first mature published poem, *Heroic Stanzas* (1659), shortly after Cromwell's death, dedicating the work "to the Glorious Memory of Cromwell." Every line evidences Dryden's mastery of his craft. The subject matter, too, is significant, as it was to become a preoccupation of Dryden in his later heroic tragedies and poems: the necessity for a man of stature, who, transcending the mob, can lead his society from chaos to order. With this poem, Dryden's literary career began.

LIFE'S WORK

When he began his career as a poet, Dryden was in a very different situation from that of many of his contemporaries. A portrait shows him as a handsome, well-dressed aristocrat, secure in his social position, yet with warm eyes and a generous mouth, which predict his later kindness to those less fortunate. Dryden had a comfortable income. He also had contacts that would propel him into the highest circles of English society. For example, the

John Dryden. (Library of Congress)

friendship of Sir Robert Howard, the son of the earl of Berkshire and a tested Royalist, proved helpful now that Charles II had returned from France as king.

Dryden's next poem, *Astraea Redux* (1660), promised a new golden age in England, under the reign of Charles II. Other poems followed, including "To His Sacred Majesty," on the coronation (1661); "To My Lord Chancellor" (1662), a tribute to Edward Hyde, first earl of Clarendon, a loyal supporter of both Charles I and Charles II who now had received his reward; and "To My Honor'd Friend Dr. Charleton" (1663), published along with the scientist Walter Charleton's book on Stonehenge. It was Charleton who recommended Dryden for inclusion in the newly chartered Royal Society. Thus, despite his Puritan background, Dryden became a member of the inner circle of Restoration society, known to the court as a loyal supporter of Charles II.

Dryden's association with the Howards was important both in his personal life and in his literary career. In 1663, he married Sir Robert's sister, Lady Elizabeth, and by 1669, they had three sons. Meanwhile, he was also involved in Sir Robert's theatrical ventures. When the English theaters were reopened after their suppression by the Puritans, it was Sir Robert Howard who joined with Thomas Killigrew to construct a new building for the Theatre Royal company. For that company, Dryden wrote his first play, a comedy titled *The Wild Gallant* (pr. 1663, pb. 1669). Although the play was not successful, it did start Dryden on his career as a dramatist. The playwright would go on to create comedies, tragedies, tragicomedies, and operas.

After the production of a rhymed tragicomedy and a collaboration with Howard, *The Indian Queen* (pr. 1664, pb. 1665), a highly successful and lavishly staged play about Montezuma, Dryden wrote *The Indian Emperor: Or, The Conquest of Mexico by the Spaniards* (pr. 1665, pb. 1667), which also dealt with the Aztecs. In it appeared Nell Gwyn, who was to become a famous actress and the favorite mistress of Charles II. At this point, bubonic plague hit London, sending the Drydens fleeing to the country. After the Great Fire burned much of London in 1666, Dryden wrote one of his finest poems, *Annus Mirabilis* (1667), which celebrated the incontestable courage of Charles and his leadership of the country in times of crisis.

As the decade concluded, Dryden's fortunes continued to rise. Financially, he was doing so well that he could lend a considerable sum to Charles II. His plays were successful. In 1668, he was created poet laureate of England (there had been others who were informally considered poets laureate by virtue of a royal stipend, but Dryden was the first to hold the official title). Shortly afterward, he was made historiographer royal, with a sizable pension. In 1670, the ten-act *The Conquest of Granada by the Spaniards, Part I* (pr. 1670, pb. 1672), Dryden's most famous heroic play, was the talk of London. Meanwhile, Dryden defended his literary practice with critical works that are still among the most lucid ever produced. *Of Dramatic Poesie: An Essay* (1668) presented various aesthetic viewpoints in dialogue form, arguing about whether ancient or contemporary works, French or English, were superior. "A Defence of *An Essay of Dramatic Poesy*" (1668) followed later in the year.

Although he and his works were criticized and satirized—for example, in *The Rehearsal* (pr. 1671, pb. 1672), by George Villiers, second duke of Buckingham—Dryden continued to write successful plays and criticism. *All for Love: Or, The World Well Lost* (pr. 1677, pb. 1678), perhaps his finest heroic tragedy, deals with Marc Antony's conflict between love and honor, represented by his Egyptian mistress Cleopatra and his virtuous Roman wife Octavia. The following year's production was not notable, perhaps because the Theatre Royal, with which Dryden had been so long associated, was in the process of disintegration.

Meanwhile, Dryden found means of retaliating against his enemies. In his satirical poem *Mac Flecknoe: Or, A Satyre upon the True-Blew-Protestant Poet, T. S.* (wr. 1678, pb. 1682), he attacked Thomas Shadwell and other inferior writers. With *Absalom and Achitophel, Part I* (1681), Dryden turned to a political subject, satirizing the opponents of Charles II who had plotted to remove Charles from the throne and to replace him with his illegitimate son, the duke of Monmouth. Although the topical references in the poem require some knowledge of Restoration political and religious parties, the character-types are timeless, from the Machiavellian Achitophel to his mindless, egotistical puppet Absalom, from the Bible-quoting fanatics to the ignorant, irrational followers of the elusive Inner Light—indeed, to all the disloyal groups in England.

Dryden's preoccupation with the need for order prompted his defense of the Anglican Established Church, *Religio Laici* (1682). In 1685, Charles II died, acknowledging Roman Catholicism on his deathbed, and his Roman Catholic brother James II came to the throne. Late that year, Dryden became a Roman Catholic. He defended his new faith, at the expense of Anglicanism, in *The Hind and the Panther* (1687). Dryden has often been accused of having changed his religion when-

ever his rulers changed theirs. Certainly he moved from Puritanism to mainstream Anglicanism to Roman Catholicism at convenient times. It should be pointed out, however, that when James II revealed his stubborn intolerance and was dethroned in favor of the Protestants William III and Mary II, Dryden did not return to Anglicanism. As a result, he lost the posts of poet laureate and historiographer royal, along with considerable income.

In the last eleven years of his life, Dryden depended on the theater and on translation for much of his income. He wrote two tragedies, a comedy, an opera, a tragicomedy, and a masque. He translated works by Juvenal, Persius, Ovid, Tacitus, Geoffrey Chaucer, and Giovanni Boccaccio. In addition, he wrote odes and short poems, as well as publishing a volume of fables. His translation of *The Works of Vergil* (1697), which is still much admired, was a great financial success. Living in London, Dryden presided at Will's Coffee House, where writers thronged to pay him homage. From time to time, he returned to Northamptonshire for a round of visits with relatives. His health, however, was declining. Although he continued to work, after 1697 he was seldom well. In the spring of 1700, his condition worsened, and on May 12, Dryden died. On May 13, his funeral procession, including more than one hundred coaches, moved slowly through London to Westminster Abbey, where he was buried next to Chaucer, whom he had always loved.

SIGNIFICANCE

The Restoration was the Age of Dryden. He towered above his contemporaries, more than Alexander Pope in the first part of the following century or Samuel Johnson in the last. Furthermore, Dryden was the major influence on the neoclassicists of the eighteenth century, and after the heroic couplet went out of fashion, Dryden's translations and his criticism continued to be models of their kind.

In a period of religious and political conflict, when schemers, fanatics, and visionaries continued to threaten not only the throne but also the rule of reason itself, Dryden's voice urged careful skepticism in thought, sanity in decision, and decorum and dignity in action. His poetic practice mirrored his mind. It was Dryden who established the heroic couplet as a means of distilling passion and speculation into a brief, clear truth. It was he, too, who adapted the heroic couplet to highly effective satire, which could sum up venality, irrationality, or stupidity in two or four lines.

Dryden's continuing self-criticism is exemplified by the fact that he was willing to change his own practice;

DRYDEN'S MAJOR WORKS

1659 *Heroic Stanzas*

1660 *Astraea Redux*

1662 "To My Lord Chancellor"

1663 *The Wild Gallant*

1664 *The Indian Queen* (with Sir Robert Howard)

1664 *The Rival Ladies*

1664-1700 *Prologues and Epilogues*

1665 *The Indian Emperor: Or, The Conquest of Mexico by the Spaniards*

1667 *Annus Mirabilis*

1667 *Secret Love: Or, The Maiden Queen*

1667 *Sir Martin Mar-All: Or, The Feign'd Innocence* (with William Cavendish, duke of Newcastle; adaptation of Molière's *L'Étourdi*)

1667 *The Tempest: Or, The Enchanted Island* (with Sir William Davenant; adaptation of William Shakespeare's play)

1668 "A Defence of *An Essay of Dramatic Poesy*"

1668 *An Evening's Love: Or, The Mock Astrologer* (adaptation of Thomas Corneille's *Le Feint Astrologue*)

1668 *Of Dramatic Poesie: An Essay*

1669 *Tyrannic Love: Or, The Royal Martyr*

1670 *The Conquest of Granada by the Spaniards, Part I*

1671 *The Conquest of Granada by the Spaniards, Part II*

1671 "Preface to *An Evening's Love: Or, The Mock Astrologer*"

1672 *Marriage à la Mode*

1672 "Of Heroic Plays: An Essay"

1672 *The Assignation: Or, Love in a Nunnery*

1673 *Amboyna: Or, The Cruelties of the Dutch to the English Merchants*

1675 *Aureng-Zebe*

1677 "The Author's Apology for Heroic Poetry and Poetic License"

1677 *The State of Innocence, and Fall of Man*, pb. 1677 (libretto; adaptation of John Milton's *Paradise Lost*)

1677 *All for Love: Or, The World Well Lost*

1678 "Preface to *All for Love*"

1678 *The Kind Keeper: Or, Mr. Limberham*

1678 *Oedipus* (with Nathaniel Lee)

1679 "The Grounds of Criticism in Tragedy"

1679 *Troilus and Cressida: Or, Truth Found Too Late*

1680 *Ovid's Epistles* (translation)

1680 *The Spanish Friar: Or, The Double Discovery*

1681 *Absalom and Achitophel, Part I*

1682 *Absalom and Achitophel, Part II* (with Nahum Tate)

1682 *The Duke of Guise* (with Lee)

1682 *The Medall: A Satyre Against Sedition*

1682 *Mac Flecknoe: Or, A Satyre upon the True-Blew-Protestant Poet, T. S.*

1682 *Religio Laici*

1684 *The History of the League* (translation of Louis Maimbourg's *Histoire de la Ligue*)

1685 *Albion and Albanius* (libretto; music by Louis Grabu)

1685 "Preface to *Sylvae*"

1685 *Threnodia Augustalis*

1687 *The Hind and the Panther*

1687 "A Song for St. Cecilia's Day"

1688 *Britannia Rediviva*

1688 *The Life of St. Francis Xavier*, 1688 (translation of Dominique Bouhours's *La Vie de Saint François Xavier*)

1689 *Don Sebastian, King of Portugal*

1690 *Amphitryon: Or, The Two Socia's*

1691 *King Arthur: Or, The British Worthy* (libretto; music by Henry Purcell)

1692 *Cleomenes, the Spartan Hero*

1692 *Eleonora*

1693 *A Discourse Concerning the Original and Progress of Satire*

1693 "Dedication of *Examen Poeticum*"

1693 *The Satires of Juvenal and Persius* (translation)

1694 "To My Dear Friend Mr. Congreve"

1694 *Love Triumphant: Or, Nature Will Prevail*

1695 "A Parallel of Poetry and Painting"

1697 *Alexander's Feast: Or, The Power of Music, an Ode in Honor of St. Cecilia's Day*

1697 "Dedication of the *Aeneis*"

1697 *The Works of Vergil* (translation)

1700 "To My Honour'd Kinsman, John Driden"

1700 "Preface to *Fables Ancient and Modern*"

1700 *The Secular Masque* (masque)

1711 "Heads of an Answer to Rymer"

when he decided that the couplet was not appropriate for heroic tragedy, he admitted his earlier mistake and wrote *All for Love* in blank verse. Operating out of his profound knowledge of the classics and of Renaissance writers, Dryden analyzed and synthesized, rather than imitating. Thus his odes differ in form and subject from their classical models. Original and magnificent, they became models for the writers of the eighteenth century.

The precision of Dryden's mind was also evident in his prose works. As a translator, he was accurate in tone, as well as in meaning. Thus his 1697 translation of Vergil's *Georgics* (c. 37-29 B.C.E.; English translation, 1589) is still believed to recreate the original as well as any translation can do. As a critic, Dryden was brilliant and lucid. Making his own evaluations of earlier writers, he did much to convince his own age of the glories of Chaucer and the Elizabethans, who should not be jettisoned, he believed, simply because they were not neoclassical. Again, his emphasis was rational: Critics should see the whole, not the parts, the work itself, not their own prejudices.

Although Dryden's integrity has been questioned because of his changing religious allegiances, biographers now believe that his life was as honest as his works. Loathing anarchy, whether literary, political, or religious, Dryden did not, however, find order by settling into a narrow rigidity. His willingness to change as his reason prompted is illustrated by the years of religious questioning that preceded his final conversion. His courage, once he was convinced, is attested by the years when, having found the order that he had sought, he stood firm.

—*Rosemary M. Canfield Reisman*

FURTHER READING

Dryden, John. *The Letters of John Dryden: With Letters Addressed to Him.* Edited by Charles E. Ward. Durham, N.C.: Duke University Press, 1942. This slender volume contains the few letters of Dryden that are extant, along with careful scholarly notes by the author of a Dryden biography.

Fisk, Deborah Payne, ed. *The Cambridge Companion to English Restoration Theatre.* New York: Cambridge University Press, 2000. Selection of essays about theater, performance, and the various types of plays produced in Restoration England.

Hammond, Paul. *John Dryden: A Literary Life.* New York: St. Martin's Press, 1991. One of the titles in the Literary Lives Series.

Miner, Earl, ed. *John Dryden.* Athens: Ohio University Press, 1972. Essays on Dryden by major critics, including Jean H. Hagstrum, John Loftis, and Miner himself. Topics range from the political climate that produced *Absalom and Achitophel* to Dryden's translations and his comedies. A major collection.

Owen, Susan J. *Restoration Theatre and Crisis.* New York: Oxford University Press, 1996. Describes how works by Dryden, Aphra Behn, and other playwrights both reflected and intervened in the highly politicized environment of Restoration theater.

Schilling, Bernard N., ed. *Dryden: A Collection of Critical Essays.* Englewood Cliffs, N.J.: Prentice-Hall, 1963. Among others, includes T. S. Eliot's important essay on Dryden and Louis I. Bredvold's "The Intellectual Milieu of John Dryden." Some of the essays deal with single poetic works; particularly recommended are Earl Wasserman on "To My Honor'd Friend Dr. Charleton" and E. M. W. Tillyard on the ode to Anne Killigrew.

Ward, Charles E. *The Life of John Dryden.* Chapel Hill: University of North Carolina Press, 1961. The standard biography of Dryden, this work is clear, scholarly, and extremely readable. Much interesting material was relegated to the notes, so that the narrative itself would proceed without digression. Indispensable for an understanding of the writer and his works.

Winn, James Anderson. *John Dryden and His World.* New Haven, Conn.: Yale University Press, 1987. Winn used public records, recollections of Dryden's contemporaries and friends, and Dryden's works to compile this biography.

Zwicker, Steven N., ed. *The Cambridge Companion to John Dryden.* New York: Cambridge University Press, 2004. Collection of essays examining Dryden's role as a poet, dramatist, and commentator, Dryden's London, Restoration theater, and Augustan culture.

SEE ALSO: Charles I; Charles II (of England); First Earl of Clarendon; Oliver Cromwell; Nell Gwyn; James II; Mary II; Duke of Monmouth; William III.

RELATED ARTICLES in *Great Events from History: The Seventeenth Century, 1601-1700:* 1601-1672: Rise of Scientific Societies; December 6, 1648-May 19, 1649: Establishment of the English Commonwealth; May, 1659-May, 1660: Restoration of Charles II; Spring, 1665-Fall, 1666: Great Plague in London; September 2-5, 1666: Great Fire of London.

SIR ANTHONY VAN DYCK
Flemish painter

Along with Rubens, van Dyck was one of the major Flemish artists of the seventeenth century. Recognized as a painter of portraits and religious subjects, he also was known for his etchings and landscape watercolors. He was knighted and appointed court painter to Charles I of England.

BORN: March 22, 1599; Antwerp, Spanish Netherlands (now in Belgium)
DIED: December 9, 1641; London, England
ALSO KNOWN AS: Anthonie/Antonie/Antoon/Anton van Dijck
AREA OF ACHIEVEMENT: Art

EARLY LIFE

Anthony van Dyck was born the seventh of twelve children. His father, Frans, was a prosperous Antwerp textile merchant. His mother, Maria Cuypers, was known for her skill in embroidery. In 1609, the ten-year-old Anthony was apprenticed to one of the city's leading painters, Hendrick van Balen. It is speculated that the young artist was working independently prior to his acceptance as a painting master in the Guild of St. Luke in 1618. One of his first known works, *Self-Portrait* (1613-1614), was executed when he was about fourteen or fifteen. It displayed a sense of immediacy and technical facility.

Antwerp's preeminent painter, Peter Paul Rubens, recognized Anthony's talent. The celebrated master had developed a powerful visual language noted for heroic nude figures, dynamic compositions, and intense drama that appealed to secular rulers as well as leaders of the Counter-Reformation. He had an overwhelming impact on the art of his time and particularly on the young van Dyck, who could blend his work seamlessly with that of the older artist. The date of Anthony's entry into Rubens's studio is unknown, but it is believed that they were collaborating on works from about 1615 to 1620.

Van Dyck enjoyed early success in painting religious subjects. *Saint Jerome*, his first known large-scale religious painting, was produced about 1615. Many of these early works were altered versions of the compositions of Rubens. This was exemplified by van Dyck's early apostles series as well as his composition for *The Emperor Theodosius Is Forbidden by Saint Ambrose to Enter Milan Cathedral* (c. 1619-1620).

The young artist struggled to emerge from Rubens's shadow. Whereas the older master visualized figures in the round, van Dyck became more interested in surface pattern and texture. When he went to England in late 1620 to serve as a painter for King James I, he had the opportunity to study original Italian works. Paintings by Titian and other sixteenth century Venetian masters had an immediate impact on his style.

Few of van Dyck's works from this period are documented, but characteristics of the mature artist began to emerge. In his portrait of *Thomas Howard, Second Earl of Arundel* (1620-1621), van Dyck used a freer technique and adopted Venetian portrait backdrops. Although it was a modest work, it showed van Dyck's interest in portraying casual aristocratic elegance.

LIFE'S WORK

In 1621, van Dyck returned to Antwerp, where he produced some of his best early works. He broke with the conventions of Flemish portrait painting and began to portray distinctive personalities characterized by their elegant movements and detailed costumes. Neutral backgrounds were discarded for landscape vistas. Curtains and accessories were introduced to enrich the settings. These changes were exemplified in the portrayal of *Isabella Brandt* (1621), the young wife of Rubens. This is considered to be among the best of van Dyck's pre-Italian portraits.

From 1621 to 1627, van Dyck resided in Italy where he visited major art centers such as Genoa, Rome, Venice, Florence, and Palermo. His stay was documented in his sketchbook, now in the collection of the British Museum. By this time, van Dyck was recognized as a painter of both portraits and religious subjects. Major works from this period included the seated portrait of *Cardinal Guido Bentivoglio* (1623). He also executed *Madonna of the Rosary*, an altarpiece that he started in 1624 for the Oratorio del Rosario in Palermo and completed in 1627. It is regarded as one of the outstanding religious works of his Italian period. This painting, like many of his portrayals of the Madonna and Child, reflected the coloristic and expressive refinement of Titian's Venetian altarpieces.

Van Dyck was in Genoa from 1625 to 1627. With commissions from local patricians, he further developed his portrait style. He depicted his subjects with slender figures and expressive hands. Although they were accurate likenesses, they had a look of remote grandeur and ease. His subjects were richly dressed, with careful renderings of lace, silk, satin, and velvet. They were posed against the backdrop of their opulent palaces and gardens. Cascades of background drapery created a sense of movement. These characteristics were exemplified in his multifigure depiction of *The Lomellini Family* (1625-1627).

Van Dyck was back in Antwerp from 1627 to 1632. Commissions for altarpieces, large-scale portraits, smaller devotional images, and mythologies were so numerous he had to employ assistants. Altarpieces from this period included the large-scale *Saint Augustine in Ecstasy* (1628), and the smaller *Vision of the Blessed Herman Joseph* (1630). He also painted *The Crucified Christ with Saint Dominic and Saint Catherine of Siena* (1629), considered to be among his best works. Antwerp was a Catholic city, and van Dyck's intense emotionalism and mystical fervor reflected the religious intensity fostered by the Counter-Reformation.

While in Antwerp he was appointed court painter to Archduchess Isabella. His noted technical facility, smooth flowing brush strokes, and sensuous textures were evident in portraits such as *Maria Louisa de Tassis*

(c. 1629) and *Philippe le Roy* (1632). Although each work was distinctive, he developed some standardization of form and created a repertoire of portrait types.

In 1632, van Dyck returned to England and the highly cultivated court of Charles I. The king, who admired the artist's social graces as well as his work, appointed him to the position of principal painter. In addition to his salary and commissions, van Dyck was knighted, given a studio on the Thames at Blackfriars, and provided with a summer residence.

He worked in Antwerp and Brussels in 1634. At this time he began a series of small, monochrome portraits of famous contemporaries. They included princes, military commanders, politicians, scholars, artists, and collectors. He etched many of these himself. Plates of his drawings were issued individually, but the works were published posthumously as *Icones principum vivorum doctorum pictorum . . .* (1645), more commonly known as *The Iconography*. It became an important visual record of the time.

Van Dyck returned to England early in 1635. Working primarily on portraits of Charles I, Queen Henri-

Engraved depiction of Sir Anthony van Dyck painting his famous portrait of King Charles's family. (F. R. Niglutsch)

etta Maria, and members of the aristocracy, he devised additional ways to dignify his subjects. *Charles I on Horseback* (c. 1637-1638) was reminiscent of the statue of Marcus Aurelius in Rome and Titian's portraits of Charles V. *Charles I at the Hunt* (c. 1635) portrayed the king with an air of matchless elegance and unquestioned authority. Van Dyck depicted the royal children with great sensitivity; although they were formally posed, he captured their innocence and charm. He also painted *Cupid and Psyche* (c. 1637), one of his few mythologies. The sensuous figures, delicate colorations, and rich textures were highly acclaimed.

In 1639, he married Lady Mary Ruthven, lady-in-waiting to Queen Henrietta Maria. The following year the political situation in England was disintegrating and van Dyck, possibly preparing to re-establish himself on the Continent, undertook a series of travels between Antwerp, Paris, and London. He suffered ill health, perhaps from tuberculosis, and returned to London. His daughter Justiniana was born just before his death. He died December 9, 1641 at the age of forty-two and was honored with burial in St. Paul's Cathedral in London.

SIGNIFICANCE

Although van Dyck created dramatic religious works, he is remembered primarily for his genius as a portrait painter. He borrowed techniques that had been pioneered by artists such as Titian and Rubens, but he developed an elegant portrait style that had international impact. He was a brilliant colorist, combined formality with a sense of ease, and dignified his subjects, yet managed to capture their individuality. Opulent settings and suggestions of movement made them seem resplendent and alive.

Van Dyck transformed portraiture wherever he worked; painters throughout Europe emulated his style. He provided English history with an image of aristocratic society in the early part of the seventeenth century. His style resounded in works of great eighteenth century English portraitists such as Thomas Gainsborough and Joshua Reynolds. Whether painting the rulers and aristocrats of the Netherlands, Italy, or England, he depicted the celebrities of his time and created a testament to the elegance of seventeenth century aristocratic and courtly life.

—*Cassandra Lee Tellier*

FURTHER READING

Blake, Robin. *Anthony van Dyck: A Life, 1599-1641*. Chicago: Ivan R. Dee, 2000. A carefully researched chronicle about the painter's life and work. Notes, bibliography, and index.

Brown, Christopher, and Hans Vlieghe. *Van Dyck, 1599-1641*. New York: Rizzoli, 1999. This book was published to coincide with the exhibition of van Dyck's major works in Antwerp and London. It includes high quality reproductions, comparative illustrations, and essays on the development of van Dyck's work. Also includes a chronology, a bibliography, and an index.

Depauw, Carl, and Ger Luijten. *Anthony van Dyck as a Printmaker*. New York: Rizzoli, 1999. This work discusses van Dyck as a gifted draughtsman and printmaker. Includes reproductions, comparative illustrations, and a bibliography.

Meij, A. W. F. M. *Rubens, Jordaens, Van Dyck, and Their Circle*. Rotterdam, the Netherlands: NAI, 2001. A study of drawings by seventeenth century Flemish masters from the Museum Boijmans van Beuningen in Rotterdam. Generously illustrated with pertinent essays.

Wheelock, Arthur K., Jr. *Dutch Paintings of the Seventeenth Century*. New York: Oxford University Press, 1995. Catalog of the collection of seventeenth century Dutch paintings at the National Gallery of Art in Washington, D.C., including Hals and many of his contemporaries.

SEE ALSO: Charles I; Frans Hals; Henrietta Maria; James I; Nicolas-Claude Fabri de Peiresc; Rembrandt; Peter Paul Rubens; Jan Vermeer.

RELATED ARTICLES in *Great Events from History: The Seventeenth Century, 1601-1700*: c. 1601-1620: Emergence of Baroque Art; March, 1629-1640: "Personal Rule" of Charles I.

JOHN ELIOT

English-born colonial American theologian and missionary

The Puritan clergyman Eliot is known as the Apostle to the Indians for his close to fifty years of work among the Indians of Massachusetts. He assisted in the production of the first book published in North America, the 1640 Bay Psalm Book, *and translated the first Bible printed in North America, an Algonquian language version.*

BORN: August 5, 1604 (baptized); Widford, Hertfordshire, England

DIED: May 21, 1690; Roxbury, Massachusetts Bay Colony (now in Massachusetts)

AREAS OF ACHIEVEMENT: Religion and theology, linguistics

EARLY LIFE

John Eliot was the third of seven children born to Bennett Eliot and Lettese Eliot. He was baptized August 5, 1604, in the parish church of Saint John the Baptist. Within six years of John's birth, the Eliot family moved to the village of Nazeing, Essex. At the time, many of the clergy and laity of Essex felt strong sympathy for the Puritan cause, a fact that would prove significant for the later development of Eliot's religious beliefs.

In January of the year Eliot was born, King James I of England refused to allow Puritan reforms within the established Church of England. After the accession of Charles I in 1625, the situation worsened for the Puritans: The archbishop of Canterbury, Archbishop William Laud, held that conformity to the practices of the Church of England was not optional. Although many Puritan leaders did not see themselves as separatists from the established church, they nevertheless saw exile from England as their only alternative. The colonists who founded the Massachusetts Bay Colony in 1629 belonged to this group of nonseparatist Puritans, and many Puritans from the County of Essex who moved to the colony about the same time as Eliot did were motivated by the same religious reasons.

Eliot lived with his family in Nazeing until 1618, when he entered Jesus College, Cambridge University. He received a B.A. in 1622. The master of Jesus College at the time was the brother of Lancelot Andrewes, Roger Andrewes, who had helped translate the 1611 King James Bible. In later life, Eliot demonstrated his continued respect for his school by sending his alma mater an inscribed copy of the Bible that he had translated into the Algonquian language from the King James Bible.

There is some debate as to where and when Eliot was ordained a clergyman, but it seems likely that he received ordination from the bishop of Ely before he departed for New England in 1631. After his ordination and before his journey to Massachusetts, Eliot served for a time as an usher in the Puritan Thomas Hooker's private school in Little Baddow. In July, 1630, Hooker fled Archbishop Laud's persecution for the safety of Holland. In the summer of 1631, Eliot sailed to New England aboard the ship *Lyon* to begin a new chapter of his life.

LIFE'S WORK

Eliot is best remembered for his work among the Native Americans of Massachusetts; however, from his arrival in New England on November 2, 1631, until his death in 1690, Eliot primarily served as a clergyman for the Puritan settlers. After his arrival, he conducted worship and preached for the church of Boston until its minister returned from England in May, 1632. He then became the second pastor of the church in Roxbury, Massachusetts, where he would remain for fifty-eight years.

By the time Eliot assumed his post in Roxbury, a number of settlers from Nazeing had arrived, including Eliot's fiancée, Hanna Mumford, and several of Eliot's sisters and their husbands. Later, they would be joined by Eliot's brother Philip. Eliot and his fiancée were married in Roxbury's first recorded marriage ceremony in October, 1632.

Eliot was very much involved in the education of the young in Roxbury and helped found the Roxbury Latin School (Eliot's brother Philip was the first schoolmaster). In 1637, he was involved with other Boston-area clergy in the trial, excommunication, and banishment of Anne Hutchinson on charges of sedition. Eliot also contributed to the first book published in North America, the *Bay Psalm Book* (1640; printed by Stephen Day in Cambridge). The *Bay Psalm Book* provided translations in English meter of the entire Psalter for use in congregational singing.

From the initial days of the founding of the Massachusetts Bay Colony, the settlers had expressed interest in performing Christian missionary work among the Massachusetts Indians. The seal of the colony portrayed an Indian speaking these words: "Come over and help us." The colony's charter enjoined the colonists to bring to the Native Americans the "knowledge and obedience of the onlie true God and Savior of mankinde." After learn-

John Eliot. (Library of Congress)

and in 1658, he published Algonquian translations of the Book of Exodus and the Gospel of Matthew. Interestingly, two specially bound copies of Eliot's Indian Bible were presented to King James II, whose grandfather (James I) had authorized the translation of the Bible Eliot used as the basis for his Algonquian version, and under whose father (Charles I) Eliot had felt compelled to leave England.

The local New England clergy supported Eliot throughout his missionary work, and he received support from England through the Society for the Propagation of the Gospel in New England and Parts Adjacent in North America, established by an act of Parliament in 1649. This organization was the first Protestant missionary society and provided funds for supplies, Eliot's translation work, and the education of Indian students. For 120 years, this missionary society worked among the native peoples of New England.

In 1650, the first village of "praying Indians" was organized. The Christian Indians of Nonantum moved to Natick and were organized by Eliot around Old Testament patterns. A common assumption of the seventeenth century New England Puritans was that the native peoples around them were the lost ten tribes

ing the Algonquian language from an Indian named Cockenoe, Eliot started preaching to the Massachusetts Indians in the fall of 1646. He began modestly, in the village of Nonantum (now Newton) within the wigwam of an Indian chieftain named Waban. In the Algonquian language, Eliot read a Bible verse (Ezekiel 37:9), preached, and asked some theological questions of those present.

Eliot's preliminary effort was well received, and it was the beginning of many years' work among the Massachusetts Indians. In the course of his work with the Algonquian language, Eliot produced *The Indian Grammar* (1666), an incomplete introductory grammar of the language of the Massachusetts Indians. Eliot's work with the Algonquian language was crowned with the publication in 1663 of his Indian Bible, printed by Samuel Green and Marmaduke Johnson in Cambridge. Eliot had translated the psalms into the Algonquian language in 1653,

of Israel. Whether Eliot fully accepted this theory is not known, but in any event, he found in the Old Testament story of Jethro's advice to Moses a model for the villages of Christian Indians that sprang up under his guidance. Senior members of the community were chosen to be leaders of groups of ten, fifty, and a hundred individuals. The towns pledged a "civil covenant" that bound them together as a Christian community.

In outward appearance, these Native American towns were organized on a European model. They had meeting houses, organized streets, and even some English-style homes, although the majority of the Indians preferred wigwams. Schools were opened, and English was taught along with European crafts so that the villages, which were self-governing under Massachusetts law, could be self-supporting. From these villages, Eliot drew and trained preachers and teachers to help catechize and lead worship in the communities. In all, Eliot helped organize fourteen Christian villages, which grew to contain around four thousand individuals. These communities eventually became casualties in Metacom's War (1675-1676, also known as King Philip's War) during which the followers of Metacom (or King Philip), the son of Massachusetts Indian chief Massasoit, fought the English settlers. The four Christian Indian villages that were not destroyed during the conflict were not able to recover economically once it was over. Nevertheless, Eliot's work among the Indians continued. A second edition of his Indian Bible was published in 1685 to replace those lost in Metacom's War. Eliot died in Roxbury on May 21, 1690.

SIGNIFICANCE

In 1894, 204 years after his death, a stained-glass window was dedicated to the memory of Eliot in the church of St. John the Baptist, Widford, England. To this day, he is remembered as the Apostle to the Indians for his missionary work in Massachusetts.

Eliot is also remembered for his enlightened views on the rights of the Indians. His attitude toward the Massachusetts Indians and their plight stands in contrast to the indifference or outright hostility toward the Indians displayed by many of his fellow New England Puritans. He took the time and energy to learn their language and customs. He helped the villages of Christianized Indians become self-sufficient and taught them trades that made them less reliant on the English colonists. He taught individual Indians to read both English and Algonquian and promoted the development of Native American schools. With his Indian grammar, the two editions of his Indian Bible, and the publication of a number of other works in the language of the Massachusetts Indians, Eliot helped foster the study of Indian languages and has provided researchers with invaluable insights into the linguistic heritage of one branch of Native American peoples.

—*J. Francis Watson*

FURTHER READING

Adams, Nehemiah. *The Life of John Eliot: With an Account of the Early Missionary Efforts Among the Indians of New England.* Boston: Massachusetts Sabbath School Society, 1847. Offers details of Eliot's work in New England, plus an appendix with samples of his correspondence.

Clark, Michael P., ed. *The Eliot Tracts: With Letters from John Eliot to Thomas Thorowgood and Richard Baxter.* Westport, Conn.: Praeger, 2003. The majority of these tracts were written by Eliot and published in London between 1643 and 1671. The tracts describe British missionary activity in New England.

Cogley, Richard W. *John Eliot's Mission to the Indians Before King Philip's War.* Cambridge, Mass.: Harvard University Press, 1999. A comprehensive examination of the Puritans' mission in New England, combining an analysis of Eliot's theological writings with a historical account of the mission's development. Includes biographies of Native Americans who accepted the mission, histories of settlement towns, and an appendix of primary sources.

Eliot, John. *John Eliot and the Indians, 1652-1657: Being Letters Addressed to Rev. Jonathan Hanmer of Barnstaple, England.* Edited by Wilberforce Eames. New York: The Adams and Grace Press, 1915. Provides details of Eliot's work with the Indians and of his relations with neighboring clergy and the Society for the Propagation of the Gospel in New England. Includes facsimiles of title pages from a number of Eliot's published works.

_____. *John Eliot's Indian Dialogues: A Study in Cultural Interaction.* Edited by Henry W. Bowden and James P. Rhonda. Contributions in American History 88. Westport, Conn.: Greenwood Press, 1980. Contains the text of Eliot's "training manual," intended for use by Indian preachers and teachers. An introduction places this work in context to help readers understand seventeenth century Puritan and Indian cultural interactions.

Moore, Martin. *Memoirs of the Life and Character of Rev. John Eliot, Apostle of the N. A. Indians.* Boston: T. Bedlington, 1822. An insightful account of Eliot's work written by a minister of the church in Natick, Massachusetts. Presents a number of letters from Eliot about his work with the Indians.

Tinker, George E. *Missionary Conquest: The Gospel and Native American Cultural Genocide.* Minneapolis: Fortress Press, 1993. A revisionist history, maintaining that missionaries reaped personal gain from policies of colonial genocide. Focuses on four missionaries, including John Eliot in a chapter entitled "John Eliot: Conversion, Colonialism, and the Oppression of Language."

Winslow, Ola Elizabeth. *John Eliot: "Apostle to the Indians."* Boston: Houghton Mifflin, 1968. A very insightful biography, offering information on Eliot's upbringing, his Puritan background, and his work in Massachusetts. Has a useful appendix of Eliot's published works.

ELIZABETH OF BOHEMIA
German philosopher

Elizabeth of Bohemia is best known for her correspondence with the French philosopher Descartes, in which she challenged his dualist interactionism. She is an example of a seventeenth century woman who succeeded in overcoming the barriers that prevented women from engaging in rational discourse.

BORN: December 26, 1618; Heidelberg, Lower Palatinate (now in Germany)
DIED: February 8, 1680; Herford, Brandenburg (now in Germany)
AREA OF ACHIEVEMENT: Philosophy

EARLY LIFE

Elizabeth of Bohemia was born into an illustrious family. Her parents were Elizabeth Stuart, the daughter of King James I of England, and Frederick V, elector of the Palatinate. Her father's mother was a member of the Dutch House of Orange. Frederick was king of Bohemia, briefly, but was ousted in 1620 by the same Protestant rebels who had installed him. The dethronement of Frederick and the confiscation of his lands resulted in one of the early campaigns of the Thirty Years' War (1618-1648), which brought death and destruction to many German principalities.

Elizabeth's parents and her older brother escaped to The Hague (now in the Netherlands), under the protection of the prince of Orange, while she and her younger brother remained with their grandmother and aunt. In 1628, the two children joined their parents in Holland and were sent to Leyden to be educated by royal tutors and professors at the university there. Elizabeth excelled in her studies, which included ancient and modern languages, logic, history, and mathematics.

In 1632, Elizabeth's father died while involved in attempts to regain his kingdom. Thereafter, her mother, who showed little interest in her daugh-

ters, became a champion of the Protestant cause. At the age of sixteen, Elizabeth received a marriage proposal from King Władysław IV Vasa of Poland, but she refused because she would have had to convert to Catholicism. Elizabeth and, later, her much younger sister Sophie, both of whom were fascinated by philosophy, participated in the intellectual circle hosted by her mother in their home. Guests included poet and government official Constantijn Huygens (1596-1648), philos-

Early seventeenth century portrait of Elizabeth of Bohemia. (The Granger Collection, New York)

opher René Descartes (1596-1650), and philosopher Franciscus Mercurius van Helmont (1614?-1699).

LIFE'S WORK

Descartes included six sets of objections and his replies in *Meditationes de prima philosophia* (1641; *Meditations on First Philosophy*, 1680). A mutual acquaintance informed Descartes that the intelligent, well-educated princess was interested in metaphysics, and the two met in 1642 or 1643. Their correspondence lasted from June of 1643 until 1649 and covered a number of philosophical topics, including the nature and relationship of the mind and body, ethics, free will and moral responsibility, God's existence and nature, and the emotions. Elizabeth's initial letters concerned Descartes's exposition of interactionist dualism in the *Meditations on First Philosophy*. In particular, she wrote that she could not understand how nonextended, nonphysical substance—the mind or soul—and physical, extended substance—body or matter—could causally affect each other. Descartes's answers did not satisfy her, so in July, 1643, she proposed her own solution: that the mind had some kind of extension and therefore could cause motion in material bodies. Descartes made no response to her idea.

In 1643, Elizabeth solved a difficult geometrical problem posed by Descartes. During the next year, Descartes traveled and oversaw the publication of *Principia philosophiae* (1644; *Principles of Philosophy*, 1983), which he dedicated to Princess Elizabeth. Elizabeth wrote one letter only during this period, but in characteristic fashion, she asked him for explanations of several points she found inconsistent. Although Descartes did not like criticism, their correspondence was quite friendly. It has been suggested that Descartes was in love with Elizabeth, but the differences in their ages, social class, and religion would have made a romantic relationship impossible.

Elizabeth's susceptibility to repeated illness concerned Descartes, concerns he expressed in his letters.

ELIZABETH OF BOHEMIA IN PASSIONATE CORRESPONDENCE WITH RENÉ DESCARTES

Princess Elizabeth of Bohemia's inquisitive, thoughtful, and extraordinary letters to René Descartes helped inspire him to write about the passions and mind/body dualism, for which he is especially known. Elizabeth's letter of May 16, 1643, her first to Descartes, questions his separating the thoughts of the mind from the actions and feelings of the body. Correspondence between the two continued for several years.

Princess Elizabeth (Letter of May 16, 1643): How can the soul of a man determine the spirits of his body so as to produce voluntary actions (given that the soul is only a thinking substance)?

Descartes (Letter of May 21, 1643): So I believe that up to now we have confused the idea of the power with which the soul acts in the body with the power by which one body acts in another body. And that we have attributed both the one and the other, not to the soul . . . but to various qualities of bodies, such as heaviness, heat, and others, which we have imagined to be real. . . .

Princess Elizabeth (Letter of September 13, 1645): I would like to see you define the passions, in order to know them better, because those who call them disturbances of the soul would persuade me that their force only consists in shattering and subjecting the reason if my reason didn't also show me that there are some that lead to rational actions.

Descartes (from *The Passions of the Soul*, 1649): I consider that all that which occurs or that happens anew, is by the philosophers, generally speaking, termed a passion. . . . [I]n order to understand the passions of the soul its functions must be distinguished from those of body. . . . [T]he heat and movement of the members proceed from the body, the thoughts from the soul.

Source: Letters excerpted in *The Princess and the Philosopher: Letters of Elisabeth of the Palatine to René Descartes*, by Andrea Nye (Lanham, Md.: Rowman & Littlefield, 1999), pp. 9, 19, 59. Descartes excerpt from *Passions* in *Descartes: Selections*, edited by Ralph M. Eaton (New York: Charles Scribner's Sons, 1927), pp. 361-363.

---

cause motion in material bodies. Descartes made no response to her idea.

Though not a physician, he attributed her fever of 1644 to sadness, that is, to depression, and he advocated the neo-Stoical view that a superior soul could overcome and control the passions (and thus her depression). Consistent with his dualism, Descartes recommended that Elizabeth separate rational thought from the corporeal functions of imagination and emotions and advised her to view her problems with rational detachment, perform her duties, and then seek enjoyments. She was preoccupied, however, because some of her family members were embroiled in both Continental wars and English politics. She also had to maintain her household and act as mother to her numerous siblings. So Elizabeth found it impossible to comply with Descartes's recommendations.

These issues led to another phase of their correspondence, which focused on the emotions and morality. For

Elizabeth, in stark contrast to Descartes, the soul and body were the same, and one could not so easily detach reason from passion. Moreover, she was concerned with the relationships between the self and others, topics she believed were not adequately treated by Descartes. Elizabeth did convince Descartes that his ethics required a theory of emotion to support it. He brought her a manuscript in March, 1646, which elaborated on the viewpoints he expressed in his letters to her. Elizabeth then asked him to clarify obscure points. In particular, she noted that passions do not occur in isolation, as Descartes seemed to think, but instead were connected with other passions, as love is associated with desire and either joy or sadness. One passion, in other words, led to another passion, and so forth. Furthermore, she inquired how Descartes came to believe that the general movements of the blood could account specifically for the five basic passions he identified.

Finally, she judged as inadequate the morality he espoused, in which reason must be used to *control* the passions, She argued that since life was unpredictable—and that some desires, such as the desire to live, were not grounded in free will—some passions therefore could not be easily controlled.

Elizabeth's troubles with her family multiplied during this period. Her mother was deeply in debt and still trying to regain the Palatine lands. In October, 1645, Elizabeth received the shocking news that her brother Edward had married the sister of the queen of Poland and had converted to Catholicism. In June of 1646, another brother, Philip, and several of his men killed a French captain who had boasted of successful dalliances with another sister, Louise, and with their mother. Threatened with arrest, Philip fled Holland and Elizabeth was banished to Berlin by her enraged mother, who believed that she had encouraged Philip to revenge the captain's insults and, thus, had brought infamy to the family.

The Thirty Years' War ended in 1648, and Elizabeth's family recovered part of its lost land. Her brother Charles and his wife moved to Heidelberg, where he formed an illicit liaison with another woman. Her uncle, English and Scottish king Charles I, was beheaded in England in 1649. Also in 1649, Descartes traveled to Sweden to tutor Queen Christina in philosophy, but he died a year later.

Unwilling to live in the house of her brother Charles, Elizabeth made arrangements to enter the Protestant convent in Herford, a retreat for aristocratic women and one of the four female ecclesiastical principalities in Germany. During her years there, she corresponded with

many notable individuals, including philosophers Nicolas de Malebranche, Henry More, Gottfried Wilhelm Leibniz, and Anne Conway, as well as the Quaker convert William Penn. She was abbess at the convent from 1667 until her death in 1680.

SIGNIFICANCE

Elizabeth of Bohemia did not publish her writings and refused to allow her letters to be part of a publication of Descartes's correspondence. Her letters were lost and did not resurface until the nineteenth century.

She is an important figure for several reasons. First, she raised objections to Descartes's interactionism and his views on the passions, on what makes a happy life, and on morality, to which, according to some scholars, he had inadequate responses. Moreover, she formulated views alternative to Descartes's interactionism and moral theories. In her own right she was a philosopher whose ideas require scholarly analysis. As the subject of much modern research, her life and ideas have been used to illustrate feminist ideologies that focus on the importance of subjectivity to thinking, in contrast to Descartes's insistence on objectivity in thinking and on questions of morality.

She represents the life of an intellectual woman during the seventeenth century, burdened by domestic duties while wanting to participate in the life of the mind, outside the university setting. In this regard, she is an example of Descartes's belief, unusual for the time perhaps, that reason is a human, and not an exclusively male, characteristic. Her responses to Descartes, however, were challenges to a tradition of philosophy that called for a life of reason separated from and unaffected by ordinary, daily life.

—*Kristen L. Zacharias*

FURTHER READING

Broad, Jacqueline. *Women Philosophers of the Seventeenth Century*. New York: Cambridge University Press, 2002. Chapter 1 presents an overview and critique of modern scholarship on Elizabeth and argues that Elizabeth's moral outlook was based not on her life experiences but on her metaphysics.

Findlen, Paula. "Ideas in the Mind: Gender and Knowledge in the Seventeenth Century." *Hypatia: A Journal of Feminist Philosophy* 17, no. 1 (Winter, 2002). Using modern critical editions of the writings of women in the seventeenth century, the author analyzes the works to explore the connections between gender and knowledge.

Graukroger, Stephen. *Descartes: An Intellectual Biography*. Oxford, England: Clarendon Press, 1995. A lengthy analysis of the development of Descartes's philosophy. Chapter 10 examines his correspondence with Elizabeth and how it influenced his *Les Passions de l'âme* (1649; *Passions of the Soul*, 1650).

Harth, Erica. *Cartesian Women: Versions and Subversions of Rational Discourse in the Old Regime*. Ithaca, N.Y.: Cornell University Press, 1992. Chapter 2 discusses the relationship between Descartes and Elizabeth and explains how Elizabeth came to be recognized as *cartésienne*, attempting to break the gender barrier against women participating in rational discourse during the seventeenth century.

Nye, Andrea. *The Princess and the Philosopher: Letters of Elisabeth of the Palatine to René Descartes*. New York: Rowman and Littlefield, 1999. Includes a translation of the letters written by Elizabeth to Descartes, along with a somewhat novelistic commentary that places them within contemporary cultural and political contexts.

Tollefsen, Deborah. "Princess Elisabeth and the Problem of Mind-Body Interaction." *Hypatia: A Journal of Feminist Philosophy* 14, no. 3 (1999): 59-77. A philosophical analysis of Elizabeth's metaphysics and her critique of Descartes.

SEE ALSO: Charles I; Christina; Anne Conway; René Descartes; Pierre de Fermat; Frederick V; Gottfried Wilhelm Leibniz; Ninon de Lenclos; Duchess of Newcastle; William Penn; Elena Cornaro Piscopia; Anna Maria van Schurman.

RELATED ARTICLE in *Great Events from History: The Seventeenth Century, 1601-1700*: 1637: Descartes Publishes His *Discourse on Method*.

ELIZABETH STUART
Queen of Bohemia (r. 1619-1620)

The daughter of King James I of England, Elizabeth married Palatine elector Frederick V in 1613. When she was exiled from the Palatinate and Bohemia in 1620, Elizabeth established herself as a symbol of the Protestant cause in Europe.

BORN: August 19, 1596; Falkland Castle, Fifeshire, Scotland

DIED: February 13, 1662; Leicester House, London, England

ALSO KNOWN AS: Elizabeth of Bohemia

AREA OF ACHIEVEMENT: Government and politics

EARLY LIFE

Elizabeth Stuart was the second child and oldest daughter of James VI of Scotland (later James I of England) and Anne of Denmark. She was placed in the care of Alexander—seventh Lord Livingston and, from 1600, the first earl of Linlithgow—and his wife, Helen, daughter of the eighth earl of Erroll. Elizabeth spent her early years at Linlithgow Palace, Scotland, a lovely residence midway between Stirling and Edinburgh.

When James was proclaimed king of England in 1603, Elizabeth was given a new guardian, Lady Frances Howard, widow of Henry Fitzgerald, eighth earl of Kildare, and wife of the eighth Lord Cobham. Lady Kildare's guardianship was over almost as soon as it began, however. Her husband was implicated in two plots against the throne, the Main Plot, a conspiracy that aimed at putting Arbella Stuart on the English throne instead of James, and the Bye Plot, a plan to kidnap the king and force him to repeal anti-Catholic laws. Elizabeth became the ward of Lord Harington of Exton and his wife Anne and resided at Combe Abbey. Her new guardians provided her with an excellent education, as is indicated by her surviving childhood letters, written in English, French, and Italian.

Elizabeth's marriage was important to England's foreign policy. Although her parents, especially her mother, may have favored a Spanish marriage, James accepted a Protestant, Frederick V, elector Palatine of the Rhine, as his daughter's suitor. Shortly before the wedding, Prince Henry, Elizabeth's beloved older brother, died on November 6, 1612. His tragic death raised the possibility that the marriage might be postponed and that Elizabeth would remain in England. Frederick assured James that the wedding must proceed as scheduled, and the couple was married on February 14, 1613. John Donne wrote an epithalamion for the occasion, and Shakespeare's *The Tempest* was performed as part of the wedding festivities. The choice to marry on Saint Valentine's Day was pointedly symbolic. According to her admiring contemporary, James Howell, Elizabeth, because of her "winning princely comportment," was known to her contemporaries as the Queen of Hearts.

LIFE'S WORK

Elizabeth was accompanied to her new home by her former guardians, Lord and Lady Harington; to Elizabeth's sorrow, Lord Harington became ill and died on the return journey. The new electress was welcomed to Heidelberg on June 17, 1613. Elizabeth had never managed her own household, and she incurred huge debts because of her generosity to servants and her expenditures on her wardrobe. During her residence in Germany, she mastered the language and later learned Dutch as well. She was then able to converse in six languages: English, French, Italian, German, Dutch, and Latin. Elizabeth's first child, Frederick Henry (1614-1629) was born on January 14, 1614; her second son, Charles Lewis followed on January 1, 1618, and her eldest daughter, Princess Elizabeth of Bohemia, was born of December 26 of that year.

In 1619, the Bohemian estates deposed Archduke Ferdinand II of Austria and offered Frederick the crown. Elizabeth was supposed to have pressed him to accept this offer because of her commitment to Protestantism, but this rumor was actually circulated by Elizabeth's enemies. Christian of Anhalt, Frederick's chief minister, was responsible for shaping foreign policy. The risk of taking the Bohemian crown was immense, because the deposed Bohemian king was a Habsburg, and the resources of both Spain and Austria would be used to oppose Frederick. Elizabeth was encouraged by George Abbott, archbishop of Canterbury, to believe that Frederick would enjoy the full support of England, but the promised support never materialized.

The royal couple left Heidelberg and arrived in Prague on October 31. Frederick was crowned king of Bohemia on November 4, and Elizabeth's coronation occurred a few days later. On December 18, 1619, Elizabeth gave birth to her fourth child, christened Rupert. Frederick and Elizabeth were nicknamed the Winter King and Queen by the Jesuits, who accurately prophesied that their rule would last only through the winter: When the spring came, they would vanish as the winter snows themselves melted.

Frederick probably counted too much on the support of Great Britain, Denmark, Holland, and the German Protestant princes. He was decisively defeated on November 8, 1620, at the Battle of the White Mountain near Prague. Frederick lost not only Bohemia, but also his own lands in the Palatinate; his capital at Heidelberg was overrun by Spanish troops. Elizabeth's fifth child,

Maurice, was born on January 16, 1621, as the couple fled to the Netherlands. Frederick and Elizabeth took refuge at The Hague, where they were supported by grants from the Dutch and English governments.

Elizabeth became a Protestant heroine, encouraging the cult of the Queen of Hearts. The diplomat Sir Thomas Roe swore to serve her until death, with the added pledge that he would be converted to dust and ashes at her feet. Aristocrats like Christian of Brunswick-Wolfenbuttel, Germany, and the third earl of Essex in England became devoted to her cause.

Elizabeth's already large family continued to grow even larger, and she ultimately gave birth to twenty children. In 1629, her eldest son was drowned, and in 1631, she lost her daughter Charlotte, aged three. In 1632, the Swedish king Gustavus II Adolphus fell at Lützen, and a few days afterward, Frederick died at Mainz on November 29, 1632. Charles I invited Elizabeth to England after Frederick's death, but Elizabeth declined, because she realized that if she went to England she would be giving up all dynastic claims to the Palatinate. Elizabeth's sons, Charles Lewis and Rupert, continued to fight to regain the Palatinate.

When civil war broke out in England between the Parliament and the king, Charles Lewis supported the Parliamentary side, while Rupert and his younger brother Maurice fought for the Royalists. Charles Lewis was in England when Charles I was executed. Even after the restoration of the Palatinate dynasty by the Treaty of Westphalia in 1648, Elizabeth remained in The Hague. She never returned to the Palatinate because of a disagreement with Charles Lewis over lands relating to her jointure.

In 1661, after the Restoration of the Stuart monarchy, Elizabeth returned to England against the wishes of Charles II, staying initially with her old friend, William, earl of Craven. After attempting to move to a residence of her own, she died on February 13, 1662, at Leicester House. On February 17, 1662, she was buried in Westminster Abbey near her beloved brother, Prince Henry.

SIGNIFICANCE

As the female head of an exiled dynasty, Elizabeth Stuart had few material resources and no real political power. Nevertheless, by personality and charm, she managed to create for herself a romantic image that inspired great loyalty. Perhaps her greatest legacy, however, lies in the many paths followed by her many children.

Elizabeth's son Edward converted to Catholicism, as did her daughter Louise Hollandine. Princess Elizabeth, the elder Elizabeth's brilliant namesake, studied philosophy and science and became a devoted friend to René Descartes. After his death, the princess went to Brandenburg and became an abbess of the Protestant ecclesiastical community of Herford. Sophia, Elizabeth Stuart's youngest daughter, portrayed her mother in her memoirs as more concerned about her dogs and monkeys than her children. Elizabeth had opposed Sophia's marriage to Ernst August of Brunswick in 1658, not foreseeing that the suitor she thought unsuitable would become elector of Hanover. The son of Sophia and Ernst became King George I of England. Prince Rupert became the first lord of the British admiralty after serving as a naval commander in the Second and Third Anglo-Dutch Wars. He was the first governor of the Hudson's Bay Company.

—*Jean R. Brink*

FURTHER READING

Barroll, Leeds. *Anna of Denmark, Queen of England: A Cultural Biography*. Philadelphia: University of Pennsylvania Press, 2001. Excellent biography of Anna, consort to James I and mother of Elizabeth Stuart. Important discussion of the politics surrounding Elizabeth's marriage to Frederick.

Elizabeth, Queen of Bohemia. *Letters of Elizabeth, Queen of Bohemia*. Compiled by L. M. Baker with an introduction by C. V. Wedgwood. London: The Bodley Head, 1953. Illustrates the warm childhood relationship between Elizabeth and Henry, Prince of Wales, Elizabeth's older brother, and her interest in European politics.

Green, Mary Anne Everett. *Elizabeth: Electress Palatine and Queen of Bohemia*. Rev. ed. London: Methuen, 1909. Pioneering work on Elizabeth's biography with extensive quotes from the State Papers of Great Britain.

Norbrook, David. "The Masque of Truth: Court Entertainments and International Protestant Politics in the Early Stuart Period." *Seventeenth Century* 1 (1986): 81-110. Study of the politics of court masques and other entertainments presented at the Stuart court.

Oman, Carola. *Elizabeth of Bohemia*. Rev. ed. London: Hodder and Stoughton, 1964. Standard biography of Elizabeth with useful genealogical table.

Ross, Josephine. *The Winter Queen: The Story of Elizabeth Stuart*. New York: St. Martin's Press, 1979. Sympathetic portrait of Elizabeth's life.

Schreiber, R. E. *The First Carlisle: Sir James Hay, First Earl of Carlisle as Courtier, Diplomat, and Entrepreneur, 1580-1636*. Philadelphia: American Philosophical Society, 1984. Biography of an important political supporter to the exiled queen.

Smuts, R. Malcolm. *Culture and Power in England, 1585-1685*. New York: St. Martin's Press, 1999. Discussion of the social and political events transpiring in England during Elizabeth's lifetime.

Strachan, M. *Sir Thomas Roe, 1581-1644: A Life*. Salisbury, Wiltshire, England: Michael Russell, 1989. Biography of British diplomat who corresponded with Elizabeth during her years in exile.

Werner, H. "The Hector of Germanie: Or, The Palsgrave, Prince Elector and Anglo-German Relations of Early Stuart England: The View from the Popular Stage." In *The Stuart Court and Europe*, edited by R. Malcolm Smuts. New York: Cambridge University Press, 1996. Analysis of the iconography and symbolism that developed around Elizabeth and her husband Frederick.

SEE ALSO: Charles I; Elizabeth of Bohemia; Ferdinand II; Frederick V; Gustavus II Adolphus; James I; Prince Rupert.

RELATED ARTICLES in *Great Events from History: The Seventeenth Century, 1601-1700:* March 24, 1603: James I Becomes King of England; 1618-1648: Thirty Years' War; May 23, 1618: Defenestration of Prague; November 8, 1620: Battle of White Mountain; 1642-1651: English Civil Wars; July, 1643-October 24, 1648: Peace of Westphalia; May, 1659-May, 1660: Restoration of Charles II; March 4, 1665-July 31, 1667: Second Anglo-Dutch War; April 6, 1672-August 10, 1678: French-Dutch War.

JOHN EVELYN
English writer and scientist

A pioneer in the field of botanical writing, Evelyn wrote Sylva *and many other works on the flora of his native land. He was also instrumental in founding the Royal Society.*

BORN: October 31, 1620; Wotton, Surrey, England
DIED: February 27, 1706; Wotton
AREA OF ACHIEVEMENT: Science and technology

EARLY LIFE
John Evelyn (EEV-luhn) was the second son of Richard Evelyn, a large landed proprietor in Wotton, Surrey. Richard was himself the grandson of George Evelyn, who was the first proprietor of gunpowder mills in the England of Elizabeth I. In 1589, he had secured a patent on the method of manufacturing gunpowder, which had previously been imported from the Continent. The method, involving the mixing of saltpeter, sulphur, and charcoal, produced black powder. The family business flourished until King Charles I converted it into a royal monopoly, essentially robbing the Evelyns of their livelihood.

Fortunately, the Evelyns had already used their profits from gunpowder manufacturing to buy significant land holdings, thereby converting the family into members of the landed gentry. By the time of John's birth, the Evelyns had become wholly integrated into the class of large landowners who were able to live entirely from their land rents. The estate at Wotton owned by Richard Evelyn encompassed some 7,500 acres (3,035 hectares) and produced rents of around £1,150 per year, a sum that enabled its owner to live in some comfort. As a second son, however, Evelyn did not initially inherit the estate; he received instead the income from some lesser properties owned by the family. Only following the death of his older brother in 1699 did John Evelyn become the proprietor of Wotton Estate.

Evelyn was raised in large measure by his maternal grandparents, who lived in Lewes, Sussex, in the hope that he would thus be distanced from the plague that was ravaging London and its surroundings. He attended some local schools but did not go to Eton; instead he went directly to Balliol College, Oxford, in 1637. Evelyn appears to have enjoyed the relative freedom of a college student and not to have applied himself much to his studies. In 1639 he joined his older brother in London at the Inns of Court, supposedly to acquire training in the law. Evelyn was more interested in politics than the law, however, and never developed any serious legal professionalism.

LIFE'S WORK
The beginnings of the Puritan Revolution happened to coincide with Evelyn's young adulthood, and the crisis turned Evelyn into a passionate Royalist. Although he occasionally took part in some of the military exercises of the adherents of Charles I, however, Evelyn did not join a Royalist regiment. Instead, most of the critical years of the Puritan Revolution Evelyn spent on the Continent, which he visited for the first time in 1641. He spent much of the decade of the 1640's there, traveling extensively in the Low Countries, France, and Italy.

In 1643, in Paris, Evelyn paid his respects to Charles I's resident envoy, Sir Richard Browne, and first encountered Browne's daughter, Mary, whom he married in 1647. Shortly thereafter he "reconnoitred" the Browne's estate, Sayes Court, just south of London. After the execution of Charles I in 1649 and the creation of the Commonwealth, Sayes Court was confiscated by the government and sold. Evelyn was successful in buying it back in 1653, and after his return to England in 1654, it became the residence of John and his new wife, Mary Browne. He devoted much of his time to restoring the grounds of the estate, and this work became the foundation of his knowledge of botany.

Evelyn had already begun his career as a writer, with an ephemeral pamphlet championing royal power, in 1649. He had previously written *The State of France* (1652), a perceptive pamphlet that was published in London. Other pamphlets championing royalty followed, including *A Character of England* (1659) and *An Apology for the Royal Party* (1659). These paved the way for Evelyn's friendship with the restored Stuart monarch, Charles II, who returned to England in 1660. His friendship with the king was a major factor in one of Evelyn's most significant achievements: He brokered royal support for the Royal Society, the group of thinkers in London that became the source of the new scientific knowledge. It was thanks to Evelyn that the Royal Society became an established entity under royal patronage in 1662.

During the decade of the 1660's, Evelyn participated actively in the meetings of the Royal Society, and it was on October 15, 1662, that Evelyn made a presentation to the Society of his manuscript on sylva, the forest trees of

England. The work that Evelyn had done in restoring the grounds of Sayes Court formed the basis of this study, together with a concern prevalent in governing circles that the rapid destruction of the forests of England then going on could, in the future, damage the British Navy, which relied on wood, especially oak timbers, for its vessels. *Sylva: Or, A Discourse on Forest Trees and the Propagation of Timber* (1664) was published at the instigation of the Royal Society; it was the first of their sponsored publications. It was far and away the most successful of Evelyn's writings, with new editions appearing in his lifetime and well after.

Evelyn continued to be involved in the activities of the Royal Society. In 1678, he secured the donation of a valuable library to the society. In 1680, he joined in the campaign to elect Robert Boyle, the distinguished scientist and inventor of the airpump, president of the society, and he himself served as vice president of the society in 1685. Among its major concerns, the society placed agriculture high on the list, and Evelyn was involved in the many ongoing discussions of how to improve agriculture in England. These in turn fed into his botanical writings,

including *Kalendarium Hortense: Or, The Gardener's Almanack* (1664) and *Acetaria* (1699), about salad greens. He gathered material for a book to be entitled *Elysium Britannicum*, but much of what he had intended for that work appeared under other titles.

Evelyn's interest in things botanical led him to an environmental concern, namely, the state of the atmosphere in London, which was heavily polluted at the time, as coal was being burned at a high rate to heat London's houses. Evelyn's concern led him to publish a pamphlet attacking the poor condition of the air, *Fumifugium* (1661), in which he proposed that all industrial activities in London be banished to the outskirts of the city. He even helped prepare a bill to this effect to be submitted to Parliament, but it never made it that far. The pamphlet was dedicated to King Charles II.

In the late 1660's, Evelyn renewed his connection to Oxford University. He persuaded Henry Howard, later the duke of Norfolk, to present to Oxford the Arundel marbles, some 130 stone slabs, many of which were covered with chronologies of ancient Greek events and other engravings. Howard responded by hiring Evelyn to do some landscaping on one of his estates, and Oxford responded by awarding Evelyn an honorary doctorate in June of 1669.

Evelyn's connections with the royal family led to his being given several largely honorary appointments, including commissioner of the privy seal. Charles II nominated him to the commission in charge of caring for the sick and wounded in the Second Anglo-Dutch War (1665-67), and a similar appointment during the Third Anglo-Dutch War (1672-1674). This activity, which entailed Evelyn's personal involvement, led to his being named in 1695 to the post of treasurer of Chelsea Hospital, a hospital for wounded war veterans.

SIGNIFICANCE

Much more is known of Evelyn than many of his contemporaries because of the diary that he kept throughout much of his life. It provides insight into the world of the seventeenth century country gentleman, as well as to English politics during that period. His *Sylva* is in many ways the first ecological treatise of the modern era, and his role in the foundation and activities of the Royal Society earn him a place in the history of science.

—*Nancy M. Gordon*

John Evelyn. (Hulton Archive/Getty Images)

FURTHER READING

Bowle, John. *John Evelyn and His World: A Biography.* London: Routledge & Kegan Paul, 1981. A good biography of Evelyn, making clear the many faceted life he led.

Brimblecombe, Peter. *The Big Smoke: A History of Air Pollution in London Since Medieval Times.* New York: Methuen, 1987. A long range look at one of the ecological problems Evelyn tackled.

Eamon, William. *Science and the Secrets of Nature: Books of Secrets in Medieval and Early Modern Culture.* Princeton, N.J.: Princeton University Press, 1994. Portrays Evelyn as an advocate of scientific exclusivity.

Hiscock, W. G. *John Evelyn and His Family Circle.* London: Routledge & Kegan Paul, 1955. Another biography, particularly useful because it includes a bibliography of Evelyn's writings.

Lynch, William T. *Solomon's Child: Method in the Early Royal Society of London.* Stanford, Calif.: Stanford University Press, 2001. The second chapter deals specifically with Evelyn's role in the early Royal Society.

SEE ALSO: Robert Boyle; Charles I; Charles II.

RELATED ARTICLES in *Great Events from History: The Seventeenth Century, 1601-1700:* 1601-1672: Rise of Scientific Societies; December 6, 1648-May 19, 1649: Establishment of the English Commonwealth; May, 1659-May, 1660: Restoration of Charles II; March 4, 1665-July 31, 1667: Second Anglo-Dutch War; April 6, 1672-August 10, 1678: French-Dutch War.

DAVID AND JOHANNES FABRICIUS
German astronomers

David Fabricius discovered the first periodic variable star, and his son, Johannes, was the first to make telescopic observations of sunspots, although some contend it was Galileo who did so before Johannes. Johannes was, however, the first to publish on the subject of sunspots. Also, David and Johannes determined that the Sun rotates on its axis.

DAVID FABRICIUS

BORN: March 9, 1564; Esens, East Frisia (now in Germany)
DIED: May 7, 1617; Osteel, East Frisia (now in Germany)
ALSO KNOWN AS: David Faber

JOHANNES FABRICIUS

BORN: January 8, 1587; Resterhafe, East Frisia (now in Germany)
DIED: March 19, 1616; Osteel, East Frisia (now in Germany)
ALSO KNOWN AS: Johann Goldsmid
AREAS OF ACHIEVEMENT: Astronomy, science and technology, religion and theology, scholarship, geography

EARLY LIVES

Not much is known about the early lives of David and Johannes Fabricius (fah-BREET-see-uhs). "Fabricius" is a Latin form of the surname "Faber." In the early 1580's, David Fabricius studied in Resterhafe to become a Lutheran pastor. By 1585, he was serving as a pastor in the small town of Osteel. He was the father of seven children, four daughters and three sons.

In addition to being a respected clergyman, David was an adept cartographer and compiled the first map of East Frisia in 1589. He was very interested in science, particularly astronomy, and through correspondence and personal visits became good friends with astronomers Tycho Brahe and Johannes Kepler. He met with Brahe to discuss astronomy and astrology at Wandsburg Castle (in southwestern Germany) in 1598 and also in Prague in 1601.

Johannes Fabricius, David's second child and first son, studied medicine between 1604 and 1610 in Helmstedt and Wittenberg, then in Leyden. While at Leyden, his interest in astronomy developed. He became very interested in using a telescope to make observations of stars and planets. In 1610, he returned to Osteel and began to practice as a physician, taking with him a telescope. He apparently continued some further medical studies at Wittenberg in 1611.

LIVES' WORK

By the mid-1590's, David Fabricius, by this time an accomplished pastor and mapmaker, also was an astute observational astronomer. On August 3, 1596, he discovered without a telescope a star originally named Omicron Ceti. The star was later renamed Mira, meaning "wonderful." Because of the star's brightness, David thought initially that Mira was a nova. With subsequent observations, he noticed that the star was sometimes bright enough to be easily seen with the naked eye, while at other times it faded out of sight. He had discovered the first periodic, pulsating variable star, a discovery that refuted Aristotle's notion that the heavens were constant and perfect.

From an observatory that he established in Osteel, David observed the supernova of 1604 near the conjunction of Jupiter and Mars and reported his findings in both German and Latin publications. Kepler referred to David in some of his writings as the second best astronomer in Europe next to Tycho Brahe.

As a practicing physician in Osteel, Johannes Fabricius devoted much of his spare time to astronomical observations using the telescope that he had obtained in Leyden. On March 9, 1611, he made the first telescopic observations of sunspots. Apparently, his father, David, had observed sunspots many years earlier without a telescope, as had Korean and Chinese astronomers and early English astronomer John of Worcester. Shortly after his first observations of sunspots, Johannes made geometrical drawings of his findings and shared them with his father. Subsequently, they made numerous additional observations, typically just after sunrise and just before sunset. Finding moving blemishes on the Sun was another refutation of Aristotle's premise that the heavens were perfect and constant.

Because of the eye inflammation and pain that came from viewing the Sun directly, David and Johannes soon adopted and perfected the camera obscura technique. With this method, an image of the Sun is projected onto a suitable surface in a darkened room by passing sunlight through a pinhole opening that is made in the covering of

DAVID AND JOHANNES FABRICIUS LOOK AT THE SUN

David and Johannes Fabricius looked directly at the morning and late afternoon sun through a telescope to see sunspots. Even through a telescope, the sun's rays were powerful, causing their work to be painful and debilitating. They describe this experience here, in a translation published in 1916 in Popular Astronomy.

Having adjusted the telescope, we allowed the sun's rays to enter it, at first from the edge only, gradually approaching the center, until our eyes were accustomed to the force of the rays and we could observe the whole body of the sun. We then saw more distinctly and surely the things I have described [sunspots]. Meanwhile clouds interfered, and also the sun hastening to the meridian destroyed our hopes of longer observations; for indeed it was to be feared that an indiscreet examination of a lower sun would cause great injury to the eyes, for even the weaker rays of the setting or rising sun often inflame the eye with a strange redness, which may last for two days, not without affecting the appearance of objects.

Source: W. M. Mitchell, "The History of the Discovery of Solar Spots." *Popular Astronomy* 24 (1916). Cited on the Web site of the National Center for Atmospheric Research, High Altitude Observatory, "Johann Fabricius (1587-1616)." http://www.hao.ucar.edu/public/education/sp/images/fabricius.html. Accessed December, 2004.

a window in the room. The camera obscura was a safe way to observe the sun, and, also, it gave a clearer view of the solar disk. Between March and June of 1611, David and Johannes recorded numerous observations of sunspots. They noted that spots appearing on the western edge of the Sun would reappear on the eastern side after approximately twelve days. They made the correct interpretation of sunspot movement by concluding that the Sun must rotate on its axis. The two differed in their opinion as to where the spots were located, however. Johannes believed the spots to be on the surface of the sun, whereas his father thought that they might be clouds or planetary objects passing by the Sun and not part of the Sun itself.

Johannes wrote *De maculis in sole observatis* (narration on spots observed on the sun) and published the booklet in 1611 using the name "Johann Goldsmid," a version of his name evidently used while he was studying in Leyden. Unfortunately, observation times and dates, as well as sketches of the spots, were not included in the treatise. Although it was sold at a book fair in Frankfurt in the fall of 1611, it remained in obscurity until it was rediscovered and publicized in 1723. In the meantime, Galileo and Christoph Scheiner had each claimed credit for making the first telescopic observations of sunspots dur-

ing the latter part of 1611 or early 1612. Due credit was not given to David and Johannes Fabricius until more than one hundred years after their important work.

Johannes died of unknown causes in 1616 at the very young age of twenty-nine. Almost one year later, David suffered a surprising death at the hands of an irate member of his Lutheran congregation. While presenting a sermon, the elder Fabricius had chastised farmer Frerik Hoyer for stealing a goose. Later, Hoyer confronted David in the church yard and struck him in the head with a shovel, killing the pastor. David was depicted in a novel by nineteenth century French writer Jules Verne. In Verne's *Autour de la lune* (1870; *From the Earth to the Moon . . . and a Trip Around It*, 1873), David is portrayed as an astronomer who viewed inhabitants on the moon with his telescope.

In honor of the contributions of David and Johannes to astronomy, a large impact crater on the Moon was named "Fabricius." The crater is located within the northeastern part of the Janssen walled plain in the southern hemisphere of the Moon and has a diameter of approximately 90 kilometers. It is not known, however, if the crater was named originally to honor both David and Johannes Fabricius, or to honor just one.

SIGNIFICANCE

Astronomical observations made by David Fabricius initiated the study of periodic variable stars by other astronomers, leading to an explanation of pulsating star phenomena in terms of varying luminosity and surface temperature. Observations of sunspot phenomena made by Johannes and David Fabricius advanced the use of the camera obscura method for investigating the Sun and motivated other astronomers to study sunspots. Interpretation of the day-by-day movement of sunspots by David and Johannes Fabricius led them to conclude correctly that the Sun rotates on its axis. The younger Fabricius was the first astronomer to publish the results of such findings. Their discovery of pulsating variable stars and telescopic observations of sunspots led many astronomers to revise their own theories that the heavens were perfect and constant, as originally thought by Aristotle.

The work of David and Johannes Fabricius was noted by many contemporary astronomers, including Johannes Kepler, Michael Mästlin, and Simon Marius. David and Johannes Fabricius were instrumental in stimulating the curiosity of other astronomers to carefully study and correctly interpret observations of the stars.

—Alvin K. Benson

FURTHER READING

Brody, Judit. *The Enigma of Sunspots: A Story of Discovery and Scientific Revolution.* Edinburgh: Floris Books, 2002. Brody relates the fascinating story of the discovery of sunspots by David and Johannes Fabricius and the efforts that have been made since their time to describe and understand sunspots. Includes bibliographical references and color illustrations.

Christianson, John Robert. *On Tycho's Island: Tycho Brahe, Science, and Culture in the Sixteenth Century.* New York: Cambridge University Press, 2002. This work tracks the history of Tycho Brahe—philosopher, chemist, and astronomer—and discusses his interaction with David Fabricius. David corresponded and visited with Brahe and discussed some of his astronomical discoveries with him. Includes bibliographical references and index.

Drake, Stillman, Noel M. Swerdlow, and Trevor Harvey Levere. *Essays on Galileo and the History and Philosophy of Science.* Vol. 1. Toronto: University of Toronto Press, 1999. This volume includes a discussion on the controversy over who discovered sunspots—David and Johannes Fabricius, Galileo, Christoph Scheiner, or someone else. Includes bibliographical references and index.

Kepler, Johannes, and Edward Rosen. *Kepler's Somnium: The Dream: Or, Posthumous Work on Lunar Astronomy.* New York: Dover Books, 2003. Recounts some of Kepler's accomplishments and ideas, including his dream about a trip to the Moon, and tells of the friendship of David and Johannes Fabricius with Kepler.

SEE ALSO: Galileo; Francesco Maria Grimaldi; Edmond Halley; Johannes and Elisabetha Hevelius; Christiaan Huygens; Hans Lippershey; Wilhelm Schickard.

RELATED ARTICLES in *Great Events from History: The Seventeenth Century, 1601-1700:* 17th century: Advances in Medicine; 1617-1628: Harvey Discovers the Circulation of the Blood.

THIRD BARON FAIRFAX
English military leader

Fairfax commanded the Parliamentary army during the crucial phase of the English Civil War, ensuring the defeat of the Royalist forces of King Charles I.

BORN: January 17, 1612; Denton, Yorkshire, England
DIED: November 12, 1671; Nun Appleton, near Bilborough, Yorkshire, England
ALSO KNOWN AS: Thomas Fairfax (given name)
AREAS OF ACHIEVEMENT: Military, warfare and conquest, government and politics

EARLY LIFE

Thomas Fairfax, third Baron Fairfax, was born into a family that had won military distinction during Queen Elizabeth I's reign. His grandfather, Thomas, first Baron Fairfax, had as a young man served in the Low Countries under Sir Francis Vere, the greatest English commander of his day, as well as with the queen's favorite, the earl of Essex. In 1607, Lord Fairfax saw to it that his eldest son, Ferdinando, married the daughter of Lord Sheffield. Thomas, third Baron Fairfax, was their son.

In 1620, as England was drawn into the Thirty Years' War, Sir Horace Vere led a regiment of volunteers to aid the Protestant cause in Germany. Young Thomas's uncles William and John served under Vere in the Low Countries. Later, his uncle Peregrine was killed at the Siege of La Rochelle (1627-1628). It was natural, then, for the junior Fairfax to spend some time as a soldier early in his life. Not only was military service a family tradition, but it was also a common means at the time for a young gentleman to complete his education.

After spending three years at St. John's College, Cambridge (1626-1629), Fairfax himself traveled to the Low Countries, where he served as a volunteer under Vere at the Siege of Bois-le-Duc. The Dutch, aided by English volunteers and mercenaries, besieged this great fortress from May to September, 1629, when they finally compelled the Spanish to surrender it. Fairfax returned to

England in 1632, hoping to secure permission to serve under the Swedish king, Gustavus II Adolphus, the principal champion of the Protestant cause. It seems that Fairfax did not pursue his purpose, however, perhaps having been dissuaded by his grandfather. In June, 1637, he married Ann Vere, the daughter of his old commander, presumably intending to settle down in Yorkshire, but he was to have anything but a quiet life in the next decade. A surviving portrait of Fairfax shows a handsome figure (dark enough to have been nicknamed Black Tom), clean-shaven, with hair worn to his shoulders.

LIFE'S WORK

In 1639, Fairfax went to war again, this time in England, commanding a troop of dragoons in the First Bishops' War between England and Scotland. King Charles I, in his attempt to impose religious uniformity and episcopacy on all of his kingdoms, provoked a rebellion in Presbyterian Scotland. The Scots defended themselves vigorously and forced the king to conclude a truce with them. In January, 1640, Fairfax was rewarded with a knighthood for his efforts in the Scots War. The Scots rebellion could not be quashed, however, and it provoked a political crisis in England that proved to be insoluble and

Third Baron Fairfax. (Library of Congress)

led, in due course, first to a complete rupture between the king and Parliament and then to a civil war. Though at first the king was isolated politically, eventually, as he gave ground on some of the issues that divided the country, he was able to build the Royalist Party.

The Fairfaxes, father and son, were leaders on the Parliamentary side in Yorkshire. The moderation, even the ambiguity, of their position is suggested by the fact that only weeks before the outbreak of serious fighting, in September, 1642, the Fairfaxes were trying to negotiate a neutrality pact to keep Yorkshire out of the struggle. When the truce broke down, Lord Ferdinando took charge of the Parliamentary troops in Yorkshire with the younger Fairfax as his chief cavalry officer. For the remainder of 1642 and 1643, though both sides could claim their victories, the war was essentially a stalemate. A good part of Yorkshire was controlled for the king by the duke of Newcastle, but the Fairfaxes, though seriously outnumbered, prevented the Royalists from striking south against London. Much of the credit for this belongs to Sir Thomas, who distinguished himself in a series of bold skirmishes in 1643. That summer, however, Newcastle defeated the senior Fairfax in a major battle and besieged the Parliamentary forces in Hull, the nadir of Parliamentary fortunes in the north.

In the fall, joined by the troops of the Eastern Association under the earl of Manchester and Oliver Cromwell, the Fairfaxes recovered, winning a crucial victory at Winceby. The siege of Hull was broken, and the immediate danger ended. Taking the offensive, Parliament broke the stalemate by negotiating an alliance with the Scots. In the summer of 1644, the Scots marched down into Yorkshire. Joining with Fairfax, Manchester, and Cromwell, they fought a great and decisive battle against the duke of Newcastle and Prince Rupert, the king's nephew, at Marston Moor, near York. Utterly defeated, Newcastle went into exile, and the back of the resistance to Parliament in the north was broken.

Fairfax was now seen to be one of the leading commanders on the Parliamentary side. In the winter of 1644-1645, Parliament agreed to create a national army, rather than a local one, based on the highly successful model of the Eastern Association's force. The command of this New Model Army was given to Fairfax, with Cromwell as its chief cavalry officer. Fairfax accepted with some reluctance. In May, he began, under Parliamentary orders, to blockade the king's capital at Oxford, but once allowed a free hand, in June, he and Cromwell promptly brought the king to battle at Naseby and won another great and decisive victory, sealing the Royalists' fate.

In the succeeding weeks, Fairfax turned westward into the king's last region of support, destroying Lord Goring's army at Langport and storming Bristol, held by Prince Rupert. The war was then reduced to a series of sieges of isolated Royalist strongholds, which maintained their loyalty to the king to the bitter end.

Oxford fell in June, 1646. Though the fighting was over, the problems that had caused the Civil War—at bottom, an inability to define the limits of royal power—remained unresolved. King and Parliament were no closer to agreement than they had been in 1641, for the king, though militarily defeated, declined to yield, to surrender any of his traditional rights and powers.

In the spring of 1647, Parliament voted to disband much of the army, with Fairfax to continue as commander. The soldiers were still awaiting their pay and were reluctant to disband until they were satisfied. Once disarmed and dispersed, the urgency of their demands would diminish. The moderate majority in Parliament, for its part, feared the intervention of the army into politics. Fairfax, responsible for the army's discipline, found himself in the middle, mediating between Parliament and his troops for the settlement of their grievances. Unlike Cromwell, he was far less comfortable as a politician than as a general.

In June, 1647, the virtual mutiny of the army against parliamentary control was formalized by the creation of an Army Council, made up of senior officers and elected representatives of each of the regiments, some of whom, especially the more junior officers, had been influenced by radical political ideas such as democracy, a revolutionary proposition. Against this usurpation of power (that of Parliament and his own), Fairfax struggled. In July, to his profound disapproval, the king was seized by radical army officers, but he could do little to restrain them or secure the king's release.

In the latter half of 1647, Fairfax's energies were spent largely in trying to maintain discipline in the army, prevent outright mutiny, and restrain the Army Council from any further direct intervention in politics. Late in the year, he had succeeded in restoring the army to a reasonable measure of discipline but had made little progress in mediating between Parliament and the more radical army officers. On the contrary, Cromwell and other senior officers pressed Fairfax to support them in purging Parliament of its most conservative members, who

were preventing the army from imposing a hard settlement on the king.

The outbreak of the Second Civil War in the summer of 1648 deferred the issues. The Royalist attempt to resume the Civil War was encouraged by the fact that the victors in the first round were unable to agree on a new course. In purely military terms, however, the swift triumph of the Parliamentary forces showed that the outcome of the First Civil War was no accident. Fairfax succeeded in restoring discipline so successfully that the Royalist risings were quickly crushed everywhere. He personally commanded at the Siege of Colchester (1648) and had the Royalist commanders shot, abandoning his usual leniency to prove his determination to end the conflict.

With the military issues definitively settled, attention now returned to the insoluble political problems presented by a king who, perceiving that the victors remained profoundly divided, declined to surrender to their demands for changes in the "ancient constitution." With the danger from the radicals (among whom were the Levellers, who favored social equality and religious toleration) behind them, Cromwell now believed that he could move against the conservatives in Parliament. Striking quickly, the army excluded those members in Pride's Purge and, the Parliament thus altered, moved to try the obdurate king. Though the king was convicted, sentenced, and publicly executed in January, 1649, however, Cromwellian republicanism did not carry the nation with it.

Fairfax resisted participating in this sequence of events. He disowned responsibility for purging Parliament. Though appointed one of the king's judges, he did not attend the trial. When it became clear that the king would be condemned, he used his influence, in vain, to defer the sentencing and execution.

After the dissolution of the monarchy, Fairfax continued to serve for a time as commander of the army and a member of the Council of State, the new executive body. In May, 1649, he suppressed a final Leveller mutiny in the army. Nevertheless, he was not genuinely committed to the Commonwealth. He resigned his commission in the summer of 1650 rather than invade Scotland, for he was wavering toward royalism. He retired to private life. Thereafter, throughout the 1650's, he played little part in public life except to serve in the Parliament of 1654. The Cromwellians suspected him of plotting with the Royalists, though apparently they were incorrect. Suspicion was also aroused against Fairfax by the marriage of his daughter to a Royalist peer.

After Cromwell's death, Fairfax maintained an uneasy middle-road position in the movement to restore the monarchy. Ultimately, however, his reservations were swept aside and Charles II came to the throne with relatively free hands. As a result of his moderate and ambiguous position in the Restoration, Fairfax was neither rewarded for making it possible nor punished for his part in the previous rebellion. He spoke out against the punishment of many who had done far less than he to oppose the king during the Civil War. Unmolested by the restored regime, he lived quietly in Yorkshire until his death in November, 1671.

SIGNIFICANCE

The third Baron Fairfax's religious commitments as a devout Presbyterian made his adherence to the Parliamentary cause inevitable. His military experience, dashing courage, fierce energies, and utter devotion to victory made him a striking success in the field. Early in the war, though consistently outnumbered, he won a string of local victories that were substantially the product of his personal bravery and determined leadership. He contributed as much in the complex and decisive triumphs at Marston Moor and Naseby, where the outcome of the Civil War was essentially decided. Fairfax's great gifts were military ones, headed by a valor that commanded respect. He was not so well suited, however, for the baffling politics of a revolutionary era when, for the first time, ordinary men, who had loyally followed their social superiors to make war on a king whom both believed to be acting unlawfully, demanded after their victory that the future be different and that those who had risked their lives to defeat the king should be consulted about how the country was to be governed.

Like Cromwell and the other grandees of the army, Fairfax was no modern democrat. The justice he sought for his men was merely that they should be treated fairly and allowed to worship freely. Like moderate men on both sides, he hoped to alter the existing political arrangements as little as possible, to see to it only that the king lived within the bounds of the ancient constitution as understood and defined by Parliament and that he secured its consent to any substantial change. He had no wish to see English society changed in a "levelling" (democratic) fashion. To secure political stability and preserve the social order, he accepted, as Cromwell did not in the end, the need for a king and the ancient constitution.

Having negotiated his own way through the shoals of the Restoration to safety, however, Fairfax disapproved of its terms. The vindication of his views may be seen in the terms upon which, a generation later, the monarchy had to be reestablished, bound this time by a constitution, a constitution that could only take hold after a second, if bloodless, revolution in 1688.

—S. J. Stearns

FURTHER READING

Bell, Robert, ed. *Memorials of the Civil War*. 2 vols. London: Bentley, 1849. Completes the work begun by scholar George Johnson of compiling the Fairfax correspondence.

Cromwell, Oliver. *The Writings and Speeches of Oliver Cromwell*. Edited by Wilbur Cortez Abbot. 4 vols. Cambridge, Mass.: Harvard University Press, 1937-1947. Reprint. New York: Russell & Russell, 1970. The standard edition, together with a full biography, of the dominant figure of the age.

Firth, Charles H. *Cromwell's Army*. London: Methuen, 1921. Reprint. Novato, Calif.: Presidio Press, 1992. An examination of pro-Cromwell military organization and institutions by one of the great scholars of the period.

Gardiner, Samuel R. *History of the Great Civil War*. 4 vols. New York: Longmans, Green, 1893. Reprint. London: Windrush Press, 1987. Still the definitive narrative account by the greatest scholar of the period, though much corrected in detail by subsequent scholarship.

Hooper, A. J. *The Readiness of the People: The Formation and Emergence of the Army of the Fairfaxes, 1642-1643*. York, North Yorkshire, England: Borthwick Institute of Historical Research, University of York, 1997. A history of the Fairfaxes' military campaign in Yorkshire.

Johnson, George W., ed. *The Fairfax Correspondence*. London: Bentley, 1848. Selections from the correspondence and papers of the Fairfax family in the early seventeenth century until the outbreak of war. Continued by scholar Robert Bell.

Wilson, John. *Fairfax: A Life of Thomas, Lord Fairfax, Captain-General of All the Parliament's Forces in the English Civil War, Creator and Commander of the New Model Army*. London: J. Murray, 1985. A useful biography of Fairfax.

Young, Peter, and A. H. Burne. *The Great Civil War*. London: Eyre and Spottiswoode, 1959. A concise military history. A revised edition of this work, written by Young with Richard Holmes, was published in 1974.

FRANÇOIS DE SALIGNAC DE LA MOTHE-FÉNELON
French religious leader and writer

A major figure in the religious controversies of seventeenth century France, Fénelon was also an accomplished novelist and an early advocate of women's education. As archbishop of Cambrai, he exhibited tolerance and concern in an era of religious and political conflict.

BORN: August 6, 1651; Château de Fénelon, Périgord, France

DIED: January 7, 1715; Cambrai, France

AREAS OF ACHIEVEMENT: Religion and theology, literature, education

EARLY LIFE

François de Salignac de La Mothe-Fénelon (frah-swah duh sah-leen-yahk duh lah-moht-fayn-loh) was born to poor but aristocratic parents. He completed his studies at the Jesuit College du Plessis and the seminary of St. Sulpice in Paris and was ordained in about 1675. After early parish work, he directed for ten years the Nouvelles Catholiques, a Parisian school for the education of young female converts from Protestantism.

When the Edict of Nantes was rescinded in 1685, Fénelon became a missionary for six months to the Protestants in the districts of Saintonge and Aunis. His experience at the Nouvelles Catholiques contributed to his *Traité de l'education des filles* (1687; *Instructions for the Education of a Daughter*, 1707), an early essay on the importance of the education of girls, for which some have termed him an early feminist. A year later, Fénelon met the mystic Madame Guyon. Struck by her intense personal devotion, he was drawn to her practice of mystical prayer, thus becoming linked to the quietist movement, a branch of mysticism first established in Spain by Father Miguel de Molinos (1640-1696) and promoted by Guyon.

After being inducted into the French Academy in 1693, in 1695 Fénelon became the tutor to King Louis XIV's rebellious grandson, the duke of Burgundy, and his influence at court broadened. Instrumental in the educational reform of this difficult child was Fénelon's *Les Aventures de Télémaque* (1699; *The Adventures of Telemachus, the Son of Ulysses*, 1699), a work of utopian fiction. The king was so pleased with his grandson's improvement that he made Fénelon the archbishop of Cambrai in 1695, a prestigious position that further expanded his spiritual influence across France.

However, his allegiance to Guyon and quietism began to erode his prominence. Even though he did not agree with the emotional excesses that sometimes marked her work, he nevertheless issued *L'Explication des maximes des saints sur la vie intérieure* (1697; *The Maxims of the Saints Explained, Concerning the Interiour Life*, 1698) as a defense against growing criticism that her doctrines were heretical. This work, however, incurred the opposition of Jacques-Bénigne Bossuet (1627-1704), bishop of Meaux, and Fénelon finally lost all royal support. In 1699, he was banished from court, removed as a royal tutor, and (at the urging of the king and Bossuet) censured by Pope Innocent XIII for his seemingly quietist views.

Throughout this controversy he gained the admiration of many by vigorously defending himself while not descending to the harsh animosity shown by his accusers. In the last two decades of his life, he distinguished himself by exemplary work in his own diocese, leaving it once in eighteen years. His devout life, impressive sermons, and concern for his parishioners were noteworthy. When his diocese was ravaged by the War of the Spanish Succession (1701-1714), he gave generously of his resources for care of the injured. Fénelon died in 1715 of complications resulting from a carriage accident.

LIFE'S WORK

Fénelon's work spanned the fields of religion, education, politics, and literature. Though he opposed both the *absolute* quietism of Molinos and the doctrines of Jansenism (a reformist Catholic movement that advocated a system of doctrine based on moral determinism opposed by the Catholic Church and considered heretical), he acquired a reputation for being more tolerant than many of the prominent Catholics who clustered around the king, such as Bossuet or Father Michel Le Tellier, King Louis XIV's confessor after 1709.

Fénelon's emphasis upon the faith of an individual soul and its relationship with God, rather than upon intellectual assent to particular doctrines, now seems a precursor to what was called "enthusiasm" in the eighteenth century, an emotional devotion aroused by the "the god within" (*en-theos*), which came to characterize such groups as the Methodists and the Quakers. For traditionalists at the royal court this smacked too much of a reliance upon *sola fides* (the Protestant emphasis upon being saved by faith alone), without benefit of the Church's hierarchy. Although Fénelon readily acknowledged the authority of the pope and king, he displayed a tolerance for a variety of practices that, without making him a rationalist, seems to link him with the coming period of the Enlightenment.

His association with Madame Guyon, his wide network of influential friends, and his close relationship with the wife of King Louis XIV, Madame de Maintenon—whose school for girls at St. Cyr had at one time also come under Guyon's influence—all suffered when Bossuet, Maintenon's close associate, judged Fénelon and Guyon to be advocating unorthodox beliefs. The rigidly doctrinaire Bossuet viewed their devotional practices with suspicion, even though Fénelon was not a thoroughgoing quietist and had condemned what he called the "damnable teachings of Molinos." Although it had been Bossuet who had consecrated Fénelon a bishop, the conflict between the two grew bitter, and Bossuet even implied an illicit relationship between Fénelon and Guyon.

The theological principles of quietism were reviewed in a conference at Issy in 1695; the result was a list of thirty-four articles condemning the movement. Bossuet, Fénelon, and Guyon all signed the document, but Fénelon and Bossuet quarreled again two years later upon appearance of Fénelon's *The Maxims of the Saints Explained, Concerning the Interiour Life*, whose publication led to Fénelon's banishment to Cambrai.

Several works mark Fénelon's importance in education. His *Instructions for the Education of a Daughter* especially rejected the more inflexible practices of educating women in favor of a broad grounding in religion and classical literature, combined with lessons in moral uprightness and practical domestic skills for the management of households and servants. His schooling of the duke of Burgundy also was grounded in the educational value of literature.

From 1689 to 1699, Fénelon composed several books that were graduated to match a child's growing maturity: *Contes et fables, Dialogues des morts, Demonstration de l'existence de Dieu, Direction pour la conscience d'un roi*, and *The Aventures of Telemachus, the Son of Ulysses*. The last, an epic novel in which Telemachus, son of Odysseus, follows the advice of his teacher Mentor, is a didactic work whose young hero is the model of youthful behavior. Through a series of adventures, they visit Salente, a new city for which Mentor offers guidance and instruction. Mentor's comments are Fénelon's own thinly disguised beliefs on the design of an ideal political state. Critical of absolutist rulers and praising humanitarian practices in peace and war, the novel was seen as a critique of Louis XIV's administration, and it contributed to Fénelon's fall from influence in 1699. The year before he died, Fénelon also wrote the *Dialogues sur l'éloquence. Mémoire sur les occupations de l'Académie Française* (*Dialogues Concerning Eloquence in General, and Particularly That Kind Which Is Fit for the Pulpit*, 1760), one of several works of literary criticism that praised the virtues of classical literature.

SIGNIFICANCE

Fénelon was a major figure in the religious controversies of seventeenth century France, supporting, especially, the quietism of the mystic Madame Guyon, for which he was deeply criticized. A critic of royal absolutism, he was an accomplished author and an early advocate of women's education. He acquired a reputation for tolerance, and as a bishop showed a saintly concern for those under his care.

—Christopher Baker

FURTHER READING

Carcassonne, Elie. *Fénelon: His Life and Works*. Translated by Victor Leuliette. Port Washington, N.Y.: Kennikat, 1970. An English translation of a detailed French biography, which includes an introduction and notes.

De la Bedoyere, Michael. *The Archbishop and the Lady: The Story of Fénelon and Madame Guyon*. New York: Pantheon, 1956. A popular account of Fénelon's friendship with Madame Guyon. Contains a short bibliography, with most entries in French.

Fénelon, François de Salignac de la Mothe-. *The Adventures of Telemachus, the Son of Ulysses*. Translated by Tobias Smollett, edited by O. M. Brack, Jr. Athens: University of Georgia Press, 1997. A modern translation of Fénelon's epic novel, with an introduction and notes by Leslie A. Chilton, a map, a bibliography, and an index.

_____. *Instructions for the Education of a Daughter.* Translated by George Hicks. Bristol, England: Thoemmes Press, 1994. A facsimile reprint of the first English translation (1707) of Fénelon's treatise on the education of girls, with an introduction by Jeffrey Stern and with illustrations.

Hillenaar, Henk. *Nouvel etat present des travaux sur Fénelon.* Atlanta: Rodopi, 2000. A collection of essays, in French, discussing Fénelon's views on such topics as politics, religion, and pedagogy. Contains a bibliography of works about Fénelon that appeared from 1940 to 2000.

Kanter, Sanford B. "Archbishop Fénelon's Political Activity: The Focal Point of Power in Dynasticism." *French Historical Studies* 4, no. 3 (Spring, 1966): 320-334. Argues that Fénelon is more accurately termed a political activist than a political theorist because of his efforts to influence Louis XIV's regime through his personal friendships and his role as royal tutor.

Leduc-Fayette, Denise, ed. *Fénelon: Philosophie et spiritualité.* Geneva: Droz, 1996. An anthology of essays, in French, on various aspects of Fénelon's life and work, covering such topics as his education, spirituality, and his links with Gottfried Wilhelm Leibniz, Guyon, and Augustinianism.

Lougee, Carolyn C. "Nobelesse, Domesticity, and Social Reform: The Education of Girls by Fénelon and Saint-Cyr." *History of Education Quarterly* 14, no. 1 (Spring, 1974): 87-113. Reviews the nature and purpose of Fénelon's treatise on the education of girls.

Ward, Patricia A. "Fénelon Among the New England Abolitionists." *Christianity and Literature* 50, no. 1 (Autumn, 2000). Traces Fénelon's influence among American antislavery figures, Unitarians, Transcendentalists, and Quakers. Comments on his influence upon Harriet Beecher Stowe and her novel *Uncle Tom's Cabin.*

SEE ALSO: Jacques-Bénigne Bossuet; Innocent XI; Cornelius Otto Jansen; Louis XIV; Madame de Maintenon; Anna Maria van Schurman.

RELATED ARTICLES in *Great Events from History: The Seventeenth Century, 1601-1700:* 1638-1669: Spread of Jansenism; 1689-1694: Famine and Inflation in France.

FERDINAND II
Holy Roman Emperor (r. 1619-1637)

While emperor of the Holy Roman Empire, Ferdinand II sought to restore Roman Catholicism to the Protestant areas of the empire and to assert the empire's Habsburg political hegemony. His efforts directly resulted in the Thirty Years' War in Germany, one of history's most devastating wars.

BORN: July 9, 1578; Graz, Styria (now in Austria)
DIED: February 15, 1637; Vienna, Holy Roman Empire (now in Austria)
AREA OF ACHIEVEMENT: Government and politics

EARLY LIFE

Ferdinand II was born the eldest son of Archduke Charles of Inner Austria (Styria) and Maria of Bavaria. The Europe into which he was born was filled not only with political struggles between dynastic, territorial states but also with religious strife between various Protestant denominations and Roman Catholics. The Holy Roman Empire itself was a microcosm of these conflicts. German princes, especially Protestant ones, and the Roman Catholic Habsburg emperor were continually at odds over the definition of the empire. Further complicating this situation was the dream of a catholicized, consolidated Europe and empire held by both the Austrian and the Spanish branches of the Habsburg family.

Ferdinand's father, a devout Roman Catholic and brother of Emperor Maximilian II, was archduke of a principality that was predominantly Protestant. Of necessity, in 1578, he had granted religious guarantees in the form of a "religious pacification" to the Lutheran dominated Estates, the representative assembly of nobles of Inner Austria. Yet he was determined that his son would not be influenced by Lutheranism, which he viewed as dangerous not only spiritually but also politically. He sent Ferdinand to the Jesuit University of Ingolstadt, where the young man studied between 1590 and 1595. Also attending the university was his cousin and future brother-in-law, Maximilian I of Bavaria. It was there that

Ferdinand II. (Library of Congress)

Ferdinand learned the fundamental tenets that were to guide him throughout his life: unswerving loyalty to the Roman Catholic church, the responsibilities of a Christian prince, and a belief in the divine right doctrine of "one ruler, one religion." It was also there that he learned to depend upon the Jesuits for their advice and counsel, something he was to do for the remainder of his life.

With his father's death in 1590, Ferdinand, as a minor, ruled through a regency until 1596. Upon gaining power, he immediately demonstrated that he had learned his Ingolstadt lessons well. His first action was to refuse to confirm the "religious pacification" that his father had issued. He then set about restoring Roman Catholicism in his lands by expelling the Protestant preachers and teachers, closing or destroying the Protestant churches, confiscating the property of Protestant nobles, and offering nonnoble Protestants a choice of exile or conversion. This confessional absolutism resulted in Ferdinand's establishing religious uniformity within his domain within a relatively short period of time. By removing the base of support for his Protestant nobles, he was able simultaneously to destroy potential opposition to his absolutism by forcing the Estates to accede to his demands. In this undertaking, Ferdinand was confident that his was a mission in the service of the Church. His success led him to

intrigue to gain the succession to the imperial throne, where he could continue his mission on a broader scale.

LIFE'S WORK

The Holy Roman Empire of the early seventeenth century was an empire in name only. Since the mid-fourteenth century, the crown of emperor had been elective, and the princes' jealously guarded their prerogatives, won at great cost. The Reformation, which had begun with Martin Luther's declarations in Saxony, had accelerated the forces of fragmentation. Religious coalitions of princes resulted in frequent wars; by 1555, the empire was on the verge of political and religious anarchy. In that year, the Peace of Augsburg fixed the limits of Lutheranism but ignored Calvinism altogether. Afterward, weak or otherwise occupied emperors were neither able to enforce the treaty nor to enhance the power of either the Habsburgs or Roman Catholicism.

When Emperor Rudolf II died heirless in 1612, and his brother and successor Matthias appeared destined to do the same, it was deemed imperative by the Spanish-Bavarian factions at the imperial court that the best candidate be elected emperor. With Ferdinand's record of devotion to Roman Catholicism and his strong-willed leadership with his own domain to recommend him, the Archduke of Inner Austria was the obvious choice. To the German princes of all religions, the move was greeted with trepidation. Still, as the result of no small degree of behind-the-scenes manipulation, Ferdinand was crowned king of Bohemia in 1617 and of Hungary in 1618. He was elected Emperor of the Holy Roman Empire in 1619. When he moved to Vienna, he took with him his closest associates, especially his Jesuit confessor, William Lamormaini, and those who had served him well in catholicizing Inner Austria.

That such a person would be crowned particularly concerned Bohemian Protestant nobles, who had little influence on the choice of their king. Fearing the loss of their religious privileges, held since the time of John Hus, in May, 1618, they revolted and declared the Calvinist Frederick V, elector of the Palatinate, as their choice for king of Bohemia. That was the opening event of the Thirty Years' War. Although the Bohemians briefly besieged Vienna, they were soon placed on the defensive. Ferdinand was supported by Spanish Habsburg troops and by the Catholic League of German princes under the leadership of Maximilian I of Bavaria. Opposing the Catholic forces was the Protestant Union, an amalgam of Lutheran and Calvinist princes who were divided in their support of the Bohemian rebels. Accordingly, Ferdinand was able to crush the rebels as well as to occupy the Palatinate.

During the Bohemian phase of the Thirty Years' War, many Lutheran princes had remained neutral. Ferdinand's actions after his victory were to send a corporate chill of horror through their ranks. As he had once done in Inner Austria, he now restored Bohemia to Roman Catholicism and instituted political absolutism through the Jesuits, the Inquisition, and confiscation. He executed the leaders of the revolt, destroyed the Bohemian Estates, confiscated vast tracts of land, ruined the town-centered economy, and expelled Protestants by the thousands. What had been a vibrant, Protestant, town-oriented society was transformed into a rural, agricultural latifundia under Jesuit domination. The thoroughness of the undertaking resulted in the Protestant princes of the empire allying themselves with the Lutheran king of Denmark and declaring war on the emperor.

The Danish phase of the Thirty Years' War resulted in the virtual ascendancy of the Habsburgs over the Holy Roman Empire, something that had not existed for centuries. The long-standing weaknesses of the Austrian Habsburgs had been a shortage of income and a reliance upon the military strength of allies. The confiscations of land and the concomitant destruction of the burgher class in Bohemia had greatly added to the imperial treasury. The large-scale economic depredations resulted in a disastrous inflation that Ferdinand's advisers used to his financial advantage. Just as significant was the emergence of Albrecht Wenzel von Wallenstein as general of the imperial army. That lessened Ferdinand's reliance upon the military forces provided by his Spanish Habsburg cousins and the Catholic League. Wallenstein was a great general who completely defeated the Protestant forces by 1629 and dominated the entire German area of the empire. He was also able to implement a system of support for his army that cost the emperor virtually nothing, thereby freeing him from dependence upon the generosity of the Catholic League.

Ferdinand, as undisputed master of the empire, now sought to apply his fundamental tenets to the empire itself. In March, 1629, he issued the Edict of Restitution, which ordered the return to the Roman Catholic Church of all property confiscated by Protestants since the Peace of Augsburg. Had this been successful, Ferdinand would have established imperial ascendancy throughout the empire. His action, however, succeeded only in uniting Protestant and Catholic princes against him. Their combined efforts resulted in Wallenstein's dismissal in 1630, thereby depriving the emperor of a major factor in his

successes. The Edict of Restitution also resulted in further consequences. The French, who wanted to block the Habsburgs wherever possible, agreed to support financially the efforts of Gustavus II Adolphus of Sweden, who was alarmed by the strong Habsburg forces on the Baltic shoreline. In 1630, the Swedish king invaded the empire, driving imperial and Catholic League forces back to Austria. Ferdinand recalled Wallenstein, who checked the Swedish advance. The death of Gustavus II Adolphus at Lützen in 1632 ended the brilliant skein of victories for the Protestants, and the Swedish phase of the Thirty Years' War became a virtual stalemate.

The strains of war and rule left Ferdinand prematurely aged. He acquiesced to the dismissal and assassination of Wallenstein in 1634. He then turned much of the work of government over to his very capable son, Ferdinand III. As the war had degenerated into a desultory conflict during which the civilian population suffered greatly, his son was largely responsible for the Peace of Prague (1635), which reconciled most of the German princes with the emperor. This peace effectively terminated Ferdinand's dream of a Catholic, Habsburg Holy Roman Empire. Sadly for Germany, the war, which began as a religious/political struggle within the empire, had become a part of a European-wide war between the Bourbons and the Habsburgs. The Thirty Years' War would not end until France, Sweden, and Spain were in agreement; that would not occur until 1648. Ferdinand himself died in Vienna on February 15, 1637.

While the Thirty Years' War dominated most of Ferdinand's actions during his life as monarch, there were other aspects of his life that are worth mentioning. He was a stout, blond, blue-eyed man who was kind and benevolent to those he loved. He was devoted to his family. He was twice married, in 1600 to Maria Anna of Bavaria, sister of Maximilian I, and, following her death in 1616, in 1622 to Eleonora Gonzaga, sister of Vincenzo II of Mantua. He was the father of six children. In his personal life, he was frugal; in his public life, he was as ceremonious as the occasion demanded. He was also a patron of the arts, especially music and the theater. He did not look the part of a zealot, but he most assuredly was as far as his religion was concerned.

SIGNIFICANCE

The significance of Ferdinand II in history is based upon his unyielding belief in the Roman Catholic faith. Although he could be kind and benevolent on some matters, his Catholic convictions were an all-consuming passion. He lived the Catholic life; he was pious and virtuous. He attended masses at all hours of the day and night; he favored priests and relics; he went on pilgrimages; and he relied on his Jesuit confessors and advisers.

Just as devoutly as he believed in his faith, so too did he devoutly believe that Protestantism meant heresy and disloyalty. Therefore, Protestantism had to be ruthlessly extirpated. Had he been in a position of insignificance, his zealotry would have perhaps been inconvenient, but not dangerous. As an archduke and an emperor, his actions led to great changes in Central Europe.

While the Thirty Years' War was for many a political conflict, there is no disputing that for Ferdinand it was for Catholicism first and political gain second. Other powers may have used the war for political gains; Ferdinand used it for the Counter-Reformation. No other explanation of his activities in Inner Austria, his crusade in Bohemia, or his issuance of the Edict of Restitution can suffice. Perhaps naïve, and certainly bigoted, Ferdinand missed a golden opportunity to unite or at least to control the Holy Roman Empire for the Habsburgs. In sum, Ferdinand II was an exceptionally diligent monarch who worked long hours with his ministers in an effort to carry through his fundamental tenets.

—*William S. Brockington, Jr.*

FURTHER READING
Asch, Ronald G. *The Thirty Years' War: The Holy Roman Empire and Europe, 1618-1648.* New York: St. Martin's Press, 1997. Asch describes how a crisis of the Habsburg monarchy and the Holy Roman Empire were among the causes of the war.
Coxe, William. *History of the House of Austria, from the Foundation of the Monarchy by Rhodolph of Hapsburgh, to the Death of Leopold the Second, 1218 to 1792.* 3d ed. London: Bell & Daldy, 1873. This standard work, although older, remains significantly valuable for those interested in Austrian history. Propounds both thought-provoking analyses and interesting details of court and personal life.
Evans, R. J. W. *The Making of the Habsburg Monarchy, 1550-1700: An Interpretation.* New York: Oxford University Press, 1984. Evans focuses upon the Central European Counter-Reformation and its socioeconomic consequences, as well as upon the interaction between regions of the empire and the imperial government. His prime focus is upon intellectual and social history.
Fichtner, Paula Sutter. *The Habsburg Monarchy, 1490-1848: Attributes of Empire.* New York: Palgrave Macmillan, 2003. Sutter argues that the expansion of the Habsburg Empire constituted a form of European imperialism.
Guthrie, William P. *Battles of the Thirty Years' War: From White Mountain to Nordlingen, 1618-1635.* Contributions in Military Studies 213. Westport, Conn.: Greenwood Press, 2003. This first volume of two books describes the battles fought in the early years of the war.
_____. *The Later Thirty Years' War: From the Battle of Wittstock to the Treaty of Westphalia.* Contributions in Military Studies 222. Westport, Conn.: Greenwood Press, 2003. Guthrie concludes his examination of the Thirty Years' War with a description of the battles fought between 1636 and 1648.
Ingrao, Charles W. *The Habsburg Monarchy, 1618-1815.* 2d ed. New York: Cambridge University Press, 2000. This revised and updated history of the monarchy traces the Habsburg state's emergence as a military and cultural power of tremendous influence. Includes a chapter on the Thirty Years' War.
Parker, Geoffrey, ed. *The Thirty Years' War.* 2d rev. ed. New York: Routledge, 1997. Several historians collaborated to provide this account of the war. It is the best single work for providing the reader with an overview of the conflict and with pertinent bibliographical information.
Wandruszka, Adam. *The House of Habsburg: Six Hundred Years of a European Dynasty.* Translated by Cathleen Epstein and Hans Epstein. Westport, Conn.: Greenwood Press, 1975. An excellent overview of the role of the Habsburg Dynasty in European affairs, containing good character sketches of its members.

PIERRE DE FERMAT
French mathematician

Fermat made several pivotal discoveries in the foundations of analytical geometry, differential calculus, and probability theory, serving as an intellectual catalyst for René Descartes, Gottfried Wilhelm Leibniz, and Sir Isaac Newton. His main achievements, however, were in number theory, in which he established the basis of the modern theory and formulated two fundamental theorems that still bear his name.

BORN: August 17, 1601; Beaumont-de-Lomagne, France
DIED: January 12, 1665; Castres, France
AREA OF ACHIEVEMENT: Mathematics

EARLY LIFE

Pierre de Fermat (pyehr deh fehr-mah) was born in a provincial village northwest of Toulouse in the Gascony region of southern France. His father, Dominique, was a well-to-do leather merchant and petty official; his mother, Claire, née de Long, belonged to a prominent family of jurists. Pierre, his brother Clement, and his two sisters acquired primary and secondary education at the local monastery of Grandselve. Pierre then attended the University of Toulouse, from which, having decided on a legal career, he entered the University of Law at Orléans, where he earned a bachelor of civil laws degree in 1631. Shortly before graduation, he purchased an office in the *parlement* of Toulouse; shortly after, he married a distant cousin, Louise de Long, and settled down to a long and apparently uneventful career as a civil official and legislator. For the next thirty-four years, he fathered five children, served capably in office, and overtly did little to distinguish himself. Few records remain of his life, beyond the normal transactions of the bourgeois.

The single remaining portrait of Fermat, apparently done when he was around forty-five, shows a round, somewhat fleshy face, with arched brows, a large straight nose, and a small, rather delicate mouth. The large eyes, the most prominent feature of his face, seem unfocused, as though staring at something deep within. On the whole, he looks remote, withdrawn, aloof, and a bit patrician—a proper image for a provincial jurist.

He looked undistinguished largely because he wanted to. His life spanned a turbulent period in French history, when distinction often led to disgrace or at least to difficulty. Fermat avoided this adroitly, and he therefore gained stability and a measure of leisure, allowing him to pursue his real interest: mathematics. Mathematics had not yet become a profession, hence, it could be pursued as a hobby. Fermat became one of the greatest mathematical hobbyists of his or of any other time. His correspondence is filled with the most daring mathematical speculations ever recorded, all the more striking because he strenuously resisted publication or any kind of public recognition. Publication might have jeopardized his stability, his security, and his serenity.

LIFE'S WORK

Fermat's major achievements lie in the field of his great love, number theory; but he anticipated these with striking discoveries in other analytical areas, which, characteristically, he neglected to publish, thereby allowing others—notably René Descartes and Blaise Pascal—to gain credit that was properly his. Thus, for example, he anticipated the fundamental discovery underlying the differential calculus thirteen years before the birth of Sir Isaac Newton and seventeen years before that of Gottfried Wilhelm Leibniz; yet they are commonly given independent credit for that finding. He did this in a characteristic way.

The basic problem of differentiation is to determine the rate of change of a system at a particular instant in time. This is commonly represented by the attempt to draw the straight-line tangent to the graph of a continuous function—that is, to discover how to construct a line tangent to any point of a given curve. After Descartes had invented a coordinate system, constructing the graph itself was relatively easy. The difficulty lay in determining the tangent, for it changed at every point in the curve. The inventors of the calculus solved this simply by visualizing what would happen to a given tangent as it approached a given point—that is, by seeing how the tangent changed as the distance between it and the point dwindled to nothing. Once they had seen this in their imagination, they could proceed to create algebraic or graphical means of specifying it; this was done by determining the limiting values of the y-component divided by the x-component as both approached zero simultaneously. This sounds complicated and is extremely difficult to visualize without graphic demonstration and some knowledge of trigonometry, but these problems had real physical applications that had to be determined before modern physics and the technology based on it could be carried out.

Fermat made a second discovery in this new differential calculus closely related to the first. Basic algebra presents equations in which one quantity is expressed in terms of another: $y = 4t$ for example. This means that the value of y can be determined by calculating the value of $4t$. From another point of view, the value of y depends on t, or y depends on t, or y is a function of t: $y = f(t)$, in algebraic notation. In this particular instance, the function can be graphed as a straight line, and the calculations for applications are quite simple. When the graph is a complex curve, however, in many practical applications it is necessary to find the maximum and minimum values of the function. Fermat derived a way to do this simply, both graphically and algebraically. Beginning with his earlier observations about tangents, Fermat reasoned that the highest and lowest values of any function would be found at the highest and lowest points of the curve. Observation would show this easily on a graph. Furthermore, these tops and bottoms would occur only where the tangents became parallel to the horizontal axis—that is, where the equation of the tangent became zero. To find them, he had only to set the tangent equation equal to

Pierre de Fermat. (Library of Congress)

zero and calculate the point. This discovery, relatively simple, had vital and far-reaching effects.

Fermat himself occasionally dabbled in particular applications of his general theorems. In one case, he turned his attention to optics and the problems of determining how a ray of light will behave when it reflects from or is refracted through a surface. In the process of studying this, he discovered what has come to be called the principle of least time, which is the fundamental principle of quantum theory, particularly in its mathematical aspect of wave mechanics. A ray of light passes from point A to point B, undergoing several reflections and passing through several surfaces. Fermat proved that regardless of deviations, the path the ray must take can be calculated by a single factor: The time spent in passage must be a minimum. On the strength of this theorem, Fermat deduced that, in reflection, the angle of incidence equals the angle of reflection and, in refraction, the sine of the angle of incidence equals a constant multiple of the angle of refraction in moving from one medium to another.

Fermat was also an innovator in analytic geometry, anticipating Descartes in the process but characteristically refusing to declare his precedence by publishing his findings. In fact, he went beyond Descartes and made the crucial applications on which all further progress in the discipline depended. Fermat was the first to postulate a space of three dimensions, thereby laying the basis for modern multidimensional analytic geometry. Like most of his other discoveries, this marked a true turning point, for the great difficulty in this method of analysis is going from two to three dimensions. Moreover, in making this transition, Fermat also corrected Descartes in the classification of curves by degrees of equation. Descartes, assuming proprietary rights as the assumed inventor of the system, at first balked at accepting the corrections of an amateur but had to concede in the end. Yet true credit for this invention was denied Fermat for centuries. Similarly, not until 1934 did anyone discover that Newton had borrowed the fundamental theorem of the differential calculus from Fermat.

Any of these discoveries alone would have sufficed for the life's work of any mathematical genius. For Fermat, however, these were mere incidents; his principal mathematical occupation was the theory of numbers, a field in which he made his major achievements. This field concerns itself with the most basic of all topics in mathematics: the simple whole numbers and their common relationships and properties. Although basic to mathematics and simple in the beginning, the problems presented here have led to the most abstract theories.

Fermat began by concentrating on prime numbers—those numbers greater than one that have no divisors other than 1 and the number itself: 2, 3, 5, 7, 11, and the like. In working with these numbers, Fermat routinely presented his theorems without proofs, or without proving them completely, or simply with hints about the methods he used to discover them. Furthermore, he sometimes happened to be completely—or partly—wrong. Something like that took place in his formulation of what came to be known as Fermat's numbers: the series 3, 5, 17, 257, 65537. All of these numbers are found by the same process of raising 2 to a further power of 2 itself raised to a sequential power of 2. Fermat asserted that every number so found is a prime. He was right for the first five numbers, but the next two that follow are not primes. Thereafter in the sequence, there seems to be no general rule, though that could not be determined until the development of modern computers. The amazing point is this: Fermat was wrong, but these numbers still turned out to have significant applications in physics.

Fermat's greatest accomplishments in number theory are found in two theorems that still bear his name: Fermat's theorem and his last theorem. The first can be stated simply: If n is any whole number and p is any prime, then $n^p - n$ is divisible by p. Typically, he gave this without proof, and one was not presented until fifty years after his death. Yet the proof depends on only two facts: that a given whole number can be made only by multiplying primes, and that if a prime divides a product of two numbers then it divides at least one of them. Yet it also depends on the use of the principle of mathematical induction, which was first formulated during Fermat's lifetime. That Fermat had formulated this principle independently is clear from this theorem and from his description of a method he called "infinite descent," already suggested in the account given of his method of tangents.

Fermat's so-called last theorem, which states that there are no solutions to equations of the type $x^n + y^n = z^n$ when n is greater than 2, grew out of his fascination with the kind of equations called Diophantine—equations with two or more unknowns requiring whole number solutions. Fermat accomplished much with these equations. For example, he asserted that the equation $y^3 = x^2 + 2$ has only one solution: $y = 3$, $x = 5$. As usual, he gave no proof; yet he must have had one, since one eventually emerged.

SIGNIFICANCE

The significance of someone such as Fermat is difficult to state directly or simply, since he worked solely in the area of abstract mathematics and produced few tangible or readily measurable results. It is even more difficult with him than with other mathematicians because he refused publicity; at his death, few could have been aware that one of the world's truly seminal minds was passing away. Furthermore, many of his discoveries were paralleled by other workers; it would be easy to dismiss him as interesting but not particularly significant, but such a judgment would not do him justice.

So many of his discoveries were pivotal, providing a necessary impetus to the opening of several new and rich fields of inquiry. While it is true that others paralleled some of his work, in most cases he provided the catalyst. In analytic geometry, for example, Descartes preceded him in print, but Fermat made the absolutely necessary transition to the third dimension; he also corrected Descartes's formulation of the degrees of the equations. Without these contributions, Cartesian analysis could not have become a formidable instrument in the development of mechanics and the incipient engineering of the Industrial Revolution. Similarly, Newton and Leibniz could not have begun differential calculus without Fermat's work on tangents and slopes. Finally, whole areas of analysis in physics remain indebted to Fermat.

—James Livingston

FURTHER READING

Beiler, Albert H. *Recreations in the Theory of Numbers: The Queen of Mathematics Entertains*. 2d ed. New York: Dover, 1966. Beiler provides a solid introduction to the problems that Fermat attacked and his methods of solution. This work is less technical in approach than many books in number theory, but it requires some knowledge of advanced mathematics.

Bell, Eric T. *Men of Mathematics*. New York: Simon & Schuster, 1986. An excellent general introduction to the major figures in classical mathematics. Bell's discussion of Fermat covers all major topics with style and wit.

Burton, David M. *The History of Mathematics: An Introduction*. Boston: Allyn & Bacon, 1984. A standard text, written for readers with some knowledge of advanced mathematics. Burton re-creates the process of problem solving, which is particularly good for understanding Fermat.

Kline, Morris. *Mathematical Thought from Ancient to Modern Times*. New York: Oxford University Press,

1972. An excellent general history of mathematics, with a clear, succinct account of Fermat's contributions.

Krizek, Michal, Florian Luca, and Lawrence Somer. *Seventeen Lectures on Fermat Numbers*. New York: Springer, 2001. These lectures provide an overview of the properties of Fermat numbers and their various mathematical applications.

Mahoney, Michael Sean. *The Mathematical Career of Pierre de Fermat (1601-1665)*. Princeton, N.J.: Princeton University Press, 1973. The quality of writing and clarity of exposition makes this book a good work for general readers as well as historians of mathematics or science. The mathematical explanations are fully detailed and not overly technical.

Ribenboim, Paulo. *Fermat's Last Theorem for Amateurs*. New York: Springer, 1999. Intended for students, teachers, and amateur mathematicians, the book explains the proofs related to Fermat's last theorem.

Simmons, George Finlay. *Calculus Gems: Brief Lives and Memorable Mathematics*. New York: McGraw-Hill, 1992. This collection of biographies includes a chapter about Fermat's discovery of analytic geometry and his founding of modern numbers theory.

Singh, Simon. *Fermat's Enigma: The Epic Quest to Solve the World's Greatest Mathematical Problem*. New York: Walker, 1997. Recounts how scientists and mathematicians during a 350-year period attempted to solve Fermat's last theorem, concluding in Andrew Wiles's eventual solution.

SEE ALSO: Pierre Bayle; The Bernoulli Family; Robert Boyle; Tommaso Campanella; Anne Conway; René Descartes; Elizabeth of Bohemia; Galileo; Pierre Gassendi; Thomas Hobbes; Gottfried Wilhelm Leibniz; John Locke; Marin Mersenne; Duchess of Newcastle; Sir Isaac Newton; Blaise Pascal; Wilhelm Schickard; Baruch Spinoza; Wang Fuzhi.

RELATED ARTICLES in *Great Events from History: The Seventeenth Century, 1601-1700:* 1615-1696: Invention and Development of the Calculus; 1637: Descartes Publishes His *Discourse on Method*; 1654: Pascal and Fermat Devise the Theory of Probability; 1673: Huygens Explains the Pendulum; Summer, 1687: Newton Formulates the Theory of Universal Gravitation.

NICHOLAS FERRAR
English religious leader

Turning away from his worldly success in London society, business, and politics, Ferrar found a richer life on the borders of the Fen country at Little Gidding, in a tiny Christian community that he designed for his extended family. Although he performed no great deeds, Ferrar's example of religious everyday family life had an impact on future generations.

BORN: February 22, 1592; London, England
DIED: December 4, 1637; Little Gidding, Huntingdonshire, England
AREA OF ACHIEVEMENT: Religion and theology

EARLY LIFE

Nicholas Ferrar's (FUR-uhr) father was a wealthy and prominent London merchant, a business associate of the Elizabethan adventurers Sir John Hawkins, Sir Francis Drake, and Sir Walter Ralegh, and director of the Virginia Company. His mother, Mary Woodnoth Ferrar, a deeply religious woman, was the daughter of Cheshire gentry, but she found her vocation in homemaking and child rearing. Nicholas was their third son and fifth child.

From infancy, Nicholas displayed a remarkable aptitude for learning and religious sensitivity. The Ferrar family nicknamed the boy "Saint Nicholas" and told tales about his piety. For example, at age five Nicholas was so taken with his confirmation ceremony that afterward he slipped into another group of candidates and had the bishop confirm him a second time. Before he was six and went away to grammar school, Nicholas had read the Bible and John Foxe's *Actes and Monuments* (1563). He attended grammar school in Newbury and when he was fourteen matriculated at Clare Hall, Cambridge, where he distinguished himself through learning, temperance, and piety. In 1610, when he graduated at the age of eighteen, he was elected to a fellowship and as a fellow of Clare Hall began the study of medicine.

Ill health interrupted Ferrar's medical studies. He had never been robust and now suffered from malaria or some other form of ague. In 1612, his physician advised him to travel abroad, and in 1613, on the recommendation of the master of Clare, he was placed in the entourage of the daughter of James I, Princess Elizabeth

Stuart, who was then starting her ill-fated career as the Winter Queen by going to the Continent to join her husband, the Palatine elector Frederick V. Ferrar traveled with her party to Holland and there departed on his own grand tour, which took him through Germany, Italy, France, and Spain between 1613 and 1618. He mastered the languages of these countries and studied their religious practices, but his travels overtaxed his strength, and at Marseilles in 1616, he nearly died of a severe fever.

In 1618, he came home to London, where his father was dying, and the resulting disarray of the family firm required Ferrar to enter business and take charge of the firm. He would have preferred to return to Cambridge or to accept the academic post that was offered to him at Gresham College, but he dutifully agreed to manage the Ferrar business interests. He tried energetically to save the Virginia Company, but it was dissolved in 1623 despite his efforts and largely for political reasons. In 1624, he was elected a member of Parliament. In the House of Commons he was active in the impeachment of Lionel Cranfield, first earl of Middlesex, who had led the attack on the Virginia Company.

By 1625, Ferrar had distinguished himself in business, politics, and London society, but his many successes seemed only to disillusion him deeply. A wealthy young bachelor, he was offered in marriage many rich city heiresses and blue-blooded daughters of gentry and nobility, but he had decided never to marry. Years later, he would explain his disillusionment by saying that in worldly callings there were diverse perplexities, distractions, and utter ruin. Knowing Scripture as he did, he might have cited Luke 10:38-42 to the point: He had been anxious and troubled about many things and yet in his eyes one thing only was needful, to serve the Lord by heeding his word.

Ferrar's father had died in 1620, and his widowed mother was unhappy in the city and wished for a religious retreat and retirement in the country. During the mid-1620's, Ferrar liquidated the family business interests. Ferrar and his mother looked for a suitable refuge in the country. The manor of Little Gidding in Huntingdonshire had come on the market in 1620 after the suicide in the Tower of London of Gervase, first Baron Clifton. Clifton had neglected his properties, and Little Gidding was in a state of ruin. The manor house was dilapidated, the church was used for a hay barn and pigsty, and a sole shepherd's hut stood where many cottages had once been. Mary Ferrar bought the manor in 1625. The London plague of 1625 provided the occasion for the move of the whole Ferrar family from London to Little Gidding in 1626.

LIFE'S WORK

Ferrar's most important work occurred during the eleven years between his arrival at Little Gidding in 1626 and his death there in 1637. His accomplishment was the religious community of Little Gidding, and it was his legacy to the Church of England and to humanity. Many contemporary Englishmen misunderstood Little Gidding, and the community has puzzled historians as well. Puritan critics attacked it as a Protestant nunnery. Modern historians have described it variously as papist, Puritan, Platonic, familial, Utopian, and Anglo-Catholic. Ferrar was neither a Puritan nor a crypto-Roman Catholic: He was an Anglican. A well-informed contemporary described the residents of Little Gidding correctly as "orthodox, regular, puritanical protestants."

Upon their arrival, the members of the new community first repaired the fabric of Little Gidding, giving the church priority. Next, Ferrar designed a rule for religious living, a regime of continual prayer, day and night, and wide community service, providing education and medical care for the neighborhood. Ferrar believed that everyone ought to have a trade, and so the community took up bookbinding and produced handsome volumes of religious works. They followed the old Benedictine principle of *ora et labora:* Everyone was occupied in meaningful prayer and labor for the greater good and greater glory of God.

Ferrar took neither side in the great religious, political, and social conflicts that would result, in 1642, in the English Civil War. He had been brought up on Foxe's *Actes and Monuments* to believe that the pope was the Antichrist. He was a Royalist, because he loved King Charles I, and he was a high churchman, because he espoused Archbishop William Laud's religious aesthetics of "the decency of divine worship" and "the beauty of holiness." Yet he allowed both Roman Catholics and Puritans to visit Little Gidding and join in its devotions. He befriended both Laud and Laud's enemy, Bishop John Williams of Lincoln.

Visitors were welcome at Little Gidding, so long as they neither interfered in nor interrupted the community's religious activities. Ferrar became accustomed to harmonizing the discordant interests of members of the three-generational extended family that formed the community. Far from homogenous, the community included not only his two saintly virgin nieces but also the black sheep, his younger brother Richard, not to mention everyone from the holy to the rakehell. The family of Little Gidding had the problems that any family has, exacerbated by its size of thirty to forty members.

Ferrar did not rule as a tyrant, nor was he the pseudo-messiah of a cult. He scorned worldly success, political power, ecclesiastical preferment, and academic honors. In the wider world, he was content to remain a deacon of the Church of England. At Little Gidding, he was content to obey his aged mother, and until her death in 1634, she was matriarch of the community. In his many literary endeavors, Ferrar always sought anonymity. His published works were all printed without his name. Most of his works remained unpublished, because he wrote them for the instruction and entertainment of his community or of particular friends outside Little Gidding. These works were either manuscripts or editions privately printed at Little Gidding.

In fact, Ferrar's literary modesty was such that he considered his works to be those of community, and he made no distinction between the art of authorship and the craft of book production. Ferrar never traveled to court to curry favor of the great; instead, he was happy to permit the great, including King Charles I himself, to visit Little Gidding and participate in community religious life. In his attitude there was no perverse pride, reverse snobbery, or false humility. He started no religious movement, no Anglican monastic order, no school of Ferrarian theology. Rather, his monument was the example of his life, which has endured long after 1646, when Puritan fanatics destroyed Little Gidding and scattered the surviving members of the religious community.

Ferrar's life at Little Gidding was not uneventful. The Metaphysical poets George Herbert and Richard Crashaw visited and corresponded with him. He designed the rule for the community and coordinated community activities. He studied and wrote, worked and prayed, and suffered from his chronic fevers. Ferrar profoundly influenced Herbert, other Metaphysical poets, many Anglican churchmen, King Charles I, and many others, neither by what he wrote nor by his great deeds but by how he lived.

Indeed, Ferrar was so self-effacing that his biographers write not about his personality but about his "impersonality." Few of his contemporaries seem even to have noticed his appearance. It was as if Ferrar really existed only insofar as he was in the Little Gidding community and had no existence apart from it. His portrait as a young man, which hangs in Magdalene College, Cambridge, shows an intense and very Italianate, unshaven Englishman with dark hair and large, wide-set, dark eyes.

Like the anonymity of his writings, his impersonality reflected humility and his merging identity with the Little Gidding community. Ferrar's variety of religious experience resembles that of another merchant's son who felt himself unworthy to take Holy Orders, Saint Francis of Assisi, but Saint Francis's medium was nature, while Ferrar's was family life. His biographer A. L. Maycock rightly called Ferrar "one of the most saintly men that has ever adorned the Church of England."

SIGNIFICANCE

Ferrar achieved rapid success in academic life, business, politics, and social life, but at the age of thirty-two, he renounced worldly callings and retired to Little Gidding in Huntingdonshire, where he established a religious community for his extended family. Ferrar's example had tremendous impact on his age and has continued to influence Christian spiritually for centuries, especially in the Church of England, Anglo-Catholicism, and the works of English poets from Herbert to T. S. Eliot.

—*Terence R. Murphy*

FURTHER READING

Ferrar, John. *Materials for the Life of Nicholas Ferrar: A Reconstruction of John Ferrar's Account of His Brother's Life Based on All the Surviving Copies.* Edited with an introduction by Lynette R. Muir and John A. White. Leeds, West Yorkshire, England: Leeds Philosophical and Literary Society, 1996. A modern edition of John Ferrar's biography of his brother, Nicholas.

Ferrar, Nicholas. *The Ferrar Papers.* Edited by B. Blackstone. Cambridge, England: Cambridge University Press, 1938. Important primary source materials including an early biography of Ferrar. Contains useful commentary.

Maycock, A. L. *Nicholas Ferrar of Little Gidding.* London: Society for Promoting Christian Knowledge, 1938. Reprint. Grand Rapids, Mich.: W. B. Eerdmans, 1980. The standard biography; workmanlike and scholarly, but with a literary flair. Maycock also wrote the *Chronicles of Little Gidding* (1954).

Moore, William W. *The Little Church That Refused to Die.* Princeton Theological Monograph Series 35. Allison Park, Pa.: Pickwick, 1993. A history of the Little Gidding community.

"Nicholas Ferrar and George Herbert." In *The Criterion, 1922-1939,* edited by T. S. Eliot, 18 vols. London: Faber and Faber, 1967. The fourth of Eliot's *Four Quartets* (1943) is titled "Little Gidding" and was inspired by Ferrar's theology and a pilgrimage that Eliot had made one winter in the 1930's to Little Gidding. Several of Eliot's essays, such as "George Herbert" and "The Metaphysical Poets," are also pertinent.

Ransome, Joyce. "Prelude to Piety: Nicholas Ferrar's Grand Tour." *Seventeenth Century* 18, no. 1 (Spring, 2003): 1. Describes Ferrar's travels in Europe while he was a fellow at Clare College and the impact of these travels upon his later life.

Summers, Joseph H. *George Herbert: His Religion and Art.* Cambridge, Mass.: Harvard University Press, 1968. Important study of the complexity of early Stuart religion.

Thomas, Keith. *Religion and the Decline of Magic: Studies in Popular Beliefs in Sixteenth and Seventeenth Century England.* New York: Charles Scribner's Sons, 1971. Reprint. New York: Oxford University Press, 1997. Indispensable and brilliant discussion of systems of belief current in Tudor and Stuart England.

Trevor-Roper, H. R. *Archbishop Laud, 1573-1645.* 2d ed. London: Macmillan, 1963. Reprint. London: Phoenix Press, 2000. Important for background and for some fascinating comments on Ferrar, especially on pages 137-139.

SEE ALSO: Charles I; Richard Crashaw; Elizabeth Stuart; Frederick V; George Herbert; James I; William Laud.

RELATED ARTICLE in *Great Events from History: The Seventeenth Century, 1601-1700:* 1642-1651: English Civil Wars.

JOHN FLETCHER
English playwright

John Fletcher was the leading playwright for the King's Men theatrical company and the most widely imitated dramatist of the post-Shakespearean English theater. Along with Francis Beaumont, he introduced to the stage the genre of the tragicomedy, which attracted unprecedented numbers of elite spectators to London's private theaters.

BORN: December 20, 1579 (baptized); Rye, Sussex, England
DIED: August, 1625; London, England
AREAS OF ACHIEVEMENT: Literature, theater

EARLY LIFE

John Fletcher came from a family of distinction, though details of his early life are few. Fletcher's father, Richard Fletcher, had a successful ecclesiastical career, attaining the positions of dean of Peterborough, bishop of Bristol, bishop of Worcester, chaplain to Queen Elizabeth I (r. 1558-1603), and finally bishop of London. On February 8, 1587, Richard Fletcher, then dean of Peterborough, officiated at the execution of Mary, Queen of Scots (r. 1542-1567). He gained notoriety for the vehemence with which he harassed the undeterred Mary about her Catholic convictions, even when she was upon the scaffold. Little is known about John Fletcher's mother, Elizabeth Fletcher.

John Fletcher. (Library of Congress)

FLETCHER'S MAJOR WORKS

c. 1604	*The Woman's Prize: Or, The Tamer Tamed*
c. 1606	*The Woman Hater* (with Francis Beaumont)
c. 1608-1609	*The Faithful Shepherdess*
1608-1610	*The Coxcomb* (with Beaumont)
c. 1609	*Philaster: Or, Love Lies A-Bleeding* (with Beaumont)
c. 1609-1612	*The Captain* (with Beaumont)
1609-1614	*Bonduca*
1610-1614	*Valentinian*
1610-1616	*Monsieur Thomas*
1611	*A King and No King* (with Beaumont)
c. 1611	*The Maid's Tragedy* (with Beaumont)
c. 1611	*The Night Walker: Or, The Little Thief*
1612	*Cupid's Revenge* (with Beaumont)
c. 1612	*Four Plays, or Moral Representations, in One* (commonly known as *Four Plays in One*) (with Beaumont)
c. 1612-1613	*The Two Noble Kinsmen* (with William Shakespeare)
1613	*Henry VIII* (with Shakespeare)
1613	*The Masque of the Inner Temple and Grayes Inn* (with Beaumont)
c. 1614	*Wit Without Money*
1615-1616	*The Scornful Lady* (with Beaumont)
1616?	*Love's Pilgrimage*
c. 1616	*The Mad Lover*
1616?	*The Nice Valour: Or, The Passionate Madman*
1616-1617	*The Queen of Corinth*
1616-1618	*The Knight of Malta*
c. 1617	*The Chances*
1617?	*The Tragedy of Thierry, King of France, and His Brother Theodoret* (commonly known as *Thierry and Theodoret*) (with Beaumont)
1618	*The Loyal Subject*
1619	*The Humourous Lieutenant*
1619	*Sir John van Olden Barnavelt* (with Philip Massinger)
c. 1619-1620	*The Custom of the Country* (with Massinger)
1619-1621	*The Island Princess: Or, The Generous Portugal*
1619-1623	*The Little French Lawyer* (with Massinger)
1619-1623	*Women Pleased* (pb. 1647)
c. 1620	*The False One* (with Massinger)
c. 1621	*The Double Marriage* (with Massinger)
1621	*The Pilgrim*
1621	*The Wild-Goose Chase*
before 1622	*The Beggars' Bush* (with Massinger)
1622	*The Prophetess* (with Massinger)
1622	*The Sea Voyage*
1622	*The Spanish Curate* (with Massinger)
1623	*The Lover's Progress* (revised by Massinger, 1634)
1623	*The Maid in the Mill* (with William Rowley)
1624	*Rule a Wife and Have a Wife*
1624	*A Wife for a Month*
1625	*The Elder Brother* (with Massinger)
1626	*The Fair Maid of the Inn* (with Massinger?)
1647	*Wit at Several Weapons* (possibly with Beaumont)

John Fletcher's extended family included a number of literary artists. Fletcher's uncle, Giles Fletcher the Elder (c. 1548-1611), was both an envoy to Russia for Elizabeth I and a minor poet. Fletcher's first cousins, Giles Fletcher the Younger (c. 1585-1623) and Phineas Fletcher (1582-1650), were both poets who, producing compositions heavily influenced by Edmund Spenser (c. 1552-1599), attained minor celebrity in Cambridge University circles.

On October 15, 1591, Fletcher was accepted as a student at Benet College (now known as Corpus Christi), Cambridge University. In 1593, Fletcher became a Bible clerk, but he does not seem to have pursued an ecclesiastical career with much earnestness. Though few details of his life in Cambridge are known, Fletcher clearly benefited from the university town's vibrant literary scene. At some point after his father's death in 1596, Fletcher moved to London.

LIFE'S WORK

In London, Fletcher appears to have become part of the literary circle centered around the Mermaid Tavern, in Cheapside, London. Frequenters of the Mermaid included some of the key dramatists of the day, such as Ben Jonson and William Shakespeare. It was probably in this environment that Fletcher met Francis Beaumont (c. 1584-1616), with whom he would establish a highly successful partnership and, according to anecdotal accounts, a fast friendship. Beaumont and Fletcher's names first appeared together in print in 1607, when each contributed commendatory verses for Ben Jonson's *Volpone: Or, The Fox* (pr. 1605, pb. 1607).

Possibly the first publically produced work of which Fletcher was the sole author was a pastoral play, *The Faithful Shepherdess* (pr. c. 1608-1609, pb. c. 1610, corrected ed. 1629), probably performed by the Children of the Queen's Revels at the Blackfriars Theatre, in London. Though there is no consensus as to when Fletcher began to collaborate with Beaumont, scholars see signs of Fletcher's hand in *The Woman Hater* (pr. c. 1606, pb. 1607), an unsuccessful play performed by one of the troupes of boy actors at the Blackfriars. By 1609, the two playwrights seem to have been working together in earnest. Their first success was *Philaster: Or, Love Lies a-Bleeding* (pr. c. 1609, pb. 1620), an early tragicomedy. By 1611, the pair of playwrights, whose works were now being performed by the King's Men company, had produced two more theatrical triumphs, *The Maid's Tragedy* (pr. c. 1611, pb. 1619) and the tragicomical *A King and No King* (pr. 1611, pb. 1619).

In the preface to the first printed edition of *The Faithful Shepherdess*, Fletcher offers his definition of what he calls the new genre of tragicomedy, which became the primary offering at the private Blackfriars Theatre after its lease was acquired by Richard Burbage, the leading actor of the King's Men. Beaumont and Fletcher's tragicomedies featured exotic settings, upper-class protagonists, and highly romanticized plots designed to appeal to the Blackfriars audience, which consisted largely of the upper classes and the highly educated, as opposed to the largely lower middle class patrons of the public Globe Theatre.

In 1613, Beaumont married Ursula Isley, a wealthy heiress, and retired to the Kent countryside. Despite the fact that Beaumont wrote little after his marriage, numerous plays still carried his name as coauthor with Fletcher; evidently, the collaborators' relationship was highly marketable. Though it is often difficult to assess authorship in the seventeenth century, in which collaboration seems to have been common, scholars have been able to identify the work of Fletcher through idiosyncrasies in his writing style, such as the very high percentage of end-stopped lines in the blank verse in which he regularly composed.

In 1613, Fletcher was selected as the successor to Shakespeare as the principal playwright for the King's Men company. Fletcher seems to have been the sole author of some 10 plays in this period, including the tragicomedy *The Mad Lover* (pr. c. 1616, pb. 1647), the comedy *The Wild Goose Chase* (pr. 1621, pb. 1652), and the exoticized *The Island Princess: Or, The Generous Portugal* (pr. 1619-1621, pb. 1647). Among English playwrights of the seventeenth century, Fletcher stands as the

most influenced by Spanish drama, as can be seen in his *The Pilgrim* (pr. 1621, pb. 1647).

Tragicomedies in the style Beaumont and Fletcher had introduced proved to be eminently popular, ensuring that Fletcher was constantly in demand. Fletcher typically composed with other playwrights during his final years. Around 1613, Fletcher seems to have collaborated with Shakespeare on *Henry VIII* (pr. 1613, pb. 1623) and *The Two Noble Kinsmen* (pr. c. 1612-1613, pb. 1634). The list of playwrights with whom Fletcher composed includes many of the leading dramatists of his time, such as Thomas Middleton, James Shirley, Nathan Field, John Ford, John Webster, and Ben Jonson.

However, Fletcher's principal collaborator after the retirement of Beaumont was Philip Massinger (1583-1640), who also came from upper-class origins. Fletcher and Massinger composed at least twelve plays together, including the tragedy *The Prophetess* (pr. 1622, pb. 1647), tragicomedies such as *The Custom of the Country* (pr. c. 1619-1620, pb. 1647), and the romantic comedy *The Beggar's Bush* (pr. before 1622, pb. 1647). Fletcher and Massinger continued to use the exotic settings, extravagant plots, and romantic language with which Beaumont and Fletcher had won over the well-heeled patrons of the Blackfriars Theatre.

Sometime in August of 1625, Fletcher died of the plague. He was buried in Saint Saviour's, in Southwark, London, on August 29, 1625.

SIGNIFICANCE

Fletcher stands as one of the key figures of seventeenth century drama, having been the leading force behind the explosion in popularity of plays performed in London's private theaters. In partnership with Beaumont, Fletcher produced plays that spoke in the idiom of wealthy and educated theater patrons, spurring the King's Men acting company to shift its primary venue from the Globe to the Blackfriars Theatre.

Besides having introduced the highly successful genre of tragicomedy, Fletcher is responsible for a considerable canon of drama. Working alone or in collaboration, Fletcher had a hand in some fifty plays, including perhaps fifteen of which he was the sole author. Fletcher also introduced elements of Spanish literature to English playwrights by turning to sources such as the playwright Lope de Vega Carpio.

Numerous playwrights imitated Fletcher's penchant for exotic settings, farcical situations, and aristocratic protagonists speaking in highly romanticized language. Fletcherian tragicomedy thus became the preeminent style that shaped English drama in the decades after Shakespeare's period.

—*Randy P. Schiff*

FURTHER READING

Bowers, Fredson, ed. *The Dramatic Works in the Beaumont and Fletcher Canon*. Vol. 9. New York: University of Cambridge Press, 1994. Part of a ten-volume collection of critical editions of works assigned to Beaumont and Fletcher in 1679, this volume focuses on plays composed with Massinger, Fletcher's key collaborator in his later years.

Cone, Mary. *Fletcher Without Beaumont: A Study of the Independent Plays of John Fletcher*. Salzburg, Austria: Insitut für Englische Sprache und Literatur, Universität Salzburg, 1976. Offers in-depth analysis of works often attributed to the sole authorship of Fletcher, highlighting his influences both from English and Spanish drama.

Glover, Arnold, and Alfred Rayney Walker, eds. *The Works of Francis Beaumont and John Fletcher*. Vol. 1. Cambridge, England: Cambridge University Press, 1905. First of a ten-volume series. This volume presents editions of Beaumont and Fletcher's first major successes, including *Philaster* and *A King and No King*.

Masten, Jeffrey. *Textual Intercourse: Collaboration, Authorship, and Sexualities in Renaissance Drama*. New York: Cambridge University Press, 1997. Analysis of the cultural context for collaborative composition in early modern dramatic circles. Includes detailed analysis of Fletcher's interactions with Beaumont and with Massinger.

Shakespeare, William, and John Fletcher. *The Two Noble Kinsmen*. 2d ed. Edited by Eugene M. Waith. New York: Oxford University Press, 2002. Includes an extensive introduction to the play, with an emphasis on the process of collaborative composition and on the question of determining relative authorship. Includes a full and annotated text of the play.

Squier, Charles S. *John Fletcher*. Boston: Twayne, 1986. Biography of Fletcher that sets his works in the sociohistorical context of Early Modern drama. Includes bibliographical data.

SEE ALSO: Richard Burbage; Ben Jonson; Thomas Middleton; James Shirley; Lope de Vega Carpio; John Webster.

RELATED ARTICLES in *Great Events from History: The Seventeenth Century, 1601-1700:* c. 1601-1613: Shakespeare Produces His Later Plays; June 29, 1613: Burning of the Globe Theatre.

ROBERT FLUDD
English physician and philosopher

A physician of encyclopedic learning, Fludd compiled a systematic account of the old cosmology, in which the heavens and earth mirrored each other and man was the epitome of all things. He defended this cosmology against attacks from thinkers who wanted science to be more strictly empirical and more fully separated from religion. He supported the Rosicrucian movement but had no personal contact with Rosicrucians.

BORN: January 17, 1574 (baptized); Bearsted, Kent, England
DIED: September 8, 1637; London, England
AREAS OF ACHIEVEMENT: Medicine, philosophy, religion and theology, science and technology

EARLY LIFE

Robert Fludd was born into a wealthy family, the son of a landowner who had been knighted for service to Queen Elizabeth I. Fludd received the best available education: After earning two degrees in arts from Saint John's College, Oxford, he traveled on the Continent for six years, making many connections in the Protestant states and collecting books on subjects little known in England. He returned to Oxford, where he earned two degrees in medicine from Christ Church College. He then settled in London, where he spent the rest of his life.

In 1606, Fludd applied for membership in the elite Royal Society of Physicians of London, but he did not gain admission for several years, because he was too enthusiastic about new chemical medicines and too dismissive of older herbal medicines in the eyes of several examiners. He was finally admitted in 1609 and formed close professional associations with several members, including William Harvey. Fludd prided himself on being the first writer to defend Harvey's discovery of the circulation of the blood.

Fludd enjoyed considerable popularity as a physician to London's wealthy citizens. He could afford the services of a secretary to take careful notes on his cases and an apothecary to prepare chemical remedies. He could also sit with his patients and try out his religious and philosophical ideas, which had the consoling effects of a good bedside manner.

LIFE'S WORK

Once back from his European travels, Fludd began work on a wide-ranging study of all the arts and sciences. He made notes on music and acoustics, theater and optics, drawing and geometry, and divination of all sorts, from astrology to palmistry. He published nothing, however, until a literary event in Germany began to influence thinkers all over Europe.

In 1614 and 1615, two manifestos were published in Germany, purporting to contain the story of Christian Rosenkreutz and the philosophy of his secret society, the Fraternity of the Rosy Cross. The Rosicrucian manifestos have been traced to a circle of Lutheran scholars in Tübingen and are sometimes attributed to a member of that circle, the young Johann Valentin Andreae. They were published anonymously, however, and offered no means of contacting the Fraternity other than publishing a new book or pamphlet. Intrigued by the promise of universal knowledge based on the signs of nature and the message of the Bible, hundreds of educated people published appeals over the next decade. Meanwhile, many religious and academic officials denounced the fraternity. At a time when witch trials were still common, several alleged Rosicrucians were tried for heresy.

Thanks to his European contacts, Fludd followed the polemics surrounding the Rosicrucians in print. Writing in Latin, the universal language of scholarship, he prepared a short apology for the Rosicrucian ideals in 1616 and expanded it in 1617. In *Tractatus apologeticus integritatem societatis de Rosea Cruce defendens* (1617; apologetic tract defending the integrity of the society of the Rosy Cross), Fludd tried to move beyond contemporary controversy and place Rosicrucian ideals in the context of European philosophy from antiquity to the present. Fludd claimed no familiarity with the Rosicrucians, and later lamented that he never heard from them. (He did not conclude that the Fraternity was a literary hoax, as Andreae later claimed.) Meanwhile, however, readers of Fludd's other books assumed that the "Fluddean philosophy" (*philosophia Fluddana*) was Rosicrucian.

By the time that he revised his apology for the Rosicrucians, Fludd had found a publisher for the first and largest of his own books. This was no easy task, for he specified that the book must be illustrated with dozens of engravings. He found a remarkable firm of printers and engravers in Oppenheim, Germany, which produced his *Utriusque cosmi maioris scilicet et minoris metaphysica, phsycica atque technica historia* (part I 1617, part II 1618, combined edition 1619; metaphysical, physical, and technical history of both worlds).

The two worlds referred to in Fludd's opus are the greater and lesser cosmos. The controlling idea of the work is that the macrocosm is mirrored in the microcosm, the great world of God's creation in the little world of humanity. This idea underlies the two-part structure of the work and is presented visually in some of the book's most famous engravings. Fludd elaborated the basic distinction in Latin works on medicine such as *Medicina Catholica* (1629; universal medicine). He found most of his readers outside England, but an English translation appeared of his final, posthumously published work, *Philosophia Moysaica* (1638; *Mosaicall Philosophy*, 1659).

Although Fludd never claimed to speak for the Rosicrucians or any other group, his statements were generally assumed to be representative of a Rosicrucian or occult tendency in European thought and were attacked by some prominent scientists of the age. The Dutch scholar Isaac Casaubon challenged Fludd's too easy acceptance of the extreme antiquity of occult figures like Hermes Trismegistus, the legendary founder of alchemy. The French monastic Marin Mersenne rejected Fludd's use of the Bible in scientific arguments, as did several of Mersenne's scientific associates. Most famously, the German astronomer Johannes Kepler began a private correspondence with Fludd that led to public debate over the relative importance of music and mathematics in the study of astrology and astronomy, conducted in weighty books at a time when astronomy and astrology were often hard to distinguish.

Culminating these exchanges was a response to Mersenne by a purported friend, one Joachim Fritzius, that made a comprehensive case for the occult sciences and, at the same time, a final apology for the Rosicrucians. Some scholars think that *Summum Bonum, quod est verum magiae, cabalae, alchymae verae, Fratrum Roseae Crucis verorum subjectum* (1629; the supreme good, which is the true subject of the magic, cabala, and true magic of the Fraternity of the Rosy Cross), though attributed to Fritzius, is actually a pseudonymous book by Fludd. Meanwhile, Fludd was challenged at home for championing such occult theories of medicine as the "weapon-salve," a sympathetic cure for wounds made by treating the instruments that caused them. *Doctor Fludd's Answer* (1631) to this challenge was one of his last books.

When Fludd died in 1637, printing was closely regulated in England and included none of the Rosicrucian works associated with Fludd. As freedom of the press emerged with the English Civil War in the next decade, many books on Rosicrucian themes appeared in English translation, including the original manifestos, which appeared as *The Fame and Confession of the Fraternity of R:C:* (1652). To alchemists and philosophers of this generation, Fludd was a leading light.

SIGNIFICANCE

History has proved Fludd to be on the losing side in the debates that launched the Scientific Revolution. He celebrated scientific discoveries, such as the circulation of blood, but tried to place them in a "macrocosmic" scheme that is now considered pseudo-scientific. He defended freedom of thought, but did so by defending the believer's right to interpret scripture rather than the separation of science and religion. His highly schematic mind found its most lasting expression in the illustrations he specified for his works, engravings that are now familiar, even to many who have never heard of Robert Fludd.

—Thomas Willard

FURTHER READING

Debus, Allen G. *The Chemical Philosophy.* 1977. Reprint. Mineola, N.Y.: Dover, 2002. A comprehensive study of Paracelsian medicine. Includes a long chapter on Fludd.

Godwin, Joscelyn. *Robert Fludd: Hermetic Philosopher and Surveyor of Two Worlds.* London: Thames and Hudson, 1979. A large-format review of Fludd's major publications on man and the cosmos. Includes 126 illustrations from his books with a brief commentary on each illustration.

Huffman, William H. *Robert Fludd and the End of the Renaissance.* New York: Routledge, 1988. The fullest study yet of Fludd's life and works. Traces both his personal and intellectual connections.

_____, ed. *Robert Fludd.* Berkeley, Calif.: North Atlantic Books, 2001. Seven selections from Fludd's writings, with helpful introductions. Also includes excerpts from a classic study of Fludd's controversy with Kepler, written by C. G. Jung's associate Wolfgang Pauli.

Yates, Frances A. *The Rosicrucian Enlightenment.* London: Routledge, 1972. A lively study of the Rosicrucian manifestos, reprinted in translation, with attention to sources of the ideas and major proponents. Includes a chapter on Fludd and his engraver.

_____. *Theatre of the World.* Chicago: University of Chicago Press, 1969. A study of memory theaters in the Renaissance, by the leading authority, with two chapters on Fludd. Makes fascinating claims for Fludd's influence on the Elizabethan stage, some of which have been qualified or disproved by subsequent research.

SEE ALSO: William Harvey; Johannes Kepler; Marin Mersenne.

RELATED ARTICLE in *Great Events from History: The Seventeenth Century, 1601-1700:* 1642-1651: English Civil Wars.

GEORGE FOX
English religious leader

Fox founded the Religious Society of Friends (Quakers) and then spent the remainder of his life defending and sustaining the new sect during one of England's most tumultuous periods.

BORN: July, 1624; Drayton-in-the-Clay (now Fenny Drayton), Leicestershire, England
DIED: January 13, 1691; London, England
AREA OF ACHIEVEMENT: Religion and theology

EARLY LIFE

George Fox's father, Christopher Fox, was a successful weaver. The family of Fox's mother, Mary Lago, was more socially prominent than his father's family. Although it is unclear exactly how many siblings Fox had, at least four sisters and one brother have been verified.

Fox was an unusually serious-minded child. Given to reflection, he was convinced of the need for a religiously centered life even in his youth. Indeed, he records in his journal—published as *The Journal of George Fox* (1694)—that "When I came to eleven years of age, I knew pureness and righteousness, for while I was a child I was taught how to walk to be kept pure. The Lord taught me to be faithful in all things." Modern biographers and scholars confirm that the Foxes' neighbors were also apparently keenly aware of this unusual boy's "godliness" from an early age.

Apprenticed in his early teens to a shoemaker, Fox learned quickly all aspects of the business, which flourished, yet he grew increasingly dissatisfied with his existence and the life his peers and mentors led. Feeling more and more a stranger in his hometown, Fox left Drayton-in-the-Clay at nineteen and wandered, eventually reaching London. Disturbed by the tumultuous life he observed in London and concerned for his anxious parents, Fox returned to Leicestershire for about a year.

In his early twenties, Fox felt himself tempted by despair and increasingly alienated by the values of his society. During the mid-1640's, Fox spoke at length with ministers from several denominations, struggling against his own despair to find spiritual strength in the religion of his youth. Eventually, however, in 1647, Fox experienced what he terms in his journal, "a great opening," detailed in one of the most famous passages from his writings:

And when all my hopes in [ministers and preachers] were gone, so that I had nothing outwardly to help me, nor could tell what to do, then, Oh then, I heard a voice which said, "There is one, . . . Christ Jesus, that can speak to thy condition," and when I heard it my heart did leap for joy.

Given fresh hope and a new purpose by this conversion experience, Fox moved toward attaining a full understanding of his life's vocation and ministry.

Feeling suddenly that "all things were new," Fox began to share openly the powerful spiritual discernment his years of wandering and intense soul-searching had finally brought him to at age twenty-four. He was arrested at Nottingham in 1649 and at Derby in 1650 for disrupting worship services in churches. In these instances, Fox was moved to take issue with the "priests" (as he referred to all professional, paid clergy) and their explication of

George Fox. (Library of Congress)

283

scriptural texts. Fox emphasized to the congregations that all they needed in order to understand Christ's message ("Truth") could be theirs through "inward revelation" of the indwelling Christ.

This message of inward reflection and revelation at the heart of all of Fox's preaching increasingly fell on receptive ears. People began to attend Fox's public sermons in large numbers, much to the consternation and then fury of the traditional clergy. Fox, a muscular, striking young man with almost shoulder-length curly locks, fascinated crowds with his booming voice and theologian's understanding of the Bible. Many local ministers, intending to rebuke him in public, quailed in front of his piercing eyes. Hundreds of Independents, Baptists, and Puritans were convinced of the truth and wisdom of Fox's message, even though Fox continued frequently to be arrested or beaten by hostile clergy, congregations, and townspeople. Especially threatening and offensive to them were Fox's arguments against forced tithing and his Pauline insistence that the Christian church lived in its people and not in buildings, which Fox and his followers dismissed as "steeplehouses."

In June, 1652, following another mystical vision atop Pendle Hill in Lancashire, Fox traveled to an area near the border of Westmorland (now in Cumbria) and Yorkshire, in western England. From a great rock in Firbank Fell, near the village of Sedbergh, Fox addressed more than one thousand people. For several hours, Fox spoke "under the power of the Lord," explaining at length his understanding of Christ's message and of the Christian life. Emphasizing his listeners' ability to hear the message of Christ in their own hearts, free of creeds, doctrines, and paid cleric-interpreters, Fox laid the groundwork for an organized new religion, one with a nonviolent message for a period of universal strife in English history. Fox, founder and chief exponent of this new religion, was not yet twenty-eight years of age.

LIFE'S WORK

From the early 1650's to the end of his life, Fox knew little rest or outward peace. His call to the Westmorland Seekers and their heady response did not lessen the furor of religious and political upheaval that characterized the larger society for all but the last several years of Fox's life. The beatings, stonings, imprisonments, and illegal detentions did not merely continue but intensified steadily after the restoration of Charles II to the English throne in May, 1660.

Successive acts of Parliament between 1662 and 1668, intended primarily to punish Puritans for their sup-

port of Oliver Cromwell, resulted also in systematic, ferocious persecutions of the pacifist Quakers, who by that time were officially called the Religious Society of Friends. Quakers became martyrs in England, and between 1659 and 1661, four Friends were hanged in Boston. Between imprisonments and persecutions on one hand and the inevitable factionalization within the society itself on the other hand, Fox's resolve and resources were tested severely during from 1652 to 1688. His tasks required all of his prodigious talents of physical endurance, shrewd courtroom rhetoric, and a sustaining religious faith.

In spite of this seemingly withering opposition and oppression, Fox and the Society of Friends thrived. In October, 1669, at age forty-five, Fox married Margaret Askew Fell of Swarthmoor Hall, Lancashire. Fell, the widow of Judge Thomas Fell, had been a principal supporter of Fox since 1652 and had long lent her social prominence and considerable wealth to the Quaker cause. Historians credit Margaret Fell and her first husband—who never actually became a Quaker—with protecting the movement in its vulnerable first years. The Society of Friends, meanwhile, grew as it sent missionaries to France, Holland, Scotland, Ireland, the American colonies, and even to Turkey.

By the time George Fox died, in London, in January, 1691, William III and Mary II had acceded to the throne of England, and the Toleration Act of 1689 had brought a final halt to the persecutions of the Quakers and other non-Anglicans. With his message of the Inner Light, of Christ's presence and love; with his refusal to take up arms or to espouse any violent cause; with his prophetic vision of a healed world, Fox had outlived violent opposition. When he died, he left behind an established religious sect committed to realizing his vision of revivified Christian love.

SIGNIFICANCE

As the founder of Quakerism, George Fox had an enormous impact on religious and cultural history. Indeed, in the judgment of the eminent British historian G. M. Trevelyan, "George Fox made at least the most original contribution to the history of religion of any Englishman." This originality manifests itself in the central tenets of Quakerism. With his prophetic visions and promptings to guide and empower him, Fox derived a system of belief based upon the concept of continuing revelation, which holds that the spirit of Christ lives within the hearts of the truly faithful and that the will of God is thus continuously revealed as human history unfolds. Fox therefore offered seventeenth century Christians a newly invigorated faith that made immediately accessible a living, dynamic Christ who could speak to the condition and lives of Christians caught in the religious undercurrents of the English Civil War and its bloody aftermath (1641-1660).

Fox's insistence on the equality of women and men in spiritual matters tapped sources of talent and leadership unprecedented in the history of Christianity. Such spiritual equality encouraged and anticipated wider educational and social opportunities for women—not only in Britain but also in America. Fox's uncompromising integrity—he always refused bail bonding, for example, because he thought it was an implied admission of guilt—inspired Quakers to advocate reforms against slavery, labor conditions, punitive judicial sentences, harsh prison conditions, and so on. Further, Fox's refusal to seek revenge, either physical or legal, against his persecutors inspired the Quaker belief in nonviolence, pacifism, and conscientious objection to participation in wars.

Historically, it is amazing that Fox and his early followers survived at all, yet eventually, even preeminent national leaders such as Oliver Cromwell (1599-1658), Charles II (1630-1685), and James II (1633-1701) came to credit (if not agree with) the unusual vision of Christian love that Fox and the Society of Friends espoused. Combining the visionary clarity of a prophet, the intuitive discernment of a mystic, the organizational ability of a political leader, and the integrity and stamina of a hero, Fox founded a religious sect whose influence reverberated far beyond the doors of its meetinghouses.

—*David W. Pitre*

FURTHER READING

Bailey, Richard. *New Light on George Fox and Early Quakerism: The Making and Unmaking of a God*. San Francisco, Calif.: Edwin Mellen Press, 1992. Bailey interprets Fox's belief in Inner Light, arguing the Inner Light was the celestial Christ who inhabited and made the believer divine.

Bori, Pier Cesare. "The Vision of Paradise in *The Journal of George Fox*." In *The Earthly Paradise: The Garden of Eden from Antiquity to Modernity*, edited by F. Regina Psaki and Charles Hindley. Birmingham, N.Y.: Global, 2002. An examination of the original Quaker conception of Paradise, as articulated by Fox in his journal.

Brinton, Howard H. *Friends for Three Hundred Years: The History and Beliefs of the Society of Friends Since George Fox Started the Quaker Movement*. London: Allen and Unwin, 1953. Reprint. Wallingford, Pa.: Pendle Hill, 1983. Perhaps the most accessible and authoritative history of Quakerism. Brinton's gift is combining scholarly insight with readability.

_____. *The Religious Philosophy of Quakerism: The Beliefs of Fox, Barclay, and Penn as Based on the Gospel of John*. Wallingford, Pa.: Pendle Hill, 1973. Brinton concisely outlines the scriptural and theological roots of Quakerism. Although brief (115 pages), the book reflects both insight and broad learning.

Fox, George. *The Journal of George Fox*. London: Thomas Northcott, 1694. Rev. ed. Cambridge, England: Cambridge University Press, 1952. Reprint. London: Religious Society of Friends, 1975. An authoritative edition of Fox's journal, incorporating the emphases and deletions of previous editions.

Gwyn, Douglas. *Apocalypse of the Word: The Life and Message of George Fox*. Richmond, Ind.: Friends United Press, 1986. An excellent scholarly biography that places Fox and Quakerism in historical and theological context. Background discussions are informative, concise, and helpful.

Ingle, H. Larry. *First Among Friends: George Fox and the Creation of Quakerism*. New York: Oxford University Press, 1994. A scholarly biography, placing Fox's life within the upheavals of the English Civil War, the Puritan Revolution, and the Reformation.

Monaghan, Hanna Darlington. *"Dear George": George Fox, Man and Prophet*. Philadelphia: Franklin, 1970. An unusual, well-researched study of Fox, this book is based on the author's comparative study of Fox's journal and the questionable liberties the first editors and compilers took with it. Especially interesting is Monaghan's discussion of the healing performed by Fox, a subject ignored by most modern biographers.

Munro, Oliver Fyfe, ed. *George Fox, 1624-1691: Our Living Contemporary*. London: Farrand Press, 1991. Contains transcripts of five lectures given to mark the tercentenary of Fox's death. The lectures outline Fox's life, the development of the Society of Friends, and the society's current and future position in the world.

Vipont, Elfrida. *George Fox and the Valiant Sixty*. London: Hamish Hamilton, 1985. Focusing on the sixty missionaries who first carried Fox's message through England and abroad. The book's content displays historical understanding and familiarity with Quaker historical geography, but its style too often borders on irksome quaintness.

West, Jessamyn. *The Friendly Persuasion*. New York: Harcourt, Brace, 1945. Reprint. San Diego, Calif.: Harcourt Brace Jovanovich, 1991. West's engaging collection of short stories about a Civil War era American Quaker family offers a human embodiment of Quaker principles, traditions, and behavior in a society that does not share those views. As such, the stories present a tangible portrait of traditional Quakerism in America.

_____, ed. *The Quaker Reader*. New York: Viking Press, 1962. Reprint. Wallingford, Pa.: Pendle Hill, 1992. A helpful anthology of Quaker thought and writing from the seventeenth to the twentieth century.

Offers a good introductory survey of Quaker theology in journals, letters, treatises, and books, but its abridgements are sometimes unsatisfactory.

SEE ALSO: Charles II (of England); Oliver Cromwell; James II; Mary II; William III.

RELATED ARTICLES in *Great Events from History: The Seventeenth Century, 1601-1700:* 1642-1651: English Civil Wars; 1652-1689: Fox Organizes the Quakers; May, 1659-May, 1660: Restoration of Charles II; 1688-1702: Reign of William and Mary; November, 1688-February, 1689: The Glorious Revolution; May 24, 1689: Toleration Act.

FREDERICK HENRY
Dutch military leader and politician

Frederick Henry, through his military and diplomatic abilities, completed successfully the Dutch Wars of Independence for the independence of the Dutch United Provinces from Spain and established the House of Orange as the hereditary sovereign of the new nation.

BORN: January 29, 1584; Delft, Holland, United Provinces (now in the Netherlands)

DIED: March 14, 1647; The Hague, Holland, United Provinces (now in the Netherlands)

ALSO KNOWN AS: Frederick Henry, count of Nassau; Frederick Henry, prince of Orange

AREAS OF ACHIEVEMENT: Military, diplomacy, government and politics

EARLY LIFE

The seventh child of William the Silent by William's fourth wife, Louise de Coligny, daughter of the French Huguenot leader Gaspard de Coligny, Frederick Henry, count of Nassau and prince of Orange, was born less than six months prior to the assassination of his father on July 10, 1584, at Delft by Balthasar Gerard. Although his mother probably intended him for a career in France, his half brother Maurice of Nassau, who was also William the Silent's successor in the struggle against Spain, directed him toward a life of service to the Dutch.

Educated at the University of Leiden, elected a member of the Council of State while still a very young man, a participant in foreign negotiations, and a close companion of his brother on the latter's military campaigns, Frederick Henry acquired at an early age a firm founda-

tion in the twin arts of diplomacy and military matters. Handsome, with a mustache and a small beard beneath thick black hair, a high forehead, and dark piercing eyes, possessed of noble bearing, renowned early for his gallantry in arms, and the first of his house with the ability to speak the Dutch language without a foreign accent, he endeared himself quickly both to the army and to the Dutch people. Unfortunately, during most of his life he suffered grievously from gout, ultimately dying of its complications.

In 1624, at the age of forty, largely on the urging of his brother Maurice, who had no children of his own, Frederick Henry married the intelligent and ambitious Amalia von Solms, who was perhaps Frederick Henry's shrewdest adviser throughout the remainder of his career.

LIFE'S WORK

The Netherlands, originally under the dominance of the Catholic Habsburg Dynasty of Spain, was divided at the time of the death of Maurice on April 23, 1625, into two parts: the southern part, primarily Roman Catholic (now Belgium and Luxembourg), under the control of Spain, and the northern part, primarily Dutch Protestant (now the Netherlands) but containing many Roman Catholics and consisting of eight provinces, struggling for its independence. Seven of the eight northern provinces were loosely bound together in a confederation congress called the Estates-General, which tried, sometimes successfully, sometimes not so successfully, to unite all eight provinces into uniform action against the Habsburg Spanish overlord.

On the death of his brother, Frederick Henry was quickly elected by five of the eight northern provinces of Holland, Zeeland, Utrecht, Overyssel, and Gelders as stadtholder (chief executive officer) to replace Maurice and was appointed by the Estates-General captain-general and admiral-general of the confederation or union, as well as head of the Council of State. Friesland, Groningen, and Drente retained their own stadtholders, while Drente, although a northern province, was not then a member of the Estates-General.

Where William the Silent had been the spirit of the revolution of the Dutch northern provinces, he lacked the military ability to go with it; where his son Maurice had the military ability, he lacked the gift of diplomacy that would have made the military struggle easier. In Frederick Henry, both military ability and diplomacy were present, so that on occasion he was able to make the conflicting interests of Calvinists and Roman Catholics work together in the northern provinces, persuade the proud province of Holland to work together with the Estates-General, and convince Cardinal de Richelieu of France to give aid to the Protestant Dutch struggle against the Catholic Habsburgs.

His first consideration lay in securing the southern and eastern borders of the union against Spanish attack, and here he demonstrated his enormous ability in besieging fortresses with success. The 1627 campaign was marked by the brilliant capture of Grol, a town on the eastern frontier, and in 1629 the even more brilliant conquest of 's Hertogenbosch. In this campaign, Frederick Henry exhibited an ability not only to obtain the highest efficiency from his soldiers but also to win their hearts, something made all the more difficult by the fact that where the Dutch Wars of Independence had become a training ground for military men from a variety of countries, of the eighteen regiments under him at 's Hertogenbosch, three were Netherlanders, one Frisian, one Walloon, two German, four French, three Scottish, and four English. Although he was unable to take Dunkirk in 1631, a Spanish fleet of thirty-five large vessels and a number of smaller ships carrying stores and munitions were destroyed on September 12 in the Battle of the River Slaak, while in 1632 the eastern frontier was strengthened by the capture of the city of Maastricht. These setbacks brought the archduchess Isabel, Habsburg regent of the Netherlands, to an effort at negotiations.

Frederick Henry. (Library of Congress)

Matters of religion and trade, however, interfered with the negotiations, as the Spaniards insisted upon the elimination of heresy in the Netherlands, and the Calvinists in the United Provinces pressed for the restriction of Roman Catholicism. Furthermore, the merchants of Amsterdam wished an elimination of trading restrictions against them that Spain was not willing to grant.

The failure of these negotiations and the need for money led Frederick Henry to achieve an almost miraculous alliance with Richelieu's France. Spain and France were both Catholic, but as they were political enemies, France was loath to see the Netherlands in Spanish hands. Although the Dutch were primarily Protestants and heretics in the eyes of Richelieu, he needed the Dutch fleet to help blockade the French Huguenot port of La Rochelle, which he was besieging. Despite the objections of French Catholics on one side and Dutch Calvinists on the other, a defensive and offensive alliance was concluded between the Dutch and the French in the early part of 1635. By the terms of the agreement, any conquests in the southern Netherlands were to be divided between them; neither nation was to conclude peace without the consent of the other; and each was to provide for field action an army consisting of twenty-five thousand foot soldiers and five thousand cavalry.

In 1637, the important city of Breda in the province of Brabant fell to the Dutch, giving the Dutch Republic the security of three great frontier fortresses: 's Hertogenbosch, Maastricht, and Breda. The following year, at the great Battle of the Downs, Lieutenant-Admiral Maarten Tromp debilitated a powerful Spanish fleet under the command of Antonio de Oquendo. For the Dutch, this battle was comparable to England's defeat of the Spanish Armada of 1588, and it ended any attempt of the Spaniards toward dominance on the sea. The following year, however, Frederick Henry's campaign against the frontier town of Hulst ended in failure, made even more disappointing by the death in that campaign of Count Henry Casimir of Nassau-Dietz, who was stadtholder of the three provinces of Groningen, Friesland, and Drente. Groningen and Drente chose Frederick Henry to be their stadtholder in place of Henry Casimir, which strengthened the union, but Friesland chose to elect William

Frederick, the younger brother of Henry Casimir, as its stadtholder. On May 12, 1640, Frederick Henry had gained sufficient prestige to enable him to marry his son William to Mary, the eldest daughter of Charles I of England, by which he hoped to add England's aid to that of France. The rift between the two branches of the House of Nassau eventually was healed when, three or four years after the death of Frederick Henry, William Frederick in 1651 married Frederick Henry's daughter Albertine Agnes.

During the Civil War in England, in which the Puritan Parliament under the leadership of Oliver Cromwell rebelled against Charles I, Frederick Henry's sympathies were with Charles. Henrietta Maria, Charles's wife, who resided at The Hague during the early stages of that revolt, pressured Frederick Henry to come to the aid of her husband, but that statesman was much too prudent not to know that the Calvinists in the northern provinces would never do again as they did in France—come to the aid of a non-Calvinist king against their fellow Calvinists. They were already dissatisfied with an alliance that in its ultimate effects permitted France to enlarge itself in the southern Netherlands at the expense of Spain, and Frederick Henry himself came to realize that it was far too dangerous to his country to permit a powerful France to take the place of a much weaker Spain in the southern Netherlands.

When religion was involved, Frederick Henry always had to be prudent. The insistence by Spain that the Inqui-

sition be introduced into the Netherlands to crush the Protestants was the original spark that inflamed the Protestants of the northern provinces to their wars for independence under William the Silent beginning in 1568. That portion of the Reformed church in the northern provinces, the Calvinists, demanded the complete suppression of Roman Catholicism. Those Protestants of the Dutch provinces who were more worldly and more tolerant of Catholicism so long as they themselves could practice their own religion were called Remonstrants, or Arminians, after the Amsterdam preacher Jacobus Arminius, while the Calvinists were called Counter-Remonstrants.

The Synod of Dort, under the dominance of the Counter-Remonstrants and Maurice's armed forces, condemned the Remonstrants and had their major leader, Johan van Oldenbarnevelt, put to death. Yet the realities of the situation outweighed the theories of the Calvinists, and in the course of time the Dutch of the northern provinces, and Frederick Henry, came to see that Catholics and Protestants could live together as Dutch folk, tolerant of one another's religious beliefs, in a country independent of Spain. Therefore, like the merchant-burghers of Amsterdam, Frederick Henry concluded that so long as the northern Dutch provinces had secured their borders, it would be better to make peace with Spain.

In the meantime, the Dutch were expanding both in the West and East Indies (the Americas and Southeast Asia, respectively). On May 9, 1624, under Piet Hein, a Dutch fleet captured Bahia in Brazil from the Portuguese, who were then under Spanish domination, then lost Bahia to the Spaniards on April 28, 1625; Hein recaptured it on March 23, 1627. The following year, Hein started attacking the treasure ships bringing gold and silver from the New World back to Spain, while other attacks on Spanish shipping led the way toward a gradual extension of Dutch control in Brazil. In the East Indies, Dutch naval supremacy over all European rivals became especially evident, so that soon rich cargoes were flowing back to Amsterdam from Amboina, Banda, the Moluccas, Java, Formosa, and even Japan. Where the Dutch West India Company had been successful in planting colonies, the Dutch East India Company had been successful in planting colonies as well as developing a rich trade in the spices and jewels that Europe prized most, both companies acting with the encouragement of Frederick Henry.

After the campaign against Hulst, Frederick Henry, age sixty-three, was broken in health, suffering badly from gout, with rapidly failing faculties of mind, spirit, and body. On March 14, 1647, he died and was buried with great pomp beside his father William and his brother Maurice in Delft. By the Acte de Survivance of April 19, 1631, almost sixteen years before, the Estates-General had declared the son of Frederick Henry, William, to be heir to his father's offices of captain-general and admiral-general of the United Provinces, giving Frederick Henry something of the position of a sovereign prince. Therefore, on Frederick Henry's death, his son succeeded him in his various offices and honors as William II.

Spain, its treasury empty; its gold galleons attacked by Dutch, French, and English buccaneers; and facing French armies at the Pyrenees, Portugal, and Catalonia in revolt, was ready for the peace that came about at Münster, on January 30, 1648, in which Spain recognized the independence of the Dutch Republic and brought an end to the Dutch Wars of Independence.

SIGNIFICANCE

The stadtholdership of Frederick Henry has been called the Golden Age of the Dutch Republic, in that Netherlanders were enormously productive in many fields of learning: law, philosophy, painting, letters, science, and seafaring. As a human being, Frederick Henry, with his natural characteristics of military ability, tolerance, and humanity, was able not only to win for his country its independence but also to stand as a model of the religious tolerance, kindliness, and practical wisdom for which the Dutch people have became so well known.

—*Robert M. Spector*

FURTHER READING

Edmundson, George. "Frederick Henry, Prince of Orange." In *The Cambridge Modern History*, edited by A. W. Ward, G. W. Prothero, and Stanley Leathes. Vol. 4. Cambridge, England: Cambridge University Press, 1906. Although there is little information about his life prior to 1625, this is still the best survey in English of Frederick Henry's career from 1625 until his death. The portion of the book dealing with the Dutch overseas activities in the Western Hemisphere and the East Indies is concise and understandable.

Geyl, Pieter. *The Netherlands in the Seventeenth Century*. Rev. ed. London: Ernest Benn, 1961. For the seasoned student of history, volume 1 of this multivolume collection deals with Dutch history from 1609 through the Peace of Westphalia in 1648, of which the

Treaty of Münster, which ended the Dutch Wars of Independence, was a portion. Contains little on the life of Frederick Henry prior to his becoming stadtholder in 1625.

_____. *Orange and Stuart, 1641-1672*. Translated by Arnold Pomerans. New York: Charles Scribner's Sons, 1970. Chapter 1, "Frederick Henry of Orange and King Charles I, 1641-47," deals more with the politics of the marriage of Frederick Henry's son William than with the life and personality of Frederick Henry. Yet the book does address Frederick Henry's difficult position between the Calvinists on one side and the non-Calvinist Stuarts on the other, both of whom he sought to please.

Memegalos, Florence S. "Breda 'Bravely Besieged.'" *Military History* 19, no. 4 (October, 2002). Recounts how Frederick Henry's leadership enabled the Dutch to capture the city of Breda from Spanish forces. Describes the battle's significance to the Netherlands.

Rowen, Herbert H. *The Princes of Orange: The Stadholders in the Dutch Republic*. New York: Cambridge University Press, 1988. Describes the lives, minds, and personalities of Frederick Henry and other members of the House of Orange-Nassau who helped develop the unique institution of stadtholderate.

Schama, Simon. *The Embarrassment of Riches: An Interpretation of Dutch Culture in the Golden Age*. New York: Alfred A. Knopf, 1987. Although this book does not discuss Frederick Henry and the military situation in the Dutch Republic, it presents an extensive kaleidoscope of Dutch society during that period, including domestic life, eating habits, business, trade, the making of money, child care, and the general Dutch mentality.

SEE ALSO: Charles I; Oliver Cromwell; Frederick William, the Great Elector; Piet Hein; Maurice of Nassau; Peter Minuit; Friedrich Hermann Schomberg; Peter Stuyvesant; Maarten and Cornelis Tromp.

RELATED ARTICLES in *Great Events from History: The Seventeenth Century, 1601-1700:* 1617-1693: European Powers Vie for Control of Gorée; March 31, 1621-September 17, 1665: Reign of Philip IV; 1625: Grotius Establishes the Concept of International Law; 1640-1688: Reign of Frederick William, the Great Elector; June-August, 1640: *Bandeirantes* Expel the Jesuits.

FREDERICK WILLIAM, THE GREAT ELECTOR
Prussian military leader and ruler

Frederick William was the first gifted ruler of the Hohenzollern family. He was the founder of the Prussian army and bureaucracy, and laid the basis for the future strength of the Brandenburg-Prussian state.

BORN: February 16, 1620; Berlin, Brandenburg-
Prussia (now in Germany)
DIED: May 9, 1688; Potsdam, near Berlin,
Brandenburg-Prussia
ALSO KNOWN AS: Friedrich Wilhelm von Hohenzollern,
Kurfürst von Brandenburg (full name)
AREAS OF ACHIEVEMENT: Government and politics,
military

EARLY LIFE

Frederick William was born in Berlin, the son of the elector of Brandenburg George William of the House of Hohenzollern, and Elizabeth Charlotte, the granddaughter of William I of the House of Orange. Frederick William's early years were clouded by Brandenburg's financial exhaustion and military vulnerability during the Thirty Years' War (1618-1648). When the electorate of Brandenburg was threatened by Albrecht Wenzel von Wallenstein's imperial soldiers, Frederick William, then seven years old, was moved for safety into the fortress of Küstrin. For five years, he remained at the fortress, growing both physically and intellectually under the direction of his Rhenish tutor. When Frederick William was fourteen, he was sent to continue his education in the security of the Netherlands, where his relative, Frederick Henry of Orange was stadtholder.

Frederick William became elector of Brandenburg upon his father's death on December 1, 1640. The prospects of the twenty-year-old elector were dim. His territories had been devastated by the Thirty Years' War, the population of Brandenburg had been cut nearly in half, agriculture and commerce had collapsed, and much of his land was occupied by foreign armies. The local estates in all the elector's territories continued their resistance to any increase in taxation or strengthening of the central government. This sad state was compounded by the fact that the army that was passed on to the young elector consisted of only five thousand largely worthless men.

LIFE'S WORK

Even before his father's hated Catholic adviser Adam von Schwarzenberg died in March, 1641, Frederick William reappointed Schwarzenberg's Lutheran and Calvinist opponents to the Privy Council. To these the new elector added his young and energetic friends, Conrad von Burgsdorf, Joachim Friedrich von Blumenthal, Count Georg Friedrich von Waldeck, and Otto von Schwerin. In the face of overwhelming Swedish power, Frederick William placed his army on the defensive. At the same time that he sought an armistice with the Swedes, he purged the chaff from his army and, with a remaining core of about twenty-five hundred men, began rebuilding his army numerically and morally. By the end of the Thirty Years' War, the force had grown to almost eight thousand disciplined, loyal, and well-paid men. This credible army won respect for Brandenburg in the deliberations leading to the Treaty of Westphalia.

Frederick William, at the beginning of his reign, had gone to Warsaw and given homage to Władysław IV Vasa to ensure his status in the duchy of Prussia, which was held as a fief of Poland. He then went to Königsberg and, after confirming the traditional rights of the Prussian Estates, received their support. After winning a truce with Sweden in July, 1641, he attempted to gain Swedish-occupied Pomerania and the Baltic coast by marrying the Swedish queen Christina. Rebuffed by her, Frederick William in 1646 turned to the Netherlands, from which he gained an alliance and a wife, Louise Henriette, the daughter of Frederick Henry of Orange.

At Westphalia in 1648, Frederick William was able to win legal recognition for his fellow Calvinists and the termination of the princes' right to compel religious conformity. He failed, however, to secure his claim to all of Pomerania. The Swedes retained western Pomerania and the port of Stettin, while Frederick William received only the eastern half and the lesser port of Colberg. He did receive some compensating parcels of territory, including Minden and a future claim to Magdeburg, which contributed to the expansion and strengthening of Brandenburg.

During the Northern War between Sweden and Poland, Frederick William pursued a vacillating and self-serving course, switching from neutrality to the side of Sweden and finally to that of Poland. As a result of these maneuvers, he was able to win from Poland the recognition of his sovereignty in Prussia, which was confirmed in the Treaty of Oliva in 1660. With his expanded army, which had grown to twenty-seven thousand men during the war, and the recognition of sovereignty in Prussia, which lay outside the Holy Roman Empire, Frederick William increased his stature to that of a European sovereign.

Realizing the importance of his army for both his external and internal policies, Frederick William maintained a strong standing force in peace time, which could be doubled in size at time of war. The elector's army in 1686 numbered thirty thousand, second only to the Austrian army among the German states. During peace, the soldiers were utilized for public-works projects, such as the construction of the canal linking the Oder and Elbe rivers, which made Berlin the center of transportation in north Central Europe. Frederick William established for the army a central command, which developed into a permanent general staff. The officials and bureaus, which he initiated to provide financial support for the army, developed into a centralized and professional bureaucracy.

State interest and shifting alliances continued to characterize Frederick William's subsequent military policy but with much less success than in the Northern War. During the Franco-Dutch Wars, Frederick William ran Louis XIV's Swedish allies out of western Pomerania, winning for himself the appellation "Great" for his victory at Fehrbellin on June 28, 1675. However, he was betrayed at the peace conference by his Dutch and imperial allies. Forced to return his conquests, the great elector turned to the French, until he was repelled by Louis's revocation of the Edict of Nantes in 1685 and Louis's increasingly aggressive anti-German policy.

If the Northern War raised Frederick William's external status, it also enabled him to augment his power within his territories and advance the cause of centralization. When he assumed the electorship, Frederick William had conciliated the local estates. Taking advantage of the unsettled foreign scene in 1653, he was able to extract a six-year tax grant from a united Diet of the Brandenburg Estates. In 1655, at the outbreak of the Northern War, when the Brandenburg Estates refused an additional tax, Frederick William used his army to collect his desired tax and to extort additional funds from the chastened estates. When the six-year tax of 1653 expired in the middle of the war,

Frederick William merely continued to collect the tax, and never again called together the Brandenburg Diet.

Frederick William coopted the district directors, who had acted as elected representatives of the estates, by simultaneously appointing them war commissioners. These local administrative officers were thus gradually transformed into loyal agents of the central government. He also appointed war-tax commissioners to collect taxes in the towns. These officials gradually took total control over the town administration and thus destroyed the self-government that the towns had exercised. The western territories of Kleve and Mark were able to resist this centralizing destruction of local traditional rights and representation somewhat more successfully than Brandenburg, but Frederick William asserted his right to station troops permanently in those territories, and their estates, though they continued to meet, did grant the taxes requested by the elector.

Frederick William, the Great Elector. (Library of Congress)

It was in eastern Prussia that the struggle between Frederick William and the estates was most bitter. The estates there had won broad rights by appealing to the kings of Poland against their Hohenzollern dukes. The Prussian estates claimed that these privileges recognized by Frederick William in 1640 had not been erased by the Treaty of Oliva. Frederick William's close associate Otto von Schwerin summoned a Great Diet and offered to recognize most of the privileges of the estates in return for their recognition of the elector's sovereignty. The estates, led by Hieronymus Roth, a leading magistrate of Königsberg, rejected the offer. Eventually Frederick William himself went to Königsberg and had Roth arrested and tried before a special commission. Despite pleas for clemency, Frederick William condemned Roth to life imprisonment. Persuaded by Frederick William's forcefulness, the estates in 1663 recognized his sovereignty and in return had their privileges confirmed.

The next Diet, which met in 1669, haggled over the elector's tax request. This Diet, however, was cowed when another leading dissident, Christian Ludwig von Kalckstein, was executed for treason. After 1680, Frederick William collected a regular military tax from Prussia through a rural land tax and an excise tax in Königsberg. With city and countryside divided, the estates atrophied and in 1705 ceased to function.

SIGNIFICANCE

Frederick William, the Great Elector, was the first truly gifted Hohenzollern ruler. He laid the foundations for the greatness of Brandenburg-Prussia. When he became elector in 1640, he faced a formidable challenge. He had to establish internal order and to secure his territories against predatory foreign powers. He also had to build a credible military from practically nothing. With the army, he secured Brandenburg against outsiders and asserted the authority of the central government over the defenders of local interests and rights. Having forcibly asserted his power to tax at will, he was able to expand his army and enlarge the state's developing bureaucracy. He ran roughshod over traditional rights but did establish the order and security craved by many of his subjects after the calamity of the Thirty Years' War, and he laid the foundations of later Prussian absolutism.

—*Bernard A. Cook*

FURTHER READING

Carsten, F. L. *The Origins of Prussia*. Oxford, England: Clarendon Press, 1954. Carsten's book is a first-rate scholarly study, more than one-third of which is devoted to Frederick William and his accomplishments. Carsten details the elector's use of his army to replace the power of the provincial *Landtag* with his own absolute authority.

Fay, Sidney Bradshaw. *The Rise of Brandenburg-Prussia to 1786*. New York: Holt, Rinehart and Winston, 1937. This is an excellent introduction to and summary of Prussian history, including the reign of Frederick William. Fay clearly summarizes both internal and external developments under Frederick William and describes the bureaucracy the elector developed.

Holborn, Hajo. *A History of Modern Germany*. Vol. 2. New York: Alfred A. Knopf, 1968. In this second of his three-volume history of Germany, Holborn gives a brief but perceptive overview of Frederick William's career and achievements.

Koch, H. W. *A History of Prussia*. New York: Longman, 1978. Koch presents an uncritical and rather old-fashioned treatment of Prussian history. The chapter on Frederick William emphasizes that while he did not make Prussia a great power, he laid the foundation for future Prussian greatness.

McKay, Derek. *The Great Elector: Frederick William of Brandenburg-Prussia*. New York: Longman, 2001. The first English biography in fifty years, McKay's study does not view Frederick William as a precursor to Frederick the Great. Instead, McKay describes Frederick William as a product of his time—an unusually tough and opportunistic ruler able to overcome the hostility of local nobles and surrounding nations.

Nelson, Walter Henry. *The Soldier Kings: The House of Hohenzollern*. New York: G. P. Putnam's Sons, 1970. Nelson's study of the Hohenzollerns is intended for general readers. The work stresses the improbable accomplishments of the elector, laying the basis for a great state in his poor, sparsely populated, disjointed, and exposed territories.

Schevill, Ferdinand. *The Great Elector*. Chicago: University of Chicago Press, 1947. Schevill is largely noncritical and laudatory, excusing Frederick William's deviousness and violation of traditional privileges. Schevill maintains that Frederick William's willfulness and brutal pursuit for additional power were justified by the end result: the groundwork for the modern Prussian state.

Shennan, Margaret. *The Rise of Brandenburg-Prussia*. New York: Routledge, 1995. Surveys the rise of Prussia from the early seventeenth century until 1740, focusing and evaluating the role of its rulers, Frederick William and his two successors.

FREDERICK V
Elector of the Palatinate (1610-1623) and king of Bohemia (r. 1619-1620)

Though an effective ruler in the Palatinate, Frederick's decision to accept the offer of the Bohemian Estates to become the first Protestant king of Bohemia in 1619, and his flight from Prague a year later, triggered the opening stage of the Thirty Years' War.

BORN: August 26, 1596; Amberg, Upper Palatinate (now in Germany)
DIED: November 29, 1632; Mainz (now in Germany)
ALSO KNOWN AS: Friedrich Wittelsbach (given name); Frederick I of Bohemia; the Winter King
AREAS OF ACHIEVEMENT: Government and politics, religion and theology

EARLY LIFE

Frederick was the first-born son of Elector Palatine Frederick IV and his wife, Luisa Juliana, the daughter of William of Orange, leader of the United Provinces of the Netherlands. The Palatinate (Pfalz in German), was an important principality in the Holy Roman Empire with about 600,000 inhabitants. It was divided into the fertile Lower Palatinate, which stretched between the Moselle and Neckar Rivers, and the mineral-rich Upper Palatinate, located to the north of Bavaria; the two were separated by the territories of Württemberg and Bamberg.

The elector was second only to the emperor in authority and was one of seven men responsible for electing each new emperor. Frederick was raised Calvinist and educated in the courtly arts and Latin at Sedan with his uncle Henry de La Tour, duke of Bouillon, and academically at the University of Heidelberg, a city that served as the capital of the Lower Palatinate. His father died when Frederick was fourteen (1610), and Frederick took full control of his territories four years later. On February 14, 1613, he married Elizabeth Stuart, daughter of King James I of England. While in London, James made Frederick a Knight of the Garter. During the next nineteen years, Elizabeth would bear thirteen children in a marriage that was by all accounts genuinely loving.

LIFE'S WORK

As elector palatine, Frederick was a fair and tolerant ruler in an often intolerant age. Though a Calvinist, he tried to foster good relations among all Protestants, retaining members of several denominations at his court. Tied by birth and marriage to the two major Protestant powers outside the empire, he was a kind of natural confessional linchpin.

From his father he inherited leadership of the Protestant Union, a loose defensive alliance of Lutheran and Calvinist German states, England, and the United Provinces, which sought to protect Protestant liberties in the empire and foil the power of the antagonistic Roman Catholic Austrian and Spanish Habsburg Dynasty. In response, the Austrian Habsburgs and Maximilian I Wittelsbach of Bavaria formed the Catholic League to protect their religious and dynastic interests. On May 23, 1618, the Protestant estates in Bohemia openly rebelled against the Habsburg king of Bohemia, Ferdinand II (elected in 1617), in the Defenestration of Prague, the third such revolt in a decade.

Though desirous of peace, Frederick did not want it to be at the price of Protestant liberties or the extension of Habsburg power. With financial help from Charles Emmanuel I, the duke of Savoy, Frederick sent troops to aid the insurgents. Led by Count Peter Ernst von Mansfeld, this army drove Ferdinand's forces from Bohemia and neighboring Austria, and the estates formally deposed Ferdinand in August of 1619. Six days later they elected Frederick their new king (as Frederick I).

Frederick pondered the honor for nearly a month. The idea was enthusiastically supported by Christian of Anhalt, one of his closest advisers, a fine general, and the administrator of the Upper Palatinate. The Bohemian king was also an imperial elector, and at the next election Frederick would have two votes, which, combined with those of the Calvinist elector of Brandenburg and Lutheran elector of Saxony, would ensure a Protestant emperor.

Even so, the risks were great. Ferdinand had just been elected Holy Roman Emperor (August 28), and without doubt would reject his deposition as Bohemian king and attack his erstwhile successor. Spain would certainly aid the imperial cause, as would powerful Catholic Bavaria. Frederick, like other Protestant princes and rulers, feared an all-out war within the empire, but feared and detested Habsburg power even more. Frederick could expect little aid from the Protestant Union, while his powerful father-in-law offered nothing beyond a few thousand men to help defend the Palatinate itself. Nonetheless, feeling that God was calling him to his destiny, Frederick accepted the offer in late September, 1619. Escorted by 800 cavalrymen, the elector, his family, and a baggage train of some 153 wagons left Heidelberg and arrived in Prague on October 31. Frederick was crowned the first Protestant king of Bohemia four days later, on November 4. With this he assumed leadership of the Bohemian rebellion, which had been successful to that point.

In the dead of winter, he traveled throughout his new territories, introducing himself to his more powerful subjects and extracting promises of support and loyalty. He was able to procure little else in the way of military aid from the estates of Lusatia, Moravia, and Upper and Lower Austria. As in the Palatinate, he was evenhanded and professed tolerance of all types of Christianity. He demanded the reformation of only one Catholic church in his new capital, the palace church of St. Vitus. He did, however, expel the Catholic Jesuits from Bohemia, since he saw them as the main agents provocateurs of the pope and militant Catholicism. He favored Protestant Bohemian leaders for local positions, but little else changed.

With the spring of 1620 came little in the way of good news for Frederick. Despite his successful installation, none of Europe's Protestant powers offered support for the Bohemian cause, and the Protestant Union, at a meeting in Nuremberg, formally rejected military aid. The Dutch, however, did plan to send troops to help defend the Lower Palatinate when the time came. European princes of all stripes called on Frederick to abandon the Bohemian cause, and Ferdinand threatened the imperial ban, which would formally label Frederick an outlaw who forfeited all of his rights to titles and property and even the safety of himself and his family. Strengthened by his faith in God, Frederick persevered, even as the ban

went into effect on June 1. He felt that he could fight its legality, but Emperor Ferdinand had other ideas.

The emperor had informally promised Maximilian the Palatinate and its electorship and placed him in command of the Catholic League's multinational army. Led by Flemish general Johan Tserclaes, count of Tilly, they cleared the Bohemian and allied rebel forces from Austria and much of Bohemia in the summer of 1620 and approached Prague in the fall. In August, Italian general Ambrosio de Spínola, in Spanish service, marched 25,000 Spanish troops from Brussels across the Rhine River into the Palatinate to secure it for the emperor. Frederick joined his Bohemian army, but had little to offer beside moral support. General Tserclaes smashed this army at White Mountain on November 8, causing Frederick to flee Prague with his family the very next day. In their haste they left behind virtually everything, including state and personal papers and even the crown jewels. His short reign earned him the derisive nickname the Winter King.

For the next dozen years, Frederick and his family lived as exiles at various Protestant courts, as Frederick sought to regain what he had lost. Maximilian replaced him as elector in 1623, and Ferdinand reasserted his authority in Bohemia. Frederick, however, never lost hope in his cause. During his last years, he clung to the successful King Gustavus II Adolphus of Sweden, who might have been able to reinstate Frederick in the Palatinate. Frederick died of plague in 1632, only thirty-six years old.

SIGNIFICANCE

Historians have generally been harsh with Frederick's legacy, blaming his obstinacy or foolishness for triggering one of Europe's most devastating wars. His utter defeat and the Spanish occupation of the Palatinate could not go unanswered, and soon the conflagration began. Frederick's motives were mixed, and they included the defense of imperial constitutionalism and Protestantism, both of which he saw threatened by Habsburg control of Bohemia. To many he became a romantic martyr for a lost but just cause, to others simply an egotistic failure.

—*Joseph P. Byrne*

FURTHER READING

Clasen, Claus-Peter. *The Palatinate in European History, 1559-1660.* Oxford, England: Basil Blackwell, 1963. A close study of Frederick's territory.

Parker, Geoffrey. *The Thirty Years' War.* 2d ed. New York: Routledge, 1988. The fullest treatment of the political and diplomatic aspects of the entire war, including Frederick's participation in its opening phase.

Pursell, Brennan. *The Winter King: Frederick V of the Palatinate and the Coming of the Thirty Years' War.* Burlington, Vt.: Ashgate, 2003. A detailed narrative and analysis of Frederick's role in the early stages of the Thirty Years' War. This work is the only monograph on Frederick in English.

Sutherland, N. M. "The Origins of the Thirty Years' War and the Structure of European Politics." *English Historical Review* 107 (1992): 587-625. A succinct discussion of the broader context of Frederick's decision to aid Bohemia.

Wedgwood, C. V. *The Thirty Years' War.* New York: Methuen, 1982. A classic narrative treatment of the war and Frederick's early adventure.

SEE ALSO: First Duke of Buckingham; Charles I; Charles II (of England); Elizabeth of Bohemia; Elizabeth Stuart; Ferdinand II; Gustavus II Adolphus; James I; Prince Rupert; Friedrich Hermann Schomberg.

RELATED ARTICLES in *Great Events from History: The Seventeenth Century, 1601-1700:* 1618-1648: Thirty Years' War; May 23, 1618: Defenestration of Prague; November 8, 1620: Battle of White Mountain; 1640-1688: Reign of Frederick William, the Great Elector.

GIROLAMO FRESCOBALDI
Italian composer

Frescobaldi was one of the most innovative and imaginative keyboard composers of the early Baroque period and a brilliant organ improviser. He is credited with having created an instrumental style that was the equivalent of the emotionally charged seconda pratica *promoted by Claudio Monteverdi in his vocal madrigals.*

BORN: September, 1583; Ferrara, Papal States (now in Italy)
DIED: March 1, 1643; Rome, Papal States (now in Italy)
AREA OF ACHIEVEMENT: Music

EARLY LIFE

Information about Girolamo Frescobaldi (jee-RAW-lah-moh fray-skoh-BAHL-dee), especially his early years, is scarce, but his training and musical activities as a composer and performer can be learned from two major sources: the dedications the composer wrote for the numerous volumes of works published in his lifetime, which frequently included autobiographical references; and a collection of manuscripts, once in the possession of the Chigi family (major art patrons), appearing to be in his own hand. The manuscripts, which were uncovered in the 1990's, include small-scale pieces and exercises composed by Frescobaldi and his contemporaries, and they probably were used in conjunction with his teaching of counterpoint, composition, and improvisation at the Cappella Giulia in Rome in the early decades of the seventeenth century.

Like Mozart before him, Frescobaldi was a child prodigy, equally gifted as a singer and a keyboard player. Much of his musical education, especially the portion having to do with achieving incredible dexterity in organ playing, was accomplished under the direct guidance of his father. Frescobaldi, though, considered that his mentor was the organist Luzzasco Luzzaschi, one of the best musicians at the ducal court of Ferrara. By the time he was fourteen years old, the young Girolamo was already succeeding the organist Ercole Pasquini at the Ferrarese Accademia (Ferrara Academy).

Before leaving the city in 1607, Frescobaldi was immersed in the rich cultural life of the Ferrarese court—something that served to both improve his playing and to forge personal relationships that were very useful in the furthering of his musical career. His patrons from Ferrara included Guido Bentivoglio (1579-1644) and Enzo Bentivoglio (1575-1639), the sons of singer Isabella Bendidio (1546-after 1610), who were intensely involved with music themselves; Enzo went on to become an important impresario of the seventeenth century. Furthermore, it was Guido Bentivoglio whom Frescobaldi followed to Rome, then to Brussels, in 1607.

LIFE'S WORK

Frescobaldi distinguished himself as a composer of instrumental works, but his vocal and vocal-instrumental output are significant as well. His first published volume was a collection of nineteen five-part madrigals, *Il primo libro de' madrigali* (1608; English translation of text,

Eighteenth century engraving of Girolamo Frescobaldi by James Caldwall. (Hulton Archive/Getty Images)

then proceeded to develop them in a series of successive sections of increasing complexity.

In 1614 and 1615, Frescobaldi, perhaps unhappy with the terms of his employment with Enzo Bentivoglio, began a series of negotiations for a position with the ducal court of Mantua. The toccatas in *Toccate e partite d'intavolatura di cimbalo* (toccatas and partitas, or suites, for harpsichord; English summary of preface, 1977) were published during these negotiations, and the composer believed that dedicating this volume to Duke Ferdinando Gonzaga would be a wise move on his part.

With the toccatas Frescobaldi set the foundations of a keyboard style that was radically different from that of his contemporaries. These pieces represent a distinct second stylistic category, known in modern scholarship as the instrumental "equivalent of the *seconda pratica*" (the second practice, or style, a concept introduced by Claudio Monteverdi in his madrigals). The *seconda pratica* focuses on dramatically expressing the whole gamut of human emotions. Like their vocal counterpart found in the madrigals of Monteverdi, Carlo Gesualdo, and Luca Marenzio, Frescobaldi's toccatas are full of musical color derived from abrupt changes in harmony, rhythm, and meter, with many passages looking like improvisations frozen on page. In reality, both the larger contrapuntal frame and the details of each piece were lucidly and thoroughly planned.

Frescobaldi fashioned several revised editions of the *Toccate e partite*, one of which, published 1615-1616, included a number of stylized *correntes*—settings of popular dance tunes that were at the height of fashion throughout the Renaissance and early Baroque periods. This was the inauguration of a different stylistic direction. The dance-tune settings in his interpretation—the so-called popular style—were unlike those of his predecessors or even contemporaries: Frescobaldi's were elaborate, elegant, refined, and rather aristocratic.

The fantasias had set a precedent in terms of Frescobaldi's preference for a specific formal design, and after his return to Rome, where he remained until 1628, he reprised this design in composing the capriccios in *Il primo libro di capricci*, first published early in the 1620's (English preface, 1984. Still in Rome, and still playing on more than one occasion for a variety of churches, Frescobaldi continued to compose and began preparation for *Il secondo libro di toccate, canzone, versi d'hinni, Mag-*

1983), composed during the period he was in the service of Guido Bentivoglio. From 1608 to 1615, while living in Rome, Frescobaldi was appointed organist at the Cappella Giulia at Saint Peter's Cathedral. In addition to his duties as an organist, he gave private keyboard lessons to members of the Roman aristocracy and higher clergy, was frequently called upon to perform in religious musical events, and, between 1608 and 1609, was hired to teach the singers associated with the household of his former patron Enzo Bentivoglio, now living in Rome.

A true perfectionist, Frescobaldi was constantly engaged in revising his works, thus many of his collections of instrumental music were published twice or even three times under his supervision. His style can generally be divided into three categories: The works written in the so-called *stile antico* are infused with the restraint and gravity found in the "old," or "antiquated" style" of Renaissance vocal music. *Il primo libro delle fantasie* (1608; English summary of preface, 1995), contemporary with the book of madrigals, contains twelve four-part instrumental pieces representative of this style. Yet even in these early works, Frescobaldi's unique approach began to shine through: As a novelty, he introduced several themes at the beginning of each piece, and *nificat, gagliarde, correnti et altre, partite d'intavolatura di cembalo et organo* (1627; English preface, 1979), dedicated to Bishop Luigi Gallo. As the title implies, this publication included a generous mix of both harpsichord and organ pieces, both secular and sacred, and covered a rather large variety of genres and forms. Of these, the partite include sets on the chaconne and passacaglia, and modern scholarship has credited Frescobaldi with bringing these two forms together.

In November of 1628, Frescobaldi was appointed organist at the court of Ferdinand II de' Medici, grand duke of Tuscany, to whom he dedicated his next published volume, *Il primo libro delle canzoni, accomodate per sonare con ogni sorte de stromenti* (the first book of canzonas adapted to be played on any type of instruments). The years 1629-1630 marked two important events in his career. First, he was appointed organist for the Baptistery in Florence, and second, he published two books of *Arie musicali per cantarsi*—a collection of vocal arias for several parts, with theorbo and harpsichord accompaniment (*Two Sacred Songs for Voice and Piano*, 1961). It was during his Florentine period that Frescobaldi began collaborating with Marco da Gagliano (1582-1642), a well-known early opera composer. Together they wrote the music for two major events: the celebration of the canonization, in 1629, of Andrea Corsini (1302-1373) and the consecration of the cathedral at Colle di Val d'Elsa.

Frescobaldi spent the last decade of his life (1634-1643) in Rome, under the protection and patronage of Cardinal Francesco Barberini, nephew of Pope Urban VIII. He retook his post as an organist at the Cappella Giulia, played the harpsichord at the Oratorio del Crocifisso, and continued composing and publishing. The volume of *Fiori musicali di diverse compositioni: Toccate, kyrie, canzoni, capricci e recercari* (English preface and notes, 1997), a collection dedicated to Cardinal Antonio Barberini, was followed, in 1637, by several additions to the earlier published *Toccatas*.

He died on March 1, 1643, and was buried in the Basilica of the Twelve Apostles in Rome.

SIGNIFICANCE

Frescobaldi was a player of genius, as recognized by many of his contemporaries who spoke highly of his brilliant, astounding improvisations on the keyboard. Many of his numerous compositions were at the forefront of a new style of writing for the keyboard, a style that he pioneered and championed. His style was an expressive, dramatic, impassioned, and emotionally involved instrumental response to the novelties introduced by his contemporaries in the vocal music of the period.

—*Luminita Florea*

FURTHER READING

Annibaldi, Claudio, and Laura Callegari Hill. "Musical Autographs of Frescobaldi and His Entourage in Roman Sources." *Journal of the American Musicological Society* 43, no. 3 (1990): 393-425. An important large-scale study of some of the Chigi manuscripts and other manuscripts uncovered in Rome, including autograph works by Frescobaldi.

Arnold, Denis, et al., eds. *The New Grove Italian Baroque Masters: Monteverdi, Frescobaldi, Cavalli, Corelli, A. Scarlatti, Vivaldi, D. Scarlatti*. New York: W. W. Norton, 1984. A revised version of biographical studies first published in the 1980 edition of *The New Grove Dictionary of Music and Musicians*. Includes facsimile reproductions, portraits, lists of works, and bibliography.

Hammond, Frederick. *Girolamo Frescobaldi*. Cambridge, Mass.: Harvard University Press, 1983. A detailed biographical study and in-depth analysis of Frescobaldi's contribution to the development of Italian organ music.

_____. *Girolamo Frescobaldi: A Guide to Research*. New York: Garland, 1988. An authoritative reference source for the life and works of Frescobaldi, especially notable for its inclusion of a large discography.

Schulenberg, D. "Some Problems of Text, Attribution, and Performance in Early Italian Baroque Keyboard Music." *Journal of Seventeenth-Century Music* 4 (1998). Available at http://www.sscm.harvard.edu/jscm/v4no1.html. Accessed September, 2004. Examines the problems of attribution in the assumed works of Frescobaldi and other composers of the period.

Silbiger, A. "From Madrigal to Toccata: Frescobaldi and the Seconda Prattica." In *Critica Musica: Essays in Honor of Paul Brainard*, edited by J. Knowles. Amsterdam, 1996. Explores a range of work by Frescobaldi.

SEE ALSO: Francesca Caccini; Arcangelo Corelli; Jean-Baptiste Lully; Claudio Monteverdi; Johann Pachelbel; Barbara Strozzi; Urban VIII.

RELATED ARTICLES in *Great Events from History: The Seventeenth Century, 1601-1700:* c. 1601: Emergence of Baroque Music; February 24, 1607: First Performance of Monteverdi's *La favola d'Orfeo*; c. 1673: Buxtehude Begins His Abendmusiken Concerts.

GALILEO
Italian astronomer and mathematician

Galileo helped establish the modern scientific method through his use of observation and experimentation. His work in mathematics, astronomy, and physics made him a leading figure of the early scientific revolution.

BORN: February 15, 1564; Pisa, Republic of Florence (now in Italy)
DIED: January 8, 1642; Arcetri, Republic of Florence (now in Italy)
AREAS OF ACHIEVEMENT: Astronomy, mathematics, physics, science and technology

EARLY LIFE

Galileo (gahl-ih-LAY-oh) was the first of seven children born to Vincenzo Galilei and Giulia Ammanati. His father was a cloth merchant and a noted musician who wrote several treatises on musical theory. The Galileis were a noble Florentine family that over the years had lost much of its wealth. It was for financial reasons that Vincenzo left Florence and moved to Pisa to establish his textile trade.

Galileo. (Library of Congress)

At the age of ten, Galileo and his family returned to Florence. His early education was directed by his father with the help of a private tutor. He also spent some time at the monastery of Santa Maria di Vallombrosa. The content of Galileo's elementary education is unknown, but it was probably humanistic in character. His father urged him to pursue university studies that would lead to a lucrative profession.

Following his father's wish, Galileo enrolled as a student of medicine at the University of Pisa in 1581. He showed little interest in his medical studies; it was mathematics that captured his attention. A year after enrolling at the university, Galileo made his legendary discovery of the isochronal movement of pendulums by observing a chandelier in the Pisa cathedral. He confirmed his theory regarding the equal movement of pendulums by conducting a series of experiments. He continued an independent study of science and mathematics, finally convincing his father to allow him to abandon his medical studies. Galileo withdrew from the University of Pisa in 1586 without receiving a degree, and he returned to his family.

Upon his return to Florence, Galileo studied a wide range of literary and scientific texts. In addition, he delivered a series of popular lectures on the *Inferno* of Dante's *La divina commedia* (c. 1320; *The Divine Comedy*, 1802) at the Florentine Academy. In 1589, he used the influence of friends to obtain an appointment as a lecturer of mathematics at the University of Pisa. His return to Pisa marked a productive and enjoyable time for the young scholar. He conducted a series of experiments relating to falling bodies and wrote a short manuscript that challenged many traditional and generally accepted teachings about physics. In addition to his scholarly activities, Galileo was known for his quick wit, biting sense of humor, and excellent debating ability. Once again his friends intervened on his behalf to arrange an appointment, in 1592, to a more prestigious chair of mathematics at the University of Padua.

LIFE'S WORK

It was at Padua that Galileo began his life's work, which would bring him both fame and controversy. He quickly established himself as an excellent and popular teacher, both in terms of public lectures and private tutoring. He also wrote a series of short manuscripts on a variety of technical and practical issues. In 1597, he constructed a "military compass" to assist artillery bombardments and army formations.

Although Galileo's invention of the military compass brought him acclaim and a good source of additional income, it was his work in the study of motion and astronomy that firmly established his reputation as a leading scientist. In 1604, a new star could be seen, and its sudden appearance prompted a fierce debate. According to the dominant theory of the time, Earth was the immovable center of the universe. Based on the work of Aristotle and Ptolemy, most scholars believed that the planets, Sun, and stars rotated around a stationary Earth. The universe was thought to reflect a perfect and unchangeable order that had been created by God. The new star raised a problem of how to account for its presence in an already complete and perfectly ordered universe.

The intensity of this debate reflected a larger controversy regarding the work of Nicolaus Copernicus. Copernicus claimed that Earth and the other planets orbited the Sun, and the stars were fixed or stationary. The appearance of a new star provided a tangible point of reference to settle a much larger scientific and theological debate on the structure and nature of the universe. It was a debate Galileo wanted to enter. As his correspondence with the astronomer Johannes Kepler indicated, Galileo found Copernicus's thesis convincing, but he lacked the necessary instrument to test the theory. This problem was remedied in 1609 when on a visit to Venice, Galileo learned about a new "eye-glass by means of which visible objects, though very distant from the eye, were distinctly seen as if nearby." Based on this limited information, Galileo returned to Padua to design and build his own telescope.

With this new instrument, Galileo turned his gaze toward the sky. He saw that the Moon was not a smooth sphere, as previously assumed, but had many craters and mountains. These geological characteristics implied that Earth was not a unique or central planet in the universe. While observing Jupiter, he discovered four moons, disproving the assumption that Earth was the only planet to be orbited by a natural satellite. His observations of Venus forced Galileo to conclude that its phases could not be accounted for within the traditional geocentric model of the universe but could only be explained in terms of

---

GALILEO ON THE PENDULUM'S MOTION

Galileo used dialogue to present his ideas on motion in Dialogue Concerning the Two Chief World Systems, Ptolemaic and Copernican *(1632), a work banned by the Catholic Church. Two of the book's "interlocutors," Sagredo and Salviati, were close friends of Galileo, and here they set the stage for a discussion of the motion of a pendulum by wondering about the to-and-fro movement of a hanging church lamp.*

Sagredo. A thousand times I have given attention to oscillations, in particular those of lamps in some churches hanging from very long cords, inadvertently set in motion by someone, but the most that I ever got from such observations was the improbability of the opinion of many, . . . that motions of this kind are maintained and continued by the medium, that is, the air. It would seem to me that the air must have exquisite judgment and little else to do, consuming hours and hours in pushing back and forth a hanging weight with such regularity. . . .

Salviati. First of all, it is necessary to note that each pendulum has its own time of vibration, so limited and fixed in advance that it is impossible to move it in any other period than its own unique and natural one. Take in hand any string you like, to which a weight is attached, and try the best you can to increase or diminish the frequency of its vibrations; this will be a mere waste of effort. On the other hand, we [can] confer motion on any pendulum, though heavy and at rest, by merely blowing on it. This motion may be made quite large if we repeat our puffs; yet it will take place only in accord with the time appropriate to its oscillations. If at the first puff we shall have removed it half an inch from the vertical, by adding the second when, returned toward us, it would commence its second vibration, we confer a new motion on it. . . .

Source: Galileo, *Two New Sciences* (1638), translated and introduced by Stillman Drake (Madison: University of Wisconsin Press, 1974), pp. 98-99.

---

the Copernican heliocentric system. His study of the Sun revealed its spots, implying that it was spherical and rotated on its axis as did Earth.

In 1610, Galileo published his findings in his *Sidereus nuncius* (*The Sidereal Messenger*, 1880). The book was quite popular and was translated and reprinted in a wide variety of languages. The book implied a strong support of the Copernican solar system. The vast number of stars and movement of planets Galileo observed could be explained only in the context of a heliocentric model wherein Earth and the other planets orbit the sun, and the stars are fixed points of light that appear to move only because of Earth's orbital path.

The Sidereal Messenger brought Galileo international fame and set the stage for future controversy. The University of Padua granted him a professorship for life. Instead of accepting the offer, however, he resigned so that he could return to Florence and become the grand duke's chief philosopher and mathematician. The move marked a fateful change for the scientist.

A year after his return to Florence, Galileo made a triumphant visit to Rome. He lectured widely, demonstrated his telescope, and debated a variety of scientific issues. Although he was well received by both the pope and papal court, there were signs of growing opposition to his work. Some theologians claimed that Copernicus, and therefore Galileo, was in conflict with the Bible and the doctrines of the Church regarding the central role and location of Earth in God's created order. Galileo was warned that he should teach and discuss the Copernican system only as a speculative theory and not as a truthful representation of the universe. In 1615, Copernicus's book, *De revolutionibus orbium coelestium* (1543; *On the Revolutions of the Heavenly Spheres*, 1939; better known as *De revolutionibus*), was placed on the Catholic Church's Index of Forbidden Books. In response to this censorship, Galileo refrained from any public comment on astronomy for a number of years, turning his attention to navigational problems. In 1618, however, three comets appeared, and a Jesuit astronomer maintained that their appearance disproved Copernicus. Galileo broke his silence with the publication of *Saggiatore* (1623, the assayer; partial English translation, 1990). The brief tract not only refuted the attack against Copernicus but also presented an elegant argument in behalf of free scientific inquiry.

As the controversy surrounding this episode subsided, Galileo began writing his most important and controversial book, *Dialogo sopra i due massimi sistemi del mondo, tolemaico e copernicano* (1632; *Dialogue Concerning the Two Chief World Systems, Ptolemaic and Copernican*, 1661). Its purpose was to present an "inconclusive" comparison between the Ptolemaic and Copernican models of the universe. Although Galileo carefully presented the various claims in terms of competing theories, it was apparent that he believed that the Ptolemaic geocentric theory was false and that the Copernican heliocentric theory was true. Although the book had received the Catholic Church's imprimatur, it was placed on the Index of Forbidden Books shortly after its publication. A few months later, the Office of the Inquisition summoned Galileo to Rome to stand trial for heresy. What was at stake was whether he had defied a papal ban

"to hold, defend, and teach the Copernican doctrine." More important, the Church's authority and ability to enforce compliance with its teachings were also at issue.

After a five-month trial, Galileo was convicted because he "held and believed false doctrine, contrary to the Holy and Divine Scriptures." The punishment would be a public prohibition of *Dialogue Concerning the Two Chief World Systems* and a prison sentence. Galileo, however, was given an opportunity to recant, which he accepted, swearing, "I will never again say or assert . . . anything that might furnish occasion for a similar suspicion." Theological authority, for the time being, had silenced the claims of scientific observation.

SIGNIFICANCE

For the rest of his life Galileo remained under house arrest, first in the village of Siena and later in Arcetri. He was not allowed to take any extensive trips or to entertain many guests. Following the death of his favorite daughter in 1634, he lived a lonely life and became blind in 1637. Despite the attempt to isolate him from the world, his fame grew—such noted figures as Thomas Hobbes and John Milton went out of their way to visit him shortly before his death.

His legacy was to establish science, based on observation and experimentation, as an important intellectual and social force in the world. Unlike Copernicus or Kepler, he was not a systematic or speculative thinker, preferring to base his work on a careful inquiry into the causes of natural phenomena. As indicated by his various inventions, he also was interested in applying his knowledge to practical problems.

Galileo marked an important break between theology and science that was not easily or quickly bridged—Copernicus and he were not removed from the Church's Index of Forbidden Books until 1835. Yet despite his conviction for heresy, history has judged his right to seek after truth quite differently. According to legend, as Galileo signed his recantation following his trial, he mumbled, *"Eppur si muove"* (and yet it [Earth] moves). Although Galileo never spoke these words, the legend's existence and endurance is a fitting indication of the eventual support he received not only for his work but also for the right of the scientist to engage in free and open inquiry.

—*Brent Waters*

FURTHER READING

Boas, Marie. *The Scientific Renaissance, 1450-1630.* New York: Harper & Row, 1962. A detailed historical account of the major scientific discoveries and conflicts during the Renaissance. Provides good background material regarding the work and accomplishments of Galileo.

Fermi, Laura, and Gilberto Bernardini. *Galileo and the Scientific Revolution*. New York: Basic Books, 1961. A concise and highly sympathetic biography. Includes a limited number of illustrations and a translation of Galileo's first tract, "The Little Balance."

Freedburg, David. *The Eye of the Lynx: Galileo, His Friends, and the Beginnings of Modern Natural History*. Chicago: University of Chicago Press, 2002. Galileo was a member of the Academy of Lynxes, a group of scientists who edited and published his work. This book describes how the group used microscopes and other tools to study and illustrate plants and animals, aiming to represent all of nature in pictures.

Geymonat, Ludovico. *Galileo Galilei*. New York: McGraw-Hill, 1965. A highly detailed biography focusing on the development of Galileo's thinking. Particular attention is placed on reconstructing his emerging philosophy of science.

Koyré, Alexandre. *Galileo Studies*. Translated by J. Mepham. Atlantic Highlands, N.J.: Humanities Press, 1978. A highly technical and critical examination of the scientific and mathematical principles used by Galileo in his various observations and experimentations.

Kuhn, Thomas S. *The Copernican Revolution: Planetary Astronomy in the Development of Western Thought*. Cambridge, Mass.: Harvard University Press, 1957. A detailed historical review of the debate inspired by Copernicus. The intellectual and social implications of the change from a geocentric to a heliocentric worldview are also examined.

Redondi, Pietro. *Galileo: Heretic*. Translated by Raymond Rosenthal. Princeton, N.J.: Princeton University Press, 1987. A comprehensive and critical examination of Galileo's trial before the Inquisition. Particular attention is directed toward examining the motivations and issues at stake for the Catholic Church.

Reston, James, Jr. *Galileo: A Life*. New York: HarperCollins, 1994. A character study and political biography, written in the present tense. The major portion of the book is devoted to Galileo's trial.

Ronan, Colin A. *Galileo*. New York: G. P. Putnam's Sons, 1974. A standard biography that not only provides numerous details about Galileo's life but also places them within the larger context of the intellectual changes taking place. Contains numerous illustrations and photographs.

Rowland, Wade. *Galileo's Mistake: A New Look at the Epic Confrontation Between Galileo and the Church*. New York: Arcade, 2003. Rowland argues that Galileo and church officials disagreed about something more significant than whether Earth revolved around the sun; they were disputing the nature of truth and how people acquire the truth.

SEE ALSO: Giovanni Alfonso Borelli; Tommaso Campanella; Gian Domenico Cassini; René Descartes; David and Johannes Fabricius; Pierre Gassendi; Francesco Maria Grimaldi; Edmond Halley; Johannes and Elisabetha Hevelius; Johannes Kepler; Hans Lippershey; Cosimo II de' Medici; Marin Mersenne; Nicolas-Claude Fabri de Peiresc; Santorio Santorio; Evangelista Torricelli; Urban VIII.

RELATED ARTICLES in *Great Events from History: The Seventeenth Century, 1601-1700:* 1601-1672: Rise of Scientific Societies; September, 1608: Invention of the Telescope; 1609-1619: Kepler's Laws of Planetary Motion; 1610: Galileo Confirms the Heliocentric Model of the Solar System; 1617-1628: Harvey Discovers the Circulation of the Blood; 1620: Bacon Publishes *Novum Organum*; 1623-1674: Earliest Calculators Appear; 1632: Galileo Publishes *Dialogue Concerning the Two Chief World Systems, Ptolemaic and Copernican*; 1637: Descartes Publishes His *Discourse on Method*; 1643: Torricelli Measures Atmospheric Pressure; 1655-1663: Grimaldi Discovers Diffraction; February, 1656: Huygens Identifies Saturn's Rings; 1660's-1700: First Microscopic Observations; 1660-1692: Boyle's Law and the Birth of Modern Chemistry; 1665: Cassini Discovers Jupiter's Great Red Spot; 1669: Steno Presents His Theories of Fossils and Dynamic Geology; Late December, 1671: Newton Builds His Reflecting Telescope; 1673: Huygens Explains the Pendulum; December 7, 1676: Rømer Calculates the Speed of Light; 1686: Halley Develops the First Weather Map; Summer, 1687: Newton Formulates the Theory of Universal Gravitation.

GIOVANNA GARZONI
Italian painter

Garzoni, one of the most important artists of the early modern period, was a miniaturist who specialized in still-life and floral paintings. She synthesized art and science with a skill almost unequaled by artists in her genre. Her works were sought by famous art collectors and patrons, and her talent helped her find patronage and employment at Italy's principal courts.

BORN: 1600; Ascoli, Piceno, Papal States (now in Italy)
DIED: February, 1670; Rome, Papal States (now in Italy)
AREA OF ACHIEVEMENT: Art

EARLY LIFE

Little is known about the life of Giovanna Garzoni (jo-VAHN-uh gahr-ZOHN-ee), and there is no precise information about the date and place of her birth. Newer archival documents have revealed that her father was a Venetian who resided in the marches, or border regions, at the turn of the century, making Ascoli the most probable birthplace of Giovanna. Nothing is known about her childhood and early training, however, it is likely that she grew up in Venice, and that while there, she was introduced to the art world by either her maternal grandfather (a goldsmith) or her uncle (a painter and printmaker).

Garzoni's only known paintings from her teen years include the small *Holy Family*. The painting bears a date of 1616 and an inscription that mentions that she was sixteen years old, thus confirming her birth year in 1600. She also painted a large canvas representing *Saint Andrew* (c. 1616). Both works demonstrate similarities with the works of Jacopo Palma the Younger (Palma Il Giovane) in style and composition, suggesting that she spent time in the workshop of this important Venetian painter. Despite this start as a traditional painter, a document dated February, 1630, places her in the calligraphy school of Giacomo Rogni, indicating that she also was a miniaturist. An extant letter that she wrote to Cassiano del Pozzo, dated June 15, 1630, and sent from Naples, shows that Garzoni left Venice a few months later. Although several scholars have speculated that she had visited Rome in 1616, it is more likely that Garzoni met Cassiano, a famous intellectual and art collector in Rome (who will later prove to be an important acquaintance), on her way to Naples.

LIFE'S WORK

Garzoni's mature career began in Naples, where she remained for more than a year having found a patron in the duke of Alcalà, the Spanish viceroy. Although she quickly achieved great fame in Naples, there are no extant works securely attributed to her from this period. In 1632, the duke of Alcalà returned to Spain, leaving Garzoni without a stipend. In November, 1632, she moved to Turin in Piedmont, after finding protection and employment from Christina of France, the duchess of Savoy. The Savoy court was particularly interested in contemporary Dutch and Flemish art, numbering in its collections many still-life paintings as well as masterpieces by Peter Paul Rubens and Sir Anthony van Dyck. Garzoni found this environment congenial and so remained in the service of the Savoy until Duke Vittorio Amadeo I died in 1637.

In Turin, she produced portraits and miniatures of various subjects, as well as the first documented still-life paintings attributed to her. Three extant portraits exemplify her painting style: Although the portraits generally recall mannerist examples, dominating these portraits are the qualities of lifelikeness and preciosity, both dependent on her miniaturist training and epitomized by the remarkable details in the treatment of the garments and armatures. Her choices of medium and technique underscore her technical abilities: Tempera on parchment—the medium in which she executed the majority of her later works—does not allow for correcting mistakes. Moreover, the paint in these portraits is applied primarily by means of stippling, minute marks painstakingly created with the point of the brush. The only still-life composition securely attributed from the Turin period, a bowl of casually arranged fruit on a table that includes several insects, suggests that her prototypes were similar paintings by Lombard artists, such as Ambrogio Figino and Fede Galizia. Examples of their style existed in the Savoy court's collections.

Documentation for the years 1638-1641 is scant, but it is very likely that Garzoni went to the royal courts of France and perhaps even of England, thanks to the direct contacts of the Savoy with the French and English royal families. She returned to Italy in the summer of 1642, taking up residence in Florence, where she worked primarily for the grand duke Leopold. Although she was very much appreciated at the Medici court, she often left Florence to visit Rome. (The Medici court had patronized Jacopo Ligozzi, allowing him to flourish in the final decades of the sixteenth century and to establish a local tradition for miniaturists and painters of botanical subjects, painters such as Garzoni.)

These trips brought her again in direct contact with Cassiano and with other members of the Academy of Lynx, the Lincei. They employed Garzoni for their scientific pursuits focused on natural history, but also studies of fossils and mushrooms and astronomy. Garzoni was one of the artists the Lincei hired to draw portraits of specimens, images that they used to document, study and classify their findings. To fit the "scientific" aim of these drawings, Garzoni adapted her style. The best collection of such drawings are the fifty plates she painted for an illustrated herbal, which was attributed to the artist only in 1984. It is now conserved in Washington in the collections of Dumbarton Oaks.

These botanical illustrations are astonishing for their verisimilitude and attention to detail. Although they undoubtedly reflect the direct observation of the specimens, aided by magnifying lenses more than through direct observation without a visual aid, they are programmed pictures that provide a wealth of botanical information. In fact, each plant portrait, set against a blank background, not only includes the roots but also leaves and flowers in various states of development and, crucial from the scientific perspective, examples of the plant's means of reproduction, usually seeds.

The illustrations of these plants embody an aesthetic dimension, exemplified in the play of light and shadows on petals and leaves; however, the descriptive, scientific aspects undoubtedly take precedence. This is readily revealed by comparing the herbal's plates with her other works, whether paintings of flower vases and of fruit bowls. For either type, she carefully arranged the composition to create a pleasing accumulation of forms and juxtaposition of colors while also manipulating the perspectival space, which "bends" around the flower vase or the fruit bowl. Moreover, in these still lifes and floral paintings, beyond the realization of microscopic details of flowers or fruits, Garzoni's patrons would have appreciated her representation of reflected and transmitted light, usually seen in the glass vase but occasionally present even in the leaves.

In 1651, Garzoni moved to Rome permanently. Like most of her life, the last years are not well documented. She died in Rome sometime in February of 1670. The detailed account of her will—she donated most of her wealth and properties to the Accademia di San Luca, the painters' academy—indicates that she was wealthy and

successful and that she was a patron of aristocratic elites throughout Italy, who paid her well.

SIGNIFICANCE

The fame enjoyed by Garzoni during her life demonstrates not only that female artists could be successful in the male-dominated art world but also that Baroque art is not simply about the portrayal of heightened emotions and dramatic chiaroscuro. The same patrons that admired Gian Lorenzo Bernini, Peter Paul Rubens, and Nicolas Poussin eagerly bought Garzoni's still lifes and floral paintings. Her miniatures were valued for more than their astonishing verisimilitude: Her compositions are particularly pleasing, projecting onto the beholder a distinctive calmness.

Her botanical portraits and still-life paintings respond to preexisting traditions, but they were not Baroque inventions. Instead, the scientific dimensions of the realism of some of her pictures depended exclusively on seventeenth century ideas. Garzoni's art extends traditions championed by famous northern and Italian artists during the two preceding centuries, including Jan van Eyck, Leonardo da Vinci, Albrecht Dürer, Ligozzi, Caravaggio, and Frans Snyder. Although she certainly found inspiration in the paintings and drawings of these great masters, her work should be seen as a development of the Lombard tradition of naturalism, indebted to Leonardo. The Lombard tradition of painting produced the two dominant schools of Italian seventeenth century painting, that of the Carraccis and that of Caravaggio.

—*Renzo Baldasso*

FURTHER READING

Bayer, Andrea, ed. *Painters of Reality: The Legacy of Leonardo and Caravaggio in Lombardy.* New Haven, Conn.: Yale University Press, 2004. This well-illustrated catalog is helpful for its explanation of the concept and varieties of naturalism in late-Renaissance Italian painting. Includes an extensive bibliography.

Casale, Gerardo. *Giovanna Garzoni: "Insigne miniatrice," 1600-1670.* Rome: Jandi Sapi, 1991. The standard monograph on Garzoni and her works. Includes a chronology and a biography. Complete and well-illustrated.

Freedberg, David. *The Eye of the Lynx: Galileo, His Friends, and the Beginnings of Modern Natural History.* Chicago: University of Chicago Press, 2002. This award-winning book provides the intellectual context for understanding the scientific aspects of the Garzoni's realism and the choice of subject of the artist's still-life compositions, floral paintings, and portraits of animals and plants. Extensive bibliography and numerous color illustrations.

Fumagalli, Elena, and Silvia Meloni Trkulja. *Giovanna Garzoni: Still Lifes/Geilleben/Natures Mortes*. Paris: Bibliotheque de l'Image, 2000. This catalog of Garzoni's works is particularly useful for its reproductions.

Spike, John T. *Italian Still Life Paintings from Three Centuries*. Florence: Stiav, 1983. An exhibition catalog that provides comparative material and a context for Garzoni's still-life paintings. The author's intro-

duction and catalog entries are offer insightful analyses of this genre of painting.

Tongiorgi Tomasi, Lucia. *The Flowering of Florence: Botanical Art for the Medici*. Washington, D.C.: National Gallery of Art, 2002. An exhibition catalog with informative essays and excellent illustrations. Includes a separate section on the Garzoni.

SEE ALSO: Gian Lorenzo Bernini; Artemisia Gentileschi; Nicolas Poussin; Peter Paul Rubens; Elisabetta Sirani; Sir Anthony van Dyck.

RELATED ARTICLE in *Great Events from History: The Seventeenth Century, 1601-1700:* Mid-17th century: Dutch School of Painting Flourishes.

PIERRE GASSENDI
French scientist, philosopher, and religious leader

Although best known for his Christianization of Epicurean atomism, Gassendi also advanced science through his discoveries in physics and astronomy, and he promoted Catholicism through his pastoral and administrative work.

BORN: January 22, 1592; Champtercier, Provence, France

DIED: October 24, 1655; Paris, France

ALSO KNOWN AS: Pierre Gassend

AREAS OF ACHIEVEMENT: Science and technology, mathematics, philosophy, scholarship

EARLY LIFE

Pierre Gassendi (pyehr gah-sahn-dee) was born in a Provençal village in the south of France. His father, Antoine Gassendi, was a peasant farmer, and his mother, Françoise (Fabry) Gassendi, came from similar provincial roots. The mental abilities Pierre manifested as a child convinced his parents that he was not suited to farm labors, and his uncle, Thomas Fabry, the village priest, took care of his early education.

From the age of seven to fourteen, Pierre attended schools at Digne and Riez, neighboring towns to the east and south of Champtercier. After leaving school he spent two years on his father's farm while teaching rhetoric at Digne. He resumed his formal education in 1609 at Aix-en-Provence, where he studied philosophy and theology. In 1612, he returned to Digne to teach theology. Having decided to become a priest, he traveled to Avignon and

received his doctorate in theology in 1616. Shortly thereafter, he was ordained to the priesthood and said his first Mass.

For the next six years Gassendi taught philosophy at the university in Aix-en-Provence. During this time he began making the astronomical observations that would continue for more than three decades and constitute more than four hundred pages of his collected works. For example, in 1621, he observed luminous, multicolored, and shifting shapes in the northern sky, to which he gave the name "aurora borealis." On his travels around France he met influential intellectuals and learned from them new scientific and philosophical ideas. Particularly important was his association with Nicolas-Claude Fabri de Peiresc, the priest, politician, and Humanist who became Gassendi's friend and patron.

LIFE'S WORK

Gassendi saw his life's task as reconciling Christianity and science by resurrecting an ancient atomic theory and making it compatible with his deeply held religious convictions. In his first book, *Exercitationes paradoxicæ adversus Aristoteleos* (1624; unwelcome essays against the Aristotelians), he was highly critical of Aristotle's claim to know the essences of things. For example, Aristotle reasoned from the nature of sound to the conclusion that high tones travel more rapidly than low tones, but seventeenth century scientists discovered that a sound's velocity was independent of its pitch. In contrast to the authoritarianism of the Aristotelians, Gassendi favored a middle way between dogmatism and skepticism, in which genuine scientific knowledge arose from the astute description of phenomena. During the 1620's, Gassendi visited Paris and deepened his friendship with Marin Mersenne, a Minim friar who was a proponent of the new science and a foe of the occult sciences. Gassendi, too, became an opponent of astrology, alchemy, divination from dreams, and natural magic.

When the Jesuits took over the university at Aix-en-Provence, Gassendi returned to Digne where, for the next several years, he devoted himself to his clerical duties, his scientific studies (by using the newly invented telescope, microscope, and barometer), and his philosophical and theological inquiries. He corresponded with Galileo, whose Copernicanism he shared. He also traveled to Paris, Flanders, and Holland, where he met many leading scholars and scientists. François Luillier, a government official, sometimes accompanied Gassendi, and he became another of his important patrons.

Throughout the 1630's, Gassendi made many astronomical observations. Particularly important was his telescopic observation of Mercury crossing the face of the Sun in 1631. He was the first to see this transit of Mercury, and in his *Mercurius in sole visus* (wr. 1632; Mercury seen in the Sun; pb. 1658 in his *Opera omnia*) he used his data to support the heliocentric systems of Copernicus and Johannes Kepler, although, like Galileo, he was critical of Kepler's theory of elliptical planetary orbits.

By this time Gassendi had become convinced that the only way to solve the skeptical crisis confronting Christianity was through the atomic theory of Epicurus, a Greek philosopher who had lived three centuries before the time of Christ. Gassendi once stated that he chose Epicurus as his exemplar because his system of the world could be more easily consolidated with Christianity than any other ancient philosophy. Epicurus was an unlikely choice, since this polytheist believed in a purposeless and uncreated universe inhabited by humans with mortal souls, whereas Gassendi, a believer in Divine Providence and the immortal human soul, understood that God had created a purposeful world composed of a finite number of atoms whose properties and aggregations accounted for all natural phenomena. Peiresc and Luillier, Gassendi's patrons, supported his attempt to Christianize Epicurean atomism, but Peiresc's death in 1637 had a devastating effect on Gassendi. Setting aside his studies of Epicureanism, he devoted himself to writing a biography of his friend, which was published in 1641.

Returning, in the 1640's, to his scientific work and ecclesiastical duties, Gassendi traveled to Paris and taught philosophy to the nineteen-year-old Jean-Baptiste Poquelin, who would later become the famous playwright Molière. In 1642, he published a short work on motion that contained the first correct statement of the principle of rectilinear inertia, that is, the tendency of an object to remain in motion in a straight line. At the request of Mersenne, Gassendi published, in 1644, a critique of René Descartes's *Meditationes de prima philosphia* (1641; *Meditations on First Philosophy*, 1680). Contrary to Descartes, Gassendi believed that, regardless of how clear and distinct ideas were, there was no guarantee that they represented anything real. Furthermore, Gassendi disagreed with the Cartesian identification of matter with extension, and he opposed Descartes's theory of a voidless universe filled with matter, since Gassendi needed empty spaces for atomic motions.

In 1645, Gassendi became a professor at the Royal College in Paris. Here, in 1647, he published a book, dedicated to yet another patron, Cardinal de Richelieu, on the astronomical theories of Ptolemy, Copernicus, and Tycho Brahe. In the late 1640's, he began to publish his ideas on Epicurean atomism, suitably revised to assure their compatibility with Catholic doctrines.

Mersenne died in 1648 and Gassendi's own health declined. He returned to Provence where he continued his work on science and Epicurean philosophy under the patronage of Henri-Louis Habert de Montmor. In Provence and, after 1653, in Paris, he wrote biographies of the astronomers Copernicus, Brahe, Regiomontanus, and Georg von Peurbach. He also reinterpreted Epicurean ethics in a Christian way. Epicurean hedonism sought to maximize pleasures and minimize pains, but for Gassendi the greatest pleasure attainable by a human being was the beatific vision of God, attainable after death only if individuals followed the rules of Christian morality. He did not live to see the publication of his chief work, *Syntagma philosophicum* (published in his *Opera omnia*, 1658). The disease from which he suffered, most likely tuberculosis, weakened his health, and he died at the home of Lord Montmor in 1655. Three years after his friend's death, Montmor had all of Gassendi's works published in six volumes.

SIGNIFICANCE

Those scholars who admire Gassendi see him as laying the foundations of modern scientific thought. Though his contributions to science were not on the same level as those of Galileo, Kepler, or Newton, he performed some interesting experiments, such as analyzing falling objects from the mast of a moving ship, and he did introduce some important scientific ideas, such as rectilinear inertia, which went beyond Galileo's erroneous circular inertia. Furthermore, by avoiding the dogmatism of the Cartesians and the nihilism of the skeptics, he devised a reformed atomism acceptable to both Christians and scientists.

Critics of Gassendi argue that his reformed atomism did little to stimulate new observations and experiments. Karl Marx, the nineteenth century materialist and socialist, characterized Gassendi's attempt to Christianize atomism as cloaking a courtesan in a nun's habit. However, a few scholars see Gassendi as a cryptomaterialist, whereas some Catholic scholars see a contradiction between his strong empiricism (nothing is in the mind that is not first in the senses) and his belief in an immaterial, immortal soul (how did such an idea get into the mind?).

Despite these differences, general agreement exists about Gassendi's importance to seventeenth century thought. To many Christians, including some influential Jesuits, Gassendism was preferable to Cartesianism as an alternative to Scholasticism. To Protestants such as John Locke and Thomas Hobbes, Gassendi's empiricism, hedonistic ethics, and theory of the social contract were important influences on their political theories. Gassendi's ideas also influenced such scientists as Robert Boyle, Isaac Newton, and John Dalton. His contemporaries, especially those who knew him best, testify that he was comfortable with his Catholicism. Like the priest-scientist Pierre Teilhard de Chardin in the twentieth century, who Christianized evolution, Gassendi, through the cross-fertilization between his natural and supernatural milieus, created new views concerning Humanism, religion, and science that helped to create the intellectual foundations of the modern Western world.

—*Robert J. Paradowski*

FURTHER READING

Lindberg, David C., and Ronald L. Numbers, eds. *When Science and Christianity Meet*. Chicago: University of Chicago Press, 2003. This book emphasize the complexity of the relationship between science and Christianity throughout history, and William B. Ashworth, Jr.'s, essay, "Christianity and the Mechanistic Universe," shows how Gassendi's life and work was an important part of this story in the seventeenth century. Includes a further-reading guide and an index.

Osler, Margaret J. *Divine Will and the Mechanical Philosophy: Gassendi and Descartes on Contingency and Necessity in the Created World*. New York: Cambridge University Press, 1994. Osler argues that the differences between Descartes and Gassendi grew out of their different theological presuppositions. Includes an extensive bibliography and an index.

Sarasohn, Lisa T. *Gassendi's Ethics: Freedom in a Mechanistic Universe*. Ithaca, N.Y.: Cornell University Press, 1996. In this analysis of the relationship between Gassendi's natural philosophy and his ethics, Sarasohn shows how Gassendi found a middle way between Hobbesian materialism and Cartesian rationalism. Index.

SEE ALSO: Robert Boyle; René Descartes; Pierre de Fermat; Galileo; Thomas Hobbes; Johannes Kepler; Gottfried Wilhelm Leibniz; John Locke; Marin Mersenne; Sir Isaac Newton; Nicolas-Claude Fabri de Peiresc; Cardinal de Richelieu.

RELATED ARTICLES in *Great Events from History: The Seventeenth Century, 1601-1700:* 1601-1672: Rise of Scientific Societies; 1610-1643: Reign of Louis XIII; 1625: Grotius Establishes the Concept of International Law; 1637: Descartes Publishes His *Discourse on Method*; 1660-1692: Boyle's Law and the Birth of Modern Chemistry.

ARTEMISIA GENTILESCHI
Italian painter

At an early age Artemisia began producing paintings in the strong, bold manner of chiaroscuro popularized by Caravaggio, and she painted in the history style, which had been traditionally closed to women. She was the first Italian woman whose works were praised by contemporaries and whose paintings were influential in the work of other artists.

BORN: July 8, 1593; Rome, Papal States (now in Italy)
DIED: 1652 or 1653; Naples, Kingdom of Naples (now in Italy)
AREA OF ACHIEVEMENT: Art

EARLY LIFE

Following the death of their mother, Prudentia Montoni, in 1605, Artemisia Gentileschi (ahrt-eh-MIHZ-ee-ah jayn-tee-LEHS-kee) and her brothers were raised by her father Orazio Gentileschi in the Roman home that combined their family living quarters with his very active painting studio. Artemisia was exposed to the workshop and to painting from an early age, although critics still debate the extent to which social decorum prevented her from coming into contact with other artists, apprentices, and models. Women of the period were banned from life-drawing, but she might have had the opportunity in the privacy of her father's studio, and she herself served as a model for some of her father's paintings. She received no formal education. She did not learn to read and write until she was an adult, and she was seldom seen outside the Gentileschi family home.

In 1610, at the age of seventeen, she produced her first painting, *Susanna and the Elders*. It is possible to see the coercion of the elders in the Susanna story as Artemisia's commentary on personal experience. In 1611, artist Agostino Tassi, a teacher of perspective who had been hired by her father, raped Gentileschi. A suit was brought by Orazio Gentileschi against Tassi for raping his daughter. Tassi was already an accused criminal (accused of incest with his sister-in-law and conspiracy to murder his wife), but it is uncertain whether Orazio knew his background before hiring him. The violence of the initial rape is clearly evident from Artemisia's testimony, but the situation was complicated because the two had a sexual relationship after the rape on the understanding that Tassi would marry her. Orazio might have pressed the lawsuit not because of the rape of his daughter but because Tassi had reneged on the marriage.

Although Tassi was the accused, it was Artemisia who was subjected to questioning under torture. In the end, Tassi was found guilty and Artemisia was vindicated. On November 29, 1612, Artemisia effectively regained her status in the community by marrying an acquaintance of her father.

LIFE'S WORK

After moving to Florence, Artemisia began her independent career. She received assistance from Michelangelo Buonarotti, the Younger, who provided her with the social entrée necessary to win patrons. She also began to correspond with Galileo. With the help of intermediaries such as Buonarotti, Artemisia's works, including the *Penitent Magdalene* (c. 1617-1620) and *Judith Slaying Holofernes* (c. 1613-1614), were purchased by Cosimo II de' Medici, grand duke of Tuscany. King Philip IV of Spain, the collector Cassiano del Pozzo, and Prince Karl Eusebius von Liechtenstein all owned paintings by her. She was commissioned, with several male contemporaries, to paint an *Allegory of Inclination* for the decoration of the Casa Buonarotti (1615-1617). It was this commission that led to her matriculation in the Florentine Academy.

Many of her paintings are remarkable for her exploitation of the emotional possibilities of relatively compressed spatial composition and chiaroscuro. *Judith Slaying Holofernes* features a muscular Judith in the actual act of decapitation, literally holding down a struggling Holofernes whose large hand, at the center of the spiraling trio of figures, grasps ineffectually upward toward Judith's maidservant accomplice. The instinctive patterning of the brightly spotlighted actors against the dark, murky background contributes to the psychological and physical tension. A later version of *Judith and Her Maidservant* (1625-1627) is almost like a sequel, in which an alert and listening Judith, lit by the flickering candlelight in the enemy's chamber, calls for silence with her upraised hand, while still grasping in her right the scimitar of Holofernes and cautioning her crouching maidservant. One almost feels their fear of discovery, while the decapitated head of the mute Holofernes, at the lower foreground edge, turns pleadingly to the viewer. In both paintings Judith is draped in the remarkable yellow gold that Artemisia preferred for her draperies in the 1620's and 1630's, and which she, like her father, often combined with a clear, cool, cobalt blue.

In 1623, Artemisia appears to have broken with her husband. By 1626, she was living on the Via del Corso in Rome with her eldest daughter, Prudentia. A second daughter died almost immediately after birth, and two sons (Giovanni Battista and Cristofano) disappear from the record with her husband (he is only mentioned again in 1637, when Artemisia asked a correspondent if he were still alive). In 1634, an English visitor to Naples noted that Prudentia was a painter in her own right (no extant works are attributed to her).

After becoming independent from her husband, Artemisia embarked on a peripatetic career, moving first to Genoa and then to Venice. Some of Artemisia's paintings made their way into premier European collections, but she seems to have lacked direct patronage, relying on intermediaries to broker deals for her.

In 1627, a pamphlet published in Venice praised three of her works, and while there she completed a *Hercules and Omphale* for Philip IV, king of Spain, and painted other works for the duke of Alcalà. By 1630, she was in Naples. In a famous self-portrait of this period she appears as the *Allegory of Painting* (1630). In this image, Artemisia fashions herself in a traditionally male role, as master of the heroic physical labor of painting, combining a view of herself at work at her easel with symbolism that alludes to the intellectual foundation of the painter's art (although her intellectualism is often questioned, she did possess a ready grasp of standard classical and biblical subject matter). Artemisia's self-presentation as a somewhat masculine working painter is entirely appropriate given that she did live entirely off the proceeds of painting.

It is difficult to know how she established and maintained the succession of studios that she must have required to complete her work. Her only assistant might have been her daughter Prudentia. In 1635, although clearly in financial straits in Naples and looking for patronage, she resisted a summons to England from Charles I. She was forced by circumstances to leave Italy for London and was there when her father, who had worked in England since 1626, died in 1639. Some of her works entered the royal collections. Despite success in England, by 1640-1642, Artemisia was back in Naples, where she died in 1652 or 1653. Although she did complete works for Neapolitan patrons in this final decade, her last years are poorly documented.

SIGNIFICANCE

For many years, the transcripts concerning the rape trial against Tassi were more widely known than any of Artemisia Gentileschi's paintings. They provided the basis for an early, fictionalized biographical account and for more recent novels and even a biographical film. Her artistic personality and her painterly oeuvre have therefore largely been constructed by feminist scholarship stemming from the biographical details. For this reason, her bold, decisive treatment of historical or biblical accounts of female victimization, subjugation, and often heroic virtue (subjects not uncommon to the period), and especially her tendency to present her female subjects as frank, heroic nudes, have been widely read in terms of her own physical and psychological trauma.

Such a reading privileges only one aspect of her subject matter, and it has tended to overshadow serious treatment of her talents as a painter. She did overcome the notoriety that resulted from the trial, and the rampant misogyny of the period and the profession, to become a successful independent painter. She became a member of the Design Academy established by artist and writer Giorgio Vasari in Florence, and she went on to work all over Italy and for Charles I in London.

As is the case with Caravaggio, modern scholarship has made it difficult to separate the circumstances of Gentileschi's life from her art. The many versions of the story of *Judith Slaying Holofernes* made by male painters of the Baroque period have not received nearly so much scrutiny as those by Artemisia, because hers are read in the context of her rape, subsequent trial, and her relationship with her father. Such readings tend to obscure her talents as a painter in general, claiming that her work addressed feminist concerns mainly, while ignoring her more-general portraits and religious and allegorical works.

Given the limitations on women in this period, it is remarkable that Artemisia was able to successfully adapt herself to the business of painting, earning commissions, communicating with patrons, moving from city to city, establishing a series of studios, and earning her living through her work. She deserves to be further studied for her technical mastery and eye for clarity of color and purity of form.

—*Sally Anne Hickson*

FURTHER READING

Banti, Anna. *Artemisia*. 1947. New ed. Translated by Shirley D'Ardia Caracciolo. Introduction by Susan Sontag. Lincoln: University of Nebraska Press, 2004. A biographical novel of Artemisia based on available archival sources, which brought to light the remarkable circumstances of her life.

Bissell, R. Ward. *Artemisia Gentileschi and the Authority of Art: Critical Reading and Catalogue Raisonné.* University Park: Pennsylvania State University Press, 1999. An examination of Artemisia's complete oeuvre, with a thorough catalog of works and exhaustive transcriptions of all relevant documents. Contains a valuable appendix with a technical examination of her works, discussing pigments, varnishes, and techniques.

Christiansen, Keith, and Judith W. Mann, eds. *Orazio and Artemisia Gentileschi.* New Haven, Conn.: Yale University Press, 2001. An exhibition catalog and excellent study of the complete Gentileschi oeuvre, and the first exhibition to consider father and daughter together. Adds new documents concerning Orazio's career and new inventories of Artemisia's household effects in Florence. Contains a particularly incisive, thoughtful, and eminently sensible reassessment of Artemisia's career by Rona Goffen.

Garrard, Mary D. "Artemesia and Susanna." In *Feminism and Art History: Questioning the Litany*, edited by Norma Broude and Mary D. Garrard. New York: Harper & Row, 1982.

_____. *Artemisia Gentileschi Around 1622: The Shaping and Reshaping of an Artistic Identity.* Berkeley: University of California Press, 2001. This work examines two little-known paintings by Artemisia.

_____. *Artemisia Gentileschi: The Image of the Female Hero in Italian Baroque Art.* Princeton, N.J.: Princeton University Press, 1989. All three works provide a feminist reading of Artemisia's subjects and her life. The 1989 book offers valuable English translations of documents relevant to her trial, and is a thorough iconographical study of selected works.

SEE ALSO: Giovanna Garzoni; Georges de La Tour; Philip IV; Elisabetta Sirani.

RELATED ARTICLES in *Great Events from History: The Seventeenth Century, 1601-1700:* c. 1601-1620: Emergence of Baroque Art; Mid-17th century: Dutch School of Painting Flourishes.

ORLANDO GIBBONS
English musician and composer

An honored organist of the Chapel Royal and personal musician to Prince Charles, Gibbons helped perfect and significantly expanded the musical genres of the verse anthem, keyboard music for the virginal, consort music for viols, and English madrigals.

BORN: 1583; Oxford, England
DIED: June 5, 1625; Canterbury, England
AREAS OF ACHIEVEMENT: Music, religion and theology

EARLY LIFE

Although he was born in Oxford, England, Orlando Gibbons's family moved to Cambridge when he was very young. Several members of his family were musicians, including his father, William, who performed at civic events in his office as a wait, or town musician, for Cambridge. Orlando's brother Edward, the eldest of Orlando's ten siblings, earned academic degrees in music at both Cambridge and Oxford and was appointed as master of the choristers at King's College, Cambridge. Orlando was listed as a member of this choir from 1596 until 1599.

In 1598, Orlando, under an arrangement in which his fees were waived or reduced in exchange for some labor, matriculated at King's College, where he continued to serve as a chorister. In 1603, he became a musician in the Chapel Royal, an affiliation he maintained for the rest of his life, serving under James I (1566-1625) for a period closely matching that monarch's reign. He was officially appointed in 1605, Soon after this appointment, Gibbons married Elizabeth Patten; they had seven children.

LIFE'S WORK

In England during the time of Gibbons, the Renaissance practice of performing consort music, music written for groups of similar instruments, was still very popular, especially music written for the viol (a fretted, softer relative of the modern violin). Gibbons contributed a great deal to the consort music repertoire and added organ accompaniments. At some point within the years 1606-1610, Gibbons became the first English composer to have his music printed from engraved plates, using a technology that had been developed in continental Europe during the previous two decades. His work *Fantasies of Three Parts* (1621) was dedicated to Edmund Wray, then groom of the privy chamber, although he was exiled from the court the following year. Another friend and patron was Sir Christopher Hatton, to whom he dedi-

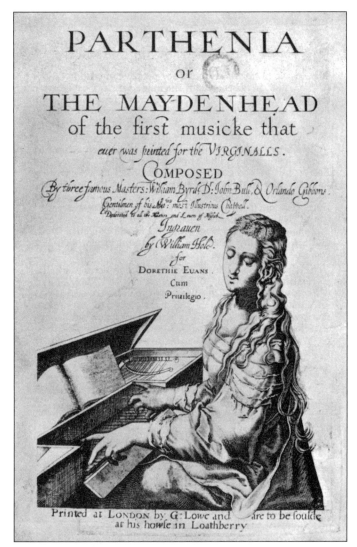

Title page of Parthenia, *composed by William Byrd, John Bull, and Orlando Gibbons, and published about 1612.* (Hulton Archive/Getty Images)

and Baroque (the theme and variations structure favored in English virginal music, harmonic clarity) can be heard.

Gibbons was honored by having his works included in *Parthenia* (c. 1612), the first printed collection of works for the virginal, a small harpsichord especially favored in England. The other two contributors were much older and more famous; William Byrd, the late Queen Elizabeth's favorite, and Dr. John Bull, an organist of the Chapel Royal. The pieces were written to honor the marriage of Princess Elizabeth Stuart and Frederick V, elector of the Palatinate.

Gibbons's great skill as an organist was eventually recognized, and in 1615, he was first listed as an organist in the Chapel Royal. In addition to his continued service in the Chapel Royal, Gibbons accepted appointments with Westminster Abbey, and he was able to hold these joint positions, because many of the duties and musical responsibilities of each position were rotated among the same group of musicians. As a member of the Chapel Royal, he accompanied the king on his visit to Scotland in 1617, for which he composed the anthem "Great King of Gods" and a secular song, "Do not repine, fair sun."

Gibbons wrote a great deal of sacred music, although his major polyphonic works were not published until after his death. Unlike his older predecessors, who had participated in the musical transition from Catholic to Anglican services, Gibbons's own development as a composer of sacred music was completely within the liturgy of the Church of England. He is especially known for his pieces in the verse anthem genre, which contrasts the full chorus with solo passages, often with instrumental accompaniment by a consort of viols or an organ. In addition to the anthems, he composed two services, the Anglican equivalent of the great masses of Giovanni Pierluigi da Palestrina (c. 1525-1594). Because of this, he was sometimes referred to as the English Palestrina, and his polyphonic style for these large works evoked the Renaissance techniques, but with more emphasis on the syllables of the text. His choruses sometimes extended to as many as eight voices, as in his well-known piece "O clap your hands."

Although he was certainly recognized by King James I, who had awarded him two grants in 1615, it was the

cated *The First Set of Madrigals and Mottets* (1612), a collection of songs that included "The Silver Swan," one of Gibbon's most famous compositions.

An important characteristic of Gibbon's style as a secular composer is the ability of many of his melodies to serve either as instrumental or vocal parts. This flexibility would have been very useful in adapting his music to changing performance conditions and the contingencies of musician availability. In Gibbons's compositional style, coming at a period of transition between the Renaissance and Baroque musical periods, characteristic elements of both the Renaissance (use of viol consorts, conservative control of dissonance, flowing polyphony) young Prince Charles, later King Charles I, who, after becoming the prince of Wales, hired Gibbons as one of his personal staff of musicians in 1617. Two years later, Gibbons was given an additional appointment to serve as King James's virginalist. In 1623, Gibbons was given yet another set of musical duties, when he and Thomas Day, a colleague who served with him in Prince Charles's household as well as the Chapel Royal, were given shared appointments as organists and masters of the choristers at Westminster Abbey.

In 1625, James I died, and the new King Charles prepared to meet his bride, Henrietta Maria of France, in Canterbury. Gibbons was to attend, but on May 31, he suddenly fell ill and went into a coma, dying just a few days later. His life was cut short when he was at the peak of his musical powers, just as his major patron had risen to supreme power in England.

SIGNIFICANCE

Gibbons made lasting contributions to the repertoire of several distinctively English genres, including consort songs, keyboard music for the virginal, and verse anthems. His serious, polyphonic compositions represented a continuation of the major techniques and motifs of Renaissance music, of which he was undisputedly a master. At the same time, Gibbons's music was undeniably modern and helped to shape the development of early Baroque compositions in England: For all his facility with Renaissance high seriousness, Gibbons eschewed Renaissance chromatic harmonies and decorative tropes in favor of periodic harmony and modern rhythmic figures. He influenced later English composers, including Henry Purcell (1659-1695). His sacred music remained in use within the Anglican church, and was eventually adopted by other denominations.

—*John Myers*

FURTHER READING

Ashbee, Andrew, and Peter Holman, eds. *John Jenkins and His Time: Studies in English Consort Music.* New York: Oxford University Press, 1996. Essays by various experts in English consort music. John Jenkins (1592-1678), a composer of instrumental music, was an important contemporary of Gibbons, who is also given extensive coverage in this work, including detailed discussion of patronage, the use of instruments (viols, lutes, organ, etc.); and musical manuscripts.

Fellowes, Edmund H. *Orlando Gibbons and His Family: The Last of the Tudor School of Musicians.* Hamden, Conn.: Archon Books, 1970. First published in 1925 as *Orlando Gibbons: A Short Account of His Life and Work.* Biographical information on Gibbons, with separate chapters on his church, secular vocal, and instrumental music. Illustrated. Includes appendices and genealogical chart of the Gibbons family.

Harley, John. *Orlando Gibbons and the Gibbons Family of Musicians.* Brookfield, Vt.: Ashgate, 1999. Detailed accounts, including many musical examples with analysis and commentary. An entire chapter on Christopher Gibbons. Appendixes, extensive musical examples, illustrations, list of works, historical documents, bibliography.

Morehen, John, ed. *English Choral Practice, 1400-1650.* New York: Cambridge University Press, 2003. Nine essays focus on performance practice (including pitch), the evolution of the church choir, musical training, pronunciation, and research of manuscripts. Twelve references to Gibbons.

Silbiger, Alexander. *Keyboard Music Before 1700.* 2d ed. New York: Routledge, 2004. After a general article on the evolution of of European keyboard music, chapters by specialists focus on composers and regional developments, including France, Germany, the Netherlands, Italy, Spain, and Portugal, as well as England, with several references specifically to Gibbons. This edition adds a chapter on performance practice by Silbiger, updated bibliographies and new information. Places Gibbons's keyboard music in an international context.

SEE ALSO: Charles I; Elizabeth Stuart; Frederick V; Henrietta Maria; James I; Henry Purcell.

RELATED ARTICLES in *Great Events from History: The Seventeenth Century, 1601-1700:* c. 1601: Emergence of Baroque Music; March 24, 1603: James I Becomes King of England.

LUIS DE GÓNGORA Y ARGOTE
Spanish poet

Regarded as the poet's poet of the Spanish Golden Age of literature, Góngora introduced the highly stylized, baroque manner into Spanish poetry.

BORN: July 11, 1561; Córdoba, Spain
DIED: May 23, 1627; Córdoba
AREA OF ACHIEVEMENT: Literature

EARLY LIFE

Luis de Góngora y Argote (lew-EES day GAWNG-eh-rah ee ahr-GOH-tay) was born to a patrician family in Córdoba, one of the principal towns of Andalusia, the coastal Mediterrean region of Spain. Built by the Romans, Córdoba had been conquered in the Middle Ages by the Islamic Moors. Though Spanish Christians under Ferdinand III had reconquered Córdoba in 1236, the city retained the flavor of its Moorish past, including a vibrant oral tradition of poetry and song that synthesized Arab, Berber, and Spanish elements. While still a boy, Góngora composed his first poems and songs in imitation of oral tradition. At the same time, he became became steeped in classical Greek, Latin, and Italian literatures—thanks in large part to his father's ample library.

He continued his studies at the Universidad de Salamanca, following a course in law. Upon graduation, he returned to Córdoba, where he assumed his uncle's prebendary at the city's cathedral. This allowed him a portion of the church's revenues in return for minimal clerical duties. To the consternation of his bishop, Góngora indulged more in temporal than religious pursuits. A "man about town," he attended bullfights, took an active part in the city's nightlife and spent much of his free time composing songs and poems to the women that caught his fancy. He also became addicted to gambling, which led him to financial ruin late in life.

LIFE'S WORK

Góngora's early lyrical poetry, songs, and romances first won him popular recognition in Córdoba and beyond. Though these works were not officially published until after his death in 1627, they were disseminated by manuscript and word of mouth during his lifetime. Many became—and remain—classics. The style is light and the wordplay fanciful, as Góngora tackles time-honored themes such as the fickleness of Fortune or the mutability of romantic love.

Typical of this manner is a ballad on Fortune with the refrain *"cuando pitos, flautas/cuando flautas, pitos"*

(which translates freely as when you want a whistle, [Fortune gives you] a flute, when a flute, a whistle). Similarly, his well-known sonnet opening *"la dulce boca que a gustar convida"* (the sweet mouth which offers a taste) ends with an image of thwarted love turned to venom. This latter poem is said to have been inspired by one of Góngora's own ill-starred love affairs. Indeed, one of the hallmarks of Góngora's early work is its grounding in observation and experience. His sonnet on his native Córdoba has a painterly quality that celebrates the region's *"Oh fertil llano, oh sierras levantadas,/que privilegia el cielo y dora el dia!"* (oh fertile planes, oh rising mountains, that the sky smiles down on and colors gold). His poem "La mas bella nina" vividly records the bitter experience of a peasant girl, newly married and widowed as her groom is called off to war.

In the early 1600's, Góngora moved from Córdoba to Madrid (to be near the Spanish royal court). He gradually departed from his early style, evolving a much more mannered approach indebted to his classical learning more so than to his oral tradition. In the parlance of the day, Góngora gave up the *estilo llano* (or plain style) for the *estilo culto* (or high-culture style). In place of ballads, sonnets, and the short romances, he attempted longer, more consciously "literary" works with complex narrative structures, convoluted latinate syntax, and tangles of metaphors and classical allusions. In short, he began to compose works to be read (and reread), rather than to be read aloud or sung.

His new style found an appreciative audience in the highly literate court of Phillip III, but it also engendered the furious opposition of Góngora's chief poetic rivals: Lope de Vega Carpio and Francisco Gómez de Quevedo y Villegas, who proudly hailed themselves common "geese" in opposition to Góngora's self-styled group of high culture "swans." This bitter literary feud continued to the end of Góngora's life, taking a particularly vicious turn in 1625, when Quevedo y Villegas bought at auction the Madrid home of Góngora, who was nearly bankrupt because of his gambling losses.

The culminating works that mark Góngora's new style were *Fábula de Polifemo y Galatea* (1627; *Fable of Polyphemus and Galatea*, 1961) and *Soledades* (1627; *The Solitudes of Don Luis de Góngora*, 1931; *The Solitudes*, 1964). Both works retain a semblance of narrative: The former is a reworking of Ovid's tale of the cyclops Polyphemus's thwarted love for the nymph Galatea; the latter is a dreamy idyll in which the shipwrecked protagonist encounters the simple life of island folk and marries a beautiful maiden.

A web of intertextuality, built upon description, metaphor, and allusions, however, almost overwhelm the narrative—and defy easy translation. For example, Góngora transforms the crude and violent one-eyed goatherd of Ovid and Homer into an aesthete who in his love song to Galatea drops learned references from the Queen of Sheba to the King of Java. At times, Polyphemus's metaphors metastasize. He develops elaborate conceits in which the antlers of an aged deer become "*de Helvecias picas*" (Helvetian pikes) and his own single eye becomes a sunlike orb. Similarly, the first stanza of *Soledades* begins simply enough with "Era del ano la estacion florida" (literally, it was of the year the flowery season) but soon morphs into a complex net of sexual allusions to Europa, Ganymede, and Jupiter. While the poem demands much of its reader, it generally repays the effort. *Soledades* is not so much a narrative poem but an ambitious interior journey that calls into question the traditional dichotomies of poet and reader, subject and object, and word and thing. Though he planned a series of four installments, Góngora abandoned the *Soledades* project after completing the first part. Yet its "unfinished" status is somehow appropriate to such an "open-ended" work that is still being "written" in the act of contemporary creative interpretation.

SIGNIFICANCE

Góngora's highly mannered late work—a poetry for poetry's sake seemingly divorced both from common speech patterns and objective reality—gave rise to a European literary style, *gongorismo*. *Gongorismo* has often been likened to the Euphuistic tradition of a particular sixteenth century English literature (whose foremost practitioner was the prosodist John Lyly): Both are baroque in nature, highly ornamental, and self-consciously artful. However, *gongorismo* surpasses mere Euphuism in its intellectual concentration (similar to that of the Metaphysical School of seventeenth century English poetry) and its radical aestheticism that promotes the idea of a poem as a self-referential object rather than an Aristotelian "imitation" of some external reality.

Góngora can be seen as an important precursor to the nineteenth century French Symbolist poetry of Charles Baudelaire, Arthur Rimbaud, and, most particularly, Stéphane Mallarmé. He also became a rallying figure to twentieth century Spanish poets such as Federico García Lorca and Rafael Alberti, who saw in the *estilo culto* a

prefiguration of high literary modernism. In the 1920's Góngora's work again became the locus of a fierce literary argument: Proponents held up *Soledades* as a world masterpiece while detractors decried the work as unintelligible, self-absorbed, snd ostentatious in its use of classical allusions (charges similar to those laid by antimodernists against works such as T. S. Eliot's *The Waste Land* (1922) and James Joyce's *Ulysses* (1922). Nor has the fascination with Góngora's late work lessened for postmodernist critics, who have explored its deconstruction of authorial "voice," subversion of gender roles, and reliance on liminal settings.

—Luke A. Powers

FURTHER READING

Brenan, Gerald. "Gongora and the New Poetry." *The Literature of the Spanish People: From Roman Times to the Present Day*. London: Cambridge University Press, 1951. This magisterial work remains a key English-language overview of Spanish literature. The chapter on Góngora does an excellent job of providing the historical and social context of the poet's "light" and "dark" periods and recognizes his primacy as the poet's poet of Spain's literary Golden Age.

Collins, Marsha. *Soledades, Gongora's Masque of the Imagination*. Columbia, Mo: University of Missouri Press, 2002. In an ambitious defense of Góngora's famously difficult "masterwork," Collins reinterprets the poem in the tradition of the literary court masque—effectively opening up the poem written for the "closed" literary clique of the Spanish Hapsburg monarchy.

Foster, David William, and Virginia Ramos Foster. *Luis Gongora*. New York: Twayne, 1973. A thorough reconsideration of Góngora's entire literary output, including the early work. Also a good place to start for biographical material on the poet.

Lehrer, Eve. *Classical Myth and "Polifemo" of Gongora*. Potomac, Md.: Scripta Humanistica, 1989. This work examines the use of classical mythology in *Fabula de Polifemo y Galatea* as a contemporary literary code accessible to the educated reader of Góngora's day.

Picasso, Pablo. *Gongora*. New York: George Braziller, 1985. This work, originally published in Paris in 1948, features Picasso's calligraphic renderings and illustrations of selected sonnets by Góngora (translated into English by Alan S. Trueblood). Picasso's graphic intensity mirrors Góngora's lyric intensity in a manner similar to William Blake's illustrated lyrics.

Woods, Michael J. *Gracian Meets Gongora: The Theory and Practice of Wit*. Oxford, England: Aris & Philips,

1995. Woods analyzes the play of Góngora's language through the theories of wit and tropes of his contemporary admirer Baltasar Gracián y Morales.

SEE ALSO: Pedro Calderón de la Barca; Baltasar Gracián y Morales; Philip III; Francisco Gómez de Quevedo y Villegas; Tirso de Molina.

RELATED ARTICLES in *Great Events from History: The Seventeenth Century, 1601-1700:* c. 1601-1682: Spanish Golden Age; 1604-1680: Rise of Criollo Identity in Mexico; 1605 and 1615: Cervantes Publishes *Don Quixote de la Mancha*; June 8, 1692: Corn Riots in Mexico City.

MARIE LE JARS DE GOURNAY
French writer and translator

Known mainly as the posthumous editor of the Essais *of Michel Eyquem de Montaigne, Gournay also was a writer, translator, and feminist. Her aesthetic theories contributed to the contemporary debate on the development and expansion of the French language and literature. Conversations at her salon helped influence the creation of the Académie Française.*

BORN: October 6, 1565; Paris, France
DIED: July 13, 1645; Paris
AREAS OF ACHIEVEMENT: Literature, patronage of the arts

EARLY LIFE

Marie le Jars de Gournay (mah-ree leh-zhahr deh guhr-neh) was the eldest daughter of Guillaume le Jars and Jeanne d'Hacqueville. When the family fortunes were affected by the French Wars of Religion, they relinquished their ownership of the town of Le Jars and left their estates to move to Paris, where, in 1561, Marie's father was appointed a court official. After his death in 1577, financial difficulties compelled Marie's mother to move with Marie and her five younger siblings to their country castle of Gournay-sur-Aronde, Picardy. It was here that Marie began her study of Latin, which led to her work as a literary translator.

She pursued her education against her mother's wishes, studying the classics, not with a tutor, but by comparing the originals with French translations. She never received the formal education she so craved because of her mother's conservative opposition; in consequence, perhaps, she spent a lifetime advocating educational opportunities for women.

LIFE'S WORK

At age eighteen, Gournay opened the book that would change her life: Montaigne's *Essais*. Although her initial excitement was so great that her family thought she

needed sedation, her interest evolved into a lifelong devotion to the work and to memory of its author. In 1588, she met Montaigne in Paris and began her correspondence with him. He called her his *fille d'alliance*, his "adopted [literary] daughter," and he welcomed her incisive insights into his work. After Montaigne's visits to the Gournay estate, Gournay wrote *Le Proumenoir de Monsieur de Montaigne* (1594; *The Promenade of Monsieur de Montaigne*, 2002; better known as *The Promenade*), a novel based on a story she supposedly told him during their walks.

Gournay's mother died in 1591, leaving Gournay responsible for her younger siblings in straitened circumstances, which were to continue throughout her life. Montaigne died in 1592, but it was many months before Gournay was notified of his death by the great Flemish Humanist, Justus Lipsius, a mutual friend, who appreciated Gournay's work. In 1594, Montaigne's widow sent the manuscripts of the *Essais* to Gournay, asking her to serve as his posthumous editor. Gournay brought out an edition within nine months, prefaced by her defense of his writing; the 1598 revised edition was based upon work at the Montaigne home in Bordeaux, which she visited in 1595. She continued her editorial work on the *Essais* over the course of her lifetime.

Gournay published *The Promenade*, a psychological romance-tragedy, in 1594. The work argued against forced marriages and for a woman's right to choose a spouse and to pursue an education. Her digressions treat themes she would develop over her lifetime: gender equity, love affairs, and the condition of women in society, as well as the nature of wisdom, political integrity, and responsibility. All of her arguments were accompanied with quotations from Latin, Greek, and French writers. This first of what would be many editions of *The Promenade* also included specimens of her poetry and her translation extracts from Vergil's *Aeneid*.

After staying with the Montaigne family for about a year and a half, Gournay had to attend to her family's disorganized finances. Although she was well-connected with influential circles and although she received funds throughout her life from friends, family, and the royal court, financial matters remained a source of worry.

In 1597, she traveled to the Netherlands, perhaps to meet Lipsius, perhaps to promote Montaigne's work, or perhaps to advance her own literary reputation. She was well received by people of eminence in Brussels and Antwerp, and it was at this point that she may have decided to devote her life to literary pursuits.

Gournay was a staunch defender of the older poetic theories and practice of Pierre de Ronsard (1524-1585) and the literary circle La Pléiade. She debated with the representative of new poetics, François de Malherbe (1555-1628), probably in the circle of Marguerite of Valois, the repudiated wife of King Henry IV of France, and in other centers of conversation that preceded the salon at the Hôtel de Rambouillet, hosted by the marquise de Rambouillet. She won the favor of the duke of Névers, who presented her to Henry IV, from whom she hoped to gain a pension, a hope that was dashed by the assassination of the king in 1610. Gournay's *"Adieu de l'am du Roy de France et de Navarre, Henry le Grand à la Royne, avec la Defence des pères Jesuites"* (farewell to the soul of Henry the Great, king of France and Navarre, to the queen, with the defense of the Jesuit fathers) led to vitriolic attacks against her by those hostile to the Jesuits.

In a 1619 publication, *Versions de quelques pièces de Virgile, Tacite et Saluste, avec l'Institution de Monseigneur, frère unique du Roy* (some fragments translated from Virgil, Tacitus, and Sallust, with the institution of Monseigneur, the only brother of the king), she laid out literary positions that she would treat in detail seven years later and would spend most of her life defending. In print, she criticized Malherbe and the new poetic theory, extolling Ronsard and La Pléiade, thus establishing herself both as dated in her ideas and as an advocate of La Pléiade notions of the inspired nature of poetic creation.

Her 1622 essay, *"Egalité des Hommes et des femmes"* ("The Equality of Men and Women," 2002) argues that without social repression, women would be the moral and intellectual equals of men. She published another feminist essay, *"Grief des dames"* ("The Ladies' Complaint," 2002) in 1626, and would continue advocating against the oppressive social condition of women.

In 1626, Gournay published a large collection of works called *"L'Ombre de la demoiselle de Gournay"* (the shadow of Miss de Gournay), which contained detailed studies of poetics; the *"Apologie pour celle qui escrit"* (*Apology for the Woman Writing and Other Works*, 2002); moral and autobiographical essays; original poetry; a defense of a new edition of *The Promenade*; translations of classical authors, including Tacitus, Sallust, Ovid, Cicero, and Vergil; and an essay on the art of translation, asserting that modern translators of classics must use language that can transfer nuances of feeling and subject matter to the translation. In her several essays on language and literature, she discusses further her aesthetic theories, claiming, among other things, that for Malherbe and the new poets, poetry ceased to be an inspired, sacred art, and instead became a craft, which inhibited the flourishing of French literature.

Her third-floor Parisian apartment on the rue de l'Arbre sec, where she lived until around 1628, became Gournay's salon, where she received many distinguished visitors. She moved to the rue St. Honoré with her lifelong attendant and friend, Nicole Jamyn. Her residence became one of several centers of discussion that led to the founding of the Académie Française. From this address she assembled her last collection, *Les Advis: Ou, Le Présens de la demoiselle de Gournay* (the opinions and writings of Miss de Gournay), published in 1634 and revised 1641, and a last edition of the Montaigne's *Essais*, dedicated to and made possible by Cardinal de Richelieu.

SIGNIFICANCE

Gournay was both admired and satirized in her own time for her aesthetic vision, her lifestyle, and her association with the Académie Française. *The Promenade* is considered a forerunner of French psychological and feminist novels, featuring a female protagonist who defies convention to strive for self-fulfillment. Her essays on women's equality were very much ahead of their time, with arguments taken up and expanded upon by later generations. Her life as an independent woman of letters, which she surely had to defend, helped pave the way for other women. Her translation theory, evidenced in her own poetic translations, was that translation is an art that should produce a work of beauty as aesthetically satisfying as the original. In a time when new poetic theory discarded much figurative language, Gournay's insistence on the necessity of extreme metaphor and other figures anticipated later practice. Within a generation, several aspects of Gournay's literary agenda became standard practice in many circles, prefiguring the Baroque age.

—Donna Berliner

FURTHER READING

Bauschatz, Cathleen M. "Marie de Gournay's Gendered Images for Language and Poetry." *Journal of Medieval and Renaissance Studies* 25, no. 3 (Fall, 1995): 489-500. Assesses Gournay's feminizing of language and images as an act of literary feminism. This edition of the journal is a special issue on Gournay and Montaigne.

Bijvoet, Maya. "Marie de Gournay, Editor of Montaigne." In *Women Writers of the Seventeenth Century*, edited by Katharina M. Wilson and Frank J. Warnke. Athens: University of Georgia Press, 1989. Translation of Gournay's two feminist essays, with evaluations of each. Includes a biography.

Dezon-Jones, Elyane. "Marie le Jars de Gournay (1565-1645)." In *French Women Writers: A Bio-Bibliographical Source Book*, edited by Eva Martin Sartori and Dorothy Wynne Zimmerman. Westport, Conn.: Greenwood Press, 1991. Contains a survey of criticism from Gournay's lifetime to the present.

Gournay, Marie le Jars de. *Apology for the Woman Writing and Other Works*. Edited and translated by Richard Hillman and Colette Quesnel. Chicago: University of Chicago Press, 2002. Contains the first English translations of Gournay's *The Promenade* and *The Apology for the Woman Writing*, along with translations of other texts. Includes introductory material for each essay and a bibliography.

Holmes, Peggy. "Marie de Gournay's Defense of Baroque Imagery." *French Studies* 8 (April, 1954): 122-131. Analysis of Gournay's theories concerning poetic practice.

Ilsely, Marjorie H. *A Daughter of the Renaissance: Marie le Jars de Gournay, Her Life and Works*. The Hague, the Netherlands: Mouton, 1963. Still the most authoritative biography in English.

SEE ALSO: Madame de La Fayette; Duchesse de Longueville; François de Malherbe; Marquise de Rambouillet; Madame de Sévigné.

RELATED ARTICLE in *Great Events from History: The Seventeenth Century, 1601-1700:* 1610-1643: Reign of Louis XIII.

BALTASAR GRACIÁN Y MORALES
Spanish writer

Gracián was a major thinker in Spanish Golden Age letters. His writings provide well-defined theories about aesthetic techniques, politics, language, and social behavior. His work is key to understanding artistic and intellectual production during the Baroque period.

BORN: January 8, 1601; Belmonte de Calatyud, Saragossa, Spain
DIED: December 6, 1658; Tarazona, Saragossa
ALSO KNOWN AS: Baltasar Gracián; Lorenzo Gracián (pseudonym); García de Morales (pseudonym)
AREAS OF ACHIEVEMENT: Literature, art, philosophy, religion and theology, education

EARLY LIFE

Baltasar Gracián y Morales (bahl-tah-SAHR grahth-YAHN ee moh-RAH-lays) was born into a family whose religious beliefs had a decisive impact on his education. Several of his brothers were members of religious orders. His father, physician Francisco Gracián, had a brother, Antonio Gracián, who was a cleric. Baltasar Gracián was educated in Toledo with his uncle and entered the Society of Jesus (Jesuits) in 1619. In 1635, he took the four solemn vows the Jesuits required.

Gracián studied philosophy and humanities in the Jesuit College of Calatayud, and theology in Saragossa, where he moved to in 1623. After finishing his studies, he was named presbyter and began teaching Latin grammar in the College of Calatayud. From 1631 to 1636, he taught moral theology and philosophy in Lérida, Gandía, and Valencia. After this, he was sent to the convent of Huesca as a preacher and a confessor. The years in Huesca afforded him ample occasion for reflection and intellectual stimulation. It was there that Gracián met his future patron, the erudite nobleman Vicente Juan de Lastanosa, whose social entourage and impressive library gave Gracián the opportunity to strengthen both his intellectual training and his knowledge of the human condition.

LIFE'S WORK

Gracián's first book was *El héroe* (pb. 1637; *The Hero of Lorenzo: Or, The Way to Eminencie and Perfection, a Piece of Serious Spanish Wit*, 1652; better known as *The*

Hero), which he published under the name Lorenzo Gracián to hide his real identity. This text, a reaction to Niccolò Machiavelli's *Il principe* (wr. 1513, pb. 1532; *The Prince*, 1640), depicts the different qualities that a gentleman must possess to lead a virtuous life, among which are good judgment, taste, wit, and grace. This was to become the basis for his philosophy unifying the intellect and aesthetics.

It was during the years after the publication of *The Hero* that the first disputes arose between Gracián and other members of his order. He was sharply criticized for publishing his work without the required authorization from the members of the order. Yet, in 1640, even with this dispute, he became the confessor of Francesco Carafa, the duke of Nocera, with whom he moved to Saragossa and traveled to Madrid. In Madrid, he encountered for the first time the society of politicians and courtesans he would later criticize. Nocera was imprisoned soon after for opposing the policy of the count-duke of Olivares (court favorite of King Philip IV) regarding the war in Catalonia. Olivares's severity, in part, pushed Gracián to write his harshly critical treatises attacking a corrupt political world governed by hypocrisy, intrigues, and dissimulation.

Gracián's next treatise, *El político Don Fernando el Católico* (1640; the statesman Ferdinand the Catholic), which was published under the same pseudonym, offers an example of a virtuous man based on the figure of the Catholic king Ferdinand II (1578-1637). Ferdinand served as a model for Gracián because of his good judgment as a statesman and because he had an idealized vision of the past. Gracián approved of Ferdinand's character because the values that the king symbolized were difficult to find in Gracián's own time period.

Gracián spent several years in Madrid preaching, and he soon won fame among the intellectual elite. In the 1640's, he frequented the literary and aristocratic circles of the capital. He moved to Catalonia during the war and served as a chaplain for the army. From the battlefields, he went to Tarragona, where he served as rector of the Jesuit College and continued to preach.

In 1644, in Valencia, he worked on the publication of *El discreto* (1646; *The Compleat Gentleman: Or, A Description of the Several Qualifications, Both Natural and Acquired, That Are Necessary to Form a Great Man*, 1726; better known as *The Compleat Gentleman*), again under his pseudonym. As he did in his last work, he explores here the notion of "prudence" and the qualities necessary to be discrete. He pursues the theme of prudence in his collection of three hundred aphorisms entitled *Oráculo manual y arte de prudencia* (1647; *The Courtiers Manual Oracle: Or, The Art of Prudence*, 1685).

His treatise *Agudeza y arte de ingenio* (pb. 1648; *The Mind's Wit and Art*, 1962) is a reworking and an expansion of *Arte de ingenio* (pb. 1642; art of the mind). Here he codifies the rhetorical theories and perspectives of different authors from classical antiquity to his time period, including Seneca, Cicero, Camoens, Quevedo y Villegas, and Góngora. *Arte de ingenio* sheds lights on not only Gracián's work but also the poetics, the rhetoric, and aesthetics of Baroque literature in general. The key element for this rhetoric lies in the notion of "wit," which can be viewed as an intellectual and aesthetic method to reveal the illusions of a deceitful reality.

Gracián was in Saragossa when he published the first part of one of his most important works, considered by many his masterpiece, the novel *El criticón*, which was published in three parts (1651, 1653, 1657; complete translation, *The Critick*, 1681). For this work, he used the pseudonym García de Marlones, an anagram of his name. *The Critick* moved into the realm of allegory, following the model established by John Barclay in *Euphormionis lusinini satyricon* (1603, 1607; *Euphormio's Satyricon*, 1954). In this ambitious text, Gracián condensed all of his thought. Divided into three different ages of life, the novel satirizes society's artificiality, placing reason and willfulness high on the scale of values. Here, Gracián defines the "ideally virtuous man," while closely examining the morals and traditions of his time as well as its hypocrisy and corruption. Here again he shows the importance of prudence and sought to unmask a world of deceit. *The Critick* is a clear example of Baroque disillusionment and can be viewed as a philosophical novel, which allegorically depicts human life as a journey. It mixes genres including elements of satire, the picaresque, and the Byzantine novel.

During the writing of *The Critick*, Gracián wrote *El comulgatorio* (pb. 1655; *Sanctuary Meditations*, 1875), a devotional text signed with his real name, most likely because of its religious content. This work did not erase the damage that the publication of *The Critick* had caused Gracián, though it did bring him international praise. In fact, for *The Critick*, he was severely punished by his superiors and sent into forced confinement and a diet of bread and water in Huesca, while a jurist published a highly critical pamphlet attacking *The Critick*, entitled "Crítica de reflexión" (1658; reflective criticism). With his health weakened from his predicament and tarnished reputation, Gracián died that year in Tarazona.

SIGNIFICANCE

Though Gracián was not a prolific writer (he published seven books during his lifetime), he is considered one of the most important thinkers of Spanish letters. His relevance went beyond national borders, mostly because his books have been widely translated. Among his most fervent admirers were Voltaire, François de La Rochefoucauld, Friedrich Nietzsche, and Arthur Schopenhauer, who translated *Oráculo manual y arte de prudencia* into German.

Gracián's life serves as an excellent example of the life of a Baroque thinker who was able to synthesize the movements of his time in a didactic project. His interest in pedagogy, which was in accordance with the ideals of his order, can be found throughout his texts and his career. Furthermore, his work is clear evidence of the solid literary and religious culture that he possessed.

—*Victoria Rivera-Cordero*

FURTHER READING

Acker, Thomas S. *The Baroque Vortex: Velázquez, Calderón, and Gracián Under Philip IV.* New York: Peter Lang, 2000. Acker examines similarities found in the works of Diego Velázquez and Pedro Calderón de la Barca and Baltasar Gracián. The study shows how the literature and painting of the time drew from the same sources.

Gracián y Morales, Baltasar. *The Mind's Wit and Art.* Translated by Leland Hugh Chambers. Unpublished Ph.D. dissertation. University of Michigan, 1962. A Gracián treatise, translated as part of a doctoral dissertation. Includes a bibliography.

Sanchez, Francisco J. *An Early Bourgeois Literature in Golden Age Spain: Lazarillo de Tormes, Guzman de Alfarache and Baltasar Gracián.* Chapel Hill: University of North Carolina Press, 2003. Sánchez examines works by Baltasar Gracián and well-known picaresque narratives including the anonymous *Lazarillo de Tormes* and Mateo Aleman's *Guzman de Alfarache*. This study analyzes the concepts of the Christian person, culture and life as well as wealth and the "bourgeois self" while revealing the historical underpinnings of the new bourgeois literature.

Spadaccini, Nicholas, and Jenaro Talens, eds. *Rhetoric and Politics: Baltasar Gracián and the New World Order.* Minneapolis: University of Minnesota Press, 1997. Edited volume of essays that examine Gracián's writings on rhetoric and public life in the light of current events and the "New World Order." The collection includes studies that analyze Gracián's modernity, the concept of the modern subject, the art of public representation, symbolic wealth as well as ethical concerns.

Woods, Michael J. *Gracian Meets Gongora: The Theory and Practice of Wit.* Oxford, England: Aris & Philips, 1995. Woods analyzes the influence of Gracián's theories of wit and tropes on the play of language by poet Luis de Góngora y Argote, a contemporary.

Zárate Ruiz, Arturo. *Gracian, Wit, and the Baroque Age.* New York: Peter Lang, 1996. Examining Gracián's theories on wit, Zárate Ruiz argues that these moral and logical theories are designed to furnish a system for the mind's apprehension of ideas. The study includes an analysis of Gracián's complete works concluding that Gracián's system is an important contribution to the theory of rhetoric.

SEE ALSO: Pedro Calderón de la Barca; Ferdinand II; Luis de Góngora y Argote; Count-Duke of Olivares; Philip IV; Francisco Gómez de Quevedo y Villegas; Tirso de Molina; Diego Velázquez.

RELATED ARTICLES in *Great Events from History: The Seventeenth Century, 1601-1700:* c. 1601-1620: Emergence of Baroque Art; c. 1601-1682: Spanish Golden Age.

JAMES GREGORY
Scottish astronomer and mathematician

Gregory designed the first practical reflecting telescope and proposed utilizing light intensity to estimate stellar distances. He formulated methods anticipating the discovery of calculus, developed infinite series representations for various trigonometric functions, and was the first person to propose and prove the rudimentary theoretical proposition today known as the fundamental theorem of calculus.

BORN: November, 1638; Drumoak, near Aberdeen, Scotland
DIED: October, 1675; Edinburgh, Scotland
ALSO KNOWN AS: James Gregorie
AREAS OF ACHIEVEMENT: Astronomy, mathematics, science and technology

EARLY LIFE

James Gregory was born in the Manse of Drumoak, 9 miles (15 kilometers) west of Aberdeen, to the Rev. John Gregory, an Episcopalian clergyman, and Janet Anderson. The youngest of three children, James was often sick as a child. Perhaps for this reason, his mother, an intelligent, educated woman, taught him mathematics and geometry. Following their father's death in 1650, James's twenty-three-year-old brother, David Gregory (an amateur mathematician), gave James a copy of Greek mathematician Euclid's *Elementa* (c. 300 B.C.E.; *Elements*, 1570) to encourage his latent talent. Easily mastering the material, James was sent on to the Aberdeen Grammar School. He then proceeded to Marischal College, Aberdeen, where he focused his studies on astronomy and mathematical optics.

After graduating in 1657, Gregory devoted his energy to studying optics and telescope construction. Encouraged by his brother David, he wrote a treatise summarizing five years of original research. Titled *Optica Promota* (1663, the advance of optics), this work proved theorems on the reflection and refraction of light, presented propositions on mathematical astronomy, and discussed photometric methods to estimate stellar distances.

The book's greatest contribution, however, was an exposition of the first practical reflecting telescope utilizing a concave mirror to focus light. Gregory's innovation employed a small concave mirror near the top of the telescope to reflect light from the focusing mirror back down the telescope tube through a small aperture in the center of the primary mirror, where it formed an image that could be examined with an eyepiece. Gregory's design had two advantages over refracting telescopes: The tube was more compact and the color distortion (chromatic aberration) introduced by an objective lens was nonexistent. Because Gregory did not possess the skill to grind and polish a mirror to the correct shape, he abandoned his concept in 1664 and journeyed to Padua, Italy, devoting himself exclusively to mathematical studies.

LIFE'S WORK

Enrolling at the University of Padua in 1664, Gregory spent the next four years studying geometry, mechanics, and mathematical astronomy under the tutelage of Stefano degli Angeli. While studying at Padua, Gregory produced his first mathematical treatise, *Vera Circuli et Hyperbolae Quadratura* (1667; the true squaring of the circle and of the hyperbola). This text was the first to distinguish between an infinite series of summed terms that converge and those that diverge. (When all the terms of a converging series are added, a finite limit is approached, unlike a diverging series, whose sum approaches infinity.) Gregory used convergent infinite series to calculate, respectively, the areas of circles and hyperbolas.

The succeeding year saw the publication of a second insightful treatise, even more general and abstract than the first. Titled *Geometriae Pars Universalis* (1668; the universal part of geometry), this opus presented rules for finding the areas of curves and the volumes of their solids of revolution (that is, the volume generated when a two-dimensional curve is rotated about an axis). In the process of producing this work, Gregory formulated two key aspects of calculus, differentiation and integration, in a consistent systematic manner. Although Sir Isaac Newton has been given priority for inventing the calculus, Gregory and several other mathematicians were working out the ideas independently at about the same time.

Gregory returned to England in the spring of 1668. Based on his books, Gregory had acquired a sufficient commendatory reputation in mathematics that he was elected a fellow of London's prestigious Royal Society soon after his return. Through Gregory's connections in the Royal Society, King Charles II was persuaded to create an endowed chair of mathematics at the University of Saint Andrews, Scotland, to provide Gregory a professorship from which he could continue his distinguished mathematical research. His reputation now secured,

James Gregory. (The Granger Collection, New York)

Gregory took up residence at Saint Andrews late in 1668. The succeeding year, he married a young widow, Mary Jamesome, who would bear him two daughters and a son.

During his tenure at Saint Andrews, Gregory carried out much important mathematical and astronomical work. In his *Exercitationes geometricae* (1669; geometrical exercises), Gregory developed an analytical method of drawing tangents to curves (in the parlance of calculus, this would become known as differentiation). He kept in touch with current research by corresponding with other members of the Royal Society, including Newton, whom Gregory greatly admired. Based on this correspondence, Gregory incorporated many of Newton's ideas into his own teaching, even though these concepts were considered quite controversial at the time.

Due to an earlier controversy with Christiaan Huygens, who falsely claimed authorship of sections of *Vera circuli et Hyperbolae Quadratura*, Gregory was reluctant to publish much of his work or disclose the methods by which he made discoveries. Consequently, it was not until the James Gregory Tercentenary in 1938, when his papers were exhumed from the archives of Saint Andrews's library, that the full extent of his brilliance was realized. For example, had discovered the principle now

known as Taylor's theorem in February, 1671; it was not published by Brook Taylor until 1715.

Gregory made another important scientific discovery when he utilized the feather of a sea bird to observe the diffraction of light, a phenomenon explicable only if light consisted of waves. Because Newton believed light had a corpuscular nature and Gregory had an enormous respect for Newton, he pursued this concept no further. Consequently, Gregory received only a fraction of the credit he deserved during his lifetime and even less during the ensuing centuries. The true magnitude of his achievements was not acknowledged until the 1930's, when, in the wake of the tercentenary, his notes and correspondence were examined and published by H. W. Turnbull as *James Gregory: Tercentenary Memorial Volume* (1939).

Increasing prejudice against the brilliant mathematician by Saint Andrews's classically oriented faculty and administration caused Gregory to resign his position at the end of the 1674 spring term. Eager to acquire this young, productive scholar, Edinburgh University created a new position for him, their first chair of mathematics. Unfortunately, this was a post he was to occupy for only one year. In October, 1675, while observing the moons of Jupiter through a telescope, Gregory suffered a blinding stroke, dying several days later at the age of thirty-six.

SIGNIFICANCE

Gregory was one of the most important mathematicians of the seventeenth century, significant especially in the steps that led to the calculus. Unfortunately, like so many other scientific luminaries of the seventeenth century, his brilliance was eclipsed by that of Isaac Newton. His lack of historical appreciation was further exacerbated by his reluctance to publish his methods and his relatively short life. Some of his remarkable contributions, only recently brought to light, include his discovery of the general binomial theorem several years before Newton and his exposition of so-called Taylor expansions forty years before Taylor. He studied infinite series and elucidated one of the earliest examples of a test for a series's convergence.

In calculus, Gregory's definition of the integral was well formulated in a completely general form, and he had acquired a profound understanding of the various solutions possible for differential equations. He was the first mathematician who attempted to prove that π and e are irrational numbers, and he knew how to express the sum of the nth powers of the roots of an algebraic equation in terms of their coefficients. His correspondence also suggests that at the time of his death he had begun to realize that algebraic equations of degree greater than four could not be solved by equations in closed form.

Although possessing an enormous talent for mathematics and exhibiting tremendous promise for outstanding future accomplishments, Gregory's relatively short life precluded him from realizing any major discoveries, publishing them, and receiving the critical acclaim he most definitely deserved. During his last years of life, Gregory was reluctant to publish important results, and he was reticent to engage in controversy or proprietary arguments with Newton once he heard of Newton's advances in calculus and infinite series. This reluctance posthumously exacted a heavy toll upon his place in history.

—*George R. Plitnik*

FURTHER READING

Dehn, M., and E. Hellinger. "Certain Mathematical Achievements of James Gregory." *American Mathematical Monthly* 50 (1943): 149-163. This article discusses Gregory's anticipation of important mathematical discoveries in number theory, differential calculus, and infinite series.

Malet, A. "James Gregorie on Tangents and the 'Taylor' Rule for Series Expansions." *Archives for History of Exact Science* 46 (1993-1994): 97-137. Explains how Gregory's tangent rule is essentially equivalent to differentiation and how Gregory proposed, but never published, the famed Taylor expansion decades before Taylor.

Scriba, C. J. "Gregory's Converging Double Sequence: A New Look at the Controversy Between Huygens and Gregory Over the 'Analytical Quadrature of the Circle.'" *Historia Math* 10, no. 3 (1983): 274-285. A critical account of Huygens's attack on Gregory's *Vera circuli*, as well as Gregory's rebuttal, which proves that Huygen's aggressive assault was unfounded and unnecessary.

Simpson, A. D. C. "James Gregory and the Reflecting Telescope." *Journal of the History of Astronomy.* 23, no. 2 (1992): 77-92. A brief account of Gregory's design for a practical telescope and his futile search for a London optician who could correctly grind and polish the mirrors.

Turnbull, H. W. "James Gregory." In *James Gregory Tercentenary Memorial Volume*, edited by H. W. Turnbull. London: G. Bell & Sons, 1939. In addition to articles discussing Gregory's major works and the Gregory/Huygens controversy, this volume contains copies of Gregory's letters and posthumous manuscripts.

SEE ALSO: Charles II (of England); Christiaan Huygens; Sir Isaac Newton.

RELATED ARTICLE in *Great Events from History: The Seventeenth Century, 1601-1700:* 1615-1696: Invention and Development of the Calculus.

FRANCESCO MARIA GRIMALDI
Italian physicist and astronomer

Grimaldi is best known for his experiments with light, being the first to describe its diffraction. Light diffraction is a phenomenon that indicates that light consists of waves, and is not, as previously thought, corpuscular in nature. He also detailed and named prominent features on the Moon's surface.

BORN: April 2, 1618; Bologna, Papal States (now in Italy)
DIED: December 28, 1663; Bologna
AREAS OF ACHIEVEMENT: Physics, science and technology, astronomy

EARLY LIFE

Francesco Maria Grimaldi (frahn-CHAYS-koh mah-REE-ah gree-MAHL-dee) was the fourth son of Paride Grimaldi, a wealthy silk merchant, and his second wife, Anna Cattani. After his father's death, Francesco and an older brother left their family to devote their lives to God as Roman Catholic priests. In March of 1632, they entered the Society of Jesus (Jesuits), a religious order devoted to helping others through education. After a three-year training course as a novitiate, Francesco took advanced training in philosophy between 1635 and 1638, consecutively attending Jesuit colleges in Parma, Ferrara, and Bologna.

From 1638 through 1642, Grimaldi taught humanities and rhetoric at the College of Santa Lucia, Bologna. From 1642 through 1645, he studied theology at the same school; additional study in philosophy earned him a doctorate in 1647. He was then appointed as a professor of philosophy, but ill-health forced him to assume a less demanding position teaching mathematics, a post he occupied for the remainder of his life. His studies in philosophy had prepared him well for teaching mathematics because natural philosophy at the time included geometry, optics, mechanics, geography, and astronomy.

Although Grimaldi was ostensibly a professor of belles lettres, his academic interests were predominantly in science. Even as a student, but particularly after beginning his teaching career at Santa Lucia, he created time to study and to engage in research in basic physics and astronomy. During the latter part of his life he devoted himself almost entirely to these subjects, eventually teaching astronomy and optics.

LIFE'S WORK

When Grimaldi began his teaching career at the Jesuit university in Bologna, his immediate supervisor, or dean, was Giambattista Riccioli, an amateur scientist with considerable interest in physics and astronomy. Encountering a kindred spirit in Grimaldi, he enlisted his aid in scientific endeavors. In the period from 1640 through 1650, Grimaldi conducted experiments on falling bodies for Riccioli, and was able to verify that for a freely falling body vertical displacement is proportional to the square of the time the object has been falling from rest.

Commencing in 1645, Grimaldi engaged in mathematical analyses and geographic surveys, which he employed to accurately determine the meridian line for Bologna. During the course of these measurements, many made with instruments he had constructed, Grimaldi distinguished himself as both a meticulous observer and a person with consummate skill in constructing scientific instruments. These instruments included an efficient quadrant to measure the heights of lunar mountains, which were to be included in the accurate map he compiled from telescopic observations during different lunar phases. In preparing this map, Grimaldi inaugurated the procedure of naming prominent craters after illustrious philosophers, scientists, and astronomers; these names, still in use, include a crater named Grimaldi. All of his work had been incorporated into Riccioli's *Almagestum novum* (1651), and he also arrayed most of the astronomical tables and measurements on fixed stars that are featured in the second volume of Riccioli's *Astronomia reformata* (1665).

Although Grimaldi and Riccioli worked together as peers, Grimaldi's most successful research on his own was in the emerging field of optics. Grimaldi's most important discovery was that rays of light could be diffracted, or bent, when passing through a small aperture or around objects. It had been assumed earlier that light always traveled in perfectly straight lines, lending credence to the then-prevalent theory that light consisted of small rapidly moving particles called corpuscles.

Grimaldi projected a bright beam of sunlight into a darkened room through a small circular hole. The cone of light produced was projected onto a white screen at an oblique angle, thus creating an elliptical image of the sun. He then inserted a narrow opaque rod into the cone of light, casting a shadow that was considerably larger than rectilinear projection predicted. Furthermore, the shadow did not have clearly defined borders, but instead consisted of alternating dark and light bands with colored fringes. The bright band nearest the principal shadow also contained a narrow violet band close to the shadow and a narrow red band on the edge farther away.

Another experiment allowed the beam to pass through a second, somewhat larger, aperture before being projected onto the screen. The resulting spot of light was larger than the second aperture and also contained colored fringes. Grimaldi correctly concluded that the light rays had diverged slightly, becoming bent outward after passing through the second aperture. Because these phenomena cannot be explained by a corpuscular theory of light, Grimaldi deduced that light had a fluid nature that allowed it to bend around objects. He coined the word "diffraction," based on a Latin root meaning "a breaking up," by analogy to the manner in which a stream of water splits apart when it encounters an obstacle.

Although sound was known to be a wave phenomena that bent around obstacles analogously to the manner by which water waves diffracted around rocks, it seems that the notion that light might also consist of periodic waves never occurred to Grimaldi. He conceived of light rays as a column of fluid in vibration, but the vibration was not repetitive; it did not possess the periodicity exhibited by sound waves. To explain the varieties of color he had observed, he proposed that what has occurred was a change in the agitation of the luminous flow of light.

Grimaldi died in Bologna on December 28, 1663, after suffering from a fever for eight days. Only months before his death, he had completed his book that described his experiments. *Physico-mathesis de lumine, coloribus, et iride* (1665; physico-mathematical thesis on light, colors, and the rainbow; English translation, 1963) included a brief eulogy for Grimaldi by Riccioli.

SIGNIFICANCE

Grimaldi's most important scientific work was in optics, where his careful innovative experiments laid the foundation for the wave theory of light, a theory that was not accepted by scientists fully until the nineteenth century.

Two seventeenth century scientists greatly influenced by Grimaldi's book were Isaac Newton, who championed the corpuscular theory of light, and the Dutch scientist Christiaan Huygens, who favored a wave theory. Huygens proposed a principle demonstrating how waves progressed through a material medium from any initial position, and he used this principle to derive the known laws of reflection and refraction. Newton, on the other hand, incorporated Grimaldi's results along with his own careful measurements into a comprehensive corpuscular theory. Newton explained Grimaldi's fringes as the result of attractive and repulsive forces imposed by material obstacles when light rays glazed the surface. Newton's scientific eminence was so momentous that his viewpoint dominated throughout the eighteenth century, despite mounting evidence supporting the wave theory.

Although Grimaldi's discovery and documentation of the diffraction of light was of fundamental importance, it was too far ahead of the known theory to be conclusive and, given Newton's opposition to a wave theory, did not provide the impetus to advance Huygens's ideas that it should have. The true significance of Grimaldi's experiments was not recognized until more than a century later. He showed that the colored fringes could not be caused by reflection or refraction, but he failed to realize that they were indicative of periodic wave phenomena. Grimaldi's diffraction experiments were posited and explained by the French physicist Augustin Fresnel in 1821.

—George R. Plitnik

FURTHER READING

Batorska, Danuta Stefania. *Giovanni Francesco Grimaldi.* Ph.D. dissertation, University of California, Los Angeles, 1972. An unpublished study of Grimaldi's work.

Busacchi, V. "F. M. Grimaldi (1618-1663) e la sua opera scientifica." In *Actes du VIIe Congress International d'Histoire des Sciences.* Paris: Académie Internationale d'histoire des Sciences, 1958. A survey of Grimaldi's scientific career, including his lunar observations, mathematical and geographic measurements, and optics. In Italian.

McGrath, F. A. *Grimaldi's Fluid Theory of Light.* Master's thesis, University College, London, 1969. An unpublished but complete and effectual discussion of Grimaldi's life and career in science.

Savelli, R. *Nel terzo centenario del "De lumine" di F. M. Grimaldi.* Ferrara: Università degli studi di Ferrara, 1966. Issued in honor of the tercentenary of Grimaldi's book, this brief tract contains significant information on his life and his personality.

Sommervogel, C., ed. *Bibliothèque de la Compagnie de Jésus.* Nouv. éd. Mansfield, Conn.: Maurizio Martino, 1998. Grimaldi's entire academic career is summarized in this work about the Jesuits.

Tabarroni, G. *P. F. M. Grimaldi, bolognese iniziatore della ottica-fisica.* Bologna, 1964. A brief work that nevertheless contains significant information on Grimaldi's optical research.

Waldman, G. *Introduction to Light.* Englewood Cliffs, N.J.: Prentice Hall, 1983. An easy-to-read book that covers the nature and history of light and clearly explains optical phenomena such as diffraction.

SEE ALSO: Pierre de Fermat; Galileo; Pierre Gassendi; Christiaan Huygens; Johannes Kepler; Hans Lippershey; Sir Isaac Newton; Nicolas-Claude Fabri de Peiresc.

RELATED ARTICLES in *Great Events from History: The Seventeenth Century, 1601-1700:* 1655-1663: Grimaldi Discovers Diffraction; 1673: Huygens Explains the Pendulum; December 7, 1676: Rømer Calculates the Speed of Light; Summer, 1687: Newton Formulates the Theory of Universal Gravitation.

HANS JAKOB CHRISTOFFEL VON GRIMMELSHAUSEN
German writer

Grimmelshausen's novel Simplicissimus, *a masterpiece of German literature, depicts the adventures of a rogue amidst the horrors of the Thirty Years' War. He also is well regarded for a sequel about a female rogue named Courage, and feminist scholars have embraced this work for depicting a woman controlling her own life.*

BORN: March 17, 1621?; Gelnhausen (now in Germany)
DIED: August 17, 1676; Renchen (now in Germany)
ALSO KNOWN AS: Hans Johann Jakob Christoffel von Grimmelshausen (full name); Johann Jacob Christoffel von Grimmelshausen; Hans Jacob Christoph von Grimmelshausen
AREA OF ACHIEVEMENT: Literature

EARLY LIFE

Hans Jakob Christoffel von Grimmelshausen (hahnz YAH-kohp krihs-TOH-fehl fohn GRIHM-ehls-how-zehn) was born in the small town of Gelnhausen in southwestern Germany during the Thirty Years' War (1618-1648). His father, Johannes, died when he was young, and his mother, Gertraud, left him to be raised by his grandfather when she remarried in 1627.

Evidence is scanty for the rest of Grimmelshausen's early years, but he may have been forced to flee his Protestant town in 1634, when it was captured by Catholic soldiers. In later years, he served with Catholic regiments in various capacities, including as a stableboy and a private soldier, eventually rising to positions as clerk and regimental secretary.

Grimmelshausen's formal education probably consisted of six or seven years at the local grammar school in Gelnhausen, where he would have studied religion and classical languages such as Latin, but he clearly read widely on his own.

LIFE'S WORK

After the end of the Thirty Years' War, Grimmelshausen left the military. A year later, in 1649, he married Catharina Henninger, with whom he had ten children, six of whom survived to adulthood. Before his marriage, he converted to Catholicism and also added "von" to his name, indicating his noble ancestry. His grandfather, a baker and innkeeper, had dropped the "von," which had been part of the family name for centuries.

Also in 1649, Grimmelshausen became a steward in the village of Gaisbach, near Strasbourg, in charge of the estates of his former regimental commander, thus occupying a middle position in the social hierarchy between the nobility and the peasants. He remained in charge of the Schauenburg estates until 1660, then became steward for another landowner, a physician, from 1662 through 1665. He also tried his hand at being an innkeeper, first during 1657-1658 and then from 1665 to 1667. From 1667 until his death in 1676, he served as mayor of the town of Renchen, a position whose duties included tax collecting and acting as police chief and judge.

It was during the last decade of his life that Grimmelshausen began to publish his writings, but in that decade, despite being busy as the mayor of Renchen, he issued a large number of works. The best known of these, both at the time and since, was *Der abentheuerliche Simplicissimus* (1669; *The Adventurous Simplicissimus*, 1912). Known commonly as *Simplicissimus*, the work is a tale of picaresque adventure involving an orphan boy named

---

GRIMMELSHAUSEN ON THE THIRTY YEARS' WAR

Hans Jakob Christoffel von Grimmelshausen wrote—vividly—of the devastating horrors of the Thirty Years' War in his famous novel Simplicissimus *(1669), sparing no detail in the telling.*

The air was filled with smoke and a thick dust that purposely seemed to cover the dreadful sight of the wounded and the dead. Our ears were ringing with the woeful screams of the dying and the hearty shouts of those still full of life. . . .

The earth that is wont to cover the dead was strewn itself with deceased soldiers who offered a variety of sights. Here lay heads that had lost their owners; there bodies that were short of heads. Some had their intestines hanging out, others had had their heads smashed and their brains spattered. Here the soul-bereaved bodies had been emptied of their blood; there the living were splashed with foreign blood. Here lay isolated arms whose fingers were still moving as if they wanted to get back into the fray. . . . All in all it was nothing but a wretched and miserable sight.

Source: Grimmelshausen, *Simplicissimus* (1669), excerpted in *The Age of Reason: The Culture of the Seventeenth Century*, edited by Leo Weinstein (New York: George Braziller, 1965), p. 49.

Simplicissimus who becomes a roguish prankster as well as a soldier, a court jester, a physician's assistant, a gentleman farmer, an actor, a traveler, and a quack doctor.

Simplicissimus was immediately successful, going through six editions in Grimmelshausen's lifetime and inspiring numerous imitations. Grimmelshausen followed the work with a number of sequels as part of a "Simplician" cycle. One of the most notable of these sequels was *Lebensbeschreibung der Ertzbetrügerin und Landstörtzerin Courasche* (1670; *Courage, the Adventuress*, 1964; also translated as *The Life of Courage: The Notorious Thief, Whore and Vagabond*, 2001), a story of a female rogue nicknamed Courage, who fends for herself during the Thirty Years' War.

Other sequels included *Der seltsame Springinsfeld* (1670; *The Singular Life Story of Heedless Hopalong*, 1981), about one of Courage's lovers, and *Das wunderbarliche Vogelsnest* (1672, 1675; *The False Messiah*, 1964), about a bird's nest that makes its owner invisible.

Grimmelshausen also published several non-Simplician works, including two romantic novels, *Dietwald und Amelinde* (1670) and *Proximus und Lympida* (1672), as well as *Der keusche Joseph* (1666; chaste Joseph), a novel based on the biblical story of Joseph. His first publication, *Der satyrische Pilgram* (1666, 1667; the satirical pilgrim) was a nonfiction work dealing with a number of philosophical and topical issues. Other nonfiction works include *Simplicianischer zweyköpffiger Ratio Status* (1670), an examination of the best way of governing; *Rathstübel Plutonis* (1672; Pluto's council chamber), a discussion of wealth; and *Der teustsche Michel* (1673; German Michael), a mocking contribution to discussions on reforming the German language.

Throughout his works, Grimmelshausen displays a strong interest in morality from a Christian point of view, condemning or mocking various human vices and indicating the vanity of human endeavors by showing the unpredictable ups and downs of fortune. At the end of *Simplicissimus*, he even has his hero retreat from the evil world to become a hermit. At the same time, Grimmelshausen seems to encourage his readers to enjoy the various adventures in his novels even if they involve vices, and he also seems to have a sneaking liking for rogues, such as his character Courage, despite making overt condemnations of her immorality.

In his nonfiction works, Grimmelshausen tends to espouse a strict Christian morality. For example, in *Ratio Status*, Grimmelshausen depicts David, the biblical king, as a model ruler because of his humility, his obedience to God, and his repentance for his sins.

Grimmelshausen was self-taught, and he was an outsider when it came to the literary world of his time. What also set him apart from his contemporaries, who tended to write in an ornate, dignified, baroque style about aristocratic characters, was his style and subject matter. Harking back more to the plain style of sixteenth century writers such as Hans Sachs, Grimmelshausen had a satirical, ironic approach, used folksy language, and focused on the lives of ordinary people.

SIGNIFICANCE

Grimmelshausen published most of his works under pseudonyms, and his authorship of the Simplician cycle was not discovered until the 1830's. Once his authorship became known, Grimmelshausen's name was honored in Germany. The Simplician cycle, after falling out of favor in the eighteenth century, had become a major part of Germany's cultural heritage by the nineteenth century.

Although often honored, Grimmelshausen's work also produced unease, leading editors in later centuries to revise his writing to moderate its language and remove its supposed vulgarity. There had been debate even in the Prussian parliament in 1876 on whether it was appropriate to teach *Simplicissimus* in the schools.

Despite this uneasiness in some quarters, it was *Simplicissimus* that made Grimmelshausen so highly regarded. Commentators refer to the work as Germany's major seventeenth century contribution to world literature. The novel evokes a lively combination of a number of different modes: the rogue's tale of entertaining adventures, a *Bildungsroman* or coming-of-age story about the hero's developing character, a satire on the world's foibles, a serious examination of moral issues, and a realistic portrayal of the horrors of war.

Grimmelshausen's story of the female rogue, Courage, which inspired the creation of the character Mother Courage by the twentieth century German playwright Bertolt Brecht, has also won attention. Feminist scholars have focused, especially, on Grimmelshausen's portrayal of a woman in control of her own destiny.

Finally, as one of the few writers of his time to write about the Thirty Years' War, which devastated Germany in his lifetime, Grimmelshausen's depiction of the war has been of great use to historians and has influenced how the war has been seen in later centuries.

—*Sheldon Goldfarb*

FURTHER READING

Benito-Vessels, Carmen, and Michael O. Zappala, eds. *The Picaresque: A Symposium on the Rogue's Tale.*

Newark: University of Delaware Press, 1994. A collection that analyzes picaresque literature, that is, literature with a roguish protagonist. The essay "From Duplicitous Delinquent to Superlative Simpleton: Simplicissimus and the German Baroque" examines Grimmelshausen's major novel.

Horwich, Cara M. *Survival in Simplicissimus and Mutter Courage.* New York: P. Lang, 1997. Explores the theme of survival in Grimmelshausen's major work and in Bertolt Brecht's play based on the Grimmelshausen's "courage" sequel. Part of the Studies in Modern German Literature series.

Menhennet, Alan. *Grimmelshausen the Storyteller: A Study of the "Simplician" Novels.* Columbia, S.C.: Camden House, 1997. Provides biographical information, including a useful discussion of Grimmelshausen's social status. Also analyzes his novels, focusing, perhaps excessively, on the notion of dualism.

Negus, Kenneth. *Grimmelshausen.* New York: Twayne, 1974. Provides detailed biographical information and a useful chronology. Analyzes Grimmelshausen's works, but is overly concerned to fit them into categories and prove that they are unified.

Otto, Karl F., Jr. *A Companion to the Works of Grimmelshausen.* New York: Camden House, 2003. Useful collection of articles on various aspects of Grimmelshausen's life and works. One shortcoming for readers unable to read German: The German quotations are not translated.

SEE ALSO: Madame de La Fayette; Charles Perrault; Cyril Tourneur.

RELATED ARTICLE in *Great Events from History: The Seventeenth Century, 1601-1700:* 1630-1648: Destruction of Bavaria.

HUGO GROTIUS
Dutch scholar and politician

Grotius is considered the father of international law for his groundbreaking 1625 treatise On the Law of War and Peace. *Although he favored peaceful resolution of conflicts between states, one of his best known concepts is that of the just war—war to enforce a state's legal rights and secure redress for violations of those rights in the absence of any judicial remedy.*

BORN: April 10, 1583; Delft, Holland, United Provinces (now in the Netherlands)

DIED: August 28, 1645; Rostock, Mecklenburg (now in Germany)

ALSO KNOWN AS: Huig de Groot

AREAS OF ACHIEVEMENT: Law, government and politics

EARLY LIFE

Hugo Grotius (HYEW-goh GROH-shee-uhs) was born into a prominent Dutch family on Easter Sunday, 1583. His father was burgomaster of Delft before becoming curator (member of the board of trustees) of the University of Leiden; an uncle was a professor of law at that institution. A child prodigy, Hugo began his own studies there in 1594 at the age of eleven, majoring in philosophy and classical philology. He received a doctorate of laws in 1598 from the University of Orléans while he was visiting France with a Dutch diplomatic mission. He so impressed his elders with the breadth of his knowledge that the French king, Henry IV, publicly hailed him as "the miracle of Holland."

In 1599, Grotius was admitted to the bar in his native province of Holland. In 1601, he was named Latin historiographer of Holland. In 1604, he was appointed legal counsel to the commander in chief of the armed forces of the United Netherlands, Prince Maurice of Nassau (Orange), and was appointed in 1607 *advocaat-fiscaal* for the court of Holland, Zeeland, and West Friesland (a position combining responsibility for prosecution of criminal cases with that of looking after the state's property interests). On July 7, 1608, he married Maria van Reigersbergh. The marriage produced four sons and three daughters. One of the sons and two of the daughters died in infancy.

In 1613, Grotius was sent on a special diplomatic mission to England. That same year, he was appointed pensionary (paid officer) of the city of Rotterdam, a post that included a seat in the States-General (or parliament) of Holland. In 1617, he became a member of the College van Gecommitteerde Raden (committee of councillors), which, with the *landsadvocaat* (de facto prime minister) Johan van Oldenbarnevelt, was responsible for the day-to-day administration of provincial affairs.

In these positions, Grotius became entangled in the

bitter conflict between the Arminians and the Calvinists—with himself emerging as a leader of the Arminian party. The theological issue was the Arminian affirmation of human moral freedom, in contradiction to the Calvinist doctrine of unconditional predestination. The conflict became transformed into a constitutional crisis that pitted the provincial authorities of Holland, on one side, against Prince Maurice and the central government of the United Netherlands, on the other. The result was a military coup by Prince Maurice in 1618 in which Grotius was arrested and then sentenced the following year by a special tribunal to life imprisonment for treason. In 1621, he escaped from prison, thanks to a daring plan devised by his wife, and went into exile in France with a modest pension from King Louis XIII of France.

LIFE'S WORK

Grotius was a prolific writer. While still a student, he had gained fame for his poetry in Greek and Latin, and he continued his literary endeavors throughout his life. His output included two lengthy poetic dramas in Latin on religious themes, *Adamus exul* (1601; *The Adamus Exul*, 1839) and *Christus patiens* (1608; *Christ's Passion*, 1640); editions of Greek and Latin poetic and historical texts; and patriotic histories of ancient Holland. During his later years, his major preoccupation became theology and biblical commentary. Nearly eight thousand letters to and from Grotius have survived.

Grotius is remembered primarily, however, for his legal treatises. His first, *De jure praede commentarius*, upholding on the grounds of natural law the right of captors to the proceeds of property captured during war, was written around 1604-1606 for the Dutch East India Company. The work was not published, however, until 1868, after the manuscript had been rediscovered. An English translation appeared in 1950 under the title *Commentary on the Law of Prize and Booty*. A chapter from this longer work—setting forth Grotius's arguments in favor of freedom of navigation and trade—was published anonymously in 1609 as *Mare liberum* (*The Freedom of the Seas*, 1916).

In 1622, Grotius published what was simultaneously an analysis of the public law of Holland and a defense of his own official conduct to rebut the accusations for which he had been imprisoned. The work, which appeared in Latin and Dutch editions, is entitled *Apologeticus eorum qui Hollandiae Westfrisiaeque et vicinis quibusdam*

Hugo Grotius. (Library of Congress)

natioibus ex legibus praefuerunt (defense of the lawful government of Holland and West Friesland, together with some neighboring provinces, as it was before the change occurring in 1618). Of more long-term significance was his analysis of Dutch private law—the rights that are enjoyed by individuals to and in things—in his *Inleidinge tot de Hollandsche Rechts-geleerdheid* (1631; *Introduction to Dutch Jurisprudence*, 1845). Although written during his imprisonment, the work was not published until 1631. Modeled upon Justinian's Institutes (c. 533)—and amalgamating Roman law principles with Old Dutch customs and charters—*Introduction to Dutch Jurisprudence* would enjoy in Holland the same authority that Sir William Blackstone's *Commentaries on the Laws of England* (1765-1769) would have in the Anglo-American legal world. For more than a century, the work remained the foundation of instruction in civil law in the Dutch universities. Whereas *Apologeticus* has never been translated into English, *Introduction to Dutch Jurisprudence* has appeared in three different English translations.

GROTIUS'S MAJOR WORKS
1601   *Adamus exul* (*The Adamus Exul*, 1839)
c. 1604-1606   *De jure praede commentarius* (pb. 1868; *Commentary on the Law of Prize and Booty*, 1950)
1631   *Inleidinge tot de Hollandsche Rechtsgeleerdheid* (*Introduction to Dutch Jurisprudence*, 1845)
1625   *De iure belli ac pacis libri tres* (*On the Law of War and Peace*, 1654)
1627   *De veritate religionis Christianae* (*The Truth of the Christian Religion*, 1680)
1655   *Historia Gotthorum, Vandalorum, and Langobardorum*

Grotius's most influential work was his *De iure belli ac pacis libri tres* (1625; *On the Law of War and Peace*, 1654). He appears to have written the work after his escape from prison while living in France; the first edition, in three volumes, was published in Paris. Grotius's revisions and additions were incorporated into the second edition, published in Amsterdam in 1631; that edition is generally regarded as the definitive text. Grotius's purpose, as he explains in the preface to the work, was to elucidate the laws that should govern "the mutual relations among states or rulers of states."

His starting point is the existence of a common law governing all humankind derived from three sources: the law of nature (that is, rules discovered by the right reason implanted in humans by God); the *ius gentium* (law of nations), or rules that have been accepted in the actual customs and usages of all or nearly all peoples; and God's direct commands expressed through revelation. As a result, states, like individuals, enjoy legal rights, are bound by legal duties, and are liable to punishment for violation of such rights and disregard of such obligations. Yet there is one crucial difference between individuals and states. Within an organized political society, civil law provides legal remedies for the protection of individual rights. States, however, in their relations with one another, have no superior authority to which to turn for the redress of wrongs. Therein lies the basis for Grotius's concept of the just war—war as an instrument for enforcing a state's legal rights and securing redress for violations of those rights in the absence of any judicial remedy. As he summed up his position, "Authorities generally assign to wars three justifiable causes, defense, recovery of property, and punishment."

In this sense, Grotius legitimated war. At the same time, however, he hoped that peaceful measures short of war could be developed to resolve disputes among states.

He thought that there was no practical possibility of establishing a world government. He did suggest, however, three methods by which disputes could be settled short of war: conferences, arbitration, and "single combat" by "lot." If war could not be avoided, he aspired to limit its destructiveness by laying down mitigating rules of warfare, such as those barring the killing of noncombatants. He thus emphasized that there remained in force even during war unwritten laws governing how enemies should behave, "which nature dictates or the consensus of nations has established."

In 1631, Grotius returned to Holland, but he was forced to flee to Germany early the following year. In 1634, the Swedish chancellor, Count Axel Oxenstierna, appointed him Swedish ambassador to France—a post he would retain until the end of 1644. He played a key role while in Paris in maintaining the French subsidy to Sweden in the Thirty Years' War. He died at Rostock in what is now the eastern part of Germany on August 28, 1645. His last words, reportedly, were, "By undertaking many things, I have accomplished nothing."

SIGNIFICANCE

Grotius underestimated his legacy. More than one hundred editions and translations of *On the Law of War and Peace* have appeared since its first publication. The work has had a dual significance. On one hand, Grotius accepted—and legitimated—the modern system of sovereign states that was emerging at the time out of the breakdown of the former legal unity of Christendom under the Papacy and the Holy Roman Empire. On the other hand, he put forth the vision of a still law-bound world to limit, or at least to mitigate, the potential anarchy of the new state system. That vision struck a responsive chord not only among many of his contemporaries but with later generations as well.

The revival of Grotian ideas in the nineteenth century owed much to Henry Wheaton's *History of the Law of Nations* (1841). The influence of those ideas can be traced through The Hague Peace Conferences of 1899 and 1907, Woodrow Wilson's attempt to establish the League of Nations, the establishment of the World Court, and the peace-through-law activists of modern times.

—*John Braeman*

Further Reading

Bull, Hedley, Benedict Kingsbury, and Adam Roberts. *Hugo Grotius and International Relations*. New York: Oxford University Press, 1992. Examines Grotius's contributions to the field of international relations. Reappraises his ideas, compares them to previous theories of international relations, and places his philosophy within the context of the wars and controversies of his time.

Chappell, Vere, ed. *Grotius to Gassendi*. New York: Garland, 1992. Collection of essays about the ideas of Grotius and other early modern philosophers, including Pierre Gassendi.

Dumbauld, Edward. *The Life and Legal Writings of Hugo Grotius*. Norman: University of Oklahoma Press, 1969. A brief (less than fourteen pages of text) biographical sketch, with an examination of Grotius's major legal treatises.

Edwards, Charles S. *Hugo Grotius, the Miracle of Holland: A Study in Political and Legal Thought*. Chicago: Nelson-Hall, 1981. A valuable examination of the sources for the ideas in *On the Law of War and Peace*, successfully placing Grotius in the larger intellectual context of his time. Edwards downplays the novelty of Grotius's ideas, demonstrating how Grotius synthesized themes found in the thought of the late Middle Ages.

Gellinek, Christian. *Hugo Grotius*. Boston: Twayne, 1983. A self-styled exercise in literary analysis. Although Gellinek has a chapter on the legal treatises, the bulk of his text deals with Grotius's poetic works, philological texts, and patriotic histories.

Knight, W. S. M. *The Life and Work of Hugo Grotius*. 1925. Reprint. Dobbs Ferry, N.Y.: Oceana, 1962. A comprehensive, detailed, and balanced treatment of Grotius's life and work. The book requires revision, however, in light of the large body of scholarly research conducted since its publication, most of which remains accessible only to those with a knowledge of the Dutch language.

Nellen, Henk J. M., and Edwin Rabbie, eds. *Hugo Grotius, Theologian*. New York: E. J. Brill, 1994. Discusses Grotius's main theological works, his relationship to Dutch Humanist scholar Desiderius Erasmus, his opinions on Jews and Judaism, and the reception of Grotius's theological thought in the seventeenth and eighteenth centuries. An appendix provides a bibliography of works that explore Grotius as a theologian.

Ter Meulen, Jacob, and P. J. J. Diermanse. *Bibliographie des écrits imprimés de Hugo Grotius*. The Hague, the Netherlands: Martinus Nijhoff, 1950. The standard bibliography listing more than twelve hundred items with accompanying annotations. The indispensable work for all serious research on Grotius.

Tuck, Richard. *The Rights of War and Peace: Political Thought and the International Order from Grotius to Kant*. New York: Oxford University Press, 1999. Examines the history of thinking on international law with chapters on Humanism, scholasticism, Grotius, Thomas Hobbes, Immanuel Kant, and others.

Vollenhoven, Cornelis van. *The Framework of Grotius' Book "De Iure Bellis ac Pacis," 1625*. Amsterdam: Noord-Hollandsche, 1931. A perceptive and detailed analysis of *On the Law of War and Peace* by a scholar who was probably the foremost modern Dutch expert on Grotius.

See also: Sir Edward Coke; Frederick Henry; Pierre Gassendi; John Locke; Louis XIII; Maurice of Nassau; Axel Oxenstierna; Samuel von Pufendorf; Anna Maria van Schurman.

Related articles in *Great Events from History: The Seventeenth Century, 1601-1700:* 1625: Grotius Establishes the Concept of International Law; 1667: Pufendorf Advocates a Unified Germany.

GUARINO GUARINI
Italian architect

Guarini's fusion of medieval and Moorish architectural vaulting systems, his theologically symbolic geometric floor plans, and his dramatic use of light allowed him to create structures that are perennially fascinating and influential.

BORN: January 17, 1624; Modena (now in Italy)
DIED: March 6, 1683; Milan (now in Italy)
AREA OF ACHIEVEMENT: Architecture

EARLY LIFE

Guarino Guarini (gwah-REE-noh gwah-REE-nee) joined the Theatine priesthood in 1639, at the age of fifteen. His decision catapulted him from the small north Italian town of Modena to Rome, the dynamic cultural center of Baroque Italy. Guarini remained in Rome studying theology, philosophy, mathematics, and architecture in the monastery of Silvestro al Quirinale until 1647.

During Guarini's Roman years, Francesco Borromini and Gian Lorenzo Bernini created the buildings and sculpture that defined the Roman baroque style. The precise conditions of Guarini's early training as an architect are unknown. Nevertheless, his biographers all agree that Borromini was Guarini's primary architectural inspiration. Borromini's Church of San Carlo alle Quatro Fontane is in the same district of Rome as the monastery where Guarini was a student. In addition to being in Rome at the same time, Borromini and Guarini have in common a youthful contact with medieval architecture. Borromini worked on the fabric of the Gothic cathedral at Milan before he came to Rome, and Guarini was reared in a town dominated by the splendid Romanesque cathedral of St. Germinian.

Guarini's membership in the Theatine order and his training in mathematics as well as philosophy and theology set him on a path toward a theologically complex and expressive multinational style of architecture. The Theatines were one of the new orders created in the sixteenth century known as the Clerks Regular. These orders devolved out of the Roman Catholic Church's Counter-Reformation, advocated in the sixteenth century by Gian Pietro Carafa, one of the founders of the Theatines. Carafa became Pope Paul IV in 1555.

The Theatines, recognized by Pope Leo X in 1524, were the first of the Clerks Regular, setting the model for other sixteenth and seventeenth century Counter-Reformation orders, including the Barnabites, Somaschi, Caracciolini, and the well-known Jesuits. All these groups needed new churches, and all moved freely throughout Europe since Clerks Regular were not bound to a single parish.

Cajetan, one of the founders of the Theatines, sought to reform both clergy and laity with ideals much like those of the thirteenth century reformers Saint Dominic and Saint Francis. Therefore it is not surprising that Guarini would feel a kinship with the architecture of the thirteenth century as well as the theology of that age. As the Gothic church functioned as a bible of the poor in the Middle Ages, so Baroque Counter-Reformation architects such as Borromini, Bernini, and Guarini created an architecture to inspire and amaze the worshiper through the use of startling visual effects designed to make the intervention of the divine in the natural world a concrete event.

The illusionistic use of light is paramount in Italian Baroque architecture, and Guarini probably learned this lesson from Bernini. He was in Rome when Bernini began his sculpture *Saint Theresa in Ecstasy* (1645-1652). For this work, Bernini designed the space of the Coronaro Chapel in Santa Maria della Vittoria so that it seems as if the worshiper has suddenly come face to face with the living saint in an intimate spiritual moment. Above and behind the figures, Bernini concealed a window so that the impression of a sudden, light-filled visionary moment is made all the more believable. Guarini would use just such dramatic illusionistic lighting in his domes in Lisbon, Sicily, Paris, and Turin, making them appear to float on slender, interlaced ribs.

From Borromini, Guarini learned the use of complex geometry as a basis for floor plans. Borromini's Church of San Carlo alle Quatro Fontane is an oval inscribed in a rectangle, an elongated version of the circle inscribed in a square that was the geometric basis for much Gothic decoration. Borromini's second Roman church, Saint Ivo della Sapienza, was a star hexagon plan created by superimposing two equilateral triangles. Guarini used such a format in the presbytery dome of San Lorenzo in Turin.

LIFE'S WORK

After completing his studies in Rome, Guarini returned to Modena in 1647, where he worked with Giovanni Castiglione on the Church of San Vincenzo and the Theatine monastery. For some reason he left Modena in 1657 and his activities are not documented again until

1660, when he appears as a teacher of mathematics and philosophy at Messina, in Sicily. It seems quite likely that during the years 1657-1660, Guarini went to Spain. Juan Antonio Ramirez's well-argued conclusion that Guarini traveled on the Iberian Peninsula is based on Guarini's use of the twisted or salomóniac column in his published designs for Santa Maria della Divina Providenza in Lisbon. Unfortunately this church was lost in an earthquake in 1755.

Another frequently suggested proof that Guarini was in Spain is the similarity between the vaulting system he developed in his mature work and the Moorish design of the vaults of the mosque at Cordova. In any case, Guarini knew the Talvera Chapel in the old Cathedral of Salamanca, for he cited it in his treatise on architecture.

Although few of his buildings remain standing, Guarini did leave major monuments in the north Italian city of Turin and records of his intellect and designs in his books. His interest in philosophy resulted in *Placita philosophica* of 1665. He wrote a mathematical treatise, *Euclides adauctus et methodicus*, in 1671; his architectural drawings were published three years after his death as *Desegni d'architettura civile e ecclesiastica* in 1686; and his best-known and most influential book, *Architettura civile*, was published posthumously by Bernardo Vittone in 1737 ("Civil Architecture," 2004). The architectural books document Guarini's international reputation, because they contain plans for churches in Prague as well as Lisbon, Nice, and Paris. No other books by him have been translated into English, but they found a wide readership in eighteenth century Western Europe, and twentieth century editions of the architectural works were published in London and Milan in 1964 and 1968.

By 1662, Guarini was in Paris, a fully mature, well-traveled architect, uniquely suited to design the Theatine Church of St. Anne-la-Royale. He had assimilated the influences of Borromini, Bernini, and the lessons of medieval and Moorish vault construction. The Theatines, invited to Paris by Cardinal Jules Mazarin, had royal protection, but David R. Coffin attributes their popularity in seventeenth century Paris to their dramatic liturgies. Guarini set the stage for those practices with a floor plan for St. Anne-la-Royale consisting of four diamond shapes that overlapped the corners of a fifth central diamond. Above the central space rose a dome laced with eight overlapping semicircular ribs pierced with kidney-shaped windows. On the exterior, this startling shape was expressed as an octagon with concave faces. While the exterior reveals the influence of Borromini, the interior was Guarini's invention. He experimented with this kind

of vault in the hexagonal Church of the Somaschi in Messina before he came to Paris and presumably just after he returned to Italy from Spain. Unfortunately, all of his works in Messina were destroyed by an earthquake in 1908, and St. Anne-la-Royale was demolished by 1823.

The final phase of Guarini's development took place in northern Italy. In 1666, Guarini became the chief architect of the House of Savoy, making their capital city, Turin, the most progressive architectural center in Italy at the close of the seventeenth century. His secular commissions there consisted of additions to the Palace of Racconigi, the unfinished Collegio dei Nobili, and the main wing of the Palazzo Carignano. Guarini's contribution at Carignano was a sophisticated rippling facade of concave and convex pattern that Rudolf Wittkower notes is suggestive of Bernini's rejected plans for the Louvre. The facades of Borromini's San Carlo and St. Ivo are also recalled at Carignano. A most unique feature of this palace is Guarini's use of cast brick ornament around the windows and in dense vertical bands of eight-pointed stars on the courtyard facade. Carignano was completed in the nineteenth century and so does not as fully represent Guarini's mature style as do his ecclesiastical commissions in Turin.

San Lorenzo was the Theatine church in Turin and received the full measure of Guarini's intellectual and visual complexity. It is an octagon that at the second floor area becomes a four-sided Greek cross and then metamorphoses into an eight-pointed star floating between the floor and a secondary dome. Guarini intensified his illusory space by piercing the wall between the first and second domes with windows. A six-pointed star formed by two overlapping equilateral triangles crowns the adjoining dome of the presbytery, giving visual form to the theological concept of the Trinity. Guarini's floating domes at San Lorenzo are matched only by his Chapel of the Holy Shroud, also built at Turin.

With this dome/tower, Guarini captured the illusion of a telescope focused on infinity, which brings a vision of the Holy Spirit to the congregation. Using spaces and structures based on multiples of three, he raised six hexagons of increasingly smaller dimensions toward an apparently free-floating, twelve-edged golden star upon which he depicted a white dove in flight. The hexagons are set at angles to one another, adding to the mystery of the space, while the walls between the hexagons are pierced by windows framed with segmental arches. Christian Norberg-Schulz termed the Chapel of the Holy Shroud "one of the most mysterious and deeply stirring spaces ever created."

SIGNIFICANCE

Guarini's arguments that one could create a miraculous architecture with Gothic vaulting were persuasively presented in his commentary on Gothic building in his *Architettura civile* and in his buildings. His book was widely circulated in eighteenth century Austria and Germany, contributing to the development of such architects as Johann Lucas von Hildebrandt, Johann Bernhard Fischer von Erlach, and Johann Balthasar Neumann. In the twentieth century, his understanding of skeletal construction and window-pierced walls has appealed to architects who use steel and reinforced concrete to support their curtain-walled constructions. Guarini's ability to activate a spiritual space remains a model for all designers.

—*Alice H. R. H. Beckwith*

FURTHER READING

Blunt, Anthony, ed. *Baroque and Rococo: Architecture and Decoration.* New York: Harper & Row, 1978. A general introduction to seventeenth and eighteenth century architecture in Europe and the Americas. Excellent for setting Guarini's work in historical context.

Cannon-Brookes, P., and C. Cannon-Brookes. *Baroque Churches.* Feltham, N.Y.: Hamlyn, 1969. Contains a chapter on Guarini in Turin and specific information on Guarini's early training.

Coffin, David R. "Padre Guarino Guarini in Paris." *Journal of the Society of Architectural Historians* 15, no. 2 (1956): 3-11. Focused on the Parisian church of St. Anne-la-Royale. Excellent coverage of contemporary judgments of the church with extensive footnotes.

Guarini, Guarino. "Civil Architecture." In *The Emergence of Modern Architecture: A Documentary History from 1000 to 1810*, edited by Liane Lefaivre and Alexander Tzonis. New York: Routledge, 2004. Part of a collection of primary source documents by architects and others writing between 1000 and 1810.

Meek, H. A. *Guarino Guarini and His Architecture.* New Haven, Conn.: Yale University Press, 1988. The first book-length English-language biography, providing a comprehensive survey of Guarini's life and architectural achievements. Includes illustrations of Guarini's work, many of them in color.

Müller, Werner. "The Authenticity of Guarini's Stereotomy in His *Architettura civile*." *Journal of the Society of Architectural Historians* 27, no. 3 (1968): 202-208. Analysis of the mathematical content of Guarini's treatise on architecture. Müller notes the errors Guarini's publisher or editor made in transcribing parts of his text on Euclidian geometry into the architectural treatise. Excellent discussion of sixteenth and seventeenth century mathematical theory and the science of stone cutting.

Norberg-Schulz, Christian. *Baroque Architecture.* Reprint. New York: Rizzoli, 1986. Many very clear photographs of pages from Guarini's architectural writings as well as good photographs of most extant buildings. Interesting discussion of Guarini's concept of architecture as a union of spatial units.

Ramirez, Juan Antonio. "Guarino Guarini, Fray Juan Ricci, and the 'Complete Salomonic Order.'" *Art History* 4 (1981): 175-185. A well-argued case for Guarini's visit to Spain in the late 1650's. Useful information about seventeenth century Spanish architectural theory.

Scott, John Beldon. *Architecture for the Shroud: Relic and Ritual in Turin.* Chicago: University of Chicago Press, 2003. An architectural history of the Chapel of the Holy Shroud, including information on Guarini's design and construction of the church.

Wittkower, Rudolf. *Art and Architecture in Italy, 1600-1750.* Revised by Joseph Connors and Jennifer Montagu. 3 vols. New Haven, Conn.: Yale University Press, 1999. Frequently revised, this is the most readily available general text on Italian Baroque architecture in English. Analysis of Guarini is superb for its balanced insights on his engineering innovations and sensitivity to his theological symbolism.

SEE ALSO: Gian Lorenzo Bernini; Francesco Borromini; François Mansart; Jules Hardouin-Mansart; Jules Mazarin.

RELATED ARTICLE in *Great Events from History: The Seventeenth Century, 1601-1700:* 1656-1667: Construction of the Piazza San Pietro.

OTTO VON GUERICKE
German physicist and engineer

Guericke's experiments with electricity and, especially, air pressure make him a foundational figure in the era of the scientific revolution. His experiments attempted to prove the existence of void, or a vacuum, in nature. His work on atmospheric pressure was significant for the development of the steam engine in the mid-eighteenth century.

BORN: November 20, 1602; Magdeburg, Saxony (now in Germany)
DIED: May 11, 1686; Hamburg (now in Germany)
AREAS OF ACHIEVEMENT: Physics, engineering, science and technology

EARLY LIFE

Otto von Guericke (OHT-toh fawhn GAY-rihk-eh) was the only son of Hans Guericke (or Gericke) and his second wife, Anna von Zweidorff. The elder Guericke was a prominent citizen and important city official of Magdeburg, who could afford to provide tutors for the elementary education of his son. In 1617, the fifteen-year-old Otto went to Leipzig and then, in 1620, to Helmstedt for studies that would prepare him for a higher education in philosophy.

The death of his father may have changed his plans, as he went to Jena to study law between 1621 and 1622. In 1623, he was in Leiden, the Netherlands, where he studied foreign languages, mathematics, geometry, mechanical arts, and the like. He completed his education with a tour through England and France before returning to Magdeburg to marry Margarethe Alemann in 1626. At about the same time, he entered city government as director of public works and soon became Magdeburg's director of military affairs as well.

The Thirty Years' War had begun in 1618, and Magdeburg was spared none of the evils of that particularly horrible war. Guericke warned that the city was in danger of attack by imperial Catholic troops and that it could not withstand such an attack. In May of 1631, his predictions came true as forces under Johan Tserclaes seized Magdeburg and forced the conversion of its forty thousand inhabitants to Catholicism. During the process, many people were killed and much of the city, including Guericke's house, was sacked and burned. His youngest son was wounded and his family threatened with death. Finally, after paying a ransom of three hundred talers, he managed to leave for Erfurt, where he became an engineer for the Swedish army. In the spring of 1632, he returned to Magdeburg to help in the rebuilding of the city.

From about 1642, Guericke was diplomatic representative of Magdeburg in the negotiations for the reconstitution of Germany. In that capacity, he was successful in obtaining recognition of the former rights of the city and in completing other diplomatic missions for the next twenty years. In 1646, he began his thirty-year tenure as mayor of Magdeburg. An imperial patent of nobility dated January 4, 1666, allowed him to attach "von" to his name as an indication of noble status. In view of his active political life, it is remarkable that he was able to find time for the scientific experiments that are his greatest claim to fame.

LIFE'S WORK

Guericke was interested in cosmology and, consequently, in two particular subjects—magnetism and the nature of space. Experiments concerning the latter subject led to his theories and famous experiments regarding atmospheric pressure.

In the seventeenth century, there was a continuing argument between the Aristotelian and the "new" natural philosophers concerning the emptiness of space. The Aristotelians maintained that forces of nature, such as magnetism or heat, could not operate through empty space. This view was a result of Aristotle's explanation of physics, which was based on the notion that mechanical contact is necessary for an object to influence another object. The Aristotelians, therefore, believed that a true vacuum is impossible and that all space is filled with the aether—an undetectable but real substance. René Descartes had adopted the Aristotelian view and asserted that space is, in fact, matter.

On the other side of the issue, by inventing the barometer, the Galilean Evangelista Torricelli had shown that a vacuum could exist. He filled a glass tube open at one end with mercury and inverted it in a container of mercury. The mercury in the tube fell to an approximate height of thirty inches, leaving a space at the top of the tube that could contain nothing, since everything in the tube had been previously displaced by the mercury. Another aspect of the demonstration was the indication that the weight of the atmosphere suspended the column of mercury in the tube by acting on the surface of the liquid in the open container.

Since his student days at Leiden, Guericke had taken the side of the anti-Aristotelians. Torricelli's experiments were apparently unknown to him, but he determined to conduct experiments of his own that would demonstrate the possibility of a vacuum and that space and matter were not the same. If Descartes and Aristotle were correct, the evacuation of the air from a hollow object should lead to its collapse, as it would be impossible to create a vacuum. Pursuing this line of reasoning, Guericke first invented the vacuum pump. It resembled a modern bicycle pump except that it worked in reverse. With this pump, he tried to evacuate a sealed barrel filled with water. The seals were insufficient, however, and air could be heard whistling into the barrel as the water was removed. He then tried placing a water-filled barrel inside a larger barrel also filled with water. His hope was that the outer barrel would act as a seal, but he could not prevent the surrounding water from leaking into the inner barrel as it was evacuated.

Having failed with wooden barrels, he turned to metal

Otto von Guericke. (Library of Congress)

spheres. His first attempt was with a copper ball, but the copper proved too weak and collapsed as the air was pumped out of it. Although this seemed to substantiate the Aristotelian view, Guericke tried again with a stronger vessel, and this time he succeeded in creating a vacuum without collapsing its container. After this success, he proceeded to perform a number of experiments that were to shed light on the nature of atmospheric pressure and the properties of air.

At first he assumed from the example of water that the air sank as it was removed from the valve in the bottom of the vessel; changing the location of the valve seemed to make no difference in any of his results, however, and he concluded that the air remained evenly distributed in the sphere regardless of how little there was of it. He showed that a candle flame is extinguished and the sound of a bell becomes muffled as the air around them is depleted. Further experiments showed that floating objects sank lower as the density of the air was reduced.

His most famous experiments showed the effect of air pressure. They became famous because of their scientific importance and, perhaps more significant, because of their dramatic appeal. Guericke's travels within Germany as a representative of Magdeburg also helped spread his reputation as he performed his experiments before several dignitaries. One of his demonstrations involved a piston closely fitted inside a tube. When an air valve at the bottom of the closed end of the tube was open, the piston could be lifted easily by means of a rope passing through a pulley and attached to a ring on top of the piston. With the valve closed, several men could lift the piston only part of the way up in the cylinder and, as the air was pumped from the bottom of the tube, they could not prevent its descent. Guericke performed this demonstration before the imperial court in 1654.

Another of Guericke's devices was a water barometer. He constructed brass tubes, filled them with water, and used them in the same way that Torricelli had used his smaller mercury-filled tubes. Guericke realized that changes in the weather produced changes in the height of the water and used his device to make weather predictions. Yet the experiment with which his name is most often associated utilized the so-called Magdeburg hemispheres. These were two copper hemispheres about 20 inches in diameter and constructed in such a way that they could be placed together to form a sphere with surfaces matching so well that a gasket between them formed an airtight seal. He first wrote of the hemispheres on July 22, 1656, when he described how "six strong men could not separate them" after he had evacuated the air from them. In 1657, he repeated the experiment with two teams of horses attempting the separation. He demonstrated the phenomenon for the imperial court in Berlin in 1663.

Guericke's purpose in these experiments was to understand the nature of space. In this connection, he became interested in magnetism because of the argument about how forces could act across empty space. He was inspired by the work of William Gilbert to construct a variety of spheres with magnetic properties. Finally, he made a sphere of pure sulfur that could be caused to act as a magnet by rubbing it while it was spinning. He noted that objects such as feathers were attracted to it but were also repelled after they had touched it. Gilbert had denied the existence of repulsion and believed that gravity was actually magnetism with the earth acting as a huge magnet. Guericke, on the other hand, concluded that gravity is related to electricity because his sphere had to be rubbed to induce its magnetic properties. He realized that electricity was different from magnetism because he saw sparks and heard the crackling of electrical discharge. He also demonstrated that a charge could be made to travel through a linen string coming from the ball.

Guericke's cosmological conclusions from these experiments were that the universe consists of a large number of stars (suns), each with its own planetary system; these solar systems are held together by a gravitational force centered in each system; and the space in which they are contained is empty and infinite. Earlier speculations on the infinity of space had run into religious objections because only God was believed to be infinite and his creations finite. Guericke neatly solved this problem by maintaining that nothingness (space) already existed when God began filling it with creations. In 1681, Guericke retired and went to live in Hamburg with his son. He died there in 1686 at the age of eighty-three.

SIGNIFICANCE

In his day, Guericke was an important political figure in his own small sphere of central Germany. During a long and productive life, he led his city of Magdeburg through some of the most troubled years in its history. In addition to his political activities, he was able to establish a reputation as an ingenious inventor of experiments that became famous throughout Europe.

He also offered scientific theories about the nature of the universe, but his scientific theories were to prove much less important than his experiments. Many more famous scientists, such as Irish chemist Robert Boyle and Dutch scientist Christiaan Huygens, were stimulated by his work with air pressure and vacuum pumps to duplicate and continue it with important results. It may be said that those who speculated about the possibility of creating an engine that worked by means of atmospheric pressure were inspired by Guericke. This line of inquiry led directly to the steam engine, without which the Industrial Revolution would have been impossible.

Although writers in the eighteenth century noted his importance, Guericke's work with electricity has not been recognized as much as it deserves because it has been maintained that he did not fully understand his observations. As with the experiments regarding atmospheric pressure, the example of his investigations of electrical phenomena is more important than his conclusions. The hints about conduction and induction, generation of electricity, transmission lines, and the construction of a crude generator led to the works of Benjamin Franklin and later experimenters.

—Philip Dwight Jones

FURTHER READING

Barrow, John D. *The Book of Nothing: Vacuums, Voids, and the Latest Ideas About the Origins of the Universe*. New York: Pantheon Books, 2000. Includes a six-page discussion of Torricelli's influence on Guericke, and Guericke's experiments with vacuums.

Genz, Henning. *Nothingness: The Science of Empty Space*. Translated by Karin Heusch. Reading, Mass.: Perseus Books, 1998. An account by a German theoretical physicist of theories of the void from the time of the Greeks to modern theory of superstrings. Includes discussion of Guericke's infamous experiment trying to prove the existence of empty space (a vacuum) in nature. Bibliography, index.

Guericke, Otto von. *The New (So-Called) Magdeburg Experiments of Otto von Guericke*. Translated by Margaret Glover Foley Ames. Boston: Kluwer Academic, 1994. The first English translation of *Experimenta nova (ut vocantur) Magdeburgica de vacuo spatio* (1672), Guericke's account of his vacuum experiments. Also contains a foreword examining Guericke and his work.

Karwatka, Dennis. "Otto von Guericke." *Tech Directions* 51, no. 4 (November, 1997): 14. Profile of Guericke and explanations of his experiments with vacuum pumps and space.

Krafft, Fritz. "Otto von Guericke." In *Dictionary of Scientific Biography*, edited by Charles Coulston Gillispie, vol. 5. New York: Charles Scribner's Sons, 1972. Reprint. 1981. The entry on Guericke includes very little biographical information but provides a concise overview of his scientific work. Describes Guericke as a "convinced Copernican" and emphasizes the extent to which his Copernicanism directed his "attempt to reach a complete physical world view."

Lindberg, David C., and Ronald L. Numbers, eds. *When Science and Christianity Meet*. Chicago: University of Chicago Press, 2003. Emphasizes the complexity of the relationship between science and Christianity throughout history. Includes a guide to further reading and an index.

SEE ALSO: Robert Boyle; René Descartes; Pierre Gassendi; Christiaan Huygens; Denis Papin; Evangelista Torricelli.

RELATED ARTICLES in *Great Events from History: The Seventeenth Century, 1601-1700:* 1612: Sanctorius Invents the Clinical Thermometer; 1643: Torricelli Measures Atmospheric Pressure; 1660-1692: Boyle's Law and the Birth of Modern Chemistry; July 25, 1698: Savery Patents the First Successful Steam Engine.

GUSTAVUS II ADOLPHUS
King of Sweden (r. 1611-1632)

Gustavus was one of the greatest military commanders in the history of warfare. He was responsible for brilliant military innovations in strategy and tactics, and in the development of modern weaponry. He also transformed Sweden into one of the leading nations in Europe by implementing wide-ranging domestic reforms in the fields of government administration, economic development, and education.

BORN: December 9, 1594; Stockholm, Sweden
DIED: November 6, 1632; Lützen, Saxony (now in Germany)
ALSO KNOWN AS: Gustav II Adolf; Gustavas Adolphus
AREAS OF ACHIEVEMENT: Military, warfare and conquest, government and politics

EARLY LIFE

Gustavus II Adolphus (geh-STAY-vuhs ah-DAWL-fuhs) was born the first son of Charles IX and Christina of Holstein. As a youthful member of the royal family, he received a traditional education, and his childhood was largely uneventful. When his father died in 1611, however, Gustavus found himself king of Sweden at the age of sixteen. As the new king, Gustavus inherited what appeared to be unsurmountable problems. In 1600, his father had usurped the throne and deposed his nephew Sigismund, who was also king of Poland at the time. That resulted in a dynastic dispute between Sweden and Poland that continued for almost sixty years; for twenty years of his own reign, Gustavus always had to confront the possibility of a legitimate invasion by Poland to restore the vanquished monarchy. As if that were not

enough, Charles IX also precipitated a war in Russia to place his own candidate on the vacant Russian throne; while his troops were deeply inside foreign territory, he recklessly started a war with Denmark.

Charles's domestic policies were no less harmful. His rule of Sweden after taking the throne was harsh and arbitrary; soon afterward, he did away with the aristocratic constitutionalism that had functioned under the previous king, and he executed five leading members of the aristocracy. In addition, although Charles had replaced a Catholic sovereign who had threatened the very existence of Swedish Lutheranism, his strict religious views, most probably a form of Calvinism, put him into endless conflict with the Lutheran church. When Charles died, the country suffered from religious strife, the monarchy was unpopular, and the people themselves were tired of the incessant warfare. Gustavus was only permitted to succeed his father as king and assume control of the government by agreeing to important constitutional concessions demanded by the Swedish Estates (or assembly).

LIFE'S WORK

When Gustavus therefore assumed the throne in 1611, he was faced not only with three major foreign wars but also with a constitutional crisis in Sweden. Since he regarded the war with Denmark as lost, he immediately decided to end it. The terms stated in the Peace of Knäred (1613) required Sweden to give its only North Sea port to Denmark to function as a guarantee for the payment of an extremely large war idemnity. The war with Poland could not be concluded as easily, and it continued intermittently for years.

The consequences of the war with Russia were much more serious for Gustavus—it was here that he learned the strategy and tactics of warfare. His father had initally invaded Russia to prevent a Polish candidate from being crowned czar, but with the election of Michael Romanov, a Russian, this threat had ended. Gustavus, however, continued the war with the intention of occupying as much Russian land as possible. He was driven by the fear that, once Russia's political situation had stabilized, the country might become a major military and naval power in the Baltic region. The Treaty of Stolbovo (1617) rewarded his efforts; according to the terms of the treaty, Sweden annexed Ingria and Kexholm and established a continuous strip of occupied territory from Finland to Estonia. The result—Russia was denied access to the Baltic and turned back toward Asia, thereby delaying its emergence as a major power in Europe for more than one hundred years.

In the meantime, the domestic situation in Sweden had improved markedly. The concessions demanded from Gustavus by the Estates might have resulted in the nobility dominating the monarchy. That did not happen, because the man who had actually drawn up the demands, Chancellor Axel Oxenstierna, became Gustavus's confidant and collaborator for the entire duration of his reign. These two men complemented each other's capabilities and temperaments; the result was a unique and historic partnership that led to sweeping domestic reforms.

In 1614, a new Swedish supreme court was established along with a permanent treasury and chancery four years later; both an admiralty and a war office were founded by the end of Gustavus's reign. For the first time in Sweden's history, the Council of State became a permanent fixture of the government and assumed responsibilities for the nation's affairs while the king was fighting overseas. While one reform professionalized local government and subsumed it under the control of the king, another limited the number of estates at four, including the nobles, clergy, peasants, and burghers. By 1634, Sweden had the most progressive and efficient central government administration in all Europe. Yet the most impressive of Gustavus's domestic accomplishments was in the field of education. He provided financial security to the University of Uppsala so that it could continue its development; he founded the University of Dorpat (modern Tartu State University); and, during the 1620's, he was deeply involved in the creation of the *Gymnasia* in Sweden.

Gustavus renewed the war with Sigismund in 1621 with the intention of ending the continual Polish claim to

Gustavus II Adolphus. (Library of Congress)

the Swedish throne; by 1626, he had concentrated his main point of attack in Prussia, where he hoped to control the Vistula River and defeat the Polish commanders. Yet his attention was gradually directed toward the danger posed to German Protestantism by the brilliant and successful Catholic generals of the Habsburg Empire, Albrecht Wenzel von Wallenstein and Johan Tserclaes. Thus, for Gustavus, the war in Poland became part of the Protestant resistance against the Catholic Counter-Reformation; if Sigismund were victorious, all of Scandinavia would be recatholicized. When the Protestant cause in Germany began to experience one military defeat after another, its leaders looked to Gustavus as the one person who could save Europe from complete Catholic domination.

The Polish struggle ended with the Truce of Altmark in 1629; in June of 1630, Gustavus landed with his Swedish force at Peenemünde to enter the Thirty Years' War (1618-1648). What had been an inconclusive war waged by traditional strategies, tactics, and weapons was now revolutionized by Gustavus's presence. In Germany, the king completed the transformation of the art of warfare started by Maurice of Nassau, prince of Orange, and one of the greatest military commanders in the early seventeenth century. Gustavus adhered to Maurice's idea that a professional army should be paid on a regular basis; that prevented looting in time of war and desertion in time of peace. He also followed Maurice's advice on discipline: The Swedish army under Gustavus's command was instilled with a sense of corporate discipline, which meant that each soldier was thoroughly prepared for large-scale maneuvers, reorganization on the battlefield, and coordination among artillery, cavalry, and infantry units. Largely as a result of Gustavus's articles of war, his army was one of the best behaved in all Europe: Swearing, blasphemy, fornication, looting, and drunkenness were strictly forbidden. In arming his men with weapons he thought necessary to fight a modern war, Gustavus decreased the weight of the musket to make it less cumbersome and made large strides in standardizing powder and caliber. These reforms and innovations gave the Swedish army extraordinary power and mobility— Europe was both amazed and frightened by the unusual quality of Gustavus's forces.

At Breitenfeld, in September of 1631, Gustavus's army routed Tserclaes's Catholic forces in a battle that forever changed the course of German history. This one battle ensured the survival of Protestantism in Germany and is regarded by historians as a textbook example of the art of war. Over the next few months, Gustavus swept through central Germany rather easily, consolidating his control as he advanced. By the end of the year, he was being called the "Lion of the North," the Protestant hero of the Thirty Years' War.

At the end of 1631, with the liberation of north and central Germany complete and the plans for a campaign in southern Germany well under way, Gustavus broadened his strategy. He was now convinced that the only means whereby the German Protestant princes could guarantee their security against the Catholic forces lay in the formation of a Corpus Evangelicorum, or Protestant Union. This union would consist of a comprehensive and permanent association of all the German princes for their mutual defense. Most important, Gustavus would become its political leader and military director.

The formation of the union and its establishment depended to a large extent upon the result of Gustavus's campaign of 1632; the Catholic control over Bavaria was to be broken as a prelude to the conquest of Vienna in 1633. At the River Lech in Bavaria, Gustavus brilliantly managed to cross boats over a bridge while concealing his exact location by burning damp straw for a smokescreen and to rout Tserclaes's new army on the opposite bank. The road was now open to Munich.

Wallenstein, however, appeared to threaten the Swedish-controlled city of Nürnberg. To relieve the city, Gustavus attacked Wallenstein's forces in the Battle of the Alte Feste but failed because of the Catholic commander's prepared fortifications and the inability of the Swedish calvary and artillery to play their part. After a period of maneuvering by both armies, Gustavus finally met Wallenstein in the open field at Lützen on November 6, 1632. Mist and bad weather deprived Gustavus of the advantage of surprise, but the Swedish army fought fiercely and appeared to be gaining ground. At the very moment when victory seemed certain, Gustavus led a calvary charge against the enemy, was separated from his men, and was shot in the back. He fell from his horse and lay in the mud until one of Wallenstein's men killed him with a pistol.

SIGNIFICANCE

The Swedish army won a tactical victory at the Battle of Lützen; Gustavus II Adolphus's innovations in strategy and tactics, logistics, and weaponry made it the most powerful armed force in Europe—and it continued to influence the course of German history even after his death. Yet, with Gustavus gone, the army lost its vital spark, and Sweden's presence in European affairs began gradually to diminish. Less than a century later, Sweden's military and political influence on the Continent was negligible. Yet Gustavus had personally guided the course of history for the few short years before his death and had transformed Sweden into one of the most modern and powerful nations of the era. Not the least of his accomplishments were the domestic reforms in the areas of government administration, education, and economic development that he bequeathed to his country.

—Thomas Derdak

FURTHER READING

Dupuy, Trevor N. *The Military Life of Gustavus Adolphus: Father of Modern War*. New York: Franklin Watts, 1969. A good description of Gustavus's military genius and technical innovations. Focuses on his development as the first great modern commander.

Fletcher, C. R. L. *Gustavus Adolphus and the Struggle of Protestantism for Existence*. New York: G. P. Putnam's Sons, 1890. An account of the king's participation in the Thirty Years' War. Fletcher contends that Gustavus actually saved Protestantism in Central Europe because of his involvement.

Garstein, Oskar. *Rome and the Counter-Reformation in Scandinavia: The Age of Gustavus Adolphus and*

Queen Christina of Sweden, 1622-1656. New York: E. J. Brill, 1992. Completes Garstein's earlier study of the Counter-Reformation in Scandinavia from 1537 until 1622. This book recounts an underground campaign, funded by the Holy See, to lure Scandinavian students to attend Jesuit colleges. Campaign supporters hoped the students would return to Scandinavia and infiltrate themselves into the area's political and religious life. Garstein evaluates the success of this campaign.

Parker, Geoffrey, ed. *The Thirty Years' War.* London: Routledge & Kegan Paul, 1984. An excellent treatment of the Swedish influence on Europe during the Thirty Years' War. Deals with the diplomatic and economic elements of Swedish influence as well as Swedish military prowess.

Roberts, Michael. *Gustavus Adolphus.* London: Longman, 1992. A well-written biography that places Gustavus's life and actions within the context of European historical events. Examines Gustavus's foreign policy, domestic and military reforms, and other aspects of his reign.

_____. *Gustavus Adolphus: A History of Sweden, 1611-1632.* 2 vols. London: Longmans, Green, 1953-1958. The standard work in English on Gustavus's relationship to his own nation and his influence on an era. A masterfully written study, placing Gustavus's military achievements in a rich historical perspective.

_____. *Gustavus Adolphus and the Rise of Sweden.* London: English Universities Press, 1973. A classic study on selected aspects of Sweden's rise to power in Europe. Emphasizes the personal traits and characteristics that contributed to the king's leadership.

Wedgwood, C. V. *The Thirty Years' War.* New York: Doubleday, 1961. Includes an examination of Gustavus's motives for declining to intervene in the Thirty Years' War and a discussion of his contribution to the art of warfare up to that time.

SEE ALSO: Alexis; Charles X Gustav; Christina; The Great Condé; Ferdinand II; Frederick Henry; Frederick William, the Great Elector; Frederick V; Maurice of Nassau; Axel Oxenstierna; Michael Romanov; Albrecht Wenzel von Wallenstein.

RELATED ARTICLES in *Great Events from History: The Seventeenth Century, 1601-1700:* 1610-1643: Reign of Louis XIII; 1618-1648: Thirty Years' War; May 23, 1618: Defenestration of Prague; November 8, 1620: Battle of White Mountain; March 6, 1629: Edict of Restitution; 1630-1648: Destruction of Bavaria; November 10, 1630: The Day of Dupes; 1640-1688: Reign of Frederick William, the Great Elector; July, 1643-October 24, 1648: Peace of Westphalia; Spring, 1645-1660: Puritan New Model Army; July 10, 1655-June 21, 1661: First Northern War; November 30, 1700: Battle of Narva.

MADAME GUYON
French mystic and writer

Guyon's advocacy of a religious doctrine known as quietism, the absolute reliance upon God's will and belief in the perfection of the passivity of the soul, made her both a prominent and a scorned mystic of the seventeenth century. Her convictions sparked a major theological debate in France.

BORN: April 13, 1648; Montargis, France
DIED: June 9, 1717; Blois, France
ALSO KNOWN AS: Jeanne-Marie Bouvier de La Motte (given name); Madame de Guyon du Chesnoy
AREAS OF ACHIEVEMENT: Religion and theology, literature

EARLY LIFE
Madame Guyon (mah-dahm gwee-ohn) was born Jeanne-Marie Bouvier de La Motte in Montargis, France. After an unhappy childhood, at age sixteen, she married Jacques Guyon du Chesnoy, who was twenty-two years her senior. He died in 1676, leaving her with a son and daughter.

Her troubled domestic life encouraged her love of prayer, which was often accompanied by mystical experiences. During this period she befriended the duchesse de Béthune and was introduced to François de Salignac de La Mothe-Fénelon (1651-1715), archbishop of Cambrai beginning in 1695, at the duchesse's home. After her husband's death, she met François Lacombe (1643-1715), a Barnabite priest with whom she began to travel throughout France, Switzerland, and Italy, espousing her quietistic concepts of prayer and spirituality. Her doctrines aroused opposition from Jacques-Bénigne Bossuet (1627-1704), bishop of Meaux, but she gained support from Fénelon. Upon their return to Paris in 1686, she and Lacombe were imprisoned on suspicion of heresy, and Guyon's years of controversy began. The next year Lacombe was sentenced to prison for life, and she was held in a Parisian convent until released through the intervention of Madame de Maintenon (1635-1719), who regarded her mystical events as genuine.

In 1695, at the Conference of Issy, her works were condemned despite Fénelon's defense. His argument, published two years later as *Explication des maximes des saints sur la vie intérieure* (*The Maxims of the Saints Explained, Concerning the Interior Life*, 1698), contended that her religious practices were valid. For this, he was ejected from the royal court by King Louis XIV at the urging of Bossuet, who felt that Guyon's ideas advocated a kind of antinomianism, an originally Gnostic belief that Christians by grace were not obligated by any moral law, including those of the Old Testament. Guyon, and Fénelon's book, were censured by Pope Innocent XII in 1699, and Guyon was imprisoned in Vincennes (1695-1696), Vaugirard (1696-1698), and the Bastille (1698-1703), ending her days at the home of her son-in-law in Blois, where she died on June 9, 1717.

LIFE'S WORK

Madame Guyon must be understood within the context of mysticism, the form of religious experience in which a believer seeks for a direct, personal realization of the existence of God. There is a mystical strain in all of the great religions; in Christianity, mysticism's goal might be summarized in Saint Augustine's famous statement, "Our hearts are restless until they rest in thee." Mystical practices such as prayer, fasting, meditation, and a retired life of solitude and self-abnegation have historically been held to prepare the soul for a vision or experience of the divine, which is believed to be God's own gift of himself.

Guyon is remembered for having helped foster a mystical current in early modern French Catholicism. She was certainly aware of the great Spanish mystics of the sixteenth century—Saint Teresa of Ávila (1515-1582) and Saint John of the Cross (1542-1591)—but she went beyond them in the stringency of her extreme reliance upon God's will alone, negating the operation of personal volition or rationality.

A prolific but not distinguished author, Guyon's collected works (pb. 1767-1791) filled forty volumes. She is one of the foremost proponents of what came to be known as quietism, a mystical doctrine first advanced by the Spanish priest Miguel de Molinos (1628-1696),

whose followers had been derisively termed "quietists." Molinos taught that Christian perfection is achieved only when the soul is utterly passive or quiet before God, completely expectant and dependent upon nothing other than the desire to do his will. Activity of any kind, even mental or emotional, is eschewed on the grounds that it might interfere with or obscure God's action within the soul. While quietists encouraged prayer, they believed that the highest form of prayer is a complete mental silence and obedience before God. As Guyon said in one of her poems, "I am as nothing, and rejoice to be/ Emptied and lost and swallowed up in thee." The Church's opposition to quietism and its adherents stemmed from the following:

- Quietism's apparent underemphasis on the doing of good works;
- The belief that such a complete passivity could lead to a moral laxity in which sin is not sufficiently resisted (both Molinos and later Guyon were accused of immorality, she especially as a result of her extensive travels with La Combe); and
- That the self-sufficiency aroused in the believer by the quietistic attitude in the believer renders irrelevant the function and authority of the Church and its hierarchy.

Guyon's own efforts to advance this doctrine were further complicated by the Church's criticism of her being a woman.

Her most notable works are the *Moyen court et très facile de faire oraison* (1685; *The Worship of God in Spirit and in Truth: Or, A Short and Easy Method of Prayer*, 1789), *Le Cantique des cantiques de Salomon* (1688; *The Song of Songs of Solomon*, 1879), and her autobiography, *Les Torrents spirituels* (1682; *Spiritual Torrents*, 1853). She also composed a commentary on the Bible. Her volume on prayer proved quite popular among mystically inclined Protestants, such as Quakers, for whom it offered a personal guidebook for seeking a direct apprehension of the divine. This was achieved through study, silence, and what Guyon called the "prayer of simplicity," a wordless state in which one focuses deeply upon the reality of God and seeks only to do his will. Like Teresa of Ávila and John of the Cross before her, she counseled patience in dealing with temptations, distractions, and in those periods of spiritual aridity in which it seemed one was making no spiritual progress at all. These are forms of suffering to be patiently borne as part of religious growth. Guyon's ideas were strongly attacked by Bishop Bossuet, most notably in his *Relation sur le quiétisme* (1698; *Quakerism A-la-mode: Or, A History of Quietism*, 1698), which satirizes her by portraying her work as the defiant outpouring of an unruly woman, resistant to proper religious authority. By the time of her death, she had spent seven years in prison and been interrogated by Church authorities on some eighty separate occasions.

SIGNIFICANCE

Madame Guyon is the greatest French mystic of her era and perhaps of any era. She asserted the importance of apophatic, or "negative," theology, which stressed God's unknowability through rational means, at a time when the French Catholic hierarchy favored a theology that stressed reasonable propositions about the faith that could be apprehended logically rather than emotionally.

In her defiance of male Church authority, she looks toward such later Enlightenment concerns as the rejection of political absolutism, the assertion of the validity of individual religious experience, and the advocacy of women's religious views. Her protofeminist stance, challenging patriarchy in both church and state, has drawn attention from modern feminist historians.

Her struggles with the antimystical and promonarchical church hierarchy of her time made her an attractive figure to pietistic Scottish, German, and Dutch Protestant groups, for whom her doctrines of personal prayer offered a fresh avenue for personal devotions and a private experience of God, without a necessary reliance upon clergy. Evidence of her impact is seen in the fact that she initially sought Archbishop Fénelon as an adviser, yet he came to regard her as one of his most important spiritual models.

—Christopher Baker

FURTHER READING

Bruneau, Marie-Florine. *Women Mystics Confront the Modern World: Marie de l'Incarnation (1599-1672) and Madame Guyon (1648-1717)*. Albany: State University of New York Press, 1998. Pages 135-219 examine Guyon's life and work within the context of female mysticism, feminism, and the intellectual emergence of modern Europe. Pays special attention to the methods used by Bossuet to discredit her.

De La Bedoyere, Michael. *The Archbishop and the Lady: The Story of Fénelon and Madame Guyon*. New York: Pantheon, 1956. A popular account of the friendship between Guyon and Archbishop Fénelon. Contains a bibliography, mostly of French sources.

Goldsmith, E. "Mothering Mysticism: Mme. Guyon and Her Public." In *Women Writers in Pre-Revolutionary France: Strategies of Emancipation*, edited by Collette H. Winn and Donna Kuizenga. New York: Garland, 1997. Discusses Guyon's efforts to gain a reading public and the methods she used to retain a community of adherents to her doctrines despite official opposition to her ideas.

Guenin-Lelle, Dianne. "Jeanne Guyon's Influence on Quaker Practice: A Guiding Voice in Silence." *La Spiritualité/L'Epistolaire/Le Merveilleux au grand siécle*, edited by David Wetsel and F. Canovas. Tübingen, Germany: Narr, 2003. Contends that Guyon's influence upon *A Guide to True Peace*, an important work of Quaker spirituality published in the early nineteenth century, is greater than that of Fénelon or Molinos.

Randall, Catherine. "'Loosening the Stays': Madame Guyon's Quietist Opposition to Absolutism." *Mystics Quarterly* 26, no. 1 (March, 2000): 8-30. Reviews the major events and controversies of Guyon's life, emphasizing her challenge to the divine-right monarchy of Louis XIV and the antimystical Church policies of Bishop Bossuet.

Ward, Patricia A. "Madame Guyon and the Democratization of Spirituality." *Papers on French Seventeenth Century Literature* 23, no. 45 (1996): 501-508. Defends Guyon's merit as a significant nonconformist thinker of her time, worthy to be called "modern" in outlook. Written in English, with quotations from Guyon's works in French.

_____. "Madame Guyon in America: An Annotated Bibliography." *Bulletin of Bibliography* 52, no. 2 (June, 1995): 107-112. A list of fifty-nine works by and about Guyon, all published in the United States from the early eighteenth century until the present. Many entries are annotated.

SEE ALSO: Jakob Böhme; Jacques-Bénigne Bossuet; François de Salignac de La Mothe-Fénelon; George Fox; Innocent XI; Louis XIV; Madame de Maintenon; Elena Cornaro Piscopia.

RELATED ARTICLES in *Great Events from History: The Seventeenth Century, 1601-1700:* 1638-1669: Spread of Jansenism; 1661: Absolute Monarchy Emerges in France; 1685: Louis XIV Revokes the Edict of Nantes.

NELL GWYN
English actress

Nell Gwyn was a celebrated actress of the prestigious Drury Lane Theatre. The most famous of the numerous mistresses of King Charles II, she was the only royal mistress to be popular with the public.

BORN: February 2, 1650; London, England
DIED: November 14, 1687; London
ALSO KNOWN AS: Eleanor Gwyn (given name)
AREAS OF ACHIEVEMENT: Government and politics, theater

EARLY LIFE

On February 2, 1650, Nell Gwyn (GWIHN), née Eleanor, was born into poverty in London. Her father was Thomas Gwyn, a former Welsh soldier who died in the debtor's prison at Oxford. Her mother Rose managed a brothel, where Nell spent her childhood. Nell never learned to read or write, but she became known for her natural charm, singing, and conversational talents in London taverns.

On May 7, 1663, Theatre Royal Drury Lane (better known as the Drury Lane Theatre) was opened by Thomas Killigrew for his company, the King's Men (or King's Company), one of two official theater companies sanctioned by King Charles II. Gwyn became an orange-seller at this theater and soon attracted the attention of the company's leading actor, Charles Hart. Gwyn became his mistress, and he trained her for an acting career. In 1665, at the age of fifteen, she joined Killigrew's company and made her stage debut as Cydaria, Montezuma's daughter, in John Dryden's *The Indian Emperor: Or, The Conquest of Mexico by the Spaniards* (pr. 1665, pb. 1667). That same year, the Great Plague (1665) reached London, and theaters were closed. In 1666, after the plaque left, theaters reopened, and the royal court returned to London. That year, Gwyn played the role of Lady Wealthy in James Howard's comedy, *The English Monsieur* (pr. 1663, pb. 1674), and her talent for comedy was immediately obvious.

LIFE'S WORK

Gwyn's wit, charm, and sprightliness made her a favorite of audiences and the leading comic actress of the King's Company from 1666 to 1669. Except for a short break in the summer of 1667, when she was the mistress of Charles Sackville, Baron Buckhurst (later sixth earl of Dorset and first earl of Middlesex), Gwyn performed continually with the company during those years. The great diarist Samuel Pepys was so enthusiastic about Gwyn's comic performances that he dubbed her "pretty, witty Nell." She was especially in demand as a speaker of bawdy prologues and epilogues. Some of her leading roles were Euphrasia, also known as Bellario, in *Philaster: Or, Love Lies A-Bleeding* (pr. c. 1609, pb. 1620), by Francis Beaumont and John Fletcher; Flora in *Flora's Vagaries* (pr. 1663, pb. 1670), by Richard Rhodes; and Samira in *The Surprisal* (pr. 1662, pb. 1665), by Sir Robert Howard.

Gwyn also impressed John Dryden, the leading English dramatist of the time, who was appointed poet laureate of England in 1668. Dryden created numerous roles

Eleanor "Nell" Gwyn. (Hulton Archive/Getty Images)

to showcase Gwyn's personality and talent. In 1667, Gwyn played Florimel in Dryden's comedy, *Secret Love: Or, The Maiden Queen* (pr. 1667, pb. 1668). In 1669, he produced *Tyrannic Love: Or, The Royal Martyr* (pr. 1669, pb. 1670), a rhymed heroic tragedy. This play dealt with the serious subject of the persecution of Christians, but at the end of the play, he had Nell, whose character had been stabbed to death, come back to life and recite a humorous epilogue as she was carried off the stage.

Also in 1669, at the age of nineteen, Gwyn became one of King Charles II's many mistresses. Charles's marriage to Catherine of Braganza, was childless, but the so-called Merry Monarch fathered at least fourteen illegitimate children with his mistresses. Gwyn herself had two sons by the king. She gave birth to the first on May 8, 1670, naming him Charles Beauclerk (1670-1726). King Charles acknowledged Charles Beauclerk as his illegitimate but natural child, awarding him a number of noble titles. The king created Beauclerk Baron Heddington and earl of Burford in 1676, and in January, 1684, after the death of the earl, Beauclerk became the first duke of Saint Albans.

Gwyn gave her last stage performance in 1670, appearing as Almahide in Dryden's greatest heroic tragedy, *The Conquest of Granada by the Spaniards, Part I* (pr. 1670, pb. 1672). In 1671, she moved to a Pall Mall estate, a lavish gift from the king, and formally retired from the stage. On December 25, 1671, James, Lord Beauclerk, her second child by King Charles, was born. This second son died while still a child in 1679. In the same year, Gwyn's mother passed out from intoxication and drowned in a pond in Chelsea. In 1681, the king gave Burford House, Windsor, to Gwyn.

Although the king gave her many gifts and provided well for her, Gwyn was not demanding or greedy. By all accounts, she was generous, gave to the needy, and never forgot her less fortunate friends from the theater. Tradition also maintains that it was Gwyn who persuaded the king to build a hospital for the old soldiers who had fought for Charles and his father, Charles I, during the English Civil War. Gwyn had encountered many old soldiers begging in the streets and perhaps was also reminded of her own father, who had died an impoverished ex-soldier. These unfortunate war veterans were now old, needy, and neglected. As a result of her efforts, in 1682, work began on the Royal Hospital, Chelsea, a refuge for old war veterans.

Gwyn was faithful to Charles II, both while he lived and after his death. For Charles's part, although the king had other mistresses, his commitment to Gwyn never ended. On his deathbed, Charles made this request to his brother and successor, James II: "Do not let poor Nelly starve." After Charles died on February 6, 1685, James obeyed his brother's last wish by generously paying off Gwyn's debts and setting up an annual pension for her. However, Gwyn survived Charles by only two years. She died of apoplexy on November 14, 1687, at the age of thirty-seven. On November 17, Vicar Thomas Tenison (1636-1715), later the archbishop of Canterbury, preached the funeral sermon for Gwyn, who was buried in the Church of Saint Martin-in-the-Fields, at the corner of Trafalgar Square, London.

SIGNIFICANCE

"Pretty, witty" Gwyn was the most popular and admired actress of her time. Although illiterate and poor, she was able to overcome her background and become England's preeminent comedic actress, often playing roles created especially for her by Dryden, one of the foremost dramatists of the Restoration period. Her ready wit, audacity, frankness, and generosity appealed to a public weary of Puritanical austerity. The public also embraced Gwyn as a representative of the common person. Gwyn is remembered, moreover, for her exceptional, natural wit. She referred to King Charles II as her own "Charles the Third," because her previous lovers were Charles Hart (her Charles the First) and Charles Sackville, Lord Buckhurst (her Charles the Second).

Finally, Nell is historically significant as the only royal mistress to have been genuinely loved by the English public. At the same time, she is also legendary as the only one of Charles's mistresses who truly loved him, was faithful to him, and cared about others. Old veterans called her their benefactress, for her part in the establishment of the Royal Hospital in Chelsea, and an inn near the hospital created a commemorative inscription in her honor.

—*Alice Myers*

FURTHER READING

Bax, Clifford. *Pretty Witty Nell: An Account of Nell Gwyn and Her Environment*. New York: Benjamin Blom, 1969. A full biography, with chapters in chronological order. Illustrated, with numerous portraits of Nell Gwyn. Appendices and bibliography.

Bevan, Bryan. *Nell Gwyn: Vivacious Mistress of Charles II*. New York: Roy, 1970. A complete biography of Nell Gwyn. Includes illustrations, notes and a bibliography.

Dasent, Arthur. *Nell Gwynne, 1650-1687*. New York:

Benjamin Blom, 1969. Provides detailed descriptions of the theaters and buildings where Gwyn lived and a chronological list of the Drury Lane plays in which she performed.

Gleichen-Russwurm, Alexander Von. *The World's Lure: Fair Women, Their Loves, Their Power, Their Fate*. Translated by Hannah Waller. New York: Alfred A. Knopf, 1927. This work about "Queens of love and courtesans" contains an informative chapter on Nell Gwyn. Illustrated, including her portrait.

Hopkins, Graham. *Nell Gwynne*. London: Robson, 2000. A well-researched biography, with numerous illustrations, extensive chapter notes and a comprehensive bibliography, including both primary and secondary sources.

Masters, Brian. *The Mistresses of Charles II*. London: Constable, 1997. Examines the character and roles of Charles's mistresses, including Nell Gwyn. Illustrated.

Parker, Derek. *Nell Gwyn*. Stroud, Gloucestershire, England: Sutton, 2001. An important biography, including a chronology of events, bibliography, detailed chapter notes, and seven appendices.

Wilson, Derek A. *All the King's Women: Love, Sex, and Politics in the Life of Charles II*. London: Hutchinson, 2003. Historical accounts of the women in Charles II's life, including his relationship with Nell Gwyn. Illustrated, including many colorplates. Bibliography and index.

SEE ALSO: Catherine of Braganza; Charles I; Charles II (of England); John Dryden; Samuel Pepys.

RELATED ARTICLES in *Great Events from History: The Seventeenth Century, 1601-1700:* February 24, 1631: Women First Appear on the English Stage; 1642-1651: English Civil Wars; Spring, 1665-Fall, 1666: Great Plague in London.

MATTHEW HALE
English lawyer, scholar, and judge

Hale, a lawyer, scholar, and author, who climaxed a brilliant legal career by serving as lord chief justice of the Court of the King's Bench, was one of the three or four most important contributors to the seventeenth century evolution of English common law.

BORN: November 1, 1609; Alderley, Gloucestershire, England
DIED: December 25, 1676; Alderley
AREAS OF ACHIEVEMENT: Law, government and politics

EARLY LIFE

Matthew Hale was born on November 1, 1609, at Alderley Grange, his parents' country home in Gloucestershire. The Hale family had moved up into the ranks of the landed gentry half a century earlier after making a fortune in the cloth industry. His mother, née Jane Poyntz, came from an old Gloucestershire family that claimed descent from one of William the Conqueror's Norman knights. His father, Robert Hale, had been called to the bar at London's Lincoln's Inn but soon after gave up his legal practice for the life of a country squire. Matthew, their only child, was left an orphan by 1614. His Puritan guardian and kinsman, Anthony Kingscot, had him educated first by the equally Puritan local vicar and then, in 1626, sent him to Magdalen College, Oxford, to be trained for a career in the church. Hale's tutor at Oxford was Obadiah Sedgwick, a noted Puritan preacher and enemy of episcopacy.

Unusually tall, well built, and physically strong, the young Hale read Thomas Aquinas, John Duns Scotus, and the other major medieval philosophers, but he also found plenty of time for keeping up with the latest fashions in dress, going to the theater, and engaging in sports such as fencing, at which he excelled. Feeling no call to an ecclesiastical career, Hale thought of becoming a professional soldier in the Dutch service. Then, a business visit to London in the spring or summer of 1628 altered the course of his life. Visiting Lincoln's Inn, Hale got into conversation with some of his father's old friends, who aroused in him a fascination with the field of law. The result was that he enrolled as a student there on November 8, 1628.

Hale's proclivities for sports, fine clothes, and entertainment were gradually abandoned as he began to master the mysteries of his new calling. Studying at least eight and sometimes sixteen hours each day, he read deeply not only in English law but also in Roman law and history. His new studious habits and sober lifestyle in time attracted the favorable attention of one of the governing benchers of the Inn, William Noy. The older man took Hale into his chambers, showing him such favor that friends and colleagues began referring to him as "Young Noy."

LIFE'S WORK

The patronage of Noy, who became King Charles I's attorney general in 1631 (though he died three years later) must have been very valuable to Hale in launching his career. Called to the bar on May 17, 1636, Hale rapidly won a reputation as a skillful conveyancer and was employed by many clients attached to the royal court. During the early 1640's, as the political confrontation between the king and Parliament developed into the English Civil War, he was called upon to counsel a number of eminent Royalists who were being indicted or impeached. Evidence suggests that he advised the first earl of Strafford with regard to his impeachment in 1641, and he actually represented Archbishop William Laud at the archbishop's impeachment trial in 1643. There is reason to believe that it was Hale who advised King Charles I not to recognize the jurisdiction of the special court that, without his cooperation, convicted him and sentenced him to death in January, 1649.

His Royalist connections did not hinder Hale's professional advancement—a very unusual situation in the anti-Royalist London of the 1640's and 1650's that, more than any other evidence, indicates just how skilled and esteemed a lawyer Hale must have been. In 1648, he was elected a bencher of Lincoln's Inn. During the period of the Commonwealth (1649-1660), he continued to represent accused Royalists such as the duke of Hamilton, commander of the Scottish Royalist army that had invaded England in August, 1648, and the Reverend Christopher Love, a Presbyterian minister accused of plotting to restore the monarchy. In 1650, at a hearing in London's Guildhall, he argued for the conservative point of view that the lord mayor and sheriffs ought to be elected by only the liverymen of the guilds rather than by all the freemen of the city.

Despite these Royalist and conservative activities, in January, 1652, Hale was named by the members of the Rump Parliament to a special commission charged with making recommendations for legal reform. He even

Matthew Hale. (Library of Congress)

public life and began to devote his time to study and writing.

Elected to the Convention Parliament in April, 1660, Hale actively supported the Restoration of the monarchy a month later and, on June 22, was reappointed a sergeant. In that capacity, he assisted in the prosecution of the surviving regicides who had been responsible for Charles I's execution. On November 7, 1660, Charles II appointed him to preside over the Court of Exchequer (the highest revenue court) in Westminster Hall as lord chief baron and at the same time made him a knight. After the Great Fire, which destroyed much of the old city of London in the first week of September, 1666, it was apparently Hale who drafted the act passed by Parliament the following February establishing a Court of Fire Judges, and, during the next few years, he was one of the most active members of the court, hearing some 140 of the cases that were brought before it. On May 18, 1671, he was appointed chief justice of the Court of King's Bench, the country's highest criminal court.

Hale's Puritan background was reflected in his general lifestyle in his mature years. He believed in wearing clothes of plain brown or black English cloth, and he continued for the rest of his life to dress in the manner that had been in fashion when he was thirty. A strict Sabbatarian, he was also abstemious in eating and drinking. He was not interested in either music or art, and he never traveled abroad. Apparently he knew no foreign language beyond the smattering of French that all lawyers had. Although he was very interested in scientific research, he once told a Suffolk jury from the bench that "that there were such creatures as witches, he made no doubt at all; for . . . the scriptures had affirmed so much." The general moral climate of Restoration England he found deplorable: "It is rare to find a temperate or sober master, or a sober and faithful servant, a sober and discreet husband, or a prudent or modest wife," he remarked close to the end of his life.

By his first wife, Anne Moore, Hale had ten children, of whom four sons and two daughters lived to adulthood. His second marriage, in 1667, to Anne Bishop, a woman of humble origin said to have previously been his housekeeper, caused a small scandal. Nevertheless, all of his contemporaries agreed that he was a good and faithful husband and a kindly and dutiful father and grandfather. He was also a good landlord to his tenants and an almost fanatical believer in kindness to animals.

served as chairman of the commission, sometimes referred to as the Hale Commission, for the first few weeks of its work, though he was afterward an infrequent attender of its meetings. Although Hale supported removing jurisdiction over the probating of wills from the church courts and giving it instead to the common law courts, he disapproved, like most professional lawyers, of most of the commission's recommendations as either too radical or too impractical.

Under the Protectorate (1653-1659), Hale fared even better, being appointed a sergeant-at-law on January 25, 1653, and five days later a justice of the Court of Common Pleas, England's highest civil court. The promotion meant leaving Lincoln's Inn and moving into new quarters in the Sergeant's Inn in Chancery Lane, where he stayed for the remainder of his career. Although he refused to preside at the trial of Penruddock and other Royalists at Exeter in April, 1655, seven months later Hale was appointed a member of the Committee on Trade, which advised Oliver Cromwell on mercantile matters. After Cromwell's death in September, 1658, apart from serving briefly for Oxford University in Richard Cromwell's only Parliament, Hale retired temporarily from

By the autumn of 1675, Lord Chief Justice Hale was in very poor health. He would not resign, because he believed that justices should serve at the king's pleasure. In February of the following year, however, the king reluctantly agreed to accept his retirement. Hale spent the remaining months of his life reading and writing at his country home, Alderley. He died there on Christmas Day, 1676, and was buried in the parish churchyard ten days later.

SIGNIFICANCE

In spite of the strong Puritan influences on his youth and a lifelong distaste for pomp and ceremony in worship, Hale always supported the principle that the Church of England should be governed by its bishops. After the Restoration in 1660, however, he was among those who wanted to compromise with the Presbyterians by having the bishops administer their dioceses with the aid of elected synods. He also tried, as a judge, to protect Protestant Noncomformists from the harshest aspects of the new set of penal laws called the Clarendon Code by taking the position that dissent that was not seditious or in any way criminal. One of his close neighbors at Acton, the London suburb where he purchased a residence in 1667, was the noted Dissenting preacher and writer Richard Baxter, with whom he spent many hours discussing books and philosophers.

As a judge, Hale contributed to the development of modern ethical standards for the English judiciary, both by his own personal example of fairness and firmness and by his insistence that he, and everyone who worked under his supervision, be completely above suspicion of favoritism or corruption. He was reckoned more learned in the law than any other judge of his day; more important, however, he was also well-read in both science and philosophy. As a result, he approached the study of law in an orderly and systematic manner. He tried to learn and understand how the common law had evolved from its primitive origins into the complex system of his own day and how it could best be adapted and improved.

One of the fruits of his researches was a large collection of books and manuscripts, most of which went to the Lincoln's Inn library at his death. Though only two short essays by him on scientific topics were published in his lifetime, in the century after his death some two dozen additional titles culled from his manuscript notes were published, on scientific and sociological as well as legal topics. Various essays have been issued in more than two hundred editions down to the present day. Most important is his *History of the Pleas of the Crown* (1736) and *History of the Common Law* (1713), which deal with criminal and civil law respectively. Described by a modern commentator as "the first book with any pretense to be a comprehensive account of the growth of English law," the latter work is still in print today.

—Michael de L. Landon

FURTHER READING

Campbell, Lord. *The Lives of the Chief Justices of England.* Vol. 2. New York: Cockcroft, 1878. Reprint. Holmes Beach, Fla.: Gaunt, 1997. Includes a short biography of Hale.

Cotterell, Mary. "Interregnum Law Reform: The Hale Commission of 1652." *English Historical Review* 83 (October, 1986): 689-704. This article, based almost entirely on primary source materials, covers the work of the commission in greater detail than does Heward or other Hale biographers.

Cromartie, Alan. *Sir Matthew Hale, 1609-1676: Law, Religion, and Natural Philosophy.* New York: Cambridge University Press, 1995. Examines Hale's theories about law, politics, religion, and natural science.

Hale, Sir Matthew. *The History of the Common Law of England.* Edited by Charles M. Gray. Chicago: University of Chicago Press, 1971. The editor, in an introductory essay, discusses in detail Hale's place among seventeenth century legal writers and his contributions to the development of modern common law concepts. Explains why this particular work is considered to be the first great classic in the literature of English legal history.

Heward, Edmund. *Matthew Hale.* London: Robert Hale, 1972. Written by a lawyer, for lawyers, but interesting to other readers as well. Includes a complete list of, and commentary on, all of Hale's published works. Like most Hale biographies, it is primarily based on Bishop Gilbert Burnet's *Life and Death of Sir Matthew Hale*, and Richard Baxter's *Additional Notes on the Life and Death of Sir Matthew Hale*, both published in London in 1682.

Holdsworth, Sir William Searle. *A History of English Law.* 9 vols. London: Methuen, 1903-1932. Reprint. London: Sweet and Maxwell, 1966. A brief account of Hale's life, together with a survey of his legal writings and his contributions to legal thought. The best short modern treatment. Thoroughly footnoted.

Hostettler, John. *The Red Gown: The Life and Works of Sir Matthew Hale.* Chichester, West Sussex, England: Barry Rose Law, 2002. Biography of Hale written by a British legal historian and former magistrate.

Shapiro, Barbara J. "Law and Science in Seventeenth Century England." *Stanford Law Review* 21 (April, 1969): 727-766. Discusses how Hale's research into scientific and legal problems were interrelated, and how he reflected and affected the intellectual climate of his age.

SEE ALSO: Richard Baxter; Charles I; Charles II (of England); Oliver Cromwell; William Laud; First Earl of Strafford.

EDMOND HALLEY
English astronomer

Among his many scientific achievements, Halley's best-known accomplishment was to solve the riddle of the orbits of comets. In particular, he predicted that the one seen in 1682 would return in 1759. This comet was later named for him.

BORN: November 8, 1656; Haggerston, near London, Shoreditch, England
DIED: June 14, 1742; Greenwich, near London, England
AREAS OF ACHIEVEMENT: Astronomy, science and technology

EARLY LIFE

The details of the life of Edmond Halley (HAL-ee) are only sketchily known, since most of his private papers and correspondence have been lost. Some facts have been collected from the papers of colleagues, relations, and friends, but many gaps remain. It is known that he was born on November 8, 1656, in Haggerston, on the outskirts of London. His father, a soap boiler, belonged to the monied merchant class and provided for Halley throughout his education. Halley attended St. Paul's School, where he became the school captain, and furthered his studies at Queen's College, Oxford, in 1673. It was there that he first formally studied astronomy, beginning a regular correspondence with John Flamsteed, who was then astronomer royal. The older man took the young Halley under his wing, and with Flamsteed's guidance, Halley made one or two minor contributions to the mathematics of astronomy.

In 1676, Halley ventured to Saint Helena in the Southern Hemisphere on an expedition to study the stars there. He was supported during this time by his father, who was still comparatively wealthy, despite having suffered some property losses during the 1666 Great Fire of London. Halley had an allowance of three hundred pounds a year. Although conditions at Saint Helena were overcast, he achieved his aim and on his return published the *Catalogus Stellarum Australium* (1678; Australian stellar catalog) and a planisphere. His work found favor with King Charles II, since Halley regrouped a particular constellation of stars and renamed them Charles's Oak in his honor.

Halley was awarded an M.A. at Oxford for this work, and his endeavors brought him to the attention of the Royal Society (the somewhat august body to which all the leading scientists of the day belonged). The society made him a fellow. He was asked by the Royal Society to visit the Dutch astronomer Johannes Hevelius at Danzig to investigate his methods of star observation. With telescopic sights now in vogue, the society believed that Hevelius's methods were old-fashioned and therefore inaccurate. Halley reported in Hevelius's favor (much to Flamsteed's annoyance and causing a breach of friendship between the two that lasted some forty years).

While Halley's scientific reputation soared with these projects, however, his personal reputation was surrounded by rumor and innuendo. On the Saint Helena expedition, his name was coupled with that of a married woman who found herself pregnant on Halley's departure, and during the Danzig trip, gossip abounded about Halley's relationship with Elisatetha Hevelius, Johannes's wife. In the coffeehouses, Halley appears to have been labeled a womanizer, and his reputation offended some of his more straitlaced colleagues.

In 1680, Halley traveled to Paris to work with Gian Domenico Cassini, the director of the Paris Observatory. The two made detailed observations of a new comet that had appeared. This was not the comet that would later bear his name, but this kind of painstaking observational work was to be Halley's hallmark throughout his scientific career. He returned to London, perhaps because his father could no longer support him, and married Mary Tooke in 1682. They settled in Islington, London, and remained married until her death in 1736. Little is known about her or about their life together.

LIFE'S WORK

The next period of Halley's life was bound up with his own meticulous observations, the continual wranglings of the Royal Society, and his friendship with Sir Isaac Newton, undoubtedly the greatest scientist of that generation. The Royal Society at that time contained some of the most prominent men of the seventeenth century—Sir Christopher Wren, Samuel Pepys, Robert Hooke, Flamsteed, and Newton—and the papers and theories that were presented at its meetings were in the vanguard of scientific research.

The late seventeenth century was an exciting period in the history of astronomy. Following the pioneering observational work of Galileo and Johannes Kepler, planets were known to travel in regular, elliptical orbits around the sun. The problem facing the scientists of the Royal Society was to explain the mechanics of this occurrence, demonstrating from first principles, mathematically, why it should be so. Many of the eminent men of the day were tackling the challenge, and the race was on to reach the solution first. Halley played no small part in this story.

In 1684, Halley became the clerk of the Royal Society, a post that was later accompanied by a stipend of fifty pounds a year, although there is some evidence to suggest that he rarely actually got paid. This post involved much organizational work for the society, but it also placed Halley in the thick of its debates. Around this time, wanting to confirm some of his observations on comets, Halley went to visit Newton at Cambridge. During their discussions, Newton claimed to have solved the elliptical problem, asserting that the elliptical shape of planetary orbits was a result of the inverse square law of attraction, which states that bodies are attracted to one another in proportion of the inverse square of their distance from one another. Newton said, however, that he had mislaid the proof, so Halley was not totally convinced.

On Halley's second visit, Newton successfully produced a nine-page paper explaining the elliptical orbits of the planets, and Halley, recognizing the overwhelm-

ing importance of Newton's work, persuaded him to publish it. Through Halley's offices, Newton published first a short tract, *De motu corporum in gyrum* (1684; on the motion of bodies in an orbit), which demonstrated Kepler's laws of planetary motion, and then his famous book *Philosophiae Naturalis Principia Mathematica* (1687; *Mathematical Principles of Natural Philosophy*, 1729), in which he elaborated his three laws of mechanics and his theory of gravity.

This work was, perhaps, the most important scientific work to be published in the century and, throughout, Halley was Newton's friend, confidant, editor, and publisher, encouraging him to continue, adding the occasional helpful comment to the manuscript, and even finally paying for its publication. He also had the difficult and diplomatic task of mediating between Newton and Hooke, who were rivals, the latter claiming that Newton had not credited his contribution to the discovery of the inverse square law. Halley's involvement in this dispute made Hooke his enemy too, and Hooke tried to remove him from his post of clerk to the Royal Society. Halley's efficiency and popularity won the day, however, and Hooke's motion was defeated.

Edmond Halley. (Library of Congress)

During this period of his life, Halley, who had numerous diverse interests, wrote a paper trying to explain the causes of the biblical Flood. This paper was to have disastrous consequences for his career. He argued that the Flood had occurred for natural, not miraculous reasons, possibly from a close encounter with a comet. (It is interesting to note that speculation about the effects of comets on the Earth has flourished ever since.) The result of Halley's reasoning was to place the date of the Flood somewhat earlier than the accepted orthodoxy of 4004 B.C.E.

Halley's theory of the Flood offended his more religious colleagues, and rumors abounded that Halley might be a skeptic or, worse still, an agnostic. In 1691, a vacancy opened for the Savilian Chair of Astronomy at Oxford. Were it not for this paper and the question concerning Halley's religious beliefs, he would certainly have been appointed. Flamsteed, however, argued vehemently against him, and not even Newton came to his protégé's defense. Later, in 1694, when he finally presented the offending paper to the Royal Society, he added the explanation that he was not actually referring to the Flood itself but speculating on what might have happened given the proper circumstances—thus mitigating some of the damage to his reputation.

Although Halley is best known for his work in astronomy, he made contributions in a number of other areas during his life, perhaps motivated by his persistent lack of money. He was interested in nautical problems, designing various practical instruments: a prototype diving bell, a device for measuring the path of a ship, and another device for measuring the rate of evaporation of seawater. This latter device had consequences for another interest of his, chronology. Indeed, it led to some of his conclusions about the date of the Flood.

Between 1696 and 1698, Halley's career took another turn. He became the deputy comptroller of the Royal Mint at Chester, a post offered him by Newton, who was then the warden of the Mint. (At the time, there was much trouble with "clipped" gold and silver coins, and scientists were being used to supervise the minting.) Administration did not prove to be one of Halley's many talents, however, and Newton found himself having to defend his friend against the Lord's Commissioners. In 1698, Halley set out on another expedition, this time to the South Seas to study the magnetic variations of the earth's compass. The journey was abandoned (with the ship's first lieutenant facing a court-martial on their return), but Halley tried again a year later with more success. He also went on a secret mission in 1701, about which little is

known, traveling to France for the Admiralty on the pretext of yet another scientific expedition.

While Halley's accomplishments were many, the achievements for which he is best known are in the field of astronomy, particularly regarding the orbits of comets. This was a field on which he had already begun detailed work when he first met Newton. By 1695, he had undergone a thorough search of historical records on the subject, examining the figures with scrupulous attention. Recognizing that comets, too, were affected by the gravitational influence of the planets (following Newton's work), Halley calculated their possible orbits from the available data. That led him to disagree with Newton, who, in book 3 of *Mathematical Principles of Natural Philosophy*, had argued that comets' orbits should be parabolic. Halley concluded that they must, in fact, be elliptical like the planets themselves.

In 1703, Halley became a member of the Council of the Royal Society in recognition of his work, and in the same year, he was appointed to the Savilian Chair of Geometry at Oxford, previous doubts about his religion being now forgotten. Two years later, he published *Astronomie cometicae synopsis* (1705; synopsis of cometary astronomy), in which he outlined his theory of elliptical orbits for comets and asserted that the particular comet seen in 1682 would, as part of its periodic cycle, return in 1758. Although he did not live long enough to test his hypothesis, when the comet did come into view in 1759 (Halley made a minor miscalculation), it was seen not only as a verification of Halley's prediction but also as a major confirmation of the truth of Newton's mechanics. The comet was named for Halley. In 1719, on Flamsteed's death, Halley succeeded to the post of astronomer royal, a position he held until his death in 1742.

SIGNIFICANCE

Halley lived at a time when the old theories of the structure of the universe, which were still based on the teachings of Aristotle, were being overturned. Experimentally, Galileo and Kepler had led the way, but it took the work of Newton to provide a theoretical underpinning to it all. Halley, in publishing Newton's work, had been largely responsible for bringing it to the attention of scientists and the public. Newton's theories turned the scientific world upside down, causing debate, discussion, and disagreement for nearly a century after their publication. One of the major triumphs of the new theories, helping eventually to bring about their universal acceptance, was the reappearance of Halley's comet, which he had predicted using Newton's work and his own observations. Halley's meticulous recording of observational detail and his ready grasp of contemporary theories had enabled him to become the champion of Newtonian science. In this way, he was central to one of the most exciting periods of scientific history.

—*Sally Hibbin*

FURTHER READING

Armitage, Angus. *Edmond Halley*. Camden, N.J.: Thomas Nelson and Sons, 1966. A detailed historical evaluation of Halley's scientific research, mainly based on the papers he contributed to *Philosophical Transactions*, with relevant biographical information. Illustrated with plates and figures.

Calder, Nigel. *Comets: Speculation and Discovery*. New York: Dover, 1994. A popular account of the science, facts, and legends related to Halley's comet, and the people involved in its discovery and observation. Originally published in 1981 as *The Comet Is Coming! The Feverish Legacy of Mr. Halley*.

Cook, Alan. *Edmond Halley: Charting the Heavens and the Seas*. New York: Oxford University Press, 1998. A full-length biography drawing upon recently acquired information to discuss Halley's life and his contributions to science.

Halley, Edmond. *Correspondence and Papers of Edmond Halley*. Edited by Eugene Fairfield MacPike. Oxford, England: Clarendon Press, 1932. Reprint. New York: Arno Press, 1975. An edited collection of Halley's surviving papers and letters, with a memoir of his life by one of his contemporaries, and the "Éloge" by d'Ortous de Mairan. The best, although necessarily incomplete, primary source for students of Halley.

Lancaster Brown, Peter. *Halley and His Comet*. Poole, Dorset, England: Blandford Press, 1985. Occasioned by the anticipated appearance of Halley's comet in 1986, a modern reappraisal of Halley's life and work, its relevance to the origins of life on Earth, and its significance to the space age. Highly informative for specialists and lay readers.

Newton, Sir Isaac. *A Dissertation on Comets*. London: c. 1750. Describes the mechanical principles of the motions of planets, using Newton's new theory of gravity, from which Halley developed his own theory that comets travel in ellipses and will therefore return.

_____. *The Mathematical Principles of Natural Philosophy*. Translated by Andrew Motte. London: B. Motte, 1729. Originally published by Halley, who, recognizing the importance of Newton's theories of gravity and motion, persuaded him to put it into book form. Motte's translation remains the standard text.

Thrower, Norman J. W., ed. *Standing on the Shoulders of Giants: A Longer View of Newton and Halley*. Berkeley: University of California Press, 1990. A collection of essays by astronomers, historians of science, and other writers that re-examine the professional relationship of Newton and Halley, describing their influence upon each other and on subsequent generations of scientists.

SEE ALSO: Gian Domenico Cassini; Galileo; Johannes and Elisabetha Hevelius; Robert Hooke; Johannes Kepler; Sir Isaac Newton; Samuel Pepys; Sir Christopher Wren.

RELATED ARTICLES in *Great Events from History: The Seventeenth Century, 1601-1700:* 1601-1672: Rise of Scientific Societies; September 2-5, 1666: Great Fire of London.

FRANS HALS
Flemish-Dutch painter

Hals, and Rembrandt, were two of the most celebrated northern painters of their era. Hals specialized in painting group scenes and individual portraits in which his highly original use of grays provided his work with a chromatic unity that in the work of artists such as Leonardo da Vinci was achieved through chiaroscuro, the play of light and dark.

BORN: c. 1583; Antwerp, Spanish Netherlands (now in Belgium)
DIED: September 1, 1666; Haarlem, United Provinces (now in the Netherlands)
AREA OF ACHIEVEMENT: Art

EARLY LIFE

The first record of the family of Frans Hals (frahns hahls) is dated March 19, 1591, the day on which Dirck Hals, Frans's younger brother, who was also a painter, was baptized in Haarlem. It is thought that Hals's parents, Franchoys and Adriaentgen van Geertenrijk Hals, came from Mechelen but settled in Antwerp before 1580. They are known to have fled Antwerp for the north during Frans's early childhood to avoid religious persecution. By 1591, they had settled in Haarlem, where Hals spent most of his life.

Hals's father was a weaver and maker of cloth; his wife probably assisted him in his work when she was able. Hals is thought to have begun studying art with Karel van Mander, cofounder of the Haarlem Academy, around 1600. By 1610, five years after van Mander's death, Hals was a member of the Guild of St. Luke, part of whose charge was to regulate the duties and privileges of Haarlem's painters.

Hals married Annetje Harmansdr in 1610. She died in 1615, leaving Hals with two children. One of them, Harmen, baptized in Haarlem on September 2, 1611, became a painter. Annetje was buried in land that Haarlem reserved for the burial of its poor, so it is clear that Hals was not prosperous at the time of his wife's death. Hals married Lysbeth Reyniers on February 12, 1617, nine days before their first child, Sara, was baptized. Their union produced eight children, of whom his sons Frans, Nicolaes, and Jan became painters. Hals's daughter Adriaentgen married Pieter Roestraten, a noted still-life painter.

Between the death of his first wife and his marriage to his second, Hals apparently visited Antwerp, where, it is speculated, he first encountered the paintings of Peter

Paul Rubens. Shortly before he remarried, Hals was commissioned by members of the St. George Civic Guard Company to paint a picture of their banquet, a group portrait whose composition presented problems comparable to those Leonardo da Vinci faced in the composition of *The Last Supper* (1498) more than a century earlier. The general tone of the Hals painting, however, depicts revelry rather than the reflective contemplation of *The Last Supper*.

Hals, nevertheless, had to present reasonable likenesses of each of the twelve people in the picture, because each was paying for this recognition. Those who paid the most or who had important positions in the company had to be most prominently presented. Hals struck on the brilliant unifying technique of placing slightly left of the center of the picture a boy carrying the company's standard over his shoulder, so that its horizontal axis forms about a twenty-degree angle. Hals coordinates the colors in the standard with the colors in each member's sash and enhances the perspective and dimensionality by the placement of the figures and by placing immediately behind the standard a window opening onto an obscure cityscape. A vertical standard at the far right of the painting and highlighted drapery toward the top of the far left portion reinforce the dimensionality of the total work. Each figure is clad in black but wears a white ruff that ties in with the white damask tablecloth, intricately reproduced in all its detail, that covers the table at which the company has feasted.

LIFE'S WORK

Hals was essentially a portrait painter. Flourishing two centuries before even the crudest cameras existed, Hals, like his contemporaries, was called upon to preserve the memories of people by painting them as accurately as he could, either singly or in groups. Because it was generally the subjects of his paintings who paid for them, he had to make them look as good as possible, a limitation he shared with his contemporaries.

That Hals, a fun-loving man given to free spending and serious drinking, was popular among the painters of Haarlem is attested by his having been given six separate commissions to paint the officers of the Civil Guard Company in slightly more than two decades, as well as by the number of paintings he produced during his lifetime, nearly all of them painted on commission.

Hals worked rapidly and painted with a sure hand. At

a time when many artists worked in pairs, Hals preferred to work alone, although on rare occasions he collaborated with such fellow artists as Nicolaes van Heussen, Willem Buytewech, and Pieter de Molyn. Hals was particularly adept at reproducing exquisitely and intricately detail in cloth and jewelry. More important, he was able to produce recognizable likenesses of his subjects while simultaneously probing their inner beings and capturing, much as Rembrandt was able, what can best be called their "inner lights."

Unlike many artists of his day, Hals seldom painted himself into his group portraits. He did, however, depict himself as a background figure in his Civic Group Company painting of 1639. He appears in the upper left of the painting and, judging from a close examination of this single self-portrait of him when he was at least fifty-five years old, he had long, dark hair, dark eyes, a mustache, and a goatee. At first glance, the picture, like that of his most celebrated portrait, *The Laughing Cavalier* (1624), seems to be of a happy-go-lucky, self-assured person. Closer examination of both pictures, however, reveals that the seemingly upturned lips are really not upturned. It is the mustache that gives the illusion that the figure in each case is laughing. In actuality, Hals's cavalier has at best a Gioconda smile, a quizzical smirk. The self-

Reproduction of a drawn portrait of Frans Hals. (Library of Congress)

portrait reveals a melancholy figure, one whose mustache is laughing but whose eyes and lips reveal someone quite the opposite.

It is at least in part Hals's ability to have painted enigmatically that has helped to assure his position among the leading painters of the world. Leonardo's *Mona Lisa*, begun in 1503, and Hals's *The Laughing Cavalier* each put a burr in the minds of those who see them, establishing them not only as unforgettable but also as intellectually provoking. It is unlikely that Hals was imitating Leonardo when he painted *The Laughing Cavalier*; rather, he was revealing the sardonic nature inherent in his own temperament.

Although one can point to pockets of prosperity in Hals's life, it can generally be said that he almost constantly lived near the edge financially. As his children, four of them artists, grew older, they could contribute little to the household. Hals and his family moved from one rented dwelling to another, often being evicted when they could not pay their rent. In 1654, a Haarlem baker to whom Hals owed two hundred guilders seized his furniture and five of his paintings to satisfy the debt. Seven years later, the Guild of St. Luke's waived the payment of Hals's annual dues because of the artist's poverty. The following year, the burgomasters of Haarlem granted Hals's request for a subvention of fifty guilders, and they followed that gift shortly with one three times as large. In 1663, they agreed to pay him two hundred guilders a year for the rest of his life. Nine years after his death, the city fathers had to grant his widow a pittance on which to live. Hals continued to paint until the year of his death, completing some of his finest work in 1664, when he undertook a commission to paint the regents of the Haarlem Almshouse. This commission brought him a modicum of prosperity, so that when he died in 1666 he was in less dire straits than he had been during much of his life.

Among Hals's greatest artistic inventions was that of controlling his work by infusing it with color values obtained by his use of grays. The chiaroscuro perfected by Leonardo and Masaccio in Italy in the early fifteenth century had been widely imitated. Hals, however, sought a new means of handling light and of bringing chromatic unity to his work. Like Rembrandt and Jan Vermeer, he experimented extensively with light and its sources, finally developing, through the use of grays, his unique way of solving the problem.

SIGNIFICANCE

Despite his persistent penury, Frans Hals was recognized as a leading citizen of Haarlem. The two hundred guilder annual subvention the town fathers settled on him was a munificent sum in its day. In the Groot Heiligland, from which Hals and his family once had to move because they could not pay their rent, the Frans Hals Museum, a significant tourist attraction, now stands. The artist's place in the history of art is secure. He ranks only slightly below Rembrandt, and his influence has been substantial.

Among those who imbibed directly of his artistic spirit are Hieronymous Bosch, Pieter Brueghel (the Elder), Pieter Brueghel (the Younger), and Jan Brueghel, all of whom painted in a popular style infused with wit. What was sardonic wit in Hals became a broader, puckish—sometimes outrageous and scatological—wit in Bosch. Paintings such as Hals's *The Lute Player* (c. 1621) or *Seated Man Holding a Branch* (1645) could easily have been incorporated into any of Bosch's or the Brueghels' busy, crowded paintings.

On September 1, 1666, Hals's body was placed in its grave in the choir of St. Bavo's Church in Haarlem, an honor accorded only to those who had brought honor to the town. Perhaps the final irony in the Hals story is that despite the poverty in which he lived, Hals's paintings, which seldom come on the market, have commanded prices in excess of ten million dollars.

—R. Baird Shuman

FURTHER READING

Baard, H. P. *Frans Hals*. Translated by George Stuyck. New York: Harry N. Abrams, 1981. This oversize volume has excellent color plates of most of Hals's major paintings. The text gives perceptive commentary on specific paintings and valuable biographical detail, dispelling the myth that Hals's work was essentially humorous. Includes a chronology of Hals's life.

Beeren, Willem A. *Frans Hals*. Translated by Albert J. Fransella. London: Blanford Press, 1962. While providing accurate information about Hals's life and the lives of his artist children, this book is at its best in relating Hals to the artistic milieu of his day. Presents sensitive interpretations of Hals's style and artistic method.

Gratama, Gerrit D. *Frans Hals*. 2d ed. The Hague, the Netherlands: Oceanus, 1946. Gratama understands Hals in relation to other artists such as Jan Steen, Peter Paul Rubens, and Rembrandt. Hals's paintings are discussed from a technical viewpoint, indicating how he captured intricate details despite the boldness of his heavy textures. Hals emerges as a highly original craftsman who solved artistic problems in singular ways.

Grimm, Claus. *Frans Hals: The Complete Work*. Trans-lated by Jürgen Riehle. New York: H. N. Abrams, 1990. Contains 471 plates, one-third of them in color, with interpretation by Grimm, a German scholar who has spent years studying Hals's art. Grimm argues that only 145 of Hals's paintings have survived, and repudiates the authenticity of about 80 paintings commonly attributed to Hals. Grimm also describes how Hals's painting techniques anticipated the styles of Manet, Cezanne, and other nineteenth century French painters.

Hals, Frans. *The Civic Guard Portrait Groups*. Text and foreword by H. P. Baard. New York: Macmillan, 1950. A slim volume that discusses Hals's six paintings of the Civic Guard Company, executed between 1616 and 1639, comparing and contrasting them to the paintings of his contemporaries who also were commissioned to paint the Company. Clearly demonstrates the uniqueness of Hals's work.

_____. *Like Father, Like Son? Portraits by Frans Hals and Jan Hals*. Raleigh: North Carolina Museum of Art, 2000. An illustrated catalog of an exhibition held at the North Carolina Museum of Art in 2000. Includes bibliographical references.

_____. *The Paintings of Frans Hals*. Text by Numa S. Trivas. New York: Oxford University Press, 1942. Trivas's discussions of Hals's major paintings remain pertinent. The accompanying illustrations are appropriately chosen and of acceptable quality, considering the difficulties of printing art books during World War II.

Valentiner, Wilhelm R. *Frans Hals Paintings in America*. Westport, Conn.: F. F. Sherman, 1936. Although dated, this book lists, and has reproductions of, Hals paintings in collections in the United States. Most of the paintings listed here remain in the same collections that held them in 1936, although additional Hals acquisitions have been made since the publication of this valuable catalog.

Wheelock, Arthur K., Jr. *Dutch Paintings of the Seventeenth Century*. New York: Oxford University Press, 1995. Catalog of the collection of seventeenth century Dutch paintings at the National Gallery of Art in Washington, D.C., including Hals and many of his contemporaries.

SEE ALSO: Georges de La Tour; Rembrandt; Peter Paul Rubens; Sir Anthony van Dyck; Jan Vermeer.

RELATED ARTICLES in *Great Events from History: The Seventeenth Century, 1601-1700:* c. 1601-1620: Emergence of Baroque Art; Mid-17th century: Dutch School of Painting Flourishes.

WILLIAM HARVEY
English physician

Observation, dissection, and experimentation led Harvey to conclude that blood follows a circular path through the body, outward through the arteries and back to the heart through the veins. His publication of this theory and his methodology in formulating and supporting it contributed to the advent of the Scientific Revolution.

BORN: April 1, 1578; Folkestone, Kent, England
DIED: June 3, 1657; London, England
AREAS OF ACHIEVEMENT: Medicine, science and technology

EARLY LIFE

William Harvey was the first of nine children of Thomas Harvey and his second wife, Joan Halke. The Harveys were a family of farmers who had become merchants during the reign of Queen Elizabeth I. Five of William's six brothers became prosperous international merchants. From his father, William got his energy, his capacity for hard work, and his painstaking and careful attention to detail; from his mother came his charitable disposition and his faith.

Like most middle-class children of the sixteenth century, Harvey studied at home with a preacher or an itinerant schoolmaster. At age ten, he was admitted by examination to the King's School in Canterbury as a fee-paying day scholar and lived with an uncle while he went to school.

When he was sixteen, Harvey received a Matthew Parker scholarship to Gonville and Caius College, Cambridge University. Although he was the first Parker scholar to study medicine, he did not decide to make medicine his career until he was at the University of Padua. Most medical education in the late sixteenth and early seventeenth centuries was still based on the writings of ancient authorities such as Aristotle and Galen. Gonville and Caius College had an excellent reputation as a medical school. The program not only emphasized the classical authorities but also provided informal medical lectures and discussions and occasional anatomical demonstrations. Harvey remained at Cambridge for almost six years. At this time, he was a rather small man with raven hair, dark eyes, and a somewhat sallow complexion. A keen observer and an enthusiastic naturalist interested in the causes and relations of things, he was quick to make comparisons, to theorize, and to contrive tests of his theories.

In December, 1599, Harvey went to study at the University of Padua, Italy's foremost school of medicine, which was noted for its experimental research, freedom of thought, and religious toleration. Protestants were welcome, and Harvey's fellow students paid him the honor of electing him in three consecutive years to be their representative in the governing system of the university. At Padua, Harvey studied comparative anatomy, embryology, and experimental physiology. One of his most famous teachers was Hieronumus Fabricius ab Aquapendente (known as Fabricius), who had constructed a unique, almost vertical anatomy theater capable of seating as many as 240 viewers to observe anatomical demonstrations. Fabricius's interest was in the heart and blood. His treatise on the valves of the veins, *De venarum ostiolis* (1603), was central to Harvey's own research. Even before Fabricius's book was published, however, Harvey had received his degree as a doctor of medicine and departed from Padua. At twenty-four, he was ready to begin his life's work.

LIFE'S WORK

Returning to England from Padua, Harvey applied as a candidate for a fellowship at the College of Physicians and was provisionally permitted to practice medicine while awaiting his examination for candidacy. Finally admitted as a candidate in 1604, he was elected a fellow in 1607.

Soon after being admitted as a candidate for the fellowship, Harvey married Elizabeth Browne, the daughter of Dr. Lancelot Browne, first physician to Queen Elizabeth until her death in 1603. The Harveys had no children and lived most of their lives in Saint Martin's Parish near Saint Paul's Church in London. Until Harvey became a fellow in the College of Physicians, his opportunities for income and study were limited to his private practice. In 1609, his reputation as a physician and a letter of recommendation from King James I secured for him the post of physician for Saint Bartholomew's Hospital, a charity hospital for the London poor. His duties were to visit once a week and treat the patients. During those years, Harvey also served as a censor on a committee of the College of Physicians that monitored doctors practicing within seven miles around London.

All these professional activities were essential for a young man ambitious for success. Throughout this period, however, it was Harvey's innate medical curiosity and his

William Harvey. (Library of Congress)

rigorous research—resulting in voluminous notes based upon both observation and experiment—that would prove most significant both to his life and to his legacy. Although the seeds of his discovery had been germinating in his mind since Padua, it was his appointment as Lumleian Lecturer on anatomy and surgery that finally brought to light his theory of the circulation of blood. On Wednesday, April 17, 1616, Harvey announced his belief that blood traveled through the arteries to all parts of the body and returned to the heart through the veins.

Harvey's logic was complex, based on his observations of the volume and speed with which blood moved through the body, the muscular action of the heart as it propelled the blood, and Fabricius's treatise describing one-way valves in veins. Since the liquid from food and drink then commonly believed to generate blood could not easily create as much blood as passed through the system, and since the volume of blood was certainly more than that necessary to nourish the extremities of the body, Harvey saw that the blood moving out into the body through the arteries had to be the same blood that returned to the heart through the veins with their one-way valves. Otherwise, the arteries would quickly become

flooded and distended with so much blood and the veins would empty.

Harvey's observations and experiments since Padua were directed at determining the mechanism controlling this flow of blood. Observations of living animals and the dissections of dead and living animals confirmed his hypothesis. The pulsating motion, the thickening and constriction of the wall of the heart, and the forcible expulsion of the blood by contractions of the ventricles all occurred so rapidly as to appear to be simultaneous. Even so, Harvey believed movement began in the auricles, with the left ventricle being the key to the propulsion of the blood through the lungs. The pulse was caused by the pumping action of the blood in the arteries, and when the flow was hindered, the pulse decreased.

The heart and blood, Harvey concluded, were the agents of life. If the heart failed or if blood did not flow to some part of the body, life in the whole body or in part of it would also fail. If the blood flow were restored, life would be restored. One of the major difficulties for Harvey in this investigation was that many of his observations were based on dissection of animals, but dissection in the sixteenth century quickly led to death. A modern scientist in his conceptions, Harvey lacked the technology necessary to test his theories adequately.

The theory of the circulation of blood was Harvey's great contribution to science. He published this theory in *Exercitatio anatomica de motu cordis et sanguinis in animalibus* (1628; *The Anatomical Exercises of Dr. William Harvey . . . Concerning the Motion of the Heart and Blood*, 1653). How far or fast his revolutionary idea traveled is uncertain, however. For twelve years, he had tested his theory, presenting his ideas for discussion and criticism until he had the approval of each of the fellows of the College of Physicians.

Harvey believed that most of his scientific colleagues accepted his theory even though it contradicted Galen, the ancient authority on blood. Other scientists, including Fabricius, Andreas Vesalius, and Michael Servetus, had already come close to challenging Galen's theories of oscillation and the separation of blood in the veins and arteries. Nevertheless, Harvey's theory was attacked by enough eminent scholars to cause the scientific world to be divided into circulators and noncirculators. This may be one reason that Harvey later declared that it was better to study and think than to publish too quickly and risk stirring up trouble. Like Galileo, Harvey had little respect for authorities. He believed anatomy should be taught by dissection and observation, not by books and other authorities. Scientists, he said, should test every hypothesis with their own eyes, trusting authorities only if their conclusions could be corroborated by firsthand observation and experiment.

After the publication of his treatise on the circulation of blood, Harvey's life entered a more public and political phase in his job as physician to King Charles I and the royal household. Not only did he continue his experiments and observations of many species of animals, insects, and plants, but he also made several trips, at the king's request, to Europe, Scotland, and even the Holy Roman Empire. Harvey's connection with the royal court gave him unusual opportunities for observations. Asked to examine seven Scottish women accused of witchcraft, he determined that they had no unusual anatomical characteristics and cleared them of the charge. Performing an autopsy on Thomas Parr, reputed to be 152 years old when he died, Harvey concluded that the cause of death was his move from Shropshire, where he had worked outdoors in cool, clean air, to London, where he sat, ate, and got little exercise while breathing unclean, sooty air.

Seventeenth century London, desperately overcrowded and growing fast, was in the midst of a medical crisis period. Several recurrences of the plague motivated medical research on the disease's causes and treatment. In the 1630's, England was also moving closer to a civil war between Royalist and Parliamentary interests. As the king's physician, Harvey was directly touched by these two national crises. When London and Parliament turned against the king, Harvey was dismissed as chief physician of Saint Bartholomew's Hospital. The hostility of his former London colleagues was less disturbing to Harvey than was the plundering of his house and the destruction of his files, which included valuable observations on the generation of insects. To Harvey, politics was insignificant compared with the excitement of scientific investigation. In 1646, at age sixty-eight, he resigned his position as royal physician and was fined two thousand pounds for assisting the Royalist army. He spent the rest of his life making scientific observations and performing experiments.

Harvey's wife, Elizabeth, died sometime between 1645 and 1652, when he wrote his will—probably before he returned to London from Oxford. His last years were spent quietly at his work at the home of one of his brothers. Science occupied his personal life and was his legacy. His studies, observations, and experiments were a solace that invariably resulted in new and unexpected information. In his studies of animals, he found not only the lesser secrets of nature but even an inkling of the Supreme Creator as well. Harvey, the natural philosopher, claimed that nature in its infinite variety, rather than books, was the true source of knowledge. He was confident that no matter how many discoveries were made by scientists, much still lay hidden for future investigation.

In 1649, he published another book on the circulation of the blood, *De circulatione sanguinis* (1649; *The Circulation of the Blood*, 1847). This volume was a reply to Galenist criticisms of his theory. His final publication, *Exercitationes de generatione animalium* (1651; *Anatomical Exercitations, Concerning the Generation of Living Creatures*, 1653), on the generation of animals, was his major contribution to embryology, offering a new view of foetal development as epigenetic, that is, caused by changes in the egg or womb occurring over several days or weeks. In 1651, Harvey arranged to build a library for the College of Physicians and made a gift to the college of his patrimonial estate in Kent. On June 3, 1657, he died in London, where his memorial service took place. He was buried in Hampstead, Kent.

SIGNIFICANCE

Harvey, like his contemporaries Galileo, Johannes Kepler, Thomas Hobbes, Francis Bacon, and René Descartes, was an early figure in the scientific revolution. For these men, knowledge depended on human observation, rational analysis of that observation to create workable hypotheses, and tests to prove or disprove those hypotheses. These men of the early seventeenth century believed in their own ability and were confident that nature was a God-given authority superior to any ancient philosopher.

What Harvey did naturally, earlier scientists and some of Harvey's contemporaries thought revolutionary. Consumed with curiosity, Harvey collected specimens, observed the natural world, painstakingly recorded his observations, and made copious, detailed notes. He dissected countless animals and performed innumerable autopsies. All of his work was done before the invention of the microscope. This method of meticulous observation and scrupulous record-keeping was new to the seventeenth century and became the basis of the scientific method, which is the foundation of all scientific inquiry today. Perhaps, in the long run, Harvey's most important contribution lay in his introduction of that method to future generations of scientists.

—Loretta Turner Johnson

FURTHER READING

Aubrey, John. "William Harvey." In *Aubrey's Brief Lives*. Reprint. Boston: D. R. Godine, 1999. A colorful personal impression of Harvey, whom Aubrey knew. Valuable as a picture of seventeenth century England and of Harvey's behavior and idiosyncrasies.

Bylebyl, Jerome J., ed. *William Harvey and His Age: The Professional and Social Context of the Discovery of the Circulation*. Baltimore, Md.: Johns Hopkins University Press, 1979. This collection of three scholarly papers discusses the discovery of circulation in the context of the health crises created by the plague and fire in seventeenth century London. The papers also examine the general practice of medicine in London and the reaction to Harvey's theories among his contemporaries.

Dickinson, C. J., and J. Marks, eds. *Developments in Cardiovascular Medicine*. Baltimore, Md.: Johns Hopkins University Press, 1978. A collection of papers presented at a symposium celebrating the four hundredth anniversary of Harvey's birth. Papers by Gweneth Whitteridge, a medical historian, and H. Trevor-Roper, a social historian, relate Harvey to seventeenth century England.

French, Roger. *William Harvey's Natural Philosophy*. New York: Cambridge University Press, 1994. Explains how Harvey devised a method for structuring knowledge, formulating questions and arriving at answers and how he used this system to discover how blood circulates.

Fuchs, Thomas. *The Mechanization of the Heart: Harvey and Descartes*. Translated by Marjorie Grene. Rochester, N.Y.: University of Rochester Press, 2001. Compares and contrasts the two men's views on the circulation of blood and the action of the heart. Examines how their opposing opinions were received and revised in subsequent generations.

Gregory, Andrew. *Harvey's Heart: The Discovery of Blood Circulation*. Lanham, Md.: Totem Books, 2001. Describes Harvey's discovery and how it challenged existing theories of blood circulation.

Keynes, Geoffrey. *The Life of William Harvey*. Oxford, England: Clarendon Press, 1966. The standard biography. Attractive, illustrated, and well documented, written by a medical historian whose previous works include a number of articles on Harvey. Detailed and interesting, although dated by style and format.

McMullen, Emerson Thomas. *William Harvey and the Use of Purpose in the Scientific Revolution: Cosmos by Chance or Universe by Design?* Lanham, Md.: University Press of America, 1998. A biography focusing on how Harvey and his contemporaries thought about purpose and chance in the universe. Thomas maintains that Harvey held deeply religious beliefs that influenced his scientific work.

Pagel, Walter. *William Harvey's Biological Ideas: Selected Aspects and Historical Background*. New York: S. Karger, 1967. This book by a medical historian balances Harvey's medical discoveries and innovations with his speculative natural philosophy and use of symbolism in ways compatible with medieval science.

Rogers, John. *The Matter of Revolution: Science, Poetry, and Politics in the Age of Milton*. Ithaca, N.Y.: Cornell University Press, 1996. Examines how Harvey's ideas about blood circulation and other novel beliefs of the seventeenth century influenced Milton's thoughts and writings.

Whitteridge, Gweneth. *William Harvey and the Circulation of the Blood*. New York: American Elsevier, 1971. A scholarly biography placing Harvey in the context of fellow seventeenth century scientists. Presents Harvey as a more medieval than modern scientist.

SEE ALSO: Charles I; René Descartes; Galileo; Thomas Hobbes; James I; Johannes Kepler.

RELATED ARTICLES in *Great Events from History: The Seventeenth Century, 1601-1700:* 1617-1628: Harvey Discovers the Circulation of the Blood; 1642-1651: English Civil Wars.

PIET HEIN
Dutch military leader

Hein aided the Netherlands substantially in its breakaway from Spanish control. He defeated the Spanish and Portuguese several times in naval combat, including the most celebrated capture of treasure ships in the history of the Spanish Main.

BORN: November 15, 1577; Delfshaven, Holland, United Provinces (now in the Netherlands)

DIED: June 18, 1629; at sea, near Dungeness, off the coast of England

AREAS OF ACHIEVEMENT: Military, warfare and conquest, diplomacy

EARLY LIFE

Piet Hein (peet hin) was born in the small port town of Delfshaven on the Meuse River near Rotterdam. He was christened Pieter Pieterszoon Heyn but is known to history simply as Piet Hein. His father was an ordinary Dutch fisherman, but he secured additional income from privateering and trade and earned a modest living for his family. Piet learned seamanship from his father, whom he accompanied on voyages into the North Sea. The fishing boats of that period were small but were armed with two or three cannons and sailed in fleets for mutual protection against both Spanish and French corsairs.

The Dutch had declared their independence from Spain in 1581, but maintaining that independence took decades. Catholic Spain refused to accept the Reformed Protestant faith of the United Provinces or their self-governing constitutional autonomy. With valor and determination, the Dutch prevented the most powerful nation in the world in the sixteenth century from controlling the small country of Holland. In 1609, a Twelve Years' Truce began, but war between Spain and Holland resumed in 1621, culminating in Hein's celebrated capture of the combined treasure fleet in 1628 off the coast of Cuba. By then, the Spanish knew that they were not going to regain control of the Netherlands. Nevertheless, it was not until the Treaty of Westphalia in 1648 that Spain officially recognized the independence of the Netherlands.

That was the international situation that faced Hein during his entire life. The Dutch had always been a seafaring people, but in the seventeenth century they had the largest merchant marine in the world, well in excess of the combined merchant fleets of Spain, Portugal, France, Scotland, and Germany. Spain, however, had a large navy while the Dutch relied on privateers, armed vessels that were also involved in fishing and trade. Some 10 percent of the adult male population of Holland made their living on the ocean.

Every time Hein ventured from shore, usually merely to catch fish to help support his family, he risked armed confrontation with the Spanish or with privateers authorized by the Spanish to attack Dutch ships. At the age of twenty, he was captured at sea and spent the next four years as a Spanish galley rower. He gained his freedom in 1601 in an exchange of Dutch and Spanish prisoners.

LIFE'S WORK

Hein became a director of the Dutch West India Company in 1621, the same year Spain renewed hostilities with the Netherlands. In 1623, he was appointed vice admiral of the fleet of the Dutch West India Company and sailed with twenty-six ships with five hundred guns, sixteen hundred sailors, and seventeen hundred soldiers to attack São Salvador on the coast of Brazil. Spain ruled Portugal at the time, so Brazil was also controlled by Spain. The Dutch objective was to secure a base there for depredations against Spanish shipping in the Caribbean.

São Salvador was the first capital of Brazil and was strongly fortified by three forts. Fifteen large Spanish ships defended the bay. Into that strong position Hein led his column of ships and fought a three-hour gun battle and then boarded the Spanish ships. Seven Spanish ships were burned, but the Dutch captured the other eight. This sudden disaster enabled the intrepid Hein and his aggressive fighters to climb to the top of the nine-foot walls and, with darkness closing in, spike the Spanish guns and blow up the ammunition depot.

Hein left behind a garrison of troops and set sail with his eight Spanish ships heavily loaded with sugar, wines, oils, and spices. Though greatly outnumbered, the Dutch had defeated a Spanish fleet and captured a Spanish stronghold. The reception at home in the Netherlands was joyful; Hein was promoted to admiral. For two years, the new admiral sailed the Caribbean, capturing whatever Spanish prizes he could find. He returned to Holland and then was given the assignment that resulted in one of the greatest losses ever inflicted on the Spanish and made Piet Hein's name known throughout the European and American worlds.

The Spanish had four main ports—Veracruz, Havana, Porto Bello, and Cartagena—in which to rendezvous the two annual treasure fleets, the one from Peru and the other from Mexico. The Dutch knew that all four ports were too strong to permit an attack in port. The best place, they judged, to waylay the fleet was outside Havana harbor. With surprising ease, Hein and his thirty ships caught nine Spanish treasure ships from Mexico running along the Cuban coast and trapped six more in Matanzas Bay. The treasure taken and sent to Holland included 177,537 pounds of silver in chests and bars, 135 pounds of gold, 37,375 hides, 2,270 chests of indigo, 7,691 pieces of logwood, 735 chests of cochineal, 235 chests of sugar, and some pearls, spices, and various tropical products. The total value of the booty was 11,509,524 Dutch florins, the greatest theft in the history of the Spanish-American Empire. The profits enabled the Dutch West India Company to pay a phenomenal dividend of 50 percent to stockholders that year. The sailors involved were given a rather small share, and Hein received only seven thousand guilders. The unfortunate Spanish admiral was imprisoned for two years by the Spanish king and then executed. Hein, however, was given a hero's welcome and wined and dined in many parts of Holland and even with the Prince of Orange and the king of Bohemia. His admirers even wrote a little song to Piet which has become part of Dutch folklore:

> Piet Heyn, Piet Heyn, Piet Heyn,
> His name is small,
> His deeds are great, his deeds are great.
> He has won the Silver Fleet.
> Hurrah, hurrah, hurrah,
> He has won the Silver Fleet.

That same year, Hein, at fifty, decided that he had had enough of action and retired from the sea to a comfortable home in Delft. His retirement ended less than a year later, when Hein was appointed admiral-in-chief and lieutenant general of Holland. His first task was to clear the English Channel of privateers who were wreaking havoc with Dutch shipping. In May of 1629, the new admiral-in-chief sailed in a single reconnaissance ship along the Channel off Dunkirk. He sighted three privateers on June 18, and, following his lifelong habit of aggressive daring, he immediately attacked the three ships and was killed by an enemy shot. His enraged men captured the privateers and threw all survivors overboard. The jubilation of the previous year was reversed as the Spanish rejoiced and the Dutch mourned.

SIGNIFICANCE

In the seventeenth century, the Dutch could not maintain their independence, culture, and maritime economy without a strong fleet. The entire nation owed much to Hein and the men who served with him in protecting Dutch trade routes worldwide. They left their mark all over the world as many of the place names in both the East Indies and West Indies were given permanent Dutch names, such as Spitsbergen, Cape Hoorn, and New Zealand. Superior seamanship and superior ships enabled the tiny nation to influence events far more than would be expected by the population figures of that small nation along the coast of Europe. That Hein played a significant role in persuading the Spanish to recognize finally the independence of the Netherlands should be obvious.

—*William H. Burnside*

FURTHER READING

Allen, Thomas B. "Cuba's Golden Past." *National Geographic* 200, no. 1 (July, 2001): 74. Describes the gold coins and other treasures from shipwrecked pirate ships that are now displayed at a museum in Havana, Cuba. Recounts Hein's capture of a treasure fleet off the coast of Cuba in 1628.

Geyl, Pieter. *The Netherlands in the Seventeenth Century.* Rev. ed. London: Ernest Benn, 1961. Provides information about the seventeenth century Dutch maritime system, a detailed description of Hein's maritime exploits, and an explanation of his significance during that period of history.

Haley, K. H. D. *The Dutch in the Seventeenth Century.* London: Thames and Hudson, 1972. The 158 illustrations, including sketches, maps, coins, monuments, and portraits, make this a particularly attractive book. Describes the Dutch civilization and economy of the seventeenth century, placing Hein in this historical setting.

Israel, Jonathan I. *The Dutch Republic and the Hispanic World, 1606-1661.* Oxford, England: Clarendon Press, 1982. Describes life in Spain and the Dutch Republic during the seventeenth century and examines the relationship of the two countries. Features a lengthy section on the war between the Spanish and Dutch in the Caribbean, including a detailed description of Hein's victory at Matanzas Bay in Cuba.

Parker, Geoffrey. *Spain and the Netherlands, 1559-1659.* Short Hills, N.J.: Enslow, 1979. An important interpretive study of the diplomatic relations of Spain and Holland. Deals with such topics as why the Dutch revolt lasted so long, the larger world of international politics to which this conflict belonged, and the economic consequences of the revolt.

Peterson, Mendel. *The Funnel of Gold.* Boston: Little,

Brown, 1975. The best treatment in English of the protracted war for treasures in the Caribbean in the sixteenth and seventeenth centuries. Discusses in detail the ships, weaponry, and tactics of that era, including a description of Hein's fighting abilities and techniques. Also includes an account of the capture of 1628 in Hein's own words.

SEE ALSO: Frederick Henry; Maurice of Nassau; Michiel Adriaanszoon de Ruyter; Abel Janszoon Tasman; Maarten and Cornelis Tromp.
RELATED ARTICLES in *Great Events from History: The*

Seventeenth Century, 1601-1700: 17th century: Age of Mercantilism in Southeast Asia; December, 1601: Dutch Defeat the Portuguese in Bantam Harbor; Beginning Spring, 1605: Dutch Dominate Southeast Asian Trade; 1606-1674: Europeans Settle in India; October, 1625-1637: Dutch and Portuguese Struggle for the Guinea Coast; June-August, 1640: *Bandeirantes* Expel the Jesuits; January 14, 1641: Capture of Malacca; August 26, 1641-September, 1648: Conquest of Luanda; April, 1652: Dutch Begin to Colonize Southern Africa; Beginning 1680's: Guerra dos Bárbaros; Early 1690's: Brazilian Gold Rush.

JAN BAPTISTA VAN HELMONT
Flemish chemist, physician, and mystic

Helmont was among the first to introduce the methods and results of chemistry into the science of medicine. He discovered carbonic acid and carbon dioxide, coined the term "gas," invented gravimetry for urinalysis, and made several advances in physiology and pharmacology.

BORN: January 12, 1580; Brussels, United Provinces (now in Belgium)
DIED: December 30, 1644; Vilvoorde, Spanish Netherlands (now in Belgium)
ALSO KNOWN AS: Johannes Baptista van Helmont; Joan Baptista van Helmont; Johann Baptista van Helmont; Jean Baptiste van Helmont
AREAS OF ACHIEVEMENT: Science and technology, medicine

EARLY LIFE
Jan Baptista van Helmont was born to privilege in the Flemish landed gentry, the son of Brabant state counselor Christian van Helmont and Brussels socialite Marie de Stassart. His marriage to Margerite van Ranst in 1609 connected him to the influential Merode family, but he never used his rank for personal gain.

He was always intellectual, inquisitive, otherworldly, and skeptical almost to the point of iconoclasm. His quest for knowledge led him to travel throughout Europe and to experiment with different paths of learning. He studied with the Jesuits, but was more strongly influenced by magic and alchemy. He finally settled on a life that related mystical spirituality to natural science.

After immersing himself in a variety of subjects, including philosophy, geography, and law, Helmont

earned his medical degree in 1599 at the University of Louvain and taught surgery there briefly. His medical career was voluntarily short. He opposed bloodletting and other violent but popular therapies. One story says that he gave up medicine when an Italian Paracelsian cured his scabies by applying sulfur and mercury after Galenic physicians had failed to cure it with emetics, purgatives, and herbal remedies. He quit practicing medicine around 1605, proclaiming that he would no longer make his living from the sufferings of others. Thereafter he dedicated his life to biomedical and biochemical research.

LIFE'S WORK
Helmont's main influences were the philosopher Nicholas of Cusa and the physicians Hippocrates and Paracelsus. He distrusted Galen and most medieval medical authors, especially the Arabs. His method was empirical, but tempered by metaphysics. With his concepts of disease derived as much from speculation as from experience, he relied on Paracelsus regarding the importance of chemistry and alchemy in the practice of medicine. He adopted from Paracelsus the concept of "archaeus," the governing spirit of each physiological process. The archaeus initiates and regulates the production of bodily ferments that work like enzymes to produce physiological results. The process is entirely chemical. Helmont additionally claimed that the soul was the ultimate source of physiological change, which meant that, to take care of the body, one must first take care of the soul.

Iatrochemistry, the brainchild of Helmont and German physician Franciscus Sylvius (Franz Deleboe), is a kind of bioscience based on the axiom that physiological processes are essentially chemical. Iatrochemistry was one of two major movements in seventeenth century medical research. The other, iatromechanism, whose main drivers were René Descartes and Giovanni Alfonso Borelli, reduced physiology to mechanics and concentrated on musculoskeletal relations, nerve reflexes, heart motion, digestive action, and optical physics. Both sides achieved much, but remained at odds. Moreover, dissension existed within each movement. Sylvius remained a Galenist, while Helmont's departure in a Paracelsian direction led eventually to German physician Georg Ernst Stahl propounding medical animism, the theory that the soul directly causes all physiological events.

Helmont was the first to recognize that there are different kinds of gases, which he believed were different aspects of spirit. He coined the word "gas" as an alteration of the Greek and Latin word *chaos*, which means space, emptiness, boundlessness, or shapelessness. His experiments on fermentation and combustion advanced the knowledge of the products of these processes, especially the invisible products. He isolated carbon dioxide, which he called "gas sylvestre," from wine fermentation, but did not distinguish adequately between carbon dioxide and carbon monoxide. He also identified and described but misnamed and imperfectly understood chlorine, methane, sulfur dioxide, hydrogen sulfide, and several other gases, as well as carbonic acid.

Much of Helmont's research concerned the chemical properties and physiological effects of acids, and he verified that digestion occurs because of acid. His experiments on digestive system acids dovetailed with his research into the effects of other acids on other organic tissues. He noticed that acid contributes to the formation of pus and that acids are involved in the formation of bodily gases. He devised methods of using specific gravity to test for the presence of metals in solution and to determine the contents of urine. He also conducted pathological research, where his most important results related to asthma, catarrh, and epilepsy.

Since he preferred medical to surgical and gentle to aggressive methods in medicine, most of Helmont's practical clinical advances were in pharmacology. Like Paracelsus, he favored mercury as a therapeutic agent. The focus of most of his drug research was to improve the Paracelsian formulary.

Beginning in 1622, the Spanish Inquisition and other Roman Catholic authorities challenged the religious orthodoxy of Helmont's science, mainly because of his adherence to Paracelsus. In 1625, the Inquisition cited twenty-seven of his assertions as heretical. The Church impounded his 1621 book, *De magnetica vulnerum*

curatione (English translation in *A Ternary of Paradoxes: The Magnetick Cure of Wounds, Nativity of Tartar in Wine, Image of God in Man*, 1650). His teachings were officially banned by the University of Louvain from 1622 to 1634 because he was suspected of advocating or practicing magic. He was placed under house arrest from 1634 to 1636 and was not cleared until 1642. He conducted extensive research for the last four decades of his life, but because he could not receive an imprimatur between 1622 and 1642, he published very little.

The ecclesiastical persecution made Helmont's writings that appeared during his lifetime scattered and unsystematic. In his last two years of life, he attempted to break out of that pattern, notably in 1644 with four essays published together as *Opuscula medica inaudita* (*Unheard of Little Works on Medicine*, 1664). The essays cover "diseases of the stone," fevers, humours, and the plague.

His son, Franciscus Mercurius van Helmont, collected and edited his father's works and published them in 1648 as *Ortus medicinae* (*A Ternary of Paradoxes: The Magnetick Cure of Wounds, Nativity of Tartar in Wine, Image of God in Man*, 1650). These two books are the foundation points of iatrochemistry. Although extracting Helmont's scientific content from his mystical language is often difficult, this posthumous book is the basis of his fame as a scientist.

SIGNIFICANCE

Helmont's influence has proceeded in disparate ways. Because he blurred the distinction between natural science and mysticism to the extent that his metaphysical speculations and prejudices sometimes obscured the useful scientific results in his writings, his reputation as a scientist is less than it deserves to be. His emphasis on soul, spirit, and vital forces influenced animistic scientists such as Stahl, vitalist philosophers such as Henri Bergson, and, through Bergson, twentieth century process philosophy.

Despite his mysticism, Helmont is rightly regarded as one of the most important founders of biochemistry. His experiments with gases laid some of the groundwork for Joseph Black's investigations of respiration in the eighteenth century. His iatrochemistry was a powerful bioscientific force in the second half of the seventeenth century, especially in Britain and the Low Countries, including among its adherents Thomas Willis, Jan Swammerdam, and Regnier de Graaf. His ontological views of diseases as separate entities helped to prepare the way for the nosological movement of the eighteenth century.

Like most physicians and others of his era, Helmont condescended to women, but his disdain for women's ailments and even their nature was more explicit than most. In 1826, American obstetrician and gynecologist William Potts Dewees quoted with disapproval Helmont's assertion that a woman is what she is only because of her uterus, a view common into the twentieth century.

—*Eric v.d. Luft*

FURTHER READING

Coulter, Harris L. *The Origins of Modern Western Medicine: J. B. van Helmont to Claude Bernard.* Vol. 2 in *Divided Legacy: A History of the Schism in Medical Thought.* Berkeley, Calif.: North Atlantic Books, 2000. The second of four volumes of a provocative view of the hegemony of regular medicine by an expert in the history of alternative medicine. Coulter sees Helmont as an important figure in the development of modern empiricism.

Debus, Allen G. *Chemistry and Medical Debate: Van Helmont to Boerhaave.* Canton, Mass.: Science History, 2001. From the point of view of the history of chemistry, this innovative reinterpretation of the rivalries among early modern medical philosophies sets them in their larger cultural context and breaks stereotypes about them.

Ettinger, Jacqueline Erbrecht. *J. B. van Helmont's Heuristic Wound: Trauma and the Subversion of Humoral Theory.* Ph.D. dissertation. University of Washington, 2001. Analyzes the concept of traumatic injury in Helmont's writings to show that his theory of disease emerged from the paradox of iatrogenic wounds, that is, injuries caused by doctors.

Pagel, Walter. *Joan Baptista van Helmont: Reformer of Science and Medicine.* New York: Cambridge University Press, 1982. The standard biography of Helmont.

Pagel, Walter, and Marianne Winder, eds. *From Paracelsus to van Helmont: Studies in Renaissance Medicine and Science.* London: Variorum Reprints, 1986. A collected reissue of fifteen of Pagel's scholarly articles, most of which concern Helmont in some way.

Schott, Heinz. "Paracelsus and van Helmont on Imagination: Magnetism and Medicine Before Mesmer." In *Paracelsian Moments: Science, Medicine, and Astrology in Early Modern Europe,* edited by Gerhild Scholz Williams and Charles D. Gunnoe, Jr. Kirksville, Mo.: Truman State University Press, 2002. An examination of Helmont's work from the perspective of the history of medicine, the natural sciences, and religion. Includes illustrations, a bibliography, and an index.

SEE ALSO: Johann Joachim Becher; Jakob Böhme; Giovanni Alfonso Borelli; Robert Boyle; René Descartes; Marcello Malpighi; Santorio Santorio; Jan Swammerdam; Thomas Willis.

RELATED ARTICLES in *Great Events from History: The Seventeenth Century, 1601-1700:* 17th century: Advances in Medicine; 1612: Sanctorius Invents the Clinical Thermometer; 1660's-1700: First Microscopic Observations; 1672-1684: Leeuwenhoek Discovers Microscopic Life.

HENRIETTA MARIA
French-born queen consort of England (r. 1625-1649)

Henrietta Maria's Catholicism and her influence over her husband, Charles I, aroused distrust and animosity not only toward her, but toward the king as well, contributing to the outbreak of the English Civil War. As the mother of the future kings Charles II and James II, however, Henrietta Maria helped ensure the English succession.

BORN: November 25 or 26, 1609; Louvre Palace, Paris, France

DIED: September 10, 1669; Chateau de Colombes, near Paris, France

AREA OF ACHIEVEMENT: Government and politics

EARLY LIFE

Henrietta Maria (hehn-ree-EHT-uh muh-RI-uh), the sixth child and third daughter of King Henry IV of France and his wife, Marie de Médicis, was named after both of her parents. Just before she was six months old, on May 14, 1610, Henrietta Maria's father was assassinated. Her eldest brother then succeeded to the throne as Louis XIII, but, since he was only eight years old, his mother acted as regent for him until he came of age.

Ruling France left Marie de Médicis little time for motherhood, but it was the custom of the time anyway for royal and noble children to be raised by governesses. Henrietta Maria and her brothers and sisters, excluding her brother the king, resided in a château outside Paris under the care of Madame de Montglat. Henrietta Maria grew up seeing very little of her mother or eldest brother. She was, perhaps naturally, closest to the sibling that was nearest her in age, her brother Gascon. All of the children were well-cared-for but not coddled by Madame de Montglat and her staff.

Henrietta Maria's education was typical for a young princess of her day: She learned religion, court etiquette, riding, dancing, and singing. Academic subjects like history were mostly neglected. Her chief and only purpose, after all, was to marry according to the dictates of French foreign policy, and potential matches were being seriously considered before she even reached adolescence. In 1624, the English approached Marie de Médicis about her youngest daughter's hand after a proposed match between then-Prince Charles and a Spanish princess fell through. The marriage took place when Henrietta Maria was just fifteen, in May of 1625, shortly after Charles had become king.

LIFE'S WORK

As queen of England, Henrietta Maria's most important job was to secure the succession by producing a male heir, but the first four years of her marriage were childless. This may have been due, in part, to her young age, but it might also have been because of a certain coldness that existed between husband and wife in the first years of their marriage, a coldness that can be blamed on Charles's deep attachment to George Villiers, first duke of Buckingham. After Buckingham was assassinated in 1628, however, relations warmed between the royal spouses, with Charles becoming as emotionally dependent on Henrietta Maria as he had been on Buckingham.

The couple's first child, a boy, was born prematurely in May of 1629, dying shortly after birth. A year later, though, Henrietta Maria gave birth to a healthy son, the future Charles II, on May 29, 1630. She eventually had five more surviving children with Charles: Mary, born December 4, 1631, who married William II of Orange; James (the future James II), born October 14, 1633; Elizabeth, born December 28, 1635; Henry, born July 8, 1639; and Henrietta Anne, known in the family as "Minette," born June 16, 1644, and later married to Philip, duke of Orléans.

Throughout the 1630's, Henrietta Maria was her husband's close companion and confidante, advising him on many matters, including political issues and affairs of state. Her influence over the king, however, aroused distrust and concern among the English. The primary reason for this was that Henrietta Maria, a Roman Catholic, openly practiced her religion at court, and this caused fears that she was leading her husband into "popish" policies, a fear not lessened by the increase in ceremony and ritual that Charles was bringing into the Anglican Church during this period.

Another reason for the suspicion was that the queen was French and in many ways remained very French in her tastes and habits, despite living in England. The English associated France with the sort of divine right absolute monarchy that Henrietta Maria's brother, king Louis XIII, was establishing there, and they believed the queen was influencing the king to adopt similar policies. In actuality, Charles needed little persuasion, as he was already a firm believer in royal divine right, but Henrietta Maria was an easy target, especially as she led the court in masques and pageants on royal absolutist themes.

Beloved by her husband, Henrietta Maria was increasingly hated by the English, who blamed her, along with Charles's other "evil counselors," for the distasteful royal policies imposed on them during the eleven years Charles ruled without a Parliament.

It was, in fact, to prevent Henrietta Maria from being impeached by the Long Parliament in January, 1642, that Charles attempted to arrest five members of the House of Commons, a violation of parliamentary privilege. The next month, Henrietta Maria sailed to the Netherlands to be a fund-raiser, recruiter, arms-supplier, and advocate for the royal cause abroad.

Henrietta Maria made two trips to the Netherlands, each of which also had the benefit of removing her from the dangers posed to her by the hostile Parliamentarians. In her first trip, the more successful one, she amassed a considerable sum of money by securing loans for the king and selling or pledging royal jewels. She also procured a large supply of weapons and other war materiel, in addition to mercenary troops. Upon returning to England in February, 1643, however, Henrietta Maria was unable to join her husband at his court in Oxford until July. Fears for her safety soon prompted her to flee England again, this time for her native France, in July of 1644. She took up residence just outside Paris and tried to

Henrietta Maria. (Hulton Archive/Getty Images)

garner support for Charles's cause from the French and the Irish.

Charles I was ultimately defeated, tried, and executed by Parliament. Afterward, Henrietta Maria helped establish the court-in-exile of her son, now King Charles II, but she found that she did not have the political influence with him that she had had with her husband. Moreover, her Catholicism continued to be controversial and divisive among the British Royalists. After her son's Restoration to the throne, she made two visits to England, but she returned to France in 1665 and died there in 1669.

SIGNIFICANCE

In addition to giving birth to the future kings Charles II and James II, Henrietta Maria's main historical significance lies in her contribution both to the political problems that helped cause the English Civil War and to the failure to find a negotiated peace between king and Parliament. Her open Catholicism and her nationality led the English to take an overwhelmingly negative view of the influence that she wielded over her husband, arousing increasing hostility and suspicion toward both her and Charles I, which did much to help bring on the war. Henrietta Maria's actions abroad did provide crucial financial and military support for the Royalist cause, but they were construed by many of the English as nothing less than treason, impugning the king's loyalty to England as well. Moreover, whether separated from Charles or by his side, Henrietta Maria encouraged him to be resolute in his absolutist positions, insisting that no compromise could be made with "rebels." She was thus the chief voice of absolutism among the Royalists whose views strengthened Charles's intransigence in the face of opposition.

—*Sharon Arnoult*

FURTHER READING

Bone, Quentin. *Henrietta Maria: Queen of the Cavaliers*. Urbana: University of Illinois Press, 1972. An older but scholarly biography of Henrietta Maria.

Coote, Stephen. *Royal Survivor: A Life of Charles II*. London: Hodder & Stoughton, 1999. A biography of Henrietta Maria's eldest son.

Morrah, Patrick. *A Royal Family: Charles I and His Family*. London: Constable, 1982. A portrait of the marriage and family life of Charles and Henrietta Maria.

Plowden, Alison. *Henrietta Maria: Charles I's Indomitable Queen*. Stroud, Gloucestershire, England: Sutton, 2001. A useful biography of Henrietta Maria.

Quintrell, Brian. *Charles I, 1625-1640.* New York: Longman, 1993. A relatively brief and accessible biography of the king.

SEE ALSO: First Duke of Buckingham; Charles I; Charles II (of England); James II; Louis XIII.

RELATED ARTICLES in *Great Events from History: The Seventeenth Century, 1601-1700:* March, 1629-1640: "Personal Rule" of Charles I; November 3, 1640-May 15, 1641: Beginning of England's Long Parliament; 1642-1651: English Civil Wars; May, 1659-May, 1660: Restoration of Charles II.

GEORGE HERBERT
English poet and cleric

George Herbert is among the most important British religious lyricists of all time. His influence extends not only to other Metaphysical poets but also to major writers of the nineteenth and twentieth centuries. His life, moreover, reflected the same unwavering dedication to his faith that is evident in his poetry.

BORN: April 3, 1593; Montgomery, Wales
DIED: March 1, 1633; Bemerton, near Salisbury, Wiltshire, England
AREAS OF ACHIEVEMENT: Literature, religion and theology

EARLY LIFE

Richard Herbert, the father of George Herbert, came from a long line of military leaders and courtiers; George's mother, Magdalen Herbert, was descended from a prominent Shropshire family, the Newports. Magdalen was known for her piety, and she had need of all her spiritual resources when, in 1596, her husband died, leaving Magdalen with nine children and a tenth on the way. This redoubtable woman immediately took steps to settle the estate and arrange for the welfare of her children.

Shortly after the birth of her son Thomas in 1597, Magdalen moved the family to the home of her mother, Margaret Bromley Newport, at Eyton-upon-Severn in Shropshire. She then arranged an advantageous marriage for her oldest son, Edward, who was at Oxford University. The following year, Lady Newport died, and Magdalen moved to Oxford, where she took a house for herself and her children, along with Edward's young bride. There, the younger boys, including George, were probably taught by tutors. According to Herbert's biographer Isaak Walton, it was at Oxford that Magdalen Herbert first met the poet and priest John Donne, who became a close friend.

In 1601, Magdalen moved to London and established a permanent home at Charing Cross. She attended divine

services regularly, supervised a large household, and entertained often. In 1608, she married Sir John Danvers, a young man half her age. It was evidently a happy match, and Danvers later became one of George's closest friends. Among Magdalen's regular guests in London was the new dean of Westminster Abbey, Lancelot Andrewes, a learned Anglican divine. Andrewes probably helped place George in the prestigious Westminster School, where he was so outstanding a student that he was awarded one of three Westminster nominations to Trinity College, Cambridge. George was admitted to Cambridge on May 5, 1609, a month after his sixteenth birthday. He would be associated with the university for the next fifteen years.

LIFE'S WORK

During his years at Cambridge, Herbert remained undecided as to what course he should pursue in life. His aristocratic rank, his family background, and his education equipped him for a role at court, perhaps as a diplomat like his brother Edward, who in 1619 became ambassador to France. However, George's correspondence indicates that as early as 1618 he was planning to study divinity. In any case, Herbert meant both his life and his poetry to be a testament to his faith. In 1610, Herbert had sent two sonnets as a gift to his mother. In the poems and in the letter dispatched along with them, he promised to use his poetic talents solely to glorify God. Nevertheless, while he was at Cambridge, in addition to his devotional poems, Herbert also wrote occasional poems, some of them addressed to friends like John Donne and the scholar and philosopher Francis Bacon.

Herbert received a B.A. and an M.A. from Cambridge and became a fellow of Trinity College. In 1620, he was appointed university orator. As Cambridge's official spokesperson, he conducted official correspondence with the king and other important personages and delivered Latin orations at public occasions. The position could have opened the way to a bright future at court.

HERBERT'S MAJOR WORKS

1620	*Musae Responsoriae* (printed 1662)
1623	*Passio Discerpta*
1623	*Lucus*
1627	*Memoriae Matris Sacrum*
1633	*The Temple*
1634	*A Treatise of Temperance and Sobrietie of Luigi Cornaro* (translation)
1640	*Outlandish Proverbs Selected by Mr. G. H.*
1652	*A Priest to the Temple: Or, The Country Parson His Character and Rule of Holy Life*

However, several months after he was elected to Parliament from the borough of Montgomery in 1623, Herbert was granted leave from his duties as orator, and later the appointment expired. By now, he had evidently decided against a secular life. His biographer, Amy M. Charles, has found evidence that he was ordained a deacon in 1624; at that time, he was presented with several minimal church livings. However, Herbert would not become a priest until 1630.

The intervening years were difficult for Herbert. Though never robust, in 1627 he became so ill, perhaps from consumption, that it took him the better part of a year to recuperate. That same year, his mother died, and Herbert published *Memoriae Matris Sacrum* (1627), the only collection to appear during his lifetime. The work consisted of nineteen Greek and Latin poems and appeared on July 7 along with John Donne's funeral sermon.

After Herbert's health improved, he began courting Jane Danvers, a relative of his stepfather. Their wedding took place on March 5, 1629. The following year, Herbert was presented the living of Fugglestone-with-Bemerton. Shortly thereafter, he was installed as rector, and on September 19, 1630, he was ordained to the priesthood. Contemporary accounts and his own prose description of a country parson's life indicate that, modeling his life on that of his Master, Herbert devoted himself to his flock. Unfortunately, he would remain with them for only three years. After a short illness, he died on March 1, 1633; on March 3, he was buried in the church at Bemerton.

Since the great poetic work for which Herbert is best known was not published until after his death, scholars can only conjecture as to dates of composition. *The Temple: Sacred Poems and Private Ejaculations* (1633) is divided into three parts. The first part, "The Church-porch," is a long poem in stanzaic form, probably written early in Herbert's life, that advises his readers both as to how best to comport themselves in society and how to lead a moral Christian life. The final section, "The Church Militant," is also believed to be an early work. This poem, which is written in heroic couplets, is satirical in tone; its theme is that wherever the Christian Church goes, sin is close behind, bent on corrupting the institution and its members. The lyric poems that make up the impressive central section of *The Temple*, which is entitled "The Church," are far more profound. Evidently they were composed and revised throughout Herbert's lifetime.

SIGNIFICANCE

Before he died, Herbert had arranged for the completed manuscript of *The Temple* to be delivered to his friend Nicholas Ferrar at the religious community of Little Gidding. Ferrar immediately made arrangements for it to be published along with his own brief account of the life of the author, a man he considered a saint. In 1670, Isaak Walton's lengthier biography of Herbert further enhanced the reputation of the poet-priest. By that time, *The Temple* had become one of the most admired devotional works of its time. Eleven editions of the book appeared before the end of the seventeenth century, and it is credited with having influenced some of the major Metaphysical poets of the period, including Thomas Traherne and Henry Vaughan.

As literary tastes changed and the Metaphysical poets fell out of fashion, *The Temple* became less well known. However, the critic Stanley Stewart points out that from Emily Dickinson and Gerard Manley Hopkins to T. S. Eliot, W. H. Auden, and Elizabeth Bishop, poets sensitive to the life of the spirit have found much to admire and emulate in the poetry of Herbert. Moreover, in an era of unbelief, many readers find solace in reading the work of a man who believed his faith and lived his belief.

—*Rosemary M. Canfield Reisman*

FURTHER READING

Charles, Amy M. *A Life of George Herbert*. Ithaca, N.Y.: Cornell University Press, 1977. The standard biography. Includes chronology and several appendixes. Illustrated.

Eliot, T. S. *George Herbert*. Writers and Their Work 152. London: Longmans, Green, 1962. A seminal study by a major poet, one of Herbert's most ardent admirers.

Malcolmson, Cristina. *George Herbert: A Literary Life*. New York: Palgrave Macmillan, 2004. Argues that the poet was not a recluse but a man engaged in the religious and political controversies of his time. Bibliography and index.

Patrides, C. A., ed. *George Herbert: The Critical Heritage.* Boston: Routledge & Kegan Paul, 1983. Excerpts comments and criticism from the seventeenth century through the twentieth. Appendix of musical settings. Index.

Ray, Robert H. *A George Herbert Companion.* New York: Garland, 1995. Includes chronology, biography, and discussion of the works, as well as a Herbert dictionary, suggestions on research procedures, and extensive bibliography. Despite some errors, this is an invaluable work.

Summers, Joseph H. *George Herbert: His Religion and Art.* London: Chatto and Windus, 1954. A major study of the life and works. Extensive notes.

Tuve, Rosemond. *A Reading of George Herbert.* London: Faber and Faber, 1952. A highly respected scholar examines the liturgical background and the iconography of Herbert's poetry.

Walton, Isaak. *The Lives of John Donne, Sir Henry Wotton, Richard Hooker, George Herbert, and Robert Sanderson.* 1670. Rev. ed. Reprint. London: Oxford University Press, 1927. Though not always factually accurate, Walton's lively biography is an accurate portrait of Herbert's character.

Young, R. V. *Doctrine and Devotion in Seventeenth-Century Poetry: Studies in Donne, Herbert, Crashaw, and Vaughan.* Studies in Renaissance Literature 2. Cambridge, England: D. S. Brewer, 2000. Chapters on "The Presence of Grace," "Meditation and Sacrament," and "Biblical Poetics" contain numerous references to Herbert's poems. Bibliography and index.

SEE ALSO: Lancelot Andrewes; John Donne; Nicholas Ferrar.

RELATED ARTICLES in *Great Events from History: The Seventeenth Century, 1601-1700:* c. 1601-1613: Shakespeare Produces His Later Plays; 1611: Publication of the King James Bible.

ROBERT HERRICK
English poet and cleric

Herrick produced a body of poetic works that expresses a distinctively seventeenth century carpe diem philosophy, portrays English country life during the Civil War and Restoration, and both represents and comments upon those and other historical events.

BORN: August 24, 1591 (baptized); London, England
DIED: October, 1674; Dean Prior, Devonshire, England
AREA OF ACHIEVEMENT: Literature

EARLY LIFE

Born in 1591 as the seventh child of parents Nicholas and Julia, Robert Herrick (HUR-ik) began his life in London. His father, a banker and goldsmith, is believed to have committed suicide in 1592. After some early education and an apprenticeship at age sixteen to his uncle, a goldsmith, Robert Herrick was able to attend Cambridge University. He began at Saint John's College but transferred to Trinity Hall to cut down on his overspending. He received a B.A. in 1617 and an M.A. in 1620. Originally hoping to become a lawyer, Herrick studied the Greek and Roman classics, texts important for law that would come to influence his poetry as well.

Three years after graduating from Cambridge, Herrick was ordained a priest in the Church of England. Soon after, he was admitted to the Tribe of Ben, a group of poets who met with and were influenced by famed poet and playwright Ben Jonson. Jonson and his followers are often called Cavalier poets, a term associated with men at the royal court who enforced traditional political values and enjoyed food, drink, sport, and women. Herrick apparently circulated his early poems privately, in manuscript form, to a small London audience, although a few did appear in print. A connection to the court came for Herrick in 1627, when he was appointed as one of the first duke of Buckingham's army chaplains on an ill-fated expedition to the Isle of Rhé.

When that short-lived military excursion ended, Herrick was nominated to a parish in 1628, the same year his mother died, but the rural parish proved quite unlike the urban environment of London where he felt most comfortable. Instead, his church was to be in Dean Prior in Devonshire, part of the countryside in the far west of England. In September, 1630, Herrick became vicar of the small country Church of Saint George the Martyr, miles away from the London pubs where he had met and discussed poetry with his witty friends. A few of his poems grumble about the isolation of this locale, particularly "Discontents in Devon."

Herrick, moreover, was not a conventional Anglican priest. He threw his Bible during the service to gain his congregation's attention. A popular legend from Devonshire holds that Herrick kept a pet pig. At some point, he left the parish for a while without permission to live in Westminster with a young woman named Thomasin Parsons; they may have had a daughter together.

LIFE'S WORK

In some ways, Herrick was born at the wrong time. While his politics, experience, and education prepared him to be a clergyman for the nobility, the dynamics of the seventeenth century prevented that him from achieving that aspiration. With the Puritan Revolution of 1642, those who sided with the nobility were displaced, either literally forced to leave England or involuntarily removed from positions. Within a few years, Herrick lost his small, primarily Puritan parish because of his Royalist sympathies. He returned to London, presumably living off the support of family.

Although there is evidence that he tried to have his poetic work published in London as early as 1640, the major collection of Herrick's poetry, *Hesperides: Or, The Works Both Humane and Divine of Robert Herrick, Esq.* (1648), was not printed until 1648. It was dedicated to Prince Charles, the son of Charles I, the latter of whom would be executed one year later in the Puritan revolt. Even Herrick's dedication was politically perilous in this antimonarchical period, but his allegiances ultimately paid off: When Prince Charles returned to England from France in 1660, he was crowned Charles II, and Herrick, no longer a political outcast, regained his Dean Prior vicarage. The Restoration had vindicated Herrick, but he did no further publishing.

Hesperides, a largely secular collection, also contained *Noble Numbers*, a compendium of Herrick's religious verse. The title *Hesperides*, which signifies both the Western Maidens who were the mythical daughters of Night and a garden guarded by those maidens, refers to Herrick's location in the West of England, as well as to his metaphorical garden of poetry. In his apology, or overview, to the collection, Herrick announces the sub-

Seventeenth century engraving of Robert Herrick. (Hulton Archive/ Getty Images)

ject matter of this vast collection of 1,130 poems. The wide-ranging overview includes the delights and drawbacks of the countryside, folk myth, love, the beauty of women, and mortality.

Time represents one major of the volume's major topics, incorporating the cycles of nature, the seasonal holidays, and the fleetingness of life, which is also related to the concept of *carpe diem*. Literally meaning "seize the day" and originating in the ancient Roman poetry of Horace and Martial, this concept was revived in the Cavalier poetry of the seventeenth century and refers to enjoying life, especially the favors of young women, while one can, as life is short but precious. Herrick's most famous poem, "To the Virgins, To Make Much of Time" (1648), espouses this philosophy, an unusual point of view for a clergyman. His focus on time also alludes to the political changes the years have wrought, as in the shift from monarchy to parliamentary rule.

Petrarchan and Ovidian poetry heavily influence Herrick's often-playful presentation of love, and he addresses poems to numerous female characters named for those in classical Latin pastoral poetry. Herrick's other well-known poems include "Delight in Disorder" (1648), reinforcing the Cavalier aesthetic of art that seems effortless, and "Corinna's Gone A-Maying" (1648), celebrating the English May festival, a celebration of spring and fertility that the Puritans condemned.

There are more somber poems in *Hesperides* as well, dealing with the waning of the year and the deaths of Herrick's brother and his friend and mentor, Ben Jonson. Herrick also wrote frequently about his housekeeper, Prudence Baldwin, who took care of him for numerous years. A number of his poems are even addressed to himself. The variety of verse forms includes epigrams—compact, witty poems, some humorous, some serious; epithalamia, or wedding poems; shaped poems, in which the printed poem resembles its subject matter; and celebratory songs. Herrick's friend, the composer Henry Lawes, set some of Herrick's poems to music, making the most of the verses' melodic qualities.

SIGNIFICANCE

Herrick's significance lies entirely in the poetry he published; however, throughout the years, critics have argued over just how important that poetry is. The scholar and poet T. S. Eliot made Herrick famous in the mid-twentieth century by branding *Hesperides* minor poetry, and it has gone through periods of being regarded as entertaining ephemera. Contemporary evaluations see the poems as more culturally sophisticated, reflecting the seventeenth century's conflicts in religion and politics. Critics interested in cultural history have traced Herrick's material to a variety of classical sources, seventeenth century intellectual movements, and artistic aesthetics. Feminist critics discuss the numerous poems to anonymous women composed by this never-married poet. New formalist poets celebrate Herrick's carefully crafted poetic style. The quantity of poems and range of subject matter in *Hesperides* allow it to continue to be both enjoyed and analyzed by many different sorts of readers with different points of view and critical agendas.

—*Carol Blessing*

FURTHER READING

Coiro, Ann Baynes. *Robert Herrick's "Hesperides" and the Epigram Book Tradition*. Baltimore, Md.: Johns Hopkins University Press, 1988. Argues that Herrick created *Hesperides* as a unified work that has a well-thought-out structure, following the pattern of epigram writing from classical poets and Ben Jonson. Portions of Herrick's life are interwoven with discussions of his art.

Deneef, A. Leigh. *"This Poetick Liturgie": Robert Herrick's Ceremonial Mode*. Durham, N.C.: Duke University Press, 1974. Theorizes that the poems are united by their speakers' emphases on four types of ritual celebration: pastoral, courtly, realistic, and artistic. This is an advanced study, primarily for literary specialists.

Ingram, Randell. "Robert Herrick and the Makings of *Hesperides*." *Studies in English Literature, 1500-1900* 38, no. 1 (Winter, 1998): 127. Focusing on seventeenth century print culture and its difference from our own, Ingram takes to task critics who try to apply current ideas of coherence to *Hesperides*. He asserts that Herrick desired to preserve his poems beyond the printed page, in part by engaging the reader to make them his or her own.

Martin, L. C., ed. *The Poems of Robert Herrick*. New York: Oxford University Press, 1965. Often considered the standard edition of Herrick's works, the introduction has a brief overview of Herrick's life, and reproductions of the frontispieces of *Hesperides* and *Noble Numbers*.

Patrick, J. Max, ed. *The Complete Poetry of Robert Herrick*. Reprint. New York: W. W. Norton, 1968. A carefully edited edition that includes a biographical chronology, brief introductory material on Herrick's critical reception, and extensive footnotes to the poems, incorporating information on people, places, and events in Herrick's life. Also contains some poetry that may be attributed to Herrick but that is not traditionally printed with *Hesperides*.

Roe, John. "'Upon Julia's Clothes': Herrick, Ovid, and the Celebration of Innocence." *The Review of English Studies* 50, no. 199 (August, 1999): 350. Traces Herrick's important response to the ancient Roman poet Ovid in his construction of the erotic.

Rollin, Roger B. *Robert Herrick*. Rev. ed. New York: Twayne, 1992. An excellent starting point for a study of Robert Herrick and his work; contains an opening chronology of the poet's life, as well as sustained discussion of the *Hesperides*' language, genres, sources, historical context, and critical reception.

Rollin, Roger B., and J. Max Patrick, eds. *"Trust to Good Verses": Herrick Tercentenary Essays*. Pittsburgh: University of Pittsburgh Press, 1978. These essays by literary scholars were written for a 1974 conference memorializing the three hundredth anniversary of Herrick's death, covering such diverse subjects as Herrick's politics, imagery, literary influences, and poetic musicality. Includes a good annotated bibliography.

SEE ALSO: First Duke of Buckingham; Charles I; Charles II (of England); Ben Jonson; Henry Lawes.

RELATED ARTICLES in *Great Events from History: The Seventeenth Century, 1601-1700:* 1642-1651: English Civil Wars; May, 1659-May, 1660: Restoration of Charles II.

JOHANNES AND ELISABETHA HEVELIUS
German-Polish astronomers

Johannes and Elisabetha Hevelius compiled the most accurate nontelescopic catalog of the stars. Johannes established an observatory in Gdansk, compiled detailed maps of the Moon, and published a book describing many comets, including four that he discovered. Elisabetha published a collection of engravings of constellations, including eleven new constellation groupings, seven of which are still in use.

JOHANNES HEVELIUS

BORN: January 28, 1611; Gdansk, Poland
DIED: January 28, 1687; Gdansk
ALSO KNOWN AS: Johann Hewel or Howelcke; Jan Heweliusz

ELISABETHA HEVELIUS

BORN: c. 1647; Gdansk?
DIED: 1693; Gdansk?
ALSO KNOWN AS: Catherina Elisabetha Koopman (given name)
AREAS OF ACHIEVEMENT: Astronomy, science and technology, scholarship

EARLY LIVES

Johannes Hevelius (hay-VAY-lee-uhs) was born to a noble family of at least ten children. His father was a prosperous property owner who operated a brewery. His early education was at a gymnasium in Gdansk from 1618 to 1624. He then spent three years at a school near Bromberg, Poland, before returning to the Danzig gymnasium for three more years. There he studied under a tutor who gave him private lessons in astronomy and instrument-making, in addition to the regular curriculum.

Johannes traveled to the University of Leiden in the Netherlands in 1630, where he studied law for one year, plus some mathematics and optics. During the next two years, he visited several scientists in Paris. He then re-

turned to Gdansk to work in his father's brewery and to study the constitution of Gdansk. In 1635, he married Katharina Rebeschke, the daughter of a wealthy Gdansk landowner. After observing the solar eclipse of June 1, 1639, Johannes began a lifetime of astronomical work and a long career of civic responsibilities.

In the year following his first wife's death in 1662, Johannes married Catherina Elisabetha Koopman, the well-educated sixteen-year-old daughter of a wealthy merchant. Although she was thirty-six years younger than her husband, she became his chief assistant in his astronomical work while hosting many visiting astronomers and raising three daughters.

LIVES' WORK

Johannes devoted his life to civic duties, corresponded with foreign astronomers, and worked on astronomy. His first civic office in Gdansk, begun in 1641, was honorary magistrate; in 1651, he became a city councillor. The astronomers he communicated with included the Dutchman Christiaan Huygens, who discovered the rings of Saturn in 1656; John Flamsteed, who was the first royal astronomer in England; and Edmond Halley, who first demonstrated the elliptical orbits of comets and became the second royal astronomer in England. His major occupation, however, was astronomy.

Starting with a small upper room as an astronomical observatory, Johannes added a small roofed tower in 1644, and later built a platform on his house with both a stationary and a rotating observatory. In 1644, he was the first to observe the phases of Mercury, further confirming the heliocentric system. After his father died in 1649, he took over the brewery and used the extra funds for telescopes and other astronomical equipment, which made his observatory, called Sternenburg, one of the finest in the world. He also manufactured his own instruments in his own workshop and had a printing press for publishing his observations.

In 1647, Johannes published his first important work, an atlas of the Moon called *Selenographia: Sive, lunae descriptio* (reproduced map, with English translation, 1966). In the introduction to this book, he illustrates and describes his optical lathe for grinding telescope lenses. He also describes several telescopes, including the largest one, which was some 11 feet long and had about a 50-power magnification. He includes a drawing of Saturn with two semicircular handles, records of the movements of the moons of Jupiter, and observations of sunspots and eclipses. In the rest of the book, he describes lunar markings, the apparent lunar motions called librations, and drawings in his own hand of the Moon. His engravings of the lunar surface are among the best of the seventeenth century and introduce many of the names of lunar craters, mountains, and other features that are still used today.

Johannes's second great work, *Cometographia* (study of comets), published in 1668, twenty-one years after his first book. Following some introductory engravings, including one of his house and observatories, he turns to discussion of the comet of 1652 and gives evidence contrary to Aristotle that it is located in space beyond the Moon. He also provides extensive information about comets of the two preceding centuries, including four that he discovered, and suggests that they move on parabolic paths around the Sun at the focus.

Johannes described his work in designing and making his astronomical instruments (celestial machines) in a two-volume work called *Machina coelestis* (1679), partially translated as *The Illustrated Account Given by Hevelius in His "Machina celestis" of the Method of Mounting His Telescopes and Erecting an Observatory* (1882). The two volumes describe more than a dozen large (up to 6 feet) quadrants and sextants made of copper and wood for measuring celestial positions, many of them based on designs of the Danish astronomer Tycho Brahe but with even greater accuracy than those of Brahe. He also described the design of several long telescopes with focal lengths ranging from about 25 to nearly 150 feet and lenses up to 8 inches in diameter, including the difficulties of mounting such large instruments. His longest telescopes turned out to be nearly useless, however.

After several assistants either died or were found to be unsatisfactory, Johannes opened his observatory to his second wife Elisabetha, who became his most accurate and diligent observer. She is shown in two plates of *Machina coelestis* assisting in Johannes's observatory. For about ten years, she helped to run the observa-

tory; in 1679, Johannes's house, observatories, instruments, workshop and most of his papers were destroyed by a fire. By the end of 1681, the observatory was rebuilt, but with fewer and inferior instruments. He labored for five more years in declining health before dying on his seventy-sixth birthday.

Elisabetha Hevelius carried on with the work after Johannes died and completed his most important collection of observations. Three years after his death, she published a catalog of the positions and magnitudes of 1,564 stars, a work called *Prodromus astronomiae* (1690; *The Star Atlas*, 1968), the largest star catalog to that date and the last one compiled without the aid of the telescope. It gave star positions to an accuracy of about one minute of arc, about twice as accurate as Brahe's measurements. Also in 1690, Elisabetha published a volume of fifty-six engravings of constellations. Her *Uranographia* (study of the heavens) included eleven new constellation groupings with seven names that are still used.

SIGNIFICANCE

Although Johannes Hevelius was one of the leading astronomers of the mid-seventeenth century and the most accurate of the declining breed of nontelescopic observers, he represents more of a transitional figure in the inevitable trend toward telescopic astronomy. He was challenged to use telescopic sights in place of plain sighting instruments by John Flamsteed and later by Robert Hooke. Hooke wrote a critical work on Hevelius's *Machina coelestis* called *Animadversions on the First Part of the Machina coelestis of the Honourable, Learned, and Deservedly Famous Astronomer Johannes Hevelius* (1674). The resulting controversy led the Royal Society in England to sponsor a 1679 visit to Gdansk by Edmond Halley, who concluded that Johannes could determine stellar positions without a telescope as accurately as Halley could with one at that point in time. Seven years later, in private correspondence, Halley altered this conclusion in favor of telescopic sights.

In his lunar studies, Johannes produced the first true atlas of the lunar surface and the best descriptions of librational cycles up to his time, providing a sound basis for further work in this area. His comet studies were especially useful to Halley in determining the elliptical orbits of comets. His most valuable contribution was his catalog of stars, which was reprinted by Flamsteed in 1725 and used well into the eighteenth century. The completion of this catalog by Elisabetha Hevelius, along with fifteen years of work with her husband before he died, established her as one of the rare women who was in a position to make important contributions to science in the seventeenth century.

—Joseph L. Spradley

FURTHER READING

Bell, Louis. *The Telescope*. New York: McGraw-Hill, 1922. The first chapter of this book on "The Evolution of the Telescope" has several pages on the contributions of Johannes Hevelius to the early development of the telescope.

Field, J. V., and Frank A. J. L. James, eds. *Renaissance and Revolution: Humanists, Scholars, Craftsmen, and Natural Philosophers in Early Modern Europe*. New York: Cambridge University Press, 1993. This collection on issues in the scientific revolution includes an essay entitled "Johannes Hevelius and the Visual Language of Astronomy," by Mary Winkler and Albert van Helden, with several copies of engravings from Johannes's *Selenographia*.

Hevelius, Johannes. *The Star Atlas*. Introduced and edited by V. P. Sheglov. Tashkent, Uzbekistan: FAN Press, 1968. A reproduction of 56 plates of Johannes

and Elisabetha's star catalog, compiled in cooperation with the Institute of Astronomy at the Academy of Sciences of the Uzbek, formerly part of the Soviet Union. Includes bibliographic footnotes.

McPike, Eugene Fairfield. *Hevelius, Flamsteed, and Halley: Three Contemporary Astronomers and Their Mutual Relations*. London: Taylor & Francis, 1937. This book reviews the controversy over telescopic versus nontelescopic sighting instruments.

Montgomery, Scott L. *The Moon and the Western Imagination*. Tucson: University of Arizona Press, 1999. This book describes Johannes's studies of the Moon in Chapter 11, "Johannes Hevelius: A Moon of Higher Origins," including several copies of engravings from the *Selenographia*.

SEE ALSO: David and Johannes Fabricius; Galileo; Edmond Halley; Robert Hooke; Christiaan Huygens; Johannes Kepler; Hans Lippershey.

RELATED ARTICLE in *Great Events from History: The Seventeenth Century, 1601-1700:* February, 1656: Huygens Identifies Saturn's Rings.

THOMAS HEYWOOD
English dramatist

Heywood was one of the most active playwrights in seventeenth century England, composing or contributing to almost two hundred plays, including the century's most popular translation of Ovid's Ars amatoria.

BORN: c. 1573; Lincolnshire, England
DIED: August, 1641; London, England
AREAS OF ACHIEVEMENT: Literature, theater

EARLY LIFE

Thomas Heywood (HAY-wood) was born in Lincolnshire county sometime between 1573 and 1575. Little else is known about his early life. He entered Cambridge for a brief period in 1591, where he was reportedly a fellow of Peterhouse. Given Heywood's adeptness at translating the works of classical Latin authors throughout his career, it is likely that his studies at Cambridge focused at least partly on Latin literature. Shortly after his time at the university, Heywood moved to London and soon began a career writing for the theater.

The earliest record of Heywood's activity in London indicates that his *The Four Prentices of London*

(pr. c. 1594, pb. 1615) was produced by Lord Admiral's Men, one of the leading theatrical companies in London, around 1594. By 1598, Heywood was established as a regular writer for the Lord Admiral's Men, an association that he maintained until 1599. During this time, he was mostly employed as a hack writer for the company, revising and tweaking scripts or literary sources for performance as well as contributing his own work. Heywood had associations with other theatrical companies in London around the same time, and his play *Edward IV, Parts I and II* (pr. 1599, pb. 1600) was premiered by the sixth earl of Derby's company in 1599.

LIFE'S WORK

Collaboration was a frequent practice in the writing of plays in Elizabethan and Jacobean England, and playwrights often did not take care to publicize their authorship of, or contribution to, any particular play—Ben Jonson being a notable exception. It is therefore difficult to determine authorship for most of the plays Heywood wrote either fully or partially; he claimed to have "had a hand in" over two hundred plays. It is known, however, that around 1600, Heywood became a member of the earl of Worcester's theatrical company, and he immediately became the company's most prolific source of dramatic material, providing on average one or more plays each month.

As a playwright for the Lord Admiral's Men and Worcester's company, Heywood developed a reputation as a popular writer of comedies. In actuality, Heywood showed a great deal of proficiency in all dramatic genres. One of his most popular plays during his lifetime, *If You Know Not Me, You Know Nobody: Or, The Troubles of Queen Elizabeth* (Part I pr., pb. 1605, Part II pr. 1605, pb. 1606), which recounts the early years of Queen Elizabeth I and the defeat of the Spanish Armada, is most accurately characterized as a chronicle history play, similar in scope to William Shakespeare's *Henry V* (pr. c. 1598-1599). *A Woman Killed with Kindness* (pr. 1603, pb. 1607), a tragedy that deals with the punishment of an unfaithful wife, was also one of Heywood's most successful efforts: It was published several times after its initial performance, and it is still regularly performed. Heywood's other plays during this period included *The Royal King and the Loyal Subject* (pr. c. 1602, pb. 1637), *The Wise Woman of Hogsdon* (pr. c. 1604, pb. 1638), and *The Fair Maid of the Exchange* (pb. 1607).

Heywood was an accomplished classicist throughout his lifetime, and his expertise with Latin texts inflected nearly every aspect of his literary career. His long poem *Troia Britannica* (1609) is essentially a compendium of several tales from classical mythology. Heywood composed a number of similar translations or adaptations for the stage in a set of plays that deal directly with classical stories: *The Golden Age: Or, The Lives of Jupiter and Saturn* (pr. before 1611, pb. 1611), *The Silver Age* (pr. 1612, pb. 1613), *The Brazen Age* (pr., pb. 1613) and *The Iron Age, Parts I and II* (pr. C. 1613, pb. 1632). Homer is the major source for the material in these plays, although Virgil and Ovid are drawn from as well. Although Heywood's adaptation of classical tales for the stage tended to be fairly straightforward, these plays also bear the indelible mark of Britain's attempt to see itself as a cultural descendant of the classical tradition (for example, London was sometimes called Troynovant, or "New Troy"), an idea that Heywood seems to have taken to heart.

In addition to his remarkable production of plays and translations, Heywood was active as a writer of pamphlets, or treatises. He injected himself into the debates over the theater by publishing *An Apology for Actors* (1612), a treatise that attempted to defend the moral validity of the London theaters. The English theater had

been a regular object of attack by Puritan polemicists, and a number of treatises vilifying the theater had been published, beginning with Stephen Gosson's *The Schoole of Abuse* (1579).

Heywood's treatise has often been regarded by modern scholars as inept, in part because of its utter mishandling of classical sources. However, it is more likely that Heywood, who was one of England's most capable Latinists, was deliberately parodying the Puritan treatises (especially since some of Heywood's "mistranslations" are exaggerated imitations of specific Puritan texts). At any rate, Heywood's tract was considered significant enough to warrant a full-fledged refutation, which was published only one year later by the anonymous author "J. G."

Heywood stopped writing plays for a few years starting in 1616, possibly because of his company's financial difficulties. He took up writing again in 1624, around the time he joined Queen Henrietta Maria's theatrical company. Over the next several years, Heywood produced a number of plays, including *The English Traveler* (pr. c. 1627, pb. 1633) and *The Late Lancashire Witches* (pr., pb. 1634; cowritten with Richard Brome). He also composed a number of masques for the court during this time, as would have been typical for a dramatist in the queen's company. He continued to produce masques until 1639, and he authored several works of nonfiction in the final decade of his life, including a study of the prophesies attributed to the wizard Merlin. Heywood died in London in August, 1641.

SIGNIFICANCE

Although Heywood never attained the status of other Renaissance and seventeenth century dramatists like Christopher Marlowe or Ben Jonson, his plays demonstrate command of a remarkable range of genres and styles. Many of his plays, particularly those based on classical literature or English history, offer a rich source of material for studying the production of history in early modern England, particularly as it relates to Britain's burgeoning nationalism.

In recent years, as Heywood's expertise in Latin literature has received more attention, his contribution to Renaissance Humanism has finally started to gain the recognition that it deserves. In particular, consideration of his translation of Ovid's *Ars amatoria* (c. 2 B.C.E.; *Art of Love*, 1612) is indispensable for any serious study of Ovidianism in seventeenth century England. Finally, Heywood's participation in contemporary debates over the theater and morality provides scholars with a unique vantage point for understanding the English reception of Puritan ideology, since Heywood was one of the few pamphleteers who actually had direct experience with the English theater.

—Joseph M. Ortiz

FURTHER READING

Barish, Jonas. *The Antitheatrical Prejudice*. Berkeley: University of California Press, 1981. The chapter on Puritan antitheatricalism contains a substantial discussion of Heywood's *An Apology for Actors*, although it misunderstands the parodic nature of the text. Nonetheless, this is the preeminent study of the early modern attacks on the theater, making it an important work for understanding the historical context of Heywood's writings on the theater.

Clark, Arthur Melville. *Thomas Heywood: Playwright and Miscellanist*. Oxford, England: Basil Blackwell, 1931. Although this book predates much of the twentieth century critical work on Heywood, it remains the most comprehensive biography of the playwright's life and career. The details of Heywood's professional life are well-researched and copiously documented.

McLuskie, Kathleen. *Dekker and Heywood: Professional Dramatists*. New York: St. Martin's Press, 1994. This book analyzes the dramatic careers of Heywood and Dekker, with particular regard to the social and cultural context of London in the early seventeenth century. Bibliography and index.

Stapleton, M. L., ed. *Thomas Heywood's "Art of Love."* Ann Arbor: University of Michigan Press, 2000. This is an excellent, carefully annotated modern edition of Heywood's translation of Ovid's *Ars amatoria*. Stapleton's introduction to the text provides a lucid and informative discussion of Heywood's career as a translator, as well as some more general thoughts about the status of translation in the Renaissance. Bibliography.

SEE ALSO: Henrietta Maria; Ben Jonson.

RELATED ARTICLE in *Great Events from History: The Seventeenth Century, 1601-1700:* c. 1601-1613: Shakespeare Produces His Later Plays.

HISHIKAWA MORONOBU
Japanese painter and printmaker

The founder of the ukiyo-e *school of printmaking, Hishikawa Moronobu was skilled in traditional Japanese painting styles. His basically monochrome prints, in the form of book illustrations, single sheets, and posters, served as the prototypes for the more colorful* ukiyo-e *prints developed by his successors a century later.*

BORN: 1618; Hota, Japan
DIED: 1694; Edo, Japan (now Tokyo, Japan)
ALSO KNOWN AS: Kichibe
AREA OF ACHIEVEMENT: Art

EARLY LIFE

Hishikawa Moronobu (hee-shee-kah-wah moh-roh-noh-boo) was born in the seaside town of Hota, in what is now Chiba Prefecture, east of Edo. His father, Kichizaemon, was a textile designer and brocade artisan who taught Moronobu skills he would later apply to woodcuts. After his father's death in 1662, Moronobu left the local textile business and went to Edo to become an artist. He apparently spent some time studying the traditional painting techniques of the Kano school and occasionally produced scroll paintings and standing-screen paintings for wealthy Edo merchants.

Moronobu's early years in Edo focused, however, on learning the art of producing woodcut illustrations with popular themes, first as illustrations for books, and then for picture albums (*ehon*), single prints (*ichimai-e*), and posters. The painter Iwasa Matabe, who died about a decade before Moronobu came to Edo, had painted pictures on popular themes commissioned by the shogun and other Edo notables. Iwasa is regarded by art historians as a forerunner of *ukiyo-e* because of his depiction of scenes from ordinary life, though both he and his audience were aristocratic. Iwasa's work may have inspired early woodcut artists such as Kambun Kyōshi (Master of the Kambun Period), an otherwise nameless artist credited with producing fifty or more sets of book illustrations and several dozen early prints on popular themes.

Emulating these recent masters, Moronobu began producing prints focusing on Kabuki actors (*yakusha-e*), courtesans, and exceptionally beautiful Edo women (*bijinga*). Most of the people depicted were actual persons well known in Edo, and the prints served as a form of publicity. They were popular with fans, who might lack the opportunity to see these celebrities in person. Since these actors and courtesans lived in the artificial environment of the entertainment world, the prints came to be called *ukiyo-e*, or pictures of the floating world, because they depict an unstable, insecure, unanchored social order. Some of Moronobu's entertainment prints were erotic or even pornographic, part of an *ukiyo-e* subgenre known by the euphemistic name *shunga*, or springtime pictures.

LIFE'S WORK

Hishikawa Moronobu's extant works are fairly sparse and are scattered in museums throughout the world, but his original output was very large. One of his famous *ehon* is *Buke hyakunin isshu* (1672; one hundred poems by one hundred samurai), a set of illustrations accompanying the poetry of noted samurai aristocrats. This picture album was designed to appeal to a merchant-class audience interested in martial arts figures. Moronobu also painted *byōbu*, paintings covering multiple panels or standing screens. His *Ueno hanami zu oshiebari byōbu* (c. 1688-1694; cherry-blossom viewing at Ueno), a six-panel set of folding screen paintings on silk using ink, color, and gold dust, is a panorama of parkland in Ueno, with character studies of people out to enjoy the scenery. Another screen shows scenes at an Edo Kabuki theater, the Nakamuraza, complete with a man at the entrance trying to attract customers and a view of a curtain call with the entire cast on stage.

Seventeenth century Japanese books and prints were generally produced from wooden block impressions. During the sixteenth century, woodblock printing was primarily used to produce copies of Buddhist scriptures and religious pictures, distributed by major Buddhist temples. Toward the end of the sixteenth century, however, illustrated books with secular themes began to appear in the Kyōto-Ōsaka area, as well as in Edo, after the latter city became the capital of the shogunate in the early seventeenth century.

While conventional illustrated books predominated in the Kyōto-Ōsaka area, a market developed in Edo for topical picture-books and for illustrations printed as separate sheets. By the mid-seventeenth century, there were a number of woodblock illustrators working for publishers in Edo. Moronobu is credited with having been the first such illustrator to persuade a publisher to print significant quantities of single-sheet illustrations without accompanying texts. These illustrations sold quite well, creating a public demand for more, and this early

achievement by Moronobu is regarded as the origin of Japanese woodblock prints as a distinct artistic genre.

Moronobu's hand-scrolls, long horizontal scrolls of sequential scenes designed for tabletop viewing, are also outstanding works of art. His *Henge ga maki* (fantastic transformation hand-scroll) is a curious combination of unwitting humans and menacing demons. His *Shokunin zukushi emaki* (craftspeople of various trades) is a pair of hand scrolls that show details of the work of various types of Edo artisans. This is a valuable source of information on the applied technology of the time and on modes of work and craftsmanship in late seventeenth century Edo. These scrolls include scenes from more than fifty different crafts and trades, including brush makers, street entertainers, swordsmiths, and sake brewers. In some cases, Moronobu's hand-scroll pictures derived from prints, since he sometimes both printed related scenes as separate sheets and pasted them together onto hand-scrolls.

Among Moronobu's woodblock prints are scenes from the Yoshiwara licensed quarters and the Edo Kabuki district, generally regarded as most typical of his work. These prints provide insights into the entertainment world of the time, which was frequented by merchants *(chōnin)* and samurai *(bushi)* alike. Since Moronobu's pictures are believed to have been faithful to reality, it is possible to identify individual theaters or cabarets of the time. In addition, individual woodcuts that were originally designed as book illustrations have also survived, including Moronobu's illustrated version of stories from the *Ise monogatari* (c. 980; *Tales of Ise*, 1968). Moronobu also sometimes portrayed religious themes, as in a surviving woodcut of the Buddhist sect founder Nichiren, praying for rain along with his followers.

While some artists may tend to underestimate their own importance, Moronobu seems not to have been one of them. He did not think of himself only as an *ukiyo-e* genre artist but referred to himself more broadly, as a Japanese artist *(Nihon-e shi)*. Actually, the first recorded use of the term *ukiyo-e* appeared in a *haiku* poem in a collection published in 1681, when Moronobu was already more than sixty years old. Moronobu himself first used the term in writing in 1682, in the expression *Yamato ukiyo-e* (Japanese *ukiyo-e*), apparently emphasizing that this form was part of Japan's national artistic heritage.

Moronobu's final years extended into the first part of the Genroku Era (1688-1704), a time regarded by many Japanese historians as the high point of Tokugawa art, theater, and literature. Although he was already seventy when the Genroku Era began, Moronobu is ranked by historians as one of the greatest artists of this era, along with the screen painter Ogata Kōrin and Kōrin's younger brother, the great potter and ceramic artist Ogata Kenzan (1663-1743).

SIGNIFICANCE

While most people today think of Japanese prints as being outstanding in their gradations and juxtapositions of vivid colors, woodcut technology in Moronobu's time was capable of producing little more than black-on-white, monochrome depictions. Since Moronobu was an accomplished traditional painter as well, he was able to paint over the main figures and details in color after the fact, transforming individual monochrome prints into color paintings. As a result, people today often do not realize that the pioneering Moronobu never made actual color prints.

After Moronobu's time, some prints came to be made using just a few colors, but it was not until the time of Suzuki Harunobi (1725-1770), more than half a century later, that it became technically possible to produce multicolor prints, known as *nishiki-e* (brocade prints), that were as striking in their use of color as the brocades that Moronobu had begun his career designing and creating, when he had first started out back in Hota.

Moronobu's own greatest contribution to the development of *ukiyo-e* art is thought to be his unique creation of a series of inventive subgenres, depicting various aspects of daily life and nightlife in Edo. The manner of depiction originated by Moronobu came to be first accepted, and then expected, by the general public. By the time Suzuki Harunobi began his creative career, he was able to focus his attention on technical improvements in the production values of *ukiyo-e* prints, since Moronobu

had already explored and developed most of the artistic themes used in them during the Edo Period.

—*Michael McCaskey*

FURTHER READING

Clark, Timothy. *The Dawn of the Floating World, 1650-1765: Early Ukiyo-e Treasures from the Museum of Fine Arts*. London: Royal Academy of Arts, 2001. A detailed catalog and analysis of a collection shown at the Boston Museum of Arts and then at the London Royal Academy.

Fahr-Becker, Gabriele. *Japanese Prints*. London: Taschen, 2002. An illustrated history of the development of Edo prints.

Gentles, Margaret. *Masters of the Japanese Print: Moronobu to Utamaro*. New York: Arno Press, 1976. An illustrated and annotated catalog of prints, beginning with the work of Hishikawa Moronobu.

Gerhart, Karen M. *The Eyes of Power: Art and Early Tokugawa Authority*. Honolulu: University of Hawaii Press, 1999. Focuses on art patronage by the Tokugawa shogunate in the seventeenth century.

Guth, Christine. *Art of Edo Japan: The Artist and the City, 1615-1868*. New York: H. N. Abrams, 1996. An illustrated general history of art in the Tokugawa shogunal city of Edo.

Kobayashi, Tadashi. *Ukiyo-e: An Introduction to Japanese Woodblock Prints*. New York: Kodansha International, 1997. A concise guide to woodblock prints by a Japanese prints expert.

SEE ALSO: Ogata Kōrin.

RELATED ARTICLE in *Great Events from History: The Seventeenth Century, 1601-1700:* 1688-1704: Genroku Era.

THOMAS HOBBES
English philosopher

A pioneer of modern political principles, Hobbes wrote Leviathan, *the English language's first great work of political philosophy.*

BORN: April 5, 1588; Westport, Wiltshire, England
DIED: December 4, 1679; Hardwick Hall, Derbyshire, England
AREA OF ACHIEVEMENT: Philosophy

EARLY LIFE

In his autobiography, Thomas Hobbes (HOBZ) tells a story, possibly apocryphal, regarding the circumstances of his birth and the relation of those circumstances to his political ideas. His mother, Hobbes says, was much alarmed by the approaching Spanish Armada, and her disquiet led to his premature birth on April 5, 1588. Thus, Hobbes claimed, he was born with an especially keen aversion to violence; he and fear were born twins. If his mother's timidity explains his reverence for peace, however, what explains the ardor and stubbornness with which Hobbes later developed and presented his political theory? The personality of Hobbes's father may present the answer. A "choleric man," Hobbes's father was a vicar who abandoned his family after taking part in a brawl in the doorway of his church.

Along with an older brother and sister, Hobbes was reared in the household of his uncle, Francis Hobbes. At the age of four, Thomas was sent to school at the Westport church, where he proved to be an able student. Subsequently, his education was put into the hands of Robert Latimer, a classicist with an extraordinary knack for teaching. Latimer took special pains to develop Hobbes's natural abilities. In 1603, Hobbes set off for Magdalen Hall, Oxford. He was put off by Oxford's archaic curriculum, however, and as a result, he did not always attend lectures. Instead, he chose to haunt bookshops in search of materials that would better stimulate and satisfy his curiosity.

After receiving a bachelor's degree in 1608, Hobbes took a position as tutor in the household of William Cavendish, who later became the second earl of Devonshire. This arrangement was an extraordinarily happy one and an important one for Hobbes's further intellectual development: The Devonshire house was far more stimulating an environment than Oxford had been, and Hobbes thrived there, deepening his study of various subjects within the liberal arts. In 1610, Hobbes accompanied his pupil on a tour of Europe, where he studied French and Italian. Back in England, Hobbes continued his explorations of the life of the mind, making the acquaintance of Francis Bacon in the early 1620's. A significant figure in the history of science, Bacon championed the inductive method. Hobbes's irreverence for Scholasticism was probably reinforced by Bacon's.

In 1629, Hobbes completed an English translation of Thucydides' account of the Peloponnesian War. Some Hobbes scholars have concluded that this work was selected because of the suspicion it casts on democracy. While there is little evidence to support this theory, the translation does tend to indicate that Hobbes was primarily a classicist at this point in his life. His intellectual focus, however, was about to undergo the first of two important changes.

Devonshire had died in 1628, after which Hobbes left the Cavendish household. In 1629, though, Hobbes again traveled to Europe, this time as a companion to the son

Thomas Hobbes. (Library of Congress)

of Sir Gervase Clifton. It was on this trip, according to seventeenth century author John Aubrey's *Lives of Eminent Men* (1813; also known as *Brief Lives*, 1898), that Hobbes fell "in love with geometry." This not only altered the course of Hobbes's intellectual efforts but also was to have a substantial effect on the form in which he later chose to express his political ideas. In 1630, Hobbes was called back into the service of Devonshire, this time as tutor to the third earl. In 1633, Hobbes again was able to visit Europe, where he renewed his interest in geometry and science and where he reportedly met briefly with Galileo.

In 1637, Hobbes returned to an England that was on the eve of a bitter and bloody civil war, its government and guiding political beliefs about to undergo more than a half-century of ferment. These historical events again shifted the focus of Hobbes's work, combining with his background and personality to make him both a notorious and a respected political theorist.

LIFE'S WORK

The political strife in England led Hobbes to proceed with what was to be the third part of an all-embracing work of natural philosophy and ethics. *The Elements of Law, Natural and Politic* (1640) was circulated in manuscript form by Hobbes. Written in Latin, the work begins with a theory of humankind, moving on to a discussion of the citizen. Given the unruliness of human nature, Hobbes concluded, human beings could live together in peace only if they submitted to an absolute sovereign. In the context of the time, this seems to make Hobbes a clear monarchist, but Hobbes based his defense of absolutism not on divine right but rather on expediency and consent. Expediency causes men to enter into a contract with the sovereign in which they exchange most of their natural freedom for the security of stable (that is to say, *absolute*) government. Thus, Hobbes put forward a version of social contract theory.

This type of philosophy did not please the Royalists any more than it did Parliamentarians. The latter rejected Hobbes, because his theory supported absolute monarchy. The former understood all too well the dangerous

---

HOBBES ON THE STATE OF NATURE

Hobbes argues in Leviathan *that people must submit to the rule of an absolute monarch, because without such a figure to establish and govern a society of law, people would be consigned to the state of nature, in which everyone is at war with everyone else and they must constantly fear for their lives. The following is Hobbes's most famous description of this undesirable natural state.*

Whatsoever therefore is consequent to a time of war, where every man is enemy to every man, the same consequent to the time wherein men live without other security than what their own strength and their own invention shall furnish them withal. In such condition there is no place for industry, because the fruit thereof is uncertain: and consequently no culture of the earth; no navigation, nor use of the commodities that may be imported by sea; no commodious building; no instruments of moving and removing such things as require much force; no knowledge of the face of the earth; no account of time; no arts; no letters; no society; and which is worst of all, continual fear, and danger of violent death; and the life of man, solitary, poor, nasty, brutish, and short.

Source: From *Leviathan*, by Thomas Hobbes (London: Andrew Crooke, 1651), Chapter 13. http://oregonstate.edu/instruct/phl302/texts/hobbes/leviathan-contents.html. Accessed April 19, 2005.

---

implications of social contract theory, for consent, unlike divine right, can be withdrawn. Thus, when the momentum toward civil war began to increase in 1640, Hobbes quickly exiled himself to the safety of Paris, "the first of all that fled," as he himself put it. In Paris, Hobbes took up the relatively safe project of writing "objections" to the work of René Descartes—but his political pen had been far from quieted.

In the year the First English Civil War finally broke out, Hobbes published the first edition of *De Cive* (1642, revised edition 1647; *Philosophical Rudiments Concerning Government and Society*, 1651), in which he argued that, rightly understood, a Christian state and a Christian church were united under the leadership of the sovereign. Hobbes was responding to a world in which religious radicalism had become a source of acute political strife. To Hobbes, the stewardship of religion by the secular ruler was a safeguard against religious fanaticism, holy wars, and even intolerance. In 1647, an expanded version of *De Cive* was published, and in 1650 the manuscript of *The Elements of Law, Natural and Politic* was published in two parts, *Human Nature* (1650) and *De Corpore Politico* (1650; of the body politic).

The following year, Hobbes published the centerpiece of his political philosophy, *Leviathan* (1651). Wonderfully written in the brash, colorful English of the day, *Leviathan* is remarkably consistent with Hobbes's

HOBBES'S MAJOR WORKS
1642   *De Cive* (revised 1647; *Philosophical Rudiments Concerning Government and Society*, 1651)
1650   *Human Nature*
1650   *De Corpore Politico*
1651   *Leviathan*
1656   *The Questions Concerning Liberty, Necessity, and Chance*
1679   *Behemoth: The History of the Causes of the Civil Wars of England*

earlier political treatises. Like them, it seeks to establish his political theory on a scientific basis, proceeding from point to point nearly in the manner of a geometric proof. Nor had Hobbes's substantive position changed: He still argued that absolute rule was needed in order to ensure civil peace, but also that the sovereign's power was based on consent. Where *Leviathan* broke new ground was in its unforgettably graphic portrayal of the "state of nature" (that is, the situation that precedes and leads to the social contract) and the addition of two lengthy sections in which Hobbes complements his secular arguments with an examination of the political principles suggested by Scripture and by true Christianity.

Life in the state of nature, according to Hobbes, is "solitary, poore, nasty, brutish, and short." Everywhere there is the fear of violent death. Indeed, the state of nature is actually a state of war, with each man the potential enemy of every other. There is equality in the state of nature, but it is an equality based on mortality, since even the strongest can be overcome by force or guile. There is also an abundance of liberty, since man has a right to anything he can take and hold. With this natural liberty, however, comes acute insecurity: One's possessions (and indeed one's very life) are constantly in jeopardy. Given these conditions, humans are not likely to prosper or grow comfortable enough to develop and enjoy the arts, letters, and other advantages afforded by civilization.

It is this bleak picture, Hobbes asserts, that demonstrates the need for voluntary submission to an absolute sovereign. Man's fear of violent death propels him toward a state of peace. Natural laws, based in reason, show how peace can be achieved—that is, by entering into a contractual relationship with an absolute sovereign. The establishment of such a common power alone can ensure civil peace. In Hobbes's view, stability could be achieved only where sovereignty was undivided and

absolute. Otherwise, civil authority would come undone, and the brutishness of the state of nature would reassert itself.

To this justification of absolute rule, rooted in human psychology and rational argument, Hobbes added two lengthy sections based on Scripture. In "Of a Christian Commonwealth," he argues that a theologically pure city of God is not possible in this life and a truly Christian commonwealth is that which effectively preserves peace. In "The Kingdom of Darkness," Hobbes cites scriptural evidence to refute the arguments of those who would in fact subordinate civil peace to theological purity, using the metaphor of darkness to suggest both the absence of truth and the presence of Satan. Thus, Hobbes argues for a secular state with a minimalist public religion aimed at ensuring popular allegiance to the sovereign, who in turn ensures civil peace.

What people wished to believe privately was of no interest to Hobbes, nor should it be of interest to the state in his eyes. This position challenged both Papists and Presbyterians, who argued that ecclesiastical authority ought to be supreme. To Hobbes, however, religion was too great a source of social conflict and schism to be elevated to a station of sovereignty. Though religion is interestingly absent from Hobbes's portrayal of the state of nature, it certainly did play a prominent role in the English Civil War. Such divisiveness, Hobbes believed, must be minimized by keeping public religion under the control of civil authority.

Hobbes closed *Leviathan* with a section titled "Review and Conclusions," in which he handled the tricky question of where one's allegiance belongs, should a sovereign be successfully overthrown or conquered. For Hobbes, obligation ended when the sovereign could no longer honor his side of the contract. At this point, a new contract comes into force with the newly established sovereign. Some observers have accused Hobbes of taking this position because of the imminent victory of Oliver Cromwell over the Royalists. Indeed, Hobbes did return to England shortly after Cromwell came to power, despite the fact that he had maintained close contact with Charles II while both were in France. Nevertheless, Hobbes's position regarding conquest is consistent with the rest of his political theory. The establishment and maintenance of stable political authority is the first priority for Hobbes. Forming a resistance movement to prolong conflict instead of allowing for the emergence of a new order clearly contravenes the goal of civil peace.

In any case, Hobbes's return to England was harmonious and remained so after the restoration of the English monarchy under Charles II in 1660. To be sure, Hobbes had his enemies; he was accused of being an atheist, and "Hobbism" became a term of abuse, denoting the worst kind of freethinking and godlessness. Nevertheless, Charles II extended to Hobbes the protection of the Crown and the security of a very decent pension. For his part, Hobbes avoided writing openly on politically sensitive topics, though he continued to answer personal charges and wrote extensively on mathematics and philosophy.

Not surprisingly, Hobbes did return to political themes in his writing on occasion, most conspicuously in a dialogue entitled *Behemoth: The History of the Causes of the Civil Wars of England* (1679), but he allowed this and other political works to be suppressed in order to avoid a new round of accusations. Instead, notorious at home and a celebrity abroad, Hobbes kept what was for him a low profile, constantly writing, engaging in lively discourse over the philosophical issues of the day, and, late in his life, returning to the classics to produce translations of Greek poet Homer's epics, the *Iliad* (c. 750 B.C.E.; English translation, 1611) and the *Odyssey* (c. 725 B.C.E.; English translation, 1614). Hobbes died at Hardwick Hall in Derbyshire on December 4, 1679.

SIGNIFICANCE

Hobbes failed to establish an authoritative methodology for political discourse, and his defense of absolutism was soon neutralized by various constitutional theorists, John Locke's *Two Treatises of Government* (1690), and the course of English history. Hobbes's legacy is nevertheless substantial, however, in terms of both his general approach to political theory and his conclusions about human nature and political institutions. Many college courses in modern political philosophy begin with Hobbes, who was a distinctively modern thinker, especially by virtue of his fundamentally secular methodology. Hobbes based his political theory on observation and reason rather than revelation or metaphysics. As such, he can be seen as a founding father of modern political inquiry and social science in general.

Also distinctly modern is Hobbes's emphasis on individualism and self-interest, or egoism. For Hobbes, a convincing political prescription must recognize the essential selfishness of human nature and also be consistent with the dictates of rational, or "enlightened," self-interest. In fact, Hobbes utilizes self-interest as an ordering principle of his argument. This formula for human harmony serves as the basis for contemporary free market economics and liberal democracy (or, as it is called

by some, interest-group liberalism). It is the foundation of the dominant and pervasive ideology of the United States and other Western nations: liberal individualism. Hobbes can also be linked to the development of utilitarianism and legal positivism, solidifying his status as a source of many disparate branches of modern thought.

All this, however, refers primarily to Hobbes's *approach* to questions of human conduct rather than to his conclusions. Have his answers become completely obsolete? There is no doubt that absolutism has gone out of vogue. Indeed, the concept of absolutism has been relegated to the junk heap of history, with authoritarianism, totalitarianism, corporatism, and other designations (some more or less scientific, others clearly ideological) being put forward. Hobbes's absolutism was both conceptually and practically tame compared to modern-day dictatorships. Hobbes was speaking of a form of government with natural limitations. His sovereign, bereft of contemporary propaganda devices and free of modern political religion, lacked both the power and the incentive to exercise totalitarian control. Alas, the natural limits on power assumed by Hobbes are no longer operative, if they ever were. (Elizabeth I, for example, may have lacked the power to enforce full modern totalitarian rule, but she clearly did not lack the desire, were it but possible.)

Nevertheless, there is a profound validity to Hobbes's political theory. There are, first, some political situations that resemble the Hobbesian state of nature enough to recommend Hobbes's conclusions. True, in these instances, there is usually the confusion of faction and fanaticism, and there is—almost without exception—a family structure, all elements not present in Hobbes's conception of the state of nature, but these complexities do not contravene the clear need for a well-established common power to maintain peace and order as a prerequisite for further political progress. As Hobbes pointed out, a minimum of civil order is a prerequisite for a liberty that is truly secure.

There is also something universal about Hobbes's realism. Indeed, there is even a discernible Hobbesian element in American politics, reflected, for example, in the 1787-1788 series of papers known as *The Federalist*, in which James Madison wrote (in number 51) that government is "the greatest of all reflections of human nature," since "if men were angels, no government would be necessary." Like many other American statesmen, Madison feared tyranny and sought an effective form of limited government as a safeguard, but, like Hobbes, Madison also feared anarchy and lawlessness. Without effective government, the vicious side of human nature would create a situation in which neither property nor individuals were secure. Thus, while he did not demonstrate the need for absolute government, Hobbes did provide a powerful argument for the necessity of stable government, given the dark side of human nature.

—Ira Smolensky

FURTHER READING

Bowle, John. *Hobbes and His Critics: A Study in Seventeenth Century Constitutionalism*. London: Jonathan Cape, 1951. Reprint. New York: Barnes & Noble, 1969. Gives a detailed account of the response to Hobbes's theory of absolutism from those who, laying the groundwork for the Glorious Revolution, were formulating mechanisms and principles aimed at imposing legal limitations on government.

Hobbes, Thomas. *Leviathan*. Baltimore: Pelican Classics, 1968. A handsome, unabridged edition of Hobbes's most famous political work. Includes a detailed introductory essay by C. B. Macpherson and reproduces the illustration on the title page of the 1651 edition.

Mace, George. *Locke, Hobbes, and the "Federalist Papers": An Essay on the Genesis of the American Political Heritage*. Carbondale: Southern Illinois University Press, 1979. A controversial work, in which Mace argues that *The Federalist* reflects a more Hobbesian than Lockean view. Places both Locke and Hobbes in the context of the founding of the United States.

Macpherson, C. B. *The Political Theory of Possessive Individualism: Hobbes to Locke*. New York: Oxford University Press, 1962. Macpherson argues that both Hobbes and Locke reflected the possessive individualist premises of emerging capitalist society, mistaking these premises for eternal principles of human nature. The book, therefore, constitutes a critique of Hobbes's realism about human nature.

Martinich, A. P. *Hobbes: A Biography*. New York: Cambridge University Press, 1999. A more recent scholarly biography, providing extensive detail about Hobbes's life, writings, and times.

Sorrell, Tom, ed. *The Cambridge Companion to Hobbes*. New York: Cambridge University Press, 1996. A collection of essays that show the wide range of Hobbes's intellectual preoccupations, including science and mathematics as well as political theory.

Sullivan, Vickie B. *Machiavelli, Hobbes, and the Formation of a Liberal Republicanism in England*. New York: Cambridge University Press, 2004. Sullivan argues that Hobbes and other seventeenth and eighteenth century writers were more liberal in their defense of republicanism than is commonly believed.

Tuck, Richard. *Hobbes: A Very Short Introduction*. New York: Oxford University Press, 2002. In this 148-page book, Tuck re-evaluates Hobbes's philosophy, maintaining that Hobbes was not a pessimist but was passionately concerned with the refutation of skepticism.

Wolin, Sheldon. *The Politics of Vision: Continuity and Innovation in Western Political Thought*. Boston: Little, Brown, 1960. Expanded ed. Princeton, N.J.: Princeton University Press, 2004. A popular and stylish textbook on the history of political philosophy, Wolin's work devotes a lengthy chapter to Hobbes. Hobbes is seen as a prophet of modern society, in which impersonal rules and competition between interests have come to replace notions of a close-knit political community.

SEE ALSO: Charles I; Charles II (of England); Oliver Cromwell; Galileo.

RELATED ARTICLES in *Great Events from History: The Seventeenth Century, 1601-1700:* 1642-1651: English Civil Wars; 1651: Hobbes Publishes *Leviathan*; May, 1659-May, 1660: Restoration of Charles II; 1690: Locke Publishes *Two Treatises of Government*.

ROBERT HOOKE
English scientist

As curator of experiments for England's Royal Society, Hooke proved to be one of the greatest experimentalists and inventors of the seventeenth century, contributing to a wide range of scientific fields. As city surveyor for London, he helped rebuild the city after the great fire of 1666.

BORN: July 18, 1635; Freshwater, Isle of Wight, England
DIED: March 3, 1703; London, England
AREAS OF ACHIEVEMENT: Science and technology, architecture

EARLY LIFE

Robert Hooke was born into the household of John Hooke, a minister, and his second wife, Cecelie. He was so sickly as a child that his parents did not expect him to survive, and frequent headaches later kept him from attending school. As a result, Hooke was schooled at home and largely left to his own interests. These included drawing and the inner workings of machines, which he disassembled and used as guides for making his own devices; for instance, he constructed wooden clocks and a working model of a warship, complete with firing cannons.

Hooke's father died in 1648, whereupon the thirteen-year-old collected his inheritance and went to London. At first he intended to become the apprentice of Sir Peter Lely (né Pieter Van der Faes), a celebrated painter of miniature portraits, but he soon changed his mind and entered Westminster School, a premier preparatory school. There Hooke impressed the headmaster, Richard Busby, with his talent for language and geometry and his mechanical skills. With Busby's special tutelage and support, Hooke entered Christ Church College, Oxford, in 1653.

At Oxford, Hooke eventually joined a group of natural philosophers who viewed nature as a vast mechanism and wanted to reveal how it worked. Some members of this group, including Sir Christopher Wren and Robert Boyle, became Hooke's lifelong friends and collaborators. In 1657, Boyle hired Hooke to construct laboratory equipment and help with experiments. Hooke's vacuum pump, a famous instrument of its day, permitted Boyle to explore the properties of air, part of the research that led to Boyle's law (published 1662). At the same time, Hooke began his lasting interest in chronometers as he sought to invent a durable shipborne watch for use in determining longitudes.

LIFE'S WORK

Hooke's first solo publication was a 1661 pamphlet explaining capillary action. The work so impressed contemporary scientists that, with the help of Wren and Boyle, Hooke was hired as curator of experiments for the newly founded Royal Society in 1662 and was elected a full member the following year. His duties for the society were onerous: For the benefit of members, he was to perform "three or four considerable experiments" of his own at each weekly meeting, as well as any that members themselves suggested. This he did with ingenuity and gusto, setting a high intellectual standard for the Royal Society.

During the next twenty-six years, in hundreds of experiments, Hooke investigated the nature of light, air, gravity, magnetism, gunpowder, comets and other celestial phenomena, optics, chronometers (particularly the use of springs and pendulums), lightning, earthquakes, respiration, circulation, fossils, and medical treatments, while also inventing carriages, the iris diaphragm, meteorological instruments, watches, and a wide variety of scientific tools. In 1677, he began a five-year term as secretary of the Royal Society, and he later served on its council, while also caring for the society's collection of rarities and its library.

Hooke found yet further scientific posts, each with a considerable workload. In 1664, John Cutler, a wealthy merchant, endowed a lecture series especially for Hooke in which he was to discuss the practical sciences and trades. In 1665, Hooke became Gresham College's professor of geometry; the appointment included an apartment in the college's London premises, which remained his home from then on. Amid these manifold duties, Hooke published one of the masterpieces of seventeenth century science literature, *Micrographia* (1665). It quickly became a best-seller, admired for the wide range of topics discussed, including new theories of light and combustion, as well as for the beautiful drawings of objects and creatures that Hooke had examined under his improved microscope. The book established the importance of the microscope as a scientific instrument and embodied Hooke's guiding principle, drawn from the ideas of Francis Bacon, that philosophers must base their understanding of the world on rigorous observation and experimentation; theory must arise from demonstrable fact.

In subsequent publications, Hooke formulated the

law of elasticity (now known as Hooke's law), which states that stress in springs is directly proportionate to strain. That is, the force applied to and released by coiling and uncoiling a spring is directly proportionate to the amount of deformation undergone by that spring. Hooke also conducted an early analysis of harmonic motion, helped found the fields of meteorology and crystallography, proposed an explanation for celestial dynamics, and advanced explanations (broadly correct) for the origin of fossils and the evolution of species during environment change.

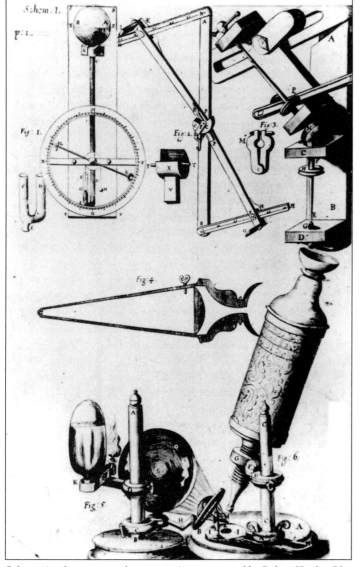

Schematic of a seventeenth century microscope used by Robert Hooke. (National Library of Medicine)

Following the Great Fire of London in 1666, Hooke helped to rebuild the devastated central city. He was appointed city surveyor in 1667, responsible for laying out the new streets, designing many new public buildings and overseeing their construction, enforcing building codes, and settling property disputes. He executed these many tasks in coordination with his friend Wren, who had been appointed royal surveyor. This partnership broadened when Hooke became an assistant and virtual partner in Wren's architectural firm. Hooke designed private houses and public buildings on his own, including Bedlam Hospital, the Royal College of Physicians, and the towering monument memorializing the fire; he assisted Wren in many other projects, including designing the new Saint Paul's Cathedral.

Hooke's official posts and private projects left him a wealthy man when he died at Gresham College in 1703, but not a happy one. He was a long-standing hypochondriac, and continual experiments in self-dosing, as well as overwork, impaired his health. Furthermore, bitter disputes with other scientists over priority in making discoveries and stating theories had gradually changed him from a gregarious, collegial genius to a suspicious, prickly recluse.

SIGNIFICANCE

Hooke has an unfortunate, undeserved distinction. His memory was almost immediately and completely eclipsed by the reputations of both his friends and his foes. During his lifetime, he had an international reputation as the premier experimentalist in England, and his biographers have called him the first professional scientist in an era when most people interested in research were aristocratic dabblers. Science historians view Hooke as a key figure in the early development of the Royal Society. In fact, Hooke was so thoroughly associated with science and the Royal Society that when Thomas Shadwell satirized the society in his play *The Virtuoso* (pr., pb. 1676), he based his main character on Hooke.

Despite his experimental genius and mechanical talent, however, Hooke's energies were scattered, and he seldom had the time or the mathematical skill to investigate topics fully. His insights were usually remarkably accurate and his suggested solutions to problems basically correct; still, he left it to others to supply proof. Accordingly, Hooke failed to get credit for many ideas that others pursued and developed largely or solely on the basis of his work. Even his architectural achievements were frequently attributed to Wren. Until a revival of interest in him around the three-hundred-year anniversary of his death, he was known almost solely for Hooke's law. Even some histories of the Royal Society omitted or glossed over his role in its founding.

Hooke quarreled with the great Dutch scientist Christiaan Huygens over the invention of a spring-driven watch for use at sea and, worse still, with Sir Isaac Newton over the nature of light and the theory of universal gravitation. Hooke held that light was composed of waves; Newton insisted it was made up of tiny particles (both were later shown to be right). Hooke claimed to have first stated that gravity was centered in bodies and decreased in strength by the square of the distance between those bodies (the inverse-square law), but he could not demonstrate it mathematically. Newton did so in *Philosophiae Naturalis Principia Mathematica* (1687; *The Mathematical Principles of Natural Philosophy*, 1729; best known as the *Principia*) and ridiculed Hooke's claim to the discovery. After Newton became president of the Royal Society, Hooke's influence quickly waned. At the same time, Newton's insistence upon rigorous mathematical demonstration in scientific investigations became the intellectual standard instead of Hooke's style of hypothesis and experimentation. Nevertheless, Hooke's scientific methods and ideas were pervasively influential during his lifetime, affecting the work even of such rivals as Newton.

—*Roger Smith*

FURTHER READING

Cooper, Michael. *"A More Beautiful City": Robert Hooke and the Rebuilding of London After the Great Fire*. Stroud, Gloucestershire, England: Sutton, 2003. Offers a brief sketch of Hooke's life and work in science, while discussing in detail his architectural work and role in rebuilding London. Maps, illustrations, and manuscript reproductions.

'Espinasse, Margaret. *Robert Hooke*. Berkeley: University of California Press, 1956. This brief biography proposes that Hooke's conflict with Isaac Newton entailed a change in how science was pursued in England, from broad, practical empirical studies to narrower, mathematical induction.

Inwood, Stephen. *The Forgotten Genius: The Biography of Robert Hooke, 1635-1703*. San Francisco, Calif.: MacAdam/Cage, 2003. Inwood explains Hooke's varied scientific achievements lucidly and discusses the attendant controversies evenhandedly, suggesting that a tendency in Hooke to overstate his claims led him into conflicts.

Jardine, Lisa. *The Curious Life of Robert Hooke: The Man Who Measured London*. New York: HarperCollins, 2004. Jardine discusses Hooke's grueling schedule of work for the Royal Society, his partnership with Christopher Wren, and his official duties for London and how these affected his research, professional standing, and health.

Robinson, Henry W., and Walter Adams, eds. *The Diary of Robert Hooke, 1672-1680*. London: Wykeham, 1968. This immensely detailed record of eight years in Hooke's life testifies to the variety, intensity, and burden of his workload.

SEE ALSO: Robert Boyle; Christiaan Huygens; Antoni van Leeuwenhoek; Sir Isaac Newton; Sir Christopher Wren.

RELATED ARTICLES in *Great Events from History: The Seventeenth Century, 1601-1700:* 1601-1672: Rise of Scientific Societies; 1660's-1700: First Microscopic Observations; 1660-1692: Boyle's Law and the Birth of Modern Chemistry; September 2-5, 1666: Great Fire of London.

THOMAS HOOKER
English-born colonial American theologian

Hooker was a major theologian within the Calvinist tradition. In addition to writing a cogent defense of the Congregational form of church government, he advocated democratic ideals and made a significant contribution to the framing of Connecticut's first constitution.

BORN: probably July 7, 1586; Markfield, Leicestershire, England
DIED: July 7, 1647; Hartford, Connecticut
AREAS OF ACHIEVEMENT: Religion and theology, government and politics

EARLY LIFE

Thomas Hooker was born the son of a head servant of the powerful Digby family. He most likely attended the grammar school at the nearby Market Bosworth. In 1604, Hooker was awarded a fellowship to attend Cambridge University. By then, he had already been attracted to the Protestant movement called Puritanism, which was influenced by the austere teachings of John Calvin. After briefly studying at Queens College, Cambridge, Hooker transferred to Emmanuel College, whose members were known to include many Puritan sympathizers. He was awarded a B.A. in 1608 and an M.A. in 1611. For the next seven years, he taught religion and catechism at Emmanuel College.

While teaching at Emmanuel, Hooker had a profound religious experience. Convinced of his divine calling, he preached a series of sermons on the nature of spiritual rebirth, which would remain a major theme throughout his career. In 1618, a man named Francis Drake, the patron of Saint George's parish in Esher, Surrey, appointed Hooker to be the church rector. One of his major tasks at Esher was to attend to the spiritual welfare of Drake's wife, Joan, who was profoundly depressed and had attempted suicide. His apparent success in helping the distraught woman promoted Hooker's reputation as a caring minister. In 1621, Hooker married Mrs. Drake's maid, Susanna Garbrand. The couple had at least six children, of whom four survived their father.

LIFE'S WORK

In 1625, following the death of Joan Drake, Hooker moved to Chelmsford, Essex, where he preached and lectured in the Church of Saint Mary. He also began a school. Essex had a large network of Puritan ministers. Hooker quickly became one of the respected leaders of the movement, and his sermons on conversion attracted considerable attention. He had developed a perspective called preparationist theology, arguing that spiritual rebirth occurs gradually over an extended period rather than in a single flash of insight. Like other Puritans, he believed the Church of England had not sufficiently purified itself of Catholic doctrines and practices, including continuation of the title "priest" and the sign of the cross. Committed to the local autonomy of congregations, Hooker began to criticize the authority and power of the bishops.

At this time, William Laud, the future archbishop of Canterbury, was already leading a crusade against the Nonconformists. In 1629, he required Hooker to appear before a church court to defend his teachings and criticisms of the Anglican Church. Although released on bond, Hooker was recalled the next year to appear before Laud's Court of High Commission. To avoid prison, Hooker went into hiding. In 1631, he fled England, joining other Puritan refugees in Holland. While working as an assistant minister in Delft, he published his first book, *The Soules Preparation for Christ* (1632), which was essentially a collection of sermons. He also met some of the organizers of the Massachusetts Bay Colony, and he decided to join a group from Essex that was establishing residence in Newtown (now Cambridge).

On September 4, 1633, Hooker arrived in New England with John Cotton and his future assistant, Samuel Stone. In Newtown, Hooker and Stone led in the foundation of a church based on Congregational principles. Hooker was soon involved in local controversies. A skillful mediator, he helped to resolve some of the differences between civil leaders and the colony's governor, John Winthrop. In 1634, the magistrates asked him for advice about John Endicott's mutilation of the English flag. Endicott had cut out the cross from the flag, based on the idea that the image of the cross was an idolatrous relic of papal superstition. In a thirteen-page discussion, "Touching the Cross in the Banners" (1634), Hooker concluded that the cross was a mere symbol rather than an idol or object of worship.

The religious ideas of Anne Hutchinson and John Wheelwright proved to be of greater consequence for the colony than those of Endicott. In 1637, Hooker and Peter Bulkeley of Concord presided over a synod convened to consider the antinomian doctrine of Hutchinson and Wheelwright, which basically asserted that those Christians directly guided by the spirit might disregard civic laws. The synod condemned eighty-two errors taught by Hutchinson and Wheelwright, providing a basis for their eventual expulsion from Massachusetts. The synod also endorsed the preparation theology of Hooker and his colleagues.

As the Newtown congregation grew, its members began to need more land for farming. They decided to sell their property to a new group of immigrants and to relocate on the fertile banks of the Connecticut River. In 1636, Hooker moved to the new settlement, which was named Hartford after the birthplace of Samuel Stone. About the same time, other groups also left Massachusetts to begin other settlements along the river. Because Connecticut was outside the Massachusetts charter, the new towns had the task of forming a new government, a task that was delayed in part by the 1637 war with the Pequot Indians.

In 1638, representatives from the towns held a general court to write a framework for a new system of government, called the Fundamental Orders. Hooker addressed the delegates with a sermon declaring that the people had the ultimate authority to decide the powers of a government and to choose the public magistrates. Historical sources are unclear about the extent to which he participated in the actual drafting of the Fundamental Orders.

Hooker was increasingly recognized as one of the spiritual leaders of New England. His published sermons, with titles like *The Soules Humiliation* (1637) and *The Soules Possession of Christ* (1638), were highly respected. During the 1640's, the religious upheavals in England led to considerable debate about church government. In 1643, Hooker and other ministers of Massachusetts and Connecticut were invited to attend the Westminster Assembly of Calvinist theologians. They declined because the assembly was dominated by Presbyterians unsympathetic to New England's system of independent congregations. An assembly of Congregational ministers requested Hooker to defend their position. Hooker's influential response, *A Survey of the Summe of Church-Discipline* (1648), was published posthumously, as was his defense of infant baptism, *The Covenant of Grace Opened* (1649).

SIGNIFICANCE

As historian Perry Miller has demonstrated, Hooker probably did not invent any new doctrines, but he did articulate, lucidly and with conviction, religious and political views widely held by moderate Puritans of the time. Nevertheless, Hooker defended democratic values more

than most of his contemporaries, and he apparently had some influence over the formation of the Fundamental Orders of Connecticut, which some historians consider the first written constitution in America.

Hooker's *A Survey of the Summe of Church-Discipline* was a highly respected defense of New England's system of church government. It allowed for more tolerance for diversity and human imperfection than many Puritan works, and it was widely cited in the discussions that resulted in the Cambridge Platform of 1648.

—*Thomas Tandy Lewis*

FURTHER READING

Ball, John H. *Chronicling the Soul's Wandering: Thomas Hooker and His Morphology of Conversion.* Lanham, Md.: University Press of America, 1992. Presents Hooker as a physician of the soul who specialized in the psychology of conversion.

Bremer, Francis. *The Puritan Experiment: New England Society from Bradford to Edwards.* Boston: University Press of New England, 1995. A helpful study that emphasizes the social aspects of Puritanism.

Bush, Sargent, Jr. *The Writings of Thomas Hooker: Spiritual Adventurer in Two Worlds.* Madison: University of Wisconsin Press, 1980. A good selection of Hooker's sermons and other theological works, with an excellent introduction that summarizes his ideas.

Hall, David, ed. *Puritans in the New World: A Critical Anthology.* Princeton, N.J.: Princeton University Press, 2004. Includes a helpful up-to-date introduction to the topic and two well-chosen selections from Hooker's writings.

LaPlante, Eve. *American Jezebel: The Uncommon Life of Anne Hutchinson, the Woman Who Defied the Puritans.* New York: HarperCollins, 2004. An interesting study of the antinomian controversy, with a very unflattering view of Hooker and other Puritan leaders.

Mather, Cotton. *Magnalia Christi Americana.* Reprint. New York: Russell & Russell, 1967. A classic Puritan work of 1702 that includes a biography under the title "The Light of the Western Churches: Or, The Life of Mr. Thomas Hooker."

Miller, Perry. *The New England Mind.* 2 vols. Boston: Beacon Press, 1939. A classic study of Puritanism, with many interesting comments on Hooker.

Shuffelton, Frank. *Thomas Hooker, 1586-1647.* Princeton, N.J.: Princeton University Press, 1977. A valuable full-length biography that emphasizes doctrinal and political controversies.

Taylor, Robert. *Colonial Connecticut: A History.* Millwood, N.Y.: KTO Press, 1979. Useful summary that has an especially good account of the writing of the colony's constitution.

Williams, George, and Sargent Bush, Jr., eds. *Thomas Hooker: Writings in England and Holland, 1626-1633*. Cambridge, Mass.: Harvard University Press, 1975. In addition to Hooker's early writings, the book contains useful essays by the editors and a comprehensive bibliography.

SEE ALSO: John Cotton; Anne Hutchinson; William Laud; John Winthrop.

RELATED ARTICLES in *Great Events from History: The Seventeenth Century, 1601-1700:* May, 1630-1643: Great Puritan Migration; Fall, 1632-January 5, 1665: Settlement of Connecticut; July 20, 1636-July 28, 1637: Pequot War; March-June, 1639: First Bishops' War; 1642-1651: English Civil Wars.

JEREMIAH HORROCKS
English astronomer

Horrocks's observation of the transit of Venus, in 1639, is the earliest on record. He applied Kepler's laws of planetary motion to the Moon, comets, and planets.

BORN: c. 1619; Toxteth Park, England
DIED: January 3, 1641; Toxteth Park
ALSO KNOWN AS: Jeremiah Horrox
AREAS OF ACHIEVEMENT: Astronomy, science and technology

EARLY LIFE

Jeremiah Horrocks (jur-uh-MI-uh HAWR-uhks) was born in Toxteth Park, near Liverpool, England, around 1619, but the records from Toxteth Park for that year have been lost. There has been some speculation that his father may have been William Herrocks, a farmer, but historical research suggests that his father was actually James Horrocks, a watchmaker. James Horrocks was married to Mary Aspinwall, who was from a family of influence in Toxteth Park. Horrocks entered Emmanuel College, Cambridge University, as a sizar, or poor scholar, in 1632. At that time, the curriculum included mostly the arts, divinity, and classical languages, although it is likely Horrocks also learned geometry and some classical astronomy. He studied at Cambridge until 1635, when he returned to Toxteth Park, where he is believed to have become a tutor.

In Horrocks's time, ideas about planetary motion were in transition. Since the ancient Greeks, it had generally been accepted that the earth was the center of the universe. In 1543, however, Nicolaus Copernicus published *De revolutionibus orbium coelestium* (1543; *On the Revolutions of the Heavenly Spheres*, 1952; better known as *De revolutionibus*), which argued that it was the Sun that was at the center, with the heavenly bodies, including the

earth, moving around the Sun. In 1608, Johannes Kepler's analysis of careful position measurements of the planets and the stars, taken by the Danish astronomer Tycho Brahe, demonstrated that the planet Mars moved in an elliptical path around the Sun, and Kepler developed a series of laws that described planetary motion.

The precision of Kepler's laws of planetary motion may have appealed to Horrocks's uncle, who is believed to have been a clockmaker. Tradition says it was this uncle who first stirred Horrocks's interest in astronomy. Shortly after returning to Toxteth Park, Horrocks constructed his own telescope, and he developed projection techniques that enabled him to view the Sun. He used his telescope to measure the positions of the planets and used these measurements to correct errors in existing astronomical tables.

LIFE'S WORK

As Horrocks's interest in astronomy deepened, he constructed simple instruments to measure the size of the Moon, Venus, and the Sun. To measure the size of Venus, he made a pinhole in a piece of paper and mounted the paper on the end of a stick. He determined the size of the pinhole by measuring the size of the pin, using an ingenious technique. Horrocks wrapped thread around the pin many times, then unwound the thread and measured its length. By dividing this length by the number of times he had wrapped the thread around the pin, he was able to accurately determine the circumference of the pin. Then he looked at Venus through the pinhole, adjusting the distance of the pinhole from his eye until Venus just filled the hole. By measuring the distance of the card from his eye, he calculated the angular size of Venus.

The passage of a planet across the disk of the Sun is called a transit, and the prediction of the exact date and time when a transit will occur requires a very precise calculation of the motion of the planet. Only transits of the two inner planets, Mercury and Venus, can be observed from the earth. These transits occur much less frequently than eclipses of the Sun by the Moon. There are generally about thirteen transits of Mercury each century. However, because Venus's orbit is considerably larger than Mercury's orbit, transits of Venus are far rarer, occurring in pairs separated by eight years. More than a century elapses between each transit pair. Seven transits of Venus have occurred since the invention of the telescope (1631, 1639, 1761, 1769, 1874, 1882, and 2004).

The French astronomer Pierre Gassendi was the first person to record that he had observed a planetary transit, that of the planet Mercury in 1631, but the time of this transit differed by six hours from that predicted by Kepler. A transit of Venus occurred just one month later. Gassendi attempted to observe it, but he failed because this transit was visible from America but not visible from Europe. According to Kepler, this was to be the only transit of Venus of the seventeenth century. While the planet would come close to making a transit in 1639, by Kepler's calculations, it would just miss moving across the face of the Sun as seen from Earth: The next transit of Venus would not occur until 1761.

Kepler's calculations in this regard were the basis of Horrocks's most important discovery. Horrocks made his own precise observations of the position of Venus over a four-year period, and he observed slight deviations from the positions predicted by Kepler. In 1639, Horrocks, who had just moved to Much Hoole, near Preston, used his measurements to calculate that a transit of Venus would occur at about 3:00 P.M. on November 24, 1639, and that this transit would be visible from Much Hoole.

On the day of the predicted transit, Horrocks projected the image of the Sun onto a sheet of paper in a darkened room. Late November is not generally a time of clear skies in that part of England, but Horrocks was able to view the Sun. However, November 24, 1639, was a Sunday, which meant that, as a good Puritan, he was expected to be in church at the time of the transit. Further, since Horrocks's calculation of the exact time of the transit might be in error, as he suspected Kepler's calculation was, Horrocks intended to observe the Sun for as much of the day as possible, beginning at sunrise. He was called away several times in the morning but maintained his vigil until mid-afternoon.

The transit began at about 3:15 P.M., and Horrocks watched Venus move across the Sun for about thirty min-

---

HORROCKS VIEWS VENUS'S TRANSIT

Jeremiah Horrocks predicted that Venus would travel in front of the Sun at around 3:00 P.M. on November 24, 1639. He knew, however, that his calculations might be off, and he was eager to watch the Sun, projected onto a screen, for the entire day. Reproduced below is Horrocks's journal entry for that day, describing the moments leading up to his greatest discovery.

I watched carefully on the 24th from sunrise to nine o'clock, and from a little before ten until noon, and at one in the afternoon, being called away in the intervals by business of the highest importance which, for these ornamental pursuits, I could not with propriety neglect. But during all this time I saw nothing in the sun except a small and common spot. . . . This evidently had nothing to do with Venus. About fifteen minutes past three in the afternoon, when I was again at liberty to continue my labours, the clouds, as if by divine interposition, were entirely dispersed, and I was once more invited to the grateful task of repeating my observations. I then beheld a most agreeable spectacle, the object of my sanguine wishes, a spot of unusual magnitude and of a perfectly circular shape, which had already fully centred upon the sun's disc on the left, so that the limbs of the Sun and Venus precisely coincided, forming an angle of contact. Not doubting that this was really the shadow of the planet, I immediately applied myself sedulously to observe it.

Source: From "The Transit of Venus over the Sun," by Jeremiah Horrocks. Translated by Arundell Blount Whatton in his *Memoir of the Life and Labors of the Rev. Jeremiah Horrox* (London, 1859), p. 124.

---

utes before the sun set. By observing the projection of the Sun with Venus moving across its face, Horrocks was able directly to compare the angular diameter of Venus with that of the Sun. His observations showed the apparent diameter of Venus to be only 1' 12," compared with the Sun's diameter of 30'. This was much smaller than the 11' angular diameter reported for Venus by Kepler.

In 1640, Horrocks returned to Toxteth Park, where he wrote his *Venus in sole visa* (1662; *The Transit of Venus over the Sun*, 1859) and started work on his next treatise on solar dimensions. He had begun essays on comets, tides, and the Moon as well. On January 3, 1641 Horrocks died suddenly. Much of his work was lost, but the surviving material was published much later as *Opera posthuma* (1678).

SIGNIFICANCE

Horrocks is generally regarded as the father of British astronomy. He excelled at both making precise observations and using those observations to predict planetary motion. Although Kepler recognized that transits of Mercury and Venus could be used to determine the distance from Earth to the Sun, he was unable to measure this distance because he died before the 1631 transits of Mercury and Venus took place. While Horrocks obtained only a rough estimate of the distance from Earth to the Sun, because he had observed the transit of Venus from only a single location, his value of 59 million miles (95 million kilometers) was significantly more accurate than previous estimates. It was not until a century later, following the transits of Venus in 1761 and 1769, that a more accurate value, about 93 million miles (150 million kilometers), was obtained. His results were used extensively by later astronomers, and even Sir Isaac Newton cited Horrocks's measurement of the diameter of the earth in the first edition of his *Philosophiae Naturalis Principia Mathematica* (1687; *The Mathematical Principles of Natural Philosophy*, 1729; best known as the *Principia*).

—*George J. Flynn*

FURTHER READING

Aughton, Peter. *The Transit of Venus: The Brief, Brilliant Life of Jeremiah Horrocks, Father of British Astronomy*. London: George Weidenfeld & Nicholson, 2004. A two-hundred-page account of Horrocks's contributions to astronomy, focusing on his observation of the transit of Venus across the Sun.

Chapman, Allan. "Jeremiah Horrocks, the Transit of Venus, and the 'New Astronomy' in Early Seventeenth-Century England." *Quarterly Journal of the Royal Astronomical Society* 31 (1990): 333-357. A detailed account of Horrocks's research methods and his scientific accomplishments, which attempts to correct myths about Horrocks's life story.

Van Helden, Albert. *Measuring the Universe: Cosmic Dimensions from Aristarchus to Halley*. Chicago: University of Chicago Press, 1985. Includes an account of Horrocks's observations, detailing his effort to determine the distance from Earth to the Sun.

_____. *Transits of Venus: New Views of the Solar System and Galaxy*. Proceedings of IAU Colloquium 196. Cambridge, U.K.: Cambridge University Press, 2004. Includes articles by Allan Chapman and John Walton detailing Horrocks's life and his astronomical observations.

SEE ALSO: Pierre Gassendi; Johannes Kepler; Sir Isaac Newton.

RELATED ARTICLES in *Great Events from History: The Seventeenth Century, 1601-1700:* September, 1608: Invention of the Telescope; 1609-1619: Kepler's Laws of Planetary Motion.

HENRY HUDSON
English explorer

Hudson led four expeditions in search of the Northwest Passage. Although he failed to find the fabled route to China, he did, by his explorations, clarify the contours of Canada's northern territories and make known in Europe the locations of several natural resources of the New World.

BORN: 1560's?; England
DIED: 1611; Hudson Bay?, North America
AREA OF ACHIEVEMENT: Exploration

EARLY LIFE

Apart from his four voyages of exploration, Henry Hudson is a shadowy figure in history. Almost nothing is known for certain about his early life, not even the year of his birth or the names of his parents. A boy named John Hudson sailed with him on his last voyage (1610-1611), and it is assumed that the boy was probably one of Hudson's sons. On this slender evidence, it has been thought that Henry may have been born in the 1560's. Henry Hudson might have been the grandson of an alderman of London with the same name, although some scholars object to this assumption. The London alderman Henry Hudson was one of the founders of the Muscovy Company, which sought to open trade routes to Russia in the far north.

Hudson was married to a woman named Katherine and had three sons and one daughter. The marriage is confirmed by the existence of a contract with the Dutch East India Company, which provided for payment of money to his wife and children and a further payment to the widow should Hudson not return from his voyage for the Dutch. At some time prior to his appearance on the stage of history, Hudson had become an experienced seaman and, like his presumed grandfather, he dreamed of discovering new sea routes for trade.

By the time of his first voyage of exploration, Hudson was a skilled and bold navigator. He was a man who was not easily deterred from his goals. Seen in the best light, he was persevering and committed; from a darker point of view, he might be considered obstinate and willful. He could ignore the sailing orders given him by the company outfitting his expedition in order to further his own plans for exploration. He had heard geographers discuss their belief that because the sun shone twenty-four hours a day in the Arctic summertime, there must be a warm area in the far north, and that once one had found a way to penetrate the ice barrier, one could sail through warm seas all the way to the Far East. Hudson became obsessed with the dream of finding this warm region that would provide an easy route from Europe to China, India, and the Spice Islands (Moluccas). He was determined to be the first person to find this fabled passage.

Perhaps Hudson's greatest fault was an inability to hold his men under the firm authority necessary for an expedition into such remote and uncivilized regions. On his third voyage, he permitted the ruffians aboard his ship to land on the New England coast and with their firearms to enter a peaceful Indian village to seek plunder. This lack of discipline, along with a tendency to show either favoritism or prejudice toward certain members of his crew, seems to have contributed to the mutiny on his fourth voyage, which cost him his life.

Hudson was a pious man. He liked to assign religious names to the areas he discovered. After fighting ice and contrary winds for a month after his entrance into Hudson Bay on his fourth voyage, he found a group of islands, which he named Isles of God's Mercies. Before setting sail on his first voyage of exploration, he took ten members of his crew with him to attend services at Saint Ethelburga's Church in London.

LIFE'S WORK

On May Day in 1607, Hudson, under the auspices of the Muscovy Company, set sail from Gravesend, England, to find a polar passage to China. With ten men and a boy aboard the small ship *Hopewell*, he vainly sought an opening in the ice barrier along the east coast of Greenland. On June 27, the intrepid explorers reached the island of Spitsbergen, known to the Dutch as Newland. Hudson did not find any previously undiscovered land on

this voyage, but he did report sighting an abundance of whales and walruses at Spitsbergen, a discovery that led to the development of the Spitsbergen whaling industry. On his return to England, the expedition passed by an island that they named Hudson Touches (Jan Mayen Island), although it actually had been previously discovered.

In April, 1608, again with the sponsorship of the Muscovy Company and with the same ship, Hudson set out to find a northeast passage. On this second voyage, he intended to sail into the polar area by finding an opening in the ice pack to the west of Novaya Zemlya (east of Spitsbergen). According to Hudson, two of the men saw a mermaid in the icy waters alongside the ship and described her as having white skin, long black hair, and a tail shaped like a porpoise but speckled like a mackerel. A more credible report was the entry in the record of finding birds and eggs on Novaya Zemlya to replenish the store of goods on the ship. As on the first voyage, ice forced the return of the ship to England, and in August, the *Hopewell* docked once more at Gravesend.

Because Hudson's English investors refused to outfit a third expedition, Hudson turned to the Dutch for support. When the suspicious Amsterdam merchants dallied with Hudson, he began secret negotiations with the French to sail under their flag. The Dutch East India Company suddenly came to terms with Hudson when it discovered the French connection. He was ordered to sail from Holland to the northeast and, if unsuccessful, to return directly to the Netherlands. The instructions clearly restricted Hudson to a northern or northeastern search, yet the wily mariner had a different view of things.

In Hudson's opinion, the search for a passage to Asia should be conducted in the northwest, and while in Amsterdam, he pondered two tempting theories, the belief of Captain John Smith, communicated to Hudson by a letter with maps, that there was a water channel to the Pacific at about 40° latitude (in the area from Chesapeake Bay to New York) and the view of Captain George Weymouth that a passage existed at 62° latitude (at the present-day Hudson Strait). Hudson had earlier heard of John Davis's discovery of a "furious overfall" in the 62° area. The rapid current seemed to suggest that beyond the strait lay a very large body of water—possibly the Pacific Ocean. The possibility of a passage to the northwest rather than to the northeast appealed to Hudson, but he did not reveal his inclinations to his Dutch backers.

On April 6, 1609, Hudson sailed from Amsterdam aboard the *Half Moon* with a mixed crew of Dutch and

English sailors. In the ice at Novaya Zemlya, the crew grew mutinous and easily induced Hudson to abandon the Dutch orders. The *Half Moon* turned toward North America to pursue the mythical passage suggested by Captain Smith. Sailing along the coastline of North America, Hudson entered the river that now bears his name. One of Hudson's officers, Robert Juet, described it as a broad, deep, and easily navigable river, full of salmon and other fish, which led into a scenic mountainous country. Hudson followed the river, until he reached a point near present-day Albany where it was no longer navigable. On its return voyage, the *Half Moon* harbored at Dartmouth, England. The English government forbade Hudson and the English members of his crew to return to Holland and to sail under the Dutch flag in the future.

On April 17, 1610, Hudson made his last voyage. Now under the sponsorship of English entrepreneurs, he made his way to the "furious overfall." In August, he passed through the strait that now bears his name and into what is now known as Hudson Bay. He explored the east coast of Hudson Bay and then entered James Bay. The harsh northern winter then forced him to find shelter and wait for the winter months to pass. With provisions in short supply, the crew spent a miserable winter. The sailors grew mutinous as rumors spread that the captain had been showing favoritism in the distribution of the meager provisions. Historians depend on the prejudiced accounts of the mutineers, intent upon self-justification, for a record of the events. These scanty accounts are interesting but only partly credible. Whatever the true course of events or reasons, the crew seized Hudson, his son, and seven others, including the sick and disabled, and on June 23, 1611, set them adrift in Hudson Bay. Nothing was ever again heard from the castaways. Presumably, Hudson and his small band died a wretched death in the cold bay region.

SIGNIFICANCE

Hudson's name has been immortalized by its attachment to a river, a strait, and a bay. He was not the first explorer to discover the great northern river that would bear his

Imaginative depiction of Henry Hudson abandoned by his crew in the Canadian bay that now bears his name. (Library of Congress)

name—that honor belongs to Giovanni da Verrazano. Yet Hudson deserves credit for making the river known to the Dutch, who then colonized the area they called New Amsterdam. Hudson's work paved the way for Dutch colonization and influence in North America. Similarly, Hudson was not the first to pass through Hudson Strait and into Hudson Bay, but his ill-fated expedition publicized the region's resources, and in later decades the area would see a flourishing fur trade. Hudson's achievement was not so much the discovery of new areas as it was the careful exploration of and reporting on regions scarcely known.

Spitsbergen would not bear Hudson's name, but his expedition there revealed the presence of whales, seals, and walruses in the region. The Dutch explorations had not reported on the abundance of whales at Spitsbergen. As a result of Hudson's reports, English, Danish, and Dutch whalers plied the waters off Spitsbergen for three centuries.

Perhaps one of Hudson's greatest achievements came by way of his greatest disappointment. His failure to find a northwest passage after careful search helped finally to dispel the persistent myth that a navigable waterway through or around the North American continent existed.

—*Richard L. Niswonger*

FURTHER READING

Asher, George M., ed. *Henry Hudson the Navigator*. London: Hakluyt Society, 1860. Reprint. New York: Burt Franklin, 1964. Asher collected a number of original accounts of Hudson's voyages and added them to the 1625 account of Samuel Purchas. This collection includes the bulk of the narratives that were available up to 1860.

Barrow, John. *A Chronological History of Voyages into the Arctic Regions: Undertaken Chiefly for the Purpose of Discovering a North-East, North-West, or Polar Passage Between the Atlantic and Pacific*. London: John Murray, 1818. Reprint. New York: Barnes & Noble, 1971. Though an old work, it provides a useful narrative of the search for the Northwest Passage. Hudson's journeys are described and set in the context of the ongoing search for a passage. The author, a

secretary of the Admiralty, sought to stimulate further English exploration.

Janvier, Thomas A. *Henry Hudson*. New York: Harper and Brothers, 1909. Janvier appraises the aims and achievements of Hudson. One of the book's chief claims to importance is the fact that it provides the previously unpublished testimony of six mutineers.

Johnson, Donald S. *Charting the Darkness: The Four Voyages of Henry Hudson*. Camden, Maine: International Marine, 1993. Reprint. New York: Kodansha Globe, 1995. The author uses Hudson's original logs to recount his voyages.

Millman, Lawrence. "Looking for Henry Hudson." *Smithsonian* 30, no. 7 (October, 1999): 100. Describes Hudson's search for a northwest passage, providing information on the *Half Moon*'s voyage, the mutiny on Hudson's final trip, and Hudson's impact on the fur trade.

Murphy, Henry Cruse. *Henry Hudson in Holland*. New York: B. Franklin, 1972. A reprint of Murphy's 1859 account of Hudson's third voyage, along with notes, documents, and a bibliography.

Powys, Llewelyn. *Henry Hudson*. New York: Harper and Brothers, 1928. A well-written biography that makes the various characters in the drama of Hudson's life come alive. Powys not only narrates the gripping story of a mariner's adventures but also describes the personality of each of the mutineers.

Shuster, Carl. "Into the Great Bay." *Beaver* 79, no. 4 (August/September, 1999): 8. The article, published in the journal of the Canadian National Historical Society, recounts Hudson's exploration in Canada.

Thomson, George Malcolm. *The Search for the North-West Passage*. New York: Macmillan, 1975. A fascinating adventure narrative of the men who pursued the myth of a channel through the polar regions. There are only two chapters on Hudson, but they are among the most readable and accurate summaries available.

SEE ALSO: Pierre Esprit Radisson; John Smith.

RELATED ARTICLE in *Great Events from History: The Seventeenth Century, 1601-1700:* Beginning June, 1610: Hudson Explores Hudson Bay.

ANNE HUTCHINSON
English-born colonial American religious leader

By challenging the orthodox theology of the Massachusetts Bay Colony, Hutchinson precipitated the Antinomian Crisis of 1637, which questioned the very basis of the New England theocracy.

BORN: July 20, 1591 (baptized); Alford, Lincolnshire, England
DIED: August 20, 1643; Pelham Bay, New Netherland (now in New York)
ALSO KNOWN AS: Anne Marbury (given name)
AREAS OF ACHIEVEMENT: Religion and theology, government and politics

EARLY LIFE

Anne Hutchinson was born Anne Marbury in Alford, a small town northeast of Boston in Lincolnshire, England. At the time of her birth, her father, Francis

Marbury (1556-1611), was master of Saint Wilfred's School in Alford, having been deprived of his pulpit for his unorthodox preaching. Thus, Hutchinson was born into the very species of religious repression that would drive her out of New England half a century later. Her mother, Bridget Dryden Marbury (1563-1645), was a midwife and the great-great-aunt of poet John Dryden (1631-1700).

Anne learned to read by studying publications (two plays and three sermons) written by her father, a Cambridge scholar whose library of theological texts soon became Anne's refuge. Francis begged to have the ban on his preaching lifted, and by 1602, he was preaching again at Alford. Three years later, when Anne was fourteen, the family moved to London, where Marbury was made rector of Saint Martin's Vintry. Anne left behind everyone she had ever known, including a nineteen-year-old merchant tailor named William Hutchinson. When Anne's father died in 1611, however, Hutchinson moved to London, and on August 9, 1612, they were married at the chapel-rectory of Saint Martin's.

Returning to Alford with his bride, William resumed his tailoring business and Anne her mother's practice of midwifery. Over the next two decades, Anne bore and raised thirteen children in Alford. The same year the Hutchinsons returned to Lincolnshire, a young pastor named John Cotton began preaching in nearby Boston, and Anne soon heard about his teaching, reminiscent of her father's. When Cotton immigrated to New England in 1633, Anne convinced her husband to turn his shop over to his brother. The following year Anne, William, and their eleven surviving children sailed for America.

LIFE'S WORK

The New England Puritan theocracy into which Cotton and Hutchinson immigrated was no more open to religious diversity than was the Anglican England they had left behind. Although founded on the premise that the ecclesiastical hierarchy in the Church of England was contrary to the "freedom of the gospel," the Congregationalist ideal of the Massachusetts Bay still depended on the deliberations of its ministers to ensure the proper interpretation of Scripture. Ministers who deviated

Anne Hutchinson. (Library of Congress)

from the teachings of the synods—periodic meetings of church elders—were deprived of their pulpits, just as Hutchinson's father had been.

One of the major sources of controversy in Hutchinson's time was Antinomianism, a doctrine involving the individual's role in salvation. The Roman Catholic Church taught that salvation was achieved by a combination of faith and good works. That is, Catholicism held that practices such as giving alms and penance prepared a sinner for salvation, and the Puritans of New England believed that remnants of this error persisted in English Protestantism. The orthodox Calvinist position, by contrast, was that God's grace alone brought salvation. The practical concern for the American Puritan was this: If I know I am saved by God's grace, why do I need to live a moral life? One Boston theologian, Thomas Shepard (1605-1649), put forward an answer that came to be called preparationism. Preparationists believed that if salvation were freely given by God, through no merit of one's own, then one could at least meet God halfway by *preparing* oneself spiritually for the gift.

By the mid-1630's, however, Hutchinson and some others in New England extended the role of the individual in salvation well beyond the approved limits of the colony's leading ministers. Hutchinson became a target of these ministers not only because they considered her position to be Antinomian, but also because she was teaching it to others in increasingly well-attended prayer meetings at her home. Her teaching was problematic for colonial authorities for two reasons. First, it bordered on preaching, which was strictly licensed (and forbidden to women under any circumstances). Second, both women and men were present at these meetings, an intermingling thought improper in a private home.

Hutchinson's threat to ministerial authority was not theoretical but direct, particularly after 1636, when colonial governor Sir Henry Vane the Younger began attending her meetings and defending her views. With such important political backing, Hutchinson herself began to move beyond simply defending her views and openly attacked the views of her opponents as constituting a Covenant of Works. She accused every minister in New England, with the exception of her brother-in-law John Wheelwright, of preaching error.

Beginning with the colony's elections in May of 1637, circumstances began to turn against Hutchinson. Former governor John Winthrop, one of her most prominent opponents, was reelected, defeating Vane in the governor's race, and immediately afterward, the ministers called a synod to define the errors of the Antinomian

---

THE TRIAL OF ANNE HUTCHINSON

Anne Hutchinson was tried for sedition as a heretic against the authority of the theocracy ruling the Massachusetts Bay Colony. In the following excerpt from her trial testimony, Hutchinson provides a personal narrative explaining how she came to hold the views she held in contradiction of the colony's religious leaders.

If you please to give me leave I shall give you the ground of what I know to be true. Being much troubled to see the falseness of the constitution of the Church of England, I had like to have turned Separatist. Whereupon I kept a day of solemn humiliation and pondering of the thing; this scripture was brought unto me—he that denies Jesus Christ to be come in the flesh is antichrist. This I considered of and in considering found that the papists did not deny him to be come in the flesh, nor we did not deny him—who then was antichrist? Was the Turk antichrist only? The Lord knows that I could not open scripture; he must by his prophetical office open it unto me. So after that being unsatisfied in the thing, the Lord was pleased to bring this scripture out of the Hebrews. He that denies the testament denies the testator, and in this did open unto me and give me to see that those which did not teach the new covenant had the spirit of antichrist, and upon this he did discover the ministry unto me; and ever since, I bless the Lord, he hath let me see which was the clear ministry and which the wrong.

Since that time I confess I have been more choice and he hath left me to distinguish between the voice of my beloved and the voice of Moses, the voice of John the Baptist and the voice of antichrist, for all those voices are spoken of in scripture. Now if you do condemn me for speaking what in my conscience I know to be truth I must commit myself unto the Lord.

Source: From http://www.annehutchinson.com/anne_hutchinson_trial_010.htm. Accessed February 5, 2005.

---

teachings. Armed with the synod's theological findings, which in Puritan New England had legal status, the Winthrop administration called a special election in October and turned Hutchinson's supporters out of the General Court. This ecclesiastical-political purge gave Winthrop's court the clout to banish Wheelwright, who had preached sermons against his sister-in-law's opponents, and, in November, 1637, to bring Hutchinson herself to trial.

Hutchinson was charged with sedition, because an attack on church authority was an attack on the government in theocratic New England. The only minister who spoke in Hutchinson's favor was John Cotton, who testified that her conversations with him on the covenant of grace had been more nuanced than the Antinomian diatribes reported by her detractors, suggesting that Hutchinson had been quoted out of context, and with prejudice. When Hutchinson herself was called to testify, however, she defied the authority of the church leaders and claimed "immediate revelation" from God as her authority—a concept directly forbidden by Calvinist orthodoxy.

The court found Hutchinson guilty. She and her family, as well as many of her followers, were banished to Rhode Island, and in March, 1638, she was formally excommunicated. When William Hutchinson died in 1642, their older children having moved on, some with families of their own, Anne moved her six youngest children with her to Long Island (then part of New England) and later in the year to Dutch New Netherland (now New York). She died there in an Indian attack on August 20, 1643, along with five of her six remaining children.

SIGNIFICANCE

Hutchinson has been called the first feminist in the New World. The laws of Puritan New England did not allow for religious freedom in the sense that we think of it today, and the concept would not have legal status in America until a century and a half after her death. Despite these facts, however, Hutchinson's assertion of the primacy of conscience in religious discourse and the right to hold that discourse in public anticipated the principles of religious toleration enshrined in the Establishment Clause of the First Amendment to the United States Constitution. Hutchinson is remembered mostly as a model for American religious freedom, but her clash with Puritan theocracy also demonstrated the need for two other basic freedoms many Americans take for granted: the freedom to assemble and the freedom of speech. In American religious history, moreover, she represents one of the earliest proponents of personal revelation, which, while antithetical to the Calvinism of the 1630's, would sweep New England a century later in what would be called the Great Awakening.

—John R. Holmes

FURTHER READING

Hall, David D., ed. *The Antinomian Controversy, 1636-1638*. 2d ed. Durham, N.C.: Duke University Press, 1990. Updated version of what had already been, in the first edition (1968), the most complete collection of primary sources on Hutchinson's trial.

Huber, Elaine. *Women and the Authority of Inspiration*. Lanham, Md.: University Press of America, 1985. A detailed analysis of the religious background to Hutchinson's conflict with church authorities as a paradigm for similar conflicts in later times.

Hutchinson, Thomas. *History of the Colony and Province of Massachusetts Bay*. Reprint. Cambridge, Mass.: Harvard University Press, 1936. A republication, for the three hundredth anniversary of Hutchinson's trial, of her grandson's account of the history of that era, first published in 1865 by her great-grandson John Hutchinson. Includes transcripts of the trial.

LaPlante, Eve. *American Jezebel: The Uncommon Life of Anne Hutchinson, the Woman Who Defied the Puritans*. San Francisco, Calif.: Harper, 2004. An exhaustive biography by a twenty-first century descendant of Hutchinson.

Lewis, M. J. "Anne Hutchinson." In *Portraits of American Women*, edited by G. J. Barker-Benfield and Catherine Clinton. New York: St. Martin's Press, 1991. Presents new information on Anne Hutchinson's death.

Pagnattaro, Marisa Ann. *In Defiance of the Law: From Anne Hutchinson to Toni Morrison*. New York: Peter Lang, 2001. The historical case of Anne Hutchinson is used as a foundation to explore the fates of similar fictional women in American literature.

SEE ALSO: John Cotton; John Dryden; Sir Henry Vane the Younger; John Winthrop.

RELATED ARTICLES in *Great Events from History: The Seventeenth Century, 1601-1700:* May, 1630-1643: Great Puritan Migration; June, 1636: Rhode Island Is Founded.

CHRISTIAAN HUYGENS
Dutch astronomer and mathematician

Huygens was one of the greatest minds of the scientific revolution. His wave theory of light became highly influential in the nineteenth century. He discovered through his improved telescope the rings of Saturn, wrote the first formal treatise on probability, and invented the pendulum clock, which was the first truly accurate timepiece.

BORN: April 14, 1629; The Hague, United Provinces (now in the Netherlands)

DIED: July 8, 1695; The Hague

AREAS OF ACHIEVEMENT: Astronomy, mathematics, physics, invention, science and technology

EARLY LIFE

Christiaan Huygens (KRIHS-tee-ahn HI-ghehnz) was born in The Hague. His father, Constantijn Huygens, was a diplomat in Dutch government service and a poet who is still better known in the Netherlands than his son. Constantijn attracted many notables to his house, among them the philosopher René Descartes. Christiaan and his brother were, until the age of sixteen, tutored at home in Latin, Greek, and the classics. In fact, all the learning available at that time was offered to them.

Christiaan studied for two years (1645-1647) at the nearby University of Leiden, where the supporters of the Aristotelian view of science were battling with the followers of the new Cartesian approach. Young Huygens joined the discussions before transferring to the new University of Breda, where Cartesianism was unopposed and the views of the Scholastics were not to be found. Huygens, after two years of study at Breda, had absorbed all the mathematical and scientific learning then available. He then went home and devoted himself for several years to advancing the frontiers of mathematics. He proved, for example, that the catenary formed by a chain hanging from two points was not a parabola, as Galileo had asserted.

In 1655, Huygens made his first extended visit to Paris. France and England were the countries where the scientific revolution was centered. Huygens's greatest periods of achievement were to be spent in France, where his precocious publications on mathematics and his family connections afforded him entrée into the highest intellectual circles.

LIFE'S WORK

Huygens's first plunge into scientific research took place in 1655 and after, when he and his brother built improved telescopes, grinding their own lenses. With these instruments, the best made up to that time, Huygens found a satellite of Saturn, Titan, and discovered that Mars has a varied surface. He gradually discerned a ring around Saturn that nowhere touched the planet, thus improving on Galileo's more primitive observation. In order to protect the priority of this discovery while continuing his viewing, he announced by the publication of a coded message that he had found the ring.

Christiaan Huygens. (Library of Congress)

HUYGENS CONSIDERS LIFE ON OTHER PLANETS

Christiaan Huygens was one of the first scientists to consider the possibility of life on other planets. In his work Cosmotheoros *(1698), published the same year in English, he writes about the inhabitants ("the Planetarians"), social composition, flora and fauna, weather, and built landscapes of these other worlds.*

A Man that is of *Copernicus*'s Opinion, that this Earth of ours is a Planet, carried round and enlightened by the Sun, like the rest of them, cannot but sometimes have a fancy, that it's not improbable that the rest of the Planets have their Dress and Furniture, nay and their Inhabitants too as well as this Earth of ours.

There may arise another Question, whether there be in the Planets but one or more sorts of rational Creatures possessed of different degrees of Reason and Sense.

But some body may perhaps object, and that not without reason at first sight, that the Planetarians it's likely are destitute of all refined Knowledge, just as the Americans were before they had Commerce with the Europeans.

What I am now going to say may seem somewhat more bold. . . . For if these new Nations live in Society, as I have pretty well showed they do, 'tis somewhat more than probable that they enjoy not only the Profit, but the Pleasures arising from such a Society: such as Conversation, Amours, Jesting, and Sights.

[W]e have good reason to believe they build themselves Houses, because we are sure they be not without their Showers. . . . To protect themselves from these [weather conditions], and that they may pass their Nights in quiet and safety, they must build themselves Tents or Huts, or live in holes of the earth.

Source: Huygens, *The Celestial Worlds Discovered* (London: Cass, 1968), pp. 1-2, 56, 66, 80, 81. Rendered into modern English by Desiree Dreeuws.

Huygens continued his work in mathematics, which he had begun in the early 1650's with publications on hyperbolas, ellipses, and circles, and he published in 1657 the world's first formal treatise on probability.

Seeking greater scientific precision by the more accurate measurement of time, Huygens in 1656 built a pendulum clock, his greatest original invention, and with it he inaugurated modern, accurate timekeeping. Galileo had experimented with pendulums and with escapement mechanisms but had not actually constructed a clock. Huygens described the clock in his *Horologium* (1658), not to be confused with his later and greater *Horologium oscillatorium* (1673; English translation, 1966).

Huygens was preoccupied after 1660 with attempting to use his clock to solve the problem of determining longitude at sea, as the Dutch, with the world's largest mer-

chant fleet, were intensely interested in navigational advances. Latitude could be ascertained easily by quadrant or sextant, but calculating longitude required an extremely accurate time measurement. Huygens had great hopes for his pendulum mechanism, and his marine clocks were given extensive sea trials but proved an ultimate failure in determining longitude. Not until well into the eighteenth century was the problem actually solved by the invention of a superbly accurate spring-driven chronometer. In an attempt to subject space as well as time to greater quantitative precision, Huygens built a micrometer in 1658. With it he could establish, within a few seconds of arc, the position of a heavenly body.

In 1661, the year he joined the Royal Society, Huygens returned to Paris, where King Louis XIV's chief minister, Jean-Baptiste Colbert, eager to retain Huygens's services for the French, procured for the Dutchman a significant government grant for scientific work.

Scholars interested in science had been meeting in Paris for years in the salons, or drawing rooms, of intellectuals and the wealthy. The Crown wished to formalize such gatherings, and so it founded the Académie Royale des Sciences (Royal Academy of Sciences) in 1666. Huygens's scientific reputation was so formidable that he was made a charter member of the academy, given a regular salary larger than that of any other member, and handed the keys to an apartment in the Bibliothèque Royale. Thus, he commenced, in 1666, a period of residence in Paris lasting until 1681. Except for two extended visits home to The Hague, Huygens remained in Paris. Still, when Huygens left Paris in 1681 for a third trip to the Netherlands, he never returned. His patron Colbert died in 1683, and anti-Protestant sentiment was growing in France, making Huygens's position difficult, as he was nominally a Calvinist.

Huygens's philosophy of science was intermediate between those of the two giants of his day: René Descartes in France and Sir Isaac Newton in England. Huygens grew up a Cartesian but broke with his mentor over the latter's extreme devotion to the mathematical, or deductive, approach to science. Descartes attempted to explain all phenomena by use of deductive logic alone. Newton, on the contrary, relied on observations and experiments as the bases for his laws.

Huygens's basic approach to the universe was mechanistic, an impact or billiard ball physics, in which he denied all action at a distance. He did prefer, however, Descartes's supposedly more tangible "vortices" of "subtle matter" to Newton's "gravity" in explaining the movements of heavenly bodies. Gravity worked unseen and over distance, moving bodies without apparently touching them. In the matter of relativity, however, Huygens was in advance of Newton. For Huygens, all motion in the universe was relative. Huygens, in this regard, was closer to the later work of Albert Einstein.

Huygens and Newton also differed over what constituted the nature of light. Newton considered light to be composed of particles or corpuscles emitted in steady streams from a light source; Huygens regarded the transmission of such particles through empty space to be mere Newtonian "action at a distance" again and incompatible with a mechanistic view of nature. Huygens propounded a wave theory of light, maintaining that a medium, an ether, must exist in space and that light is transmitted with a rapid but finite speed as shock waves in this medium. The ether, he believed, was composed of tiny, closely spaced, elastic particles, which vibrate and pass on the waves of light. Thus he did not view light itself as a substance as did Newton, nor did he consider it to be instantaneously transmitted as did Descartes.

Huygens remained in communication with Newton, although his relations with the Royal Society dwindled after 1678. He visited England again in 1689, conversing with Newton and addressing the Royal Society on his non-Newtonian theory of gravity, a theory published the following year as *Discours de la cause de la pesanteur* (1690; discourse on the cause of gravity). Huygens's last years were spent in The Hague, where he died in 1695.

SIGNIFICANCE

Huygens would have been a great intellect in any age, but the magnitude of his brilliance was not as apparent as it might have been had he not been so close in space and time to such luminaries as Newton and Descartes. Nevertheless, his achievements were considerable.

As an astronomer he not only discovered the rings and a satellite of Saturn but also was the first to notice the nebula in the constellation Orion. In his work on centrifugal force, he was the first to theorize that Earth must be an oblate spheroid. He worked with microscopes as well as telescopes and translated some of the letters of the great Dutch microscopist Antoni van Leeuwenhoek. His work in mechanics of systems led him to invent the pendulum clock, the world's first truly accurate timepiece.

Huygens originated the wave theory of light and thereby established the science of physical optics, although the wave theory was not accepted in his own century or the next one as the fundamental explanation of the nature of light. In the seventeenth and eighteenth centuries, Newton's theory of the corpuscular or particulate nature of light held sway, but nineteenth century scientists focused on the diffraction of light, which can be explained only by wavelength. Thus, the ether enjoyed a renewed popularity, and in the nineteenth century Huygens's theory was the prevailing view.

In the early twentieth century, the physics of Max Planck and Einstein led to a synthesizing of Newton's and Huygens's views into the quantum theory, in which both concepts were correct. Light today is considered indeed to have various wavelength properties, but it is also seen as moving in packets of energy called photons. A mathematical genius, Huygens improved on the work of Galileo in mechanics and astronomy, and he conferred and contested with the giants of his own generation. Always the pure scientist, he never dabbled in the metaphysical and was uninfluenced by religion—either the Calvinism of the Netherlands or the Catholicism of France. He died as he had lived, sure of only one thing: that there is in this universe no ultimate certainty.

—*Allan D. Charles*

FURTHER READING

Bell, Arthur E. *Christian Huygens and the Development of Science in the Seventeenth Century*. New York: Longmans, Green, 1947. This scholarly, well-written volume has long been the standard biography of Huygens in the English language. Bell gives a thorough and interesting account of Huygens's life, his theoretical approach to science, and his actual scientific work.

Chappell, Vere, ed. *Seventeenth-Century Natural Scientists*. New York: Garland, 1992. A collection of essays about Huygens, Robert Boyle, and Sir Isaac Newton, describing their individual scientific contributions and the wider philosophical and intellectual world in which they worked. Also explores the influence of Descartes on their conceptions of scientific method.

Dijksterhuis, Fokko Jan. *Lenses and Waves: Christiaan Huygens and the Mathematical Science of Optics in the Seventeenth Century*. Dordrecht, the Netherlands: Kluwer Academic, 2004. Intended for a reader with some knowledge of physics, this work provides an overview of Huygens's contributions to the science of optics and a broader discussion of that science during the seventeenth century.

Elzinga, Aant. *On a Research Program in Early Modern Physics*. New York: Humanities Press, 1972. Originally a doctoral dissertation, this work contains a lengthy chapter devoted to Huygens's theory of research and how he broke with the system of his mentor, Descartes.

Huygens, Christiaan. *The Celestial Worlds Discovered: Or, Conjectures Concerning the Inhabitants, Plants, and Productions of the Worlds in the Planets*. London: Childe, 1698. Reprint. London: Cass, 1968. Short, nontechnical, and readable, this continually popular book gives excellent insight into Huygens's thinking. He was one of the first scientists to conjecture about life on other planets.

Simmons, George Findlay. *Calculus Gems: Brief Lives and Memorable Mathematics*. New York: McGraw-Hill, 1992. Huygens is one of the mathematicians included in this collection of brief biographies, which discusses his mathematical theories and his relationship with Gottfried Wilhelm Leibniz, his mathematics student.

Struik, Dirk J. *The Land of Stevin and Huygens: A Sketch of Science and Technology in the Dutch Republic During the Golden Century*. Boston: D. Reidel, 1981. A short, illustrated volume, this book centers on Huygens as the chief claim to fame of the Netherlands in the scientific revolution of the seventeenth century. Struik not only describes Huygens's scientific work but also shows how Huygens was influenced by technological demands and commercial pressures.

Tabak, John. *Probability and Statistics: The Science of Uncertainty*. New York: Facts On File, 2004. The chapter about the nature of chance includes a brief discussion of Huygens's ideas on this subject.

Yoder, Joella G. *Unrolling Time: Huygens and the Mathematization of Nature*. New York: Cambridge University Press, 1988. This book describes how Huygens used mathematics to substantiate his mechanistic view of the universe. Details Huygens's discoveries, including his invention of the pendulum clock, and describes how these discoveries are linked to his mathematical universe.

SEE ALSO: Gian Domenico Cassini; Jean-Baptiste Colbert; René Descartes; David and Johannes Fabricius; Edmond Halley; Johannes and Elisabetha Hevelius; Galileo; Francesco Maria Grimaldi; Johannes Kepler; Antoni van Leeuwenhoek; Gottfried Wilhelm Leibniz; Denis Papin; Wilhelm Schickard.

RELATED ARTICLES in *Great Events from History: The Seventeenth Century, 1601-1700:* 17th century: Advances in Medicine; 1601-1672: Rise of Scientific Societies; September, 1608: Invention of the Telescope; 1610: Galileo Confirms the Heliocentric Model of the Solar System; 1632: Galileo Publishes *Dialogue Concerning the Two Chief World Systems, Ptolemaic and Copernican*; 1637: Descartes Publishes His *Discourse on Method*; 1654: Pascal and Fermat Devise the Theory of Probability; 1655-1663: Grimaldi Discovers Diffraction; February, 1656: Huygens Identifies Saturn's Rings; 1660's-1700: First Microscopic Observations; 1665: Cassini Discovers Jupiter's Great Red Spot; Late December, 1671: Newton Builds His Reflecting Telescope; 1672-1684: Leeuwenhoek Discovers Microscopic Life; 1673: Huygens Explains the Pendulum; December 7, 1676: Rømer Calculates the Speed of Light; Summer, 1687: Newton Formulates the Theory of Universal Gravitation.

PIERRE LE MOYNE D'IBERVILLE
French-born colonial Canadian military leader and explorer

Iberville's success as a military leader helped to secure French colonial claims around Hudson Bay. In 1699, he founded the first French settlement on the Gulf of Mexico, and he later established the colony of Louisiana.

BORN: July 20, 1661 (baptized); Ville-Marie de Montréal, Quebec (now Montreal, Canada)
DIED: July 9, 1706; Havana, Cuba
ALSO KNOWN AS: Pierre Le Moyne (given name)
AREAS OF ACHIEVEMENT: Government and politics, warfare and conquest

EARLY LIFE

Pierre Le Moyne d'Iberville (pee-ayr luh-mwan dee-bur-veel) was the third of thirteen children born to Charles Le Moyne and his wife, Catherine Thierry-Primot, one of colonial Quebec's most illustrious families. Charles Le Moyne had come to New France in 1641 as an indentured servant of Jesuit missionaries, but his proficiency in native languages and his political savvy soon made him one of the wealthiest men in the colony. The family's high social status was exemplified by the seigneurial titles that Charles was able to obtain for his sons, all of whom distinguished themselves through military service or exploration, or as colonial administrators. Pierre's own title, sieur d'Iberville, came from a fief held by the Le Moyne family in Charles's native Normandy.

Iberville attended the school in Montreal staffed by the Sulpicians, but when he was only twelve years old, his father obtained a position for him in the navy and his formal education ended. For the next ten years, he trained for his career as a seaman by sailing on the Saint Lawrence River and making multiple trips to France. On one of these trips, he was designated the official courier for dispatches between the governor of Quebec and the minister of marine and colonies, but even the governor's strong endorsement failed to gain for him a formal commission from the ministry. Upon his return to Quebec, however, Iberville received the opportunity to prove his military skills when he joined in the assault upon the British trading posts of the Hudson's Bay Company.

LIFE'S WORK

Iberville's determination to drive the British out of the Hudson Bay area and gain a French monopoly over the lucrative fur trade occupied his attention for more than a decade. During his first Hudson Bay campaign in 1686,

Iberville captured the post at Moose Fort and then, with only a handful of men in two canoes, managed to seize the ship that carried the British governor of the colony. These exploits won him an appointment as administrator of three of the captured posts, and he used this opportunity to begin his own involvement in fur speculation. Many of his subsequent military adventures likewise carried some promise of economic advantage.

At the outbreak of the War of the League of Augsburg (also known as King William's War), Iberville led an attack in 1690 on the British settlement of Corlaer (now Schenectady, New York). Arriving to find the village unguarded and the stockade gates open, he led an assault that resulted in the death or capture of more than one hundred inhabitants, while the French suffered only two casualties. For the remainder of the 1690's, Iberville split his time between policing the posts on Hudson Bay, ferrying furs between Quebec and France, and raiding British settlements along the maritime coast. Although shifting European alliances often annulled his military conquests, he was always careful to protect his own financial interests. His raids along the Newfoundland coast in 1695, for example, not only destroyed thirty-six British settlements but also produced a financial windfall for Iberville in his sale of captured codfish.

In September, 1697, Iberville fought his last and most celebrated naval battle in the Hudson Bay area. Separated from the rest of his fleet and surrounded by three British warships, he managed to sink one ship, capture another, and drive the third away before he had to beach his own damaged ship. Once reunited with the French fleet, he also participated in the capture of Fort Nelson. The victory proved ephemeral, however, when the Treaty of Ryswick restored the Hudson Bay region to its antebellum status.

The end of hostilities gave the French government the opportunity to consolidate its claims along the northern shore of the Gulf of Mexico, claims first established almost two decades earlier by the explorations of Sieur de La Salle. La Salle had been unable to colonize the area because he could not locate the mouth of the Mississippi River from the gulf; this task was now assigned to Iberville, who, with his brother Jean-Baptiste Le Moyne de Bienville, set sail for the Gulf of Mexico in the winter of 1698-1699.

In March of 1699, Iberville and a small crew entered the North Pass of the Mississippi, attempting to match

401

their observations with the accounts from the La Salle expeditions. Near present-day Natchez, Iberville was satisfied that he was indeed on the Mississippi, and he returned to the Gulf and constructed fortifications along the entrance to Biloxi Bay. Leaving behind a small garrison, he returned to France to report his success to King Louis XIV and to argue for the immediate colonization of Louisiana. Despite the reluctance of the Crown to support such an expensive undertaking, he received sufficient provisions to return to the Gulf in order to cultivate alliances with the Louisiana Indians, to inhibit Spanish expansion, and to gain a foothold against the British.

Iberville returned to Biloxi in January, 1700, and fortified a second location on the Mississippi at a point about thirty miles below the future site of New Orleans. When hostilities again erupted between France and England later that year (the War of the Spanish Succession or Queen Anne's War), Iberville again traveled to France to stress the strategic military value of a colony in Louisiana. When he returned to Louisiana in early 1702, he brought not only fresh supplies for the garrison at Biloxi but also the first colonists. In order to be closer to the Mississippi, the colony was established at Mobile Bay rather than Biloxi; Mobile thus became the first permanent colony in French Louisiana. Iberville negotiated an alliance with the Chickasaw nation and sent a request to the bishop of Quebec for missionaries. Confident that he had fulfilled his mission to plant a colony, he returned to France.

Iberville never returned to Louisiana, but his interest in the success of the colony led him to develop ambitious proposals intended to secure its stability, as well as increasing his personal wealth. His grandiose plans, however, were met with skepticism by the French crown and outright hostility by the Canadians, who resented Iberville's attempts to keep Louisiana independent from Quebec. Returning to service as a naval commander, Iberville led an assault upon the British colony on Nevis, in the Caribbean, but he succumbed soon after to yellow fever. He died onboard his ship while it was anchored in Havana harbor.

SIGNIFICANCE

Iberville has often been termed Canada's first great national hero, and certainly his military skills helped to preserve the French empire in North America during years of conflict with the British. To the French, he was a man of valor and determination; to the British, he was little more than a pirate and an unmerciful foe. Beyond such biased portrayals, however, Iberville must be judged objectively as a man committed to the French colonial enterprise and a brilliant, if sometimes ruthless, military commander.

Although his contributions to French Canada were considerable, it is as the founder and chief promoter of the Louisiana colony that Iberville should be remembered. Unfortunately, the French impulse to colonize North America was beginning to wane even during his lifetime, and Louisiana would never achieve the place of significance within the fading French empire that Iberville imagined. However, his skills as a sailor and administrator and his persistent support of the colonial effort left an indelible French culture in the region that stretched from Mobile to Natchitoches and beyond.

—Rodger Payne

FURTHER READING

Crouse, Nellis M. *Lemoyne d'Iberville: Soldier of New France*. 1954. Reprint. Baton Rouge: Louisiana State University Press, 2001. Still the best biography in English, although often criticized for relying too heavily on secondary resources. This edition has an introduction by Daniel H. Unser that contains a brief survey of the biographical literature.

Frégault, Guy. *Pierre LeMoyne d'Iberville*. Rev. ed. Ottawa, Ont.: Fides, 1968. A revised and updated version of *Iberville le conquerérant* (Montreal, 1944); generally considered to be the best biography of Iberville but available only in French.

Giraud, Marcel. *The Reign of Louis XIV, 1698-1715*. Vol. 1 in *A History of French Louisiana*. Baton Rouge: Louisiana State University Press, 1974. A revision of Giraud's original history, which was published in French in the 1950's. Although Iberville is mentioned in all five volumes (not all of which have been translated), he figures most prominently in this volume.

Higginbotham, Jay. *Old Mobile: Fort Louis de la Louisiane, 1702-1711*. Mobile, Ala.: Museum of the City of Mobile, 1977. A massive and detailed history of Iberville's colonization efforts in Mobile Bay based on original documentation.

McWilliams, Richebourg Gaillard, trans. and ed. *Iberville's Gulf Journals*. University: University of Alabama Press, 1981. English translations of three separate journals that recount Iberville's explorations of the Gulf Coast, prefaced by a brief biography.

O'Neill, Charles Edwards. *Church and State in French Colonial Louisiana: Policy and Politics to 1732*. New Haven, Conn.: Yale University Press, 1966. Contains substantial information on Iberville's policies in Louisiana based on extensive use of primary documents.

SEE ALSO: Sieur de La Salle; Louis XIV; Pierre Esprit Radisson.
RELATED ARTICLES in *Great Events from History: The Seventeenth Century, 1601-1700:* 1611-1630's: Jesuits Begin Missionary Activities in New France; May 2, 1670: Hudson's Bay Company Is Chartered; Beginning 1673: French Explore the Mississippi Valley; December, 1678-March 19, 1687: La Salle's Expeditions; September 20, 1697: Treaty of Ryswick; May 1, 1699: French Found the Louisiana Colony.

IHARA SAIKAKU
Japanese writer, poet, and playwright

Saikaku was the first major Japanese writer to focus primarily on the lives of common people in his fiction and poetry. He also dealt with sexual relationships with a frankness new to Japanese literature.

BORN: 1642; Ōsaka, Japan
DIED: September 9, 1693; Ōsaka
ALSO KNOWN AS: Hirayama Tōgo (given name)
AREAS OF ACHIEVEMENT: Literature, theater

EARLY LIFE

Ihara Saikaku (ee-hah-rah si-kah-kew) was born Hirayama Tōgo to a merchant family in Ōsaka, one of the chief commercial centers in Japan in the Genroku period (1688-1704). His family were probably sword makers and belonged to Ōsaka's *chōnin*, or townspeople class. He was brought up in the family business and eventually took it over. He married and is said to have sired a daughter who was blind. (Another tradition speaks of multiple daughters.)

Saikaku's business and familial duties did not prevent him from composing poetry, particularly *rengae*, or linked verse. He became known both for his prodigious output and for his willingness to tackle traditionally vulgar subjects (for which he earned the disdain of a contemporary, Matsuo Bashō). Although he used a number of literary pseudonyms, "Saikaku" (which translates freely as a "quick plan to make money" and suggests his *chōnin* background) is the one by which he is remembered. Saikaku was unusual in his refusal to collaborate with other poets in writing linked verse. In a single day, he is said to have composed by himself more than twenty thousand linked verses (a record that apparently still stands).

When he was approaching forty, Saikaku's beloved wife died suddenly. He commemorated her in a linked verse elegy, one of the few written on the loss of a wife in Genroku Japan. He is said to have lost his daughter not long after that. He turned his business over to associates and retired. Just as his poetry was unorthodox, so was his retirement. A man in his station might have been expected to join a monastic community or take on the role of a wandering Buddhist monk. After his wife's death, however, although Saikaku did travel incessantly around Japan, particularly to the urban areas such as Edo (modern Tokyo), he did so as a decidedly secular observer rather than as a spiritual pilgrim.

LIFE'S WORK

Saikaku was likely Japan's first professional writer. He used his retirement to begin a second career as prose chronicler of the *ukiyo*, or "floating world," the dynamic, rapidly expanding, and unstable urban culture of Genroku Japan. Although the term *ukiyo* was originally derived from the Buddhist notion of the transience of all things, it quickly came to connote the secular hustle and bustle of a city life built upon the pursuit of fleeting pleasures. Saikaku's *ukiyozoshi* (literally, stories of the floating world) departed from the upper-class setting and characters of Japan's classic narrative traditions. Rather than recount the distant exploits of the samurai class, he recorded the contemporary *chōnin* society centering on the Kabuki theater, the marketplace, the urban slums, and even the brothel.

Saikaku did not abandon poetry for prose; rather, he redirected his poetic attention to detail in order to paint vivid prose portraits of his contemporary society. His first work in prose was the novel *Kōshoku ichidai otoko* (1683; *The Life of an Amorous Man*, 1964). Its subject, the sexual biography of its hero, and its structure, divided into fifty-four chapters, is modeled on the classic *Genji monogatari* (1021; *The Tale of Genji*, 1921-1933). However, its hero, Yonosuke, is a sort of anti-Genji, whose exploits are often comic rather than heroic, frankly sexual rather than romantic. In one episode, Yonosuke attempts to ravish a woman who will not submit to him; in another, he marries a prostitute. At the end of the novel, the confirmed libertine sets sail on a quixotic quest for an island of amazon women.

Saikaku later authored a companion work, *Kōshoku ichidai onna* (1696; *The Life of an Amorous Woman*,

IHARA SAIKAKU'S MAJOR WORKS

1673	*Ikudama manku*
1675	*Dokugin ichinichi senku*
1677	*Saikaku haikai ōkukazu*
1681	*Saikaku ōyakazu*
1683	*Kōshoku ichidai otoko* (*The Life of an Amorous Man*, 1964)
1683?	*Yakusha hyōbanki*
1684	*Shoen ōkagami*
1685	*Gaijin Yashima*
1685	*Koyomi*
1685	*Saikaku shokoku-banashi*
1685	*Wankyū isse no monogatari*
1686	*Kōshoku gonin onna* (*Five Women Who Loved Love*, 1956)
1686	*Honchō nijū fuko*
1687	*Futokoro suzuri*
1687	*Nanshoku ōkagami* (*The Great Mirror of Male Love*, 1990)
1687	*Budō denraiki*
1688	*Buke giri monogatari* (*Tales of Samurai Honor*, 1981)
1688	*Nippon eitaigura: Daifuku shin chōja-kyō* (*The Japanese Family Storehouse: Or, The Millionaire's Gospel Modernised*, 1959)
1689	*Honchō ōin hiji* (*Tales of Japanese Justice*, 1980)
1692	*Seken munezan' yō* (*Worldly Mental Calculations*, 1965)
1693	*Saikaku okimiyage*
1694	*Saikaku oridome* (*Some Final Words of Advice*, 1980)
1695	*Saikaku zoku tsurezure*
1696	*Kōshoku ichidai onna* (*The Life of an Amorous Woman*, 1963)
1696	*Yorozu no fumihōgu*

1963). The heroine of this work is a female Yonosuke, whose picaresque adventures include stints as court concubine, dancer, nun, tea server, and prostitute. As in Daniel Defoe's *The Fortunes and Misfortunes of the Famous Moll Flanders, Written from Her Own Memorandums* (1722, commonly known as *Moll Flanders*), the heroine confesses the error of her ways at the end of the novel, but an aura of irony prevents the reader from accepting this confession at face value.

Although Saikaku's protagonists pay lip service to the Buddhist notion that desire is at the root of suffering, they live life to the hilt, actively pursuing their desires to the end. In this respect, his work seems quite modern, as his protagonists rely on personal codes rather than received traditions to give their lives meaning and value. A note of pessimistic absurdity creeps into *Kōshoku gonin onna* (1686; *Five Women Who Loved Love*, 1956), a collection of stories about the loves and travails of working-class women. In one of the stories, which Saikaku adapted from a tawdry popular ballad, he reimagines the heroine as an almost existential figure who loves her husband

dearly but commits adultery and then suicide as a way of controlling her destiny.

Saikaku was also an innovator in his frank and nuanced depiction of homosexuality in Tokugawa Japan. Prior to the criminalization of homosexuality during the Meiji restoration in the 1860's, Japanese culture exhibited considerable tolerance, and even encouragement, of same-sex love—particularly in the idealized relationships between mentor and student, samurai and page, and priest and novice. The Kabuki theater (in which men played female roles) became a locus for an emerging gay subculture. Saikaku's *Nanshoku ōkagami* (1687; *The Great Mirror of Male Love*, 1990) is a virtual compendium of this subculture, but as with heterosexual love, Saikaku maintains an ironic perspective on the divagations of human desire.

Not all Saikaku's works can be strictly classified as poetry or narrative prose fiction. He exploited the epistolary form in a number of works, most notably *Yorozu no fumihōgu* (1696; partial translation as "A Miscellany of Old Letters," 1985), published after his death. The introduction to *Yorozu no fumihōgu* claims the work was derived from a packet of random letters found tied up in a broom, and this gimmick allows Saikaku to create a series of fictional vignettes in epistolary form, some of which tell complete stories, while others merely adumbrate them. Within the strict confines of the epistolary form, Saikaku reveals the inner life and longings of the *chōnin* class.

Other works dispense with narrative altogether. Saikaku ventured into broad social satire with *Nippon eitaigura: Daifuku shin chōja-kyō* (1688; *The Japanese Family Storehouse: Or, The Millionaire's Gospel Modernized*, 1959) and even wrote travel books that mixed poetry with descriptions of various places. As a professional writer, he exhibited both innovation and productivity, clearly living up to a pseudonym that meant "quick plan to make money."

SIGNIFICANCE
Saikaku influenced the form and content of Japanese literature. He transformed the linked verse form from a

game-like interplay of various poets into an extended meditation by a single writer. He also fathered the *ukiyozoshi* form, presenting realistic fictional stories of the floating world. He even flirted with the epistolary novel. In terms of content, Saikaku tackled formerly taboo subjects, such as homosexuality and prostitution. As Japan's first professional writer, he was driven by novelty to provide literary works that were exciting and accessible to the newly literate *chōnin* class and that reflected its lives and values. He combined a journalist's narrative zest with a poet's eye for details and a master storyteller's ability to transform the mundane into the magical. Moreover, he did not exploit taboo subjects so much as portray them with a realism and depth of understanding that allowed his socially marginalized characters to speak for themselves.

—Luke A. Powers

FURTHER READING

Drake, Christopher. "Collision of Traditions in Saikaku's Haikai." *Harvard Journal of Asiatic Studies* 52, no. 1 (June, 1992): 5-75. A good place to start to review Saikaku's achievements as a poet and literary innovator. Includes a detailed comparison of Saikaku and Bashō.

Hibbett, Howard. *The Floating World in Japanese Fiction*. London: Oxford University Press, 1959. Excellent introduction to the Genroku period and the development of *ukiyozoshi*, with a major focus on Saikaku. Includes reproductions of *ukiyo-e* illustrations that accompanied Saikaku's original Japanese texts.

Richie, Donald. *Japanese Literature Reviewed*. New York: ICG Muse, 2003. This history of Japanese literature from the beginnings to the present includes a chapter on Saikaku and Edo literature.

Schalow, Paul Gordon. "Introduction." In *The Great Mirror of Male Love*. Stanford, Calif.: Stanford University Press, 1990. Schalow's fifty-page introduction to his translation of Saikakus's *Nanshoku ōkagami* is one of the best scholarly works on Saikaku in English. It both provides an overview of homosexuality in Tokugawa Japan and offers a detailed cultural context that illuminates his translation.

SEE ALSO: Matsuo Bashō.

RELATED ARTICLES in *Great Events from History: The Seventeenth Century, 1601-1700:* 1603-1629: Okuni Stages the First Kabuki Dance Dramas; 1617: Edo's Floating World District; 1688-1704: Genroku Era.

INNOCENT XI
Italian pope (1676-1689)

Innocent XI was noted for his austere, exemplary life and his zeal for reforming church administration and rooting out nepotism. He repeatedly clashed with France, Europe's strongest power, and attempted to frustrate the Gallican and expansionist designs of King Louis XIV. Ultimately, he took part in the grand coalition against the French monarch in 1688.

BORN: May 16, 1611; Como, duchy of Milan (now in Italy)
DIED: August 12, 1689; Rome, Papal States (now in Italy)
ALSO KNOWN AS: Benedetto Odescalchi (given name)
AREAS OF ACHIEVEMENT: Religion and theology, church reform, government and politics

EARLY LIFE

The Odescalchi family was of comfortable, upper-middle-class background, and Benedetto's (Innocent XI's) father owned a bank in Genoa, to which Innocent was apprenticed in 1626. Having been educated by the Jesuits, he and his younger brother, Guilio Maria (who would enter the Benedictine order) were religiously inclined. Rather than go into the family business, Innocent studied jurisprudence at Rome and Naples, receiving his doctorate in law in 1639.

Innocent soon drew the attention of Pope Urban VIII (1623-1644), who appointed him protonotary, then president of the Apostolic Chamber, commissary of the Marco di Roma, governor of Macarata, and papal legate to the duchy of Ferrara. Pope Innocent X (1644-1655) named him cardinal-dean of Saint Cosmas and Damien Church in 1645, cardinal-priest in 1647, and bishop of Novara in 1650. During the six years that he pastored at Novara, he gained considerable fame as an energetic and compassionate bishop who was particularly concerned with fostering works of charity and relief for the impoverished. He resigned in 1656 for reasons of health, and from that time on he stayed mainly in and around Rome itself, undertaking various special tasks and projects for Popes Alexander VII (1655-1667), Clement IX (1667-1669), and Clement X (1670-1676).

LIFE'S WORK

Innocent XI, as Cardinal Odescalchi, had become so respected that, after Pope Clement IX died of a stroke on December 9, 1669, he was considered by the conclave as the leading candidate to succeed Clement on the papal throne. However, King Louis XIV of France held a virtual veto on the eventual choice and, believing that Odescalchi might prove to be too independent-minded and therefore potentially difficult to deal with, blocked the cardinal's candidacy. After weeks of political maneuvering and negotiations, a seventy-nine-year-old cardinal, Emilio Altieri, was elected and crowned as Clement X.

During the pontificate of Clement X, Odescalchi played a prominent, but behind the scenes, role. Most notably, he fostered a united effort by Christian European powers against the revitalized Ottoman Turks, who were steadily advancing into Austrian lands and threatening Vienna. Clement X died on July 22, 1676, but it was not until September 21 that the College of Cardinals, after another contentious round of meetings, elected Odescalchi. This time, Louis XIV did not firmly oppose the decision, and the cardinals agreed to endorse reforms that Odescalchi had demanded as a precondition of acceptance. His coronation took place on October 4, and he assumed the name of Innocent XI, after Pope Innocent X, who had conferred him with the rank of cardinal.

With singular determination, the new pontiff embarked upon a program of reform, which reduced the papal budget and vastly increased the level of administrative efficiency in the Papal States. Within his domain, he outlawed gambling and closed down all gaming houses. Also, he tried to eliminate nepotism and appointments that were based on favoritism by setting a good example. However, he never succeeded in completely eradicating these practices among the cardinals and the Vatican bureaucracy.

With his strict code of morality and his restraint and self-denial, he was suspected by many of harboring Jansenist sympathies. He seemed to have tendencies in that direction, and he certainly never criticized Jansenism as energetically as he proscribed Laxism and quietism, two other breakaway tendencies operating within the Church. Laxism, which would have relaxed many moral and ethical guidelines on the faithful within the Church

and was favored by some of the Jesuits, was repudiated in 1679. Miguel de Molinos, the foremost advocate of quietism (which favored a philosophy of inaction and acceptance), was convicted of heresy in 1687 and sentenced to perform life penance.

Just as he had done when he was Cardinal Odescalchi, Pope Innocent adamantly opposed the spread of Islamic rule into Central Europe and made every effort to secure assistance for the beleaguered Holy Roman Emperor Leopold I against the Ottomans. The crucial campaign occurred in 1683, when Turkish armies advanced to the gates of Vienna and laid siege to the Austrian capital. The Christian alliance that Innocent was instrumental in fashioning between Leopold, Venice, and John III Sobieski, king of Poland, ultimately turned back the Ottoman threat. In Innocent's estimation, no thanks were to be given to King Louis XIV, who had rebuffed the pope's pleas for assistance and even had spurned an offer to establish a Christian state at Constantinople, to be governed by his son. Innocent never quite got over this and, henceforth, was always suspicious of the king and his motives.

However, what really poisoned Vatican-French relations throughout Innocent's pontificate was the issue of the *regale*, that is, the right of the king of France to draw upon the income from dioceses and monastic houses during times when the leadership had fallen vacant and until such time as a new bishop, abbot, abbess, or other person might be appointed to take charge. Under the terms of the Concordat of Bologna of 1516, the French monarchy also claimed the prerogative to nominate candidates to fill these positions, subject to final approval from the pope. In order for the government to derive maximum benefit, the tendency was to move very slowly through the nomination process. The *regale* originally applied only to northern France, but in 1673, Louis extended it into the southern provinces, requiring that all bishops swear an oath acknowledging the legality of this initiative. When two Languedocian bishops protested, Innocent condemned the king's policy.

In 1682, Louis convened a French Catholic Council, which drew up the Declaration of Gallican Liberties. The declaration denied the pope's infallibility, asserted the independence of the French Church, and subjected all papal decisions to review by each individual bishop. Innocent invalidated the declaration and threatened Louis and his ministers with excommunication. The controversy remained at a standoff as long as Innocent XI was alive, but Louis was the eventual winner: Years later, he secured what he wanted from Pope Innocent XII.

Another serious rift occurred in 1687, when the pope tried to do away with the right of foreign ambassadors to extend asylum to persons of their choice. (Asylum was extended often to criminals who were willing to bribe their way to safety.) To the deep annoyance of Innocent XI, France alone refused to comply with his request.

Some scholars believe that one of the reasons that Louis XIV launched a ferocious persecution of Huguenots from 1681 to 1685 was to demonstrate how Catholic he was, that by showing he could eradicate Protestantism in France, he could get into the pope's good graces. If so, it backfired on Louis because Innocent, appalled by atrocity reports coming out of France, denounced the persecution and joined in the effort of the Calvinist stadtholder William III of the Netherlands to forge an anti-French coalition of European powers, which became known as the League of Augsburg (1686). In 1688, Innocent pointedly rejected Louis's nominee for the important post of archbishop of Cologne in favor of Emperor Leopold's nominee, and he would not support the Catholic king James II in his struggle over the English throne against William III: Innocent considered James to be too closely tied to Louis. The following year, the War of the League of Augsburg (1689-1697), or War of the Grand Alliance, broke out, pitting almost every European power against France.

SIGNIFICANCE

Pope Innocent XI earned admiration for his integrity and strength in maintaining his convictions, and he also earned admiration from powerful enemies for his unyielding stance and refusal to compromise. Attempts to canonize him as a saint from 1714 to 1744 met with failure because of French opposition, and it was not until 1956 that he was beatified and the Feast Day of August 12 set aside in his memory.

Innocent did much to restore and enhance the prestige of, and respect for, the Papacy, and the victories over the Turks to which he contributed in no small measure changed the course of history in Central and Eastern Europe.

—Raymond Pierre Hylton

FURTHER READING

La Due, William J. *The Chair of St. Peter: A History of the Papacy*. Maryknoll, N.Y.: Orbis Books, 1999. La Due considers Innocent to be a crypto-Jansenist and stresses the importance of his efforts to rescue Vienna.

Lossky, Andrew. *Louis XIV and the French Monarchy*. Princeton, N.J.: Princeton University Press, 1994. This work explains the complex relationship between the French monarchy and the Vatican, setting forward the basis for Gallican claims and chronicling the bitter, yet restrained struggle of bluff and counterbluff between Louis XIV and Innocent XI in a comprehensible manner.

McBrien, Richard P. *Lives of the Popes: The Pontiff from St. Peter to John Paul II*. New York: HarperCollins, 2000. Contains a chronology of the events surrounding the development of the Papacy and biographies of each individual pope. Rates Innocent XI as the most significant pope of the seventeenth century.

Maxwell-Stuart, P. G. *Chronicles of the Popes*. London: Thames and Hudson, 1997. A well-illustrated volume that emphasizes Innocent's piety in a materialistic age and the consequences of his quarrels with Louis XIV.

Wright, A. D. *The Early Modern Papacy: From the Council of Trent to the French Revolution, 1564-1789*. Harlow, England: Longmans, 2000. A detailed period study that sets Innocent aside as one of the strongest-willed pontiffs of his era.

IZUMO NO OKUNI
Japanese actress

Izumo no Okuni is credited with the creation of a new dramatic form, combining song, dance, and other varieties of performance, called Okuni Kabuki. This art eventually developed into Japan's internationally famous Kabuki theater.

BORN: 1571; Izumo, Japan
DIED: 1658; Izumo
ALSO KNOWN AS: Okuni
AREAS OF ACHIEVEMENT: Theater, music

EARLY LIFE

Very little is known concerning the early life of Izumo no Okuni (ee-zoom-oh noh oh-koon-ee), the woman normally credited with the creation of Kabuki. Those accounts of her younger days that remain combine traditions, folktales, and obvious inventions. At present, most scholars agree that it is nearly impossible to ascertain the facts of her upbringing with any certainty. Nevertheless, tradition holds that she was born in the town of Izumo in what is now Shimane prefecture. Izumo was centered on the Izumo Grand Shrine, one of the oldest and holiest sites of Japan's native Shinto religious tradition. It is believed that Okuni was born to a family with connections to the shrine and that her father may have been a metalworker in the service of the priests there. It is also held that she was trained in song and dance in connection with the festivals of the Izumo Grand Shrine. There are reports that she was a miko or priestess of the shrine. What is more certain, however, is that she, along with a troop of other dancers connected to the shrine, adapted these religious dances, including those influenced by the Buddhist tradition, to meet popular tastes and traveled in order to appeal for alms.

LIFE'S WORK

Surviving accounts indicate that Izumo no Okuni may have studied music and dance at the famous Kasuga Shrine, another important Shinto institution, in the city of Nara. It is also believed that she accompanied a troop of dancers who gave performances all over central Japan. Her travels certainly brought her to the imperial capital of Kyōto in the early seventeenth century. It was there that her fame was established.

Izumo no Okuni's fame is mostly derived from a series of performances that she delivered in Kyōto, beginning in 1603. She performed at the Shinto Kitano

Tenmangu shrine, as well as on the banks of the river Kamogawa, the main river running through the city of Kyōto, and achieved tremendous popularity. Her performances included skits, longer dramatic performances, song, dance, and musical accompaniment and are said to have employed some risqué material. The men of Kyōto greatly enjoyed her performances, and the fame of Izumo no Okuni spread beyond the boundaries of the city.

Originally, these performances were thought of as being a type of *nembustsu odori*, a form of popular Buddhist dance and performance. Their unique character was soon recognized, however, and it is held that Izumo no Okuni herself applied the name *kabuki* to her novel variety of performance. Scholars believe that the word was originally the noun form of the verb *kabuku* and referred to a form of physical transformation. It is believed that in her dances and dramatic sketches, Izumo no Okuni wore her hair short, danced in male clothing, and employed swords in the performance, and it is assumed that the name originated from this enacted gender transformation. In any case, the performances that Izumo no Okuni gave in Kyōto in 1603 are considered to be the beginning of what is now known as Okuni Kabuki, and of the Kabuki tradition in general.

In 1603, Tokugawa Ieyasu, a powerful general, received the title of shogun from the imperial court in Kyōto. Ieyasu's stronghold at Edo, in eastern Japan, became the new power base in the country, and a period of political disorder and bloodshed that had lasted since the beginning of the Ōnin War in 1467 was brought to an end. While Tokugawa endeavoured to strengthen the rule of law, the climate of uncertainty, transience, and chaos of the previous era continued to exercise a strong hold on the imagination of the townsfolk of cities such as Kyōto. These urban areas were also becoming increasingly prosperous, and the desire for entertainment asserted itself more forcefully in people's lives. It is because of this popular climate that Izumo no Okuni's performances, characterized by an irreverent disregard for authority and taboos, garnered such popular attention in the early seventeenth century.

Although her explosive popularity in Kyōto in the early 1600's is well documented, far less is known about Izumo no Okuni's successive career. As the Tokugawa political order began to consolidate itself, the authorities took an unfavorable view of the new phenomenon. Edicts concerning frugality and morality were issued.

Sexual morality was a particular concern of the new government, and along with efforts to control prostitution came a move to control the theater as well. In 1629, actresses, considered a threat to the public morality, were banned from the stage. The fear was that the actresses' profession had become related to prostitution and that racy material on the stage was stirring up troubles away from the theater. The Kabuki theater survived but was fundamentally changed as female parts were taken over by men—the *onnagata*. It is assumed that this brought an end to the careers of Izumo no Okuni and women like her, but tradition has it that Izumo no Okuni enjoyed a long life and died at the age of eighty-seven, very old by the standards of the time. It is thought that she was buried in a small graveyard near the Izumo Grand Shrine.

SIGNIFICANCE

Most modern scholars refuse to speculate as to how great an influence Izumo no Okuni's brand of early seventeenth century Kabuki had on the later Kabuki tradition. Relatively little is known about the methods of Izumo no Okuni's brand of performance, and the content of the dramatic material that she presented is also unclear compared to the canon of plays written after women were banned from Kabuki performances in 1629. What is clear, however, is that Okuni Kabuki helped to establish the musical drama as the preeminent form of entertainment for Japan's townsmen classes, a trend that lasted until the late nineteenth century.

It is also clear that, although the subject matter may have changed, the colorful costuming and radical dance that have proven to be Kabuki's most recognizable trademarks originated with Okuni Kabuki. Kabuki remains an important traditional art to this day, and its troupes, which remain all male, continue to pay tribute to Izumo no Okuni, the Kabuki theater's female founder. In Japan, her life has been the subject of a number of works of fiction. Kabuki has been praised by international dramatists

as one of the most complete and innovative theatrical traditions, and Izumo no Okuni is widely acknowledged as an important innovator by critics the world over.

—*Matthew Penney*

FURTHER READING

Ariyoshi, Sawako. *The Kabuki Dancer*. New York: Kodansha International, 1994. Although it is a fictional account of Izumo no Okuni's life, it is a major work of one of Japan's most prominent female authors and offers insight into Izumo no Okuni's continued influence.

Brandon, James R. *Studies in Kabuki: Its Acting, Music, and Historical Context*. Honolulu: University of Hawaii Press, 1978. An important book concerning the historical development of Kabuki.

De Ferranti, Hugh. *Japanese Muscial Instruments*. New York: Oxford University Press, 2000. A detailed study of the Japanese musical tradition of which Kabuki is a part. Gives insight into the religious and secular musical traditions that went into Izumo no Okuni's style of performance.

Leiter, Samuel L. *New Kabuki Encyclopedia*. New York: Greenwood, 1997. This has become the standard reference work on Kabuki in English, and all aspects of Izumo no Okuni's life and the early Kabuki tradition are covered in detail.

_____, ed. *A Kabuki Reader: History and Performance*. New York: M. E. Sharpe, 2002. A fascinating collection of works of importance to the history of Kabuki. Contains references to Izumo no Okuni and the development of the Kabuki tradition.

SEE ALSO: Tokugawa Ieyasu.

RELATED ARTICLES in *Great Events from History: The Seventeenth Century, 1601-1700:* 1603: Tokugawa Shogunate Begins; 1603-1629: Okuni Stages the First Kabuki Dance Dramas.

JAHĀNGĪR
Emperor of India (r. 1605-1627)

Jahāngīr was an emperor with musical, poetic, artistic, intellectual, culinary, and sartorial tastes and sensibilities. With his penchant for courtly rituals, as well, he contributed immensely to what came to be hallmarks of Mughal culture.

BORN: August 31, 1569; Fatehpur Sīkri, India
DIED: October 28, 1627; Chingarhsiri, India
ALSO KNOWN AS: Jehangir; Salīm (given name);
Nūruddīn Muḥammad Jahāngīr (full royal name)
AREAS OF ACHIEVEMENT: Government and politics, patronage of the arts, warfare and conquest

EARLY LIFE

Jahāngīr (jeh-HAHN-geer) was born Prince Salīm, the eldest son of one of India's greatest Mughal emperors, Akbar (r. 1556-1605), and his Rājput queen Jodha Bai (d. 1623). Reportedly, Salīm's birth was hailed by his parents as the gift of the sixteenth century Muslim saint Sheik Salīm Chishti and was, therefore, a blessing for them, as they had desperately desired a male successor. The royal child, given the royal name Nūruddīn Muḥammad Jahāngīr (light of the faith of Muḥammad, the world conqueror) was educated beginning at age four, under the guidance of important tutors such as Akbar's courtier Abdur Rahim Khankhanan, who taught him Persian, Arabic, Hindi, history, arithmetic, geography, and other sciences.

From an early age, Jahāngīr displayed a kind of schizophrenic personality. On one hand, he was romantically inclined and had an artistic sensibility and an intellectual bent of mind. On the other hand, he had a violent temper, was intolerant of religion, and had bouts of bacchanalian frenzy, aggravated no doubt by his abuse of opium and alcohol, typical of his family. As early as 1591, Jahāngīr had been estranged from his royal father, who feared being poisoned by his son.

Around 1599, Jahāngīr, though married to several wives and the father of three sons, became involved in a scandalous love affair with one of his father's wives, the teenaged Anarkali (pomegranate kernel). After being caught in bed with the prince, Anarkali was buried alive, and the offending prince was bypassed by his eldest son Khusru in succession to the throne. Khusru was born in 1587 to Jahāngīr and his Rājput wife Man Bai. Akbar's choice of Khusru for the throne disconcerted Jahāngīr, and he sought to procure his rightful succession through the use of force. His opportunity came in the fall of 1599, when Akbar had left for a campaign in the Deccan (central India), which put Jahāngīr in the charge of the capital.

In July of 1600, Jahāngīr, who tried unsuccessfully to seize control of Āgra fort, confronted his father when he returned to Āgra. He spurned his father's conciliatory of-

Jahāngīr, seated center right, drinks wine under a canopy in an eighteenth century painting by Manohar. (Hulton Archive/Getty Images)

fer of the governorship of Bengal and Orissa and instead retreated to Allahabad, where he began to have the *khutba* (the Friday sermon in the mosque) read and to have coins struck in his name. He also had his father's trusted councillor Abu-l Fazl ʿAllāmī assassinated in 1602. (Abu-l Fazl ʿAllāmī had been sent from the Deccan to deal with Jahāngīr.) Ultimately, the terminally ill, old Emperor Akbar had a change of heart and forgave his renegade son, recognizing him as his successor before he died on October 16, 1605.

LIFE'S WORK

Jahāngīr's reign began with his son Khusru's revolt on April 6, 1606. The rebellion was crushed easily and cruelly. Khusru was confined, though his life was spared at first. When, in August, 1607, Khusru was implicated in a plot to assassinate Jahāngīr, the emperor had his son partially blinded and kept under strict surveillance.

Jahāngīr's reign was markedly affected by his marriage to Mihr-un-Nisāʿ (d. 1645), the daughter of a Persian place-seeker at Akbar's court. She earlier had married a court noble, but he died in service in Bengal. She relocated to the imperial court, where she attracted Jahāngīr's attention, and married the emperor in 1611, thus obtaining her famous sobriquet, Nūr Jahān (light of the world). She was also known as Nūr Mahāl (light of the palace). Possessed of immense charm, charisma, and cunning, Nūr Jahān, along with her father (who received the title of Itimad-ud-daula, pillar of the state) and her brother, emerged as the real sources of power and policy in Jahāngīr's government between 1611 and 1622.

The rise of this Persian junta coincided with the emperor's increasing obsession with opium, wine, poetry, music, dance, and other pastimes, to the utter neglect of the more prosaic and practical art of government. A rival faction at court emerged under the Afghan soldier-statesman Mahabat Khan toward the end of Jahāngīr's reign.

Jahāngīr continued the Mughal policy of territorial conquest and expansion. In the northeast, he subdued the warlike Ahoms (immigrants from upper Burma) in 1612. In 1614, the Hindu maharaja Amar Singh of Mewar capitulated and became a friendly tributary ruler under the Mughals. In 1616, Jahāngīr's third son, Khurram (1592-1666), conquered Ahmadnagar in the Deccan and obtained from his royal father the title of Shah Jahan (ruler of the world), reigning from 1628 to 1658. In 1618, Jahāngīr defeated the raja of Kangra, one of the Rājput chiefs whose valley kingdoms cordoned the Himalayan foothills.

LIFE AT JAHĀNGĪR'S COURT

Sir Thomas Roe, King James I's ambassador to the Mughal court beginning in 1614, chronicled the life of Jahāngīr's court, especially its theatrical qualities, depicted here.

Three times a day he sits out in three places: once to see his Elephants and beasts fight, about noon; after, from four to five or six, to entertain all that visit him; at night, from nine till mid-night, with all his great men, but none else, where he is below with them, in all familiarity. I visited him in the second of these, where I found him in a Court, set above like a King in a Play, and all his Nobles and my self below on a state covered with carpets—a just Theater; . . . Canopies over his head, and two standing on the heads of two wooden Elephants, to beat away flies.

Source: Quoted in *Nur Jahan: Empress of Mughal India*, by Ellison Banks Findly (New York: Oxford University Press, 1993), p. 63. Rendered into modern English by Desiree Dreeuws.

During the Mughal operation in the Deccan, Jahāngīr spent more than five years away from the capital at Āgra, traveling to Mandu and Gujarat. When he returned to the capital in April of 1619, his health failed and his court came under the control of Nūr Jahān's faction. Nūr Jahān, originally a favorer of Khurram's succession, feared losing her hold over the empire because she disliked the prince's imperious attitude. In search of a pliable successor, she had her own daughter from her first marriage, Ladli Begum, married to Jahāngīr's youngest son, Shahryar (1605-1628). Her first effective move against Shah Jahan was made in 1622, when the empire's ongoing clashes with the Ṣafavid ruler of Persia, Shah ʿAbbās the Great (r. 1587-1629), over Qandahār had taken a bad turn. Nūr Jahān wanted Khurram to lead the expedition to Qandahār, where he would either be defeated by the shah or, because he would have to stay far away, lose his clout at the imperial court.

Shah Jahan's expected refusal played into Nūr Jahān's hands, and he was hunted by the imperial army as a traitor. Mahabat Khan, the commander in chief of the imperial army, was able to bring the rebellious prince under control, but he did not surrender him to the court, fearing that such a move would strengthen Nūr Jahān's position. Mahabat allowed his prisoner to escape to far-off Bengal, where Shah Jahan began to regroup his forces. When Nūr Jahān accused Mahabat of embezzling government funds and violating imperial protocol, the enraged commander in chief retaliated by placing both the emperor and his queen under his surveillance in March of 1626, while the royal couple was encamping at Lahore. Mahabat's move did not succeed because Nūr Jahān still enjoyed the complete support of the court at Āgra, which was under the control of her family. In October of 1626, Mahabat's protégé Parvez, Jahāngīr's second son, died, so Mahabat decided to join forces with Shah Jahan in Bengal to prepare for a final showdown of power between the ailing emperor and his renegade son.

Meanwhile, Jahāngīr's illness, which had become serious since 1621, rapidly worsened. During the hot weather of 1627, he traveled to his beloved Kashmir for relief and rest. Within days of arrival there, both he and his accompanying youngest son, Shahryar, fell ill, terminally. Shahryar's condition compelled him to return to the warmer climate of Lahore. Jahāngīr, too, was persuaded to leave Kashmir and stay near his ailing son. On October 28, 1627, on the way back to Lahore from Kashmir, at Chingarhsiri, Jahāngīr died at age fifty-eight, after having reigned for a little more than twenty-one years.

SIGNIFICANCE

Jahāngīr was an accomplished individual, "an aristocrat with the eye of a naturalist, the vision of a poet, the taste of connoisseur and the philosophy of an epicurean," in the estimation of an eminent scholar. Arguably, his reign was of little note politically—he merely carried on the policies of his predecessor—though it registered a cultural triumph. Thanks to the influence of his queen Nūr Jahān, Persian culture affected almost every aspect of refined life, from cuisine, calligraphy, and costumes to art and architecture, and it became a part of Indian civilization.

Though seen generally as a lazy and indulgent libertine, jealous of his brothers and sons, Jahāngīr nevertheless was a self-conscious monarch with a vision of majestic grandeur. He prescribed the parameters of an ordered society upon commencing his reign (witness his *dastan ul-amal*, twelve edicts for the conduct of his subjects). He also had a "chain of justice" fastened at one end of the battlements of Āgra fort and to a stone post on the Yamuna River at the other end. Anyone seeking justice or the attention of the emperor could pull the chain of bells.

In the realm of religion, Jahāngīr was a marked eclectic and was even occasionally seen as a favorer of Christianity. It was during his reign that the British East India Company received the imperial *farman* (decree or license) in 1619 to open a factory at Surat, Mughal India's principal port on the western coast, after the arrival of Sir Thomas Roe, King James I's ambassador to the Mughal court, in 1614.

—Narasingha P. Sil

FURTHER READING

Edwardes, S. M., and H. L. O Garrett. *Mughal Rule in India*. 2d ed. Delhi, India: S. Chand, 1962. A solid and succinct account of the Mughal period in India.

Findly, Ellison B. *Nūr Jahān: Empress of Mughal India*. New York: Oxford University Press, 1993. This work is elegant as well as erudite, offering an excellent read and valuable analysis of both Nūr Jahān and Jahāngīr.

Husain, Afzal. *The Nobility Under Akbar and Jahāngīr: A Study of Family Groups*. New Delhi: Manohar, 1999. Details the kinship structures of nine noble families and the social structure of Mughal culture in general. Explains the relationship between family, politics, and religion.

Prasad, Beni. *History of Jahāngīr*. 1922. 5th ed. Allahabad: Indian Press, 1962. A standard and reliable account of Jahāngīr's life and reign.

Richards, John F. *The Mughal Empire*. Vol. 5 in *The New Cambridge History of India*. 1993. Reprint. New York: Cambridge University Press, 1996. A standard scholarly overview of the Mughal Empire in the context of India's history.

Wolpert, Stanley. *A New History of India*. 7th ed. New York: Oxford University Press, 2004. This frequently updated general history, written by one of the leading historians of India, provides an accessible introduction.

Yunus, Mohammed, and Anuradha Parmar. *South Asia: A Historical Narrative*. New York: Oxford University Press, 2003. A helpful text for beginners but lacking in important details.

SEE ALSO: ꜥAbbās the Great; Aurangzeb; Kösem Sultan; Murad IV; Shah Jahan; Śivājī.

RELATED ARTICLES in *Great Events from History: The Seventeenth Century, 1601-1700:* 17th century: Rise of the Gunpowder Empires; 1602-1639: Ottoman-Ṣafavid Wars; 1605-1627: Mughal Court Culture Flourishes; 1606-1674: Europeans Settle in India; 1632-c. 1650: Shah Jahan Builds the Taj Mahal; 1658-1707: Reign of Aurangzeb; c. 1666-1676: Founding of the Marāthā Kingdom; 1679-1709: Rājput Rebellion; March 30, 1699: Singh Founds the Khalsa Brotherhood.

JAMES I
King of England (r. 1603-1625) and king of Scotland as James VI (r. 1567-1625)

Overcoming the tragedies that characterized his tumultuous formative years, James I founded the Stuart Dynasty in England and provided continuity in English politics for a generation after the death of Elizabeth I.

BORN: June 19, 1566; Edinburgh Castle, Edinburgh, Scotland
DIED: March 27, 1625; Theobalds, Hertfordshire, England
ALSO KNOWN AS: James VI; James Stuart (given name)
AREA OF ACHIEVEMENT: Government and politics

EARLY LIFE

James I was the son of Mary, Queen of Scots, and Henry Stewart, Lord Darnley. In February, 1567, Darnley died violently as a result of an explosion that destroyed his house; fifteen years later, James organized the execution of the earl of Morton for the murder of his father. A few months after Darnley's death, Mary married her third husband, James Hepburn, earl of Bothwell. Mary's forces were defeated by dissident Scottish aristocrats, and Mary abdicated the throne. The infant James was crowned James VI of Scotland on July 24, 1567. In 1568, Mary fled Scotland and abandoned her son.

During his youth, James VI was controlled politically by a succession of regents, the earls of Moray, Lennox, Mar, and Morton. His education was provided by his tutors, George Buchanan and Peter Young; through their influence, James acquired a sound education based on the classics and an interest in intellectual pursuits, and he began to consider himself as a philosopher-king. Although James continued to exhibit a propensity for the study of theology and literature, his mind was not of the first rank.

James VI experienced a traumatic childhood and adolescence. The absence of parents, the frequent political intrigues and upheavals that were focused on him, and his seemingly endless series of temporary and artificial relationships produced a young man who was complex and unsettled. He was interested in poetry and philosophy but not in the workings of government; he was nervous, insecure, and ill-mannered, yet he projected an image of confidence and fancied himself a trendsetter. During his early years, he produced two volumes of poetry, *The Essayes of a Prentise in the Divine Art of Poesie* (1584) and *His Maiesties Poeticall Exercises at Vacant Houres* (1591).

In 1589, James married Anne of Denmark, the daughter of King Frederick II of Denmark and Norway. In 1594, she gave birth to a son, Henry. During the late 1580's and early 1590's, John Maitland served as James's principal adviser. Maitland worked to enhance royal power and prestige in Scotland. James believed that he exercised power and held office by divine right and that he was responsible only to God. These sentiments were expressed by James in his *The True Law of Free Monarchies* (1598). Other works that James produced during the late 1590's were *Daemonologie* (1597), an expression of the king's fear of the mysterious spiritual world, and *Basilikon Doron* (1599), consisting of a series of rambling passages on politics and theology intended as instruction for Prince Henry.

Since the late 1580's, James, interested in the English throne, had followed a policy of accommodation in his dealings with Elizabeth I. Even when his mother, Mary, was executed in 1587 for her involvement in a conspiracy to overthrow Elizabeth, James's only response was to file a complaint. His diplomacy was rewarded when Elizabeth I died on March 24, 1603, and James VI of Scotland became James I of England while retaining his Scottish crown.

James I. (Library of Congress)

JAMES I ON THE DIVINE RIGHT OF KINGS

English politics in the seventeenth century were largely defined by the struggle between the Stuart kings and Parliament over the distribution of power. Parliament advocated a limited, or constitutional, monarchy, whereas the Stuarts believed that the monarch's power should be absolute, because he ruled by divine right. Reproduced below is an excerpt from a speech of James I to Parliament in 1609 setting out his theory of monarchy.

Kings are justly called gods, for that they exercise a manner or resemblance of divine power upon earth; for if you will consider the attributes to God, you shall see how they agree in the person of a king. God hath power to create or destroy, make or unmake at his pleasure, to give life or send death, to judge all and to be judged nor accountable to none, to raise low things and to make high things low at his pleasure, and to God are both soul and body due. And the like power have kings: they make and unmake their subjects, they have power of raising and casting down, of life and of death, judges over all their subjects and in all causes and yet accountable to none but God only.

Source: From *Readings in European History*, edited by James Harvey Robinson (Boston: Atheneum Press, 1906), pp. 349-350.

LIFE'S WORK

Initially, those Englishmen who traveled north to greet the new monarch as he progressed south were impressed; the exuberant James I was liberal in his promises, and indeed, he elevated more than two hundred men to the peerage before he even arrived in London. In appearance, James I was not attractive; his legs were not formed properly, and he spoke with a Scottish accent, which was rendered nearly incomprehensible by his larger-than-normal tongue. Nevertheless, the English nation greeted the new king with a sense of hope and expectation. Many problems that had been ignored or deferred during the later years of Elizabeth I's reign quickly surfaced. The financial condition of the realm was jeopardized by the continuing war with Spain, inflation, and the fixed nature of governmental revenues. Another problem soon manifested itself when Nonconformists expressed their dissatisfaction with Anglican theology and the episcopal organization of the Church of England.

Under the able and astute guidance of Robert Cecil, earl of Salisbury, James appeared to confront these issues willingly. In 1604, James permitted Puritans to address the Hampton Court conference. He concluded that most of the Puritan recommendations were not accept-

able, however, because he feared that they would lead to a presbyterian form of religion, which would weaken the Crown. He defended the episcopal arrangement and demanded conformity to a uniform church service. James also thwarted the efforts of the English Catholics (the Recusants) to improve their standing before the law. Disappointed Recusant Radicals formulated the Gunpowder Plot in 1605. The conspiracy was designed to eliminate Parliament and the king by blowing up Parliament on November 5, 1605, when James was scheduled to appear. Through Salisbury's network of spies, the plot became known before it could be implemented.

The most significant problem James encountered was the deteriorating relationship between the Crown and Parliament. He never recognized that the primary source of this difficulty was his own lack of understanding of the English constitutional process and the interrelationship and interdependence of the monarch and Parliament. As a consequence, James came into conflict with Parliament when he tried to bypass Parliament and simply rule without one.

The severity of the hostility between James I and his Parliaments mounted after the death of Salisbury in 1612. James would not find another efficient minister for the remainder of his reign; instead, he allowed his personal favorites, Robert Carr, earl of Somerset, and George Villiers, first duke of Buckingham, to assume positions of great power.

Both of James's favorites were individuals of limited intelligence and talent who were motivated by personal gain. Their policies and actions exacerbated rather than improved the Crown's relationship with Parliament. James further alienated the English legal community by his attacks on Sir Edward Coke, a staunch defender of the common law. In 1616, James arranged for Coke's dismissal from the Court of Common Pleas.

James's pro-Spanish foreign policy also was not well received by the English people in the wake of the crisis of the Spanish Armada in the late 1580's and the subsequent war with Spain. James concluded a peace treaty with Madrid in 1604. The king planned to reconcile with both Madrid and Paris, the two traditional enemies of England. The influence of the Spanish ambassador, Diego Sarmiento de Acuña, count of Gondomar, upon the king was so extensive that James ordered the execution of Sir Walter Ralegh at Gondomar's suggestion. Near the end of his reign, James urged his heir, Charles (Prince Henry had died in 1612), to enter into a Spanish marriage. After Charles and Buckingham traveled to Madrid for this purpose in 1623, however, they returned with hostile attitudes toward Spain.

In 1618, the Thirty Years' War broke out on the Continent. The English expected their king to support the Protestant side, especially since his son-in-law, Frederick II, elector of the Palatinate, was one of the leaders of the Protestant League during the Bohemian phase of the war. Instead, because of his interest in maintaining good terms with Spain, James tried to serve as a diplomatic mediator. His problems were then compounded by the Spanish invasion of the Palatinate in 1620. During the 1620's, James's foreign policy and financial problems emerged as the principal issues in his continuing conflict with Parliament.

During the last decade of his life, James became increasingly decadent and allowed Buckingham to assume extensive powers. Buckingham in turn corrupted the royal government: He demanded and received bribes from everyone involved in its business. The corruption became pervasive and caused scandal; attempts to introduce reform in administration met with failure. As the 1620's progressed, James's health continued to decline. He died at his country estate in Hertfordshire, the Theobalds, on March 27, 1625.

SIGNIFICANCE

During the reign of James I, the antagonism between the Crown and Parliament was heightened, and the king was in large part responsible for this development. The king chose his advisers poorly after 1612, and those advisers both made significant political errors and spread corruption through the royal administration. James, moreover, failed to recognize the dynamic forces of the period and the seriousness of their impact on English politics. His reign, then, witnessed the emergence of a polarized English society with Royalists and Anglicans on one side and Parliamentarians and Puritans on the other. As he aged, James became less involved with the mounting crises and retreated into his preoccupation with personal matters. He bequeathed to his son, Charles I, a kingdom that was in financial disarray and politically and religiously divided.

—William T. Walker

FURTHER READING

Ashley, Maurice. *England in the Seventeenth Century.* 3d ed. New York: Penguin Books, 1963. Portrays James I as an effective, if not glorious, governor of the realm. Ashley's James I was clever and bright, but vain and weak in dealing with his personal retinue.

Ashton, Robert. *The English Civil War: Conservatism and Revolution, 1603-1649.* New York: W. W. Norton, 1979. James I emerges as a monarch of limited managerial ability who was instrumental in establishing the separate, insular society of his court culture.

Croft, Pauline. *King James.* New York: Palgrave Macmillan, 2003. Balanced and perceptive account of James's life and reign, emphasizing his attempts to rule Scotland and Ireland as well as England.

Gardiner, Samuel Rawson. *The First Two Stuarts and the Puritan Revolution, 1603-1660.* New York: Longmans, Green, 1876. Reprint. New York: Thomas Y. Crowell, 1970. In this classic interpretation of James I and Charles I, Gardiner portrays James I as an intelligent but indolent and indecisive monarch who lacked an understanding of English political and constitutional processes.

Hill, Christopher. *Puritanism and Revolution: Studies in Interpretation of the English Revolution of the Seventeenth Century.* New York: Schocken Books, 1964. This study of the decades leading to the English Revolution of the 1640's portrays James as an indecisive politician, limited by finances and influenced by close confidants at court.

_____. *Society and Puritanism in Pre-Revolutionary England.* 2d ed. New York: Schocken Books, 1967. In this book by a renowned English Marxist historian, James I is seen as an intelligent individual who was influenced and restricted by the rise of Puritanism.

Kenyon, J. P., ed. *The Stuart Constitution: Documents and Commentary.* 2d ed. New York: Cambridge University Press, 1986. Kenyon's interpretation of James's relationship with Parliament is more tempered than traditional analysis of this subject. Kenyon examines the relationship within the context of a continuing debate between Crown and Parliament, and traces the difficulties in the relationship to the failure of the king's ministers and advisers.

Lockyer, Roger. *Tudor and Stuart Britain, 1471-1714.* 2d ed. New York: St. Martin's Press, 1985. Explains how anticipation of a more prosperous era during James I's rule was unrealized because of the government's continuing financial problems and the pervasive corruption of public life. Lockyer examines how the resulting disillusionment led to the beginnings of a constitutional crisis.

Patterson, W. B. "King James I and the Protestant Cause in the Crisis of 1618-21." In *Religion and National Identity*, edited by Stuart Mews. Oxford, England: Basil Blackwell, 1982. Describes James's attempts to help the Protestant cause and mediate conflict during the Bohemian phase of the Thirty Year's War. These attempts led to increasing criticism of James's regime.

Stewart, Alan. *The Cradle King: The Life of James VI and I, the First Monarch of a Unified Great Britain*. New York: St. Martin's Press, 2003. Focuses on how James VI of Scotland became James I of England. Stewart maintains James was an able ruler of Scotland, but the tactics that served him well in that country were not applicable for governing England and a unified Great Britain.

Wilson, David Harris. *King James VI and I*. London: Jonathan Cape, 1956. Wilson's biography is considered the definitive work on James I. The king emerges as a complex individual who was greatly influenced by the chaos that characterized his early life.

Woolrych, Austin. "The English Revolution: An Introduction." In *The English Revolution: 1600-1660*, edited by E. W. Ives. New York: Barnes and Noble Books, 1969. Depicts James I as an incompetent administrator, preoccupied with personal affairs. Woolrych attributes the general stability that characterized James's reign until 1612 to Cecil's influence.

SEE ALSO: First Duke of Buckingham; Robert Carr; Charles I; Sir Edward Coke.

RELATED ARTICLES in *Great Events from History: The Seventeenth Century, 1601-1700:* November 5, 1605: Gunpowder Plot; 1618-1648: Thirty Years' War; 1642-1651: English Civil Wars.

JAMES II
King of England (r. 1685-1688)

Although he was not a successful king, James II had a fruitful career as duke of York before he reached the throne. He was a distinguished soldier and sailor and an efficient, industrious naval administrator. His pro-Catholic policies as monarch, however, led directly to the Glorious Revolution and the end of the Stuart Dynasty.

BORN: October 14, 1633; London, England
DIED: September 16, 1701; Saint-Germain, near Paris, France
AREA OF ACHIEVEMENT: Government and politics

EARLY LIFE

The future James II was born on October 14, 1633, at Saint James's Palace in London. He was the second surviving son of King Charles I and Queen Henrietta Maria. Three and one-half years younger than his elder brother, the future Charles II, James was created duke of York when he was only three months old.

James lived his childhood and youth in the midst of dramatic and shattering political events. Charles I's autocratic rule steadily antagonized Parliament, and civil war broke out in 1642. When James was only eight years old, he found himself a witness to the first battle of the war, at Edgehill. After the battle, James was sent to Oxford, where he remained until the end of the first phase of the war. Because of the disruption the war caused, James received an inadequate and incomplete education, and he received little direct attention from his parents.

When the Parliamentary forces triumphed, James was confined to Saint James's Palace in London. In 1648, however, Royalists planned his escape: Disguised in girl's clothing, the young duke slipped out of the country and gained sanctuary in Holland. The following year, having traveled to Saint-Germain, near Paris, to be with his mother, he heard the news that his father had been tried and executed. It needs little imagination to grasp the devastating effect of such an event on a fifteen-year-old boy. The stubbornness and inflexibility that were to mark his brief reign as king arose in part because of his belief that his father might have saved his throne had he acted more firmly in his dealings with Parliament.

In 1652, after serving a brief period as governor of the Channel Islands while his brother, now Charles II, fought in Scotland to regain his kingdom, James became a soldier. He fought in four campaigns in France—on the Royalist side in the civil war, and then against the invading Spanish—under the command of the famous Henri de La Tour d'Auvergne, viscount de Turenne. Brave and resourceful, he became at the age of twenty the youngest of Turenne's lieutenants general.

James's years in France were to prove the happiest and most successful of his life. Tall, fair, handsome, and charming, he made a strong impression on his contemporaries. In 1655, he first met Anne Hyde, daughter of the earl of Clarendon, and she became his wife in 1660. She later bore him two daughters.

In 1657, James reluctantly changed sides and took up service with the Spanish army. Spain was supporting the English Royalist cause in opposition to the alliance between the English Protectorate (1653-1659) and France. The Battle of the Dunes (1658), in which James fought, resulted in a defeat for the Spanish and victory for the French.

In 1660, the republican factions in England quarreled, and Charles II was invited to return. James was appointed lord high admiral, a post that he had nominally held since he was a child. At the age of twenty-six, he was back in his homeland and heir presumptive to the throne.

LIFE'S WORK

As lord high admiral, James was a hardworking and efficient naval administrator, and he also involved himself with trade and colonial affairs. He was responsible for sending an expeditionary force to New England that captured New Amsterdam from the Dutch, renaming it New York in his honor. When trade rivalries with Holland resulted in the Second Anglo-Dutch War of 1665-1667, James was joint commander of the English fleet, and he distinguished himself in the victorious sea battle of Lowestoft. It was his first experience of war at sea. In 1672, when war with the Dutch broke out again, he became supreme commander of the fleet and defeated the Dutch at the Battle of Southwold Bay.

It was during this period of his greatest successes, however, that the seeds of James's downfall were being sown. He had become sympathetic to Catholicism during his years in France, and sometime between 1660 and 1671 he finally converted. James ceased to take the sacraments of the Church of England in 1672, and in 1673, he married his second wife, Mary of Modena, an Italian Roman Catholic. These developments were of enormous significance in Protestant England, where Catholicism was disliked and feared. Events came to a head in 1678, when rumors of a Jesuit plot to kill the king (which became known as the Popish Plot) led to a movement to ban Catholics from Parliament and to exclude James from succession to the throne. Charles II felt compelled to send his Catholic brother into exile until the storm died down. It was three years before James was recalled to England in March, 1682, at a time of comparative peace and

James II. (Library of Congress)

quiet. By 1684, James had rejoined the Privy Council and had resumed his position as lord high admiral.

When Charles II died in 1685, James duly acceded to the throne. His position appeared secure. The new Parliament was composed mostly of loyal monarchists; the anti-Papacy phase appeared to be over. Parliament voted James II a large revenue for life. A brief rebellion in June by the duke of Monmouth, the illegitimate son of Charles II, was quickly put down. The rebellion actually strengthened James's position, enabling him to justify the establishment of a standing army.

James then began to press ahead with a policy of religious toleration, to include Protestant Nonconformists as well as Catholics. He allowed Catholics to hold important positions in the universities and in the army and appointed a Jesuit to the Privy Council. His policy of toleration culminated in the first Declaration of Indulgence in 1687, but his ultimate goal was the repeal of the two Test Acts (under which Catholics were not allowed to hold public office) and of the penal laws against Dissenters. He was unprepared for the fears and opposition that his policy was to arouse, however, and he proceeded far too quickly. He did not appreciate that he was alienating important members of the Church of England, whose support he needed if his policies were to succeed. He took that support too much for granted. Many of his subjects believed that it was James II's secret plan eventually to compel the entire country to embrace Roman Catholicism.

James's instruction that the Declaration of Indulgence should be read out in the churches in May, 1688, precipitated a chain of events that led to his downfall. When the majority of the clergy refused to do as he wished, James imprisoned seven bishops, including the archbishop of Canterbury, and charged them with seditious libel. This action antagonized the entire Church of England.

Then in June, the queen gave birth to a son, greatly increasing the prospects of a Catholic dynasty being established, prospects that the country as a whole found deeply disturbing. The situation deteriorated to such an extent that prominent English noblemen invited the Protestant William III of Orange, the king's nephew and son-in-law (he was married to Mary, the king's daughter), to intervene in England. When James discovered that a Dutch invasion force was being mounted against him, he belatedly tried to reverse his policies and pacify the Church of England, but these were panic measures and had little effect.

William of Orange landed in November, 1688, and immediately there were massive defections from James's own military forces. Even his two daughters and his two sons-in-law deserted him. In December, seeing no other course of action, James joined his queen in exile in France. Because no blood was spilled in the course of this seizure of power by William, the event came to be known as the Glorious Revolution. The following year, James tried to regain his throne by leading an expedition to Ireland, planning afterward to invade Scotland, where support for him remained strong. James, however, was defeated by the larger army of William III at the Battle of the Boyne in June, 1690. He again fled to France and spent the remainder of his life at Saint-Germain, near Paris, with an allowance provided by the French government. During his exile he devised various unlikely schemes to win back his kingdom, and he became increasingly occupied with practicing his religious faith. He died on September 16, 1701.

SIGNIFICANCE

History has judged James II harshly, as one of the least effective English kings. When he came to the throne, he was hailed by his countrymen with enthusiasm and goodwill: His record as soldier, sailor, and administrator had been exemplary. Within four years, however, he managed to alienate so many important groups in the country that he was forced ignominiously to abandon his own kingdom. In the crisis of 1688-1689, his military skill and courage deserted him, and his indecisiveness prevented him from asserting his authority at a time when he might still have prevailed.

James's central error as king lay in his failure to appreciate the need for subtlety and diplomacy in his dealings with Parliament. He was an arrogant and stubborn man who tended to treat his advisers as mere servants; he badly miscalculated in his belief that the Church's traditional loyalty to the Crown would hold no matter what he did. He did not realize that in granting personal exemptions to the Test Acts so that he could appoint Catholics to high positions, he was flouting the authority of Parliament, a course of action that had plunged the country into civil war only forty years previously.

James's inflexibility was rooted in other aspects of his character. He was an honest and straightforward man, without guile. He was unable, for example, to conceal his enthusiasm for his Catholic faith—unlike Charles II, who had also been a Catholic, but who had upheld the rights and privileges of the Church of England. It is likely, however, that James genuinely believed in the principle of religious toleration, the freedom of all Christians to worship as they chose. In this, he was certainly ahead of his time, because the emancipation he proposed was not fully achieved until the nineteenth century. The contemporary fear—which was endorsed by historians right up to the nineteenth century—that he aimed forcibly to bring Great Britain once more under papal authority, was probably unfounded. The tragedy of James II was that a highly principled man of genuine religious feeling, who was not without courageous achievement, should have become so inexplicably obtuse on so many important occasions and issues in his short-lived mismanagement of his kingdom.

—Bryan Aubrey

FURTHER READING

Ashley, Maurice. *The Glorious Revolution of 1688*. New York: Charles Scribner's Sons, 1967. The best account of the year in which James was deposed, by a senior historian of the Stuart period. Concise, reliable, and balanced.

_____. *James II*. Minneapolis: University of Minnesota Press, 1978. Sober, fair, and objective portrait that does not minimize James's faults but nevertheless gives full weight to his positive qualities.

Belloc, Hilaire. *James the Second*. Philadelphia: J. B. Lippincott, 1928. Enthusiastic, Roman Catholic defense of James, but lacking in objectivity and balance. Contains an excellent account of the Battle of the Boyne.

Clarke, James. *Life of James II*. 2 vols. London: Carlton House, 1816. Primary source, used by all subsequent biographers. Much of it consists of the official life, based in part on James's memoirs, which William Diccoonson compiled shortly after James's death.

Haswell, Jock. *James II: Soldier and Sailor*. New York: St. Martin's Press, 1972. Study of James as soldier and sailor, much of which closely follows the account in Clarke (see above). It supplements Turner's biography (see below), which does not adequately cover James's military and naval career.

Miller, John. *King James*. New Haven, Conn.: Yale University Press, 2000. Explores the political, diplomatic, and religious issues that shaped James's brief reign.

_____. *Popery and Politics, 1660-1688*. New York: Cambridge University Press, 1973. Valuable and unprejudiced study. Miller shows how anti-Catholicism was a major force in late seventeenth century English politics, but argues it was not the threat that English Protestants considered it to be.

Mullett, Michael A. *James II and English Politics, 1678-1688*. New York: Routledge, 1994. Focuses on the central role of James, duke of York and later king of England, during this crucial decade within the wider context of political and religious developments.

Turner, Francis Charles. *James II*. New York: Macmillan, 1948. A scholarly, solid, and thorough attempt to understand James II in the context of his time. Turner treats James more kindly than some historians but unconvincingly argues that James suffered from a mysterious mental disease.

SEE ALSO: Charles I; Charles II (of England); Henrietta Maria; Mary II; Duke of Monmouth; Viscount de Turenne; William III.

RELATED ARTICLES in *Great Events from History: The Seventeenth Century, 1601-1700:* 1642-1651: English Civil Wars; December 6, 1648-May 19, 1649: Establishment of the English Commonwealth; December 16, 1653-September 3, 1658: Cromwell Rules England as Lord Protector; May, 1659-May, 1660: Restoration of Charles II; March 4, 1665-July 31, 1667: Second Anglo-Dutch War; April 6, 1672-August 10, 1678: French-Dutch War; 1673-1678: Test Acts; August 13, 1678-July 1, 1681: The Popish Plot; April 4, 1687, and April 27, 1688: Declaration of Liberty of Conscience; November, 1688-February, 1689: The Glorious Revolution.

CORNELIUS OTTO JANSEN
Dutch theologian and church reformer

Jansen created a new and challenging interpretation of the theology of Saint Augustine for the Catholic Reformation. Out of the controversy over his book Augustinus *emerged Jansenism, a powerful church reform movement bearing his name.*

BORN: October 28, 1585; Accoi, Holland (now in the Netherlands)

DIED: May 6, 1638; Ypres, Spanish Netherlands (now in Belgium)

AREAS OF ACHIEVEMENT: Church reform, religion and theology

EARLY LIFE

Cornelius Otto Jansen (kohr-NAY-lee-uhs oh-toh JAHN-sehn) was born in Accoi, a village near Leerdam in southern Holland. Although the district was Calvinist, Jansen's family was Roman Catholic. After an elementary education at Culemborg, he attended the Latin school of Saint Jerome in Utrecht. In 1602, he entered the University of Louvain, where he resided in the Falcon College. An assiduous and intelligent student, he earned first honors among his colleagues in the liberal arts.

In 1604, he began theological studies under the direction of Jacobus Jansonius, a fellow Dutchman from Amsterdam, who introduced him to the Augustinian views of Michael Baius, a controversial sixteenth century Flemish theologian who had been condemned by Rome in 1567. At Louvain, Jansen also became familiar with the debate caused by the treatise of the Jesuit Luis de Molina on divine grace and free will. As a student, Jansen had adopted Augustinian in contrast to Jesuit positions on the points at issue. Nevertheless, while criticizing the theology and ecclesiastical privileges of the Society of Jesus, he learned to appreciate its religious spirit, zeal for the Church, and scholarly attainments.

After receiving the bachelor's degree in theology in 1609, Jansen left Louvain for Paris. This change of place was most likely the result of his growing desire to devote himself to the study of the Bible and the writings of the Fathers of the Church rather than to dogmatic theology. In Paris, while studying Greek, he met Jean Du Vergier de Hauranne, later Abbé de Saint-Cyran. Thus began a most influential friendship. Sharing a common love for the basic sources of theology, the two men continued their studies together at the estate of Du Vergier's mother, near Bayonne in southern France. Ordained priest in Mechelen in 1614, Jansen returned to France for two more years until obliged to return to the Low Countries, following his father's death. Chosen to lead a newly organized college for Dutch ecclesiastical students at Louvain, he earned a doctor's degree in theology at the university in October, 1617. He became a professor of theology in May of that year.

Cornelius Otto Jansen. (Library of Congress)

LIFE'S WORK

In 1623, Jansen began an extensive, systematic treatment of Saint Augustine's views on the subject of divine grace. This project, the principal occupation of his life, was soon interrupted. He was called upon by the university to represent its interests at the Spanish court in Madrid. Resigning his post as head of the Dutch college, he traveled to Spain in 1624 and again in 1626 to protect the university's monopoly on instruction from attempts by Jesuits to offer courses in Louvain. In those years, he was also drawn into controversies with Calvinists. From 1624 to 1626, and occasionally thereafter, Jansen disputed the Calvinists' theological positions as laid down in the decrees of the Synod of Dordrecht.

In 1628, he returned to his work on Saint Augustine with a celebrated sermon on the spiritual life based on Augustinian principles. Two years later, appointed regius professor of Holy Scripture, he undertook heavy instructional as well as administrative duties. The lectures that he prepared for his classes were published posthumously as commentaries on the books of the Bible. Based on patristic writings, his commentaries explain the literal meaning of the text and avoid excessive use of allegory. These commentaries were well received because of their author's clarity and sound erudition.

Jansen continued to pursue his scholarly goals despite distractions caused by the progress of the Thirty Years' War (1618-1648) in the Low Countries. Alarmed by the invasion of his country by French and Dutch forces, he helped organize the defense of Louvain in 1635. In that same year, he also composed *Mars gallicus* (1636), an attack on Cardinal de Richelieu's policy of seeking Protestant allies in France's war against Spain. Translated into Spanish and French, the tract angered Richelieu and set off a polemic, which Jansen left to his friends to continue.

Nominated bishop of Ypres by the Spanish government in October, 1635, Jansen was consecrated the next year. A zealous pastor, he improved the administration of the diocese and cultivated good relations with the Society of Jesus. Neither the dignity nor the burdens of his new office, however, could draw him from his study of Saint Augustine. By this time, he had composed his thoughts in a large manuscript, *Augustinus* (1640), which was known only to Du Vergier and a few other close friends. The great project was brought to a conclusion at the same time that

Jansen was struck by the plague and died in 1638. *Augustinus* was published at Jansen's request in Louvain in 1640 by two friends, Calenus and Froidment, who had witnessed the treatise's development over many years.

Augustinus is a serious, logically constructed treatise, whose arguments are well buttressed with references to sources and by the author's own explanatory notes. It is written in a classicist Latin that reflects Jansen's intimate familiarity with the fourth century idiom of Saint Augustine. Jansen organized the treatise in three parts. In the first part, he describes Saint Augustine's critique of the positions taken by Pelagian and semi-Pelagian theologians on the relationship between divine grace and free will. In his introduction to the second part, Jansen examines the relationship between philosophy and theology. Rejecting the excessively rationalistic methods of Scholastic schools of theology, he declares that he intends to follow Saint Augustine on the doctrine of grace. The bulk of the second part is devoted to an examination of the effects of original sin on humankind and the fallen angels. These creatures have been completely alienated from their creator; their wills tend without fail toward evil. Even the most estimable achievements of unredeemed human nature are morally tainted at their root. Denying the concept of a state of pure nature to which Jesuit theologians argued that humans had been originally called, Jansen contended that, by creation, humans were called to a supernatural level of existence.

The third and most important part of the treatise explains Saint Augustine's concept of Christ's restoration of human nature by his redeeming grace. Although Christ's action heals the evil effects of sin and restores true human freedom, his grace remains continually necessary for any human work to be pleasing to God. Even when redeemed, humans remain powerless to reconcile themselves with God. Salvation, according to Jansen's reading of Saint Augustine, is profoundly paradoxical, for humankind's free will is neither forced nor compromised, although God's saving grace is irresistible and unfailingly effective. Human freedom consists in a voluntary compliance with the will of God.

Perhaps the most characteristic of the concepts that Jansen develops in this part of the treatise is his view that human existence is dominated by two conflicting delights or desires. *Delectatio coelestis*, or heavenly desire, is a product of divine grace working in a person, leading him or her to love God and to do good works. *Delectatio terrena*, in contrast, is a product of fallen human nature, inclining a person to love of the world and to sin. The inclination that prevails in a person's life is called by Jansen *delectatio victrix*, or the victorious desire.

Although Jansen focused the body of *Augustinus* on the doctrines of the great Father of the Church rather than on contemporary theological controversies, he appended to the treatise an epilogue, attributing to Molina and other Jesuits the Pelagian and semi-Pelagian doctrines condemned by Saint Augustine. Even without this polemical appendix, the *Augustinus* was certain to provoke powerful opposition from the Jesuits, because it implicitly claimed the enormous authority of Saint Augustine in support of contemporary teaching on grace and free will that the Jesuits assiduously opposed. Jansen anticipated that the Jesuits would resort to any means to suppress his treatise, so he made elaborate arrangements to have it printed secretly. His unexpected death delayed, but did not prevent, Calenus and Froidment from having the treatise printed and widely distributed.

SIGNIFICANCE

Jansen was an outstanding representative of the Reformation of the Roman Catholic Church that took place in the Spanish Netherlands at the beginning of the seventeenth century. A devout priest of austere character, he worked loyally for the improvement of the Church as teacher, university rector, and bishop. As a scholar, he adhered to the best contemporary standards, attempting to reach truth in complex theological issues that aroused intense religious passions.

The historical impact of his treatise, *Augustinus*, was enormous. It was received favorably by persons who identified themselves with the Augustinian theological tradition. Jesuits and their allies, however, accused Jansen of falling into heresy. *Augustinus*, they contended, virtually denied human free will and repeated other errors taught by John Calvin and Baius, which the Church had already condemned. Prodded by Jansen's critics, Pope Urban VIII condemned *Augustinus* in 1643.

Conflict over the treatise spread from the Spanish Netherlands to France soon after its publication. Jansen's bitter enemy, Richelieu, died in 1642, but his hostility to Jansen and his work lived on in Jules Mazarin, who assumed control of the royal government. Jansen's friend Du Vergier nevertheless won support for *Augustinus*. In 1649, anti-Jansenists at the University of Paris drew several propositions, allegedly from the treatise, and demanded that they be condemned. A confusing debate ensued in which *Augustinus* was effectively defended by Antoine Arnauld. The disputed propositions were eventually limited to five that Pope Innocent X condemned in 1653.

The controversy over Jansen's work generated a movement, Jansenism, that waged war against his critics and enemies over a broad range of issues. Arnauld charged the Jesuits with laxity in regard to the proper disposition for reception of the sacraments, while philosopher and mathematician Blaise Pascal ridiculed Jesuit casuistry. Although Jansenism's antiauthoritarian implications led Mazarin to seek its condemnation by Rome, its followers won support among magistrates in the high courts of law. Jansenist concepts of church reform, based on principles of Christian Humanism and the decrees of the Council of Trent, also proved attractive to some religious orders.

The growth of Jansenism provoked King Louis XIV to adopt a policy of ruthless extermination. From 1661 to 1667, the clergy of the kingdom were required to sign a condemnation of the five propositions. The resistance of Jansenists to this persecution led Pope Clement IX to acknowledge tacitly that the condemned propositions were not in fact representative of Jansen's views. By the end of the seventeenth century, Jansenism had developed a life of its own, pursuing causes other than the vindication of Jansen and his *Augustinus*.

—*Charles H. O'Brien*

FURTHER READING

Cognet, Louis, et al. *The Church in the Age of Absolutism and Enlightenment*. Vol. 6 in *History of the Church*, translated by Gunther J. Holst, edited by Hubert Jedin and John P. Dolan. New York: Crossroad, 1981. Cognet, an authority on Jansenism in seventeenth century France, includes several chapters on French Jansenism during that era. His discussion contains a brief explanation of Jansen's background and work at Louvain.

Delumeau, Jean. *Catholicism Between Luther and Voltaire: A New View of the Counter-Reformation*. Philadelphia: Westminster Press, 1977. Includes a chapter on Jansenism, providing modern interpretations of the religion. Briefly discusses the issues raised by Jansen in his principal work, *Augustinus*, and the conflicts arising from its publication.

Doyle, William. *Jansenism: Catholic Resistance to Authority from the Reformation to the French Revolution*. New York: St. Martin's Press, 1999. A brief, balanced view of Jansenism, including a discussion of Jansen's *Augustinus* and how the book's publication deepened the feud between French Jesuits and more-established Catholic orders.

Gonzalez, Justo L. *From Protestant Reformation to the Twentieth Century*. Vol. 3 in *A History of Christian Thought*. Nashville, Tenn.: Abandon Press, 1975. A brief but clear analysis of Jansen's theological concepts and the course of Jansenism up to the French Revolution. Gonzalez discusses Jansen's belief that the methods of philosophy and theology are radically different; only the method of theology can attain knowledge that is certain.

Hargreaves, Kevin John. *Cornelius Jansenius and the Origins of Jansenism*. Ann Arbor, Mich.: University Microfilms, 1974. A thorough investigation of the contributions Jansen made to the movement that bears his name and to theology. A doctoral dissertation from Brandeis University, this book is the most extensive study of Jansenism available in English. The neglected sources examined by the author include Jansen's treatise on theological method, his introduction to *Augustinus*, and his works on spirituality. Jansen's theological concepts are analyzed and placed in the context of the history of religious ideas from Saint Augustine to Calvin. Hargreaves contends that Jansen's theology represents an extreme critique of the rational, Scholastic tradition of theology.

Lubac, Henride. *Augustinianism and Modern Theology*. Translated by Lancelot Sheppard. New York: Crossroad, 2000. Discusses Jansen's principal work, *Augustinus*, and his role in creating a new religious movement. Originally published in 1969, this reprint includes a new introduction with information about Jansenism.

Mosse, George L. "Changes in Religious Thought." In *Cambridge Modern History*. Vol. 4. New York: Cambridge University Press, 1970. Places Jansen and Jansenism in a general historical context. Mosse regards Jansenism as a challenge to orthodoxy within Catholicism analogous to Puritanism within Protestantism. He also argues that Jansen played a role in the beginning of modern rationalism.

SEE ALSO: François de Salignac de La Mothe-Fénelon; Innocent XI; Jan Komenský; Duchesse de Longueville; Blaise Pascal; Jean Racine; Urban VIII; Saint Vincent de Paul.

RELATED ARTICLES in *Great Events from History: The Seventeenth Century, 1601-1700*: 1610-1643: Reign of Louis XIII; November 10, 1630: The Day of Dupes; 1638-1669: Spread of Jansenism.

SAINT ISAAC JOGUES
French-born colonial Canadian priest and missionary

The Jesuit Jogues served as a missionary to the Hurons and Iroquois in New France (Canada). His prolonged torture by the Iroquois made him a celebrity and a symbol of French Counter-Reformation spirituality, and his later death at their hands rendered him a martyr in the eyes of the Catholic Church.

BORN: January 10, 1607; Orléans, France
DIED: October 18, 1646; Ossernenon, near Fort Orange, New Netherland (now Auriesville, New York)
AREA OF ACHIEVEMENT: Religion and theology

EARLY LIFE

Saint Isaac Jogues (ee-zahk zhawg) was the third son born to Laurent Jogues and his second wife, Françoise. Both parents were from prominent and prosperous Orléans families, and five of their six sons entered business or professional careers. Isaac, however, was drawn to the religious life, and at the age of seventeen, he entered the newly founded Jesuit College in Orléans.

The Jesuits were rapidly expanding their missionary work in Asia and the Americas at the time, and young Jogues was enraptured by the accounts he heard of missionaries suffering in the cause of religion. In 1624, he entered the Society of Jesus as a novice in Rouen and began his formal study of philosophy and theology there before moving to the College of La Flèche in Anjou in 1626. At La Flèche, Jogues met for the first time some of the Jesuits who had labored in New France (Canada), and it was probably during this time that he determined his own calling lay as a missionary in the wilderness of North America. In 1634, he moved to Paris to continue his studies at the College of Clermont but became impatient to enter the missionary life. He requested and obtained from his superiors his release from further study, and in January of 1636, he was ordained to the priesthood. Four months later, Jogues set sail for New France.

LIFE'S WORK

Jogues arrived in the colony of Quebec during the summer of 1636 and from there traveled to Ihonatiria, the largest of the villages of the Huron nation. The Jesuit mission to the Hurons had been expanded, and Jogues's first assignment was to minister to the natives who had succumbed to smallpox and the other diseases inadvertently brought by the colonists. Native suspicions that the

"Blackrobes" were themselves the cause of "the fever" placed the Jesuits in great danger, even though Jogues himself was afflicted. The Hurons' death threats against the missionaries were never executed, however, and in 1639, Jogues was chosen to open a mission among the Petun (Tobacco) Nation on the shore of Georgian Bay. Two years later, he and Brother Charles Raymbault traveled to the western end of Lake Huron to preach among the Algonquians and Ojibway, becoming, during this journey, the first Europeans to visit Lake Superior.

Upon their return to the Huron villages in June, 1642, Raymbault fell ill, and Jogues was chosen in his stead to accompany a group of Huron converts to Quebec for supplies. On the return journey, Mohawk warriors from the Iroquois confederation ambushed the company; three Hurons were killed and twenty-two were captured, along with René Goupil, a lay assistant. Jogues and another lay assistant, Guillaume Coûture, initially escaped and hid in the woods but then surrendered themselves to remain with their companions. Their captors immediately began to torture the prisoners, chewing off their fingernails and beating them with fists and clubs, before beginning the two-week journey to the village of Ossernenon.

Jogues's account of his captivity among the Iroquois—versions of which were included in the periodical *Jesuit Relations*—became a classic narrative of missionary literature. The tortures inflicted by the Iroquois were designed to make their captives cry out and so allow the captors to gain superiority over both body and spirit, but Jogues's thirst for physical mortification and desire for martyrdom proved to be an equal match for his captors' cruelty.

At Ossernenon, the prisoners were forced to run the gauntlet and then were brought to a platform for public mutilation. Jogues and Goupil each had a thumb sliced off with a sharpened oyster shell, and hot coals were placed on their wounds; such tortures continued intermittently for a number of days. Coûture was eventually adopted into a Mohawk family, but Goupil was killed after a few weeks of captivity by a hatchet blow to the head. Jogues himself became a virtual slave, although as something of a curiosity he was allowed to travel among the Mohawk villages to meet with other Christian captives and even to preach to the Iroquois.

Although Jogues found spiritual gratification in his condition, after thirteen months of captivity, he took advantage of an opportunity to escape when he accompanied a trading party to the settlement of Fort Orange (now Albany). Hidden by Dutch sympathizers, Jogues was eventually smuggled to New Amsterdam (now New York City) and from there traveled incognito to Europe. He landed on the coast of Brittany on Christmas Day, 1643, and early in the new year made his way to the Jesuit community in Rennes, where he presented himself to the surprised rector.

In France, Jogues found himself an instant celebrity. The regent, Queen Anne of Austria, requested an audience with the "living martyr," and Pope Urban VIII granted him a special dispensation to continue to say Mass despite his deforming injuries. By the spring of 1644, however, Jogues obtained permission to return to Quebec, although he was denied his request to return to the missions. Finally, he was permitted to travel to Ossernenon as a member of a peace delegation, and the success of the trip and the warm reception he received from his former captors renewed his determination to open a mission among the Iroquois. In autumn of 1646, Jogues and a lay assistant named John Lalande, while on their way to the Mohawk villages, were intercepted and brought again as captives to Ossernenon. Although a tribal council urged that the missionaries be released in honor of the recently concluded peace, Jogues and his companion were ambushed and decapitated.

SIGNIFICANCE

On June 29, 1930, Pope Pius XI canonized Jogues and seven others—including René Goupil and John Lalande—as the North American martyrs. Thus honored as a Catholic saint, the powerful story of his captivity, mutilation, and death make objective analysis of his life difficult. Most biographical accounts offer little more than hagiography; even the strongly anti-Catholic historian Francis Parkman was forced to salute Jogues's heroic virtue, even if he never quite comprehended his motivation.

Although Jogues aided in the establishment of numerous mission posts and probably baptized some two thousand Hurons (as well as a few dying Iroquois), his real significance is as a symbol of the Counter-Reformation piety of seventeenth century France. After surviving a century of civil war provoked by religious differences, French Catholicism found renewed confidence in the willingness of Jesuits such as Jogues to submit themselves to torture for the sake of the Church. In 1940,

Jogues and the other North American martyrs were collectively proclaimed the patron saints of Canada.

—Rodger Payne

FURTHER READING

Greer, Allan. "Colonial Saints: Gender, Race, and Hagiography in New France." *William and Mary Quarterly*, 3d ser. 57 (2000): 323-348. Although Jogues is not the focus of this study, Greer examines some of the issues concerning the genre of hagiographic narratives, including those of the North American martyrs.

Parkman, Francis. *The Jesuits in North America in the Seventeenth Century*. Vol. 2 in *France and England in North America*. Reprint. Lincoln: University of Nebraska Press, 1997. Recounts the efforts of Jogues and others in New France. As a historian, Parkman can be justly criticized for anti-Catholic and ethnocentric sentiments, but his prose remains vivid.

Roustang, François. *An Autobiography of Martyrdom: Spiritual Writings of the Jesuits in New France*. St. Louis, Mo.: Herder, 1964. Although the introductory material is very hagiographic, the long section on Jogues contains translations of letters and other original documents that are not otherwise easily available in English.

Talbot, Francis, S. J. *Saint Among Savages: The Life of Isaac Jogues*. Reprint. New York: Image Books, 1961. Probably the best biography in English, but still encumbered by hagiographic concerns and outdated attitudes toward Native American cultures.

Thwaites, Reuben Gold, ed. *The Jesuit Relations and Allied Documents*. 73 vols. Cleveland, Ohio: Burrows Brothers, 1896-1901. Criticized for occasional sloppiness in its transcription of original French, Latin, and Italian documents and their English translations, this still remains the definitive source collection for the Jesuit missions. Contains both letters written by Jogues to his superiors and accounts of his work by others; the most famous account of his capture and torture is in volume 31.

SEE ALSO: Anne of Austria; Marie de l'Incarnation; Pierre Esprit Radisson; Urban VIII.

RELATED ARTICLE in *Great Events from History: The Seventeenth Century, 1601-1700:* 1611-1630's: Jesuits Begin Missionary Activities in New France.

JOHN OF AUSTRIA
Spanish military leader

Through military and political endeavors, John of Austria attempted to sustain the power of the Spanish realm and its Habsburg Dynasty in the midst of its declining hegemony in Europe and around the world.

BORN: April 7, 1629; Madrid, Spain
DIED: September 17, 1679; Madrid
ALSO KNOWN AS: Don John of Spain, the Younger; Don Juan de Austria; Don Juan José de Austria; John Joseph of Austria
AREAS OF ACHIEVEMENT: Military, government and politics

EARLY LIFE

John of Austria was the son of noted actress Maria Calderón (La Calderona), a mistress of King Philip IV. Even though Calderón had been intimate with other lovers, Philip recognized his paternity of John. John, thereby, entered the vastly powerful Habsburg family of the king and received the education of a prince. He matured into a handsome and vibrant young man, was given an independent income, and attracted a faithful following. As an illegitimate son, he could not inherit the throne and become the Habsburg ruler. Fate, however, made him a principal defender of the family's realms.

LIFE'S WORK

The Habsburgs, whose ancestral realm lay in south-central Europe, in Austria, and in neighboring territories, ruled over vast territories throughout Europe. The family also ruled in the Netherlands and in southern Italy and Sicily. Most important were its dynastic holdings on the Iberian Peninsula. As the monarchs, beginning in the sixteenth century, of the kingdoms of Castile and Aragon, they presided over the birth of modern Spain. Eventually, they also ruled Portugal. These kingdoms had pioneered vast and wealthy discoveries in the Americas and Asia, which provided the Habsburgs with unprecedented wealth.

By the seventeenth century, however, this wealth was declining, which weakened the dynasty's ability to maintain a hold on its European territories. This decline had begun under King Philip III, the predecessor of John's father. As an older though illegitimate son of Philip IV, John was fated to have a military career. He would have to confront ever increasing rebellions against Habsburg rule with ever decreasing resources from the dynastic territories.

To meet the huge expenses of maintaining a vast realm while confronting the reality of diminishing wealth from overseas colonies, the Habsburgs had recourse to raising old taxes and creating new ones. Opposition to oppressive Habsburg policy grew under Philip IV, and John was given responsibilities for suppressing rebellion and maintaining order.

Provoked by a new tax on fruit, a mob took power in Naples in 1647, led by fisherman Tommaso Aniello, popularly referred to as Masaniello. Together with the local Habsburg administrators and military forces, the young John helped to suppress this rebellion. The following year, though still a teenager, John was appointed viceroy of Sicily. This island had been under the rule of Aragon, making it inheritable by the Habsburgs when they took over the monarchy of Spain. John continued Spanish policy for Sicily, which was to obtain maximum tax revenue from the island while allowing its local aristocracy to assume all necessary powers to suppress any opposition.

The most important region of Aragon was Catalonia, its trade centered in the rich Mediterranean port of Barcelona. Since 1640, both Catalonia and Portugal had been in revolt against Spanish rule. Portugal had reestablished its own monarchy under the Braganza Dynasty and its head, King John IV. Catalonia's strategy to free itself from Spain was to establish an alliance with France and its king, Louis XIII, naming him the count of Catalonia.

The Catalan uprising was steadily suppressed, however, by Castile, because the French alliance proved unreliable. Louis XIII died in 1643 and was succeeded by an unsteady regency: his five-year-old successor, Louis XIV, who was too young to rule. John was sent to wipe out the last stages of the Catalan rebellion during 1651-1652.

In 1656, John was appointed governor of the Spanish Netherlands in the middle of the Franco-Spanish Wars (1635-1659). This war was ultimately won by the French and sealed the fate of Spain as a defunct power in Europe. Near Dunkirk in 1658, in the Battle of the Dunes (June 14), an alliance of French and English forces, led by the canny French general, Henri de La Tour d'Auvergne, viscount de Turenne, defeated John's Spanish forces. The following year, in the Treaty of the Pyrenees, the national boundaries of France were extended to border Spain through the Pyrenees mountains. Spain also ceded to France its territory of Flanders, in the Spanish Netherlands.

Don John of Austria. (Library of Congress)

In 1656, John, the rebellious king of Portugal, died. Confronting its losses along the Pyrenees, Spain at this time set its sights on regaining the kingdom along its western border. John was given charge of the assault. In 1663, he advanced into Portugal as far as Évora, occupied it, and then moved farther into the country. However, John had overextended himself, and, as he tried to return to his base, the Portuguese pursued him, defeating the Spanish in the Battle of Ameixal. Two years later, he confronted and was defeated by Portuguese forces in the Battle of Montes Claros. The Portuguese were led by the skilled German general Friedrich Hermann Schomberg, who was sponsored by the English and French

governments. The ineffectiveness of John's campaign in Portugal was confirmed by the Treaty of Lisbon (1668), whereby Spain recognized the independence of Portugal.

The final phase in the life of John occurred in Spain and within the confines of Spanish court politics. With the death of Philip IV in 1665, the stepbrother of John became King Charles II. This sibling was not yet five years old when their father died. Moreover, Charles was physically feeble and mentally disabled, so that his mother, Queen Mother Mariana de Austria, ruled in his stead. She was consumed with jealousy, foreboding, and loathing before the powerful general, aristocrat, and stepbrother, John.

Because the Queen Mother's loyalties and power base lay more in Austria than in Spain, John had her exiled in 1677. He then assumed the reins of the Spanish government. The following year, Spain was forced by the Treaty of Nijmegen to cede the region of Franche-Comté (Burgundy) to France, a territory in northern Europe that the Habsburgs had occupied since the previous century. In 1679, John died. Mariana returned and continued to rule for her son, Charles II. He had no heirs, so upon his death in 1700, the Spanish Habsburg dynasty ended. The Bourbons of France, archenemies of Spain, inherited the Spanish throne.

John of Austria was a dashing military figure who recalled his namesake, the first John of Austria. The earlier John was an illegitimate son of the first Spanish Habsburg monarch and the legendary hero of the Battle of Lepanto (1571). However, unlike his predecessor, who waged war at the zenith of Habsburg power in Europe, John the Younger struggled in the waning shadows of John the Elder's earlier brilliance.

SIGNIFICANCE

John of Austria was a military and political figure of late Habsburg Spain engaged in trying to maintain the regime's withering grasp over its extended dynastic holdings in Europe. He was caught in a historical geopolitical quandary that was essentially without solution. He was a key military and administrative member of a declining dynasty ruling over a widely dispersed realm in Europe with ever decreasing financial and military resources. The dynasty's position was contested globally by rising Dutch and English naval powers. On the Continent, it was defeated and then absorbed by the steady ascendancy in Europe of the military might of the French Bourbon Dynasty and its most powerful monarch, Louis XIV.

—Edward A. Riedinger

FURTHER READING

Brown, Jonathan, and John H. Elliott. *A Palace for a King: The Buen Retiro and the Court of Philip IV*. New Haven, Conn.: Yale University Press, 2003. With extensive illustrations, this work examines the environment in which John matured, exploring the architectural and stylistic details of the palace built by Philip IV on the outskirts of Madrid beginning in the 1630's.

Corteguera, Luis R. *For the Common Good: Popular Politics in Barcelona, 1580-1640*. Ithaca, N.Y.: Cornell University Press, 2002. This work examines the sociopolitical conditions of Catalonia within the context of the Iberian Peninsula, conditions that led to rebellion against Habsburg rule. The rebellion was suppressed by John and other Spanish leaders.

Elliott, John H. *Imperial Spain, 1469-1716*. New York: St. Martin's Press, 1964. The author places the life of John within the context of the history, economy, society, and politics of the Habsburg Dynasty and of its successor, the Bourbon Dynasty.

Lynch, John. *The Hispanic World in Crisis and Change, 1598-1700*. Oxford, England: Blackwell, 1992. A revised edition of volume 2 of *Spain Under the Habsburgs*, by a noted English historian. Lynch places the life of John within the context of Spanish imperial decline in seventeenth century Spain.

Stradling, R. A. *Philip IV and the Government of Spain, 1621-1665*. New York: Cambridge University Press, 1988. An authoritative analysis of the philosophical and political assumptions, ambitions, policies, and practices of government of the father of John, King Philip IV.

SEE ALSO: Charles II (of Spain); John IV; Louis XIII; Louis XIV; Philip III; Philip IV; Friedrich Hermann Schomberg; Viscount de Turenne.

RELATED ARTICLES in *Great Events from History: The Seventeenth Century, 1601-1700:* March 31, 1621-September 17, 1665: Reign of Philip IV; May, 1640-January 23, 1641: Revolt of the Catalans; February 13, 1668: Spain Recognizes Portugal's Independence; February, 1669-January, 1677: John of Austria's Revolts; October 11, 1698, and March 25, 1700: First and Second Treaties of Partition.

JOHN III SOBIESKI
King of Poland (r. 1674-1696)

In lifting the Turkish siege of Vienna, Sobieski halted the Ottoman conquest of Europe, helping to preserve Western culture and Christendom. The status of women, in particular, differs so profoundly in Christian societies from that in Islamic societies that the significance of Sobieski's generalship to women's equal rights in the West can hardly be overstated.

BORN: August 17, 1629; Olesko Castle, Poland (now in Ukraine)

DIED: June 17, 1696; Castle Wilanów, near Warsaw, Poland

ALSO KNOWN AS: Jan Sobieski (given name)

AREAS OF ACHIEVEMENT: Military, warfare and conquest, government and politics, women's rights

EARLY LIFE

John III Sobieski was born in Olesko Castle, near Zolkiew, then in southeastern Poland. During the first thirty years of his life, Poland was involved in two wars with Sweden, two wars with Russia, and virtually continuous strife in the Ukraine. Two reigning kings died, and two replacements were elected by the uniquely Polish system that was in 1674 to crown Sobieski himself.

Sobieski's reputation as the most cultivated of all Poland's seventeenth century kings, and its greatest military hero, is in the tradition of his family, which descended from Poland's first ruler, Piast. Sobieski's highly educated father, Jakób, was the descendant of Dinarian country squires and prosperous Lechite nobles. He had become castellan of Kraków, Poland's highest ranking secular senator, before Sobieski was twenty. Governing and fighting, especially Turks, were Sobieski's predictable spheres.

Sobieski's intellect was appropriate to his remarkably large head. By middle age, his belly had expanded to match this head, which, taken with his surprisingly tiny feet, gave him rather an oval shape. The French ambassador wrote that he looked from a distance like a gigantic egg. Closer, he granted Sobieski an aquiline nose and a pleasant voice. Because of the rigors of his final campaign, Sobieski was in ill health for the last five years of his life, but for the preceding sixty-two his immense vitality had informed his every aspect. His mental capacities, his physical appetites, and his capacity for rage and for sweetness, for thoughtful and for impulsive behavior, all were exaggerated.

Through the death of an elder brother, Sobieski inherited a great estate. Like most young Renaissance Poles of his class, he concluded his studies (at the University of Kraków) by touring Western Europe (1646-1647). He then joined the Polish army, fighting a Cossack uprising in the Ukraine, an area that was to be a grief and trouble to him throughout his life.

LIFE'S WORK

In 1569, the Ukraine was transferred from Lithuania to Poland. Lithuania had been unable to protect the Ukrainians from the Tatar troops that regularly plundered them, taking so many captives to Crimean ports for sale as slaves to the Muslims that the Ukraine had become seriously underpopulated. This underpopulation had brought refugees from Polish Lithuanian feudalism, people willing to defend themselves from Tatars for the sake of freedom from taxes and serfdom. These Cossacks evolved into a distinct people, farmers and soldiers, resistant to Polish authority. Their military ventures into

Moldavia (part of modern Romania), the Crimea, and Turkey were blamed on the Polish crown, which sometimes tried to subdue them and other times employed them against foreign enemies. Between Sobieski's birth and his first military service, the Polish army had marched against the Cossacks five times.

In 1648, Poland's king died. The Polish nobility elected John II Casimir Vasa, a Swede with a French wife (Marie Louise), to replace him. Sobieski's early military career was to benefit from Marie Louise's patronage, and he was to marry a woman from her court.

Like Sobieski when he became king, Marie Louise tried and failed to reform Poland's laws of succession. Poland's magnates enjoyed immense power, which they guarded so jealously as to keep their king too weak to pursue Poland's interests. Reasoning that a living king could influence the choice of his successor in favor of a son or close relative, which risked development of a despotic hereditary monarchy, the magnates would not designate a king's successor during his lifetime. Every reign ended with a dangerous interregnum. The result was that the Vatican and Poland's neighbors competed through bribery and intrigue to choose Poland's kings, each of whom was then his foreign patron's tool. Even so strong a character as Sobieski, who, like John II Casimir Vasa, began his reign with the backing of Louis XIV of France but who developed a foreign policy independent of French interests, was in the end unequal to the combination of domestic intransigence and foreign intrigue.

Casimir proved unable to achieve a compromise between the Ukrainians and Poland's magnates, and in 1654 the Cossacks sought Russian help. Czar Alexis declared the Ukraine a Russian protectorate and sent troops against the Polish army there. Taking advantage of this, Sweden invaded Poland in 1655. Increased Swedish power on the Baltic was such a threat to the czar that he signed an armistice with Poland and directed his army against the Swedes. Sobieski continued fighting the Russians by joining the Swedish army.

The Protestant Swedes intended to destroy Catholicism in Poland. The wanton destruction, pillage, and massacres united the fractious Poles against them. In 1656, Sobieski rejoined the Polish army and took a leading part in fighting the Swedes. By the Treaty of Oliva in 1660, Sweden acquired Poland's last Baltic territories but otherwise withdrew. Poland was in ruins and again at war with the Russians and Cossacks in the Ukraine.

In 1665, Sobieski married the ambitious French widow Marie Casimire de la Grange d'Arquien, who at once began maneuvering to make Sobieski Casimir's

John III Sobieski. (Hulton Archive/Getty Images)

successor. Marysieńka, as the Poles called her, was beautiful, brilliant, devoted to Sobieski, and one of history's most avaricious women. Influenced by her, Sobieski in the latter half of his reign sold every possible office, amassing an awesome fortune. This cupidity, plus her foreign birth, made Marysieńka unpopular in Poland, contributing to the Sobieskis' failure to secure Poland's crown for their eldest son.

In 1665, through the favor of Queen Marie Louise, Sobieski was made grand marshal, rising to field commander the following year. The Cossacks, having found Russian aid against the Poles insufficient, turned to the Tatars and Turkey. The threat of Turkish intervention in the Ukraine so alarmed the czar that he made a truce with Poland (Andruszów, January, 1667). Only Sobieski recognized in time that the Tatars marching into the Ukraine that summer meant to fight Poles, not Cossacks. With an army funded almost entirely by himself, he turned back Tatar troops numbering ten times his own at Podhajce in October, 1667. In 1668, he became grand hetman. Efforts by Marie Louise to reform the crippling features of Poland's constitution ended upon her death in 1667, and her discouraged widower abdicated. The Habsburgs' influence prevailed in the consequent election, and Michal Wiśniowiecki was crowned in 1669.

Sobieski's victories against the Cossacks continued, but the Seym (parliament) did not take his advice about the Turkish threat, and when Turkey invaded, Poland was forced to sign the Peace of Buczacz (1672), losing territory and, most galling, promising annual tribute. When Michal's death (1673) nearly coincided with Sobieski's tremendous victory over the Turks at Khotin, Sobieski became too popular in Poland for the Habsburgs' next candidate; in 1674, with lukewarm French support, he was elected king.

Louis XIV, almost continuously at war with the Holy Roman Empire (hence Turkey's ally), hoped to use Poland in this connection. By the secret Treaty of Jaworów (1675), Louis promised to Sobieski that he would mediate a peace between Poland and Turkey to Poland's advantage and to subsidize a Polish campaign to recover Prussia from the elector of Brandenburg, a subsidy that would double if Poland fought Austria. The Prussian venture attracted Sobieski not only because of Poland's interest in the Baltic but also because he wanted the Prussian throne for his eldest son, Jakób. Yet the vaunted settlement with Turkey (signed at Żórawno, 1676) left half of the Ukraine a Turkish protectorate, and Sobieski's Baltic hopes were also disappointed. Turkey remained Poland's greatest enemy, making Austria rather than France

her natural ally. Sobieski's initial rapport with France was also strained by Louis's unwillingness to do as much as Marysieńka expected for her immediate and extended family. In 1683, Sobieski signed a treaty with Austria whereby either would come to the aid of the other's capital should it be besieged by Turkey. That summer, Turkey marched 115,000 men on Vienna. Sobieski, as ranking officer, commanded the several armies that cooperated to lift the siege with half the Turks' manpower in one of the most brilliant and important battles of European history (Battle of Kahlenberg, September 12, 1683).

Sobieski's subsequent campaigns against the Turks, in Hungary and Moldavia, were unsuccessful. He dreamed of a "Holy League" of Christian nations to drive Turkey out of Europe, and in 1686 he signed the Treaty of Moscow whereby Poland ceded Kiev to Russia in return for Russia's less tangible agreement to join this league. His sons competed to succeed him, while Poland's magnates continued to be adamantly and successfully opposed to all three. The satisfactory marriage of his only daughter, Kunegunda, to the elector of Bavaria (1694) alleviated the disappointments of his final years. He died in the most lavish of his castles, the last great king of Poland.

SIGNIFICANCE

John III Sobieski's aims as king were to strengthen Poland's government, especially by making the monarchy hereditary; to regain Polish territories lost in various wars; and, through his Holy League, to free Europe from Islam. Poland's kings, who could not tax or raise armies, were further weakened in 1652 by the magnates' successful assertion of the right of any single one of them to dissolve any session of the Seym upon demand. Moreover, when a magnate exercised this right (the *liberum veto*), all business conducted by the Seym up to that point was obviated. Foreign governments paid enormous sums for the timely exercise of the *liberum veto*. Of the Seym's forty-four sessions during the latter half of the seventeenth century, fifteen were dissolved by the *liberum veto*.

Constitutional reform was doomed by the narrow self-interest of Poland's magnates and by the vast sums Poland's neighbors made available to any of them who would block such reforms. Poland's inability to pacify the Ukraine, either militarily or by granting and securing justice to its inhabitants, was again chiefly a result of its weak central government. Sobieski perceived the lack and foresaw the consequences, making his administrative failures bitter. His dream of restoring Poland's Baltic power was similarly doomed. The great accomplishment of Sobieski's life was the deliverance of Poland from Tatar and Turk.

—*Martha Bennett Stiles*

FURTHER READING

Davies, Norman. "Sobieski: Terror of the Turk, 1674-1696." In *The Origins to 1795*. Vol. 1 in *God's Playground: A History of Poland*. New York: Columbia University Press, 1982. Davies includes a chapter on Sobieski in his insightful and well-written survey of Polish history, a two-volume work many critics consider the best book on Poland in the English language.

_____. *Sobieski's Legacy: Polish History, 1683-1983, a Lecture*. London: Orbis, 1985. In addition to Davies's lecture delivered at London University's School of Slavonic and East European Studies, the book contains English translations of letters and documents relating to Sobieski's life and times.

Dyboski, Roman. *Outlines of Polish History*. 2d ed. London: George Allen & Unwin, 1931. Reprint. Westport, Conn.: Greenwood Press, 1979. A concise overview of Polish history.

Gronowicz, Antoni. *The Piasts of Poland*. Translated by Joseph Vetter. New York: Charles Scribner's Sons, 1945. A brief history of the Polish struggle for independence. Modern portions are subjective.

Halecki, Oskar. *A History of Poland*. Translated by M. M. Gardner and Mary Corbridge-Patkaniowska. Chicago: Henry Regnery, 1966. A revised, enlarged edition of the author's 1933 survey of Polish history. Chapter 16, "John Sobieski," is a clear, worthwhile treatment.

Michener, James A. *Poland*. New York: Random House, 1983. A perfunctory fictional thread is woven through this clear, vivid history of Poland from Genghis Khan to Lech Wałęsa. Chapter 5 deals with Sobieski's administration, especially the rescue of Vienna.

Prazmowska, Anita J. *A History of Poland*. Basingstoke, England: Palgrave Macmillan, 2004. A survey of Polish history.

SEE ALSO: Charles X Gustav; Innocent XI.

RELATED ARTICLES in *Great Events from History: The Seventeenth Century, 1601-1700*: 1632-1667: Polish-Russian Wars for the Ukraine; August 22, 1645-September, 1669: Turks Conquer Crete; July 10, 1655-June 21, 1661: First Northern War; Summer, 1672-Fall, 1676: Ottoman-Polish Wars; 1677-1681: Ottoman-Muscovite Wars; July 14-September 12, 1683: Defeat of the Ottomans at Vienna; 1684-1699: Holy League Ends Ottoman Rule of the Danubian Basin; Beginning 1687: Decline of the Ottoman Empire; 1697-1702: Köprülü Reforms of Hüseyin Paşa; January 26, 1699: Treaty of Karlowitz; November 30, 1700: Battle of Narva.

JOHN IV
King of Portugal (r. 1640-1656)

As duke of Braganza, John accepted the leadership of the Portuguese nobility in rebellion against King Philip IV of Spain and broke the Iberian Union, ending a nearly sixty-year period known as the Babylonian Captivity. As king, he restored Portuguese independence, recovered significant territories lost during the union, and established the Braganza Dynasty, which lasted until the formation of a republic in 1910.

BORN: March 18, 1604; Vila Viçosa, Portugal
DIED: November 6, 1656; Lisbon, Portugal
ALSO KNOWN AS: John the Fortunate; John the Restorer; Duke of Bragança; João IV; Duke of Braganza
AREAS OF ACHIEVEMENT: Government and politics, music, patronage of the arts

EARLY LIFE

John IV was descended on his father's side from the first duke of Braganza, the illegitimate son of King John I (r. 1385-1433), the first king of the Aviz Dynasty. John IV's grandmother, Catherine, was the granddaughter of King Manuel I (r. 1495-1521). John grew up at the Braganza palace at Vila Viçosa in the Alentejo, the most productive region of Portugal. Educated to be a nobleman, John was tutored in general education, riding, hunting, and fencing. He preferred hunting to military skills, but his real passion was music.

Having mastered several instruments, he and his brothers performed at their father's funeral in 1630. While a young man, he established contacts with some of the leading composers of his era and maintained those contacts throughout his life. He collected musical manuscripts, including his own compositions, in a personal library that reputedly was one of the largest in Europe until it was destroyed by fires spawned by the Lisbon earthquake of 1755.

In 1633, John married Luisa de Guzmán, daughter of Spain's duke of Medina-Sidonia. Their daughter, also named Catherine, was born in 1638 and married King Charles II of England in 1662. Hoping to make the Braganza family a firm supporter of the Habsburg rule of Portugal, the count-duke of Olivares, Spain's prime minister, persuaded King Philip IV to give the duchy of Guimarães to the Braganzas as a wedding gift. Because he had thousands of people on his combined estates, John was the wealthiest nobleman in Portugal. His enhanced economic status reminded the nobility that the Braganzas had legitimate regnal claims. The duchy of Guimarães had belonged to King Manuel's son Edward, the father of John's grandmother. The Aviz Dynasty had come to an end when King Henry died in 1580. After examining the claims of seven candidates, the University of Coimbra concluded that Catherine, not Spain's King Philip II, had the best claim to the throne. King Philip II's bigger army trumped Catherine's better claim, and the Portuguese Cortes crowned the invading Philip II of Spain as King Philip I of Portugal, thus uniting the Iberian Peninsula.

LIFE'S WORK

Portugal, now a viceroyalty of Spain, suffered greatly during the Iberian Union. By contributing ships to the Spanish Armada (1588), Portugal participated in the attack against its longtime ally England. England responded by smuggling and raiding at will Portuguese overseas possessions. The Bourbon monarchy of France united with Protestant states in a series of wars called the Thirty Years' War (1618-1648) to prevent the expansion of Habsburg Spain and the Holy Roman Empire in central Europe. The Dutch, in a state of rebellion against Spain since the 1560's, were attacking Portuguese colonies around the world. Portugal eventually lost to the Dutch the sugar-producing region of Brazil, Elmina and part of Angola in Africa, much of the Malabar and the Coromandel coastal possessions in India, and control of the Spice Islands. Attacks from English and Dutch ships drastically reduced Portuguese travel across the Indian Ocean to Macao and Formosa. The Netherlands was now situated as the "grocery provider of Europe."

The loss of revenue combined with the wars to trigger an economic depression that provoked social unrest and widespread dissatisfaction with the increasingly Cas-

tilian character of Spain's rule. Philip II had pledged to staff civil and military positions in the viceroyalty with Portuguese nationals. His two successors increasingly ignored that pledge and gradually but steadily filled vacancies with Spaniards. Hoping to capitalize on Portuguese troubles and weaken Spain, France sent, in 1638, a provocateur to encourage the nobility to rebel. Encouraged by a promise of French material support, forty dukes conspired to break from Spain and restore Portugal's independence. They asked the duke of Braganza, regarded as the legitimate ruler of Portugal, to lead the rebellion. John demurred, but his wife, Luisa, the duchess of Braganza, wanted to be queen. For the next two years, she acted as a cutout between the conspiracy and its reluctant leader.

Apparently sensing that the discontent in Portugal could provoke rebellion, the count-duke of Olivares, the favorite of King Philip IV, tried to identify the duke of Braganza closely with the Spanish crown, or to discredit him with Portuguese nationalists. He appointed Olivares the Governor of the Arms of Portugal. He was to introduce himself in this new capacity to the viceroyalty while on an inspection tour of fortifications. Furthermore, he was to raise a personal army of one thousand men. Before this task was completed, the Catalonians rebelled against Spain in June of 1640. King Philip IV commanded his feudal lords and vassals to take up arms and suppress the rebellion. The Portuguese nobility were to report to their Governor of Arms and proceed to Spain as quickly as possible.

Rather than fight for Spain, John gave the conspirators permission to act on his behalf. On December 1, 1640, forces led by the conspirators overpowered the guards at the royal palace in Lisbon and arrested the viceroy. Simultaneously, conspirators seized or isolated all Spanish garrisons in Portugal. Before the day was over, conspirators and an approving population declared Portugal free of Spain and pledged their loyalty to the House of Braganza. The duke came to Lisbon and was crowned King John IV on December 15. Realizing that he could not remain king if Spain invaded, John sought recognition from the international community and alliances with Spain's enemies. A treaty with England in 1642 renewed the old alliance but paid few dividends because of the English Civil War. The Dutch suspended an early treaty after Portuguese who were living in newly captured Dutch possessions celebrated John's accession by rising in rebellion. Brazil and many of the African and Indian possessions eventually returned to the Portuguese fold. France quickly signed an offensive and defensive treaty but delivered little military assistance beyond vigorously supporting the Catalonian rebellion and pursuing its war against Spain.

Spain had few military resources to use to suppress the Portuguese rebellion. The most significant engagement took place near the Spanish town of Montijo in 1644, where a larger Spanish army was scattered with heavy losses. The victory gave heart to the Portuguese nation. Additional naval victories over the Spanish fleets in African waters combined with the Brazilian rebellion to strengthen Portuguese resolve to restore its independence.

SIGNIFICANCE

When John died in Lisbon in 1656, Spain had yet to accept the loss of Portugal. His successors completed his diplomatic initiatives, resulting, finally, in Spain's recognition of Portugal's independence through the Treaty of Lisbon of 1668, ending the War of Restoration.

Although a reluctant rebel, John established and maintained a government that justified the confidence of the Portuguese nobility and population that were thrust upon him. His abandonment of a comfortable personal life to accept and endure the strains of challenging Spain has not been forgotten. December 1 is still a national holiday in Portugal, and John the Restorer's musical compositions are being performed to appreciative audiences still.

—Paul E. Kuhl

FURTHER READING

Ames, Glenn Joseph. *Renascent Empire? The House of Braganza and the Quest for Stability in Portuguese Monsoon Asia, c. 1640-1683*. Amsterdam: Amsterdam University Press, 2000. Based on extensive archival research, Ames describes Portugal's imperial losses in Asia and the attempts of the Braganzas, largely after John, to recover their lucrative possessions in South Asia and Southeast Asia.

De Oliveira Marques, A. H. *From Lusitania to Empire*. Vol. 1 in *History of Portugal*. New York: Columbia University Press, 1972. This volume moves confidently through the complications of the court intrigues and dynastic rivalries of the Iberian kingdoms.

Livermore, H. V. *A New History of Portugal*. 2d ed. New York: Cambridge University Press, 1976. Livermore provides careful coverage of Portugal's dynastic history.

Russell-Wood, A. J. R. *A World on the Move: The Portuguese in Africa, Asia, and America, 1415-1808*. New York: St. Martin's Press, 1992. This work examines John's efforts to recover and develop the Portuguese empire.

Ryan, Michael. "John IV of Portugal, King and Musician: An Anniversary Assessment." *Musical Times* 145, no. 1887 (2004): 58-62. An interesting treatment of the education and enduring contributions of John in the field of music.

SEE ALSO: Catherine of Braganza; Charles II (of Spain); John of Austria; Njinga; Count-Duke of Olivares; Philip III; Philip IV; Friedrich Hermann Schomberg.

RELATED ARTICLES in *Great Events from History: The Seventeenth Century, 1601-1700:* 17th century: Age of Mercantilism in Southeast Asia; Beginning Spring, 1605: Dutch Dominate Southeast Asian Trade; March 31, 1621-September 17, 1665: Reign of Philip IV; May, 1640-January 23, 1641: Revolt of the Catalans; June-August, 1640: *Bandeirantes* Expel the Jesuits; January 14, 1641: Capture of Malacca; August 26, 1641-September, 1648: Conquest of Luanda; 1644-1671: Ndongo Wars; October 29, 1665: Battle of Mbwila; February 13, 1668: Spain Recognizes Portugal's Independence.

LOUIS JOLLIET
Colonial Canadian explorer

Along with Father Jacques Marquette, Jolliet led an expedition to determine the course of the Mississippi River, descending to the mouth of the Arkansas River before being certain that the Mississippi flowed into the Gulf of Mexico. The journey paved the way for later French exploration of the area.

BORN: September 21, 1645 (baptized); probably in Beaupré, near Quebec, New France (now in Canada)

DIED: May, 1700; Quebec Province, New France

AREA OF ACHIEVEMENT: Exploration

EARLY LIFE

Louis Jolliet (lwee zhawl-yeh) was born in New France ten years after the death of Samuel de Champlain, the founder of the colony, and was baptized in the Roman Catholic Church near the city of Quebec on September 21, 1645. When he was six years old, his father, a wheelwright and wagon maker, died. Jolliet was educated for the priesthood in a Jesuit seminary in Quebec and received minor orders as a Roman Catholic priest. He was also a music master at the seminary and the organist in the cathedral. In 1666, he presented a master of arts thesis in philosophy. He was proficient in logic, metaphysics, and mathematics. He also studied briefly in France. By 1667, Jolliet was well qualified for a career in the service of his church, but he had shown no transcendent quality of character that would inspire such service.

By 1668, Jolliet had left the Jesuit seminary and abandoned the life of a priest for that of a trapper, fur trader, and explorer. In 1669, after his brother Lucien had disappeared, Jolliet led an unsuccessful French expedition to find copper along the shore of Lake Superior and then from Lake Huron south to Lake Erie. He became friends with Native Americans in the region and learned much about the area. Jolliet also met missionaries, including Jesuit father Jacques Marquette, who in 1671 founded the Saint Ignace Mission on Mackinac Island between Lake Huron and Lake Michigan. In 1670, Jolliet joined French explorer Simon François Daumont, sieur de Saint Lusson, on another Great Lakes copper-finding mission. At Sault Sainte Marie, between Lake Superior and Lake Huron, Saint Lusson, in the presence of a large number of Native Americans, claimed all land from the Arctic Ocean to the Gulf of Mexico and from Labrador on the Atlantic Ocean west to the Salt Sea (Pacific Ocean) in the name of French monarch Louis XIV.

LIFE'S WORK

Spanish explorer Hernando de Soto had first discovered the lower Mississippi River near Memphis, Tennessee, in 1541, but the Spanish were looking for gold and did not recognize the significance of de Soto's discovery. French exploration of the upper Mississippi Valley began with Jean Nicolet in 1634. The French were interested in the possibility that the river might flow to the Pacific Ocean and thus provide a route to the Far East. Nicolet reached Green Bay on the west side of Lake Michigan and learned much about the river from Native American tribes such as the Winnebagos, Potawatomis, and Mascoutens.

In 1669, Father Claude-Jean Allouez founded the Mission of Saint Francis Xavier on Green Bay. He was the first Frenchman to record the name Messipi (father of waters), which the Chippawas had given to the Mississippi River. Father Allouez and Father Claude Dablon, a trained geographer, ascended the Fox River and portaged to the Wisconsin River. Although they never reached the Mississippi, they did initiate the route later followed by Jolliet and Father Marquette.

In April, 1672, Louis de Buade, comte de Frontenac, became governor of New France. He soon endorsed a plan by Jean-Baptiste Talon, the intendant of New France, to send Jolliet on an expedition to explore the Mississippi River. Jolliet quickly agreed to go, even though the government of the colony had no funds to finance his trip and he had to buy his own supplies. In December of that year, Jolliet was on Mackinac Island delivering orders for Father Marquette from his Jesuit superior, Father Dahlon, to join the expedition.

On May 17, 1673, Jolliet, Marquette, and five French woodsmen left Mackinac Island in two birch-bark canoes. Their food supplies consisted primarily of dried corn and smoked buffalo meat. The first Native Americans encountered were the Folles-Avoines, who were already known to Father Marquette. Although friendly, they warned of the dangers ahead: hostile tribes who killed all intruders, monsters in the Great River that devoured both persons and canoes, and heat so great that it would surely cause death. The Frenchmen thanked them for their warnings but declined to heed them. A few days later, they entered Green Bay.

During the first week in June, the Frenchmen ascended the Fox River. The most difficult part of this phase of their journey was having to carry their canoes past the rapids and into Lake Winnebago, a natural lake on the Fox. On June 7, they arrived in the land of the Mascoutens, who agreed to send two guides to lead them toward the big river. On June 10, the day they resumed their journey, they portaged two and one-half miles to the Wisconsin River. This route was made up of small lakes and swamps so confusing that Marquette gave full credit for the successful crossing to the Mascouten guides, who even carried the two canoes.

After putting the canoes into the Wisconsin, the Mascouten guides turned back, having gone as far as their knowledge could take them. Jolliet and Marquette were now entering a world unknown to other Frenchmen and the Native American tribes they knew. The descent of the Wisconsin was difficult at times because of sandbars and small islands. Marquette named this river "Mesconsing," later changed to "Ouisconsin" and finally anglicized to "Wisconsin." To the mild surprise of the Frenchmen, they saw no Native Americans along the Wisconsin, although hidden eyes no doubt watched them from the shore. This journey reached its climax near the end of the day on June 17, when the expedition members saw the big river, the goal of Frenchmen since Nicolet. Exactly one month after leaving Mackinac, they floated into the peaceful waters of the upper Mississippi River near the site of the modern town of Prairie du Chien, Wisconsin.

The first sign of human occupancy along the Mississippi, a little path on the west side, was spotted on June 25. The expedition followed the path to a village of the Illinois on the bank of the Des Moines River in present-day Iowa. The Illinois had heard of the French and gave them a warm welcome. The Iroquois from the east, who were allies of the British, had been raiding Illinois towns. The Illinois were hoping for an alliance with the French to stop the Iroquois raids. Jolliet and Marquette were escorted back to their canoes by about six hundred Illinois. They were also given a calumet, a feathered pipe of peace, for protection from more hostile tribes farther south. They soon passed the mouth of the Illinois River on the east side of the Mississippi River. This discovery would facilitate their return trip.

Farther down the river, near the mouth of the Missouri River, Jolliet and Marquette saw the monsters described by the Folles-Avoines painted on high rocks above the east bank of the river. The waters of the Missouri, entering the Mississippi from the west, brought mud, tree limbs, and great turbulence that polluted the peaceful blue waters the travelers had enjoyed to this point. After passing the mouth of the Ohio River on the east, along the

present Illinois-Kentucky state line, they came to the mouth of the Arkansas River from the west. Here they found the Quapaw and indications that their southern journey was about to end.

At this point, the Frenchmen faced their first threat of violence from Native Americans. Only when Quapaw elders recognized the Illinois calumet being waved by Jolliet from his canoe were young Quapaw braves prevented from capsizing the canoes and massacring the inhabitants. From the Quapaw, Jolliet and Marquette confirmed what they already suspected, that the Mississippi flowed south to the Gulf of Mexico rather than to the Pacific Ocean. They also heard about Spanish activity to the south and realized they were in danger of being captured or killed, which would mean that France would not reap the benefit of their discoveries. Assured about the course of the Mississippi, the hard decision was made to turn around and return to New France.

For the return trip beginning on July 17, Jolliet and Marquette chose a route up the Illinois River, a portage to the Chicago River into Lake Michigan, and back to Green Bay, arriving in late September. The journey of about twenty-five hundred miles had taken four months.

Jolliet remained at Green Bay, compiling his notes and drawing a map of the Mississippi River, until the spring of 1674, when he returned to give his report to Frontenac in Montreal. In his ascent of the Saint Lawrence River, he tried to hasten his journey by shooting the Lachine Rapids. His canoe capsized, a slave boy given to him by the Illinois drowned, the box containing his reports and map was lost, and Jolliet was barely rescued by two fishermen. Despite the loss of his papers, Jolliet was warmly welcomed by the governor and was able to reproduce most of his report and map from memory.

Jolliet was denied permission to establish a trading post among the Native Americans along the Mississippi River. Instead, he became involved in the fur trade on the lower Saint Lawrence River, on the coast of Labrador, and on Hudson Bay. In 1694, Jolliet led the expedition that charted the coast of Labrador. In 1697, he was appointed royal hydrographer for New France and mapped the sea approaches to the Saint Lawrence. Jolliet died near Quebec in May, 1700.

SIGNIFICANCE

Jolliet, along with Father Jacques Marquette, traveled uncharted waters, making maps and writing journals, on a journey in search of the Mississippi River. They not only found the river but also traveled down it to the mouth of the Arkansas River, establishing that the river flowed not to the Pacific Ocean but to the Gulf of Mexico and paving the way for future French explorers.

The name of the river explored by Jolliet and Marquette was a topic of debate for several years. The Spanish had named it River of the Holy Spirit. Marquette called it Conception River in honor of the Virgin Mary. Jolliet preferred Buade, the family name of Frontenac. In the end, no more fitting name could be found than the Chippewa's name for the river, "Messipi," meaning "father of waters."

The loss of Jolliet's records in the Lachine Rapids denied him much-deserved recognition for his voyage. The narrative kept by Father Marquette, which emphasized more the missionary potential of their discoveries, became the standard reference. This narrative can be found in *History and Exploration of the Mississippi Valley* by J. G. Shea. The expedition of René-Robert Cavelier, sieur de La Salle, down the Mississippi to the Gulf of Mexico in 1682 was greatly facilitated because of the journey of Jolliet and Marquette. However, historical evaluation and significance soon elevated the latter expedition over the former.

—*Glenn L. Swygart*

FURTHER READING

Balesi, Charles John. *The Time of the French in the Heart of North America, 1673-1818.* Chicago: Alliance Française Chicago, 1992. The book focuses on French settlements in Illinois and Wisconsin, providing information on Jolliet's exploration in these states.

Caruso, John Anthony. *The Mississippi Valley Frontier.* Indianapolis, Ind.: Bobbs-Merrill, 1966. Chapter 10 provides full coverage of the journey of Jolliet and Marquette as well as the background and results of their work. Includes good descriptions of the Native American tribes throughout the Mississippi Valley.

Fiske, John. *New France and New England.* Boston: Houghton Mifflin, 1902. Reprint. Washington, D.C.: Ross and Perry, 2002. This book covers the expeditions of trailblazers such as France's Jacques Cartier and Italy's Giovanni da Verrazano, Jolliet and Marquette's mission, and other topics dealing with the region up to the end of the French and Indian War in 1763.

Hartsough, Mildred. *From Canoe to Steel Barge on the Upper Mississippi.* Minneapolis: University of Minnesota Press, 1934. Good coverage of Jolliet and Marquette; puts the emphasis on Marquette and his missionary goals. Discusses the results of the journey, both religious and economic, and future uses of the Mississippi River.

Ogg, Frederic Austin. *The Opening of the Mississippi: A Struggle for Supremacy in the American Interior.* New York: Macmillan, 1904. Reprint. New York: Greenwood Press, 1969. Discusses the importance of the Mississippi Valley to American development. Covers Spanish and French discoveries, including those of Jolliet and Marquette, and the subsequent struggle between France and Great Britain for control of the valley. Has several good maps.

Parkman, Francis. *France and England in North America.* Edited by David Levin. Vol. 2. New York: Viking Press, 1983. In 1856, Parkman published his seven-part history of North America. Part 5, *Count Frontenac and New France Under Louis XIV*, is included in the second volume of this revised edition published in 1983. The book recounts historical developments in New France during the period when Jolliet and Marquette explored the Mississippi River Valley.

Severin, Timothy. *Explorers of the Mississippi.* New York: Alfred A. Knopf, 1968. Includes a good description of the Mississippi River from its source to its mouth. Covers de Soto's discovery. Chapter 4 provides full coverage of the journey of Jolliet and Marquette. Also includes a summary of the latter years of Jolliet's life.

SEE ALSO: Samuel de Champlain; Sieur de La Salle; Louis XIV; Jacques Marquette.

RELATED ARTICLES in *Great Events from History: The Seventeenth Century, 1601-1700:* Spring, 1604: First European Settlement in North America; April 27, 1627: Company of New France Is Chartered; Beginning 1673: French Explore the Mississippi Valley; May 1, 1699: French Found the Louisiana Colony.

INIGO JONES
English theatrical designer and architect

Jones designed the sets, costumes, and machinery for many of the most important English plays of the seventeenth century. In addition, he contributed greatly to the urban planning done under Charles I and gradually changed the architectural design and appearance of the city of London.

BORN: July 15, 1573; London, England
DIED: June 21, 1652; London
AREAS OF ACHIEVEMENT: Theater, architecture

EARLY LIFE

Inigo Jones (IHN-uh-goh JOHNZ) was born July 15, 1573, and baptized four days later in the Church of Saint Bartholomew the Less in London. His father, a destitute cloth worker, attempted to provide for his son and three daughters until his death in 1597. Little is known about Jones's life before 1605, but it is believed that members of the wealthy gentry were alerted to his artistic promise when he was quite young. At some point, this artistic promise recommended itself to William Herbert, the third earl of Pembroke, under whose patronage Jones traveled through Italy and other parts of Europe. According to his own assertion, Jones studied the ruins of ancient buildings while in Italy. The first existing records of his later life in London indicate that he had already attained a powerful cultural position, having negotiated his way through the patronage system.

The English court masque had come into prominence in Jones's youth. The masque was designed solely for performance in the royal court, usually with only one performance. It was in this respect quite unlike the public theater exemplified by the plays of William Shakespeare. The court considered, and theatrical producers agreed, that the masque should mirror the stature and nobility of the king—it should represent the king and his royal authority, and consequently, any change in the art form would affect the way the king asserted his power.

The dominant architectural style in England during Jones's apprenticeship was high Gothic. Jones is credited with ushering in an architectural style influenced by designs from classical antiquity. This development in English cultural history appeared gradually over a fifty-year period, but because Jones occupied the court-appointed positions of surveyor and surveyor general, he has been credited with a central role in the development.

LIFE'S WORK

During the reigns of King James I and his heir, Charles I, the court masque became a primary means for royalty to display its power and prestige. Such was the nature of the production in 1605, on Twelfth Night—the evening before January 6, the day of Epiphany—of Ben Jonson's *The Masque of Blackness* (pr. 1605, pb. 1608). The production, mounted for James's queen, Anne, was staged at Whitehall and marked Jones's first appearance in London alongside Ben Jonson, who was the most prominent court poet and playwright of his day.

The long working relationship of Jones and Jonson that followed was at the center of the development of the masque as an art form—a form that was unique to the Renaissance and that reflected English social and political history. It is in this context that the significance of Jones's life and art emerges. The first edition of *The Masque of Blackness*, which Jonson prepared for publication, included a full description of the design, scenes, machines, and dress used by Jones in the original production. Though Jonson's inclusion of these details marks his recognition of Jones's contribution, the two men did not share the same view of the nature of the masque. For Jonson, the masque's informing spirit was his poetry, and all the rest was mere show; for Jones, the immediacy of the visible spectacle of the masque was its essential quality. His later career in architecture emerged from this strong conviction about the importance of theatrical design.

Over the next ten years, the contributions of these two artists resulted in increasing prominence for the masque in the royal court. With prominence came larger and larger budgets. The masque's success was in large part a result of Jones's introduction of recent Italian artistic developments. In the queen's masque of 1605, as well as in his commission from Oxford University that same year, he employed movable scenery, which had not previously been done in England. Three-dimensional scenic background produced a visual illusion of reality. Jones also used various mechanical "Italianate devices"—exploding lights and similar contraptions. The most lasting feature was the proscenium arch, a curtained partition between the stage and the audience. By framing the action on the stage, the proscenium provided depth and perspective.

One outcome of Jones's innovations was the advent of the hierarchically organized theater. The masque developed into a new emblem of state for the king, an idealized projection of his power. Its drama was not confined to the actual performance but extended to the seating of the spectators. The best seat was the point from which the scenery's perspective achieved its full effect. The king sat there. Around this point a courtly drama developed, based on the seating position of courtiers. The closer the courtier was to the king, the greater was his favor with the king, or his potential to seek it.

In 1613, Jones returned to Italy to study architecture, painting, and sculpture. He also purchased works of art for English aristocrats; he had become the agent for the first private art collections in England. It was on this trip that Jones created his own major architectural opus, a collection of sketches with annotations of Andrea Palladio's *I quattro libri dell'architettura* (1570; *Architecture: In Four Books*, 1736). In October, 1615, Jones rose to the office of surveyor general of the works, a position that assured for him a sufficient income until the op-

position to and eventual overthrow of Charles I during the 1640's.

The collaboration and friendship of Jonson and Jones waned toward the end of the decade, though they worked together as late as 1631. The development is explained in part by the commencement in 1619 of a second career for Jones. It was in that year that his prolific production of court masques prompted the king to appoint him the royal surveyor of the works. Jones held the position during the emergence of a new architectural style, King James Gothic. His industrious application to his duties led to the incorrect attribution to him of the designs of many buildings. In reality, most of his duties consisted of ordinary repairs to public buildings.

Until about 1620, Jones embarked on numerous projects of building and repair. The royal treasury was, however, rapidly emptying, and most of Jones's designs were never executed. Few works of architecture by Jones remain. The most celebrated is the repair of the southwest corner of Saint Paul's Cathedral in London. Other works include theaters, churches, and other public buildings.

One of Jones's duties during his tenure as surveyor general had significant consequences. In 1620, King James commanded Jones to investigate the history of Stonehenge. After his death, Jones's successor and heir, John Webb, used Jones's notes to pursue his master's inquiries, although most of the notes he ascribed to Jones in a publication were wholly concocted. Webb reacted to criticism of his farfetched and erroneously attributed theories by publishing a defense in which he provided considerable fruit for Jones biographers. The credibility of the information on Jones's life also is questionable, however, because it confirms Webb's initial claims.

Jonson repeatedly created unflattering depictions of Jones throughout the 1620's and 1630's. Jones, however, enjoyed more harmonious relations with other collaborators, including George Chapman, William Davenant, Richard Fletcher, and Thomas Carew. His fortune changed with the increasing opposition to Charles I. Jones took refuge with members of the nobility in 1643, remaining enclosed for more than two years until Oliver Cromwell's forces captured and imprisoned him. As he had taken no part in the fighting, he was pardoned; he recommenced his work of building

Engraving of Inigo Jones, from a portrait by Sir Anthony van Dyck. (Library of Congress)

and repair, though by this time his health, which had never been good, was failing. He died on June 21, 1652.

SIGNIFICANCE

With Jones's introduction to English court masques of Italian theatrical innovations, the art form became a token of the political climate of his day. Jones's contributions to the short-lived theatrical form also profoundly influenced the mainstream theater from which it initially distinguished itself.

Jones also is significant for his contribution, as royal surveyor and surveyor general, to a revival of classical architecture and the founding of numerous private art collections in England. Evidence shows, for example, that after his second visit to Italy, Jones convinced Charles I to commission Peter Paul Rubens to paint the ceiling of the banquet hall at Whitehall. Ironically, it was concern for the preservation of Rubens's work from the effect of candle grease that led to the suspension of the presentation of masques in the hall for three years until masques were again performed at Whitehall, beginning in 1637, in a temporary room designed by Jones.

—Peter Monaghan

FURTHER READING

Cunningham, Peter. *Inigo Jones: A Life of the Architect*. London: Shakespeare Society, 1848. Remarks on some of his sketches for masques and dramas. Accompanied by many facsimiles of Jones's drawings.

Goldberg, Jonathan. *James I and the Politics of Literature: Jonson, Shakespeare, Donne, and Their Contemporaries*. Baltimore: Johns Hopkins University Press, 1983. Focuses on the images deployed by the rulers and the way in which these reveal the rulers' conceptions of their own roles and stature.

Gotch, J. Alfred. *Inigo Jones*. London: Methuen, 1928. Reprint. New York: B. Blum, 1968. The authoritative biography of both the historical and the mythical Inigo Jones. Written in a high Victorian style, it is a fine example of historical biography.

Greenblatt, Stephen. *Renaissance Self-Fashioning: From More to Shakespeare*. Chicago: University of Chicago Press, 1980. One of the main texts of the "New Historicism." Incorporating modern semiotic and historical theories, Greenblatt analyzes the development of various conceptions of the self and their role in the art and politics of Jones's time.

Leapman, Michael. *Inigo: The Troubled Life of Inigo Jones, Architect of the Renaissance*. London: Review, 2003. Jones's life is recounted in an accessible style with a wealth of details, anecdotes, and description.

Mowl, Timothy, and Brian Earnshaw. *Architecture Without Kings: The Rise of Puritan Classicism Under Cromwell*. New York: St. Martin's Press, 1995. A general survey of buildings constructed in England between 1642 and 1660, using Jones as a benchmark for the move away from architectural chaos to order.

Orgel, Stephen. *The Jonsonian Masque*. Cambridge, Mass.: Harvard University Press, 1965. Traces the development of the court masque, with particular emphasis on Jonson's major role in it. Orgel's contributions to this field of inquiry are enormous, and his studies illustrate a comprehensive grasp of the era.

Orrell, John. *The Theatres of Inigo Jones and John Webb*. New York: Cambridge University Press, 1985. Contains all of the drawings that Jones and his pupil, Webb, prepared as designs for public theaters.

Shaw, Catherine. *"Some Vanity of Mine Art": The Masque in English Renaissance Drama*. Salzburg, Austria: University of Salzburg, 1979. This doctoral thesis places the masque in the context of the more public theater in which Shakespeare, for example, worked. The author notes the mutual influences and relationships between these two art forms.

Summerson, John. *Inigo Jones*. New Haven, Conn.: Yale University Press, 2000. A reprint of the 1964 biography, with a new introduction. Summerson reassessed Jones's life and career, unearthing many previously unknown examples of Jones's architecture.

SEE ALSO: Charles I; Oliver Cromwell; James I; Ben Jonson.

RELATED ARTICLE in *Great Events from History: The Seventeenth Century, 1601-1700:* 1642-1651: English Civil Wars.

BEN JONSON
English playwright and poet

The comic plays Jonson wrote in the 1600's remain landmark works of the English Jacobean theater. As a mentor to younger writers, moreover, he influenced the course of poetry in the seventeenth century and beyond.

BORN: June 11, 1573; London, England
DIED: August 6, 1637; London, England
ALSO KNOWN AS: Benjamin Jonson (full name)
AREAS OF ACHIEVEMENT: Literature, theater

EARLY LIFE

Between his birth in 1573 and his death in 1637, Ben Jonson was at different times a soldier, an actor, a playwright, a poet, an essayist, and a translator. His fortunes were equally varied: from branded felon to poet laureate, from lionized man of letters to impoverished pensioner. Though he was influential as a mentor to young writers (the "tribe of Ben"), Jonson is remembered primarily as a dramatist, not for his tragedies and dozens of masques but for such comedies as *Volpone: Or, The Fox* (pr. 1605-1606, pb. 1607), *Epicœne: Or, The Silent Woman* (pr. 1609, pb. 1616), *The Alchemist* (pr. 1610, pb. 1612), and *Bartholomew Fair* (pr. 1614, pb. 1631).

Benjamin Jonson was born on June 11, 1573, in or around London. His Protestant father (a descendant of Lowland Scots) had lost his property under Catholic Mary I, was imprisoned for a time, and then became a minister. The elder Johnson (*sic*) died a month before his son was born. (The playwright always styled himself Ben—and gave this shortened name to three sons, all of whom died young—and also changed the spelling of his surname to make it distinctive.) The widowed Mrs. Johnson remarried, to a Westminster bricklayer who may have been named Robert Brett. Young Jonson first attended a private school in Saint Martin's Church, his stepfather's parish, but he soon came to the attention of William Camden of the Westminster School, and by 1580 he had become a student there.

Much of the substantial scholarship that is characteristic of Jonson's works has its origin in the careful tutelage of the eminent Camden, who was to remain Jonson's close friend and mentor until the elder man died in 1623. Years later Jonson (in "Epigram 14") wrote: "Camden, most reverend head, to whom I owe/ All that I am in arts, all that I know. . . ." In addition to providing its boys a thorough grounding in the classics, the school also had stressed dramatics since the time when Nicholas

Udall, author of the comic play *Ralph Roister Doister* (pr. c. 1552, pb. 1566?), had been its headmaster. The boys did three plays a year in English and Latin, and these Westminster experiences constituted Jonson's apprenticeship for the stage.

By 1590, when he had left the school, he may have spent some time at Saint John's College, Cambridge, but there is no firm evidence for this. It is certain, though, that on July 19, 1619 (by which time he was regarded as highly as was William Shakespeare), Oxford University conferred upon him the master of arts degree, Jonson telling his friend William Drummond, "he was Master of Arts in both the universities, but by their favour, not his studie."

After Westminster School, perhaps with an interlude at Cambridge, Jonson worked for a while as a bricklayer with his stepfather, but then he joined the English army on the Continent. During his brief military career he challenged an enemy soldier to a one-on-one fight and killed him, but he decided against a military career and

Ben Jonson. (Library of Congress)

returned to London and his stepfather's trade, eventually completing a seven-year apprenticeship and becoming a freeman of Brett's company of bricklayers. Also during this period, Jonson married, on November 14, 1594. Of Anne Lewis Jonson practically nothing is known, except for her husband's description of her (in 1618-1619) as "a shrew yet honest." They had at least four children but lived apart from 1602 to 1607, and perhaps at other times, and by 1612 Mrs. Jonson may have died.

LIFE'S WORK

What led Jonson to turn to the theater for a career is not known, but he began as an actor, perhaps as early as 1594, and played the leading role—of the mad Hieronimo—in Thomas Kyd's *The Spanish Tragedy* (pr. c. 1585-1589, pb. 1594?), probably for touring companies as a journeyman player but also with the earl of Pembroke's Men at the Swan Theatre. Jonson's physical appearance was such that he could not reasonably aspire to a wide range of major roles, for his tanned, moon-shaped face was badly pockmarked. Further, though he was very thin, almost skeletal, as a young man, later in life he was, by his own testimony, "fat and old, laden with belly."

Even though the stage was a relative newcomer on the English cultural scene, it already had become a major force. Not only Shakespeare and Kyd, but also such men as Christopher Marlowe, Robert Greene, George Peele, and Thomas Nashe had turned out popular plays, and Sir Philip Sidney's *Defence of Poesie* (1595), which greatly influenced Jonson, provided a philosophical basis for the verse that was common in the comic as well as the tragic drama. From its earliest incarnation in Elizabethan England, the theater was caught up in political and religious controversies, as Jonson experienced early with the production of *The Isle of Dogs* (pr. 1597).

Begun by Thomas Nashe, the satirical play, which no longer is extant, was completed by Jonson and probably others. The queen's Privy Council said that it contained "very seditious and slanderous matter," denounced it as "lewd," and issued a warrant for the arrest of Jonson "not only an actor but a maker of part of the said play." He spent more than two months in Marshalsea Prison for his alleged offense. In the aftermath of this affair, the queen decided to license only two companies of players: Shakespeare's Lord Chamberlain's Men and Philip Henslowe's Admiral's Men. Jonson joined the latter; an early reference in Henslowe's accounts describes Jonson as a "player," but he soon was solely a writer.

Only two other Jonson plays from 1597-1598 sur-

vive—*The Case Is Altered* (pr. 1597, pb. 1609) and *Every Man in His Humour* (pr. 1598, pb. 1601, revised pr. 1605, revised pb. 1616)—but he must have had a hand in more, for Francis Meres in *Palladis Tamia* (1598) calls Jonson a leading dramatist and "among our best for tragedy." Of these two extant plays, *The Case Is Altered* is a comic exercise that draws on the Roman dramatist Plautus, not unlike what the young Shakespeare did in fashioning *The Comedy of Errors* (1592-1594).

The more distinguished of the two plays is *Every Man in His Humour*, first produced on September 20, 1598, not by Henslowe but by the Lord Chamberlain's Men, with Shakespeare in the cast. The temporary break with Henslowe may have been caused by a conflict between Jonson and Gabriel Spencer, an actor in the company, which led to a duel on September 22, 1598, in which Jonson killed his adversary. When he went from Newgate Prison to the Old Bailey in October, Jonson admitted his guilt but pleaded benefit of clergy, a dispensation granted to the literate since the Middle Ages. In the event, his property was confiscated, and he was branded on the left thumb (identifying him as a murderer who had been spared by pleading benefit of clergy).

Every Man in His Humour has many of the plot conventions of ancient Roman comedy (for example, mistaken identity and jealous husbands), but it also is an innovative play, a realistic comedy of contemporary London life, written in accordance with Jonson's own humors theory, which he explains in the induction to *Every Man Out of His Humour* (pr. 1599, pb. 1600):

> As when some one peculiar quality
> Doth so possess a man, that it doth draw
> All his affects, his spirits, and his powers,
> In their confluctions all to run one way,
> This may be said to be a humour.

In the prologue to the first comedy, he expresses his intent to dramatize "Deeds and language such as men do use,/ And persons such as Comedy would choose,/ When she would show an image of the times,/ And sport with human follies, not with crimes." The result is a play whose characters have dominant traits that make them comic caricatures, and their names usually highlight their personalities.

At the start of 1599, flush with the popular and critical success of *Every Man in His Humour* and newly converted to Catholicism, Jonson again found himself in Marshalsea Prison, this time as a debtor. He was released after paying the complainant and was reconciled with

JONSON'S MAJOR WORKS

1597	*The Isle of Dogs* (with Thomas Nashe; no longer extant)
1597	*The Case Is Altered*
1598	*Every Man in His Humour* (revised pr. 1605)
1598	*Hot Anger Soon Cold* (with Henry Chettle and Henry Porter; no longer extant)
1599	*Every Man Out of His Humour*
1599	*The Page of Plymouth* (with Thomas Dekker; no longer extant)
1599	*Robert the Second, King of Scots* (with Chettle and Dekker; no longer extant)
c. 1600-1601	*Cynthia's Revels: Or, The Fountain of Self-Love*
1601	*Poems*
1601	*Poetaster: Or, His Arraignment*
1603	*The Magnificent Entertainment Given to King James* (with Dekker and Thomas Middleton)
1603	*Sejanus His Fall* (commonly known as *Sejanus*)
1605	*Eastward Ho!* (with George Chapman and John Marston)
1605-1606	*Volpone: Or, The Fox*
1609	*Epicœne: Or, The Silent Woman*
1610	*The Alchemist*
1611	*Catiline His Conspiracy* (commonly known as *Catiline*)
1614	*Bartholomew Fair*
1616	*The Devil Is an Ass*
1616	*Epigrams*
1616	*The Forest*
1616	*The Workes of Benjamin Jonson*
1626	*The Staple of News*
1629	*The New Inn: Or, The Light Heart*
1632	*The Magnetic Lady: Or, Humours Reconciled*
1633	*A Tale of a Tub*
1640	*The English Grammar*
1640	*Horace His Art of Poetry* (translation of Horace's *Ars poetica*)
1640	*The Sad Shepherd: Or, A Tale of Robin Hood* (fragment extant)
1640	*Underwoods*
1641	*Timber: Or, Discoveries Made upon Men and Matter*
1640-1641	*The Works of Benjamin Jonson* (2 volumes)

upon career successes. For reasons that are unknown, Jonson and Dekker, his erstwhile collaborator, became adversaries, and a third playwright, John Marston, joined the fray against Jonson. The result was the War of the Theaters, in the course of which the men attacked one another through such plays as Marston's *Jack Drum's Entertainment* (pr. 1600, pb. 1601) and *What You Will* (pr. 1601, pb. 1607), Jonson's *Cynthia's Revels: Or, The Fountain of Self-Love* (pr. c. 1600-1601, pb. 1601) and *Poetaster: Or, His Arraignment* (pr. 1601, pb. 1602), and Dekker's *Satiromastix: Or, The Untrussing of the Humorous Poet* (pr. 1601, pb. 1602), the last of which seemed to be the final word in the conflict and made Jonson the object of ridicule through much of the city.

Because of this stage warfare, Jonson refrained from writing comic plays for almost four years, instead doing hack work for Henslowe in a continuing struggle against poverty. He also turned in earnest to tragedy. According to his "Apologetical Dialogue," "since the comic muse/ Hath proved so ominous to me, I will try/ If Tragedy have a more kind aspect./ Her favours in my next I will pursue." *Sejanus His Fall* (pr. 1603, pb. 1605; commonly known as *Sejanus*) was the result, and in 1603, Shakespeare's company, now called the King's Majesty's Servants, presented it.

Though Burbage and Shakespeare appeared in this first of Jonson's Roman tragedies, which George Chapman helped him to write, *Sejanus* failed on the stage, "the people's beastly rage" unequivocally "adjudging it to die," probably because of the dearth of action and the great number of similar characters. In the published version (received more favorably), Jonson says in a preface that tragic drama should focus upon "truth of Argument, dignity of Persons, gravity and height of Elocution, fullnesse and frequencie of Sentences." Whereas his comic theory may have served him well on the stage, his tragic theory mitigated against theatrical appeal. Written

Henslowe, for whom he collaborated with Thomas Dekker and others on tragedies, while at the same time working on *Every Man Out of His Humour*, which was performed for the queen at Christmastime, 1599. It also was one of the first plays staged at the new Globe Theatre by the Lord Chamberlain's Men, with Richard Burbage taking the lead, as he had in the earlier companion piece. The play was so popular that a printed version went through three editions in 1600.

Already a well-known and highly regarded man of the theater, Jonson now moved to broaden his reputation, by writing dedicatory verses and commendatory epistles; but as happened before, personal difficulties intruded to edify, the play was too erudite for most of the Globe audience. His second Roman tragedy, *Catiline His Conspiracy* (pr., pb. 1611; commonly known as *Catiline*), also failed on the stage; among the educated, however, it was highly regarded through much of the seventeenth century.

Jonson rebounded quickly from the public rejection of *Sejanus*, creating the well-received *Part of King James, His Royall and Magnificent Entertainment* (pr. 1604), a civic pageant honoring the new king in March of 1604. Two months later, he prepared a May Day entertainment for James I and Queen Anne. Thus began Jonson's career as a court writer, and over the years he wrote for the royal family dozens of masques (elaborately staged entertainments composed of songs, dances, and rhetorical speeches). The first of these, *The Masque of Blackness* (pr. 1605, pb. 1608) was performed at Whitehall on January 6, 1605, with the queen and her ladies in blackface as Moors amid elaborate Inigo Jones scenery.

Soon after his triumph at court, though, Jonson again was in prison, this time for his part in writing the play *Eastward Ho!* (pr., pb. 1605), which was largely by Marston and Chapman. In *Eastward Ho!*, speakers ridicule the king's Scottish accent and his practice of selling knighthoods. Jonson's friends at court came to his aid, however, and he was exonerated.

The Gunpowder Plot, led by Guy Fawkes later in the year, was fortuitous for Jonson, since it gave him (a Catholic) an opportunity to demonstrate his allegiance by engaging in an undercover investigation for the government. He enjoyed life and work in the court, but the public stage continued to attract him, and most likely in February of 1606, his comedy *Volpone* premiered at the Globe, followed by performances at Oxford and Cambridge. It was a great triumph. The least realistic of his plays, it marks an advance for him as a comic playwright, because instead of sporting with folly, he castigates vice, and rather than mocking eccentricity, he exposes deceit and greed. Only in the subplot does he retain unaltered the elements of his humors comedy.

Epicœne: Or, The Silent Woman, Jonson's next comedy, reached the stage about four years later, done by the Children of the Queen's Revels at the Whitefriars. The play is set in London and focuses upon a young man's efforts to get his eccentric uncle to name him heir. Subplots introduce licentious women, gulled men, and foolish courtiers: the standard mix of irrational characters for satiric comedy, and all labeled by appropriate humor names. John Dryden later praised the construction of the play.

Samuel Taylor Coleridge said that Jonson's next play, *The Alchemist*, had one of the best plots in literature. A popular success from its initial performance, it was first acted by the King's Men at the Globe in the spring of 1610, was done at Oxford several months later, and was revived at court in 1613. Set in Jacobean London during a visitation of the plague, *The Alchemist* is similar to *Volpone* in that its characters are people whose desire to get rich leads to their being deceived and exploited. Although the play presents alchemy and the occult as sophisticated confidence games, Jonson uses them mainly as his means of satirizing people whose greed makes them easy prey for the unscrupulous.

After the success of *The Alchemist* came the failure in 1611 of *Catiline His Conspiracy*, and Jonson again became disaffected from the stage. As a change of pace he signed on as tutor to Sir Walter Ralegh's dissolute son (in years past, Jonson probably had tutored young men in the classics on several occasions) and took him to the Continent, a journey (spent mainly in France) that lasted about fifteen months. Upon their return, Jonson resumed the writing of masques and turned again to the theater. The Lady Elizabeth's Men introduced *Bartholomew Fair* at the new Hope Theatre on October 31, 1614, and performed it at court the next day. It was a success, and according to tradition the familiar appellation "O rare Ben Jonson" was first uttered by someone at the Hope when the opening performance ended. Most of the action of this prose play takes place at the annual summer fair, and Jonson uses the opportunity to develop a realistic panorama of Jacobean life. There is a satiric note, primarily aimed at religious hypocrisy, but the play is more determinedly lighthearted than the earlier comedies.

By any measure, 1616 was a landmark year for Jonson. First, King James gave his "well-beloved servant" a lifetime pension "in consideration of the good and acceptable service done by him," and Jonson thereby became England's first poet laureate. He was lucky that the king bestowed the honor in February, for six months later Jonson's satiric *The Devil Is an Ass* (pr. 1616, pb. 1631) was done by the King's Men at the Blackfriars. The mockery of influence peddling and other courtly abuses led the king to censure Jonson.

The second notable event of 1616 was the death of Shakespeare, which event—more so than the pension—made Jonson his country's leading man of letters. Third was the publication of Jonson's collected works, which he had given to the printer three full years earlier. The folio volume included masques, satires, epigrams, epistles, and nine plays, all meticulously edited. The inclusion of the last genre (normally regarded at that time as ephemeral) in such a volume was an innovation, and it may have been the precedent that led to the publication in 1623 of the First Folio of Shakespeare's works (for which Jonson wrote the prefatory statement to the reader).

The king's visit in 1617 to his native Scotland (the first since he had ascended the throne fourteen years earlier) may have encouraged Jonson to make his own journey in 1618 on foot to the land of his forebears. In Edinburgh the council gave him a banquet and made him an honorary burgess. Jonson also spent several weeks at the castle of William Drummond of Hawthornden, the Scottish poet, scholar, and bibliophile, whose record of their conversations is a major source of information about Jonson's life and thought. Soon after he returned to England in 1619, Jonson traveled to Oxford, visiting the poet Richard Corbett and receiving an honorary degree.

Jonson clearly had become a celebrity, whether in Edinburgh, Oxford, or London, where he presided over a group of younger poets at the Devil Tavern. Among this "sealed tribe of Ben" were William Cartwright, Robert Herrick, Richard Lovelace, and Thomas Randolph—who have come to be known as the Cavalier poets. In 1621, there was talk in London that the king had offered a knighthood to Jonson; he apparently refused, but he continued to write masques for the court and frequently turned out occasional verses as poet laureate. In November of 1623, Jonson suffered a major calamity, the burning of his library, possibly the most valuable in England at the time. Two years later, with the death of James and the accession of Charles I, Jonson's relations with the court became strained.

When the theaters reopened in November of 1625 (after having been closed for months to mourn the old king and to slow the spread of the plague), Jonson's *The Staple of News* (pr. 1626, pb. 1631) was presented, a combination of topical satire and allegory that John Dryden later included among those plays of Jonson's "dotage." An unsuccessful work, it was one of his last. Still to come were two more failures, *The New Inn: Or, The Light Heart* (pr. 1629, pb. 1631) and *The Magnetic Lady: Or, Humours Reconciled* (pr. 1632, pb. 1640), both written after Jonson had suffered a stroke in 1628.

These fiascoes of his later years encouraged lesser men of letters to step up their attacks on the old man, whose illness made it hard for him to respond with his characteristic biting invective. During this period, too, he was replaced as writer of the court's masques, and he even became estranged for a time from his protégé (and former servant) Richard Brome, whose first play was

staged in 1629. Two bits of good news were that King Charles increased his poet laureate's annual stipend, and the next year engaged Jonson to write the Christmas masque, his first for the Caroline court; but a break with Inigo Jones brought an early end to this activity, and he thus lost his last major source of income.

Weak though Jonson was, his will remained formidable, and during the last years of his life his fortunes improved. Whereas *The Magnetic Lady* was a failure, other projects fared somewhat better. In 1633, he resurrected an early play, *A Tale of a Tub* (rev. ed. pr. 1633, pb. 1640), and rewrote it to include an attack on Inigo Jones; it was presented at the Cockpit (without the anti-Jones parts, which the Lord Chamberlain had stricken), and it was popular enough to be done later at court with the satiric barbs reinstated, where it was "not likte." In addition, both in 1633 and in 1634, the duke of Newcastle had Jonson write masques for visits of the king, and Charles was sufficiently pleased to order that Jonson's London pension (withheld since 1631) be reinstated.

SIGNIFICANCE

Jonson died on August 6, 1637, in his mid-sixties. According to a contemporary account, when he was buried in Westminster Abbey on August 9, 1637, "he was accompanied to the grave with all or the greatest part of the nobility and gentry then in town." A suitable tomb was proposed but was not built; instead, over his burial place on the north side of the nave, a small slab of pavement has carved in it "O rare Ben Jonson." Simple though this monument is, interment in the Abbey was an honor that in at least one singular way set him above William Shakespeare.

For forty years Jonson had been the primary literary force in England: the leading comic playwright of Jacobean England, the preeminent creator of masques, a highly regarded poet, a cultivator of new talent, and an arbiter of literary taste. Nevertheless, during the important early years—indeed, when his talent was at its peak—Jonson labored in the shadow of his more eminent contemporary. From the perspective of history, Shakespeare is the greater writer; the range of his work for the theater and the lasting successes he achieved in so many different dramatic and poetic forms are testimony to this fact. Shakespeare, however, was not the man of letters, the important critical force, that Jonson was for so long. Through quarrels, rivalries, and withdrawals, Jonson remained the person to be reckoned with, the man of letters to whom all others ultimately deferred, personality disputes notwithstanding.

Centuries after his death, Jonson's dramatic and poetic legacy remains considerable. *The Alchemist* and *Volpone* are frequently produced, and *Bartholomew Fair* is attracting renewed attention; also, the more ambitious poems have taken their place alongside the lyrics as products of an inspired imagination. In the pantheon of English authors, there are few whose works have withstood the passage of centuries as successfully as have those of Jonson.

—*Gerald H. Strauss*

FURTHER READING

Barton, Anne. *Ben Jonson, Dramatist.* New York: Cambridge University Press, 1984. An authoritative study of the full range of Jonson's works, providing detailed analyses of his entire output. Departs from earlier critics' view that after *Bartholomew Fair*, Jonson's powers faded. Believes that the later plays "are works of substance and delight," though *The Alchemist* is his greatest achievement.

Cave, Richard Allen, Elizabeth Schafer, and Brian Wolland. *Ben Jonson and the Theatre: A Critical and Practical Introduction.* New York: Routledge, 1999. A collection of essays written from the view of theater practitioners, including actor Geoffrey Rush and director Sam Mendes.

Chute, Marchette. *Ben Jonson of Westminster.* New York: E. P. Dutton, 1953. A singularly readable biography. Although the focus of the narrative is on Jonson's life, there are useful summaries and analyses of key plays. Helpful, too, for Chute's description of the social, intellectual, and political milieu of London during Jonson's lifetime.

Harp, Richard, ed. *Ben Jonson's Plays and Masques.* 2d ed. New York: W. W. Norton, 2001. Contains several plays, including *Volpone* and *The Alchemist*; masques; analysis; and critical essays.

Harp, Richard, and Stanley Stewart, eds. *The Cambridge Companion to Ben Jonson.* New York: Cambridge University Press, 2000. A collection of essays by theater historians and critics analyzing Jonson's plays and the theater and court in Jonson's London.

Jonson, Ben. *Ben Jonson.* Edited by C. H. Herford, Percy Simpson, and Evelyn Simpson. 11 vols. Oxford, England: Clarendon Press, 1925-1952. The definitive edition, providing scholarly texts of the full range of Jonson's dramatic and nondramatic works. The lengthy introduction, both biographical and critical, has served as an important source for later scholars.

Kay, W. David. *Ben Jonson: A Literary Life.* New York: St. Martin's Press, 1995. Concise biography, placing Jonson's career within the context of Jacobean politics, court patronage, and his literary rivalries.

Maclean, Hugh, ed. *Ben Jonson and the Cavalier Poets: Authoritative Texts, Criticism.* New York: W. W. Norton, 1974. A varied selection of Jonson's poetry as well as poems by such heirs and followers as Thomas Carew, Richard Corbett, Abraham Cowley, Robert Herrick, Richard Lovelace, James Shirley, and John Suckling. Also contains representative criticism from the twentieth century and earlier periods. The poetry is annotated to clarify allusions and archaic language.

Miles, Rosalind. *Ben Jonson: His Life and Work.* New York: Methuen, 1986. A comprehensive and admiring treatment of Jonson's life. Provides a wealth of details about Jonson and his environment, but no critical study of the works. Excellent for Jonson's personal and professional relationships with his fellow playwrights.

SEE ALSO: Richard Burbage; Charles I; Thomas Dekker; John Dryden; Robert Herrick; James I; Inigo Jones; Richard Lovelace.

RELATED ARTICLE in *Great Events from History: The Seventeenth Century, 1601-1700:* November 5, 1605: Gunpowder Plot.

ENGELBERT KÄMPFER
German explorer and writer

Based on his own travels, Kämpfer wrote detailed and highly accurate accounts of Japan and other areas of Asia, the Middle East, and Russia. In addition, he wrote on Asian natural history, diseases, and medical practices.

BORN: September 16, 1651; Lemgo, duchy of Lippe, Westphalia (now in Germany)
DIED: November 2, 1716; Lemgo
AREAS OF ACHIEVEMENT: Literature, scholarship, medicine, science and technology

EARLY LIFE

Born the son of Johannes Kämpfer, a teacher and minister, Engelbert Kämpfer (eng-ehl-behrt KEHMP-fehr) was provided ample opportunity to study. As a youth, Kämpfer studied the sciences and the humanities at a number of Swedish, Polish, German, and Dutch schools and universities. Enrolled at Danzig in 1672, he wrote a thesis on the politics of monarchy; the following year, he earned a degree in philosophy from Kraków. He then studied medicine and natural history at Königsberg. Although his early education included the study of medicine, he did not take a formal medical degree until some twenty years later.

Throughout his early education, Kämpfer was an avid student of foreign languages. He learned French, Greek, and Latin, the primary languages of intellectual discourse in his day, and also English, Swedish, Portuguese, Spanish, Aramaic, Russian, and Polish. In his later medical and scientific investigations, he often had occasion to draw on his multilingual background.

By 1681, Kämpfer had traveled to Uppsala, Sweden, to study medicine and anatomy with the famous physician Olof Rudbeck. His excellent scholarship and ties to Rudbeck and other professors presented him with the chance to travel to Persia, an opportunity that ultimately led him to journey to the Southeast Asian lands of Java and Siam (modern Thailand) en route to Japan.

LIFE'S WORK

At the age of thirty-two, Kämpfer joined a Swedish embassy to Persia. Departing in 1683, he began a series of travels throughout the Middle East and Asia that continued for ten years. Serious illness during this time did not deter him from energetic investigation of the exotic lands he explored.

Throughout his travels, he wrote detailed diaries that proved useful sources of information for contemporary adventurers and later scholars alike. Prior to his travels through Russia and Persia, Kämpfer's notebooks contained largely personal memorabilia—greetings from friends and relatives, fellow students, and famous people he had met. Beginning with his entry into Russia in 1683, Kämpfer's diaries reveal a boundless curiosity about the lands and cultures through which he now passed.

Russian officials stalled the Swedish embassy because the Russian diplomatic ego was bruised by the fact that the embassy's itinerary listed Persia before Russia. It took two months for Swedish officials to resolve the dispute. During this time, Kämpfer absorbed all the new information he could acquire. His diaries include descriptions of a meeting with the young man who became Czar Peter the Great, reports of conditions in Siberia, and copies of letters to Czarina Sophia.

In January, 1684, the embassy finally reached Persia. Although the official business of the embassy was delayed for several months while permission for an audience with the shah (king) was arranged, Kämpfer found plenty to occupy his time. At Baku, on the Caspian Sea, he collected specimens representative of the flora and fauna of the area, explored the local geographic wonders, and practiced medicine.

The embassy's business was completed in a relatively short time, but when it returned to Sweden in 1685, Kämpfer decided to stay. He remained in Persia for three more years, working as an employee of the Dutch East India Company. While traveling to ports on the Strait of Hormuz, Kämpfer was stricken by serious illness—high fever, malaria, and dropsy. For a while, his life was clearly in danger, but he managed to recover by leaving the humid lowlands for the healthier climate of the hills.

Finally, in 1688, Kämpfer boarded ship for Southeast Asia. Traveling along the coast of Arabia, he crossed the Indian Ocean to Malabar, Ceylon, Bengal, and, ultimately, Sumatra. Throughout his voyage, he wrote a number of medical treatises. Among them, his essay on perical, the swollen foot ulcers unique to the inhabitants of Malabar, was the first to describe this ailment. In 1689, he arrived in Batavia (modern Jakarta). Staying there only a few months, he departed for Siam and Japan in May, 1690. He arrived in Japan that fall, on September 26, to spend a year as the resident physician to the Dutch trading community in Nagasaki.

At this time, opportunities for Europeans to travel to

KÄMPFER ON THE ART OF TEA

Engelbert Kämpfer, in his History of Japan, *documented the Japanese art and custom of tea, including how to prepare it, how to present it to guests, and how to properly drink it in the company of others. He also wrote of the tea ceremony and how tea was used by the poor and the resourceful, so that no tea went to waste.*

It is a particular art to make the Tea, and to serve it in company, which however consists more in certain decent and agreeable manners, than in any difficulty as to the boiling or preparation. This art is call'd Sado and Tsianoi. As there are people in Europe, who teach to carve, to dance, to fence, and other things of the like nature, so there are masters in Japan, who make it their business to teach children of both sexes, what they call Tsianosi, that is, to behave well, when in company with Tea-drinkers, and also to make the Tea, and to present it in company, with a genteel becoming and graceful manner.

The poorer sort of people, particularly in the province Nara, sometimes boil their rice, which is the main sustenance of the natives, in the infusion or decoction of the Tea, by which means, they say, it becomes more nourishing and filling, insomuch that one portion of rice, thus prepared, will go so far with them as three portions, if it were boil'd only in common water.

I must not forget to mention another external use of the Tea, after it is grown too old, and hath lost too much of its virtues, to be taken inwardly: It is then made use of for dying of silk-stuffs, to which it gives a brown, or chestnut colour. For this purpose vast quantities of the leaves are sent almost every year from China to Gusarattam (or Suratta).

Source: Engelbert Kämpfer, "The Natural History of the Japanese Tea," in *The History of Japan* (1727-1728). Online edition by Wolfgang Michel (1997). http://flcsvr.rc.kyushu-u.ac.jp/~michel/serv/ek/hj/6appendix1-text.html. Accessed April, 2005.

Japan were rare. After a major rebellion in which the Portuguese were implicated, Japan limited Western visits to Dutch traders in 1639—even the Dutch could enter and leave only on specified days of the year, regardless of weather conditions. Their business activity in Japan was restricted as well, and they could only establish an office (factory) on a small island (called Deshima) in Nagasaki harbor in southern Japan. Although the Dutch were allowed to trade with Japan, suspicion of them remained high, and it was difficult for the Dutch traders to become intimate with any Japanese.

At the time of Kämpfer's arrival, Japan was enjoying a period of cultural expansion and economic prosperity. One hundred years of peace had given birth to bustling cities that supported an unprecedented array of poets, artists, bibliophiles, and theatrical troupes. Wealthy merchants as well as members of the ruling samurai (warrior) class supported the arts and demonstrated a high degree of intellectual curiosity.

Soon after his arrival, Kämpfer resolutely set about the task of overcoming Japanese reserve toward foreigners and began to explore the excitement of end-of-the-century Japan. Liberally dispensing European remedies to Japanese interpreters and their acquaintances, and treating them to large quantities of liquor, he gained their confidence. Through these people and in the course of his travels, he learned much about the natural history of Japan and its customs.

Kämpfer finally departed Japan in November, 1692. When he left, he took with him a wide variety of suspiciously acquired Japanese memorabilia, in addition to his extensive notes. During his stay, he had managed to obtain a substantial number of Japanese books and other materials, despite the fact that such purchases were flatly illegal. These treasures included maps of Japan—maps that foreigners were not permitted to have because they provided information that the Japanese believed compromised their national security.

Upon his arrival in Europe, Kämpfer resumed his medical studies. In April, 1694, he received a doctorate in medicine from Leiden. His doctoral thesis was composed of ten essays based on his studies during his travels in Asia. Returning to his home near Lemgo, he engaged in the practice of medicine as physician to the prince of Lippe. His medical responsibilities made it impossible for him to prepare his journals for publication. Only one collection of essays was published before he died, *Amoenitatum exoticarum*, which appeared in 1712.

Kämpfer did not marry until he was fifty-one. The marriage appears to have been little more than an attempt to acquire his bride's estate. He hoped that her wealth would provide him with the financial wherewithal to escape some of the burdens of his medical practice and free him to devote more time to his writing. His marriage to a woman thirty-five years his junior proved to be an unhappy one, and even Kämpfer's financial expectations were disappointed when his bride's estate proved to be considerably smaller than he had thought. The tragedy of his marriage was compounded by the deaths in infancy of each of his three children.

In 1716, at the age of sixty-five, Kämpfer died at Lemgo. His dreams of publishing the findings of his world travels remained unfulfilled. All of his books, artworks, maps, and notes were left with a nephew, Johann Herman Kämpfer, with whom they remained for almost a decade.

SIGNIFICANCE

Kämpfer died an unhappy man. His life's ambitions in many respects were unfulfilled. True, he ranked as one of the seventeenth century's great explorers, but he had never had the opportunity to publish accounts of his travels and explorations in the depth and to the extent that he desired. Nevertheless, these pessimistic self-evaluations should not obscure the direct impact his travels, writings, and collections of Asiatica had in stimulating European curiosity about the Far East and the incisive understanding of Japan that he conveyed to his fellow naturalists and explorers. Unfortunately, much of the evidence of this success followed Kämpfer's death. The spread of Kämpfer's work and the preservation of his collections were almost accidental.

Kämpfer's collections might have remained at Lemgo and his most famous work, *The History of Japan*, might never have been translated and published were it not for the efforts of Sir Hans Sloane. Sloane never met Kämpfer but knew of him through his one publication, *Amoenitatum exoticarum*. Seven years after Kämpfer's death, Sloane negotiated with Johann Kämpfer for the purchase of the Kämpfer manuscripts, artworks, maps, books, and botanical specimens. Shortly thereafter, Sloane used his influence in the Royal Society of London to arrange for the translation of Kämpfer's manuscripts on Japan into English. The work was first published in two volumes in 1727. Ultimately, the Kämpfer collection, plus others gathered by Sloane, became part of the founding collection of the British Museum in 1759.

The most accessible of Kämpfer's work, *The History of Japan*, is much more than a survey of Japanese history and mythology. In addition, it includes an extensive, detailed account of Japan's geography and climate, Kämpfer's travels in Japan, and his experiences during audiences with the shogun, the most powerful man in the land. An appendix includes Kämpfer's argument in favor of Japan's policy of limiting contact with the West. When copies of *The History of Japan* entered Japan some years after it was published, it was translated into Japanese and used to bolster the arguments of political con-servatives who wished to limit severely Japan's relations with Western nations.

—*Philip C. Brown*

FURTHER READING

Bodart-Bailey, Beatrice M., and Derek Massarella, eds. *The Furthest Goal: Engelbert Kämpfer's Encounter with Tokugawa Japan*. Sandstone, England: Japan Library, 1995. A collection of essays focusing on Kämpfer's trip to Japan and his historical account of that country. Includes essays about his Japanese collaborator, the plants that bear Kämpfer's name, the purchase and publication of his history book, and his drawings to illustrate his text.

Bowers, John Z. *Western Medical Pioneers in Feudal Japan*. Baltimore: Johns Hopkins University Press, 1970. Chapter 2, "The Early Years at Deshima: Willem Ten Rhijne and Engelbert Kämpfer," presents a lively and descriptive account of Kämpfer's life and travels. Bowers credits Kämpfer with being the first great German explorer and the scientific discoverer of Japan. Bowers is strongest in his assessment of Kämpfer's impact on Europe as opposed to Japan.

Boxer, C. R. *Jan Compaigne in Japan, 1600-1817: An Essay on the Cultural, Artistic, and Scientific Influence Exercised by the Hollanders in Japan from the Seventeenth to Nineteenth Centuries*. 2d rev. ed. The Hague, the Netherlands: Martinus Nijhoff, 1950. Boxer's book is a general treatment of Dutch activities and influence in Japan. He presents little material that concentrates directly on Kämpfer and his activities in Japan, but his work is useful background for understanding the impact Europeans such as Kämpfer made on Japan.

Gardner, K. B. "Engelbert Kämpfer's Japanese Library." *Asia Major* 7 (December, 1959): 74-78. Gardner identifies the specific parts of the British Museum collections that were the result of Kämpfer's efforts and discusses the unique characteristics of these materials. Helpful in gaining an understanding of Kämpfer's interests and the kinds of Japanese materials he introduced to Europe.

Goodman, Grant K. *Japan: The Dutch Experience*. Atlantic Highlands, N.J.: Humanities Press, 1985. Goodman devotes little space to Kämpfer's activities but provides a good account of the Dutch scientific and medical impact on Japan. Because Goodman draws rather heavily on Kämpfer's descriptions of Japan, this book itself is a good example of how Kämpfer influenced Western understanding of late seventeenth century Japan.

Haberland, Detlef. *Engelbert Kämpfer, 1651-1716: A Biography*. Translated by Peter Hogg. London: British Library, 1996. An English translation of a modern German biography, recounting Kämpfer's life and travels. Illustrated with some of Kämpfer's drawings.

Kämpfer, Engelbert. *The History of Japan*. Reprint. Translated by J. G. Scheuchzer. 3 vols. Glasgow, Scotland: J. MacLehose, 1906. Originally published in 1727-1728, multiple reprints of this work are widely available. Kämpfer's history is a remarkably accurate compendium of information and the most

widely quoted source on seventeenth century Japan. Includes numerous illustrations, as well as extensive appendices discussing the history of tea in Japan, medical practices, and other interesting aspects of Japanese life and customs. The introductory material includes a biography of Kämpfer.

SEE ALSO: Charles X Gustav.

RELATED ARTICLE in *Great Events from History: The Seventeenth Century, 1601-1700:* April 29, 1606: First European Contact with Australia.

KANGXI
Emperor of China (r. 1661-1722)

Kangxi, the fourth emperor of the Qing Dynasty, is considered one of the greatest emperors of any Chinese dynasty. Blending knowledge and action in his leadership, he consolidated Manchu power and legitimated the Manchus' rule in China.

BORN: May 4, 1654; Beijing, China
DIED: December 20, 1722; Beijing
ALSO KNOWN AS: K'ang-hsi (Wade-Giles)
AREA OF ACHIEVEMENT: Government and politics

EARLY LIFE

Kangxi (kahng-shee), the third son of the Shunzhi emperor, was born on May 4, 1654, in Beijing, the capital city of the Manchu (Qing) Empire. The Manchus, a branch of the nomadic Jurchen tribe, arose in the twelfth century in Manchuria, where they subsisted by hunting and fishing. By the sixteenth century, however, they had absorbed so many Chinese cultural, economic, and technological influences that their previously nomadic existence had been thoroughly transformed. By the early seventeenth century, the Chinese Ming Dynasty (1368-1644) had fallen into steep decline. This allowed the Manchus, who had established powerful armies, to defeat the Ming and establish the Qing Dynasty in Beijing in 1644.

Although Kangxi eventually became the fourth Manchu emperor of China, he was actually less than half Manchu; his parents were of mixed Mongol, Chinese, and Manchu ancestry. Kangxi was conscious of his multiple ethnic heritage and worked throughout his life to create a government representing all the diverse races and nationalities within his empire. As a youth, Kangxi probably had as little experience of a happy, shared fam-

ily life as any imperial prince of his time. His father took little interest in him, his daily care was entrusted to wet nurses, and palace eunuchs attended him in nearly all of his activities. It was impossible for him to be alone, and he rarely saw his mother and father. As a youngster, Kangxi survived smallpox, one of the most dreaded diseases of the time, and this virtually ensured that he would lead a long life. This may have been the main reason for his being named the heir apparent. When his father died in 1661, Kangxi assumed the throne at age seven.

A four-man regency, headed by the powerful Manchu general Oboi, ruled in Kangxi's name for the next eight years. Oboi used his position to secure a nearly impregnable hold on the imperial court. Kangxi's tutors, meanwhile, used these years to prepare him to rule the empire. A voracious reader from the age of four, he eventually committed large sections of the Confucian classics to memory. He studied calligraphy, composed poetry, and later experimented with Western science and music.

LIFE'S WORK

Two court controversies in the late 1660's offered Kangxi the opportunity to wrest control of the throne from Oboi and the other regents. The first involved the making of the dynastic calendar. To the Chinese, a correct calendar was more than a method of reckoning time; it was a powerful symbol of imperial authority. An appropriate calendar would help to legitimate Manchu authority in the eyes of the Chinese. Early in the dynasty, the Manchus employed a German Jesuit missionary, Adam Schall, to prepare an official calendar. Schall created an astronomically correct document, but in doing so, he relied on Western methods and unwittingly violated certain key elements of court etiquette. This exposed him to attacks by court factions opposed to Western influence.

Oboi took advantage of the calendar controversy to embarrass the Jesuits and solidify his own position. Kangxi recognized Oboi's strategy, however, and conducted his own investigation of the matter. In time, he vindicated the Jesuits, who thereafter served as important advisers to him. Oboi's critics welcomed Kangxi's independent actions and began to attack Oboi openly. Kangxi, in turn, used the anti-Oboi factions to reshape the balance of power in the court to a point where, on June 14, 1669, he was able to arrest Oboi and take personal control of the government. Oboi died in prison shortly thereafter, and Kangxi remained the uncontested ruler of China until his own death in 1722.

Kangxi's long reign of sixty-one years was characterized by courage, sagacity, and decisiveness. Under him, the Manchu state stabilized, the people prospered, and both the territories and the administrative infrastructure of the empire expanded to an unprecedented extent. Kangxi completed the military conquests begun by his Manchu predecessors and laid the foundations for the largest empire China had known, save for that of the Mongols. To consolidate Manchu control of China, though, he had to overcome threats from both the south and the north.

In the south, Kangxi was confronted by three Chinese generals who had helped the Manchus conquer China and then were rewarded with virtually independent control over the Yunnan (Yün-nan), Guangdong (Kwangtung), and Fujian (Fukien) provinces. Together, these vast domains were known as the Three Feudatories (San-Fan). Shunzhi had tolerated the autonomy of the Feudatories, because he felt too weak to risk a civil war. Kangxi, however, was determined to put an end to their independence. Consequently, he maneuvered them into open rebellion, and in 1681, after long and bitter campaigning, he narrowly defeated the three princes.

Also plaguing the Manchus in the south was a Ming loyalist movement under the control of Zheng Chenggong and his son, Zheng Jing. After fighting against the Qing in central China for many years, the Zheng forces retired to Taiwan, where they eliminated Portuguese claims to the island and continued their resistance to the Manchus until 1683, when Qing armies finally vanquished them and turned Taiwan into a prefecture of the neighboring Fujian Province. This completed the Qing conquest of the south and allowed Kangxi to turn his attention to the north.

In the north, Kangxi also confronted two threats, the Olod Mongols in the northwest and the Russians in the northeast. Both of these powers had expanded their control after the 1640's: Russian settlers had moved into Siberia and the Amur regions of northern Manchuria, and the Olod had expanded into Eastern Turkestan and Outer Mongolia. It appeared possible that the Olod and the Russians might form an alliance against the Qing. To prevent this, Kangxi pursued a divide-and-conquer policy.

Kangxi campaigned first against the Russians, defeating them at their advance base of Albazin and then offering them a generous settlement in the Treaty of Nerchinsk (1689). This first modern treaty between China and a Western nation established the frontiers of the Amur region and permitted the Russians to trade with Beijing. It ensured Russian neutrality in any conflict between the Olod and the Qing. Kangxi then turned his attention to the Olod, who had expanded across Outer Mongolia as far as the Kerulen River. After many years of desultory fighting, he finally defeated them in 1696. Thereafter, he extended Qing rule to Outer Mongolia and as far west as Hami. After his death, his successors continued the westward expansion, eventually conquering Chinese Turkestan in the 1750's.

Within China, Kangxi's administration was marked by extraordinary energy, diligence, and wisdom. Most Chinese believe that he possessed the characteristics of the ideal emperor. He was, above all, a capable administrator who provided just and benevolent rule for all of his subjects. Unlike many later Qing emperors, Kangxi repeatedly toured his far-flung empire, assessing for himself the needs of the people and ensuring that his officials met those needs. These excursions acquainted him with local conditions and solidified the presence of the central government in even the remotest parts of the empire.

Kangxi broadened the ethnic base of his government by encouraging his Chinese subjects to take the civil service examinations and by appointing them to key bureaucratic posts. He named his own Chinese bond servants to high positions and used them as sources of information, independent of normal bureaucratic channels. To ensure the support of the masses, he reduced the land and grain taxes numerous times, set customary rates of taxation, cleaned up government corruption, built water-conservancy works, and reversed the policy that had allowed the Manchus to take good Chinese farms in exchange for inferior Manchu lands. All this and more he accomplished by dint of extraordinary labor. He typically arose at four o'clock in the morning and usually did not retire before midnight. Few of his advisers could match his prodigious energy and capacity for hard work.

Contemporaries described Kangxi as above average in height, with large ears, a sculpted mouth, and a long, aquiline nose. He had a stentorian voice, and his face was handsome, though heavily pockmarked by smallpox. His unusually bright eyes gave his features great vivacity. Physically active even in his old age, he kept himself fit by a daily regimen of exercises and by vigorous riding and hunting trips.

Kangxi was also extraordinarily cultured and learned. Well versed in the Confucian classics, he also patronized other branches of Chinese learning. As a result of his patronage, scholars wrote the history of the preceding Ming Dynasty, compiled authoritative editions of the works of the great Neo-Confucian scholar Zhu Xi (Chu Hsi), and composed several landmark dictionaries and encyclopedias. His personal interests included painting, calligraphy, and Western learning. He studied Western music, geography, science, and mathematics with the Jesuit missionaries at his court. Although there is some doubt that he mastered these subjects, his openness to them is one measure of the remarkable breadth of his intellectual pursuits.

SIGNIFICANCE

Kangxi was a conscientious ruler with extraordinarily broad interests. He created an integrated Manchu-Chinese government, broke down ethnic barriers, ended the civil war in the south, protected China's northern frontiers, opened China to Western scientific knowledge, and laid the foundations for a century of peace in East Asia. Under Kangxi, Manchu rule in China became a settled fact. Kangxi was keenly aware of the richness and variety of the China he ruled. He claimed to have traveled 700 miles (1,125 kilometers) in each direction from Beijing, hunting, collecting flora and fauna, and preparing his troops for combat by shooting, enduring camp life, and practicing formation riding. Ultimately, he traveled so that he could personally gather information about his realm. He was always reluctant to credit secondhand intelligence.

Kangxi took seriously his rule over his 150 million subjects. His empire was the largest in the world at that time, and he was aware that his decisions often dictated the fates of millions. The immense suffering caused by his war against the Three Feudatories made him aware of how fateful his decisions could be. His concern for individual justice led him to review every sentence of death in the entire empire every year. In an attempt to gather accurate information from his government, Kangxi invented the palace memorial system, through which his ministers and officials wrote to him directly, thus circumventing possible censoring by other officials. He possessed an inquiring mind that was remarkably responsive to new intellectual phenomena. Although he was not profoundly philosophical, he had an irrepressible curiosity. This is demonstrated by his patronage of the Jesuits, who brought Western learning to his court, and his demand that the writing of the Ming Dynasty history conform as much as possible to the facts, even if they damaged the reputations of his Manchu ancestors.

Kangxi, despite his admirable personal characteristics, could not escape the intrigues and tragedies of court politics. In the early decades of his reign, he could postpone problems caused by the misbehavior of his sons and the machinations of the pretenders to his throne, but he could not escape these difficulties as he grew old. As he became aware of the limitations of his heirs and as court factions jockeyed for position in the succession struggle, Kangxi's judgment faltered, and he sometimes behaved in hysterical and cruel ways. These tragedies, however, do not detract from the fact that Kangxi was one of China's greatest emperors. He was at once a scholarly man of reflection and a man of action. He protected his subjects' livelihoods and provided competent, predictable government in the largest empire in the world at that time. It is appropriate that he is often compared with Louis XIV and that he is remembered not only as a great conqueror but also as a conscientious, enlightened monarch.

—*Loren W. Crabtree*

FURTHER READING

Kessler, Lawrence D. *K'ang-hsi and the Consolidation of Ch'ing Rule, 1661-1684.* Chicago: University of Chicago Press, 1976. This thin, scholarly volume deals with the rise of Kangxi to the throne and his subsequent consolidation of power. His dealings with Oboi are clearly explained, as is his vanquishing of his internal and external enemies.

Lee, Robert H. G. *The Manchurian Frontier in Ch'ing History.* Cambridge, Mass.: Harvard University Press, 1970. Lee's book explains the problems the Manchus had with their northeastern frontier. In particular, Lee describes how the Qing coped with the Russians.

Lux, Louise. *The Unsullied Dynasty and the K'ang-hsi Emperor.* Philadelphia: Mark One, 1998. An examination of the relationship of Kangxi to the Qing Dynasty and to the Jesuits. Genealogy, bibliography, maps, index.

Oxnam, Robert B. *Ruling from Horseback: Manchu Politics in the Oboi Regency, 1661-1669.* Chicago: University of Chicago Press, 1974. A detailed study of the period between Kangxi's accession to the throne and his taking over of the government. Discusses such issues as the calendar controversy and the elimination of Oboi's regency.

Spence, Jonathan D. *Emperor of China: Self-Portrait of K'ang Hsi.* New York: Alfred A. Knopf, 1974. Reprint. New York: Vintage Books, 1988. This beautifully written and illustrated book makes Kangxi come alive as a man, not simply a grand historic figure. Spence presents Kangxi in his own words, describing his methods of ruling and his relationship to his sons, among other topics.

_____. *Ts'ao Yin and the K'ang-hsi Emperor: Bondservant and Master.* 1966. Reprint. New Haven, Conn.: Yale University Press, 1988. Spence here describes the way Kangxi used his Chinese bond servants as his own eyes and ears within the government bureaucracy. Reveals much about the inner workings of Kangxi's government.

Struve, Lynn A., ed. and trans. *Voices from the Ming-Qing Cataclysm: China in Tigers' Jaws.* New Haven, Conn.: Yale University Press, 1993. Personal accounts of Chinese life from the waning years of the Ming Dynasty through the Manchu takeover and eventual Qing rule.

Wakeman, Frederic E., Jr. *The Great Enterprise: The Manchu Reconstruction of Imperial Order in Seventeenth-Century China.* 2 vols. Berkeley: University of California Press, 1985. This massive work is indispensable for a detailed reconstruction of Kangxi's reign. Extremely detailed and offers keen insights into the ways Kangxi and others conceived and practiced their control of China.

SEE ALSO: Abahai; Chen Shu; Chongzhen; Dorgon; Liu Yin; Shunzhi; Tianqi; Wang Fuzhi; Zheng Chenggong.

RELATED ARTICLES in *Great Events from History: The Seventeenth Century, 1601-1700:* 1616-1643: Rise of the Manchus; April 25, 1644: End of the Ming Dynasty; June 6, 1644: Manchus Take Beijing; 1645-1683: Zheng Pirates Raid the Chinese Coast; February 17, 1661-December 20, 1722: Height of Qing Dynasty; 1670: Promulgation of the Sacred Edict; December, 1673-1681: Rebellion of the Three Feudatories; August 29, 1689: Treaty of Nerchinsk Draws Russian-Chinese Border.

MERZIFONLU KARA MUSTAFA PAŞA
Ottoman grand vizier (1676-1683)

Heir to two previous reform-minded Köprülü grand viziers, Kara Mustafa Paşa failed to take Vienna in an infamous 1683 battle, which led to the loss of major European provinces for the Ottomans and to the empire's further decline.

BORN: 1634 or 1635; Merzifon, Ottoman Empire (now in Turkey)

DIED: December 25, 1683; Belgrade, Serbia

AREAS OF ACHIEVEMENT: Warfare and conquest, military, government and politics

EARLY LIFE

The date of birth and even the origins of Kara Mustafa Paşa (ka-RAH-mew-stah-FAH-pah-SHAH) are uncertain. One tradition maintains that he was the son of a cavalryman killed during Sultan Murad IV's siege of Baghdad in 1638 and that, following the father's death, the son was admitted into the household of the future grand vizier Köprülü Mehmed Paşa (d. 1661), who had been his father's friend.

Another tradition holds that Kara Mustafa was the son of a cavalryman from Merzifon and that his father presented him to Mehmed Paşa as an *içoghlan* (page) and then rose steadily in the pasha's household. A third tradition links Kara Mustafa to the vicinity of Trabzon, where Mehmed Paşa was governor (c. 1656-1661).

All of these traditions link him to Mehmed Paşa and attribute his rise to Köprülü family patronage. When Mehmed Paşa became grand vizier in 1656, Kara Mustafa's fortunes rose with those of his patron, and in 1658, campaigning beside Mehmed Paşa in Transylvania, Kara Mustafa was sent to the sultan, Mehmed IV, to announce the capture of the important fortress of Jenö. Shortly afterward, he was taken into the sultan's service, and in 1660, he was appointed *beylerbey* (governor) of Silistria. A year later, he performed the important task of arranging the transfer of the *valide sultan* (queen mother) from Edirne to Constantinople. Subsequently, he rose to the rank of vizier (minister of state) and was appointed *vali* (governor) of Diyarbakır.

Merzifonlu Kara Mustafa Paşa. (F. R. Niglutsch)

Köprülü Mehmed Paşa's eldest son, Fazıl Ahmed Paşa (1635-1676), replaced Mehmed Paşa as grand vizier after his death in 1661. Sustained by Köprülü's good will, Kara Mustafa was appointed *kapudan-i derya* (grand admiral).

When, in 1663, Ahmed Paşa set off to campaign in Hungary, Kara Mustafa stayed behind and was appointed *kaymakan* (deputy vizier), an office that gave him direct access to the sultan. After Ahmed Paşa, returning from Hungary, captured Candia, Kara Mustafa carried the news of the island's fall to the sultan. In 1672, Ahmed Paşa invaded Podolia in southeastern Poland, and Kara Mustafa participated in the sieges of Chocim and Kamieniec-Podolski. He personally captured the fortress of Buczacz and was the chief Ottoman plenipotentiary in the peace negotiations that followed. Podolia became an Ottoman province (the last territorial addition to the empire), and the western Ukraine became an Ottoman protectorate.

Although Kara Mustafa was an Anatolian Turk and the Köprülüs were Albanians, Kara Mustafa and Ahmed Paşa must have been very close: They are described as foster brothers, and later Kara Mustafa married one of Ahmed Paşa's sisters. He also was high in the sultan's favor, however, and in 1675, he was betrothed to the sultan's daughter. Thus, as he approached his early forties, he had a reputation as an ambitious administrator and an experienced soldier. He was also known for his extreme hostility toward Europeans in Constantinople. The Venetian *bailo* (consul) described him as corrupt, cruel, and unjust, presumably in contrast to his suave brother-in-law.

LIFE'S WORK

Near the end of 1676, Kara Mustafa was appointed grand vizier following the death of Ahmed Paşa. Succeeding his father-in-law and brother-in-law as the third Köprülü (by adoption) to guide the empire, he was exceptionally well placed to continue their work.

His immediate concern was Podolia, which had been ceded by Poland in the Treaty of Żórawno (1676). The security of this new acquisition depended upon support from the sultan's vassal, the Crimean khan Selim Giray I (r. 1671-1678, 1684-1691), with whom the grand vizier was soon on bad terms. Kara Mustafa also needed the support of the hetman (chieftain or leader) of the Ukrainian Cossacks, Petro Doroshenko, an exceptionally able leader who had come to power in 1666 and ruled until 1698.

A year later, Poland and Muscovy had in effect partitioned the Ukraine between them (Treaty of Andrusovo, 1667), a disaster for Cossack aspirations, thus forcing Doroshenko into the arms of the sultan, whom he recognized as suzerain. By 1668, he was hetman of both the Dnieper River Left-Bank and Right-Bank Cossacks, but his ties to Constantinople provoked both Polish and Muscovite enmity.

More dependent than ever on the Ottomans, in 1672, Doroshenko was forced to bring 12,000 Cossacks to support the 100,000 Ottoman troops with which Ahmed Paşa invaded Podolia. Alliance with the Muslim infidels destroyed Doroshenko's credibility with his Cossacks. In 1675-1676, Muscovy contrived an uprising of the Left-Bank Cossacks, and the denouement that followed led to Doroshenko's deposition and exile. This was the position facing Kara Mustafa, who was forced in 1677 to appoint, as hetman of the Right-Bank Cossacks, Yurii Khmelnytsky, the inept son of the famous Cossack leader Bohdan Khmelnytsky (c. 1595-1657).

During 1677 and 1678, Kara Mustafa campaigned against the Muscovites, and, in August of 1678, he took and dismantled the Cossack stronghold of Chyhryn, beginning the construction of new forts on the Bug and the Dnieper Rivers in 1679. A fourth season's campaigning in 1680 proved inconclusive, however, leading to the Treaty of Bakchisaray, or Baghchesaray (1681), brokered by the Crimean khan. Thereby, the Right Bank remained under Ottoman suzerainty, while the Left Bank became a Muscovite dependency. The hapless Khmelnytsky was executed in 1685.

Kara Mustafa returned to Constantinople and, prompted by French diplomats, turned to Hungarian affairs. The twenty-year truce negotiated at Vasvár (1664) was due for renewal, but the grand vizier declined to renegotiate. Both his predecessors had earned laurels in Hungary, and he intended to do the same. In Transylvania, the prince, Michael Apaffy, an Ottoman vassal, had proved ineffective, and Constantinople suspected that he would be disloyal if it served his interests. He needed replacing. Across the frontier, in Habsburg-controlled Hungary, Kara Mustafa saw excellent prospects. In recent years, Emperor Leopold I, in his capacity as Hungarian king, had fiercely harassed his Protestant subjects and the independent-minded Hungarian magnates, who had reacted with conspiracy and rebellion, giving Leopold an excuse to abrogate the Hungarian constitution in 1673. Hungarian resistance was then to take the form of irregular bands known as *kuruc*—ruthless freebooters comparable to the *hajduks* of the time of Hungarian national leader and prince of Transylvania István Bocskay—under a daring young leader, Count Imre Thököly, who by 1678 was raiding into Hungarian territory from Transylvania, and receiving modest French and Polish subsidies.

Kara Mustafa saw in Thököly an ideal instrument for his ambitions, and the grand vizier granted him the title of prince of Hungary. Initially, it was to support Thököly that Kara Mustafa began to plan a great expedition into Hungary, rumored to have Gyor and Komárom as its objectives. However, at some point, Kara Mustafa raised his sights, and the goal became Vienna. Süleyman the Magnificent, greatest of sultans, had failed to take Vienna in 1529. Now, Kara Mustafa would lead a jihad, a holy war, against the capital of the infidel emperor, and by his triumph outshine even Süleyman.

The great expedition was mobilized in the spring of 1683, commanded by Kara Mustafa: 100,000 Ottoman troops, including the crack Janissary regiments, to be joined by Thököly, with his *kuruc* forces, and Selim Giray, with his highly mobile Tatar cavalry. The outcome is well known to many. Leopold and his court abandoned Vienna, which was closely invested from July to September 12, 1683, when the city was relieved by the Polish king, John III Sobieski, and his German allies. Kara Mustafa made serious mistakes, holding back his cavalry from intercepting the advancing Poles and quarreling with the Crimean khan, who withdrew in disgust. The rout that followed proved an overwhelming disaster for the Ottomans.

Kara Mustafa may not have seen his defeat as so apocalyptic an event as did Christendom. Much of his army was intact, and he fell back on Buda, convinced that, with the sultan's support, he would renew the assault in the following spring. Here, he received ceremonial robes of honor and a bejeweled sword, traditional gifts of sultanic approbation, sent by Mehmed IV. By November 18, 1683, he was in winter quarters in Belgrade with a substantial part of the army, but his enemies had poisoned the sultan's mind against him, and on December 13, his death warrant was drawn up in Edirne and dispatched to Belgrade, where the grand vizier was strangled on December 25, 1683. His head, brought to the sultan, was subsequently interred beneath a tombstone in Edirne's Sariça Pasha mosque.

SIGNIFICANCE

Until the denouement at Vienna, Kara Mustafa Paşa enjoyed the reputation of an able and energetic administrator in the Köprülü tradition, which earned him the highest office in the empire. Ostentatious and arrogant in his public persona, he was known as a pious Muslim who established religious foundations in Constantinople, Galata, Edirne, and his birthplace of Merzifon. Yet the assault on Vienna was a huge blunder. He clearly overestimated the extent of the military revival achieved by his two predecessors, and he underestimated recent European advances in military technology. His failure led directly to the loss of Hungary and Transylvania, the Morea, and Podolia, confirmed in the Treaty of Karlowitz of 1699. By his recklessness, he accelerated Ottoman decline, which no subsequent Köprülü grand viziers could reverse.

—*Gavin R. G. Hambly*

FURTHER READING

Barker, Thomas W. *Double Eagle and Crescent*. Albany: State University of New York Press, 1967. A well-written, detailed account of the siege of Vienna in 1683, presenting an account of not only the military but also the diplomatic and political aspects of the siege.

Kurat, A. N. "The Ottoman Empire Under Mehmed IV." In *The New Cambridge Modern History*. Vol. 4. Cambridge, England: Cambridge University Press, 1961. An excellent overview of the empire during the time of Mehmed IV.

Murphey, Rhoads. *Ottoman Warfare, 1500-1700*. New Brunswick, N.J.: Rutgers University Press, 1999. A useful work that examines seventeenth century Ottoman military campaigning.

Stoye, John. *Siege of Vienna*. London: Collins, 1964. A scholarly narrative that explores the siege.

Turnbull, Stephen. *The Ottoman Empire, 1326-1699*. New York: Routledge, 2004. A history of Ottoman rule, imperial expansion, and military tactics that focuses especially on Ottoman battles against European powers and on control of the Balkans. Includes illustrations, maps, index.

Wheatcroft, Andrew. *Infidels: A History of the Conflict Between Christendom and Islam*. New York: Random House, 2004. Examines the continuing religious conflicts between the Christian West and the Islamic Middle East.

SEE ALSO: Innocent XI; John III Sobieski; Leopold I; Murad IV.
RELATED ARTICLES in *Great Events from History: The Seventeenth Century, 1601-1700:* 1603-1617: Reign of Sultan Ahmed I; September, 1605: Egyptians Rebel Against the Ottomans; September, 1606-June, 1609: Great Jelālī Revolts; November 11, 1606: Treaty of Zsitvatorok; 1623-1640: Murad IV Rules the Ottoman Empire; 1638: Waning of the *Devshirme* System; August 22, 1645-September, 1669: Turks Conquer Crete; 1656-1676: Ottoman Empire's Brief Recovery; 1677-1681: Ottoman-Muscovite Wars; July 14-September 12, 1683: Defeat of the Ottomans at Vienna; 1684-1699: Holy League Ends Ottoman Rule of the Danubian Basin; Beginning 1687: Decline of the Ottoman Empire; 1697-1702: Köprülü Reforms of Hüseyin Paşa; January 26, 1699: Treaty of Karlowitz.

KÂTIB ÇELEBÎ
Turkish scholar

Kâtib Çelebî, the first Ottoman intellectual to urge the exploration of Western knowledge and technology and its incorporation into Eastern scholarship, was one of the greatest secular scholars of the Ottoman Empire. He wrote books on geography, history, politics, and literature and set the course for future scholars in the empire.

BORN: February, 1609; Constantinople, Ottoman Empire (now Istanbul, Turkey)
DIED: September 24, 1657; Constantinople
ALSO KNOWN AS: Khatib Chelebi; Khatib Shalabī; Ḥājī Khalīfa; Haçi Halife; Muṣṭafa ibn ʿabd Allāh (Turkish given name)
AREAS OF ACHIEVEMENT: Scholarship, geography, government and politics, historiography, literature

EARLY LIFE

Kâtib Çelebî (kah-TEHB-chay-lay-BEE) was born Muṣṭafa ibn ʿabd Allāh to a poor family. His father was either a Janissary or *sipahi*, a member of the palace's cavalry unit. Kâtib Çelebî received his early education at his father's side and went with him on military expeditions to Baghdad and Erzurum. During these childhood travels, he acquired a taste for the military, travel, and geography. Even though he was taught to read and write at an early age, his family was too poor to send him to one of the madrasas, Muslim schools that taught theology, jurisprudence, and rhetoric with a concentration on Muslim sacred studies. This turned out to be a blessing.

As the world moved through the Renaissance, the Islamic fundamentalist movement opposed any form of innovation and rationalism. The madrasas reacted by refusing to teach mathematics, science, or medicine, subjects condemned as Western heresies. Because he was self-taught, and thereby not influenced by the madrasas, Kâtib Çelebî remained open-minded toward Western learning. His scholarship was to urge others to learn from Western thinking and ideas.

After his father died, in 1623, he entered the civil service and became a *katib*, or scribe. In service to Sultan Murad IV, Kâtib Çelebî rose through the ranks to become a chief scribe, or *khalfah*. At age twenty-five, he entered the office of the chief historiographer at the palace and attended the Persian campaigns in Hamadān and Baghdad with the Ottoman army. When the army wintered at Aleppo, Kâtib Çelebî took the time off to make a pilgrimage to Mecca and Medina, which earned him the title Hajji, or pilgrim. After his pilgrimage, he performed one last duty for the chief historiographer and attended the siege of Erivan (Yerevan). Once he returned to Constantinople, in 1645, he resigned from the civil service and began to study in earnest.

LIFE'S WORK

Kâtib Çelebî sought out the principal professors in Constantinople and spent ten years studying languages, law, logic, rhetoric, interpretation of the Qurʾān, mathematics, and geography. After suffering ill health, he embarked on a study of medicine, and then added foreign religions to his studies as well.

Near the beginning of his studies, Kâtib Çelebî took what little money his father had left him and purchased a variety of books. He had always loved books and had read every manuscript he could find during his travels. Later, a well-to-do relative died, leaving Kâtib Çelebî quite well off financially, providing for his daily living. He was able to add to his personal library and often sat up all night reading. His study and devotion to learning eventually made him the most learned individual of his time. As a natural outgrowth of his studies, Kâtib Çelebî began to publish his writings.

Kâtib Çelebî wrote the first major Ottoman work on geography, the *Jihannuma* (world mirror, or, view of the world) in 1648. In the preface, he discusses his inability to find works in Turkish, Persian, or Arabic that describe the British Isles or Iceland accurately. He used connections, without much success, to try to find information available in Western works. Just as he was about to give up, he found a copy of the *Theatrum orbis terrarum* (1570; *Atlas Minor*) by Flemish cartographer Abraham Ortelius (1527-1598). Also, he met a French priest who had converted to Islam. The French convert helped him translate the *Atlas Minor*, and Kâtib Çelebî used the information in his *Jihannuma*.

In addition to the *Jihannuma*, Kâtib Çelebî wrote, by 1655, a geography of Asia that was the most widely read geography in the Ottoman Empire, and a description of European Turkey. Also, he translated Ortelius's *Atlas Minor*, the first translation of a European geography book into Turkish. These geographies, considered the best geographical works from the Ottoman era, helped significantly in changing Ottoman ideas on the science of geography. They were also some of the first books printed on the first Turkish printing press in 1729.

After his first foray into geography, Kâtib Çelebî indulged his love of books in his greatest work, the bibliographic and encyclopedic dictionary *Kashf al-ẓunūnʿan asāmī al-kutub wa al-funūn* (1652?; the removal of doubt from the names of books and the sciences). This work, which captured the best of Eastern literature and ideas and preserved their record for future generations, was a massive bibliography of thousands of works in Arabic, Persian, and Turkish. The work included biographies of each listed author.

In addition to *Kashf al-ẓunūnʿan asāmī al-kutub wa al-funūn* and his geographies, Kâtib Çelebî wrote five major histories: a universal history, in Arabic, from "creation" to 1655 (1656?); a detailed account, in Turkish, of Ottoman history from 1591 to 1655 (1656?); *Tuhfat al-Kibar fi Asfar il-Bihar* (1651; English translations of chapters 1-4 in *The History of the Maritime Wars of the Turks*, 1831), a history of the Ottoman fleet and the main Ottoman naval campaigns through 1651, plus biographies of the Ottoman naval heroes; a history of Constantinople; and a chronology (1650?) of the principal historic events and dynasties of countries around the world, from "creation" to 1648. Kâtib Çelebî deliberately included information about Europe's role in Ottoman history in these works to educate the Islamic world by providing accurate information about the Europeans, who were conquering the seas, taking over Muslim areas, and introducing Christianity to the world. He addressed these same issues in an outline of European systems of government (1648?); in a guide on Greek, Roman, and Christian history (1655?); and in his many short treatises.

In *Dustūr al-amal li islah al-khalal* (1653; instructions for the reform of abuses), a book on the causes and remedies of Ottoman imperial debt, and in his final work, *Mizan al-ḥaqq fi lkhtijārī al-ahaqq* (1657?; *The Balance of Truth*, 1957), which contains a short autobiography, Kâtib Çelebî discusses the reasons for the decline of the Ottoman Empire and criticizes the madrasas for ignoring European sciences, mathematics, history, logic, medicine, and other scholarship. He urged the Ottomans to learn and teach the Western disciplines or face the fact that these subjects would be mastered by the intellect and technology of the West. After publishing his final plea in *The Balance of Truth*, he died on September 24, 1657.

SIGNIFICANCE

Kâtib Çelebî spent thirty years studying and writing, and he was known as a deliberate and impartial historian with a versatile and unconventional mind. In *Tuhfat al-Kibar fi Asfar il-Bihar*, Kâtib Çelebî plainly stated that the Ottomans needed to study and master geography, both their own and that of the nations with whom they were at war, to avoid the many battlefield errors made by the Ottomans during the shifting of troops, ships, and supplies.

In his history books and books on politics, Kâtib Çelebî bravely complained that the educational focus of the madrasas on law and theology engendered an intense prejudice against the secular courses of learning. Again and again, he pleaded with his fellow Muslims to recognize and incorporate Western intellectual, scientific, and technological advances. He argued that the Europeans knew much more about the Ottomans and Islam than did the Ottomans about the Europeans.

Kâtib Çelebî also made great efforts to obtain accurate information on Western scholarship from what sources were available to him. His sources were not always good, and he knew it, so he condemned them as such in his manuscripts.

—Peggy E. Alford

FURTHER READING

Goffman, Daniel. *The Ottoman Empire and Early Modern Europe*. New York: Cambridge University Press, 2002. A reconsideration of the Ottoman Empire, arguing that it should be understood as part of Renaissance Europe, rather than as a "world apart," isolated and exotic. Includes illustrations and maps.

Greene, Molly. *A Shared World: Christians and Muslims in the Early Modern Mediterranean*. Princeton, N.J.: Princeton University Press, 2000. Examines the interrelationship between the Muslims and Christians of the Mediterranean region.

Haji Khalifeh [Kâtib Çelebî]. *The History of the Maritime Wars of the Turks*. Translated by James Mitchell. New York: Johnson Reprints, 1968. Reprint of the 1831 translation of *Tuhfat al-Kibar fi Asfar al-Bihar*. Mitchell's preface contains a short but very informative biography of Kâtib Çelebî.

Imber, Colin. *The Ottoman Empire, 1300-1650: The Structure of Power*. New York: Palgrave Macmillan, 2002. Imber includes extensive information about the life and works of Kâtib Çelebî as part of his overall treatment of the Ottoman Empire.

Lewis, Bernard. *The Muslim Discovery of Europe*. New York: W. W. Norton, 2001. Lewis examines Kâtib Çelebî's works, including those based on European scholarship and those about the West itself.

Turnbull, Stephen. *The Ottoman Empire, 1326-1699*. New York: Routledge, 2004. This history of Ottoman rule, imperial expansion, and military tactics focuses especially on battles against European powers and on control of the Balkans. Includes illustrations, maps, index.

Wheatcroft, Andrew. *Infidels: A History of the Conflict Between Christendom and Islam*. New York: Random House, 2004. Examines the continuing religious conflicts between the Christian West and the Islamic Middle East.

SEE ALSO: Merzifonlu Kara Mustafa Paşa; Murad IV.
RELATED ARTICLES in *Great Events from History: The Seventeenth Century, 1601-1700:* 1603-1617: Reign of Sultan Ahmed I; September, 1605: Egyptians Rebel Against the Ottomans; 1623-1640: Murad IV Rules the Ottoman Empire.

JOHANNES KEPLER
German astronomer

Through the application of his exceptional intellect, faith, and tenacity, Kepler created the science of modern astronomy—the fusing together of physics and astronomy—and provided the solid foundation upon which Isaac Newton built his laws of universal gravitation. He also is considered the father of modern optics.

BORN: December 27, 1571; Weil, Swabia (now Weil der Stadt, Germany)

DIED: November 15, 1630; Regensburg, Bavaria (now in Germany)

AREAS OF ACHIEVEMENT: Astronomy, physics, mathematics, science and technology

EARLY LIFE

Johannes Kepler (yoh-HAHN-ehs KEHP-lehr) was born prematurely, the first child of Heinrich and Katharine Kepler, and his childhood was exceptionally difficult. He was small and sickly, with thin limbs and a large, pasty face surrounded by dark hair. It is one of the ironies of history that the child who would one day revolutionize astronomy had poor eyesight. His mother was a small woman with a nasty disposition; his father appears to have had no established trade and, in 1574, simply left the family to fight for the Catholic duke of Alva in the Netherlands. His mother followed a year later, leaving Kepler in the care of his grandparents, who treated him badly. In 1576, his parents returned, but this provided only a dubious improvement in his family life.

Under such circumstances, it is not surprising that Kepler's self-image as a child was terrible; he described himself once as a "mangy dog." Possibly in response to the instability in his life, Kepler developed a pronounced religious disposition at a young age. Indeed, of all his childhood memories only two stood out as pleasant. When he was six, Kepler's mother took him to a hill to see a comet, and at age nine his parents took him outside to observe an eclipse of the Moon. The seeds were planted that would influence the direction of his life.

Yet it was obvious even to his parents that Kepler was a bright child, and school provided a way for him to divert himself from the suffering of family life while building his self-assurance and developing his intellect. Kepler was fortunate that the Lutheran dukes of Württemberg provided generous educational scholarships for the intelligent sons of poor parents.

Kepler began his schooling at age seven at the Latin school in Leonberg. He completed the curriculum at age twelve, and his intellect, poor health, and pious nature preordained him to a clerical career. After passing a competitive exam on October 16, 1584, Kepler continued his studies at the higher seminary at Maulbronn. On September 17, 1589, he entered the University of Tübingen, where he was particularly influenced by his professor of astronomy, Michael Mästlin. Mästlin was unique in that he believed that Nicolaus Copernicus's heliocentric theory was essentially true. Influenced by this exceptional teacher, Kepler accepted the Copernican view of the universe—an act that would have a profound impact on his life and the future of scientific thought.

At the age of twenty, Kepler was matriculated at the Tübingen Theological School. His career path seemed assured, but circumstances fatefully intervened. In 1593, the mathematician of the Lutheran high school of Graz died, and the school requested Tübingen to recommend a replacement. Kepler was nominated and agreed to accept the position.

His job was to teach mathematics and to publish the annual calendar of astrological forecasts. Kepler was lucky with his first calendar, correctly predicting a cold spell and a Turkish invasion. He would be involved with astrology all of his professional life, but he did it primarily to supplement his income. Still, while he considered popular astrological forecasts a "dreadful" superstition, Kepler believed that astrology could become an exact empirical science, and with that aim in mind, he would write several treatises on the subject.

Kepler was a terrible teacher. He was often unintelligible, launching into obscure digressions whenever a thought occurred to him. Yet it was during one of these lectures that the event happened that set Kepler on the path that would ultimately lead him to reinterpret the prevailing view of the universe.

LIFE'S WORK

Kepler found his first year at Graz very trying. To escape its frustrations, he turned to the astronomical studies he had experimented with at Tübingen. The more he contemplated the Copernican system, the more he became convinced of its truth, but he was also aware that it was not the final, definitive explanation of the operation of the universe.

Already in 1595, Kepler was beginning to ask the questions that would determine that course of his scientific inquiry. Why are there only six planets? What determines their distances from the sun? Why do the planets move more slowly the farther away they are from the sun? These and other queries had been coursing through his mind when, on July 19, 1595, as he was teaching, an incredible thought struck him. On the blackboard, he had drawn a figure showing an outer circle circumscribing a triangle, which enclosed an inner circle. As Kepler looked at the two circles, he was suddenly dumbfounded by the realization that the ratios of the two circles were the same as those of the orbits of Saturn and Jupiter. Could it be that there were only six planets because planetary orbits were related to the five regular solids—the tetrahedron, cube, octahedron, dodecahedron, and icosahedron—of Euclid's geometry?

This revelation was the basis of Kepler's first major work, *Mysterium cosmographicum* (1596; *The Secret of the Universe*, 1981). His thesis was that one of the five regular solids fit between each of the invisible spheres that carried the six planets. The key insight of this book, however, revolved around his search for a mathematical relationship between a planet's distance from the Sun

Johannes Kepler. (Library of Congress)

and the time necessary for it to complete its orbit. Kepler concluded that there must be a force emanating from the Sun that swept the planets around their orbits. The outer planets moved more slowly because this force diminished in a ratio to distance, just as light did. Here is found the first hint of celestial mechanics, the joining of physics and astronomy, that would lead to the laws of planetary motion.

Kepler sent copies of the work to a number of scientists in Europe, including Tycho Brahe, who had spent several years making painstakingly accurate observations of planetary orbits and who would shortly become the imperial mathematician of the Holy Roman Empire. Although he did not agree with the Copernican underpinning of Kepler's work, Brahe was impressed by Kepler's knowledge of mathematics and astronomy, and he invited Kepler to join his staff in the observatory at Benatek, just outside Prague. Kepler was flattered by the invitation, but he had just been married and was too poor to afford the trip. The deteriorating religious situation in Graz, in which Protestants were being forced either to convert to Catholicism or to emigrate, compelled Kepler to make a decision. In 1600, Kepler joined Brahe in Prague, where he would remain until 1612. This period would be the most productive of his life.

Kepler's first publication after arriving at Prague, *De fundamentis astrologiae certioribus* (1601; the more reliable bases of astrology), while rejecting the belief that celestial bodies direct people's lives, supported the mystical view that there is a harmony between the universe and the individual. In 1606, after observing a supernova, Kepler published *De stella nova in pede serpentarii* (the new star in the foot of the serpent bearer), which argued that the universe of fixed stars was not pure and changeless, as had been believed. In 1604, Kepler authored a major work on optics, *Ad Vitellionem paralipomena, quibus astronomiae pars optica traditur* (*Optics: Paralipomena to Witelo and Optical Part of Astronomy*, 2000). The main subject was the atmospheric refraction, or bending, of light as it enters Earth's atmosphere from space. An understanding of this phenomenon was vital if Kepler was to make optimum use of Brahe's observational data. In this work, Kepler for the first time explained the fundamental structure and function of the human eye. Although he was unsuccessful in developing the law of refraction, he was able to create an improved table of refraction.

Kepler concluded his work in optics with *Dioptrice* (1611; partial translation of the preface, 1880), which not only restated his concept of refraction but also covered such subjects as reflections, images, magnification, and the optical principles of the astronomical telescope. These two works have justifiably established Kepler as the father of modern optics. That same year, Kepler wrote the *Dissertatiocum nuncio sidereo* (1610; *Kepler's Conversation with Galileo's Sidereal Messenger*, 1965), placing his then-considerable scientific prestige in support of Galileo's astronomical discoveries. Kepler's great magnum opus, published in 1609 after years of painstaking effort, was the *Astronomia nova* (*New Astronomy*, 1992).

When Kepler first arrived at Prague in 1600, Brahe immediately assigned him to investigate the orbit of Mars, which Brahe and his assistant, Danish astronomer Longomontanus (Christian Severin), had been unable to determine. The selection of Mars was particularly fortuitous because of all the planets, Mars has the most elliptical orbit and, therefore, provided the best opportunity for discovering the secrets of planetary motion. Once Kepler had full use of Brahe's observational data following Brahe's death in 1601—for now Kepler was the imperial mathematician—he became completely immersed in this project.

As he began the study of Mars, Kepler had a thoroughly Copernican concept of planetary motion. Each planet revolved around the Sun at a uniform speed in a perfectly circular orbit, considered the perfect geometrical shape. Accordingly, Kepler first tried to show that the Martian orbit was circular. After three years of intense, repetitive calculations, Kepler believed that he had proved Mars had a circular orbit, only to discover that two of Brahe's innumerable observations of the planet differed from Kepler's orbit by only 8 minutes of arc. (The width of a pinhead held at arm's length approximately equals 8 minutes of arc.) Previous scientists would have made the evidence fit the theory, but Kepler would not. Believing that God would not create anything imperfect, Kepler knew that he could not ignore those 8 minutes of arc. The orbit of Mars could not be circular but had to be some other geometrical curve.

Kepler now had to redetermine the Martian orbit, but first he had to recalculate the orbit of Earth. Earth was his observatory, and if there were any misconceptions regarding its motion, then all conclusions regarding other planetary motion would be in error. He discovered that Earth did not revolve around the Sun at a uniform speed, but rather moved faster or slower depending upon its distance from the sun. Obviously, the Platonic and Copernican concept of uniform motion was incorrect. Kepler, however, discovered a new type of uniform motion:

With the Sun as its focus, the planet, while revolving along the periphery of its orbit, will sweep out, in equal intervals of time, equal areas of the orbit, and unequal arcs along the periphery of the orbit.

The second law determined the variations of the planet's speed along its orbit but not the shape of the orbit itself. For two more years, Kepler worked on that problem before coming upon the solution: an ellipse. This led to his first law (discovered after his second law): A planet moves in an ellipse with the Sun at one of the two foci.

Kepler's third law was not published until 1619 in the *Harmonices mundi* (partial translation as *Harmonies of the World*, 1952). Here Kepler states that the squares of the planetary periods (the time it takes a planet to complete its orbit) are proportional to the cubes of their average distance from the Sun (the 3/2 ratio). The farther from the Sun an object is, the slower it moves.

These two works, the *New Astronomy* and *Harmonies of the World*, completed Kepler's work on planetary motion and provided the basis for Isaac Newton's explanation of universal gravitation, which affects every material object in the universe.

In the meantime, Kepler's life underwent much upheaval. In 1610, his wife died, and the next year his patron, Holy Roman Emperor Rudolf II, slipped into insanity and was deposed by his brother, Matthias, who became the new king of Hungary. Although he was reappointed imperial mathematician, Kepler left Prague and moved to Linz, Austria. In 1623, he was married to Susanna Reuttinger, who although several years younger than Kepler and of lower social status, proved to be one of the few joys of his later life.

While in Linz, Kepler published his *Epitome astronomiae Copernicanae* (1618-1621; partial translation as *Epitome of Copernican Astronomy*, 1939). This relatively unknown and underrated work is highly significant, ranking next to Ptolemy's *Almagest* (second century) and Copernicus's *De revolutionibus* (1543) as the first systematic elaboration of the concept of celestial mechanics established by Kepler. In it, he not only conclusively proved the validity of the Copernican view of the universe but also revealed all the knowledge he had uncovered during his many years of research.

As he worked on *Epitome of Copernican Astronomy*, Kepler heard that his mother was going to be tried as a witch, a capital offense. Self-interest as well as familial devotion led him to conduct a successful defense. Had she been convicted, not only would there be severe consequences for her, including possible death, but Kepler's status as imperial mathematician also could have been imperiled.

Kepler also planned to publish *Tabulae Rudolphinae* (English translation, 1675), named in honor of Rudolf II, in Linz, but a peasants' rebellion and religious unrest forced Kepler to move to Ulm, where the work was first published in 1627. Based on Brahe's observations, *Tabulae Rudolphinae* is a book on practical astronomy. It became an indispensable astronomical tool for more than a century, and Kepler considered it the crowning achievement of his life.

The last three years of Kepler's life were a struggle. Albrecht Wenzel von Wallenstein, the famous mercenary general of the Thirty Years' War (1618-1648), promised to meet Kepler's financial needs, but the general was unreliable. In 1628, Kepler moved to Żagań, Silesia, and late in 1630 he left for Austria to collect some funds he was owed. He stopped at Regensburg, where the Imperial Diet was meeting, fell ill, and died on November 15, 1630. Scientists throughout Europe mourned his death.

SIGNIFICANCE

Kepler's impact on the development of astronomy and general science was enormous. By the sheer force of his intellect and the tenacity of his spirit, he forged ahead in the understanding of the cosmos, further than any of his contemporaries. Kepler not only provided the mathematical proof of the Copernican system but also went far beyond it, creating the science of modern astronomy, in which physics, the concept of physical force, and astronomy were fused together. He discovered the famous three laws, created the science of optics, and came very close to discovering gravity. His determination that the theory must fit the facts and not vice versa established the standard for future scientific inquiry. Without Kepler, there would not have been Newton's laws of universal gravitation.

Kepler also had a more abstract impact on Western society. A society's perception of the cosmos is reflected in the way it views itself. By demonstrating conclusively for the first time that the universe operates according to fixed, natural laws, Kepler assisted Western society in freeing itself from the shackles of superstition and ignorance.

Basic to Kepler's success was his Christian faith. Although his belief in the harmony of the worlds led him into many mystical conjectures, Kepler's firm belief that God would only have created a harmonious universe, where there had to be a predetermined reason for the oc-

currence of certain events, provided the proper attitude for discerning the existence of natural laws. Indeed, Kepler's faith, rather than being a hindrance, was a creative force pushing him ever forward.

—Ronald F. Smith

FURTHER READING

Armitage, Agnus. *John Kepler*. London: Faber & Faber, 1966. Although not as detailed as other biographies, this is a very good introduction to Kepler and his work. It is lucid, includes excellent illustrations, and provides clear explanations of Kepler's calculations.

Bishop, Philip W., and George Schwartz, eds. *Moments of Discovery*. Vol. 1 in *The Origins of Science*. New York: Basic Books, 1958. Pages 265-277 contain the first partial translation of *Astronomia nova*, specifically Kepler's explanation of his first law.

Caspar, Max. *Kepler*. New York: Abelard-Schuman, 1959. This translation of the 1947 German edition is the definitive work on Kepler, thoroughly investigating every aspect of his life and work. Well written and lucid, this work is a must for any study of Kepler.

Connor, James A. *Kepler's Witch: An Astronomer's Discovery of Cosmic Order Amid Religious War, Political Intrigue, and the Heresy Trial of His Mother*. San Francisco, Calif.: HarperSanFrancisco, 2004. A biography of Kepler, placing him within the context of seventeenth century life. Depicts him as one deeply driven by his Lutheran faith and one who was trying to survive the politics of the Counter-Reformation.

Gilder, Joshua, and Anne-Lee Gilder. *Heavenly Intrigue: Johannes Kepler, Tycho Brahe, and the Murder Behind One of History's Greatest Scientific Discoveries*. New York: Doubleday, 2004. Depicts the troubled relationship of Kepler and his mentor, Brahe, contending Kepler murdered Brahe to obtain the scientific data Kepler needed to complete his laws of planetary motion. Portrays Kepler as a virtual sociopath, consumed with anger and beset with illness.

Kepler, Johannes. *New Astronomy*. Translated by William H. Donahue. New York: Cambridge University Press, 1992. The first full translation in English of Kepler's major work. Includes a bibliography and an index.

_____. *Optics: Paralipomena to Witelo and Optical Part of Astronomy*. Translated by William H. Donahue. Santa Fe, N.Mex.: Green Lion Press, 2000. The first English translation of Kepler's major work on optics. Includes a bibliography and an index.

Koestler, Arthur. *The Watershed: A Biography of Johan-*

nes Kepler. Garden City, N.Y.: Anchor Books, 1960. This Science Study series volume is a fine introduction to Kepler and his work. The discussion on Kepler and Galileo is excellent, showing that Kepler had a much greater impact on the development of astronomy and physics than Galileo.

Small, Robert. *An Account of the Astronomical Discoveries of Kepler.* London: J. Mawman, 1804. Reprint. Madison: University of Wisconsin Press, 1963. Until the translation of Caspar, this was the best work on Kepler in English. It remains the best English work for readers interested in the mathematical details of Kepler's theories. Contains reproductions of many of Kepler's geometric figures.

Spiller, Elizabeth. *Science, Reading, and Renaissance Literature: The Art of Making Knowledge.* New York: Cambridge University Press, 2004. Studies literary works and the works of Kepler and other scientists to examine the changing disciplines of literature and science during the Renaissance.

SEE ALSO: Giovanni Alfonso Borelli; Gian Domenico Cassini; David and Johannes Fabricius; Galileo; Pi-

erre Gassendi; Johannes and Elisabetha Hevelius; Christiaan Huygens; Hans Lippershey; Nicolas-Claude Fabri de Peiresc; Wilhelm Schickard; Albrecht Wenzel von Wallenstein.

RELATED ARTICLES in *Great Events from History: The Seventeenth Century, 1601-1700:* 1601-1672: Rise of Scientific Societies; September, 1608: Invention of the Telescope; 1609-1619: Kepler's Laws of Planetary Motion; 1610: Galileo Confirms the Heliocentric Model of the Solar System; 1615-1696: Invention and Development of the Calculus; 1618-1648: Thirty Years' War; 1620: Bacon Publishes *Novum Organum*; 1623-1674: Earliest Calculators Appear; 1632: Galileo Publishes *Dialogue Concerning the Two Chief World Systems, Ptolemaic and Copernican*; 1637: Descartes Publishes His *Discourse on Method*; February, 1656: Huygens Identifies Saturn's Rings; 1665: Cassini Discovers Jupiter's Great Red Spot; 1673: Huygens Explains the Pendulum; December 7, 1676: Rømer Calculates the Speed of Light; Summer, 1687: Newton Formulates the Theory of Universal Gravitation; June 2, 1692-May, 1693: Salem Witchcraft Trials.

BOHDAN KHMELNYTSKY
Ukrainian Cossack hetman (r. 1648-1657)

Between 1648 and 1654, Khmelnytsky led the Zaporozhian (Dnieper) Cossacks in a successful uprising against the Polish-Lithuanian Commonwealth, permanently changing the balance among Eastern European powers and advancing the cause of Ukrainian nationalism.

BORN: c. 1595; Subotiv?, Ukraine
DIED: August 16, 1657; Chyhyryn, Ukraine
ALSO KNOWN AS: Bohdan Zinoviy Mykhaylovych Khmelnytsky (full name); Bohdan Chmielnicki
AREAS OF ACHIEVEMENT: Government and politics, warfare and conquest

EARLY LIFE

Bohdan Khmelnytsky (BAWG-dahn khmyehl-NYIHT-skuhih), hetman (chieftain) of the Zaporozhian Cossack Host and founder of the Hetman state (1648-1781), was the son of a member of the Cossack gentry. Khmelnytsky's father came from the Pereyaslavl region and served the Polish crown hetman Stanislaw Zolkiewski and later the Polish provincial governor of Chyhyryn. It

was in Chyhyryn that the elder Khmelnytsky acquired his estate, Subotiv, where Bohdan was probably born. During the Polish-Ottoman War of 1618-1621, Bohdan's father commanded recruits from Chyhyryn under his old mentor, Zolkiewski, until he was killed in the battle of Cecora (September, 1620).

Bohdan Khmelnytsky was raised Orthodox and spoke Ukrainian as his first language. By the time he lost his father, he had completed his education under the Jesuits, probably at L'viv, and was fluent in Polish and Latin, to which he later added a knowledge of Turkish, Tatar, and French. His first experience of war was at Cecora, beside his father, where he was taken prisoner and spent two years of captivity in Constantinople, before his mother ransomed him.

Little is known about Khmelnytsky's movements between 1622 and 1637, but at some point in the 1620's, he became a "registered Cossack," in effect a member of the Polish-officered Cossack militia first instituted by King Stephen Báthory in 1578 for frontier defense. In 1638, he was part of a Cossack delegation that went to Warsaw to request the restoration of former Cossack privileges, and in 1645, he served with a Cossack detachment in France. On Khmelnytsky's return from France in 1646, King Władysław IV Vasa (r. 1632-1648), seeking to put Poland at the head of an anti-Ottoman alliance, summoned him to Warsaw to discuss ways to enlist the support of the Zaporozhian Host. He was thus a person of some note in the eyes of the Warsaw court. Around this time, Khmelnytsky lost his first wife, with whom he had had three sons, including Tymish (1632-1653) and Yurii (1641-1685), and four daughters.

LIFE'S WORK

In the southeastern lands of the Polish-Lithuanian Commonwealth where Khmelnytsky lived, the Catholic Polish magnates and landowners were intent upon reducing the overwhelmingly Orthodox local population, both peasants and Cossacks alike, to virtual serfdom on their vast estates. They hated the free spirit of the Cossacks and by the 1640's were determined to break the independent-minded members of the Cossack gentry, such as Khmelnytsky.

With the complicity of the provincial authorities, several landowners descended upon the Khmelnytsky estate at Subotiv and destroyed it. In the course of the attack, a small son of Khmelnytsky was beaten to death in the marketplace at Chyhyryn, and his fiancée was abducted. His own arrest and execution were ordered, but thanks to the intervention of the Chyhyryn garrison, he escaped in January of 1648 and fled beyond the Dnieper River with such followers as he could muster.

The events of 1647—a dead wife, a murdered child, an abducted fiancée, and a devastated estate—turned what had hitherto been a middle-ranking fifty-year-old Cossack officer with a record of loyalty to the Polish crown into a terrifying nemesis to Poland, dedicated to the destruction of the Polish elite and all who aided them. These events changed forever the history of eastern Europe. However much Khmelnytsky was driven by a lust for revenge, though, he could not have achieved what he did had his treatment been an isolated experience. Khmelnytsky's tribulations were merely the most extreme examples of injustices to which all the Cossacks, both the elite and the rank and file, had been exposed. His rebellion became a means for channeling their collective resentments.

Khmelnytsky's revolt was the greatest and bloodiest of the insurrections that tore apart the Polish-Lithuanian and Russian borderlands. Against the Poles, the Cossacks' greatest weakness was a lack of trained cavalry,

but Khmelnytsky appealed for support from the traditional enemies of the Cossacks, the Crimean Tatars. His timing was perfect, for Tatar-Polish relations were at a low ebb, and the khan, Islam Giray III (r. 1644-1654), sent four thousand Tatars to support the Cossack rebellion. On May 6, 1648, an advance guard of six thousand Poles, riding ahead of the main force of twenty thousand, was ambushed at Zhovti Vody, near the Sich, the Zaporozhian Cossack headquarters. Almost three weeks later, on May 26, 1648, the main Polish army was annihilated near Korsum, where many Polish leaders and magnates were taken prisoner.

A few days later, King Władysław died and was succeeded by his half brother, John II Casimir Vasa (r. 1648-1668). Thereafter, on both banks of the Dnieper River, Cossacks, burghers, and peasants, joined by runaway serfs, bandits, and Tatars, rose up against their oppressors in a *jacquerie* (peasant revolt) of unparalleled savagery. The Jews were particular objects of the rebels' hostility. The Polish magnates responded to the savage rebellion in kind, torturing and slaughtering Cossack peasants, women, and children wherever they found them. Meanwhile, the Poles assembled a formidable force of thirty-two thousand Polish troops and eight thousand German mercenaries, which Khmelnytsky's troops met at Pyliavtsi (September 23, 1648), midway between Kiev and L'viv, winning a resounding victory.

Khmelnytsky now entered Volhynia and Galicia, where the peasants rose in his support. In early October, he besieged L'viv but was bought off by an enormous ransom. He then turned north to Zamosc, where he learned that the new king, John II, was offering him an armistice. He accepted it, for his troops, as well as the population in general, were stricken by plague and famine, and his Tatar allies were deserting him. Khmelnytsky turned east again and marched to Kiev, where he was given a tumultuous welcome by the citizens and the Orthodox hierarchy, who acclaimed him as a new Moses delivering his people from Polish bondage (January, 1649).

The Poles renewed the fighting later in 1649, advancing through Volhynia only to be ambushed near Zboriv. At his moment of triumph, however, Khmelnytsky was abandoned by Khan Islam Giray and forced to negotiate. The Treaty of Zboriv (August 18, 1649), was a triumph, but it left neither party satisfied: The Cossacks thought that Khmelnytsky had given too much away, and the Poles, that they had gained too little.

In 1651, the Poles sent another army to crush Khmelnytsky's Cossacks and Tatars, and in a two-week battle

(June 18-29, 1651) near Berestechno in Volhynia, Khmelnytsky experienced total defeat, again as a result of Tatar treachery. The subsequent Treaty of Bila Tserkva (September 28, 1651) was much less favorable to Cossack interests than the Treaty of Zboriv had been, although Khmelnytsky countered this blow by a decisive victory against the Poles at Batih on May 1, 1652. By that time, it was clear that both sides had taken, as well as given, terrible punishment and had fought each other to a stalemate.

Prevailing discontent throughout the Ukraine and conflict between the ruling Cossack elite and the rank and file, whose aim was the abolition of serfdom, underscored Khmelnytsky's problems. Further, his unstable alliance with the Tatars was bitterly unpopular with most Cossacks. Khmelnytsky had long recognized that the Cossacks could not stand alone, however, so he decided to compel Moldavia, an Ottoman vassal, into an alliance. In 1650, he sent his eldest son, Tymish, into Moldavia with a force of Cossacks to compel Prince Vasile (r. 1634-1653) to abandon his Polish alliance. In 1652, Tymish married Vasile's daughter, Roksana, perhaps intending by this marriage to claim the succession. However, the marriage aroused the rulers of Transylvania and Walachia, and Tymish was killed in battle at Suceava (September 15, 1653), attempting to defend his father-in-law's interests.

With the failure of the Moldavian adventure and still mistrusting the Tatar khan, in 1651, Khmelnytsky negotiated for the Zaporozhian Host to become a vassal state of the Ottoman sultan on terms similar to those extended to Moldavia, Walachia, and the Crimea. His Cossacks, however, could not stomach a Muslim overlord. Reluctantly, Khmelnytsky turned to Russian czar Alexis, and in January, 1654, he agreed to the momentous Treaty of Pereyaslavl, by which the czar became overlord of the Zaporozhian Host. With the southwestern Ukraine ravaged mercilessly by the Tatars, allies no longer, and with Cossack tensions growing in response to Muscovite high-handedness, an embittered Khmelnytsky died in Chyhyryn in 1657.

SIGNIFICANCE

Few men of such comparatively obscure origins and advanced age have done so much to change history as did Khmelnytsky. Khmelnytsky's campaigns brought massacre, famine, and depopulation to vast areas of eastern Europe, marking the beginning of the decline of the Polish-Lithuanian Commonwealth, which had been at its prime when the century began and was in its dotage by century's end. The Commonwealth's Jewish communities, in particular, would never fully recover from the destruction wrought by the Cossacks.

Khmelnytsky's epic struggle against the Poles forced him into the arms of Muscovy, which, thereafter, inexorably advanced into the fertile, underpopulated grasslands of Russia's future bread bowl, but Khmelnytsky also gave the Cossacks a sense of national pride, providing the foundation for today's Ukrainian national identity. His legacy is, therefore, complex: A monster to Poles and Jews, he is praised by Russian historians for advancing the union of the Ukraine with Muscovy, and he was praised by Soviet historians as a great revolutionary (which he was not), while to Ukrainians, he is the father of their nation.

—Gavin R. G. Hambly

FURTHER READING

Davis, Norman. *God's Playground: A History of Poland.* 2 vols. New York: Columbia University Press, 1982. Khmelnytsky's revolt is described from a Polish point of view.

Hrushevsky, Michael. *A History of Ukraine.* New Haven, Conn.: Yale University Press, 1970. A classic statement of a leading Ukrainian historian.

Longworth, Philip. *The Cossacks.* New York: Holt, Rinehart and Winston, 1970. General introduction to the Cossack phenomenon.

Subtelny, Orest. *Ukraine: A History.* 3d ed. Toronto: University of Toronto Press, 2000. Authoritative overview of Ukrainian history.

Vernadsky, G. *Bohdan: Hetman of Ukraine.* New Haven, Conn.: Yale University Press, 1941. A biography of Khmelnytsky by a great Russian historian.

SEE ALSO: Alexis; Ivan Stepanovich Mazepa.

WILLIAM KIDD
Scottish privateer

At the time of his death, Kidd was probably the most notorious pirate of the age, but he was also a victim of the changing political and administrative practices of an increasingly modern era.

BORN: c. 1645; Greenock, Renfrew, Scotland
DIED: May 23, 1701; London, England
AREAS OF ACHIEVEMENT: Government and politics, military

EARLY LIFE

Little is known of William Kidd's early life. He was born in Greenock, on the Firth of Clyde, and his father was possibly a Presbyterian minister in the Scottish national church. The young Kidd turned his back on the land, choosing the sea rather than the national church for his career.

The late seventeenth century was a world in transition. Scotland was an independent kingdom, although the same monarchs ruled both that nation and England. Kidd's future would be tied to those monarchs, particularly William III, who succeeded James II, a Catholic king in a Protestant land and an advocate of royal absolutism, in the Glorious Revolution of 1688. James took refuge in France, England's traditional enemy.

Politically, England was divided into Whigs and Tories, factions made up of members of the ruling classes, including aristocrats, merchants, and bankers—old and new wealth. At the time, no European nation could be described as democratic, and the common people had little say in politics. Differences existed between the two factions—the Whigs were in favor of placing controls on the monarchy, the Tories were more royalist—but politics largely revolved around the quest for power, place, and patronage. The Whigs' willingness to support William's war against France after 1688 gave them an advantage over their Tory rivals.

Under Louis XIV, France had become Europe's leading power, threatening in particular William's United Provinces of the Netherlands. In addition, considerable imperial rivalry existed over trade and colonies, both in the Americas and in Asia. War was the norm on both land and sea, and on the latter, privateers—ships licensed by a particular government—preyed on those of the enemy. Often only a fine line separated legal privateering and illegal piracy, and Kidd sailed back and forth across that line.

LIFE'S WORK

Kidd first appeared in the historical record in 1689 as part of a pirate crew in the Caribbean. The Glorious Revolution of the previous year brought England into the wars against Louis XIV, continuing the English-French rivalry that would not end until the nineteenth century. Like other former pirates, Kidd became an English privateer, captain of his own ship, *The Blessed William*, but shortly after an engagement against the French, for which he was praised for his fighting skills, his men stole both his ship and his money, a not uncommon experience in such a risky profession.

He was given another vessel in recompense, and by 1691, he was in colonial New York, a volatile environment split by personalities, factions, and political upheavals. Kidd gained both money and recognition by assisting the newly appointed governor against the previous one. He married a wealthy widow, Sarah Bradley Cox Oort, eventually had two children, and settled in New York.

By 1695, Kidd had had enough of urban respectability. Because of the war with France, the economy was in the doldrums. One of the few areas of prosperity was privateering. Whatever Kidd's motives—money, boredom, adventure—he sailed to England to obtain a commission as a privateer. He had few contacts but did obtain the favor of Richard Coote, the earl of Bellamont, a Whig politician with connections to the major Whig figures who had recently been appointed governor of both Massachusetts Bay and New York. Kidd soon received a privateering commission to hunt down pirates. As a former pirate, who could be more qualified? Piracy was a problem, but the aim was also financial: Several of the Whig lords invested in the scheme, and King William was to receive a share of the profits. Political patronage had paved Kidd's path.

Sailing from England in April, 1696, on the *Adventure Galley* with a crew of seventy on a no-prey, no-pay basis (they were paid only from what they seized), Kidd's destination was New York. In transit, Kidd captured a French fishing boat, hardly a major prize. In New York, he saw his family, then set sail in September for the Indian Ocean, where, according to his privateering commission, he would pursue pirates.

While still in the Atlantic, Kidd came into contact with several Royal Navy ships, who coveted, with legal justification, some of the *Adventure Galley*'s crew. At first chance, Kidd deserted the flotilla, earning the wrath of the English commander, who passed the word that Kidd was likely to be more pirate than privateer, an accusation that was to dog Kidd.

The island of Madagascar, notorious for its piratical associations, was Kidd's first destination in the Indian Ocean, where the British East India Company was the regional economic power. Its ships were tempting prizes for pirates but were off limits to English privateers such as Kidd, for the company had considerable economic and political influence in England. After obtaining food, water, and additional sailors, Kidd sailed north to the Arabian Sea, although there were pirate bands nearby that he might have pursued. Pushed by the economic demands of his London backers as well as his crew, he decided instead to seize a ship of Islamic pilgrims, one of many that traveled annually from India to Arabia and back again. These ships were not English, but for economic and political reasons, the East India Company took a decided interest in their safety, and when Kidd attempted a capture in August, 1697, he was forestalled by an English vessel.

After failure in the Red Sea, Kidd sailed to India. He was not yet a pirate, but only because he had not been successful. That changed with the capture of an English ship, which he took although it had little economic value. He next attempted to capture a wealthy merchantman but was driven off by two Portuguese ships. An East India Company boat was seized, but Kidd, still straddling the line between piracy and privateering, freed it, in spite of considerable opposition from his crew. Thus far, the voyage had been a disaster: no captured pirates, no wealthy cargoes. Kidd's frustration cumulated in October, 1697, when, in a fit of anger, he struck and killed William Moore, one of his sailors.

Luck finally turned in November with the appearance of a Dutch-owned merchantman. Flying a French flag on his own vessel, Kidd skillfully manipulated the captain into showing a French pass, thus technically allowing the vessel to be seized under Kidd's commission. Two smaller ships were soon apprehended, on an even more tenuous legal ground. Finally, in January, 1698, a wealthy Indian merchantman, the *Quedah Merchant*, was captured. The economic goals of the voyage had at last been achieved, but Kidd had definitely crossed the line from privateer to pirate.

That status was soon compounded when he tried but failed to seize two East India Company ships.

With the monsoon season imminent, Kidd abandoned India for Madagascar. The *Adventure Galley* was in poor shape, and Kidd's success in reaching that large island in April, 1698, speaks for his sailing ability. There Kidd parted company from the majority of his crew, who preferred to stay in the Indian Ocean, shipping out on other pirate vessels. Kidd decided to return to New York in the hope of legitimizing his voyage, his profits, and himself, as others before him had often done in the murky political environment of the colonies and the mother country. After destroying his log and preparing his explanation that it was his crew who forced him into illegal activities, Kidd set sail in November on the *Quedah Merchant*—the *Adventure Galley* was no longer seaworthy—with a small crew.

William Kidd oversees the burying of his treasure on Gardiner's Island. (Library of Congress)

The political world had changed since he left. Reflecting both the long-range tendencies of European governments toward administrative centralization and the monopolization of political and military power against private interests as well as short-range necessities, not least of all pressure from the East India Company, a new statute against piracy had been adopted. Back in the Caribbean in April, 1699, Kidd learned that he was wanted for piracy. With care, Kidd disposed of much of the valuable bulk goods, obtained a new ship, and sailed to the mainland.

The governor of New York and Massachusetts Bay was Lord Bellamont, Kidd's onetime partner. In order to please his London patrons and the government that appointed him, with complications from ever-increasing Tory and East India influence, Bellamont was committed to eliminating piracy. Kidd arrived in New York in the midst of an antipirate campaign. Cautiously, he landed on Long Island, saw his family, and contacted Bellamont, promising to surrender if given a pardon. Initially, the governor seemed sympathetic, but after several meetings between Kidd and Bellamont in Boston, Kidd was arrested on July 6, 1699. When the news reached England in September, his notoriety was such that even King William was informed, and a special ship was dispatched to bring him to London for trial.

The Tory opposition in Parliament used Kidd's connection with the Whigs to attack the government. Kidd had become more than just a marginally successful pirate; he was a symbol and a pawn. Because of winter storms, the prisoner did not reach London until April, 1700. After being examined by the Admiralty Board, he was incarcerated in the pesthole prison of Newgate. There, he languished for months while the legal and political process slowly ground on. The leading Whigs, some of whom were his partners, saw the necessity of throwing a minor figure, a Jonah, overboard, and Kidd was their man.

Parliament interviewed Kidd in March, 1701. On two days in May, in separate trials, he was condemned for the murder of Moore and for piracy. His trial, although extraordinarily swift for a later age, met the norms for the times. He was taken from Newgate by cart to the Thames. Arriving drunk, he castigated his former patrons, and although the rope broke the first time, he was successfully hanged on the second attempt.

SIGNIFICANCE

Before he died, Kidd had already become a legendary figure who would become the subject of numerous biog-

raphies and novels. For some, he epitomized the notorious pirate; for others, he was a victim of a perverted legal system. In fact, Kidd was neither. He was a pirate, although not particularly successful: His known career spanned only the single voyage to the Indian Ocean, and there his deeds were hardly of legendary proportions; his trial was as fair as the times allowed. He was, however, a victim, or a symbol, of changing conditions in the emergence of the modern administrative state, and he was a pawn, though not an innocent one, of the powerful politicians of his day. Kidd's career is proof of the adage that when forced to choose between the facts and the legend, it is advisable to print the legend.

—Eugene Larson

FURTHER READING

Bonner, William Hallam. *Pirate Laureate: The Life and Legends of Captain Kidd*. New Brunswick, N.J.: Rutgers University Press, 1947. A scholarly work that sees Kidd as an innocent victim of politics and a corrupt judiciary.

Clifford, Barry, and Paul Perry. *Return to Treasure Island and the Search for Captain Kidd*. New York: William Morrow, 2003. Undersea explorer Clifford went to Madagascar to find and excavate the *Adventure Galley*, Kidd's legendary pirate ship. His book tells the story of his trip as well as recounting Kidd's life and voyages in the Indian Ocean.

Cochran, Hamilton. *Freebooters of the Red Sea*. Indianapolis, Ind.: Bobbs-Merrill, 1965. A sympathetic account of Kidd and other pirates. Written for a general audience, it contains many fascinating details, including those surrounding Kidd's execution.

Harris, Graham. *Treasure and Intrigue: The Legacy of Captain Kidd*. Toronto: Dundurn Press, 2002. Examines Kidd's life within the context of piracy in the Indian Ocean. The author concludes Kidd was thrust into a life of piracy by wealthy investors who made him a scapegoat for their crimes.

Pringle, Patrick. *Jolly Roger*. London: Museum Press, 1953. A popular work about the great age of piracy. It includes a chapter on Kidd, in which the author argues that Kidd did not receive a fair trial.

Ritchie, Robert C. *Captain Kidd and the War Against the Pirates*. Cambridge, Mass.: Harvard University Press, 1986. This is the definitive work on Kidd and his times, rich in Kidd's own story and also in illuminating the emerging modern state.

Seitz, Don C. *The Tryal of Capt. William Kidd for Murther and Piracy*. New York: Rufus Rockwell

Wilson, 1936. An interesting account of Kidd's trial told through a combination of narration and documents.

Zacks, Richard. *The Pirate Hunter: The True Story of Captain Kidd*. New York: Hyperion, 2003. A popular history of Kidd's life and sea voyages. The author debunks the myth that Kidd was a cutthroat pirate, arguing he was actually a successful New York sea captain who was hired by the English government and New World investors to track down pirates and retrieve their stolen wares.

SEE ALSO: James II; Louis XIV; William III.

RELATED ARTICLE in *Great Events from History: The Seventeenth Century, 1601-1700:* November, 1688-February, 1689: The Glorious Revolution.

EUSEBIO FRANCISCO KINO
Italian priest and missionary

Kino was a Jesuit priest who founded missions in present-day Arizona and northern Mexico. An important cartographer and a bold explorer, he produced some of the first European maps of the northern frontier of New Spain and Baja California.

BORN: August 10, 1645; Segno, Tirol (now in Italy)

DIED: March 15, 1711; Magdalena, Sonora, New Spain (now in Mexico)

ALSO KNOWN AS: Eusebio Francesco Chini (given name); Eusebio Francesco Chino (given name); Eusebio Francesco Kühn

AREAS OF ACHIEVEMENT: Religion and theology, exploration, geography

EARLY LIFE

Born to Francesco Chini and Margherita Lucchi, Eusebio Francisco Kino (ow-SAYB-yoh frahn-THEES-koh KEE-noh) was one of five children raised on the Chini family farm in northern Italy. A talented student, he studied in Trento, Italy, as well as at universities in Austria and Germany, taking courses in languages, theology, mathematics, and astronomy. At the age of nineteen, Kino fell gravely ill. Praying to Saint Francis Xavier, he vowed that if he recovered, he would devote his life to being a missionary. After recuperating, in 1665 Kino joined the Society of Jesus, or Jesuits, a Catholic religious order dedicated to education, preaching, and missionary work. He hoped to be sent on a mission to China, following in the footsteps of a cousin, Father Martino Martini.

LIFE'S WORK

In 1677, Kino was ordained a priest at Eistady, Austria. The following year, he received his assignment as a missionary to the Americas. He left Genoa, Italy, with nineteen other Jesuits for Cádiz, Spain, port to the New World. As a result of bad weather conditions, however, the group arrived late, missing the ship, and they remained in Seville, Spain, for two years waiting for the next fleet to leave. While in Seville, Kino learned Spanish. He also studied Halley's comet, eventually publishing a treatise on the subject in 1682. Kino's ship finally left Spain in 1681, arriving at Veracruz, Mexico, after three months. He was thirty-six years old.

In Mexico City, Kino joined the expedition of Admiral Isidro Atondo Antillón to Baja California as rector of the mission and royal cartographer. Kino was to be the first missionary in the area. In 1682, the group set sail from the west coast of Mexico. Although they established a mission and fort at San Bruno in 1683-1684, their attempts to colonize Baja California eventually failed because of the challenging geography and the resistance of the native population. The group withdrew from the region in 1684.

Kino's next assignment was as a missionary to the Pima Indians, or O'odham ("the people"), in the Pimería Alta region (now Arizona and the Mexican state of Sonora). It was hoped that missionaries could pacify this area, the site of continued conflict between the Pima and Apache tribes. In addition, the Spanish feared that the Pima might join forces with the Pueblo Indians of New Mexico, who already, in 1680, had staged the most successful native uprising of the colonial era, the Pueblo Revolt.

Kino arrived at the Sonoran town of Cucurpe in 1687. Shortly thereafter, he established his first mission in the nearby settlement of Cosari, giving it the name Nuestra Señora de los Dolores (Our Lady of Sorrows). He remained in Pimería Alta for twenty-four years, from 1687 until his death in 1711, founding more than twenty other missions in Sonora and Arizona.

Eusebio Francisco Kino. (Arizona Historical Society)

Kino's missions were typical of those founded by the Jesuits. He located them near preexisting native settlements, frequently on rivers, and in close proximity to other missions for support. After first erecting a cross on the site, they constructed a simple lean-to in which to say Mass, followed by a small adobe chapel. Once the site was well established, a more substantial church was built, usually by native laborers using local materials under the priest's direction.

Kino's missions lie along a 75-mile (120-kilometer) chain extending from Sonora north into Arizona, in the area of the Sonoran Desert. Some of the best known of the missions he founded include the churches at San Ignacio, Magdalena, Cocóspera, and Caborca in Sonora and San Xavier del Bac and Tumacácori in Arizona. Virtually nothing remains, though, of Kino's original structures. Shortly after his death in 1711, the missions fell into disuse and eventual ruin. After the expulsion of the Jesuits from the Spanish empire in 1767 as a result of conflict with King Charles III of Spain, the Franciscans took over the Jesuit missions on the northern frontier. At most sites, they rebuilt larger, more elaborate churches of fired brick. The famous mission church of San Xavier del Bac, near Tucson, Arizona, is the best known of all, a gleaming white Baroque edifice rebuilt in 1783-1797 by

the Franciscans on the foundations of Kino's simple adobe church of 1700. It still serves Native American worshipers today.

Kino is also remembered for establishing European agricultural methods at his missions. For example, he introduced European foodstuffs such as wheat and fruit trees to the Pima. He also imported domesticated animals such as cattle and sheep and taught the Pima carpentry and ironworking techniques. His goal was for each mission to become a self-supporting community.

Despite Kino's great success at founding missions among the Pima peoples, his twenty-four-year residence in the Pimería Alta was not without difficulties. The most dramatic of these was the Pima Uprising, or the Tubutama Revolt, of 1695. The rebellion occurred when, after brutal mistreatment by Spanish settlers and their Indian overseers at Tubutama, angry Pimas rose up, destroyed several missions, and killed the Jesuit priest at Caborca, Father Francisco Xavier Saeta. Father Kino intervened, putting an end to Spanish retaliation, and he was able to broker a peace between the Spanish and the Pima. He then undertook the rebuilding of the destroyed missions.

To this day, Kino is remembered as a peacemaker and advocate for the Pimas. He helped unite the various Pima peoples in their ongoing battles with the Apache. He also defended them from the abuses of Spanish settlers in the area. To that end, he enforced a royal decree prohibiting the colonists from enslaving local Indians in the silver mines of northern Mexico. Admittedly, the decree protected only Christian Indians and thus was clearly designed to facilitate conversion. Facing the choice between enslavement or Christianity, most Pimas were inclined to choose the latter. The same decree also exempted native neophytes from paying tribute.

In addition to his missionary activities, Father Kino is also remembered as an intrepid explorer. He made numerous trips on horseback into the desert Southwest, where no previous Europeans had ventured, including about forty trips into Arizona. In 1694, he was the first European to visit and report on the impressive Hohokam ruins of Casa Grande. He charted rivers in the region, including the Colorado, Gila, and Río Grande. In 1700, he determined that Baja California was a peninsula, not an island, as the Spanish had previously thought. As a result of his explorations, he produced about thirty maps that charted the Pimería Alta, Baja California, and the Sea of Cortez. They became the standard sources on the area.

Since the failed expedition of 1682-1684 to Baja California, Kino had longed to return to the first site of his missionizing. The head of the Jesuit order in Rome, General Tirso González, finally sent him there again in 1697. Jesuit attempts to convert Native Americans in the area recommenced. At the same time, Kino continued to evangelize in the Pimería Alta, traveling back and forth between the two areas for the next decade. He died on March 15, 1711, in Magdalena, Sonora, after dedicating yet another chapel, this one honoring his patron saint, Saint Francis Xavier. Since the discovery of Father Kino's body in 1966, Magdalena has become a pilgrimage site for devotees from Sonora, Chihuahua, and the southwest United States. In the early twenty-first century, plans were afoot to canonize the so-called Padre on Horseback.

SIGNIFICANCE

Because of Father Kino's energy, persistence, and talents, the Pimería Alta missions were the most successful Jesuit missions in the Americas, despite their location in an area that had long resisted Spanish colonization. Kino is revered to this day by many Pima peoples as an advocate and peacemaker. He was responsible for the introduction of European farming and ranching techniques on the northern frontier. As an explorer and cartographer, moreover, Kino produced the first maps of the Pimería Alta region and Baja California, maps that continued in use through the late nineteenth century.

—*Charlene Villaseñor Black*

FURTHER READING

Bolton, Herbert Eugene. *The Padre on Horseback*. Chicago: Loyola University Press, 1963. Still the definitive biography of Kino.

Polzer, Charles W. *Kino, a Legacy: His Life, His Works, His Missions, His Monuments*. Tucson: Jesuit Fathers of Southern Arizona, 1998. One of the best-detailed studies, by the authority on Kino. Written from a Catholic point of view.

_____. *Kino Guide II: A Life of Eusebio Francisco Kino, S. J., Arizona's First Pioneer, and a Guide to His Missions and Monuments*. Tucson: Southwest Mission Research Center, 1982. A short version of Kino's life with helpful information on the history of the mission churches. Written from a Catholic point of view by the current authority on Father Kino.

Poole, Stafford. "Iberian Catholicism Comes to the Americas." In *Christianity Comes to the Americas, 1492-1776*, by Charles H. Lippy, Robert Choquette, and Stafford Poole. New York: Paragon House, 1992. Provides an excellent overview of the work of Kino and the Jesuits on the northern frontier and places their activities within a wider historical context.

SEE ALSO: Saint Isaac Jogues; Jacques Marquette.

RELATED ARTICLE in *Great Events from History: The Seventeenth Century, 1601-1700:* August 10, 1680: Pueblo Revolt.

JAN KOMENSKÝ
Moravian theologian, educator, and philosopher

A Humanist reformer and Protestant bishop, Komenský believed in the unity of all knowledge as well as ecumenical unity. His writings in support of compulsory universal education and his pedagogical theories influenced education in Europe and North America for centuries.

BORN: March 28, 1592; Nivnice, Moravia (now in the Czech Republic)
DIED: November 15, 1670; Amsterdam, Holland, United Provinces (now in the Netherlands)
ALSO KNOWN AS: Jan Amos Comenius; Johann Amos Comenius; John Amos Comenius; Jan Ámos Komenský (full name)
AREAS OF ACHIEVEMENT: Education, religion and theology, philosophy

EARLY LIFE

Jan Komenský (yahn kaw-MEHN-skee) was born in southeastern Moravia near the Hungarian border. Although under the rule of the Habsburg Empire at the time, the area was known for religious tolerance, and a concentration of Protestants had settled there. Komenský's family members were devout Protestants, attending the Church of the United Brethren, a Protestant sect founded on the principles of the medieval Czech martyr Jan Hus.

By the turn of the century, however, mounting conflict between Catholics and Protestants reached Komenský's village, and when he was ten years old, a Hungarian Protestant army invaded the region. That same year, Komenský's parents and two sisters died of pestilence, and he was sent to live with an aunt. Soon after, he began his formal schooling, which he later described as brutal, characterized by rote learning and corporal punishment.

At age sixteen, he advanced to the Latin school run by the United Brethren, where he became enthralled with the study of classical language. As was the custom, he adopted the Latinate version of his name, Comenius. Seeking to continue his religious studies, he enrolled at the Herborn Academy, a Calvinist institution where he studied with the theologian Johann Heinrich Alsted. Comenius completed his religious studies at Heidelberg University under the tutelage of David Pareus, a noted religious scholar and leader who hoped to unite all Protestants under a broad Reformed Church.

In 1614, Comenius returned to Moravia to teach at his former Latin school, and he began writing prolifically, producing a Czech-Latin dictionary and textbook (*Janua linguarum reserata*, 1631; English translation, 1641) and beginning a Czech language encyclopedia. In 1616, he was ordained, and two years later he moved to his own parish in Fulnek with his new wife, Magdalena Vizovská. Also in 1618, a Protestant rebellion in Prague, known as the Defenestration of Prague, led to an invasion of imperial forces and the outbreak of the Thirty Years' War (1618-1648). Following the defeat of Czech resistance at the Battle of White Mountain in 1620, Protestants were driven from their homes. Comenius's home and library were razed, and he was forced to go into hiding. In 1628, he fled to Poland, never to return to his native land.

LIFE'S WORK

In spite of a life continually disrupted by war, religious persecution, and personal tragedy, Comenius retained his faith in God and his hope for humanity. In the 1620's, having lost his wife and children to the plague and his home to imperial forces, he embarked on a reexamination of his life that culminated in both a deeper religious conviction and an affirmation of the ability of the individual to improve the human condition through the practice of Christianity. *Labyrint světa a Ráj srdce* (1623; *Labyrinth of the World and the Paradise of the Heart*, 1901), a satirical allegory written in 1623, reflects his journey in the figure of a pilgrim who overcomes the folly of the world through introspection.

A progressive thinker, Comenius was able to combine his religious faith, his humanistic convictions, and his educational theories into a comprehensive system that he believed would lead to a better world. Known as pansophy, this system advocated universal education, an idea to which he was first exposed during his studies at Herborn with Alsted.

Comenius sought to make universal education a reality by instituting broad reforms. To facilitate educating children, he proposed abolishing corporal punishment and, instead, incorporating play, presenting material in increments geared to the child's capacity to learn, teaching Latin in the vernacular, and making lessons relevant to everyday life. His text *Orbis sensualium pictus* (*Visible World: Or, A Picture and Nomenclature of All the Chief Things That Are in the World*; better known as *Visible World*), which incorporates his pedagogical strategies, is considered the first effective illustrated textbook. Published in 1658, it was translated into English the following year and was in common use throughout Europe and North America for nearly two hundred years.

While the Thirty Years' War continued in his homeland, Comenius's reputation as both a religious leader and as an innovative educator spread across Europe, extending to the newly established North American colonies. In 1632, he was elected a bishop of the Unity Church by an international synod. Believing that Christianity is more a matter of practice than of orthodoxy, he attempted to unify Protestant sects with differing views on Christian doctrine. In 1641, he was invited to England to assist in instituting educational reform; he planned to found a pansophic college dedicated to Sir Francis Bacon, an English philosopher whom Comenius considered a role model. The proposed college would bring together, in pursuit of common goals, people of different religions. Although his plans were interrupted by the outbreak of civil war in England, he is credited with laying the groundwork for the English Royal Society, an independent organization devoted to promoting study of mathematics and the natural sciences, subjects that were in the seventeenth century considered less important than classical studies.

In 1642, Comenius received three extraordinary offers: Governor John Winthrop of Massachusetts invited him to assume the presidency of Harvard University; Cardinal de Richelieu, chief minister of King Louis XIII of France, requested his assistance in establishing a pansophic college in Paris; and a wealthy industrialist offered to finance extensive educational reform in Sweden. Believing that Sweden would support the interests of Czech exiles, Comenius accepted the latter offer and spent the next six years in Sweden, where he designed programs of instruction and continued to work toward attaining his ecumenical ideals.

In 1648, the Treaty of Westphalia brought an end to the Thirty Years' War, but the victorious Catholics refused to acknowledge the legitimacy of the Moravian

Church; consequently, Comenius was never able to return to his homeland, moving from Sweden to Poland to Transylvania and, finally, to Amsterdam. In the years before his death in 1670, he became immersed in mysticism but maintained his hope in the potential for humankind to improve the world.

SIGNIFICANCE

Comenius is known as the father of modern education. His influence can be seen in the work of twentieth century thinkers such as Jean Piaget and Lev Vygotsky, in contemporary liberal arts curricula, and in student-centered learning practices. His belief in the integration of knowledge is reflected in the proliferation of interdisciplinary studies in the late twentieth century.

In his homeland, whose history is one of foreign domination and oppression, Comenius is revered as a model of hope and courage. Echoes of his belief that humanity can achieve a far better world through individual responsibility can be heard in the writings and speeches of Václav Havel, former president of the Czech Republic, and in the novels of Czech writers Milan Kundera, Ivan Klíma, and Joseph Škvorecký. In Prague, he is commemorated with a museum and a statue by František Bílek, and his likeness appears on the twenty-crown note in Czech currency.

Internationally, Comenius is well remembered. He continues to draw scholarly interest, and in 1992, the 400th anniversary of his birthday was celebrated with symposia in Prague, Moravia, and Amsterdam, and with an exhibition at Oxford University in England.

—*K. Edgington*

FURTHER READING

Komenský, Jan Ámos. *The Great Didactic of John Amos Comenius*. Translated by M. W. Keatinge. 2d ed. London: A. & C. Black, 1910. Comenius began composing this work in Czech in the 1630's. In it he sets out his theories of child development and pedagogical strategies. Biographical introduction by the translator.

_____. *The Labyrinth of the World and the Paradise of the Heart*. Translated by Howard Louthan and Andrew Sterk. New York: Paulist Press, 1998. A modern translation of Comenius's satirical allegory and his only work of fiction, which draws on his early life and educational experiences.

Mitchell, Linda. C. *Grammar Wars: Language as Cultural Battlefield in Seventeenth and Eighteenth Century England*. Burlington, Vt.: Ashgate, 2001. An impressively researched expansion of the author's dissertation that examines Comenius as a radical thinker whose ideas were controversial and underappreciated by mainstream grammarians in seventeenth century England. Illustrations, bibliography, index.

Murphy, Daniel. *Comenius: A Critical Reassessment of His Life and Work*. Portland, Oreg.: Irish Academic Press, 1995. This study focuses on the role of Moravian Christianity in shaping Comenius's educational and pedagogical theories. It includes a biographical portrait, a chapter on cultural and historical influences, and a highly developed discussion of his theories and contributions. Index and bibliography.

Peprnik, Jaroslav. "Jan Amos Comenius." In *Fifty Major Thinkers on Education: From Confucius to Dewey*, edited by Joy A. Palmer. New York: Routledge, 2001. Peprnik, a professor at University Olomouc in the Czech Republic, provides insight into Comenius's importance to the Czech and the Slovak peoples.

Spinka, Matthew. *John Amos Comenius: That Incomparable Moravian*. 1943. Reprint. New York: Russell & Russell, 1967. A comprehensive biography with background information on conflicts between Protestants and Catholics leading to the Thirty Years' War. Bibliography and index.

Wolfe, Jennifer. *Learning from the Past: Historical Voices in Early Childhood Education*. Mayerthorpe, Alta.: Piney Branch Press, 2000. An entry-level college text that features a chapter on Comenius's contributions to education, including sample pages from his text *Orbis sensualium pictus*. Illustrations, bibliography, index.

SEE ALSO: Jakob Böhme; Cornelius Otto Jansen; Cardinal de Richelieu; John Winthrop.

RELATED ARTICLES in *Great Events from History: The Seventeenth Century, 1601-1700:* November 8, 1620: Battle of White Mountain; 1638-1669: Spread of Jansenism.

KÖSEM SULTAN
Queen consort, queen mother, and concubine

Kösem Sultan, the Queen Mother of two sultans and the grandmother of another, wielded sweeping powers in public decision making, in domestic and foreign policy, and in political appointments up to the time of her assassination.

BORN: c. 1585; place unknown

DIED: September 2, 1651; Constantinople, Ottoman Empire (now Istanbul, Turkey)

ALSO KNOWN AS: Kösem Mahpeyker/Maypeyker Sultan; Anastasya; Anastasia (given name)

AREA OF ACHIEVEMENT: Government and politics

EARLY LIFE

Originally christened Anastasia, Kösem Sultan (koh-SEHM-sool-TAHN) came to the palace in Constantinople in her childhood as a slave of Greek or Bosnian origin. She was attractive, intelligent, and witty, and had an excellent voice. She joined the harem at Sultan Ahmed I's Topkapi Palace. Kösem quickly attracted the sultan's eye, so he made her his *haseki*, or concubine. As his *haseki*, she bore three of the sultan's sons—Murad, İbrahim, and Kasim. She was thus entitled to special privileges, such as a private apartment in the palace, a *seray*. As the sultan's favorite and as the Queen Mother, given her dynamic persona, and with the cooperation of the black eunuch in charge of the harem (the *harem agasi*), Kösem acquired nearly absolute authority until Ahmed I's death in 1617.

After Ahmed's death, Kösem succeeded in having Mustafa I, the son of Mehmed III, take Ahmed's place, thereby outmaneuvering Osman, the son of Ahmed I and his bitter rival concubine, Mahfiruz. Sultan Mustafa I (r. 1617-1618 and 1622-1623) was soon deemed insane, however, and was deposed by Kösem's adversaries in favor of Osman II (r. 1618-1622). According to tradition, Kösem and her entourage were then relegated to the old palace, but when Osman II in turn became demented and was deposed and then assassinated, Murad IV, the son of Ahmed and Kösem, was installed and Kösem returned to Topkapi Palace as his guardian. Murad IV (r. 1623-1640), however, managed to shake off his mother's domination until his alcoholism got the better of him and he died early from cirrhosis. (Ironically, Murad had forbidden his subjects from using alcohol under the penalty of death.) Kösem then engineered the takeover by another son, İbrahim (1640-1648).

LIFE'S WORK

Kösem Sultan assumed the regency for her son Murad, who was then just eleven years old. At that time, given that Süleyman the Magnificent's stress on merit had long been abandoned, the empire was rife with graft, bribery, corruption, and favoritism. Wars by the Ottoman Empire continued with Persia in the east and Austria in the west. With his mother's help, Murad restored law and order, increased state revenues (mostly by taxing), and cut state spending. Some of the sultan's authority was also reinstated.

When Ahmed and Kösem's other son, İbrahim, assumed office in 1640, however, like his brother Murad, he turned out to be paranoid and degenerate, a trend Kösem encouraged because she did not wish to see another woman compete with her. İbrahim's debauchery and alcoholism made his rule ineffective, correspondingly increasing Kösem's influence in public affairs. With Kösem's consent, İbrahim, called "the Mad," was deposed and then strangled a few days later by members of the palace in 1648.

Mehmed IV (1648-1687), Kösem's six-year-old grandson, succeeded as sultan. According to tradition, Hadice Turhan Sultan, one of İbrahim's concubines and also Mehmed's mother, should have become the boy's guardian, but the young Turhan was unable to match Kösem's dominance and rivalry. Thus, Kösem managed to promote herself and become the *buyuk valide*, or Grand Queen Mother, and, instead of moving off-site as was traditional, remained at Topkapi.

Turhan, though, may have had her own political ambitions, and, also, she felt marginalized by her mother-in-law. (Turhan's yearly stipend was smaller than Kösem's.) Turhan started to build her own network inside and outside the palace, which was never a political monolith. On getting wind of the situation, Kösem decided to replace Turhan's son, Mehmed IV, with Süleyman II, the son of Saliha Dilasub Sultana, another of İbrahim's concubines, whom Kösem considered more pliant. Turhan, however, came to know of the plot. On September 2, 1651, Turhan's followers strangled Kösem with her own braids, an assassination that Turhan may have sanctioned if not instigated. Turhan was the one who, in her long career as guardian of princes, had protected her sons from the traditional practice of fratricide.

Kösem Sultan is buried in the shrine near Sultan Ahmed I in the Ahmediye Mosque—the Blue Mosque—

next to Ahmed's tomb, even though Ahmed never formalized his relationship with Kösem through marriage, as two of his forebears had done in the sixteenth century. There was great public mourning at Kösem's death.

Even though the record does not show that Kösem Sultan was a particularly good or caring parent—she had mercenary political motives in marrying off her daughters to the powerful, despite the tradition of arranged marriages at the time—she nevertheless seemed to have had her "soft" side. For example, one of Kösem's several personal charities consisted in seeking out orphaned or freed slave girls who were unable to marry for lack of a dowry and to provide them with money, lodgings, and furnishings for their home. This action, incidentally, extended her clientele network outside the palace.

SIGNIFICANCE

Kösem, the last of the great Queen Mothers, colorful and influential, managed to establish a powerful regency for herself despite the fact that regencies were not provided for by Ottoman law. Through intrigue and by astutely marrying off her daughters— Ayse, Fatma, and Handan (Hanzade)—to ministers (viziers) in high places, she bolstered her reputation with political allies essential to sustaining her regency. She wielded much of her power behind the throne to the very end, despite challenges.

Kösem Sultan left great wealth to charity, personal and institutional, and to religious endowments such as a mosque complex at Uskudar and elsewhere. The complexes represent Kösem's major architectural legacy. Her estate originated from crown domains assigned to her from freehold property to which she had title, yielding greater income than that of any Queen Mother before her. Some have suggested, however, that her riches represented an abuse of the empire's fiscal management.

Whatever the case, though, Kösem is remembered by Turks as the most powerful among sultanas, even greater than Roxelana, the favorite concubine and later wife of Süleyman the Magnificent. After Kösem's death, the position of Queen Mother was to lose its special status.

—Peter B. Heller

FURTHER READING

Bon, Ottaviano. *The Sultan's Seraglio: An Intimate Portrait of Life at the Ottoman Court*. London: Saqi Books, 1996. Introduced and annotated by Godfrey Goodwin. A seventeenth century Venetian ambassador's serious attempt to describe life at the Ottoman palace during Kösem Sultan's time. Originally published as *A Description of the Grand Seignor's Seraglio* in 1650. Includes endnotes and a glossary.

Cicek, Kemal, et al., eds. *The Great Ottoman-Turkish Civilisation*. 4 vols. Ankara, Turkey: Yeni Türkiye, 2000. The chapter in volume 2 by Fariba Zarinebat-Shahr, "The Wealth of Ottoman Princesses During the Tulip Age," is especially helpful. The text describes the growing importance of Queen Mothers and their internal rivalries, such as the one between Kösem and her daughter-in-law, Turhan.

Goodwin, Godfrey. *The Private World of Ottoman Women*. London: Saqi Books, 1997. Topical treatment highlighting the exclusion and thus waste of potential female talent—with major exceptions such as Kösem Sultan's—in personal and public development. Illustrations, genealogy, glossary, bibliography, index.

Goodwin, Jason. *Lords of the Horizon: A History of the Ottoman Empire*. New York: Henry Holt, 1998. A topical survey focusing on places, people, structures, and events, including the circumstances surrounding the death of Kösem. Illustrations, chronology, glossary, bibliography, index.

Inalcik, Halil. *The Ottoman Empire: The Classical Age, 1300-1600*. Translated by Norman Itzkovitz and Colin Imber. New York: Praeger, 1973. A good background study that describes the empire's rise and decline, presented from historical, political, administrative, religious, cultural, social, and economic perspectives. Illustrations, genealogy, chronology, glossary, endnotes, bibliography, index.

Peirce, Leslie P. *The Imperial Harem: Women and Sovereignty in the Ottoman Empire*. New York: Oxford University Press, 1993. Originally a Princeton University dissertation (1988), this scholarly work explains the Ottoman harem as a complex combination of social, political, and administrative structures and the role played by women in these hierarchies. Peirce's book corrects the negative image of the harem previously depicted by Western authors as a nest of sensuality and intrigue. Illustrations, glossary, maps, genealogy, endnotes, bibliography, index.

Wheatcroft, Andrew. *The Ottomans*. New York: Viking, 1993. Highlighting the evolution of the harem in the seventeenth century Ottoman Empire, the author discusses the relationship between Kösem and her sons Murad IV and İbrahim and her grandson Mehmed IV. Illustrations, chronology, map, endnotes, bibliography, index.

SEE ALSO: ʿAbbās the Great; Merzifonlu Kara Mustafa Paşa; Kâtib Çelebî; Murad IV; Mustafa I.

RELATED ARTICLES in *Great Events from History: The Seventeenth Century, 1601-1700:* 1602-1639: Ottoman-Ṣafavid Wars; 1603-1617: Reign of Sultan Ahmed I; September, 1605: Egyptians Rebel Against the Ottomans; November 11, 1606: Treaty of Zsitvatorok; 1609-1617: Construction of the Blue Mosque; May 19, 1622: Janissary Revolt and Osman II's Assassination; 1623-1640: Murad IV Rules the Ottoman Empire; 1632-c. 1650: Shah Jahan Builds the Taj Mahal; September 2, 1633: Great Fire of Constantinople and Murad's Reforms; 1656-1676: Ottoman Empire's Brief Recovery; 1658-1707: Reign of Aurangzeb; c. 1666-1676: Founding of the Marāthā Kingdom; 1679-1709: Rājput Rebellion; 1697-1702: Köprülü Reforms of Hüseyin Paşa.

JEAN DE LA BRUYÈRE
French essayist

La Bruyère wrote Les Caractères: Ou, Les Moeurs de ce siècle, *which documented the sentiments, manners, hypocrisy, idiosyncrasies, characteristics, and traits of French society and culture during the last years of the reign of King Louis XIV.*

BORN: August 16, 1645; Paris, France
DIED: May 10, 1696; Versailles, France
AREA OF ACHIEVEMENT: Literature

EARLY LIFE

Jean de la Bruyère (zhahn deh lah bree-yehr) was born into a modest bourgeois family. Educated at the University of Orléans, he was admitted to the bar in Paris in 1665. In 1673, he bought a post in the revenue department at Caen, which provided him with the status of nobility and with a certain income, but he sold the office in 1687. A lonely, meditative man from a middle-class family who tutored Louis, the duke of Bourbon, he stayed on at court in Chantilly after the tutorship ended, where he continued to observe the world of courtiers. When his pupil married, he was kept on as secretary and librarian of Chantilly, but was treated as a servant and made to feel insignificant.

LIFE'S WORK

Les Caractères: Ou, Les Moeurs de ce siècle was the only work written by La Bruyère. Nine editions were published during his lifetime, with many more published since. Social historians often use 1685—three years before the publication of *Les Caractères*—as a convenient date for "the beginning of the end" of the seventeenth century. The revocation of the Edict of Nantes, an edict that granted Protestants' limited freedom of religion symbolized the second half of the reign of King Louis XIV, marked by costly and unsuccessful military campaigns, financial crises and destitution, and an aura of religious severity at court.

An administrative and financial hierarchy was emerging. The literary public made up a small part of the upper echelon of society. In the early years of the century, those interested in discussing literary and intellectual matters gathered at houses of socially prominent women, gatherings that were later called salons. The social revolution worked toward refinement, so that aesthetic pleasure came to result from the *avoidance* of excess. At the same time, works of the period contained frequent allusions to the contemporaneous social and political situation.

La Bruyère's sharp vision of French society set him in a major literary tradition in which he commented on humankind as an explicit subject. His portraits brought him many readers as well as many enemies. *Les Caractères*, as a whole, is a compilation of remarks, and its themes are historical and part of the social commentary of the time: love, women, the powers of deception, the court, religious hypocrisy, and social idiosyncrasies. A second

Jean de La Bruyère. (Hulton Archive/Getty Images)

LA BRUYÈRE'S MAJOR WORKS	
1688	*Les Caractères: Ou, Les Mœurs de ce siècle* (*The Characters: Or, The Manners of the Age*, 1699)
1688	*Les Caractères de Théophraste* (translation of Theophrastus's essays)
1693	*Discours de réception à l'Académie française* (*M. Bruyère's Speech upon His Admission into the French Academy*, 1713)
1699	*Dialogues posthumes du sieur de La Bruyère sur le quiétisme*

group of themes deals with merit, wealth, favor, infirmity, and death.

The word *caractère* is ambiguous, for it can refer to personal psychology, force of character, moral fiber, characteristics, character types, or social role. La Bruyère often used it to designate two meanings at once, that is, dealing with different but related usages on different levels. Various concrete and specific, observed details were accumulated in series, creating choppy sentences that are nevertheless precise and finely chiseled. The presentation of the portraits varies from anecdote to dialogue, and his frequent use of the pronoun "I" predominates. He used metaphor and an oratorical presentation to create a viewpoint from which to criticize and judge. La Bruyère perceived and projected a vision of the relationship between humans and their social and concrete surroundings. Each subsequent edition of his work contained details and realistic observation of men and women attached to appearances as a means of achieving status and prestige, viewed by La Bruyère as self-serving. His subjects are composites of types and social groups.

SIGNIFICANCE

La Bruyère's depiction of French society during the reign of Louis XIV and his commentary on the traits of ambition, pride, and sentimentality in France during the period of Louis's reign earned him a place in the Académie Française, to which he was elected in 1693. As a moralist, he was concerned with analysis of character: morals, manners, customs, and sentiment. His *caractères* tended toward abstraction, and many stand alone as commentaries on behavior without any personalized reference.

—*Marcia J. Weiss*

FURTHER READING

Fowlie, Wallace. *French Literature: Its History and Its Meaning*. Englewood Cliffs, N.J.: Prentice-Hall, 1973. A classic text containing a concise survey of French literature.

Harth, Erica. *Ideology and Culture in Seventeenth Century France*. Ithaca, N.Y.: Cornell University Press, 1983. Considers the manner in which ideology dictated French society and culture in the seventeenth century.

Knox, Edward C. *Jean de La Bruyère*. New York: Twayne, 1973. A detailed study of the work of La Bruyère, including historical and literary references.

SEE ALSO: Madame de La Fayette; Louis XIV; Marquise de Rambouillet; Madame de Sévigné.

RELATED ARTICLES in *Great Events from History: The Seventeenth Century, 1601-1700:* 1661: Absolute Monarchy Emerges in France; 1664: Molière Writes *Tartuffe*; 1682: French Court Moves to Versailles; 1685: Louis XIV Revokes the Edict of Nantes; 1689-1694: Famine and Inflation in France.

MADAME DE LA FAYETTE
French writer

La Fayette, a prominent figure in Parisian literary salons, wrote heroic and historical novels, a biography of Henrietta Anne of England, and other works. Her The Princess of Clèves *has been hailed as the first modern French novel.*

BORN: March 18, 1634 (baptized); Paris, France
DIED: May 25, 1693; Paris
ALSO KNOWN AS: Marie-Madeleine Pioche de la Vergne (given name); Mademoiselle de la Vergne; Comtesse de Lafayette, de La Fayette, de LaFayette; Segrais (pseudonym)
AREA OF ACHIEVEMENT: Literature

EARLY LIFE

Marie-Madeleine Pioche de la Vergne, later known as Madame de La Fayette (mah-dahm deh lah-fah-yeht), grew up in the fashionable Parisian district of Saint-Germain. She was baptized in the neighborhood church of Saint-Sulpice. Her father, Marc Pioche de la Vergne, a military engineer and member of the lower nobility, died in December of 1649, when La Fayette was only fifteen years old. Her mother, Isabelle Pena, the daughter of a royal physician, remarried the following year. Under the guidance of a mentor, La Fayette learned the rudiments of Latin and Italian, read works by Petrarch and by Torquato Tasso, and associated with poets and literati at the Hôtel de Rambouillet, hosted by the marquise de Rambouillet, and other locales. She became close friends with Marie de Rabutin-Chantal, better known as Madame de Sévigné, and became acquainted with the French novelist Madeleine de Scudéry, whose works were popular at the time.

Probably around 1651, at the age of seventeen, La Fayette became one of Queen Anne of Austria's hand-maidens. As a result of her stepfather's involvement in the Wars of the Fronde (1648-1653), she was forced to leave the capital in 1653 and spend most of the following year in Anjou. On February 15, 1655, at the age of twenty, she married François Motier, comte de La Fayette, a widower almost twice her age, and accompanied him to his estates in Auvergne. Accustomed to the intellectual charms of Parisian high society, however, she grew weary of life in the province and returned with her husband to the French capital, giving birth there to two sons, the first in 1658 and the second in 1659.

After November, 1561, she and her husband, to a large extent, led separate lives. He managed the estates in Auvergne while she looked after their interests in Paris. With infinite discretion, she also cultivated her talent as a writer.

LIFE'S WORK

Following her return to Paris in 1658, Madame de La Fayette assumed a prominent role amid the Parisian aristocracy. She was again seen at court; attended cultural salons in the company of her mentor, scholar Gilles Ménage; and hosted similar gatherings in her own spacious residence at Rue Férou.

Her first published work, a brief descriptive portrait of her friend Madame de Sévigné, appeared under her own name in *Divers portraits* (pb. 1659), a collection of fifty-nine literary portraits commissioned for publication by the duchess de Montpensier, Anne-Marie-Louise d'Orléans. All of La Fayette's subsequent writings, letters excluded, circulated either anonymously or under the name of a male "coauthor," leaving historians with the difficult task of determining not only what works to attribute to her but also the extent of her authorship in each. Prominent guests at her house—Ménage, poet Jean Regnault de Segrais, scholar and prelate Pierre-Daniel Huet, and writer François de La Rochefoucauld—assisted her by appraising, proofreading, and correcting her drafts, and perhaps, to some extent—as extant manuscript documents suggest—by teasing out some of her ideas on paper. All this was, however, common practice for both men and women writers of the period.

By the time La Fayette began writing, the French *nouvelle* (prototype of the modern novel or novella) was already in the process of supplanting the heroic romance as a dominant form of narrative prose fiction. Plausibility was a prime concern among theorists of the modern novel. Her friend Segrais, theorist and author of *Les Nouvelles françaises* (pb. 1656-1657; French novels), recommended looking to history and, in particular, to recent French history, for inspiration and guidance. Published anonymously in 1662, La Fayette's first novella, *La Princesse de Monpensier* (*The Princess of Monpensier*, 1666) did just that. Recounting the tragic fate of an unhappily married woman and her adulterous passion, this novella is set during the turbulent events of the French Wars of Religion one century earlier. Readers and critics readily presumed that hidden beneath the veneer of this historical romance was a chronicle of contemporary society.

Her following novel, *Zaïde, une histoire espagnole* (pb. 1669 and 1671; *Zayde, a Spanish History*, 1678), is a heroic romance set in medieval Spain. Its pages are full of chivalric episodes, digressions, and improbable events common in the baroque novel. Although the work appeared under Segrais's name, with no mention of La Fayette's central role, documents suggest it was indeed the product of collaboration between La Fayette and her entourage.

In *The Princess of Clèves* (1679), La Fayette's masterpiece of fictional prose, a faithful wife torn between reason and passion naively confesses to her husband her attraction to another man. Such an idea had surfaced already in a *nouvelle* by Marie-Cathérine Desjardins (Madame de Villedieu) some three years earlier, yet the success of La Fayette's version was far greater. In the months following the anonymous publication of *The Princess of Clèves*, readers and critics avidly debated in various public forums its tantalizing moral issues and pioneering aesthetic qualities. As in *The Princess of Monpensier*, the action takes place in sixteenth century France. In this case, however, La Fayette enhanced the psychological complexity of her characters and developed the art of suggestion through abstract language and symbols. Published anonymously, it was not until 1780 that *The Princess of Clèves* appeared for the first time with La Fayette's name, and it was the last work to be published during her lifetime, albeit without her name.

In 1680, she mourned the loss of her dear friend, La Rochefoucauld, and four years later that of her husband. At the time of her own death in 1693, few beyond her circle of friends and literary acquaintances suspected that La Fayette would come to be remembered as one of France's most innovative novelists. Works attributed to her posthumously include the anonymously published novella *La Comtesse de Tende* (pb. 1718; *The Comtesse de Tende*, 1992), *Histoire de Madame Henriette d'Angleterre* (wr. 1664-1669, pb. 1720; *Fatal Galantry: Or, The Secret History of Henrietta, Princess of England*, 1722), and *Mémoires de la cour de France pour les années 1688 et 1689* (pb. 1731; *Memoirs of the Court of France for the Years 1688-1689*, 1929). A modern editor of her works, Roger Duchêne, considers the latter work apocryphal. Her correspondence, consisting of some 250 extant letters, provides valuable insight into the culture of Parisian salons.

SIGNIFICANCE

For various reasons—aesthetic qualities, narrative techniques, moral and philosophical concerns, questions of

---

MADAME DE LA FAYETTE'S PASSIONATE PRINCESS

The heroine in La Fayette's novel The Princess of Clèves *is overcome by a passion for the duke of Nemours, a man not her husband who loves her in return. She confesses to her husband not that she is in love with another man but that she is being overcome by her passion. Still, he suspects she has a lover. The princess's husband dies, and she spends her days in turmoil because she feels her confession played a part in his passing. She cannot come to bear the emotion that would arise if she were to marry the duke, so she renounces his marriage proposal as a way to control her feelings.*

Monsieur de Nemours threw himself at [the princess's] feet, and gave way to all the feelings that agitated him. He showed by his words and by his tears the tenderest passion with which a heart has ever been touched; Madame de Clèves was not insensible, and, looking at the Duke with eyes somewhat swollen with tears, she cried: "Why is it that I must accuse you of the death of Monsieur de Clèves [her husband]? Why did I not meet you for the first time after I was free, or why did I not know you before I was married? Why does fate separate us with such an insurmountable obstacle?"

"There is no obstacle, Madame," replied Monsieur de Nemours: "you alone oppose my happiness, and you alone impose on yourself a law that virtue and reason could not impose on you."

"It is true," she said, "that I am sacrificing much to a duty that exists only in my imagination. Wait and see what time can do. Monsieur de Clèves has only just died. . . . [R]est assured that the feelings I have for you will be eternal, and that they will remain unchanged whatever I do. Good-bye—this conversation shames me. . . ."

With these words, she left the room, without Monsieur de Nemours' being able to retain her.

Source: Excerpted in *The Age of Reason: The Culture of the Seventeenth Century*, edited by Leo Weinstein (New York: George Braziller, 1965), pp. 238-239.

---

authorship, and historicity, to name a few—Madame de La Fayette's novels, historical memoirs, and letters have intrigued generations of readers and critics. Turning to the collaborative model of salon writing common in her day, she produced highly refined fictional works capable of appealing to readers on their own merit. As a memorialist and a letter writer, she had firsthand knowledge of many of the people and events she described, so she offers unique insight into Parisian salon culture and life at court.

Her attention to historical detail and emphasis on subtle character analysis in *The Princess of Clèves* greatly contributed to its stunning success and led the way in the transition from heroic romance to the modern novel. Generations of students and scholars have debated, and will likely continue to debate in the foreseeable future, the plausibility of the princess's singular confession and the reasons for her ultimate refusal to marry the man she loved. The novel's underlying dichotomy of reason and passion, a typical theme in classical French theater and poetry, places La Fayette's masterpiece in the philosophical mainstream of seventeenth century European literature.

—Jan Pendergrass

FURTHER READING

Beasley, Faith Evelyn. *Revising Memory: Women's Fiction and Memoirs in Seventeenth-Century France.* New Brunswick, N.J.: Rutgers University Press, 1990. In chapter 3, Beasley examines La Fayette's activity as a memoirist, and in chapter 5, she discusses how, as a novelist, La Fayette challenged the normative poetic concept of "plausibility."

_____. "The Voices of Shadows: Lafayette's *Zaïde.*" In *Going Public: Women and Publishing in Early-Modern France*, edited by Elizabeth C. Goldsmith and Dena Goodman. Ithaca, N.Y.: Cornell University Press, 1995. Beasley suggests that the multiplicity of narrative voices in *Zayde* reflects the collaborative model of writing practiced in the literary salons of Paris.

Beasley, Faith E., and Katherine Ann Jensen. *Approaches to Teaching Lafayette's "The Princess of Clèves."* New York: Modern Language Association of America, 1998. Contributions from eighteen specialists in this volume offer a wide spectrum of views and analyses focusing on La Fayette's novel.

DeJean, Joan. *Tender Geographies: Women and the Origins of the Novel in France.* New York: Columbia University Press, 1991. In chapter 3, Dejean describes the collaborative practice of "salon writing" during La Fayette's time.

Green, Anne. *Privileged Anonymity: The Writings of Madame de Lafayette.* Oxford, England: Legenda, 1996. Green focuses on La Fayette's work as a novelist as well as historian.

Haig, Stirling. *Madame de Lafayette.* New York: Twayne, 1970. This work provides an overview of La Fayette's life and work.

Henry, Patrick, ed. *An Inimitable Example: The Case for the Princesse de Clèves.* Washington, D.C.: Catholic University of America Press, 1993. In this volume, fourteen specialists discuss various aspects of *La Princesse de Clèves.*

Lyons, John D., ed. *The Princess of Clèves: Contemporary Reactions, Criticism.* New York: Norton, 1994. Articles by eleven literary historians accompany this English translation of *La Princesse de Clèves.*

Racevskis, Roland. *Time and Ways of Knowing Under Louis XIV: Molière, Sévigné, Lafayette.* Lewisburg, Pa.: Bucknell University Press, 2003. In chapter 4, Racevskis discusses the perception of time in La Fayette's *La Princesse de Clèves.*

SEE ALSO: Anne of Austria; Jacques-Bénigne Bossuet; Marie le Jars de Gournay; Jean de La Fontaine; François de La Rochefoucauld; Duchesse de Montpensier; Marquise de Rambouillet; Madeleine de Scudéry; Madame de Sévigné.

RELATED ARTICLES in *Great Events from History: The Seventeenth Century, 1601-1700:* 1637: Descartes Publishes His *Discourse on Method*; 1661: Absolute Monarchy Emerges in France; 1664: Molière Writes *Tartuffe*; 1682: French Court Moves to Versailles; 1685: Louis XIV Revokes the Edict of Nantes; 1689-1694: Famine and Inflation in France.

JEAN DE LA FONTAINE
French writer

La Fontaine is recognized as one of the major writers of the French classical period. He wrote drama, ballet, popular tales, and various forms of poetry, but he is best known in France and abroad for his verse fables, a genre he developed to perfection.

BORN: July 8, 1621; Château-Thierry, Champagne, France
DIED: April 13, 1695; Paris, France
AREAS OF ACHIEVEMENT: Literature, theater

EARLY LIFE

Jean de La Fontaine (zhahn deh lah-fohn-tehn) was born in a small farming town in Champagne located about fifty miles east of Paris. His father, Charles de La Fontaine, was a local administrator of forests and waters. His mother, Françoise Pidoux, belonged to a respected middle-class family from Poitiers. The widow of a wealthy merchant, she had one daughter when she married Charles in 1617.

Although little is known about La Fontaine's early years, most scholars believe he attended school in Château-Thierry before going to college in Paris. During his school years, he learned Latin rhetoric and grammar and was introduced to ancient works that would provide subjects for his later creative endeavors. He was most likely a sensitive student who liked to daydream and who perhaps found his teachers boring and authoritarian. Several uncomplimentary references to schoolboys and schoolmasters in his fables suggest that his school years were not entirely pleasant.

On April 27, 1641, La Fontaine entered the Oratory, a religious seminary in Paris. By October, his teachers had discovered his preference for popular love stories and wrote that he should be strongly urged to study theology. After eighteen months, La Fontaine withdrew from the seminary and returned to Château-Thierry to read and daydream. Although many writers refer disparagingly to this idle period, La Fontaine was becoming familiar with ancient and modern authors, especially the poets François de Malherbe and Vincent Voiture, François Rabelais, and the Latin writers Horace, Vergil, and Terence.

From 1645 to 1647, La Fontaine studied law in Paris, spending much of his time, however, with aspiring young writers (François Maucroix, Paul Pellisson, and Antoine Furetière) who would influence and support him throughout his career. In this formative period, La Fon-

taine continued to increase his knowledge of ancient and modern literature.

In 1647, at the age of twenty-six, La Fontaine was married to Marie Héricart, who was fourteen and a half years of age, and who brought him a dowry of thirty thousand livres, a considerable sum. Although amiable at first, the couple drifted apart. Absorbed for weeks in his reading, La Fontaine ignored both his family and his duties as forest warden, a position he obtained in 1652. Although he appeared idle and absentminded, the extent of his voracious reading and keen observation would become evident in his later works.

LIFE'S WORK

During the classical period, which flourished in France from 1660 to about 1685, writers were expected to imitate and to adapt works of ancient authors, not by radically changing the originals but by presenting them in new styles to please contemporary audiences. As his first major work, La Fontaine tried to adapt a racy Latin comedy by Terence to the refined tastes of Parisian high society, but the necessary changes destroyed the flavor

Jean de La Fontaine. (Library of Congress)

and unity of the original. Although *L'Eunuque* (1654; the eunuch) was never produced, its lively dialogue demonstrates his narrative skills.

For the next few years, La Fontaine was occupied by family affairs. The income from his administrative position and similar positions inherited from his father in 1658 was insufficient to pay family debts, forcing La Fontaine to annul his marriage in order to sell property held jointly with his wife. From this time on, he lived mostly apart from his family, relying on wealthy patrons to support his life's work.

His first patron was Nicolas Fouquet, a wealthy and ambitious minister of finance whose estate at Vaux-le-Vicomte was being built as a showplace of the arts, and whose eighteen thousand employees included the leading artists, architects, gardeners, musicians, and writers. In addition to occasional verse to entertain the society at Vaux, La Fontaine wrote *Adonis* (1658), a six-hundred-line love story in rhymed couplets, which merges three distinct genres (heroic, idyllic, and elegiac) in a creative synthesis of earlier sources. La Fontaine was also working on *Le Songe de Vaux* (1659; the dream of Vaux), a mixture of poetry and prose in which the muses of painting, gardening, architecture, and poetry describe the wonders of Fouquet's magnificent estate, then under construction. The work reveals La Fontaine's remarkable ability to communicate visual imagery in verse.

When the young Louis XIV had Fouquet imprisoned for plundering the treasury, La Fontaine demonstrated his uncompromising loyalty to the finance minister in a short poem circulated anonymously among Fouquet's supporters, deploring the minister's downfall and asking the nymphs of Vaux to make the king merciful. A year later, in "Ode au Roi" (1663; ode to the king), La Fontaine urged Louis XIV to pardon his disgraced minister.

Forty years of age, without a patron and in disfavor with the young monarch who had taken Fouquet's role as parton of the arts, La Fontaine traveled to Limoges with his wife's uncle, Jacques Jannart, who had been exiled for supporting Fouquet. La Fontaine describes this trip, the longest he ever took, in six letters later published as *Relation d'un voyage en Limousin* (1663; account of a trip to Limoges). Returning to Paris after a few months, La Fontaine found protection with the duke and duchess

LA FONTAINE'S MAJOR WORKS	
1654	*L'Eunuque*
1658	*Adonis*
1659	*Le Songe de Vaux*
1663	*Relation d'un voyage en Limousin*
1664	*Contes et nouvelles en vers (Tales and Short Stories in Verse,* 1735)
1666	*Deuxième partie des "Contes et nouvelles en vers"* (*Part Two of "Tales and Short Stories in Verse,"* 1735)
1668-1694	*Fables choisies, mises en vers (Fables Written in Verse,* 1735)
1669	*Les Amours de Psyché et de Cupidon (The Loves of Cupid and Psyche,* 1744)
1671	*Clymène*
1671	*Troisième partie des "Contes et nouvelles en vers"* (*Part Three of "Tales and Short Stories in Verse,"* 1735)
1674	*Nouveaux Contes (New Tales,* 1735)
1679	*Discours à Mme de La Sablière*
1682	*Daphné* (libretto)
1682	*Galatée* (libretto)
1687	*Épître à Huet*
1692	*L'Astrée* (libretto)
1697	*Poèmes et poésies diverses*

of Bouillon, perhaps discovering an appreciative audience for his licentious tales inspired by Giovanni Boccaccio, Ludovico Ariosto, and other writers.

Accepting an undemanding post as gentleman servant to the duchess of Orléans in 1664, La Fontaine began his most productive period. His licentious *Contes et nouvelles en vers* (1664; *Tales and Short Stories in Verse,* 1735) became immediately popular among sophisticated society, accomplishing his chief goal: to entertain his readers. He published several more collections of tales.

La Fontaine's method of shaping new works from old sources, artfully departing from established rules of versification to create a studied negligence, and carrying on a dialogue with the reader worked even better in his fables. His first edition of *Fables choisies, mises en vers* (1668-1694; *Fables Written in Verse,* 1735), a collection of 124 fables in six books, was an immediate success. In the introduction, La Fontaine declared that his fables presented important truths in amusing stories, adding that they were "portraits in which all of us are depicted."

In the fables, La Fontaine drew upon all of his previous reading and experience to present an overview of French society that included kings and nobles, lawyers and judges, students and teachers, doctors and philosophers, and the lowliest laborers. His goal, even when his characters were animals or plants, was to portray human nature and, like his friend Molière, to hold vices up to ridicule.

When the duchess of Orléans died in 1672, La Fontaine was taken in by the intelligent and witty Madame de La Sablière, who introduced him to scientists, philosophers, and other intellectuals. Under her influence, La Fontaine published five more books of fables, widening his sources to include fables by the Indian sage Pilpay. He also treated philosophical questions in the 237-line *Discours à Mme de La Sablière* (1679), refuting René Descartes's claim that animals were a kind of machine.

Unable to limit himself to a single genre, La Fontaine experimented with a variety of hybrid works. *Les Amours de Psyché et de Cupidon* (1669; *The Loves of Cupid and Psyche*, 1744) was a fairy tale in prose and poetry related to three friends during a visit to Versailles. The four friends—traditionally identified as Molière, Jean Racine, Nicolas Boileau-Despréaux, and La Fontaine (because they were constantly together when the piece was composed around 1664)—are now considered composite characters reflecting views discussed at length by La Fontaine and his many friends. Although the work was not popular, it inspired a successful play with music and ballet by Molière, Pierre Corneille, and Jean-Baptiste Lully in 1671.

Other works include a religious poem about the temptation of Saint Malc, a scientific epic about the fashionable drug quinine, an opera rejected by the composer Lully, a ballet with only two acts, a comedy that was performed only four times, and the opera *L'Astrée* (1692), which ran for six performances.

In 1683, La Fontaine was elected to the prestigious Académie Française, but Louis XIV refused to accept the vote until Boileau-Despréaux was elected in 1684 and La Fontaine had promised to write no more works such as *Tales and Short Stories in Verse*. As a member of the Académie, La Fontaine entered the Quarrel of the Ancients and Moderns with his *Épître à Huet* (1687; letter to Huet), which praised both ancient and modern writers while discouraging a slavish imitation of earlier works.

With the publication of his last collection of fables in 1694, La Fontaine completed his life's work. In his last years, he experienced a religious conversion, disavowed *Tales and Short Stories in Verse*, and destroyed a play he had been writing. La Fontaine died April 13, 1695, in Paris at the age of seventy-three.

SIGNIFICANCE

Although he tried his hand at many literary forms, La Fontaine is remembered for his fables, which have survived translation into many languages. Except for *Tales and Short Stories in Verse*, his other works are relatively unknown outside his own country, even to students of French literature. One exception, his poem *Adonis*, has received much scholarly attention since its brilliant analysis by the French poet Paul Valéry in 1921.

A careful writer even when trying to appear casual, La Fontaine was totally dedicated to his craft, despite a reputation for idleness and an eagerness to please the audience of his day. Forced to seek patrons to support his work, he firmly but diplomatically maintained his independence as a writer, rejecting suggestions to write the fables in prose or to follow his sources more closely. His fables are a synthesis of his extensive reading, keen observation, and years of poetic experimentation. With his unerring ear for dialogue, his insight into human nature, and his skill as a poet and storyteller, La Fontaine carried the classic art of imitation to its highest extreme by molding the fable into a new poetic genre. More than three centuries later, his accomplishment remains unsurpassed.

—*Richard M. Shaw*

FURTHER READING

Fumaroli, Marc. *The Poet and the King: Jean de La Fontaine and His Century*. Translated by Jane Marie Todd. Notre Dame, Ind.: Notre Dame Press, 2002. Examines La Fontaine's struggle to maintain artistic integrity against the oppression of Louis XIV's regime.

Guiton, Margaret. *La Fontaine: Poet and Counterpoet*. New Brunswick, N.J.: Rutgers University Press, 1961. Examines La Fontaine's competing visions of comedy and imaginative poetry, with English translations of his work. Includes chronology of La Fontaine's life and works.

La Fontaine, Jean de. *The Complete Fables of Jean de La Fontaine*. Edited and translated by Norman B. Spector. Evanston, Ill.: Northwestern University Press, 1988. A bilingual edition in clear, crisp rhymed verse. Closer to the original language and imagery than many other versions.

Lapp, John C. *The Esthetics of Negligence: La Fontaine's "Contes."* New York: Cambridge University Press, 1971. Refutes previous disparaging studies by demonstrating how La Fontaine's wit, eroticism, lyricism, and charm make the *Tales and Short Stories in Verse* superior to their sources.

Mackay, Agnes Ethel. *La Fontaine and His Friends: A*

Biography. New York: Braziller, 1972. Examination of La Fontaine's relationship with intimate friends and influential patrons, with French passages translated in chapter endnotes.

Powell, Kirsten. *Fables in Frames: La Fontaine and Visual Culture in Nineteenth-Century France*. New York: Lang, 1997. Powell examines why La Fontaine's fables became the subject of artists in the nineteenth century and how these artists used the poems to comment on topical issues.

Runyon, Randolph Paul. *In La Fontaine's Labyrinth: A Thread Through the Fables*. Charlottesville, Va.: Rockwood Press, 2000. Demonstrates the connections between La Fontaine's individual fables.

Slater, Maya. *Craft of La Fontaine*. Madison, N.J.: Fairleigh Dickinson University Press, 2001. A detailed analysis of La Fontaine's fables, examining the humor, representation of animals, literary qualities, and moralistic core of the works.

Sweetser, Marie-Odile. *La Fontaine*. Boston: Twayne, 1987. A good place to begin a study of La Fontaine, Excellent review of his life, description of his major works, and concise summary of important studies. Lists selected critical articles, many in English.

Wadsworth, Philip A. *Young La Fontaine*. Evanston, Ill.: Northwestern University Press, 1952. A detailed study of La Fontaine's growth as a poet up to publication of his first fables in 1668.

SEE ALSO: Nicolas Boileau-Despréaux; Pierre Corneille; Jean-Baptiste Lully; Molière; Jean Racine.

RELATED ARTICLE in *Great Events from History: The Seventeenth Century, 1601-1700:* 1693: Ray Argues for Animal Consciousness.

JOHN LAMBERT
English general and politician

After serving as one of Parliament's leading officers in the English Civil War, Lambert emerged as a central figure in the Protectorate. After Oliver Cromwell's death, Lambert led the army's unsuccessful attempt to maintain a republic and prevent the Stuart Restoration.

BORN: September 7, 1619 (baptized); Calton, West Riding, Yorkshire, England
DIED: March, 1684; St. Nicholas Isle, Plymouth Sound, Devon, England
AREAS OF ACHIEVEMENT: Warfare and conquest, government and politics

EARLY LIFE

John Lambert's family was part of the rising British gentry class, having gained several manors after Henry VIII's dissolution of the monasteries during the Reformation. Lambert was probably educated at the grammar school in Kirby Malham and then at Trinity College, Cambridge. He then appears to have attended one of the Inns of Court, probably the Middle Temple. This pattern was typical for a young gentleman of the time, and Lambert's later performance indicates that he was well educated and familiar with the law.

Lambert's father, Josiah, died in 1632, four years before his son entered Cambridge. Just after his twentieth birthday, John married Frances Lister, the daughter of a prominent Yorkshire family. The match tied Lambert to two additional leading county families, the Fairfaxes and the Bellasises. These connections would aid Lambert in future years, both as the First English Civil War began and after the Restoration.

Until the strains between Charles I and the Long Parliament brought England to the verge of civil war, Lambert's life was that of a successful young country squire. Handsome and charming, he had married well and could anticipate improving his position through active participation in the affairs of the county community. The outbreak of war, however, transformed him into a national figure who rose to be the second most powerful man in England within a dozen years.

When Yorkshire was divided in 1642, Lambert followed the third Baron Fairfax in support of Parliament. Despite Lambert's youth and lack of military experience, Fairfax made him a captain in his cavalry regiment. Like Oliver Cromwell, Lambert proved to be a natural-born soldier and an excellent leader of men. His courage, dashing appearance, and amiable personality served him well, and he quickly gained a reputation as a soldier's soldier that lasted throughout his career. Always concerned for his men's welfare, he came to be known throughout the parliamentary army as "Honest" John Lambert.

Lambert rose quickly during the war. By the end of 1643, he commanded his own regiment. His first major triumph as an independent commander came at Bradford in his home county in March, 1644. Fighting a larger Royalist force commanded by his wife's relative, Colonel John Bellasis, Lambert won the battle with a cavalry charge after most of his men had run out of powder. At Marston Moor, he distinguished himself while serving under Fairfax in July, 1644. Toward the end of the first part of the war, he negotiated the surrender of Oxford and for a time served as governor of the city. When he returned to Yorkshire, he was a major general and one of the outstanding parliamentary commanders.

LIFE'S WORK

Charles I's defeat opened a new phase in the English Revolution and in Lambert's life. The struggle for power shifted from the battlefield to the political arena, and, like many of his colleagues, Lambert was transformed into a soldier-politician. For the remainder of his career, politics became his main focus, even though he took to the field several more times. Unlike Oliver Cromwell and his main rival during the early 1650's, Major General Thomas Harrison, Lambert was not concerned primarily with religion. Little, indeed, is known about his personal religious views, an unusual situation for so central a figure in this religious conflict. Lambert was motivated by a desire for political change and personal ambition. He did not, however, seek the sweeping social and economic changes desired by the radicals.

As tension grew between Parliament and the army, Lambert was chosen by his fellow officers to help Henry Ireton draft a statement of the army's political and constitutional goals, the Heads of Proposals. This was Lambert's first venture into developing political positions and statements.

When the second phase of the Civil War flared in 1648, Lambert again took to the field for Parliament. Given command of the north, he defeated local Royalists but was forced to fall back when the Scots invaded. He distinguished himself at the climactic Battle of Preston and was left in charge of eliminating lingering resistance after Cromwell returned to London. The siege of the last Royalist garrison at Pontefract caused him to miss the trial and execution of Charles I in January, 1649. Lambert later claimed that he opposed these acts, but in any case, his duties in the north saved his life at the Restoration by freeing him from the taint of regicide.

Lambert was now second only to Fairfax and Cromwell in the army. In the campaigns against the Scots and Prince Charles in 1650 and 1651, Lambert was Cromwell's second-in-command. With Harrison, he drove

John Lambert. (Library of Congress)

Prince Charles's forces toward Worcester and defeat when they crossed into England. For his services at Worcester, he received lands worth one thousand pounds per annum from Parliament.

By 1653, many in England and the army were calling for the ouster of the "Rump" of the Long Parliament. Lambert led those officers pressing Cromwell to move against the Rump and set up a government more responsive to the landowning classes. Harrison and the radicals simultaneously urged Cromwell to replace the Rump with an "Assembly of Saints" and usher in a "Godly Commonwealth." In late April, Cromwell did dismiss the Rump, but Harrison's views prevailed and Lambert withdrew to his residence to prepare for future opportunities.

Lambert's residence at that time was the former royal estate at Wimbledon. In addition to monies gained through parliamentary grants and the fruits of command and office, Lambert had earned great wealth by buying Royalist and church lands and speculating in the debentures soldiers received when their pay was in arrears.

As Lambert expected, Cromwell soon became disenchanted with the saintly Barebones Parliament over its reformism and objections to ending the costly war with the Dutch. In December, Lambert engineered the Barebones' dissolution and presented his new plan for governing England, the Instrument of Government.

England's first and only written constitution, the Instrument of Government established the Protectorate. While providing for a parliament, the Instrument placed power in the hands of the Lord Protector, Cromwell, and a Council of State. Because the council had to approve most actions and was not simply appointed and controlled by the Lord Protector, it had considerable influence. With a solid group of allies on the council, Lambert enjoyed substantial power between 1654 and 1657. He was regarded widely as Cromwell's viceregent and heir apparent.

Still in his thirties, Lambert had risen to unexpected heights in a manner unmatched by any of his contemporaries. Despite his political and administrative skills, he lacked patience and, at times, sound judgment. He was principally responsible for two policies that brought great criticism from many loyal Englishmen, the 1655 rule by major generals and the purge of unfriendly Members of Parliament after the election of 1656. These mistakes, coupled with signs that he had forgotten that Cromwell was still the true source of authority, brought Lambert's influence to an abrupt halt.

In 1657, many moderates were urging Cromwell to take the crown. Lambert and many other leading officers opposed this, calling on Cromwell to reject Parliament's Humble Petition and Advice embodying the plan. When Cromwell refused the crown but accepted the concept of a hereditary lord protectorship, most officers and civilian moderates consented. This support strengthened the Lord Protector's position considerably. Cromwell was now king in all but name, the council lost most of its power, and Lambert was no longer the protector-designate.

Claiming loyalty to the cause, Lambert refused the oath to the new order. He was stripped of his offices and commissions and forced into retirement. He did receive, however, a stipend of two thousand pounds per annum. Lambert's eclipse proved only temporary. Following Cromwell's death in September, 1658, England gradually slipped toward chaos. Richard Cromwell proved unable to maintain his father's position, and Lambert slowly returned to politics. Still popular in the army, he received his regiment back in time to suppress the pro-Royalist rebellion led by George Booth in August, 1659, for the now-restored Rump Parliament.

Lambert emerged as the most dynamic, able, and ambitious of the senior officers challenging the Rump for power. When Parliament moved to dismiss him along with eight other officers on October 12, 1659, he padlocked the Houses of Parliament and dispersed its members. This coup was typical of Lambert. Bold and sudden, it also displayed a disdain for civilians and their sensibilities and a lack of thought about long-term consequences. Lambert's action provided General George Monck, the English commander in Scotland, with the necessary pretext to intervene in English politics to restore constitutional rule and end military tyranny. What Monck restored was the monarchy.

Because he had not signed Charles I's death warrant, Lambert was not executed or jailed at the Restoration. In 1662, however, he was tried and condemned for causing rebellion. His real crime was being able, popular, and ambitious. In 1659, Charles II's advisers had considered using Lambert as a means to restore the king by arranging a marriage between Charles and Lambert's daughter. Lambert may have been an acceptable royal father-in-law then, but by 1662 he was an unacceptable royal risk.

Thanks to quiet activity by Yorkshire friends such as Fairfax and Bellasis, and also because of his humble manner at his trial, Lambert was reprieved almost immediately after being sentenced. He could not, however, go free. Until 1670, he was held in comfortable confinement on Guernsey, usually with his wife and family. Then he was transferred to the less comfortable but more secure St. Nicholas Isle in Plymouth Sound. Here, too, Lambert enjoyed the company of his wife, until her death in 1676. He reportedly received two visits from Charles II and James, duke of York. During his imprisonment, Lambert occupied himself with botany and painting. He died in late March, 1684, and was buried on March 28.

SIGNIFICANCE

Lambert represented several forces shaping English life in the middle of the seventeenth century. He also embodied characteristics the English have long regarded with great suspicion. His charisma, ability, and ambition caused him to stand out to his and future generations.

Lambert personified the social and economic mobility and dynamism within the English ruling classes. The Civil War and revolution simply made his rise faster and easier than would have been possible during normal times. Members of the nation who enjoyed good connections, significant ability, and luck could go far. Thanks to his times, his personality, and his instinctive flair for military leadership, Lambert provides a meteoric example of the rising gentleman.

At the same time, Lambert exemplified the overambitious military man entering politics and using the sword to thwart the will of the nation. He relied on force to reach his goals, showed scant respect for political forms and traditions, and often displayed a clear lack of principles. As the most successful of the officer-politicians after Cromwell, and lacking his superior's redeeming sense of mission, Lambert personified a most un-English type, the would-be military despot.

Lambert's greatest political accomplishment, the Instrument of Government, struck many as also essentially un-English. It was a thoughtful effort to provide a legal basis for a regime trying to consolidate the gains of a successful revolution. It was, in the abstract, a good example of a written constitution. Thanks to the course of events between 1653 and 1660, however, Lambert's effort helped confirm the English disdain for written constitutions.

Lambert had the ability to take advantage of his times and the ambition to press his advantages to the limit. In the end, he pressed too hard and ended by helping to destroy the republic he had worked so hard to create, and restoring the Stuarts he had fought so skillfully. Perhaps his youth and lack of prewar political experience caused him to ignore too much that was essential to political success in seventeenth century England. As dashing as any Cavalier, Honest John Lambert ultimately helped ensure that England would remain a monarchy. He also helped keep England a constitutional monarchy, through both his successes and his excesses.

—Vinton M. Prince, Jr.

FURTHER READING

Ashley, Maurice Percy. *Cromwell's Generals.* New York: St. Martin's Press, 1955. Provides a summary of Lambert's career with emphasis on the creation of the Protectorate. Also contains chapters on other key army figures.

Davies, Godfrey. *The Early Stuarts, 1603-1660.* 2d ed. Oxford, England: Oxford University Press, 1959. A solid and thorough account of the context of Lambert's career and a reliable narrative of his times.

Dawson, William H. *Cromwell's Understudy: The Life and Times of General John Lambert and the Rise and Fall of the Protectorate.* London: William Hodge, 1938. Until recently, the only full biography of Lambert of even reasonably modern vintage. Provides an accurate account of his actions but is quite laudatory and at times exaggerates his role.

Durston, Christopher. *Cromwell's Major-Generals: Godly Government During the English Revolution.* Manchester, England: Manchester University Press,

2001. Reevaluates the rule by major-generals, a form of government that Lambert advocated and that later contributed to his loss of influence within Cromwell's government.

Farr, David. *John Lambert, Parliamentary Soldier and Cromwellian Major-General, 1619-1684.* Rochester, N.Y.: Boydell Press, 2003. The first biography of Lambert to be published in recent years, this is a thorough account of his life and military career.

Fraser, Antonia. *Cromwell: The Lord Protector.* New York: Alfred A. Knopf, 1973. Reprint. New York: Grove Press, 2001. An exhaustive and often insightful account of Oliver Cromwell's life and the events and figures surrounding him.

Heath, George D., III. "Cromwell and Lambert, 1653-1657." In *Cromwell: A Profile*, edited by Ivan Roots. New York: Hill and Wang, 1973. Argues that Lambert was the central figure in the first Protectorate and provides an excellent analysis of the Instrument of Government.

Hill, Christopher. *God's Englishman: Oliver Cromwell and the English Revolution.* New York: Dial Press, 1970. A lively and provocative analysis of Cromwell and his era, but not simply a life-and-times narrative. Requires some understanding of the period for full appreciation.

Hutton, Ronald. *The Restoration: A Political and Religious History of England and Wales, 1658-1667.* New York: Oxford University Press, 1985. Gives the most complete account of the power struggles following Oliver Cromwell's death. Very good on the contest between Lambert and Monck and Lambert's last months of political activity.

Jones, J. R. *Country and Court: England, 1658-1714.* Cambridge, Mass.: Harvard University Press, 1978. Provides a summary of the latter part of Lambert's career and a shrewd assessment of his character.

SEE ALSO: Charles I; Charles II (of England); Oliver Cromwell; Third Baron Fairfax; James II; George Monck.

FRANÇOIS DE LA ROCHEFOUCAULD
French moralist and essayist

La Rochefoucauld immersed himself in the life of the seventeenth century Parisian salons after a failed political career. His chief literary work, Maximes, *best exemplifies the predilection of the salons for the genre of maxims and set the standard of excellence for maxim writers during his century and later.*

BORN: September 15, 1613; Paris, France
DIED: March 16 or 17, 1680; Paris
ALSO KNOWN AS: Prince de Marsillac; François VI de
   La Rochefoucauld (given name)
AREA OF ACHIEVEMENT: Literature

EARLY LIFE

François VI de La Rochefoucauld (frah-swaw deh lah-rawsh-foo-koh) was born into an ancient aristocratic French family. He bore the title of Prince de Marsillac until he inherited the title of duke de La Rochefoucauld at his father's death in 1650. He grew up in the family château at Verteuil, in Angoumois in western France, and, at the age of fourteen, married thirteen-year-old Andrée de Vivonne, who would bear five sons and three daughters.

Having joined the army when he was fifteen, he entered court life the next year with hopes for a great political career. However, he soon became embroiled in court conspiracies, partly because of the women with whom he was involved, such as Marie de Rohan, duchesse de Chevreuse, and Anne-Geneviève de Bourbon Condé, the duchesse de Longueville (who had a son with him). He sided with Queen Anne of Austria (the regent for her young son, Louis XIV) against Armand-Jean du Plessis, Cardinal de Richelieu, and later opposed Richelieu's successor, Cardinal Jules Mazarin. After being involved in military campaigns in Italy, the Netherlands, and Flanders, he played an active role in the Wars of the Fronde (1648-1653), the armed uprising of nobles against the French monarchy's increasing power. In 1652, he was shot in the face during a skirmish in Paris's Faubourg Saint-Antoine, losing an eye and becoming blind for a few months.

By the end of 1652, disillusioned by years of court intrigue, failed love affairs, and broken promises at court, he abandoned his political career. Accepting Cardinal Mazarin's offer of amnesty in October to the rebel nobles, La Rochefoucauld retired from the court and withdrew to his country estates in Angoumois.

LIFE'S WORK

Although his political career was laid to rest, La Rochefoucauld was about to enter a new, unexpected career that would make him famous. During his retirement, he wrote his *Les Mémoires sur la régence d'Anne d'Autriche*, first published anonymously in 1662 (*The Memoirs of the Duke de La Rochefoucault*, 1683), detailing his experiences of intrigue in the court of Louis XIV. His objective account of then-recent political events and the personalities involved foreshadowed the aloof tone and the close psychological observation of his future masterpiece.

He returned to Paris in 1656 and entered into a new social milieu, the salons. Salons were the meeting places for the aristocratic intelligentsia of France, whose discussions ranged from literature to theology. Although he visited many salons, including that of Madeleine de Scudéry, by 1659, he participated primarily in the salon of Madeleine de Souvré, the marquise de Sablé. Here he became close friends with Marie Madeleine Pioche de la Vergne, Madame de La Fayette, and Madame de Sévigné, and met such contemporaries as the playwright Molière and the mathematician and theologian Blaise Pascal.

In this atmosphere emerged La Rochefoucauld's most important literary work. One of the salons' favorite pastimes was formulating maxims—thoughtful, witty, concise statements concerning human nature or behavior. Unlike a proverb or an adage, which expresses an obvious, commonplace truth, a maxim presents a universal truth about a social, psychological, or moral principle, expressed in a profound but elegant way. Salon participants would choose a particular idea and contribute suggestions as to how to best formulate the thought, polishing it and revising it as a group. Although several participants, including the marquise de Sablé, published maxims, the master of this genre was unquestionably La Rochefoucauld.

La Rochefoucauld's *Réflexions: Ou, Sentences et maximes morales* (1665; *Epictetus Junior: Or, Maximes of Modern Morality*, 1670), better known as *Maximes*, demonstrates the high point of the maxim writing of seventeenth century salons. La Rochefoucauld oversaw four more editions of this work, augmenting, polishing, and sometimes revising maxims more than thirty times for phrasing and succinctness. The fifth edition, published in 1678, contains 504 maxims—each almost always ex-

LA ROCHEFOUCAULD'S GENERAL MAXIMS

La Rochefoucauld refined and revised his maxims repeatedly, actions that perhaps unwittingly particularize statements meant to be general and universal. His maxims include the following eleven randomly selected pieces. He published his major work Maximes *five times during his lifetime, adding new maxims and rewriting old ones with each edition.*

26. Neither the sun nor death can be looked at steadily.
38. We make our promises according to our hopes, and keep them according to our fears.
43. Man often believes he leads, when indeed he is being led; and while his mind directs him toward one goal, his heart drags him unconsciously toward another.
98. Each speaks well of his heart, and no one dares speak so well about his mind.
102. The head is forever fooled by the heart.
210. As we grow old, we become sillier and wiser.
326. Ridicule hurts our honor more than does dishonor itself.
384. We ought never to be surprised, save that we can still be surprised.
439. We would scarcely wish zealously for things, if we really understood the things we wanted.
464. There exist extremes of well-being and misery that go beyond our sensibility and imagination.
496. Quarrels would not last long, if the wrong were only on one side.

Source: From *The Norton Anthology of World Masterpieces*, vol. 2, edited by Maynard Mack (New York: W. W. Norton, 1980), pp. 125-127.

pressed as a single sentence—grouped together by general categories (love, marriage, self-love, vices and virtues, and so forth). The reflections, which make up a short portion of the book, are very brief essays on a variety of topics related to the maxims.

La Rochefoucauld's maxims probe the source of people's actions. His overriding theme is that social and moral behavior often is based on self-interest or self-love. All noble virtues, sentiments, and actions are mixed, consciously or unconsciously, with pride, envy, or other ulterior motives. In addition, habit, fashion, temperament, heredity, and circumstances also contribute to people's motives, thus making virtues and vices often the predetermined products of unconscious motives. Like his seventeenth century contemporaries, La Rochefoucauld did not believe in the goodness of human nature, and his maxims seek to expose lies disguised as truth, vice disguised as virtue, and the selfishness underlying good deeds. However, he went further than his contemporaries by questioning the validity of free will and the existence of uncontaminated virtue and good works.

His pessimism, cynicism, and determinism were considered subversive by some but approved by others.

In addition to his perceptive insights, La Rochefoucauld's style also makes him the prime example of a seventeenth century French moralist. As the omniscient, detached observer who penetrates below the surface, he almost always uses the words "we" or "people" rather than "I" to emphasize the shared commonality of all human beings in whatever truth is being expressed. Through his masterful use of oxymora and parallelisms, he startles the reader out of conventional thinking patterns, illuminating in a sudden flash something that lies hidden. Because each maxim is a self-contained unit on a single, in-depth aspect of people's behavior or motivation, the work can appear contradictory and fragmentary, but this in fact mirrors the contradictory and complex nature of human beings.

When he died of gout in 1680 in the arms of the French orator Bishop Jacques-Bénigne Bossuet, La Rochefoucauld was already famous. His *Maximes* continued to be appreciated not only by the French but also by English writers such as Jonathan Swift and Samuel Johnson, and they would go on to influence many thinkers in the centuries that followed.

SIGNIFICANCE

Although he fulfilled the moralist's task of exposing human weaknesses, La Rochefoucauld cannot be categorized as a philosopher, a theologian, or a moral reformer: He presented no coherent system, had no specific methodology, and expressed no interest in religion or desire to change people's behavior. As a perceptive observer of facts concerning people's behavior, however, he was a forerunner of modern psychology, sociology, and behavior theory. He laid the groundwork for basic concepts about the unconscious that were later developed by Sigmund Freud and others, and his insights on the multifaceted and contradictory nature of the self contributed to the history of social ethics and to modern studies on human behavior and motivation.

La Rochefoucauld's *Maximes* remains one of the most penetrating works on the hidden life of the human heart because it offers an accurate, impartial assessment of the human condition that transcends his century. His insights—on self-interest in particular—were expanded by various European thinkers, including the Scottish economist Adam Smith and the German philosopher Friedrich Nietzsche, and led to a reevaluation of the concept of self-love as an attitude that can be appropriate and acceptable, rather than a vice.

—*Marsha Daigle-Williamson*

FURTHER READING

Clark, Henry C. *La Rochefoucauld and the Language of Unmasking in Seventeenth-Century France*. Geneva, Switzerland: Librairie Droz, 1994. A helpful discussion of the context of French politics and of Jansenism, and arguments against religious content in the maxims. Includes a brief biography and analysis of La Rochefoucauld's main themes and philosophy. Translations for French quotations are simultaneous in the text. Includes a bibliography of French and English sources and an index.

Conley, John J., S. J. *The Suspicion of Virtue: Women Philosophers in Neoclassical France*. Ithaca, N.Y.: Cornell University Press, 2002. Interesting reevaluation of the role and influence of intellectual women and salons in seventeenth century France. Includes detailed arguments in chapter 2 on the marquise de Sablé's underestimated contribution to La Rochefoucauld's maxims. Extensive notes, bibliography, and index.

Epstein, Joseph. *Life Sentences: Literary Essays*. New York: W. W. Norton, 1997. A positive overview in this book on nineteen famous writers of La Rochefoucauld's life and works in the chapter "La Rochefoucauld: Maximum Moralist."

Hodgson, Richard G. *Falsehood Disguised: Unmasking the Truth in La Rochefoucauld*. West Lafayette, Ind.: Purdue University Press, 1995. Focuses on the theme and style of La Rochefoucauld's maxims, with acceptable arguments for their baroque elements. Multilingual bibliography, index. Translation of maxims often only in appendices.

La Rochefoucauld, François de. *Moral Maxims*. Newark: University of Delaware Press, 2003. A dual language edition of La Rochefoucauld's classic work. Includes an introduction and further notes by Irwin Primer. Based on the 1749 English translation.

Levi, Anthony. *Louis XIV*. New York: Carroll & Graf, 2004. Very readable description of the political and social atmosphere of the seventeenth century, including La Rochefoucauld's role in court intrigues and the salons he later visited. Chronology, genealogy, maps, substantial notes, and index.

Thweatt, Vivien. *La Rochefoucauld and the Seventeenth-Century Concept of Self*. Geneva, Switzerland: Librairie Droz, 1980. A good discussion of the function and worldview of salons. Includes analysis of La Rochefoucauld's philosophy and style, as well as his manuscript changes and revisions. French quotations and phrases not translated. Bibliography of primary, secondary, and critical sources, and an index.

SEE ALSO: Anne of Austria; Jacques-Bénigne Bossuet; Duchesse de Chevreuse; Marie le Jars de Gournay; Madame de La Fayette; Jean de La Fontaine; Duchesse de Longueville; Jules Mazarin; Molière; Blaise Pascal; Cardinal de Richelieu; Madeleine de Scudéry; Madame de Sévigné; Viscount de Turenne.

RELATED ARTICLES in *Great Events from History: The Seventeenth Century, 1601-1700:* 1637: Descartes Publishes His *Discourse on Method*; 1661: Absolute Monarchy Emerges in France; 1664: Molière Writes *Tartuffe*; 1682: French Court Moves to Versailles; 1685: Louis XIV Revokes the Edict of Nantes; 1689-1694: Famine and Inflation in France.

SIEUR DE LA SALLE
French explorer

La Salle was the first European to traverse fully the Mississippi River. He exited into the Gulf of Mexico, where he later attempted unsuccessfully to found a French colony on the coast of what is now Texas.

BORN: November 22, 1643; Rouen, France
DIED: March 19, 1687; on the Brazos River (now in Texas)
ALSO KNOWN AS: René-Robert Cavelier (given name)
AREA OF ACHIEVEMENT: Exploration

EARLY LIFE

René-Robert Cavelier was born in Normandy. He preferred to use as his name the noble title sieur de La Salle (syuhr duh lah-sahl). His father, Jean Cavelier, was a wealthy landowner. La Salle's mother, née Catherine Geest, came from a family of wholesale merchants. The parents wanted René-Robert and his older brother, Jean, to take priestly vows in the Catholic Church. Jean joined the Order of Saint Sulpice and went to French Canada. Young René-Robert entered the Jesuit College of Rouen several years later, at the age of nine.

At Rouen, the youth showed an aptitude for mathematics and philosophy. He thus proved to be a capable student in his academic work. René-Robert, however, had problems with the Jesuit teachers. His large physical size and athletic prowess, coupled with a lusty desire for adventure and excitement, did not suit him for a life of prayer and scholarship. Although no specific physical description of him survives, La Salle seems to have been a handsome and personable youth who made friends easily. At times, however, young La Salle proved to be moody, hot-tempered, and stubborn. His rebellious spirit and strong sense of independence made it difficult for him to succeed in the Jesuit brotherhood. This calling demanded introspection, moderation, tolerance, and austerity. Nevertheless, the youth completed his education at Rouen, although he refused to take full vows as a Jesuit brother upon reaching adulthood.

Instead, young Cavelier renounced his novitiate vows in 1667 and decided to emigrate to New France. He was penniless upon leaving the Jesuits because his father had died while he was a novitiate in the order. Under French law, René-Robert had thus been ineligible to inherit the family property. Canada might therefore provide the young man a chance to earn fortune and fame for himself. In addition, La Salle already had connections in the colony through his brother Jean at Montreal. Also, his uncle had been a member of the Hundred Association of New France and a heavy investor in French development of Canada.

La Salle used these family connections to secure a seigniory (a large landed estate) along the St. Lawrence River. There, he began living the life of a gentleman planter. He traveled in the best social circles of the colony, meeting the rich and powerful of New France. La Salle soon became fascinated with the Indians of Canada and learned some of their major languages. He realized that fur trading with the Indians would provide for him the fastest route to wealth and riches. This desire to enter the fur trade caused La Salle to sell his seigniory and move to the frontier.

LIFE'S WORK

La Salle joined an expedition sent by the Sulpicians in 1669 to found new missions and trade in furs along the western Great Lakes. He visited the Ohio River Valley and familiarized himself with much of the Great Lakes region. This expedition established La Salle as a successful explorer who had the potential for expanding the French fur trade into new areas of North America. His activities on the western frontier caught the attention of New France's governor, Louis de Baude, the comte de Frontenac. The governor was eager to enrich himself personally in the fur trade. He recognized that a partnership with La Salle would provide a means of doing so. The governor dispatched La Salle to France in 1674 to obtain for them a royal fur-trading monopoly in the Ontario region of the St. Lawrence River. This the two partners soon secured from the French king. From his base at Fort Frontenac on the eastern end of Lake Ontario, La Salle spent the next three years exploring and trading with the Indians in the upper Great Lakes region.

All the while, La Salle dreamed of greater triumphs. He had heard rumors of the mighty unexplored river to the west, which the Indians called "Messi-Sipi." He had also talked with Louis Jolliet, another Frenchman who had earlier visited its upper reaches. La Salle decided to secure a grant from the king permitting him to descend the river to its mouth, explore its course in the process, and, in so doing, obtain a fur-trading monopoly with the Indians along its banks. In 1677, he returned to France in the company of his faithful lieutenant Henry de Tonty and secured such a concession from the king. By the summer of 1678, La Salle was back in Canada, busily engaged in organizing an expedition for this purpose.

Events, however, moved slowly. It took more than a year to raise the necessary money and secure all the supplies. Further delays came when La Salle suffered various financial reverses. Finally, early in 1682, he and his expedition began their descent of the Mississippi, reaching the Gulf of Mexico on April 9. In formal ceremonies held on that date near the mouth of the river, La Salle laid claim for France to all lands that the river drained. He named the region "Louisiana," in honor of the French king. La Salle and his men then returned whence they had come, making the laborious journey back up the river to Canada.

During his absence on the Mississippi expedition, Frontenac left the governor's office, and Antoine Lefebre, the sieur de la Barre, assumed the position. He was one of La Salle's enemies in the competitive fur trade of French Canada. The new governor removed La Salle from his position in absentia and accused him of various minor crimes. La Salle returned to France to clear his name. The king, pleased with the explorer's accomplishments, restored his monopoly and trading rights in the Mississippi Valley. La Salle thereupon set about organizing a major colonizing expedition that would found a French settlement on the Gulf of Mexico at the mouth of the Mississippi. This expedition left France in July of 1684. Its voyage across the Atlantic was not auspicious. Food and water were in short supply, and La Salle quarreled incessantly with the sieur de Beaujeu, the naval officer who commanded the ships of the expedition.

Morale was low and illness had ravaged the colonists by the time they stopped at French Hispañola, their stepping-stone to the Gulf of Mexico. La Salle, suffering from a fever, was indecisive in his leadership, and Captain Beaujeu refused to cooperate with the explorer. Under these circumstances, they continued their journey. The reconnaissance to find the mouth of the Mississippi did not go well. La Salle missed the river entirely, instead leading his expedition almost due west to Matagorda Bay on the shores of Texas.

Nevertheless, La Salle decided to establish his colony in this uncharted territory and use it as a base to search for the Mississippi. He had a small fort constructed while the colonists built modest huts in which to live. Conditions in the colony were harsh and forbidding, made worse by La Salle's quarrel with Captain Beaujeu. Acrimony with Beaujeu became so bitter that the naval commander sailed home, leaving the colonists on their own. Moreover, La Salle was not clear about his intentions. At times he talked of harassing the Spanish to the south in Mexico, while on other occasions he maintained that finding the Mississippi was his chief objective.

During 1686, La Salle led several exploring parties into various parts of the surrounding region. The only result of these journeys was increased dissatisfaction among the colonists. In January, 1687, La Salle and a small band of men departed on foot for the Mississippi, leaving behind most of the colonists at Fort St. Louis. By March, several members of this traveling party had become frustrated with La Salle's authoritarian style of command. These individuals plotted to assassinate La Salle by ambush, which they did on March 19, 1687.

The death of La Salle ended the French colony at Fort St. Louis, which did not long survive his passing. Within months, some of the colonists made their way back to Canada via the Mississippi (which they eventually found), while others died at the hands of hostile Indians who attacked the settlement. A handful, including several children, lived with friendly Indians along the Texas coast. Spanish Captain Alonso de León, whom the authorities in Mexico City had sent to destroy the French settlement, found the few remaining survivors when he arrived at Fort St. Louis in 1689.

Sieur de La Salle. (Library of Congress)

SIGNIFICANCE

La Salle's greatest triumph was his exploration of the Mississippi River in 1682, which established claim to Louisiana for France. This acquisition more than doubled the territory held by the French king in North America. Yet the spirit of independence and single-mindedness that permitted La Salle to excel as an explorer made him poorly suited to be a colony builder. He sometimes treated his subordinates dogmatically and imperiously. He could be moody and withdrawn, to the extent that one modern biographer, E. B. Osler, maintains that La Salle was a manic-depressive personality type. Moreover, the explorer was a poor financial manager and spent most of his career deeply in debt.

Nevertheless, La Salle ranks as one of history's best-known explorers. His accomplishments include a number of "firsts" that certainly justify this reputation: the first European to sail down the Mississippi to the Gulf, the first person to advocate the founding of a major city at the mouth of that river, and the first colonizer to attempt a settlement on the western coast of the Gulf of Mexico. It is because of La Salle that the French fleur-de-lis is one of the six flags that have flown over Texas during its history.

—Light Townsend Cummins

FURTHER READING

Bruseth, James E., and Toni S. Turner. *From a Watery Grave: The Discovery and Excavation of La Salle's Shipwreck, La Belle*. College Station: Texas A&M University Press, 2004. The frigate *La Belle* was stranded near Matagordo Bay in Texas during La Salle's ill-fated final voyage. Archaeologists in the 1990's excavated the shipwreck, uncovering a human skeleton and one million artifacts intended for use in a newly constructed colony. The book examines La Salle's dream of building a colony, the excavation and artifacts unearthed, and *La Belle*'s legacy.

Caruso, John Anthony. *The Mississippi Valley Frontier: The Age of French Exploration and Settlement*. Indianapolis, Ind.: Bobbs-Merrill, 1966. A standard scholarly survey of expansion of French Canada into Louisiana. Examines La Salle and the colonizing activities that came after him, in the eighteenth century.

Cox, Isaac Joslin. *The Journeys of René-Robert Cavelier, Sieur de La Salle*. 2 vols. New York: A. S. Barnes, 1905-1906. A lengthy collection of documents, personal memoirs, and contemporary reports dealing with La Salle's career. All in English translation.

Galloway, Patricia, ed. *La Salle and His Legacy: Frenchmen and Indians in the Lower Mississippi Valley*. Jackson: University of Mississippi Press, 1982. A series of historical papers on La Salle presented at the 1982 meeting of the Mississippi State Historical Society, in celebration of the three hundredth anniversary of La Salle's voyage.

Johnson, Donald S. *La Salle: A Perilous Odyssey from Canada to the Gulf of Mexico*. New York: Cooper Square Press, 2002. Johnson recounts La Salle's expeditions in the New World.

Joutel, Henri. *Joutel's Journal of La Salle's Last Voyage*. London: A. Bell, 1714. Reprint. Edited by Melville B. Anderson. Chicago: Caxton Club, 1896. Joutel accompanied La Salle on the Texas expedition and was among the survivors.

La Salle, Nicolas de. *The La Salle Expedition on the Mississippi River: A Lost Manuscript of Nicolas de La Salle, 1682*. Translated by Johanna S. Warren, edited by William C. Foster. Austin: Texas State Historical Association, 2003. Nicolas de La Salle (no relation to the explorer) was one of the men on Sieur de La Salle's 1682 Mississippi River expedition. A rare copy of Nicolas's journal of that voyage was recently discovered at the Texas State Archives. This translation and analysis of the journal reveals new information about the historic exploration.

Osler, E. B. *La Salle*. Don Mills, Ontario: Longmans Canada, 1967. An excellent modern biography, full of detail, taking the position that La Salle was sometimes mentally unstable, thereby explaining his erratic leadership style.

Parkman, Francis. *La Salle and the Discovery of the Great West*. Boston: Little, Brown, 1879. Parkman ranks as one of the greatest nineteenth century narrative historians. The study, in spite of minor inaccuracies, is a literary work.

Weddle, Robert S. *The Spanish Sea*. College Station: Texas A&M University Press, 1985. A lengthy examination of European efforts to explore the Gulf of Mexico in the sixteenth and the seventeenth centuries. Based on extensive manuscript research in European archives.

_____. *Wilderness Manhunt: The Spanish Search for La Salle*. Austin: University of Texas Press, 1973. Examines the La Salle colony in Texas from the Spanish viewpoint, as a threat to Spain's control of the Gulf of Mexico. Contains much detail about Spanish efforts to locate and destroy La Salle's ill-fated colony.

See also: Samuel de Champlain; Pierre Le Moyne d'Iberville; Louis Jolliet; Louis XIV; Jacques Marquette; Pierre Esprit Radisson.

Related articles in *Great Events from History: The Seventeenth Century, 1601-1700:* March 15, 1603-December 25, 1635: Champlain's Voyages; April 27, 1627: Company of New France Is Chartered; 1642-1700: Westward Migration of Native Americans; Beginning 1673: French Explore the Mississippi Valley; December, 1678-March 19, 1687: La Salle's Expeditions; May 1, 1699: French Found the Louisiana Colony.

GEORGES DE LA TOUR
French painter

La Tour, whose realist religious and genre scenes uniquely combined the baroque style and classicism, is best known for his use of light—candles, lamps, torches, and daylight—contrasted with shadow, to create a contemplative atmosphere. Within this baroque setting, La Tour imbues his characters with classicism's reserve to create intimate scenes of silent communication.

Born: March 13, 1593; Vic-sur-Seille, Lorraine, France
Died: January 30, 1652; Lunéville, Lorraine
Area of achievement: Art

Early Life

Georges de La Tour was born to Jean de La Tour, a baker in Vic, and Sybille de La Tour. Jean de La Tour traded land and wholesaled grain, practices that placed him in the town's bourgeoisie. Although it was in Lorraine, Vic nevertheless was under the jurisdiction of the bishopric of Metz and was its administrative center. The city provided a rich cultural and intellectual life for the young La Tour. Vic had a lieutenant general, major administrative personnel, a mint, schools, and printers. The presence of rich salt mines brought wealth to the town.

The first archival mention of La Tour after his baptism on March 14, 1593, is 1616. Nothing conclusive is known about his activity in the twenty-three years between 1593 and 1616. During this period, he would have completed his apprenticeship and postapprenticeship study. The young La Tour may have apprenticed in Nancy with mannerist Jacques Bellange, the court painter of Charles IV, the duke of Lorraine. Because the greatest influence on the artist was the Italian Baroque painter Caravaggio, La Tour might have gone to Rome after his initial apprenticeship; he also might have pursued his studies in Catholic Utrecht (now in the Netherlands) with one of the several followers of Caravaggio.

In 1617, La Tour married Diane Le Nerf, the daughter of wealthy nobleman Jean Le Nerf, minter to the duke of Lorraine. In 1620, the La Tours settled permanently in Lunéville, an important ducal headquarters in Lorraine and also Diane's hometown. Her family probably had contacts important for La Tour's artistic career. Lunéville was undergoing a period of rapid growth during this time. Duke Henry II had been building a château that needed the work of artists and artisans. It appears also that Lunéville had no established painter.

Life's Work

La Tour began his successful career in the 1620's. He hired an apprentice in 1620 and another in 1626. Duke Henry II commissioned two paintings. The La Tours also were able to buy the Le Nerf family mansion. This is the period of La Tour's daylight genre and religious works, paintings whose light source is outside the work. In the 1620's, he painted his early religious portraits, such as the series of apostles and his genre scenes of hurdy-gurdy (medieval stringed instrument) players, brawling musicians, and common people. A hallmark of La Tour's style, the realistic and noble treatment of both commoners and saints, already can be seen in these early paintings.

The 1630's were tragic years for Lorraine and Lunéville. The duchy became the battleground of the Thirty Years' War (1618-1648) between France and the Habsburg Empire, with which Charles IV was an ally. French troops battled for Lorraine starting in 1630, and King Louis XIII annexed the duchy in 1634. Famine and plague were rampant. The two sackings of Lunéville by French troops in September and October of 1638 were most tragic for the La Tours. Art historians believe these attacks wiped out a large part of La Tour's production, especially the daylight paintings.

Despite the calamities of war, La Tour's commercial and artistic success grew. The La Tours remained in Lunéville during the French occupation. Georges was friendly with the French occupiers and often served as a godfather or as an official witness for them. He profited by selling grain to both sides of the conflict and bought land from those forced to leave the city. Although details about commissions are sketchy, they appear to have come from French collectors in Paris or in Lorraine. La Tour stayed at the Louvre in 1639 as a guest of Louis XIII, presumably as thanks for a painting, and was granted the title *peintre ordinaire du roi*.

La Tour painted his most complex daylight subjects and the first of his nocturnal works before and during the 1630's. Large narrative genre scenes such as *Fortune Teller* and two paintings of card cheats (*Cheat with the Ace of Diamonds* and *Cheat with the Ace of Clubs*) are among the seventeenth century's greatest genre scenes. His two paintings of the penitent Saint Jerome are his most ambitious daylight religious scenes and are the first expression of the Franciscan mysticism that would become the major force in the painter's work for the remainder of his career.

In the mid-1630's, he stopped painting daylight genre scenes and concentrated on nocturnal religious subjects. These nocturnal religious works, paintings whose light source is within the painting, are the works for which La Tour is best known. A candle, a lamp, or a torch within the work produces the dramatic contrast of light and shadow known as chiaroscuro. La Tour's chiaroscuro creates an intimate atmosphere conducive to meditation and spirituality. His most famous nocturnal composition from this decade is the horizontal *Saint Sebastian Tended by Saint Irene*, a subject that La Tour apparently presented to both King Louis XIII and Charles IV of Lorraine.

La Tour reached the summit of his success during the 1640's, even in the face of continuing warfare in Lorraine. A new governor, Henri, maréchal de La Ferté-Sénectère, was installed in Nancy in 1643. Lunéville paid tribute to the governor annually by presenting him with a painting by La Tour. The six paintings La Ferté received between 1645 and 1652 are the best-documented commissions in the artist's oeuvre.

La Tour's most refined and moving nocturnal religious works come from this productive decade. *Adoration of the Shepherds*, *The New-born*, the vertical *Saint Sebastian Tended by Saint Irene*, *Christ with Saint Joseph in the Carpenter's Shop*, and *Repentance of Mary Magdalene* are all contemplative scenes of silent and intimate communication.

SIGNIFICANCE

La Tour was a successful artist in his lifetime but was quickly forgotten after his death. Little of La Tour's

work is signed or dated, so his work remained unidentified until the beginning of the twentieth century, when German art historian Hermann Voss began to reconstruct La Tour's oeuvre. His standing grew steadily throughout the century. In the 1990's, a biography and two major retrospectives of the artist's work in the United States and Paris solidified La Tour's reputation as one of the great seventeenth century French artists.

Mystery still surrounds the artist, though. Little is known about commissions or the number of paintings he made. Approximately fifty works by La Tour have been identified to date. They divide almost equally between religious and genre scenes. Art historians disagree, however, on the dates and chronological order of the works. Also, there is disagreement about the subject and meaning of two paintings: *The Flea Catcher* and *Payment of Dues* (1630's to 1640's). Most important, the artist left behind no explanation of any kind about his work.

La Tour treated the most traditional religious and genre subjects in a unique style. He painted the Counter-Reformation religious scenes recommended by the Council of Trent, such as the founding fathers of the Church, the early apostles and martyrs, and subjects the Reformation Church criticized, such as the practice of penitence.

The subjects of his genre paintings are the same as those that were found all over Europe at that time: scenes of card cheats, fortune-tellers, and traveling musicians and beggars. La Tour stands out from his contemporaries, however, with both his realism and his unique style, which combine elements of the Baroque and of French classicism. La Tour's characters, whether saints or commoners, are not idealized; they look like everyday people (even the saints), with all their imperfections, but still given dignity by the artist.

True to his realism, La Tour represents the divine symbolically with his use of light rather than through the use of halos and hovering angels. His nocturnal religious works combine the Baroque's chiaroscuro with classicism's reserve. The chiaroscuro creates an atmosphere conducive to contemplation or worship, so that it appears his characters experience some form of silent epiphany, perhaps even the mystical union with God, in a calm and inner-directed way.

—Stuart McClintock

FURTHER READING
Conisbee, Philip, et al. *Georges de La Tour and His World*. New Haven, Conn.: Yale University Press,

1996. A catalog from the 1996-1997 La Tour exhibition in Washington, D.C., and Fort Worth, Texas. A thorough study of all facets of La Tour's work.

Grossman, Fritz. "Some Observations on Georges de La Tour and the Netherlandish Tradition." *Burlington Magazine* 115 (1973): 576-583. This article theorizes that because La Tour studied in Catholic Utrecht after his initial apprenticeship, there are striking similarities between the paintings of La Tour and those of the Utrecht masters, Gerrit van Honthorst, Hendrik Terbrugghen, and Dirck van Baburen.

McClintock, Stuart. *The Iconography and Iconology of Georges de La Tour's Religious Paintings, 1624-1650.* Lewiston, N.Y.: Edwin Mellen Press, 2003. This study interprets twenty-one of La Tour's religious paintings in the light of the religious, political, and artistic movements of the time.

Nicolson, Benedict, and Christopher Wright. *Georges de La Tour.* London: Phaidon Press, 1974. An Anglo-Saxon perspective of La Tour's work.

Thuillier, Jacques. *Georges de La Tour.* London: Flammarion, 1993. An extensive biography of La Tour.

SEE ALSO: Artemisia Gentileschi; Frans Hals; Rembrandt; Peter Paul Rubens; Sir Anthony van Dyck; Jan Vermeer.

RELATED ARTICLES in *Great Events from History: The Seventeenth Century, 1601-1700:* c. 1601-1620: Emergence of Baroque Art; 1610-1643: Reign of Louis XIII.

WILLIAM LAUD
English archbishop

As archbishop of Canterbury and as a martyr for his conception of the Church of England, Laud contributed powerfully to the Anglo-Catholic tradition in English religion. The severity of his anti-Puritan policies led directly to the exodus of many Puritans, including the Pilgrims, to the New World.

BORN: October 7, 1573; Reading, Berkshire, England
DIED: January 10, 1645; London, England
AREAS OF ACHIEVEMENT: Religion and theology, government and politics

EARLY LIFE

The son of a clothier, William Laud (LAWD) was born in Reading, halfway between London and Oxford, and those two places, capital and university town, were to be the poles around which most of his life revolved. After an early education at Reading Grammar School, at age sixteen he went to what was then one of Oxford's newer colleges, Saint John's. It had been founded in 1555 by a wealthy Reading man who also funded a scholarship for Reading boys that benefited Laud. Laud received bachelor and master of arts degrees in 1594, a bachelor of divinity in 1604, and a doctor of divinity in 1608. He remained at Saint John's, first as a fellow (faculty member) of the college and then as its president from 1611 to 1621. He later showed his love for Oxford and Saint John's with magnificent gifts, including valuable manuscripts and a beautiful new quadrangle.

Although laymen were present in Elizabethan Oxford and Cambridge in growing numbers, the universities continued to be primarily concerned with educating men for careers in the church. Theology was the most important discipline, and the dominant theological outlook in the late Elizabethan church was not merely Protestant but Calvinist. Calvinists all over northern Europe were playing leading roles in the struggle to defend Protestantism against Roman Catholic efforts to regain lost souls and lands. Only a year before Laud went to Oxford, the Spanish had attempted an invasion of England, the centerpiece of a plan to snuff out the Protestant cause in England, France, and the Netherlands. In 1618, the Thirty Years' War broke out in Bohemia, it eventually spread through most of central Europe. English Protestants were deeply worried that Catholic victory on the Continent would be followed by an assault upon England, and those fears over the survival of the Protestant religion and national independence formed the backdrop to Laud's career and were the source of much of the opposition that he faced.

In his early days in Oxford, Laud associated himself with a small party of anti-Calvinists, men who rejected Calvin's doctrine of predestination in favor of belief in the importance of free will in the process of salvation. In 1604, he further angered the Calvinist Party in Oxford by publicly maintaining the need for bishops in a true Christian church. This and similar episodes during his days in Oxford illustrate significant aspects of his character: He held his views strongly, stated them truculently, and clung to them regardless of the consequences.

Laud was a man of small stature with a round, florid face and closely clipped hair. His personal habits were austere; in an age in which men in high office frequently exploited those positions for private advantage, he was incorruptible. An intensely hard worker who insisted on efficiency and thoroughness, he was an able administrator, and he put all of his considerable energies into the achievement of his goals for the Church of England. Furthermore, in his mind an orderly church meant an orderly society in which people would obey the king as well as the bishops. Anyone who attacked episcopacy was also attacking monarchy.

LIFE'S WORK

The key to Laud's rise to power was the friendship that he formed with George Villiers, first duke of Buckingham. Buckingham, the favorite of both James I and his

William Laud. (Library of Congress)

successor, Charles I, convinced James to make Laud bishop of Saint David's in 1621. James had reservations about Laud, but Charles I admired him and promoted him rapidly: to dean of the Chapel Royal (1625), bishop of Bath and Wells (1626), bishop of London (1628), chancellor of the University of Oxford (1630), and archbishop of Canterbury (1633). Laud was, in fact, Charles's principal adviser on religious matters from the beginning of the reign in 1625, as Charles had no use for the Calvinist archbishop he inherited from his father.

Laud saw to it that virtually all appointments to higher positions in the church went to anti-Calvinists (who were known as Arminians by the 1620's). These clergymen quickly spoke up in support of Charles's policies, urging Englishmen to pay the taxes that Parliament had refused to vote. Laud's influence was not limited to clerical matters; he was a commissioner for the Treasury, a privy councillor, and a judge on the Court of Star Chamber. Because one of Laud's goals was the restoration of churchmen to the kind of political power they had often exercised in the Middle Ages, he was pleased to have such duties. Many people, however, believed that churchmen should concentrate exclusively on religious tasks and be denied authority in civil matters.

Once in power, Laud endeavored to suppress theological controversy, and he was behind the royal order prohibiting preaching or writing about the doctrine of predestination (November, 1628). He worked hard to establish what he called "the beauty of holiness," by which he meant that the outward worship of God should be conducted in complete conformity with the Book of Common Prayer by priests wearing the required vestments. Following in the footsteps of Lancelot Andrewes, bishop of Winchester, Laud was a great advocate of ceremonies. He believed that although the truest worship was inward, "the external worship of God in his church is the great witness to the world, that our heart stands right in the service of God."

For many Calvinists, whether moderate or more zealous (such as the Puritans), Laud's ban on disputation about predestination and his drive to restore ceremonies smacked of "popery." Because Charles I's French-born queen, Henrietta Maria, was encouraging conversion to Catholicism at court with some success, Laud's activities were even more suspect. Puritans were infuriated by his policy of suspending and depriving their preachers because of their refusal to wear the surplice or otherwise abide by ceremonial requirements. Some went abroad to escape them, even as far as New England. Their quarrel with Laud was fundamentally simple, for they believed that the heart of worship was the hearing of the word of God read and preached. Laud said, however, that "the altar is . . . greater than the pulpit" because "a greater reverence" is due to God's body than to God's word. Thus, sacraments took precedence over preaching. For many of Laud's enemies, the Protestant Reformation in England had not gone far enough; too many remnants of "popery" were not yet expunged.

For Laud himself, the problem was that the Reformation had gone too far. In his view, greedy laymen had seized authority and property that rightfully belonged to the clergy, and his aim was to restore the clerical estate to its former glory. Laud had a particularly exalted notion of the calling of bishops, insisting, against Elizabethan tradition, that they held their authority by divine right. He employed the Court of Star Chamber to punish the opponents of episcopacy with fines, imprisonment, and even publicly inflicted mutilation. His most famous victim, a Puritan lawyer and pamphleteer named William Prynne, suffered branding on the cheeks and the loss of his ears.

Although always active in the effort to improve the Church's financial resources, Laud tried to prevent laymen from having anything to say about how the money was spent. He forced the dissolution of the Feoffees for Impropriations, an organization established by Puritans to finance preaching, and confiscated the money they had raised. His program inevitably led to clashes with the common lawyers; they wanted to narrow the jurisdiction of church courts, whereas he wanted to increase it. When punishing a lawyer who had justified his destruction of a stained-glass window on the grounds that the parish vestry had approved, Laud commented: "Thus much let me say to Mr. Sherfield, and such of his profession as slight the ecclesiastical laws and persons, that there was a time when churchmen were as great in this kingdom as you are now; and let me be bold to prophesy, there will be a time when you will be as low as the church is now, if you go on to contemn the church."

At least in the short run, Laud proved a poor prophet. His attempt to extend liturgical uniformity to Calvinist Scotland provoked a massive rebellion in 1637. Charles I, his efforts to quell the Scots having failed, was forced to call his first Parliament in eleven years in 1640. Although it was soon dismissed, its successor, the Long Parliament, was more durable. The majority of its members, convinced that Laud had been among the leaders of a plot to overthrow Protestantism and Parliament, voted to impeach the archbishop on December 18, 1640. Imprisoned in the Tower of London, Laud watched as the nation stumbled toward civil war and as laymen took

over decision making in the church. His trial was delayed until 1644, and the prosecutor was William Prynne. Sentenced to death under an act of attainder, Laud was beheaded on Tower Hill on January 10, 1645.

SIGNIFICANCE

Laud was not guilty of the charge that he had planned to subvert Protestantism in England, but he had pursued his goals of imposing a uniform and "High Church" style of ritual and restoring clerical authority and power in such a way as to make the charges against him credible to many members of the Long Parliament. To understand his fate, it is important to realize that to his contemporaries his program was innovative. He was trying to overthrow the Calvinist theological consensus and the "Low Church" liturgical style in which his enemies had been reared and which they wished to retain. Laud also was struggling to extirpate lay influence and authority that had come into the Church with the Reformation.

The Restoration of the Stuart monarchy in 1660 brought episcopacy and the Book of Common Prayer in its train, but the restored Church was a pale shadow of the politically powerful one that Laud had tried to build. Not until the Oxford Movement in the nineteenth century, which stressed the Church of England's continuity with Catholic Christianity, did Laud and his ideas find admirers and advocates.

—*J. Sears McGee*

FURTHER READING

Collinson, Patrick. *The Religion of Protestants: The Church in English Society, 1559-1625*. New York: Oxford University Press, 1982. Building on the foundation of his important book on the Elizabethan Puritan movement, Collinson surveys the religious scene in England during James I's reign.

Como, David. R. "Predestination and Political Conflict in Laud's London." *Historical Journal* 46, no. 2 (June, 2003): 263. Examines the policies Laud pursued while he was bishop of London, focusing on how he enforced royal edicts against a discussion of predestination.

Fincham, Kenneth. "William Laud and the Exercise of Caroline Ecclesiastical Patronage." *Journal of Ecclesiastical History* 51, no. 1 (January, 2000): 69. Describes Laud's role in formulating ecclesiastical policy during the reign of Charles I.

Fincham, Kenneth, and Peter Lake. "The Ecclesiastical Policy of James I." *Journal of British Studies* 20 (1986): 169-207. Shows how James shrewdly maintained a careful balance in church patronage by preferring moderates and excluding radicals from either side.

Hibbard, Caroline. *Charles I and the Popish Plot.* Chapel Hill: University of North Carolina Press, 1983. A carefully researched account of Catholic influence at the court of Charles I. Shows how Laud resisted that influence, but that the fears of Protestants were not unfounded.

Lake, Peter. "Calvinism and the English Church, 1570-1635." *Past and Present* no. 114 (February, 1987): 32-76. Establishes a distinction between "credal" and "experimental" Calvinists that is helpful in understanding Laud's opponents.

McGee, J. Sears. "William Laud and the Outward Face of Religion." In *Leaders of the Reformation*, edited by Richard L. DeMolen. London: Associated University Presses, 1984. Offers a narrative account of Laud's career with analysis of his program and the opposition to it. Includes a bibliographical essay.

Sharpe, Kevin. "Archbishop Laud and the University of Oxford." In *History and Imagination*, edited by Hugh Lloyd-Jones, Valerie Pearl, and Blair Worden. London: Duckworth, 1981. Stresses Laud's dislike for theological controversy and discusses the reasons for it.

Trevor-Roper, Hugh. *Archbishop Laud.* London: Macmillan, 1940. 2d ed. 1962. Reprint. London: Phoenix Press, 2000. The only modern biography, a pleasure to read. Better, however, on the political than the religious aspects of the subject.

Tyacke, N. R. N. *Anti-Calvinists: The Rise of English Arminianism, c. 1590-1640*. Oxford: Oxford University Press, 1987. Supplies an important dimension missing from Trevor-Roper's biography: the theological and intellectual background and basis for Laud's program. Tyacke also traces the influences and relationships among the anti-Calvinists.

White, Peter. *Predestination, Policy and Polemic: Conflict and Consensus in the English Church from the Reformation to the Civil War*. New York: Cambridge University Press, 1992. White disagrees with historians who maintain the English Civil War was the result of a Laudian and Arminian attack on Calvinism. He denies that Calvinism was predominant in England before the war, and maintains that theologians with contrasting beliefs contributed to the evolution of church doctrine.

SEE ALSO: Lancelot Andrewes; First Duke of Buckingham; Charles I; Henrietta Maria; James I.

RELATED ARTICLES in *Great Events from History: The Seventeenth Century, 1601-1700:* 1618-1648: Thirty Years' War; March-June, 1639: First Bishops' War; November 3, 1640-May 15, 1641: Beginning of England's Long Parliament; 1642-1651: English Civil Wars; May, 1659-May, 1660: Restoration of Charles II.

FRANÇOIS LAVAL
French-born colonial Canadian bishop

As the first bishop of Quebec, Laval worked with the governors of New France to convert the Native Americans to Christianity and to establish the parish structure of the Roman Catholic Church in Canada. Laval's work also preserved French influence in Canada, even after the English conquest in 1763.

BORN: April 30, 1623; Montigny-sur-Avre, near Chartres, France

DIED: May 6, 1708; Quebec, New France (now in Canada)

ALSO KNOWN AS: François-Xavier de Laval-Montmorency (given name)

AREA OF ACHIEVEMENT: Religion and theology

EARLY LIFE

François Laval (frahn-swah lah-vahl) was born François-Xavier de Laval-Montmorency, at Montigny-sur-Avre, in the department of Eure-et-Loir in the diocese of Chartres, on April 30, 1623. His father was a descendant of the cadet branch of an important family of the French upper nobility noted especially for its military service to the Crown. As the third son, François was expected to find his life's work in the Church. Consequently, at age nine, he was tonsured as a cleric and sent by his family to La Fleche, a Jesuit college in Paris, where he was educated in the humanities by the devout Jesuit Father Bogot. Bogot, one of the two most influential persons in Laval's life, taught him the militant

Jesuit virtues of discipline, asceticism, and persistence.

At age fifteen, Laval was appointed a canon of the Cathedral of Évreux. This post enabled him to continue his studies at the College of Clermont in Paris even after his father died. The deaths of his two older brothers threatened to change Laval's life even more, because his family expected him to marry and perform his duty as head of the family. Whether from ambition for more power than a minor noble could command or from religious devotion, Laval chose to renounce his patrimony in favor of a younger brother and take holy orders—saying his first Mass in Paris on September 23, 1647.

From 1647 to 1653, Laval served at Évreux. He then resigned his position to go to Rome, expecting to be sent by the pope as a bishop to Asia. When Portuguese opposition prevented this, Laval returned to Caen in France, where Jean de Bernières de Louvigny, with a group of disciples, prayed and lived in piety and charity in a mystical community called the Hermitage. These men practiced a sort of transcendental devotion resulting in visions and revelations. Zealous advocates of the Jesuits, they believed that God had chosen them to monitor the orthodoxy of the clergy.

These two men and institutions—Bogot and the Jesuits, and Bernières and the Hermitage mystics—formed the character of Laval. His zeal and devotion, his austere and ascetic religious practice, and his willingness to endure and even seek out deprivation were characteristic of the mystics of Caen. The hard, cold, combative side of his nature was built into the Jesuit educational system. Austerity and the habit of authority are apparent in Laval's portrait. The large, aristocratic nose, well-formed forehead, and strongly arched brow frame his small bright eyes and thin compressed lips to convey a haughty self-confidence. It is not so easy to see in his portrait the affable manner and charm also noted by his contemporaries.

In seventeenth century France, bishops were nominated by the king and approved by the pope. Laval's character and breeding made him a perfect Jesuit candidate when King Louis XIV of France asked them to suggest nominees to be the first bishop to New France. Clergy going to Canada had traditionally been chosen and approved by the archbishop of Rouen. Laval broke that pattern. The pope accepted the royal nomination, but in the interests of papal supremacy he made Laval vicar apostolic for Canada. Thus, the bishop would be subject to no authority other than the pope's and could be recalled only by the pope. Consecrated as the bishop of Petraea with the official title of vicar apostolic, Laval

embarked for Quebec in April, 1659, arriving in June as the first bishop in New France.

LIFE'S WORK

Laval, age thirty-six, reached Canada during its transition from a mission and trading station to a colony. New France was populated mainly by Algonquians, Hurons, and Iroquois. In 1659, the Iroquois remained the only persistent native enemies of the French. The French settlers did not exceed twenty-five hundred, including priests, nuns, traders, farmers, and merchants. Shortly after Laval arrived, Louis XIV began sending approximately three hundred settlers per year, mostly peasants but also marriageable young women. Soldiers sent to Quebec and Montreal from France were often given land grants in Canada to encourage them to remain as settlers after their term of service was completed. When Laval arrived in Canada, the creation of institutions and communities was more important than exploration and martyrdom.

The civilizing of Canada was Laval's life's work. During his early years in Quebec, he fought two major battles in the interests of Christianizing and unifying New France. The first of these was his struggle with other clergy and missionaries to establish himself as the head of the church and to create an orderly ecclesiastical hierarchy. The second struggle was a common one of the time—the contest between the powers of the Church and those of the state.

Almost immediately after Laval arrived in the New World, Sulpician priests in Montreal and the archbishop of Rouen in France challenged the new bishop's claims to authority over them. Difficulties in communication between Canada and Rome, as well as the seventeenth century contest between the king of France and the pope over control of the French clergy, complicated Laval's efforts to establish his preeminence. Nevertheless, by 1661 the archbishop of Rouen had been transferred to Paris and the Sulpician priests had accepted the authority of the vicar apostolic. A later attempt in 1670 to limit the power of the clergy by sending Franciscan missionaries—the Recollects—to challenge Laval's support from the Jesuits had little impact.

In the early conflicts between Laval and political leaders in New France, Laval proved his diplomatic ability. Before 1663, one governor resigned and another was recalled by the king in the dispute over selling brandy to the Canadian Indians. The official trading company policy tolerated the sale of brandy to the Indians because brandy was the most desired exchange for beaver furs. If

French traders did not offer alcohol, so the company reasoned, English and Spanish interlopers would. Rejecting such rationalizations, Laval proscribed the brandy trade and excommunicated offenders, forcing one governor to impose the death penalty for that crime. When a subsequent governor refused to prosecute offenders, however, alcohol was again sold freely, and violence among Indians and against Europeans increased.

Unable to control traders and hostile Indians, the Company of New France resigned its claims to Canada, and royal officials created new political institutions to govern the colony. The first Sovereign Council in Quebec was chosen jointly by Laval and Governor Augustin de Saffray, chevalier de Mézy, newly appointed in 1563 on Laval's recommendation. This council was pro-Laval, favoring strong control of the liquor trade and the preeminence of the clergy in decision making. The governor could not tolerate such disregard for his authority and, although Mézy had been chosen by Laval because of ties with Bernières and the Hermitage mystics, conflict erupted between the governor and the bishop. No governor, with a tenure of only three years, could successfully challenge the power of a noble papal appointee holding office for life, one who was also supported by the Jesuits.

Having successfully faced the challenges of other clergy and, at least temporarily, of the royal officials, Laval turned his attention to transforming rustic Canada into a civilized colony. He began by founding schools. A seminary established in 1663 to educate priests and to care for old and sick clergy was the first. From this seminary issued a supply of priests to serve among the Canadian Indians and French wherever they were needed by the growing and shifting population. This school also enhanced Laval's power by creating a clergy at his command. The second stage of this educational system was a lesser seminary opened in 1668 to educate boys, including some Indian pupils, for the upper seminary; a boarding school at Saint Joachim trained boys in agriculture and the trades. Young women in Montreal, including some Huron and Algonquian women, were educated by the Congregation of Notre Dame; young women in Quebec, by the Ursulines, who were connected with the Hermitage mystics. These religious and educational institutions established New France as a viable community separate from its European roots.

By 1674, New France was secure and civilized enough, with sufficient French settlers, to warrant the appointment of Laval as the first permanent bishop of Quebec. The pope and Louis XIV clashed over the method of appointment, but they eventually compromised: The king would nominate the candidate; the pope would rule him. To avoid disruption of Roman Catholic worship in the event that Canada was conquered by another power, the bishop of Quebec would be directly subordinate to the pope.

Laval's staunchest opponent was Governor Louis de Buade, count of Palluau and Frontenac, who arrived in Quebec in 1672. This powerful leader promoted the economic development of the colony by supporting the sale of masts to shipbuilders in France, trade with the West Indies and American colonists when feasible, and the strengthening of French control of the fur trade. Forts were built in the interior, and the exploration of the Mississippi Valley and points west resumed. During this period of colonial competition with England and Spain in the New World and increasingly serious European military conflicts that spilled over into colonies, Frontenac's military abilities made him an indispensable representative for Louis XIV.

Governor Frontenac was a match for the new bishop of Quebec. The rivalry between these two men was carried on through a struggle to control the appointment of the members of the Sovereign Council and by appeals to the king and his ministers. The issues that they disputed were the sale of brandy to the Indians and the creation of a fixed parish system with permanent parish priests, who would not be controlled by the bishop. By 1679, both issues had been settled by compromise. Although the sale of alcohol to Native Americans was tolerated in the interests of trade and in order to treat the Indians the same as the French, the king forbade traders to carry alcohol to the interior for sale. Further, the king required fixed appointments of priests to clearly defined parishes. Although Laval did not control the movement of priests, the seminary allocated royal funds for the priests, and Laval was responsible for defining the parishes.

Finally, in 1684, Bishop Laval created a cathedral chapter at Quebec with twelve canons, five born in the colony, and four chaplains. This made his episcopal seat the equal of a European bishopric. Having accomplished this goal, Laval returned to France to resign as bishop and select a successor.

Laval chose to spend his last years, from 1688 to 1708, in a small room of his seminary in Quebec, in prayer and poverty. Although Laval's strong will often led to clashes with the new bishop, he continued to serve his former parishioners as they endured Indian attacks, the 1690 bombardment by the English fleet, fires, and epidemics. Occasionally, when the new bishop was abroad,

Laval served as his substitute. The venerable cleric died of diabetic gangrene on May 6, 1708, and was buried in the Cathedral of Quebec.

SIGNIFICANCE

In many ways, Laval played a major role in defining the North American character as humanitarian and tolerant. Although his first duty as bishop was to the French settlers in the colony, he challenged all abuses of the Indians by traders, whether the abuse was acquiring furs by fraud or subterfuge or the selling of alcohol. The schools Laval founded were open to French settlers and Indians alike.

To Laval, French Canada owes much, including the strength of French influence in Canada. His success in creating a strong centralized Roman Catholic church at Quebec with jurisdiction throughout North America ensured that French culture would survive even after the English conquest in 1763. Laval University in Quebec not only bears the bishop's name but also is a direct descendant of the lesser seminary founded in 1668 by Laval. Laval not only labored fiercely to mold a civilized colony in the New World but also left an indelible mark on his adopted land.

—*Loretta Turner Johnson*

FURTHER READING

Cather, Willa. *Shadows on the Rock*. New York: Random House, 1931. A novel of Quebec during the last days of Frontenac. Although Laval is not the central character, he is portrayed by Cather as the Old Man beloved by his parishioners.

Delanglez, Jean, S.J. *Frontenac and the Jesuits*. Chicago: Institute of Jesuit History, 1939. Depicts Frontenac as a powerful but poor governor because he was unable to reconcile religious and official power groups to achieve the monarchy's goals.

Eccles, William John. *Canada Under Louis XIV, 1663-1701*. London: Oxford University Press, 1964. Although this book covers the period of Laval's tenure in France, it focuses primarily on political issues. Laval appears as a strong supporter of royal views.

_____. *Frontenac the Courtier Governor*. Toronto: McClelland and Stewart, 1959. Reprint. Lincoln:

University of Nebraska Press, 2003. This picture of Frontenac belies Parkman's mythical strongman (see below). Frontenac is seen as less important than the competing claims of nationalism, mercantilism, and religion.

Leblond de Brumath, Adrien. *Bishop Laval*. Toronto: Morang, 1910. A typical hagiographical biography largely based on the collection of documents sent to Rome to promote Laval's beatification. In an outdated and uninteresting style, Laval is presented as the moral conscience of New France.

Moogk, Peter N. *Le Nouvelle France: The Making of French Canada, a Cultural History*. East Lansing: Michigan State University Press, 2000. Moogk traces the roots of the current conflict between English- and French-speaking Canadians to the political and social developments that occurred in New France in the seventeenth century.

Parkman, Francis. *France and England in North America*. Edited by David Levin. Vol. 2. New York: Viking Press, 1983. In 1856, Parkman published his seven-part history of North America. Part 5, *Count Frontenac and New France Under Louis XIV*, is included in the second volume of this revised edition published in 1983. Parkman examined the role Laval played in Canada's exploration, trade, war, and missionary activity, emphasizing the political nature of Laval's achievements. The well-written book provides a balance to other, primarily religious accounts.

Rudin, Ronald. *Founding Fathers: The Celebration of Champlain and Laval in the Streets of Quebec, 1878-1908*. Toronto: University of Toronto Press, 2003. From 1878 to 1908, Quebec City celebrated its founding at four commemorative events. Although Rudin's book focuses on the staging of these celebrations, and it describes Quebecers' perceptions of the historical significance of Champlain and Laval.

SEE ALSO: Alexander VII; Saint Isaac Jogues; Louis XIV; Marie de l'Incarnation.

RELATED ARTICLE in *Great Events from History: The Seventeenth Century, 1601-1700*: April 27, 1627: Company of New France Is Chartered.

HENRY LAWES
English musician

Henry Lawes was arguably the most prolific composer of songs in seventeenth century England, and his musical output helped to establish the declamatory song as the principal style for solo music in the period. He composed music for several court masques, and he was among the favorite musicians of the Cavalier poets for his talent at setting texts to music.

BORN: January, 5, 1596 (baptized); Dinton, Wiltshire, England
DIED: October 21, 1662; London, England
AREA OF ACHIEVEMENT: Music

EARLY LIFE

Thomas Lawes, the father of Henry Lawes (LAWZ), was appointed to the position of lay vicar at Salisbury Cathedral in 1602, a post that he kept until 1632. In addition to its famous cathedral, Salisbury boasted a rich cultural and musical environment, and it is likely that in this respect Henry benefited from his family's move to Salisbury: All of the Lawes children eventually pursued careers as musicians or composers.

Although records of Henry Lawes's early education are unavailable, he would most likely have received musical training as a boy chorister in the cathedral. At some point he received training on the lute, an instrument on which he later excelled both as a performer and a composer. John Dowland's lute works were at the peak of their popularity during Henry's childhood, and his later works show that he had been deeply influenced by Dowland's style. By the time he was twenty years old, Lawes moved to London, where his brothers John and William were already establishing themselves as prominent musicians. Possibly, he received instruction there from Giovanni Coperario, the English musician who had studied in Italy and was responsible for bringing many continental methods to the English musical scene.

LIFE'S WORK

Although Henry's brother William was the first of the two to distinguish himself as a composer (he had already composed a number of court masques by 1632), Henry did manage to procure a number of royal appointments, largely on the basis of his performing talents, by the time he was thirty-five years old. In 1625, Henry Lawes was admitted to the Chapel Royal as an epistoler, or reader. In 1626, he was effectively promoted to gentleman of the Chapel Royal, a position that would have given him some musical duties in the Anglican service. In 1630 or 1631, Lawes was named a member of the King's Private Musick, a prestigious position that he held throughout his lifetime, except during the rule of Oliver Cromwell's Commonwealth, when the Chapel Royal and King's Musick were temporarily dissolved.

As was typical for an aspiring musician in seventeenth century England, Lawes sought patronage from influential figures at court, a sphere to which he had greater access following his appointment to the Chapel Royal. Sometime before 1630, Lawes had set to music certain poems written by the earl of Pembroke, a nobleman who was well known for his patronage of writers, artists, and musicians. Although it is unclear how much support Lawes received from Pembroke, his courtly connections were well established by 1630, when he was hired by the Egerton family to contribute music for an entertainment held in honor of the countess of Derby, the Egerton matriarch.

Lawes's association with the Egerton family directly led to one of the most important artistic collaborations of his career, his composition of the music for John Milton's *Comus* (pr. 1634, pb. 1637 as *A Maske Presented at Ludlow Castle*). The masque had been commissioned as part of the entertainment surrounding the ceremonial installment of the earl of Bridgewater at Ludlow Castle, and both Lawes and Milton were directly involved in the preparation and presentation of the masque (in fact, Lawes appeared as one of the singer-actors in the work).

Court masques in seventeenth century England were typically loosely structured presentations of verse, song, and dance, all contributing to a simple, usually mythological, plot that served as a thinly veiled compliment to a royal figure. As might have been expected from a poet of Milton's stature, *Comus* far exceeded previous masques in its complexity and dramatic design, and the music Lawes composed for the masque was more integral to its dramatic structure than would have been expected from a simple entertainment. For this reason, *Comus* has occasionally been designated as a precursor to English opera.

Although little record of Lawes's involvement with other masques survives, he is generally recognized as the musical contributor to Sir William Davenant's *The Triumphs of the Prince d'Amour* (pr., pb. 1636), a project to which his brother also contributed. Lawes provided the music for a number of plays performed at Oxford in 1636. During this time, he was gaining a remarkable reputation for his ability to set poems to music. Milton immortalized Lawes in one his later poems, citing the composer's talent for making words and music "agree." Moreover, Lawes's acquaintance with Oxford playwright William Cartwright led to their collaboration on "Ariadne's Lament" (pb. 1651), a long solo recitative on the myth of Ariadne and Theseus. Over the next several years, Lawes became a favorite among poets who wished to see their work set to music, including Thomas Carew, Richard Lovelace, John Suckling, John Harington, Edmund Waller, and Aurelian Townshend.

Lawes was very active in the publication of his music, a fact that most likely helped sustain his popularity during his lifetime. In addition to collaborating with Milton on the publication of *Comus*, Lawes worked with the prominent music publisher Humphrey Mosley to publish an edition of his own lyrics in 1645. This edition was followed by Lawes's *Choice Psalms Put into Music* (1648), which posthumously included settings by his brother William, and multiple volumes of the *Ayres and Dialogues* (1653-1658). The publication of his music also invariably helped Lawes remain productive during England's rule by the Commonwealth, when Lawes's royal associations effectively became defunct. Although Lawes lived to see the Restoration of Charles II, he did not enjoy the level of court patronage under the restored monarch that he had under Charles I. Lawes died in London on October 21, 1662, and was buried in Westminster Cathedral.

SIGNIFICANCE

Although Henry Lawes was deeply admired and respected during his lifetime, most twentieth century critics dismissed his musical contributions as insipid or simplistic. However, twenty-first century scholars and musicians have recognized this negative attitude as reflective of modern preferences for music that is structurally complex and that places less value on the accompanying text. Lawes often composed music with the opposite goals in mind, and in terms of the solo music of his time, his compositions are unrivaled in their melodic lyricism and in their unique ability to join words with music. Moreover, the fact that Lawes was directly active in having much of his later music published, including many of his contributions to masques and plays, ensured that a great body of seventeenth century solo music is available for performance today. For this reason (as well as for the inherent beauty of his works), much of Lawes's music is recorded and available to modern listeners.

—Joseph M. Ortiz

FURTHER READING

Buhler, Stephen M. "Counterpoint and Controversy: Milton and the Critiques of Polyphonic Music." *Milton Studies* 36 (1998). An excellent article, which cogently discusses the debates over music in seventeenth century England in which Henry Lawes was directly implicated. The essay offers a corrective view on Lawes's reputation as a composer of mainly homophonic music. Illustrations, musical examples.

Evans, Willa McClung. *Henry Lawes: Musician and Friend of Poets*. London: Oxford University Press, 1941. This is the only available book-length biography of Lawes. Because of the paucity of records of Lawes's personal life (particularly concerning the early years), this study often relies heavily on speculation, although it offers interesting details about musical life in seventeenth century England. Illustrations, bibliographical note.

Ortiz, Joseph M. "'The Reforming of Reformation': Theatrical, Ovidian, and Musical Figuration in Milton's *Maske*." *Milton Studies* 44 (2004). This essay reconsiders Henry Lawes's most well-known contribution to the English masque tradition, in light of seventeenth century Reformist ideas about music. The article particularly considers Lawes's reputation as a composer who "married" poetry and music better than any of his contemporaries.

Shawcross, John T. "Henry Lawes's Settings of Songs for Milton's *Comus*." *The Journal of the Rutgers University Library* 28 (1964): 22-28. A brief article that traces the manuscript evidence for Lawes's collaboration with Milton on the masque. This is a bibliographic rather than interpretive study and therefore not likely to be as useful for purely critical study of Lawes's music.

Spink, Ian. *Henry Lawes: Cavalier Songwriter*. New York: Oxford University Press, 2000. This is a well-argued and lucid analysis of Lawes's musical achievement throughout his career, paying particular attention to the musical settings of Cavalier poetry. The discussion is interspersed throughout with biographical details. Several musical examples, bibliography.

SEE ALSO: Charles I; Charles II (of England); Oliver Cromwell; Richard Lovelace; John Milton; Sir John Suckling.

RELATED ARTICLES in *Great Events from History: The Seventeenth Century, 1601-1700:* 1642-1651: English Civil Wars; December 6, 1648-May 19, 1649: Establishment of the English Commonwealth; May, 1659-May, 1660: Restoration of Charles II.

CHARLES LE BRUN
French painter and designer

One of the greatest French painters of the seventeenth century, Le Brun helped design and decorate the Palace of Versailles; directed the Gobelin factories that supplied tapestries, art, and furnishings to Louis XIV; and cofounded France's Royal Academy of Painting and Sculpture and the French Academy in Rome.

BORN: February 24, 1619 (baptized); Paris, France
DIED: February 12, 1690; Paris
AREAS OF ACHIEVEMENT: Art, architecture, patronage of the arts

EARLY LIFE

Charles Le Brun (shahrl luh bruhn) was one of eight children born to the sculptor Nicolas Le Brun. Charles's brothers Nicolas and Gabriel became a noted sculptor and a painter and engraver, respectively. Young Charles showed signs of talent as a sculptor and draftsman, and his father had him apprenticed at the age of thirteen to the Parisian painter François Perrier. The youth was more interested in Perrier's collection of sketches of Roman antiquities than he was in his master's lessons, however, and the association was short-lived.

Charles's mother, Julienne Lebé, had family in the king's service, and his father was working for Chancellor Pierre Séguier during Charles's youth. When he was fifteen, Charles was introduced formally to Séguier, who in turn placed him in the care of Simon Vouet, who was then painting the chancellor's library in the Hôtel de Bellegarde. Charles learned what he could, quickly grew bored, and moved to the royal palace of Fontainebleau, where he sketched and painted the masterpieces in the king's collection. He was rapidly becoming a master imitator of others' styles, including late mannerism, early Baroque, and early classical, while slowly developing a style that was distinctly his own. Le Brun returned to Séguier's employ and completed three major classical canvases for Cardinal de Richelieu, which hung in the royal palace. On June 26, 1638, he was named painter to the king.

With Séguier's financial support, letters of introduction to Pope Urban VIII and Cardinal Antonio Barberini, and the companionship of the famed French painter Nicolas Poussin, who was twenty-five years his senior, Le Brun set off for Rome in the summer of 1642. During his three-year stay, he read voraciously and created some five hundred sketches and paintings of ancient and Renaissance masterworks. He also learned to imitate Poussin's style deftly and to appreciate the mundane elements of Roman material life through his study of archeological discoveries that were finding their way into local collections. These bits of everyday life would add authenticity and a clearly classical flavor to his later historical and mythological canvases.

LIFE'S WORK

During the decade after his return from Rome, Le Brun produced numerous works, predominantly religious, for churches and convents in Paris. For the queen mother, he produced a *Crucifixion with Angels* that she considered a true masterwork. He also designed and executed secular decorative programs for several of Paris's major private palaces, or *hôtels*, including the palaces of De la Rivière, D'Aumont, and La Bazinière. His marriage to Suzanne Butay (February 26, 1647), a fellow artist's daughter, produced no children.

In 1648, with the patronage of Cardinal Jules Mazarin, Le Brun and eleven other artists created the Royal Academy of Painting and Sculpture. Centered in Paris, the academy was a direct challenge to the ancient guild system that tightly controlled the arts in the French capital. From the beginning, it provided an artistic education that supplanted the traditional apprentice system and even replaced the need for French art students to visit Rome. Le Brun played a major role in the life of the Royal Academy over the next four decades. He was elected its chancellor in 1655, rector "for life" in 1668, and director in 1683.

Le Brun oversaw a major reorganization of the academy that opened up the membership ranks in 1663, founded a series of regular lectures on theory and criticism in 1666, and established biennial exhibitions of members' work in 1667. His own lectures in 1668 and 1671 on human faces and expressions (physiognomy) were accompanied by some 250 drawings and, when printed, became a classic embodiment of seventeenth century psychology through art. Le Brun also established the French Academy in Rome (1666) as a center of art education and attempted to use the two academies to link the artistic fortunes of France and Italy.

Le Brun's decoration of the compartmented ceiling of the long gallery in the residence of Nicolas Lambert de Thorigny brought the artist to the attention of Nicolas Fouquet, King Louis XIV's ostentatious and ill-fated finance minister. From 1658 to 1660, Le Brun supervised the decoration of Fouquet's château at Vaux-le-Vicomte. He designed every detail of the building's decoration, from cabinet doorknobs to entire rooms. It was a unified artistic tour de force that rivaled contemporary *palazzi* in Florence or Rome. The expense was enormous, and shortly after Louis was fêted there, on August 17, 1661, he had Fouquet arrested for misuse of public funds.

Le Brun, on the other hand, entered Louis's service directly and was named first painter to the king (unofficially in 1661, confirmed in 1664). Already in 1660, Le Brun had produced for Louis a huge canvas, often considered his masterpiece, the *Queens of Persia at the Feet of Alexander*. It was to be the first in a series of enormous works that glorified Louis by celebrating Alexander the Great. In 1662, Le Brun received a patent of nobility, and in 1664 he was given control over all the king's art and artistic commissions. In 1663, Minister Jean-Baptiste Colbert, effectively Le Brun's protector, named him director of the Gobelin Manufactory. Though best known for its glorious tapestries, Gobelin had a virtual monopoly on the production of art, furnishings, and decorative pieces for the royal palaces, and Le Brun controlled the design process and the nearly 250 craftspeople. It was Le Brun's unified vision guiding the work of these 250 individuals that enabled Gobelin to achieve a stylistic unity that became known simply as the Louis XIV style.

Le Brun is best known as one of the three principal designers of Louis's enormous palace and grounds at Versailles. The artist worked on decorative schemes for the royal palaces in Paris (the Louvre and the Tuileries) and the royal château at Marly-le-Roi (1679-1686), and from 1671 he was the chief of decoration at Versailles. He oversaw the work on the royal apartments and personally created the magnificent Hall of Mirrors, the Salons of War and Peace, and Ambassadors' Staircase, which was destroyed during eighteenth century remodeling. He also provided a plethora of ephemeral decorations, from fireworks to triumphal arches, used in ceremonies in Paris and Versailles.

With the death in 1683 of Colbert, for whom he had decorated the château at Sceaux (finished in October, 1677), Le Brun lost his protector. His opponents, most notably Pierre Mignard, were now able to marginalize the heretofore commanding figure, despite Louis's continuing support. Though he retained his positions in the Academy and Gobelins, Le Brun's personal artistic output dwindled along with his inspiration and energy. He now spent much of his time at his château at Montmorency, which he lavishly decorated. He died one of the century's wealthiest and most influential artists.

Charles Le Brun. (Library of Congress)

SIGNIFICANCE

As Alain Merot points out, Charles Le Brun's significance has ebbed and flowed with the reputation of the academic style he helped create and champion. After a period of critical neglect, his specific contributions were rehabilitated by an exhibition of his work at Versailles in 1963 and the renewed scholarship it sparked. Versailles itself, whatever one may think or feel about its monumentality, remains a testament not only to Louis XIV but also to the genius of André Le Nôtre, Louis Le Vau, and Le Brun, whose individual visions and successful collaboration created the controversial masterpiece.

Le Brun's management of the Gobelin works ensured a stylistic unity and outstanding quality of production that mark all of the royal commissions of the first half of Louis XIV's reign. Le Brun's work with the Royal Academy, however, transcends even these achievements. In his various roles, he helped create the major national institution for the training and education of generations of French artists, an institution that eventually became the

École des Beaux Arts. His reforms strengthened the academy itself and broadened its impacts on society, laying the groundwork for the great nineteenth century *salons*. His lectures and theoretical texts established a framework for teaching and criticism that long outlived his personal influence and even that of the academic style he created by carefully toeing a line between cool classicism and sumptuous baroque.

—*Joseph P. Byrne*

FURTHER READING

Duro, Paul, ed. *The Academy and the Limits of Painting in Seventeenth-Century France.* New York: Cambridge University Press, 1997. Discussion of the Royal Academy of Painting and Sculpture, Le Brun's various roles in it, and its impact on artistic style, subject matter, and education.

Gareau, Michel. *Charles Le Brun: First Painter to King Louis XIV.* Translated by Katrin Sermat. New York: Abrams, 1992. Only monographic treatment of Le Brun in English; well illustrated in color and black and white.

Le Brun, Charles. *A Method to Learn to Design the Passions.* Los Angeles: William Andrews Clark Memorial Library, University of California, 1980. Facsimile of 1743 edition of Le Brun's work on depicting emotions.

_____. *Resemblances: Amazing Faces.* New York: Harlin Quist, 1980. Collection of plates illustrating the resemblances of human to animal physiognomy.

Merot, Alain, and Caroline Beamish. *French Painting in the Seventeenth Century.* New Haven, Conn.: Yale University Press, 1995. Chapter 11 covers Le Brun and Pierre Mignard as directors of the royal artistic programs.

Pérouse de Monclos, Jean-Marie. *Versailles.* New York: Abbeville Press, 1991. Lavishly illustrated treatment of the great palace, its landscaping, and the campaigns of building and decoration that involved Le Brun.

SEE ALSO: Jean-Baptiste Colbert; André Le Nôtre; Louis Le Vau; Louis XIV; Jules Mazarin; Nicolas Poussin; Cardinal de Richelieu; Urban VIII.

RELATED ARTICLES in *Great Events from History: The Seventeenth Century, 1601-1700*: c. 1601-1620: Emergence of Baroque Art; Mid-17th century: Dutch School of Painting Flourishes; 1661: Absolute Monarchy Emerges in France; 1673: Renovation of the Louvre; 1682: French Court Moves to Versailles; 1689-1694: Famine and Inflation in France.

FIRST DUKE OF LEEDS
English politician and statesman

Under King Charles II, Osborne was instrumental in bringing about the British two-party system by creating a court party in Parliament, which developed into the Tory Party. Later, he was the subject of two impeachment proceedings and played a pivotal role in the Glorious Revolution of 1688.

BORN: February 20, 1632; Kiveton, Yorkshire, England
DIED: July 26, 1712; Easton Neston, Northamptonshire, England
ALSO KNOWN AS: Thomas Osborne (given name); Marquis of Carmarthen; First Earl of Danby
AREA OF ACHIEVEMENT: Government and politics

EARLY LIFE
Thomas Osborne's father, the first Baronet Osborne, was a staunch Royalist from Yorkshire, where his son was born. The younger Osborne spent much of his formative years in Paris. After his father's death in 1647 and his succession to the estates and to the title of second Baronet Osborne, however, he spent more time in Yorkshire. In 1653, Osborne married Lady Bridget Bertie, daughter of the earl of Lindsay.

While in Yorkshire, Osborne became a protégé of George Villiers, second duke of Buckingham, and as the duke's star rose, so in turn did Osborne's. As an openly acknowledged monarchist, Osborne's political career did not, of course, begin until after the Restoration of Charles II in 1660. Moreover, his family's experiences during the English Civil War and the Cromwellian Protectorate had left him with a firmly Anglican viewpoint and a lifelong aversion to Protestant Dissent, which he associated with the anti-Royalist radicalism of the 1640's and 1650's and, hence, with treasonous beliefs and actions.

LIFE'S WORK
In 1661, Osborne was named to his first public office, high sheriff of Yorkshire. In 1665, he was elected member of Parliament for York. An ardent Cavalier parliamentarian, he allied himself to the high Anglican faction

and was among those who persistently assailed the comparatively moderate positions of Edward Hyde, first earl of Clarendon, and James Butler, first duke of Ormond, who were, respectively, the lord chancellor of England and the lord lieutenant of Ireland. Osborne's first significant government position was joint treasurer to the Royal Navy.

Osborne's attacks on Clarendon became progressively more strident, and in 1667, he joined with Buckingham and others to press for the lord chancellor's impeachment. Following Clarendon's flight and exile to France, Buckingham formed the famous ruling committee known as the Cabal with Henry Bennet, first earl of Arlington; Anthony Ashley Cooper (later first earl of Shaftesbury); John Maitland, second earl (later first duke) of Lauderdale; and Thomas Clifford (later first Baron Clifford of Chudleigh). Ormond was dismissed as lord lieutenant of Ireland in 1669, by which time the Cabal's grip on British political life had tightened. Throughout the Cabal's years of dominance, Osborne was never far from the seat of power, though he was not yet within the inner circle. The king granted him the titles of Baron Osborne of Kiveton, Viscount Osborne of Dunblane, and Viscount Latimer of Danby.

In 1673, Osborne became lord treasurer, and the next year, he was created earl of Danby. When the Cabal fell apart in 1674, Osborne was well-positioned, with the support of King Charles, effectively to function as the nation's chief political power broker. He became a sort of proto-prime minister. During the time he was in the ascendant (1674-1678), Osborne developed a basic political party structure that was anchored around his supporters in Parliament and at court, who adhered to a high Anglican and anti-French ideology.

It was not long before Osborne's pro-Anglican and anti-Dissenter policies provided the impetus for the formation of an organized opposition. Those who, loosely speaking, followed Osborne's orientation would eventually solidify into the Tory Party. Those, on the other hand, who favored constitutional limits on royal power enforced by Parliament, and who subscribed to pro-Dissenter policies or favored religious toleration, formed the kernel of what became the Whig (or "Country") Party. The Whigs would be led by the first earl of Shaftesbury, a former member of the Cabal.

The most controversial measure in the early years of these parties' evolution was the Test Act of 1673, which excluded all non-Anglicans from public office. The act was aimed in the first instance at Catholics, but Protestant Dissenters who refused to take Anglican Communion and

First Duke of Leeds. (Library of Congress)

affirm that the British monarch was the head of the Church of England were also disenfranchised by the law.

Osborne was equally anti-Catholic and anti-French; his primary ally was Sir William Temple, British ambassador to the United Provinces of the Netherlands. It was at this time that, through Temple, Osborne began to cultivate a close working relationship with William III, stadtholder of the Netherlands. In 1678, he was in large part responsible for bringing about William's marriage to Princess Mary, daughter of King Charles II's brother, James, duke of York, the heir to the English throne.

The strength of Osborne's commitment to the Protestant alliance with the Dutch was demonstrated during the Franco-Dutch Wars, when he persuaded the king to mobilize an army to be sent to the aid of the Netherlands. These troops were to be dispatched to protect Dutch territory from further attacks by King Louis XIV of France. The troops were not used, however, and a large number of them remained in England. It was considered necessary to avoid disbanding the units, in case the peace negotiations then under way (which ultimately resulted in the Treaty of Nijmegan) broke down. However, the continued presence of a mobilized army on English soil aroused suspicions that a Royalist, Pro-Catholic coup was in the making. Osborne was a major object of these suspicions.

The hysteria engendered by the Popish Plot of 1678 and the full disclosure of Osborne's role in the Crown's secret negotiations with France proved to be his downfall: He was impeached, attainted for treason, and held in the Tower of London. Only the king's intervention prevented his execution, and he remained incarcerated until 1685, when the duke of York acceded to the throne as King James II and issued an amnesty.

Osborne was never able to regain favor with the new monarch and became increasingly disgruntled over James II's pro-Catholic, anti-Anglican tendencies. By 1687, Osborne was in contact with agents of the king's Protestant son-in-law, William III, stadtholder of the Netherlands. By this time, too, he had rekindled his influence in Parliament, especially in the House of Lords, and had once again become a principal Tory leader. During the crisis of 1688, Osborne was among seven significant parliamentary leaders to sign an invitation to William III to invade England, an event that precipitated the Glorious Revolution and paved the way for the accession of William and Mary to the throne.

Receiving some measure of favor from the new joint monarchs, Osborne was made marquis of Carmarthen (1689), first duke of Leeds (1694), and lord president of the Privy Council. However, he would never approach the prestige and power that he had enjoyed in the 1670's as Charles II's chief minister.

In 1695, Daniel Finch, second earl of Nottingham, launched a determined campaign in Parliament against the government's foreign and domestic policies. As allegations of incompetence and corruption became ever more widespread, Osborne was included in the net. He was again impeached, this time on charges of bribery in collusion with officials of the British East India Company. As Charles II had done earlier, King William rescued Osborne (and others) by ordering the adjournment of Parliament in 1696. Though Osborne remained for a while as president of the Privy Council, relations between him and the king became increasingly strained. In 1699, after voting in favor of dismissing William's Dutch Guards, Osborne was dismissed from office. Although he continued to be sporadically active in politics and even reestablished some small measure of influence upon the succession to the throne of Queen Anne (1702), he proved to be a spent force, and his death in 1712 attracted little notice.

SIGNIFICANCE

Though in the end he was tarnished by scandal and politically marginalized, at the height of his power, Thomas Osborne, first duke of Leeds, played the pivotal, pioneering role in bringing together the dual-partisan political system of England. His actions, at the very time when Parliament decisively assumed a dominant role in the British government and put an end to the threat of absolutist monarchy, shaped the form that Parliament was to take and the means by which political power would function in Britain from then on. Moreover, Osborne's presence as a supporter of William III and Mary II contributed significantly to the legitimacy and success of the Glorious Revolution.

—Raymond Pierre Hylton

FURTHER READING

Coward, Barry. *The Stuart Age: England, 1603-1714.* Harlow, England: Pearson Education, 2003. Considering that this is mainly intended as a general work on the Stuart era, it contains an astonishingly thorough depiction of Danby's political career.

Miller, John. *The Restoration and the England of Charles II.* New York: Addison Wesley Longman, 1997. Views Danby's overall policy as nostalgic and extremely divisive and stresses his role as a champion of high church Anglicanism.

Prall, Stuart. *The Bloodless Revolution: England, 1688.* Garden City, N.Y.: Doubleday, 1972. A study that actually goes beyond the narrow scope of the title and includes a good analysis of Danby's virtues and shortcomings as a government minister political manager, plus his pivotal role in the events of 1688-1689.

Seaward, Paul. *The Restoration, 1660-1688.* London: Macmillan Education, 1991. Holds a fairly negative few of Danby's methods of parliamentary management and concludes that these methods were, in the end, more counter-productive than effective.

SEE ALSO: Charles II (of England); First Earl of Clarendon; Oliver Cromwell; James II; Louis XIV; Mary II; First Earl of Shaftesbury; William III.

RELATED ARTICLES in *Great Events from History: The Seventeenth Century, 1601-1700:* 1642-1651: English Civil Wars; December 16, 1653-September 3, 1658: Cromwell Rules England as Lord Protector; May, 1659-May, 1660: Restoration of Charles II; April 6, 1672-August 10, 1678: French-Dutch War; 1673-1678: Test Acts; August 13, 1678-July 1, 1681: The Popish Plot; 1688-1702: Reign of William and Mary; November, 1688-February, 1689: The Glorious Revolution.

ANTONI VAN LEEUWENHOEK
Dutch inventor and scientist

Leeuwenhoek discovered a new world of living organisms never before seen by human eyes after he made the undeveloped microscope a significant tool for scientific research. Considered the founder of modern microscopy, his microscope was used for more than two centuries because of its accuracy.

BORN: October 24, 1632; Delft, Holland, United Provinces (now in the Netherlands)
DIED: August 26, 1723; Delft
AREA OF ACHIEVEMENT: Science and technology

EARLY LIFE

Antoni van Leeuwenhoek (ahn-TOHN-ee vahn LAY-vehn-hewk) was the son of a basket maker, Philips Antonyszoon van Leeuwenhoek, and Margaretha. Antoni's father died when the boy was about seven, and about two years later his mother remarried. About that time, young Leeuwenhoek was sent to school at Warmond, just north of Leiden. Subsequently, he lived with an uncle, who was a lawyer serving as town clerk of Benthuizen.

Leeuwenhoek's early education must have provided a good foundation in geometry, trigonometry, and natural science, but his later writings show that he had received no instruction in Latin or modern foreign languages, and thus he had never been intended for the university.

At the age of sixteen, Leeuwenhoek was sent to Amsterdam to learn the cloth trade. After some six years, he returned to Delft as a draper, residing there for the rest of his life. In 1660, he was named chamberlain of the city hall. It was a well-paying sinecure, leaving him with a fair income, even after hiring the personnel and supplies necessary to clean, heat, and light the building.

Testifying to his mathematical ability, he was made municipal surveyor in 1677, and in 1679, he was named inspector of weights and measures. Eventually, as a result of his microscopy, he would become an "institution" in Delft, and the city would award him a special pension. As time went on, Leeuwenhoek spent fewer hours selling cloth out of the ground-floor shop in his house and more time in what today would be called his laboratory.

Leeuwenhoek was married twice, the first time to Barbara de Mey, a draper's daughter, in 1654. They had five children, but only one, Maria, survived. She kept house for her father in later years. Daughter Barbara died in 1666, and Leeuwenhoek married a clergyman's daughter, Cornelia van der Swalm, in 1671. Cornelia may have borne a child who failed to survive, but in 1694, she too died, leaving Leeuwenhoek with no new children.

Numerous writers have agreed that Leeuwenhoek grew interested in lenses because drapers used magnifying glasses to check the weave and to count the number of threads per inch in cloth. Yet a later researcher, Brian J. Ford, credits Leeuwenhoek's acquaintance with *Micrographia* (1665), by the English scientist Robert Hooke as the inspiration for Leeuwenhoek's move into microscopy. Leeuwenhoek apparently studied the illustrations and had sections of the book translated for him by friends.

The ingenious and meticulous Leeuwenhoek was self-taught. He seems to have done virtually everything on his own and owed little except his mathematical and drapery training to anyone else. Even his Dutch, his only language, was colloquial and nonliterary. The learned world would have paid no attention to such a man, unless his work was undeniably brilliant.

LIFE'S WORK

Leeuwenhoek was a proper, middle-class Dutch burgher. He wore respectable clothing and a wig, had the

Antoni van Leeuwenhoek. (Library of Congress)

delicate hands of a craftsperson, and possessed the keen eyesight and patience needed for detailed observation through the microscope. He was a man of presence, with a broad face and a large nose, and must have possessed an excellent constitution, for he lived to be almost ninety-one years of age.

It was apparently a Delft research physician and friend who enabled Leeuwenhoek to make connection with the Royal Society, a newly formed scientific organization in England. Leeuwenhoek had begun experimenting with microscopes in the late 1660's, and by 1673 he had made enough startling observations that it was time for him to be discovered. He wrote his findings in lengthy, rambling letters that for the remaining fifty years of his life were regularly published in *Philosophical Transactions of the Royal Society*. The first selection of extracts from these letters were published by the society as *A Specimen of Some Observations Made by a Microscope* (1673).

Thus, the scientific world became aware of the work of the amazing Dutchman. He had not invented the microscope—indeed, microscopes had been used for at least half a century—but Leeuwenhoek's skill at lens grinding, along with his patient and insightful mind, made him the father of modern microscopy.

In his first letter to the Royal Society, Leeuwenhoek anonymously criticized famous scientist and society member Hooke for accepting the idea of spontaneous generation of life. Leeuwenhoek had already seen that life comes from life and that maggots in meat, for example, do not simply appear but are produced from eggs laid by adult flies. He later extended his research debunking spontaneous generation by work on fleas, weevils, shellfish, and eels.

In 1680, the then secretary of the Royal Society, Hooke, proposed Leeuwenhoek for actual society membership, and he was unanimously elected. Cognizant of the honor, Leeuwenhoek remained devoted to the English organization and to no other for the rest of his life.

Leeuwenhoek's countryman Christiaan Huygens, the greatest educated scientist whom the Netherlands produced in the seventeenth century, spent many years in France and translated many of Leeuwenhoek's early letters into French for publication.

Hooke's microscopic work dealt primarily with insects and plant and animal tissue, and he is mainly famous for using his low-power microscope to discern and name the cells in cork. Later, under Leeuwenhoek's influence, he built a microscope of Leeuwenhoek's description and did additional work. No "regular" scientist of that century—including Hooke, Huygens, and Leeuwenhoek—was both able and willing to grind the lenses and stare through them for the uncounted hours necessary to discern what was really happening in the microscopic world.

Leeuwenhoek was very accurate at estimating the relative and absolute sizes of the things he observed. The great Italian microscopist Marcello Malpighi had demonstrated in 1660 the existence of blood capillaries, but he could not see red blood cells clearly. It would be Dutch naturalist Jan Swammerdam who most likely was the first to clearly observe red blood cells through a microscope (between 1658 and 1665, although the precise date is unknown). Leeuwenhoek, however, not only gave the world's first accurate description of red corpuscles but also correctly calculated the diameter of the red blood cell at one three-thousandth of an inch—amazingly close to the modern value. He described his findings in a 1688 letter to the society (reprinted as *On the Circulation of the Blood*, 1962).

The instrument Leeuwenhoek employed was the simple microscope, one with a single, beadlike lens

LEEUWENHOEK RESPONDS TO A MISCONCEPTION

Antoni van Leeuwenhoek happened upon a book that mentions a claim by Cornelis Bontekoe, a contemporary, that Leeuwenhoek believed human sperm cells are made up of "little infants and so on." In a letter dated March 30, 1685, Leeuwenhoek counters Bontekoe's recollection of his visits with Leeuwenhoek.

Recently a little book is fallen into my hands, named *Collectanea Medico Physica*, in which C[h]apt. 5. Pag[e]. 8 among others is said: "But the most strangiest story is, that the scholar [M]r. Cornelis Bontekoe told us (on good authority) from the curious Leeuwenhoek, that the human sperm is abundant of little infants and so on in the nature of things." Indeed, it is true that mister Bontekoe has visited me several times; However, I never have used such arguments to him, nor to anybody in the world, namely that human sperm is abundant of little infants: but I did say that there were plenty of living animals or verms [worms] in it, having long tails, and it is just that construction I showed in the figure.

Source: Warnar A. W. Moll, "Antonie van Leeuwenhoek." http://www .euronet.nl/users/warnar/leeuwenhoek.html. Accessed April, 2005.

mounted in a hole between two small metal plates riveted together. An arrangement of three screws moved the object to the proper position in front of the lens, and the entire apparatus, no bigger than the palm of one's hand, was held to the eye for viewing. There were no tubes and no compound lenses. Hooke, with a compound lens, could achieve only a magnification of around fifty diameters, but Leeuwenhoek's instruments have been calculated to have attained some 266 power. It has been estimated that some of his microscopes no longer in existence must have attained about 500 power magnification in order for him to have discerned the detail that he described.

Leeuwenhoek's microscopes were so simple that he made more than five hundred of them, of which there are about nine known to be extant. Rather than disturb an interesting specimen that was properly mounted, he would often construct another microscope. His lenses were ground, never blown, and were convex on both sides. Leeuwenhoek kept his best observation technique secret, but it has been surmised from an obscure comment in one letter that he used dark field illumination for contrast. He did not employ any staining method.

Leeuwenhoek devoted much time to scrutinizing plant and animal tissue, but his best efforts were made observing microbes. He watched the movements of every kind of "animalcule," as he termed the tiny creatures that danced, darted, floated, and vibrated under his lens. He saw protozoa, smaller organisms called bacteria, and human spermatozoa, and he studied algae, yeasts, and molds. He found these organisms everywhere—in his rain barrel, in his mouth, in nearby ponds and canals, and in the soil. He was better at verbal than at artistic description, and so he retained the services of draftsmen to produce pictures of what he saw. In this effort, it is possible that his early work was assisted by his friend and neighbor Jan Vermeer, one of the best and most precise artists of all time.

The homegrown scientist not only studied how animalcules and insects reproduced but also experimented with what would kill them. He found that pepper water would kill many microbes, that nutmeg would kill mites, and that sulfur dioxide would kill moths. He never seems to have suspected, however, that some of these tiny animals would be able to kill him. Leeuwenhoek was even visited by Hermann Boerhaave of nearby Leiden University, and the august personage gravely peered through the microscopes. Professor of medicine, botany, and chemistry, and a cofellow of the Royal Society with Leeuwenhoek, Boerhaave had turned Leiden into Europe's best-known medical center of the time. Thus, as

---

LEEUWENHOEK EXPLAINS THE STUFF BETWEEN AND UPON TEETH

In a 1683 letter titled "Containing Some Microbial Observations, About Animals in the Scurf of the Teeth...," Leeuwenhoek explains the "animals" he saw in human mouths when looking through a microscope. The letter was abstracted and then published in a journal of the Royal Society of London.

The Spittle of an old Man that had lived soberly, had no Animals in it; But the substance upon and between his Teeth, had a great many living Creatures, swimming nimbler then I had hitherto seen. . . .

The Spittle of another old man and a good fellow was like the former, but the Animals in the scurf [surface flakes or foul remnants] of the teeth, were not all killed by the parties continual drinking Brandy, Wine, and Tobacco, for I found a few living Animals of the 3d. sort, and in the scurf between the Teeth I found many more small Animals of the 2 smallest sorts. I took in my mouth some very strong wine-Vinegar, and closing my Teeth, I gargled and rinsed them very well with the Vinegar, afterwards I washt them very well with fair water, but there were an innumerable quant'ty of Animals yet remaining in the scurf upon the Teeth, yet most in that between the Teeth, and very few Animals of the first sort A.

I took a very little wine-Vinegar and mixt it with the water in which the scurf was dissolved, whereupon the Animals dyed presently. From hence I conclude, that the Vinegar with which I washt my Teeth, kill'd only those Animals which were on the outside of the scurf, but did not pass thro the whole substance of it.

Source: From "An Abstract of a Letter from Anthony Leewenhoeck at Delft, Dated Sept. 17, 1683." *Philosophical Transactions of the Royal Society of London* 14, no. 159 (May 20, 1684), pp. 569, 570.

---

he drew no medical conclusions from observing the animalcules, Leeuwenhoek can certainly be forgiven for not doing so. That microbes were the source of many human diseases remained virtually unknown for another two centuries.

Asking himself how microbes came to inhabit a previously sterile medium, Leeuwenhoek concluded that they were borne on the very dust motes of the air. In fact, there were few questions that Leeuwenhoek did not ask, but as a solitary and untutored investigator ahead of his time, the miracle is that Leeuwenhoek did what he did in the first place.

SIGNIFICANCE

Leeuwenhoek is recognized as having founded the disciplines of bacteriology and protozoology. Strangely, however, he established no school of followers. He had no disciples, and he refused to train younger men to succeed him. Even though Leeuwenhoek did not train others and establish a tradition of excellent microscopy, posterity does know what he did in his half-century of research, as he wrote some two hundred lengthy and illustrated letters to the Royal Society, letters that were published in English translation. The Royal Society also received twenty-six microscopes bequeathed in Leeuwenhoek's will—the only instruments he ever relinquished so far as is known. The society treasured them for years but eventually lost them. Luckily, the original letters were preserved.

Some of Leeuwenhoek's best work was done when he was in his seventies and early eighties, mainly dealing with nonparasitical protozoa living in water. By that time, Leeuwenhoek was an international institution, a phenomenon to whom all paid tribute. The University of Louvain sent Leeuwenhoek a silver medal in 1716 to honor him for his work, and he was visited by numerous potentates and crowned heads of state.

Several editions of Leeuwenhoek's collected letters appeared in Dutch and in Latin while he was still alive. He was not a man who was forgotten until he had been long dead. He had looked deeper and longer into the microscopic universe than had any other person of his time, and his world honored him. He was largely overlooked by the next several generations, until he was rediscovered in the nineteenth century, an enigmatic precursor of a science regarded as absolutely fundamental to an understanding of nature.

—*Allan D. Charles*

FURTHER READING

Bender, George A., and Robert A. Thom. *Great Moments in Medicine: A History of Medicine in Pictures*. Detroit, Mich.: Northwood Institute Press, 1966. Contains an excellent chapter on Leeuwenhoek, recounting his life and work. There is an excellent illustration of the microscopist and his workshop based on the four life portraits that were actually made of Leeuwenhoek and on other surviving artifacts and information.

De Kruif, Paul. *Microbe Hunters*. London: Jonathan Cape, 1926. Reprint. New York: Pocket Books, 1950. This well-written work provides a long chapter on Leeuwenhoek, whom de Kruif justifiably labels "first of the microbe hunters." De Kruif conveys the excitement Leeuwenhoek must have felt at making humankind's first forays into the subvisible world.

Dobell, Clifford. *Antoni van Leeuwenhoek and His "Little Animals": Being Some Account of the Father of Protozoology and Bacteriology and His Multifarious Discoveries in These Disciplines*. 1932. Reprint. New York: Russell & Russell, 1958. The standard biography of Leeuwenhoek in English. Dobell, himself a microscopist and also an excellent linguist and scholar, researched old Dutch records to uncover everything that could be found on Leeuwenhoek. He quotes and comments on Leeuwenhoek's letters and provides ample footnotes to explain sources and methods.

Ford, Brian J. *Single Lens: The Story of the Simple Microscope*. New York: Harper & Row, 1985. This book gives the history of the development and use of the simple microscope from the period before Leeuwenhoek's discoveries through the nineteenth century. More than half of the book is devoted to Leeuwenhoek. The author, also a microscopist, performed research that provided him information not available in earlier publications.

Fournier, Marian. *The Fabric of Life: Microscopy in the Seventeenth Century*. Baltimore, Md.: Johns Hopkins University Press, 1996. Examines the work of Leeuwenhoek and four other scientists to explain the reasons for the microscope's appearance and eventual eclipse in the seventeenth century.

Huerta, Robert D. *Giants of Delft: Johannes Vermeer and the Natural Philosophers: The Parallel Search for Knowledge During the Age of Discovery*. Lewisburg, Pa.: Bucknell University Press, 2003. Although this book focuses on Vermeer's perception of the world, it describes how that perception was influenced by the microscope and other discoveries in the science of optics. Several chapters describe how Leeuwenhoek, Galileo, and other scientists created a "more optical" way of viewing the world.

Palm, L. C., and H. A. M. Snelders, eds. *Antoni van Leeuwenhoek, 1632-1723: Studies on the Life and Work of the Delft Scientist Commemorating the 350th Anniversary of His Birthday*. Amsterdam: Rodopi, 1982. A collection of articles exploring Leeuwenhoek's enduring legacy and topics such as his education, his microscopes, his mechanistic worldview, and intellectual opposition to his work. Bibliography, index.

Ruestow, Edward G. *The Microscope in the Dutch Re-*

public: *The Shaping of Discovery*. New York: Cambridge University Press, 1996. Describes the work of Leeuwenhoek and Jan Swammerdam, discussing how their uneasiness with their social circumstances spurred their discoveries. Ruestow describes how their discoveries were both aided and impeded by some aspects of contemporary Dutch culture.

Schierbeek, Abraham. *Measuring the Invisible World: The Life and Works of Antoni van Leeuwenhoek*. London: Abelard-Schuman, 1959. An abridged translation of a two-volume biography written in Dutch, containing a biographical chapter written by Maria Rooseboom. Provides a good overview of Leeuwenhoek's life and work.

SEE ALSO: William Harvey; Jan Baptista van Helmont; Robert Hooke; Christiaan Huygens; Marcello Malpighi; Nicolaus Steno; Jan Swammerdam; Jan Vermeer.

RELATED ARTICLES in *Great Events from History: The Seventeenth Century, 1601-1700:* 17th century: Advances in Medicine; 1660's-1700: First Microscopic Observations; 1672-1684: Leeuwenhoek Discovers Microscopic Life.

GOTTFRIED WILHELM LEIBNIZ
German philosopher and mathematician

Leibniz contributed to the development of rationalist metaphysics and a dynamic theory of motion. Contrary to Descartes, he believed that activity, and not extension, is essential to substance. He coined the term "monad" to refer to these fundamental units of existence, metaphysical entities that are not extended and are not of a material nature but are dynamic units of psychic activity.

BORN: July 1, 1646; Leipzig, Saxony (now in Germany)

DIED: November 14, 1716; Hanover (now in Germany)

AREAS OF ACHIEVEMENT: Philosophy, mathematics

EARLY LIFE

Gottfried Wilhelm Leibniz (GAWT-freet VIHL-hehlm LIP-nihts) was born into an academic family; his mother's father was a professor, as was his own father (who died when Leibniz was six). Leibniz was intellectually gifted; he taught himself Latin and read profusely in the classics at an early age. When he was an adolescent, Leibniz began to entertain the notion of constructing an alphabet of human thought from which he could generate a universal, logically precise language. He regarded this language as consisting of primitive simple words expressing primitive simple concepts that are then combined into larger language complexes expressing complex thoughts. His obsession with this project played an important role throughout his life.

Leibniz was formally educated at the University of Leipzig, where he received his bachelor's and master's degrees for theses on jurisprudence, and at the University of Altdorf, where he received a doctorate in law in 1666. He declined a professorship at Altdorf and entered employment as secretary of the Rosicrucian Society. Even-

Gottfried Wilhelm Leibniz. (Library of Congress)

tually he was employed as a legal counsel by Johann Philipp von Schönborn, a governing official of Mainz.

LIFE'S WORK

Leibniz's philosophy was rationalist. According to this theory, human knowledge has its origins in the fundamental laws of thought instead of in human experience of the world as in the doctrine of empiricism. In fact, Leibniz argued that the laws of science could be deduced from fundamental metaphysical principles and that observation and empirical work were not necessary for arriving at knowledge of the world. What was needed instead was a proper method of calculating or demonstrating everything contained in certain fundamental tenets. For example, he believed that he could deduce the fundamental laws of motion from more basic metaphysical principles. In this general conception, he followed in the intellectual footsteps of René Descartes. The great problem with interpreting Leibniz's contribution to this tradition of thought is that he published only one major book during his lifetime, and it does not contain a systematic account of his full philosophy. Accordingly, it is necessary to reconstruct his system from his short articles and his more than fifteen thousand letters.

Leibniz's youthful dreams of constructing a perfect language quickly evolved into a theory of necessary and contingent propositions. He claimed that in every true affirmation the predicate is contained in the subject. This idea evolved from his conception of a perfect language that (in all of its true, complex statements) would perfectly reflect the universe. The true propositions of this language are necessarily true, and all necessary proposi-

tions are, according to Leibniz, ultimately reducible to identity statements. Such a conception was more plausible in the case of purely mathematical statements since, for example, $4 = 2 + 2$ can be equated with $4 = 4$.

Yet this conception seemed impossible in the case of contingent statements such as "the house is blue." Leibniz avoided this problem by arguing that the necessity in what appears as contingent truths can be revealed (or resolved) only through an infinite analysis and therefore can be carried out in full only by God. It follows that, for humans, all contingent truths are only more or less probably true. Such truths are guaranteed by the principle of sufficient reason, which states that there must be some reason for whatever is the case. Necessary truths, or truths of reason, on the other hand, are guaranteed by the principle of contradiction, which states that the denial of such a truth is a contradiction (though this can be known only by God). A logical principle closely related to the principle of sufficient reason is the notion of the "identity of indiscernibles," now known as Leibniz's law. This principle states that it is impossible for two things to differ only numerically, that is, to be distinct yet have no properties that differ; if two things are distinct, there must be some reason for their distinctness.

Leibniz had elaborated the rudiments of his metaphysical system while at Mainz, but it was during his sojourn in Paris that his philosophy matured. In 1672, he was sent to Paris on a diplomatic mission for the German princes to persuade King Louis XIV to cease military activities in Europe and send forces to the Middle East. Leibniz remained in Paris for four years, and, though he failed to even gain an audience with the monarch, he met frequently with the greatest minds of the day, such as Christiaan Huygens, Nicolas de Malebranche, Antoine Arnauld, and Simon Foucher. He also carried out studies of the mathematics of Blaise Pascal and René Descartes, and built one of the first computers—a calculating machine able to multiply very large numbers. While residing in Paris, he also made a brief trip to England, where he met with Irish chemist Robert Boyle and visited the Royal Society, to which he was elected.

When he returned to Hanover, he accepted a post as director of the library to John Frederick, the duke of Brunswick, where he remained for the next ten years. It was only after working with Huygens in Paris on the nature of motion that Leibniz finally came to grips with the problem of the continuum. On his

---

LEIBNIZ'S MAJOR WORKS	
1666	*Dissertatio de arte combinatoria*
1686	*Discours de métaphysique* (pb. 1846; *Discourse on Metaphysics*, 1902)
1704	*Nouveaux essais sur l'entendement humain* (pb. 1765; *New Essays Concerning Human Understanding*, 1896)
1710	*Essais de théodicée sur la bonté de Dieu, la liberté de l'homme et l'origine du mal* (*Theodicy: Essays on the Goodness of God, the Freedom of Man, and the Origin of Evil*, 1951)
1714	*La Mondologie* (pb. 1840; also published as *Lehrsütze über die Monadologie*, 1720; *Monadology*, 1867)
1714	*Principes de la nature et de la grâce fondés en raison* (pb. 1768?; *The Principles of Nature and of Grace*, 1890)

return trip from Paris, during which he visited philosopher Baruch Spinoza in Holland, he composed "Pacidius Philalethi" (1676), an extended analysis of this subject. This issue is traced back to the ancient Greeks and concerns the problem of resolving the motion of an object into its motions over discrete parts of space. If the body must pass through each successive parcel of space between two points, then it can never get from one point to another, since there are an infinity of such discrete parcels between any two points. It was in the context of this problem of motion and the continuum that Leibniz developed, in 1676, the differential calculus, publishing his results in 1684. Sir Isaac Newton had already discovered the calculus but did not publish his results until 1693, several years after Leibniz published his discoveries. Priority of discovery is accorded to Newton though the consensus now is that they arrived at the calculus independently.

Leibniz argued that Cartesian physics renders motion ultimately inexplicable on the basis of fundamental concepts, since it is grounded in the notion of matter as extension and does not accommodate dynamic properties. For Leibniz, the fundamental tenet is that activity is essential to substance. Substantial being is what is simple—what can be conceived by itself and what causes itself. The term "monad" was adopted by Leibniz to refer to this fundamental unit of existence. Monads are metaphysical entities that are not extended and are not of a material nature but are units of psychic activity. All entities are monadic, from God, the supreme monad who has created all the other grades of monads, to the lowest grade of being. The universe of monads is divided into two realms on the scale of perfection, that of nature and that of grace.

Because monadic substances are psychic rather than material, Leibniz's philosophy has been labeled "panpsychistic idealism." On the level of phenomena, Leibniz retained a mechanical model: Matter in the phenomenal realm is "secondary matter," composed of monadic substances and having mass. Yet, according to Leibniz, substances and monads do not interact with each other. The universe consists of an infinity of such monadic substances, individuated by the principle of indiscernability and each of which undergoes changes. This change in the monad occurs entirely because of its own nature, according to a logically necessary law and not because of effects coming to it from outside. All these changes in the monads have been harmonized by God into what appears as a causal order. Leibniz referred to this as the "way of preestablished harmony" and likened it to the synchronized sounding of two clocks. Since each monad/substance is

---

LEIBNIZ'S METHOD OF REASON

Gottfried Wilhelm Leibniz believed foremost in the power and necessity of reason for solving all problems, not just mathematical or scientific ones. He wanted to find a way to calculate and note philosophical, moral, and ethical thoughts, beliefs, and concerns with precision and certainty by using signs and characters.

It is manifest that if we could find characters or signs appropriate to the expression of all thoughts as definitely and as exactly as numbers are expressed by arithmetic or lines by geometrical analysis, we could in all subjects, in so far as they are amenable to reasoning, accomplish what is done in Arithmetic and Geometry.

All inquiries which depend on reasoning would be performed by the transposition of characters and by a kind of calculus which would directly assist the discovery of elegant results. We should not have to puzzle our heads as much as we have to-day, and yet we should be sure of accomplishing everything the given facts allowed.

Moreover, we should be able to convince the world of what we had discovered or inferred, since it would be easy to verify the calculation either by doing it again or by trying tests similar to the of casting out nines in arithmetic. And if someone doubted my results, I should say to him "Let us calculate, Sir," and so by taking pen and ink we should soon settle the question.

Source: Leibniz, *On Method* (1677), excerpted in *The Age of Reason: The Culture of the Seventeenth Century,* edited by Leo Weinstein (New York: George Braziller, 1965), pp. 88-89.

---

completely independent of all the others, Leibniz said (in his later writings) that they are "windowless"; that is, they do not look out on the world. Though this conception may appear to be rather unusual, it does account for the plurality of existents in the universe, since the substances are infinite and independent of one another.

The changes of a monad are changes in the degree to which it expresses the universe. This expression or "perception" occurs on all levels of being; all individuals express the rest of the universe through the changes that occur in it. Since each individual represents all individuals, metaphysical accommodation is made of the unity of the universe in the diversity of an infinity of monads. An exhaustive specification of the nature of one substance/monad would give an exhaustive specification of the natures of all other substances/monads (from a particular point of view). Since such a specification would be logically necessary (in any true assertion the predicate is contained in the subject), the complete description of the universe is a tautology, though this could only be fully known by God.

The characteristics of the monad, activity and perception, are analogous to the features of the mental lives of human beings. In connection with the notion of perception, Leibniz later introduced the notion of "apperception." In *Principes de la nature et de la grâce, fondés en raison* (1714; *The Principles of Nature and of Grace*, 1890), he distinguished between perceiving the outer world and apperceiving the inner state of the monad (which is self-consciousness in a human being). In fact, differences between monads relate to their degree of clarity of perception and the presence of perception or apperception. At the bottom of the hierarchy of being are monads with confused perception and unselfconscious appetition. Leibniz's theory of human understanding is developed in his *Nouveaux essais sur l'entendement humain* (1765; *New Essays Concerning Human Understanding*, 1896), written in response to English philosopher John Locke but not published in his lifetime. The perceptions of the human soul are expressions of the perceptions occurring in the body and are confused and unclear. Since all changes occur according to internal principles, all the ideas of the human mind are innate.

Leibniz was the first thinker to employ explicitly the notion of the unconscious, which he did in connection with the distinction between apperception and perception—not all perceptions are apperceived. These perceptions he refers to as "petites perceptions" and gives as his favored example the sound of a wave crashing on the beach; the sound is composed of tiny perceptions of droplets hitting the beach; although one is *unaware* of the droplets hitting the beach, one still *perceives* them (hears the sounds they make).

During his years in Hanover, Leibniz grew very close to Sophia, the wife of his patron Ernest Augustus, first elector of Hanover, and to Sophia's daughter, Sophia Charlotte, who became the first queen of Prussia. Leibniz discussed many philosophical ideas with them, and from these conversations arose his only published book, *Essais de théodicée sur la bonté de Dieu, la liberté de l'homme, et l'origine du mal* (1710; *Theodicy*, 1951). In this text, Leibniz argued along Augustinian lines that evil exists in the world because the world could not be as good as it actually is without the evil that it contains. In fact, out of all the possible universes, Leibniz believed, this universe contains the greatest amount of good. This

conception earned for Leibniz's theories the appellation a "philosophy of optimism."

Toward the end of his life, Leibniz became embroiled in an intellectual dispute with Samuel Clarke, a disciple of Newton. Leibniz claimed that Newtonian physics had contributed to a general decline of religion in England. Clarke defended Newtonian physics against this charge, while Leibniz attacked Newton's conceptions on philosophical grounds in a series of letters. Leibniz asserted that the notions of absolute space and absolute time violated the principle of sufficient reason and that the concept of gravity introduced the incomprehensible notion of action at a distance. Leibniz had earlier argued that space and time have no substantive existence and are only the ordered relations between coexistent entities and the ordering of successively existent entities, respectively. The death of Leibniz ended the debate with Clarke, who immediately published the correspondence. In spite of his extensive contacts with savants throughout Europe, Leibniz's death on November 14, 1716, was relatively unnoticed.

SIGNIFICANCE

Leibniz remained in the humble employ of royal patrons his whole life, though at one point he was offered the position of head librarian at the Vatican, which he declined to accept. In 1700, the Berlin Society of Sciences was founded, and Leibniz was elected president for life. Throughout his life, Leibniz speculated about grandiose social-intellectual projects. He advocated the Christian conquest of the pagan lands, the compilation of a universal encyclopedia of human knowledge, the reuniting of the Protestant and Catholic churches, and the restoration of peace in Europe under the Holy Roman Empire. In a true Enlightenment spirit, Leibniz also advocated the establishment of scientific academies throughout the world and actually corresponded with Peter the Great concerning such an academy for Russia. In spite of such visionary plans, Leibniz was very conservative politically; he did not criticize existing institutions and was opposed to innovation in moral and religious matters. Yet he was friendly to all, avid of learning of the world from everyone he encountered.

Leibniz had a tremendous influence on his contemporaries. Virtually all philosophers in Germany were Leibnizian during the years after his death. One early Leibnizian who proved to be equally influential in Germany was Christian von Wolff. Wolff had corresponded with Leibniz from 1704 to 1716 on mathematical and philosophical topics. Wolff taught the Leibnizian system to Martin Knutzen, who in turn taught it to Immanuel Kant, who long remained a Leibnizian. One of Kant's early essays in metaphysics was on the principle of sufficient reason and its relation to the logical principles of identity and contradiction.

Writing in the light of the Lisbon earthquake of 1756, Voltaire bitterly satirized the philosophical optimism of Leibniz (along with Alexander Pope) in his work *Candide: Ou, L'Optimisme* (1759; *Candide: Or, All for the Best*, 1759). Leibniz's philosophical influence is still evident to this day. His law concerning the identity of indiscernibles is the starting point of much of the work done in the twenty-first century on semantics, and his notions of necessity and possibility are the ancestors of work by contemporary modal logicians on the nature of necessity.

—*Mark Pestana*

FURTHER READING

Broad, C. D. *Leibniz: An Introduction*. New York: Cambridge University Press, 1975. A compilation of the lecture notes used by Broad, published after his death. Reconstructs and analyzes the whole of Leibniz's philosophy.

Hostler, John. *Leibniz's Moral Philosophy*. New York: Barnes & Noble Books, 1975. A full study of the metaethical dimensions of Leibniz's metaphysics. Argues that the metaphysics is worked out in the framework of his systematic moral ideas.

Jolley, Nicholas. *Leibniz and Locke: A Study of the New Essays on Human Understanding*. New York: Oxford University Press, 1984. A study of Leibniz's response to Locke. Attempts to substantiate the notion that the guiding motive of Leibniz in writing his study was to refute Locke's materialism.

_____, ed. *The Cambridge Companion to Leibniz*. New York: Cambridge University Press, 1995. Thirteen essays examine Leibniz's life, his theories of metaphysics, knowledge, and morality, and his reception in the eighteenth century.

Leibniz, Gottfried Wilhelm. *The Monadology and Other Philosophical Writings*. Translated with an introduction and notes by Robert Latta. Oxford, England: Clarendon Press, 1898. Contains a two-hundred-page introduction to the whole of Leibniz's philosophy. Extensive discussion of his influence on the development of psychology in late nineteenth century Germany.

McRae, Robert. *Leibniz: Perception, Apperception, and Thought*. Toronto, Canada: University of Toronto Press, 1976. Focuses on Leibniz's theory of knowledge and attempts to explain how perception and apperception combine to provide for thought.

Mates, Benson. *The Philosophy of Leibniz: Metaphysical Underpinnings*. New York: Oxford University Press, 1986. This is an excellent introductory work on Leibniz, written by a logician. Covers all aspects of his general metaphysics.

Rescher, Nicholas. *Leibniz: An Introduction to His Philosophy*. Totowa, N.J.: Rowman and Littlefield, 1979. Argues that Leibniz's unorthodox metaphysical system is ultimately aimed at providing a foundation for utterly orthodox views in ethics and religion.

_____. *On Leibniz*. Pittsburgh, Pa.: University of Pittsburgh Press, 2003. Eleven essays examine key aspects of Leibniz's philosophy, personality, and personal and scholarly development. The final chapter explores how current issues in the philosophy of science can be addressed in terms of Leibniz's principles.

Russell, Bertrand. *A Critical Exposition of the Philosophy of Leibniz*. Cambridge, England: Cambridge University Press, 1900. An important work, arguing that Leibniz's philosophy can be understood in terms of five fundamental principles that are ultimately inconsistent.

Rutherford, Donald, and J. A. Cover, eds. *Leibniz: Nature and Freedom*. New York: Oxford University Press, 2005. A collection of essays exploring Leibniz's ideas on free will, determinism, and the philosophy of nature.

SEE ALSO: Pierre Bayle; The Bernoulli Family; Robert Boyle; Tommaso Campanella; Anne Conway; René Descartes; Elizabeth of Bohemia; Pierre de Fermat; Pierre Gassendi; Thomas Hobbes; John Locke; Duchess of Newcastle; Sir Isaac Newton; Blaise Pascal; Samuel von Pufendorf; Wilhelm Schickard; Baruch Spinoza; Wang Fuzhi.

RELATED ARTICLES in *Great Events from History: The Seventeenth Century, 1601-1700:* 1601-1672: Rise of Scientific Societies; November, 1602: First Modern Libraries in Europe; 1609-1619: Kepler's Laws of Planetary Motion; 1615-1696: Invention and Development of the Calculus; 1623-1674: Earliest Calculators Appear; 1637: Descartes Publishes His *Discourse on Method*; 1654: Pascal and Fermat Devise the Theory of Probability; 1667: Pufendorf Advocates a Unified Germany; Summer, 1687: Newton Formulates the Theory of Universal Gravitation.

JACOB LEISLER
German-born colonial American merchant, politician, and religious leader

As the acting leader of colonial New York from 1689 to 1691, Jacob Leisler established a legislative assembly that was not dominated by wealthy landowners and merchants. Later proponents of democratic representation were sometimes called Leislerians.

BORN: March 31, 1640 (baptized); Frankfurt-am-Main (now in Germany)
DIED: May 16, 1691; New York, New York
AREA OF ACHIEVEMENT: Government and politics

EARLY LIFE

Jacob Leisler (YAH-kawp LIS-luhr) was born into a prominent family of Calvinist ministers and bankers. His father was the Reverend Jacob Victorian Leisler, minister of a French Huguenot congregation in Frankfurt-am-Main, Germany. After the Reverend Leisler died in 1653, the family moved to Hanau, and Jacob attended a Protestant military academy. As a member of the Calvinist elite, he had early contacts with leading Calvinist intellectuals and leaders in both Europe and New England. In 1658, he moved to Amsterdam, where he worked as a translator for a wealthy shareholder of the Dutch West India Company. In 1660, the company appointed him as an officer of troops in the Dutch colony of New Netherland.

Soon after Leisler settled in New Amsterdam, he entered into the trading business. His exports included furs, tobacco, fish, whale oil, and agricultural products. He imported spices, finished cloth, indentured servants, and slaves. He quickly acquired the reputation of a hardworking and skillful trader. In 1663, he married a wealthy widow, Elsie Tymens van der Veen, and the couple eventually had seven children. By the time of his marriage, Leisler was investing money in land, and despite his youth, he was acquiring a substantial amount of wealth.

LIFE'S WORK

In August of 1664, when the English invading fleet (led by James, duke of York and future King James II) arrived at the tip of Manhattan, Leisler was among the prominent citizens who signed a remonstrance urging Governor Peter Stuyvesant to surrender. Following the surrender on September 7, Leisler quickly swore his allegiance to the duke of York's new regime. Although the duke of York confiscated the property of the Dutch West India Company, he confirmed existing property rights of individual settlers. Leisler continued his business ventures with few changes, and he frequently served as a court-appointed arbitrator of economic disputes.

Leisler proved to be quite skillful at adapting to changing political regimes. When the Dutch recaptured New York in 1673, he became one of the advisers to the Dutch governor, and he also worked as a tax assessor. The next year, when New York was returned to the British, Leisler obtained the position of New York agent for Maryland governor Thomas Notely. Becoming increasingly active in civic affairs, Leisler was appointed commissioner to the Admiralty Court in 1683 and a New York County justice of the peace in 1685. For many years, he also served as a militia captain and was recognized by the mid-1680's as the senior captain of the militia.

Leisler also remained an enthusiastic member of the Dutch Reformed Church in New York. By 1670, he was a deacon and a member of the consistory. In 1676, he became embroiled in a religious controversy when he declared that the preaching of a minister in Albany, Reverend Nicholas Van Rensselaer, did not conform to the orthodox creeds of the Reformed faith. When the minister sued him, the suit divided the citizens of New York until the governor ordered its end. In 1685, when Louis XIV terminated the rights of French Huguenots in France, Leisler led in the establishment of a refuge for them in New Rochelle. At this time, he left the Dutch Church and became a founding elder of the first French Huguenot Church in New York City.

In July of 1688, when King James II annexed New York to the Dominion of New England, committed Protestants such as Leisler were infuriated by the centralizing and pro-Catholic tendencies of the Stuart monarchy. In early 1689, most colonists were delighted to learn of the Glorious Revolution, in which King James II was replaced by William III and Mary II. In April, 1689, Bostonians took matters into their own hands by overthrowing the unpopular Dominion governor, Sir Edmond Andros. The lieutenant governor of New York, Francis Nicholson, tried to maintain his position by appointing an expanded council, which included Leisler and other strong Protestants. After Nicholson hesitated to recognize the abdication of James II, however, Leisler resigned from the council.

On May 31, 1689, the New York militia revolted and occupied Fort James. Leisler probably did not participate in the initial revolt, but within two days he emerged as the recognized leader of the anti-Nicholson faction. Nicholson was forced to flee for his life. He left behind his three chief counselors, Stephanus Van Cortlandt, Nicholas Bayard, and Frederick Philips, who still refused to acknowledge the monarchy of William and Mary. In the provinces of New York and New Jersey, supporters of the revolution, called Orangists, sent representatives to establish a special Committee of Safety, which attempted to restore orderly government. In June, the committee named Leisler as captain of Fort James. On August 16, it promoted him to be the commander in chief of the province.

In December, Leisler assumed the title of lieutenant governor and sent a letter to King William III pledging his support to the new regime. In 1690, Leisler called for elections to an assembly based on direct popular representation, and he initiated the first codification of New York's laws. His Orangist faction initially had the support of a broad coalition of Dutch settlers, workers, yeoman farmers and middle-class merchants. A rival Regent faction was supported by members of the wealthy elite and most Englishmen. Nicholas Bayard and other members of the Regent faction organized an anti-Leisler government in Albany. Faced with this opposition, Leisler increasingly acted in an arbitrary and autocratic manner. He dismissed the Committee of Safety, formed an executive council, and imprisoned Bayard as well as other leaders of the opposition.

Leisler's letter of allegiance to King William was intercepted by the French and never delivered. In London, Francis Nicholson convinced the king that Leisler was disloyal and not to be trusted. In September, 1689, William appointed a new governor, Henry Sloughter, who had an unfavorable view of Leisler and his regime. The Board of Trade, composed of conservative Tories, was even more hostile. Meanwhile, in February, 1690, a French and Indian attack on the frontier town of Schenectady confirmed the colonists' fears of a Papist threat from Quebec. Leisler called for an intercolonial conference, which met in June to organize an invasion of Canada. The delegates from New York, Massachusetts, and Connecticut agreed to dispatch a two-pronged expedition, but it proved to be a fiasco.

In January, 1691, Sloughter's military assistant, Captain Richard Ingoldsby, arrived in New York and demanded that Leisler turn over control of the fort. Leisler refused, in part because Ingoldsby did not have any written evidence of his authority. Leisler's enemies supported Ingoldsby. After a stand-off of two months, fighting broke out, which resulted in six deaths. Two days later, Sloughter arrived, and Leisler agreed to surrender the fort. Sloughter ordered him to be arrested and tried for treason. Leisler protested that he had not sought personal power but had only acted to oppose "popery" and heresy. Found guilty in a hasty trial, both he and his brother-in-law, Jacob Milborne, were hanged and then beheaded on May 16, 1691.

Many people in America and Europe denounced the executions of Leisler and Milborne. In 1695, the English Parliament, with the encouragement of William III, reversed the judgments of the New York trials and recognized Leisler's administration as legitimate. In 1702, the New York assembly voted an indemnity to his heirs.

SIGNIFICANCE

For many historians, Leisler's most lasting influence was his call for an intercolonial conference, independent of English authority. Although the Canadian expedition failed to achieve its objective, it helped prepare for future cooperation between Puritan New England and Dutch Reformed New York. It also provided inspiration for Benjamin Franklin's Plan of Union, which was adopted at the Albany Conference of the next century.

Leisler was one of the strongest proponents of a representative assembly in seventeenth century New York. Following his death, he became a symbol for the idea of democratic government. During the next half a century, the division between the Leislerians and their conservative opponents continued to divide the politics of New York. Thomas Hutchinson (1711-1780), the last colonial governor of Massachusetts from 1771 to 1774, identified Leisler as one of the forerunners of the movement for American independence. Some historians have argued that the Leisler controversy contributed to the development of a two-party system in New York.

—*Thomas Tandy Lewis*

FURTHER READING

Andrews, Charles A. *Narratives of the Insurrections.* New York: Barnes & Noble, 1915. Includes three important seventeenth century documents—two that are anti-Leislerian and one that defends the rebellion.

Archdeacon, Thomas. *New York City, 1664-1710: Conquest and Change.* Ithaca, N.Y.: Cornell University Press, 1976. A detailed and useful account of the politics and culture of the colony during the turn of the century.

Burrows, Edwin, and Mike Wallace. *Gotham: A History of New York City to 1898.* New York: Oxford University Press, 1999. In this large and impressive volume, chapters 7 and 8 include excellent accounts of the rebellion and its legacy.

Christoph, Peter, ed. *Leisler Papers, 1689-1691*. Syracuse, N.Y.: Syracuse University Press, 1999. A scholarly collection of original documents with a helpful introduction and background information.

Hoffer, Peter Charles. *The Brave New World: A History of Early America*. Boston: Houghton Mifflin, 2000. A succinct summary of Leisler's rebellion within the broad context of colonial government and history.

Kammen, Michael. *Colonial New York: A History*. New York: Oxford University Press, 1996. Scholarly work that places Leisler and the rebellion within the historical context of colonial New York.

McCormick, Charles Howard. *Leisler's Rebellion*. Ithaca, N.Y.: Taylor & Francis, 1989. Scholarly account of the rebellion and its significance.

Osgood, H. *The American Colonies in the Seventeenth Century*. Vol. 3. Gloucester, Mass.: Peter Smith, 1957. An old but still useful account of the colonial

period, with a good account of Leisler and his rebellion.

Reich, Jerome. *Leisler's Rebellion: A Study of Democracy in New York*. Chicago: University of Chicago Press, 1953. A standard work on Leisler's rebellion, with an emphasis on its democratic aspects.

SEE ALSO: James II; Louis XIV; Mary II; Peter Stuyvesant; William III.

RELATED ARTICLES in *Great Events from History: The Seventeenth Century, 1601-1700:* March 20, 1602: Dutch East India Company Is Founded; Beginning c. 1619: Indentured Servitude Becomes Institutionalized in America; 1619-c. 1700: The Middle Passage to American Slavery; July, 1625-August, 1664: Founding of New Amsterdam; March 22, 1664-July 21, 1667: British Conquest of New Netherland; 1685: Louis XIV Revokes the Edict of Nantes; June, 1686-April, 1689: Dominion of New England Forms; 1688-1702: Reign of William and Mary; November, 1688-February, 1689: The Glorious Revolution.

NINON DE LENCLOS
French courtesan and writer

Lenclos was a feminist intellectual and a courtesan who scorned marriage and prized her independence. She founded a fashionable salon where some of the most prominent men and women in France gathered for discussions, especially of literature and philosophy. She contributed immeasurably to the intellectual development of seventeenth century French society.

BORN: November 10, 1620; Paris, France
DIED: October 17, 1705; Paris
ALSO KNOWN AS: Anne de Lenclos (given name)
AREAS OF ACHIEVEMENT: Philosophy, literature, women's rights, patronage of the arts

EARLY LIFE
Ninon de Lenclos (nee-nohn deh lahn-kloh) was named Anne at birth. She was the third child and only daughter of Henri de Lenclos, a pleasure-loving, free-thinking cavalry officer, and his pious wife, Marie-Barbe de La Marche. It was her father who gave Anne the name "Ninon," and she would use it the rest of her life. Henri also taught his daughter to play the lute, and he supervised her reading. Despite her mother's best efforts, Ninon soon turned away from Catholicism, preferring the Epicurean,

libertine philosophy her father embraced. Many of the principles she would live by came from one of his favorite writers, the sixteenth century French essayist Michel Eyquem de Montaigne.

Unfortunately, Henri became involved in a love affair with a married woman. He was tried for adultery and had attempts made on his life. After killing one of his persecutors, Henri fled from France, and with his property confiscated, the family was left in straitened circumstances. Marie-Barbe moved to a small house in the Marais, which was the new social and cultural center of Paris. It was here that Lenclos became the "pet" of aristocratic ladies and learned how society operated.

By the time the voluptuous, flirtatious girl was fifteen, it seemed to her mother that her daughter's marriage should be arranged. What Marie-Barbe did not realize, however, was that none of the young men who flocked to her house would even consider marrying a girl without a dowry. Also, both Lenclos and her mother naively believed the promises of the sieur de Saint-Étienne, a worthless playboy, who seduced Lenclos and then abandoned her. There was another liaison, but this time Lenclos did not let herself fall in love, and she broke off the affair to nurse her dying mother. After Marie-Barbe's death, Lenclos retreated to a convent, but evidently she decided that she could never take the veil. When she emerged in 1643, she had decided to support herself by becoming a courtesan.

LIFE'S WORK

Over the next four decades, Lenclos received money for her maintenance from five men she referred to as "payeurs." In return, they were occasionally admitted to her company and some of them to her bed. From among the many men who sought her company, Lenclos chose her lovers, but she never accepted a sou (a trifle) from any of them. In each case, after Lenclos's passion cooled, she ended an affair, but usually her former lovers remained in her circle of friends, which would become her salon. That circle also included a number of men, and some women, who simply enjoyed her company. Lenclos set the tone for what would become her salon, insisting that her guests behave with the utmost decorum and consider topics of real significance.

Even before her mother's death, Lenclos had made some impressive friends. At the salon of her friend Marion Delorme, who for a time was the mistress of the powerful Cardinal de Richelieu, Lenclos had met the young abbé Paul Scarron, who would become a famous writer, as well as the distinguished courtier, wit, and writer Saint-Évremond (Charles de Marguetel de Saint-Denis). Both men became mainstays of Lenclos's salon, and they remained her lifelong friends. Through her conversations with Saint-Évremond, Lenclos came to understand her place in life. She would live not as the women around her—dependent upon tyrannical men—but like an *honnête homme*, an independent person governed by a keen sense of honor.

However, no one in France could live unaffected by politics. Lenclos lost a number of her friends during the Wars of the Fronde (1648-1653), in which France saw serious internal challenges to royal power and national unity. That uprising also cost the life of her father, who had evidently slipped back into Paris in 1647; it is not known whether he saw Lenclos during the two years before his death. With Paris intermittently under siege and conditions there almost intolerable, Lenclos fled to a convent. There, however, she did not find the serenity she sought. Instead, she was so hounded by a relative of Richelieu, in this case, the lecherous older brother of the famous statesman, that she decided to return to Paris, where she again maintained her salon, entertained her friends, and indulged in short-lived affairs, including one

with the comte de Sévigné, the husband of the brilliant letter writer, Madame de Sévigné.

Then, in 1652, when she was twenty-nine, Lenclos fell deeply in love with Louis de Mornay, marquis de Villarceaux. The two left Paris and spent most of the next three years together in the countryside, where, in 1653, their son Louis-François de Mornay was born. By 1655, the affair had run its course, and Lenclos went back to Paris, her friends, and her salon. However, the following year, the religious party at court finally succeeded in having Lenclos sent to a convent dedicated to the reform of wayward women. After nine months in captivity, she received a visit from Queen Christina of Sweden, who used her powerful influence to have Lenclos released.

Lenclos's friendship with the playwright Molière, which began at about this time, was almost inevitable, given their mutual passion for honesty. He is known to have consulted her regularly about his works. In his comedy *Les Précieuses ridicules* (pr. 1659, pb. 1660; *The Affected Young Ladies*, 1732), Molière ridiculed prudish court ladies, such as those who had intrigued against Lenclos. That same year, in her epistle *La Coquette vangée*, Lenclos's only significant literary work, she exposed two seemingly pious men who had been sent to her salon as spies. When Molière finished *Tartuffe: Ou, L'Imposteur* (pr. 1664, pb. 1669; *Tartuffe*, 1732), a play about a religious hypocrite, he read the play to Lenclos. After it was banned, she joined him in the five-year struggle for permission to return it to the stage.

Lenclos's final liaison was with Charles Sévigné, the twenty-three-year-old son of one of her earlier lovers. However, her affairs had always been mere amusements to her; it was her social and intellectual life that was always of primary importance. In her later years, Lenclos became the person to whom young aristocrats were sent to be polished, while established intellectual and political leaders continued to frequent her salon. When Lenclos was in her eighties, the young François-Marie Arouet (the writer and philosopher Voltaire) was taken to meet her. She encouraged him to write poetry, and she left him a substantial bequest. Long after he had become famous, Voltaire would often refer to her kindness. Lenclos died on October 17, 1705. She was buried in Paris, at the church of Saint Paul.

SIGNIFICANCE

Over the course of her life, Lenclos was well respected for her opinions. It has been said that when King Louis XIV took a new mistress, he wanted to know what Lenclos might say about his decision.

Though her sense of decorum had made her a preeminent social arbiter, Lenclos also functioned as an intellectual lightning rod. She contributed to the thought of Saint-Évremond, as recorded in their correspondence during his long exile in England; she commented on Molière's works-in-progress. Voltaire was to later make references to her.

Perhaps even more significant, however, is that she was a woman who rejected a masculine culture, society, and Church. She was a courtesan who refused to sell sexual favors, and she was a feminist who was able to bring the great men of her era into her presence, and into the presence of other women, proving that women, too, could be great thinkers.

—*Rosemary M. Canfield Reisman*

FURTHER READING

Austin, Cecil. *The Immortal Ninon: A Character-Study of Ninon de L'Enclos*. London: G. Routledge, 1927. A fictionalized biography in which the author speculates about the thoughts and feelings of his characters, assumptions generally in line with historical facts. Illustrated.

Cohen, Edgar H. *Mademoiselle Libertine: A Portrait of Ninon de Lanclos*. Boston: Houghton Mifflin, 1970. The standard biography, which provides a useful list of principal persons, a chronology, a bibliography, an index, and illustrations.

Magne, Émile. *Ninon de Lanclos*. Edited and translated by Gertrude Scott Stevenson. New York: Holt, 1926. A readable study, though lacking in dates. Includes list of Lenclos's works. Extensive bibliography. Illustrated.

Robinson, Charles Henry, ed. and trans. *Life, Letters, and Epicurean Philosophy of Ninon de L'Enclos, the Celebrated Beauty of the Seventeenth Century*. 1903. Reprint. Whitefish, Mont.: Kessinger, 2004. A paperback reprint of one of the earliest biographies of Lenclos written in English.

Sainte-Beuve, C. A. "Mademoiselle de l'Enclos." In *Portraits of the Seventeenth Century, Historic and Literary*. Translated by Katharine P. Wormeley. Vol. 1. New York: Frederick Ungar, 1964. This work points out the qualities in Lenclos's character that drew men and women to her and her salon.

Waddicor, Mark. "Voltaire and Ninon de Lenclos." In *Woman and Society in Eighteenth-Century France: Essays in Honour of John Stephenson Spink*, edited Eva Jacobs, W. H. Barber, Jean H. Bloch, F. W. Leakey, and Eileen Le Breton. London: Athlone, 1979. The writer examines evidence of Voltaire's association with Lenclos and his continuing fascination with her.

SEE ALSO: Christina; The Great Condé; Elizabeth of Bohemia; Madame de La Fayette; Marie le Jars de Gournay; Madame de Maintenon; Molière; Marquise de Rambouillet; Cardinal de Richelieu; Anna Maria van Schurman; Madame de Sévigné.

RELATED ARTICLES in *Great Events from History: The Seventeenth Century, 1601-1700:* 1637: Descartes Publishes His *Discourse on Method*; 1661: Absolute Monarchy Emerges in France; 1664: Molière Writes *Tartuffe*; 1682: French Court Moves to Versailles; 1685: Louis XIV Revokes the Edict of Nantes; 1689-1694: Famine and Inflation in France.

ANDRÉ LE NÔTRE
French architect

Le Nôtre's designs for great public gardens complement the architecture of many of the most important buildings in seventeenth century France. He virtually created the French formal garden, which subordinated nature to reason and order while maintaining a fascination with and awareness of nature's beauty and delight.

BORN: March 12, 1613; Paris, France
DIED: September 15, 1700; Paris
AREAS OF ACHIEVEMENT: Architecture, art

EARLY LIFE

André Le Nôtre (ahn-dray leh noh-treh) was born in his father's home, adjoining the Tuileries Gardens. His father, Jean Le Nôtre, royal master gardener, served the king, as had his father, and was in charge of a specific part of the royal gardens. Like all tradespeople of the time, gardeners were a close-knit group, handing their jobs from father to son for generations. Le Nôtre's christening records substantiate that, for his godmother was the wife of Claude Mollet, a member of another third-generation gardening family that was then better known than the Le Nôtres.

Growing up amid this coterie of amateur and professional landscape architects and gardeners, the young Le Nôtre was undoubtedly influenced by their standards, and they probably even discussed his training and education. A prominent author, Jacques Boyceau de la Barauderie, had set forth the qualifications needed by gardeners: literacy, mathematical training, and drawing skill. Drawing was necessary in order to reproduce embroidery patterns on the ground to serve as designs for flower beds. Geometry was necessary to measure paths and flower beds. If he wished, a gardener might study architecture to enable him to design structures for his garden. This theoretical training would be accompanied by the more practical study of seeds, soils, transplanting, and weather prediction.

Apparently, the youthful Le Nôtre showed such skill in drawing that his family arranged for him to study with Simon Vouet, the chief painter to King Louis XIII. This natural skill is apparent in Le Nôtre's carefully executed and delicately colored garden plans, which exhibit draftsmanship and proportion characteristic of an artist. It is generally accepted that he must also have studied architecture, either with Jacques Lemercier or François Mansart. Judging by his later life, this education in painting and architecture must have been of a highly academic quality, accompanied by extensive reading in subjects such as optics, Turkish art, and Italian garden design.

After two years of architectural study, Le Nôtre began training as a gardener, serving as an apprentice to his father, who applied to Louis XIII to have his position passed to his son. The younger Le Nôtre went to work in the Tuileries, receiving his appointment, with a salary and a lodging in the park, in 1637. He remained in charge of these gardens all of his life, arranging for his nephews to inherit this responsibility after his death.

Even though Le Nôtre was a dashing and vivacious young man and lived in a notoriously amoral court atmosphere, no scandal was ever attached to his name. In 1640, he married Françoise Langlois, and his energies thereafter seem always to have been directed to his own family and to his work. He conducted both with discipline and humility. Their married life was happy as well as prosperous, although not untouched by sadness. Apparently neither their son nor their two daughters survived infancy. With no children of their own, Le Nôtre and Françoise cared for their nephews and nieces and a godchild. They also provided a home for his mother after Jean Le Nôtre's death. In their later years, both Le Nôtres inherited property and land from their parents. As Le Nôtre's reputation grew, he prospered, and ultimately he and his wife were wealthy, with an annual income equivalent to thirty-five thousand dollars.

LIFE'S WORK

Le Nôtre's work was known and admired by royalty, nobles, and his contemporaries as early as the 1640's. When only in his early thirties, he conceived a witty and original plan for an episcopal garden at Meaux in the shape of a bishop's miter. He had worked in the Luxembourg Gardens for Gaston, duc d'Orléans. His position as designer in ordinary of the king's gardens continued unchanged after the death of Louis XIII and the ascension of Louis XIV. It is generally accepted, however, that real fame came to him as the designer of the gardens at Vaux-le-Vicomte for Nicolas Fouquet.

Fouquet, superintendent of finance for the Queen Mother, had amassed a huge fortune, which he spent on a château designed to be the most magnificent that money could achieve. He seems to have been anxious to overawe the young Louis XIV and commissioned Louis Le Vau as architect, Charles Le Brun as designer of furnishings, and Le Nôtre as designer of the gardens. They created a masterpiece. The palace stood amid one thousand acres of gardens and park. During its construction, three small villages disappeared, rivers were diverted, and a whole forest was transplanted. In August of 1661, Fouquet invited six thousand people, including the king and the whole court, to a grand party. There were fireworks, illuminations, fountains arching into the sky, and a play performed in the gardens, written and directed by French playwright Molière. Although Fouquet was arrested and imprisoned twenty days later, Le Nôtre's triumph was undiminished. Furthermore, Louis XIV was apparently determined to build an even more magnificent palace at Versailles and to have the same three masters of art and architecture construct and design to their best ability, again with no regard for expense.

Ultimately, Louis XIII's unremarkable hunting lodge at Versailles was transformed into the Louis XIV's palace, the most extravagant and influential building and garden in European history. From its probable beginning date of 1662 throughout the rest of the king's life, the expansion of the buildings, parks, and gardens of Versailles became symbolic of the aggrandizement of France under his rule. The growth of his power can be charted in the growing acreage added to the gardens and parks. The king himself was active in designing his new city. The axis of the gardens and avenues designed by Le Nôtre at Versailles—eventually eight miles of them—literally converged in the king's apartment. The primary theme of the gardens and the sculptures therein is the mythology of Apollo, the original *roi de soleil* (sun king, a moniker for Louis XIV). Additionally, the four rivers of France appear as ancient water gods. The four seasons, the four parts of the day, the continents, the four elements, and the various gods of nature and mythology relate to the garden. The image of the Sun King's supremacy was eventually translated into stone and marble, fabulous water displays, bosquets (thickets or groves), and grottoes, in a symbolism that was complex and unified in its focus.

At Versailles, Le Nôtre followed an essentially orderly geometrical formula from which he rarely deviated throughout his career. The gardens and the buildings they surrounded were an architectural unit. The château was the focal point in a plan beginning with a central axis that bisected the structure and stretched westward to the horizon. Although actually on several different levels, at Versailles this long vista seemed to stretch to its vanishing point, past fountains, secondary canals, and ultimately the mile-long, sixty-foot-wide Grand Canal. Poets of the day said that this vista formed a pathway to

André Le Nôtre. (Library of Congress)

the heavens so that the sun god could descend to his earthly domain. To the architects of the palace and garden, this grand view expressed the limitless power of the king, the personification of France. At right angles across the axis were laid other vistas, geometrically balanced and equally perfect on a smaller scale.

The park at Versailles had three vistas: the main one, which extended to the west, and the ones that extended north and south. Each began at a parterre directly in front of the palace or its wings. These flower beds were planted to resemble embroidered fabric and were edged with low-growing shrubs. Rectangular green panels provided open spaces and led the eye to the many pools. Higher elements of relief, such as trees, were kept at a distance so as not to clutter the vista. The trees served to define the borders within the garden and to provide green walls for a series of cozy, intimate outdoor "rooms," the bosquets, which often served as outdoor ballrooms, theaters, or concert halls.

To the south of the château was a second series of terraces that contained the orangerie, which was designed by Le Nôtre and built by Mansart. From there, tubs holding trees laden with oranges, pomegranates, flowering jasmine, and oleanders were wheeled out in spring to form part of the planned garden. The constructed lake visible from the upper terrace was Le Nôtre's last work at Versailles, completed when he was seventy-four years old. North of the château, where the ground sloped sharply, was the third vista. Le Nôtre there showed his mastery of perspective, for he made the flower beds wedge shaped, with distant ones shorter and smaller and near ones larger, and with the longest sides of the triangles facing the château. Steps of rose-colored marble descended through a steep avenue, past two rows of fountains, through a wood, to reflecting pools, from which water rose in great spouts. This part of the garden also demonstrated the diversity of optical illusions of which Le Nôtre was capable, for when viewed from its farthest points the angle of ascent along the main axis was exaggerated by the luminous waters, the constant refraction of light, and the dazzling play of color in the greens of the woods, the sky-reflecting pools, and the gilded sculptures. All were planned and executed in a perfect harmony of proportion to be viewed from any point.

Le Nôtre's distinguished career was marked by many honors. He became a member of the French Academy of Architecture in 1681. The king honored him with the Order of Saint-Michel, a great mark of distinction. Following Le Nôtre's own whim, Louis XIV bestowed on him a coat of arms consisting of a gold chevron and three silver snails. Other architects and designers lost favor, but until his death Le Nôtre remained the honored friend of the king. Le Nôtre, as the king himself recognized, was like his gardens: honest, straightforward, balanced, and without pettiness. One painting of Le Nôtre in middle age shows a successful, bewigged man with a strong face, intelligent expression, and large dark eyes that seem about to smile. When he died at the age of eighty-seven, his obituary noted that "he was esteemed by all the sovereigns in Europe and there are few who have not requested the design of a garden from him."

SIGNIFICANCE

Le Nôtre did not invent the formal garden, but he did carry its pattern to a level of artistic grandeur that set a pattern for the rest of Europe. He advanced the architectural design of the Renaissance garden, which had been evolving in Italy for two hundred years, to its ultimate form. His imagination, coupled with his artistic perception and the mathematical clarity of his vision, created gardens that epitomized seventeenth century neoclassicism. He had traveled to Italy and conferred with the pope. He

had laid out gardens in England for Charles II and William of Orange. Besides his masterpiece at Versailles, the gardens at Hampton Court, Clagny, Triauon, Sceaux, and Pont Chavtrain further testify to his greatness.

He left no personal literary record of his ideas, but his students were influential in France as well as in the rest of Europe for many years. Many of his gardens no longer exist in original form, but those that are unchanged show his brilliance. It was partly in reaction to his highly developed formality that the so-called romantic or English garden became popular in the more emotional eighteenth and nineteenth centuries.

—Patricia A. Finch

FURTHER READING

Adams, William Howard. *The French Garden, 1500-1800.* New York: George Braziller, 1979. A work based on careful examination of documents and manuscripts of the period, as well as explorations of surviving sites. An extensive chapter tells of Le Nôtre's life and his architectural and landscaping innovations.

Fox, Helen. *André Le Nôtre: Garden Architect to Kings.* New York: Crown, 1962. A good biography that presents Le Nôtre as a symbol of seventeenth century classicism. Includes color reproductions of Le Nôtre's garden plans, sketches, and engravings of garden scenes, and a portrait of Le Nôtre.

Hadfield, Miles. *Pioneers in Gardening.* London: Routledge & Kegan Paul, 1955. Examines the evolution of gardening as different from horticulture or botany. The chapter on the formal garden is almost totally devoted to Le Nôtre.

Hazlehurst, F. Hamilton. *Gardens of Illusion: The Genius of André Le Nostre.* Nashville, Tenn.: Vanderbilt University Press, 1980. A scholarly and complete study of the life and work of Le Nôtre, whom Hazlehurst calls "Le Nostre," consistent with seventeenth century spelling. Especially remarkable are the illustrations: contemporary engravings, artists' views, and several plan and elevation drawings done to scale by a modern architect.

Jellicoe, Sir Geoffrey, Patrick Goode, Michael Lancaster, and Susan Jellicoe, eds. *The Oxford Companion to Gardens.* New York: Oxford University Press, 1986. A comprehensive quick-reference volume containing condensed biographies of Le Nôtre and his major contemporaries. Especially important for its definitions of the many specialized terms associated with gardening, past and present.

Mariage, Thierry. *The World of André Le Nôtre.* Translated by Graham Larkin. Philadelphia: University of Pennsylvania Press, 1999. Mariage, the architect in charge of Versailles Museum, Park and Gardens, examines Le Nôtre's work within a social and cultural context, and describes how seventeenth century practices of land management, surveying, and hydrology contributed to Le Nôtre's design.

Orsenna, Erik. *André Le Nôtre: Gardener to the Sun King*. Translated by Moishe Black. New York: George Braziller, 2001. Orsenna, a French novelist and head of the National School of Landscaping at Versailles, focuses on the design of the gardens of Versailles, examining the many facets of Le Nôtre's landscaping style.

Weiss, Allen S. *Mirrors of Infinity: The French Formal Garden and Seventeenth Century Metaphysics*. New York: Princeton Architectural Press, 1995. A concise intellectual history of the function and meaning of Versailles and other French formal gardens.

SEE ALSO: Charles II (of England); Charles Le Brun; Louis Le Vau; Louis XIV; François Mansart; Jules Hardouin-Mansart.

RELATED ARTICLES in *Great Events from History: The Seventeenth Century, 1601-1700:* c. 1601-1620: Emergence of Baroque Art; 1673: Renovation of the Louvre; 1682: French Court Moves to Versailles.

LEOPOLD I
Holy Roman Emperor (r. 1658-1705)

Leopold I presided over the revival of imperial and Habsburg influence after the defeats of the Thirty Years' War. He consolidated imperial authority in Germany, recovered Hungary from the Turks, and resisted the efforts of Louis XIV of France to achieve European hegemony.

BORN: June 9, 1640; Vienna, Austria
DIED: May 5, 1705; Vienna
ALSO KNOWN AS: Leopold Ignatius (given name)
AREAS OF ACHIEVEMENT: Government and politics, military, warfare and conquest

EARLY LIFE

Born during the last years of the Thirty Years' War (1618-1648) as a younger son of Emperor Ferdinand III and Maria Anna of Spain, Archduke Leopold Ignatius was originally intended for a career in the Church. The education that Leopold received from the Jesuits at the Austrian and Spanish courts, intended to prepare him for the ecclesiastical career for which he was temperamentally so well suited, remained one of the most formative influences on his subsequent development.

This formation was a blend of the traditions of the House of Habsburg with the militant and authoritarian Counter-Reformation. The Austrian monarchy, more than any other European power, was the creation of its ruling dynasty, often the sole force holding together its disparate provinces. The imperial crown was seen as the patron and defender of the Church, continuing the traditions of the Crusades and the Spanish Reconquista, ex-

emplified in Leopold's reign by the wars against the Turks. The Counter-Reformation, embodied in the Jesuits, represented an unbending aversion to all that was contained in the Protestant movement, exemplified in the harsh treatment of the Protestant inhabitants of Hungary and in Leopold's reluctance, despite pressing reasons of state, to ally with William of Orange.

With a German Habsburg father and a Spanish Habsburg mother, Leopold possessed all the family physical traits in an extreme form: the long, narrow face, the large and somewhat tired looking eyes, the slightly hooked nose, and above all the famous "Habsburg lip"—a protruding lower lip with a long, pointed chin. Quiet, withdrawn, and lacking self-confidence, Leopold was at ease only in the family circle. Despite his unprepossessing appearance and manner, however, Leopold was neither stupid nor devoid of personal resources, sharing with most members of his dynasty a great love of the arts, especially music, and possessing a high sense of duty and a tenacity of purpose that would characterize his policies.

With the death of his elder brother in 1654, this fourteen-year-old prince became the heir to one of the major thrones of Europe. He succeeded his father in the Habsburg lands in 1657 and was elected Holy Roman Emperor of the German nation, despite French opposition, on July 18, 1658.

LIFE'S WORK

The patrimony that Leopold I inherited, consisting of the Austrian lands, the lands of the Bohemian crown, and the fragments of the Kingdom of Hungary independent of the Turks, each with its own character and institutions, was exhausted from the destructive warfare of the earlier seventeenth century. The administration, defense, and augmentation of this patrimony would be Leopold's life's work.

Located in Central Europe, with few natural boundaries, the Habsburg monarchy was vulnerable to enemies from all directions. During the first portion of the seventeenth century, the Habsburg emperors had attempted to strengthen the imperial power, assisted by their Spanish cousins and the Jesuits, but had been frustrated by the victorious forces of international Protestantism personified in the king of Sweden, assisted by the revived Bourbon monarchy in France.

Because the greatness of France under Louis XIV rested on its alliance with the Protestant powers to defeat the Habsburgs of Spain and the empire in the Thirty Years' War, Leopold identified the interests of Catholicism and of his imperial office with dynastic interests. At Leopold's accession, his greatest danger still appeared to come from the Protestant challenge, as King Charles X Gustav of Sweden threatened not only to seize control of Poland but also, in alliance with Prince George of Transylvania, to partition the Habsburg possessions, taking Bohemia for himself and placing George on the Hungarian throne. Immediately after his imperial coronation, Leopold sent an army under his leading military officer, Raimundo Montecuccoli, to bring the Swedish threat under control. By the time the Treaty of Oliva ended the First Northern War in 1660, Austria had successfully asserted its integrity and its leading role in Central Europe, saving not only Bohemia but also Poland. This success, however, was more than offset by the rise of a more dangerous power to the East in the revived Turkish Empire.

As the reinvigorated Turkish forces drove toward Vienna in the year 1664, the Ottoman power posed a threat not to Leopold alone. Crete, Poland, and Transylvania were similarly threatened by the renewal of the age-old struggle between Islam and Christendom. Consequently, Leopold's appeal for help received a widespread response, culminating in Raimundo Montecuccoli's victory at Szentgotthárd on August 1. Leopold failed to follow up this victory with vigorous action. French successes in Lorraine and constant anxiety about the Spanish succession diverted his attention to the west. Hence, in the Treaty of Vasvár, Leopold obtained only a twenty-

Leopold I. (Library of Congress)

year truce, leaving important Hungarian strong points in Turkish hands.

Leopold's failure to profit from the victory of Szentgotthárd was a result of his involvement in dynastic considerations and the divided counsel received from his advisers. During the period of the 1660's and 1670's, the Habsburg Dynasty was in danger of extinction. This is well known as it applies to the Spanish branch of the family, but it is often forgotten that between 1649 and 1678, no healthy male children were born to the Austrian Habsburgs, so that Leopold was constantly faced with the prospect of being the last of his line. Hence, dynastic considerations, meaning coordination with the court of Madrid, often took precedence with Leopold over the interests of his own lands. Obsessed with these concerns but lacking self-confidence, Leopold relied heavily on the advice of his Privy Council. That body was divided between a Spanish, or western faction, which was primarily concerned with keeping the goodwill of Spain while checking the expansion of France, and an eastern faction, which saw the greatest threat to the monarchy in the revived Turkish danger and the greatest opportunities in the recovery of Hungary. With a divided council, Leopold pursued his own overriding interest, turning his attention away from Hungary as soon as the immediate danger was passed and concentrating on the French menace.

This neglect of Hungarian affairs was greatly resented by the Magyars, leading to a conspiracy led by Peter Zrínyi and others, encouraged by France. The conspirators bungled their attempts and did not obtain the expected assistance from either France or the Turks. By 1671, the leaders were executed, and royal Hungary lay prostrate at the emperor's feet. The Privy Council proposed the complete centralization of authority in Vienna, as had been done with Bohemia after the victory at White Mountain in 1620, while utilizing the opportunity to re-Catholicize the realm completely. Although Leopold regarded the Hungarians as a burden rather than an asset and, like most statesmen of the age, looked upon religious dissent as actual or potential treason in league with foreign powers, he was not prepared to accept the sweeping proposals of his advisers. He rejected complete abolition of Hungarian autonomy as contrary to his coronation oath as Hungarian king. His intolerance is seen in the harsh measures taken against Hungarian Protestants, but his humanity appears in his commutation to fines and imprisonment of the many death sentences imposed by the courts. These measures left Hungary seething with discontent, so that Leopold was never able to concentrate fully on his goals to the West.

Two factors led to a revival of imperial prestige during the middle years of Leopold's reign. In the West, the aggressive policies of Louis XIV, exemplified in the capture of Strasbourg in 1681, began to win for Leopold the position of champion of German rights, culminating in the outbreak of the Wars of the League of Augsburg in 1688, in which Leopold figured as the leader of all Germany, Catholic and Protestant, against the ambitions of France. In the east, the equally aggressive ambitions of the Turks under the Grand Vizier Merzifonlu Kara Mustafa Paşa resulted in the violation of the truce between the two empires and the siege of Vienna in 1683. Once again, Leopold stood forth as the champion of Christendom. Europe held its breath while the western forces under the emperor's brother-in-law, Charles IV of Lorraine, and the Polish king, John III Sobieski, assembled for the relief of the beleaguered Austrian capital. The great victory at Kahlenberg in September, 1683, was the beginning of the recovery of Hungary for the west.

Although the campaign in the east would eventually result in the defeat of the Hungarian Protestants, who had joined with the Turks, and Prince Eugene's splendid victory at Santa in 1697, resulting in the recovery of Hungary by the Treaty of Karlowitz in 1699, it also tied down a large portion of the resources at Leopold's disposal for sixteen years, preventing him from vigorously prosecuting the war with France and leaving him exhausted when the question of the Spanish succession came to a head at the turn of the century. Moreover, Leopold was uneasy in his conscience about his alliance with William of Orange, who had overthrown the Catholic James II of England. That unease appeared justified when his English and Dutch allies signed treaties with Louis XIV, partitioning the Spanish Empire.

Leopold believed that the Habsburg Dynasty had the best claim to the Spanish throne, grooming his younger son Charles for that dignity, thus exhibiting a grasp of the European balance of power and of the shift of strength from Spain to Austria within the dynasty. When Charles II of Spain died November 1, 1700, Leopold stood alone against the Bourbon hegemony represented by the succession of Philip of Anjou. Before Leopold's death a few years later, however, his brilliant general Prince Eugene had presented him with impressive victories in Italy and Bavaria, and the empire, the Dutch, and the English were once again allies of the House of Habsburg.

Internally, under constant pressure of war in the east and the west, the army developed into a powerful force for unity, but those same pressures prevented the formation of other organs of administration for the entire monarchy. Nevertheless, through his administrative reforms and support of mercantilist policies, Leopold left the Habsburg lands in significantly better condition than he found them in 1657 and prepared the way for the role Austria would play as the leading Central European power in the eighteenth century.

Leopold continued the long Habsburg tradition of patronage of the arts, especially of music, in which field he had the strongest personal interest, leaving behind an impressive corpus of his own compositions. After the Siege of Vienna, Leopold's patronage began the creation of the Baroque Vienna that would be the cultural focus of Central Europe for two centuries.

SIGNIFICANCE

Leopold I reigned during a critical period for the Habsburg monarchy and for Central Europe. He found that power weakened and threatened with dissolution by its defeats in the Thirty Years' War, the ambitions of its neighbors, and the revived strength of the Ottoman Empire. A man without genius, but with integrity, a highly developed sense of responsibility, and tenacity, Leopold provided sound foundations for both the political and cultural development of his state in the next century, resisting without overcoming centrifugal forces while making Austria into an essential element in the continental balance of power. Faced with dangers to the East and West, he consistently preferred to meet the French challenge, believing that Providence would guarantee his success as the defender of Christendom against the Turks. Nevertheless, he failed to recover Alsace from France or to preserve the Spanish throne in the Habsburg Dynasty. In the east, he recovered Hungary, confirmed its association with the dynasty, and presided over the beginnings of the eclipse of the Ottoman Empire as a major world power. Leopold is more significant for the forces that he embodied than for his personal contributions to their success or failure.

—*William C. Schrader*

FURTHER READING

Barker, Thomas M. *Double Eagle and Crescent: Vienna's Second Turkish Siege and Its Historical Setting*. Albany: State University of New York Press, 1967. A detailed account of the Siege of Vienna in 1683, well written and presenting an account of not only the military but also the diplomatic and political aspects of the siege.

Coxe, William. *History of the House of Austria, from the Foundation of the Monarchy by Rhodolph of Hapsburgh, to the Death of Leopold the Second, 1218 to 1792*. 3d ed. London: Bell & Daldy, 1873. Despite its age, this standard work contains significant material for those interested in Austrian history. Propounds both thought-provoking analyses and interesting detail of court and personal life.

Evans, R. J. W. *The Making of the Habsburg Monarchy, 1500-1700*. New York: Oxford University Press, 1984. A detailed study, drawing on many sources unavailable in English for the formative forces underlying the Habsburg monarchy. Especially good on the influence of the Counter-Reformation.

Fichtner, Paula Sutter. *The Habsburg Monarchy, 1490-1848: Attributes of Empire*. New York: Palgrave Macmillan, 2003. Sutter argues that the expansion of the Habsburg's empire constituted a form of European imperialism.

Frey, Linda, and Marsha Frey. *A Question of Empire: Leopold I and the War of the Spanish Succession*. New York: Columbia University Press, 1983. The authors discuss Leopold's role in the battle for control of Spain.

Goloubeva, Maria. *The Glorification of Emperor Leopold I in Image, Spectacle, and Text*. Mainz, Germany: Philipp von Zabern, 2000. Examines how artists created an image of Leopold I as a powerful and important monarch.

Ingrao, Charles W. *The Habsburg Monarchy, 1618-1815*. 2d ed. New York: Cambridge University Press, 2000. This revised and updated history of the monarchy traces the Habsburg state's emergence as a military and cultural power of tremendous influence.

Spielman, John P. *Leopold I of Austria*. New Brunswick, N.J.: Rutgers University Press, 1977. The only full-length biography of the emperor in English, giving a balanced but generally favorable account of Leopold and the people around him.

Wandruszka, Adam. *The House of Habsburg: Six Hundred Years of a European Dynasty*. Translated by Cathleen Epstein and Hans Epstein. Westport, Conn.: Greenwood Press, 1975. An excellent overview of the role of the Habsburg Dynasty in European affairs, containing good character sketches of the members. Particularly helpful on the shift of power from Madrid to Vienna during the reign of Leopold.

SEE ALSO: Charles II (of Spain); Charles X Gustav; Louis XIV; John III Sobieski; Viscount de Turenne.

RELATED ARTICLES in *Great Events from History: The Seventeenth Century, 1601-1700:* 1601-1672: Rise of Scientific Societies; November 11, 1606: Treaty of Zsitvatorok; 1630-1648: Destruction of Bavaria; 1640-1688: Reign of Frederick William, the Great Elector; August 22, 1645-September, 1669: Turks Conquer Crete; July 10, 1655-June 21, 1661: First Northern War; 1656-1676: Ottoman Empire's Brief Recovery; 1667: Pufendorf Advocates a Unified Germany; May 24, 1667-May 2, 1668: War of Devolution; August 10, 1678-September 26, 1679: Treaties of Nijmegen; July 14-September 12, 1683: Defeat of the Ottomans at Vienna; 1684-1699: Holy League Ends Ottoman Rule of the Danubian Basin; Beginning 1687: Decline of the Ottoman Empire; 1689-1697: Wars of the League of Augsburg; 1697-1702: Köprülü Reforms of Hüseyin Paşa; March 9, 1697-August 25, 1698: Peter the Great Tours Western Europe; September 20, 1697: Treaty of Ryswick; October 11, 1698, and March 25, 1700: First and Second Treaties of Partition; January 26, 1699: Treaty of Karlowitz; November 30, 1700: Battle of Narva.

DUKE DE LERMA
Spanish nobleman

The duke de Lerma inaugurated the position of válido, *or king's favored minister, in the court of King Philip III of Spain. Lerma's administration became synonymous with corruption, representing the political decline that took place in imperial Spain at the same time the empire reached the apogee of its cultural golden age.*

BORN: 1553; Seville, Spain
DIED: May 17, 1625; Valladolid, Spain
ALSO KNOWN AS: Francisco Gómez de Sandoval y Rojas (given name)
AREA OF ACHIEVEMENT: Government and politics

EARLY LIFE

Francisco Gómez de Sandoval y Rojas, who would become the duke de Lerma (LEHR-mah), was the son of the marquis de Denia and de Lerma and included in his illustrious lineage King Ferdinand of Aragon and Saint Francis Borgia. His uncle, the archbishop of Seville, supervised his education, and at first the young nobleman seemed destined for a career in the Church. However, his father held important positions in the court of King Philip II and obtained favors there for his son. At an early age, the budding courtier skillfully learned and applied the techniques and habits of ingratiating himself with those who could advance his fortune.

In 1575, Sandoval y Rojas inherited his family's lands and titles, becoming marquis de Lerma, but its fortunes were at a very low ebb. At court since adolescence, he became an intimate adviser and friend to the heir to the throne, who in 1598 became King Philip III. Pious and habituated to spectacles, indolent and indifferent to governing, the new monarch found in his wily adviser the perfect complement to himself. The marquis de Lerma proved someone in whom the king could confide, entrust royal authority, and delegate the task of manipulating the court and managing state affairs. Within hours of becoming king, Philip III conferred on Lerma the novel position of *válido*, or most favored royal minister. In 1599, the king created him duke de Lerma.

LIFE'S WORK

Supported by the king's authority and friendship, Lerma came to control vast resources of patronage and funding. Such control had previously been distributed among various councils and agencies, but they now came under the single control of the uniquely sanctioned *válido*. Moreover, as the king's principal chamberlain, Lerma controlled and restricted access to the monarch by anyone else. Lerma remained in power until 1618, the apogee of the golden age of Spanish literature and the arts. His name, however, has become a byword for corruption and venality, representative of the decay of Spanish royal authority and government.

Lerma consolidated his own power first through nepotism, having numerous members of his family appointed to government and ecclesiastical positions. His two sons were elevated in the aristocratic hierarchy and given court positions providing sizable incomes and properties. The uncle who had mentored him was raised to archbishop of Toledo. His brothers-in-law were appointed viceroys in Naples and Peru. Moreover, Lerma created a subhierarchy of *válidos* who answered only to him. These subordinates thrived on the incomes and bribes of their government appointments and operated an extensive system of spies throughout the Habsburg realms and in foreign courts, alerting Lerma of his critics and opponents.

Members and intimates of the royal family grew increasingly alarmed at the extent of Lerma's power and the voracity of his appetite for more. To protect himself from these opponents, Lerma persuaded the king to move his court from Madrid, the center of intrigues against the *válido*, to Valladolid, northwest of the capital. This was the center of Lerma's family properties. There, over the next decade, he converted the Lerma castle into a palace, stocking it with one of the largest art collections of its time. Keeping the court in Valladolid allowed the *válido* to have more of his kinsmen and intimates ingratiate themselves with Philip III and obtain royal favor.

Nonetheless, after the death in 1603 of the king's grandmother, one of Lerma's fiercest opponents, the court returned to Madrid. By 1609, Lerma shaped two of the most significant policies of the reign of Philip III. In that year and the following, all Muslims (known also as Moors) who did not convert to Catholicism were expelled from Spain. With this act, the country was consolidated as an exclusively Catholic stronghold. The king thereby strengthened his sobriquet of Philip the Pious.

In foreign policy, Lerma obtained in 1609 a peace treaty of twelve years with the Protestant United Provinces of the Netherlands. For forty years, the United

Provinces had been in rebellion against Spanish Habsburg rule. The Dutch used the peace to their advantage, augmenting their naval and commercial maritime prowess and becoming a powerful challenge to the Spanish and Portuguese empires a decade later.

A breach in the power of Lerma began to appear in 1607, when one of his closest advisers was accused of massive corruption and incompetence in office. The scandal was aggravated by the beginning of a national economic crisis that endured for the remainder of the decade. Further crises due to corruption by Lerma's subordinates followed. Moreover, the *válido* himself had amassed a fortune worth, in modern terms, hundreds of millions of dollars. Nonetheless, he continued to retain the confidence of the king. Indeed, in 1612, the king announced that Lerma's signature would be equal in authority to his own.

The phenomenon of a favored royal minister was not unique to Spain in the seventeenth century. Since the beginning of the Age of Discoveries, with growing empires, more complex global trade patterns, and expanded bureaucracies, royal governance in Europe had become ever more complex. King Louis XIII had a powerful, favored minister in Cardinal de Richelieu. King Charles I of England had one in the first duke of Buckingham. Such figures were necessary to maneuver the growing intricacies of government business and court politics, generously lubricating them with royal patronage and favor yet not directly compromising or damaging royal authority.

A powerful alliance against Lerma, however, steadily mounted. It consisted of the king's wife, his confessor, marginalized members of upper nobility and the high councils, and, ultimately, Lerma's eldest son. The nepotism and venality of Lerma's administration were abundantly apparent. Moreover, the extreme suspicion and intricacy with which he conducted state affairs had added a further dimension of morosity to the imperial Spanish bureaucracy.

Anticipating an eventual downfall, Lerma had requested from the pope, beginning in 1614, to be nominated a cardinal. Beyond the piety of an elevated ecclesiastical position, a cardinalate provided Lerma with status and protection against indictment. By the beginning of 1618, the pope made Lerma a cardinal. By the end of the year, Philip allowed him to withdraw to his now luxurious country properties in Lerma. His enemies, nonetheless, succeeded in obtaining weighty fines against him, amounting to annual payments equivalent to tens of millions of dollars.

SIGNIFICANCE

Philip III made the duke de Lerma's eldest son his next *válido*, and elevated him to duke de Uceda. The king's second *válido*, however, had nowhere near the power of the first, and the king himself soon died in 1621. Nonetheless, the position of *válido*, which Lerma had inaugurated, continued with the next king, Philip IV. Lerma died on his estates four years after Philip III. The most lasting image of Lerma is a portrait of him in gleaming body armor and mounted on a white charger, painted in 1603 by Peter Paul Rubens.

—*Edward A. Riedinger*

FURTHER READING

Allen, Paul C. *Philip III and the Pax Hispanica, 1598-1621: The Failure of Grand Strategy*. New Haven, Conn.: Yale University Press, 2000. Reviews policy making and strategies devised by Lerma for Philip III to pacify territories under Habsburg control.

Darby, Graham. *Imperial Spain, 1469-1715*. New York: St. Martin's Press, 1964. Analyzes the economic conditions and sociopolitical developments in the rise and fall of the Spanish Empire and the Habsburg Dynasty.

_____. *Spain in the Seventeenth Century*. London: Longman, 1994. Examines the economic, political, and military conditions of reign of Philip III in relation to his Habsburg predecessors and successors.

Elliot, J. H., and L. W. B. Brockliss, eds. *The World of the Favourite*. New Haven, Conn.: Yale University Press, 1999. Includes an article on Lerma as *válido* and compares his role to that of favored royal ministers at other courts in seventeenth century Europe.

Feros, Antonio. *Kingship and Favoritism in the Spain of Philip III, 1598-1621*. New York: Cambridge University Press, 2000. Revisionist assessment of the administration of Lerma and reign of Philip III, contravening standard interpretations of corruption and incompetence.

Sánchez, Magdalena S. *The Empress, the Queen, and the Nun: Women and Power at the Court of Philip III of Spain*. Baltimore, Md.: Johns Hopkins University Press, 1998. Reviews strategies and roles of major female figures around Philip III, his grandmother, wife, and an aunt, who opposed Lerma's manipulation of him.

Schroth, Sarah. *The Private Picture Collection of the Duke of Lerma*. Ph.D. dissertation. New York University, 1990. Based on archival inventories, this work estimates that the art collection of Lerma included approximately fifteen hundred paintings, inaugurating fashion for major art collecting at Spanish court.

Smith, Hilary Dansey. *Preaching in the Spanish Golden Age: A Study of Some Preachers of the Reign of Philip III*. New York: Oxford University Press, 1978. Examines objectives, styles, and methods of rhetorical eloquence in sermons and religious discourse.

SEE ALSO: First Duke of Buckingham; Philip III; Philip IV; Cardinal de Richelieu; Peter Paul Rubens.

RELATED ARTICLES in *Great Events from History: The Seventeenth Century, 1601-1700*: c. 1601-1682: Spanish Golden Age; March 31, 1621-September 17, 1665: Reign of Philip IV.

LOUIS LE VAU
French architect

Le Vau was one of the greatest French architects of the mid-seventeenth century. His blending of native French and baroque Italian styles established a new architectural idiom in buildings, from townhouses to the king's château at Versailles.

BORN: 1612; Paris, France
DIED: October 11, 1670; Paris
ALSO KNOWN AS: Louis LeVeau (given name)
AREA OF ACHIEVEMENT: Architecture

EARLY LIFE

Louis Le Vau was born to Louis LeVeau, a master mason on royal projects in Paris and at the château of Fontainebleau. He also served as an inspector of royal buildings. Little is known of young Louis's early life, though he was probably apprenticed to and trained as a mason by his father, who used his position and skills to become a successful speculative builder and developer. In this business young Louis became quite active around 1638.

By 1641, Louis and his father had built nine houses at the eastern end of the Île-St.-Louis in the Seine River, either for specific customers or on speculation. Louis's first known design (1640) was for a townhouse (*hôtel*) for Lambert de Thorigny in this development. Through his father's connections at court, Louis apparently joined the entourage of Jacques Lemercier, court architect to King Louis XIII, and participated in early work on the Louvre palace in Paris.

In 1639, Louis was named a royal architect. Shortly thereafter, he changed his name to "Le Vau," perhaps to distinguish himself from his father, with whom he lived in a fine townhouse around the corner from the Louvre. By assiduous study and application Le Vau molded himself—imitating Lemercier—into a sophisticated, learned, and well-traveled (at least within France) man of the court. In 1644, he bought the office of coun-

selor and secretary to the king, a largely symbolic title, but one that placed him firmly at the center of the court. In 1649, Le Vau designed a château for the secretary of finances, Jacques Bordier. From 1654 to 1660, Le Vau worked for Cardinal Jules Mazarin on the royal château complex at Vincennes, near Paris. Through his designs and supervision, the medieval castle was transformed into a splendid and comfortable rural retreat for both the cardinal and his royal guests. Here, for the first time, he began uniting traditional French structures with classical elements, laying the groundwork for a classicizing French Baroque. In 1657, Le Vau purchased the office of *intendant* of buildings, matching his father's highest position.

LIFE'S WORK

In 1655, Le Vau was raised to the honor of first architect to the king. Also at this time, he designed the choir and radiating chapels of the important Parisian church of St. Sulpice. The following year he began a five-year project with landscape architect André Le Nôtre and painter Charles Le Brun on the Château de Vaux-le-Vícomte for the ambitious royal *surintendant* of finances, Nicolas Fouquet. Le Vau designed a grand structure that retained the French tradition of amassing differentiated building units rather than establishing a uniform, unified whole. Its classical elements, such as pediments and pilasters, seemed rather out of place, and the whole effect was more provincial than monumental.

Le Vau became increasingly affected, however, by contemporary Italian architectural trends, as exemplified by the Romans Gian Lorenzo Bernini and Francesco Borromini. Though he never visited Italy, Le Vau collected and carefully studied through prints, books, and drawings the works of classical Roman and Renaissance Italian architects and builders, such as Vitruvius, Andrea Palladio, and Sebastiano Serlio.

Le Vau's first major royal project was the completion of the Garden of the Tuileries in Paris, which continued in stages from 1655 until 1668. In 1662, the executors of the will of Cardinal Mazarin, the regent of France, engaged Le Vau to design and build the cardinal's Collège des Quatre-Nations (now the Institut de France), a school for sixty boys that was overseen by the University of Paris. After much squabbling, Le Vau had it sited across the Seine River from the Louvre palace in such a way that it completed a major sight-line from the palace's Cour Carrée (square courtyard). Thus, this independent commission was drawn into the orbit of royal architecture that was beginning to define King Louis XIV and his capital.

The church at the center of the college's facade served as both a collegiate chapel for the scholars and as a burial chapel for the cardinal. Le Vau utilized the typically baroque oval and topped off his structure with one of Paris's earliest domes. His overall design of a domed central core with curved outstretching arms reflected the recent remodeling at the church of Sant'Agnese and St. Peter's in Rome as well as earlier designs for secular architecture, such as the Villa Trissino at Meledo by the Venetian architect Palladio. The school's library, which housed Mazarin's book collection, was adapted from the Palazzo Barberini in Rome.

If Paris was to be the capital of a great kingdom, its architects had to adorn it with buildings that echoed those of the Eternal City itself. This held true as well for the Louvre, to which, with the assistance of Le Brun and writer Charles Perrault, Le Vau added a stiff and formal neoclassical colonnade in the colossal order (1667). Le Vau also worked on the south or river wing of the palace with Perrault and Le Brun (1668-1669), though his initial plan for the Louvre's east wing never developed above the foundations, as Louis briefly engaged Bernini (1664), on loan from the pope, to leave his mark here instead.

When Louis XIV decided to expand his hunting château at Versailles, he relied on Le Vau, as well as Le Brun and Le Notre, to design it and oversee construction. Having worked at Vaux, the three brought a shared vision and sense of cohesion to the undertaking. In 1662, Le Vau began by laying out on the site the menagerie: a zoo, kennel, farmyard, and breeding center. He erected the massive water mill pumps and gravity-feed water tower (1663) that would keep the canals filled and feed the scores of fountains. Work on the château itself started with the ceremonial Marble Court and its facades from Louis XIII's day. Eventually, Le Vau enclosed the existing structure within what was called the Enveloppe (1668-1673), the new, Italiante central block that would be further expanded by architect Jules Hardouin-Mansart. Le Vau also was responsible at Versailles for the Grotto of Thetis (from about 1664) and his last architectural work, the Porcelain Trianon (1670).

Le Vau engaged also as an entrepreneur in the production of metals and finished metal products. He began in the 1650's with a small factory for tin roofing material, but in 1665, he opened the Royal Manufactory for Tin in the Niversais, with royal subsidies of 60,000 livres and a thirty-year monopoly. His was a vertically integrated organization that controlled the supply of raw materials as well as production and delivery of finished products. Despite a steady flow of government contracts, poor quality goods, such as flawed iron cannon, undermined the firm's reputation, and Le Vau died bankrupt in 1670. After his death, Le Vau was further scandalized by claims that he had misused funds (100,000 livres) from the *collège* project in supporting his failed enterprise.

Significance

As royal architect, Le Vau contributed to the design and construction of many of the most important French buildings of his era, including the Palais de Louvre, the Château de Versailles, and Mazarin's Collège des Quatre-Nations. Though largely self-educated as an architect in the latest styles, he experimented with Roman neoclassicism and helped transform French royal architecture from provincial late Renaissance to seventeenth century classicism. He also borrowed the latest in baroque from Rome, building one of Paris's first domes and uniting it with the era's trendy oval in the *collège*.

Despite his failures as an industrialist, and his fall from grace, he remained a powerful force in seventeenth century design, perhaps second only to Bernini as an architect of genius.

—*Joseph P. Byrne*

Further Reading

Ballon, Hilary. *Louis LeVau, Mazarin's Collège, Colbert's Revenge*. Princeton, N.J.: Princeton University Press, 1999. A close study of Le Vau's design and the construction of the Collège des Quatre-Nations, set in the context of his full career as an architect. The only monograph in English on Le Vau.

Berger, Robert. *The Palace of the Sun: The Louvre of Louis XIV*. College Park: Pennsylvania State University Press, 1993. An architectural study of the building campaigns at the Louvre during the mid-seventeenth century, and Le Vau's roles in those campaigns.

_____. *A Royal Passion: Louis XIV as Patron of Architecture.* New York: Cambridge University Press, 1994. A unique study in English of Le Vau as a builder, with special attention to his projects at Versailles and Paris and his effort to emulate the Roman emperors as monumental patrons.

_____. *Versailles: The Château of Louis XIV.* College Park: Pennsylvania State University Press, 1985. A brief monograph on the building of the château and the roles of the architects and artists.

Pérouse de Montclose, Jean-Marie. *Versailles.* New York: Abbeville Press, 1991. A lavishly illustrated, large-format study of the entire project at Versailles, Le Vau's early role and designs, and the accommodations to them made by later architects and contractors.

Tooth, Constance. "The Early Private Houses of Louis LeVau." *Burlington Magazine* 109 (September, 1967): 510-518. A study of Le Vau's earliest domestic designs in Paris and their place in his development as an architect.

SEE ALSO: Gian Lorenzo Bernini; Francesco Borromini; Charles Le Brun; André Le Nôtre; Louis XIV; François Mansart; Jules Hardouin-Mansart; Jules Mazarin; Charles Perrault.

RELATED ARTICLES in *Great Events from History: The Seventeenth Century, 1601-1700:* 1656-1667: Construction of the Piazza San Pietro; November 7, 1659: Treaty of the Pyrenees; 1673: Renovation of the Louvre; 1682: French Court Moves to Versailles.

JOHN LILBURNE
English political writer and activist

A leader of the Levellers, England's first organized popular political movement, Lilburne contributed to and publicized Leveller ideas and demands, such as religious freedom, the sovereignty of the people, a government answerable to the electorate, and wide access to the vote.

BORN: c. 1615; Greenwich, England
DIED: August 29, 1657; Eltham, Kent, England
AREAS OF ACHIEVEMENT: Government and politics, social reform

EARLY LIFE

John Lilburne (LIHL-burn) was the third child and second son of Richard Lilburne and Margaret Hixon. Both the Lilburnes and the Hixons were respectable gentry families with minor connections to the royal court. The Lilburnes even boasted a coat of arms, and John, although a champion of the rights of the people, always stressed his upper-class lineage. Margaret Lilburne died when her son John was very young, and he probably did much of his growing up at the Lilburne family manor near Durham. He was also sent to school, but his formal education lasted less than ten years. As the Lilburne family estate would go to John's older brother Robert, some other provision had to be made for the younger sons. So, when John was about 15, his father apprenticed him to a London cloth wholesaler named Thomas Hewson.

The city of London must have seemed dazzling to a young boy from the country, but what Lilburne himself later remembered most about his apprenticeship was all the reading that he was able to do in the empty hours spent minding his master's warehouse. Lilburne's family seem to have been Puritans, and the young man's reading reflected Puritan tastes: He read the Bible, of course, but also John Foxe's *Commentarii rerum in ecclesia gestarum* (1554; *Actes and Monuments of These Latter and Perillous Dayes*, 1563, popularly known as *Foxe's Book of Martyrs*), theological works, and books on history and law. All of this reading made a deep impression, instilling in him a concern for social justice and possibly a certain identification with martyrs. When his apprenticeship ended in 1636, however, there was not yet anything to distinguish Lilburne from any other fervent young Puritan in London, preoccupied with Bible reading and attending Puritan sermons.

LIFE'S WORK

Lilburne's public career began in 1637, when he came under the influence of the Puritan pamphleteer John Bastwick and started smuggling banned Puritan works into England. As a result, Lilburne was arrested; he was tried and convicted in 1638 and ordered to be whipped, pilloried, and imprisoned. Lilburne's first published work, written in March of 1638, was an account of his trial. He portrayed himself as a godly martyr defying cruel religious authorities. While in prison, Lilburne managed to both write and publish several such tracts, in which he denounced the bishops of the Church of England in increasingly angry terms.

Lilburne was released from prison by the Long Parliament late in 1640. He set up a brewery, married Elizabeth Dewell, and staunchly supported Parliament in its opposition to King Charles I. At the outbreak of the First English Civil War in 1642, he enlisted in the Parliamentary army, fighting with distinction and eventually rising to the rank of lieutenant-colonel. He refused, however, to sign the Solemn League and Covenant, in which the Parliamentary side officially embraced Presbyterianism, and so left the army in April of 1645. Returning to London, Lilburne, increasingly dissatisfied with the Parliamentary regime, began writing and publishing again. His new works again got him into trouble with the authorities; more often than not, his tracts were written in prison.

Lilburne's works criticizing the Parliamentarians, like his *England's Birth-Right* (1645), demonstrate both how far he had moved from religious issues to political concerns and how much more radical he was becoming in his ideas in general. Lilburne's increasing radicalism was due in part to his association with Richard Overton and William Walwyn, who were also publishing tracts and pamphlets on similar themes and concepts.

The writings of Lilburne, Overton, Walwyn, and a handful of others developed the ideas that would form the basis for the Leveller movement. Among other things, they called for sovereignty to reside solely in the House of Commons, the democratically elected representatives of the people, and for the government to remain answerable to the people. They demanded religious freedom, the reform of the legal and tax systems, a much wider distribution of the vote, and safeguards for the people's rights. By March of 1647, these demands had taken the form of a specific program for social and political reform set forth in the Levellers' Large Petition, which was formally presented to Parliament September 11, 1648. In the process of authoring the Large Petition, the Levellers had become a formal political movement, a movement that was spread throughout the army through agents known as Agitators.

From prison, Lilburne advised both the Agitators and those working on behalf of the petition. He also continued to be one of the Levellers' chief propagandists, with a knack for passionate rhetoric and an ability to dramatize political points. Lilburne probably had a hand in the Agreement of the People, drawn up in October of 1647 in

John Lilburne. (Hulton Archive/Getty Images)

a collaboration of Agitators and civilian Levellers. The agreement was nothing less than a proposed new constitution for England, with a government based on the sovereignty of the people, exercised through their elected Parliament.

At the end of 1648, Lilburne and some other Leveller leaders attempted, but failed, to persuade the army leaders to support the Agreement of the People. By February of 1649, Lilburne was denouncing the army-dominated government; in *England's New Chains Discovered* (1649), he accused that government of betraying the people of England. In May, Lilburne, Walwyn, and Overton published a revised version of the Agreement of the People, retitled *Agreement of the Free People* (1649) and representing a summation of Leveller political thought.

The *Agreement of the Free People* was the Levellers' swan song. By the end of the summer of 1649, the Leveller movement had been crushed. Lilburne was released from prison in November of 1649 but was unable to keep out of trouble. In January of 1652, he was banished from England; when he returned in 1653, he was imprisoned once again. In 1655, he was moved to Dover Castle and had begun to covert to Quakerism. The next year, although still a prisoner, he was allowed to visit his wife and children, eventually spending extended periods of time with them. He died on August 29, 1657, aged forty-two.

SIGNIFICANCE

The Leveller movement failed, but the political ideas articulated by Lilburne and the Levellers did not die: They are the foundations upon which modern democratic government rests. Lilburne's greatest significance, then, lies in his role in developing and promoting such concepts as popular sovereignty, the rightful derivation of power from the will and consent of the people, and the answerability of all governments to the people for their actions. He insisted on the supreme importance of securing the people's rights, sought an expansion of suffrage, and demanded religious freedom, as well as reform of the legal system. From his religious convictions, Lilburne drew the notion of a complete and total equality of all men and applied it to the political realm.

Lilburne's significance to the Leveller movement itself, moreover, extended beyond what he contributed in ideas. Lilburne was the heart and public face of the Levellers. A great deal of Leveller organizing activity, such as protests and petitions, centered on his trials and imprisonments. Lilburne's great gift as a political publicist was his ability to both personalize and generalize the injustices inflicted upon him so that they were understood as being inflicted on every free Englishman.

—*Sharon Arnoult*

FURTHER READING

Arnoult, Sharon L. "The Sovereignties of Body and Soul: Women's Political and Religious Actions in the English Civil War." In *Women and Sovereignty*, edited by Louise Olga Fradenburg. Edinburgh: Edinburgh University Press, 1992. Contrasts the religious and political ideas of Leveller women with those of nonradical women.

Aylmer, G. E., ed. *The Levellers in the English Revolution*. London: Thames and Husdon, 1975. Primarily a collection of the writings of John Lilburne, William Walwyn, and Richard Overton; the editor's introduction remains one of the best, brief explications of Leveller thought in the context of the times.

Frank, Joseph. *The Levellers*. Cambridge, Mass.: Harvard University Press, 1955. Provides biographical information on key Leveller leaders, including John Lilburne, and traces the development of the Leveller movement with special focus on Leveller texts.

Gregg, Pauline. *Free-born John: A Biography of John Lilburne*. London: George G. Harrap, 1961. Only full-length biography of John Lilburne.

Sharp, Andrew, ed. *The English Levellers*. New York: Cambridge University Press, 1998. A useful collection of Leveller tracts.

Woolrych, Austin. *Britain in Revolution, 1625-1660*. New York: Oxford University Press, 2002. Comprehensive history of the dramatic events that formed the context for John Lilburne and the Leveller movement.

SEE ALSO: Charles I.

RELATED ARTICLES in *Great Events from History: The Seventeenth Century, 1601-1700:* November 3, 1640-May 15, 1641: Beginning of England's Long Parliament; 1642-1651: English Civil Wars; August 17-September 25, 1643: Solemn League and Covenant; 1646-1649: Levellers Launch an Egalitarian Movement.

HANS LIPPERSHEY
Dutch inventor

Lippershey, a lens grinder and spectacle maker, generally receives credit for the invention of the telescope and binoculars. The invention of the telescope was a key technological event that gave impetus to the scientific revolution.

BORN: c. 1570; Wesel, Westphalia (now in Germany)
DIED: c. 1619; Middelburg, Zeeland, United Provinces (now in the Netherlands)
ALSO KNOWN AS: Hans Lipperhey; Jan Lippersheim; Hans Lippersheim
AREA OF ACHIEVEMENT: Science and technology

EARLY LIFE

Almost nothing is known of the early life of Hans Lippershey (hahnz LIHP-ehrs-hi), but it is apparent that between 1570 and 1608, he became a master lenscrafter and spectacle maker and established a shop in Middelburg, the capital of the province of Zeeland, in what is now the Netherlands. In Lippershey's shop, many different kinds of glass lenses were ground and sold; spectacles, or eyeglasses, were also manufactured and sold there.

The idea of using lenses to make distant objects appear closer to the viewer was suggested by the Englishman Robert Grosseteste, bishop of Lincoln, in the thirteenth century and was most likely considered even earlier. In the mid-sixteenth century, his fellow countryman and mathematician Leonard Digges appears to have devised a successful single-lens telescopic instrument. In 1585, another Englishman, William Bourne, described the use of a convex lens to magnify objects at a distance, although his device had the disadvantage of inverting the object's image in the lens. Bourne also hinted that a combination of a concave mirror with a convex lens might produce telescopic effects.

Before 1589, Giambattista della Porta seems to have arranged one convex and one concave lens into a telescopic combination of perhaps 1 or 2 magnifications, as did Raffaelo Gualterotti in 1590. These lens combinations were used by Porta and Gualterotti only in spectacles to sharpen and correct short-range vision; they were ineffective when they were applied to viewing faraway objects. By the early seventeenth century, however, lensmakers had improved their ability to grind strong concave lenses; concave lenses with short focal lengths were also increasingly manufactured. Thus, the makings of the first telescope—a strong concave lens combined with a weak convex lens—were available in the spectacle makers' shops. Yet these improved lenses remained solely confined to use in eyeglasses.

LIFE'S WORK

Extant evidence remains insufficient to answer the question of who invented the telescope, that is, by arranging a combination of one strong concave with one weak convex lens that was of appreciable use in long-distance vision. Historians still argue over assigning priority for the invention. According to some accounts of questionable validity, an early telescope was made in Italy in 1590 and was brought to the United Provinces in 1604. There is little doubt, however, that by 1608 the first working telescope—a convex objective lens combined with a concave eye lens to produce a sharp and upright image of a distant object—had been constructed. Historical records confirm that in October, 1608, three Dutchmen were in possession of such a device.

Lippershey is commonly awarded credit for inventing the telescope because he was the first to apply for a patent for such a device. The two other candidates for the title of inventor of the telescope are Zacharias Janssen and Jacob Metius. Janssen was another early seventeenth century Middelburg spectacle maker and peddler, of somewhat disreputable character. According to his son, a source many historians have discredited, Janssen constructed a telescope in 1604, after seeing an Italian model dated 1590. Metius, the son of engineer, mathematician, and burgomaster Adriaen Anthonisz, and the brother of mathematician Adriaen Metius, was a resident of Alkmaar. Historians supporting Metius's claim contend that Metius placed an order for some lenses to be ground at Lippershey's shop, and, while working with the lenses, Lippershey discovered his customer's intent. Metius's claim, however, rests more firmly on the fact that approximately two weeks after discussing Lippershey's application, the States-General (the representative assembly of the United Provinces) discussed the patent application for a telescope similar to, but not as well made as Lippershey's, which Metius had submitted.

Hieronymus Sirturus (Girolamo Sirtori), in *Telescopium: Sive ars perficiendi novum* (1618), first connected Lippershey with the invention of the instrument. In the seventeenth through the nineteenth centuries, opinion as to the device's inventor oscillated between Lippershey and Janssen. Modern historians consider Lippershey and

Hans Lippershey. (Library of Congress)

Janssen as the two likely candidates for the title of inventor of the telescope, with Lippershey possessing the strongest claim.

Those who proclaim Lippershey the inventor have related several stories describing the occasion of this invention, all with a common thread. According to the story, sometime in the summer of 1608 (or perhaps earlier) someone in Lippershey's spectacle shop looked through two lenses at once at a weather vane on a nearby church steeple and was surprised to find that the combination of lenses made the weather vane appear closer. The stories vary as to who made this discovery; two playing children, one of Lippershey's apprentices, and Lippershey himself have all been suggested. Lippershey then mounted two lenses in the same arrangement in a tube, thus constructing the first telescope. According to some sources, Lippershey's telescope was constructed using a double convex lens as the object glass and a double concave lens as the eyepiece and thus did not produce an inverted image. Other accounts describe it as a combination of two convex lenses, which did invert. This telescope probably was mounted in a paper tube about 1.5 feet long, was about 1.5 inches in aperture, and had no focusing mechanism. Both types fall into the general category of refracting telescopes.

Subsequent events in the history of the invention of the telescope are more clearly documented. After constructing his telescope, Lippershey wrote the provincial government of Zeeland about his invention. They referred him to Maurice of Nassau, stadtholder of the Dutch Republic, and to the republic's States-General. Lippershey contacted the States-General, requesting a thirty-year exclusive patent to the telescope's production and sale. According to its official records, on October 2, 1608, the States-General discussed Lippershey's petition, noting that he desired either an exclusive patent to the instrument or an annual pension, which would allow him to make telescopes solely for the use of his country. Lippershey's telescope was successfully tested by members of the States-General. On October 6, the government asked whether its manufacturer could improve the telescope so that the viewer might look through it with both eyes at once. Answering that he could, Lippershey set a price for the binocular of one thousand florins.

Shortly thereafter, the spectacle maker furnished the States-General with a telescope, which a committee tested and agreed might be useful to the republic. The committee, reiterating their request for binoculars, reached an agreement with Lippershey for the price of nine hundred florins, three hundred of which they would pay in advance. On December 15, 1608, Lippershey presented the first binoculars to the States-General, received their approval and an order for two more, and requested a patent for the binoculars as well. Ultimately, however, the Dutch government concluded that, since other persons in addition to Lippershey were able to construct telescopes and binoculars, they could not grant him patents for the devices. Instead, they awarded him monetary prizes for the invention.

In 1612, Greek mathematician Joannes Dimisiani coined the word "telescope," from the Greek "to see at a distance," for the new device, and after 1650 telescope gradually became its commonly accepted name. The type of instrument that many believe Lippershey constructed is often referred to as a Dutch telescope.

SIGNIFICANCE

By the end of 1608, news of the telescope—or Dutch trunks, perspectives, or cylinders, as they were called—had spread to France, and the devices themselves could be purchased in the Holy Roman Empire. Early in 1609, telescopes could be bought in Paris. By May, 1609, the news of the invention had reached Milan, and before the end of the year, telescopes were being manufactured in England.

The significance of the telescope in military operations was recognized immediately upon its invention, and it was quickly put to use in warfare. Only in the eighteenth century, however, did the telescope become a common part of surveying and navigational instrumentation.

Eventually, the telescope exerted its greatest, although less tangible, impact upon the European intellectual world. In May, 1609, Galileo, while visiting Venice, heard that a Dutchman had invented a device that made distant objects appear nearer and larger. Returning to Padua, Galileo immediately built his own, greatly improved telescope. Galileo turned his telescope to the skies and became the first person to view the Sun and planets other than with the naked eye. His observations and discoveries dealt a crushing blow to the old geocentric astronomy and paved the way for the acceptance of the heliocentric system.

At first, the telescope was used for qualitative astronomical observations only. Within a few decades, however, the telescope was applied to quantitative observation of the heavens, and it greatly increased the level of accuracy obtainable. Still, the instrument itself, and its relative the microscope, remained novelties and did not become widely accepted scientific instruments until a generation after their invention. It was not until about 1660 that telescopes and microscopes were regularly manufactured, and not until after 1665 was observation of the heavens with the naked eye abandoned and the telescope deemed indispensable in astronomical observation. From this time until the early twentieth century, the telescope remained the primary astronomical instrument.

—*Martha Ellen Webb*

FURTHER READING

Doorman, G. *Patents for Inventions in the Netherlands During the Sixteenth, Seventeenth, and Eighteenth Centuries, With Notes on the Historical Development of Technics.* Translated by Johann Meijer. The Hague, the Netherlands: Martinus Nijhoff, 1942. Still the best available English source of information on Lippershey's claim to the title of inventor of the telescope. Contains an essay on the telescope and a history of the patent applications for its invention. An important and detailed study.

Drake, Stillman. *The Unsung Journalist and the Origin of the Telescope.* Los Angeles: Zeitlin & Ver Brugge, 1976. This work contains a facsimile of a 1608 news sheet announcing that Maurice of Nassau had received from a spectacle-maker from Middelburg, most likely Lippershey but not named, lenses that enlarge objects seen at a distance.

King, Henry C. *The History of the Telescope.* 1955. Reprint. New York: Dover, 1979. The standard history of the telescope that should be read by everyone interested in its invention and development. Contains an excellent summary of the device's early history and what is known of Lippershey's work.

Maddison, Francis. "Early Astronomical and Mathematical Instruments: A Brief Survey of Sources and Modern Studies." *History of Science* 2 (1963): 17-50. This article contains an excellent, annotated bibliography of literature on the telescope and related instruments.

Moll, Gerard. "On the First Invention of Telescopes." *Journal of the Royal Institution* 1 (1831): 319-332, 483-496. Invaluable, though somewhat hard to find, as a source of information about the early history of the telescope. It discusses the patent applications made to the States-General of the United Provinces and provides excerpts from the official state records concerning Lippershey's and others' applications.

Singer, Charles. "Steps Leading to the Invention of the First Optical Apparatus." In *Studies in the History and Method of Science*, edited by Charles Singer. Vol. 2. Oxford, England: Clarendon Press, 1921. This essay concisely and chronologically examines developments in optical theory and technology from antiquity through the construction of the first telescopes in the early seventeenth century. Excellently documented, the work includes references to, and excerpts from, the works of a wide range of scientists and inventors. Singer presents a discussion of the claims of Lippershey and others to the instrument's invention.

Van Helden, Albert. "The Historical Problem of the Invention of the Telescope." *History of Science* 13 (1975): 251-263. An authoritative discussion of the debate over who should receive credit for the invention. Discusses the claims of Lippershey, Janssen, and Metius, based on an examination of early historical documents and treatises on the history of the telescope.

Wolf, Abraham. *A History of Science, Technology, and Philosophy in the Sixteenth and Seventeenth Centuries.* 2d ed. Vol. 1. Gloucester, Mass.: Peter Smith, 1968. An easily accessible work that gives a concise history of the invention of the telescope and its subsequent development by Galileo, Johannes Kepler, and others in the sixteenth and seventeenth centuries. The work shows the immediate and long-range consequences of the application of the telescope to astronomy and also discusses the telescope as one of several crucial technological developments of the period.

SEE ALSO: David and Johannes Fabricius; Galileo; Johannes and Elisabetha Hevelius; James Gregory; Johannes Kepler; Evangelista Torricelli.
RELATED ARTICLES in *Great Events from History: The*

Seventeenth Century, 1601-1700: 17th century: Advances in Medicine; September, 1608: Invention of the Telescope; 1610: Galileo Confirms the Heliocentric Model of the Solar System; 1632: Galileo Publishes *Dialogue Concerning the Two Chief World Systems, Ptolemaic and Copernican*; 1660's-1700: First Microscopic Observations; 1672-1684: Leeuwenhoek Discovers Microscopic Life.

LIU YIN
Chinese poet and painter

An accomplished poet, Liu Yin also cowrote poems with her husband Qian Qian Yi, and she coedited the women's section in his influential anthology of Ming Dynasty poets. Liu's paintings have met with sustained modern critical interest as a result of their originality and fresh style.

BORN: 1618; Wujiang, Jiangsu province, China
DIED: July 21, 1664; Jiangsu province
ALSO KNOWN AS: Liu Shi (Pinyin), Liu Shih (Wade-Giles); Yang Ai; Yang Ying; Madame Hedong (Pinyin), Madame Ho-tung (Wade-Giles)
AREAS OF ACHIEVEMENT: Literature, art

EARLY LIFE

In 1618, Liu Yin (lee-ew yihn) was born into a family of insufficient means to prevent her from early extramarital sexual experience. Her foremost Chinese biographer, Chen Yin Ge, holds that Liu had a romantic relationship with the married poet Chen Zilong from the time she was fourteen, in 1632, until she turned seventeen in 1635. She may even have lived with Chen Zilong for half a year in 1635, before his jealous wife made her leave. By 1636, contemporary sources identify Liu as working for the Gui family brothel in the town of Shengze, near Liu's hometown of Wujiang, near Nanjing.

As the Gui establishment was upscale, young Liu enjoyed a status comparable to a Japanese geisha. As such, education in poetry and painting was considered essential. In 1636, Liu worked at the Gui facility as an apprentice and servant to the sex worker Xu Fo, who was most likely her teacher in art and poetry. Liu's first paintings were of orchids, narcissus, and bamboo, the favorite subjects of her colleagues. Typically, courtesan artists like Liu would give their paintings to especially well-liked clients.

Resolved to escape life as a courtesan and looking for

a man with similar artistic interests, Liu Yin sought the acquaintance of male poets. According to legend, Liu asked for a date with Chen Zilong, who refused her through an intermediary. If Liu had been his lover before, this story was invented to protect Chen's reputation. In 1640, Liu cross-dressed as a male scholar and went to see the famous poet and critic Qian Qian Yi. She asked to study poetry with him, and a serious relationship ensued, despite the fact that Qian was already married. On July 14, 1641, Qian made Liu his second wife, as male polygamy was permitted. At age twenty-three, Liu ceased to be a courtesan and instead became a wife.

LIFE'S WORK

Liu Yin quickly settled into a productive artistic relationship with her husband. Qian supported and mentored Liu. He took her poetry and painting seriously, even though he lived in an age that discriminated significantly against women artists. In addition to her own work, Liu and Qian began writing poems together. They also discussed art and poetry with the intellectuals and artists who visited Qian. On these occasions, Liu wore a male scholar's dress. She chose this outfit deliberately not just to blend in, but also to show her intellectual equality.

In 1643, the building for Qian's private library was completed. Set below some hills in the province of Jiangsu, the three-story building was called Jiang Yun Lou (Crimson Cloud Mansion). It was here that Liu spent the happiest years of her life. She and Qian worked in the library together, writing poetry, editing an anthology of Ming poets, and studying art and literature. Liu also continued to paint.

Liu's surviving paintings demonstrate the growth of her artistic independence at Qian's library. An early album attributed to Liu, the exact date of which is still disputed, contains eight paintings in ink and colors on paper. These paintings copy Chinese masterpieces of an earlier period, a common practice at the time. Liu's paintings generally feature human figures embedded in landscapes and seem to tell a story, a trademark of Liu's art. They portray such figures as a tiny solitary fisherman in his boat just below imposing rocks or one person strolling through an orchard while another sits in a nearby garden pavilion.

Liu's most famous work, on permanent exhibition at the Palace Museum of Beijing, is the hand scroll ink-and-color painting *Yue di yanliu tu* (1643; misty willows at the moon dike). It was created when Liu and Qian visited Wiping Water Mountain Lodge, Qian's old villa. The painting shows this villa comfortably nestled within wind-blown willows. There is a small boat moored close to the villa, and the sickle of a newly crescent moon lies on its side above the trees and atop a red river bridge. Liu's inspiration, Qian wrote later, came from an earlier poem of his that describes this scenery. He had written the poem in 1637, before meeting Liu. Once Liu finished the painting, Qian added his earlier poem on the blank right side of the scroll.

Liu's life at the library was not limited to study and the creation of art and poetry. The Crimson Cloud Mansion was also the center for an active social life. In 1643, Huang Yuan Jie, another woman painter, lived there, at her friend Liu's invitation.

China's larger political turmoil also affected Liu's life. When the Manchus conquered China and Nanjing fell to the invaders in 1645, Liu implored Qian to commit suicide with her rather than live under the foreigners. Qian refused, however, and Liu chose life as well. Liu loved Qian loyally. Even though Qian collaborated somewhat with the Manchus, in 1647 he was thrown in jail for sheltering a Ming loyalist. Liu did everything she could to have him released and succeeded after forty days. In 1648, she gave birth to their only child, a daughter whose name is no longer known.

Liu experienced great professional success in 1649. Qian published his anthology of Ming poets, *Liechao shiji* (1649; famous poets), the women's section of which Liu had substantially edited. The book became famous, and it enhanced Liu's reputation. Her own poems were widely read as well. Disaster struck the next year, however, when Crimson Cloud Mansion burned down. Most of the books and treasure stored in the mansion were lost, and Liu and Qian's life changed dramatically. They began to focus on Buddhist studies and year by year lived an ever more religious lifestyle. In 1663, at age forty-five, Liu Yin shaved her head like a Buddhist nun.

In June, 1664, Qian Qian Yi died. He left their daughter and his son with his first wife in the care of Liu Yin. Immediately, Qian's enemies forced Liu to hand over most of Qian's fortunes. Especially vicious was Qian Zeng, whom Qian Qian Yi had supported throughout his life. He relentlessly pursued Liu and took almost everything from her that she tried to save for the children. Once land, treasure, and household staff (including slaves) were taken, Qian Zeng demanded three thousand silver taels in cash, a sum Liu no longer possessed.

On July 21, 1664, Liu Yin hanged herself. She committed suicide as a protest against Qian Zeng and his gang. Before she sacrificed her life, Liu asked her friends to intervene with the government so that some material means of their father would be left for the children. Shocked by Liu Yin's suicide, Qian's friends eventually settled with Qian Zeng, restoring a legacy for Liu's stepson, who would become a government official. Her daughter also married well. In 1808, the house where Liu Yin hanged herself, unused after her death for fear of her angry ghost, was converted into a temple honoring her life.

SIGNIFICANCE

Liu Yin's life has been celebrated for its artistic and literary triumph and for the uncompromising nature of her final act. Traditionally, her suicide out of concern for the future of her daughter and her stepson has been hallowed as exemplifying motherly love. To modern critics, it also points at the limited choices of a persecuted woman in early Qing China. In the end, Liu felt that only the most drastic, self-negating step would have any effect.

Liu Yin's paintings are respected for the originality of style and execution she brought to her subjects. Her landscapes anticipate the works of later generations of male painters and possess a lyrical propensity for storytelling. Liu's poems are collected both in widely read general anthologies and in collections of her husband Qian's works. The poems she wrote together with Qian are gathered under the title of *Dong shan chou he ji* (east mountain poetic conversations) in Qian's complete works. Her artistic spirit transcended the gender limitations of her age.

—R. C. Lutz

FURTHER READING

Cahill, James. "The Paintings of Liu Yin." In *Flowering in the Shadows: Women in the History of Chinese and Japanese Painting*, edited by Marsha Weidner. Honolulu: University of Hawaii Press, 1990. Informative discussion of the major paintings attributed to

Liu, with a brief discussion of her life. Includes reproductions of her art. The same book also contains a chapter on "Women Painters in Traditional China" by Ellen Johnston Laing that provides background for understanding Liu's life and art. Illustrated, notes, bibliography, glossary of Chinese names.

Chang, Kang-I Sun. "Ming-Qing Women Poets and the Notions of 'Talent' and 'Morality.'" In *Culture and State in Chinese History*, edited by Theodore Huters et al. Stanford, Calif.: Stanford University Press, 1997. Scholarly discussion of the standards for evaluating the artistic achievement of poets like Liu Yin, as well as their choice of subject matter and their position in Chinese society. Notes, bibliographic references.

_____. *Women Writers of Traditional China*. Stanford, Calif.: Stanford University Press, 2000. Liu Yin is referred to as Liu Shih in this excellent anthology that contains a selection of her poetry, the biographical-critical preface Liu wrote for women poets in Qian Qian Yi's anthology, and the preface to her own works written by Chen Zilong. Invaluable English source for Liu's poetry and criticism.

Weidner, Marsha, et al. *Views from the Jade Terrace: Chinese Women Artists, 1300-1912*. Indianapolis: Indianapolis Museum of Art, 1988. Catalog of the first American exhibition that included works by Liu Yin. Has reproductions of her paintings and a sketch of her life. Illustrated, notes, bibliography, index.

SEE ALSO: Abahai; Chen Shu; Chongzhen; Dorgon; Kangxi; Shunzhi; Tianqi; Wang Fuzhi; Zheng Chenggong.

RELATED ARTICLE in *Great Events from History: The Seventeenth Century, 1601-1700:* June 6, 1644: Manchus Take Beijing.

JOHN LOCKE
English philosopher

One of the first modern philosophers, Locke combined the rational, deductive theory of René Descartes and the inductive scientific experimentalism of Francis Bacon and the Royal Society. He produced one of the most significant and influential bodies of social and political philosophy of the modern era.

BORN: August 29, 1632; Wrington, Somerset, England
DIED: October 28, 1704; Oates, Essex, England
AREA OF ACHIEVEMENT: Philosophy

EARLY LIFE

John Locke was born in the small English village of Wrington, in Somerset, on August 29, 1632. His father, John Locke, Sr., was a local attorney of modest means. His mother, née Agnes Kneene, was the daughter of a local tanner. Both parents were educated Puritans, and while the home atmosphere was austere, it was also intellectual. Locke's father was a stern and taciturn man who seemed little interested in his son during his youth, but grew friendlier as Locke became an adult. Agnes Locke was ten years older than her husband and thirty-five when John, her first son, was born. She was a pious and affectionate mother. Locke had only one brother, Thomas, born August 9, 1637. Shortly after John Locke's birth, the family moved to Belluton and a larger and more comfortable farmhouse.

Locke's early education was at home. By 1647, at the age of fifteen, his father arranged an appointment to Westminster School, located next to Westminster Abbey in London. Headmaster Richard Busby was a remarkable teacher with definite conservative sympathies toward the Royalists and the Church of England. Even though Parliament had gained the upper hand in the Civil War with the king, Busby kept his post. Although he was not able to influence Locke toward either political or religious orthodoxy, Busby apparently cooled his pupil's zeal for the Puritan faith.

In 1650, Locke was elected a king's scholar. This meant that he boarded in the school instead of private quarters outside and, more important, would be eligible for a scholarship to Oxford or Cambridge when he was graduated. Locke studied Latin, Greek, Hebrew, and Arabic in order to read the great books written in those languages. In 1651, Locke's brother, Thomas, also came to Westminster. In later years, Locke criticized boarding schools severely for the cruelty and violence they encouraged, indicating that those were not happy years for him. Only four of his schoolmates remained his friends in later life.

Locke grew to be tall and slender, a handsome man with a long, sensitive, and patrician face, a high forehead, large, dark, expressive eyes, a full mouth, and a dimpled chin. In later years, he often wore a wig in the style of his times, but he never lost his own hair. Locke did not change much as he grew older, except that his hair turned white and his face grew thinner.

In May of 1652, when he was nineteen, Locke was last on a list of six Westminster students elected for scholarships to Christ Church, Oxford, where he enrolled the next November. Although Oxford had suffered greatly during the Civil War, it had become a more settled place by the time Locke arrived. The curriculum was still medieval, and three and a half years' study in logic, metaphysics, and classical languages were required for the bachelor's degree. Latin was the spoken language, and all students attended religious services twice daily. While at Oxford, Locke acquired the lifelong idiosyncrasy of using ciphers, invisible ink, code names, and other devices to keep secrets. He seems to have cultivated an aura of romantic mystery for himself, an unexpected trait for someone renowned as the founder of the Age of Reason.

When Locke earned his B.A. in 1656, he decided to begin the three years of study required for the master of arts degree. What attracted him was not the regular curriculum with its methodology of disputation (he saw little chance of finding truth in that way) but rather the new learning, just making its appearance in the sciences, with its empirical methodology. He attended meetings to discuss the discoveries of Vesalius, William Harvey, William Gilbert, and Paracelsus, among others, whose work was based on observation. This was the beginning of a lifelong study of science, medicine, and experimental philosophy.

Locke concluded that unquestioning adherence to tradition and trusting emotional convictions were the two principal causes of human error; Royalists and Puritans, respectively, were his prime examples. Locke practiced medicine throughout his adult life and seems to have had something of a gift for it, but he was never much of a scientist. As a philosopher of the empirical and rational method of the scientific search for knowledge, however, he had few peers.

For Oxford, these were hard years as the political fortunes of the Royalist and Parliamentarian factions shifted back and forth and were reflected in changes at the university. Since religion was still a matter of state at this time, each shift brought a different religious focus. Out of these struggles grew an interest in toleration

John Locke. (Library of Congress)

among the students and scholars at Oxford. Within the context of this debate, Locke concluded that toleration was a nice idea but impractical. He thought religious zealots, such as most Puritans, had proved dangerous to society's peace and security, while Catholics were always suspect because their allegiance to the pope could too easily make them traitors. Later in his life, Locke would take a more liberal stand, but the change grew out of experience, not principle. Interestingly, some of his arguments against toleration were cribbed from Thomas Hobbes's great work *Leviathan* (1651), although he never acknowledged his debt to Hobbes, which was not unusual for Locke's time.

Locke was also beginning to think seriously about the concept of natural law, especially the idea that it incorporated a moral code that was knowable to rational beings, and compelling once known. His ideas on the subject were as yet poorly formed. The theory was not new; it dated back to the Greek Stoics and had been adopted by medieval Christianity as the law of God. The idea of natural law was then reclaimed in the Renaissance by secular interests as the basis for a new theory of government and was a popular issue for scholarly debate in Locke's time. It was the Greek and Renaissance forms that interested Locke. He rejected the medieval theory that humankind innately knew the law of nature as it applied to human conduct. He was already moving toward a theory that explained all knowledge as the result of experience.

LIFE'S WORK

Locke's father died on February 13, 1661, and his one brother, Thomas, died in late 1663. That left him alone in the world, since his mother had died in 1654. Locke's father left him some land and a few cottages, which provided him a small but adequate income the rest of his life. Locke had numerous female friends throughout his life and seems to have been close to marriage at least twice. For reasons on which he chose not to comment, however, he remained a bachelor.

LOCKE'S PREFACE TO THE *SECOND TREATISE OF GOVERNMENT*

John Locke's Second Treatise of Government *is among the most influential works of modern political philosophy and is widely cited as the primary influence upon the authors of the Declaration of Independence and the framers of the United States Constitution. Despite the general applicability of this work to political theory and practice, however, Locke's treatise was written to respond in the first instance to a specific moment in English political history, as this passage from his Preface indicates.*

Reader, thou hast here the beginning and end of a discourse concerning government; what fate has otherwise disposed of the papers that should have filled up the middle, and were more than all the rest, it is not worth while to tell thee. These, which remain, I hope are sufficient to establish the throne of our great restorer, our present King William; to make good his title, in the consent of the people, which being the only one of all lawful governments, he has more fully and clearly, than any prince in Christendom; and to justify to the world the people of England, whose love of their just and natural rights, with their resolution to preserve them, saved the nation when it was on the very brink of slavery and ruin.

Source: From the Preface to *Two Treatises of Government*, by John Locke (London: Millar, Woodfall, et al., 1764). http://oregonstate.edu/instruct/phl302/texts/locke/locke2/2nd-contents.html. Accessed April 19, 2005.

Christ Church elected him lecturer in Greek the same year that his father died, and in 1663 he was appointed lecturer in rhetoric. During these early years as a teacher, Locke periodically considered becoming a clergyman to advance his career. Permanent faculty members customarily took holy orders. His dislike of theology and his interest in science, however, seem to have been the deciding factors, and he never did so. His great friend and scientific mentor, and the leading scientist of the day at Oxford, was Robert Boyle. He advised Locke to concentrate on scientific research and leave theology to those who loved disputation.

In 1665, while the Great Plague was ravaging London, King Charles II and his court came to Christ Church for an extended stay. Locke may have met the king at that time, because Locke was offered the post of secretary to the diplomatic mission in Brandenburg. What interested Locke most while on this assignment, was how easily Brandenburgers accepted religious differences. A change in his thoughts on toleration dates from this experience. Locke was offered several other posts with diplomatic missions but declined, preferring to stay at Oxford.

In the summer of 1666, Locke met Anthony Ashley Cooper, then Baron Ashley and later first earl of Shaftesbury. There immediately developed between them a deep respect and admiration, which evolved into a collaboration. Cooper invited Locke to Exeter House, his London home, first as a houseguest and then as his personal physician. Locke accepted because he liked Cooper and the city, and because many of his friends lived in London. Cooper knew most of the prominent intellectuals of his day and introduced Locke to them. In this environment, Locke, heretofore a minor Oxford scholar, amateur scientist, and unqualified medical practitioner, discovered his talent as a philosopher. While Locke did occasionally perform medical services for Cooper and his family, and in at least one instance may have saved Cooper's life, Locke was chiefly a friend, confidant, and adviser to Cooper in his many political activities, especially during his tenure as one of the king's leading ministers in 1672 and again in 1678.

Religion was a critical concern of English politics during the reign of Charles II. Although the king was personally willing to allow all Englishmen to worship as they pleased, Parliament was adamantly opposed to all but the Church of England. Complicating matters, Charles II's heir was his brother James, duke of York, who had publicly announced his conversion to Catholicism. Prompted by Cooper, who advocated toleration, Locke almost finished his *Epistola de Tolerantia* (1689;

A Letter Concerning Toleration, 1689) by 1667, although it was not published until 1689.

In fact, none of Locke's important works were published until late in his life. He was an overly cautious man in an unsettled political atmosphere. In *A Letter Concerning Toleration*, Locke distinguished between those actions and opinions that concerned politics and society, and those that did not. He argued that toleration of the latter was necessary. Locke concluded that all Christian religions except Catholicism must be tolerated. Catholic allegiance to the papacy and the threat to social peace posed by all non-Christians disqualified both groups from toleration. For his day, that was a liberal position and, as a result of Locke's later fame, influential in the evolution of full toleration in England. Locke's personal religious convictions were few. He rejected nearly all dogma except a belief in God, and he argued for a rational interpretation of Christianity in all other matters.

Also as a result of Cooper's interest, Locke had become concerned about economics and matters of trade. Through Cooper's influence, Locke received appointments to public offices related to trade and commerce and invested in various commercial enterprises. Locke was meticulously careful with money and was very knowledgeable about finance. He always made a profit from his investments. He wrote several essays to protest government policies that he thought unwise or unfair.

In 1671, as a result of ill health, Locke went to France for an extended visit. While in France, he met Samuel von Pufendorf, Gottfried Wilhelm Leibniz, and a number of others connected to the French Royal Society. Locke traveled extensively in France and later in England because of his continuing respiratory problems, which were aggravated by the London smog. While traveling, he maintained an extensive correspondence with his friends.

By 1681, Cooper was out of government and involved in a plot to overthrow Charles II in order to put the king's bastard son, the duke of Monmouth, on the throne. The purpose was to prevent the king's legitimate heir, his brother James, from succeeding him and giving England a Catholic monarch. After the plot was discovered in 1682, it became dangerous for anyone to be associated with Cooper. This included Locke, who slipped out of England secretly and by February of 1683 was in Rotterdam. He lived in various cities in the Netherlands, part of the time in hiding to avoid extradition, and did not return to England until 1690. It was, however, a productive period for Locke. He spent the winter of 1684-1685 in Utrecht beginning work on *An Essay Concerning Human Understanding* (1690), finishing it by late 1686. Before publishing it he released several short, descriptive summaries to promote sales of the essay. The essay itself was not printed until 1690.

In *An Essay Concerning Human Understanding*, Locke was addressing three questions: How do we gain knowledge? How trustworthy is that knowledge? and What is the scope or extent of what can be known? Although Locke claimed to be approaching these questions empirically, an empiricist would not attempt to answer the third question, or even perhaps the second, before all knowledge was known. Locke was more indebted to the rationalism of Descartes than he admitted. Empiricism, however, was the method he tried to use to demonstrate his conclusions, and, in the process, he presented a radically new view and definition of human nature.

Locke was certain that people were born with minds empty of any knowledge and that the mind's only links with the external world were through the senses. The mind had the capability of forming abstract ideas after reflecting on sensory perceptions it received and of constructing from those ideas even more complex abstractions. Locke made a clear distinction between knowledge by reason, which can be empirically demonstrated, and faith or opinion, which he thought was ungrounded fantasy. *An Essay Concerning Human Understanding* also contains an extensive discussion of language and the use of words. A major achievement of the essay was in separating faith from reason in types of philosophical inquiry and in demonstrating which would lead to trustworthy knowledge. Locke's was a view of human nature radically different from what Christian theologians had proposed. There was no place in Locke's scheme for original sin or predestination to evil; human behavior came from thought that was learned and subject to the influence of reason and observation.

While in the Netherlands, Locke was involved in some other minor writing projects and in editing his *Letter on Toleration*. He also spent time visiting friends including Antoni van Leeuwenhoek, the inventor of the modern microscope, and Prince William III of Orange and Mary (the future Queen Mary II), the next monarchs of England. Charles II had died in 1685 and was succeeded by James II, but by 1688 the English were so offended by their new king that they invited William and Mary to intervene and take the throne. Locke was delighted by their acceptance and the flight of James II. He made ready to return home immediately, having been offered space aboard Princess Mary's ship, and arrived in England February 20, 1689.

LOCKE'S MAJOR WORKS	
1689	*Epistola de Tolerantia* (*A Letter Concerning Toleration*, 1689)
1690	*A Second Letter Concerning Toleration*
1690	*Two Treatises of Government*
1690	*An Essay Concerning Human Understanding*
1692	*Some Considerations of the Consequences of Lowering of Interest, and Raising the Value of Money*
1692	*A Third Letter for Toleration*
1693	*Some Thoughts Concerning Education*
1695	*The Reasonableness of Christianity as Delivered in the Scriptures*
1706	*Some Thoughts on the Conduct of the Understanding in the Search of Truth*

King William offered Locke several diplomatic posts, but Locke refused to leave England and accepted only a part-time position as commissioner of appeals. Locke's Oxford position had been lost while he was in the Netherlands. He asked to have it restored but withdrew the request upon learning that someone else would be dispossessed. Locke was soon involved in finishing his great work of political philosophy, *Two Treatises of Government* (1690), publishing it anonymously in 1690.

Locke had written the first drafts of the *Two Treatises of Government* back in 1681 when Cooper was planning to overthrow Charles II. Although Cooper's activities may have been part of Locke's inspiration, the issues raised were ones that had been under discussion among Europe's intellectuals for some time, and Locke was already familiar with them. The Glorious Revolution of 1688 made the *Two Treatises of Government* apposite again. There is no evidence to support Locke's statement that there were originally three treatises and that the longer middle one had been lost, and scholars are at a loss to explain Locke's claim.

The first treatise was written as a detailed refutation of Sir Robert Filmer's *Patriarcha* (1680), an undistinguished work in defense of autocracy that had become popular in Royalist circles. Although Locke cited Hobbes as his antagonist, Hobbes was unpopular and Locke's arguments were more clearly in opposition to Filmer's than to Hobbes's. The reason for the subterfuge is unknown. The second treatise proposed an alternative theory for the origins and purpose of government based on natural law. Locke maintained that because God had given each person his or her life, it was part of God's natural law that the

individual was the only rightful owner of his life, that each had this right equally, and that the right was therefore inalienable.

Besides life, there were the other primary rights of liberty and property, which were necessary to preserve life, and without which an inalienable right to life could have little value. From these three, all other rights were derived. Locke argued that before government existed (which he called a state of nature), each person had sole responsibility for the defense of his or her own rights. For convenience and the better protection of their rights, especially property, people established societies with governments by consenting to a social contract. For Locke, if followed that the only legitimate reason a government had for existing was to preserve and protect rights. If the government then violated individual rights, it destroyed the social contract. This violation released the individual from any obligation and justified rebellion in order to establish a new social contract.

Between 1688 and 1690, the three most important of Locke's works were published. In the years following 1690, he published a number of lesser items, including a special edition of *Aesop's Fables* (1691), printed in English and Latin to help children learn Latin; his first economics essay, written in 1672, *Some Considerations of the Consequences of Lowering of Interest, and Raising the Value of Money* (1692); *A Third Letter for Toleration* (1692), in answer to a critic; *History of Air* (1692), edited for his old friend Boyle, who had died and left the manuscript in rough form; *Some Thoughts Concerning Education* (1693); second, third, and fourth editions of his *Essay Concerning Human Understanding*, in which he expanded his arguments; *The Reasonableness of Christianity as Delivered in the Scriptures* (1695); and vindications of several works that had been attacked by other writers.

Locke was also interested in current affairs. He was the dominant commissioner on the Board of Trade from 1695 to 1700 and undertook several projects to influence his friends in Parliament on economic issues. Specifically, he wanted Parliament to allow the censorship law to lapse in 1695, and to issue new coins with milled edges to prevent clipping. They did both.

Locke kept up the habit formed during the years he was a member of Cooper's household of creating discussion clubs. These usually met weekly in a tavern and discussed science, politics, or philosophy, or all three. Members of the clubs had included Cooper, John Somers, Lord Pembroke, and other important educated people. He also found time to visit his many friends, including

Sir Isaac Newton and Sir Christopher Wren. By 1695, his asthma was so bad during the London winters that he moved permanently to the home of Lady Masham, his closest female friend, where he lived out the remainder of his life. He had become a famous man of letters in England and throughout Europe. A steady stream of friends, disciples, and dignitaries came to visit and pay their respects.

Because of failing health, Locke refused, in 1697, the personal request of King William III to take the post of embassy secretary in Paris at a critical time in the negotiation of the Partition Treaties with King Louis XIV. He chose his young cousin, Peter King, as his heir and gave him help and advice to further his career as a lawyer and statesman. King became lord high chancellor of England for a time after Locke's death. In 1700, Locke began having trouble with swelling in his legs, which kept him in bed for extended periods. Locke continually prepared himself for death, which, periodically, he thought was imminent. Nothing, however, ever interfered with his mental powers. Locke kept up a voluminous correspondence and read the latest important books and papers. His physical condition grew steadily weaker throughout 1703 and 1704, and on Saturday, October 28, 1704, he was unable to rise without help and died peacefully sitting in a chair shortly after 3:00 P.M. with Lady Masham by his side. Locke was buried quickly and privately in the nearby village churchyard of High Lever, as he had requested. He was seventy-two years old.

SIGNIFICANCE

Locke left an extraordinary intellectual legacy. His essays on toleration were a major contribution on the subject and deserve some of the credit for the development of a more liberal government policy toward religious beliefs. His *Essay Concerning Human Understanding* created a new image of human nature substantiated by empirical observation. Locke objected to medieval rationalism because the premises of any disputation were determined by theology. Earlier philosophers had attempted to separate theology from rationalism but failed to provide an alternative means of substantiating their conclusions, resulting in some bizarre concepts in philosophy. Locke's insistence on empirical evidence gave the study of human nature a scientific basis, doing for the social sciences what Newton did for the natural sciences.

Locke's *Two Treatises of Government* were a synthesis of a long-standing debate among Europe's intellectuals. In his work, the combination of natural law theory and the concept of vested rights were clearly stated for the first time, transforming the latter into the principle of inalienable rights. These rights became a matter of universal principle and a specific manifestation of a new individualistic definition of liberty. Later, Enlightenment philosophers expanded Locke's ideas to create new visions of how a society should be structured and the ways in which progress could be achieved.

—*Richard L. Hillard*

FURTHER READING

Anstey, Peter R., ed. *The Philosophy of John Locke: New Perspectives.* New York: Routledge, 2003. Essays about Locke's natural philosophy, political and moral thought, and religious theories.

Berlin, Isaiah, ed. *The Age of Enlightenment: The Eighteenth Century Philosophers.* Boston: Houghton Mifflin, 1956. Selections from original sources of nine representative Enlightenment writers, one of whom is Locke. The introduction to each author and commentary on selections are useful for readers interested in sampling the variety of Enlightenment thought.

Chappell, Vere, ed. *The Cambridge Companion to Locke.* New York: Cambridge University Press, 1994. Ten essays explore Locke's life and times, various aspects of his philosophy, and his influence.

Cranston, Maurice William. *John Locke: A Biography.* New York: Macmillan, 1957. Reprint. New York: Oxford University Press, 1985. This is the best scholarly biography of Locke and the only one to make full use of the Lovelace collection of Locke manuscripts. In spite of irritatingly long and frequent quotations and sometimes poor organization, it is a readable and informative work.

Dewhurst, Kenneth. *John Locke (1632-1704), Physician and Philosopher: A Medical Biography.* London: Thames and Hudson, 1963. Reprint. New York: Garland, 1984. Dewhurst concentrates on Locke's lifelong interest in medicine but offers interesting details on Locke's life and ideas in general.

Dunn, John. *Locke: A Very Short Introduction.* Rev. ed. New York: Oxford University Press, 2003. Explains how Locke arrived at his theory of knowledge and how his advocacy of toleration and responsible government were central to eighteenth century Enlightenment thought.

Gay, Peter. *The Enlightenment: An Interpretation.* 2 vols. New York: Alfred A. Knopf, 1966. Reprint. New York: Norton, 1977. A brilliant and elegant interpretation of the Enlightenment. The first volume examines the revolt against the intellectually stifling dogma of religion and the second describes the inter-action of culture, economics, and politics to shape the programs of reform proposed. Locke is mentioned briefly but frequently as a touchstone of the era.

Gough, John W. *John Locke's Political Philosophy: Eight Studies*. 2d ed. Oxford, England: Clarendon Press, 1973. A scholarly analysis of Locke's political philosophy. Gough pays attention to Locke's personal life.

Jones, James Rees. *Country and Court: England, 1658-1714*. Cambridge, Mass.: Harvard University Press, 1978. An excellent and scholarly general history of England during Locke's adult life. Narrative and interpretive, well organized, and interestingly written. Locke is mentioned only in passing.

Locke, John. *An Essay Concerning Human Understanding*. London: E. Holt, 1690. Edited by Alexander Campbell-Fraser. 2 vols. Reprint. New York: Dover, 1959. The definitive edition of Locke's most original work with a helpful introduction and explanatory notes. For those who want to read and interpret Locke for themselves.

_____. *Two Treatises of Government*. London: A. Churchill, 1690. Rev. ed. Edited by Peter Laslett. Cambridge, England: Cambridge University Press, 1960. This is the definitive edition and is accompa-nied with many informative footnotes and a long introduction that not only summarizes Locke's life but also discusses the publication history and significance of Locke's essay.

Smith, Alan G. R. *Science and Society in the Sixteenth and Seventeenth Centuries*. London: Thames and Hudson, 1972. One of the best histories of the scientific revolution for the general reader in print. Discusses not only the specific discoveries but also the broad social context in which these discoveries were made and their impact on society.

SEE ALSO: Robert Boyle; Charles II (of England); René Descartes; William Harvey; Thomas Hobbes; James II; Antoni van Leeuwenhoek; Gottfried Wilhelm Leibniz; Louis XIV; Mary II; Duke of Monmouth; Sir Isaac Newton; Samuel von Pufendorf; First Earl of Shaftesbury; William III; Sir Christopher Wren.

RELATED ARTICLES in *Great Events from History: The Seventeenth Century, 1601-1700:* 1642-1651: English Civil Wars; May, 1659-May, 1660: Restoration of Charles II; 1688-1702: Reign of William and Mary; November, 1688-February, 1689: The Glorious Revolution; 1690: Locke Publishes *Two Treatises of Government*.

DUCHESSE DE LONGUEVILLE
French noblewoman and administrator

As an ambassador, rebel against the Crown, and inspiration for French writers, the duchesse de Longueville was one of the most politically active noblewomen of the seventeenth century. She rallied support from French aristocrats, helped negotiate treaties with both the Crown and with Spain, and rallied the province of Normandy to oppose the monarchy.

BORN: August 28, 1619; Vincennes prison, near Paris, France
DIED: April 15, 1679; Paris
ALSO KNOWN AS: Anne-Geneviève de Bourbon-Condé (given name)
AREA OF ACHIEVEMENT: Government and politics

EARLY LIFE
The birth of the duchesse de Longueville (lohng-veel), Anne-Geneviève de Bourbon-Condé, in Vincennes prison outside Paris in 1619 seemed to presage a life of political controversy. Born into the cadet branch of the reigning Bourbon family, her father, Henry II de Bourbon, prince of Condé (1588-1646), was imprisoned by King Louis XIII for suspected disloyalty. Her mother, Charlotte-Marguerite de Montmorency, gave birth to the princess in the royal prison, leaving imprisonment two months later after the family had sworn fidelity to the king.

The twenty-three-year-old duchess was married in 1642 to the forty-seven-year-old Henry II d'Orleans (1595-1663), duke of Longueville, governor of Normandy, and head of the most powerful aristocratic family in the Norman province. Memoirs universally described the couple as ill-matched; the new duchesse de Longueville was said to be far more high-spirited, daring, and intelligent than her older husband. She would soon take essayist François de La Rochefoucauld as a lover (in 1646).

LIFE'S WORK

In August, 1648, the duchesse de Longueville's restless energy found an outlet with the outbreak of the Wars of the Fronde. A complex series of rebellions against the Crown, the Fronde (French for sling or slingshot) erupted during the minority of Louis XIV and lasted until 1653. It brought together an ever-changing coalition of *parlementaires* (sovereign court judges), aristocrats, clergy, and local and provincial authorities. Most were opposed to the high royal taxes imposed during the Thirty Years' War (1618-1648); to the regency of foreign-born Anne of Austria and her minister, Italian-born cardinal Jules Mazarin to the Crown's attempts to curb the independence of the *grands*, or high nobility.

The duchess became a driving force in the aristocratic Fronde almost immediately. She cemented a small coalition of important aristocrats in Paris, who sided with the *parlement* of Paris against the Crown in late 1648. Most importantly, she secured the support of her husband, Longueville; her youngest brother, the prince of Conti (Armand de Bourbon); and her lover, La Rochefoucauld. In January, 1649, as rebellion flared in the provinces, the duke and duchess of Longueville moved quickly to the capital of Normandy. There they persuaded the *parlement* of Rouen to formally join the rebellion, adding one of the richest provinces of France to the lists of opposition. The duchess helped negotiate the Treaty of Rueil with the Crown in March, 1649, which brought a temporary end to the siege of Paris.

Her most important ally, however, would become her younger brother, Louis II, prince of Condé (later known as the Great Condé). By the age of twenty-seven, Condé had become the celebrated hero of France's battles against Spain during the Thirty Years' War. After winning the Battle of Lens (1648), he had ridden to the Crown's defense in Paris the following winter with royal troops, opposing frondeurs in the city. Embittered by the Crown's lack of recognition for his achievements, however, he was eventually persuaded by his sister and by his aristocratic pride to abandon the court, and he later entered into outright rebellion. As the scion of a family that virtually controlled Burgundy and other regions of France, his enlistment in the cause was a serious setback for the monarchy.

By January of 1650, however, the tide seemed to turn against the frondeurs. Several of the rebellious princes were arrested by the Crown, including the duchess's husband and her brothers Condé and Conti, who were imprisoned for more than a year. As the young King Louis made a royal entry into Rouen to demand allegiance from the Norman province, the duchess fled to the Longueville château with a garrison of more than one thousand soldiers. She summoned the city officers of nearby Dieppe to secure their cooperation with her troops, but within days her garrison had surrendered. The duchess then attempted to flee the port of Dieppe under male disguise in a boat, narrowly survived its sinking, and escaped by carriage out of France.

Undaunted, the duchess continued the fight from the Low Countries (now the Netherlands and Belgium). She contacted the Spanish for military support and rode to Stenay on the frontier to shore up frondeur general Henri de La Tour d'Auvergne, viscount de Turenne. On April 30, 1650, the duchess and Turenne signed a treaty with invading Spanish troops to fight in opposition to the French crown. Aided by revolts erupting elsewhere in the kingdom, their combined forces managed to keep royal troops from winning a decisive victory in the north. By February, 1651, First Minister Mazarin was in flight, and the frondeur princes were released from prison, but the lack of commonality of interests between the aristocratic rebels and the frondeurs of the *parlements* fatally weakened the rebellion. Despite Condé's capture of Paris for the rebels in July, 1652, the continued bloodshed and disorder had wearied even the many staunch supporters of the rebellion.

By 1652, even the duchess's husband and Turenne had rejoined the royalist side. The estranged couple, both with important supporters in Normandy, proceeded to fight passionately over the loyalty of the Rouen *parlementaires*. With the declaration of Louis XIV's majority in December, 1651, however, the frondeurs could no longer claim to be rebelling against the misrule of the king's regent and minister. They were now rebelling against the king himself. In October of 1652, Louis XIV re-entered Paris, and the Fronde began to dissolve. In November, the duchess was declared a rebel and a traitor, along with her brothers and La Rochefoucauld.

In December, 1654, the duchess reconciled with her husband. Two months later, he interceded with the Crown on her behalf, and she was cleared of charges of rebellion. Her brother Condé eventually was pardoned and returned to France in 1659, after the Treaty of the Pyrenees had ended continuing warfare between France and Spain. Cardinal Mazarin, the duchess's implacable foe during the Fronde, later paid her the compliment of calling her one of only three women he knew who could rule or overthrow an entire kingdom.

In later life, the duchess took an active role in administering the Longueville estates in Normandy. She handpicked seigneurial judges for the ducal courts and prosecuted court cases before the *parlement* of Rouen to protect the rights of the duchy. She was highly esteemed by royal officers, both for her intimate knowledge of the province and for her administration of the immense Longueville estates.

After the death of her youngest son in battle (widely thought to be the son of La Rochefoucauld), the private incarceration of her eldest son for mental illness, and death of her husband in 1663, she astonished everyone once more by retiring to the aristocratic convent of Port Royal. While never entirely giving up the worldly life of Paris, she became a passionate and powerful defender of the Jansenists at Port Royal. She died there in 1679.

SIGNIFICANCE

In the past, much has been made of the duchesse de Longueville's affairs (as well as her platonic flirtations) with other aristocratic political figures, especially La Rochefoucauld and Turenne. Both were men whom she strongly influenced to remain in opposition to the Crown, but in the early-modern world, where politics was almost always conducted through bonds of personal patronage, clientage, and exchanges of favors, her relationships with powerful men were part of the normal political process. Like them, she used her considerable personal wealth to help finance the Fronde, and drew on the loyalties of clients and family members. Unlike them, however, she was not allowed to lead an army into battle, or to hold political office.

Along the way, she inspired the playwright Pierre Corneille as a model for his heroines, while also inspiring some of La Rochefoucauld's most bittersweet reflections in his famous *Maximes* (1665). The duchesse de Longueville's activities as an aristocratic rebel, center of political influence, and seigneur of noble estates show us the possibilities, as well as the real limitations, of political noblewomen in the seventeenth century.

—Zoë A. Schneider

FURTHER READING

Bannister, Mark. *Condé in Context: Ideological Change in Seventeenth-Century France*. Oxford, England: Legenda/Oxford University Press, 2000. Examines the intellectual, political, and social context of the French Fronde and discusses the duchess's influence upon her brother Condé. Contains a useful chronology.

Cousin, Victor. *Madame de Longueville Pendant la Fronde*. Paris: Didier, 1863. This nineteenth century work remains the only full-length biography of the duchess in any language. Although romanticized and lacking a modern historical interpretation of the period, it captures the power of her personality.

La Rochefoucauld, François de. *Moral Maxims*. Newark: University of Delaware Press, 2003. A dual language edition of La Rochefoucauld's classic work. Many of his bitter love maxims were inspired by his several-year affair with the duchess, with whom he had a son. Includes an introduction and notes. Based on the 1749 English translation.

Moote, Lloyd. *The Revolt of the Judges: The Parlement of Paris and the Fronde, 1643-1652*. Princeton, N.J.: Princeton University Press, 1971. While focused on the parliamentary revolt in Paris, this definitive work sheds light on the revolt in Normandy and the role of the Longuevilles in the provincial Fronde.

Ranum, Orest A. *The Fronde: A French Revolution, 1648-1652*. New York: W. W. Norton, 1993. A reinterpretation of the Fronde that argues for its revolutionary character, as opposed to the standard interpretation that it was a rebellion without revolutionary goals.

SEE ALSO: Anne of Austria; The Great Condé; Pierre Corneille; Cornelius Otto Jansen; Louis XIV; Jules Mazarin; Cardinal de Richelieu; François de La Rochefoucauld; Viscount de Turenne.

RELATED ARTICLE in *Great Events from History: The Seventeenth Century, 1601-1700:* 1638-1669: Spread of Jansenism.